Microsoft® SQL Server 2000 UNLEASHED

Second Edition

Ray Rankins
Paul Bertucci
Paul Jensen

SAMS 800 East 96th Street, Indianapolis, Indiana 46240

Microsoft® SQL Server 2000 Unleashed, Second Edition

International Standard Book Number: 0-672-32467-9

Library of Congress Catalog Card Number: 2002110545

Printed in the United States of America

First Printing: December 2002

06 9 10

Trademarks

Warning and Disclaimer

Bulk Sales

Sams Publishing offers excellent discounts on this book when ordered in quantity for bulk purchases or special sales. For more information, please contact

U.S. Corporate and Government Sales
1-800-382-3419
corpsales@pearsontechgroup.com

For sales outside of the U.S., please contact

International Sales
international@pearsoned.com

Associate Publisher
Michael Stephens

Acquisitions Editor
Kim Spilker

Development Editor
Kevin Howard

Managing Editor
Charlotte Clapp

Indexer
Johnna Dinse

Proofreader
Jessica McCarty

Technical Editor
Chris Thibodeaux

Team Coordinator
Lynne Williams

Multimedia Developer
Dan Scherf

Interior Designer
Gary Adair

Cover Designer
Alan Clements

Page Layout
Ayanna Lacey

Contents at a Glance

Table of Contents

Part II SQL Server Tools and Utilities

Part IV Transact-SQL

About the Lead Authors

Ray Rankins is currently owner and president of Gotham Consulting Services, Inc. (www.gothamconsulting.com) near Saratoga Springs, New York. Ray has been working with Sybase and Microsoft SQL Server for more than 15 years as a database administrator, database designer, project manager, application developer, consultant, courseware developer, and instructor. He has worked in a variety of industries including financial, manufacturing, health care, retail, insurance, communications, public utilities, and government. His expertise is in database performance and tuning, query analysis, advanced SQL programming and stored procedure development, and database application design and development. Ray's presentations on these topics at user group conferences have been very well received. Ray is coauthor of *Sybase SQL Server 11 Unleashed, Sybase SQL Server 11 DBA Survival Guide, Second Edition*, and *Microsoft SQL Server 6.5 Unleashed* (all editions), all published by Sams Publishing, and he has written articles for publication in database-related periodicals. As an instructor, Ray regularly teaches classes on SQL, advanced SQL programming and optimization, database design, database administration, and database performance and tuning. Ray's ability to bring his real-world experience into the classroom consistently brings very high marks from students in his classes for both his instructional skills and courseware. He can be reached at rrankins@gothamconsulting.com.

Paul Bertucci is a senior director with Collaborative Consulting, LLC of Boston, Massachusetts (www.collaborative.ws). He leads the San Francisco, California database and performance engineering practices. He was formerly the founder of Database Architechs (www.dbarchitechs.com) and he has more than 20 years of experience doing database design, data architecture, data replication, performance and tuning, distributed data systems, data integration, and systems integration for numerous Fortune 500 companies including Intel, 3COM, Apple, Toshiba, Lockheed, Wells Fargo, Safeway, Texaco, Charles Schwab, Cisco Systems, Sybase, Webgain, Breg, Channell, and i2 Technologies. He has authored numerous articles, standards, and courses such as Sybase's "Performance and Tuning" course and "Physical Database Design" course. Paul is a frequent conference speaker and regularly teaches database design, performance and tuning, data modeling, OLAP, Supply Chain Management, and SQL courses. He has worked heavily with MS SQL Server, Sybase, DB2, and Oracle, and has architected several commercially available tools in the database, data modeling, performance and tuning, and data integration arena. Paul serves part-time as chief technical advisor for a data integration server software company as well as an advisory board member of a software services company in Silicon Valley. Paul received his formal education in computer science from UC Berkeley. He lives in northern California with his wife, Vilay, and five children, Donny, Juliana, Paul Jr., Marissa, and Nina. Paul can still be reached at pbertucci@dbarchitechs.com or also at pbertucci@collaborative.ws.

Paul Jensen is an MCDBA, MCT, MCSE, and OCP (Oracle Certified Professional) who has been involved with database and system administration for almost 15 years. His experience has made him a popular trainer, and the past few years have seen him bouncing around North America and Europe in his role as an MCT, bringing new SQL Server converts into the fold. Paul lives in Ottawa, Canada, and can be contacted through his Web site at www.infojen.com.

About the Contributing Authors

Bennett McEwan is president of Parry Five Consulting, LLC, in northern Virginia. Ben consults on SQL Server projects in the Washington, DC area. His top skills are in SQL Server replication, performance tuning, high availability database design, and data warehouse architecture. He is always on the lookout for challenging projects. Contact him at ben@parryfive.com.

Chris Gallelli is a database administrator working for Alltel Corporation in Latham, New York. Chris has more than seven years of experience with SQL Server and more than 15 years of computing experience. His experience is varied and includes work as both a Visual Basic developer and a DBA. He has a Bachelors degree in electrical engineering and a Masters degree in business administration from Union College. Chris currently lives near Albany, New York with his lovely wife Laura and two daughters Rachael and Kayla.

Alex T. Silverstein is a client/server developer for Alltel Information Services in New York's capital region. He specializes in thin-client enterprise software design and programming. His expertise is in Microsoft-powered Internet solutions based on SQL Server 2000 and Internet Information Server (IIS), Extensible Markup Language (XML) and Extensible Stylesheet Language for Transformations (XSLT), Active Server Pages (ASP), Dynamic HTML (DHTML), and scripting languages. He is a graduate of Rutgers University. Alex can be contacted at alexsilverstein@hotmail.com.

About the Technical Editors

Chris Thibodeaux, MCSE+I, MCDBA, is currently owner and principal consultant of Empowering Solutions, Inc. in Orange County, California. Chris has been in the IT industry for 10 years and has vast experience as a DBA, programmer, systems architect, and management consultant. He specializes in SQL Server architecture and development, Windows networking, network security, and strategic process/operational consulting. His SQL Server experience includes traditional back office databases, OLAP databases, and Web-driven databases, as well as Legacy database interaction. Chris has been a technical editor on numerous Sams Publishing publications. He can be reached at chris@empowering-solutions.com.

J. Boyd Nolan is a senior software developer working for PentaSafe Security Technologies, Inc. in Houston, Texas. Boyd has been in the computing industry for more than 15 years doing various things including system/network administration, database administration, and general development work. He has experience developing largescale n-tier and Web applications for business and engineering uses. He holds Bachelors and Masters degrees in mechanical engineering from the University of Oklahoma (Boomer Sooner!). Boyd currently lives in Norman, Oklahoma with the two loves of his life, his wife Lisa and son Justin.

Dedication

I would like to dedicate this book to my wife, Elizabeth, and my son, Jason, for their continued support and understanding during the long hours spent putting these books together.
—Ray Rankins

I would like to dedicate this book to my loving wife, Vilay. Her incredible support of any effort I pursue is flawless.
—Paul Bertucci

This book is dedicated to my wife. Mary-Lee, your tireless support and understanding made this work possible.
—Paul Jensen

Acknowledgments

I would first like to thank Kim Spilker at Sams Publishing for spearheading this second edition of *SQL Server 2000 Unleashed*, giving us the opportunity to revisit and improve upon our first efforts. Thanks also to all the other authors and editors involved in this project for their efforts in helping to turn out a quality publication.

I'd also like to thank my in-laws, John and Loretta Czachor, for helping shuttle my son around to the skate park and other activities while I was trying to meet my publishing deadlines. I extend my deepest appreciation to my parents, Peg Pinkham and Ernest Rankins, for all of their support and guidance through the years.

Most of all, I wish to thank Elizabeth and Jason for their patience and understanding during the long days and late nights as I was squirreled away in my office trying to get this book done. Thanks, too, to my budding graphic designer, Jason, for his help creating some of the figures used in this book.
—Ray Rankins

I would like to thank my family for allowing me to encroach on many months of what should have been my family's "quality time." Additional thanks must also go to Intel Corporation and 4 Points Technologies for hardware and technical assistance with Windows 2000 Advanced Server and Clustering and to Adam Greifer for a bit of BCP and DTS material. Breg Corporation helped out on a few complex performance issues and

thanks to Jason Lefebvre for help with some ADO.NET details. He and I coauthored *Sams Teach Yourself ADO.NET in 24 Hours*. Many good suggestions and comments came from the technical and copy editors at Sams Publishing, along with the other primary authors of this book, yielding an outstanding effort. I appreciate Sams Publishing for allowing us to write the way we wanted to on the subjects that we live and breathe every day of our working life, and not forcing us to pour information into a cookie cutter manuscript.
—Paul Bertucci

While writing may seem a solitary pursuit, it as actually very much a collaborative effort, and as such, I extend my thanks and appreciation to my coauthors, editors, and the staff at Sams for their support throughout this project.
—Paul Jensen

Introduction

by Ray Rankins

Well, it's been nearly a year now since I wrote the introduction to the first edition of this book. There haven't been any major changes to SQL Server 2000 in the last year, but the release of Service Pack 2 and new features like Notification Services, the .NET Framework, ADO.NET, improved XML and Web integration, and the soon to be released 64-bit version of SQL Server 2000 further solidifies its position in the marketplace as a robust enterprise-wide database system.

Many of us involved with this book began working with SQL Server when it was little more than just a database management system and a couple of basic (very basic!) query and administrative tools. Many of us cut our teeth on SQL Server doing everything through the isql command-line utility. However, with all of the enhancements and additional features that have been added to SQL Server over the years, SQL Server 2000 has become more than just a database management system.

The intended goal of the first edition of this book was for it to be the ultimate resource on SQL Server, providing comprehensive, in-depth, all-inclusive coverage of all the features of SQL Server 2000. Unfortunately, it was realized early on that this cannot be accomplished in a single book. Features like Data Transformation Services (DTS), Replication, and Analysis Services each provide enough material for a complete book. With this in mind, the goal of this book is to focus on the core database product and the day-to-day administrative and management aspects of SQL Server 2000, along with more extensive coverage of the new features of the SQL Server 2000 database engine. As for the additional features of SQL Server, such as DTS, Analysis Services, full-text search, and English Query, we have included the necessary information, along with tips and guidelines, to give you a solid understanding of these features, so you can begin working with and developing applications for these features.

In this second edition of *SQL Server 2000 Unleashed,* we've continued the approach of the first edition while adding coverage of the new features and enhancements for SQL Server. We also took the opportunity to expand coverage of some of the topics from the first edition, as in the chapters on Query Analyzer and SQL Profiler, and we revisited our material to ensure that we succeeded in meeting our goals for this book. The chapters have also been reorganized to provide better flow and more logical organization of the material.

One of the other main goals of this book is for it to be more than just a syntax reference that simply parrots the material contained in SQL Server Books Online. SQL Server Books Online is a very useful resource and provides a handy, searchable syntax reference that really cannot be beat. This book picks up where Books Online leaves off. In addition to providing the syntax, we've also provided valuable insight, tips, guidelines, and useful examples derived from our many years of experience working with SQL Server.

It is our hope that we have succeeded in meeting these goals and this book becomes an essential reference for anyone working with SQL Server 2000.

Who Is This Book's Intended Audience?

This *Unleashed* book is intended for an intermediate-to-advanced level of user, for both SQL Server administrators and developers who want to understand the SQL Server product more completely to be able to write better Transact-SQL code and applications. If you are responsible for analysis, design, implementation, support, administration, or troubleshooting of SQL Server 2000, this book will provide an excellent source of experiential information. You can think of this as a book of "applied technology." The emphasis is on the more complex aspects of the product, including using the new tools, coding Transact-SQL, server administration, query analysis and optimization, data warehousing, management of very large databases, and performance tuning.

This book is also intended to provide more of a behind-the-scenes look into SQL Server, showing you what goes on behind the various wizards and GUI-based tools so you can learn what the underlying SQL commands are. Although the GUI tools can make the average day-to-day operations much simpler, every database administrator should learn the underlying commands to the tools and wizards to fully unlock the power and capabilities of SQL Server. Besides, you never know when you'll have to manage the server with only a query window available.

The Layout of This Book

The book is divided into the following six parts:

- Part I, "Welcome to Microsoft SQL Server"—This section is intended to introduce you to the Microsoft SQL Server environment and the various editions and capabilities of SQL Server that are available in the various Windows environments. In addition, it provides an overview and introduction to the features to be found in SQL Server 2000, many of which are covered in more detail throughout the book.
- Part II, "SQL Server Tools and Utilities"—The tools and tasks provided with SQL Server 2000 to administer and manage your SQL Server environments are covered in this section. Coverage is provided on the various management tools you will use on a daily basis, such as SQL Enterprise Manager and Query Analyzer, along with chapters on the various optimization and analysis tools, such as SQL Profiler and the new

SQL Debugger available in Query Analyzer. If you are not familiar with these tools, you will want to read these chapters first as these tools are often used and referenced throughout many of the subsequent chapters in the book.

- Part III, "SQL Server Administration"— This section begins with coverage on the installation of SQL Server and the client component, and then goes on to discuss other administrative activities such as the creation and management of databases and the various database objects, security and user management, replication, database backups and maintenance, and remote and linked server management. A chapter on administering very large databases provides some expert advice, as well as a chapter on SQL Server clustering. Data Transformation Services (DTS), the BCP utility, and SQL Server Agent are also discussed in this section.
- Part IV, "Transact-SQL"—This part includes a comprehensive overview of all the Transact-SQL (T-SQL) statements. In addition to providing the syntax for the T-SQL components, it also provides expert tips and advice on optimizing the use of the various T-SQL commands along with extended coverage of the new Transact-SQL features available in SQL Server 2000. A chapter on transaction management provides information on how transactions are logged and guidelines on the correct use and management of transactions in client applications, as well as troubleshooting their use in SQL Server. A full chapter introduces you to the creation and use of user-defined functions, while other chapters provide useful tips and techniques for creating views, stored procedures, and triggers.
- Part V, "SQL Server Internals and Performance Tuning"—This section provides information to help you get the best performance out of SQL Server. It begins with a discussion on the internal architecture and storage structures of SQL Server to help you understand what goes on under the covers when you modify and query your data. It then builds on that with chapters on indexes, query optimization and analysis, database design and performance, and configuring and tuning SQL Server.
- Part VI, "Additional SQL Server Features"—This part provides detailed information on the other components and add-ons of SQL Server that further enhance and extend its capabilities. Included are chapters on using XML in SQL Server 2000, full-text search services, English Query, Analysis Services, and Microsoft Transaction Server (MTS). Additionally, chapters are provided that discuss the recently released Notification Services and the .NET Framework and ADO.NET.

Conventions Used in This Book

Names of commands and stored procedures are presented in a special `monospaced` computer typeface. We have tried to be consistent in our use of uppercase and lowercase for keywords and object names. However, because the default installation of SQL Server doesn't make a distinction between upper- and lowercase for SQL keywords or object names and data, you might find some of the examples presented in either upper- or lowercase.

Code and output examples are presented separately from regular paragraphs and also are in a monospaced computer typeface. Following is an example:

```
select id, name, audflags
from sysobjects
where type != "S"

id          name                           audflags
----------- ------------------------------ -----------
144003544   marketing_table                130
```

When syntax is provided for a command, we have attempted to follow these conventions:

Key	Definition
`command`	These are command names, options, and other keywords.
`placeholder`	Monospaced italic indicates values you provide.
`{}`	You must choose at least one of the enclosed options.
`[]`	The enclosed value/keyword is optional.
`()`	Parentheses are part of the command.
`¦`	You can select only one of the options listed.
`,`	You can select any of the options listed.
`[...]`	The previous option can be repeated.

Consider the following example:

```
grant {all ¦ permission_list} on object [(column_list)]
       to {public ¦ user_or_group_name [, [...]]}
```

In this case, the *`object`* value is required, but the *`column_list`* is optional. Note also that items shown in plain computer type, such as `grant`, `public`, or `all`, should be entered literally as shown. Placeholders are presented in italic, such as *`permission_list`* and *`user_or_group_name`*. A placeholder is a generic term for which you must supply a specific value or values. The ellipsis in the square brackets following *`user_or_group_name`* indicates that multiple user or group names can be specified, separated by commas. You can specify either the keyword `public` or one or more user or group names, but not both.

Most of the examples presented in this book are taken from either the pubs database or the Northwind database, and we have attempted to indicate which database the examples are using in the text. However, for many of the examples presented in Part V, "SQL Server Internals and Performance Tuning," larger tables than what is available in the pubs and Northwind database were needed to demonstrate many of the concepts with more meaningful examples. For many of the chapters in this section, the examples come from the bigpubs2000 database. This database has the same structure as the pubs database, but it contains significantly more data. A copy of the database is on the CD that accompanies this book.

To install the bigpubs2000 database on your system so you can try out the various examples, do the following:

1. Copy the bigpubs2000.mdf file from the CD into the SQL Server data folder where you want it to reside.

2. Ensure that the `Read-Only` property of the bigpubs2000.mdf file is not enabled. After the file has been copied to the destination folder, right-click the file in Windows Explorer and bring up the Properties dialog. Click the Read-Only check box to remove the checkmark. Click OK to save the changes to the file attributes.

3. Attach the bigpubs2000 database using a command similar to the following. (Note: You might need to edit the path to match the location where you copied the bigpubs2000.mdf file.)

```
sp_attach_single_file_db bigpubs2000,
          N'c:\Program Files\Microsoft SQL Server\MSSQL\Data\bigpubs2000.mdf'
```

Alternatively, you can attach the database using Enterprise Manager. Right-click the database folder, select All Tasks, and choose Attach Database. In the dialog presented, locate the bigpubs2000.mdf file and click OK. (Note: It may warn you that the filename for the log file is incorrect and ask if you want to continue and create a new log file. Click Yes.)

Good Luck!

If you have purchased this book, you are on your way to getting the most from SQL Server 2000. You have already chosen a fine platform for building database applications, one that can provide outstanding performance and rock-solid reliability at a reasonable cost. You now have the information you need to make the best of it.

Many of us who worked on this book have been using SQL Server for more than a decade. Writing about a new version challenged us to reassess many of our preconceived notions about SQL Server and the way that it worked. It was an interesting and enjoyable process, and we learned a lot. We hope you get as much enjoyment and knowledge from reading this book as we have from writing it.

PART I

Welcome to Microsoft SQL Server

CHAPTER 1

The Microsoft SQL Server Environment

by Bennett McEwan and Ray Rankins

IN THIS CHAPTER

- Overview of Client/Server
- SQL Server 2000 Components and Features

What is SQL Server 2000, exactly? When you first install the product, what are all the pieces you get, what do they do, and which of them do you need?

The SQL Server 2000 is a client/server database product that is actually made up of a number of different client and server programs that, together, make up the entire product, which provides a broad range of features and capabilities. This first chapter provides a brief overview of the client/server model and then describes each of the pieces that make up the SQL Server 2000 product and what role each component plays. All of the topics discussed in this chapter are dealt with in more detail in subsequent chapters in this book.

Overview of Client/Server

Client/server is a style of computing where a client process requests services from a server process. In the simplest terms, a *server* is a program that makes available any kind of service, such as e-mail, files, ftp, Web, or data in the form of a database server. A **client** is an application that connects to a server to make use of the service it provides.

Clients and servers have different jobs. Some examples of server responsibilities are providing backups to ensure data is safe, security against unwanted intrusion, timely access to the service, and maintenance of reliable storage facilities to ensure high availability of the service.

Some examples of client responsibilities are providing a pleasing user interface, making use of the limited server resources in a responsible and resource-economical way, and, of course, fulfilling the goals of the application.

Client applications include mail clients, such as Eudora and Microsoft Outlook. These applications connect to a mail server to retrieve e-mail messages. Internet Explorer is a client that connects to a Web server.

SQL Server client applications that ship with the product include the Query Analyzer, SQL Server Enterprise Manager, Profiler, SQL Agent, and even Data Transformation Services. Each of these applications connects to the database engine and uses the engine's services in a different way. To use the service, each of these clients sends a **query** to the server. The server processes the query and sends back **results.**

Glossary of Client/Server Terminology

Client: An application that connects to a server to make use of the service it provides.

Server: An application that makes available any kind of service for use by a client application.

Query: The term for the communication flowing from a client application to the SQL Server database engine.

Results: The data that returns from the database engine to the client in response to a *query*.

Although it is not a requirement of the client/server model, in almost every case, a server allows many clients to connect to it at once. A client might or might not have the ability to connect to multiple servers at once.

Figure 1.1 shows a representation of a typical client/server database environment.

Before client/server, two other important architectures ruled the world: mainframe, or host-based computing, and PC/LAN-based computing. It's informative to look back at where this all started.

Mainframe or Host-Based Computing

The original computing architecture was the **mainframe** or **host-based** architecture. In this environment, virtually all the processing power exists on a central host machine. The business logic tier and the data access tier reside centrally on the host. The user of the application interfaces with the data through a **dumb** terminal. The terminal is referred to as dumb simply because it has no inherent processing power of its own. The only processing provided by the terminal is sending keystrokes to the host and displaying data to the user. Although data is displayed on the dumb terminal, the host computer makes all the decisions about how the data is to be presented.

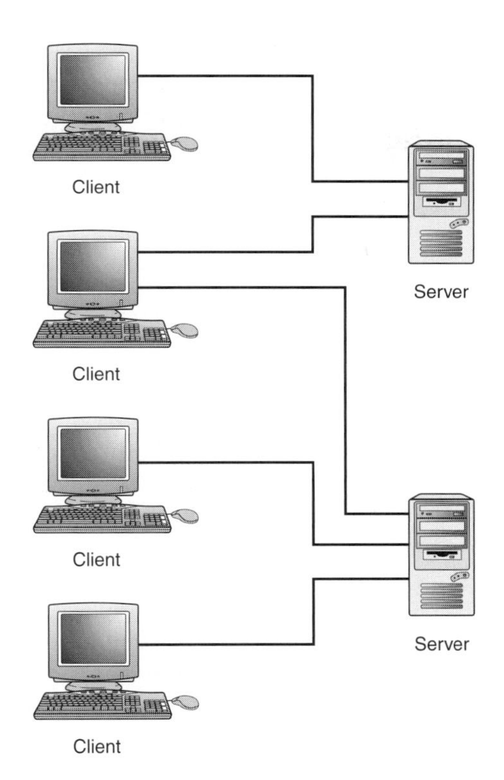

FIGURE 1.1 Typical client/server architecture.

Because these host machines were extremely expensive and maintenance costs were equally high, it made sense for an organization to centralize as much of its data and application logic as possible. Over time, organizations found that this centralized environment caused severe backlogs both in application processing and development.

In this environment, applications and data are centralized and exist solely on the host computer. Communications are virtually eliminated as a bottleneck, even when the host and the terminal are separated by hundreds of miles and only share a relatively slow asynchronous connection. Application development and maintenance is also centralized, providing an important measure of control and security. Administration of the system (backup, data maintenance) is handled centrally as well.

This highly centralized approach of data processing led to a number of issues. One of the problems was availability. If the mainframe was down, all processing ceased. Another problem was cost. The combined effect of high purchase prices and exorbitant maintenance fees was that processing cycles centralized on the host became far more expensive than the processing cycles on a PC. Another issue that arose was that end users began desiring instant access to data and information. In the mainframe environment, requesting a new report or a change to an existing report often required submission of a request to have a job written to run the report. Then the report needed to be scheduled to run and eventually the user would receive the report. This type of environment did not lend itself well to end users running ad hoc queries and reports against their data, especially to test a number of various "what if" scenarios.

End users wanted, and needed, more personal control over their data. There was also a need to offload some of the mainframe data and processing in order to reduce costs.

The first real answer to this problem was the PC.

PC/LAN-Based Computing

As the PC became affordable, it made sense to use the inherent processing power of the PC to offload data and work from the host. Many departmental users began using their PCs to perform various operations that used to rely on the host. The low cost and high availability of PC computing were extremely attractive to people who were forced to wait in line for the privilege to pay high prices for mainframe processing. The real nightmare of host processing has always been the tremendous backlog of applications waiting to be developed and maintained. PC users found that they could build their own applications (admittedly amateur, but often more usable than the enterprise applications) faster than they could fill out the forms requesting apps from the central MIS group.

> **NOTE**
>
> A popular anecdote recounts the story of a mainframe user who switched to a PC to do all his data analysis and number crunching, even though his data sets were typically large and fairly complex. His reasoning was that even though it took his PC seven minutes to do what the mainframe could do in one-half second, he didn't have to wait a week just to run the job on the mainframe.

The first widely used business applications for the PC were spreadsheet applications that could perform much of the number crunching and calculations that used to be performed on the host. Eventually, file system databases such as dBASE and FoxPro became prevalent. Users were able to create their own database-driven applications.

In this architecture, the presentation logic and the business logic typically reside on the local PC. The data could reside on the local PC as well, but often resides on another machine within the local area network, perhaps a network file server, so that the information can be shared among multiple users.

The file system databases work well for individual applications and local PC use. They are not, however, ideally suited for multiuser environments where many users need access to the same information. Using these file system databases over a LAN for shared data access can cause increasing stress on network traffic and do not scale well to the large enterprise-type applications that are needed to run a business.

Client/Server Evolves

The advent of the multiuser relational database management system (RDBMS) was really the key technology that drove the client/server computing architecture. The RDBMS served as a central storage location for an organization's data. The RDBMS was designed to handle multiuser access to a shared set of data. All the locking and connection management is handled by the RDBMS along with security. Structured Query Language (SQL) was created to be a universal programming language to request specific data from an RDBMS.

The client/server architecture was really a marriage of the best features of both the host-based environment and the PC LAN environment. This architecture utilizes the power of the PC to perform the presentation of data along with the complicated business processing that adds value to that data. The RDBMS provides a centralized storage area for data and provides the services to manage shared, concurrent access to that data. The client/server architecture can take many forms, depending on how you choose to separate the presentation, business logic, and data tiers. The following sections examine the predominant client/server architectures in more detail.

Traditional Client/Server

When you hear the term client/server, the inclination is to think of only the two sides of the transaction, the client and the server. Most of us are familiar with this traditional two-tiered view of client/server, which involves a client application running on a workstation and a server application running on a server.

In a typical two-tier client/server system, the client application connects directly to a server application, such as SQL Server. This usually means that each client workstation must be loaded with vendor-specific libraries and drivers to establish connections with the server. Client applications are also responsible for logging onto the server and maintaining connections, along with handling error messages and the like returned from the server.

The business logic layer can reside on the client, the server, or both in a two-tier system.

Three-Tier and n-Tier Client/Server

The client/server model does allow for more than just these two tiers. A **middle tier** is a program that sits between the client and server and provides beneficial services to both the client and server tiers. (One such example of a beneficial service is described in the following Note.) Applications that make use of a middle tier are called **three tier** or **n-tier** applications. When many middle tiers exist between the endpoints, each serving different functions, it is called an **n-tier model**.

The primary goal of the n-tier architecture is to separate the business logic from both the presentation and data access layers into a set of reusable objects, sometimes called business objects. Business objects are like stored procedures in that they allow you to centralize your business logic and keep it separate from your client applications.

This type of architecture has its advantages. Once an n-tier architecture is put in place, applications can be much easier to develop and maintain. You can bring new applications online relatively easily by reusing existing business objects. Database changes and business logic changes can be made without redistributing client applications. Programmers can concentrate on developing business rules without having to worry about user interface issues.

NOTE

An example of the advantages of the three-tiered architecture was demonstrated by a simple three-tier application that was used to solve a multiple-server problem for a client that had 15 database servers with identical schemas. Each database contained customer information for a different subset of customer. Because of the size of the number of customers, one server simply couldn't handle the load, so each server contained approximately one-fifteenth of the customer base.

When a new customer was added, the application had no way to know whether the customer name was already in the database without connecting to each of the 15 databases in turn and looking for it. This caused a lot of overhead.

The middle tier was designed to hold all the names and ID numbers—but not the address, e-mail, telephone number, or other extended information—of the customers, so that the client application could search against the middle tier and know instantly whether the customer was a duplicate.

The client connected to the middle tier and sent the customer information. The middle tier was responsible for maintaining a complete cache of all the customer names in the databases, plus all the names that had been added in the past 30 minutes. When a name was found as a duplicate, it was rejected; otherwise, the middle tier accessed the database to add the new customer information.

In this way, the middle tier acted as a server for the client application, providing a "duplicate check" service. It also acted as a client for the server application, inserting new customers as they flowed in from the front end.

While the n-tier architecture has a number of advantages, implementing a successful n-tier architecture requires a complex infrastructure to handle low-level services such as connection pooling, thread maintenance, and transaction monitoring. Some products, however, such as Microsoft Transaction Server (MTS) and .NET Framework, handle many of these complex infrastructure issues and reduce the complexity of implementing an n-tier solution.

SQL Server 2000 Components and Features

SQL Server 2000 is more than just the database engine. While the database engine is at the core of the product, and obviously the most important component, there are a number of additional applications bundled with the database engine, such as the tools and utilities used to manage the SQL Server environment, as well as other components and server applications that extend the capabilities and features of SQL Server 2000. This section provides an overview of the components and features that are included with the SQL Server 2000 product. Each of these components is subsequently explored in greater detail in the rest of this book.

SQL Server Database Engine

SQL Server's database engine is the primary server application in the SQL Server package. Following are the main responsibilities of the database engine:

- Provide reliable storage for data sent to the engine
- Provide a means to rapidly access this data
- Provide consistent access to the data
- Control access to the data through security
- Enforce data-integrity rules to ensure the data is accurate and consistent

Each of these points will be examined in detail later in the book. I will touch on each of these points to show how Microsoft SQL Server fulfills these core responsibilities.

Reliable Storage

Reliable storage starts at the hardware level. This isn't the responsibility of the database engine, but it's a necessary part of a well-built database. Although you can put an entire SQL database on an old IDE drive (or even burn a read-only copy on a CD), it is preferrable to maintain the data on RAID arrays. The most common RAID arrays allow hardware failures at the disk level without losing data.

To learn more about RAID arrays and database hardware planning, check out Chapter 39, "Database Design and Performance."

Using whatever hardware you have decided to make available, the database engine handles all the data structures necessary to ensure reliable storage of your data. Rows of data are stored in **pages**, each 8KB in size. Eight pages make up an **extent**, and the database engine tracks which extents are allocated to which tables and indexes.

For an in-depth discussion of data structures and how they factor into performance and reliability, see Chapter 33, "SQL Server Internals."

NOTE

Page: An 8KB chunk of a data file, the smallest unit of storage available in the database.

Extent: A collection of eight 8KB pages.

Another key feature the engine provides to ensure reliable storage is the transaction log. The transaction log makes a record of every change that is made to the database for rollback and recovery purposes. See Chapter 31, "Transaction Management and the Transaction Log."

NOTE

It is not strictly true that the transaction log records *all* changes to the database—some exceptions exist. Binary Large Objects—data of type `image` and `text`—can be excepted from logging, and inserts generated by bulk table loads can be non-logged to get the fastest possible performance.

Rapidly Accessing Data

SQL Server provides rapid access to data by utilizing indexes and storing frequently accessed data in memory.

SQL Server allows the creation of clustered and nonclustered indexes, which speed access to data by using the index pointers to find data rows rather than having to scan all the data in the table each time. See Chapter 34, "Indexes and Performance," for an in-depth discussion of indexes and how they are used to improve query performance.

Memory is allocated by SQL Server database to be used as a data cache to speed access to data by reducing the number of required physical I/Os to the disks. When pages are requested from the database, the server checks to see if they are already in the cache. If not, it reads them off the disk and inserts them into the data cache. With sufficient memory, the next time the data needs to be accessed, it should still be in cache, avoiding the need to access the disk drive(s). A separate process runs continuously and attempts to keep frequently accessed information in memory by pushing old pages that haven't been accessed recently out of the cache to make room for newly accessed pages. If the pages contain modifications, they are written to disk first before being removed from cache, otherwise the old pages are simply discarded.

NOTE

With sufficient memory, the entire database can fit completely into memory.

More information on the data cache and how it is managed is available in Chapter 33.

Providing Consistent Access to Data

Getting to your data quickly doesn't mean much if the information you receive is inaccurate. SQL Server follows a set of rules to ensure that the data you receive back from queries is consistent.

The general idea with consistent access is to allow only one client at a time to change the data, and to prevent others from reading data from the database while it is undergoing changes.

Transactional consistency has several levels of conformance, each of which provides a tradeoff between accuracy of the data and concurrency. These levels of concurrency are examined in more detail in Chapter 38, "Locking and Performance." In particular, check out the sections on "SQL Server Lock Types" and "Transaction Isolation Levels in SQL Server."

Controlling Access

The database server provides security at multiple levels. Security is enforced at the server level, the database level, and at the database object level. Access to the server is verified by either a username and password, or through integrated network security. Integrated security uses the client's network login credentials to establish identity.

SQL Server security is examined in more detail in Chapter 15, "Security and User Administration."

Enforcing Data Integrity Rules

Some databases have to serve the needs of more than a single application. A corporate database that contains valuable information might have a dozen different departments wanting to access portions of the database for different needs.

In this kind of environment, it is impractical to expect the developers of each application to agree on an identical set of standards for maintaining data integrity. For example, one department might allow phone numbers to have extensions, whereas another department does not need that capability. One department might find it critical to maintain a relationship between a customer record and a salesman record, whereas another might care only about the customer information.

The best way to keep everybody sane in this environment—and to ensure that the data stays consistent and usable by everyone—is to enforce a set of rules at the database level. This is accomplished through the database objects, including rules, defaults, triggers, stored procedures, and data-integrity constraints. See Chapter 14, "Implementing Data Integrity," for details.

SQL Server Enterprise Manager

The Enterprise Manager is the central console from which most SQL Server database-management tasks can be coordinated. SQL Enterprise Manager (hereafter referred to as SQL-EM) provides a single interface from which all servers in a company can be managed.

The SQL-EM is examined in more detail in Chapter 4, "SQL Server Enterprise Manager."

Figure 1.2 shows Enterprise Manager being used for some everyday administration tasks.

Figure 1.2 shows a list of available servers in the leftmost pane. The servers are organized into two groups: Development and Production. A connection to Palpatine has been opened, and the right pane shows the scheduled jobs on Palpatine.

The following lists some of the tasks that can be performed with SQL-EM. Most of these are discussed in detail later in the book:

- Completely manage many servers in a convenient interface
- Set server options and configuration values, such as the amount of memory and processors to use, the default language, and the default location of the data and log files

- Manage logins, database users, and database roles
- Schedule automated jobs through the SQL Agent
- Back up and restore databases and develop maintenance plans
- Create new databases
- Browse table contents
- Manage database objects, such as tables, indexes, and stored procedures
- Configure and manage replication
- Import and export data
- Transfer data between servers, SQL Server, and otherwise
- Monitor SQL Server activity and error logs
- Provide a convenient centralized front end to other applications, such as the Data Transformation Services designer, Query Analyzer, Full Text Search Services, and SQL Mail

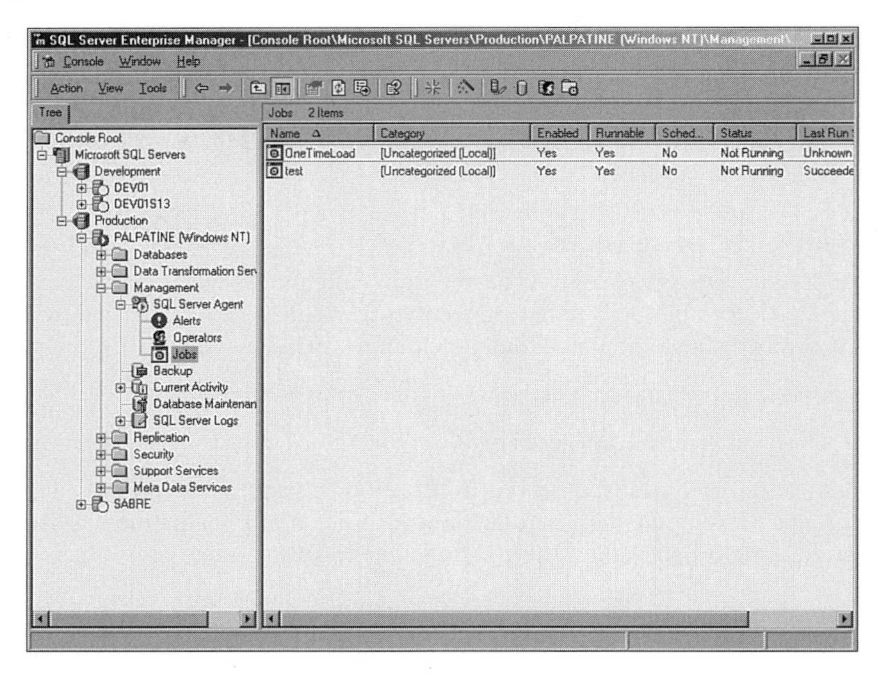

FIGURE 1.2 Enterprise Manager showing a list of scheduled jobs on the Palpatine server.

NOTE

SQL Enterprise Manager interacts with SQL Server using standard Transact-SQL commands. For example, when you create a new database through the SQL-EM interface, behind the scenes it generates a `CREATE DATABASE` SQL command. Whatever you can do through SQL-EM, you can do with the Query Analyzer or even the command line ISQL or OSQL programs.

If you're curious how EM is accomplishing something, you can run SQL Profiler to trap the commands that SQL-EM is sending to the server. I've used this technique to discover some interesting internals information. You can also use this tactic to capture SQL scripts, and then repeat tasks using the script instead of a few dozen interface clicks.

SQL Service Manager

The Service Manager is a small applet that allows easy control of several key SQL services:

- SQL Server, the database engine
- SQL Agent, a job scheduler
- SQL Search, a full-text search engine
- Distributed Transaction Coordinator
- OLAP Server, a separate service used for warehousing

The Service Manager can be used to control or monitor these services on any machine on the network. It will poll each service every few seconds (configurable through Options) to determine its state. A check box also exists for each service, which allows automatic starting of the service when Windows starts. Most servers automatically start the SQL service on system startup, but in some maintenance situations, it's important to be able to disable this property.

All services can be stopped and started. Some can also be paused. When SQL Server is paused, it continues operating normally except that new login connections are not accepted.

SQL Server Agent

The SQL Server Agent is an integrated scheduling tool that allows convenient execution of scheduled scripts and maintenance jobs. It is required to use replication services. The agent also handles automated alerts (for example, if the database runs out of space).

The Agent is a Windows service that runs on the same machine as the SQL Server engine. The agent service can be controlled through either SQL-EM, the SQL Service Manager, or the ordinary Windows service manager. The Agent is configured through SQL-EM by drilling down through the SQL Server instance | Management | SQL Server Agent.

SQL jobs can be complex. Branching is possible depending on the outcome of a query or job return status.

The Agent also handles alerting. The alert system can watch for a particular event, and then respond to this event by paging an operator, sending an e-mail, running a predefined job, or any combination of these. In the previous example of the database running out of space, an alert could be defined to watch the free space, and when it got to less than 5 percent, the database could be expanded by 100MB and the on-call DBA could be paged.

In enterprise situations in which many SQL Server machines need to be managed together, the SQL Agent can be configured to distribute common jobs to multiple servers through the use of Multiserver Administration. This is most helpful in a wide architecture scenario, in which many SQL Server databases are performing the same tasks with the databases. Jobs are managed from a single SQL Server machine. This machine is responsible for maintaining the jobs and distributing the job scripts to each target server. The results of each job are maintained on the target servers, but can be observed through a single interface.

If you have 20 servers that all need to run the same job, you can check the completion status of that job on a single server in moments, instead of logging into each machine and checking the individual status 20 times.

The SQL Agent Event also handles forwarding. Any system events that are recorded in the Windows System Event Log can be forwarded to a single machine. This gives the busy admininstrator a single place to look for errors.

More information about how to accomplish these tasks, and other information on the Agent, is available in Chapter 18, "SQL Server Scheduling and Notification."

SQL Query Analyzer

The Query Analyzer is the easiest place to run SQL scripts. Each window in the Query Analyzer represents a connection to a database. It's possible to have connections to many different servers.

Some wonderful changes have been made to the 2000 version of Query Analyzer, most notably the addition of an object browser/template manager and an integrated stored procedure debugger.

Figure 1.3 shows the Query Analyzer with the Template Manager open on the left.

The Query Analyzer tool is discussed in Chapter 6, "SQL Server Query Analyzer and SQL Debugger," along with a discussion on using its built-in SQL Debugger. See Chapter 36, "Query Analysis," for details on using the Query Analyzer to troubleshoot long-running or complex queries.

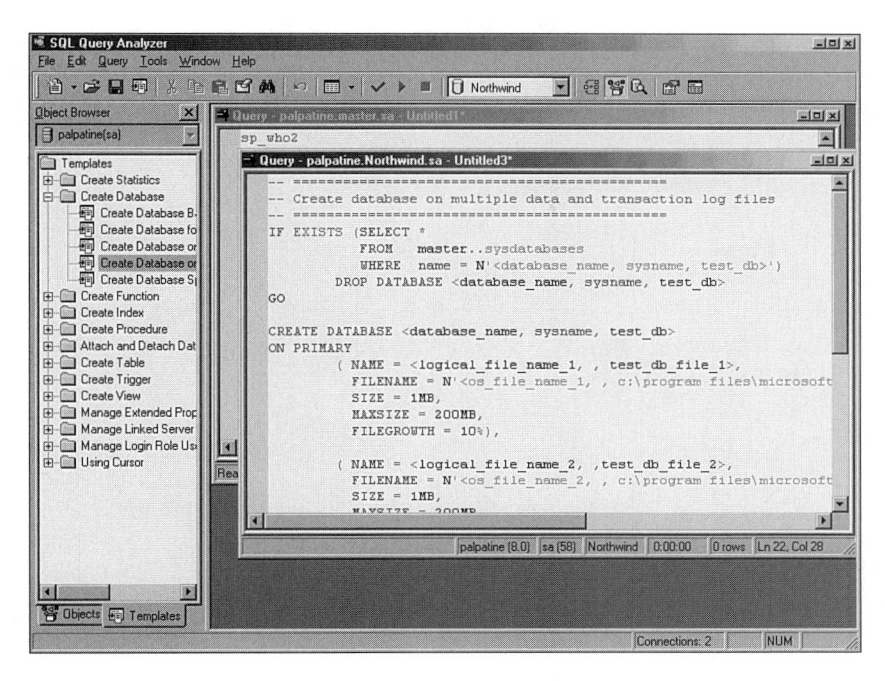

FIGURE 1.3 SQL Query Analyzer displaying the Template Manager pane on the left side, and two connections to a database server in the main window.

SQL Profiler

The SQL Profiler is a client tool that captures the queries and results flowing to and from the server. It is analogous to a network sniffer, although it does not operate on quite that low a level. The Profiler has the ability to capture and save a complete record of all the traffic passed to the server. A series of filters is useful for paring down the results when you want to drill down to a single connection or even a single query.

The SQL Profiler can be used to perform these helpful tasks:

- Capture the exact SQL statements sent to the server from an application for which source code is not available (third-party applications, for example).
- Capture all of the queries sent to SQL Server for later playback on a test server. This is extremely useful for performance testing with live query traffic.
- If your server is encountering recurring Access Violations (AVs), the profiler can be used to reconstruct what happened leading up to the AV.

- The profiler shows basic performance data about each query. When your users start hammering your server with queries that cause hundreds of table scans, the profiler can easily identify the culprits.
- For complex stored procedures, the tool can identify which portion of the procedure is causing the performance problem.
- Audit server activity in real time.

The profiler is a versatile tool; it provides functionality that is not duplicated elsewhere in the SQL Server Tools suite. More information on the Profiler is available in Chapter 7, "Using the SQL Server Profiler."

Data Transformation Services

Data Transformation Services (DTS) is a powerful tool used primarily to move data from one source to another. In the early days of client/server databases, the only way to move data from the mainframe to your shiny, new SQL Server box was to get a text file from the mainframe.

Then the fun really started. If the file was relatively uniform and straightforward, you might have been able to use a command-line BCP program to import, or bulk-copy, your data in. If not, you might have had to resort to a simple VB program to parse out each line and insert it, ever so slowly, into SQL Server.

DTS offers a simple interface, the DTS Designer, which is accessed through the SQL Enterprise Manager. DTS provides a simple means to import text files quickly, using a fast bulk insert process, and little development time. Following are some of the tasks you can do with DTS:

- Quickly import a text file into SQL Server.
- Using OLEDB or ODBC, connect to a different database (Oracle, DB2, and so forth) to use as either the source or target of the data transformations.
- Write custom scripts to cleanse/transform data to your specifications. The scripts can be written in VBScript or JScript.
- New to the 2000 version of DTS, connect to an ftp site and download files.
- Send a mail message to someone with the results of an error message or a query.
- Hook into an MS Message Queue to send or receive and process MSMQ messages.
- Read information from an ini file to drive any DTS tasks, such as the server name to which to connect, the database in which to execute specific tasks, the table name to use, or the stored procedures to call.
- Perform any of these tasks on a scheduled, recurring basis with full error control and workflow capabilities.

DTS is a wonderful tool for moving data between two places. Figure 1.4 shows a DTS Designer window inside SQL Enterprise Manager. It shows the multistep process to run a scheduled, daily import. The ini file (first step on the left) determines the name of the file to be imported and the database and table names for the destination. The truncate step empties out the table to prepare it to receive new data. If this step succeeds, the first path (colored green in the interface, though not in this screenshot) continues by running the data transformation from the text file (shown by the icon in the upper-right corner) to SQL Server (icon in the lower-left corner). If the step fails, the Log Failure step runs, which records the error and aborts the job. Finally, the GetFileDate script runs. This is a custom ActiveX script written with VBScript. It determines the date and time the file was imported, along with the date and time the file was "dropped off," and logs these details in the final step.

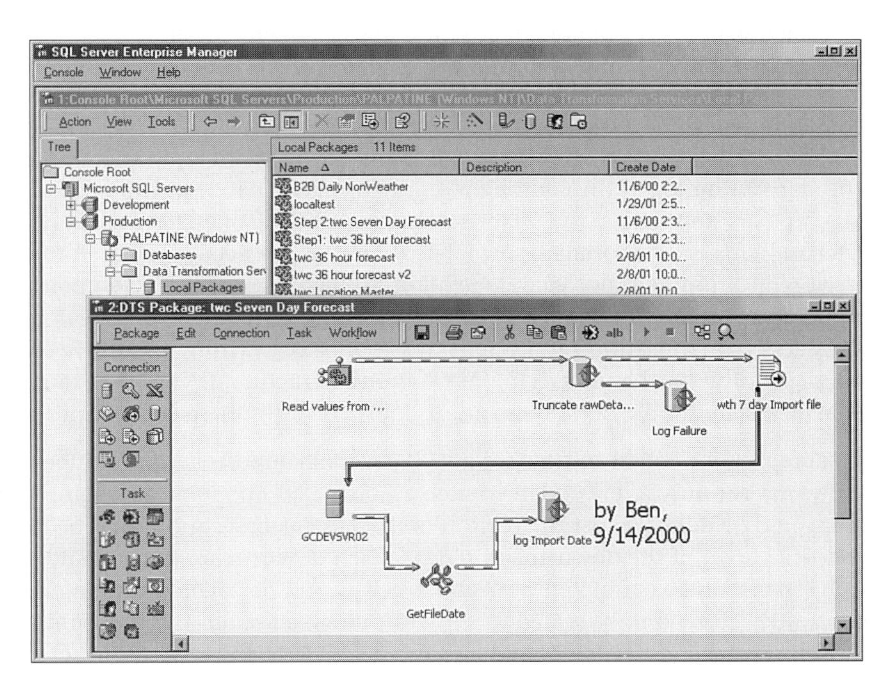

FIGURE 1.4 DTS Designer with a multistep import process example.

Replication

Replication is a server-based tool that allows data to be synchronized between two or more databases. Replication can send data from one SQL Server to another, or it can include Oracle, Access, or any other database that is accessible via ODBC or OLEDB.

SQL Server supports three kinds of replication:

- Snapshot replication
- Transactional replication
- Merge replication

The replication functionality available may be restricted depending on the version of SQL Server 2000 that you are running.

Snapshot Replication

To perform snapshot replication, the server takes a picture, or snapshot, of the data in a table at a single point in time. Usually, if this operation is scheduled, the target data is simply replaced at each update. This form of replication is appropriate for small data sets, infrequent update periods (or for a one-time replication operation), or for management simplicity.

Transactional Replication

Initially set up with a snapshot, the server maintains downstream replication targets by reading the transaction log at the source and applying each change at the targets. For every insert, update, and delete, the server sends a copy of the operation to every downstream database. This is appropriate if low latency replicas are needed. Keep in mind that transactional replication does not guarantee identical databases at any given point in time. Rather, it guarantees that each change at the source will eventually be propogated to the targets. Transactional replication can keep databases in-synch within about five seconds of each other, depending on the underlying network infrastructure. If you need to guarantee that two databases are transactionally identical, look into two-phase commit possibilities.

Transactional replication might be used for a Web site that supports a huge number of concurrent browsers, but only a few updaters, such as a large and popular messaging board. All updates would be done against the replication source database, and would be replicated in near-real-time to all of the downstream targets. Each downstream target could support several Web servers, and each incoming Web request would be balanced among the Web farm. If the system needed to be scaled to support more read requests, you could simply add more Web servers and databases, and add the database to the replication scheme.

Merge Replication

With snapshot and transactional replication, a single source of data exists from which all the replication targets are replenished. In some situations, it might be necessary or desirable to allow the replication targets to accept changes to the replicated tables, and merge these changes together at some later date.

Merge replication allows data to be modified by the subscribers and sychronized at a later time. This could be as soon as a few seconds or a day later.

Merge replication can be helpful for a sales database that is replicated from a central SQL Server box out to several dozen sales laptops. As the sales personnel make sales calls, they can add new data to the customer database or change errors in the existing data. When the salespeople return to the office, they can synchronize their laptops with the central database. Their changes are submitted, and the laptop gets refreshed with whatever new data was entered since the last sycnhronization.

NOTE

Replication will copy the data from your tables and indexed views and will even replicate changes to multiple tables caused by a stored procedure, but it will not normally re-create indexes or triggers at the target. It is common to have different indexes on replication targets rather than on the source to support different application and query requirements.

Immediate Updating

Immediate update allows a replication target to immediately modify data at the source. This is accomplished by using a trigger to run a two-phase commit transaction. Immediate updating is performance-intensive, but it does allow for updates to be initiated from anywhere in the replication architecture.

More details on replication are available in Chapter 22, "Data Replication."

Microsoft Full Text Search Services

The Microsoft Full Text Search Services provides full text searching capabilities. This is useful for searching large text fields, such as movie reviews, book descriptions, or case notes.

Full text searching works together with the SQL database engine. You specify tables or entire databases that you want to index. The full text indexes are built and maintained outside the SQL engine in special full text indexes. You can specify how often the full text indexes are updated to balance out performance issues with timeliness of the data.

NOTE

The Full Text Search Server is a separate service from the database engine. You have the option of installing it as an add-on feature when you install SQL Server. You can add it to an existing server later by running SQL Setup.

The SQL engine supports basic text searches against specific columns. For example, if you wanted to find all the rows where a text column contained the word *guru*, you might write a SQL statement like that in Listing 1.1.

LISTING 1.1 A SQL Query That Searches for the Word *Guru* in the Resume Table

```
select *
from   resume
where  description like '%guru%'
```

This will find all the rows in the resume table where the description contains the word *guru*. This method has a couple of problems, however. First, the search will be slow. Because text columns can't be indexed by the database engine, a full table scan will be done to satisfy the query. Even if the data were stored in a varchar column instead of a text column, an index wouldn't help because you're looking for *guru* anywhere in the column, not just at the beginning. (More information on avoiding situations like this one are discussed later in the book, in Chapter 34.) What if you wanted to search for the word *guru* anywhere in the table, not just in the description column? What if you were looking for a particular set of skills, such as "SQL" and "ability to work independently?"

Full text indexing addresses these problems. To perform the same search with full text indexing, you would use a query like that in Listing 1.2.

LISTING 1.2 A Full Text Query to Find the Results from Listing 1.1

```
select *
from   resume
where  contains(description, 'guru')
```

To perform the last search mentioned, use a query like that shown in Listing 1.3 in any free-text indexed column in the table:

LISTING 1.3 A More Complex Full Text Query Demonstrating Features Not Available Through the SQL Server Database Engine's Indexing Methods

```
select *
from   resume
where  contains(*, 'SQL and "ability to work independently"')
```

NOTE

Two commonly used functions are available for free text searches: `CONTAINS` and `FREETEXT`. `CONTAINS` is a better performing function and returns more exact results. `FREETEXT` will return looser results based on the meaning of the search phrase you enter. It does this by finding alternate word forms in your queries. For example, `FREETEXT(*, 'work independently')` would match `'Work Independently'`, `'Independent work preferred'`, and `'Independence in my work'`.

SQL Server Analysis Services

SQL Server Analysis Services provides essential services for using a data warehouse. These services are often referred to as OLAP, which stands for On Line Analytical Processing.

SQL Server Analysis Services connects to one or more SQL Server databases containing a data warehouse. Based on the criteria you select, data cubes are created on this data to allow powerful searches, called **data mining**. The SQL Server Analysis Services client tool assists in the addition of new data to the warehouse and allows scheduling of cube updates.

> **NOTE**
>
> SQL Server Analysis Services can be leveraged even if you do not have your data warehouse in a classical star or snowflake schema.

OLAP is commonly used to perform the following tasks:

- Perform trend analysis to predict the future. Based on how many widgets I sold last year, how many will I sell next year?
- Combine otherwise disconnected variables to gain insight into past performance. Was there any connection between widget sales and rainfall patterns? Searching for unusual connections between your data points is a typical data mining exercise.
- Perform offline summaries of commonly used data points for instant access via Web or custom interface. For example, a relational table might contain one row for every click on a Web site. OLAP can be used to summarize these clicks by hour, day, week, and month, then further categorize these by business line.

You can access OLAP services through the Analysis Services front-end application. For more in-depth analysis, make use of a SQL-like query language called Multidimensional Expressions, or MDX. MDX uses similar language to SQL, but instead of operating on tables in the from clause, it operates on data cubes.

SQL Server Analysis Services is a complex topic. For more information on MDX, data cubes, and how to use data warehousing analysis services, see Chapter 42, "Microsoft SQL Server Analysis Services."

Distributed Transaction Coordinator

With the increasing proliferation of distributed systems comes the need to access and modify data that is often in separate physical locations and in varying types of data-sources. These distributed transactions need to be treated as a single logical transaction (one "Unit of Work"). You need a way to ensure that the distributed transaction operates in the same way that a local transaction does, and that it adheres to the same ACID properties of a local transaction, across multiple servers. Microsoft provides this capability with the Distributed Transaction Coordinator.

Microsoft has implemented its distributed transaction processing capabilities using the industry standard **two-phase commit protocol**. The Distributed Transaction Coordinator Service (MS DTC) provides the means of managing distributed transactions within the SQL Server 2000 environment. Typically, each Microsoft SQL Server will have an associated distributed transaction coordinator on the same machine with it. MS DTC runs as a separate service and can be started using the SQL Sevice Manager, SQL Enterprise Manager, or it can be started via the Windows Services Control Panel.

The MS DTC allows applications to extend transactions across two or more instances of MS SQL Server and participate in transactions managed by transaction managers that comply with the X/Open DTP XA standard. The MS DTC will act as the primary coordinator for these distributed transactions. The specific job of the MS DTC is to enlist (include) and coordinate SQL Servers and remote servers (linked servers) that are part of a single distributed transaction. The MS DTC coordinates the execution of the distributed transaction at each participating datasource and makes sure the distributed transaction completes. It ensures that all updates are made permanent in all datasources (committed), or makes sure that all of the work is undone (rolled back) if it needs to be. At all times, the state of all datasources involved are kept intact.

For more information on distributed transactions and the MS DTC, see Chapter 32, "Distributed Transaction Processing."

Notification Services

SQL Server Notification Services is a platform for the development and deployment of notification applications. Notification applications send messages to users based upon subscriptions made to the notification application. Depending on how the subscriptions are configured, messages can be sent to the subscriber immediately or on a predetermined schedule. The messages sent can be personalized to reflect the preferences of the subscriber.

The Notification Services platform is a reliable, high-performance, scalable server that is built on the .NET Framework and SQL Server 2000 and runs on the Microsoft Windows Server family of operating systems. Notification Services was designed for extensibility and interoperability with a variety of existing applications.

SQL Server primarily serves as the storage location for the subscription information for Notification Services. The subscriber and delivery information is stored in a central Notification Services database, and individual subscription information is stored in application-specific databases.

For more information on the Notification Server architecture and configuring and using SQL Server Notification Services, see Chapter 45, "SQL Server Notification Services."

English Query

English Query is a framework that provides the tools to develop and deploy English Query applications, which allow end users to pose questions against your relational database in English instead of forming a query with a SQL statement.

Developing an English Query application involves creating, refining, testing, compiling, and deploying a model based on a normalized SQL database or an OLAP cube. In general, it is easiest to create English Query applications against normalized SQL databases and the resulting applications are typically more flexible and powerful than those developed against databases that are not normalized.

The English Query Model Editor runs within the Visual Studio 6.0 development environment. You can begin the creation of your English Query applications using either the SQL Project Wizard or the OLAP Project Wizard to automatically create an English Query project and model. After the basic model is created, you can refine, test, and compile it into an English Query application and then deploy it (to the Web, for example).

The basic steps for developing and deploying an English Query application are as follows:

1. Determine the questions that end users are most likely to ask. Determining the questions to be answered prior to creating a model helps you to create the appropriate entities and relationships and test your application.

2. Create a basic model using the SQL Project Wizard or OLAP Project Wizard. The wizards create a basic model by bringing in the schema of the data source (database or cube) and automatically creating entities and relationships based on the tables, columns, joins, or OLAP objects.

3. Refine the model to address any questions that cannot be answered using the basic model. This is done by adding additional entities and relationships.

4. Test and refine the model until it properly returns the answers to the questions posed.

5. Build the application and deploy it. An English Query application can be deployed as a Visual Basic or Microsoft Visual C++ application, or on a Web page running on the Microsoft Internet Information Services (IIS) as a set of Microsoft Active Server Pages (ASP).

For more detailed information on developing and deploying English Query applications, see Chapter 47, "English Query."

Summary

There is more to a successful relational database product than the database engine. The client tools and the various services and components contribute the the overall capabilities of SQL Server 2000 that sets Microsoft's database apart from its competitors. This chapter outlined the various features and components that make up the Microsoft SQL Server product and provided an overview of how those pieces can be used. More details to help you get the most from these components are contained in subsequent chapters in this book.

In the next chapter, "SQL Server 2000 Environments and Editions," you will learn about the different editions of SQL Server, and how you can choose the best version for your application.

CHAPTER 2

SQL Server 2000 Environments and Editions

by Ray Rankins

IN THIS CHAPTER

- SQL Server 2000 Environments
- SQL Server 2000 Editions
- SQL Server 2000 Licensing Models

At one time, SQL Server was a single database server product that ran on Windows NT only. Now to meet the growing needs of its customers, SQL Server is available on multiple Windows platforms and in multiple editions.

SQL Server 2000 Environments

SQL Server, in addition to being available in a number of editions, also runs on a number of Windows platforms. However, certain editions will only run on certain platforms. This section takes a look at the platforms on which SQL Server runs and the editions it supports.

Windows 98 and Windows Me

Windows 98 and Windows Me are designed primarily for the home PC user. Windows 98 is still in use on the desktop in many corporate shops as well. Windows 98 and Windows Me are intended to support mobile users who are disconnected from the network but need to run applications that require SQL Server data storage, or for users who need to run local applications that require local SQL Server data storage on the computer.

For these purposes, the Windows 98 and Windows Me platforms support the SQL Server 2000 Standard Edition and the SQL Server 2000 Desktop Engine. Although the Full Text

Search and Analysis Services are included with the Personal Edition of SQL Server, they cannot be installed on Windows 98 or Windows Me. Also, because Windows 98 and Windows Me do not support applications running as services, SQL Server and SQL Task Manager run as standard executables on Windows 98 and Windows Me rather than as services, as they do under Windows NT or Windows 2000.

The Windows 98 and Windows Me environments also support the installation of the SQL Server client tools, such as Query Analyzer, Enterprise Manager, and SQL Profiler. The connectivity components needed to connect to any SQL Server 2000 edition running on a Windows NT or Windows 2000 workstation or server can be installed on Windows 98, Windows Me, or Windows 95.

Windows NT 4.0

Windows NT is the original platform for Microsoft SQL Server versions 6.0 and later. SQL Server 2000 is still supported on all Windows NT 4.0 platforms, including Workstation, Server, and Enterprise Server. However, Windows NT 4.0 Service Pack 5 or later must be installed to run SQL Server 2000.

Windows NT 4.0 Workstation is the platform intended for the corporate desktop. It sports a Windows 95–like interface with the underlying reliability and security of Windows NT. Windows NT 4.0 Server is the server edition of Windows NT 4.0, which also sports a Windows 95-like interface as well as increased scalability. Windows NT 4.0 Server includes Internet Information Server for tighter integration with Internet and Web-based applications. The Enterprise Edition of Windows NT 4.0 Server is a more high-powered version of NT 4.0 Server, providing greater scalability (up to eight processors), clustering capability, and multinode load balancing. Windows 4.0 Server Enterprise Edition is the platform to use when deploying largescale distributed applications.

All Windows NT 4.0 platforms support the Developer, Personal, and Desktop Engine editions of SQL Server 2000. The Standard and Enterprise editions can be installed on Windows NT 4.0 Server and Windows NT 4.0 Server Enterprise Edition.

Windows 2000

Although SQL Server 2000 runs in the Windows 98, Windows Me, and Windows NT 4.0 environments, it is best suited for the Windows 2000 environments. Windows 2000 is the evolution of Windows NT 4.0 and sports a Windows 98–like user interface. Windows 2000 is available in a Professional Edition and Server Edition.

Windows 2000 Professional

Windows 2000 Professional is the version of Windows 2000 geared toward the corporate desktop and laptop. Windows 2000 provides better power management and hardware support for use on notebooks than Windows NT 4.0. Windows 2000 Professional is a more reliable and stable platform than Windows 98 or Windows Me, and even more reliable and stable than Windows NT 4.0 Workstation. Windows 2000 Professional offers high system uptime, dynamic system configuration, and resilience to application failures. It is an ideal environment for application development.

Windows 2000 Professional supports SQL Server 2000 Personal, Desktop Engine, and Developer Editions.

Windows 2000 Server Family

The Windows 2000 family supports three server platforms:

- Windows 2000 Server
- Windows 2000 Advanced Server
- Windows 2000 Datacenter Server

Windows 2000 Server

Windows 2000 Server is the next generation of Windows NT 4.0 Server, providing improved reliability and scalability. Windows 2000 Server supports up to 4GB of memory and up to four processors. Windows 2000 Server supports the installation of the Enterprise, Developer, Standard, Personal, and Desktop Engine Editions of SQL Server 2000.

Windows 2000 Server Advanced Server

Windows 2000 Advanced Server is the next generation of Windows NT 4.0 Server Enterprise Edition, providing improved reliability and scalability with support for up to 8GB of memory and eight processors. Like NT 4.0 Enterprise Edition, Windows 2000 Advanced Server provides support for clustering and multinode load balancing.

Windows 2000 Advanced Server supports the installation of all editions of SQL Server 2000, except SQL Server Windows CE Edition.

Windows 2000 Datacenter Server

The Windows 2000 Datacenter Server is a new addition to the Windows Server family. It is intended for largescale Enterprise-wide business applications. Windows 2000 Datacenter Server is like a pumped-up version of Windows 2000 Advanced Server with support for 32-way symmetric multiprocessing and up to 64GB of physical memory on systems that support it. It also provides 4-node clustering and up to 32-node network load balancing.

Windows 2000 Datacenter Server supports the installation of all editions of SQL Server 2000, except SQL Server 2000 Windows CE Edition.

Windows XP

Windows XP is the continued evolution of Windows 2000 and was designed to bridge the gap between the home and business user by being one operating system that meets the needs of both types. Windows XP is based upon the proven, reliable Windows 2000 Professional platform with improvements to the user interface for ease-of-use, home networking, and enhanced online capabilities.

Windows XP is available in two editions: Windows XP Home Edition for home use and Windows XP Professional for power users and business users. Windows XP Professional includes all the capabilities of Windows XP Home Edition plus important features to meet the demanding needs of business and power users, such as enhanced networking, security, management, and support capabilities. These features provide functionality that is critical for businesses, but might not be needed by most home users.

The advanced features of Windows XP include the following:

- Networking—Ability to belong to a domain and be centrally managed, roaming user profiles, client service for Netware, IPSecurity (IPSec)
- Corporate Security—Domain authentication, encrypting file system, group security policies, auditing tools, advanced file and folder sharing
- Corporate management—Group policy support, software management technology, improved scripting support, and management interfaces
- Mobile computing—Offline files and folders, encrypting file system, log on using dial-up connection
- Advanced/power user features—Backup utility, two-processor support, Internet Information Services, remote desktop

Both Windows XP Home Edition and Windows XP Professional support SQL Server 2000 Personal, Desktop Engine, and Developer Editions.

Windows CE

Windows CE is the modular real-time embedded operating system used in small footprint and mobile devices, such as Pocket PCs. Windows CE provides a Windows-like interface and Windows compatibility for consumer electronic devices, Web terminals, Internet access appliances, specialized industrial controllers, mobile data acquisition handhelds, and embedded communication devices. Windows CE allows developers to build applications for small footprint and mobile 32-bit devices that can integrate more seamlessly with Windows and the Internet.

Windows CE versions 2.11 and later support running SQL Server 2000 Windows CE Edition.

SQL Server 2000 Edition/Platform Matrix

Are you confused yet? Keeping track of which editions of SQL Server run on which Windows platform can be difficult. To help you, Table 2.1 summarizes the various platforms and the editions of SQL Server that are supported.

TABLE 2.1 SQL Server Editions Supported on Windows Platforms

	Personal Edition	Standard Edition	Enterprise Edition	Developer Edition	Desktop Engine	SQL Server 2000 Windows CE Edition
Windows 98 and Windows Me	✓				✓	
Windows NT 4.0 Workstation	✓			✓	✓	
Windows NT 4.0 Server	✓	✓	✓	✓	✓	
Windows NT 4.0 Enterprise Server	✓	✓	✓	✓	✓	
Windows 2000 Professional	✓			✓	✓	
Windows 2000 Server	✓	✓	✓	✓	✓	
Windows 2000 Advanced Server	✓	✓	✓	✓	✓	
Windows 2000 Datacenter Server	✓	✓	✓	✓	✓	
Windows XP Home Edition	✓			✓	✓	
Windows XP Professional	✓			✓	✓	
Windows CE						✓

SQL Server 2000 Editions

You can choose from several editions of SQL Server 2000. The edition you choose will depend on your database and data processing needs, as well as the Windows platform on which you want to install it.

For actual deployment of SQL Server in a live deployed server environment, you can only choose from two editions of SQL Server: Standard Edition and Enterprise Edition. In addition, SQL Server also is available for special uses in a Developer Edition, Personal Edition, Desktop Engine Edition, or Windows CE Edition.

This chapter will examine the different editions of SQL Server and discuss their features and capabilities. Using this information, you will be better able to choose which edition provides the appropriate solution.

SQL Server 2000 Standard Edition

The Standard Edition of SQL Server 2000 is the version intended for the masses—those running small- to medium-sized systems that don't require the performance, scalability, and availability provided by Enterprise Edition. The Standard Edition runs on any of the Windows 2000 or Windows NT 4.0 Server platforms with scalability limited to up to four processors and 2GB of memory. Standard Edition includes the following features:

- Analysis Services
- Data Transformation Services
- Full Text Search
- English Query
- Built-in XML support
- SQL Profiler and performance analysis tools
- Graphical DBA and Developer tools
- Replication
- Data mining tools

As shown in Table 2.1, the Standard Edition can be installed on any of the Windows NT 4.0 and Windows 2000 Server platforms.

The Standard Edition should meet the needs of most departmental and small- to mid-sized applications. However, if you need more scalability, availability, advanced performance features, or comprehensive analysis features, you will want to implement the Enterprise Edition of SQL Server 2000.

SQL Server 2000 Enterprise Edition

The Enterprise Edition of SQL Server 2000 is the most comprehensive and complete edition available. It provides the most scalability and availability of all editions and is intended for systems that require high performance and availability, such as large volume Web sites, data warehouses, and high throughput online transaction processing (OLTP) systems.

SQL Server 2000 Enterprise Edition supports up to 64GB of memory and up to 32 processors when it is installed on Windows 2000 Datacenter Server. It supports up to 8GB of memory and 8 processors when it is installed on Windows 2000 Advanced Server. To provide these capabilities, SQL Server 2000 Enterprise Edition can be installed only on Server versions of Windows 2000 and Windows NT.

Additionally, SQL Server 2000 Advanced Server provides performance enhancements such as parallel query, indexed views, and enhanced read-ahead scanning.

Which version is right for you? The next section explores the feature sets of Enterprise and Standard Editions so you can decide which one provides the features you need.

Differences Between Enterprise and Standard Editions of SQL Server

For deploying SQL Server 2000 in a server environment, either the Standard or the Enterprise Edition of SQL Server is a logical choice. To help decide between the two editions, Table 2.2 compares the major features supported by each edition.

TABLE 2.2 SQL Server 2000 Feature Comparison Between Enterprise and Standard Editions

Feature	Enterprise Edition	Standard Edition
Distributed partitioned views	Yes	No
Parallel index creation	Yes	No
Parallel scan	Yes	No
Parallel DBCC	Yes	No
Failover clustering	Yes	No
Failover cluster management	Yes	No
Indexed views	Yes	Yes (See Note)
Log shipping	Yes	No
Differential backups	Yes	Yes
Replication	Yes	Yes
Graphical DBA and development tools	Yes	Yes
XML support	Yes	Yes
Full Text Search	Yes	Yes
English Query	Yes	Yes
Integrated data mining	Yes	Yes
Multiple instance support	Yes	Yes
Data Transformation Services	Yes	Yes
Active Directory integration	Yes	Yes

NOTE

While all editions of SQL Server 2000 allow the creation of indexed views, only the Developer and Enterprise Editions of SQL Server 2000 will automatically consider using an indexed view in query plans. To force the optimizer to consider indexed views in other SQL Server editions, the NOEXPAND hint must be included in the query. For more information on using indexed views and how they are handled by the query optimizer, please see Chapters 27, "Creating and Managing Views in SQL Server," 34, "Indexes and Performance," and 35, "Understanding Query Optimization."

Another main difference between Enterprise and Standard Editions is scalability. Table 2.3 lists the differences in amount of memory supported by both editions depending on the platform on which it is installed.

TABLE 2.3 Maximum Number of Processors Supported by the Standard and Enterprise Editions by Platform

Operating System	Enterprise Edition	Standard Edition
Windows 2000 Datacenter	32	4
Windows 2000 Advanced Server	8	4
Windows 2000 Server	4	4
Windows NT 4.0 Server Enterprise Edition	8	8
Windows NT 4.0 Server	4	4

The amount of memory supported by each edition on the various platforms is limited, as shown in Table 2.4.

TABLE 2.4 Maximum Amount of Memory Supported by the Standard and Enterprise Editions by Platform

Operating System	Enterprise Edition	Standard Edition
Windows 2000 Datacenter	64GB	2GB
Windows 2000 Advanced Server	8GB	2GB
Windows 2000 Server	4GB	2GB
Windows NT 4.0 Server Enterprise Edition	3GB	2GB
Windows NT 4.0 Server	2GB	2GB

Other SQL Server 2000 Editions

The Standard and Enterprise Editions of SQL Server 2000 are intended for server-based deployment of applications. In addition, the following editions are available for other specialized uses:

- Developer Edition
- Personal Edition
- Desktop Engine Edition
- Windows CE Edition

Developer Edition

The Developer Edition of SQL Server 2000 is a full-featured version intended for development and end-user testing only. It includes all features and functionality of Enterprise Edition, at a much lower cost, but the licensing agreement prohibits production deployment of databases using the Developer Edition.

To provide greater flexibility during development, the Developer Edition can be installed in any of the following environments:

- Windows 2000 Datacenter
- Windows 2000 Advanced Server
- Windows 2000 Server
- Windows NT 4.0 Server Enterprise Edition
- Windows NT 4.0 Server
- Windows 2000 Professional
- Windows XP Professional
- Windows XP Home Edition
- Windows NT 4.0 Workstation

Personal Edition

The Personal Edition of SQL Server 2000 is intended for users who are running applications that require a locally installed database, often on mobile systems, and who spend at least some of the time disconnected from the network. The Personal Edition, intended for use in a single-user environment, includes all the tools and features of the Standard Edition with the following exceptions:

- It contains a workload governor that cripples performance when more than five Transact-SQL commands are executed simultaneously.
- It is limited to using a maximum of two processors (only one processor on Windows 98 and Windows Me).
- It can participate in replication but only as a subscriber.

The Personal Edition can be installed in any of the Windows 2000 or Windows NT 4.0 environments, Windows XP Professional and Home Edition, as well as Windows 98/Me. However, the Full Text Search and Analysis Services are not available under Windows 98/Me.

Desktop Engine Edition

The Desktop Engine Edition of SQL Server 2000 is a small-footprint, redistributable, database-engine-only version of SQL Server intended for distribution with applications that require an embedded or offline data store. Software developers can include it as a module for Windows Installer so it is installed with the rest of the application.

The Desktop Engine is just that—a database engine only. No administrative tools are installed. Administration must be handled through the custom application, or with graphical tools installed with another edition of SQL Server 2000. The Desktop Edition supports the same feature set as the Personal Edition with the exception of Analysis Services. The maximum database size is limited to 2GB.

Like all other editions of SQL Server 2000, the Desktop Engine Edition supports installation of multiple instances to decrease potential conflicts between instances installed by other applications or vendor products.

The Desktop Engine Edition can be installed in any of the Windows 2000 or Windows NT 4.0 environments, Windows XP Professional and Home Edition, as well as Windows 98/Me.

Windows CE Edition

The Windows CE Edition of SQL Server 2000 runs only on platforms that are running the Windows CE environment. The Windows CE Edition is a scaled-down version of SQL Server 2000 that provides Transact-SQL compatibility and a cost-based query optimizer. Developers who are familiar with SQL Server 2000 should feel comfortable developing for Windows CE Edition.

Windows CE Edition requires about a 1MB footprint on a Windows CE device, and has a maximum database size limit of 2GB. Windows CE Edition supports replication with SQL Server 2000 databases as a merge replication subscriber so that data can be accessed and manipulated offline and synchronized later with a Server version of SQL Server 2000.

SQL Server 2000 64-Bit Version

At the time of this writing, Microsoft was in the process of beginning beta testing for a 64-bit version of SQL Server 2000, code-named "Liberty." The SQL Server 2000 64-bit beta is built to take advantage of hardware enhancements of the 64-bit Itanium platform from Intel. It will offer higher levels of single-system scalability for memory-intensive data applications, such as largescale e-commerce, data warehousing, and analytics. Currently, the planned hardware offerings support up to 64GB of physical linear memory for the 64-bit version of SQL Server 2000, with up to 4 terabytes of physical linear memory planned for future hardware.

The increased memory support of the 64-bit platform will benefit database applications with memory-sensitive workloads that require working data sets larger than 4GB to be loaded in memory. In addition, the 64-bit platform may result in improved I/O performance due to larger memory buffer pools. For low-end implementations with 4-processor servers or less, some performance improvement can be expected on a 64-bit implementation over a 32-bit implementation, but higher performance gains are expected for higher-scale implementations that utilize 8 to 32 processors.

The 64-bit version of SQL Server 2000 will include a 64-bit database server, a 64-bit server agent, and 64-bit analysis server for OLAP and data mining. The 64-bit version of SQL Server 2000 will require 64-bit hardware running the 64-bit version of Microsoft Windows .NET Server Beta3.

SQL Server Licensing Models

In addition to feature sets, one of the determining factors in choosing a SQL Server version is cost. With SQL Server 2000, Microsoft has changed the licensing model to include a processor-based licensing model intended for Web-based environments in which the number of clients or user connections is indeterminate.

Processor licensing requires a single license for each central CPU in the machine running a Microsoft Server product. This type of license includes unlimited client device access. Additional server licenses, seat licenses, and Internet connector licenses are not required. You must purchase a processor license for each installed processor on the server on which SQL Server 2000 will be installed even if some processors will not be used for running SQL Server. The only exception is for systems with 16 or more processors that allow partitioning the processors into groups so the SQL Server software can be delegated to a subset of the processors.

For those who prefer the more familiar Server/Per-Seat Client Access License (CAL), or for those environments in which the number of client devices connecting to SQL Server is known, server or CAL-based licensing models are still available. This licensing model requires purchasing a license for the computer running SQL Server 2000, as well as a license for each client device that accesses any SQL Server 2000 installation. A fixed number of CALs are included with a server license and the server software. Additional CALs can be purchased as needed.

Server/Per Seat CAL licensing is ideal for those environments in which the number of clients per server is relatively low, and access from outside the firewall is not required. Be aware that using a middle tier or transaction server that pools or multiplexes database connections does not reduce the number of CALs required. A CAL is still required for each distinct client workstation that connects through the middle tier. (Processor licensing might be preferable in these environments due to its simplicity and affordability when the number of clients is unknown and potentially large.)

NOTE

The pricing listed in Table 2.5 is provided for illustrative purposes only and is based on pricing available at the time of publication. These are estimated retail prices that are subject to change and might vary from reseller pricing.

TABLE 2.5 SQL Server 2000 Estimated Retail Pricing

Licensing Options	Enterprise Edition	Standard Edition
Processor Licensing	$19,999 per processor	$4,999 per processor
Server/Per Seat CAL License with 5 CALs	N/A	$1,489
Server/Per Seat CAL License with 10 CALs	N/A	$2,249
Server/Per Seat CAL License with 25 CALs	$11,099	N/A
Product Upgrade with 5 CALs	N/A	$749
Product Upgrade with 25 CALs	$5,549	N/A

The Enterprise Edition license allows you to run multiple instances on the same machine without additional licenses. The Standard Edition requires a separate license for each instance.

The Developer Edition of SQL Server 2000 is available for a fixed price of $499 per developer.

Personal Edition Licensing

The Personal Edition is considered a client component of SQL Server 2000 and cannot be purchased separately. It is included with the Standard and Enterprise Editions of SQL Server 2000, and licensing is covered under the rules applied to Enterprise and Standard Editions. Check the End User License Agreement (EULA) Addendum for these products to learn more.

Desktop Edition Licensing

The Desktop Engine Edition of SQL Server 2000 is available with all the Enterprise, Standard, and Developer Editions of SQL Server 2000, as well as other Microsoft products, such as MDSN Universal subscription and Office Developer Edition 10. Check the EULA for these products for information on redistribution rights for the Desktop Engine. The Desktop Edition does not require a CAL when it is used on a standalone basis, or when it connects to a SQL Server instance that is licensed using the per-processor model.

Windows CE Edition Licensing

SQL Server Windows CE Edition is licensed through the Developer Edition. The Developer license allows unlimited deployment of SQL Server 2000 Windows CE Editions as long as these devices operate in standalone mode. If the device connects to a SQL Server instance that is not on the device, a separate CAL is required unless the SQL Server instance is licensed under the Per Processor model.

Choosing a Licensing Model

Which licensing model should you choose? Per Processor licensing is generally recommended for instances in which the server will be accessed from the outside. This includes servers used in Internet situations, or servers that will be accessed from both inside and outside an organization's firewall. Per Processor licensing might also be appropriate and more cost-effective for internal environments in which client-to-server processor ratios are high. An additional advantage to the Per Processor model is it eliminates the need to count the number of devices connecting to SQL Server, which can be difficult to manage on an ongoing basis.

Using the Server/Per Seat CAL model is usually the more cost-effective choice in internal environments in which client-to-server ratios are low. Table 2.6 lists the number of seats required relative to the number of server processors, where Processor licensing becomes less expensive than Server/Per Seat CAL licensing. If you will have more seats than those listed, you should consider going with Processor licensing.

TABLE 2.6 Number of Seat Thresholds in Which Processor Licensing Becomes Less Expensive Than Server/CAL Licensing

Seat Thresholds	1 Processor	2 Processors	4 Processors	8 Processors
Enterprise Edition	>80	>198	>435	>909
Standard Edition	>24	>53	>112	>229

Mixing Licensing Models

You can mix both Per Processor and Server/CAL licensing models in your organization. If the Internet servers for your organization are segregated from the servers used to support internal application, you can choose to use Processor licensing for the Internet servers and Server/CAL licensing for internal SQL Server instances and user devices. Keep in mind that you do not need to purchase CALs to allow internal users to access a server already licensed via a Processor license—the Processor licenses allow access to that server for all users.

Failover Cluster Licensing

If you are using SQL Server 2000 Enterprise Edition in a failover cluster configuration, two or more SQL Servers are clustered together to pick up each other's processing if one computer fails. Special licensing considerations exist for this type of configuration, depending on your cluster configuration. (For more information on SQL Server clustering, see Chapter 24, "SQL Server Clustering.")

If you are using an active/active cluster configuration, all servers in the failover cluster regularly process information independently unless a server fails, at which point, one server or more takes on the additional workload of the failed server. In this environment, all servers must be fully licensed using either Per Processor licensing or Server/CAL licensing.

If your cluster is an active/passive configuration in which at least one server in the cluster does not regularly process information, but simply waits to pick up the workload when an active server fails, no additional licenses are required for the passive server. The exception is if the failover cluster is licensed using the Per Processor licensing model, and the number of processors on the passive server exceeds the number of processors on the active server. In this case, additional processor licenses must be acquired for the number of additional processors on the passive computer.

Summary

This chapter examined the various platforms that support SQL Server 2000 and reviewed and compared the various editions of SQL Server 2000 that are available. The platform and edition that are appropriate to your needs depend on scalability, availability, performance, licensing costs, and limitations. The information provided in this chapter should help you make the appropriate choice.

The next chapter, "What's New in SQL Server 2000," takes at look at the new features and capabilities provided with the various SQL Server 2000 Editions.

CHAPTER 3

What's New in SQL Server 2000

by Ray Rankins

IN THIS CHAPTER

- New SQL Server 2000 Features
- SQL Server 2000 Enhancements
- SQL Server 2000 and the .NET Framework

The upgrade from SQL Server 6.5 to 7.0 was pretty significant. In addition to many new features, the underlying SQL Server architecture changed considerably. The upgrade from SQL Server 7.0 to 2000 is more of a series of enhancements, additions, and improvements. The architectural differences between the two are minimal. As a matter of fact, a database on a 7.0 SQL Server can be migrated over to SQL Server 2000 via a simple dump and restore.

On the .NET Framework front, SQL Server 2000 is at the heart of this whole new architecture movement. This book will provide a brief description of the .NET Framework and how SQL Server 2000 fits into this architectural picture. In addition, the ADO.NET (new programming data interface layer) will be outlined with working SQL Server 2000 examples.

This chapter explores the new features provided in SQL Server 2000 as well as many of the enhancements to previously available features.

New SQL Server 2000 Features

What does SQL Server 2000 have to offer over SQL Server 7? The following is a list of the new features provided in SQL Server 2000:

- User-defined functions
- Indexed views
- Distributed partitioned views

- INSTEAD OF and AFTER triggers
- New datatypes
- Cascading RI constraints
- Multiple SQL Server instances
- XML support
- Log shipping

The rest of this section takes a closer look at each of these new features and provides a reference to subsequent chapters where more information about the new feature can be found.

User-Defined Functions

SQL Server has always provided the ability to store and execute SQL code routines via stored procedures. In addition, SQL Server has always supplied a number of built-in functions. Functions can be used almost anywhere an expression can be specified in a query. This was one of the shortcomings of stored procedures—they couldn't be used inline in queries in select lists, where clauses, and so on. Perhaps you want to write a routine to calculate the last business day of the month. With a stored procedure, you have to execute the procedure, passing in the current month as a parameter and returning the value into an output variable, and then use the variable in your queries. If only you could write your own function that you could use directly in the query just like a system function. In SQL Server 2000, you can.

SQL Server 2000 introduces the long-awaited support for user-defined functions. User-defined functions can take zero or more input parameters and return a single value—either a scalar value like the system-defined functions, or a table result. Table-valued functions can be used anywhere table or view expressions can be used in queries, and they can perform more complex logic than is allowed in a view.

For more information on defining, managing, and using user-defined functions, see Chapter 30, "User-Defined Functions."

Indexed Views

Views are often used to simplify complex queries, and they can contain joins and aggregate functions. However, in the past, queries against views were resolved to queries against the underlying base tables, and any aggregates were recalculated each time you ran a query against the view. In SQL Server 2000 Enterprise or Developer Edition, you can define indexes on views to improve query performance against the view. When creating an index on a view, the result set of the view is stored and indexed in the database. Existing applications can take advantage of the performance improvements without needing to be modified.

Indexed views can improve performance for the following types of queries:

- Joins and aggregations that process many rows
- Join and aggregation operations that are performed frequently within many queries
- Decision support queries that rely on summarized, aggregated data that is infrequently updated

For more information on designing, using, and maintaining indexed views, see Chapter 27, "Creating and Managing Views in SQL Server."

Distributed Partitioned Views

SQL Server 7.0 provided the ability to create partitioned views using the `UNION ALL` statement in a view definition. It was limited, however, in that all the tables had to reside within the same SQL Server where the view was defined. SQL Server 2000 expands the ability to create partitioned views by allowing you to horizontally partition tables across multiple SQL Servers. The feature helps you scale out one database server to multiple database servers, while making the data appear as if it comes from a single table on a single SQL Server. In addition, partitioned views are now able to be updated.

For more information on defining and using distributed partitioned views, see Chapter 27 and Chapter 21, "Administering Very Large SQL Server Databases."

`INSTEAD OF` and `AFTER` Triggers

In versions of SQL Server prior to 7.0, a table could not have more than one trigger defined for `INSERT`, `UPDATE`, and `DELETE`. These triggers only fired *after* the data modification took place. SQL Server 7.0 introduced the ability to define multiple `AFTER` triggers for the same operation on a table. SQL Server 2000 extends this capability by providing the ability to define which `AFTER` trigger fires first and which fires last. (Any other `AFTER` triggers besides the first and last will fire in an undetermined order.)

SQL Server 2000 also introduces the ability to define `INSTEAD OF` triggers. `INSTEAD OF` triggers can be specified on both tables and views. (`AFTER` triggers can still only be specified on tables.) If an `INSTEAD OF` trigger is defined on a table or view, the trigger will be executed in place of the data modification action for which it is defined. The data modification is not executed unless the SQL code to perform it is included in the trigger definition.

For more information on creating, managing, and using `INSTEAD OF` and `AFTER` triggers, see Chapter 29, "Creating and Managing Triggers."

New Datatypes

SQL Server 2000 introduces three new datatypes. Two of these can be used as datatypes for local variables, stored procedure parameters and return values, user-defined function parameters and return values, or table columns:

- bigint—An 8-byte integer that can store values from -2^{63} (–9223372036854775808) through 2^{63-1} (9223372036854775807).
- sql_variant—A variable-sized column that can store values of various SQL Server–supported data types, with the exception of text, ntext, timestamp, and sql_variant.

The third new datatype, the table datatype, can be used only as a local variable datatype within functions, stored procedures, and SQL batches. The table datatype cannot be passed as a parameter to functions or stored procedures, nor can it be used as a column datatype. A variable defined with the table datatype can be used to store a result set for later processing. A table variable can be used in queries anywhere a table can be specified.

For more information on using the new datatypes, see Chapter 26, "Using Transact-SQL in SQL Server 2000."

Text in Row Data

In previous versions of SQL Server, text and image data was always stored on a separate page chain from where the actual data row resided. The data row contained only a pointer to the text or image page chain, regardless of the size of the text or image data. SQL Server 2000 provides a new text in row table option that allows small text and image data values to be placed directly in the data row, instead of requiring a separate data page. This can reduce the amount of space required to store small text and image data values, as well as reduce the amount of I/O required to retrieve rows containing small text and image data values.

For more information on specifying text and image datatypes for tables, see Chapter 12, "Creating and Managing Tables in SQL Server." For more information on how text and image data is stored in tables, see Chapter 33, "SQL Server Internals."

Cascading RI Constraints

In previous versions of SQL Server, referential integrity (RI) constraints were restrictive only. If an insert, update, or delete operation violated referential integrity, it was aborted with an error message. SQL Server 2000 provides the ability to specify the action to take when a column referenced by a foreign key constraint is updated or deleted. You can still abort the update or delete if related foreign key records exist by specifying the NO ACTION option, or you can specify the new CASCADE option, which will cascade the update or delete operation to the related foreign key records.

See Chapter 14, "Implementing Data Integrity," for more information on using the new options with foreign key constraints.

Multiple SQL Server Instances

Previous versions of SQL Server supported the running of only a single instance of SQL Server at a time on a computer. Running multiple instances or multiple versions of SQL Server required switching back and forth between the different instances, requiring changes in the Windows registry. (The SQL Server Switch provided with 7.0 to switch between 7.0 and 6.5 performed the registry changes for you.)

SQL Server 2000 provides support for running multiple instances of SQL Server on the same system. This allows you to simultaneously run one instance of SQL Server 6.5 or 7.0 along with one or more instances of SQL Server 2000. Each SQL Server instance runs independently of the others and has its own set of system and user databases, security configuration, and so on. Applications can connect to the different instances in the same way they connect to different SQL Servers on different machines.

This feature provides the ability to run an older version of SQL Server alongside SQL Server 2000, as well as the ability to run separate environments (for example, a development and test environment) on the same computer.

For more information on setting up one or more SQL Server instances, see Chapter 8, "Installing and Upgrading SQL Server."

XML Support

Extensible Markup Language has become a standard in Web-related programming to describe the contents of a set of data and how the data should be output or displayed on a Web page. XML, like HTML, is derived from the Standard Generalized Markup Language (SGML). When linking a Web application to SQL Server, a translation needs to take place from the result set returned from SQL Server to a format that can be understood and displayed by a Web application. Previously, this translation needed to be done in a client application.

SQL Server 2000 provides native support for XML. This new feature provides the ability to do the following:

- Return query result sets directly in XML format.
- Retrieve data from an XML document as if it were a SQL Server table.
- Access SQL Server through a URL using HTTP. Through Internet Information Services (IIS), you can define a virtual root that gives you HTTP access to the data and XML functionality of SQL Server 2000.

The latest version of SQLXML, version 3.0, extends the built-in XML capabilities of SQL Server 2000 with technology to create XML Web services from SQL Server stored procedures or server-side XML templates. SQLXML 3.0 also includes extensions to the .NET Framework that provide SQLXML programmability to the languages supported by Microsoft Visual Studio .NET, including C# and Microsoft Visual Basic .NET.

To help you make the most of the XML capabilities of SQL Server 2000, Microsoft provides, as a free download from its Web site, the Microsoft SQL Server 2000 Web Services Toolkit, which consists of tools, code, samples, and whitepapers for building XML Web services and Web applications with SQL Server 2000. You can find the link to download the installer file in the download area of the MSDN Web site (`http://msdn.microsoft.com/downloads`). It is currently located in the .NET Enterprise Server/SQL Server Development area.

For more information on using XML with SQL Server, see Chapter 41, "Using XML in SQL Server 2000."

Log Shipping

The Enterprise Edition of SQL Server 2000 now supports log shipping, which you can use to copy and load transaction log backups from one database to one or more databases on a constant basis. This allows you to have a primary read/write database with one or more read-only copies of the database that are kept synchronized by restoring the logs from the primary database. The destination database can be used as a warm standby for the primary database, for which you can switch users over in the event of a primary database failure. Additionally, log shipping provides a way to offload read-only query processing from the primary database to the destination database.

This capability was available in previous versions of SQL Server, but it required the DBA to manually set up the process and schedule the jobs to copy and restore the log backups. SQL Server 2000 officially supports log shipping and has made it easier to set up via the Database Maintenance Plan Wizard. This greatly simplifies the process by automatically generating the jobs and configuring the databases to support log shipping.

For more information on configuring and using log shipping, see Chapter 22, "Data Replication."

Notification Services

A new component is now available for SQL Server 2000 that makes it easy to build applications that forward messages to end users. This feature is called SQL Server Notification Services. SQL Server Notification Services is a platform for the development and deployment of notification applications. Notification applications send messages to users based upon subscriptions that they set up in advance. Depending on how the subscriptions are configured, messages can be sent to the subscriber immediately or on a predetermined schedule. The messages sent can be personalized to reflect the preferences of the subscriber.

The Notification Services platform provides a reliable, high-performance server that is built on the .NET Framework and SQL Server 2000 and runs on the Microsoft Windows Server family of operating systems. Notification Services was designed for scalability and efficiency: It can support applications with millions of subscribers and large volumes of data. As a platform, it is extensible and provides interoperability with a variety of existing applications.

SQL Server serves as the matching engine for notification applications, as well as the storage location for the subscription information. The subscriber and delivery information is stored in a central Notification Services database, and individual subscription information is stored in application-specific databases.

For more information on the Notification Server architecture and configuring and using SQL Server Notification Services, see Chapter 45, "SQL Server Notification Services."

Microsoft SQL Server 2000 Driver for JDBC

Microsoft recently released its JDBC driver for SQL Server 2000 as a free download for all SQL Server 2000 customers. The Microsoft SQL Server 2000 Driver for JDBC is a Type 4 JDBC driver that provides highly scalable and reliable connectivity for the enterprise Java environment. The current release of the SQL Server 2000 Driver for JDBC supports the JDBC 2.0 specification.

The SQL Server 2000 Driver for JDBC provides JDBC access to SQL Server 2000 from any Java-enabled applet, application, or application server. The JDBC driver provides enterprise features like support for XA transactions, server-side cursors, SQL_Variant datatypes, updateable resultsets, and more.

The SQL Server 2000 Driver for JDBC supports the Java Developer's Kit versions 1.1.8, 1.2, and 1.3 and is supported on the following operating systems:

- Microsoft Windows® XP
- Microsoft Windows 2000 with Service Pack 2 or higher
- AIX
- HP-UX
- Solaris
- Linux

For more information on the Microsoft SQL Server 2000 Driver for JDBC, see Chapter 9, "Client Installation and Configuration."

SQL Server 2000 Enhancements

In addition to the entirely new features provided by SQL Server 2000 are a number of enhancements to existing features.

Index Enhancements

SQL Server 2000 provides enhancements for defining indexes as well as enhancements to the way indexes are built.

Indexes can now be defined on computed columns, and you can specify when creating an index whether it should be built in ascending or descending index key order. SQL Server 2000 also provides an option to use `tempdb` for performing the sorting operations when creating an index. This can be specified with the `WITH SORT_IN_TEMPDB` option. When `WITH SORT_IN_TEMPDB` is specified, SQL Server performs the intermediate sorting required to build this index in `tempdb`, rather than in the current database. If `tempdb` is on a separate disk from the destination file group in the current database, building the index will take less time. For more information on the new index creation options, see Chapter 13, "Creating and Managing Indexes."

In addition to the new creation options, SQL Server now supports the use of multiple processors to perform parallel scanning and sorting when creating an index to help speed up index creation.

Collation Enhancements

In previous versions of SQL Server, all databases within a SQL Server had to use the same code page and sort order that SQL Server was configured to use. (This is typically established during SQL Server installation and is not always easy to change.) If you had to restore a database from a server using a different sort order or collation, a normal backup and restore wouldn't work and you would have to bring it over using the Database Migration utility.

SQL Server 2000 now uses collations instead of code pages and sort orders and supports multiple collations within a single SQL Server. You now can specify collations at the database level or at the column level within a table. SQL Server 2000 still supports most collations that were supported in earlier versions of SQL Server, as well as provides support for collations based on Windows collations.

DBCC Enhancements

DBCC can be run without taking shared table locks while scanning tables, thereby enabling them to be run concurrently with update activity on tables. Additionally, DBCC now takes advantage of multiple processors, thus enabling near-linear gain in performance in relation to the number of CPUs (provided that I/O is not a bottleneck).

Full Text Search Enhancements

SQL Server 2000 provides enhancements to the Full Text Search capabilities by including change tracking, which maintains a log of all changes to full-text indexed data. SQL Server 2000 also includes image filtering, which allows you to index and query documents stored in image columns.

With change tracking, you can update the full-text index by flushing the change log manually, on a schedule, or as changes occur, using the background update index option.

Image filtering allows you to specify the filename extension that a document would have had if it were stored as a file in the file system. The Full Text Search services can then load the appropriate document filter and extract textual information for indexing from the image data.

For more information on using the Full Text Search services, see Chapter 44, "SQL Server Full-Text Search Services."

Clustering Enhancements

In SQL Server 2000, Microsoft has made it much easier to install, configure, and maintain a Microsoft SQL Server 2000 failover cluster. In addition, SQL Server 2000 now provides the ability to failover and failback to or from any node in a SQL Server 2000 cluster, add or remove a node from the cluster using the SQL Server 2000 Setup utility, and reinstall or rebuild a cluster instance on any node without affecting the other cluster node instances. For more information on SQL Server clustering and failover support, see Chapter 24, "SQL Server Clustering."

Backup and Restore Enhancements

In SQL Server 2000, passwords can be defined for backup sets and media sets to prevent unauthorized users from restoring sensitive SQL Server backups. SQL Server 2000 also has improved the speed of differential database backups such that they now should complete in a time proportional to the amount of data changed since the last full backup.

SQL Server 2000 also introduces a new model for specifying backup and restore options for your database. Previous database options such as "truncate log on checkpoint" and "select into/bulk copy" have been replaced by three recovery models: Full Recovery, Bulk Logged Recovery, and Simple Recovery. These new models help clarify when you are balancing increased or decreased exposure to losing work against the performance and log space requirements of the different plans.

SQL Server 2000 also provides support for recovering transaction logs to specific points of work using named log marks in the transaction log, as well as the ability to perform partial database restores.

For more information on backing up and restoring databases and database recovery options in SQL Server 2000, see Chapter 16, "Database Backup and Restore," and Chapter 31, "Transaction Management and the Transaction Log."

Up to 64GB Memory Support

The Enterprise Editions of SQL Server 2000 can use the Microsoft Windows 2000 Advanced Windows Extension (AWE) API to support up to 8GB of memory on a Windows 2000 Advanced Data Server and 64GB of memory on a Windows 2000 Datacenter server.

Analysis Services Enhancements

What was formerly known as SQL Server OLAP Services is now called SQL Server Analysis Services. Analysis Services provides new and improved features that enhance the capabilities of the previous OLAP Services provided in SQL Server 7.0. A major new feature is the Data Mining component, which can be used to discover information in OLAP cubes and relational databases. In addition, enhancements have been made to the Cube, Dimension, and Hierarchy types to improve and extend the scalability, functionality, and analysis capabilities of cubes. Security enhancements include the ability to assign permissions on cube cells and dimension members to roles. For more information on using Analysis Services and its features and capabilities, see Chapter 42, "Microsoft SQL Server Analysis Services."

SQL Server 2000 64-Bit Version

At the time of this writing, Microsoft was in the process of beginning beta testing for a 64-bit version of SQL Server 2000, code-named "Liberty." Built to take advantage of hardware enhancements of the 64-bit Itanium platform from Intel, Liberty offers higher levels of single-system scalability for memory-intensive data applications. Currently, the planned hardware offerings support up to 64GB of physical linear memory for the 64-bit version of SQL Server 2000, with up to 4 terabytes of physical linear memory planned for future hardware.

The 64-bit version of SQL Server 2000 includes a 64-bit database server, a 64-bit server agent, and a 64-bit analysis server for OLAP and data mining. The 64-bit version of SQL Server 2000 will require 64-bit hardware running the 64-bit version of Microsoft Windows .NET Server Beta3 or the current release of Windows Advanced Server, Limited Edition running on Intel Itanium processors.

The 64-bit Windows Advanced Server, Limited Edition platform provides the ability to install up to 16 instances of SQL Server 2000 on a single machine, and supports larger numbers of users and applications. This should result in a lower cost of ownership as businesses will require fewer servers to support the same number of users.

The 64-bit components of SQL Server 2000 are code compatible with the 32-bit versions of SQL Server 2000, providing compatibility for organizations that need to maintain some of their 32-bit SQL Server deployments, while introducing new 64-bit technologies for larger, more demanding database applications. All existing 32-bit client applications, including database management and administration tools such as Enterprise Manager, Query Analyzer, and so on, can be used to remotely manage 64-bit SQL Server 2000 installations. In addition, the database storage structures are identical between the 32- and 64-bit versions of SQL Server, so databases can be exchanged between the 32- and 64-bit environments.

SQL Server and the .NET Framework

The Microsoft .NET Framework is one of the most significant technology shifts Microsoft has ever made. It is truly Microsoft's answer to J2EE/J2SE. The .NET Framework is a multi-tiered platform architecture that consists of developer tools, Web Services, a set of strongly typed programming languages that are syntactically identical whether used to program for the Web or for the desktop, a common language runtime, a set of framework classes encapsulating areas of common functionality, and a greatly improved data access model.

Microsoft SQL Server 2000 sits firmly in the heart of the .NET Framework as the major data provider for this framework. One hundred percent of the power of SQL Server can be taken advantage of within any .NET application that is developed and also with any external system as well. (Data can be transferred to and from other platforms via XML.)

Microsoft's .NET Framework ships with a set of useful built-in classes. These classes contain many of the objects you'll use to create applications, both for the Web and for the desktop, such as all built-in Web controls, Windows forms controls, and collection objects. Several of these built-in classes comprise ADO.NET (the data layer for .NET). It will be this layer that will be focused on in this book because it directly relates to how SQL Server 2000 fits into the .NET Framework.

Figure 3.1 illustrates the basic framework components that comprise the .NET Framework and the ADO.NET components.

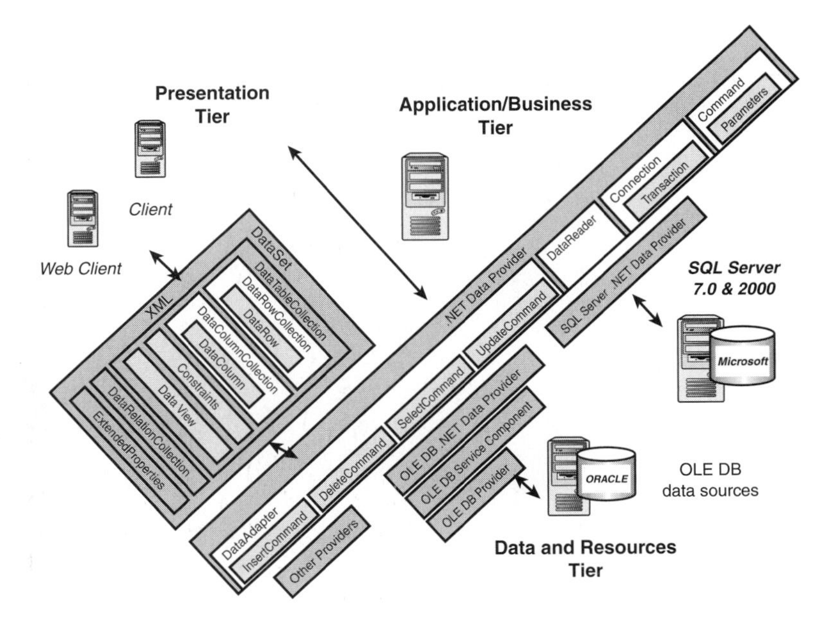

FIGURE 3.1 The Microsoft .NET Framework.

SQL Server and the .NET Framework are discussed in much more detail in Chapter 46, "SQL Server and the Microsoft .NET Framework."

Summary

Although not as significant an upgrade as SQL Server 7.0, SQL Server 2000 does provide a number of new and long-awaited features and enhancements. Since its initial release, Microsoft has continued to release new components and updated features for SQL Server 2000. This chapter provided only an overview of the new features that shipped with SQL Server 2000, add-ons, and enhancements. To learn more, please refer to the other chapters that were referenced.

PART II

SQL Server Tools and Utilities

IN THIS PART

CHAPTER **4**

SQL Server Enterprise Manager

by Paul Jensen

IN THIS CHAPTER

- Establishing Server Groups and Registering SQL Server in Enterprise Manager
- Server Configuration
- Databases
- Security
- Server Management
- Data Transformation Services
- Support Services
- System Tools
- Replication
- Using the Database Taskpad
- Using the Query Designer
- Scripting Objects
- Getting Help

Enterprise Manager (EM) is a Microsoft Management Console (MMC) plug-in used to manage SQL Server through a GUI environment. Those of you accustomed to using Microsoft's GUI tools will find it familiar and intuitive to use. For database administrators coming from a command-line environment, I encourage you to dig in and try some of its features. The more you use it, the more you appreciate how it simplifies day-to-day tasks. As EM can be used to control practically all aspects of SQL Server, this chapter could encompass the entire book. To avoid that, I will concentrate here on features specific to EM and on finding your way around the tool. For example, you will see how to use EM to create a database, but for the details on creating databases, you should reference Chapter 11, "Creating and Managing Databases."

Many database operations also can be accessed through a wizard or the Taskpad. The wizards take you through a procedure step by step and can be accessed through the Magic Wand icon on the Enterprise Manager toolbar. The Taskpad groups functions in the Details pane of EM. Therefore, you often can perform the same task three or more ways. It's up to you to choose the one with which you are most comfortable.

The best way to appreciate EM is to open it and follow along as you read through this chapter. Don't be daunted by the number of functions available. Take each one on its own, and when in doubt, right-click; if that doesn't help, refer to the supporting chapter for the feature. You will be surprised at how quickly you can manage administrative tasks using this tool.

Establishing Server Groups and Registering SQL Server in Enterprise Manager

As Enterprise Manager can manage multiple servers, it needs some way to connect to and organize the servers. Connecting to the server is done by registering the server. After the servers are registered, they can be organized into logical groups.

Server Groups

Server Groups in EM are used to group servers and named instances. When EM is first installed, a default group named SQL Server Group exists. Additional groups can be created to logically organize servers. For example, servers could be grouped by department or geographic location. Another good use of groups is to separate development servers from production; this reduces the risk of inadvertently making changes to production databases.

To create a new server group, right-click Microsoft SQL Servers or an existing server group, and select New SQL Server Group from the pop-up menu. This will open the Server Group window. Enter a name for the window and select whether it will be a top-level group or a subgroup of an existing group. Figure 4.1 shows the Server Groups window.

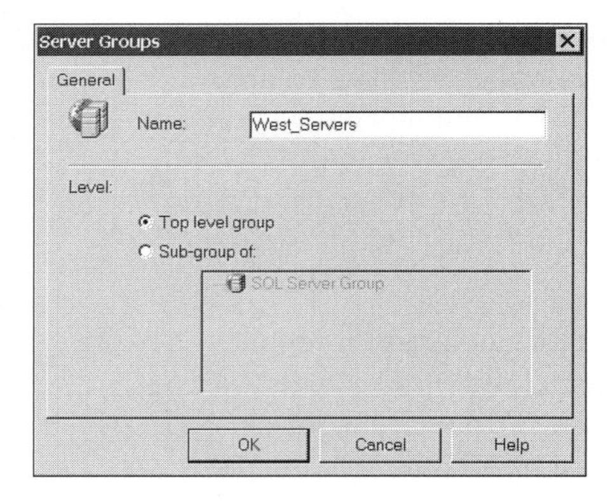

FIGURE 4.1 Creating a new server group.

Registering Servers

When accessing EM for the first time, your first task will be to register your servers. If you are running EM on the server, the local server is registered automatically in the SQL Server Group. If you want to register other servers or if you are running EM from your workstation, right-click the group to which you want to add a server and select New SQL Server

Registration. You must be a member of the sysadmin role on the server to perform the registration. The first time you run this, the Register SQL Server Wizard runs, stepping you through the registration process. If you select From Now On I Want to Perform This Task Without Using a Wizard, clicking Next will bring you directly to the Registered SQL Server Properties window, shown in Figure 4.2.

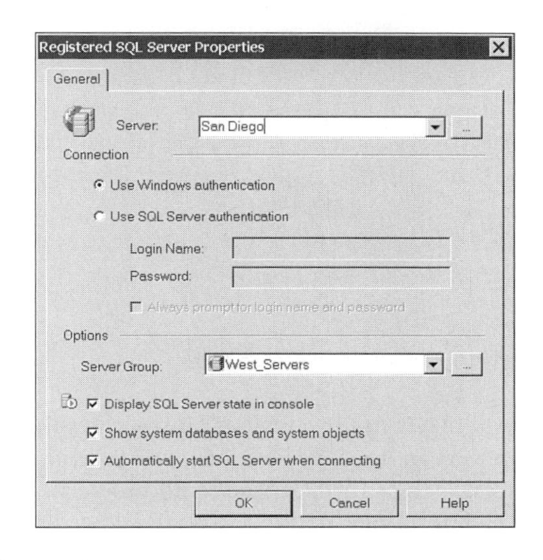

FIGURE 4.2 Registering a SQL server.

Select the server name from the drop-down box, an authentication method, the group in which you want to register the server, and the options you would like to apply to the registration. After the server is registered, if you want to change any options, right-click the server in EM and select Edit SQL Server Registration Properties.

Connecting to and Disconnecting from Servers

After a server is registered, connecting to the server is simply a matter of selecting it in Enterprise Manager. If the registration was configured to use SQL Server authentication, and to Always Prompt for a Username and Password, you will be required to provide a valid login. If you receive an error message stating `The server is not known to be running`, select Yes to connect. This is common when EM has just started and it has yet to poll the server's state. If you still can't connect to the server, check your network connectivity to the server in question. If the network connectivity is okay, try adding the server as an alias through the Client Network Utility. This might help EM to resolve a path to the server. To disconnect, right-click the server and select Disconnect from the pop-up menu.

Starting and Stopping Servers

SQL Server can be stopped and started from the EM console. Right-clicking a server will display the pop-up window shown in Figure 4.3.

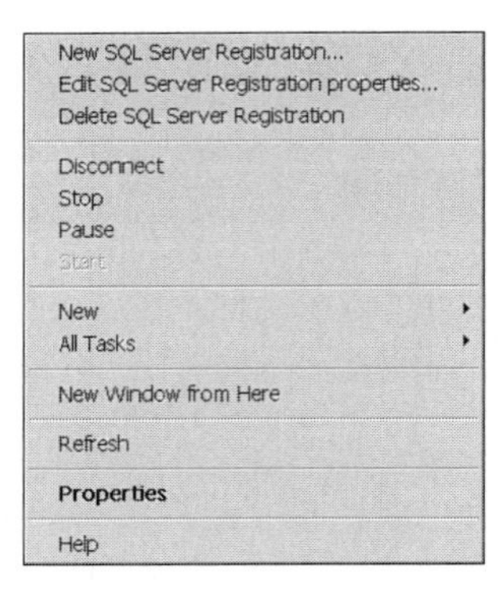

FIGURE 4.3 Starting and stopping a server from EM.

Note that Start, in this example, is not available. This indicates that the server is already running. The available options are to stop the server, which stops the SQL Server service and any dependent services, such as the SQL Agent, and to pause the server, in which case the server remains running but no new connections are allowed. If the server has been paused, then a Continue option will appear in the pop-up menu to resume SQL server in a normal connection state. If the server has been stopped, then the Start option will be available to start the server.

NOTE

Occasionally, Enterprise Manager and the taskbar Service Manager get confused as to what state the server is in and won't allow services to be stopped or started. In this case, go to the Services applet in the Control Panel, or use the net stop/net start commands to stop and restart the appropriate services.

Server Configuration

Many of the most common server configuration options are made available through EM. More advanced configuration options are available through the `SP_CONFIGURE` system-stored procedure.

CAUTION

Changing server-level settings affects all databases on the server and can adversely affect performance. When changing configuration options, consider the effect the change might have and carefully document your changes so they can be undone if required.

Server Options

EM server configuration options include memory and processor usage, connection options, default database settings, network library, and startup options. To access the server options, right-click a server in EM and select Properties. This will bring up the Server Properties page, as illustrated in Figure 4.4.

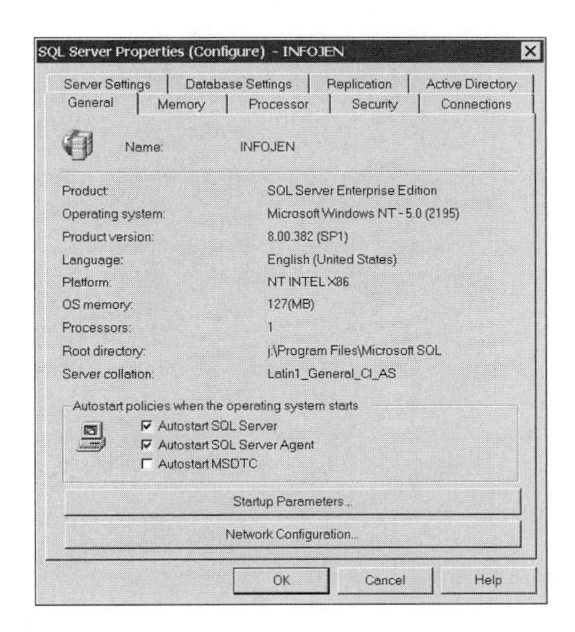

FIGURE 4.4 The Server Properties page.

Some information on each option can be accessed through the Help button on each page, but for a detailed examination of setting server configuration options, see Chapter 40, "Configuring, Tuning, and Optimizing SQL Server Options."

Security Options

The Server Properties page is also where security options for the server are set. Select the Security tab and you can switch the security mode between SQL Server and Windows or Windows Only, set an auditing level, and, if you are using EM from the Server console, you can change the account under which SQL Server runs.

Changing the Configuration

When changing server-level settings, including the Security options, you should be aware that the settings might require stopping and restarting the SQL Server service to take effect. Make sure you time your changes for the least possible disruption of service, and document them carefully. Server options that don't take effect until the service is restarted have radio buttons to select either the currently configured setting (not yet in effect) or the running value (the value to which the option was set when the service was last started). Figure 4.5 shows the configured value for memory usage.

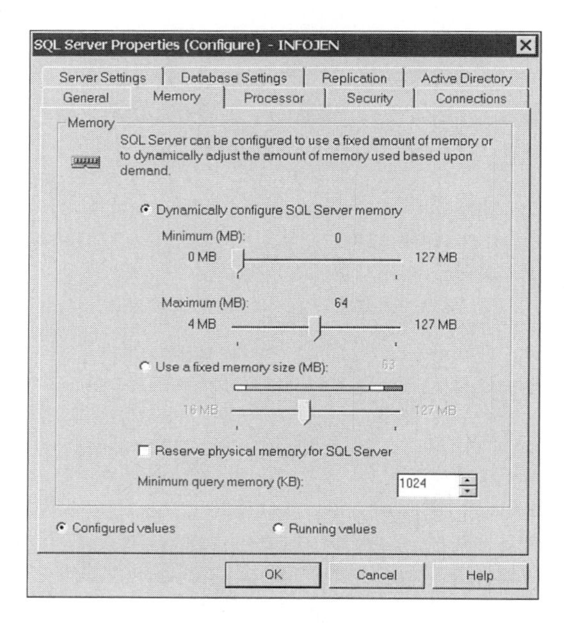

FIGURE 4.5 Displaying the configured value for memory usage.

Databases

SQL Server is all about databases, and EM is all about managing them. Using EM, it is incredibly easy to create and manage your databases. Creating a database is, if anything, too simple in EM. For example, administrators agonize for weeks over the creation of an Oracle database, carefully planning log and data file placement and setting recovery and performance options. Then they fire up EM, create a database accepting all the defaults, and complain that SQL Server is slower than Oracle. Microsoft has provided defaults—such as the path to data and log files—to simplify database creation, but in most cases, the defaults are not the best option. Before creating a database with EM, read Chapters 11 and 39, "Database Design and Performance," to get an insight into optimizing your database.

Creating and Modifying Databases

To create a database in EM, expand the server where you want the database created, right-click the Databases folder, and select New Database. This will bring up the Database Properties window, as illustrated in Figure 4.6.

From the three tabs in the Database Properties window, you can configure the database name and collation, as well as data and log filenames, size, placement, and auto grow parameters.

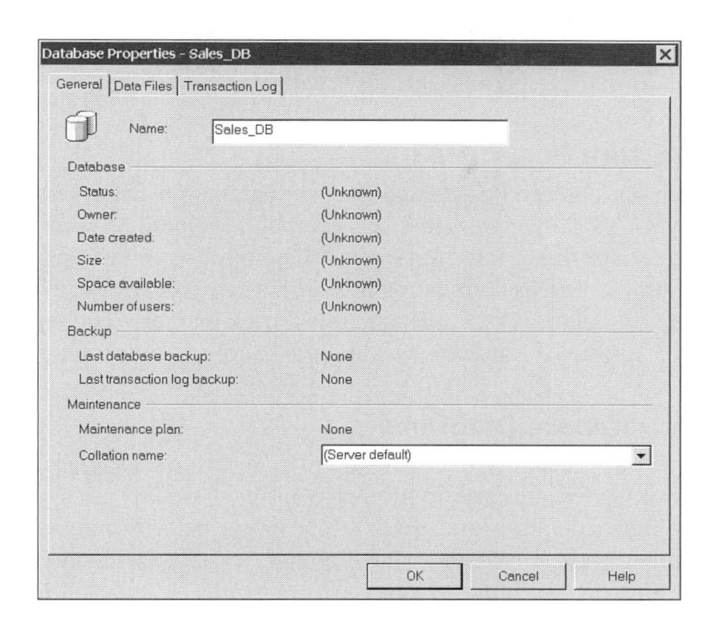

FIGURE 4.6 Creating a database.

After a database has been created, it can be modified by right-clicking the database and selecting Properties. Figure 4.7 shows the Options tab of the Database Properties window.

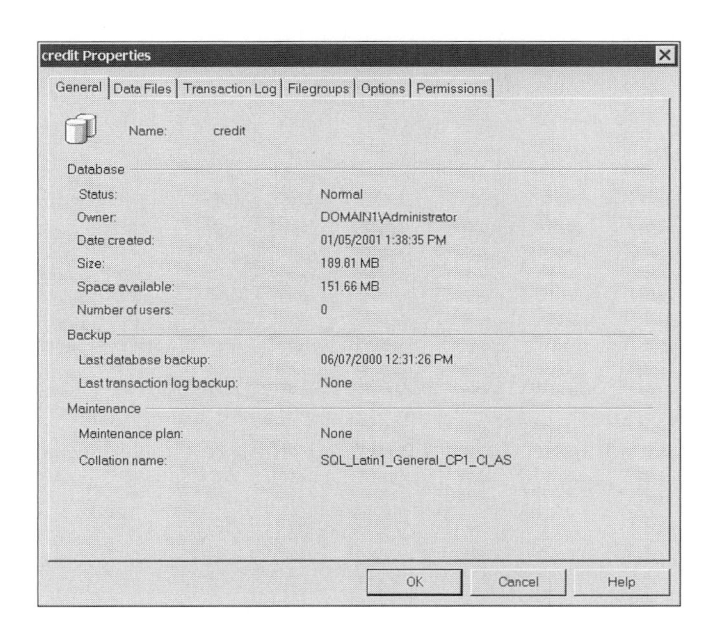

FIGURE 4.7 The Database Properties window.

In addition to changing the database options, you can alter or add log files, data files, and file groups, as well as manage permissions on the database.

Backup and Restore

Backup and restore options can be accessed on each database by right-clicking the database and selecting All Tasks. The resulting pop-up menu includes the options Backup Database and Restore Database. Selecting one of these options brings up the corresponding dialog box. For example, the Backup dialog box allows you to perform dynamic full, differential, log, and file or filegroup backups; schedule a backup; create backup devices; and set backup options. Chapter 16, "Database Backup and Restore," covers this topic in detail.

Working with Database Diagrams

Enterprise Manager has the ability to create an Entity Relational Diagram, or ERD, which allows you to not only view, but also to modify your database layout. To create a new database diagram, right-click the database, go to New, and select Database Diagram. This will start the Database Diagram Wizard, allowing you to choose which tables to add to the diagram. Figure 4.8 shows the Table Selection window of the Database Diagram Wizard.

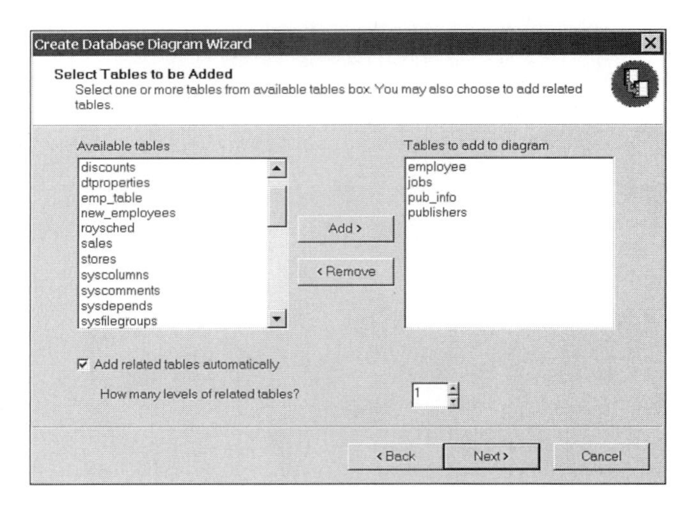

FIGURE 4.8 The Table Selection window of the Database Diagram Wizard.

After the tables have been selected, click Next and Finish to create the diagram. Figure 4.9 shows the completed diagram.

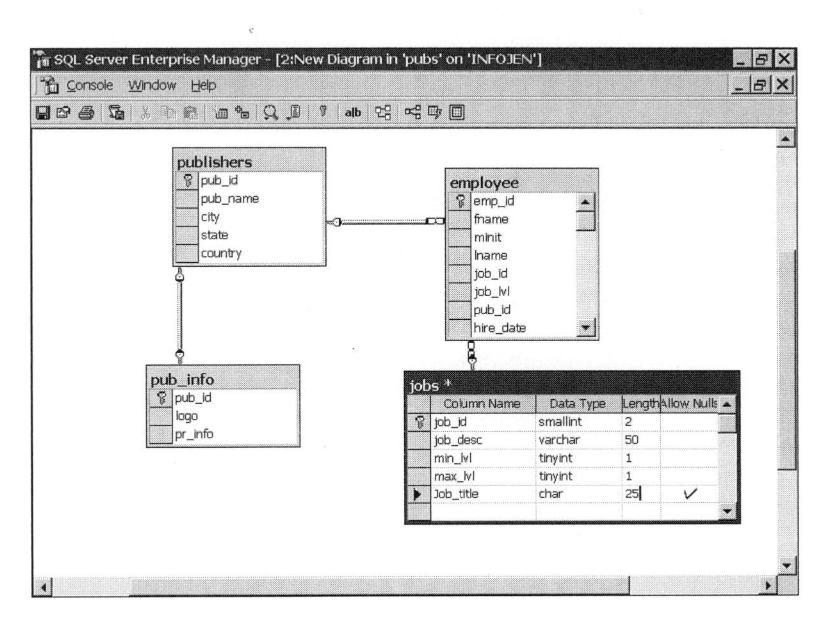

FIGURE 4.9 The database diagram.

Note that in the preceding diagram, the jobs table is displayed differently from the rest. By selecting one or more tables, a right-click brings up the various options available in the diagram window. In this case, I have selected to display the jobs table in Standard view, which displays the column properties, and I have added a column named Job_Title to the table. When changes are made to a database diagram, they are stored in memory until you select Save. Even though these changes are in memory, it is shared memory, so they are visible to anyone else working in a database diagram. When you save the changes to the diagram, they are also made permanent in the database. If you want to defer this to a later time, choose Save Change Script instead of Save. This saves the changes as a script, which can be run later and which also serves as a record of revisions. After the script is saved, exiting the database diagram window and answering no when requested to save your changes will prevent the changes from becoming effective until you run the script.

Security

The Enterprise Manager Security folder contains the objects used to manage access to SQL Server, namely Logins and Server Roles, and to define connections to other servers through Linked and Remote servers.

Managing Logins and Roles

To create a new SQL Server login, right-click Logins and choose New Login. The Login Properties dialog box will open, as shown in Figure 4.10.

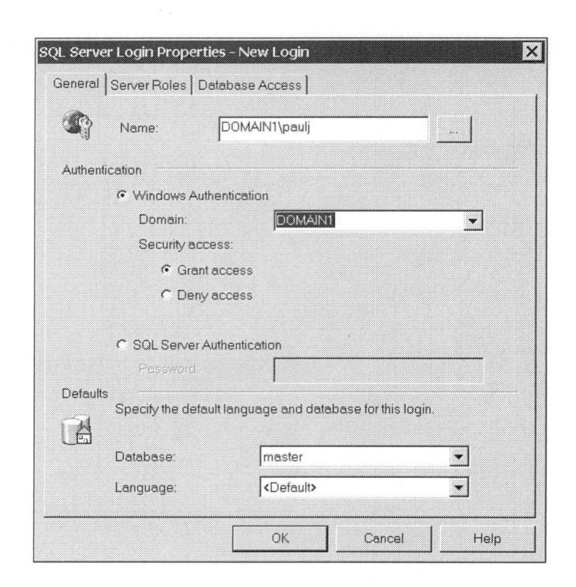

FIGURE 4.10 Creating a new login.

Enter the login name, the appropriate authentication method and database access information, and click OK.

Server roles are used to grant system privileges to logins. Server roles can't be modified, but by double-clicking one from the list, you can view the privileges associated with it and add logins to the role to enable them to perform system functions. Figure 4.11 shows the list of server roles.

Detailed information on security can be found in Chapter 15, "Security and User Administration."

Managing Linked and Remote Servers

Linked servers contain the connection properties required to access data on other servers. Remote servers are provided for backward compatibility and have, for the most part, been replaced by linked servers. For a full explanation of linked and remote servers, see Chapter 19, "Managing Linked and Remote Servers."

Server Management

The Management folder contains subfolders for the SQL Server agent, backup devices, current activity, database maintenance plans, and error logs. Each of these plays a key role in managing your server.

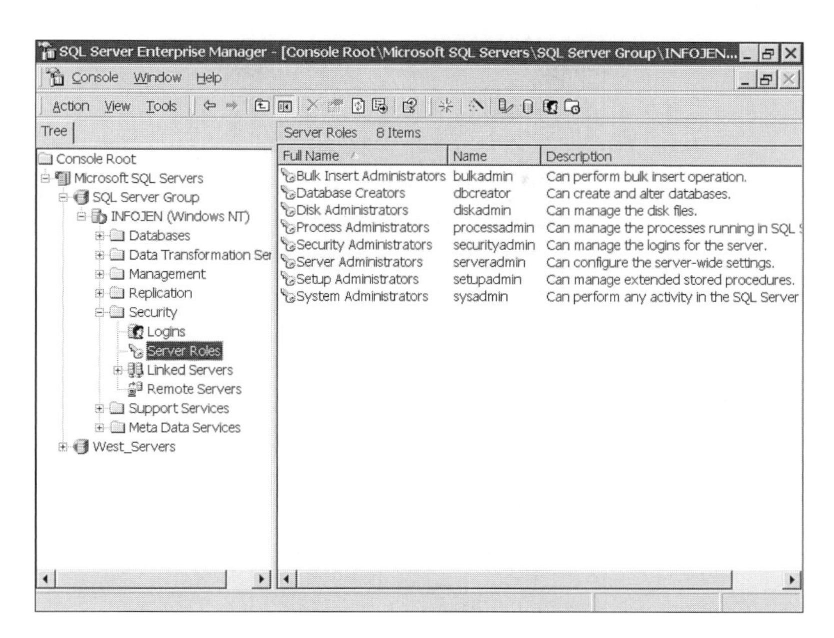

FIGURE 4.11 The server roles.

SQL Server Agent

The SQL Agent is the "quarterback" when it comes to maintenance tasks. It handles the automation of SQL Server operations. General tasks such as starting and stopping the agent can be accessed from the right-click pop-up menu, as can configuration through the Properties dialog box. Figure 4.12 displays the Agent Properties dialog box.

Subfolders for alerts, operators, and jobs exist to store and manage these respective tasks. As with other folders, the right-click menu is used to manage these specific objects. Chapter 18, "SQL Server Scheduling and Notification," provides full details on the agent's functionality.

Backup

Backup devices can be created and accessed from the Backup folder. Expanding the Management folder in EM and selecting Backup displays the backup devices in the Details pane. Right-clicking the Backup folder presents you with the options to create a new backup device or to back up a database. Double-clicking any of the backup devices in the Details pane brings up the Properties window for the device, shown in Figure 4.13, from which you can obtain file information for the device, and display the backups that the device contains. Chapter 16 covers this topic in detail.

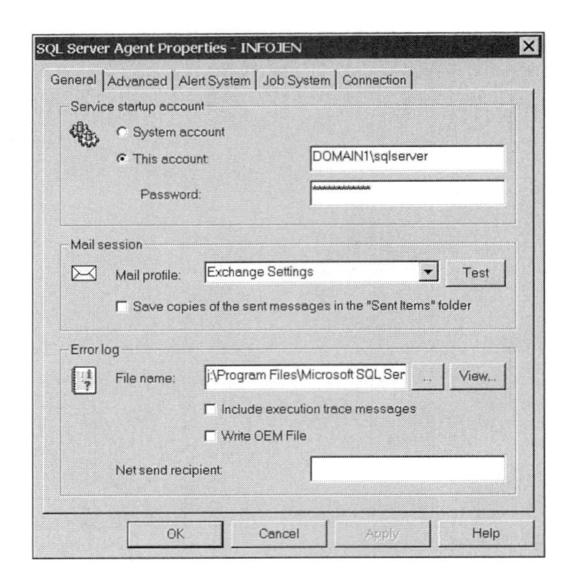

FIGURE 4.12 Configuring the SQL Server Agent.

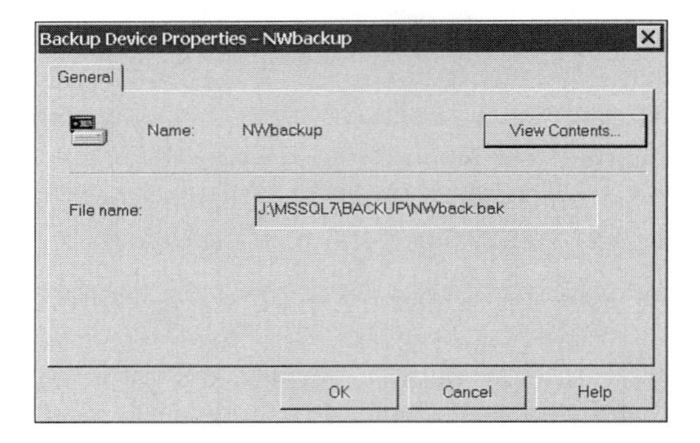

FIGURE 4.13 Displaying Backup Device properties.

Current Activity

The Current Activity folder allows you to access detailed information on processes, locks by process id, and locks by object. Note that the information provided in this folder is "point in time" information, so a refresh is required to display any changes. Clicking on any of the displayed locks or processes allows you the option of sending a message to the owner of the process, or killing the process if necessary. One of the Current Activity folder's features is its ability to display blocking and blocked processes, as displayed in Figure 4.14.

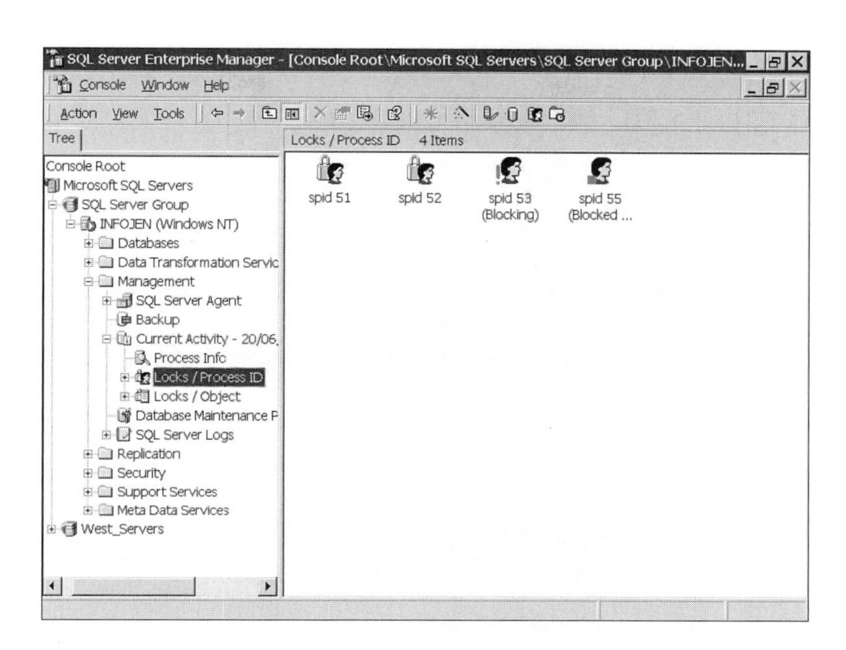

FIGURE 4.14 Displaying a blocking process.

After the blocking process is identified, it can be killed or its owner notified to complete the transaction so that the blocked process can proceed. For the full story on locking and the Current Activity folder, see Chapter 38, "Locking and Performance."

Database Maintenance Plans

This folder is used to store Database Maintenance Plans created by the Database Maintenance Plan Wizard. Right-clicking the folder and selecting New Plan activates the wizard. Stepping through the wizard allows you to create schedules for DBCCs, backups, and index reorganization. In a few minutes, you can create a complex maintenance scheme for one or all of your databases. After the scheme is completed, it is available to edit if you require changes. Figure 4.15 shows the properties for a completed maintenance plan.

Chapter 17, "Database Maintenance," will deal with the ins and outs of creating a plan with this tool. However, it is so simple and intuitive that if you are clicking along as you read this chapter, you have probably just created your first maintenance plan!

SQL Server Logs

Not to be confused with the Transaction Log, this folder contains the error, or perhaps more correctly, "information" logs. By default, seven rotating logs exist, including the current log. Each time SQL Server is taken offline, the oldest log is deleted and the current log is saved. On startup, a new current log is opened. Figure 4.16 shows the data from the current log displayed in the Details pane.

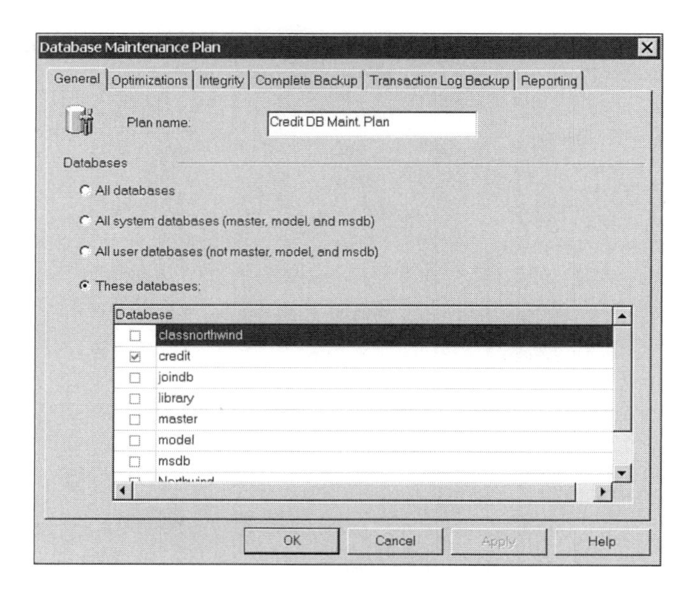

FIGURE 4.15 Displaying a maintenance plan.

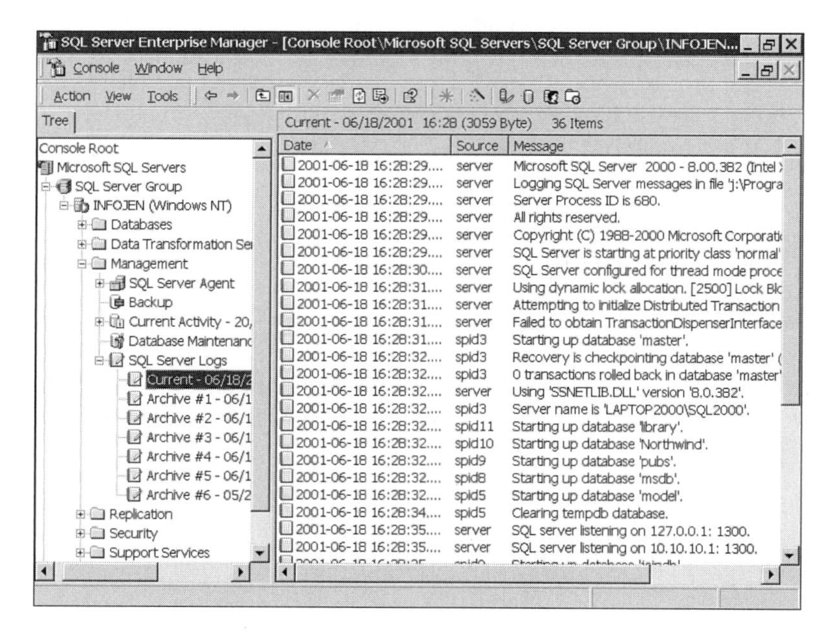

FIGURE 4.16 Displaying current log information.

By right-clicking the SQL Server Logs folder and selecting configure, you can change the number of archived logs. This is a good plan because an inexperienced administrator "bouncing" the server several times in an attempt to fix a problem could lose valuable troubleshooting information. Figure 4.17 shows the Configuration dialog box.

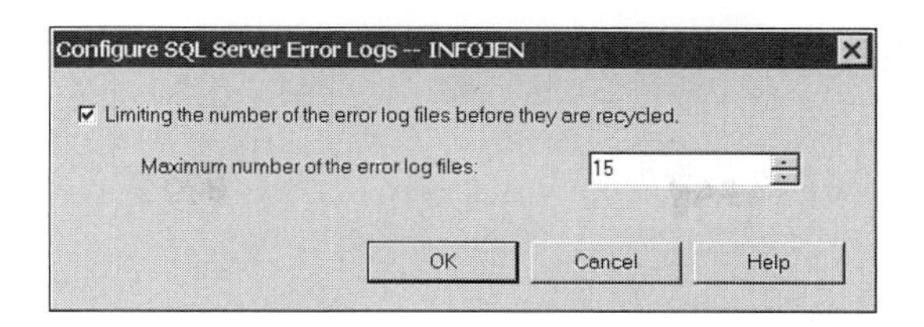

FIGURE 4.17 Configuring the information logs.

Data Transformation Services

Importing and exporting data is handled through the DTS (Data Transformation Services) folder in EM. From here, complex data transfer and manipulation tasks can be performed using the DTS Designer pictured in Figure 4.18.

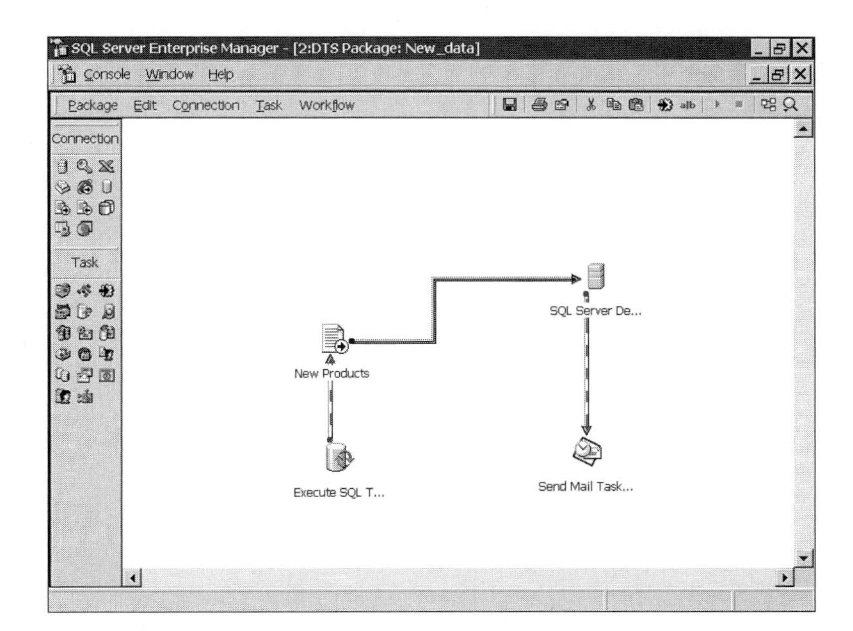

FIGURE 4.18 The DTS Designer.

Simple data import and export tasks also can be created using the Import and Export Wizards, which can be accessed from the All Tasks menus of the DTS folder, the databases, or individual tables. DTS has another associated folder in EM called Metadata Services. If DTS packages have been saved to the MSDB database, the metadata, or data about data, concerning the package can be browsed through here. Data Transformation Services is covered in detail in Chapter 20, “Importing and Exporting SQL Server Data Using BCP and DTS.”

Support Services

The Support Services folder contains the control icons for three services: Distributed Transaction Coordinator, Full-Text Search, and SQL Mail.

Distributed Transaction Coordinator

In a multi-server environment, DTC is used to ensure transactional integrity across servers. The only configuration available from EM is to start or stop the service. Chapter 32, "Distributed Transaction Processing," explains why and how you would use distributed transactions.

Full-Text Search

Full-Text Search uses indexes stored outside of SQL Server to provide fast searches on text data. The only configuration provided in EM is to start and stop the service.

SQL Mail

SQL Server has the ability to send and receive e-mail messages, but to do so, it first requires a mail profile to be set up on the server. After a mail profile is created, as Figure 4.19 shows, the Properties dialog box for SQL Mail can be used to select and test the mail profile. SQL Mail will be covered in Chapter 23, "SQL Mail."

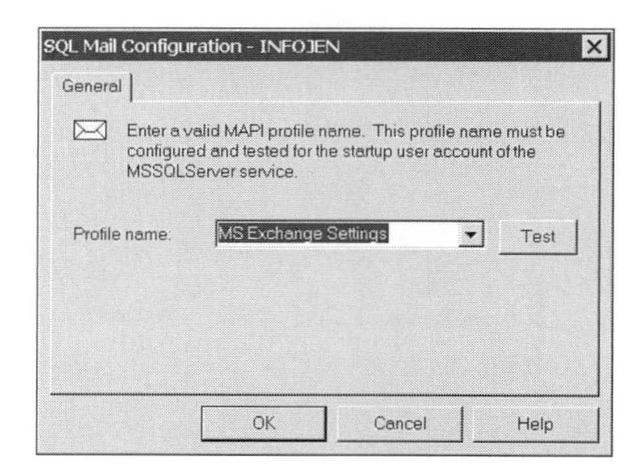

FIGURE 4.19 Configuring SQL Mail.

System Tools

The Tools menu on the EM toolbar can be used to access additional tools not necessarily related to EM, but often accessed while working with EM.

Query Analyzer

Query Analyzer, introduced in SQL 7.0, has been revamped for SQL 2000 with the addition of an object browser and templates for object creation. From this tool, queries can be built, run, saved as scripts, and analyzed for performance. Refer to Chapters 6, "SQL Server Query Analyzer and SQL Debugger," and 36, "Query Analysis," for an in-depth look at this very powerful tool. Figure 4.20 shows the Query Analyzer.

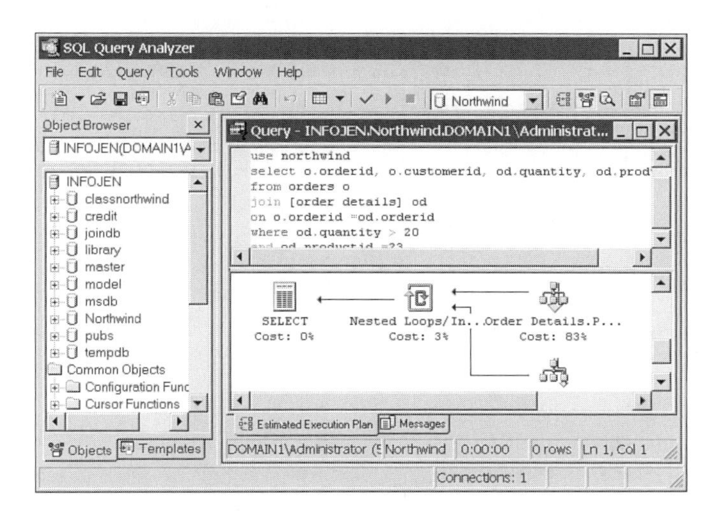

FIGURE 4.20 The Query Analyzer.

SQL Profiler

Another tool that has been updated for SQL Server 2000 is the SQL Profiler. The Profiler "records" events happening on your server and lets you save them to a file or table for later analysis. Figure 4.21 shows the Profiler with a sample trace capturing T-SQL activity. Chapter 7, "Using the SQL Server Profiler," is the place to go for details.

Managing SQL Server Error Messages

Selecting Manage SQL Server Messages from the Tools menu brings up the dialog box shown in Figure 4.22.

From here, you can search for SQL Server error messages by severity, error number, or the text it contains. After a message has been located, it appears in the Messages tab, as shown in Figure 4.23.

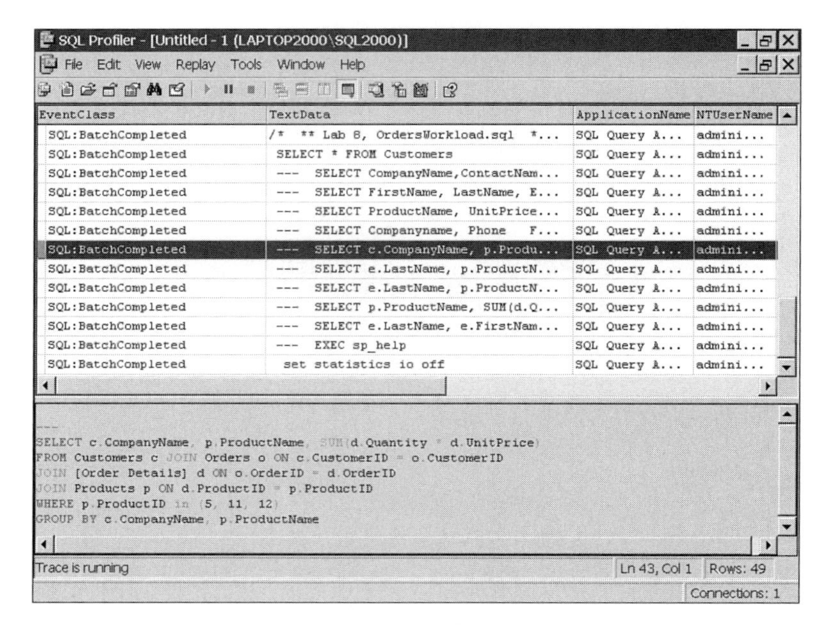

FIGURE 4.21 The SQL Profiler.

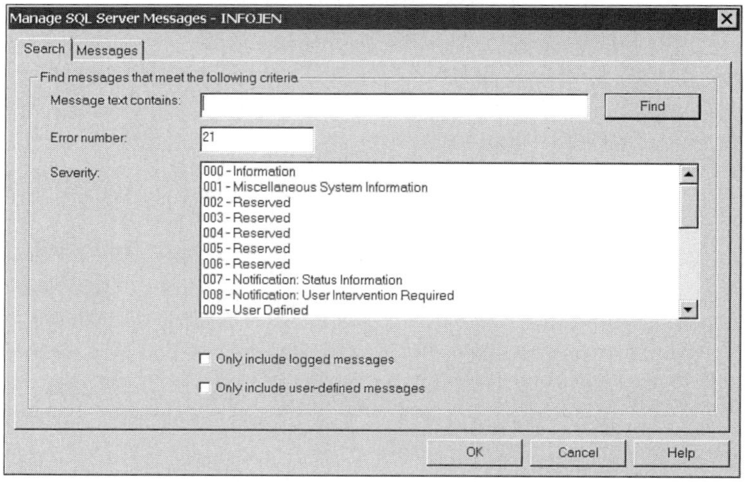

Manage SQL Server Messages - INFOJEN

Search | Messages

Find messages that meet the following criteria

Message text contains: [ ] Find

Error number: 21

Severity:
000 - Information
001 - Miscellaneous System Information
002 - Reserved
003 - Reserved
004 - Reserved
005 - Reserved
006 - Reserved
007 - Notification: Status Information
008 - Notification: User Intervention Required
009 - User Defined

☐ Only include logged messages

☐ Only include user-defined messages

OK Cancel Help

FIGURE 4.22 Managing SQL Server messages.

Messages can also be edited from here, using the Edit button; however, the only change allowed to built-in error messages is to configure whether they write to the Event Log. You can create and later edit user-defined error messages as well. These also can be set to write to the application log. This is a key point, as an error that writes to the application log can fire an alert. Because an alert can run a job, the functionality you can build in here is endless. User-defined error messages use error numbers 50,000 and above, can use substitution parameters, and are generally called with a `raiserror` statement from the application or from a trigger. Figure 4.24 illustrates creating a user-defined error.

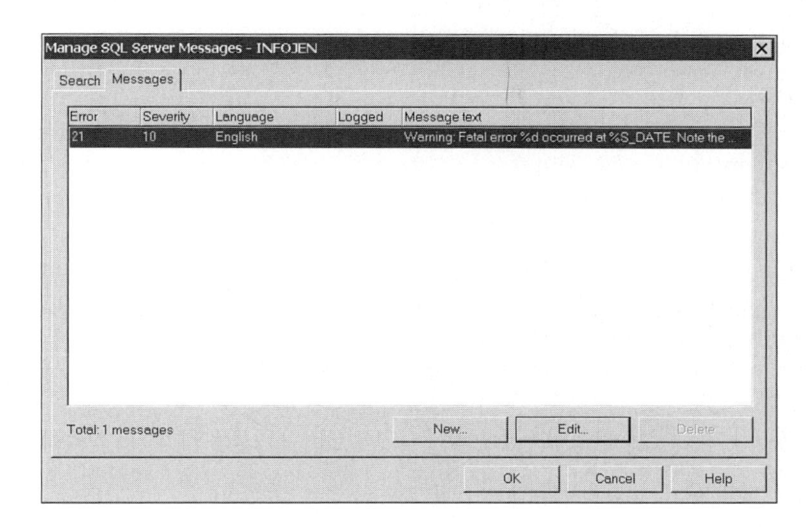

FIGURE 4.23 The SQL Server Messages tab.

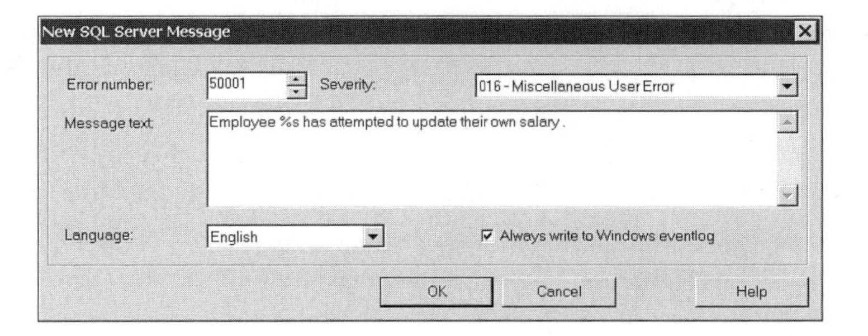

FIGURE 4.24 Creating a user-defined error.

Replication

To organize data replication tasks in SQL Server 2000, a Replication folder has been added. Replication can be configured by right-clicking the replication folder and selecting Configure Publishing, Subscribers, and Distribution. **Replication** is the process of transferring data between servers. The source of the data is known as the **publication** and the receiver is known as the **subscriber**. Two subfolders manage these entities.

Publications

To create a publication or manage an existing one, select the Publication folder. Selecting New Publication from the right-click pop-up menu will start a replication wizard to step you through the task. After a publication is created, it can be managed through its properties page.

Subscriptions

If this server is being configured to receive data in a replication scenario, its subscriptions can be created and managed from this folder. Creating subscriptions requires an existing publication server to which to connect, and you must be enabled to subscribe to the publication.

Although the Replication Wizards take care of most of the tasks associated with setting up replication, replication is a complex topic, and you should have a thorough grasp of its concepts before attempting to initiate replication. Chapter 22, "Data Replication," will help you make the proper decisions for your replication scenario.

Using the Database Taskpad

Taskpad uses the Details pane in EM to display general information and provide access to wizards and tools by function. To access Taskpad, first select a server or database, and from the View menu, select Taskpad. For a server, the Taskpad displays a General tab and a Wizards tab, from which you can launch the appropriate wizard. When Taskpad is launched at the database level, an additional tab is added for table information, displaying the table names, indexes, and the space used by each. Figure 4.25 shows the Table tab of the Taskpad.

Another interesting feature of Taskpad is the Space Allocated section of the General tab. This section gives a nice graphic view of space usage on both the data and log files.

The Space Allocated section is shown in Figure 4.26. Note also the yellow button at the top-left of each section. Hovering over this button provides a list of tools pertaining to that section.

Using the Query Designer

Don't search for the Query Designer button in Enterprise Manager. It's not there. Instead, Query Designer is accessed as the result of another operation. Select New View from the View folder and Query Designer pops up to create the Select statement for your view. In DTS Designer, selecting Build Query from an Execute SQL task will also invoke Query Designer. If you just want to design a query, then right-click one of the tables that will appear in your query, select Open Table, and then Query. The Query Designer opens, as illustrated in Figure 4.27.

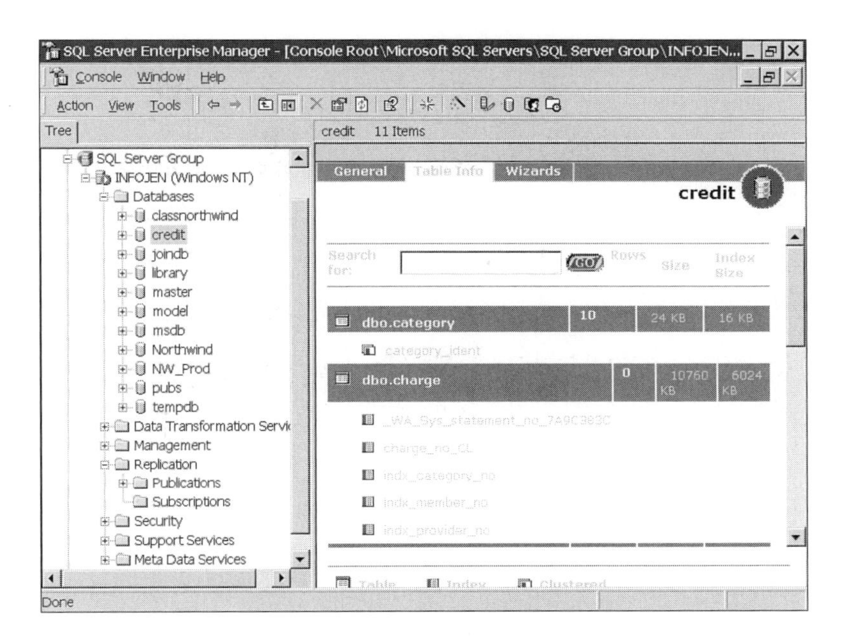

FIGURE 4.25 The Table Tab of Taskpad.

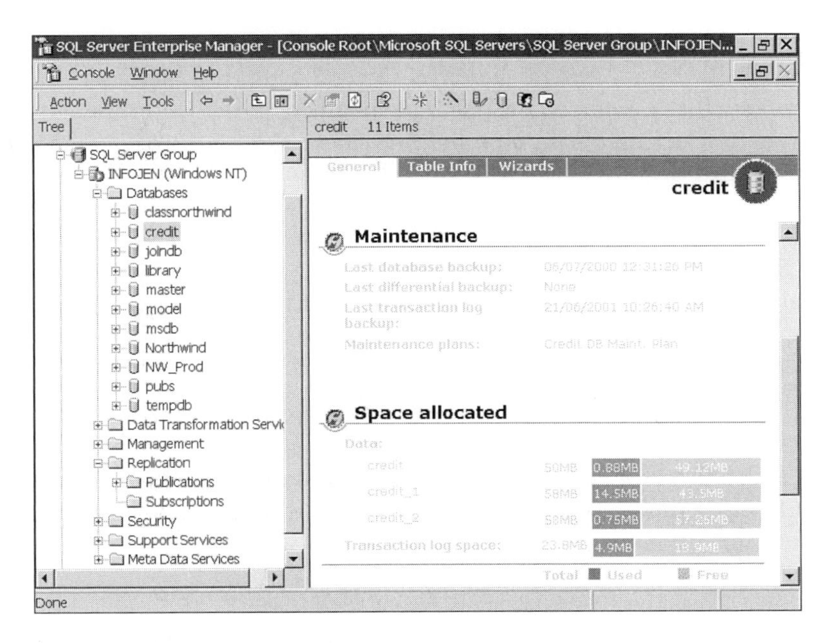

FIGURE 4.26 Viewing space allocation in Taskpad.

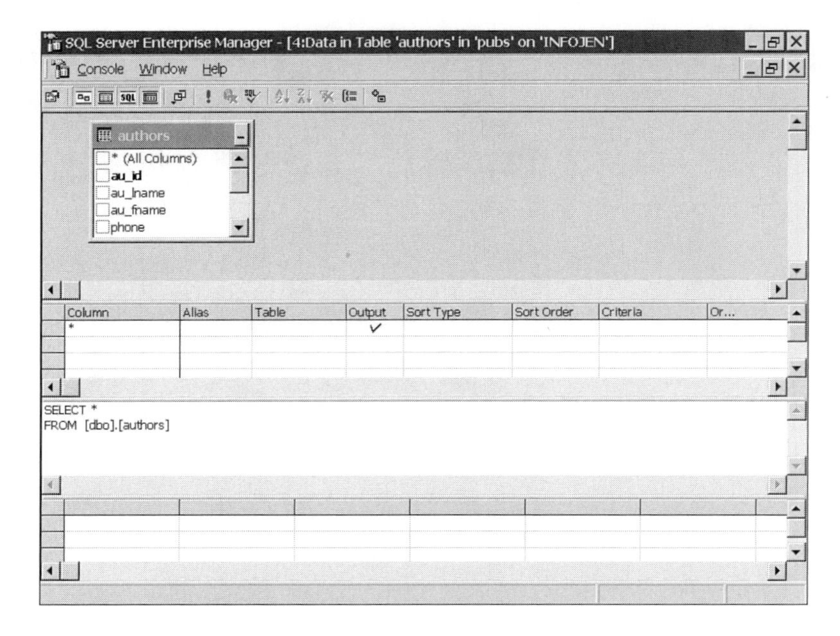

FIGURE 4.27 Accessing Query Designer.

The Query Designer has four panes. At the top is the Diagram pane, which has a graphic representation of the query. This is where you can add additional tables and build your query by checking the columns to include. The next pane is the Grid pane. This is an alternative way to select columns via drop-down boxes, and it is useful for adding `WHERE` clauses. Note that by default, * is selected for the column list. Uncheck this from the output if you want to narrow the column list. Below this is the SQL pane where the actual code generated is listed. You can edit this directly if you choose, and your changes will be reflected in the other panes. The cause and effect seen between the panes can be a great learning tool if you are new to the query language. Last is the Result pane. When you execute your query, the results will be seen here, so you can modify the query if necessary before saving it.

Actions such as adding tables, grouping, sorting, saving, and running the query can be done through the icons on the toolbar or by right-clicking in the Diagram pane. In Figure 4.28, I have added two more tables, producing a join statement to report authors' names, their book titles, and prices. Keep in mind that for this to work, the tables must have a valid relationship.

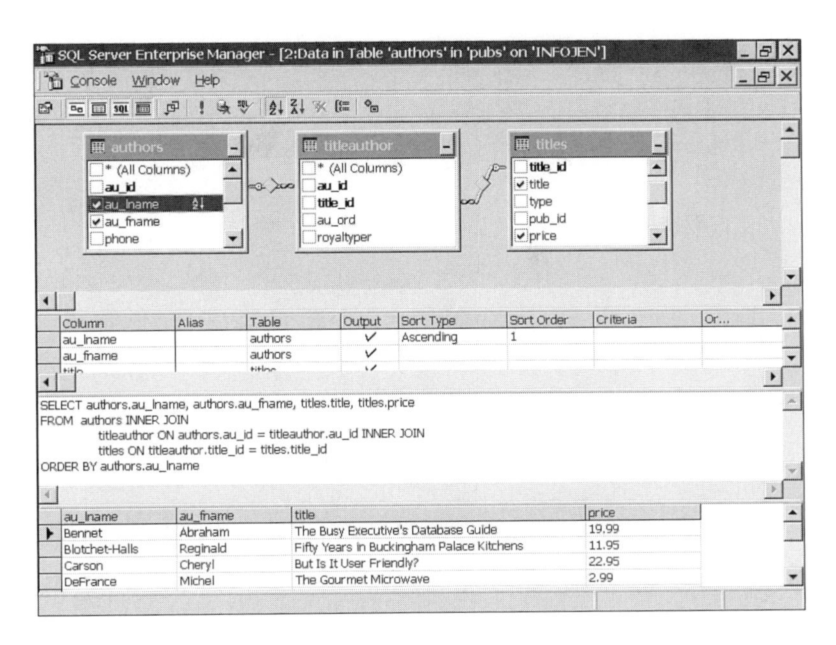

FIGURE 4.28 Expanded viewing space allocation in Taskpad.

Scripting Objects

The most common argument I hear against EM is that creating objects through a GUI as opposed to script-based management means you don't have a saved script to re-create the object if required. Fortunately, EM allows you to create and save a script to create a single object such as a view or all objects within a particular database. To create a script, select the object, right-click, and from the All Tasks menu, select Generate SQL Script. This will open the Generate SQL Scripts dialog box, as shown in Figure 4.29.

The Preview button allows you to see the format of the script, as seen in Figure 4.30.

To set up the format of the script, use the Formatting tab to set whether drop commands should be included. This is illustrated in Figure 4.31.

Additional options can be set on the Options tab. One complaint I often hear is that the objects are scripted but not the actual database. This is available under Options, but is not selected by default. As a matter of fact, if you don't select user objects and check the Script Database box, you will generate a script that just creates the database structure. Figure 4.32 shows the Options tab.

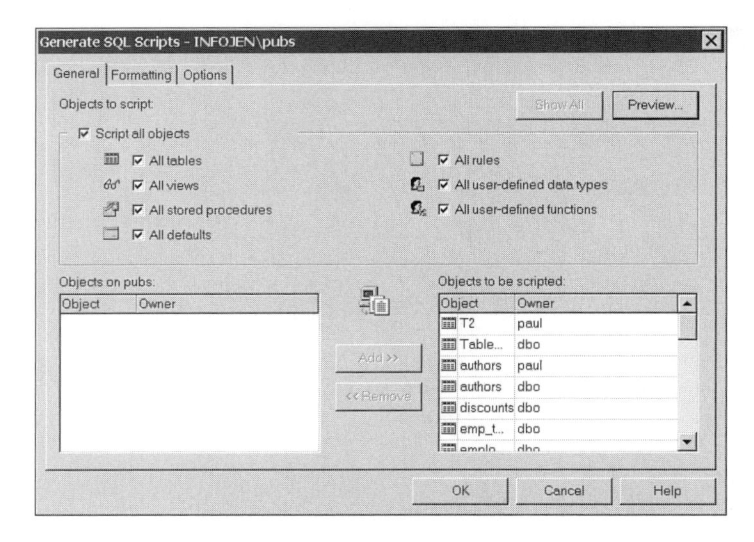

FIGURE 4.29 The Generate SQL Scripts dialog box.

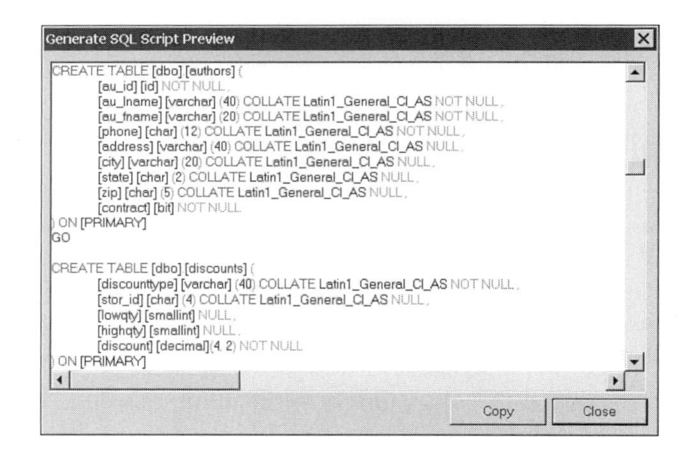

FIGURE 4.30 Previewing the script.

Getting Help

Help in Enterprise Manager is as close as the F1 key. If at any time you need information on something in EM, select the object and press F1; Books Online will open to the appropriate topic. If you need more detailed information, the search feature of BOL (Books Online) allows you to dig deeper into the topic. A Help button is available in almost every dialog box and tool, which will deliver context-sensitive help.

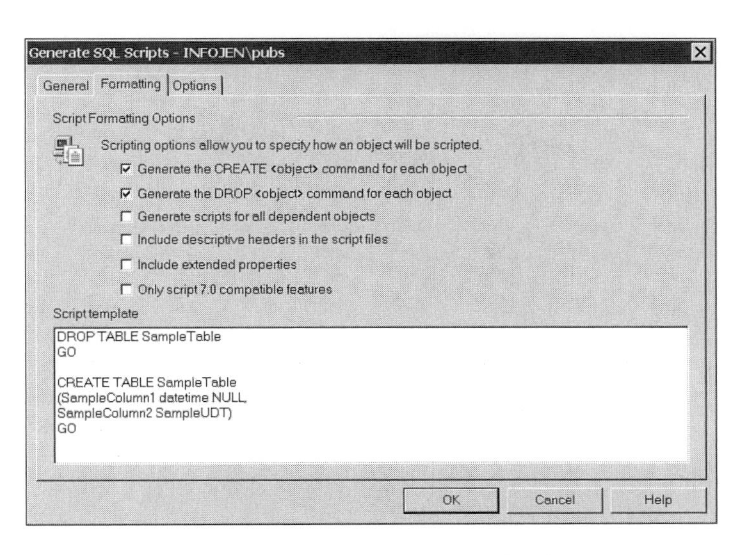

FIGURE 4.31 The Formatting tab of the Create Script dialog box.

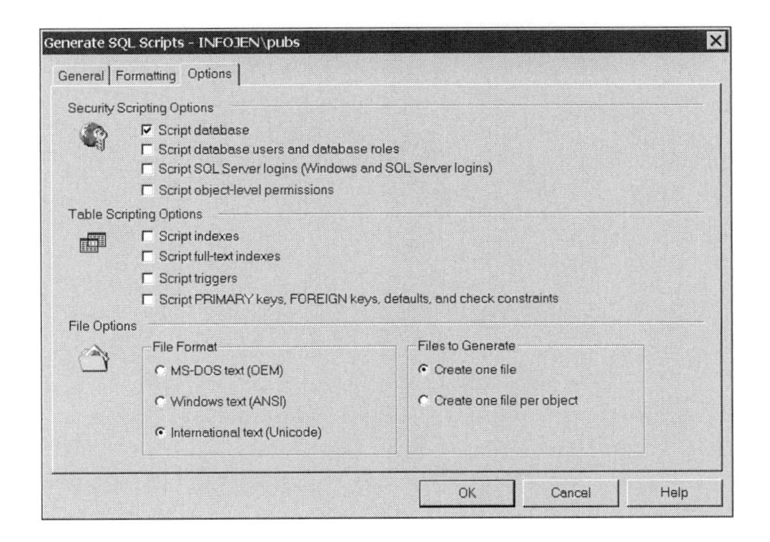

FIGURE 4.32 The Options tab of the Create Script dialog box.

Summary

As a tool you will use every day to manage your SQL Servers, I encourage you to take the time to familiarize yourself with Enterprise Manager's features. You'll be surprised at how quickly you become adept in the use of this tool. However, keep in mind it is just a tool. Just as a bigger wrench doesn't make a better mechanic, Enterprise Manager can't make you a better administrator. A sound knowledge of the principles of database management will do that. However, it's always nice to have a big wrench when you need one!

CHAPTER 5

SQL Server Command-Line Utilities

by Chris Gallelli

IN THIS CHAPTER

- BCP
- Data Transformation Services Utilities
- ISQL/OSQL
- `makepipe` and `readpipe`
- ODBCcmpt
- odbcping
- rebuildm
- regrebld
- Replication Utilities
- SQLDiag
- SQLMaint
- SQLServr
- VSwitch

This chapter explores the various command-line utilities that ship with SQL Server. These utilities provide administrators with a set of tools for such tasks as automating routine maintenance procedures and verifying client connectivity to SQL Server. In this chapter, you will explore these command-line utilities. For each utility, this chapter provides the command syntax along with the most commonly used options. For the full syntax and options available for the utility, see SQL Server Books Online.

NOTE

Four of the utilities discussed in this chapter (makepipe, readpipe, regrebld, and odbcping) are no longer installed as part of the SQL Server 2000 setup but are shipped with the installation disc. They can be run from the x:\x86\Binn directory on the SQL Server 2000 installation disc, or they can be copied from the disc to your computer for execution. The remaining command-line utilities covered in this chapter are installed in several different locations. Refer to the last section in the detailed description of each utility to find the specific location.

TIP

A batch file, typically a text file with the `.bat` extension, can be a real timesaver when executing the command-line utilities. You can create the batch file in the same directory as your executable file and specify the appropriate parameters. A PAUSE command at the end of the batch file will allow you to view the results in the command prompt window before the window disappears.

BCP

BCP (bulk copy program) is a tool that is used to address the bulk movement of data. The utility is bidirectional, allowing for the movement of data in and out of a SQL Server database.

The SQL Server 2000 version of the Bulk copy program (BCP) utilizes the ODBC bulk copy API instead of the DB-LIB API that was used in earlier versions of SQL Server. The ODBC bulk copy API was used to support new data types that the DB-Library API does not support. Backward compatibility options are provided with the SQL Server 2000 BCP utility to allow bulk copy of data types supported in earlier versions.

BCP uses the following syntax:

```
BCP {[[database_name.][owner].]{table_name| view_name} | "query"}{
    in | out | queryout | format} data_file
[-F first_row] [-L last_row]
[-t]
[-E]
```

BCP also works in conjunction with the query optimizer so that importing and exporting data is more efficient than in earlier versions. For a more detailed look at BCP, see Chapter 20, "Importing and Exporting SQL Server Data Using BCP and DTS."

Some of the commonly used options—other than the ones used to specify the database, such as user ID, password, and so on—are the `-F` and `-L` options. These options allow you to specify the first and last row of data, which is especially helpful in large batches. The `-t` option allows you to specify the field terminator that separates data elements in an ASCII file. The `-E` option allows you to import data into SQL Server fields that are defined with identity properties.

TIP

The BULK INSERT Transact-SQL statement and Data Transformation Services (DTS) are good alternatives to BCP. The BULK INSERT statement is limited to loading data into SQL Server, but has been deemed the fastest bulk copy method by Microsoft. DTS has a sophisticated GUI that allows for both data import and data export.

The BCP.EXE file is located, by default, with the SQL Server tools in `Microsoft SQL Server\80\Tools\Binn\`.

Data Transformation Services Utilities

Data Transformation Services (DTS) allows you to import, export, and transform data between Microsoft SQL Server and any OLE DB, ODBC, or text-file format. DTS saves the information and settings associated with these data movements in an object called a package. These packages can be accessed or created via the SQL Server Enterprise Manager or via the command-line utilities that ship with SQL Server 2000.

Two DTS command-line utilities are included with SQL Server: dtsrun and dtswiz. The dtsrun utility allows you to execute a DTS package without having to open the package. This is particularly useful when scheduling a DTS package for execution via the SQL Server Agent. dtsrun comes with a variety of command-line switches that allow you to customize the execution of the package. The dtsrun utility uses the following syntax to execute a package that has been saved in the SQL Server msdb database:

```
dtsrun /Sserver_name /Uuser_name /Ppassword /Npackage_name
```


TIP

The command-line text used by dtsrun can be generated using the DTS run utility. This utility is accessed by executing dtsrunui from the command prompt or the Windows run command. Upon execution, the utility presents a dialog box that allows you to enter the relative DTS information, including the DTS package name, server name, and so on. After that information is entered, you can utilize the Advanced button and generate the dtsrun command-line text that can be copied and executed via the dtsrun utility.

The dtswiz utility allows you to start the Data Transformation Services Import/Export Wizard using the options specified on the command line. You can use the Data Transformation Services Wizard to create DTS packages that can be run immediately or saved for future execution. The dtswiz utility uses the following syntax to start the wizard using Windows authentication against the database and server specified:

```
dtswiz /sserver_name /n /ddatabase_name
```

The DTS command-line utilities and the Data Transformation Services Wizard are discussed in more detail in Chapter 20.

The DTS utilities are located, by default, with the SQL Server tools in `Microsoft SQL Server\80\Tools\Binn\`.

ISQL/OSQL

The ISQL and OSQL command-line utilities can be used to execute SQL statements, stored procedures, and script files from the command prompt. Commands that can be entered interactively via Query Analyzer can be placed in batch files and executed via ISQL/OSQL. In addition, the output from these files can be routed to a file that allows daily reports and tasks of this nature to be run unattended.

The ISQL utility uses DB-LIB to communicate with SQL Server, whereas OSQL uses ODBC. Because ISQL is based on the DB-LIB interface, it does not support Unicode data. DB-Library has not been enhanced to support any of the new features in SQL Server 7.0 or 2000 and is only maintained for backward compatibility. Microsoft recommends that you use OSQL instead of ISQL for any command-line procedures.

The command-line parameters for ISQL and OSQL are similar with only a few differences. The command-line parameters for both utilities allow you to specify the query or file you want to execute, the target server and database, as well as the location for the resulting output.

TIP

According to the Books Online documentation, the ISQL utility (which is based on Db-Library) does not support named instances. Contrary to the documentation, I have been able to connect with ISQL using named instance, but you might encounter problems. If you do experience problems, one workaround is to set up an alias for the named instance using the Client Network utility. After this alias has been created, then the alias name can be used with the \S parameter in ISQL. Another alternative is to use OSQL, which does support named instances and all other SQL Server 2000 features.

A simple OSQL example follows:

```
OSQL /sserver_name /E /iinput_file  /ooutput_file
```

This example shows the basic syntax needed to run a query from a SQL script file using the default server instance. A trusted connection and an output file for the results are specified as well. The same syntax can be used for the ISQL utility.

In addition to using the utilities to run SQL queries, you can also use them by specifying the `-L` option. This option will list the names of the SQL servers currently on the network. You might want to use this option when you are troubleshooting a client's connection and you want to know which SQL servers the particular workstation can see.

The ISQL.EXE and OSQL.EXE files are located, by default, with the SQL Server tools in `Microsoft SQL Server\80\Tools\Binn\`.

makepipe and readpipe

makepipe and readpipe are a little-known pair of utilities that are useful when you want to verify a client's connectivity to SQL Server through named pipes. The utilities work in conjunction with one another. To use these utilities, you first run makepipe from a command line on the server. The basic syntax is as follows:

```
makepipe
readpipe /Sserver_name
```

You can optionally pass it a pipe name, or it will create a default named pipe on the local SQL Server with a name of \\.\pipe\abc. Next, on the client computer, you can run readpipe /*Sserver_name*. You can supply some optional parameters, but at minimum, readpipe needs the server name. If the named pipes interface is working properly between the client and the server, the client will display a message indicating that it sent data successfully to the server, and the server will echo the data sent from the client.

The following is an example of what you would see on the client machine after a successful readpipe execution.

```
SvrName:\\win2000svr
PIPE    :\\win2000svr\pipe\abc
DATA    :test
Data Sent: 1 : test
Data Read: 1 : test
```

The server also reacts to the readpipe call with the makepipe utility, showing something like this:

```
Waiting for client to send... 1
Data Read:      test
Waiting for client to send... 2
Pipe closed
Waiting for Client to Connect...
```

You can press Ctrl+C to exit the utility on the server side. The -q option for the readpipe utility enables you to specify that it poll for incoming data. If not specified, the utility will wait for incoming data.

The makepipe and readpipe utilities are not installed as part of the SQL Server 2000 installation, but they can be copied from the installation disc.

ODBCcmpt

ODBCcmpt allows you to enable or disable the 6.5 or 7.0 ODBC compatibility option, using the following syntax:

```
ODBCcmpt filename
```

The *filename* is the name of an application's executable file for which you want to set the compatibility level. This option permits the SQL Server ODBC driver (Version 3.7) to be compatible with previous drivers. You might need to enable this option when running an application that SQL Server 2000 should treat as a 6.5-level or 7.0-level application. This allows backward compatibility for applications using either the ODBC 2.*x* or ODBC 3.*x* API.

The ODBCCMPT.EXE file is located, by default, with the SQL Server tools in `Microsoft SQL Server\80\Tools\Binn\`.

odbcping

The odbcping utility is a good diagnostic tool that allows you to test a client machine's ODBC connectivity to your database server. It uses this syntax:

```
odbcping { -Sserver_name | -Ddata_source }
```

Unlike `makepipe` and `readpipe`, odbcping runs only on the client. You can use odbcping whenever you need to verify that a client's ODBC connectivity is properly configured. You can also incorporate the use of odbcping as part of an installation procedure.

You can run odbcping in two ways. You can execute `odbcping -Sserver_name` to test a client's direct connectivity to SQL Server. You can also run `odbcping -Ddata_source` to use the specified data source to connect to SQL Server. In either case, if successful, odbcping displays the version of SQL Server and the version of the SQL Server ODBC driver.

The following example shows a simple odbcping execution (using the SQL Server name) and the resulting output:

```
>odbcping –Swin2000svr\instance1

CONNECTED TO SQL SERVER

ODBC SQL Server Driver Version: 03.80.0380

SQL Server Version: Microsoft SQL Server  2000 - 8.00.384 (Intel X86)
        May 23 2001 00:02:52
        Copyright (c) 1988-2000 Microsoft Corporation
        Developer Edition on Windows NT 4.0 (Build 1381: Service Pack 6)
```

TIP

For Windows 2000 clients, a new utility named PathPing is also available for troubleshooting TCP/IP connectivity problems. Given a target server name, this utility will display the computer name and IP address for each router as it moves toward its destination. If successfully connected to the destination server, the utility echoes reply packets (messages) to the client machine to indicate that TCP/IP connectivity exists. For Windows 9.x and NT clients, the Ping utility, which has less functionality, is available instead.

The odbcping utility is not installed as part of the SQL Server 2000 installation, but it can be copied from the installation disc.

rebuildm

rebuildm is a utility that you can use to rebuild system databases, including the master, msdb, and model databases, that are shipped with SQL Server 2000.

The syntax is as follows:

```
rebuildm
```

CAUTION

rebuildm needs to be used with extreme caution because it essentially copies the original versions of these databases over the copies that you have in your database. After rebuildm has been run, all of the information that you had in these databases prior to running rebuildm (including user database information, scheduled tasks, and default database settings) will be gone.

The rebuildm utility is typically used if the following situations exist:

- A current backup of the master database is unavailable. If the backup were available, the server would need to be started in single user mode first.
- Microsoft SQL Server 2000 cannot start because the master database is severely damaged.

If you have one of these situations and you need to run the utility, then these are the basic steps involved:

1. Run the rebuildm.exe from the SQL Server 2000 installation disk or network share.
2. Re-create any backup devices.
3. Set up security including logins.
4. Restore or attach the msdb, model, and distribution databases.
5. Restore or attach any user databases.

TIP

The Northwind and Pubs databases are also restored when rebuildm is run. An alternative to running the rebuildm utility to rebuild these databases is to copy the database files (*.mdf and *.ldf) directly from the data directory located on the installation disk or network drive where you ran your install. Before doing this, you need to detach the database that you want to rebuild using Enterprise Manager; just right-click on the database and select the Detach option. After detaching the database, you can move or delete the relative database files in the DATA directory on your database server. You can then copy the files for the database that you want to rebuild from the installation disc to the DATA directory on the database server. The files are read only by default, so you must change the file properties so that they are not read only. The last step is to use Enterprise Manager to attach the database files that you have just copied.

The rebuildm.exe file is located, by default, with the SQL Server tools in `Microsoft SQL Server\80\Tools\Binn\`.

regrebld

regrebld is a utility that you can use to back up and restore the SQL Server Registry entries. It creates a set of files in the `\Microsoft SQL Server\Mssql\Binn` directory with the .RBK extension. The syntax is as follows:

```
regrebld [-Backup | -Restore ]
```

You can run regrebld with `-Backup` to back up the Registry settings or use the `-Restore` option to restore the Registry settings and verify the state of SQL Server services.

CAUTION

Be aware that if you run regrebld without specifying an option, it will restore the Registry settings. Also, be aware of the fact that regrebld, by default, targets the default instance of SQL Server.

A recommended alternative to running regrebld is to run the SQL Server 2000 setup program, select the Advanced Options button on the Installation Selection screen, and then select Registry Rebuild on the Advanced Options screen.

The regrebld utility is not installed as part of the SQL Server 2000 installation, but it can be copied from the installation disc.

Replication Utilities

You can use five utilities to configure and execute the replication functionality of SQL Server. These utilities are covered in more detail in Chapter 22, "Data Replication." The utilities include the following:

- Replication Distribution Agent partial syntax:

```
distrib -Publisher server_name[\instance_name]
-PublisherDB publisher_database
-Subscriber server_name[\instance_name]
```

  The Replication Distribution Agent is a process that transfers the replicated data held at the distributor to the various subscribers.

- Replication Log Reader Agent partial syntax:

```
logread -Publisher server_name[\instance_name]
-PublisherDB publisher_database
```

  The Replication Log Reader Agent transfers transactions marked for replication on the publisher from the transaction log to the distribution database.

- Replication Merge Agent partial syntax:

```
replmerg
-Publisher server_name[\instance_name]
-PublisherDB publisher_database
-Publication publication
-Subscriber server_name[\instance_name]
-SubscriberDB subscriber_database
```

  The Replication Merge Agent transfers the initial snapshots and any subsequent data changes in the publisher's database tables to the subscribers.

- Replication Queue Reader Agent partial syntax:

```
queueread -Publisher server_name[\instance_name]
-PublisherDB publisher_database
```

  The Replication Queue Read Agent reads messages stored in a SQL Server queue or a Microsoft Message Queue and applies those messages to the publisher. Only snapshot and transactional publications allow queued updating.

- Replication Snapshot Agent partial syntax:

```
snapshot -Publisher server_name[\instance_name]
-PublisherDB publisher_database
-Publication publication_name
```

  The Replication Snapshot Agent prepares the initial snapshots of tables in the publisher's database, stores the files on the distributor, and then maintains the status of its synchronization.

All of the replication utility files are located, by default, in `Microsoft SQL Server\80\Com\`.

SQLDiag

SQLDiag is a diagnostic tool that you can use to gather information regarding various SQL Server services. It is intended for use by Microsoft support engineers, but you might also find the information that it gathers useful in troubleshooting a problem. SQLDiag collects the information into a text file named `Sqldiag.txt` that is located in the `log` directory for SQL Server, typically `Program Files\Microsoft SQL Server\MSSQL$` *`instance_name`*`\log\`. The file contains all the SQL Server error logs, Registry data, file versions, configuration data, user and process information, and output from the Microsoft diagnostic utility (Winmsd.exe).

The syntax for SQLDiag is as follows:

```
SQLdiag
[-?] |
[-I instance_name]
[ [-U login_ID] [-P password] | [-E] ]
[-O output_file]
[-X] [-M] [-C]
```

The `-I` parameter can be used to specify the SQL Server 2000 instance name. In situations in which you have multiple versions of SQL Server running, you will want to use the instance parameter. Otherwise, it might gather information on the 7.0 server instead of the 2000 server. The `-O` option can be used to specify an alternative location for the output text file, and the `-X` option can be used to streamline the output file by excluding the error logs from the file.

A portion of a sample sqldiag.txt file follows:

```
Drives Report
----------------------------------------------------------------------
C:\  (Local - NTFS)  Total: 4,120,168 KB, Free: 1,332,071 KB
D:\  (Local - NTFS)  Total: 13,592,876 KB, Free: 3,815,028 KB
E:\  (CDROM - CDFS) X06-07018 Total: 3,959,392 KB, Free: 0 KB

Memory Report
----------------------------------------------------------------------
Handles: 6,273
Threads: 371
Processes: 58

Physical Memory (K)
   Total: 261,492
   Available: 64,420
   File Cache: 46,744
```

Again, this is just part of the output found in the text file, but you can see how useful this type of information can be.

NOTE

I am a big fan of using SQLDiag to quickly retrieve a myriad of information about the remote database servers that I support. You can execute the SQLDiag.exe program utilizing the xp_cmdshell utility from Query Analyzer and transfer the resulting file back to your office for analysis.

Realize that the file can be fairly busy with all of the error logs contained in it. However, you can easily jump past the error log data by doing a find on 'registry information' in the text file or running the SQLDiag utility with the `-X` parameter that excludes the error logs. I find the system drives and memory reports to be the most valuable sections in the text.

The SQLDIAG.EXE file is located, by default, in a path that is specific to the SQL Server instance. Therefore, one EXE is installed for each instance that is created. The path will typically be `Program Files\Microsoft SQL Server\MSSQL$`*`instance_name`*`\Binn\`.

SQLMaint

The syntax is simply the following:

```
SQLmaint
```

The SQLMaint utility is the power under the hood of the Database Maintenance Wizard. The SQL Server maintenance jobs that are created upon completion of the wizard use xp_sqlmaint to execute the SQLMaint utility with the options selected.

You can also set up and execute the SQLMaint utility independent of the wizard. All of the features and options that are available via the wizard can be manually set with the SQLMaint utility and used for setting up automated maintenance procedures for a given database.

Some of the commonly used options for SQLMaint can be grouped as follows:

`-CK` is the prefix used with any option that performs a data integrity check, such as checking the integrity of the database tables and indexes. Some of these options have the ability to bypass index checking, which speeds up the operation considerably. These options include `-CkDB`, `-CkDBNoIDX`, `-CkAl`, `-CkAlNoIdx`, and `–CkCat`.

`-UpdOptiStats` and `-RebldIdx` are options that improve query performance. The first option updates the statistics used by the query optimizer and the second option rebuilds the indexes entirely.

`-BkUp` is the prefix used with options that back up either the database or the transaction log. These options include `–BkUpDB`, `-BkUpLog`, `-BkUpMedia`, and `-BkUpOnlyIfClean`.

`-DelBkUps` determines how long the previous backups are saved before the utility deletes them. You can specify the time period that can be set for minutes, hours, days, weeks, or months.

-Rpt and -HtmlRpt are options that output the results of SQLMaint to a text file or an HTML file that can be published on a Web page.

-DelTxtRpt specifies a time period for which text reports will be deleted. Report files older than the specified time period that match the -Rpt text file pattern will be deleted.

CAUTION

Report files that are determined by the -Rpt option that have a file extention other than TXT are not deleted when the DelTxtRpt option is specified. If the report file has the TXT extention, the deletion occurs as decribed previously.

TIP

The Database Maintenance Plan Wizard can be used to generate new scheduled jobs that utilize the xp_sqlmaint extended stored procedure. The xp_sqlmaint procedure calls the sqlmaint utility with a string containing sqlmaint switches. You can change the various options available in the Plan Wizard and review the SQLMAINT options that are created in the underlying scheduled jobs. The scheduled jobs associated with the Maintenance Plan will have a name that includes the name of the new Maintenance Plan that you created with the wizard.

The SQLMAINT.EXE file is located, by default, in a path that is specific to the SQL Server instance. Therefore, one EXE is installed for each instance that is created. The path will typically be Program Files\Microsoft SQL Server\MSSQL$*instance_name*\Binn\.

SQLServr

The partial syntax is as follows:

```
SQLservr [-f] [-m]
```

The SQLServr application is the application that runs when SQL Server is started. You can use the SQLServr executable to start SQL Server from a command prompt. When this is done, all of the startup messages are displayed at the command prompt, and the command prompt session becomes dedicated to the execution of SQL Server.

CAUTION

If you start SQL Server from a command prompt, you cannot stop or pause it by using the Enterprise Manager, Service Manager, or the Services applet in the Control Panel.

Most commonly, you'll start SQL Server from the command prompt if you need to troubleshoot a configuration problem. The `-f` option starts SQL Server in minimal configuration mode. This allows you to recover from a change to a configuration setting that prevents SQL Server from starting. You can use the `-m` option when you need to start SQL Server in single-user mode, such as when you need to rebuild one of the system databases.

The SQLSERVR.EXE file is located, by default, in a path that is specific to the SQL Server instance. Therefore, one EXE is installed for each instance that is created. The path will typically be `Program Files\Microsoft SQL Server\MSSQL$`*`instance_name`*`\Binn\`.

VSwitch

The syntax for VSwitch is the following (see the Books Online Help for the full syntax of this utility):

```
vswitch -S {60 | 65 | 80}
```

You can use the VSwitch utility to switch between the currently active version of SQL Server and another version of SQL Server. This is important when SQL Server 2000 has been installed on a machine with a 6.0 or 6.5 version of SQL Server because the earlier versions of SQL Server (6.0/6.5) cannot run concurrently with SQL Server 2000. SQL Server 7.0 servers can run concurrently with SQL Server 2000 on the same machine, but they are also unable to run at the same time with 6.0 or 7.0.

It is recommended that only one version of SQL Server be installed on a given machine. Each version uses a different set of Registry keys, so configuration changes made under one version will not be made under the other version. This utility is provided primarily as a means to assist in the upgrade process.

The VSWITCH.EXE file is located, by default, in a path that is specific to the SQL Server instance. Therefore, one EXE is installed for each instance that is created. The path will typically be `Program Files\Microsoft SQL Server\MSSQL$`*`instance_name`*`\Binn\`.

Summary

SQL Server provides a set of command-line utilities that allow you to execute some of the SQL Server programs from the command prompt. Much of the functionality housed in these utilities is also available in other graphical tools such as the SQL Enterprise Manager. However, you will find the ability to initiate these programs from the command prompt is invaluable in certain scenarios.

The next chapter, "SQL Server Query Analyzer and SQL Debugger," covers two fundamental tools that you can use to create and test efficient SQL Server queries.

CHAPTER 6

SQL Server Query Analyzer and SQL Debugger

by Ray Rankins and Bennett McEwan

IN THIS CHAPTER

- Query Analyzer
- The SQL Debugger

SQL Enterprise Manager (SQL EM) is a fine tool for creating and managing databases and database objects, as well as managing and monitoring SQL Server. However, there are times when you'll want to write and execute SQL directly. For example, SQL EM provides the ability to create and modify stored procedures, triggers, functions, and views from within the database browser, but the editor window it provides is very simplistic—no search/replace capability, no ability to save or open a file from within the editor, and no way to execute and test your SQL code.

Fortunately, Microsoft provides SQL Query Analyzer. The name of SQL Query Analyzer is actually somewhat misleading. While one of its capabilities is the analysis of your queries, it also provides a number of features that really make it a tool for full-featured Transact-SQL development and interactive query execution. In this chapter, we'll take a look at the capabilities of Query Analyzer, including the ability to debug stored procedures, triggers, and functions.

Query Analyzer

Query Analyzer is a fairly straightforward and simple tool to use. Since the user interface is user-friendly and easy to navigate, the purpose of this section of the chapter is not to provide a basic tutorial on using Query Analyzer, but to help you get more out of Query Analyzer by pointing out some of its more useful features that you might not be aware of.

Establishing Connections

When Query Analyzer first starts up, you are presented with a connection dialog as shown in Figure 6.1. Within this dialog, you can choose to connect using Windows authentication or using a SQL Server specific login ID and password. The SQL Server: field provides a drop-down list of the servers you've most recently connected to, or you can simply type in the name of the SQL Server. If you click on the button to the right of the server name box, it will display a list of SQL Servers that it detects are currently running on your network. If you have the appropriate administrative privileges, a check box is available that will allow you to automatically start the specified SQL Server if it is not running.

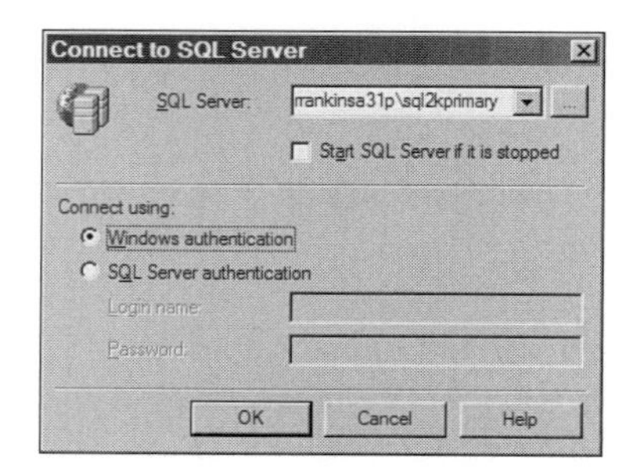

FIGURE 6.1 Query Analyzer Connection dialog.

It is important to note that each editor window opened in Query Analyzer uses a separate connection to SQL Server. If you simply open a new editor window by pressing Ctrl+N, choosing New from the File menu, or by clicking on the New Query button on the toolbar, Query Analyzer will open the new query window using the connection information from the currently active query window. If you wish to open a new connection to a different SQL Server, choose the Connect option from the File menu or press Ctrl+O.

By default, the editor opens up in the default database specified for the login ID used to connect to SQL Server. You can change your database context via the drop-down menu on the toolbar, from the Change Database dialog selected from the Query menu, or by executing the `use` *`dbname`* command within the query window.

Query Editor

The main feature of Query Analyzer is its query editing capabilities. Query Analyzer comes with a full-featured T-SQL editor that provides color coding and highlighting of different types of syntax as well as an automatic help facility. The editor includes a standard text-editing feature set, which includes cut, copy and paste, a search and replace facility, and an Undo option (the number of Undo operations allowed is configurable in the Options dialog). It also provides the ability to go to a specific line in the editor, as well as the ability to set bookmarks. Bookmarks are useful if you are working with a large SQL script. You can toggle bookmarks on and off in the Edit menu or by pressing Ctrl+F2. You can then navigate to the next or previous bookmark by pressing F2 or Shift+F2 respectively, or by selecting Next Bookmark or Previous Bookmark from the Bookmark submenu in the Edit menu.

There are some additional features under the Advanced submenu in the Edit menu that are very useful for the developer, including the ability to convert text to upper- or lowercase, comment out or uncomment a block of text, or increase or decrease the indenting for a block of text. Highlight a section of text and then choose the option you want to apply from the menu or type the appropriate shortcut key sequence. For example, to comment out a highlighted section of text, press Ctrl+Shift+C.

The editor also provides the ability to open and save SQL files. The default file type extension for SQL scripts is `.sql`. The default file extension as well as the default directory for opening and saving files can be set in the General tab on the Options dialog, which is available under the Tools menu or by pressing Ctrl+Shift+O.

Query Execution and Results

In addition to being able to edit your SQL files in Query Analyzer, you can also execute them. The SQL can be executed by choosing the Execute option on the Query menu, by clicking the green triangle in the toolbar, or by pressing F5 or Ctrl+E. you can execute the entire contents of the window, or highlight a section of text to be executed.

The results can be returned in either text format or in a spreadsheet-style grid format. The text format is most useful when executing a SQL script or stored procedure that generates print or raiserror messages that are intended to be interspersed with the resultsets, when you want to see the complete resultset fully listed and unformatted, or when you need to copy and paste the result into a text editor. Figure 6.2 shows an example of the text results for a query. Text results can be difficult to review if the columns are wide because the full column width is displayed.

When displaying results in grid format, each resultset is returned in a separate grid within the results pane. Grid format is most useful when you have resultsets that have wide columns. The columns in the result grid are initially sized to fit in the query window (if possible), and can be resized to any width. Each grid has its own set of scroll bars for scrolling through each individual resultset. Figure 6.3 shows an example of the grid results pane with multiple resultsets. Grid results are also useful if you want to save the results in a delimited text file or copy and paste the results into a spreadsheet. One downside of grid results is that the messages are displayed in a separate tabbed pane. You'll need to remember to check this pane when running a SQL script to make sure no error messages were generated.

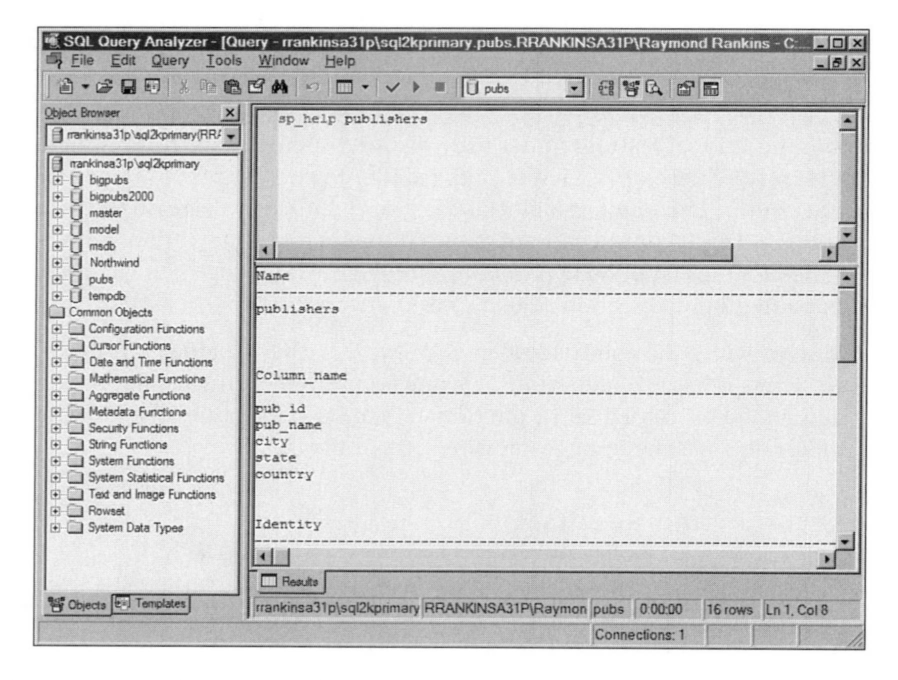

FIGURE 6.2 Query Analyzer Text Results pane.

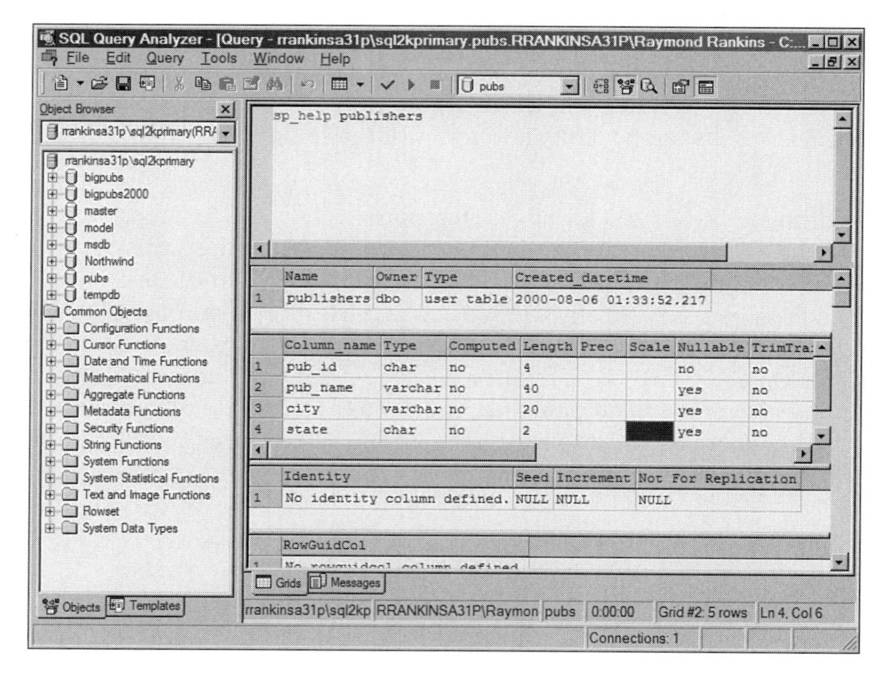

FIGURE 6.3 Query Analyzer Grid Results pane.

You can switch between grid or text results by pressing Ctrl+D or Ctrl+T respectively, or by choosing the appropriate result option from the Query menu.

To save query results to a file, place the cursor in the results pane and choose the Save option from the File menu. If saving text results, the entire results pane is saved to a file in text format. You can choose to save the text as ANSI, Unicode, or OEM (code page 437). The default file type is *.rpt, but you can override this as well if you want to save the result as *.txt. You can set a different file extension for report files globally by changing it in the General tab of the Options dialog.

When saving grid results to a file, only the currently selected grid is saved to a file. In addition to saving the text as ANSI, Unicode, or OEM (code page 437), you also have the option of saving the text as a comma- or tab-delimited file. This is useful for generating files to be imported into another database or spreadsheet tool.

To close the results pane and increase the size of the edit pane, press Ctrl+R or choose the Close Results Pane option from the Window menu.

If you don't care for the split window mode of displaying the query and results, you can switch Query Analyzer to use a tabbed mode by checking the Tabbed mode (versus Splitter mode) option on the Editor tab in the Options dialog. In this mode, each pane is the full window height, and you select the pane you want to view by clicking on the appropriate tab displayed at the bottom of the edit window. You can also cycle through the panes in an edit window using the F6 key. An example of using Tabbed mode for an edit window is shown Figure 6.4.

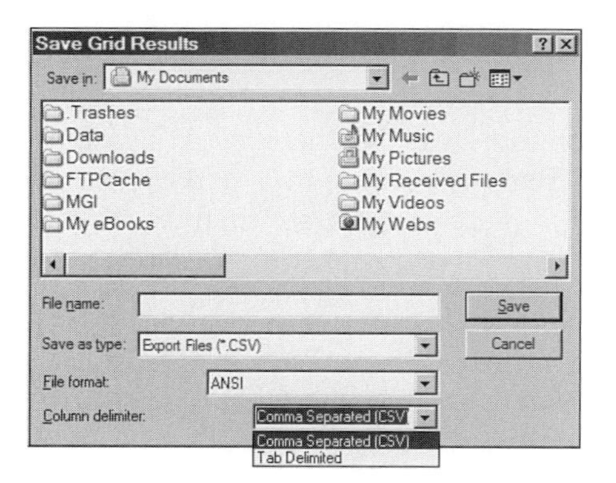

FIGURE 6.4 Query Analyzer grid results in Tabbed mode.

Query Analyzer also provides the ability to send the results directly to a file rather than to the results pane. This option can be enabled by selecting the Results to File option from the Query menu, or by pressing Ctrl+Shift+F. Once this option is turned on for an edit window, the next time you execute a query for that window, a dialog box will come up, allowing you to specify the file you want the results saved to. All query results and messages will be sent to the file and a message such as the following will be displayed in the Messages pane:

```
The following file has been saved successfully:

C:\Data\Reports\sp_help.rpt 86 bytes
```

Any error messages generated during the execution of the SQL commands will be sent to both the file and the Message pane. This feature is useful when your SQL script generates a large amount of output and you might be running Query Analyzer on a system with limited memory. Writing the result directly to a file avoids having to buffer the large resultset in memory, which could lead to paging and slow performance on the client workstation.

Query Analysis

In addition to simply executing queries, the Query menu in Query Analyzer also provides the query analysis features from which Query Analyzer derives its name. There is an option to only parse the query without executing it. This is helpful when you have a large script file and you want to validate your SQL code for syntax errors before submitting it for execution.

> **NOTE**
>
> Because SQL Server does not resolve table, column, or other object names until execution, running a parse check on your SQL code will only check for syntax errors. If the syntax is okay, but an invalid table name is specified, it will pass the parse check, but still fail during execution when the table name cannot be resolved.

The other query analysis options available include displaying the estimated execution plan, the actual execution plan, server trace info, and client statistics. For a detailed discussion on using these tools for query analysis, see Chapter 36, "Query Analysis."

Object Browser

Another great new feature in the Query Analyzer in SQL Server 2000 is the Object Browser. The Object Browser is a separate window pane that is usually displayed on the left side (you can move it to the right side by setting the option in the General tab in the Options dialog). If the Object Browser is not visible, you can invoke it by using the F8 key, or selecting the Show/Hide option from the Object Browser submenu in the Tools menu.

Note that when the Object Browser is open, it establishes a separate connection to SQL Server that is distinct from the connections made by the query windows. An Object Browser connection is made for each different server connection established in Query Analyzer. You can switch between connections to explore objects and databases on different servers by choosing the desired server from the drop-down list at the top of the Object Browser pane.

The Object Browser is very useful during development of your SQL code as a tool to display object names and object properties such as column names and datatypes, indexes, stored procedure parameters and datatypes, user-defined function arguments, and so on. The Object Browser also provides options for extracting the DDL for your database objects. It can generate code to create, alter, or drop the selected object. You can script the DDL to a new window, to a file, or to the Windows Clipboard by right-clicking on the object in the Object Browser and choosing the appropriate option (see Figure 6.5).

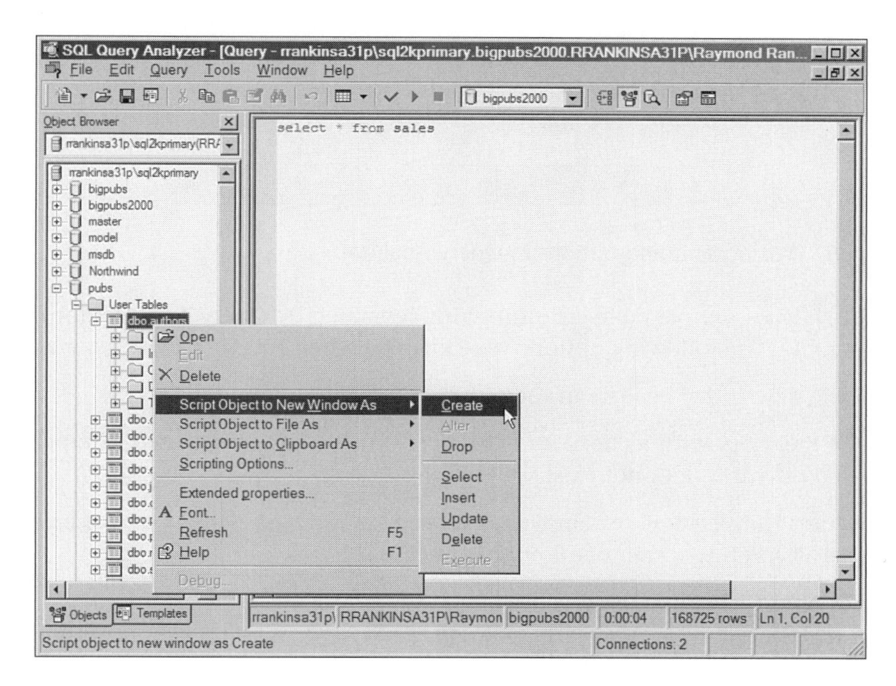

FIGURE 6.5 Extracting DDL for a table to an Editor window.

Query Analyzer provides a number of options for extracting the DDL for a database object. The script generated can automatically include the command to check for the existence of the object and automatically drop it before executing the `CREATE` command. You can also choose to include the commands to restore the existing permissions when the object is re-created.

The scripting options can be specified on the Script tab in the Options dialog box or by right-clicking on the object name in the Object Browser and choosing the Scripting Options menu option. Figure 6.6 shows the Scripting Options tab in the Options dialog.

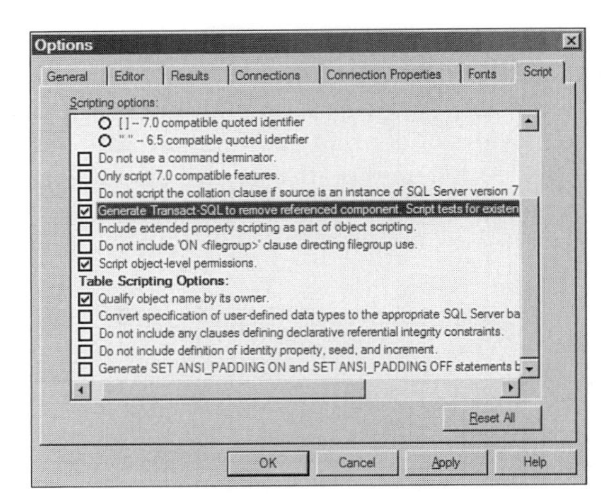

FIGURE 6.6 Setting scripting options in Query Analyzer.

Listing 6.1 shows a sample table-creation script generated by Query Analyzer for the Publishers table. The following options were enabled when this script was generated:

- Include descriptive headers in the script.
- Prefix the script with a check for existence. When script is executed, component is created only if it does not exist.
- Generate Transact-SQL to remove referenced component. Script tests for existence before attempting to remove component.
- Script object-level permissions.
- Qualify object name by its owner.

LISTING 6.1 Sample Table Creation Script Generated by Query Analyzer

```
/*** Object:  Table [dbo].[publishers] Script Date: 9/17/2002 9:34:53 PM ****/
if exists (select * from dbo.sysobjects
   where id = object_id(N'[dbo].[publishers]')
      and OBJECTPROPERTY(id, N'IsUserTable') = 1)
drop table [dbo].[publishers]
GO

if not exists (select * from dbo.sysobjects
   where id = object_id(N'[dbo].[publishers]')
     and OBJECTPROPERTY(id, N'IsUserTable') = 1)
BEGIN
CREATE TABLE [dbo].[publishers] (
        [pub_id] [char] (4) COLLATE SQL_Latin1_General_CP1_CI_AS NOT NULL ,
        [pub_name] [varchar] (40) COLLATE SQL_Latin1_General_CP1_CI_AS NULL ,
```

LISTING 6.1 Continued

```
        [city] [varchar] (20) COLLATE SQL_Latin1_General_CP1_CI_AS NULL ,
        [state] [char] (2) COLLATE SQL_Latin1_General_CP1_CI_AS NULL ,
        [country] [varchar] (30) COLLATE SQL_Latin1_General_CP1_CI_AS
          NULL CONSTRAINT [DF__publisher__count__7D78A4E7] DEFAULT ('USA'),
        CONSTRAINT [UPKCL_pubind] PRIMARY KEY  CLUSTERED
        (
                [pub_id]
        )  ON [PRIMARY] ,
         CHECK ([pub_id] = '1756' or ([pub_id] = '1622' or ([pub_id] = '0877'
           or ([pub_id] = '0736' or [pub_id] = '1389')))
           or [pub_id] like '99[0-9][0-9]')
) ON [PRIMARY]
END

GO

GRANT  REFERENCES ,  SELECT ,  UPDATE ,  INSERT ,  DELETE
    ON [dbo].[publishers]  TO [guest]
GO
```

In addition to scripting the DDL for objects, the Object Browser can also script DML statements such as SELECT, INSERT, UPDATE, and DELETE for tables and views, and EXEC for stored procedures and user-defined functions. This is useful when building a SQL script and you need to include DML statements for database objects. It can save a lot of typing and ensures proper datatypes for columns and parameters. Listing 6.2 shows DML statements generated by Query Analyzer. Once generated, the DML statements will only need editing to add values for placeholders and to remove columns or add additional conditions.

LISTING 6.2 Sample DML Statements Generated by Query Analyzer

```
SELECT [order_number], [customer_number], [order_date]
   FROM [pubs].[dbo].[orders]

INSERT INTO [pubs].[dbo].[publishers]
     ([pub_id], [pub_name], [city], [state], [country])
VALUES(<pub_id,char(4),>, <pub_name,varchar(40),>, <city,varchar(20),>,
       <state,char(2),>, <country,varchar(30),>)

UPDATE [pubs].[dbo].[jobs]
SET [job_id]=<job_id,smallint,>,
    [job_desc]=<job_desc,varchar(50),>,
    [min_lvl]=<min_lvl,tinyint,>,
    [max_lvl]=<max_lvl,tinyint,>
```

LISTING 6.2 Continued

```
WHERE <Search conditions,,>

DELETE FROM [pubs].[dbo].[stores]
WHERE <Search conditions,,>

DECLARE @RC int
DECLARE @percentage int
-- Set parameter values
EXEC @RC = [pubs].[dbo].[byroyalty] @percentage
```

The DML statements generated from the Object Browser are actually templates. You can manually edit the template code and replace the template parameter values, or you can use the Replace Template Parameters option from the Edit menu. Choosing this option brings up a dialog that lists the template parameters in a table and lets you enter data values (see Figure 6.7). When you have entered the values for the desired parameters, click the Replace All button to substitute the supplied values back into the template.

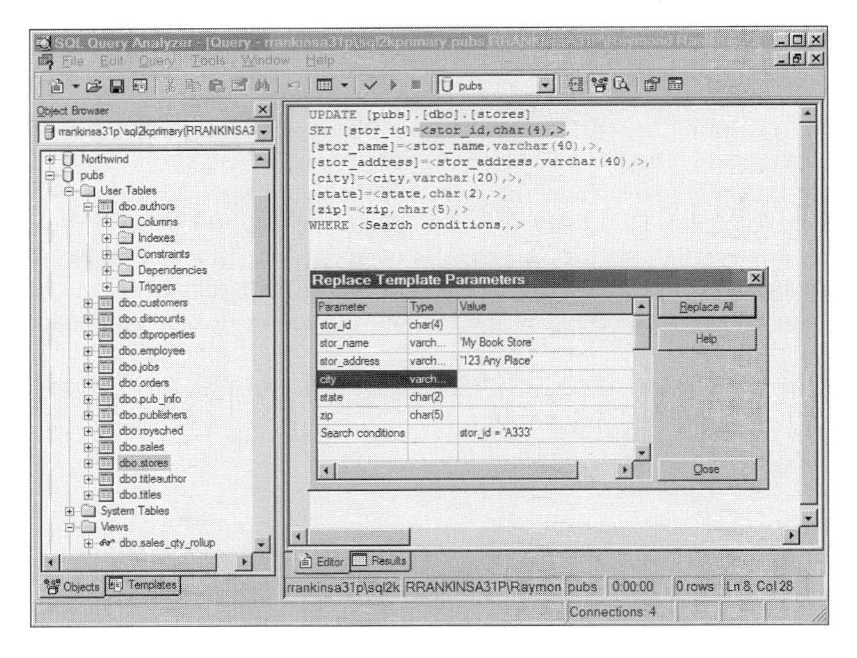

FIGURE 6.7 Replacing template parameters in Query Analyzer.

TIP

Unfortunately, there is no option to script the object information to the current window. If you want to generate the DDL or DML into the current edit window, choose the option to script to the clipboard and then paste the code into the desired location in the SQL script.

One other feature of the Object Browser is the ability to view and edit the extended properties for database objects. Extended properties are like comments that can be stored in the system catalogs for database objects and can provide application-specific or site-specific information about the database objects. The uses of extended properties are only limited by your imagination. Some examples of uses for extended properties include:

- Specifying a caption or description for a table, view, or column that applications can display in the user interface
- Specifying an input mask for a column that applications can use to validate data before submitting Transact-SQL statements
- Specifying formatting rules for displaying column data

The Design Table dialog in SQL Enterprise Manager only allows you to enter a column description that is stored as an extended property. Query Analyzer lets you create and view custom extended properties for databases, database objects, columns, and parameters. You can view, create, or edit extended properties by right-clicking on the item in the Object Browser and choosing the Extended properties option from the menu. This brings up the Extended Property dialog where you can view, add, or edit existing extended properties (see Figure 6.8).

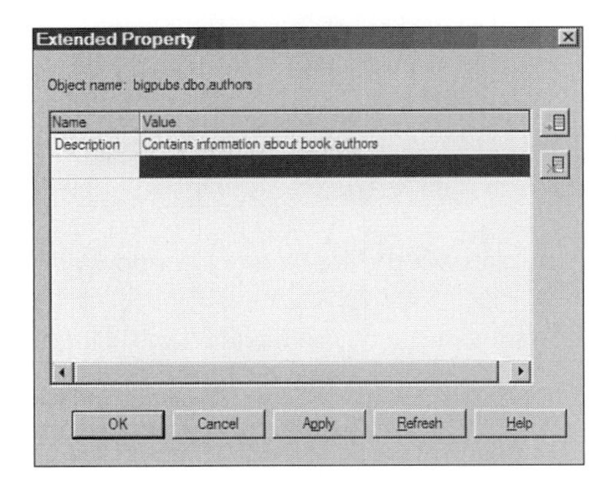

FIGURE 6.8 Managing extended properties in Query Analyzer.

SQL Script Templates

In addition to the DML template code you can generate from the Object Browser, Query Analyzer also supports the use of template files for creating SQL scripts. Query Analyzer comes with a set of predefined template files for tasks such as creating a table, stored procedure, or database, attaching and detaching a database, and managing extended properties.

You can open a blank query window or populate a new query window with the code for one of the available templates by bringing up the drop-down list for the New Document icon on the toolbar and choosing the desired template, as shown in Figure 6.9. You can also load a template by choosing the New option from the File menu and navigating through the dialog to select the desired template file.

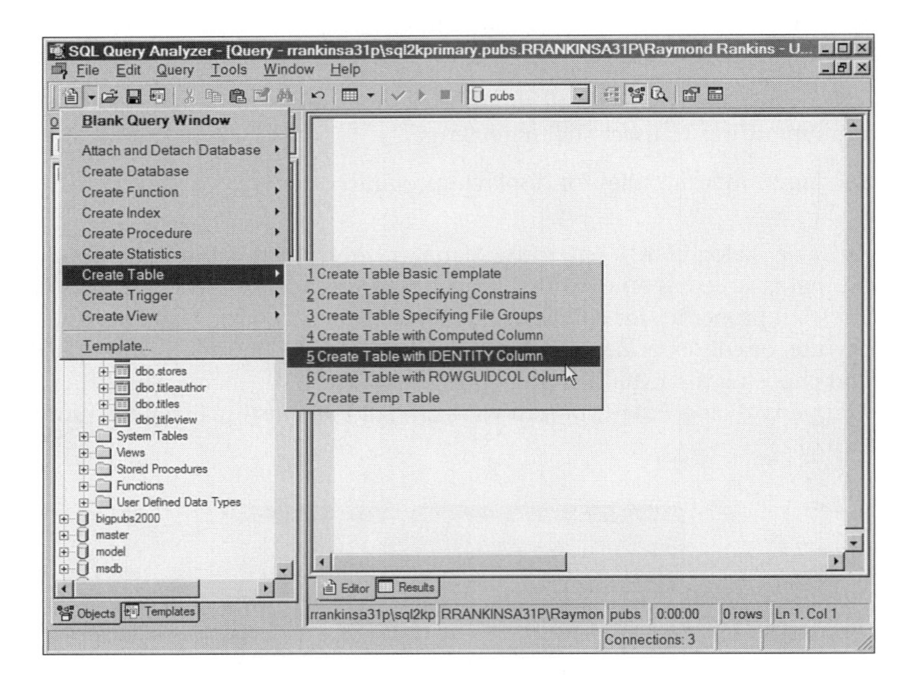

FIGURE 6.9 Choosing a template via the New Query Window dialog.

The code in Listing 6.3 shows a sample of the Create Table template for creating a table with an identity column.

LISTING 6.3 Sample Query Analyzer Template for Creating a Table with an Identity Column

```
-- =============================================
-- Create table with IDENTITY column
-- =============================================
IF EXISTS (SELECT name
           FROM   sysobjects
           WHERE  name = N'<table_name, sysname, test_table>'
           AND    type = 'U')
    DROP TABLE <table_name, sysname, test_table>
GO
```

LISTING 6.3 Continued

```
create table <table_name, sysname, test_table> (
<column_1, sysname, c1> <datatype_for_column_1, , int>
                       IDENTITY(<seed, , 100>, <increment, , 1>),
<column_2, sysname, c2> <datatype_for_column_2, , int> NOT NULL)
GO
```

You can edit the template manually, or, as with the DML templates, select the Replace Template Parameters option from the Edit menu, which will list all template parameters defined in the template. You can then enter the values for the template parameters, which can include table or column names, datatypes, stored procedure and function parameters, and so on. (Refer to Figure 6.7 for an example of this dialog.)

Templates provide a great facility for providing the basic syntax and parameters necessary for creating database objects. Templates can be used by developers to help enforce programming and database design standards. If the templates provided with SQL Server do not provide quite the structure or standards you desire, you can create your own template files. Template files are standard text files with a file extension of `.tql`. You can create them in any text editor, or create them with Query Analyzer and choose the Template SQL Files as the file type in the Save or Save As dialog.

While you can save your template files in any directory, you will have to open them manually by choosing the Template option from the drop-down list of the New File button in the toolbar. If you want your templates to be available in the menu or in the Template dialog, you need to save your templates in the default template directory. The SQL Server–provided templates are stored in the C:\Program Files\Microsoft SQL Server\80\Tools\Templates\SQL Query Analyzer directory. If you want to create a new stored procedure template that appears in the drop-down list for the New File toolbar button, create the file in the Stored Procedure subfolder in this directory.

Template files contain only SQL code and template parameters. When defining your own templates, be sure to use descriptive parameter names so users can identify what values they are filling in when using the Replace Template Parameters dialog. The format of the parameters is as follows:

```
< parameter_name, [recommended_datatype], [default_parameter_value] >
```

The *`recommended_datatype`* and *`default_parameter_value`* are optional values. If not specified, you still need to include both commas in the parameter definition. Listing 6.4 provides a sample stored procedure template that contains a procedure header, standard transaction control statements, and error handling for an update procedure.

LISTING 6.4 Sample Custom Stored Procedure Template (Proc_with_transaction_control.tql)

```
IF EXISTS (SELECT name
           FROM   sysobjects
           WHERE  name = N'<procedure_name, sysname, proc_test>'
           AND    type = 'P')
    DROP PROCEDURE <procedure_name, sysname, proc_test>
GO
-- =============================================
-- Procedure name: <procedure_name, sysname, proc_test>
-- Description:    <procedure_description, , >
-- Created By:     <creator_name, , >
-- Creation Date:  <creation_date, , >
-- Modified By:
-- Modify Date:
-- =============================================

CREATE PROCEDURE <procedure_name, sysname, proc_test>
<@param1, sysname, @p1> <datatype_for_param1, , int>
                        = <default_value_for_param1, , 0>,
<@param2, sysname, @p2> <datatype_for_param2, , int>
                        = <default_value_for_param2, , 0>
AS
DECLARE @trncnt int,
        @err_message varchar(255)

select @trncnt = @@TRANCOUNT

if @trncnt = 0 -- if no transaction current active
    begin tran <procedure_name, sysname, proc_test> -- begin transaction
else           -- transaction active
    save tran <procedure_name, sysname, proc_test>  -- set savepoint

UPDATE <table_name, sysname, t1>
   set <col_1, , > = <@param2, sysname, @p2>
   where <search_condition, , >

if @@error != 0
begin
   select @err_message = 'UPDATE of <@table_name, sysname, t1> failed'
   goto err_handler
end
```

LISTING 6.4 Continued

```
if @trncnt = 0  -- if no transaction was active, need to commit begin tran
begin
    commit tran <procedure_name, sysname, proc_test>
    return 0
end

err_handler:
rollback tran <procedure_name, sysname, proc_test>
raiserror (@err_message, 16, 1)
return -101

GO
```

Object Search

Query Analyzer also provides a basic Object Search tool to help you find instances of an object in your SQL Server databases. This tool can be invoked from the Tools menu. This can be helpful if you want to locate all instances of a specific object in one or all of your databases. The object name can include the same SQL wildcards you would use in a `LIKE` clause. Figure 6.10 shows an example of using the Object Search tool to find all user tables, procedures, and columns that contain the word `sales`.

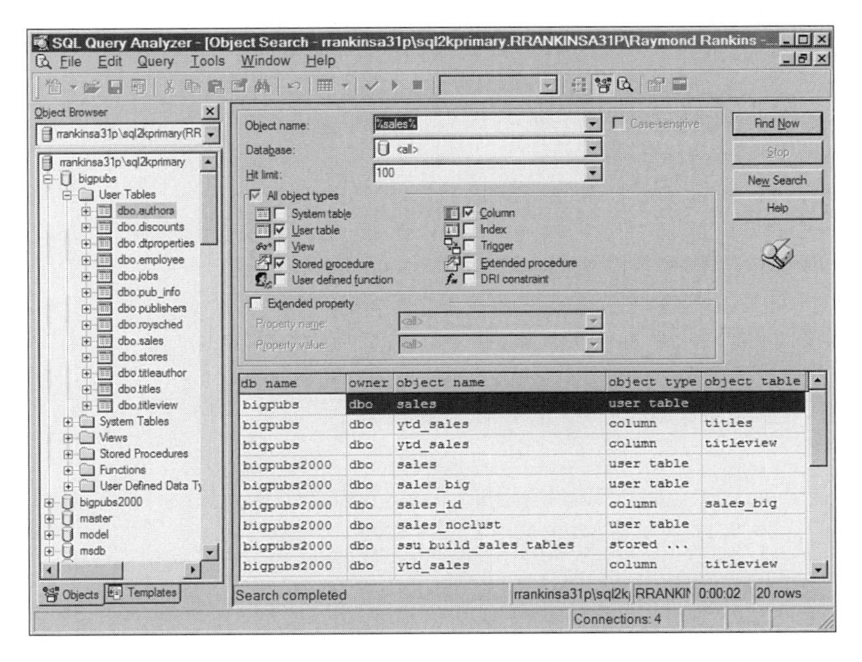

FIGURE 6.10 Using the Object Search to find all user tables, stored procedures, and columns in the SQL Server containing the keyword `sales`.

Within the list of search results, you can right-click on one of the rows and it will bring up the same dialog box as when you right-click on an object in the Object Browser, allowing you to script the object to a new window, file, or the clipboard, or to modify the extended properties of the object.

User-Defined Shortcuts

Query Analyzer provides up to 12 keyboard shortcuts for quickly executing stored procedures in Query Analyzer. SQL Server provides three predefined shortcuts:

- Alt+F1—`sp_help`
- Ctrl+1—`sp_who`
- Ctrl+2—`sp_lock`

For example, if you have a query window open and press Alt+F1, Query Analyzer will execute the `sp_help` command within the current query window context and display the results in the Results pane for that query window.

You can view or modify these shortcuts, or even add your own by selecting the Customize option from the Tools menu. On the Custom tab, you can enter the name of the stored procedure in the Stored Procedure column next to the desired keyboard shortcut you want to use to execute that stored procedure (see Figure 6.11). You might want to add your frequently executed procedures to the Custom menu to save you the trouble of having to type them every time you want to run them.

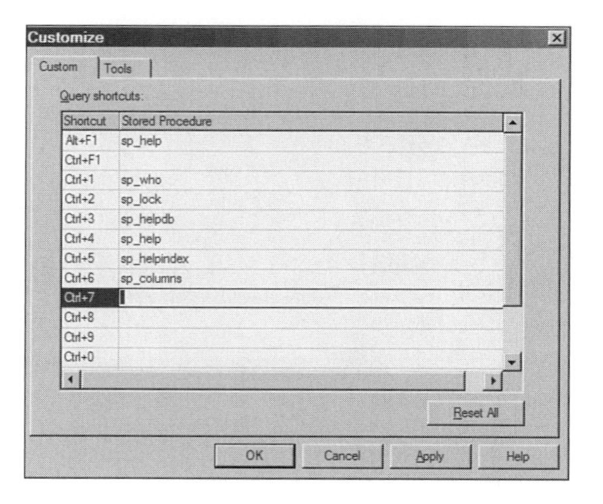

FIGURE 6.11 Adding custom keyboard shortcuts in Query Analyzer.

TIP

If you have a word, data value, or comma-separated list of values highlighted when you invoke a keyboard shortcut, Query Analyzer will pass the highlighted value(s) as parameters to the associated stored procedure.

User-Defined Tools

The Customize option in the Tools menu in Query Analyzer also provides the ability to add your own custom options to the Tools menu. In the Customize dialog, click on the Tools tab. From here, you can enter commands for programs that can then be invoked from the Tools menu, as shown in Figure 6.12.

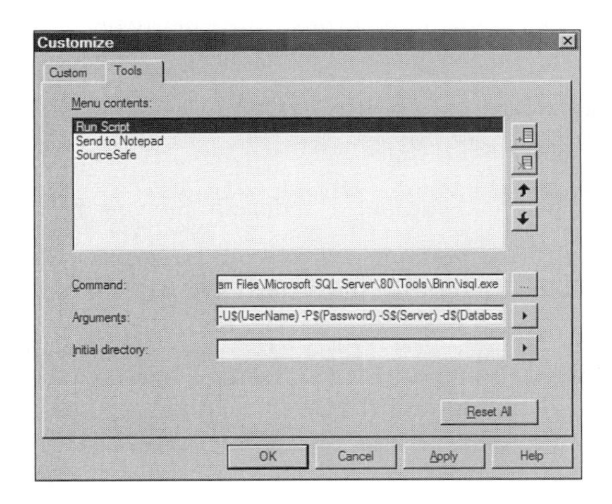

FIGURE 6.12 Adding programs to the Tools menu in Query Analyzer.

In the Command text box, you specify the full pathname of the command you want to invoke. You can click on the button to the right of the text box to browse to the command. In the Arguments text box, you specify any arguments to be passed to the command. If you click on the button to the right of the text box, you can specify variables to include in the argument string. The values of the variables are taken from the context of the currently active query window when you invoke the command from the Tools menu. The available argument variables are the following:

- File Path—The full pathname of the file currently being edited in the query window
- File Directory—The directory where the file currently being edited in the query window resides
- File Name—The name (minus the path and file extension) of the file currently being edited in the query window

- File Extension—The file extension of the file currently being edited in the query window
- Current Directory—The current directory for Query Analyzer (this is typically the directory where a file was most recently opened or saved for that query window)
- Server—The name of the SQL Server the query window is connected to
- Database—The name of the current database the query window is using
- User Name—The user name used to connect to SQL Server
- Password—The password used to connect to SQL Server

The following is an example of the argument list using the built-in argument variables that is passed to a custom command that runs the currently open SQL file via the `isql` command:

```
-U$(UserName) -P$(Password) -S$(Server) -d$(Database) -i$(FilePath)
➥ -o$(FileDir)\$(FileName).out -w1000
```

In the Initial Directory text box, you can set a default directory from which the command will be invoked.

Figure 6.13 shows the Tools menu with three custom commands added:

- Run Script—This command passes the current file being edited in the query window to `isql` for execution. It outputs the results in a file in the same directory as the script file and the output filename is the same as the input file with the file extension changed to `.out`.
- Send to Notepad—This command passes the current file being edited in the query window to Notepad.
- SourceSafe—This command simply invokes the Visual SourceSafe application as a way to provide quicker access to the tool.

Configuration Files

On the General tab of the Options dialog, you can save your Query Analyzer configuration to a file. This is especially useful if multiple people share the computer and have different preferences for how they like having Query Analyzer configured. Each person can save his or her configuration to file, and reload it to get everything back the way he or she likes it. It can also be useful if you prefer one configuration for SQL development and a different configuration for executing maintenance scripts. It's also not a bad idea to save your favorite configuration just in case you happen to really mess things up. Because the configuration is saved to a file (with file extension `.sqc`), you can even take your favorite configuration with you to another machine.

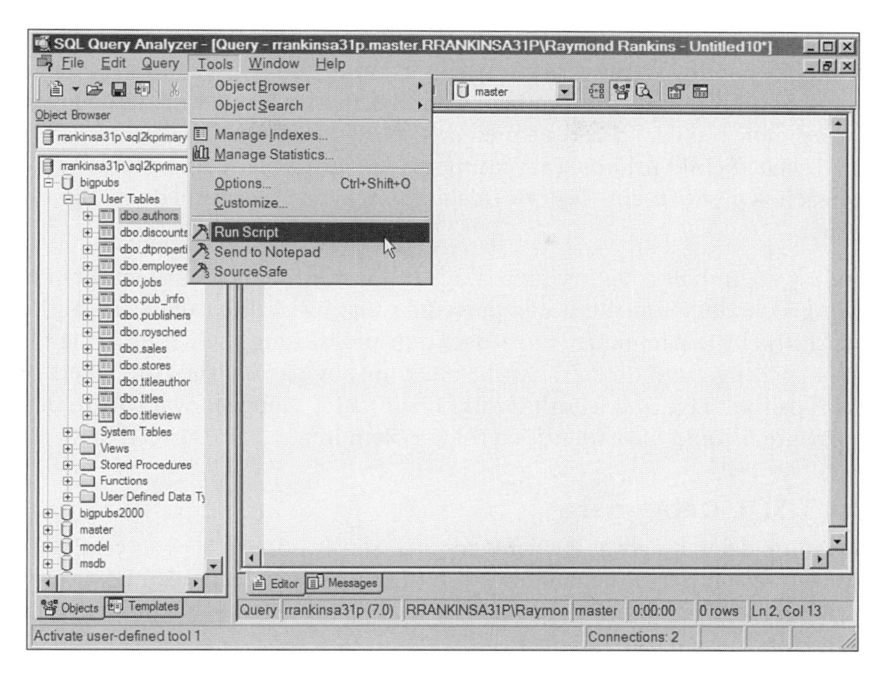

FIGURE 6.13 The Tools menu in Query Analyzer with three custom tools added.

The SQL Debugger

One of the most significant features in Query Analyzer is the SQL Debugger. With the various commands and programming constructs in Transact-SQL (T-SQL), stored procedures can perform some pretty complex operations. You might have as much programming logic built into stored procedures as in some of your other application routines written in other programming languages. As you develop and test your application code written in Visual C++ or Visual Basic (or whatever programming language you might be using), it is likely that you will use a debugger to step through the code and verify that it is working correctly or to identify where the logic is breaking. When your stored procedures are not executing correctly or they are returning the wrong result, you need to debug them as well.

In the old days, the only way to debug stored procedures and step through them line by line was to rewrite them as SQL batches and execute the statements individually or in small groups. The problem with this approach was that the contents of local variables didn't carry over between batches, so you had to redeclare and reinitialize the variables for each batch and set the values to what they were at the end of the previous batch. This process was tedious, and the SQL statements would optimize differently when passed a variable rather than what would have been a stored procedure parameter. For more information on how queries are optimized, see Chapter 35, "Understanding Query Optimization."

The only other way to track what a stored procedure was doing was to litter it with print statements to display the status of the procedure and the contents of local variables and parameters at various points. I remember using this approach one time to debug what looked like a simple problem. I had a stored procedure that needed to delete a parent record, and then all related child records. Everything worked just fine by using local variables and separating each SQL statement. My print/debug statements didn't shed any light on the matter, either.

After spending about half a day trying to track it down, I finally identified the problem—I was missing a parameter to the stored procedure that was being called within the main procedure, shifting the parameter values over one and causing the wrong value to be used to find the matching rows. (I could have avoided this by passing the parameters by name rather than position. Live and learn!) If only I had had a debugger available to debug the stored procedure, I could have identified the problem in a minute instead of a day.

The First T-SQL Debugger

Stored procedure debugging was available for SQL Server prior to SQL Server 2000, but it wasn't part of the SQL Server installation. Since the release of Visual Studio 6, Visual Interdev has included a T-SQL Debugger. Prior to this, it was available inside Visual Basic Enterprise 5.0 and Visual C++ Enterprise 4.2.

However, getting the debugger up and running was an arduous process. You had to have all the following pieces in place:

- You had to have the Enterprise Edition of Visual Studio installed.
- You had to be running at least SQL Server 6.5 with Service Pack 2 or later.
- The server running SQL Server had to be running under Microsoft Windows NT 4.0 or later.
- The client workstation had to be running Windows 95 or Windows NT 4.0 or later.

In addition, for SQL Server versions prior to SQL Server 2000, the debugging components were not installed on the server by default. To get the debugger to work, these pieces had to be installed manually. This caused a lot of headaches: Programmers who wanted to use stored procedure debugging had to bother the administrator, who might or might not have seen the need to install these pieces. It's a rare administrator who will upset the delicate balance of his smoothly running SQL Server to indulge the whim of a developer, unless some sort of bribe is involved.

You also needed to ensure Distributed COM (DCOM) was installed properly on the server and the client. You had to make sure the DCOM configuration on a Windows 98/Me machine supported debugging.

The main problem with using this debugger was that you had to install Visual Interdev. This was a pretty large, involved install if all you wanted to do was use a SQL Debugger. Also, the debugger was not part of a standard query tool like Query Analyzer, nor was it a standalone tool. It had to be brought up via a Data View window in Visual Studio.

People needed a T-SQL Debugger that could be installed along with the SQL Server Client Tools that was integrated with Query Analyzer. That finally came along in SQL Server 2000.

Using the T-SQL Debugger in Query Analyzer

Query Analyzer that ships with SQL Server 2000 now includes an integrated T-SQL Debugger. This is a full-featured debugger that lets you step through stored procedure code a line at a time, set breakpoints, view the contents of local and global variables, and see the results of the T-SQL statements as they execute.

TIP

The 2000 client brings a modern debugger to the SQL Server development environment. However, you do not necessarily need to have SQL 2000 to debug procedures. You can use a version 7 server. Instructions for making this work are available on the Microsoft support Web site at `http://support.microsoft.com/`.

The necessary steps for invoking the debugger are not easily apparent. To debug a stored procedure from within Query Analyzer, follow these steps:

- Open the Object Browser, if it is not already open, by pressing F8.
- Drill through the tree to the stored procedure you want to debug.
- Right-click on the procedure and select Debug from the context menu (see Figure 6.14).

At this stage, a couple of common problems could prevent full use of the debugger. These problems are discussed in the next section.

CAUTION

SQL debugging makes use of Distributed COM calls, which can have adverse effects on the stability and performance of your SQL Server machine. Although the debugger is a useful tool in a development environment, you should never consider using it in your production environment.

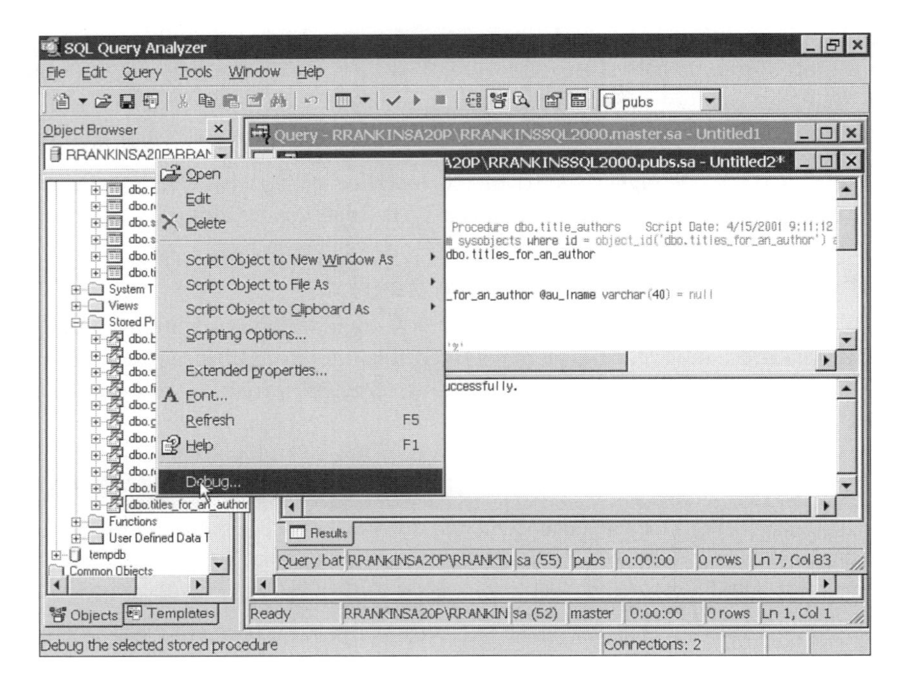

FIGURE 6.14 Invoking the SQL Debugger from the Object Browser.

Debugging a Stored Procedure

If everything is properly configured when you invoke the SQL Debugger, you will first be presented with a dialog where you can enter values for the procedure parameter(s), if any (see Figure 6.15). Click the Set to Null check box if you want to specify a NULL value for a parameter. There is also a check box that lets you specify whether you want the procedure to automatically roll back or not. Auto Rollback is the default option. This feature allows you to test and debug a stored procedure that modifies data without the data changes being permanent, so you can repeatedly debug the procedure with the same datasets each time. The debugger initiates a `BEGIN TRAN` statement before executing the procedure, and automatically issues a `ROLLBACK TRAN` when debugging is stopped. If you want to commit the changes made to data while debugging the stored procedure, uncheck the Auto Rollback option.

CAUTION

Be careful when debugging stored procedures that modify data on systems where other users or processes are executing queries. Any locks acquired during a debugging session will be held until the debugging is stopped and the changes are rolled back. This can block other users from accessing data and adversely impact system performance. For this reason, stored procedure debugging should only be performed in test or development environments where performance is not an issue.

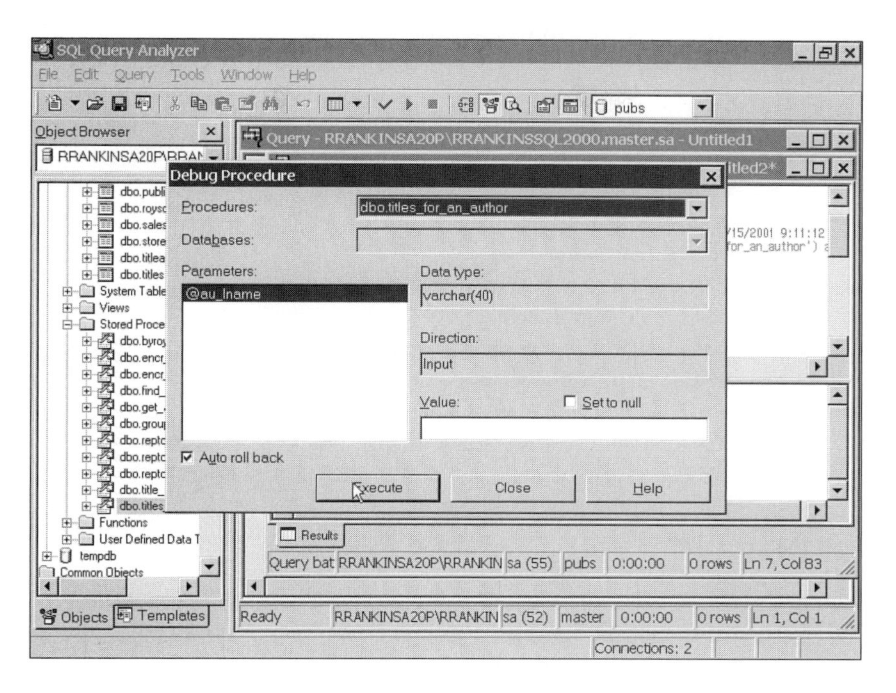

FIGURE 6.15 Providing input parameter values to the SQL Debugger in Query Analyzer.

Once you have provided any necessary input parameters and clicked the Execute button, you will next see the SQL-Debugger interface with a yellow arrow pointing to the first line in the stored procedure (see Figure 6.16). At this point, you can step through the stored procedure one line at a time, or you can set breakpoints and run to the breakpoints. All operations in the SQL Debugger are controlled by selecting the buttons on the Debugger toolbar, by right-clicking in the debugger window to bring up the command menu, or by using the keyboard shortcuts for the Debugger commands. Table 6.1 describes the available commands in the Debugger and the corresponding keyboard shortcuts.

TABLE 6.1 SQL Debugger Commands

Command	Description	Keyboard Shortcut
Go	Runs the stored procedure in debugging mode to the next breakpoint or to the end of the procedure.	F5
Toggle Breakpoint	Sets or removes a breakpoint at the current line. Breakpoints cannot be set on blank lines or lines containing nonexecutable code such as comments or declaration statements.	F9
Remove All Breakpoints	Clears all breakpoints that have been set in the current debugging session.	Ctrl+Shift+F9

TABLE 6.1 Continued

Command	Description	Keyboard Shortcut
Step Into	Executes the statement at the current execution point. If the statement is a call to a procedure or statement that contains a user-defined function or fires a trigger, the debugger positions itself on the first statement in the procedure, function, or trigger.	F11
Step Over	Executes the statement at the current execution point, but if the current statement is a call to a procedure or statement that contains a user-defined function or fires a trigger, Step Over executes the statement or procedure as a unit, and then positions the debugger at the next statement in the current procedure.	F10
Step Out	If the debugger has stepped into a procedure, user-defined function, or trigger, this command completes execution of the procedure, function, or trigger and positions the debugger at the next statement in the calling procedure.	Shift+F11
Run to Cursor	Executes all statements from the current execution point up to the position where the cursor is placed.	Ctrl+F10
Restart	Aborts the current debugging session and restarts execution from the beginning of the stored procedure.	Ctrl+Shift+F5
Stop Debugging	Aborts the current debugging session.	Shift+F5
Auto Rollback	Toggles the Auto-Rollback option on or off.	

The Debugger Window Panes

The SQL Debugger window consists of five window panes. The top pane is the Source Code window pane that displays the text of the procedure, user-defined function, or trigger that is currently being debugged. This window pane indicates the current execution point and is where you can set and display breakpoints.

NOTE

If you modify the code for the top-level stored procedure that is currently displayed in the debugger window, you will need to stop and close the debugging session and restart it to pick up and display the changes in the debugger window.

The three middle window panes are the Local Variables window pane, the Global Functions window pane, and the Callstack window pane. The Local Variables pane displays the name, value, and type of each input and output parameter and any local variables defined within the current procedure scope. You cannot add or remove any of the variables listed in this pane, but you can change the values assigned to the variables. This is useful for evaluating and testing different variable values and their impact on program flow and execution.

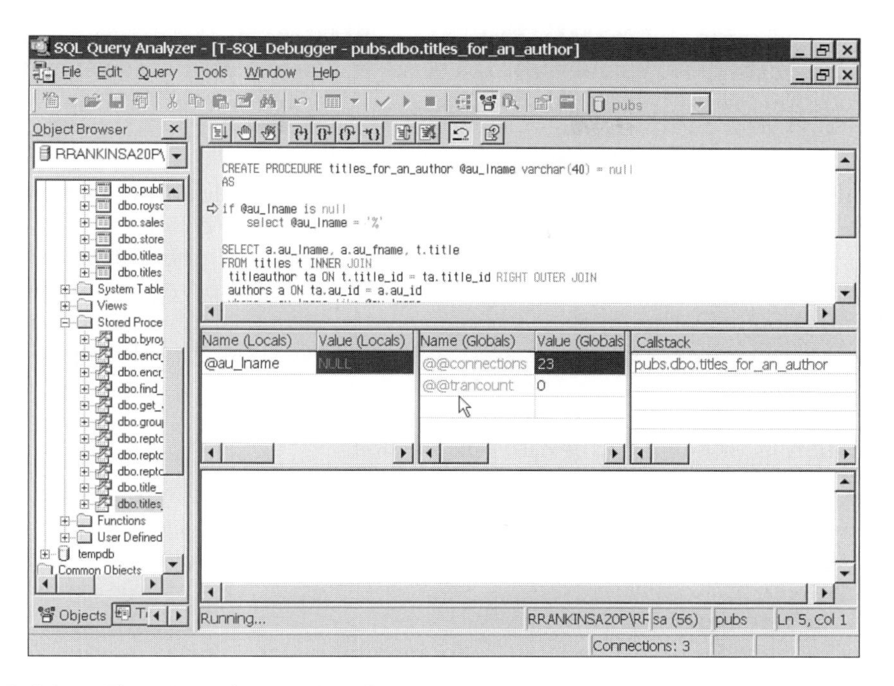

FIGURE 6.16 The SQL Debugger interface.

The Global Functions pane displays the values currently returned by the Global Functions based upon the current state of execution. You cannot modify the values for the global functions, but you can add additional global functions to the list to monitor different values, such as `@@ROWCOUNT`, `@@IDENTITY`, `@@ERROR`, or `@@NESTLEVEL`. For more information on the available global functions, see Chapter 26, "Using Transact-SQL in SQL Server 2000."

The Callstack window pane shows the list of currently open procedure calls, with the top procedure being the currently active procedure. (The currently active procedure is the one that determines the scope of the values displayed in the Local Variable and Global Function window panes.) You can change the values displayed in these panes and the Source Code window pane by clicking on the other procedures listed below the top procedure in the Callstack pane. The Callstack pane is useful to keep track of the nesting levels of the currently executing procedures.

The bottom window pane is the Results Text window pane. This window pane displays any results generated by the stored procedure being debugged as well as any print or error messages generated.

The Status Bar

The status bar at the bottom of the main Debugger window displays the current state of execution (Running, Completed, or Aborted), the name of the SQL Server the debugger is currently connected to and the login ID used to connect, the current database context, and the line number and column where the cursor is currently positioned within the Source Code window.

Debugging Triggers and User Functions

Triggers are fired only when a data modification statement runs against the table on which the trigger is defined. It isn't possible to directly invoke or debug a trigger, but you can debug triggers and user-defined functions if they are invoked from within a stored procedure you are debugging. To step into and debug a function or trigger, use the `Step Into` debugger option when invoking a command that includes a function or performs a modification on a table for which a trigger has been defined. Once the debugger is in the user-defined function or trigger, you can debug it just like debugging stored procedures, including setting break points, stepping into other user-defined functions or stored procedures, or aborting or restarting the debugging session.

If no stored procedure exists that invokes the user-defined function or trigger you want to debug, you will need to write a simple test procedure that executes a SQL statement you can step into that invokes the user-defined function or trigger you wish to debug.

Limits of the Debugger

The debugger provides a pleasing interface for monitoring local procedure variables and global variables (`@@trancount`, for example) at each stage of execution. However, the debugger has the following limits:

- Some data types cannot be monitored in the watch windows, including `table` datatypes, `cursor` variables, `sql_variant` (if the passed variable is a restricted type), and any BLOB types (`image`, `text`).
- Stored procedures larger than 64K cannot be debugged. If you need to debug procedures this large (and with so much code, it's likely you will), consider breaking up the procedure into several child procedures. The debugger can step into child procedures.
- SQL Server limits are in effect. The callstack cannot exceed 32. SQL Server 2000 limits the maximum nesting level of stored procedures to 32. The maximum number of parameters that can be passed to a procedure is 2,100.

Common Debugger Problems

The most common problem with the debugger is attempting to run the server under the local System account. If you are running the server locally on your development box, and don't expect to need to interact with network services, it is fairly common (although not recommended) to configure a server to use the local system account.

Regardless of whether the server is running locally, if the server is using the local system account and you are running a Windows 2000 or Windows NT client, you will see the following message box when you run the debugger:

SP Debugging may not work properly if you log on as 'Local System account' while SQL Server is configured to run as a service. You can open Event Viewer to see details. Do you wish to continue?

NOTE

If you are running Query Analyzer from Windows 95, 98, or Me, you will not receive this helpful warning message, but the undesirable behavior will be the same.

If you continue, the debugger will load, but you will not be able to set breakpoints or step through the procedure. If you look in the system application log using Event Viewer, you will see this error message logged, from source `SQLDebugging98`:

SQL Server when started as service must not log on as System Account. Reset to logon as user account using Control Panel.

To resolve this, change the logon account. In an enterprise setting, it is most appropriate to use a system account that restricts interactive logins, and that has been set up specifically for use by the SQL Server service. You will want to do this to take advantage of replication and multiserver administration features in any event, so take this chance to set up a separate domain account.

It is also possible to use the local Administrator account to get the debugger working. If you normally log on to your machine with an account that is different from the one under which the SQL Server service runs, you will also need to follow the instructions in the "DCOM Configuration" section later in this chapter.

Changing the Server's Logon Account

From Windows 2000, on the machine running SQL Server, follow these steps to change the logon account to local Administrator:

- From the desktop, right-click on My Computer and select Manage from the context menu.
- In the Computer Management tree, open Services and Applications and select Services.
- A list of services appears on the right. Open the MSSQLSERVER service by double-clicking it or selecting the Properties of the service.
- A service dialog box opens. Select the Log On tab.

- The window will display a choice of Local System Account or This Account. Select the This Account option. Type in the Administrator logon and the local machine's admin password.
- Restart the MS SQL Server service. (Remember to also restart SQL Agent if you have scheduled jobs on this server.)

Reconnect to the server from Query Analyzer. You should be able to use all features of the debugger.

CAUTION

There is an active bug in SQL 2000 debugging that can cause an access violation. If your server kills your connection or crashes when debugging, ensure that the server has a name. Run this query to see if your server has a name:

```
select @@servername
```

If the query returns NULL, run this query to give your server a name, and restart the SQL Server service:

```
exec sp_addserver 'MyServerName', 'local'
```

DCOM Configuration

Under Windows 2000, you can examine the distributed COM configuration by running `DCOMCNFG.EXE`. If you plan to debug stored procedures using logon accounts different from the one used by SQL Server, you will need to follow these directions on the SQL Server computer:

- Run `DCOMCNFG.EXE`, normally found in `\winnt\system32`.
- In the Distributed COM Configuration Properties window, select the Default Security tab. Under Default Access Permissions, click Edit Default.
- Add the group Everyone by selecting it and clicking Add, OK.
- Restart the SQL Server service.

Windows 98/Me might have `DCOMCNFG.EXE` in the `\windows\system` directory, but some installations do not. The most reliable way to enable DCOM on these systems is to follow these steps:

- Run `REGEDIT.EXE` to open the registry editor.
- Expand `HKEY_LOCAL_MACHINE\SOFTWARE\Microsoft\Windows\CurrentVersion\Run`.
- Add a new string value named RPCSS. Set the new string's value to the path to `RPCSS.EXE`, normally found in `C:\Windows\System\RPCSS.EXE`.

- Set the value of `HKEY_LOCAL_MACHINE\SOFTWARE\Microsoft\Ole\EnableDCOM` to 'y'.
- Set the value of `HKEY_LOCAL_MACHINE\SOFTWARE\Microsoft\Ole\EnableRemoteConnect` to 'y'.
- Restart the computer.

Summary

The SQL Server Query Analyzer has evolved into a fairly full-featured SQL development and analysis tool. It has a number of useful and advanced features that go beyond simply being able to edit and submit queries to SQL Server.

The SQL Server Transact-SQL debugger has been through a number of difficult-to-use implementations, but this time around Microsoft has a winner. The 2000 SQL Debugger is well integrated into the Query Analyzer application, and it is extremely helpful for debugging complex stored procedures, user-defined functions, or triggers. The debugger can still be somewhat difficult to configure properly, but after you have the right pieces in place, it is easy to use.

In the next chapter, "Using the SQL Server Profiler," you will read about ways to use SQL Profiler to monitor and capture the SQL and information about the SQL that is being submitted to SQL Server. If you identify any problem or poor performing queries in SQL Profiler, you can use the tools available in Query Analyzer to analyze and troubleshoot those queries.

CHAPTER 7

Using the SQL Server Profiler

by Chris Gallelli and Ray Rankins

IN THIS CHAPTER

This chapter explores the SQL Server Profiler, one of SQL Server's most powerful auditing and analysis tools. The SQL Server Profiler will give you a basic understanding of the application and help you answer questions like the following:

- Which queries are table scanning my invoice history table?
- Am I experiencing deadlocks, and, if so, why?
- What SQL queries is each application submitting?
- Which were the 10 worst-performing queries last week?
- If I implement this alternative indexing scheme, how will it affect my batch operations?

SQL Server Profiler records activity made against SQL Server. You can direct SQL Server Profiler to record output to a window, a file, or a table. You can specify which events to trace, the information to include in the trace, how you want it grouped, and what filters you want to apply.

SQL Server Profiler Architecture

SQL Server 2000 and SQL Server 7.0 were dramatically changed to allow a more granular level of auditing against SQL Server. The most dramatic of these changes came with the advent of SQL Server 7.0, but SQL Server 2000 has been further enhanced to provide even more information.

SQL Server 2000 has both a server and a client-side component for tracing activity on the server. The SQL Trace facility is the server-side component that manages queues of events that are initiated by Event Producers on the server. Extended-stored procedures can be used to define the server-side events that are to be captured. These procedures are discussed later in this chapter in the section, "Defining Server-Side Traces."

The SQL Profiler is the client-side tracing facility. It comes with a fully functional GUI that allows for real-time auditing of SQL Server events. When it is used to trace server activity, a server-side consumer sends OLE DB row sets to a client-side consumer. The basic elements involved in this process are shown in Figure 7.1.

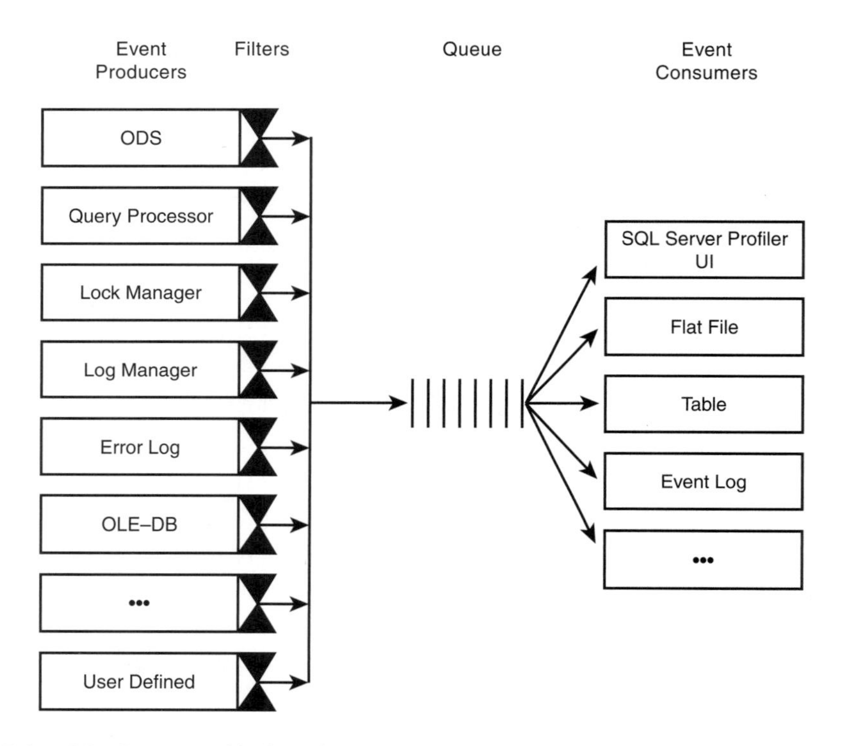

FIGURE 7.1 SQL Server Profiler's architecture.

The figure illustrates the following four steps in the process:

1. Event producers, such as the Query Processor, Lock Manager, ODS, and so on, submit events for the SQL Server Profiler.
2. The filters define the information to submit to SQL Server Profiler. A producer will not send events if the event is not included in the filter.
3. SQL Server Profiler queues all of the events.
4. SQL Server Profiler writes the events to each defined consumer, such as a flat file, a table, the Profiler client window, and so on.

In addition to obtaining its trace data from the event producers listed in step 1, you can also configure SQL Profiler so that it obtains its data from a previously saved location. This includes trace data that was saved in a file or table. The "Saving and Exporting Traces" section, later in this chapter, covers using trace files and trace tables in more detail.

Creating Traces

Because SQL Server Profiler can trace numerous events, it is easy to "get lost" when reading the trace output. You need to roughly determine the information you need and how you want the information grouped. For example, if you want to see the SQL statements that each user is submitting through his application, you could trace incoming SQL statements and group them by user and by application.

The first place you should look when creating a new trace is at the trace templates. These templates contain predefined trace settings that address some common auditing needs. The available trace templates are listed in Table 7.1.

TABLE 7.1 SQL Profiler Templates

Template	Description
SQLProfilerSP_Counts	Tracks all of the stored procedures as they start. No other event, besides the stored procedure starting, is traced.
SQLProfilerStandard	Traces the completion of SQL statements and Remote Procedure Calls (RPCs). This will include the duration of each.
SQLProfilerTSQL	Traces the start of SQL statements and RPCs.
SQLProfilerTSQL_Duration	Traces the total execution time for each completed SQL statement or RPC.
SQLProfilerTSQL_Grouped	Traces the start of SQL statements and RPCs grouped by Application, NTUser, LoginName, and ClientProcessId.
SQLProfilerTSQL_Replay	Captures profiling information that is useful for replay. It contains the same type of information as SQLProfilerTSQL, but it adds more detail, including cursor and RPC output details.
SQLProfilerTSQL_SPs	Traces detailed stored procedures, including the start and completion of each stored procedure. The SQL statements within each procedure are traced as well.
SQLProfilerTuning	A streamlined trace that only tracks the completion of SQL statements and RPCs. The completion events provide duration details that can be useful for performance tuning.

NOTE

The Trace Wizard that came with SQL Server 7.0 is no longer available in SQL Server 2000. Microsoft provides the templates instead, which can help you set up similar traces that were created with the wizard. For example, one wizard option was Find the Worst Performing Queries. You can use the SQLProfilerTuning template, which provides duration information, for this instead.

The templates that come with SQL Server 2000 are not actual traces. They simply provide a foundation for you when creating your own traces. You will see, in the next section, how to utilize these templates as you create new traces.

General Properties

You can start the SQL Server Profiler from the SQL Server Program group in the Start menu or from the Tools menu in Enterprise Manager.

Basic properties of the trace are defined in the General tab of the Trace Properties window, as shown in Figure 7.2.

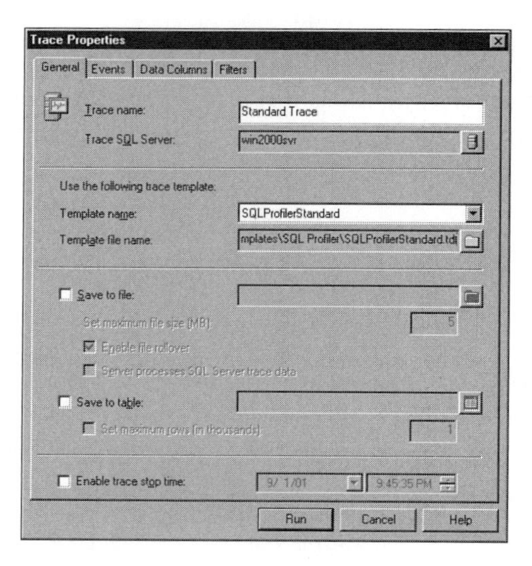

FIGURE 7.2 General properties.

To create a new trace, you can click the File menu and select New, Trace, or you can click the New Trace icon on the toolbar. This will launch the SQL Server connection screen where you specify the SQL Server that you want to trace. This is different from SQL Server 7.0. In that version, you opened the Trace Properties window first, and then you had to specify a server on the General Properties tab.

After you are connected to the server, the General tab of the Trace Properties window is displayed. This window has some of the same basic functionality as its 7.0 predecessor, including the ability to specify the trace name and the destination of the trace output (either file or table). The destination options will be discussed in more detail in the "Saving and Exporting Traces" section later in this chapter.

A new addition to the screen is the Trace Template section. This portion of the screen allows you to select a template from which to build your own trace. A template has predefined trace properties that are reflected in your trace when selected. In other words, the events, data columns, and filters that define a trace will be preselected based on the template you choose.

After a template is selected, you can modify the trace setting and customize it for your own needs. You can then save the modified template as its own template file that will appear in the template drop-down list for future trace creation.

TIP

The Trace Name is a relatively unimportant trace property for future traces. When you create a new trace, you can specify a name for the trace; however, this trace name will not be used again. For instance, if you have a trace definition that you like, you can save it as a template file. If you want to run the trace again in the future, you can create a new trace and select the template file that you saved. You will not be selecting the trace to run based on the Trace Name that you entered originally. Trace Name is useful only if you are running multiple traces simultaneously and need to distinguish between them more easily. The Trace Name is used as the window title.

Another new feature, on the General Properties screen, is the Enable Trace Stop Time option. This is a scheduling-oriented feature that allows you to specify a date and time at which you want to stop tracing. This is handy if you want to start a trace in the evening before you go home. You can set the stop time so that the trace will run for a few hours but won't affect any nightly processing that might occur later in the evening.

Events

In the Events tab, you specify the events that you want to capture in the trace. The Events tab is shown in Figure 7.3.

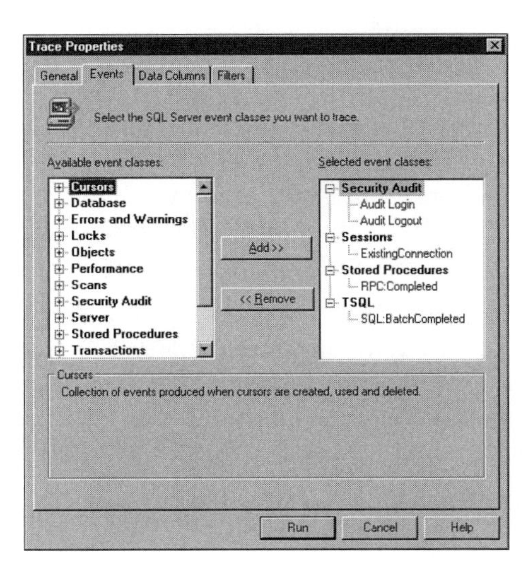

FIGURE 7.3 Event Selection screen.

TIP

If you capture too many events in one trace, the trace becomes difficult to review, especially if the auto-scroll option is enabled. Instead, you can create several traces, one for each type of information that you want to examine, and run them simultaneously.

You can choose not to capture certain events after the trace has started, but you will have to stop the trace, change the properties, and restart the trace. Be sure to save the existing trace to a table or a file before restarting the trace, or the events will be lost.

CAUTION

When a trace is initiated from the client-side Profiler application there is the possibility of missing some events that have been traced. This will typically happen when a server is under heavy load and generating a large volume of events that your Profiler trace is capturing. Under these circumstances, the Profiler GUI may be unable to process all of the events passed from the server. When this occurs, Profiler should pause and the following entry in the Profiler Message EventClass should be displayed:

```
Some trace events have not been reported to SQL Profiler because the server has reached
its maximum amount of available memory for the process.
```

This behavior is by design to minimize the risk of the Profiler GUI degrading server performance. Rather than slow down SQL Server or randomly capture intermittent commands (which would provide misleading trace information), the Profiler GUI simply stops processing events until it can again read all existing events in the Profiler queue.

Note that this is only an issue with the GUI front-end application being able to consume and display the events. The server-side SQL Trace is able to continue capturing all events. Therefore, if you need to capture events in a high volume environment, the solution is to use a server-side trace that writes to a file. A server side trace is very efficient and ensures that all of the events that you select are captured in the trace output file (information on setting up, running, and analyzing server-side traces is provided later in this chapter). Reserve the use of client-side traces for small tests on servers that are not under a heavy load.

You can choose to add an entire event group or individual events within a group. Expand an event group to list the available events within the group. You can add or remove an event group or single event by double-clicking the item or selecting it and clicking the Add/Remove button.

The available event groups and events are listed in Table 7.2. The table entries that are in bold type are new in SQL Server 2000. The Event ID column shows the corresponding event number to be specified when setting up server-side traces using the Profiler stored procedures, as covered in the "Defining Server-Side Traces" section later in this chapter.

TABLE 7.2 Event Groups and Events

Event Group	Event	Description of Captured Event	Event ID
Cursors (The cursor events are triggered only for API cursors.)	`CursorClose`	A cursor was closed.	78
	`CursorExecute`	A prepared cursor was executed.	74
	`CursorImplicitConversion`	A cursor was converted from one type to another.	76
	`CursorOpen`	A cursor was opened.	53
	`CursorPrepare`	A cursor was prepared.	70
	`CursorRecompile`	A cursor was recompiled directly or indirectly due to a schema change.	75
	`CursorUnprepare`	A cursor was deleted.	77
Database	`DataFileAutoGrow`	A data file grew automatically.	92
	`DataFileAutoShrink`	A data file was shrunk.	94
	`LogFileAutoGrow`	A log file grew automatically.	93
	`LogFileAutoShrink`	A log file was shrunk.	95
Error and Warning	`Attention`	An attention event, including client interrupts or broken connections, occurred.	16
	`Errorlog`	A message was written to the SQL Server error log.	22
	`EventLog`	A message was written to the Windows Application event log.	21
	`Exception`	A SQL Server exception occurred.	33
	`Execution Warnings`	A warning during the execution of a SQL statement or stored procedure was generated.	67
	`Hash Warnings`	A problem occurred during a hash operation.	55
	`Missing Column Statistics`	Distribution statistics for a column were not available.	79
	`Missing Join Predicate`	A join predicate was missing for the query. (This is often unintentional and results in lengthy execution time for the query.)	80
	`OLE DB errors`	An OLEDB error occurred.	61
	`Sort Warnings`	A sort operation did not fit into memory.	69
Locks	`Lock:Aquired`	A lock resource, such as a data page, was acquired.	24

TABLE 7.2 Continued

Event Group	Event	Description of Captured Event	Event ID
	`Lock:Cancel`	Acquisition of a lock resource was canceled.	26
	`Lock:Deadlock`	Processes were rolled back due to a deadlock.	25
	`Lock:Deadlock Chain`	Provides information about each deadlock participant.	59
	`Lock:Escalation`	A higher order lock was obtained. For example, a page lock converted to a table lock.	60
	`Lock:Released`	A lock was released.	23
	`Lock:Timeout`	A blocking lock caused another lock to time out.	27
Objects	`Auto Stats`	The automatic creation or update of statistics occurred.	58
	`Object:Closed`	An object was closed, such as at the end of a `SELECT`, `INSERT`, or `DELETE`.	49
	`Object:Created`	A database object was created, such as for a `CREATE TABLE` or `CREATE INDEX` statement.	46
	`Object:Deleted`	A database object was deleted, such as for a `DROP TABLE` or `DROP INDEX` statement.	47
	`Object:Opened`	A database object was closed, such as after a `SELECT` or `INSERT` statement.	48
Performance	`Degree of Parallelism1`	Description of the degree of parallelism assigned to a SQL statement. If tracing a 7.0 server, this event will trace an `INSERT` statement.	28
	`Degree of Parallelism2`	Description of the degree of parallelism assigned to a SQL statement. If tracing a 7.0 server, this event will trace an `UPDATE` statement.	29
	`Degree of Parallelism3`	Description of the degree of parallelism assigned to a SQL statement. If tracing a 7.0 server, this event will trace a `DELETE` statement.	30
	`Degree of Parallelism4`	Description of the degree of parallelism assigned to a SQL statement. If tracing a 7.0 server, this event will trace a `SELECT` statement.	31

TABLE 7.2 Continued

Event Group	Event	Description of Captured Event	Event ID
	`Execution Plan`	The plan tree generated for the SQL statement executed.	68
	`Show Plan All`	The query plan with full compile-time details for the SQL statement executed.	97
	`Show Plan Statistics`	The query plan with full run-time details, including actual number of rows for the SQL statement executed.	98
	`Show Plan Text`	The query plan text for the SQL statement executed.	96
Scans	`Scan:Started`	An index or table scan was started.	51
	`Scan:Stopped`	An index or table scan was stopped.	52
Security Audit	`Audit Add DB User`	A database user was added or dropped.	109
	`Audit Add Login to Server Role`	A login was added or dropped from a fixed server role.	108
	`Audit Add Member to DB Role`	A member was added or removed from a database role.	110
	`Audit Add Role`	A database role was added or dropped.	111
	`Audit Addlogin`	A SQL Server login was added or dropped.	104
	`Audit App Role Change Password`	The password was changed for an application role.	112
	`Audit Backup/Restore`	A `BACKUP` or `RESTORE` operation occurred.	115
	`Audit Change Audit`	A change was made to the `AUDIT` settings.	117
	`Audit DBCC`	The listed `DBCC` command was issued.	116
	`Audit Login`	A SQL Server connection was requested.	14
	`Audit Login Change Password`	A SQL Server login password was changed. (Passwords are not recorded.)	107
	`Audit Login Change Property`	A login property, other than the password, was modified.	106
	`Audit Login Failed`	A client login failed.	20
	`Audit Login GDR`	A grant, revoke, or deny action was performed on a Windows NT 4.0 or Windows 2000 account login rights.	105
	`Audit Object Derived Permission`	A `CREATE`, `ALTER`, or `DROP` command was executed.	118
	`Audit Object GDR`	A `GRANT`, `DENY`, or `REVOKE` action was performed on an object.	103

TABLE 7.2 Continued

Event Group	Event	Description of Captured Event	Event ID
	`Audit Object Permission`	A permission on an object was successfully or unsuccessfully obtained.	114
	`Audit Server Starts and Stops`	A service was shut down, started, or paused.	18
	`Audit Statement GDR`	A `GRANT`, `DENY`, or `REVOKE` statement was performed for a statement.	102
	`Audit Statement Permission`	A permission on a statement was successfully or unsuccessfully obtained.	113
Server	`Server Memory Change`	SQL Server memory usage increased or decreased by the greater of 1MB or 5% of max server memory.	81
Sessions	`Existing Connection`	A connection that was obtained before the trace started.	17
Stored Procedures	`RPC Output Parameter`	Displays information for output parameters of a previously executed RPC.	100
	`RPC:Completed`	An RPC execution completed.	10
	`RPC:Starting`	An RPC execution was started.	11
	`SP:CacheHit`	The stored procedure being executed was found in the cache.	38
	`SP:CacheInsert`	The stored procedure being executed was placed in the cache.	35
	`SP:CacheMiss`	The stored procedure being executed was not found in the cache.	34
	`SP:CacheRemove`	The stored procedure being executed was removed from the cache.	36
	`SP:Completed`	The execution of a stored procedure completed.	43
	`SP:ExecContextHit`	The execution version of a stored procedure was found in cache.	39
	`SP:Recompile`	The stored procedure was recompiled.	37
	`SP:Starting`	The execution of a stored procedure was started.	42
	`SP:StmtCompleted`	A SQL statement within a stored procedure was completed.	45
	`SP:StmtStarting`	A SQL statement within a stored procedure was started.	44
Transactions	`DTCTransaction`	A distributed transaction was coordinated between two or more databases.	19

TABLE 7.2 Continued

Event Group	Event	Description of Captured Event	Event ID
	SQLTransaction	A SQL Server transaction statement (BEGIN, COMMIT, SAVE, or ROLLBACK TRANSACTION) was issued.	50
	TransactionLog	A transaction was written to the log.	54
TSQL	Exec Prepared SQL	A prepared SQL statement was executed.	72
	Prepare SQL	A SQL statement was prepared for use.	71
	SQL:Batch Completed	A Transact SQL batch was completed.	12
	SQL:BatchStarting	A SQL batch was started.	13
	SQL:StmtCompleted	A SQL statement was completed.	41
	SQL:StmtStarting	A SQL statement was started.	44
	Unprepare SQL	A prepared SQL statement was unprepared.	73
User Configurable	User Configurable (0-9)	A user-defined event occurred.	82-91

NOTE

If you are going to use SQL Server Profiler, I recommend that you spend some time getting to know the events first. Each event has a description that is displayed when you click on it. Start a trace with a few events at a time and execute some relevant statements to see what is displayed for the events. You will soon realize the strength of the SQL Server Profiler.

Data Columns

In the Data Columns tab, you specify what information to capture and display for your events and how they will be ordered and grouped within the trace. Capturing too much data can make the trace file or trace table grow too large and can affect performance as well.

You should only include columns that make sense and are valid for the events being traced. Figure 7.4 displays the Data Columns tab.

TIP

There is a handy matrix for each event class found in the "Monitoring with SQL Profiler Event Categories" section in Books Online. This matrix shows you which data columns are valid and will be populated for each event.

Also, don't forget to use the simple help facility that is available with the *Data Columns* screens. Simply select the column that you might be interested in tracing and look at the bottom portion of the screen for a brief description of that column.

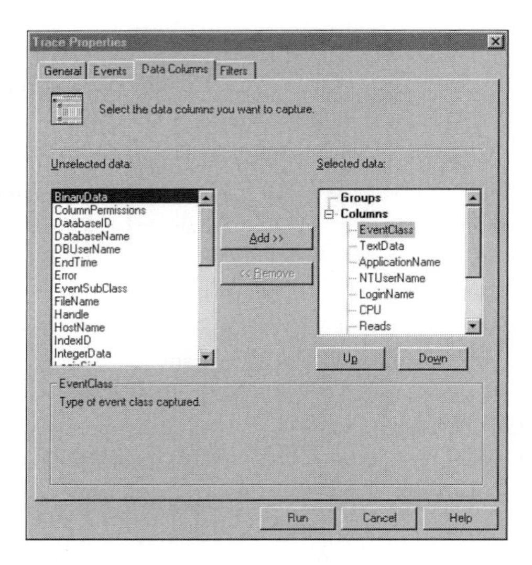

FIGURE 7.4 Defining the information to be captured in the trace.

The `EventClass` column is the name of the event you have selected. If you capture more than one event, you probably want to include this column to differentiate the source of each row of output. If you want to capture the actual text—for instance, the SQL command—include the `TextData` column. The type of information stored in this column depends on the event class.

To differentiate between activities generated from different applications, include the `ApplicationName` column; to differentiate between different users, include the `NTUserName` column or `DBUserName` column.

The `CPU`, `Reads`, and `Writes` columns are useful if you want to find out how many resources the event incurs. The `Duration` column specifies the elapsed time in milliseconds. To trace activities against a specific object, include the `ObjectName` column.

TIP

The easiest way to learn about each column is to create a trace that includes all the events and all the columns. Generate some activities against SQL Server while the trace is running and examine the information in the data columns for the different types of events. Do not run such a trace on a heavily used production server because it could significantly degrade the server's performance.

When you analyze the data, you probably want to perform some grouping with the columns. You can group all the columns you include in the trace. If you group over several columns, you should note that the column ordering makes a difference.

To specify grouping, mark the column you want to group over and choose the Up and Down button until you move the column to the desired location.

Suppose you want to find out which application performs the most table scans and then group that information by each user of the application. In that case, you group by `ApplicationName` and `NTUserName`. You might also want the reverse grouping to see which user is performing the most tables scans and which application the user is running—so then you group over `NTUserName` and `ApplicationName`.

TIP

If you save the trace to a file or a table, you can open it later and specify whatever grouping you want to reorganize output. This flexibility gives you almost endless possibilities for analyzing the trace data.

Filters

You can filter the events that are captured by the SQL Profiler via the Filters tab. SQL Server 2000 has dramatically improved this screen by giving you more items on which to filter and better filtering options. The three basic filtering options are as follows:

- Like/Not Like—This gives you the ability to include or exclude events based on a wildcard. You should use the % character as your wildcard character and separate multiple entries with a semicolon. For example, with the `ApplicationName` filter, you can specify `Like SQL Query%` and you will get only those events related to applications that match the wildcard, such as SQL Query Analyzer. This filtering option is available for text data columns and data columns that contain name information, such as `NTUserName` and `ApplicationName`.
- Equal To/Not Equal To/Greater Than or Equal/Less Than or Equal—Filters with this option have all four of these conditions available. For each condition, you can specify a single value or a series of values separated by semicolons. For example, you can filter on `DataBaseID` and input numeric values under the `Equals To` node of the filtering tree. This filtering option is available for numeric data columns such as `Duration`, `IndexId`, and `ObjectId`.
- Greater Than/Less Than—This type of filtering option is only available on time-based data columns. This includes `StartTime` and `EndTime` filters. These filters expect date formats of the form YYYY-MM-DD or YYYY-MM-DD HH:MM:SS.

Each data column is set up to have one of the three filtering options described. When you click on the data column that is available for filtering, you will expand the filter tree and expose the filtering options for that column. The values on which you want to filter are entered in the data entry area on the filter tree. This input area is shown when you select a specific filtering option. For multiple filter values, type a semicolon after each value has been entered. The semicolon will not appear in the tree text, but it acts as a carriage return that gives you another text entry node below the one you just entered.

Figure 7.5 displays the Filters tab and a text node available for input for the `DatabaseName` column.

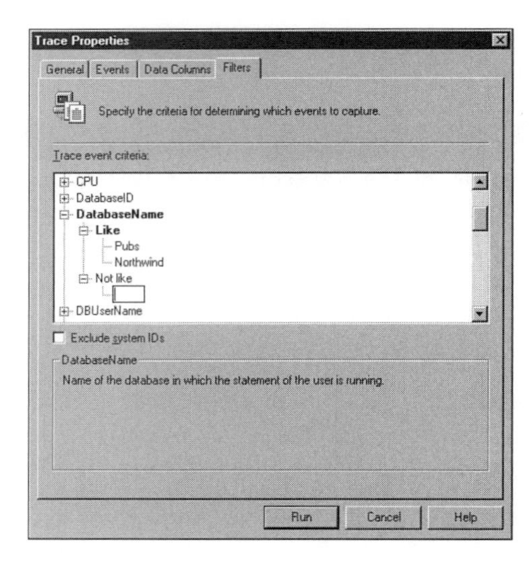

FIGURE 7.5 Producing manageable results with filters.

> **CAUTION**
>
> Be careful if you use `Like` and `Not Like` on the same data column. The filters are combined as a logical `OR` and can produce unexpected results. For example, if you use the `ApplicationName` filter and specify `Like MS%` with `Not Like SQL Profiler`, you will still get trace rows for the SQL Query Analyzer application name even though it does not match the `MS%` wildcard. The reason is because the filters condition gets rows where the name is `Like MS%` or `Not Like SQL Profiler`. In this case, the SQL Query Analyzer passes the filter because it is not like `SQL Profiler`.

Saving and Exporting Traces

You have multiple options for saving trace information. You can save the current contents of the trace window to a file or table, or, as described earlier, you can choose to save trace events to a file or table as the trace runs. This will direct the SQL Profiler to route all of the SQL statements executed during the trace to a file or table as well as to the trace window.

TIP

If you are executing a long-running trace, you should save to a file or table as the trace runs to be sure that you capture the entire trace. Saving to a file allows you to clear the current contents of the trace window and not lose the trace information.

Also, if you are saving to a trace file as the trace runs, and the trace is expected to be large, then you can utilize the Enable File Rollover option, which will create a new event file when the file reaches the size that you specify. This allows you to have smaller, more manageable trace files for your review.

If you save a trace to a table, the number of columns in the trace table depends on how many data columns you defined in the trace. Saving to a table is useful if you want to perform analysis on the trace with some other tool, such as Microsoft Access or Microsoft Query Analyzer. Because the data resides in a table, you can run more complex queries and reports on the trace data that include sorting, grouping, and more complex search conditions than are available through the SQL Profiler filters.

NOTE

Two distinct save operations are available in the SQL Profiler. You can save trace events to a file or table as just described, or you can save a trace definition in a template file. The Save As Trace Table and Save As Trace File options are for saving trace events to a file. The Save As Trace Template option saves the trace definition. Saving a trace template saves you the trouble of having to go through all the properties each time to set up the events, data columns, and filters for your favorite traces.

As an alternative to saving all the event data associated with a particular trace, you can select specific event rows from the SQL Profiler windows. You can capture all the trace information associated with a trace row by selecting a row in the trace output window of Profiler and choosing the Copy option from the Edit menu. Or, you can just copy the event text (typically a SQL statement) by selecting the row, highlighting the text in the lower windowpane, and using the Copy option.

This data can then be pasted into SQL Query Analyzer or the tool of your choice for further execution and more detailed analysis. This can be particularly useful during performance tuning. After you identify the long-running statement or procedure, you can copy the SQL, paste it into Query Analyzer, and display the Query Plan to determine why the query was running so long.

Importing Trace Files

A trace saved to a file or table can be read back into SQL Profiler at a later time for more detailed analysis or to replay the trace on the same SQL Server or another SQL Server instance. You can import data from a trace file or trace table by choosing the Open option in the File menu. Under the Open option, you will be able to choose either a trace file or trace table. If you choose to open a trace file, you will be presented with a dialog box to locate the trace file on the local machine. If you choose to import a trace table, you will first be presented with a connection dialog box to specify the SQL Server and login id and password to connect to it. Once successfully connected, you will be presented with a dialog box to specify the database and the name of the trace table you want to import from.

Once you've specified the trace file or trace table to import into Profiler, the entire contents of the file or table will be read in and displayed in a Profiler window. Sometimes the trace file or trace table can be very large and it can be difficult to analyze all the data at once, or you may just want to analyze events associated with a specific application or table, or specific types of queries.

To limit the amount of information displayed in the Profiler window, you can filter out the data displayed via the Properties dialog. You can choose which events and data columns you want to display and also specify conditions in the Filters tab to limit the rows displayed from the trace file or trace table. These options do not affect the information stored in the trace file or trace table, only what information is displayed in the Profiler window.

Importing a Trace File into a Trace Table

While you can load a trace file directly into Profiler for analysis, very large files can be difficult to analyze. Profiler will load the entire file, and if it's very large, this can take quite a while and the responsiveness of Profiler might not be the best. If the trace was split across multiple files, you'll have to open each file individually into separate Profiler windows, making an overall analysis difficult.

You can use the trace filters to limit which rows are displayed, but not which rows are imported into Profiler. The filters also don't filter out NULL values and you often end up with a bunch of rows displayed with no data in the columns you want to analyze. In addition, while the filters allow you to limit which rows are displayed, they don't really provide a means of running any more complex reports on the data like generating counts of events or displaying the average query duration.

Fortunately, SQL Server 2000 provides a way for you to import a trace file into a trace table. When importing a trace file into a trace table, you can filter the data before it goes into the table as well as combine multiple files into a single trace table. Once the data is in a trace table, you can load the trace table into Profiler, or write your own queries and reports against the trace table for more detailed analysis than is possible in Profiler.

Microsoft SQL Server includes some built-in user-defined functions for working with Profiler traces. The `fn_trace_gettable` function is used to import trace file data into a trace table. The following is the syntax for this function:

```
fn_trace_gettable( [ @filename = ] filename , [ @numfiles = ] number_files )
```

This function returns the contents of the specified file as a table result set. You can use the result set from this function just like you would a table. By default, the function returns all possible Profiler columns, even if no data was captured for the column in the trace. To limit the columns returned, specify the list of columns in the query. Table 7.3 lists the available columns in a Profiler trace. The column IDs are useful when creating a server-side trace, which is covered in the "Defining Server-Side Traces" section later in this chapter.

TABLE 7.3 Profiler Columns and Column IDs

Column Name	Column ID
TextData	1
BinaryData	2
DatabaseID	3
TransactionID	4
Reserved	5
NTUserName	6
NTDomainName	7
ClientHostName	8
ClientProcessID	9
ApplicationName	10
SQLSecurityLoginName	11
SPID	12
Duration	13
StartTime	14
EndTime	15
Reads	16
Writes	17
CPU	18
Permissions	19
Severity	20
EventSubClass	21
ObjectID	22
Success	23
IndexID	24
IntegerData	25
ServerName	26
EventClass	27
ObjectType	28
NestLevel	29
State	30
Error	31
Mode	32
Handle	33

TABLE 7.3 Continued

Column Name	Column ID
ObjectName	34
DatabaseName	35
Filename	36
ObjectOwner	37
TargetRoleName	38
TargetUserName	39
DatabaseUserName	40
LoginSID	41
TargetLoginName	42
TargetLoginSID	43
ColumnPermissionsSet	44

If you want to limit the rows retrieved from the trace file, specify your search conditions in the `WHERE` clause. If your Profiler trace used rollover files to split the trace across multiple files, you can specify the number of files you want it to read in. You can specify the default value of `default`, or `-1`, to have it read all rollover files for the trace. Listing 7.1 provides an example of creating and populating a trace table from a trace file using `select into` and then adding additional rows via `insert`. Note that the example limits the columns and rows returned by specifying a specific column list and search conditions in the `WHERE` clause.

LISTING 7.1 Creating and Inserting Trace Data into a Trace Table from a Trace File

```
/******************************************************************
** NOTE - you may need to edit the path/filename on your system if
**        you use this code to load your own trace files
******************************************************************/

select EventClass,
       EventSubClass,
       TextData = convert(varchar(8000), TextData),
       BinaryData,
       ApplicationName,
       Duration,
       StartTime,
       EndTime,
       Reads,
       Writes,
       CPU,
       ObjectID,
```

LISTING 7.1 Continued

```
      IndexID,
      NestLevel
   into TraceTable
   FROM ::fn_trace_gettable('c:\temp\sampletrace_20020826_0232.trc', default)
   where TextData is not null
      or EventClass in (16, --  Attention
                        25, -- Lock:Deadlock
                        27, -- Lock:Timeout
                        33, -- Exception
                        58, -- Auto Update Stats
                        59, -- Lock:Deadlock Chain
                        79, -- Missing Column Statistics
                        80, -- Missing Join Predicate
                        92, -- Data File Auto Grow
                        93, -- Log File Auto Grow
                        94, -- Data File Auto Shrink
                        95) -- Log File Auto Shrink

Insert into TraceTable (EventClass, EventSubClass,
            TextData, BinaryData,
            ApplicationName, Duration, StartTime, EndTime, Reads, Writes,
            CPU, ObjectID, IndexID, nestlevel)
     select EventClass, EventSubClass,
            TextData = convert(varchar(7900), TextData), BinaryData,
            ApplicationName, Duration, StartTime, EndTime, Reads, Writes,
            CPU, ObjectID, IndexID, nestlevel
        FROM ::fn_trace_gettable('c:\temp\sampletrace_20020826_0108.trc', -1)
        where TextData is not null
           or EventClass in (16, --  Attention
                             25, -- Lock:Deadlock
                             27, -- Lock:Timeout
                             33, -- Exception
                             58, -- Auto Update Stats
                             59, -- Lock:Deadlock Chain
                             79, -- Missing Column Statistics
                             80, -- Missing Join Predicate
                             92, -- Data File Auto Grow
                             93, -- Log File Auto Grow
                             94, -- Data File Auto Shrink
                             95) -- Log File Auto Shrink
go
```

Once the trace file is imported into a trace table, you can open the trace table in Profiler, or run your own queries against the trace table. For example, the following query returns the number of lock timeouts encountered for each table during the period that the trace was running:

```
select object_name(id), count(*)
    from TraceTable
    where EventClass = 27 -- Lock:Timout Event
    group by object_name(id)
go
```

Analyzing Traces with the Index Tuning Wizard

In addition to being able to manually analyze traces in Profiler, you can also use the Index Tuning Wizard to analyze the queries captured in your trace and recommend changes to your indexing scheme. You can invoke the Index Tuning Wizard from the Tools menu in SQL Profiler. The Index Tuning Wizard can read in a trace that was previously saved to a table or a file. This allows you to capture a workload, tune the indexing scheme, and rerun the trace to determine if the index changes improved performance as expected.

Because the Index Tuning Wizard analyzes SQL statements, make sure that the trace includes one or more of the following events:

```
SP:StmtCompleted
SP:StmtStarting
SQL:BatchCompleted
SQL:BatchStarting
SQL:StmtCompleted
SQL:StmtStarting
```

One of each class (one `SP:` and one `SQL:`) is sufficient to capture dynamic SQL statements and statements embedded in stored procedures. You should also make sure that the trace includes the Text data column, which contains the actual queries.

The Index Tuning Wizard analyzes the trace and gives you recommendations along with an estimated improvement in execution time. You can choose to create indexes now or at a later time or save the `CREATE INDEX` commands to a script file.

For more information on using the Index Tuning Wizard, see Chapter 34, "Indexes and Performance."

Replaying Trace Data

To replay a trace, you must have a trace saved to a file or a table. You can define a trace to be saved when you create or modify the trace definition. You can also save the current contents of the trace window to a file or table using the Save As Trace File or Save As Trace Table options in the File menu.

To replay a saved trace, you can use the File, Open menu that allows you to open a trace file or a trace table. After you select the type of trace to replay, a grid with the trace columns selected in the original trace will be displayed. At this point, you can start the replay of the trace, either step by step or complete execution of the entire trace. Either option will display the SQL Server Connection dialog box that allows you to connect to an instance of SQL Server. After you are connected, you will be given replay options as shown in Figure 7.6.

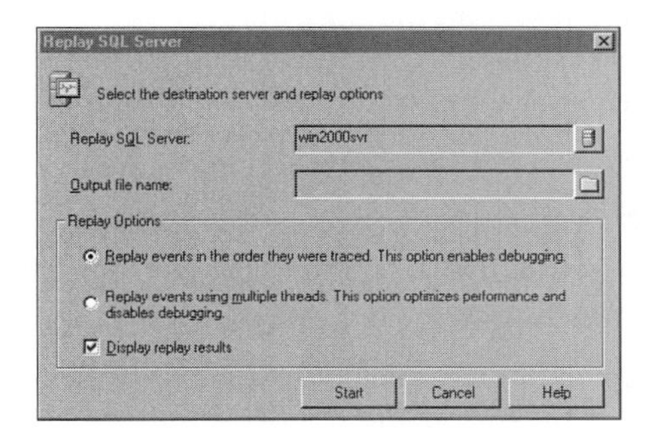

FIGURE 7.6 Options for replaying a Profiler trace.

The first option, which is enabled by default, replays the trace in the same order that it was captured and allows for debugging. The second option takes advantage of multiple threads. It optimizes performance but disables debugging. A third option involves specifying whether to display the replay results. You would normally want to see the results, but for large trace executions, you might want to forgo displaying the results and send them to an output file instead.

If you choose the option that allows for debugging, you will be able to execute the trace in a manner similar to many programming tools. You can set breakpoints, step through statements one at a time, or you can position the cursor on a statement within the trace and execute the statements from the beginning of the trace to the cursor position.

NOTE

Automating testing scripts is another important use of the SQL Profiler Save and Replay options. For instance, a trace of a heavy production load can be saved and rerun against a new release of the database to ensure that the new release has similar or improved performance characteristics and returns the same data results. The saved traces can help make regression testing much easier.

Defining Server-Side Traces

Much of the SQL Server Profiler functionality is available through a set of system-stored procedures. Through these procedures, you can define a server-side trace that can be run automatically or on a scheduled basis, such as via a Task Manager Job, instead of through the Profiler GUI. Server-side traces are also useful if you are tracing information over an extended period of time, or are planning on capturing a large amount of trace information. The overhead of running a server-side trace is less than running a client-side trace with Profiler.

To start a server-side trace, you need to define the trace using the trace-related system procedures. These procedures can be called from within a SQL Server–stored procedure or batch. You can define a server-side trace using the following four procedures:

- `sp_trace_create`—This procedure performs similarly to the General tab in the Trace Properties dialog box. It sets up the trace and defines the file to store the captured events. `sp trace create` returns a trace ID number that you'll need to reference from the other three procedures to further define and manage the trace.
- `sp_trace_setevent`—You need to call this procedure once for each data column of every event that you want to capture.
- `sp_trace_setfilter`—Call this procedure once for each filter you want to define on any of the event data columns.
- `sp_trace_setstatus`—After the trace is defined, call this procedure to start, stop, or remove the trace. You must stop and remove a trace definition before you can open and view the trace file.

You will find that manually creating procedure scripts for tracing can be rather tedious. Much of the tedium is due to the fact that many numeric parameters drive the trace execution. Tables 7.2 and 7.3 provided the ID numbers you would need to specify to for the events and data columns you would want to include in your trace. In addition, you have to call the `sp_trace_setevent` procedure once for each data column for each event in the trace. To set up filters, you must pass the column ID, the filter value, and numeric values for the logical operator and the column operator to the `sp_trace_setfilter` procedure. The logical operator can be either 0 or 1. A value of 0 indicates that the specified filter on the column should be ANDed with any other filters on the column, while a value of 1 indicates the OR operator should be applied. Table 7.4 describes the values allowed for the column operators

TABLE 7.4 Column Operator Values for `sp_trace_setfilter`

Value	Comparison Operator
0	= (Equal)
1	<> (Not Equal)
2	> (Greater Than)
3	< (Less Than)
4	>= (Greater Than Or Equal)
5	<= (Less Than Or Equal)
6	LIKE
7	NOT LIKE

Fortunately, there is an easier way of generating a trace definition script! You can set up your traces using the SQL Profiler GUI and script the trace definition to a file. Once you have the trace defined and have specified the events, data columns, and filters you want to use, select the Script Trace menu option from the File menu in Profiler to save the SQL commands to define and invoke the trace to a file. You have the option to generate a script for either SQL Server 7.0 or 2000. The script file generated contains all of the SQL, including the stored procedure executions that you will need to run to set up your server-side trace.

The SQL script generated by Profiler will only contain the commands to define the events and data columns that are contained in the Profiler trace it was generated from. If you prefer a SQL script template that is a bit more dynamic for generating your server-side traces, you can use the SQL script as shown in Listing 7.2. This script provides all the event and data column options available and lets you specify which ones to use by commenting or uncommenting out the appropriate lines. It also provides some good examples and more complete syntax for using the Profiler-related `sp_trace` stored procedures. A copy of this script is available on the accompanying CD.

LISTING 7.2 A SQL Script for Creating and Starting a Server-Side Trace

```
set nocount on
go

-- Declare needed variables
DECLARE @Trace_Name varchar(255),
        @strTraceDirectory nvarchar (1000),
        @maxfilesize bigint,
        @TraceID int ,
        @rc int,
        @strTraceFile nvarchar (245),
        @tracefile_basename nvarchar(30),
        @stoptime datetime
```

LISTING 7.2 Continued

```
-- Specify trace name, trace file directory, tracefile_basename,
--  max file size in MB, and stop time for trace
-- The trace directory is a directory on SQL Server machine
-- If you want to write from a remote SQL Server to a local drive,
--  or to a drive on another server, use UNC path and make sure SQL server has
--  write access to the specified network share
-- The tracefile_basename will be appended with a datetime stamp when
--  the trace is run
-- If stoptime if null, trace runs until manually stopped

select @Trace_Name = 'Sample Trace',
       @strTraceDirectory = 'c:\temp',
       @maxfilesize = 100,
       @tracefile_basename = 'sampletrace',
       @stoptime = NULL

-- Create table variables to hold desired events and columns
declare @trace_events TABLE (eventid int)
declare @trace_columns TABLE (columnid int)

-- Specify which events to trace
--  (uncomment insert statements for desired events)

--insert @trace_events (eventid) values (10) -- RPC:Completed
--insert @trace_events (eventid) values (11) -- RPC:Starting
insert @trace_events (eventid) values (12) -- SQL:BatchCompleted
--insert @trace_events (eventid) values (13) -- SQL:BatchStarting
insert @trace_events (eventid) values (14) -- Login
insert @trace_events (eventid) values (15) -- Logout
insert @trace_events (eventid) values (16) -- Attention
insert @trace_events (eventid) values (17) -- ExistingConnection
--insert @trace_events (eventid) values (18) -- ServiceControl
--insert @trace_events (eventid) values (19) -- DTCTransaction
--insert @trace_events (eventid) values (20) -- Login Failed
--insert @trace_events (eventid) values (21) -- EventLog
--insert @trace_events (eventid) values (22) -- ErrorLog
--insert @trace_events (eventid) values (23) -- Lock:Released
--insert @trace_events (eventid) values (24) -- Lock:Acquired
insert @trace_events (eventid) values (25) -- Lock:Deadlock
--insert @trace_events (eventid) values (26) -- Lock:Cancel
insert @trace_events (eventid) values (27) -- Lock:Timeout
--insert @trace_events (eventid) values (28) -- Degree of Parallelism1
```

LISTING 7.2 Continued

```
--insert @trace_events (eventid) values (29) -- Degree of Parallelism2
--insert @trace_events (eventid) values (30) -- Degree of Parallelism3
--insert @trace_events (eventid) values (31) -- Degree of Parallelism4
insert @trace_events (eventid) values (33) -- Exception
--insert @trace_events (eventid) values (34) -- SP:CacheMiss
--insert @trace_events (eventid) values (35) -- SP:CacheInsert
--insert @trace_events (eventid) values (36) -- SP:CacheRemove
--insert @trace_events (eventid) values (37) -- SP:Recompile
--insert @trace_events (eventid) values (38) -- SP:CacheHit
--insert @trace_events (eventid) values (39) -- SP:ExecContextHit
--insert @trace_events (eventid) values (40) -- SQL:StmtStarting
insert @trace_events (eventid) values (41) -- SQL:StmtCompleted
insert @trace_events (eventid) values (42) -- SP:Starting
insert @trace_events (eventid) values (43) -- SP:Completed
--insert @trace_events (eventid) values (44) -- SP:Statement Starting
insert @trace_events (eventid) values (45) -- SP:Statement Completed
--insert @trace_events (eventid) values (46) -- Object:Created
--insert @trace_events (eventid) values (47) -- Object:Deleted
--insert @trace_events (eventid) values (48) -- Object:Opened
--insert @trace_events (eventid) values (49) -- Object:Closed
--insert @trace_events (eventid) values (50) -- SQL Transaction
--insert @trace_events (eventid) values (51) -- Scan:Started
--insert @trace_events (eventid) values (52) -- Scan:Stopped
--insert @trace_events (eventid) values (53) -- CursorOpen
--insert @trace_events (eventid) values (54) -- Transaction Log
--insert @trace_events (eventid) values (55) -- Hash Warning
insert @trace_events (eventid) values (58) -- Auto Stats
insert @trace_events (eventid) values (59) -- Lock:Deadlock Chain
--insert @trace_events (eventid) values (60) -- Lock:Escalation
--insert @trace_events (eventid) values (61) -- OLE DB Errors
--insert @trace_events (eventid) values (67) -- Execution Warnings
--insert @trace_events (eventid) values (68) -- Execution Plan
--insert @trace_events (eventid) values (69) -- Sort Warnings
--insert @trace_events (eventid) values (70) -- CursorPrepare
--insert @trace_events (eventid) values (71) -- Prepare SQL
--insert @trace_events (eventid) values (72) -- Exec Prepared SQL
--insert @trace_events (eventid) values (73) -- Unprepare SQL
insert @trace_events (eventid) values (74) -- CursorExecute
--insert @trace_events (eventid) values (75) -- CursorRecompile
--insert @trace_events (eventid) values (76) -- CursorImplicitConversion
--insert @trace_events (eventid) values (77) -- CursorUnprepare
--insert @trace_events (eventid) values (78) -- CursorClose
```

LISTING 7.2 Continued

```
insert @trace_events (eventid) values (79) -- Missing Column Statistics
insert @trace_events (eventid) values (80) -- Missing Join Predicate
--insert @trace_events (eventid) values (81) -- Server Memory Change
insert @trace_events (eventid) values (82) -- User Configurable 0
insert @trace_events (eventid) values (83) -- User Configurable 1
insert @trace_events (eventid) values (84) -- User Configurable 2
insert @trace_events (eventid) values (85) -- User Configurable 3
insert @trace_events (eventid) values (86) -- User Configurable 4
insert @trace_events (eventid) values (87) -- User Configurable 5
insert @trace_events (eventid) values (88) -- User Configurable 6
insert @trace_events (eventid) values (89) -- User Configurable 7
insert @trace_events (eventid) values (90) -- User Configurable 8
insert @trace_events (eventid) values (91) -- User Configurable 9
insert @trace_events (eventid) values (92) -- Data File Auto Grow
insert @trace_events (eventid) values (93) -- Log File Auto Grow
insert @trace_events (eventid) values (94) -- Data File Auto Shrink
insert @trace_events (eventid) values (95) -- Log File Auto Shrink
--insert @trace_events (eventid) values (96) -- Show Plan Text
--insert @trace_events (eventid) values (97) -- Show Plan ALL
--insert @trace_events (eventid) values (98) -- Show Plan Statistics
--insert @trace_events (eventid) values (99) -- Reserved
--insert @trace_events (eventid) values (100) -- RPC Output Parameter
--insert @trace_events (eventid) values (101) -- Reserved
--insert @trace_events (eventid) values (102) -- Audit Statement GDR
--insert @trace_events (eventid) values (103) -- Audit Object GDR
--insert @trace_events (eventid) values (104) -- Audit Add/Drop Login
--insert @trace_events (eventid) values (105) -- Audit Login GDR
--insert @trace_events (eventid) values (106) -- Audit Login Change Property
--insert @trace_events (eventid) values (107) -- Audit Login Change Password
--insert @trace_events (eventid) values (108) -- Audit Add Login to Server Role
--insert @trace_events (eventid) values (109) -- Audit Add DB User
--insert @trace_events (eventid) values (110) -- Audit Add Member to DB
--insert @trace_events (eventid) values (111) -- Audit Add/Drop Role
--insert @trace_events (eventid) values (112) -- App Role Pass Change
--insert @trace_events (eventid) values (113) -- Audit Statement Permission
--insert @trace_events (eventid) values (114) -- Audit Object Permission
--insert @trace_events (eventid) values (115) -- Audit Backup/Restore
--insert @trace_events (eventid) values (116) -- Audit DBCC
--insert @trace_events (eventid) values (117) -- Audit Change Audit
--insert @trace_events (eventid) values (118) --Audit Object Derived Permission
```

LISTING 7.2 Continued

```
-- Specify which data columns to include in trace
--  (uncomment insert statements for desired columns)

insert @trace_columns (columnid) values (1) --TextData
insert @trace_columns (columnid) values (2) --BinaryData
insert @trace_columns (columnid) values (3) --DatabaseID
insert @trace_columns (columnid) values (4) --TransactionID
insert @trace_columns (columnid) values (5) --Reserved
insert @trace_columns (columnid) values (6) --NTUserName
insert @trace_columns (columnid) values (7) --NTDomainName
insert @trace_columns (columnid) values (8) --ClientHostName
insert @trace_columns (columnid) values (9) --ClientProcessID
insert @trace_columns (columnid) values (10) --ApplicationName
insert @trace_columns (columnid) values (11) --SQLSecurityLoginName
insert @trace_columns (columnid) values (12) --SPID
insert @trace_columns (columnid) values (13) --Duration
insert @trace_columns (columnid) values (14) --StartTime
insert @trace_columns (columnid) values (15) --EndTime
insert @trace_columns (columnid) values (16) --Reads
insert @trace_columns (columnid) values (17) --Writes
insert @trace_columns (columnid) values (18) --CPU
insert @trace_columns (columnid) values (19) --Permissions
insert @trace_columns (columnid) values (20) --Severity
insert @trace_columns (columnid) values (21) --EventSubClass
insert @trace_columns (columnid) values (22) --ObjectID
insert @trace_columns (columnid) values (23) --Success
insert @trace_columns (columnid) values (24) --IndexID
insert @trace_columns (columnid) values (25) --IntegerData
insert @trace_columns (columnid) values (26) --ServerName
insert @trace_columns (columnid) values (27) --EventClass
insert @trace_columns (columnid) values (28) --ObjectType
insert @trace_columns (columnid) values (29) --NestLevel
insert @trace_columns (columnid) values (30) --State
insert @trace_columns (columnid) values (31) --Error
insert @trace_columns (columnid) values (32) --Mode
insert @trace_columns (columnid) values (33) --Handle
insert @trace_columns (columnid) values (34) --ObjectName
insert @trace_columns (columnid) values (35) --DatabaseName
insert @trace_columns (columnid) values (36) --Filename
insert @trace_columns (columnid) values (37) --ObjectOwner
insert @trace_columns (columnid) values (38) --TargetRoleName
insert @trace_columns (columnid) values (39) --TargetUserName
```

LISTING 7.2 Continued

```
insert @trace_columns (columnid) values (40) --DatabaseUserName
insert @trace_columns (columnid) values (41) --LoginSID
insert @trace_columns (columnid) values (42) --TargetLoginName
insert @trace_columns (columnid) values (43) --TargetLoginSID
insert @trace_columns (columnid) values (44) --ColumnPermissionsSet


-- Build full path of tracefile
-- The format of the filename is sqltrace_YYYMMDD_hhmm.trc
-- The .trc extension will be appended to the filename automatically

IF RIGHT (@strTraceDirectory, 1) <> '\'
  SELECT @strTraceDirectory = @strTraceDirectory + '\'

SELECT @strTraceFile = @strTraceDirectory + @tracefile_basename
  + '_' +  CONVERT (varchar, GETDATE(), 112)
  + '_' +  REPLICATE ('0', 2-LEN (DATEPART (hh, GETDATE())))
  + CAST (DATEPART (hh, GETDATE()) AS varchar)
  + REPLICATE ('0', 2-LEN (DATEPART (mi, GETDATE())))
  + CAST (DATEPART (mi, GETDATE()) AS varchar)


-- Create the trace definition to get the TraceID

-- option values
--     2 - Rollover Trace File when maxfilesize reached
--     4 - Shutdown on error
--     6 - options 2 & 4
--     8 - Produce black box trace

exec @rc = sp_trace_create @traceid = @TraceID output,
                           @options = 2,
                           @tracefile = @strTraceFile,
                           @maxfilesize = @maxfilesize,
                           @stoptime = @stoptime

if (@rc != 0) goto error

-- Set the events and columns to be included in the trace
-- sp_trace_setevent must be called for each column for
--  each event, hence the nested cursors
```

LISTING 7.2 Continued

```
declare event_cursor cursor for
select eventid from @trace_events

declare column_cursor cursor for
select columnid from @trace_columns

open event_cursor

declare @event_id int,
        @column_id int,
        @on bit

select @on = 1

fetch event_cursor into @event_id

while @@fetch_status = 0 -- for each event
begin
    open column_cursor
    fetch column_cursor into @column_id
    while @@fetch_status = 0  -- for each data column
    begin
        exec sp_trace_setevent @traceid = @TraceID,
                               @eventid = @event_id,
                               @columnid = @column_id,
                               @on = @on
        fetch column_cursor into @column_id
    end
    close column_cursor
    fetch event_cursor into @event_id
end
close event_cursor

deallocate column_cursor
deallocate event_cursor

-- specify the Filters on the trace
-- Add a call to sp_trace_setfilter for each filter to apply
-- Logical operator is either 0 (AND) or 1 (OR)
-- Value Comparison operators are as follows:
--    0 = (Equal)
--    1 <> (Not Equal)
```

LISTING 7.2 Continued

```
--    2 > (Greater Than)
--    3 < (Less Than)
--    4 >= (Greater Than Or Equal)
--    5 <= (Less Than Or Equal)
--    6 LIKE
--    7 NOT LIKE

exec @rc = sp_trace_setfilter @traceid = @TraceID,
                              @columnid = 1,
                              @logical_operator = 0,
                              @comparison_operator = 7,
                              @value = N'%xp_trace%'
if (@rc != 0) goto error
exec @rc = sp_trace_setfilter @traceid = @TraceID,
                              @columnid = 1,
                              @logical_operator = 0,
                              @comparison_operator = 7,
                              @value = N'%sp_trace%'
if (@rc != 0) goto error
exec @rc = sp_trace_setfilter @traceid = @TraceID,
                              @columnid = 10,
                              @logical_operator = 0,
                              @comparison_operator = 7,
                              @value = N'%Profiler%'
if (@rc != 0) goto error
exec @rc = sp_trace_setfilter @traceid = @TraceID,
                              @columnid = 10,
                              @logical_operator = 0,
                              @comparison_operator = 7,
                              @value = N'%SQLEM%'
if (@rc != 0) goto error
-- exec @rc = sp_trace_setfilter @traceid = @TraceID,
--                               @columnid = 10,
--                               @logical_operator = 0,
--                               @comparison_operator = 7,
--                               @value = N'%Query Analyzer%'
-- if (@rc != 0) goto error
exec @rc = sp_trace_setfilter @traceid = @TraceID,
                              @columnid = 10,
                              @logical_operator = 0,
                              @comparison_operator = 7,
                              @value = N'%SQLAgent%'
```

LISTING 7.2 Continued

```
if (@rc != 0) goto error
-- exec sp_trace_setfilter @traceid = @TraceID,
--                         @columnid = 3, -- Database ID
--                         @logical_operator = 0,
--                         @comparison_operator = 0,
--                         @value = 8

-- Set the trace status to start the trace
exec @rc = sp_trace_setstatus @traceid = @TraceID,
                              @status = 1
if (@rc != 0) goto error

-- Display trace id for future references
Print 'TraceID for current trace = ' + ltrim(str(@TraceID))
goto finish

error:
Print 'Trace setup exited with return code = ' + ltrim(str(@rc))

finish:

go
```


TIP

If you want to always capture certain trace events when SQL Server is running, such as auditing-type events, you can create a stored procedure that uses the `sp_trace` stored procedures to create a trace and specify the events to be captured. You can use the code in Listing 7.2 as a basis to create the stored procedure. Then mark the procedure as a startup procedure using the `sp_procoption` procedure to set the `autostart` option. The trace will automatically start when SQL Server is started and will continue running in the background. Just be aware that although server-side traces are less intrusive than using the SQL Profiler client, some overhead is necessary to run a trace. Try to limit the number of events captured to minimize the overhead as much as possible.

Monitoring Running Traces

SQL Server 2000 provides some additional built-in user-defined functions to get information about currently running traces. Like the fn_trace_gettable function discussed previously, these functions return the information as a table result. The available functions are as follows:

- `fn_trace_getinfo(trace_id)`—This function is passed a traceid and it returns information about the specified trace. If passed the value of `default`, it returns information about all existing traces. An example of the output from this function is shown in Listing 7.3.
- `fn_trace_geteventinfo(trace_id)`—This function returns a list of the events and data columns being captured for the specified trace. Only the event and column ID values are returned. You can use the information provided in Tables 7.2 and 7.3 to map the IDs to the more meaningful event names and column names.
- `fn_trace_getfilterinfo(trace_id)`—This function returns information about the filters being applied to the specified trace. Again, the column ID and logical and comparison operator values are returned as integer IDs that you'll need to decipher. See Table 7.4 for a listing of the column operator values.

LISTING 7.3 Examples of Using the Built-In User-Defined Functions for Monitoring Traces

```
set nocount on
go
SELECT * FROM ::fn_trace_getinfo(default)
go

traceid     property    value
----------- ----------- ---------------------------------
1           1           2
1           2           c:\temp\sampletrace_20020826_0459
1           3           100
1           4           NULL
1           5           1


select * from ::fn_Trace_getfilterinfo(1)
go

columnid    logical_operator comparison_operator value
----------- ---------------- ------------------- ------------
1           0                7                   %xp_trace%
1           0                7                   %sp_trace%
10          0                7                   %Profiler%
10          0                7                   %SQLEM%
10          0                7                   %SQLAgent%
```

The property values returned by `fn_trace_getinfo` are again specified as integer IDs. Table 7.5 describes these property IDs.

TABLE 7.5 Description of Trace Property ID Values

Property ID	Description
1	Trace options specified in **`sp_trace_create`**
2	Trace filename
3	Maximum size of trace file in MB
4	Date and time the trace will be stopped
5	Current trace status

Stopping Server-Side Traces

Before you can access the trace file generated by a server-side trace, you must first stop the trace and then close and delete the trace from SQL Server. If you specified a stop time when you started the trace, it will automatically stop and close when the stop time is reached. For example, in the SQL script in Listing 7.2, if you wanted the trace to run for 15 minutes instead of indefinitely, set the value for the `stoptime` variable at the beginning of the script using a command similar to the following:

```
set @stoptime = dateadd(minute, 15, getdate())
```

To otherwise stop a running server-side trace, use the `sp_trace_setstatus` stored procedure and pass it the trace ID and a status of 0. Stopping a trace only stops gathering trace information and does not delete the trace definition from SQL Server. Essentially, it pauses the trace. You can restart the trace by passing `sp_trace_setstatus` a status value of 1.

Once you've stopped the trace, you can close the trace and delete its definition from SQL Server by passing `sp_trace_setstatus` the ID of the trace you want to stop and a status of 2. Once you've closed the trace, you must redefine it before you can restart it.

If you don't know the ID of the trace you want to stop, use the `fn_trace_getinfo` function to return a list of all running traces and select the appropriate trace ID. The following shows an example of stopping and closing a trace with a trace ID of 1:

```
-- Set the trace status to stop
exec sp_trace_setstatus 1, 0
go

-- Close and Delete the trace
exec sp_trace_setstatus 1, 2
go
```

If you want to stop and close multiple traces, you must call sp_trace_setstatus twice for each trace. Listing 7.4 provides an example of a system stored procedure that you could create in SQL Server to stop a specific trace or automatically stop all currently running traces.

LISTING 7.4 Sample System Stored Procedure to Stop Profiler Traces

```
use master
go
if object_id ('sp_OCI_stop_trace') is not null
    drop proc sp_OCI_stop_trace
go

create proc sp_OCI_stop_trace @TraceID int = null
as

if @TraceID is not null
begin
    -- Set the trace status to stop
    exec sp_trace_setstatus @TraceID, 0

    -- close and delete the trace
    exec sp_trace_setstatus @TraceID, 2
end
else  -- get a list of all current traces
begin
    declare c1 cursor for
    SELECT distinct traceid FROM :: fn_trace_getinfo(default)
    open c1
    fetch c1 into @TraceID
    while @@fetch_status = 0
    begin
        -- Set the trace status to stop
        exec sp_trace_setstatus @TraceID, 0

        -- close and delete the trace
        exec sp_trace_setstatus @TraceID, 2
        fetch c1 into @TraceID
    end
    close c1
    deallocate c1
end
```

Profiler Usage Scenarios

This chapter has covered many of the technical aspects of SQL Profiler, but what about some practical applications? Beyond the obvious uses of identifying what SQL an application is submitting, this section takes a look at a few scenarios in which the SQL Profiler can be useful. These scenarios are presented to give you some ideas of how SQL Profiler can be used. The monitoring and analysis capabilities of SQL Profiler are limited only by your creativity and ingenuity.

Analyzing Slow Stored Procedures or Queries

After you have identified that a particular stored procedure is running slow, what should you do next? You might want to look at the estimated execution plan for the stored procedure, looking for table scans and sections of the plan that have a high cost percentage. But what if the execution plan has no obvious problems? This is when you should consider using the SQL Profiler.

You can set up a trace on the stored procedure that captures the execution of each statement within it along with its duration in milliseconds. Here's how:

1. Create a new trace using the `SQLProfilerTSQL_Duration` template.
2. Add the `SP:StmtCompleted` event from the stored procedure event class to the trace.
3. Add a filter on the Duration column with the duration not equal to 0. You can also set the filter to a larger number to exclude more of the short-running statements.

If you are going to run the procedure from Query Analyzer, then you might want to add a filter on the SPID column as well. Set it equal to the process ID for your session; the SPID is displayed at the bottom of the Query Analyzer window next to your username in parentheses. This will trace only those commands that are executed from your Query Analyzer window.

When you run the trace and execute the stored procedure, you will see only those statements in the procedure that have a non-zero duration. The statements will be listed in ascending duration order. Look to the bottom of the Profiler output window to find your longer running statements. Now you can isolate these statements, copy them to Query Analyzer, and perform a separate analysis on them to determine your problem.

Auditing

Sometimes it is necessary to audit the physical changes to your database. For instance, monitor when tables are added, columns are added to a table, or stored procedures are dropped. This auditing can be accomplished with SQL Profiler as follows:

1. Create a new trace using a Blank template; this will leave the selection of all the events, data columns, and filters to you.

2. Add the Object:Created event to the trace from the Objects class and the Audit Object Derived Permission event from the Security Audit class.

3. Add the `StartTime`, `DBUserName`, `NTUserName`, `ObjectID`, `ObjectName`, and `TextData` data columns to your trace.

When you run this trace, you will capture the user and the change that he made. The object that was created or altered will be identified in the `ObjectName` column. The `TextData` column, for some of the modifications, will include the actual statement that was used to modify the database.

Identifying Ad Hoc Queries

One problem that can plague a production system is the execution of ad hoc queries against the production database. If you want to identify these ad hoc queries, the application, and the users that are running them, then SQL Profiler is your tool. You can create a trace as follows:

1. Create a new trace using the SQLProfilerStandard template.

2. Remove the `Not Like SQL Profiler` condition from the `ApplicationName` filter. Add a new `ApplicationName` filter with `Like SQL Query%` and `Microsoft%`.

When this trace is run, you will be able to identify database access that is happening via SQL Query Analyzer or Microsoft Access. The user, the duration, and the actual SQL statement will be captured. An alternative would be to change the `ApplicationName` filter to trace application access for all application names that are not like the name of your production applications, such as `Not Like MyOrderEntryApp%`.

Identifying Performance Bottlenecks

Another common problem with database applications is identifying performance bottlenecks. For example, your application is running slow, but you're not sure why. You tested all of the SQL statements and stored procedures used by the application and they were relatively fast. Yet, you find that some of the application screens are slow.

Is it the database server? Is it the client machine? Is it the network? These are all good questions, but what is the answer? SQL Profiler can help you get this answer.

You can use the same trace that was used in the previous "Identifying Ad Hoc Queries" scenario. For this scenario, you need to specify an `ApplicationName` filter with the name of the application that you want to trace. You might also want to apply a filter to a specific NTUserName to further refine your trace and avoid gathering trace information for users other than the one that you have isolated.

After you have started your trace, exercise the slow-running applications screens. Look at the trace output and take note of the duration of the statements as they execute on the database server. Are they relatively fast? How much time was spent on the execution of the SQL statements and stored procedures relative to the response time of the application screen? If the total database duration is 1,000 milliseconds (1 second), and the screen takes 10 seconds to refresh, then other factors such as the network or the application code need to be examined.

Monitoring Auto-Update Statistics

As discussed in Chapter 34, SQL Server will update index statistics automatically as data is changed in a table. In some environments, excessive auto-updating of statistics can take place and affect system performance. SQL Profiler can be used to monitor auto-updating of statistics as well as automatic statistics creation.

To monitor auto-updating of statistics, create a trace and include the `AutoStats` event in the `Object` event class. Also select the `Integer Data`, `Success`, and `Object ID` columns. When the `AutoStats` event is captured, the `Integer Data` column contains the number of statistics updated for a given table, the `Object ID` is the ID of the table, and the `TextData` column contains names of the columns together with either an `Updated:` or `Created:` prefix. The `Success` column contains potential failure indication.

If you see an excessive number of `AutoStats` events on a table or index, and the duration is high, it could be affecting system performance. You might want to consider disabling auto-update for statistics on that table and schedule statistics to be updated periodically during non-peak periods.

Monitoring Application Progress

The 10 user-configurable events can be used in a variety of ways, including tracking the progress of an application or procedure. For instance, perhaps you have a complex procedure that is subject to lengthy execution. You can add debug logic in this procedure to allow for real-time benchmarking via SQL Profiler.

The key to this type of profiling is the use of the `sp_trace_generateevent` stored procedure that enables you to launch the User Configurable event. The procedure needs to reference one of the User Configurable eventids (82 to 91) that correspond to the User Configurable event 0 to 9. If you execute the procedure with eventid = 82, then User Configurable event 0 will catch these events.

Listing 7.5 contains a sample stored procedure that will (in debug mode) trigger the trace events that SQL Profiler can capture:

LISTING 7.5 A Stored Procedure That Raises User Configurable Events for SQL Profiler

```
CREATE PROCEDURE SampleApplicationProc (@debug bit = 0)
as
declare @userinfoParm nvarchar(128)
select @userinfoParm = getdate()

--if in debug mode, then launch event for Profiler
--    indicating Start of Application Proc
if @debug =1
begin
       SET @userinfoParm = 'Proc Start: ' + convert(varchar(30),getdate(),120)
       EXEC sp_trace_generateevent @eventid = 83, @userinfo = @userinfoparm
end

--Real world would have complex proc code executing here
--The WAITFOR statement was added to simulate processing time
WAITFOR DELAY '00:00:05'

---if debug mode, then launch event indicating next significant stage
if @debug =1
begin
       SET @userinfoParm = 'Proc Stage One Complete: '
                              + convert(varchar(20),getdate(),120)
       EXEC sp_trace_generateevent @eventid = 83, @userinfo = @userinfoparm
end

--Real world would have more complex proc code executing here
--The WAITFOR statement was added to simulate processing time
WAITFOR DELAY '00:00:05' --5 second delay

---if debug mode, then launch event indicating next significant stage
if @debug =1
begin
       SET @userinfoParm = 'Proc Stage Two Complete: '
                              + convert(varchar(30),getdate(),120)
       EXEC sp_trace_generateevent @eventid = 83, @userinfo = @userinfoparm
end

--You get the idea

GO
```

Now you need to set up a new trace that includes the `UserConfigurable:1` event and also includes the `TextData` data column. After this is complete, you will be able to launch the sample stored procedure from Listing 7.5 and get progress information via SQL Profiler as the procedure executes. The execution command for the procedure follows, and the resulting SQL Profiler results are shown in Figure 7.7.

```
EXEC  SampleApplicationProc @debug = 1
```

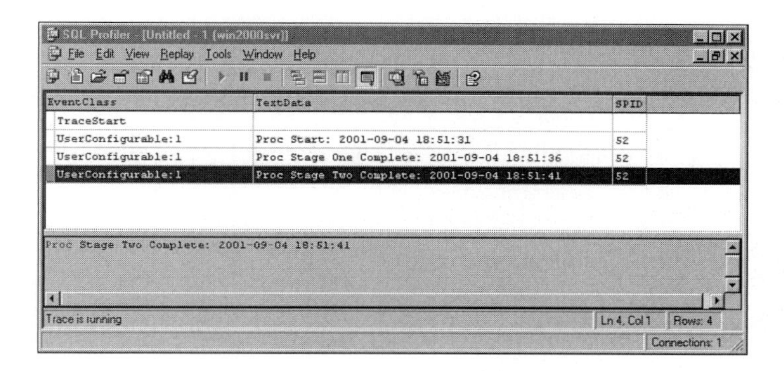

FIGURE 7.7 User-configurable trace results.

Summary

Whether you are a developer or a database administrator, do not ignore the power of the SQL Profiler. It is one of the most underused applications in the SQL Server toolkit, and also one of the most versatile. Its auditing capabilities and ability to unravel complex server processes define its value.

This chapter wraps up the introduction to the tools and utilities available with SQL Server. Now you should be equipped to start administering and working with SQL Server.

PART III

SQL Server Administration

IN THIS PART

CHAPTER 8

Installing and Upgrading SQL Server

by Paul Jensen, Paul Bertucci, and Ray Rankins

IN THIS CHAPTER

- Choosing a SQL Server Edition
- Hardware Requirements
- Software Requirements
- Selecting Installation Configuration Options
- Verifying Installation
- Starting, Stopping, and Pausing SQL Server
- Post-Installation Configuration
- Installation Troubleshooting
- Remote Installation
- Unattended Installation
- nstalling a Named Instance
- Upgrading from Previous Versions

Probably the easiest part of administering a SQL Server database is the actual installation. First, the InstallShield Installation Wizard checks that you have met the prerequisites. You are prompted to answer a few configuration questions, and finally, SQL Server starts the install. Depending on your hardware and the installation options you have chosen, the install process will take between 10 and 30 minutes. Microsoft has seen to it that this complicated product can be up and running without a major hassle, unlike both Oracle and DB2. Score one for Microsoft!

However, it would be nice to be able to supply the correct answers to the "few configuration questions" that will need to be addressed during this installation process. The good news is that most of the choices you make during installation can be changed later, and defaults are provided for many of the options. This chapter looks at the details behind each preinstallation requirement and the various options you will be prompted for during the install; this should more than allow you to make informed decisions for these selections. We will also take a look at what is needed when upgrading from previous versions of SQL Server (from 7.0 to 2000, for example) and, to wrap things up, we will cover some post-install tasks and troubleshooting of installation problems.

NOTE

You must, of course, be logged in as a member of the local administrators group to perform the install of SQL Server. Many important changes will be made, including the addition of Services entries that will require authorized windows accounts.

Choosing a SQL Server Edition

SQL Server supports five editions: Enterprise, Standard, Developer, Personal, and Windows CE. A 120-day trial version of Enterprise Edition is available for evaluation purposes, as well as a desktop data engine that can be used for data storage in any custom application. The Developer Edition has the features of the Enterprise Edition, but it is licensed for development and testing only. Personal Edition is designed as an application data store primarily aimed at the mobile computer, and Windows CE devices can use the Windows CE Edition as a local data store. The Enterprise and Standard Editions are designed for the Client/Server environment and differ from each other in their scalability and features. Standard Edition is limited to four processors and 2GB of RAM, whereas Enterprise Edition scales to 32 processors and 64GB of RAM.

In addition, you will see that Analysis Services is a separate install from SQL Server itself. In fact, it can be installed without ever installing SQL Server at all; there are no direct requirements between the two. Analysis Services is covered in great length in Chapter 42, "Microsoft SQL Server Analysis Services," and its installation will not be covered here.

Table 8.1 lists each SQL Server edition and its main usage to help you focus on which one to start from. Supported features differ in the areas of the database engine and the Analysis Services features. This will be explained shortly and will clarify your final decision on which is right for your application.

TABLE 8.1 Which SQL Server Version to Use?

Version	Used For
SQL Server Windows CE Edition	Custom desktop/CE device applications
SQL Server Personal Edition	Mobile computing usage
SQL Server Developer Edition	Development and testing only (contains most of EE's features)
SQL Server Standard Edition	Typical client/server applications (within a department)
SQL Server Enterprise Edition	Largescale client/server/Web applications across many departments or the enterprise

Table 8.2 compares the database engine features, and Table 8.3 compares the analysis features.

TABLE 8.2 Comparison of Database Engine Features

Database Engine Feature	Enterprise	Standard
Multiple-instance support	Supported	Supported
Fail-over clustering	Supported	N/A
Fail-over support in SQL Server Enterprise Manager	Supported	N/A
Log shipping	Supported	N/A
Parallel DBCC	Supported	N/A
Parallel CREATE INDEX	Supported	N/A
Enhanced read-ahead and scan	Supported	N/A
Indexed views	Supported	N/A
Federated database server	Supported	N/A
System Area Network (SAN) support	Supported	N/A
Graphical DBA and developer utilities and wizards	Supported	Supported
Graphical utility support for language settings	Supported	N/A
Full-text search	Supported	Supported

TABLE 8.3 Comparison of Analysis Services Features

Analysis Services Feature	Enterprise	Standard
Analysis services	Supported	Supported
User-defined OLAP partitions	Supported	N/A
Partition Wizard	Supported	N/A
Linked OLAP cubes	Supported	N/A
ROLAP dimension support	Supported	N/A
HTTP Internet support	Supported	N/A
Custom rollups	Supported	Supported
Calculated cells	Supported	N/A
Writeback to dimensions	Supported	N/A
Very large dimension support	Supported	N/A
Actions	Supported	Supported
Real-time OLAP	Supported	N/A
Distributed partitioned cubes	Supported	N/A
Data mining	Supported	Supported

Hardware Requirements

Microsoft supplies recommended hardware requirements for SQL Server 2000. These are the minimum requirements for running SQL Server and should be treated as such. As each installation varies, the appropriate hardware for your site will no doubt be different than these requirements. Purchase the best hardware your budget allows, and ensure that the hardware will scale with the needs of your database.

Processor

An Intel Pentium 166MHz or higher processor is required for all editions of SQL Server 2000 running on Windows NT or Windows 2000. Requirements for running on Windows 95 and Windows 98 are operating-system specific, and requirements for Windows CE are vendor specific.

If required, SQL Server 2000 can scale up to 32 processors on machines running Windows 2000 Datacenter Server. Few installations require this much processing power. For almost all of the SQL Server 2000 installations that we have seen in the last two years, at the very least, a dual-processor machine has been used. Using a dual-processor machine positions you best to handle fairly large requirements from the start, and allows you to move up with ease as loads increase.

Memory

For Standard Edition installations, the minimum recommended memory is 64MB. If you opt to run SQL Server Enterprise Edition, Microsoft recommends at least 128MB. SQL Server Personal Edition requires 64MB on Windows 2000 and 32MB on all other operating systems.

Few things will benefit a database more than adequate memory. The more memory available, the more likely that requested data will be found in memory and not have to be read in from disk. All but the smallest database installations should start with at least 256MB of RAM, with 512MB–4GB installations becoming common. On Windows 2000 Advanced or Datacenter servers, setting the /3GB switch in the boot.ini file will allow the application (SQL Server) to address 3GB of virtual memory, reserving 1GB for the operating system. Do not use the /3GB switch on systems with more than 16GB of memory because Windows 2000 needs 2GB for system purposes. If you require more than 4GB of memory, the /pae switch must be set. On systems with more than 4GB of RAM, Windows 2000 uses the Address Windowing Extension API (AWE). If more than 3GB of memory is available to SQL Server, the `SP_CONFIGURE AWE ENABLED` option must be set. If required, SQL Server 2000 Enterprise Edition running on Windows 2000 Datacenter can support up to 64GB of physical memory. See the Windows 2000 documentation for more information on supporting AWE.

NOTE

Rule of Thumb: For SQL Servers that will support less than 200 simultaneous users, you should plan on giving 25 percent of the systems memory to the operating system. For SQL Servers that will support greater than 200 simultaneous users, give a bit more (40–60 percent) of the memory to the operating system to better handle the significant increase in connections, thread management, I/O, and so on.

Disk Space and Drive Types

The required disk space for installing SQL Server 2000 and its associated options is listed in Table 8.4.

TABLE 8.4 Disk Space Requirements for Installing SQL Server

Installation Type	Disk Space Required
Full Installation	270MB
Typical Installation	250MB
Client Tools	100MB
Analysis Services	50–130MB
English Query	80MB

Of course, the preceding list doesn't take into account the storage requirements for your user databases, logs, backups, or Tempdb; these generally should be located on separate disk subsystem(s) to provide optimum performance. As databases can be extremely I/O intensive, use fast SCSI drives and quality disk controllers for your installation. If you choose to use write-caching controllers, consult your vendor to ensure they are designed for database applications to prevent potential data loss. You should also consider implementing RAID to provide fault tolerance or increased performance. Table 8.5 lists the various levels of RAID and their characteristics.

TABLE 8.5 RAID Characteristics

RAID Level	Description	Characteristics
RAID 0	Disk striping/no parity.	Excellent performance but negative fault tolerance.
RAID 1	Disk mirroring/duplexing.	Good read and write performance with excellent fault tolerance.
RAID 5	Disk striping with parity.	Excellent read performance, but only moderate write performance. Excellent fault tolerance.
RAID 10	Disk mirroring combined with disk striping (RAID 1 + 0).	Excellent performance and fault tolerance. Expensive due to the number of disks required.

For more information on RAID configurations and their use with SQL Server 200, see Chapter 39, "Database Design and Performance."

Software Requirements

The software requirements for installing SQL Server will vary according to its intended use and the version you are installing. Consideration must be given to which operating system you require, the file system you will use, and which, if any, service packs and updates must be installed.

Operating System

The various combinations of operating systems and SQL Server 2000 editions and components are listed in Table 8.6.

TABLE 8.6 Selection of the Appropriate Operating System

SQL Server Edition or Component	Operating System
Enterprise Edition	Windows NT 4.0 Server, NT 4.0 Server Enterprise Edition, Windows 2000 Server, Windows 2000 Advanced Server, and Windows 2000 Datacenter Server.
Standard Edition	Windows NT 4.0 Server, NT 4.0 Server Enterprise Edition, Windows 2000 Server, Windows 2000 Advanced Server, and Windows 2000 Datacenter Server.
Personal Edition	Windows XP, Windows Me, Windows 98, NT 4.0 Workstation, Windows 2000 Professional, and the NT 4.0 and Windows 2000 servers (all).
Windows CE	Windows CE.
Developer Edition	Windows NT 4.0 Workstation, Windows 2000 Professional, Windows XP, and the NT 4.0 and Windows 2000 servers.
Client Tools	Windows NT 4.0, Windows 2000, Windows XP, Windows Me, and Windows 98.
Connectivity only	Windows NT 4.0, Windows 2000, Windows XP, Windows Me, Windows 98, and Windows 95.

File System

SQL Server can be installed on drives formatted with FAT, FAT32, or NTFS. The NTFS file system is highly recommended for its security and recovery advantages.

When formatting partitions for data storage, additional performance gains can be achieved by using NTFS formatted with a 64KB cluster size, achieving a one-to-one ratio with the SQL Server data extent size.

NOTE

Storing SQL Servers' data and log files on compressed volumes is strongly discouraged as it can seriously degrade SQL Server performance. Compression is supported only on NTFS volumes and can be specified during the format process or later by changing the volume properties. Specific subdirectories can also be compressed within an NTFS volume. Verify that compression is *not* activated for any volume or directory that will be used by SQL Server for data and log files. If you discover an NTFS volume or directory is using compression, you might need to go through and expand operation to disable compression.

SQL Server 2000 supports the use of raw partitions for storing database files. A raw partition is a disk partition that has not been formatted with any file system. Rather than specifying a physical filename when creating a database file on a raw partition, you specify only the drive letter of the disk partition. As no filename is specified for files on raw partitions, only one file per partition is possible. The performance advantage of raw partitions over files is slight, and file manipulation operations such as copy, move, and delete are not supported. Additionally, database files on raw partitions cannot be automatically expanded. For these reasons, it is recommended that you use files created on NTFS or FAT partitions instead of raw partitions.

A great new feature for Windows 2000 is the ability to mount partitions to empty folders. By pre-creating a folder structure based on mounted partitions, you can logically group files, while keeping them physically separate to avoid contention. Consider a folder called D:\DATABASE1 with subfolders DATA1 and LOG1. If you were to mount hard drive 2 to DATA1 and hard drive 3 to LOG1, the files would be grouped logically but actually would reside physically on separate drives. The Unix folks have been using mounted disks like this for years.

Other Prerequisites

When installing SQL Server 2000 on any version of Windows NT 4.0, Service Pack 5 or higher must be installed. All installations require at least Internet Explorer Version 5.0 (IE 6.0 is out, so go ahead and move to that version if you can) to support the Microsoft Management Console (MMC); however, if only connectivity is required, IE 4.01 SP2 will suffice. For Windows 95 (connectivity only), the Winsock 2 update must be installed. This is provided on the SQL Server installation disk.

Selecting Installation Configuration Options

Having met all the hardware and software prerequisites, you are now ready to begin the install. The installation program is a wizard that steps you through a number of configuration selections, allowing you to customize your SQL Server installation.

Selecting SQL Server Components and File Locations

You will be required to choose an instance name for the SQL Server you are about to install. Use common sense when coming up with server instance names (especially if you intend to have multiple SQL Server instances up and running at the same time on a single machine). You will also choose the type of installation and the locations for the installation and data files. Figure 8.1 shows the dialog box for these selections.

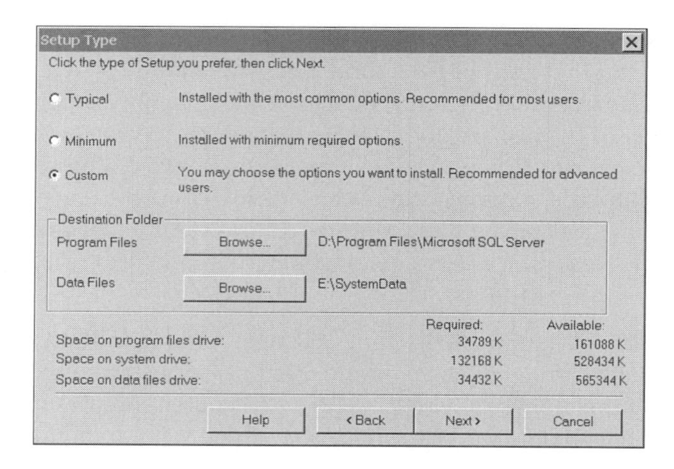

FIGURE 8.1 The Installation Type and Destination Folder dialog box.

Installation Type

The selections for installation type are Typical (the default), Minimum, and Custom. Table 8.7 compares the options available with each type.

TABLE 8.7 Comparison of Installation Options

Installation Option	Typical	Minimum	Custom
Database Server	Yes	Yes	Optional
Upgrade Tools	Yes	No	Optional
Replication	Yes	Yes	Optional
Full-Text Search	Yes	No	Optional
Client Management Tools	All	None	Optional
Client Connectivity	Yes	Yes	Yes
Books Online	Yes	No	Optional
Development Tools	Debugger only	None	Choice of tools
Code Samples	None	None	Choice of samples
Collation Settings	Yes	Yes	Choice of settings

File Location

It is at this point where you must also choose the location for the SQL Server program and data files. The default location for both the binaries and the data files is *systemroot*\Program Files\Microsoft SQL Server.

Accepting the default location for the program files is usually acceptable from a performance point of view; however, I usually prefer at least a separate partition for the SQL installation. I find it to be a cleaner separation of O/S and application from a management point of view. A 512MB partition should be fine. Note that even if you select another

partition for the SQL install, some files will be installed on the system partition. Whichever drive you choose, it is up to you whether to accept the default path. The default has the advantage of being consistent with other installs; the disadvantage is that it contains spaces, which can be a nuisance in scripting and command-line work.

On the other hand, the data files should almost always be installed on a separate disk subsystem for performance reasons. After the install, you might opt to move the `Tempdb` to its own disk system as well. For your user databases, the path you choose at this point will be the default file location when creating them through the GUI; this, of course, can be overridden. If you are installing on Windows 2000, you might also opt to pre-create a folder hierarchy using multiple disk subsystems mounted to logically grouped folders.

SQL Server and SQL Server Agent User Accounts

SQL Server runs as a service on Windows NT and Windows 2000, and as such, it can run under the context of the local system account or as a domain or local user account. If it is configured to run as the local system account, operations will generally be limited to the local server without access to network operations such as SQL mail and replication. Figure 8.2 shows the dialog box for setting up the services accounts.

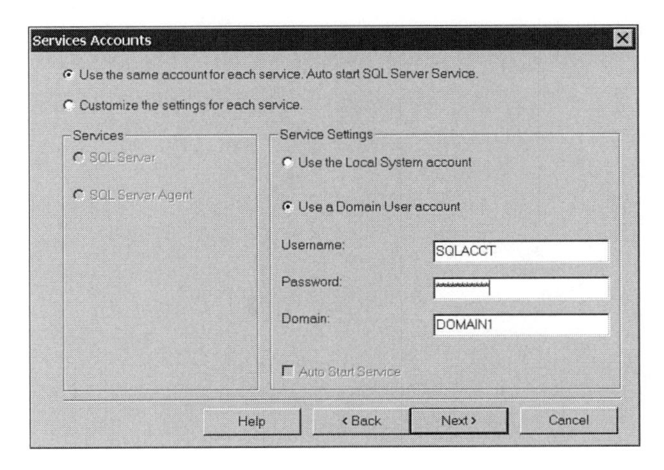

FIGURE 8.2 The Services Accounts dialog box.

The default is to set up both the SQL Server service and the SQL Server Agent service to run as the currently logged-on user. This is fine; they can share an account. This user should be a member of the domain administrators group to provide full functionality across the network. If using a domain user account, use one that is dedicated to SQL Server, not the local or domain administrator account. Using the administrator account works just fine until you change the password and discover that SQL Server can't start because it has the wrong password! If you have configured your server this way, you can fix it easily; the Services applet in the Control Panel (in Windows 2000, it is Control

Panel/Administrative Tools) allows you to configure the user account and change the password that the services use to log on. When creating an account for SQL Server, make sure you clear the User Must Change Password at Next Login and select Password Never Expires. SQL Server has no way of dealing with an expired password or with a request to change its password.

At this point, you should also ensure that the Auto Start Service check box is selected. This will set the services so that they start automatically when the operating system starts up. This can also be reset through the Services applet of the operating system after the install is complete.

Selecting the Authentication Mode

Two authentication methods are available: Windows authentication mode and mixed mode. If Windows authentication is selected, then a user connecting to SQL Server is validated through his Windows user account. In mixed mode, the user can be validated by his Windows account or by providing a SQL Server login ID. When selecting mixed mode, you will also be prompted to provide a password for the sa, or SQL Server system administration account. You can check the box to allow a blank sa password, but if you do this, you better have good backups if someone uses it to drop all your databases. The Authentication Mode dialog box is shown in Figure 8.3.

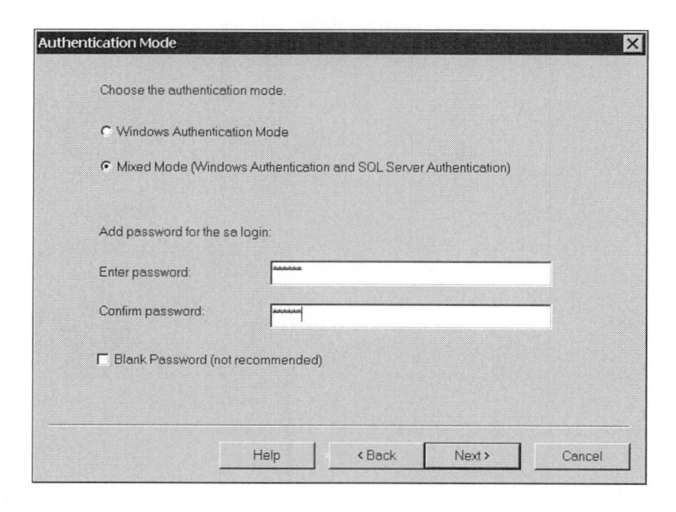

FIGURE 8.3 The Authentication Mode dialog box.

Selecting a Default Collation

During installation, you are requested to specify a default collation. The collation refers to the code page (character set) for non-Unicode data and the rules, such as sort order, that will be applied for both Unicode and non-Unicode data. In previous versions of SQL

Server, after the character set and sort order were set, they applied to all databases. In SQL Server 2000, the collation you select during install is used for the system databases and (based on the model) is the default collation unless otherwise specified at object creation. SQL Server now allows different databases—as well as tables and columns—to have different collations.

The two types of collation offered during installation are Windows locale and SQL collation. SQL collation is included for backward compatibility to allow you to match a previously installed database version 6.5 or 7.0 with which you must replicate, or if your application depends on the behavior of a previous collation. Windows locale maps to a Windows locale; by default, it maps to the one selected for the server in the Control Panel. The locale can be selected to match another server if required through the Collation Designator drop-down box, and the default sort values can be changed as required by your application. For example, the default locale for the server illustrated in Figure 8.4 is Latin1_General, and the sort order is accent sensitive.

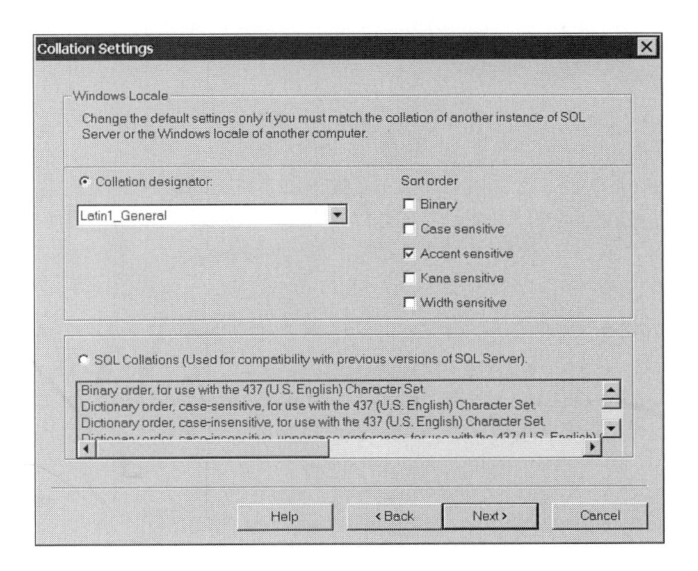

FIGURE 8.4 The Collations Settings dialog box.

Network Libraries

The network libraries are a set of DLLs that allow SQL Server to communicate over the network using a variety of protocols. Multiple network libraries can be active simultaneously to allow SQL Server to service requests from clients in a heterogeneous network environment. On Windows 2000 and NT 4.0 computers, the default network libraries are Named Pipes, TCP/IP Sockets, and Shared Memory. Shared Memory cannot be configured and is used for local client connections (same machine). If required, SQL Server also supports NWLink IPX/SPX, Banyan Vines, AppleTalk, and VIA GigaNet SAN (supported on servers only). The library the client uses to communicate with SQL Server depends on the library configuration at the client end, which must, of course, match a configured server-side library. The TCP/IP Sockets library is generally considered to be the most efficient. The Network Libraries dialog box is shown in Figure 8.5.

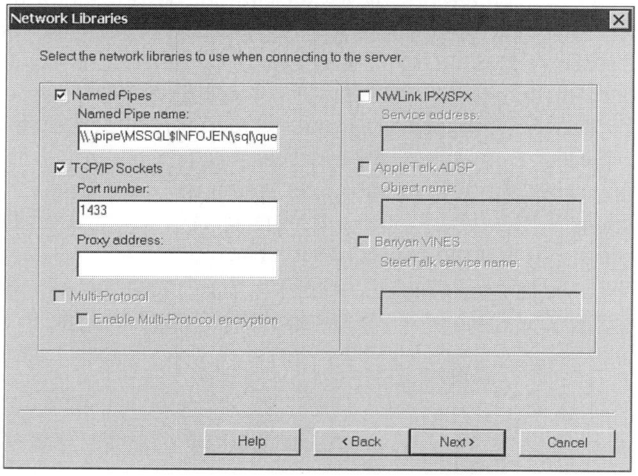

FIGURE 8.5 The Network Libraries dialog box.

Licensing Options

During the installation, you will be prompted to select a licensing mode. After SQL Server is installed, you cannot change the licensing mode. Figure 8.6 shows the Installation Licensing dialog box.

Per Seat Licensing

The Per Seat licensing option requires a seat license for each SQL Server installation and a client access license (CAL) for each workstation or "seat" that will connect to SQL Server. Per Seat licensing doesn't limit connections; each workstation can connect with multiple user connections. The Per Seat licensing mode is considered appropriate for smaller organizations, or ones with a limited, known number of users.

Per Processor Licensing

With Per Processor licensing, you acquire a license for each processor running SQL Server. No additional licenses are required, and an unlimited number of users can connect to SQL Server. This is the appropriate license mode for Web-based access or for enterprise-level access in large organizations.

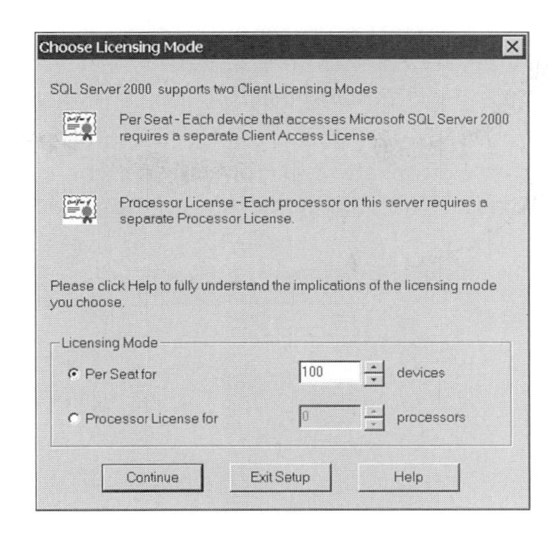

FIGURE 8.6 The Licensing dialog box.

Verifying Installation

After the installation is complete, you should verify that the SQL Server software was installed properly, that the system databases were installed in the correct location, that the management tools were installed, that you can start and stop the services, and that you can connect to a database and perform a simple query.

If SQL Server reported no errors during the install, this doesn't have to be an exhaustive check. Quickly walk through the folder hierarchy with Explorer to make sure the binaries and database are where you planned, that the Start menu has the desired tools installed, and that the services are installed and configured properly in the Control Panel. If discrepancies exist, it has been my experience that they are due to incorrect input during the install, not due to a problem with the install program.

Starting, Stopping, and Pausing SQL Server

Although SQL Server should be set to automatically start when the operating system starts, sometimes you will want to manually start, stop, or pause the SQL Server services. Pausing the SQL Server service prevents new connections but allows existing connections to remain. This is useful to prevent new connections before a planned outage, or during testing and maintenance. Pausing the SQL Server Agent suspends scheduled activities and alerts from occurring.

The SQL Server services can be started, stopped, and paused using the following:

- SQL Server Service Manager
- SQL Server Enterprise Manager

- The Services applet in the Control Panel
- The net command from the command prompt

Service manager can be accessed from the Services Manager icon on the Windows Task Bar or from the SQL Server program group. Figure 8.7 shows the Service Manager.

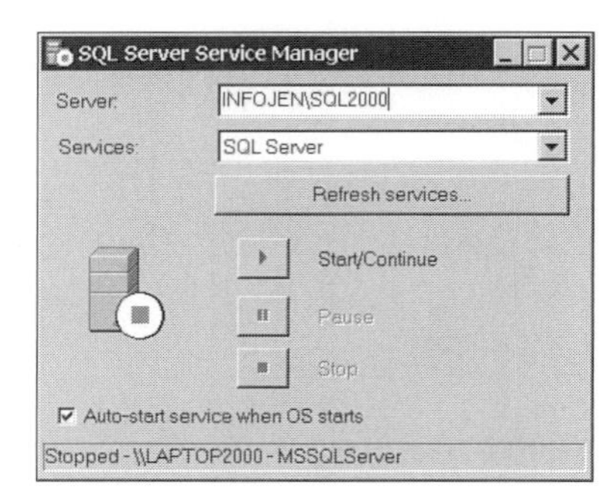

FIGURE 8.7 The SQL Server Service Manager.

From within Enterprise Manager, right-click the server name and select Start, Stop, or Pause from the pop-up menu. When using the Services applet in the Control Panel, right-clicking the appropriate service will also provide you with these options. If you choose to use the command line, the syntax for a default instance is `net start`, `net pause`, `net continue`, `net stop`, and the name of the service. For example, to start the SQL Server service, the command is `net start mssqlserver`. For a named instance, the format is `net start mssql$`*`instancename`*.

NOTE

SQL Server can also be started directly from the command prompt by running `SQLSERVR.EXE` from the binn folder of the instance you want to start. Unlike any of the previously mentioned startup options, this starts SQL Server independently of the Service Control Manager, so the application does not run as a Windows service. This means that SQL Server can't be stopped or paused from the Services applet, Service Manager, Enterprise Manager, or by using NET commands. If SQL Server is started in this manner, you must shut down SQL Server before logging off. To shut down, press Ctrl+C in the command prompt window that SQL Server was started from. This method of starting SQL Server is generally used only for troubleshooting startup or configuration problems.

Connecting to SQL Server

The final test of your installation will be connecting to SQL Server. You can choose to use either a GUI tool, such as Query Analyzer or Enterprise Manager, or a command prompt tool, such as osql. My personal preference is to fire up the Query Analyzer and run a simple query against the pubs database, first using a Windows login, and then, if the server is in mixed mode, using a SQL login.

Post-Installation Configuration

After you have determined your installation to be a success, you need to take care of a few post-install tasks.

Changing the sa Password

If you initially configured the sa account with a blank password or if you used a generic password that was shared with non-administrators assisting in the install, now is the time to change it. The sa password, like any other, can be changed from the Properties sheet for the account under the Enterprise Manager Security folder or with the `sp_password` stored procedure. For more information on changing passwords, see Chapter 15, "Security and User Administration."

Setting Up System Administrator Accounts

The sa account is not the only one with full access to your SQL Server installation. By default, when you install SQL Server, the members of the local administrators group on the server are members of the System Administrators Security Role. This is handy if you forget the sa password you used during the install; however, it also means that people who might be experienced Windows administrators, but know nothing about database management, have full access to your data. It will be up to you to decide whether the Windows administrators require this level of access.

I recommend creating additional accounts other than sa, with the appropriate levels of permissions, to be used to administer SQL Server. This provides accountability and a more granular approach to security. You can assign only the permissions required by an individual or group. Permissions can be assigned using Windows accounts or SQL Server accounts as appropriate.

Configuring the Error Log

SQL Server maintains error logs containing information and error messages. Each time SQL Server starts, it cycles a new log and saves the old log with a .1 extension. By default, six old logs, with corresponding extensions .1, .2, .3, and so on are kept. By right-clicking SQL Server logs under the Management folder in Enterprise Manager, you can configure the number of logs retained before they are recycled. The logs can also be cycled using the `sp_cycle_errorlog` stored procedure. The error logs are located by default in Program Files\Microsoft SQL Server\Mssql\Log\Errorlog, and can be viewed with Enterprise Manager or any text editor.

Server Network Utility

The Server Network Utility is located in the SQL Server program group and can be used to make changes to the Network Libraries configuration after installation. From this application, protocols can be enabled or disabled, and configuration changes such as port assignments can be made.

Installation Troubleshooting

The first place to look if you have trouble with the installation is the log files. The installation program maintains a log of the installation progress called sqlstp.log in the Winnt system directory. Reviewing the output of this log along with the system and application logs in Event Viewer will usually point you to the source of the problem. Common problems that come up after installation usually involve network connectivity or failure of the services to start.

Before banging your head against the wall troubleshooting SQL Server connectivity, make sure that network connectivity can be established using network tools appropriate to your protocol, such as ping for TCP/IP. If you can connect locally (which uses the shared memory library) but not from a client, ensure that the client and server net-libraries match.

If one or more services fail to start, check the application log in Event Viewer and the SQL Server log for the appropriate service. The most common cause of this type of error is an incorrect password for the service or a password that is set to expire on first logon. Try to log in with the account manually to ensure that it is configured correctly. If the account can log in, check that it is a member of the administrators group and that it has been granted the right to log on as a service. A good way to test if the problem is account related is to set the service to run as the local system account. If the service starts under this account, then the problem is related to the account you are using. It is also possible that a domain controller is not available to validate the account. This is not likely in production, but if you are testing SQL Server in the lab, the network for the lab is often isolated from the corporate network.

Remote Installation

The install program for SQL Server allows you to select a remote computer as the destination for the installation. When installing to a remote computer, setup collects the setup input you provide to a setup.iss file, starts a remote service on the target computer, and copies files to the computer's admin$ share. Setup then runs an unattended installation on the remote machine using the setup information in the setup.iss file. The target computer should be restarted after the setup is complete.

Unattended Installation

The unattended installation feature allows for unattended installs using a batch (.bat) file and an associated initialization (.iss) file. By placing the SQL Server compact disc in the computer or pointing to a network share and running the batch file, SQL Server will be installed with the options specified in the initialization file. Microsoft includes sample .bat and .iss files on the SQL Server compact disc for a typical, custom, and client tools only install. These can be edited with a text editor to specify options specific to your environment. An option is also available on the Advanced Installation Options screen during the install that specifies Record Unattended .ISS File. When this option is selected, the options you specify during the "install" process are saved to a setup.iss file and SQL Server is not actually installed.

The idea behind an unattended install is not that you can go for coffee instead of answering the prompts during an install, but rather that you can repeat an installation with the same options for multiple servers. If your reaction to this is anything like mine was, you are probably ready to move on to the next section because you assume you will never use this. Most sites just don't have that many servers. However, consider the advantages of having a repeatable install for even a single server. If the server ever needs to be installed, if you have saved the original unattended installation files, you can run them and be assured that all the options will be the same as for the initial install. This is especially important for the code page and sort order selections. It also will be one less thing to worry about during an already stressful system recovery. In addition, unattended install is useful for application vendors who require a certain configuration for the application to function properly. By providing the client with a set of unattended installation files to run, he is assured that the SQL Server setup is done correctly. The unattended install also ensures you can reproduce a "correct" install in the test environment when you move into production.

If there is a chance you might have to repeat an installation, I recommend using the Record Unattended .ISS file option to generate scripts to automate your install, and then running the batch file to perform the actual install. If you already have a server installed and would like the installation configuration file, the setup.iss file in the MSSQL\install folder contains the original setup options. Unattended installation—it's a good thing.

Installing a Named Instance

New for SQL Server 2000 is the capability to run more than one instance per server. Each instance has its own separate copy of the SQL Server installation files, its own system databases, and its own user databases. Microsoft supports 16 named instances per server.

Each server can have one default database, which is referenced by the server name as in previous installations of SQL Server. The default database can be version 6.5, 7.0, or SQL Server 2000. If the default is version 6.5, you must switch between the 6.5 database and SQL Server 2000 using the v-switch command-line utility. SQL 7.0 installations can function as the default database without switching. Named instances must be SQL Server 2000.

Each subsequent instance that is installed is given a name and is thereafter referenced by the combination of *server\name*. For example, let's say I installed a named instance as *unleashed* on the server *bigserver*. When connecting to that instance using query analyzer, I would select *bigserver\unleashed* in the connection window.

Why Install Multiple Instances of SQL Server?

Installing multiple instances of SQL Server allows complete separation of instances without the additional overhead of multiple servers. It can be more cost effective to run one large server as opposed to several less powerful ones. This also has implications for ASPs, or Application Service Providers, which can host multiple clients' databases on their servers. As in any given instance of SQL Server, all databases share server-wide settings such as memory and security. Named instances are required to provide for total security separation between clients and can even provide different settings for options such as memory allocation.

Upgrading from Previous Versions

SQL Server 2000 supports upgrades from SQL Server 6.5 and SQL Server 7.0. To upgrade a SQL Server 6.0 installation, you must upgrade first to version 6.5 or 7.0 and then upgrade to SQL Server 2000.

When installing SQL Server 2000 on a computer with an existing installation of SQL Server 7.0, you can choose to have the installation program overwrite the existing installation. This converts your existing installation and modifies your database files to the SQL Server 2000 format. Alternatively, you can install a named instance of SQL Server 2000, which doesn't touch the SQL Server 7.0 installation. The version 7.0 databases can now be restored to SQL Server 2000 using backups, they can be attached to the new installation using sp_attach_db, or if you choose, you can use the new Copy Database Wizard to copy your databases. This wizard uses a DTS package to copy the database and leaves the existing SQL Server 7.0 database intact. If you want, the operation can be scheduled for execution in off-normal periods. Using this option on the same server as the existing installation assumes that space exists on the server for both databases to coexist.

If you are upgrading from version 6.5, no option is available to upgrade your 6.5 databases during the installation process. After SQL Server 2000 is installed, you can upgrade using the SQL Server Upgrade Wizard. After the wizard runs, your databases will have been transferred into SQL Server 2000 and will remain intact in the SQL Server 6.5 installation as well. At this point, you can delete the previous version, or you can use the switch utility to switch between versions.

Regardless of the version from which you are upgrading, it is imperative that you perform backups immediately prior to the upgrade to prevent any data loss. No matter how well you formulate your upgrade plan, there is always the possibility for disaster when performing major software revisions. Having a good backup on hand gives you peace of mind, knowing that in the worst-case scenario, you can always go back to where you started. If you don't have a backup and problems arise, remember those six magic words for your new career: "Do you want fries with that?"

Hardware and Software Requirements for Upgrading

In addition to the hardware and software requirements for an installation of SQL Server 2000, the computer must meet some additional requirements for an upgrade. The operating system must be at least Windows NT Server or Workstation Service Pack 5 or later, Windows 2000, or Windows XP. Internet Explorer Version 5.0 or later must also be installed.

If you are upgrading SQL Server Version 6.5 to SQL Server 2000 on the same server, the SQL Server 6.5 instance must be at Service Pack 5 or later. If you are upgrading SQL Server 6.5 to an instance of SQL Server 2000 on another server, SQL Server 6.5 must be at Service Pack 3 or later.

Both servers involved in the upgrade must be configured for named pipes and be listening on the default pipe, `\\.\pipe\sql\query`. Named pipes are required even if you are upgrading the database using tape backups.

If you are upgrading the existing instance of SQL Server 7.0 to 2000, no additional disk space is required. If you plan to keep the original SQL Server 7.0 instance and migrate to SQL Server 2000, you will need additional disk space equivalent to the size of the current 7.0 databases. If you are upgrading a 6.5 SQL Server to SQL Server 2000, you will need approximately 1.5 times the space used by the 6.5 databases.

Post-Upgrade Tasks

After you upgrade from SQL Server 7.0 to SQL Server 2000, you should repopulate any full-text catalogs and update all statistics on your database tables. Both operations can be time-consuming, but will improve the performance of your SQL Server 2000 instance.

Your full-text catalogs need to be updated because the upgrade process marks your databases as full-text disabled due to a difference in formats from 7.0 to 2000. Your full-text catalogs must be repopulated after an upgrade, but this operation is not automatically run by the upgrade process. You should schedule a task to repopulate all full-text catalogs at an appropriate time. For more information, on managing full-text catalogs, see Chapter 44, "SQL Server Full-Text Search Services."

You should also update all statistics for the tables in the 7.0 databases upgraded to 2000. Again, this update might take a significant amount of time on large databases and should be scheduled to run at an appropriate time. Continuing to use SQL Server 7.0 statistics with SQL Server 2000 could result in poor query performance. For more information on index statistics and updating them, see Chapter 34, "Indexes and Performance."

In addition to updating statistics, it is also recommended that you drop and re-create all stored procedures in your upgraded databases. This will ensure that all stored procedure code behaves properly under SQL Server 2000 compatibility and also ensures that the procedures take advantage of the optimization enhancements available in SQL Server 2000.

Upgrade Compatibility Issues

The differences between SQL Server 7.0 and SQL Server 2000 are not quite as drastic as the differences between SQL Server 6.5 and 2000. The database structures in 7.0 are nearly identical to the SQL Server 2000 storage structures and there are no significant changes to the syntax or behavior of the Transact-SQL commands. Most of the changes between 7.0 and 2000 are new features and enhancements. As a matter of fact, the only real compatibility difference between versions 7.0 and 2000 is that several reserved keywords were introduced in SQL Server 2000 that can result in compatibility problems with version 7.0 databases.

NOTE

The number of enhancements and differences between SQL Server 2000 and the 6.x versions are significant and much too numerous to detail here. SQL Server Books Online provides a very detailed listing of the backward compatibility issues. It is strongly encouraged that you review this section of Books Online so that you are aware of any possible changes that might cause problems with existing applications.

One of the key differences in the 6.x versions and SQL Server 2000 is the handling of NULLs and string data in your T-SQL code. These differences often don't lead to errors, but can result in incorrect query results.

For example, in the 6.x versions of SQL Server, when you concatenate a `NULL` value with a character string, the query returns the character string. The ANSI standard states it should return a `NULL`, so the default behavior in SQL Server 7.0 and 2000 is to return `NULL`. Needless to say, this can wreak havoc with SQL code that is expecting the old behavior. To get 7.0 or SQL Server 2000 to mimic the old behavior, you need to set the database compatibility level to version 6.5 with the `sp_dbcmptlevel` *`dbname`*`, 65` statement, or turn the new behavior off with the `SET CONCAT_NULL_YIELDS_NULL OFF` command.

In addition, with ANSI NULL compatibility, when equality operators are used on NULL values, the result is `unknown`. In previous versions of SQL Server, an operator such as `@z <> 0` would return true if `@z` was null. Under ANSI NULL compatibility, the operator will resolve to unknown, causing procedural logic to behave differently. Any code that generates any sort of `= NULL` or `<> NULL` logic should be replaced with the ANSI-compliant `IS NULL` or `IS NOT NULL` syntax.

Table 8.8 provides a summary of some of the other key Transact-SQL compatibility issues between 6.x and SQL Server 2000.

TABLE 8.8 Key Transact-SQL Compatibility Issues Between SQL Server 6.x and 2000

SQL Server 6.x Behavior	SQL Server 2000 Behavior
The resultsets of `SELECT` statements with a `GROUP BY` clause are sorted by the `GROUP BY` columns.	A `GROUP BY` clause does not guarantee a sort order for the results. An `ORDER BY` clause must be explicitly specified for SQL Server to sort any resultset.
Columns can be prefixed with table aliases in the `SET` clause of an `UPDATE` statement.	Table aliases are not accepted in the `SET` clause of an `UPDATE` statement.
Warnings for invalid object names are generated when the batch is parsed or compiled, and an error message is returned when the batch is executed.	Error messages are only returned when the batch is executed.
Empty strings (`''`) are interpreted as a single blank.	Empty strings (`''`) are interpreted as empty strings.
`DATALENGTH('')` returns 1.	`DATALENGTH('')` returns 0.
`LEFT('123', m)` returns `NULL` when `m = 0`.	`LEFT('123', m)` returns an empty string when `m = 0`.
`LTRIM('     ')` returns `NULL`.	`LTRIM('     ')` returns an empty string.
`REPLICATE('123', m)` returns `NULL` when `m = 0`.	`REPLICATE('123', m)` returns an empty string when `m = 0`.
`RIGHT('123', m)` returns `NULL` when `m = 0`.	`RIGHT('123', m)` returns an empty string when `m = 0`.
`RIGHT('123', m)` returns `NULL` when *m* is negative.	`RIGHT('123', m)` returns an error when *m* is negative.
`RTRIM('     ')` returns `NULL`.	`RTRIM('     ')` returns an empty string.
`SPACE(0)` returns `NULL`.	`SPACE(0)` returns an empty string.
`SUBSTRING('123', m, n)` returns `NULL` when *m* < length of the string or when `n = 0`.	`SUBSTRING('123', m, n)` returns an empty string when *m* < length of the string or when *n* = 0.
The `CHARINDEX` and `PATINDEX` functions return null only if both the pattern and the expression are `NULL`.	The `CHARINDEX` and `PATINDEX` functions return `NULL` when any input parameters are `NULL`.

NOTE

It probably goes without saying, but you should not upgrade your production environments until you've applied the upgrade to a test or development environment first and run it through full QA cycle to identify and work out any compatibility issues that might affect your applications.

Setting Database Compatibility Level

To help ease the upgrade process, SQL Server 2000 databases provide the ability to set a database compatibility level. This capability allows you to mimic pre-2000 database behavior in SQL Server 2000 databases. Currently, SQL Server 2000 supports four compatibility levels:

- 80—SQL Server 2000 compatibility
- 70—SQL Server 7.0 compatibility
- 65—SQL Server 6.5 compatibility
- 60—SQL Server 6.0 compatibility

When you upgrade a database from SQL Server 7.0 to SQL Server 2000, the default compatibility level is set to 80. When you upgrade a SQL Server 6.5 or SQL Server 6.0 to SQL Server 2000, the original server compatibility level is retained.

In addition to supporting prior version behavior, certain newer behaviors and T-SQL syntax are not enabled at the lower compatibility levels. For example, the `LEFT OUTER JOIN` clause is not allowed if the compatibility level is set to 60. User-defined functions and indexed views cannot be created in a database if the database compatibility level is less than 80.

You can change the database compatibility level for a database using the sp_dbcmptlevel system procedure. The syntax is as follows:

```
EXEC sp_dbmptlevel dbname [, {60 | 65 | 70 | 80}]
```

If you execute the procedure without specifying a compatibility level, the current compatibility level for the database is returned.

The database compatibility level can also be viewed or set in SQL Enterprise Manager by right-clicking on a database and choosing the Properties option. In the Database Properties dialog box, click on the Options tab to display or set the database compatibility level.

Although the various `SET` options related to ANSI behavior and the ability to set compatibility levels help ease the migration process from earlier versions of SQL Server, it is strongly encouraged that you become familiar with and begin using the newer ANSI standard features in SQL Server. This is a good idea for two primary reasons:

- It allows your application code to take advantage of new capabilities available only with some of the ANSI SQL commands.
- Support for the older style syntax and behavior might no longer be supported in future releases of SQL Server.

For more information on the various ANSI-compatible `SET` options and how they affect your T-SQL code, see Chapter 26, "Using Transact-SQL in SQL Server 2000."

Setting Backward-Compatible Collation

One other key item to consider during an upgrade is the collation sequence that you are coming from and what you want it to be in the SQL Server 2000 instance. The Upgrade Wizard will inform you of your options along the way. The thing to keep in mind is how your users and programs are expecting to see the order of the result rows from queries they were using in older SQL Server versions (dictionary order, case insensitive for use with 1252 Character Set versus Latin1_General, and so on). There is a backward-compatibility option that can be specified during this process as seen in Figure 8.8

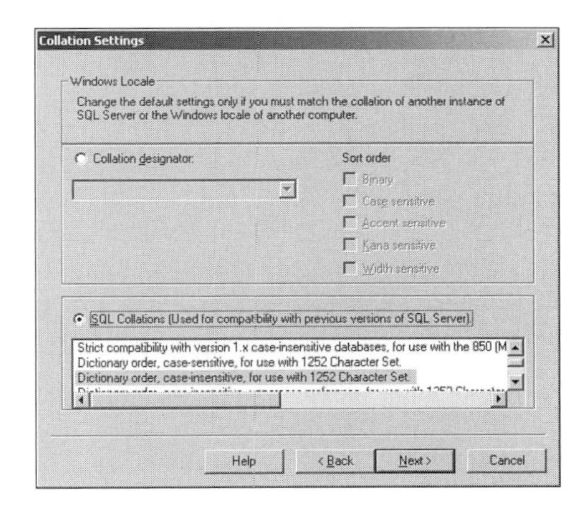

FIGURE 8.8 Backward-compatible collation sequence.

Summary

For a chapter that started out with "Probably the easiest part of administering a SQL Server database is the actual installation," we sure seem to have covered a lot of ground. The good news is that it will probably take you less time to perform the install than it did to read this chapter. The Installation Wizard presents the options in a step-by-step format that makes installation a breeze. Review your installation requirements first, check your hardware and software prerequisites, and don't forget about the unattended installation option. That way if you do get the install right the first time, you can repeat it again and again!

The next chapter dives into the client components needed to interact with SQL Server 2000. This can sometimes be a struggle if you are not already familiar with the different options available.

CHAPTER 9

Client Installation and Configuration

by Chris Gallelli

IN THIS CHAPTER

- The SQL Server Client Architecture
- Installing Client Tools
- Client Configuration
- Network Protocol Support
- Installing ODBC
- Microsoft Driver for JDBC
- Connecting to SQL Server Over the Internet

After you have completed the installation of SQL Server 2000 on your database server, it is time to think about connecting the clients. Clients, which are typically front-end applications, require their own set of software that enables them to connect to and use an instance of Microsoft SQL Server on the network.

This chapter focuses on the installation and configuration of the SQL Server client software components, including those that facilitate communications between the client computers and the server. It provides a basic understanding of the architecture that supports this communication, and then it delves into the information that you will need to get your clients connected.

The SQL Server Client Architecture

Microsoft SQL Server 2000 supports several methods for connecting client computers to a server instance. The means for connecting the computers and the software involved depends heavily on the type of client, where the client is located, and the network infrastructure that is in place.

For SQL Server 2000, several common types of clients connect to the database server. Clients, in this case, are software applications that usually fall into one of these categories:

- OLE DB consumers—These applications use one of two OLE DB providers offered by Microsoft to connect to SQL Server. The OLE DB provider for SQL Server is the recommended choice because it has been optimized for SQL Server, but the OLE DB provider for ODBC can also be used.
- ODBC Applications—Applications that rely on the open architecture of ODBC. This is an industry standard that is utilized by some of the SQL Server client tools, including Enterprise Manager and SQL Query Analyzer.
- DB-Library Applications—DB-Library is the original Application Programming Interface (API) used to connect to SQL Server. Applications that are utilizing DB-Library are typically older applications and include the ISQL command-line utility that comes with SQL Server 2000.

For these clients to connect to an instance of SQL Server 2000, they must use a client Net-Library that matches one of the server Net-Libraries that is listening for requests. The Net-Library is a dynamic-link library (DLL) that handles the communication between the client application and a network protocol. Each network protocol has a corresponding Interprocess Communication Component (IPC) API with which the Net-Library communicates.

Figure 9.1 illustrates the key components involved in the communication between the client and the server. The communication sequence from the client to the server is as follows:

1. The client application calls the OLE DB, ODBC, DB-Library, or Embedded SQL API.
2. The client API then calls a client Net-Library.
3. The client Net-Library calls an IPC API.
4. The IPC API transmits the client calls to a server Net-Library. If the client application is located on the database server, then the calls are transmitted using Windows IPC components, such as local named pipes or shared memory. If the client application is not on the server, then the network protocol stack on the client is used to communicate with the network protocol stack on the server.
5. The server Net-Library communicates with the desired instance of SQL Server 2000.

This communication scheme is fairly straightforward, but it can be complicated by the fact that some network APIs can be used over many different network protocols. Each of the Net-Libraries and the protocols they support will be addressed in more detail in the "Network Protocol Support" section later in this chapter.

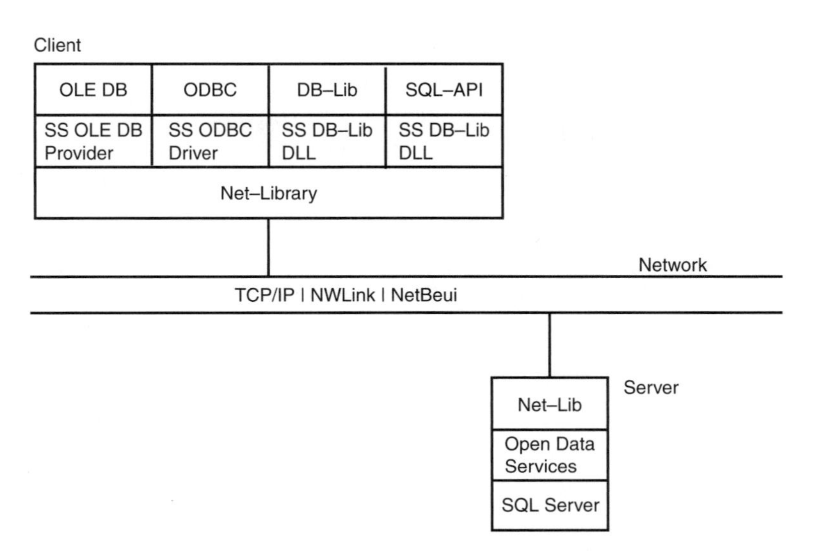

FIGURE 9.1 IPC communication architecture.

Installing Client Tools

The good news is that setting up your SQL Server clients to communicate with the database server is usually easy. The SQL Server installation program can be run on your client machines, and it will install the core data access components along with the SQL Server tools (applications) that you will need.

Client Requirements

Before you can install the SQL Server client-management tools and various library files, make sure that the computer meets the following requirements:

- Processor—Intel or compatible (Pentium 166 MHz or higher).
- Memory—32MB of RAM (minimum). Some editions of the software require 64MB.
- Hard disk space—95MB of available disk space (for client-management utilities only).
- Operating system—Windows NT 4.0, Windows 2000 (all versions), Windows Me, and Windows 98. Windows XP supports some editions of SQL Server 2000 and if you want the connectivity only, Windows 95 will work as well.
- Network software—Windows NT, Windows 2000, Windows Me, Windows 98, Windows XP, and Windows 95 have built-in networking software. (If you are using Banyan Vines or AppleTalk ADSP, you need additional network software.) Novell NetWare IPX/SPX client support is provided by the NWLink protocol in Windows Networking.

Installation Options

After you have established that you meet the minimum requirements, you are ready to start your client installation. You can install the client software in two common ways. The first, and most obvious option, is to run the SQL Server 2000 installation program. This option allows you to install both the client tools and the connectivity software you need.

The installation definition screen that is displayed as part of the SQL Server install allows you to select the components that you would like to install. On this screen, you have the option of installing the Client Tools Only, the Server and Client Tools, or the Connectivity Only (see Figure 9.2). With the Client Tools Only option, you get both the client relational database-management tools and the connectivity components. With the Connectivity Only option, only the relational database client connectivity components are installed. Included in the connectivity components is MDAC 2.6 (Microsoft Data Access Components), which is a requirement for connecting to a SQL Server 2000 named instance. A later version of the MDAC software is installed when SQL Server 2000 service packs are installed.

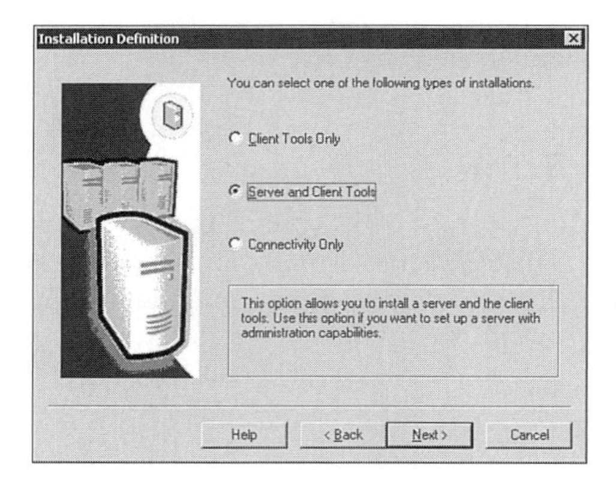

FIGURE 9.2 Installation Definition screen.

> **TIP**
>
> The SQL Server 2000 Installation program installs the client tools, by default, on the same partition on which Windows is installed. Often, this drive has the least amount of space available, but Microsoft does not support a way to change where the tools are installed.
>
> Also, be aware that the new SQL Server 2000 tools will replace any SQL Server 7.0 tools that might have been previously installed. It is possible to run both SQL Server 2000 and SQL Server 7.0 on the same machine, but the SQL Server 2000 tools will be launched instead of the 7.0 tools once the 2000 tools have been installed.

The other option for installing SQL Server 2000 client software is to utilize the sqlredis program. Sqlredis is a self-extracting executable file that can be launched independently of the SQL Server 2000 installation. It can only be used to install the client connectivity components; the client tools are not part of this install. The sqlredis executable file can be found in several directories on the SQL Server 2000 installation disc, including the ..\STANDARD\x86\other\.

The sqlredis program is often used as part of the setup process for an application that utilizes SQL Server 2000. The installation is silent and installs all of the client connectivity components needed to support a variety of application clients. OLE DB and the ODBC core components, the Microsoft OLE DB provider for SQL Server, the SQL Server ODBC driver, and the default SQL Server client Net-Libraries are all installed with sqlredis.

TIP

I highly recommend the use of the sqlredis program as part of your application's installation routine. One alternative is to include the individual connectivity component files in your application install, but this can prove to be problematic when new versions of the connectivity software (MDAC) are released. The crux of the problem is that many of the connectivity files are dependent on each other, and you might find that certain functionality on the client will not work if the complete installation is not done.

Microsoft typically releases several service packs for SQL Server. These service packs primarily contain fixes to the initial release of the software or previous service packs. It is a good practice to monitor the release of these service packs and apply them to your SQL Server environment. This includes the deployment of the service packs on your client machines. The service pack installation is very reliable and will ensure that all of the latest connectivity software, including MDAC, is in place.

Client Configuration

Client configuration is a step that might be needed to complete your client installation. It primarily consists of configuring the client's connection so that it can communicate with the server.

For most clients, the default network configuration installed with SQL Server client tools can be used without modification. These clients need only to specify the network name of the SQL Server computer to which they want to connect.

For other clients, the process can be more involved. This includes situations where connections to multiple servers running different network protocols is required. This section explores these different scenarios, the network considerations, and the configuration tools available.

Before you look at client configuration, you must have already installed the two core communication components for SQL Server. First, a pair of matching Net-Libraries (one on the server and one on the client) must be installed. Second, the correct network protocols on both the client and server must be in place.

For the most part, these prerequisites are satisfied as part of a normal SQL Server client setup. As discussed earlier, the Net-Libraries are installed as part of the SQL Server 2000 Client Tools setup. The network protocols are not installed by the SQL Server setup, but they are typically installed as part of the Microsoft Windows setup. They can also be installed via the Network applet in the Control Panel.

After you have satisfied the prerequisites, the client software is commonly configured in two different ways:

- Choice of network protocols used by the client software to connect to SQL Server. You define the names of the servers available on your network, which are used by both DB-Library and ODBC-based applications.
- The creation of ODBC datasources, which allow access to a specific server using a datasource name (DSN).

The Client Network Utility, discussed next, is the tool used for the first configuration option. The setup of ODBC and the ODBC datasources is discussed in the "Installing ODBC" section later in this chapter.

The SQL Server Client Network Utility

The SQL Server Client Network Utility screens have changed since SQL Server 7.0, but most of the core functionality is the same. This utility allows you to do the following:

- Change the default network protocol
- Create network protocol connections to specific servers with special configuration requirements (specific Net-Library choices, ports, names, and so on)
- Search for and display information about all the network libraries currently installed on a system
- Display the DB-Library version currently installed on the system and set defaults for DB-Library options

The network protocols, including the default, can be set on the first screen that is displayed after launching the Client Network Utility (see Figure 9.3).

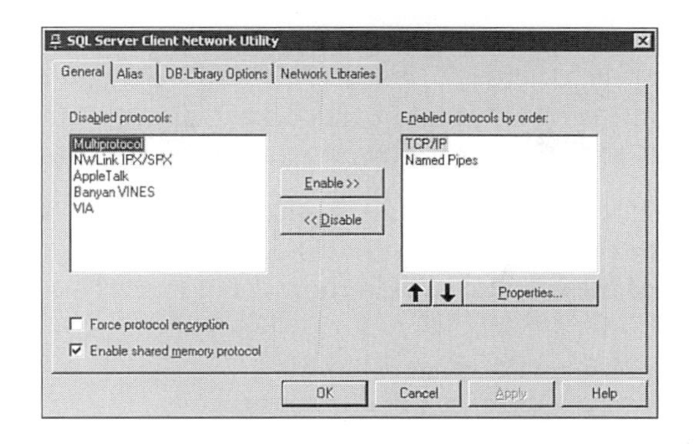

FIGURE 9.3 Client Network Utility—General tab.

The list box on the left side of the screen displays the network protocols that are not enabled. The client cannot communicate with SQL Server using the protocols that are listed here. Protocols can be enabled and disabled using the buttons in the center of the screen.

The right side of the screen displays those network protocols that have been enabled. The defaults, as shown, are the TCP/IP and named pipes protocols. These protocols are listed in priority order with the first item in the list being the default network protocol. The client will first attempt to connect to the server using the default protocol. If a connection cannot be made with it, then a connection is attempted using the next protocol on the list. This continues until a connection is established or the list of entries has been exhausted. This order can be changed using the up and down arrows found below the list box.

In most instances, no change will need to be made on the General tab of the Client Network screen. By default, clients running Microsoft Windows 2000, Windows NT 4.0, Windows 98, Windows XP, or Windows 95 use the client TCP/IP protocol. The exception is when protocols, other than the defaults, are enabled on the server. In this case, you must ensure that the client machines have the same protocols enabled as the server for a connection to be established.

TIP

The SQL Server error log is a good place to look to determine the protocols that SQL Server is listening on. You can view the error logs via the Management node in Enterprise Manager, or you can open the error log file using any text editor. The latest error log file is found by default in Program Files\Microsoft SQL Server\Mssql\Log\Errorlog. If you open the error log file with a text editor and find the word *Listening* in the error log text, you will find the relevant messages. The Server Network utility will show you what has been enabled, but there are instances when the server is unable to listen on the enabled protocol at startup.

In addition to defining the network protocols used by SQL Server, you can also define a server alias based on a specific network protocol. This can be useful when an instance of SQL Server has been configured to listen on an alternate network address or when connecting to a named instance of SQL Server 2000 using a SQL Server 7.0 client.

Figure 9.4 displays the tab where you define an alias in the Client Network Utility. Each network protocol shown on the alias definition screen has settings that correspond to that specific protocol. Each of these is discussed in more detail in the "Network Protocol Support" section that follows.

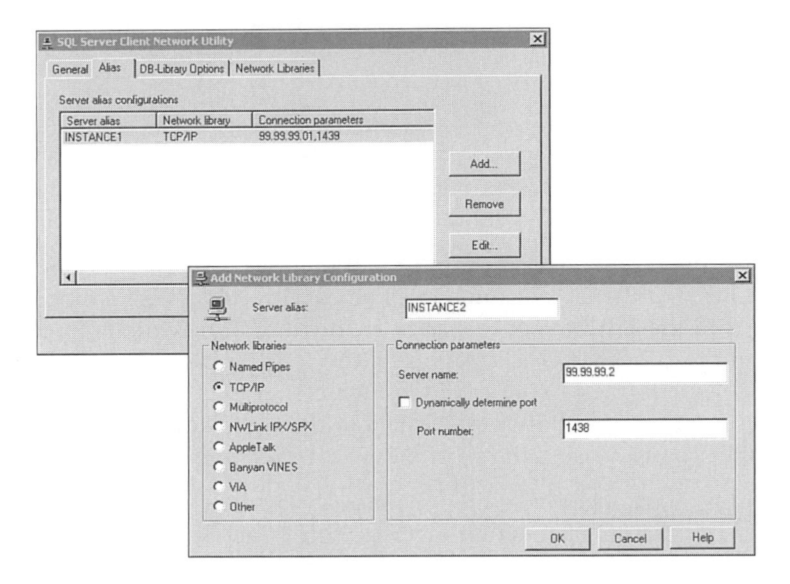

FIGURE 9.4 Client Network Utility—Alias configuration.

The alias name that you specify will be the name that you use to connect to SQL Server. It can be different from the computer name of the database server, and SQL Server will still be able to resolve the server location based on the connection information that you provide. SQL Server utilizes the configuration information and the alias names as follows:

1. If the server name used to connect to SQL Server matches the name of an alias, then the client connects with the network protocol and parameters for that alias.
2. If the server name does not match the name of an alias, then the default protocol is used.
3. If no default protocol has been defined, then TCP/IP is used.

The importance of the Alias tab in the Client Network Utility has increased with the advent of SQL Server 2000. Named instances, which have a two-part name (*server_name\ instance_name*) are not supported by several network protocols and some client applications, but an alias that maps to that instance can be used instead.

For example, in Figure 9.4, the alias name of INSTANCE2 is used when adding a new server alias via the Add Network Library Configuration screen. The actual name of the instance, in this example, is Win2000svr\INSTANCE2, but the addition of the alias will allow clients to reference the server using the abbreviated INSTANCE2 name instead.

CAUTION

The multiprotocol, Banyan VINES, and AppleTalk Net-Libraries do not support named instances for SQL Server 2000. You can connect to the default instance using the computer name of the server, but any named instance on that server will not be accessible by default using the two-part instance name.

Another SQL Server 2000 consideration that also relates to named instances is the use of ports to differentiate the network address for each instance running on the server machine. The default SQL Server instance uses port 1433, which is the same port number used in prior versions. For subsequent named instances on the same server, a different port is required for each. SQL Server does not reserve other port numbers for use by named instances. Instead, you can specify a port number of 0 (the default) during the installation of the instance that allows SQL Server to dynamically determine an available port number.

TIP

A list of port numbers registered for use can be found on the Internet at `http://www.iana.org/assignments/port-numbers`. You can look here to determine which port numbers *not* to use when setting up your alias for a SQL Server instance.

This brief review of named instances is relevant to the Client Network Utility because the alias creation screen allows you to specify a port number to connect to a particular SQL Server instance when using the TCP/IP protocol. This is required for some clients to connect to a named instance and is an easy way to specify an abbreviated server name for your named instance.

For instance, if you refer to the prior example that is displayed in Figure 9.4, you will see that a port number of 1438 was used to define an alias for INSTANCE2. The other server instance listed in this example (INSTANCE1) used port number 1439. The check box Dynamically Determine Port must be unchecked so you can enter a specific port number as in these examples. If this check box is enabled, SQL Server will dynamically determine the port number for you.

Network Protocol Support

To facilitate client-to-server communication in a variety of network architectures, Microsoft provides a choice of network libraries for use based on your network protocols. The next sections examine the different protocols available and how you can customize their use.

Table 9.1 identifies the client- and server-side Net-Libraries for each supported IPC.

TABLE 9.1 Client and Server Net-Libraries

Net-Library	Client	Server	Supported Protocols
Multiprotocol	DBMSRPCN.DLL	SSMSRP70.DLL	TCP/IP, NetBEUI, NWLink
Named Pipes	DBNMPNTW.DLL	SSNMPN70.DLL	TCP/IP, NetBEUI, NWLink
TCP/IP Sockets	DBNETLIB.DLL	SSNETLIB.DLL	TCP/IP
Novell IPX/SPX	DBNETLIB.DLL	SSNETLIB.DLL	NWLink
AppleTalk	DBMSADSN.DLL	SSMSAD70.DLL	AppleTalk
Banyan Vines	DBMSVINN.DLL	SSMSVI70.DLL	Banyan Vines
VIA GigaNet	DBMSGNET.DLL	DBMSGNET.DLL	VIA

In the case of Multiprotocol, named pipes, AppleTalk, Banyan Vines, and VIA GigaNet SAN, the DBNETLIB.DLL on the client and server routes the communications to the libraries listed.

Network Protocols

Using the Client Network Utility, you can choose the specific network library you want to use to make connections to your SQL servers. All the network libraries are implemented as dynamic link libraries (DLLs) and are used during network communication using specific InterProcess Communication mechanisms.

NOTE

With distributed computing—of which a client connection to a server is the most fundamental—a connection is made at a process-to-process level to allow communication in both directions. The foundation for this approach is an InterProcess Communication mechanism—of which Windows Sockets, Remote Procedure Calls (RPCs), NetBIOS, named pipes, and mailslots are all examples.

The following sections detail each of the available network libraries.

Named Pipes

Named pipes has historically been the default network library used by SQL Server running on NT, but it has been replaced by TCP/IP. By default, named pipes is installed to listen on a standard pipe of `\\.\pipe\sql\query`. This pipe name can be changed after installation to make it more difficult for malicious attacks against publicly accessible SQL servers.

If you do change the server's default pipe, you must use the General tab in the Client Network dialog box to connect to the new pipe name. To set up the new pipe, click the Add button on the Client Network Utility and enter the server's name and the new pipe name.

NOTE

Under Windows 95, the 32-bit named pipe network library does not support server enumeration. This is the mechanism used to create a list of available servers to which you can connect.

TCP/IP Sockets

TCP/IP Sockets is the new default protocol that allows communication over the TCP/IP protocol using standard Windows Sockets as the IPC mechanism. Using TCP/IP, the SQL Server service is assigned to port 1433; this is the official Internet Assigned Number Authority (IANA) socket number. If this value is changed on the server, you must set up a specific entry using the Client Network Utility to indicate the modified port number.

For information on connecting to a SQL server hidden behind a proxy server, see "Connecting to SQL Server Through Microsoft Proxy Server," later in this chapter.

Multiprotocol

The Multiprotocol network library allows communication over supported Windows NT IPC mechanisms. Currently, Microsoft considers only named pipes, TCP/IP sockets, and NWLink IPX/SPX to be tested and supported. The RPC service receives the server's name from the Multiprotocol network library; based on the network protocols available on the client, RPC attempts to use each protocol in turn until a connection is successfully made. The client must be using a Net-Library and protocol stack that corresponds to one on which the SQL server is listening. A client connecting with the Multiprotocol Net-Library over TCP/IP can connect to a SQL server that is running the TCP/IP protocol. If the server were running the IPX/SPX protocol stack, then no connection could be made.

Among the protocols that RPC supports are Windows-based Novell clients using SPX or IPXODI.

Multiprotocol allows authentication by Windows NT over all supported RPC protocols. Prior to SQL Server 2000, Multiprotocol was one of the only ways to get encryption over your network connection. Now, Secure Sockets Layer (SSL) encryption can be enabled over any Net-Library in SQL Server 2000 via the Server Network Utility.

The server's address is determined in the same manner as it is for named pipes: by the server's name. Multiprotocol does not support server enumeration from the client side; servers listening on just Multiprotocol do not appear in browse lists on clients able to enumerate available servers.

To map a computer name to a physical node, the RPC service makes use of the network protocol's naming service: WINS for TCP/IP, SAP for NWLink IPX/SPX, and NetBIOS broadcasts for named pipes.

NWLink IPX/SPX

Novell SPX–based clients require the NWLink IPX/SPX protocol. In a default installation of SQL Server, the service name is that of the computer. If this default is changed, you must make a customized entry for that server for each client.

The Client Network Utility allows the specification of the following items:

- Service name
- Network address, consisting of the following:
    - Address
    - Port
    - Network

Your network administrator can provide this information for you.

AppleTalk ADSP

To allow Apple Macintosh clients to use their native AppleTalk network protocol, the AppleTalk ADSP is the network library of choice.

> **NOTE**
>
> Macintosh clients can also communicate using TCP/IP.

Custom AppleTalk entries allow you to specify the object name and zone of the SQL server within the AppleTalk network.

Banyan Vines

The network library used to communicate over Banyan Vines' IP network protocol is the Banyan Vines Sequenced Packet Protocol (SPP).

When a SQL server is installed to listen on Banyan Vines, it is assigned an address of the form `servicename@group@org`. This address is what you must specify when setting up the client.

> **NOTE**
>
> Banyan Vines is currently available only on Intel-based machines.

VIA Giganet

A new Net-Library based on the Virtual Interface Architecture (VIA) was added with SQL Server 2000. It is used for fast and highly reliable data transfer between servers that are located in the same Datacenter. For VIA to work, it must be run on supported hardware provided by Giganet.

Troubleshooting Client Connections

Setting up your clients to connect to your SQL servers is not always as simple as installing the protocols on the machine. You might have to make modifications to the default settings for a protocol (as detailed in the previous sections). You might also have some additional steps or problems to overcome.

You should troubleshoot client connection problems in the same way you tackle other problems: methodically and carefully. You must first consider the different elements involved. Then isolate them, test them, and eliminate them as the source of the problem. You need to consider the following elements:

- Client hardware—Network interface card (NIC), network cable
- Network hardware—Routers, bridges, WAN links
- Server hardware—Network interface card, network cable
- Client software—Operating system, other applications, network protocol, network library, database library, SQL application, login, password
- Server software—Operating system, network protocol, network libraries, SQL Server configuration

Some of these items are obvious and easily identified: *Is* the cable plugged into the card/wall? Others require more work and other tools. Some hardware problems such as troublesome network architecture components require more sophisticated steps.

The first step is to determine whether you can see the server's name in a network browse list (look in the Network Neighborhood or use the `net view` command). If you cannot see the server, you might have a router or incompatible network protocol problem. For clients that are running TCP/IP, ping is another good starting point for determining if the client machine can connect to the server. This is discussed in more detail in the "Troubleshooting TCP/IP Connections" section that follows.

If you can see the server, then the next step is to try to make a network connection to a share on the SQL server. You can attempt to read and write a file to that location. This will establish what type of network permissions you have on the server. In some scenarios, you can still connect to SQL Server if you are unable to read and write a file, but this information is still valuable in diagnosing your problem.

Finally, you can try a different protocol from the client. If you can connect with one protocol but not another, you have eliminated at least some of the potential problem areas.

Troubleshooting TCP/IP Connections

The simplest way to check the visibility of a server is to use the ping utility, which has this form:

```
ping IPAddress|ServerName
```

You can use the name of the server if it can be identified by a DNS, WINS, or HOSTS file. If ping is successful, you should receive some feedback on the time it takes for a packet to bounce back from the server. If the server cannot be found, you receive an error message.

PathPing is another useful utility shipped with Windows 2000 that is similar to the ping command. It has similar syntax to that of ping, but it has some advanced features including the ability to see the names of computers that are connected on the way to the destination server. A simple example follows:

```
pathping dbsvr7_test
Tracing route to dbsvr7_test [00.00.00.01]
over a maximum of 30 hops:
  0  win2000svr [00.00.00.00]
  1  DBSVR7_TEST [00.00.00.01]
.....
```

This example shows partial output from the pathping command run from a Windows 2000 server named win2000svr to an NT 4.0 server named DBSVR7_TEST. The output shows the names of the servers for each network hop along with the associated IP address. In this case, only one hop was required to get between the two servers, but if additional hops are necessary, then they will be displayed as well, up to a maximum of 30.

NOTE

The Microsoft Data Access Components (MDAC) version 2.6 that is installed as part of SQL Server 2000 has a documented bug related to unusually slow connection times when using an IP address. For instance, if you have a TCP/IP alias set up for your database server with a specific IP address, you might find that connections to the server timeout take unusually long. This problem was corrected in SQL Server 2000 Service Pack 2 and MDAC 2.6 Service Pack 2. Refer to the Microsoft Knowledge Base article Q300420 for more details.

Finally, the data found in the sysprocesses system table can be useful when diagnosing TCP/IP and other network connectivity to the database server. This table contains a myriad of information, including the network library that is being used for active connections to the server. This can be helpful in circumstances where some users are able to connect to the server but others are not. You can determine if those users that are connected are using a common protocol, and if so, determine if the users that can't connect have the same client setup.

NOTE

The troubleshooting discussions in this chapter have focused on resolving network connections to SQL Server. If you are experiencing login failures, you can use a security-oriented tool to diagnose your problem. The SQL Server Enterprise Manager can be used to display security information, and the SQL Profiler can be used to audit logins and login failures.

Troubleshooting Named Pipes

You can test a network connection over named pipes with a couple different approaches. The first approach checks whether you can see a server and its resources and makes use of the `net view` command. To check the connection, enter the following statement in a command window:

```
net view \\servername
```

If this command is successful, you will see a list of resources. The next thing to try is to connect to the server's named pipe using the `net use` command:

```
net use \\servername\IPC$
```

If you can open a connection in this way but still get a failure when trying to connect a SQL tool, you can use the `makepipe` and `readpipe` command-line utilities. On the server, enter the following command:

```
makepipe
```

On the client, enter this command:

```
readpipe /Sservername /Dstring
```

In this syntax, *string* is anything you want. If the string contains a space, the string must be enclosed in quotation marks. The server process creates and manages the pipe. Then the client uses `DosOpen` to connect and then executes `DosWrite` to the pipe. After that, the server (hopefully) does a `DosRead` to receive the value sent. If the connection is a success, you should see results similar to these on the client:

```
SvrName:\\win2000svr
PIPE   :\\win2000svr\pipe\abc
DATA   :test
Data Sent: 1 : test
Data Read: 1 : test
```

The server also reacts to the readpipe call with the makepipe utility, showing something like this:

```
Waiting for client to send... 1
Data Read:      test
Waiting for client to send... 2
Pipe closed
Waiting for Client to Connect...
```

If you do not get this result, then network named pipe services are probably not loaded. You must install them before clients can make named pipe connections.

NOTE

The readpipe and makepipe utilities are not installed as part of the SQL Server 2000 installation, but they can be copied from the installation disc.

Installing ODBC

An alternative to specifying all of the connection information (including server name, user, and password) when connecting to SQL Server is to set up an ODBC datasource. Each ODBC datasource has a unique datasource name (DSN) that can be referenced by ODBC applications. The DSN definition contains all of the pertinent connection information that allows applications to simply reference the DSN to connect to the database server.

The ODBC Administration tool and SQL Server driver are installed from the SQL Server CD-ROM. After it is installed, you can use the ODBC Administrator, accessed from the Control Panel, to create user, system, or file datasources:

- User DSNs are local to a computer and can be used by only the current user.
- System DSNs are local to a computer, rather than dedicated to a user. This arrangement allows the system—or any user with the correct privileges—to use the datasource.
- File DSNs are stored in files on the client machine instead of the registry.

Configuring ODBC Datasources

To configure ODBC datasources, you can use the ODBC Datasource Administrator by selecting the ODBC applet in the Control Panel. With this tool, you can check driver versions and add and modify datasources that utilize the SQL Server ODBC driver. When you create or modify a SQL Server datasource, the Microsoft SQL Server DSN Configuration Wizard opens to help step you through the configuration.

Troubleshooting ODBC Connections

Most of the same steps described in the "Troubleshooting Client Connections" section earlier in this chapter also apply to investigating ODBC connection problems. However, there is one additional tool in your ODBC repertory: `odbcping`. `odbcping` allows you to test the visibility of a server through a datasource and to check whether ODBC is correctly installed. This 32-bit utility is not installed by default, but it can be copied from the SQL Server installation disc. The syntax for `odbcping` is shown here:

```
odbcping { -Sservername ¦ -Ddatasource } -Ulogin -Ppassword
```

In this syntax, *`servername`* is the name of the server to which you want to test the connection, *`datasource`* is the ODBC datasource name on the local machine, and *`login`* and *`password`* are valid values for that server. `odbcping` returns either the version of the SQL Server ODBC driver and the server name if successful, or an error message as specified by the ODBC driver.

Following is an example verifying a connection through a datasource:

```
odbcping /DWin2000svrDSN /Usimon /Psecret
```

Next is an example of connecting directly to a server:

```
odbcping /SWin2000svr /Usimon /Psecret
```

> **NOTE**
>
> The `odbcping` utility is not installed as part of the SQL Server 2000 installation, but it can be copied from the installation disc.

OLE DB

There is some misunderstanding about where the OLE DB interface from Microsoft fits in the grand scheme of client connectivity. OLE DB is actually a *specification for* a data access interface rather than *an interface*. It is intended to provide the basis for client access to a wide range of data storage systems.

Microsoft has provided a guide, available from its Web site, shown in Table 9.2, for which technology should be used for a given situation.

TABLE 9.2 ODBC Versus OLE DB

Situation	Technology
Accessing standard relational databases from a non-OLE environment	ODBC is the best choice.
Exposing a data interface to non-SQL data	OLE DB is the best choice.
Programming in an OLE environment	OLE DB is the best choice.
Building interoperable database components.	OLE DB is the only choice.

NOTE

An integral part of OLE DB is a driver manager that enables OLE DB clients to talk to ODBC providers.

Table 9.3 shows the actual technical differences between the ODBC and OLE DB interfaces.

TABLE 9.3 Technical Differences Between ODBC and OLE DB

ODBC	OLE DB
Data Access API	Database Component API
C-Level API	COM API
SQL-based data	All tabular data
SQL-based standard	COM-based standard
Native providers	Component architecture

Microsoft Driver for JDBC

JDBC, short for Java Database Connectivity, is similar to ODBC but is designed specifically for Java programs. Java programming has blossomed with the advent of the Internet, so Microsoft has released a new driver for JDBC that allows Java applications to access SQL Server 2000. This driver is a Type 4 JDBC driver that has been optimized for the Java environment.

All versions of SQL Server 2000 are supported for use with the SQL Server 2000 driver for JDBC, but only a limited number of operating systems are supported. The following list shows those operating systems that are supported:

- Microsoft Windows XP
- Microsoft Windows 2000 with service pack 2 or higher
- AIX
- HP-UX
- Solaris
- Linux

The Microsoft SQL Server 2000 driver for JDBC can be downloaded from the Microsoft Web site; see `www.microsoft.com/sql/downloads/default.asp` for details. The driver is available for download to all licensed SQL Server 2000 customers at no charge and is fully supported by Microsoft. The installation is fast and provides an HTML Help document and a JDBC Installation guide that is in PDF format.

Once you have Microsoft's JDBC driver installed, refer to the Microsoft Knowledge Base Article - Q313100 for information on how to get started using the driver. This article explains how to register the JDBC driver and provides some simple JAVA coding examples that indicate how the driver can be used.

NOTE

There are other third-party JDBC drivers that are available, but the Microsoft driver is free and is fully supported by Microsoft.

Connecting to SQL Server over the Internet

By making your SQL server accessible over the Internet, you can allow worldwide client access to your data. Although this permits a large degree of information sharing, it comes with the added burden of securing access to that data.

To connect your client application to a Microsoft SQL server over the Internet, both the client and server must have access to the Internet. In addition, the server must be running either TCP/IP Sockets or the Multiprotocol Net-Library. If you are using Multiprotocol, make sure that TCP/IP support is enabled. After these two requirements are satisfied, the client can then connect to a specific IP address; if the computer is registered with a domain name sever (DNS), the client can connect with its registered name.

Securing Connections over the Internet

Making your SQL server visible on the Internet should make you think carefully about the security of the server and the data it contains. One way to protect your data is to hide the server behind a firewall. A firewall system isolates your network from users who are accessing machines that are intended for Internet access. The firewall can be set up to forward only those requests that are targeted at a specific TCP/IP address. Requests for all other network addresses are blocked by the firewall.

Another consideration for protecting your data is the use of encrypted connections. You have a couple of options to ensure that your connections to SQL Server are encrypted. One option is to configure encryption on the server side. This will force SQL Server to accept only encrypted connections. You can also configure individual clients to request that their connection be encrypted. This approach allows intranet clients to connect without the added burden of encryption, while still allowing less secure Internet clients to individually ask for encryption.

Connecting to SQL Server Through Microsoft Proxy Server

If SQL Server is to be hidden behind Microsoft Proxy Server, you must specify the Remote WinSock proxy address when you set up the TCP/IP Sockets Net-Library. This can be done via the SQL Server Installation or the Server Network Utility after the installation is complete. You must enter the port number and the proxy server address (the DNS name or the IP address) in the Port Number box for the TCP/IP Sockets protocol. Then enter the DNS name or the IP address of the proxy server in the Proxy Address box.

On the client side, you follow the same configuration steps as you do for connecting directly over the Internet. You can then connect to the specified port of the proxy, which carries out the redirection to the actual port on which SQL Server is listening.

NOTE

Often, an application server will manage access to SQL Server via the Internet, and direct access to the database server by Internet clients will not be needed. Internet clients will typically access the application server, the application server will request the data from SQL Server, and then the application server will return the data to the Internet client.

Summary

This chapter presented you with the basic information that you will need to set up your client machines for SQL Server 2000. It gave you a fundamental understanding of the client architecture as it relates to SQL Server, delved into the tools and components that are installed as part of the SQL Server installation, and concluded with some advanced topics, including client configuration and Internet setup.

The next chapter, "SQL Server System and Database Administration," will give you some insight into the administration of SQL Server 2000. It covers the role of a system administrator and provides an overview of the key system information that you can use in this capacity.

CHAPTER **10**

SQL Server System and Database Administration

by Paul Jensen

IN THIS CHAPTER

- Responsibilities of the System Administrator
- System Databases
- System Tables
- System-Stored Procedures
- Useful System Procedures
- Other Methods of Querying the System Tables

This chapter outlines the role of the SQL Server system administrator, and also examines the system databases and tables and the methods the administrator can use to query system data. An understanding of these key structures is essential in administering a SQL Server database. Just like the mechanic who fixes your car, the administrator must know where to look when problems occur.

Responsibilities of the System Administrator

The administrator is responsible for the integrity and availability of the data. This is a simple concept, but it is a huge responsibility. Some large corporations place a valuation on their data as high as $1 million per 100MB. The investment in dollars is not the only issue; many companies that lose mission-critical data simply never recover.

The actual job description for a system administrator varies widely. In small shops, the administrator might lay out the physical design, install SQL Server, implement the logical design, tune the installation, and then manage ongoing tasks such as backups. Larger sites might have tasks broken out into separate job functions. Managing users and backing up data are common examples of this. However, a lead administrator should still be in place to define policy and coordinate efforts. Whether performed by an individual or as a team, the core administration tasks are as follows:

- Install and configure SQL Server
- Plan and create databases
- Manage data storage
- Control security
- Tune the database
- Perform backup and recovery

Another task that is sometimes handled by administrators is that of managing stored procedures. As stored procedures for user applications often contain complex T-SQL code, they tend to fall into the realm of the application developer. However, because stored procedures are stored as objects in the database, they are also the responsibility of the administrator. If your application calls custom-stored procedures, you must be aware of this and coordinate with the application developers.

The system administration job can be stressful, frustrating, and demanding, but it is a highly rewarding, interesting, and respected position. You will be expected to know all, see all, and predict all, but you will be well compensated for your efforts.

System Databases

The system databases exist to support the operation of SQL Server. The four system databases—master, model, msdb, and tempdb—are created by the installation program. The system databases are said to contain "metadata," or data about data. These databases cannot be dropped.

master

As the name implies, the master database is the repository for all system-wide information for SQL Server. If an object is defined at the server level, it is stored in master. Login accounts, configuration settings, system-stored procedures, and the existence of other databases are recorded in the master database. SQL Server will not run if the master database is damaged or corrupt; therefore, it is imperative that the master database is backed up on a regular basis. See Chapter 16, "Database Backup and Restore," for further information.

msdb

The msdb database holds information for the SQL Server Agent. When you define jobs, operators, and alerts, they are stored in the msdb database. Information about backup operations is also stored in msdb, so it is important to back up msdb even if you are not using the SQL Agent. In SQL Server Enterprise Edition, tables exist to support the log shipping feature.

model

The model database is a template on which all user-created databases are based. All databases must contain a base set of objects known as the database catalog. When a new database is created, the model is copied to populate the requisite objects. Conveniently, objects can be added to the model database. For example, if you want a certain table created in all your databases, create the table in the model database and it will be propagated to all subsequently created databases. If you do modify the model database, remember to back it up or your changes will be lost.

tempdb

tempdb holds temporary objects in SQL Server. Explicitly created temporary tables and temporary stored procedures, as well as system-created temporary objects, share tempdb. Think of tempdb as a workspace, or scratch pad, that SQL Server uses to hold interim data. A large sort operation, for instance, is performed in tempdb before being returned to the user process. Index creation can be set to use tempdb as well. Having tempdb on a separate disk system can vastly improve index creation time. As SQL Server re-creates tempdb each time SQL Server is started, you don't need to back up tempdb.

Distribution

The distribution database, although technically a system database, is not created by default. If you choose to set up replication, the distribution database will be installed. See Chapter 22, "Data Replication," for more information.

System Tables

SQL Server uses system tables to hold its configuration and object information. The tables are generally named with a sys prefix, such as `sysdatabases`. For this reason, system tables are often referred to as the sys tables. Some of these, such as `syslogins`, are actually implemented as views. The system tables are broken into two basic categories. The *system catalog* tables are contained in the master database and contain information common to the entire installation. The *database catalog* is contained in each database, including the master, and contains information specific to that database. The msdb database has—in addition to its database catalog—additional system tables related to SQL Agent, Backup and Recovery, and log shipping (Enterprise Edition only). When replication is configured, additional system tables are created in master, distribution, and the user databases involved in replication.

System Catalog

Table 10.1 lists the system catalog tables and views.

TABLE 10.1 The System Catalog Tables and Views

Name	Type	Description
`sysaltfiles`	Table	Contains database file information for tempdb. As tempdb is rebuilt on system startup, this information must be stored in master.
`syscacheobjects`	Table	Keeps track of compiled object usage in cache. This is a virtual table materialized each time it is queried.
`syscharsets`	Table	Contains installed character sets and sort orders.
`sysconfigures`	Table	Holds system configuration values to be used at the next system startup.
`syscurconfigs`	Table	Contains current system configuration. This is a virtual table materialized each time it is queried.
`sysdatabases`	Table	Contains information on all databases.
`sysdevices`	Table	Contains an entry for each database file, as well as disk and tape backup files.
`syslanguages`	Table	Contains an entry for each language installed on the server. There is no entry for U.S. English; however, it is always available.
`syslockinfo`	Table	Contains information on all active locks on the system.
`syslogins`	View	Contains information on each login ID, based on the `sysxlogins` table.
`sysmessages`	Table	Contains system error and warning messages.
`sysoledbusers`	View	Contains user and password mapping for linked servers. Based on sysxlogins.
`sysperfinfo`	Table	Contains performance counters that can be displayed by Performance Monitor.
`sysprocesses`	Table	Contains information on all client and system processes running on SQL Server.
`sysremotelogins`	View	Contains an entry for each remote user who can call remote stored procedures.
`sysxlogins`	Table	Contains information on each login ID.

Database Catalog

Table 10.2 lists the database catalog tables and views.

TABLE 10.2 Database Catalog Tables and Views

Name	Type	Description
`syscolumns`	Table	Contains an entry for every column in all tables and views, and a row for each parameter in a stored procedure.
`syscomments`	Table	Contains entries for each view, rule, default, trigger, CHECK constraint, DEFAULT constraint, and stored procedure. The text column contains the SQL statement to create the object.

TABLE 10.2 Continued

Name	Type	Description
`sysconstraints`	View	Maps constraints to the objects that own them. Based on the `sysobject` table.
`sysdepends`	Table	Stores relationships between dependent objects, such as the relationship of views to tables.
`sysfilegroups`	Table	Contains information about filegroups.
`sysfiles`	Table	Contains information on database files, including the logical and physical name and size.
`sysforeignkeys`	Table	Contains foreign key relationships in the database.
`sysfulltextcatalogs`	Table	Contains an entry for each full-text catalog.
`sysindexes`	Table	Contains information about indexes in the database.
`sysindexkeys`	View	Contains information about index keys.
`sysmembers`	Table	Contains member information for database roles.
`sysobjects`	View	Contains one entry for every object in the database.
`syspermissions`	Table	Contains permissions granted and denied to users, groups, and roles.
`sysprotects`	Table	Contains permissions applied to security accounts with the GRANT and DENY statements.
`sysreferences`	Table	Contains column mapping for foreign key constraints.
`systypes`	Table	Contains information on all system and user-defined datatypes.
`sysusers`	Table	Contains an entry for each Windows user, Windows group, SQL Server user, or SQL Server role that has access to the database.

Replication Catalog

The replication catalog tables are not created until replication is configured. When replication is defined, tables are created in the `master`, `msdb`, `distribution`, and user databases involved in replication. The configuration will vary depending on the replication model.

System Tables in `msdb`

In addition to the standard database catalog tables, `msdb` contains tables specific to the SQL Server Agent, backup, Log Shipping, and the Database Maintenance Plan.

Table 10.3 lists the SQL Server Agent Tables.

TABLE 10.3 SQL Server Agent Tables

Name	Description
`sysalerts`	Name, error number, and so on for all defined alerts.
`syscategories`	The categories used to organize jobs, alerts, and operators.
`sysdownloadlist`	Queue of jobs to be downloaded to other servers.
`sysjobhistory`	History table for scheduled jobs.
`sysjobs`	Information on SQL Server Agent jobs.
`sysjobschedules`	Scheduling information for jobs.
`sysjobservers`	The relationship of a job with one or more target servers.
`sysjobsteps`	Steps stored for each scheduled job.
`sysnotifications`	Notification information for each operator by job.
`sysoperators`	Operator information, such as name, e-mail address, and so on.
`systargetservergroupmembers`	The target servers that are included in a multiserver group.
`systargetservergroups`	The target server groups that are defined on the server.
`systargetservers`	The enlisted target servers.
`systaskids`	Mappings of jobs from earlier versions to current version jobs.

Table 10.4 lists the backup tables.

TABLE 10.4 The Backup Tables

Name	Description
`backupfile`	Contains information on each data or log file that is backed up.
`backupmediafamily`	Contains information on backup media families, such as name, mediaset, physical and logical filenames, and so on.
`backupmediaset`	Contains name, description, and so on for each media set.
`backupset`	Contains a row for each backup set.
`logmarkhistory`	Contains information on each committed marked transaction.
`restorefile`	Contains an entry for each file that has been restored.
`restorefilegroup`	Contains an entry for each filegroup restored.
`restorehistory`	Contains one row for each restore operation.

Table 10.5 lists the maintenance plan tables.

TABLE 10.5 Maintenance Plan Tables

Name	Description
`sysdbmaintplan_databases`	One row for each database included in the plan.
`sysdbmaintplan_history`	Maintenance plan history for executed job.

TABLE 10.5 Continued

Name	Description
`sysdbmaintplan_jobs`	One row for each job in the plan.
`sysdbmaintplans`	One row for each plan. Includes name, ID, and creation date.

Table 10.6 lists the log shipping tables.

TABLE 10.6 Log Shipping Tables

Name	Description
`log_shipping_databases`	Name and ID of the database being shipped.
`log_shipping_monitor`	Name of the log shipping monitor server.
`log_shipping_plan_databases`	Database names, enabled options for a log shipping plan.
`log_shipping_plan_history`	History information for a log shipping plan.
`log_shipping_plans`	Configuration information for a log shipping plan.
`log_shipping_primaries`	Primary server, configuration, history, and thresholds.
`log_shipping_secondaries`	Secondary server, configuration, history, and thresholds.

System-Stored Procedures

The **system-stored procedures**, created when SQL Server is installed, are integral to the administration of SQL Server. The purpose of the system-stored procedures is to shield the administrator from having to query or edit the system and database catalog tables directly. Much of SQL Server administration can now be done through the Enterprise Manager, but it pays to be familiar with the system-stored procedures as well. For instance, to add a login in Enterprise Manager, right-click Logins, select New Login from the pop-up window, and fill in the appropriate information. That's fine for one new login, but what if you want to add 200 logins? In that case, write a script that calls the system-stored procedure `sp_addlogin` and provides the appropriate values (name, password, and so on) for the new logins.

It would be impractical to list all the system-stored procedures. A quick check of the master database lists almost 1,000 procedures. Books Online and MSDN are excellent resources for information on the system-stored procedures. Another way to familiarize yourself with the procedures available is to "walk through" the list in the Query Analyzer's object browser. I often find this is enough to jog my memory when I can't quite remember which procedure I need for a particular task. If you need more info, drag the procedure into the query window, and press Shift+F1. This will open the Books Online documentation for the procedure.

Special Characteristics of System-Stored Procedures

Generally, system-stored procedures share these attributes:

- They are stored in the `master` database.
- Their name is prefixed with `sp_`.
- The owner of the procedure is dbo (database owner).
- They are global in scope. This means they can be executed from any database and will run in the context of that database.

Just as you should never directly modify system tables, the same holds true for system-stored procedures. If you want to change a system-stored procedure, copy the procedure definition from the text column of the `syscomments` table or from the procedures properties in Enterprise Manager; you can then paste it into a new stored procedure and modify it at will. If you mess it up, the original is still available.

NOTE

Be careful not to alter system-stored procedures that modify system tables. These procedures are complex and have many dependencies. If you trash your system and call Microsoft for support, don't be surprised if they tell you, "We don't support the direct modification of system objects. Have a nice day."

Useful System Procedures

Although hundreds of system-stored procedures exist, you will find a core group of 10 or 20 that you commonly use on your system. Many of the procedures prefixed as `sp_help` are, to risk stating the obvious, helpful. For instance, `sp_helpdb` returns information about all databases, or if a database name is specified, about a single database, such as `sp_helpdb 'pubs'`.

Table 10.7 lists some common system-stored procedures.

TABLE 10.7 Common System-Stored Procedures

Procedure Name	Description
`sp_help`	Lists objects in a database or returns information on a specific object. Can be used to obtain information on any database object.
`sp_helpdb`	Lists databases or returns information on a specific database.
`sp_helprotect`	Displays information on object and statement permissions.
`sp_who`	Returns information on SQL Server connections.
`sp_lock`	Locking information on all, one, or two processes. This is helpful in diagnosing locking and deadlocking problems.
`sp_configure`	Displays or changes global configuration settings.
`sp_dboption`	Displays or changes database configuration settings.

Other Methods of Querying the System Tables

So far, this chapter has focused on stored procedures to retrieve information from the database and system catalog. Two other methods, information schema views and system functions, also can be used to retrieve metadata.

Information Schema Views

Information schema views were defined by ANSI-92 as a set of views to provide system data. By using views, the actual system tables are hidden from the application. Changes made to the system tables don't affect the application because the application doesn't directly address the system tables. In this way, an application can retrieve data from an ANSI-92 information_schema–compliant system independent of the database vendor or version.

ANSI-92 and SQL Server support a three-part naming schema when referencing objects on the local server. The ANSI-92 terminology refers to *catalog.schema.object,* whereas the Microsoft equivalent is *database.owner.object.* If the database is not specified, it defaults to the current database. If the owner is not specified, it defaults to the current login ID. This is important in the context of information schema views because they are "owned" by INFORMATION_SCHEMA. Therefore, when referencing an information schema view in the current database, you must supply the *owner.object* portion of the naming schema. For example, to find out table information, the command would be as follows:

```
SELECT * FROM INFORMATION_SCHEMA.TABLES
```

Fortunately, the names of the information schema views are fairly intuitive. Some of the information schema views available are TABLES, COLUMNS, TABLE_PRIVILEGES, and VIEWS.

NOTE

Avoid writing queries that reference the system tables directly. Microsoft tries to provide backward compatibility whenever possible, but it is not guaranteed. What this means is that Microsoft reserves the right to change the names of the system tables at any time. If you have applications that call these tables, they might not migrate to the next release. The information schema views, on the other hand, will remain consistent.

System and Metadata Functions

Another way to query system information from within Transact-SQL statements is to use system or metadata functions. These are scalar functions, meaning they return single specific values. For example, to retrieve the username for the current session, use the following:

```
SELECT SUSER_NAME()
```

Some other functions that can be used to return system data are `DB_ID`, `DB_NAME`, `OBJECT_NAME`, `FILE_NAME`, and `GETDATE`.

Summary

Administering a SQL Server is a time-consuming, complex task. Understanding the structure of the system and the proper tools and methods to extract and modify system information will help you manage your databases efficiently. The next chapter, "Creating and Managing Databases," takes an in depth look at this aspect of SQL Server administration.

CHAPTER **11**

Creating and Managing Databases

By Paul Jensen and Ray Rankins

IN THIS CHAPTER

- What Makes Up a SQL Server Database?
- Data Storage in SQL Server
- Database Files
- Creating Databases
- Managing Databases
- Setting Database Options

The database is, of course, SQL Server's sole reason for existence. This chapter will examine what a database consists of, how to create one, and the ongoing management requirements of a database.

What Makes Up a SQL Server Database?

A **database** is a storage structure for database objects. It is made up of at least two files. One file is referred to as a data file, and stores the database objects, such as tables and indexes. The second file is the transaction log file that records changes to the data. A data or log file can belong to only one database, and if filegroups are created within a database, each data file can be associated with only one database filegroup.

When a new database is created, its name and other key information are recorded in the `sysdatabases` table in the `master` database. The new database will also contain the system objects required for the database to function, primarily the system catalog tables. These system objects are copied from the `model` database at the time the database is created. Because all objects in the `model` database are copied when the database is created, the initial size of a database must be at least the size of the `model` database.

NOTE

You can leverage the fact that all objects in `model` are copied to the new database by creating any objects that you want to appear in all databases in the `model` database. This is a great way to propagate common objects, such as user-defined datatypes, user-defined database roles, and user-defined functions.

Data Storage in SQL Server

Within the data files, SQL Server stores data in 8KB blocks of contiguous disk space, known as **pages**. The page is the minimum unit of IO when SQL Server transfers data to and from disk. Each of these data pages has the capacity to store up to 8060 bytes of data (8192–132 for overhead), and a single row cannot span more than one page. This is an important consideration when calculating disk usage. For example, if a table has an average row size of 4050 bytes, only one row would fit per page, essentially doubling the disk space required to store the data.

In an effort to reduce internal operations and increase IO efficiency, SQL Server, when allocating space to a table or index, allocates space in extents. An **extent** is eight contiguous pages, or 64KB of storage. There are actually two types of extents. Every table or index is initially allocated space in a **mixed extent**. As the name implies, mixed extents store pages from more than one object. When an index or table is first created, it is assigned an Index Allocation Map, or IAM, which is used to track space usage for the object, and at least one data page. The IAM and data page are assigned to a mixed extent in an effort to save space, as dedicating an extent to a table with a few small rows would be wasteful. Up to eight initial pages will be assigned this way. When an object requires more than eight pages of storage, all further space will be allocated from uniform extents. **Uniform extents** store pages for only a single index or table. This allows SQL Server to optimize read and write operations and reduce fragmentation because the data will be stored in units of 64KB (eight pages), as opposed to individual 8KB pages scattered throughout the data file.

For more detailed information on the internal storage structures and how they are managed in SQL Server databases, see Chapter 33, "SQL Server Internals."

Database Files

SQL Server needs to keep track of the allocated space in each data file; it does so by allocating special pages in the first extent of each file. As the data stored on these pages is dense and they are accessed often, they are usually found in memory; therefore, they are quickly retrieved.

The first page (page 0) in every file is the File Header Page. This page contains information about the file, such as the database to which the file belongs, the file group it is in, the minimum size, and its growth increment.

The second page (page 1) in each file is the Page Free Space (PFS) page. As its name implies, the PFS tracks free space available on the pages in a file. The PFS tracks whether a page has been allocated to an object, if it is on a mixed or uniform extent, and approximately how much free space remains. A single PFS can track 8,000 contiguous pages, and additional PFS pages are allocated as needed.

The third page (page 2) in each file is the Global Allocation Map, or GAM page. This page tracks allocated extents. Each GAM tracks 63,904 extents, and additional GAM pages are allocated as needed. The GAM contains a bit for each extent, which is set to 0 if the extent is allocated to an object, or 1 if it is free.

The fourth page (page 3) is the Secondary Global Allocation Map, or SGAM. The SGAM tracks allocated mixed extents. Each SGAM tracks 63,904 mixed extents, and additional SGAM pages are allocated as needed. A bit set to 1 for an extent indicates a mixed extent with pages available.

Primary Files

Every database will have a primary file. The primary file is the first file specified in the create database statement. It contains the system objects copied from the `model` database. These system objects are referred to as the **database catalog**. The primary file is generally identified by an `.mdf` file extension, although SQL Server does not enforce this.

The primary data file can, and often is, the only data file in the database. If this is the case, then all user objects will share the file with the database catalog or system tables.

Secondary Files

For performance, backup, and recovery purposes, additional data files can be created to store user objects separately from the database catalog. When additional files are created in the database, they are referred to as secondary data files. Secondary files, by default, are identified with an `.ndf` extension, but as with the primary file, this is not enforced. Additional files are added to accommodate storage needs greater than the size of the primary data file. By adding secondary data files, storage can be spread over multiple disks to improve IO and facilitate backing up large databases on a file-by-file basis. Allowing the database administrator to add files where and when needed to increase storage capacity also increases flexibility.

Using Filegroups

Filegroups provide for the logical grouping of files. The primary data file or files will always reside in the Primary filegroup. Additional filegroups can consist of one or more secondary files and are used to further delineate the storage of data, especially in large databases. When a filegroup consists of multiple files, SQL Server spreads the data inserts proportionally across all files in the filegroup so they are kept approximately the same percentage full. If your computer has multiple processors, it can also be advantageous to spread data across as many physical drives as possible in order to improve parallel data access throughput.

TIP

If too many outstanding I/Os are causing bottlenecks in the disk I/O subsystem, you might want to consider spreading the files across more disk drives. Performance Monitor can identify these by monitoring the `PhysicalDisk` object and `Disk Queue Length` counter. Consider spreading the files across multiple disk drives if the `Disk Queue Length` counter is greater than three. For more information on monitoring SQL Server performance, see Chapter 37, "Monitoring SQL Server Performance."

For example, a filegroup called Data could be created, consisting of three files spread over three physical drives. Another filegroup could be created named Index, with a single file on a fourth drive. Now when tables are created, they can be specified to be stored on the Data filegroup, and indexes will be stored on the Index filegroup. This will reduce contention between tables because the data is spread over three disks and between data and indexes as well. If more storage is required in the future, additional files can easily be added to the Index or Data filegroup as appropriate.

When using multiple filegroups, one filegroup will always be the default. This is not to be confused with the primary filegroup, although the primary filegroup is initially the default. If an object is created without a filegroup specified in the create statement, it will be stored on the default filegroup. If you are using two filegroups to separate the database catalog from the user objects, it would be appropriate to make the user object filegroup the default. If you have more than two filegroups, you will still have to specify where to store objects during creation because the choice for a "default" location might not be obvious. The default filegroup can be changed with the `ALTER DATABASE` command:

```
ALTER DATABASE Big_DB
MODIFY FILEGROUP User_Data DEFAULT
```

Alternatively, it can be set from the database Properties page Filegroups tab, as illustrated in Figure 11.1.

Transaction Log File

Each database also requires a transaction log file. This log file typically has an extension of `.ldf`, but once again, this is not enforced. Multiple log files can be specified; however, this is rarely done because the files will always be accessed serially; as one file fills, it switches to the next. Therefore, no performance benefit is realized because multiple data files exist. Multiple log files simply extend the potential size of the log.

Unlike data files, the log file doesn't perform IO in 8KB pages; rather, SQL Server flushes individual records of transactions being processed to log changes to data on disk as quickly as possible. As it is essential that the transaction information be flushed to the log file as quickly as possible, the log can be contentious for disk resources and, if at all possible, should be located on a disk subsystem separate from other database and server activity.

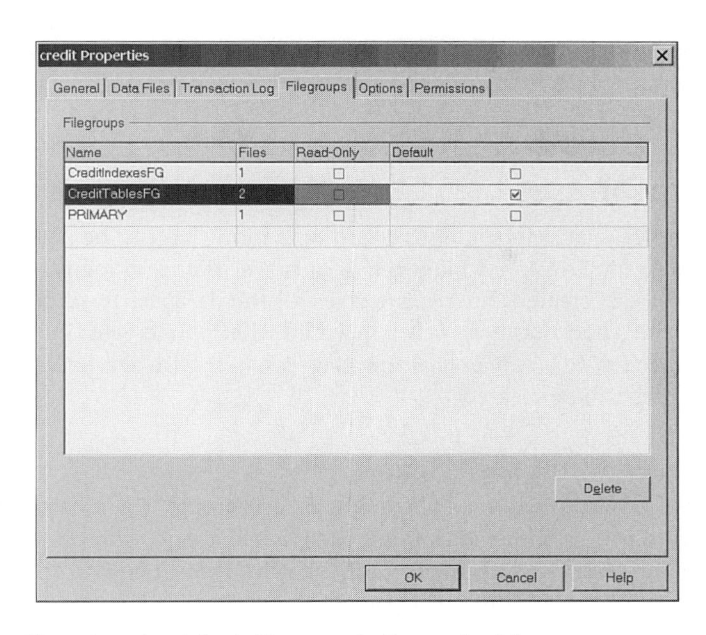

FIGURE 11.1 Changing the default filegroup in Enterprise Manager.

The Function of the Transaction Log

SQL Server is what is known as a **write-ahead database management system**. This means that as changes are made to the data through transactions, these changes are written immediately to the transaction log file once the transaction is completed. By writing each change to the transaction log before it is written to the database, SQL Server can increase IO efficiency to the data files and ensure data integrity in case of system failure.

As SQL Server performs IO to the data files in 8KB pages, it would be inefficient to flush an entire 8KB page from memory to disk every time a change was made to the page, especially because a transaction could modify the data on a page multiple times. Instead, it records to the transaction log only the changes made to the data. Because the change information for the page is now safely written to the transaction log file on disk, SQL Server doesn't have to immediately write the data page back to disk to preserve the changes. Periodically, a process called **checkpoint** runs to ensure that changed pages in memory have actually been written back to the data files. This is more efficient because it can then piggyback several page writes, making the "trip" to the disk more efficient. When checkpoint has written all the changed or "dirty" pages to the data files, it makes a note in the transaction log that all changes made up to that point have actually been flushed to the data files. If the system fails, when it is restarted, an automatic recovery process can use this checkpoint marker as a starting point for recovery. SQL Server examines all transactions after the checkpoint. If they are committed transactions, they are "rolled forward"; if they are incomplete transactions, they are "rolled back," or undone.

For more detailed information on transaction management, transaction log internals, and the recovery process, see Chapter 31, "Transaction Management and the Transaction Log," and Chapter 33.

Creating Databases

Database creation is a relatively straightforward operation that can be performed using T-SQL statements or the Enterprise Manager. Because the data and log files are created at the time the database is created, the time it takes for the database to be created will be dependent on the size and number of files specified when you create the database. If the disk space is insufficient to create any of the files specified, SQL Server will return an error and none of the files will be created.

Using the Create Database Wizard

The Create Database Wizard will take you step by step through the database creation process. This wizard can be accessed through the "magic wand" icon on the Enterprise Manager toolbar, from the Wizards menu option in the Tools menu, or from the Database Taskpad view. Figure 11.2 shows the first page of the wizard.

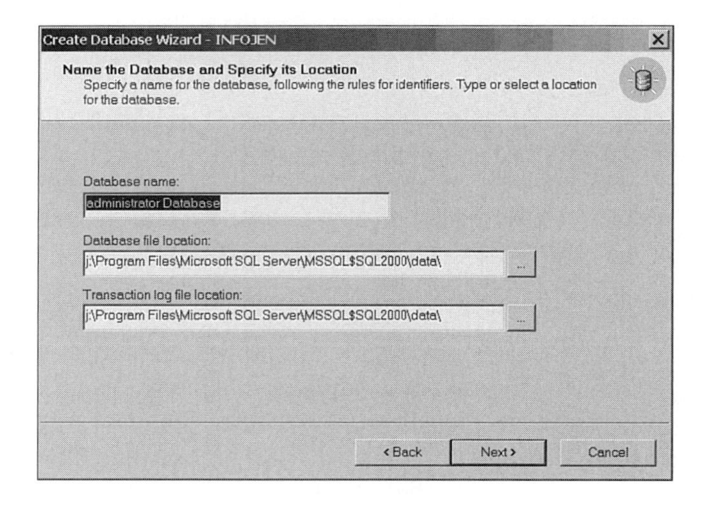

FIGURE 11.2 Creating a database with the Create Database Wizard.

Each page in the wizard provides input fields for the various options, such as database name, file location, filename, initial file size, file growth, and so on. While easy to use, this is one of my least favorite SQL Server Wizards because it takes several pages to do what you can do in three tabs or less with the Enterprise Manager Database Properties dialog box. Wizards are great for technically complex tasks, but the process of creating a database is technically quite simple. The conceptual design of file locations is the hard part, and unfortunately the wizard can't help with that.

Using Enterprise Manager

Although the Enterprise Manager Database Properties dialog box is no better than the wizard for helping with the layout of your data files, it does present more functionality in an easy-to-use format. To access the dialog box, right-click the Databases folder in Enterprise Manager and select New Database. The General tab of the Create Database dialog box is shown in Figure 11.3.

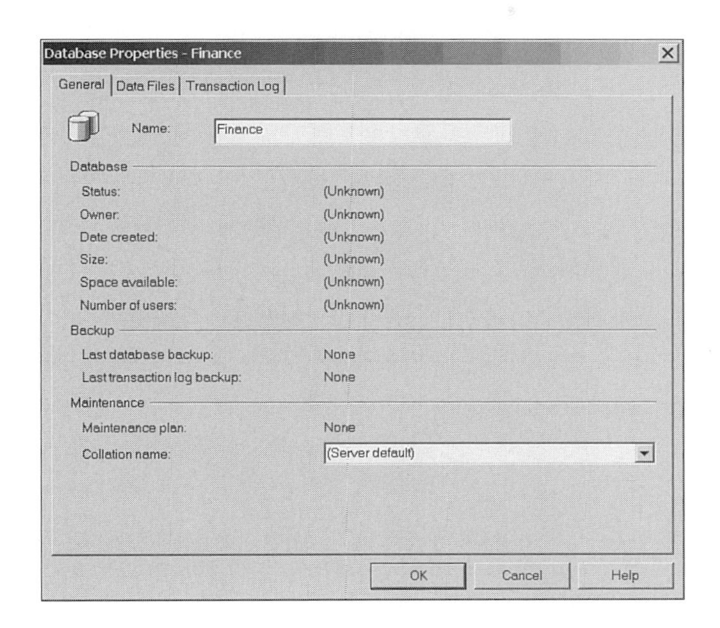

FIGURE 11.3 Creating a database with Enterprise Manager.

The General tab allows you to input a database name and select a database collation (character set and sort order). The Data Files tab allows you to input the logical filenames, the physical path and filename, the filegroup (except for the primary file), and file growth parameters. Each of these is automatically populated with defaults. For example, the filename is generated as *databasename_data*, and the path is the server default file path. The Transaction Log tab is identical to the Data Files tab except that a Filegroup column does not exist because filegroups are not valid for the log file. Figure 11.4 shows the Data Files tab.

NOTE

Although SQL Server provides default values for database options such as file size, file path, and growth increments, these values might not be appropriate for your installation. It is up to you to decide the location of data and log files, file growth parameters, and initial file size based on application requirements and hardware configuration.

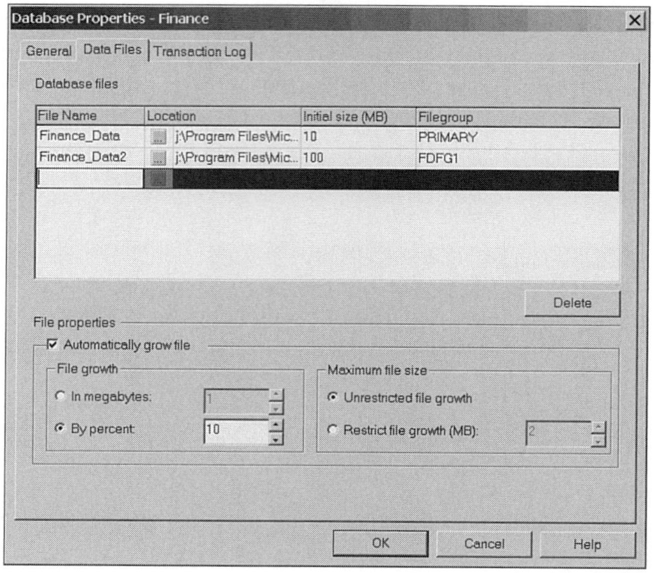

FIGURE 11.4 The Data Files tab.

Using T-SQL

Whether using the wizard or Enterprise Manager as in the previous sections, SQL Server is simply generating T-SQL statements behind the scenes. If you prefer to use T-SQL rather than the GUI, databases can be created with the `CREATE DATABASE` statement, giving you the ability to save a script for the database creation and access fully all `CREATE DATABASE` options. Listing 11.1 shows an example script to create a database called Big_DB.

LISTING 11.1 Using T-SQL to Create a Database

```
CREATE DATABASE Big_DB
ON PRIMARY
( NAME = Big_DB_dat,
   FILENAME = 'd:\data\Big_DB.mdf',
   SIZE = 10MB,
   MAXSIZE = 50MB,
   FILEGROWTH = 15% ),

FILEGROUP Big_DB_Data
( NAME = Big_DB_Data_dat,
   FILENAME = 'e:\data\Big_DB_Data.ndf',
   SIZE = 50GB,
   MAXSIZE = 100GB,
```

LISTING 11.1 Continued

```
   FILEGROWTH = 10GB )

LOG ON
( NAME = 'Big_DB_log',
   FILENAME = 'f:\log\Big_DB_log.ldf',
   SIZE = 50MB,
   MAXSIZE = 100MB,
   FILEGROWTH = 10MB )
COLLATE Latin1_General_CI_AI
GO
```

In this case, the database will be created with two filegroups: the primary filegroup and a second filegroup called Big_DB_Data. The log file is created with the `LOG ON` clause. The `COLLATE` clause specifies the collation, which determines the default Code Page (Character Set) and the sort order for the database. Note the file specification clause for each of the three files created in this example. The `NAME` parameter specifies a logical name for the file, which can be used within SQL Server to reference the file in future statements. The `FILENAME` is the actual physical filename, including the full path. The next three parameters are used to regulate the size of the file. All three parameters can be entered as `KB`, `MB`, `GB`, and `TB`, with `MB` the default if nothing is specified. The initial size of the file is controlled by `SIZE`. The `MAXSIZE` parameter controls the maximum size to which the file can grow. If `MAXSIZE` is omitted, then file growth is limited only by the available disk space. The final file parameter `FILEGROWTH` indicates the increment by which a file will increase in size if it becomes full, given available disk space, and provided the upper limit of `MAXSIZE` has not been reached; optionally, `FILEGROWTH` can also be specified as a percentage of the file size.

Managing Databases

After the database is created, you are left with the ongoing task of managing it. At the database level, this generally involves manipulating the file structure and setting options appropriate to the usage of the database.

Managing File Growth

As we saw in the previous section on creating databases, SQL Server manages file growth by automatically growing files by preset intervals when a need for additional space arises. I find this, however, to be a very loose definition of the word *manages*. What actually happens is that when the database runs out of space, it suspends all update activity, checks if it is allowed additional space and if space is available, and then increases the file size by the value defined by `FILEGROWTH`. When it fills up again, the whole process starts over.

When all the files in a filegroup are full and they are configured to autogrow, SQL Server automatically expands one file at a time in a round-robin fashion to accommodate more data. For example, if a filegroup consists of multiple files and no free space is available in any file in the file group, the first file is expanded by the specified file growth setting. When the first file is full again, and there is no more free space elsewhere in the file group, the second file is expanded. When the second file is full, and there is no more free space elsewhere in the file group, the third file is expanded, and so on.

Because `FILEGROWTH` can be defined as small as 64KB, automatically increasing the file size can be detrimental to performance if it happens too frequently. When I think of managing file growth, I think of the database administrator proactively monitoring the size of files and increasing the size before SQL Server runs out of space to allocate new extents. That's not to say automatic file growth is a bad thing; it is, in fact, a great "safety valve" to accommodate unpredictable data growth or a lack of attention on the part of the administrator.

Expanding Databases

As previously discussed, databases can be expanded automatically, or you can intervene and expand them manually. There are two methods of increasing the size of a database: by increasing the size of existing files and by adding additional files. To increase the size of a file or add an additional file using T-SQL, use the `ALTER DATABASE` command. The SQL script shown in Listing 11.2 increases the size of an existing file to 20MB and then adds a new file.

LISTING 11.2 Using T-SQL to Alter a Database to Increase the Size of a File and Add a New Data File

```
ALTER DATABASE Big_DB
MODIFY FILE
   (NAME = Big_DB_Dat,
   SIZE = 20MB)
GO
ALTER DATABASE Big_DB
ADD FILE
(
 NAME = Big_DB_Data_Dat2,
 FILENAME = 'e:\data\Big_DB_Data2.ndf',
 SIZE = 50MB,
 MAXSIZE = 100MB,
 FILEGROWTH = 5MB
GO
```

Enterprise Manager can also be used to increase the size of a file or add a new one. Access the Properties page of the database you want to modify and select the Data Files tab. In Figure 11.5, the CreditTables file is increased to 100MB, and a new file CreditTables2 is being added.

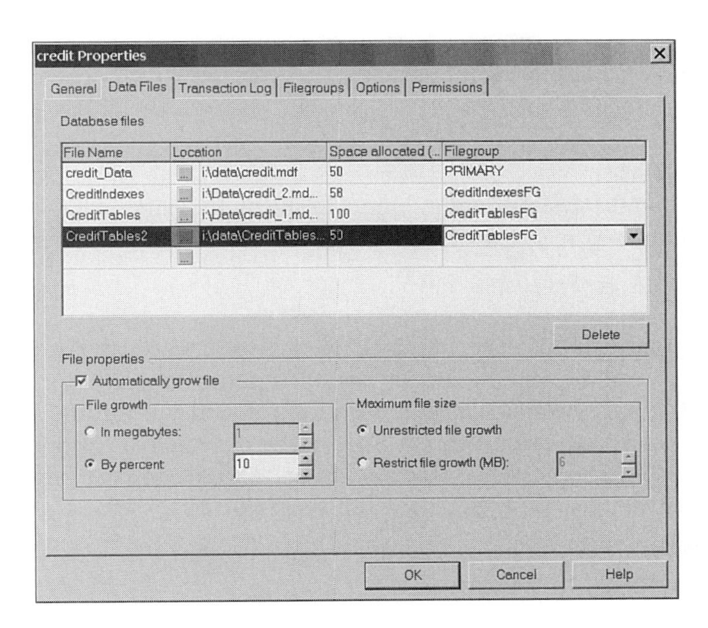

FIGURE 11.5 Increasing the database size in Enterprise Manager.

Shrinking Databases

So far this chapter has looked at expanding the database, but what if you want to make it smaller? SQL Server does provide an `AUTOSHRINK` option, which detects free space in the data files and attempts to shrink them at 30-minute intervals, leaving 25 percent free space. The problem that occurs is that the files are shrunk working back from the end of the files, and data pages might be allocated in the "upper" end of the files even though excess free space exists elsewhere in the files. When this occurs, the file cannot be shrunk until the pages are reorganized to the "front" of the file. If you have ever done an operating system disk defrag, you can picture the kind of overhead this could involve. With the exception of single-user databases running on client machines where no one manages data files, I would suggest leaving this option off, as it has been known to negatively impact the performance of production databases.

However, if you want to shrink the database manually, you can do so using the `DBCC SHRINKDATABASE` and `DBCC SHRINKDATAFILE` statements, as well as by using Enterprise Manager.

NOTE

Unless there is a definite need for the space that would be made available by shrinking a database, it is recommended that you do not shrink the database files if the space will be used again in the future. For one thing, having free space available in the database files avoids the overhead of having to autogrow the database files when they become full. Also, if a database file is repeatedly shrunk and expanded, the database file itself can become fragmented within the file system, which can degrade IO performance for the file.

DBCC SHRINKDATABASE

The `DBCC SHRINKDATABASE` statement attempts to shrink the entire database (all files) and leave a specified target percentage of free space, as shown in this statement:

```
DBCC SHRINKDATABASE (credit, 25)
```

This would attempt to shrink the credit database, leaving 25 percent free space in each file. This operation is done on a file-by-file basis. If a particular file has less than the specified amount of free space available, it is left unchanged and not shrunk. The `DBCC SHRINKDATABASE` command cannot shrink a file below the original size specified when it was created. This limitation can be overcome using `DBCC SHRINKFILE`, which can set a new minimum size for the file. Following is the full syntax for `DBCC SHRINKDATABASE`:

```
DBCC SHRINKDATABASE    ( database_name [ , target_percent ]
        [ , { NOTRUNCATE | TRUNCATEONLY } ] )
```

If the `NOTRUNCATE` option is specified, SQL Server retains the freed space in the files. The data is compacted to the front of the file, but the file size remains unchanged. This could be useful if there have been too many deleted records, causing fragmentation; however, over time you expect the number of records to increase again to the previous size. A database where records are purged, perhaps on a yearly basis, might benefit from this. Keep in mind that this operation might have extremely high overhead in a large or extremely fragmented database.

The `TRUNCATE ONLY` option is quite the opposite. This specifies that the data should not be compacted, but that unused space above the last allocated extent (referred to as the "high water mark") be released. The `target_percentage` is ignored with this option. Use this option if your data growth has stabilized, but you have too much excess space allocated in the files.

DBCC SHRINKFILE

The `DBCC SHRINKFILE` statement affords more control over file size because it shrinks individual files. `DBCC SHRINKFILE` is also useful in that it can get around the `SHRINKDATABASE` option's inability to shrink a file below its minimum specified size. This is handy if you originally allocated too much space to a file. Following is the full syntax for `DBCC SHRINKFILE`:

```
DBCC SHRINKFILE   ( { file_name | file_id } { [ , target_size ]
          | [ , { EMPTYFILE | NOTRUNCATE | TRUNCATEONLY } ] }
```

Note that with this option, a filename or ID is supplied, rather than the database name. DBCC SHRINKFILE must be run in the database that the file belongs to. The TARGET_SIZE is specified in megabytes and is the desired size for the file; if not specified, it tries to shrink the file as much as possible. The EMPTYFILE option migrates all data in the file to other files in the same filegroup. No further data can be placed on the file. The file can subsequently be dropped from the database. This can be useful to migrate a data file to a new disk. The NOTRUNCATE and TRUNCATEONLY options are functionally the same as for DBCC SHRINKDATAFILE and are outlined in the previous section.

Shrinking the Log File

The data file that is most likely to grow beyond a normal size and require shrinking periodically is the transaction log. If a user process issues a large update transaction, the log file will grow to the size needed to hold the records generated by the transaction. This could be significantly larger than the normal growth of the transaction log.

As with data files, shrinking of the log file in SQL Server 2000 can only take place from the end of the log file. However, you must first back up or truncate the log to remove the inactive log records and reduce the size of the logical log. You can then run the DBCC SHRINKFILE or DBCC SHRINKDATABASE command to release the unused space in the log file.

Transaction log files are divided logically into smaller segments called virtual log files. Transaction log files can only be shrunk to a virtual log file boundary. Because of this, it is not possible to shrink a log file to a size smaller than the size of a virtual log file, even if the space is not being used. The size of the virtual log files in a transaction log increase as the size of the log file increases. For example, a database defined with a log file of 1GB will have virtual log files 128MB in size. Therefore, the log can only be shrunk to about 128MB.

Because of the overhead incurred when the autoshrink process attempts to shrink database files, it is not recommended that this option be enabled for the transaction log as it can be triggered numerous times during the course of a business day. It is better to schedule the shrinking of the log file to be performed during normal daily maintenance when production system activity is at a minimum.

Shrinking a Database with Enterprise Manager

New for SQL Server 2000 is the ability to shrink a database or file from Enterprise Manager. Right-clicking a database, selecting All Tasks, Shrink Database will bring up the Shrink Database dialog box. This dialog box, shown in Figure 11.6, gives you the options available with DBCC SHRINKDATABASE, as well as the ability to schedule the operation.

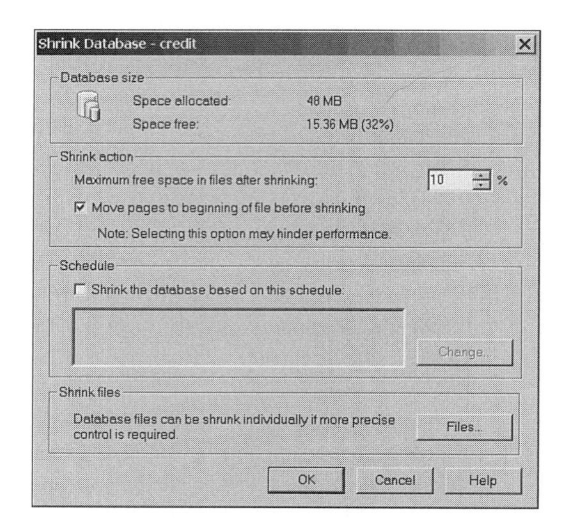

FIGURE 11.6 Shrinking the database size in Enterprise Manager.

If you want to shrink files (`DBCC SHRINKFILE`), selecting the Files button at the bottom of the page brings up the dialog box shown in Figure 11.7, allowing you to perform and schedule `DBCC SHRINKFILE` operations.

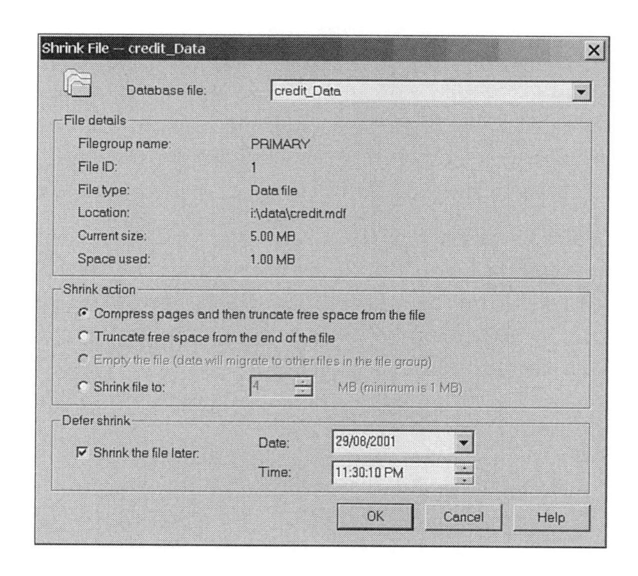

FIGURE 11.7 Shrinking file size in Enterprise Manager.

Setting Database Options

In this section, I will concentrate on how to set the various database options, as opposed to how the settings will affect your database. Many of the settings are fairly intuitively named, which helps, and are covered in detail elsewhere in this book. For example, a detailed explanation of the Recovery options can be found in Chapter 16, "Database Backup and Restore."

The Database Options

SQL Server has five categories of options that can be set to control database behavior. The categories and the associated values are listed in Table 11.1.

TABLE 11.1 Database Options

Option Category	Option
Auto Options	AUTO_CLOSE {ON|OFF}
	AUTO_CREATE_STATISTICS {ON|OFF}
	AUTO_UPDATE_STATISTICS {ON|OFF}
	AUTO_SHRINK {ON|OFF}
Cursor Options	CURSOR_CLOSE_ON_COMMIT {ON|OFF}
	CURSOR_DEFAULT {LOCAL|GLOBAL}
Recovery Options	RECOVERY {FULL|BULK_LOGGED|SIMPLE}
	TORN_PAGE_DETECTION {ON|OFF}
State Options	SINGLE_USER|RESTRICTED_USER|MULTI_USER
	OFFLINE|ONLINE
	READ_ONLY|READ_WRITE
SQL Options	ANSI_NULL_DEFAULT {ON|OFF}
	ANSI_NULLS {ON|OFF}
	ANSI_PADDING {ON|OFF}
	ANSI_WARNINGS {ON|OFF}
	ARITHABORT {ON|OFF}
	CONCAT_NULL_YIELDS_NULL {ON|OFF}
	NUMERIC_ROUNDABORT {ON|OFF}
	QUOTED_IDENTIFIER {ON|OFF}
	RECURSIVE_TRIGGERS {ON|OFF}

Using Enterprise Manager to Set Database Options

Many of the database options can be set right from the Options tab of the Database Properties page in Enterprise Manager, as shown in Figure 11.8.

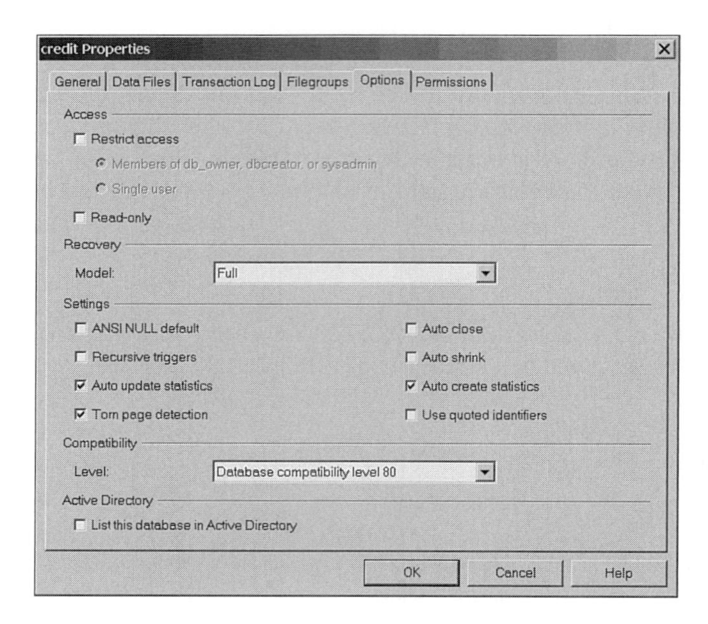

FIGURE 11.8 Setting database options in Enterprise Manager.

The `OFFLINE|ONLINE` state option is also accessible in Enterprise Manager by right-clicking a database and selecting the All Tasks menu; `OFFLINE` or `ONLINE` appears, depending on the current state of the database.

Using T-SQL to Set Database Options

If you prefer to use T-SQL, or if the option you need to set doesn't appear in Enterprise Manager, you can use the `ALTER DATABASE` command to set options as well. The following example sets `AUTO_SHRINK` to `OFF` for the Credit database:

```
ALTER DATABASE Credit
   SET AUTO_SHRINK OFF
```

The system-stored procedure `sp_dboption` is still available to check and set database options, but Microsoft advises it is available only for backward compatibility, and that you should use `ALTER DATABASE` instead. If you want to be a rebel and use it anyway, here is the syntax:

```
sp_dboption 'credit', 'autoshrink', 'false'
```

An interesting note is that if you use Enterprise Manager to generate a database creation script from an existing database, it uses `sp_dboption` to set the database options. I guess somebody missed the "We advise against using this" memo.

Retrieving Option Information

The settings for database options are best retrieved using sp_helpdb or the DATABASEPROPERTYEX function. The sp_dboption stored procedure can be used to display option information as well, but remember: It's only around for backward compatibility.

The syntax for sp_helpdb is as follows:

```
sp_helpdb databasename
```

The database options are listed, comma delimited, in the status column of the return. All Boolean options that are set to ON are returned, and all non-Boolean values are returned with the value to which they are set. Because the status column is a varchar (340), it can be difficult to view the option you are interested in. A more precise way of displaying the option information is with the DATABASEPROPERTYEX function. The function accepts input values for the database name and the property (options are properties), as shown here:

```
SELECT DATABASEPROPERTYEX ('Credit', 'IsAutoShrink')
```

This function returns a value of 1 or 0 for Boolean values—with 1 being "on" or "true"—and returns the actual value for non-Booleans. Table 11.2 lists the valid properties.

TABLE 11.2 Valid Properties for the DATABASEPROPERTYEX Function

Property	Description	Value Returned
Collation	Default collation name.	Collation name
IsAnsiNullDefault	Database follows SQL-92 rules for null values.	1 = TRUE 0 = FALSE NULL = Invalid input
IsAnsiNullsEnabled	All comparisons to a null evaluate to unknown.	1 = TRUE 0 = FALSE NULL = Invalid input
IsAnsiPaddingEnabled	Strings are padded to the same length before comparison or insert.	1 = TRUE 0 = FALSE NULL = Invalid input
IsAnsiWarningsEnabled	Error or warning messages are issued on standard error conditions.	1 = TRUE 0 = FALSE NULL = Invalid input
IsArithmeticAbortEnabled	Queries are terminated by overflow or divide-by-zero errors.	1 = TRUE 0 = FALSE NULL = Invalid input
IsAutoClose	Database shuts down after the last user exits.	1 = TRUE 0 = FALSE NULL = Invalid input
IsAutoCreateStatistics	Existing statistics are automatically updated.	1 = TRUE 0 = FALSE NULL = Invalid input

TABLE 11.2 Continued

Property	Description	Value Returned

`IsAutoShrink`	Database files are set to automatically shrink.	`1 = TRUE`
		`0 = FALSE`
		`NULL = Invalid input`

`IsAutoUpdateStatistics`	Auto update statistics are enabled.	`1 = TRUE`
		`0 = FALSE`
		`NULL = Invalid input`

`IsCloseCursorsOnCommit-Enabled`	Open cursors are closed when a transaction is committed.	`1 = TRUE`
		`0 = FALSE`
		`NULL = Invalid input`

`IsFulltextEnabled`	Database is full-text enabled.	`1 = TRUE`
		`0 = FALSE`
		`NULL = Invalid input`

`IsInStandBy`	Database is in Standby mode.	`1 = TRUE`
		`0 = FALSE`
		`NULL = Invalid input`

`IsLocalCursorsDefault`	Cursor declarations default to `LOCAL`.	`1 = TRUE`
		`0 = FALSE`
		`NULL = Invalid input`

`IsMergePublished`	The tables of a database can be published for replication.	`1 = TRUE`
		`0 = FALSE`
		`NULL = Invalid input`

`IsNullConcat`	Null concatenation yields `NULL`.	`1 = TRUE`
		`0 = FALSE`
		`NULL = Invalid input`

`IsNumericRoundAbortEnabled`	Loss of precision in expressions generates errors.	`1 = TRUE`
		`0 = FALSE`
		`NULL = Invalid input`

`IsQuotedIdentifiersEnabled`	Double quotation marks can be used as identifiers.	`1 = TRUE`
		`0 = FALSE`
		`NULL = Invalid input`

`IsRecursiveTriggersEnabled`	Recursive triggers are enabled.	`1 = TRUE`
		`0 = FALSE`
		`NULL = Invalid input`

`IsSubscribed`	Database can be subscribed for publication.	`1 = TRUE`
		`0 = FALSE`
		`NULL = Invalid input`

`IsTornPageDetectionEnabled`	SQL Server detects incomplete I/O operations.	`1 = TRUE`
		`0 = FALSE`
		`NULL = Invalid input`

TABLE 11.2 Continued

Property	Description	Value Returned

`Recovery`	Recovery model for the database.	`FULL`
		`BULK LOGGED`
		`SIMPLE`

`SQLSortOrder`	SQL Server sort order ID.	`0 = Windows collation` `>0 = Sort order ID`

`Status`	Database status.	`ONLINE`
		`OFFLINE`
		`RESTORING`
		`RECOVERING`
		`SUSPECT`

`Updateability`	Indicates whether database is read only.	`READ_ONLY` `READ_WRITE`

`UserAccess`	Indicates user access mode.	`SINGLE_USER`
		`RESTRICTED_ USER`
		`MULTI_USER`

`Version`	Internal version number of SQL Server.	`Version number = Database is open` `NULL = Database is closed`

Summary

This chapter looked at creating and managing databases and it intentionally tried to focus on the basic commands and tools that are used to accomplish these tasks. That is not because that is all you need to know about creating and managing databases. Nothing could be further from the truth. The decisions you make when creating and managing a database are key to its reliability and performance, and must be based on more than just the ability to right-click and select Create Database. Even though you are now armed with the how-to knowledge, you are strongly encouraged to read on. Several other chapters in this book provide more information to help you make informed choices when creating your databases. Especially pertinent to this topic are Chapter 16, “Database Backup and Restore,” Chapter 21, “Administering Very Large SQL Server Databases,” Chapter 31, “Transaction Management and the Transaction Log,” Chapter 33, “SQL Server Internals,” and Chapter 39, “Database Design and Performance.”

CHAPTER **12**

Creating and Managing Tables in SQL Server

by Paul Jensen

IN THIS CHAPTER

The table is the basic structure upon which the relational database is built. A table is a set of columns, having defined properties, used to store data. The stored data is represented as rows in the table. These rows are used to represent an **entity** (an employee, for example), that has a number of **attributes** (last name, salary) associated with it. These attributes are stored in the table's columns. Table 12.1 illustrates a typical table structure.

TABLE 12.1 An Example of a Table, Showing Columns and Rows

Emp_no	Lname	Fname	Phone	Dept	Salary
1	Smith	John	555-1111	20	10000
2	Jones	Jill	555-1211	20	10000
3	Johnston	Bob	555-3214	30	20000
4	Jensen	Carl	555-4321	40	12000
5	Wright	Alex	555-2156	40	14000
6	Ivings	Kris	555-3215	20	21000

The `CREATE TABLE` and `UPDATE TABLE` commands are used to create and modify tables. When you create a table, you must provide a table name, a name for each of the columns, and a datatype for each column. Optionally, but highly recommended, you can specify whether a column should allow null values. The script for creating the table in Table 12.1 is shown in Listing 12.1.

LISTING 12.1 A Simple Create Table Script

```
CREATE TABLE employee
(
  Emp_no int NOT NULL,
  Lname char(20) NULL,
  Fname char(20) NULL,
  Phone char(13) NULL,
  Dept smallint NULL,
  Salary int NULL
)
```

The example in Listing 12.1 uses three different **datatypes**—`int`, `char`, and `smallint`—to define how data will be stored. Before you learn more about the business of creating tables, it's important that you have an understanding of datatypes.

Datatypes

Datatypes define the type of data that can be stored in tables. When each column is defined, it is assigned a datatype, which enforces basic integrity by limiting the type and size of the data that can be entered. Choosing the correct datatype for each column is crucial to efficient data storage, performance, and application compliance.

SQL Server provides several base datatypes, which are grouped by the type of data that they store. Table 12.2 shows the system-supplied datatypes and their storage capacities.

TABLE 12.2 System-Supplied Datatypes

Data Type Category	SQL Server Data Type	Number of Bytes
Character	char[(n)]	0–8000
	varchar[(n)]	0–2GB
	text	
Unicode Character	nchar[(n)]	0–8000
	nvarchar[(n)]	(4000 characters)
	ntext	0–2GB
Binary	binary[(n)]	0–8000
	varbinary[(n)]	
Date and time	datetime	8
	smalldatetime	4
Integer	int	4
	bigint	8
	smallint	2
	tinyint	1
Exact Numeric	decimal[(p[,s])]	2–17
	numeric[(p[,s])]	
Approximate Numeric	float[(n)]	8
	real	4
Monetary	money	8
	smallmoney	4
Image	image	0–2GB
Global Identifier	uniqueidentifier	16
Special	Bit	1
	cursor	0–8
	timestamp	8
	sysname	256
	table	
	sql_variant	0–8016

Character and Binary Datatypes

Character datatypes are used to store strings. They can be fixed or variable length single byte or Unicode, depending on which you decide to use. The six-character datatypes are `char`, `varchar`, `nchar`, `nvarchar`, `text`, and `ntext`.

The most commonly used character datatypes, `char` and `varchar`, store data in a fixed or variable length format respectively. Use `char` if a column has a consistent length, such as a two-character State field. If `char` is defined as `char(20)`, it uses 20 bytes of storage even if only five characters are entered into the field; data is padded with blanks up to the full field size. For a variable length column, such as a Description or Name field, `varchar` would be a better choice because it doesn't pad the data with spaces, and the amount of bytes required is the actual length of the character data. `Char` and `varchar` can store up to 8,000 characters.

The Unicode variants are `nvarchar` and `nchar`. These have the same properties, but data is stored in Unicode format. Unicode supports a wider range of characters, but each character requires two bytes of storage. This limits the available storage to 4,000 characters.

`Binary` and `varbinary` also store up to 8,000 bytes, but are designed to store binary information. SQL Server interprets character data based on the sort order, whereas binary is simply a stream of bits. Binary datatypes are used to store hexadecimal values.

To store character strings and binary data that might exceed 8,000 bytes, use the `text`, `ntext`, and `image` datatypes. For example, to store large text files (.txt), you would define a column as `text` or `ntext` depending on the requirement for Unicode support. For storing images (.gif), a better choice would be the `image` datatype.

Although SQL Server has a page size of 8KB, text and image data up to 2GB can be stored. By default, these datatypes actually store a 16-byte pointer in the row, which maps to separate data pages where fragments of the large object are stored. SQL Server can retrieve these fragments and piece them back together when required. New for SQL Server 2000 is the table option text in row. This option allows you to specify that text, ntext, and image data below a certain size are stored inline. This means that rather than a pointer, the data is stored in the row. The default value for text in row is 256 bytes, and can range from 24 to 7,000 bytes. Storing the data inline will provide faster retrieval of the object, at the expense of increased row size.

The following statement specifies text in row to store objects less than 500 bytes inline for the orders table:

```
EXEC sp_tableoption 'orders', 'text in row' , '500'
```

uniqueidentifier

The `uniqueidentifier` datatype is used to generate a globally unique identifier. The datatype does not generate this value; rather, it is used in conjunction with the `ROWGUIDCOL` property and the `NEWID()` function. The value generated is guaranteed to be unique across all network computers worldwide. This is useful in situations such as merge replication, in which multiple copies of the same row must be identified as unique across multiple servers.

timestamp

`timestamp` generates an 8-byte binary number unique within the database. The primary use of `timestamp` is to determine row version. Although unique, `timestamp` is incremented with each insert, or update to a row; it is not a good candidate for a primary key. SQL Server 2000 provides a synonym for timestamp called `rowversion`. It is recommended that you now use `rowversion` because `timestamp` is an ANSI-92 keyword that is synonymous to datetime. Despite what its name implies, the value in a timestamp column has no correlation to an actual date and time when the row was last modified.

datetime Datatypes

Date and time information is stored in the datetime and smalldatetime datatypes. The difference is in the amount of precision and the storage required. Table 12.3 compares the two datatypes.

TABLE 12.3 Storing Date Information

	datetime	smalldatetime
Storage size	8 bytes	4 bytes
Precision	3/100 second	1 minute
Minimum value	Jan. 1, 1753	Jan. 1, 1990
Maximum value	Dec. 31, 9999	June 6, 2079

There are no datatypes in SQL Server that store only a date or only a time. If you insert a date value without a time into a datetime or smalldatetime field, the time will default to midnight on that date:

```
create table datetest (datecol datetime not null)
go
insert datetest values ('4/4/66')
go
select * from datetest
```

If you specify a time value without a date, the date defaults to January 1, 1900:

```
insert datetest values ('12:51:35')
go
select * from datetest
```

When inputting date values into a datetime or smalldatetime field, the value specified will be a character string containing a datetime value. SQL Server supports a number of different date formats:

- *monthname dd[,] yy[yy]*
- *dd monthname yy[yy]*
- *yyyy monthname dd*
- *mm/dd/yy[yy]*
- *mm-dd-yy[yy]*

- *mm.dd.yy[yy]*
- *[yy]yymmdd*

When U.S. English is the default language, the default date order is month day year (mdy). You can use the `SET DATEFORMAT` command to change the default date format to something else like mdy or ymd.

Time values can be specified using a 12-hour or 24-hour clock as hh[:mm[:ss[: | .]xxx]] [AM | PM].

Logical Datatype: `bit`

If you simply want to store on/off or true/false values, you can use the `bit` datatype. Valid values are `1`, `0`, or `NULL`. The `bit` datatype uses one byte of storage to hold the bit entry. That is not entirely wasteful because if you have multiple `bit` datatypes, up to 8-`bit` datatypes can share the same byte.

Numeric Datatypes

SQL Server has several datatypes to support numeric data. They can be broken into four groups:

- Integers
- Approximate numeric datatypes
- Exact numeric datatypes
- Money datatypes

Integer Datatypes

The integer datatypes—`bigint`, `int`, `smallint`, and `tinyint`—as their names imply, differ in the range of numbers they can store and the amount of storage they require. Integers are efficient to store, process, and present a wide range of unique values. This makes them ideal candidates when generating values for surrogate primary keys. Table 12.4 lists the storage requirements and capacities of the integer datatypes.

TABLE 12.4 Storing Integer Information

Integer Datatype	Storage Size	Minimum Value	Maximum Value
`tinyint`	1 byte	0	255
`smallint`	2 bytes	–32,768	32,767
`int`	4 bytes	–2,147,483,648	2,147,483,647
`bigint`	8 bytes	–9223372036854775808	9223372036854775807

What if you underestimated and used `tinyint` when you should have used `smallint`? No worries; SQL Server lets you change the datatype using the `ALTER TABLE` command or the Table Designer in Enterprise Manager.

Approximate Numeric Datatypes

The `float` and `real` datatypes are used to store values that have a large range and that you want to store with variable precision. These are generally used in scientific and statistical data where a wide range of values exists, yet absolute precision is not required. Do not use `float` and `real` when absolute precision must be maintained on the data values, especially for data values containing prices or money values. When operations on the `float` values are performed, decimal precision is not guaranteed. Use the `money` or `exact numeric` datatypes to maintain precision.

`exact numeric` Datatypes

If you require a large range of values and a high degree of accuracy, use the `decimal` or `numeric` datatype. The two are synonymous, so I'll refer to them as `decimal`. When you use the `decimal` datatype, you specify the **precision**, which is the total number of digits stored, and the **scale**, which is the number of digits stored to the right of the decimal point. For example, a `decimal` datatype specified as `decimal(5,2)` would be able to store values from –999.99 to 999.99. The amount of storage used is dependent on the precision and is listed in Table 12.5.

TABLE 12.5 Storing Decimal or Numeric Information

Precision	Storage Bytes
1–9	5
10–19	9
20–28	13
29–38	17

`money` Datatypes

For storing monetary data, SQL Server provides the `money` and `smallmoney` datatypes. These are similar to `decimal` in that they are exact datatypes, with precision to four decimal places. Table 12.6 lists the range and storage required.

TABLE 12.6 Storing Monetary Information

	`smallmoney`	`money`
Storage	4 bytes	8 bytes
Minimum value	–214,748.3648	–922,337,203,685,477.5808
Maximum value	+214,748.3647	+922,337,203,685,477.5807

Special Datatypes

SQL Server also provides additional datatypes for specialized use. These are sql variant, cursor, and table datatypes. New for SQL Server 2000, the sql variant datatype allows for the storage of multiple datatypes within a single column. This means that the storage for individual rows can vary; for example, a column could store an integer for one row, and character data for another. The cursor and table datatypes cannot be used for column definitions in a table. The cursor datatype is used when you declare variables or parameters, as in a stored procedure, and the table datatype is used in User Defined Functions and stored procedures.

For detailed discussion on sql_variant and table datatypes, see Chapter 26, "Using Transact-SQL in SQL Server 2000." For more information on the cursor datatype, see Chapter 28, "Creating and Managing Stored Procedures in SQL Server."

Datatype Synonyms

SQL Server uses different names for some datatypes than those that are specified by the ANSI-92 standard. Microsoft has accommodated this by providing synonyms for these. However, even if you specify the synonym, it will be translated and stored as the equivalent SQL Server datatype. The available synonyms are listed in Table 12.7.

TABLE 12.7 ANSI-92 Synonyms and SQL Server Equivalents

ANSI-92 Synonym	SQL Server 2000 Datatype
binary varying	varbinary
char varying	varchar
character	char
character	char(1)
character(*n*)	char(*n*)
character varying(*n*)	varchar(*n*)
dec	decimal
double precision	float
float[(*n*)] for *n* = 1-7	real
float[(*n*)] for *n* = 8-15	float
integer	int
national character(*n*)	nchar(*n*)
national char(*n*)	nchar(*n*)
national character varying(*n*)	nvarchar(*n*)
national char varying(*n*)	nvarchar(*n*)
national text	ntext
rowversion	timestamp

User-Defined Datatypes

User-defined datatypes (UDDTs) allow you to define custom datatypes based on the system datatypes. For example, you could create a name datatype defined as `varchar(30)`. Any columns you create with the name datatype would automatically be `varchar(30)`. This helps create consistent fields across the database, which is especially helpful for join columns to ensure the absence of datatype mismatches. To create more complex UDDTs, you can bind rules and defaults (see Chapter 14, "Implementing Data Integrity") to them to add even more functionality.

To create and drop UDDTs, use `sp_addtype` and `sp_droptype`:

```
Sp_addtype phone, 'char(13)'
Sp_droptype phone
```

You can also add UDDTs through Enterprise Manager. Figure 12.1 shows the UDDT Properties box.

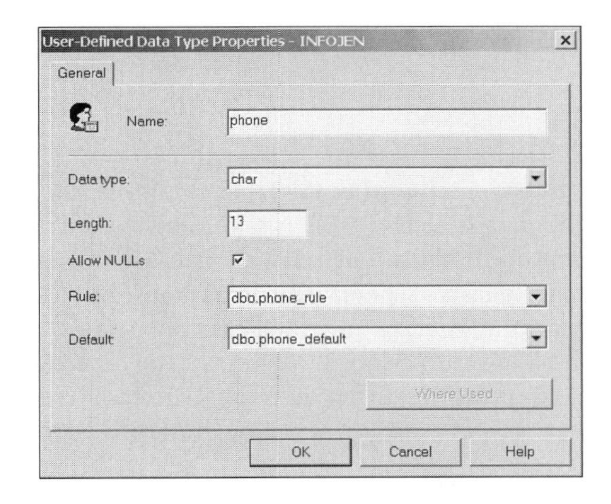

FIGURE 12.1 Using Enterprise Manager to create a UDDT.

If the system datatype expression requires parentheses, you must surround it with quotes. You cannot drop a UDDT if any tables are using it. When you want to use a UDDT, simply specify it in place of a system datatype in your `CREATE TABLE` command. Listing 12.2 illustrates using the phone UDDT when creating a table.

LISTING 12.2 Creating a Table Using a UDDT

```
CREATE TABLE call_me
(call_id int identity,
 name VARCHAR(20),
 phone_no phone)
```

The datatype allows you to define the storage for data within a column. The following section will look at creating tables to define the columns and group them in a logical fashion.

Creating Tables

Now that you've seen the various datatypes that SQL Server uses to store data, it's time to proceed with creating tables.

SQL Server 2000 supports creating tables through T-SQL, as well as the Table Designer in Enterprise Manager. Regardless of the tool you choose, creating a table involves naming the table, defining the columns, and assigning properties to the columns.

Naming Tables

When you create a table, it is always created in a database and is *generally* owned by the user creating the table. The combination of `databasename.owner.tablename` constitutes the table name. The members of the sysadmin, dbowner, and ddladmin roles can specify a different owner by using the owner's name explicitly in the `CREATE` command; for example:

```
CREATE TABLE yourdb.paul.employee
```

The preceding code fragment specifies that the table employee, owned by user Paul, be created in the northwind database. This table is said to be in Paul's **schema**, which is a fancy database term for everything Paul has created. Because the user Steve could also have a table called employee in his schema, the owner must be specified when referencing the object (unless you are Paul or Steve, in which case the default would be your own schema). One way around this is to create all objects in the database in the database owner schema. Specifying `dbo` as the owner does this. The command would then look like this:

```
CREATE TABLE yourdb.dbo.employee
```

Creating objects in the `dbo` schema is the recommended practice, as it not only simplifies things, it also has performance and security implications. If an object, such as a view, references another object, such as a table, and the two objects have different owners, permissions must be checked on each object.

By default, only members of the sysadmin, dbowner, and ddladmin roles have the `CREATE TABLE` permission. When a member of the sysadmin role or a login aliased to the `dbo` user creates a table, the owner, by default, is `dbo`. See Chapter 15, "Security and User Administration," for more information on permissions.

When naming tables, try to be descriptive without being too verbose. "Customers of Acme Limited" is a poor choice, but "customer" would be just fine. Standard table names must begin with an alphabetic character. Names should be singular, can be up to 128 characters, and can include letters, numbers, special characters, and spaces. Although including spaces and special characters is allowed, I recommend avoiding them. Also avoid using ANSI-92 or SQL Server reserved keywords. If keywords, spaces, or special characters other than the underscore (_) are included in a table name, all references to the name must use delimiters. The standard delimiter is the square bracket([]). You can also use quoted identifiers ("") if the option `SET QUOTED_IDENTIFIER ON` is enabled. Following is an example of a delimiter being used:


```
Select * from [order details]
```

Renaming Tables

After creating a table, if you find you must rename it, you can do so using Enterprise Manager or the sp_rename stored procedure. In Enterprise Manager, right-click the table name and select Rename. This will allow you to edit the name of the table from the Details window. When you press Enter to accept the change, a dialog box warns you that changes to the table name could affect dependent objects such as stored procedures, triggers, and views, and presents you with the options to accept or reject the change or to view dependencies. I recommend that you opt to view the dependencies, and if you are satisfied that the name change won't invalidate other objects, then select Yes to accept the change. If you opt to use sp_rename, the syntax is `EXEC sp_rename 'employee', 'emp'`. This statement would change the name of the employee table to emp. Before you change the table name using this method, make sure you check for dependencies, either through the Enterprise Manager, or with the sp_depends stored procedure.

Creating Tables Using T-SQL

This section examines how to use T-SQL to create tables. You will see how to define table columns and set properties for the columns. Also covered is defining a location for the table, adding constraints, and making modifications to existing tables.

Defining Columns

In defining a column, you assign a name and a datatype to the column. Depending on the datatype you choose, you might also have to assign parameters to the datatype, such as a length for a `char()` column. Listing 12.3 shows a simple `CREATE TABLE` statement defining six columns.

LISTING 12.3 Defining Columns with `CREATE TABLE`

```
CREATE TABLE yourdb.dbo.employee
(
  Emp_no int,
  Lname varchar(20),
  Fname varchar(20),
  Phone char(13),
```

LISTING 12.3 Continued

```
  Dept smallint,
  Salary money
)
```

Column Properties

Columns also can have properties assigned to them. These properties can address whether a value must be provided for a column, using `NULL` or `NOT NULL`, or whether SQL Server provides a value for the column, as is the case with the `identity` property.

NULL or NOT NULL

When writing your create table scripts, it is always good form to explicitly state whether a column should or should not contain nulls. The SQL Server default is not to allow nulls. The ANSI-92 standard is to allow nulls. To further confuse matters, the database option `'ANSI_NULL_DEFAULT'` can be set so that SQL Server matches the ANSI-92 standard. It can also be set at the session level. As a matter of fact, if you run your script from Query Analyzer, it overrides the SQL Server default and allows nulls if not specified. I hope I've made my point that it is best to explicitly specify the `NULL` property so you know for sure what it's going to be. Listing 12.4 expands on the previous example and properly specifies `NULL` or `NOT NULL`.

LISTING 12.4 Defining Column `NULL` Properties with `CREATE TABLE`

```
CREATE TABLE yourdb.dbo.employee
(
  Emp_no int NOT NULL,
  Lname char(20) NOT NULL,
  Fname char(20) NOT NULL,
  Phone char(13) NULL,
  Dept smallint NOT NULL,
  Salary int NULL
)
```

It is beyond the scope of this section to enter the debate on whether columns should ever allow nulls. That being said, I'll go ahead and put in my advice. If a column is defined as `NULL`, no value needs to be entered in that column when inserting or updating data. By defining columns as `NOT NULL` and providing a default value where possible, your data will be more consistent and easier to work with. If you allow nulls, you and the development team must always be aware of the effect nulls can have on querying the database.

Identity Columns

Another common property specified when creating tables is the IDENTITY property. This property, used in conjunction with the integer datatypes (although decimal can be used with a scale of 0), automatically generates a unique value for a column. This is extremely useful for generating what is referred to as a **surrogate primary key**. Purists will say that the primary key, or unique row identifier, should be derived from a column or combination of columns that are valid attributes of the entity. In the employee table I have been using in the examples, without an employee key being generated, I would have to combine last name, first name, and phone number as the primary key. Even then, if John Smith Jr. and John Smith Sr. had the same phone number, this combination would fail to guarantee uniqueness. This is where IDENTITY comes in. By generating a unique value for each row entered, I have satisfied the need for a unique key on the row.

When implementing an IDENTITY property, you supply a **seed** and an **increment**. The seed is the start value for the numeric count, and the increment is the amount by which it grows. A seed of 10 and an increment of 10 would produce 10, 20, 30, 40, and so on. If not specified, the default seed value is 1 and the increment is 1. Listing 12.5 adds to the script by setting an IDENTITY value that starts at 100 and increments by 10.

LISTING 12.5 Defining an Identity Column with CREATE TABLE

```
CREATE TABLE yourdb.dbo.employee
(
  Emp_no int IDENTITY (100, 10) NOT NULL,
  Lname char(20) NOT NULL,
  Fname char(20) NOT NULL,
  Phone char(13) NULL,
  Dept smallint NOT NULL,
  Salary int NULL
)
```

Defining Table Location

As databases scale in size, the physical location of database objects, particularly tables and indexes, becomes crucial. Consider two tables, Employee and Dept, which are always queried together. If they are located on the same physical disk, contention for hardware resources slows performance. SQL Server enables you to specify where a table (or index) is stored. This not only affects performance, but planning for backups as well. By dedicating a read-only table to a filegroup, you only need to back up the filegroup once. If your table contains text or image data, you can also specify where it should be stored.

The location of the table is specified with the ON clause, and TEXTIMAGE ON indicates where the text and image locaters should point. In Listing 12.6, you create the employee and dept tables, place them on two different filegroups, and store the image for the employee security photo on yet another filegroup. Note that the filegroups must exist before the tables are created. For information on filegroups, see Chapter 11, "Creating and Managing Databases."

LISTING 12.6 Syntax for Creating Tables on Specific Filegroups

```
CREATE TABLE yourdb.dbo.employee
(
  Emp_no int IDENTITY (100, 10) NOT NULL,
  Lname char(20) NOT NULL,
  Fname char(20) NOT NULL,
  Phone char(13) NULL,
  Dept smallint NOT NULL,
  Photo image NULL,
  Salary int NULL
)
ON FGDISK1
TEXTIMAGE_ON FGDISK3
GO
CREATE TABLE yourdb.dbo.dept
(
  Dept_no smallint IDENTITY (10, 10) NOT NULL,
  Name varchar(20) NOT NULL,
  Description varchar(80) NOT NULL,
  Loc_code char(2) NULL
)
ON FGDISK2
```

Defining Table Constraints

Constraints provide us with the means to enforce data integrity. In addition to `NULL`/`NOT NULL`, which was covered in a previous section, SQL Server provides five constraint types: `PRIMARY KEY`, `FOREIGN KEY`, `UNIQUE`, `CHECK`, and `DEFAULT`.

Constraints are covered in detail in Chapter 14, so in the context of creating tables, this chapter will concentrate on the syntax for adding constraints.

Listing 12.7 expands on the `CREATE TABLE` script by adding primary keys to both tables and creating a foreign key on the employee table that references the dept table.

LISTING 12.7 Syntax for Creating Constraints with CREATE TABLE

```
CREATE TABLE yourdb.dbo.employee
(
  Emp_no int IDENTITY (100, 10)CONSTRAINT EMP_PK PRIMARY KEY NOT NULL,
  Lname char(20) NOT NULL,
  Fname char(20) NOT NULL,
  Phone char(13) NULL,
  Dept smallint CONSTRAINT EMP_DEPT_FK REFERENCES dept(dept_no)NOT NULL,
  Photo image NULL,
  Salary int NULL
)
ON FGDISK1
TEXTIMAGE_ON FGDISK3
go
CREATE TABLE yourdb.dbo.dept
(
  Dept_no smallint IDENTITY (10, 10) CONSTRAINT DEPT_PK PRIMARY KEY NOT NULL,
  Name varchar(20) NOT NULL,
  Description varchar(80) NOT NULL,
  Loc_code char(2) NULL
)
ON FGDISK2
```

In the following example, CREATE TABLE is run first, and then ALTER TABLE is run to add the constraints. Listing 12.8 shows how separating constraint creation from table creation makes the script easier to read and more flexible.

LISTING 12.8 Syntax for Creating Constraints with ALTER TABLE

```
CREATE TABLE dbo.Product (
  ProductID int IDENTITY (1, 1) NOT NULL ,
  ProductName nvarchar (40) NOT NULL ,
  SupplierID int NULL ,
  CategoryID int NULL ,
  QuantityPerUnit nvarchar (20) NULL ,
  UnitPrice money NULL ,
  UnitsInStock smallint NULL ,
  UnitsOnOrder smallint NULL ,
  ReorderLevel smallint NULL ,
  Discontinued bit NOT NULL
)
GO
```

LISTING 12.8 Continued

```
ALTER TABLE dbo.Product ADD
  CONSTRAINT DF_Product_UnitPrice DEFAULT (0) FOR UnitPrice,
  CONSTRAINT PK_Product PRIMARY KEY      (ProductID),
  CONSTRAINT CK_Product_UnitPrice CHECK (UnitPrice >= 0)
GO

ALTER TABLE dbo.Product ADD
  CONSTRAINT FK_Product_Categories FOREIGN KEY
  (CategoryID) REFERENCES dbo.Categories (CategoryID)
GO
```

Adding/Removing/Modifying Table Columns Using T-SQL

The previous example touched on using `ALTER TABLE` to add constraints to an existing table. Although this is a common use of the `ALTER TABLE` command, you can actually change several properties of a table. The following lists the types of changes you can make to a table:

- Change the datatype or `NULL` property of a column.
- Add new columns or drop existing columns.
- Add or drop constraints.
- Enable or disable `CHECK` and `FOREIGN KEY` constraints.
- Enable or disable triggers.

Changing the Datatype

The `ALTER COLUMN` clause of `ALTER TABLE` can be used to modify the `NULL` property or datatype of a column. Listing 12.9 shows an example of changing the datatype of a column.

LISTING 12.9 Changing the Datatype of a Column with `ALTER TABLE`

```
ALTER TABLE product
ALTER COLUMN ProductName varchar(50)
```

You must be aware of several restrictions when you modify the datatype of a column. The following rules apply when altering columns:

- A `text`, `image`, `ntext`, or `timestamp` column can't be modified.
- The column can't be the `ROWGUIDCOL` for the table.

- The column can't be a computed column or be referenced by a computed column.
- The column can't be a replicated column.
- If the column is used in an index, the column length can only be increased in size. In addition, it must be a `varchar`, `nvarchar`, or `varbinary` datatype, and the datatype cannot change.
- If statistics have been generated using `CREATE STATISTICS`, the statistics must first be dropped.
- The column can't have a `PRIMARY KEY` or `FOREIGN KEY` constraint or be used in a `CHECK` or `UNIQUE` constraint; the exception is that a column with a `CHECK` or `UNIQUE` constraint, if defined as variable length, can have the length altered.
- A column with a default defined for it can only have the length, nullability, or precision and scale altered.
- If a column has a schema-bound view defined on it, the same rules that apply to columns with indexes apply.

NOTE

Changing some datatypes can result in changing the data. For example, changing from `nchar` to `char` could result in any extended characters being converted. Similarly, changing precision and scale could result in data truncation. Other modifications such as changing from `char` to `int` might fail if the data doesn't match the restrictions of the new datatype. When changing datatypes, always validate that the data conforms to the new datatype.

Adding and Dropping Columns

Columns are added to a table with the `ADD COLUMN` clause. Listing 12.10 illustrates adding a column to the product table.

LISTING 12.10 Adding a Column with `ALTER TABLE`

```
ALTER TABLE product
ADD ProdDesc varchar(100) NULL
```

SQL Server adds the column, and in this case allows a `NULL` value for all rows. If `NOT NULL` is specified, then the column must be an identity column or have a default specified. Note that even if a default is specified, if the column allows nulls, the column will not be populated with the default. Use the `WITH VALUES` clause to override this and populate the column with the default.

With some restrictions, columns can also be dropped from a table. The syntax for dropping a column is shown in Listing 12.11. Multiple columns can be specified, separated by a comma.

LISTING 12.11 Dropping a Column with ALTER TABLE

```
ALTER TABLE product
DROP COLUMN ProdDesc
```

The following columns cannot be dropped:

- An indexed column
- Replicated columns
- Columns used in CHECK, FOREIGN KEY, UNIQUE, or PRIMARY KEY constraints
- Columns associated with a default or bound to a default object
- A column that is bound to a rule

NOTE

Care should be taken when using ALTER TABLE to modify columns with existing data. When adding, dropping, or modifying columns, SQL Server places a schema lock on the table, preventing any other access until the operation completes. Changes to columns in tables with many rows can take a long time to complete and generate a large amount of log activity.

You should be aware that if you want to change a column's name, it is not necessary to drop it and then add a new column. Column names can be changed using `sp_rename`. As with any database object, consider the effects the rename might have on other objects or queries that reference the column. The syntax for changing a column name is `EXEC sp_rename 'northwind.[order details]', 'details', 'COLUMN'`.

Creating Tables Using Table Designer

Enterprise Manager provides a handy tool, the Table Designer, to allow you to easily create tables from the GUI. To invoke Table Designer, expand the database, right-click Tables, and select New Table. This invokes the Table Designer as shown in Figure 12.2.

After you have entered your column names and definitions, click on the Save (disk) icon and you will be prompted to name the table, as shown in Figure 12.3.

The Properties page of Table Designer allows you to create and manage constraints and indexes, as well as define ownership and filegroup placement for the table. The Properties page is shown in Figure 12.4.

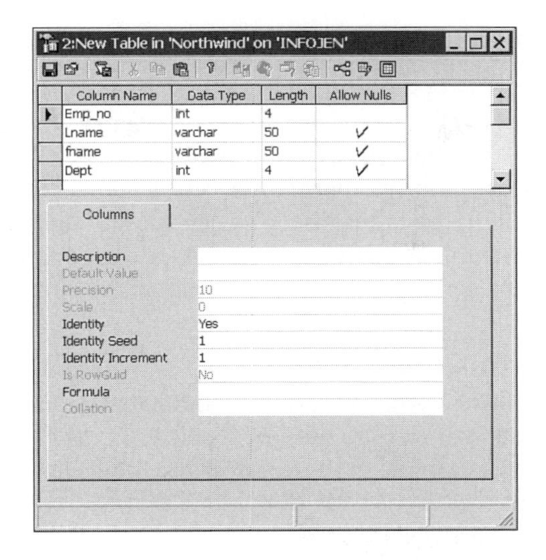

FIGURE 12.2 Using Table Designer to create a table.

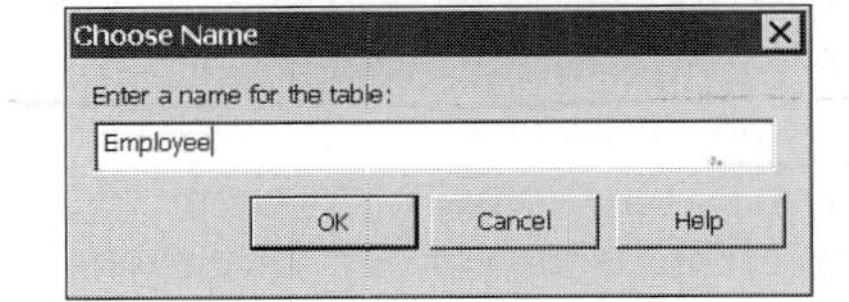

FIGURE 12.3 Naming the table in Table Designer.

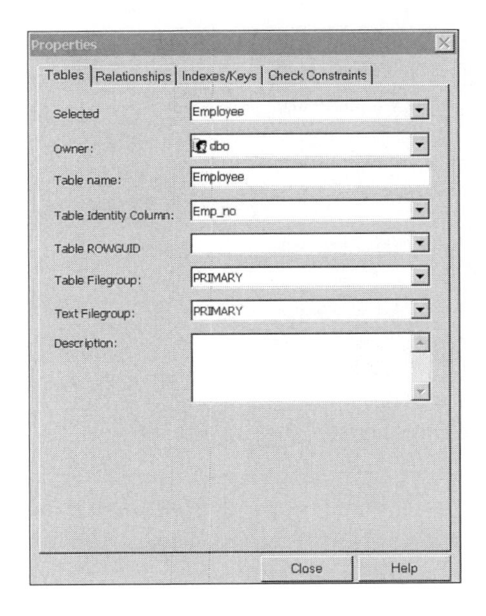

FIGURE 12.4 The Table Designer Properties page.

When you have finished defining your table, click OK, and Table Designer will generate the required Transact-SQL and create the table.

Adding/Removing/Modifying Columns Using Table Designer

After a table has been created, it is easily modified using Table Designer without having to write `ALTER TABLE` statements. In Enterprise Manager, simply right-click the table you want to edit and select Design Table. Of course, when editing a table's properties in this manner, all the restrictions pertaining to the `ALTER TABLE` command apply.

Generating Scripts to Create Tables

At this point, I suspect those of you who are new to database administration are asking yourselves why you would ever want to get into all that `CREATE TABLE/ALTER TABLE` stuff when you can use the Table Designer. On the other hand, many experienced administrators probably skipped this section because they know that the value of using scripts over GUIs to create objects is that the scripts can be saved in case the object needs to be re-created. Microsoft addressed this by including a Save Change Script icon on the Table Designer toolbar. When you have created or modified a table, click this icon (the third icon from the left) to generate the script required to re-create your changes. You also can generate complete scripts at any time for your tables and other objects from the Tools menu's Generate SQL Script item. If you use Table Designer to create or modify tables, do yourself a favor and always save your changes to a script. Figure 12.5 illustrates using Table Designer to generate a script for the addition of a Primary Key constraint.

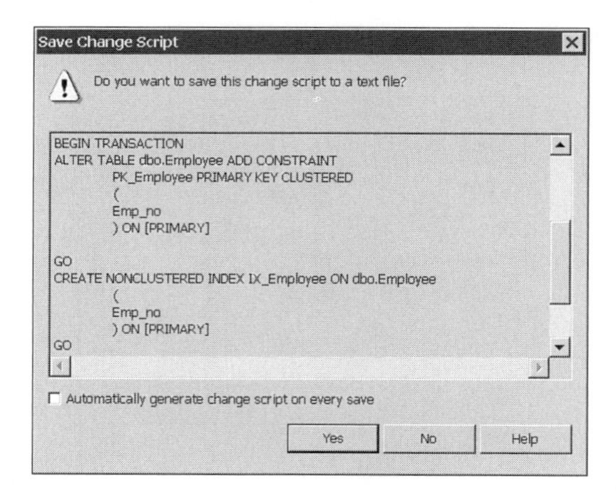

FIGURE 12.5 Using Table Designer to generate a script.

Viewing Table Properties and Data in Enterprise Manager

To view the properties for a table, right-click the table name in the Details pane of Enterprise Manager. The Properties page allows you to view the table definition and set permissions on the table. Figure 12.6 shows the Table Properties page.

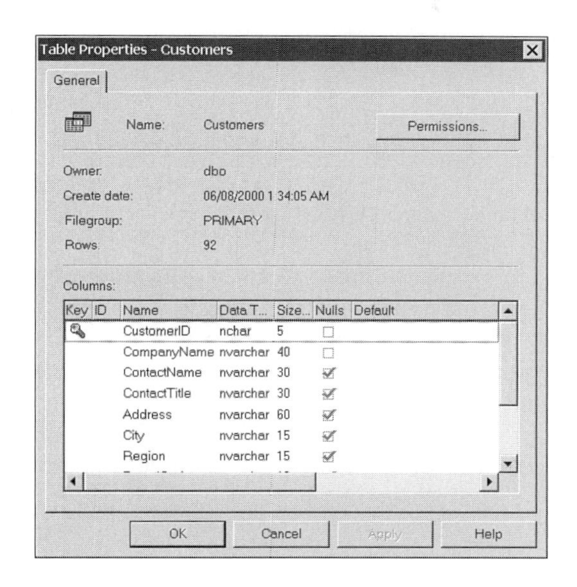

FIGURE 12.6 The Table Properties page.

Enterprise Manager also allows you to view and change table data through the GUI. In the Details pane, right-click the table and select Open Table. This will present you with three selections: Return All Rows, Return Top, and Query. The first selection returns all rows in a table, the second allows you to set a maximum return value, and the third opens a query window to write a custom select statement. Data returned in this manner can be edited from the GUI, but I don't recommend it except for perhaps one-item updates on small tables. If an update is attempted on a row, without scrolling through the entire table, the error `Transaction cannot start while in firehose mode` is generated. This is due to the way SQL Server processes the default result set, also known as a **firehose cursor**. Figure 12.7 shows the results of a query using Return All Rows.

Limitations on Table Size and Dimensions

You are limited to what you can store in a SQL Server 2000 table, but it is unlikely that you will ever reach this limit. If you are approaching the size limitations for a table, you should consider partitioning the data either vertically (split the columns into multiple tables) or horizontally (split the rows among multiple tables).

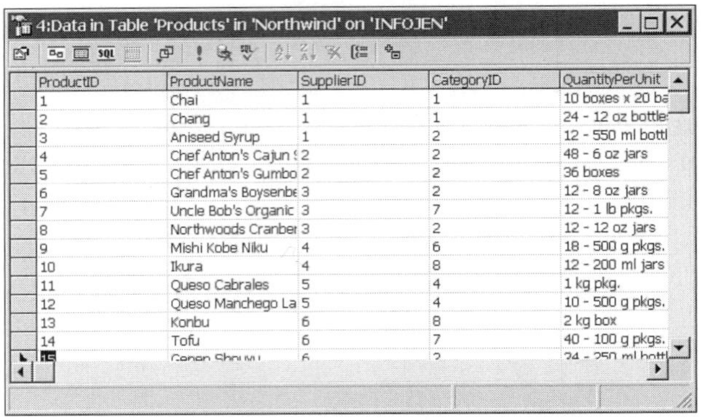

4:Data in Table 'Products' in 'Northwind' on 'INFOJEN'

ProductID	ProductName	SupplierID	CategoryID	QuantityPerUnit
1	Chai	1	1	10 boxes x 20 ba
2	Chang	1	1	24 - 12 oz bottle
3	Aniseed Syrup	1	2	12 - 550 ml bottl
4	Chef Anton's Cajun S	2	2	48 - 6 oz jars
5	Chef Anton's Gumbo	2	2	36 boxes
6	Grandma's Boysenbe	3	2	12 - 8 oz jars
7	Uncle Bob's Organic	3	7	12 - 1 lb pkgs.
8	Northwoods Cranber	3	2	12 - 12 oz jars
9	Mishi Kobe Niku	4	6	18 - 500 g pkgs.
10	Ikura	4	8	12 - 200 ml jars
11	Queso Cabrales	5	4	1 kg pkg.
12	Queso Manchego La	5	4	10 - 500 g pkgs.
13	Konbu	6	8	2 kg box
14	Tofu	6	7	40 - 100 g pkgs.
15	Genen Shouyu	6	2	24 - 250 ml bottl

FIGURE 12.7 Viewing data in Enterprise Manager.

The number of columns in a table is limited to 1,024. The amount of bytes in a row is limited to 8060KB; however, datatypes such as images can store up to 2GB because the data is stored outside the data row on separate data pages. The number of rows in a table is limited only by the available storage; this is likely to be a physical limit and not a database limit. SQL Server allows 32,767 files per database, with a maximum file size of 32 terabytes (TB). Don't bother doing the math; you don't have that much data. But hey, who knows what next year will bring. I remember when 20MB hard drives were all the rage!

Dropping Tables

Tables are dropped using the `DROP TABLE` command or through Enterprise Manager. The command to drop the sales table would be as follows:

```
Drop table sales
```

Multiple tables, separated by commas, can be referenced in a single `DROP TABLE` command. If a foreign key references a table, the referencing table or foreign key constraint must be dropped first. Any triggers and constraints associated with the table are also dropped when the table is dropped. To drop a table in Enterprise Manager, right-click the table in the Details pane and select Delete.

Temporary Tables

Temporary tables are useful as work tables to hold data while processing, such as building a table using derived data that will be referenced for further calculations.

Creating Temporary Tables

Tables are designated as temporary in SQL Server by prefacing the table name with a number sign (#). Temporary tables are created in `tempdb`; if they are not explicitly dropped, they are dropped when the session that created them ends. If a table is prefaced with a single pound sign (#table1), it is a **private** temporary table, available only to the session that created it. A table prefixed by a double pound sign (##table2) indicates that it is a **global** temporary table, which means it is accessible by all database connections. Global temporary tables exist until the session that created them terminates. If the creating session terminates while other sessions are accessing the table, the temporary table is available to those sessions until the last session's query ends, at which time the table is dropped. Tables created without the # prefix but explicitly created in Tempdb are also considered temporary, but they are a more permanent form of a temporary table. They will not be dropped automatically until SQL Server is restarted and `tempdb` is reinitialized.

Summary

Tables are the key to the Relational Database System. Careful attention must be paid when creating tables to choose the proper datatypes to ensure efficient storage of data, to add appropriate constraints to maintain data integrity, and to script the creation and modification of tables to ensure that they can be re-created if necessary.

CHAPTER 13

Creating and Managing Indexes

by Paul Jensen

IN THIS CHAPTER

The previous chapter, "Creating and Managing Tables in SQL Server," discussed the creation of tables, a structure in which to store your data. The data in a table is stored in no particular order—in fact, it's referred to as a *heap*. To find a particular piece of data, the entire heap must be scanned. This is known as a **full table scan**, and it is analgous to this book having no index or table of contents. Every time you wanted to find information on tables, for instance, you would have to start at page 1 and flip through the entire book to make sure you retrieved all the pertinent information.

An index in a database is similar to the one in this book. An index is sorted based on a key value (topics in the book, perhaps an employee number in a table). Just as the index in a book has a page number to quickly locate a topic, the index has a row identifier to drill down to the exact location of a row in a table.

Indexes can greatly improve the speed of your queries, and are also used to enforce uniqueness in data, as in the case of Primary Key and Unique Constraints. Why not index everything? Indexes require additional storage space on disk, just as the index in this book required additional pages. If you were to index every word in the book, the index would be larger than the book! Another consideration is for inserts, updates, and deletes. Indexing columns with frequently changing data means that every change to the table requires a corresponding change to the index. This additional overhead would, of course, result in performance degradation.

This chapter introduces the two types of indexes used by SQL Server and the methods you can use to create and manage them. Further information on index use by constraints appears in Chapter 14, "Implementing Data Integrity," and a detailed discussion on index structure, performance, and design can be found in Chapter 34, "Indexes and Performance." The ability to create an index on a view, a new feature for SQL Server 2000, is covered in Chapter 27, "Creating and Managing Views in SQL Server." Of course, everything will be easy to find by using the index at the back of this book!

Types of Indexes

SQL Server uses two types of indexes: clustered and nonclustered. The primary difference between the two index types is the way the data is stored in the tables—randomly for nonclustered indexes and sorted for clustered indexes. The following sections describe each type of index and suggest where one or the other might be appropriate.

Clustered Indexes

In a clustered index, the table data is actually stored sorted on the key value(s) in the index. Some would say that all table data is stored sorted in the index; others would say that the leaf, or lowest, level of the index is actually the table. Either way you look at it, the concept of a heap no longer applies. As the table data can be physically sorted only one way, only one clustered index can be created per table. Clustered indexes give fast access to values frequently searched by range, or that are accessed in sorted order. For example, for a table storing phone book data, an index on LastName, FirstName would be a better candidate for a clustered index than the PhoneNumber column. A search for Smith, John would be able to efficiently retrieve all the matching records, as they are stored "clustered" together.

Nonclustered Indexes

Nonclustered indexes, as the name implies, do not reorder the table data. They don't require the table to be reordered, so multiple nonclustered indexes can be created per table. You can create up to 249 nonclustered indexes per table, although it is doubtful you will ever need that many. Nonclustered indexes can be created on tables with clustered indexes, and in this case, use the clustered index key to locate rows in the table. As the table data is not stored sorted on the nonclustered key, range scans are inefficient, but equality searches are fast.

To continue with the phone book example, if you knew the phone number, but needed the matching name or address, creating a nonclustered index on PhoneNumber would speed the search, as this would be an equality search. Queries for a name and address to match a phone number, perhaps in response to a 911 call, would be able to use the nonclustered index to speed the response. Also, with the combination of the two indexes in place, queries to a telephone operator for the phone number of Smith, John could be efficiently handled by the clustered index, returning the last name and first name, and the nonclustered index returning the phone number. This is referred to as a covered query, as the indexes were able to return or "cover" all requested fields.

Creating Indexes Using T-SQL

This section examines the syntax used to create indexes using T-SQL. It is important to be familiar with this syntax as indexes are one of the more volatile database objects, often being dropped and re-created for performance reasons. To accommodate re-creation of indexes, it is common practice to script these actions using T-SQL.

The Transact-SQL `CREATE INDEX` Syntax

Indexes are created using the `CREATE INDEX` command. Listing 13.1 shows the complete `CREATE INDEX` syntax.

LISTING 13.1 The `CREATE INDEX` Syntax

```
CREATE [ UNIQUE ] [ CLUSTERED | NONCLUSTERED ] INDEX index_name
    ON { table | view } ( column [ ASC | DESC ] [ ,...n ] )
[ WITH < index_option > [ ,...n] ]
[ ON filegroup ]

< index_option > :: =
    { PAD_INDEX |
        FILLFACTOR = fillfactor |
        IGNORE_DUP_KEY |
        DROP_EXISTING |
    STATISTICS_NORECOMPUTE |
    SORT_IN_TEMPDB
}
```

Table 13.1 lists the `CREATE INDEX` arguments.

TABLE 13.1 Arguments for `CREATE INDEX`

Argument	Explanation
`UNIQUE`	Specifies that no duplicate rows be allowed. If duplicate rows exist in the data, the index creation fails.
`CLUSTERED | NON-CLUSTERED`	Defines the index as clustered or nonclustered. Non-clustered is the default. Only one clustered index is allowed.
index_name	Specifies the name of the index to be created.
table | view	Specifies the name of the table or view on which the index is to be based.
column	Specifies the column or columns that are to be indexed.

TABLE 13.1 Continued

Argument	Explanation
ASC | DESC	Specifies whether the index should be sorted in ascending or descending order. ASC is the default.
ON *Filegroup*	Determines on which filegroup the index should be stored.
PAD_INDEX	Specifies that a percentage of space should be left free on the non-leaf levels of the index. The percentage is determined by FILLFACTOR.
FILLFACTOR = *fillfactor*	Specifies what percentage to fill the leaf pages of the index on index creation. If inserts and updates are expected on the indexed columns, specifying a FILLFACTOR of less than 100 can improve performance by avoiding page splits. Valid values are 1–100; the default of 0 indicates a 100% fill.
IGNORE_DUP_KEY	Used in conjunction with UNIQUE. If specified, and an attempt is made to insert a duplicate key in a UNIQUE index, the duplicate key is rejected, but the statement continues. If not specified, the entire statement is rolled back when a duplicate key is encountered.
DROP_EXISTING	Used to re-create existing indexes. A performance gain can be realized when a clustered index is rebuilt, as the non-clustered indexes are not rebuilt unless the clustered keys change.
STATISTICS_NO_RECOMPUTE	Specifies that index statistics will not be automatically updated.
SORT_IN_TEMPDB	Stores the intermediate sort results used to create the index in tempdb. This increases disk space usage, but can improve index creation performance if tempdb is on a separate disk set than the user database.

Examples of Using Transact-SQL to Create Indexes

When creating an index in the current database, on the default filegroup, the minimum required syntax would be as follows:

```
CREATE INDEX emp_tel_idx ON employee (phone)
```

This creates a nonclustered index named emp_tel_idx on the phone column of the employee table.

Often, for performance reasons, it is best to separate the index from the table data. To do this, you specify a filegroup on which to create the index:

```
CREATE INDEX emp_tel_idx ON employee (phone)
ON index_fg1
```

A more complete script to create a unique clustered index that specifies several optional arguments is illustrated by the following example:

```
CREATE UNIQUE CLUSTERED INDEX emp_tel_idx
ON employee(phone)
WITH
PAD_INDEX,
FILLFACTOR = 50,
IGNORE_DUP_KEY,
STATISTICS_NORECOMPUTE
ON index_fg1
```


Creating Indexes Using Enterprise Manager

Enterprise Manager gives you several options when it comes to creating indexes. Indexes can be added with the Create Index Wizard, from the Database Diagram, or while creating or modifying a table with Table Designer.

To create an index step by step, use the Create Index Wizard. Access the wizard from the Tools menu by selecting Wizards, Database, Create Index Wizard. This will bring up the screen shown in Figure 13.1.

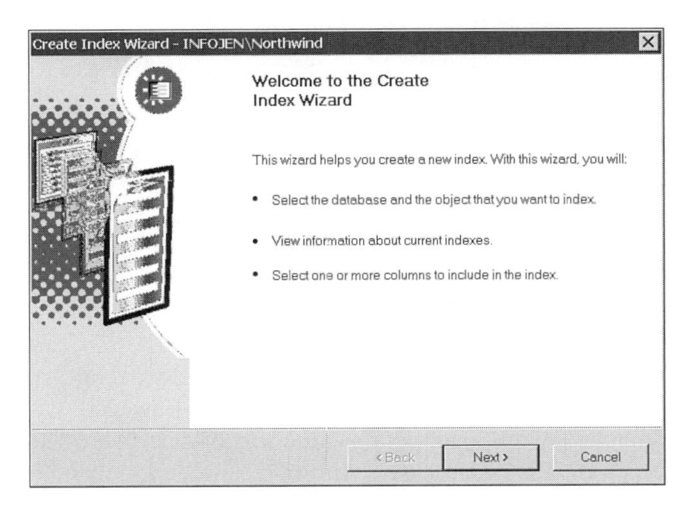

FIGURE 13.1 Using the Create Index Wizard.

Simply click Next, and the wizard will step you through the process of creating an index, from selecting the table and columns to naming the index.

If you choose not to use the wizard, you can create an index from a Database Diagram, or from Table Designer by right-clicking the table and selecting Indexes/Keys. On the Indexes/Keys tab, click New, and enter the information for your index. Figure 13.2 shows the Indexes/Keys tab.

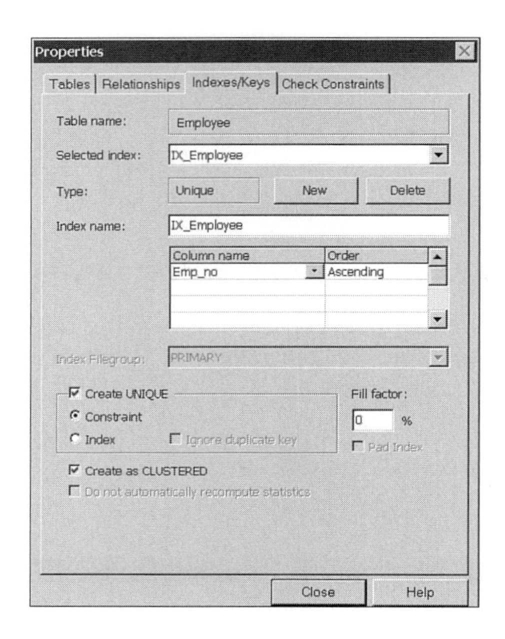

FIGURE 13.2 Creating an index from Indexes/Keys.

When creating an index through the Table Properties dialog box, you must save the table or diagram in which you are working for the index to be created.

Managing Indexes

SQL Server requires minimum interaction to manage indexes. As rows are inserted, updated, and deleted, the indexes are adjusted accordingly. By default, statistics used by the optimizer are also automatically generated. Sometimes, however, you might want to drop or re-create indexes. When loading large amounts of data, it can often be more efficient to drop any indexes, load the data, and re-create the indexes. This prevents the bulk load operation from simultaneously having to load the table and update the index.

Indexes can also become fragmented. This happens when no room is available to insert or update a row on a data page and the page "splits" into two pages. The new page will probably not be physically contiguous with the first page, and this can cause performance issues. Detecting and repairing fragmentation of indexes is covered in detail in Chapter 34.

Dropping Indexes

Indexes can be dropped through the Indexes/Keys tab in Table Designer, or by using the `DROP INDEX` command. Indexes created by Primary Key or Unique Constraints can't be dropped in this manner; see Chapter 14 for more information.

When dropping indexes with `DROP INDEX`, multiple indexes can be specified in a single statement. The command for dropping indexes is as follows:

```
DROP INDEX emp_tel_idx, emp_idx1, emp_idx2
```


Summary

Index creation is an important part of managing your database. Creating useful indexes can vastly improve query performance, but you must also consider the impact that indexes can have on data manipulation and disk space. In the next chapter, "Implementing Data Integrity," you will see how indexes are used to enforce data integrity through constraints, and subsequent chapters will show how to fine-tune your indexes for the best possible performance.

CHAPTER 14

Implementing Data Integrity

by Paul Jensen

IN THIS CHAPTER

- Types of Data Integrity
- Enforcing Data Integrity
- Constraints
- Rules
- Defaults

Ensuring the integrity of data is one of the most important tasks of an administrator. Key business decisions are often made based on information in the database; if the data is misrepresented, incorrect conclusions might be drawn. Consider a car manufacturer who uses a product code R01 (R zero one) to represent every red car sold. To predict next year's sales of red cars, they run a query on the database to count the instances of R01. They determine that they sold far fewer red cars than expected, and reduce production. Halfway through the year, they run out of red cars. On closer inspection of the data, they determine that they had actually sold plenty of red cars, but the data entry personnel had in many cases incorrectly entered the code as Ro1 (R oh one), R0l (R zero L) or Rol (R oh L). So does the blame fall on the data entry personnel? Not likely. Integrity constraints to prevent incorrect entries are the proper solution. When it comes to data integrity, the buck stops at the administrator's desk.

This chapter focuses on enforcing integrity through the use of constraints, rules, and defaults. Data integrity can also be enforced at the application level, which is a subject for a book on application design, and through stored procedures and triggers. Because stored procedures and triggers have additional functionality outside of data integrity, they are covered in separate chapters of their own. Check out Chapter 28, "Creating and Managing Stored Procedures in SQL Server," and Chapter 29, "Creating and Managing Triggers" to learn more.

Types of Data Integrity

How integrity is enforced depends on the type of integrity being enforced. The types of data integrity are Domain, Entity, and Referential.

Domain Integrity

Domain integrity refers to restricting the values that are valid for a column and the allowance or absence of nulls. Domain integrity is enforced by the datatype, restriction of the use of nulls, and validity checking such as is done with check constraints.

Entity Integrity

Entity integrity requires that all rows in a table be unique. This is enforced with a unique identifier known as the primary key.

Referential Integrity

Referential integrity maintains the dependent values between tables. Referential integrity is enforced with a primary key/foreign key relationship. Referential integrity ensures data in one table maintains its relationship with data in another table, that all foreign key, or child, records in one table relate to the valid primary key, or parent, records in another table.

Enforcing Data Integrity

Data integrity can be enforced using declarative or procedural methods. Declarative methods are generally simpler and more efficient, whereas procedural methods can enforce more complex rules.

Declarative Data Integrity

Declarative integrity is enforced within the database using constraints, rules, and defaults. This is the preferred method of enforcing integrity as it has low overhead and is programmatically simple. It is also more centrally managed and consistently enforced because it resides in the database.

Procedural Data Integrity

Procedural integrity is enforced with stored procedures, triggers, and application code. Procedural integrity generally has a higher overhead and can be quite complex, but it can enforce far more extensive business rules than declarative integrity. If implemented on the application side, procedural integrity can reduce load on the database, but it can allow discrepancies to creep into the data if data is loaded or modified with tools other than the application. For this reason, procedural integrity should be implemented to complement, but not replace, declarative integrity.

Constraints

Constraints are the primary method used to enforce integrity. The types of constraints are PRIMARY KEY, FOREIGN KEY, UNIQUE, CHECK, and DEFAULT. Defaults can be implemented as constraints or as objects in the database; these are covered in the "Defaults" section of this chapter.

PRIMARY KEY Constraints

To enforce entity integrity—in other words, to uniquely identify each row—you use a PRIMARY KEY constraint. Only one PRIMARY KEY is allowed per table, and it ensures that the column or columns that make up the key are unique and NOT NULL. When a PRIMARY KEY is created, it creates a unique index on the column(s). By default, it creates a CLUSTERED index.

When choosing a candidate for a PRIMARY KEY, try to keep it as short as possible. If you have to combine several columns to come up with a unique instance, you should consider creating a surrogate key. For example, perhaps in an employee table, you have to combine the lastname, firstname, and dept columns to come up with a unique identifier (and that combination is not necessarily guaranteed to be unique). It would be more efficient to add an Emp_no column and use the identity property to automatically generate a unique number for each employee. This would avoid having the PRIMARY KEY index cover all three columns. The following example defines a PRIMARY KEY on the Emp_no column of the employee table:

```
CREATE TABLE employee
( Emp_no int IDENTITY (100, 10)CONSTRAINT emp_pk_emp_no PRIMARY KEY NOT NULL,
  Lastname char(20) NOT NULL,
  Firstname char(20) NOT NULL,
  PayRoll char(10) NOT NULL,
  Phone char(13) NULL,
  Dept smallint )
```

UNIQUE Constraints

The UNIQUE constraint is functionally similar to the PRIMARY KEY. It also uses a unique index to enforce uniqueness, but unlike the primary key, it allows nulls. Actually, in practice, it allows NULL; if a column with a UNIQUE constraint contains a NULL value in one row, insertion of another row with a NULL in that column is blocked. It considers NULL to be a unique value. Because this behavior is unpredictable, especially if the constraint is a composite of columns, I recommend that columns with UNIQUE constraints be created as NOT NULL.

UNIQUE constraints are generally used when a column, outside of the PRIMARY KEY, must be guaranteed to be unique. A typical example would be the Social Security number or payroll number of an employee, in which an employee number was used as the PRIMARY

KEY. The example that follows shows a CREATE TABLE script that defines a UNIQUE constraint on the Payroll column:

```
CREATE TABLE employee
(  Emp_no int IDENTITY (100, 10)CONSTRAINT emp_pk_emp_no PRIMARY KEY NOT NULL,
  Lname char(20) NOT NULL,
  Fname char(20) NOT NULL,
  PayRoll char(10)CONSTRAINT emp_uk_payroll UNIQUE NOT NULL,
  Phone char(13) NULL,
  Dept smallint)
```

Referential Integrity Constraint: FOREIGN KEY

FOREIGN KEY constraints enforce referential integrity. They maintain the relations in a relational database. When a FOREIGN KEY constraint is created on a column, the column references another column in a different or even the same table. The referenced column must be a PRIMARY KEY or UNIQUE constraint. A FOREIGN KEY that references a column in the same table is said to be a self-referencing key. When changes (inserts, updates) are made to a column defined with a FOREIGN KEY, the FOREIGN KEY relationship checks if the new value matches a value in the referenced column. For example, an employee table with a Dept column could have a FOREIGN KEY referencing the Dept (PRIMARY KEY) column of the Department table. Any attempts to insert or update an employee's Dept column would be checked against the department table to ensure that the new entry was a valid department. The FOREIGN KEY constraint is also checked when deleting or updating records in the referenced table, preventing you from updating or deleting a primary key that would leave behind foreign keys with the old value in the referencing table. The following is an example of adding a FOREIGN KEY to the employee table:

```
ALTER TABLE employee
 ADD CONSTRAINT emp_dept_fk
 FOREIGN KEY (Dept)
 REFERENCES dept(dept_no)
```

When adding a FOREIGN KEY constraint, the table being referenced must already exist and the column being referenced must have a PRIMARY KEY constraint or a unique index defined via a UNIQUE constraint or CREATE INDEX statement. If you do not provide the referenced column names in a FOREIGN KEY constraint, a PRIMARY KEY constraint must be present on the appropriate columns in the referenced table. In addition, the datatypes of the referencing table columns must exactly match the datatypes of the referenced table columns.

If you need to reference a table you do not own, you will need to be granted references permission on that table by the table owner. A referenced table cannot be dropped until the referencing table or the FOREIGN KEY constraint that references the primary key table is dropped.

Cascading Referential Integrity

Cascading Referential Integrity, a feature conspicuously absent in earlier versions of SQL Server, has finally arrived in SQL Server 2000. Two new clauses, ON DELETE and ON UPDATE, have been added to the CREATE TABLE and ALTER TABLE commands to facilitate this. When CASCADE is specified for either or both of these clauses, actions against the parent table will "cascade" to the child table.

To illustrate the usefulness of this, consider the employee and department tables. If the employee table, which has a foreign key on the dept column that references the dept column of the department table, was created with ON UPDATE CASCADE, any changes to the dept column in the department table would cascade to the employee table. Therefore, if dept 20 has 5,000 employees, and you change the dept number to 200 to comply with a business rule, all 5,000 employee records are automatically updated as well. If ON DELETE CASCADE were specified for the table, then deleting dept 20 would result in the deletion of all 5,000 employees! This is a powerful, and dangerous feature, but don't let that discourage you from using it. Think of an orders/items scenario. When an order is deleted, all associated items are deleted as well. Following is the ALTER TABLE command to add a FOREIGN KEY constraint and enable cascading deletes and updates:

```
ALTER TABLE employee
 ADD CONSTRAINT emp_dept_fk
 FOREIGN KEY (Dept)
 REFERENCES dept(dept_no)
ON DELETE CASCADE
ON UPDATE CASCADE
```

You can disable the cascade feature with ON DELETE NO ACTION and ON UPDATE NO ACTION.

> **NOTE**
>
> If you plan to utilize the cascade feature, I recommend working closely with the application developers to ensure that checks and balances are in place to prevent accidental deletion of data. It is also important to note the potential overhead generated by Cascading Referential Integrity. As you saw in the preceding examples, an action on a single row was translated into an action on many rows.

CHECK Constraints

CHECK constraints provide a way to restrict the values that can be entered into a column. A CHECK constraint is implemented as a Boolean expression, which must not evaluate to false, for the insert or update to proceed. CHECK constraints can be used to ensure that data meets a certain format, as in a telephone number being expressed as (613) [0–9][0–9][0–9]–[0–9][0–9][0–9][0–9], or that the data is in a list of acceptable values such as states (AK, AL, AR, AZ, CA, and so on). A CHECK constraint can also reference a column in the same table, or a function, provided that the function doesn't require input parameters. Following is an example of implementing CHECK constraints with CREATE TABLE:

```
CREATE TABLE inventory
 (item_code char(4) not null
    constraint CK_inventory_item_code
    check (item_code like '[0-9][0-9][0-9][0-9]'),
  high_volume int not null
    constraint CK_inventory_high_volume
    check (high_volume > 0),
  low_volume int not null
    constraint CK_inventory_low_volume
    check (low_volume > 0),
      constraint CK_inventory_hi_lo_check
      check (high_volume >= low_volume
      and high_volume - low_volume < 1000)
 )
```

Creating Constraints

Constraints can be defined on a single column, which is referred to as a **column-level** constraint, or on multiple columns where it is considered a **table-level** constraint. Column-level constraints can be defined in the column definition, whereas table-level constraints must be created after the columns they reference have been defined.

When creating constraints, always provide intuitive names; if you don't, SQL Server generates a name for you. For example, a unique constraint on the Social_Security column of the employee table might be referenced as emp_ss_uk. The error `Violates constraint emp_ss_uk` is easier to troubleshoot than `Violates constraint UK__emp__5165187F`.

Although constraints are defined at the table or column level, constraint names must be unique within the current database.

Creating Constraints with T-SQL

Constraints can be created in the `CREATE TABLE` statement or after the table has been created using `ALTER TABLE`.

> **NOTE**
>
> I recommend creating your tables first, and then using `ALTER TABLE` to create the constraints. This has the twofold effect of keeping your `CREATE TABLE` syntax simpler, and providing `ALTER TABLE` scripts that can be rerun or modified as the need arises.

Listing 14.1 demonstrates creating constraints with the `CREATE TABLE` command. The script creates a PRIMARY KEY on both the employee and dept tables and creates a foreign key on the employee table that references the dept table.

LISTING 14.1 Syntax for Creating Constraints with CREATE TABLE

```
CREATE TABLE dept
(
  Dept_no smallint IDENTITY (10, 10) CONSTRAINT DEPT_PK PRIMARY KEY NOT NULL,
  Name varchar(20) NOT NULL,
  Description varchar(80) NOT NULL,
  Loc_code char(2) NULL
)


CREATE TABLE employee
(
  Emp_no int IDENTITY (100, 10)CONSTRAINT emp_pk_emp_no PRIMARY KEY NOT NULL,
  Lname char(20) NOT NULL,
  Fname char(20) NOT NULL,
  Phone char(13) NULL,
  Dept smallint CONSTRAINT emp_dept_fk REFERENCES dept(dept_no)NOT NULL,
  Photo image NULL,
  Salary int NULL
)

go
```


In the following example, CREATE TABLE is run first, and then ALTER TABLE is run to add the constraints. Listing 14.2 shows that separating constraint creation from the table creation is easier to read and more flexible. This example creates the Product table, and then alters the Product table to add a PRIMARY KEY constraint on ProductId, a CHECK constraint on UnitPrice, and a FOREIGN KEY constraint on CategoryID that references the Categories table.

LISTING 14.2 Syntax for Creating Constraints with ALTER TABLE

```
CREATE TABLE Product (
  ProductID int IDENTITY (1, 1) NOT NULL ,
  ProductName nvarchar (40) NOT NULL ,
  SupplierID int NULL ,
  CategoryID int NULL ,
  QuantityPerUnit nvarchar (20) NULL ,
  UnitPrice money NULL ,
  UnitsInStock smallint NULL ,
  UnitsOnOrder smallint NULL ,
  ReorderLevel smallint NULL ,
  Discontinued bit NOT NULL
)
```

LISTING 14.2 Continued

```
GO

ALTER TABLE Product ADD
  CONSTRAINT PK_Product PRIMARY KEY      (ProductID),
  CONSTRAINT CK_Product_UnitPrice CHECK (UnitPrice >= 0)
GO

ALTER TABLE Product ADD
  CONSTRAINT FK_Product_Categories FOREIGN KEY
  (CategoryID) REFERENCES dbo.Categories (CategoryID)
GO
```

Creating Constraints in Enterprise Manager

Previous chapters looked at using Enterprise Manager to create tables and to add indexes to those tables. Constraints are no different, in that the Table Designer is used to create and manage constraints. To access Table Designer, right-click the table you want to manage and select Design Table from the pop-up menu. The rightmost icon, as shown in Figure 14.1, is the Manage Constraints icon.

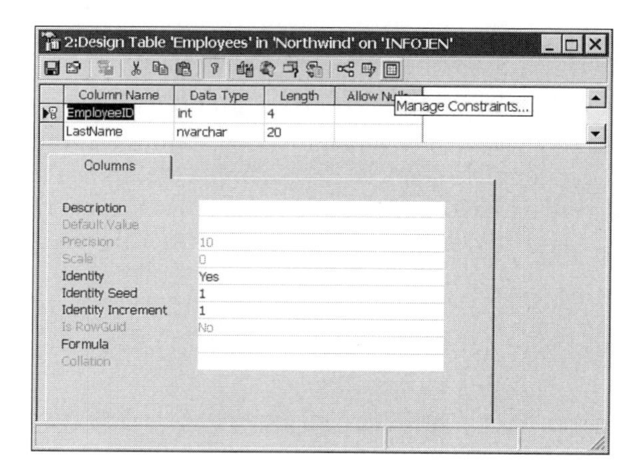

FIGURE 14.1 Using Table Designer to manage constraints.

Selecting the Manage Constraints icon brings up the Properties dialog box, as shown in Figure 14.2.

The Relationships tab manages `FOREIGN KEYS`. The Indexes/Keys tab manages `PRIMARY KEY` and `UNIQUE` constraints. The Check Constraint tab can be used to create, delete, and modify `CHECK` constraints. If you want to set `DEFAULTS`, you can do so from the Columns dialog box, as shown in Figure 14.3.

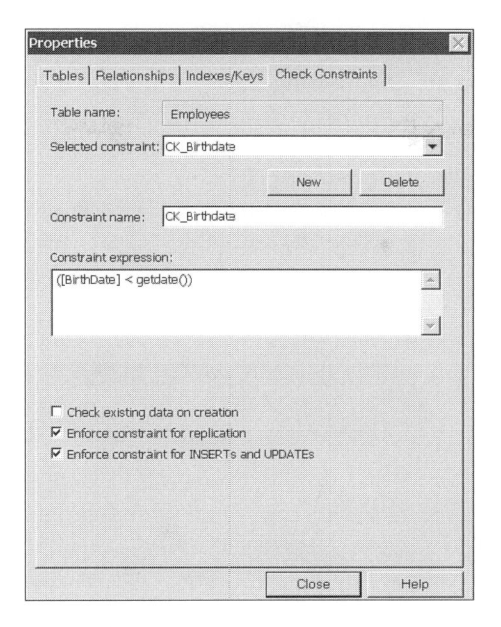

FIGURE 14.2 The Table Designer Properties dialog box.

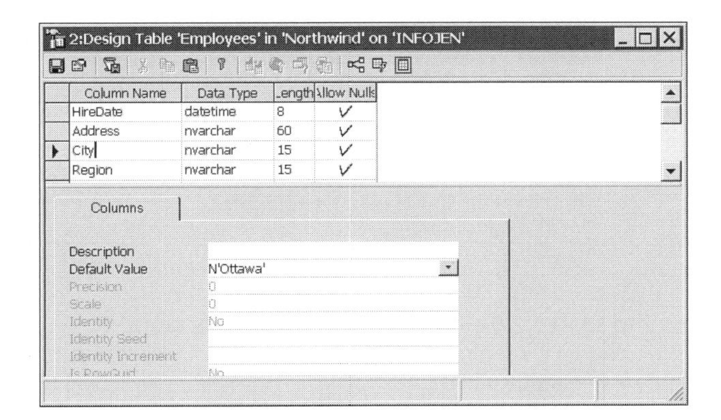

FIGURE 14.3 Adding a `DEFAULT` in the Table Designer Columns dialog box.

As with any changes made through Table Designer, changes to constraints are not saved until you exit the Designer. Before exiting the Designer, it is advisable to save your changes to a script using the Save Change Script icon (the third icon from the left).

TIP

If you plan to drop or modify constraints after business hours, perhaps to facilitate a data load, use Table Designer to generate a script for the changes. When you exit the Designer, select No when prompted to save your changes. Now you have a script you can schedule as a job, and the changes will be made when the job runs.

Managing Constraints

Managing constraints consists of gathering information about constraints, disabling and re-enabling constraints, and dropping constraints.

Gathering Information About Constraints

To get information on constraints, you can query the information_schema views: check_constraints, referential_constraints, and table_constraints. The system-stored procedures, sp_help and sp_helpconstraint, can also be executed to obtain information. Figure 14.4 shows the sp_helpconstraint output in Query Analyzer.

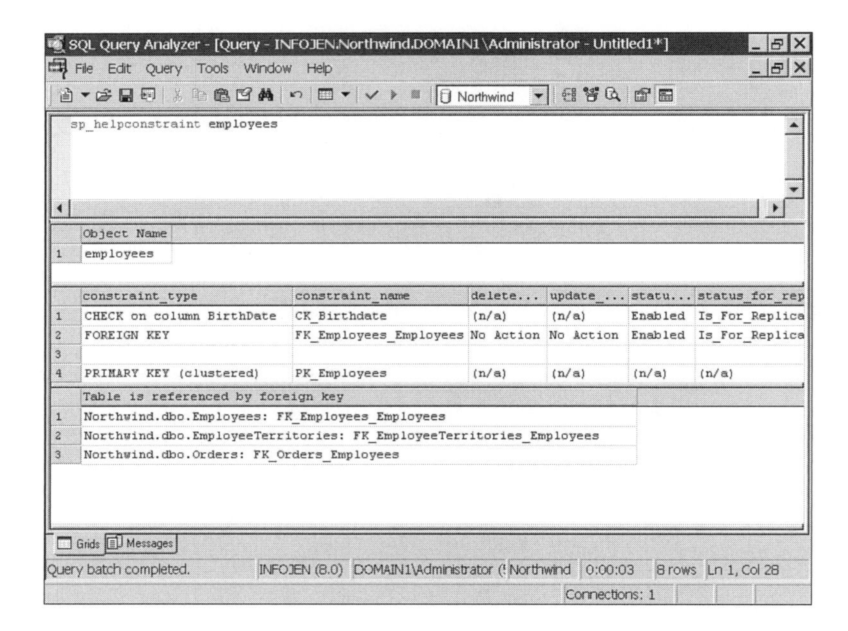

FIGURE 14.4 Executing sp_helpconstraint on the employees table.

Dropping Constraints

Constraints are dropped using the `ALTER TABLE` command. For example, to drop a constraint from the employee table, use the following:

```
Alter table employee drop constraint Ck_Product
```

You can also drop constraints from the Table Designer by selecting the constraint to be dropped and clicking Delete.

Disabling Constraints

`CHECK` and `FOREIGN KEY` constraints can be disabled from checking existing data or from checking new data to be loaded.

When adding a constraint to a table with existing data, SQL Server checks the data to make sure it doesn't violate the constraint. If you want to enforce the constraint on new data but the existing data doesn't comply (perhaps all new ZIP codes must be six digits, but the existing five digit ones don't change), you can add the constraint `WITH NOCHECK` as in the following example:

```
ALTER TABLE employee
WITH NOCHECK
ADD CONSTRAINT CK_Product_UnitPrice CHECK (UnitPrice >= 0)
```

If possible, it is better to change the existing data to meet the constraint criteria rather than use the `WITH NOCHECK`. If the data in *any* column changes at a later date, the constraint will be violated and the transaction rolled back. This can be problematic when troubleshooting because the error returns a constraint violation on ColumnB, and the update is changing data only in ColumnC.

If you want to speed the loading of data that meets the constraint criteria, or if you must load data that does not, you can disable an existing constraint using `NOCHECK`. This is illustrated in this statement:

```
ALTER TABLE employee
NOCHECK
CONSTRAINT CK_Product_UnitPrice
```

The constraint is enabled using `CHECK`. Disabling constraint checking can vastly improve the speed of large data loads, but the constraint can't be enabled if the new data violates the constraint. Once more, if possible, it is better to fix the data to be loaded before the load. However, in a less-than-perfect world, disabling constraints can be a valid option.

Rules

Rules are used to limit the range of values that can be stored in a column. They are similar to `CHECK` constraints in this regard, but they are more limited in their functionality. A rule is considered a bound object; that is, the rule is first created, and then is bound to a column or User-Defined Datatype.

Rule Usage

A rule, once created, can be bound to multiple columns or User-Defined Datatypes (UDTs). A rule can be useful to maintain consistency not just in a column, but in all columns and UDTs across the database to which it is bound. For example, if you require a standard format for telephone numbers, you could create the following rule:

```
CREATE RULE phone_rule AS
@phone LIKE '([0-9][0-9][0-9]) [0-9][0-9][0-9]-[0-9][0-9][0-9][0-9]'
```

By binding this rule to phone number columns in your database, you can ensure a consistent phone number format. This could be taken a step further by creating a UDT called Phone and binding the rule to the UDT. When creating a column for storing telephone numbers, use the Phone datatype, and the rule automatically applies.

Creating and Managing Rules

Rules are created using the `CREATE RULE` command. Rule definitions can contain anything that is valid in a `WHERE` clause. Managing rules involves binding them to columns and UDTs using `sp_bindrule` and unbinding them using `sp_unbindrule`. The following are some examples of creating and managing rules.

First, the rule must be created:

```
--Create a rule to limit product color codes
CREATE RULE ccode_rule AS
@ccode IN ('r01', 'r02', 'r03')
```

After the rule is created, it can be bound to a column or UDT:

```
--Bind a rule to a column
sp_bindrule ccode_rule, 'product.ccode'

--Bind a rule to a UDT named color
sp_bindrule ccode_rule, color
```

To unbind a rule, use `sp_unbindrule`:

```
--Unbind a rule from a UDT
sp_unbindrule color
```

Creating Rules in Enterprise Manager

If you prefer to use Enterprise Manager to create a bound rule, you simply right-click Rules in the appropriate database, then select New Rule from the pop-up menu. This opens the Rule Properties dialog box, as shown in Figure 14.5. Enter a name for the rule, as well as the rule definition in the text box, and click OK. After a rule is created, this same dialog box can be used to bind the rule to UDTs and columns.

Rule Limitations

Although rules have an advantage over `CHECK` constraints in that they can be bound to many columns or to UDTs to provide centralized rule handling, they also have limitations.

- A column or UDT can have only one rule bound to it.
- A rule cannot validate against other columns in the row.
- Rules are not ANSI-92 compliant.

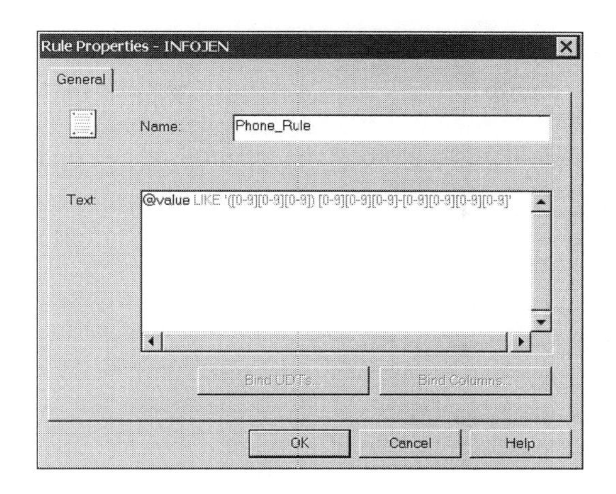

FIGURE 14.5 The Rule Properties dialog box.

The status of rules for future versions of SQL Server is also a concern. Microsoft refers to rules in the documentation as a "backward compatibility" feature. I read this to mean that rules won't be supported in the future, and could be dropped from future releases. The inference is that you should now use `CHECK` constraints where you might have used rules in the past.

Defaults

Defaults allow you to specify a value to be entered into a column, if one is not otherwise specified. Defaults can be anything that evaluates to a constant, such as a constant, a built-in function, or a mathematical expression. Defaults are of two types: declarative and bound. The two are functionally the same; the difference is in how they are implemented.

Declarative Defaults

A declarative default is just another flavor of constraint, and as such is implemented using the `CREATE TABLE` and `ALTER TABLE` commands. Following is an example of adding a `DEFAULT` constraint to the employee table that enters a value of `UNLISTED` if no phone number is specified:

```
ALTER TABLE employee ADD
  CONSTRAINT df_emp_ph DEFAULT 'UNLISTED' FOR Phone
```

To remove a declarative default constraint, use `ALTER TABLE`:

```
ALTER TABLE employee DROP CONSTRAINT df_emp_ph
```

Bound Defaults

Bound defaults are implemented in the same way rules are. The default is first created as an object in the database, and then it is bound to a column or User-Defined Datatype (UDT). The following implements the preceding example as a bound default:

```
--First create the default.
CREATE DEFAULT phone_df AS 'UNLISTED'

--Bind the default to a column
sp_bindefault phone_df, 'employee.phone'
```

As you can see, the bound default appears to require an extra step, but after it is created, it has the advantage of being able to be bound to other columns. This way, you have a consistent value of UNLISTED when no phone number is entered, rather than a mixed bag of perhaps NONE, UNKNOWN, and NULL.

Creating Bound Defaults in Enterprise Manager

If you want to use Enterprise Manager to create a bound default, right-click Defaults in the appropriate database, and select New Default from the pop-up menu. This opens the Default Properties dialog box, as shown in Figure 14.6. Enter a name for the default and the default value (don't forget the single quotes around constants), and click OK. After a default is created, this same dialog box can be used to bind the default to UDTs and columns.

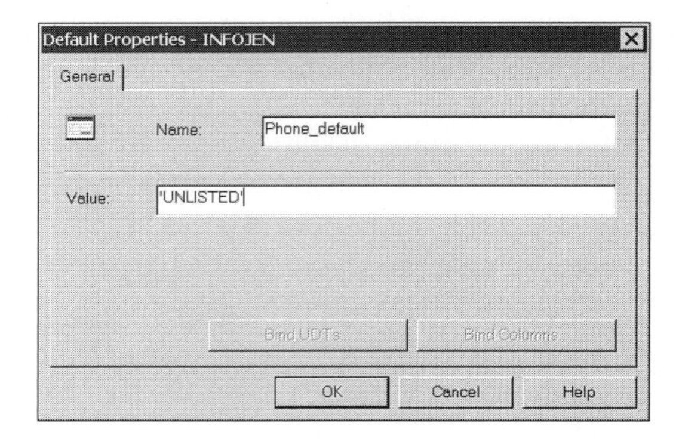

FIGURE 14.6 The Default Properties dialog box.

Default Usage

A default can act as a placeholder of sorts, perhaps with a value of NONE being entered as opposed to just allowing nulls. A default can also be used to provide the most common entry; if most of your employees live in Texas, providing 'Texas' as a default in the state column of the employee table would make sense.

Another usage of the default is to generate a value based on a system function. For instance, when inserting or updating records, it is often useful to record a timestamp, or the user ID of the person making the change. The following example adds the updtime and updby columns and provides default values for the updating user and the time using system functions SUSER_SNAME() and GETDATE().

```
CREATE TABLE employee
(
  Emp_no int IDENTITY (100, 10)CONSTRAINT emp_pk_emp_no PRIMARY KEY NOT NULL,
  Lname char(20) NOT NULL,
  Fname char(20) NOT NULL,
  Phone char(13) NULL,
  Dept smallint CONSTRAINT emp_dept_fk REFERENCES dept(dept_no)NOT NULL,
  updtime datetime DEFAULT GETDATE() NOT NULL,
  updby varchar(30) DEFAULT SUSER_SNAME() NOT NULL,
)
```


When a Default Is Applied

SQL Server can automatically generate a value for a column when a row is inserted in four ways: using a constraint or bound default, specifying the IDENTITY property for the column, using the timestamp datatype, or simply letting the column allow NULL values.

Because columns defined with the timestamp datatype or associated with the IDENTITY property automatically insert a value, they cannot allow NULL, nor can you specify the DEFAULT keyword on inserts for an IDENTITY column. The column must be omitted from the INSERT list. Just because a default is defined for a column doesn't mean that NULL values will never be in that column. If a column allows NULL, and an explicit NULL is passed in the Insert statement, a NULL will be inserted. If you implemented a default because you don't want NULL in a column, define the column as NOT NULL.

Now look at the different ways you can generate defaults in an Insert statement based on the following table:

```
CREATE TABLE test_default
(id int IDENTITY NOT NULL,
 tmstmp timestamp NOT NULL,
 phone char(13) NOT NULL DEFAULT 'UNLISTED',
 notes VARCHAR(100) NULL)
```

Because all the columns have some sort of default associated with them, the keywords DEFAULT VALUES can be used to generate values for the entire row:

```
INSERT test_default DEFAULT VALUES
SELECT * FROM test_default
```

```
id          tmstmp                phone          notes
----------- --------------------- -------------- -----
1           0x0000000000000191    UNLISTED       NULL
```

If you want a default generated for a particular column, exclude the column from the column listing. Remember that the identity column is omitted as well. The following generates an identity for id, and a default for tmstmp:

```
INSERT test_default (phone, notes)
 VALUES('(905)555-1234', 'Phone added')
SELECT * FROM test_default


id        tmstmp              phone          notes
--------- ------------------- -------------- ------------
1         0x0000000000000192  (905)555-1234  Phone added
```

Another method is to specify the keyword DEFAULT in the value listing for each column you want populated with the default value:

```
INSERT test_default (tmstmp, phone, notes)
 VALUES(DEFAULT, DEFAULT, DEFAULT)
SELECT * FROM test_default
id          tmstmp                phone          notes
----------- ------------------ ------------- -------
1           0x0000000000000193 UNLISTED       NULL
```

Binding Precedence with Rules and Defaults

A default value, rule, or check can be assigned to a column using a CHECK or DEFAULT constraint, by binding to the column a RULE or DEFAULT object, or by creating the column with a User-Defined Datatype that has a RULE or DEFAULT object bound to the UDT. To avoid conflicts between the different methods, some restrictions must apply.

The following restrictions apply for check constraints and rules:

- Only one rule can be bound to a column. Binding a new rule to a column unbinds the old rule automatically.
- Only one rule can be bound to a datatype. Binding a new rule to a datatype unbinds the old rule automatically.

- A rule bound to a column has precedence over a rule bound to a datatype. To reapply a rule bound to a datatype, unbind the rule from the column and then rebind the rule to the datatype.
- If a CHECK constraint and a rule are on the same column, the rule is validated first. If the verification for the rule fails, an error message is generated and the statement fails.

These restrictions apply for defaults:

- A column can have only one type of default apply at any one time.
- You cannot create a table with a default constraint if the column is based on a datatype to which a default object is bound.
- You cannot alter a table to add a default constraint if the column is based on a datatype to which a default object is bound or if a default object is bound to the column.
- If you have a column that uses a user-defined datatype and the column has a default constraint or default object bound to it, binding a default to the datatype will not affect that column.
- If a column is created with a datatype to which a default is bound, and subsequently, a default is bound to the column, the default bound to the column will take precedence.

Summary

This chapter examined the need to enforce data integrity, looked at the types of integrity, and explored some of the methods used to enforce it. Primary among these methods are the constraints: PRIMARY KEY, FOREIGN KEY, UNIQUE, and CHECK. This chapter also looked at rules and defaults, which can enforce integrity by limiting possible values for a column or providing a consistent default value if no other is entered.

Proper use of these features results in a consistent, reliable dataset, which is protected from accidental or malicious misrepresentation of values. As long as humans are involved in the input of data, errors will exist; however, proper implementation of integrity constraints can help keep those errors to a manageable level.

CHAPTER 15

Security and User Administration

by Paul Jensen

IN THIS CHAPTER

Managing SQL Server security involves controlling access to SQL Server and access to the databases and the objects they contain, as well as defining permissions for users who will perform administrative tasks. This chapter will examine the SQL Server security model and demonstrate the various ways to implement security.

An Overview of SQL Server Security

SQL Server security is built on a two-tier model. The first tier is access to SQL Server, which involves the person attempting to connect being authenticated as a valid SQL Server account, or **login** as it is known. Think of a login as being similar to entering an office tower and signing in with the security guard. The guard verifies that you have business in the building, and you head for the elevators. The second tier involves access to the databases. As SQL Server supports multiple databases, each database has its own security layer that provides access to that database through accounts known as **users**. These users are then mapped to the server logins to provide access. As users are created on a database-by-database basis, access can be restricted to one or many databases as needed. If you go back to the office building example, this would be like having an access card for the elevator that only allows you to get off at certain floors.

The key points to remember in SQL Server security are that logins are server-wide and give access to SQL Server, while users are database-specific and give access only to the database in which they are created. By mapping logins to users, a connection is made to SQL Server, and access is allowed to the database.

Authentication Methods

The process of being validated by SQL Server is known as **authentication**, and it can be handled in two ways. The method you choose depends on whether the operating system or SQL Server will authorize the connection.

Windows Authentication Mode

Windows Authentication mode can be used in Windows 2000 and NT 4.0 environments to facilitate connection to SQL Server. In this mode, connections to SQL Server are validated based on the Windows account requesting the connection. SQL Server checks whether an associated login account is in the sysxlogins tables, and if there is, the connection is allowed. This is known as a **trusted** connection, as SQL Server has trusted the domain controller to authenticate the connection. This has the advantage of providing a single login account and the ability to leverage domain security features, such as password length and expiration, account locking, encryption, and auditing.

Mixed Authentication Mode

As its name implies, mixed mode allows Windows and SQL Server Authentication. When running in mixed mode, an additional dialog box is presented allowing you to enter a SQL Server login account and password. Mixed mode is useful for supporting legacy applications that connect using a SQL Server account and in environments in which a Windows domain controller doesn't control network access, such as in a NetWare network.

Setting the Authentication Mode

The authentication mode can be selected during or after installation by right-clicking a server and selecting Properties, Security. The Security tab allows you to specify Windows and SQL Server (mixed) or Windows-only connections. You are also given the option to set the level of auditing you want to record on login attempts. Note that when changing the authentication mode or auditing level, the change will not take effect until SQL Server is restarted. Figure 15.1 shows the Security tab of the Server Properties dialog box.

Permissions

After you are connected to SQL Server, the actions that can be performed are dependent on the permissions that have been assigned. These permissions can be assigned directly to users or groups, or through roles, which are used to group related permissions.

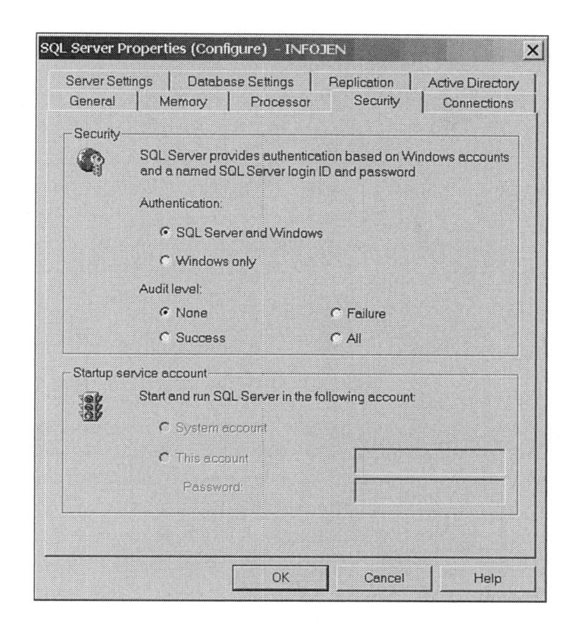

FIGURE 15.1 Changing the authentication mode.

Permissions that allow you to create and manipulate objects are referred to as statement permissions. These permissions, such as `CREATE DATABASE`, `CREATE TABLE`, and `ALTER TABLE`, are also referred to as **Data Definition Language** (**DDL**) commands. Members of the sysadmin, db_owner, and db_securityadmin roles are the only ones who can grant statement permissions.

The permissions used to access objects are referred to as **object permissions**. These permissions, such as `SELECT`, `INSERT`, `UPDATE`, and `DELETE`, are the permissions typically assigned to users of a database, and are also referred to as Data Manipulation Language (DML) permissions.

Some permissions cannot be granted through either statement or object-level permissions. These are referred to as **predefined permissions** and are obtained through membership in fixed roles or as the owner of database objects.

Fixed roles, such as the sysadmin role, have set permissions that cannot be changed or applied to other user accounts. The only way to obtain all the permissions implied by the role is to become a member of the role.

The owner of an object also has implicit permissions on the object. If, for example, a user creates a view, then that user has full permission to manage the view. No explicit permissions need to be set for a user to access or manage objects he owns.

SQL Server Security: Logins

Logins provide access to SQL Server. As they are server-wide objects, they are stored in the Master database in the table *sysxlogins*. These logins can be Windows accounts, Windows groups, or if you are running in mixed mode, they can be SQL Server logins, which are referred to as **standard logins**.

When SQL Server is installed, two accounts are created: a Windows group called builtin\administrators that allows access to anyone in the Windows local administrators group, and a standard login called sa. These accounts are both members of the SQL Server role Sysadmin, which gives them full administration privilege on SQL Server and all databases.

NOTE

As both builtin\administrators and sa have full privileges on SQL Server, be careful in their use. Remember that the local administrators group contains the domain administrators group and anyone else who has been added. If it is not appropriate that they have access to SQL Server, you can remove the builtin\administrators login. The sa account can't be removed, but you should assign it a complex password and limit its use. It is preferred to create logins for users who will administer SQL Server and assign them to the sysadmins role. This provides greater accountability.

After SQL Server is installed, you can connect using the builtin\administrator or sa login to create additional Windows user and group logins as well as SQL Server logins, to provide access to the database users and administrative staff. After logins are created, they will have to be mapped to users to provide database access. A single login can be mapped to users in multiple databases.

SQL Server Security: Users

As mentioned earlier, server access is provided by logins, but database access is provided by users. As users are database-specific, they are created in the user databases and stored in the sysusers table. When a user is created in a database, it must be mapped to a login to provide access. Typically, the user account and login would be the same, such as mapping the login "sales" to a user "sales"; however, they are separate objects, so this convention is not enforced. It should also be noted that the database "user" doesn't always represent a single person. As in the previous example, the user "sales" could be mapped to a Windows group login "sales," which could represent many actual Windows accounts. This allows you to dynamically manage potentially thousands of end users by manipulating only two SQL Server objects: the login and user.

Two users have special meaning in SQL Server: dbo and guest. The dbo user is created in every database, but guest must be manually created if required.

dbo

The dbo account is the database owner; therefore, it cannot be deleted from the database. Members of the Sysadmin server role are mapped to the dbo user in each database, which allows them to administer all databases. Objects owned by dbo can be referenced by the object name alone, such as example table1; objects with owners other than dbo or the current user must be referenced with the owner name, such as bob.table1. It is good practice for all objects in a database to be owned by dbo.

guest

The guest account is used to provide access to a database for logins that do not have a mapped user account in the database. When you create a guest account in a database (there isn't one by default), all logins that aren't mapped to a user get access through the guest account. Any permission granted to the guest account or the public role (of which all users, including guest, are members) will be granted to these logins. Use the guest account sparingly, and only in low security databases.

SQL Server Security: Roles

Roles provide a consistent yet flexible model for security administration. Roles are similar to the groups used in administering networks. Permissions are applied to the role, and then members are added to the role; therefore, any member of the role has all the permissions that the role has. A user can be a member of multiple roles and, with the exception of application roles, all permissions of all roles will apply. This makes possible a modular model for permission administration. For example, all permissions required for sales personnel can be assigned to the "sales" role. All permissions required for the managers could be assigned to the "managers" role. To implement security in the sales department, assign the sales users to the "sales" role and the sales managers to both the "sales" and "managers" roles. Roles are also useful to group permissions required for a particular application, as opposed to function or department. If a user is required to use the application, he can simply be added to its associated role.

SQL Server uses roles in three ways:

- Fixed-server and fixed-database roles, which have predefined permissions
- User-defined roles, which are created in each database to manage users
- Application roles, which have special properties useful in applying security to custom applications

Fixed-Server Roles

As the name implies, fixed-server roles are used to manage permissions at the server level and cannot be modified. Fixed-server roles are used to delegate various levels of administrative privileges by adding logins as members of the roles. This concept of delegation is important, as you can maintain security while distributing the administrative workload. A typical use of this would be to assign the network account administrators to the securityadmin role, allowing them to create logins on SQL Server. The fixed-server roles are listed in Table 15.1.

TABLE 15.1 Fixed-Server Roles

Role	Permission
sysadmin	Perform any activity
dbcreator	Create, alter, and drop databases
diskadmin	Create and manage disk files
processadmin	Manage SQL Server processes
serveradmin	Change server configuration and shut down the server
setupadmin	Set up replication and manage linked servers
securityadmin	Manage SQL Server logins and passwords, read error logs, and manage `CREATE DATABASE` permissions
bulkadmin	Execute the `BULK INSERT` statement

Managing Fixed-Server Roles

To change membership in a fixed-server role, you can use the system-stored procedures sp_addsrvrolemember and sp_dropsrvrolemember. For example, to add the Windows user domain1\bobw to the sysadmin role and drop the SQL login bwhite, the syntax would be as follows:

```
EXEC sp_addsrvrolemember 'domain1\bobw', 'sysadmin'
Go
EXEC sp_dropsrvrolemember 'bwhite', 'sysadmin'
```

If you prefer to use Enterprise Manager, in the Security folder, use either the Server Roles tab of a login's Properties dialog box or select a server role and from its Properties dialog box, click Add and select the appropriate login(s). Figure 15.2 shows the Properties page for a fixed-server role.

Fixed-Database Roles

Each database also has a predefined set of roles used to delegate permissions at the database level. As in the fixed-server roles, the permissions that apply to these roles are preset and can't be altered. The exception to this rule is the public role. The public role cannot be deleted, but permissions to access database objects can be applied to it. As all users are members of the public role, any permissions applied to the role will affect all users. Table 15.2 shows the fixed-database roles and their permissions.

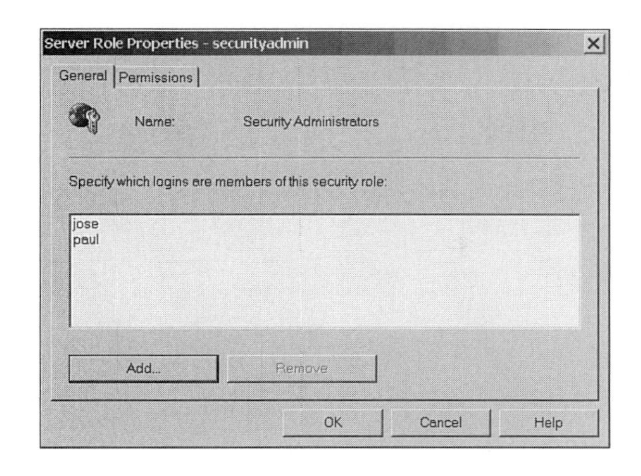

FIGURE 15.2 The Server Role Properties page.

TABLE 15.2 Fixed-Database Roles

Role	Permission
public	All default permissions
db_owner	Perform any database activity
db_ddladmin	Add, drop, or modify database objects
db_accessadmin	Add or remove database users or roles
db_securityadmin	Assign statement and object permissions, and manage role membership
db_backupoperator	Back up the database, and run DBCC statements and CHECKPOINT
db_datareader	Read (select) from any user table
db_datawriter	Insert, update, or delete on any user table
db_denydatareader	Cannot read (select) from any user table
db_denydatawriter	Cannot insert, update, or delete on any user table

Managing Fixed-Database Roles

To change membership in a fixed-database role with T-SQL, use the system-stored procedures sp_addrolemember and sp_droprolemember. The following statement adds the database user bob to the db_owner role and drops the user tom.

```
EXEC sp_addrolemember 'db_owner' , 'bob'
GO
EXEC sp_droprolemember 'db_owner', 'tom'
```

If you prefer to use Enterprise Manager, select the database you want to administer, select a user from the Users folder, and from the General tab of the User Properties dialog box, check the appropriate roles. Alternatively, select the database role from the Roles folder, and from its Properties dialog box, click Add and select the appropriate login(s). Figure 15.3 shows the Properties page for a fixed database role.

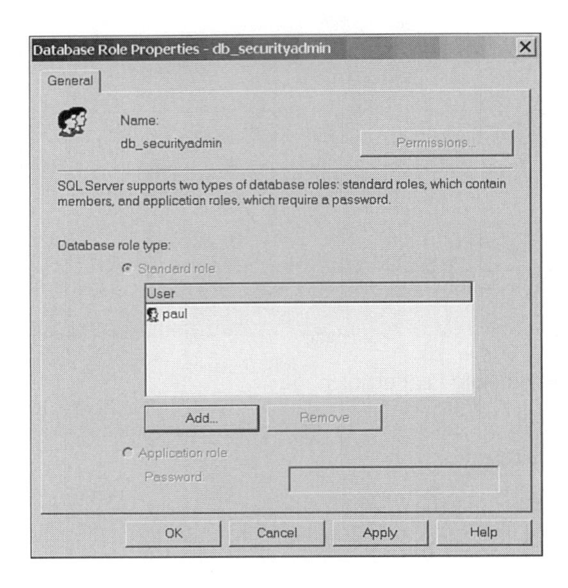

FIGURE 15.3 The Database Role Properties page.

User-Defined Roles

User-defined roles, or database roles, are used to provide a common set of permissions to a group of users. Whereas fixed roles are used to provide statement-level permissions (with the exception of public), user-defined roles are used to provide object permissions in the database. Roles can contain users and other roles, which can be useful for designing a modular security model. An example of this would be to create a role for an application—such as HR_App—and assign the permissions to it that are required to run the HR application. You could then create roles called HR_Users and HQ_Users and add the appropriate users to these roles. Now add the HR_Users and HQ_Users to the HR_App role to provide all users in those roles the needed permissions to run the application. Note that if you are using NT groups to manage users, they too could be added to the application role to facilitate permission management.

For a full discussion on creating and managing user-defined roles, see the later section, "Managing Database Roles."

Application Roles

Unlike other roles, application roles contain no database users. When an application role is created (see the later section, "Managing Database Roles"), rather than adding a list of users who belong to the role, a password is specified. To obtain the permissions associated with the role, the connection must "set" the role and supply the password. This is done using the stored procedure `sp_setapprole`. The syntax to set the role to the sales application role (with a password of "qwerty") is as follows:

```
EXEC sp_setapprole 'sales', 'qwerty'
```

You can also encrypt the password:

```
EXEC sp_setapprole 'sales', {ENCRYPT N 'qwerty'}, 'odbc'
```

When an application role is "set," all permissions from that role apply and all permissions inherited from roles other than public are suspended until the session is ended. So why is it called an application role? The answer is in how it is used. An application role is used to provide permissions on objects through an application, *and only through the application*. Remember that you must use `sp_setapprole` and provide a password to activate the role; this statement and password are not given to the users; rather, they are imbedded in the application connect string. This means that the only way the user gets the permissions associated with the role is if they are running the application. The application can have checks and balances written into it to ensure that these permissions are being used for the forces of good and not evil.

Managing SQL Server Logins

Adding, dropping, or modifying logins can be easily accomplished using Enterprise Manager or T-SQL. The tool you choose depends on your preference, but I usually reach for Enterprise Manager when dealing with one or two logins, and use T-SQL to script multiple login additions or changes. A wizard is also accessible through the Magic Wand icon on the toolbar to step you through the process.

Managing Logins with Enterprise Manager

Logins are managed through the Security folder in Enterprise Manager. Right-clicking Logins and selecting New Login brings up the General tab of the Login dialog box, as shown in Figure 15.4.

If you are creating a standard SQL Server login, enter a name, select SQL Server Authentication, and enter a password. If the login is to be associated with a Windows user or group, clicking the Ellipse button (...) beside the Name field will bring up a list box where you can select the domain and associated account. Alternatively, you can type the name and select the domain from the domain drop-down box. The account must be an existing domain user or group. From this page, you can also grant or deny access to the login and choose its default database and language.

To provide one-stop shopping, two other tabs are also available. The first tab, Server Roles, allows you to select which, if any, fixed server roles the login should belong to, as illustrated in Figure 15.5.

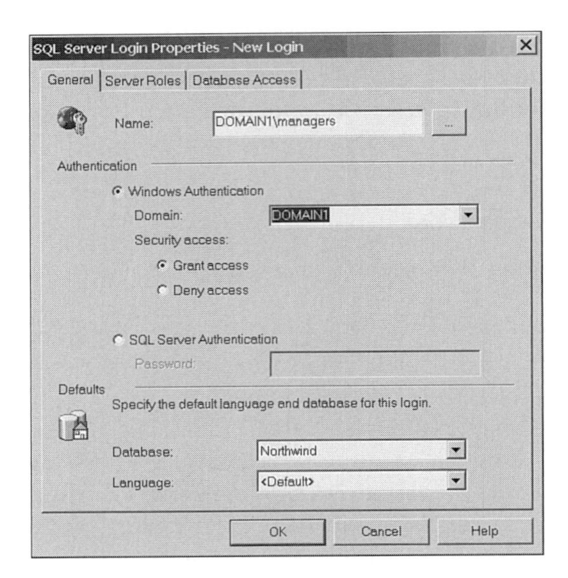

FIGURE 15.4 Creating a login in Enterprise Manager.

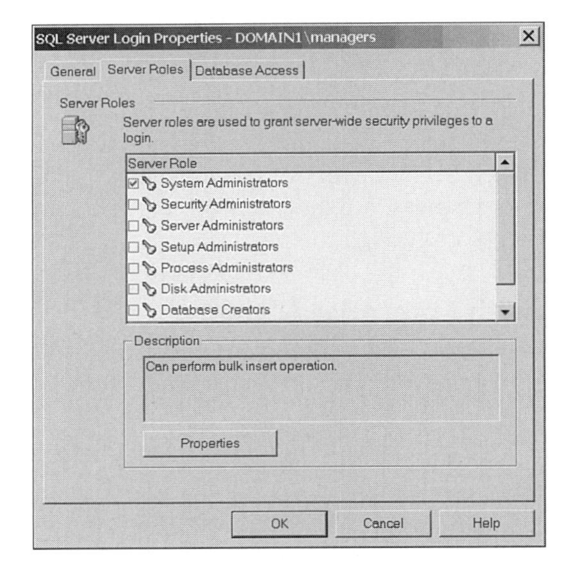

FIGURE 15.5 Choosing a server role.

The Database Access tab allows you to select the databases to which the login should have access and to select the name of the user in the database. This actually creates the user in the database for you, which is a nice feature. If desired, you can also select any roles to which the user should belong. The Database Access tab is shown in Figure 15.6.

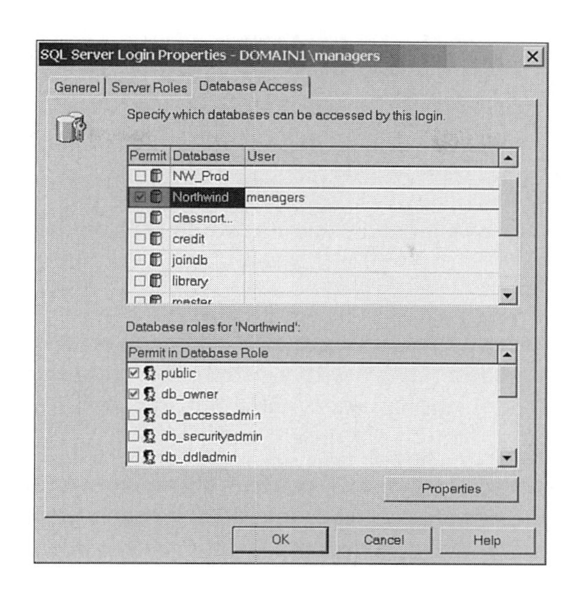

FIGURE 15.6 The Database Access tab.

If changes need to be made to an existing login, double-clicking the login in the Details pane will access the Logins Properties page again, allowing changes to all but the login name. To delete logins, highlight the login(s) in the Details pane and press the Delete key. You will be asked if you want to proceed; selecting Yes will delete the login and any associated database users.

Managing Logins with T-SQL

Managing logins through T-SQL is not as user-friendly as with Enterprise Manager; however, it does provide a way to script multiple logins and incorporate some functionality not available in the GUI. Table 15.3 lists the stored procedures used to manage logins.

TABLE 15.3 Stored Procedures for Managing Logins

Stored Procedure	Function
sp_addlogin	Add a SQL Server login
sp_grantlogin	Add a Windows login
sp_droplogin	Drop a SQL Server login
sp_revokelogin	Drop a Windows login
sp_denylogin	Deny access to a Windows login
sp_password	Change a login's password
sp_defaultdb	Change the default database
sp_defaultlanguage	Change the default language

Each of these stored procedures requires input arguments associated with the action being performed, as in the following example, which creates a new SQL Server login "Sue" with a password of "fido" and "Pubs" as the default database:

```
EXEC sp_addlogin 'Sue' , 'fido', 'Pubs'
```

If you were adding a Windows login, the syntax would be as follows:

```
EXEC sp_grantlogin 'domain1\Sue',
```

The input arguments vary depending on the procedure and are well documented in Books Online, but it is worth mentioning a few that perform functions not available through Enterprise Manager. Sp_addlogin has two input arguments—@sid and @encryptopt—to facilitate migrating logins to another SQL Server.

The @sid argument accepts a 16-byte SID, or security identifier, which will be the SID of the newly created login. This allows you to migrate logins to another server while keeping the same security identifier. The default is `NULL`, which causes SQL Server to generate a new SID.

The @encryptopt argument accepts three values: `NULL`, `SKIP ENCRYPTION`, and `SKIP ENCRYPTION OLD`. The default `NULL` causes the password to be encrypted. If `SKIP_ENCRYPTION` is used, it is assumed you are providing an already encrypted password. This encrypted password can be obtained from the sysxlogins table of the server from which you are migrating logins, and allows the logins on the new server to retain their old password. The `SKIP_ENCRYPTION_OLD` value is used during upgrade and specifies that the password was encrypted by a previous version of SQL Server.

Managing SQL Server Users

Like logins, user accounts can be managed through Enterprise Manager or via T-SQL stored procedures. The method you choose will depend on personal preference and the number of user accounts with which you are working. If you are working with multiple users, it is often more efficient to use T-SQL.

Using Enterprise Manager

In Enterprise Manager, users are managed through the Users folder in each database. Right-clicking Users and selecting New Database User brings up the New User dialog box, as shown in Figure 15.7.

From here, you can select which login to associate with the user, the name of the user, and any database roles of which they should be a member. Note that the Permissions button is grayed out; permissions to access database objects can't be added to the user until the user account is created. You must click OK to create the user and then reaccess the user's Properties page to add permissions. If you do need to add permissions or make changes to role membership, double-clicking the user in the Details pane will open the Properties dialog box.

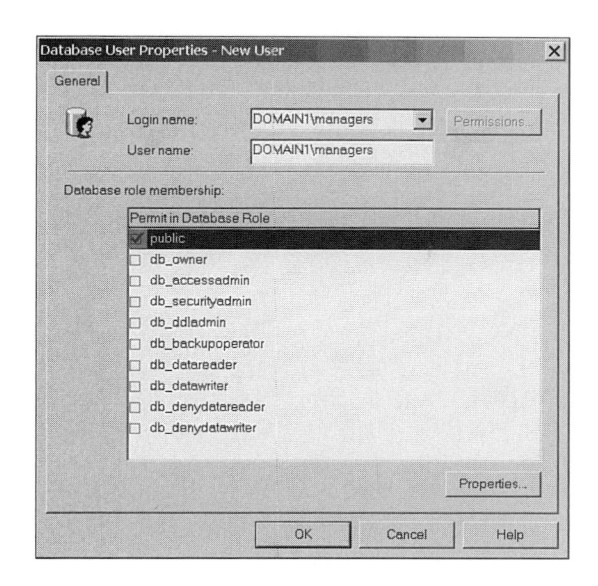

FIGURE 15.7 The New User dialog box.

Using T-SQL

To add a user to a database with T-SQL, execute the `sp_grantdbaccess` stored procedure specifying the login name and the username:

```
EXEC sp_grantdbaccess 'domain1\billw', 'billw'
```

The command for removing the user is as follows:

```
EXEC sp_revokedbaccess 'billw'
```

If you want to change the relationship between a login and user, use sp_change_users_login:

```
EXEC sp_change_users_login 'update_one', 'billw', 'domain1\bwhite',
```

The '`update_one`' argument links the specified user to a new login. This stored procedure also accepts the arguments '`report`' to list the users and their respective logins, and '`auto_fix`', which attempts to link the users with a login of the same name. This can be useful when transferring a database to a different server. The utility does a best match, so check the results to ensure you achieved the desired results.

Managing Database Roles

Besides adding logins and users to fixed server and database roles, managing roles involves creating roles to organize your users, and group application permissions.

Using Enterprise Manager

In Enterprise Manager, database roles are created in the Roles folder of the database. After roles are created, they are managed from the Property page of the role. To create a role, right-click Roles, and select New Database Role, as shown in Figure 15.8.

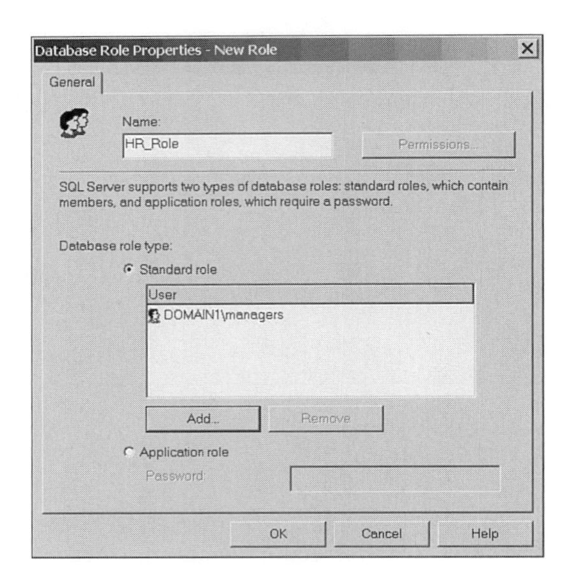

FIGURE 15.8 The New Database Role dialog box.

Enter a name for the role. If it is a standard role, you can add users to the role at this time if you want. If you select to create an application role, provide a password. Click OK and you are finished. As when creating users, permissions can't be applied until after the role is created.

Using T-SQL

Four stored procedures are used to manage roles with T-SQL. Table 15.4 lists the role-stored procedures.

TABLE 15.4 Stored Procedures for Managing Roles

Stored Procedure	Function
sp_addrole	Add a SQL Server role
sp_droprole	Drop a SQL Server role
sp_addrolemember	Add a SQL Server user to a role
sp_droprolemember	Drop a SQL Server user from a role

The syntax for adding a role called 'HR_Role', owned by 'dbo', is as follows:

```
EXEC sp_addrole 'HR_Role', 'dbo'
```

If you then wanted to add a user to that role, you could execute the following:

```
EXEC sp_addrolemember 'HR_Role', 'bobw'
```

The syntax for removing a role member and dropping the role is illustrated here:

```
EXEC sp_droprolemember 'HR_Role', 'bobw'
GO
EXEC sp_droprole 'HR_Role'
```

All role members must be dropped before the role can be dropped.

Managing SQL Server Permissions

Whether you are managing statement or object permissions, in Enterprise Manager or with T-SQL, all permission-management revolves around three commands: GRANT, REVOKE, and DENY. When a permission is granted, the user or role is given the permission to perform an action, such as creating a table. The sysprotects table keeps track of permissions, so when a GRANT command is issued, a row is added to sysprotects authorizing the action. The REVOKE command is the opposite; it deletes the associated line from sysprotects. This has the effect of removing the ability to perform the action. These permissions are cumulative, meaning that if Bob is in the sales role, and both Bob and the sales role have been granted delete permissions on the product table, Bob can delete rows from the table. If I then revoked the delete permission from Bob, he could still delete from the table, as he is in the sales role. This is where DENY fits in. If Bob must remain in the sales role, but you want to stop him from deleting records, you can DENY Bob the delete permission. Rather than deleting the row from sysprotects as the REVOKE command does, DENY changes the entry to disallow the action. If the user or any group or role with whom he is associated has a DENY entry for an action, that action is not allowed.

Managing SQL Server Statement Permissions

Statement permissions control the ability to manage objects in SQL Server. Generally, statement permissions are managed by adding users to fixed server and database roles. They can, however, also be managed on a statement-by-statement basis. An example of this might be to grant a developer the ability to create tables and views.

Using Enterprise Manager

Statement permissions are managed through the Permissions tab of the Database Properties page. A green check indicates a permission is granted, a blank box indicates the permission has not been granted or has been revoked (no entry exists in sysprotects), and a red X indicates that the permission is denied. The Permissions tab is shown in Figure 15.9.

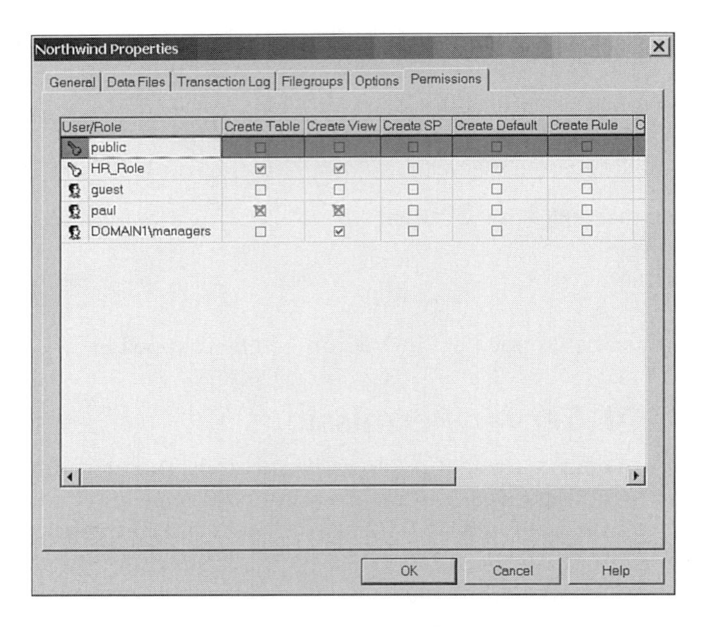

FIGURE 15.9 The Database Properties Permissions tab.

Using T-SQL

The syntax for the three T-SQL statement Permissions commands is as follows:

```
GRANT { ALL | statement [ ,...n ] }
TO {user|role} [ ,...n ]

DENY { ALL | statement [ ,...n ] }
TO {user|role} [ ,...n ]

REVOKE { ALL | statement [ ,...n ] }
FROM {user|role} [ ,...n ]
```

If `ALL` is specified, then all statement permissions are granted; otherwise, a single statement or comma-separated list can be specified. Likewise, the user or role can be single or multiple entries. The following are some examples of managing statement permissions:

```
GRANT ALL to HR_Role

GRANT CREATE TABLE to DEV_Role
```

```
REVOKE CREATE TABLE FROM HR_Role

DENY CREATE VIEW to bobw
```

Managing SQL Server Object Permissions

Object permissions or DML commands manage access to data. These are the permissions granted to users and roles to allow queries and changes in the database.

Using Enterprise Manager

Granting object permissions in Enterprise Manager can be done in one of two ways, depending on whether you want to approach permissions from a user or object perspective. From the user point of view, access the Properties page of the user or role and select Permissions. This brings up the Permissions tab, from which you can view the possible permissions on all objects, or select to view just the permissions assigned to the user or role. It is also possible to manage column-level permissions from here. Figure 15.10 shows the Permissions tab for a role.

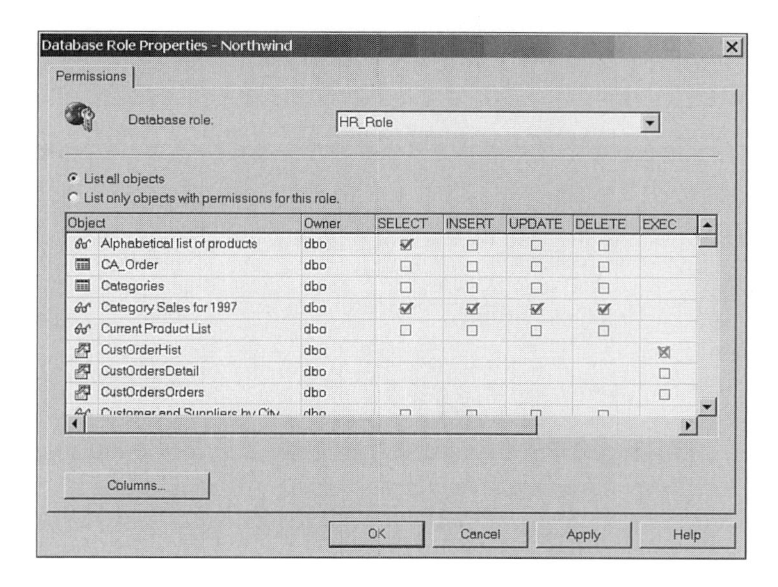

FIGURE 15.10 The Permission tab for a role.

The other approach to object permissions is from the object. From the Properties page of the object on which you want to manage permissions, select the Permissions button. This brings up the Permissions tab showing all permissions assigned to the object. Figure 15.11 shows the Permissions tab for the Categories table. Note that even though public (of which Paul is a member) has been granted delete permission, Paul will not be able to delete, as he has been denied.

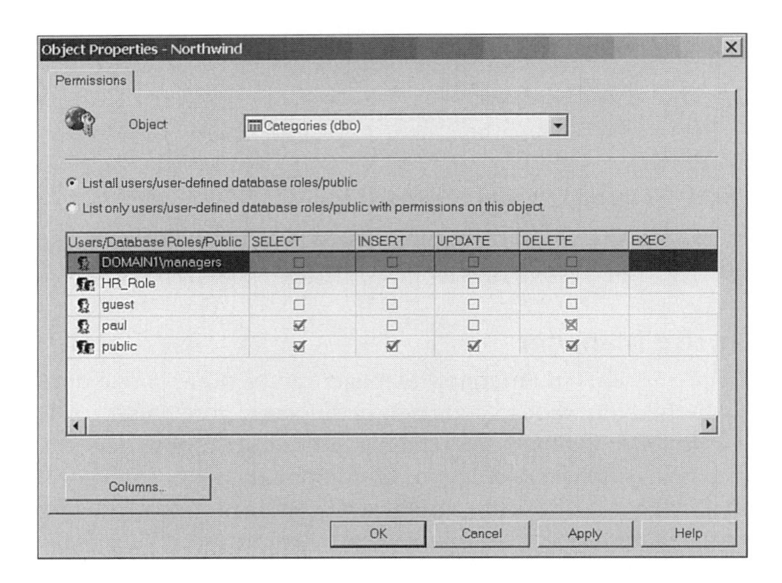

FIGURE 15.11 The Database Properties Permissions tab.

Using T-SQL

Many administrators find it easier to manage object permissions through T-SQL statements. The main advantage to this method is that if many changes need to be made, the changes can be scripted. Object permissions use an expanded version of the same syntax used to manage statement permissions. The following are some examples of statements used to manage object permissions.

To give Bill the ability to select, insert, and update data in the emp table, use the following:

```
GRANT SELECT, INSERT, UPDATE on EMP to bill
```

Following is the same statement; however, Bill can now grant the permissions to other users.

```
GRANT SELECT, INSERT, UPDATE on emp to bill  WITH GRANT OPTION
```

To `DENY` Bill the `UPDATE` permission, use the following:

```
DENY UPDATE on emp to bill
```

To remove a `DENY` from Bill (note that `REVOKE...to` is used as opposed to `REVOKE...from`), use the following:

```
REVOKE UPDATE on emp to bill
```

SQL Server Permission Approaches

Various approaches to managing permissions are available, depending on your application model and security needs. Except for databases with few users, you should try to manage permissions based on roles or groups. Managing permissions on a user-by-user basis is hard to keep track of and invariably leads to application problems and security issues.

Granting Permissions to Public

As all users are members of public, the simplest way to assign permissions common to all users is to assign them to public. This is usually only appropriate in development or on low security databases. Remember that if a guest account exists, then everyone with a SQL Server login will also be assigned any permissions granted to public. To `DENY` a permission to public denies all users.

Granting Permissions to User-Defined Roles

A common and flexible way to manage permissions is to create roles, assign the permissions to the roles, and then assign users to the roles. As roles can be assigned to roles as well, permissions can be nested, creating a module design.

Granting Permissions Using Views

Views can be used as a security layer between the users and the data. Rather than giving direct access to the tables, creating views and then assigning permissions to the views is another common practice. This also allows changes to the underlying tables without affecting the application, as long as the views present the same data to the application.

Granting Permissions Using Stored Procedures

Managing permissions through stored procedures works much the same way as through views. No permissions are assigned on the database objects—only on the stored procedures. This way, all access to the data must be through the procedures; additional functionality such as error testing can then be built into the stored procedures to protect the data.

Granting Permissions Using Application Roles

As discussed earlier, application roles protect the data by requiring a password, embedded in the application, to be handed over before the role's permissions are applied. This way, the only way a user can access the data is through the application, which can have various levels of protection built into it.

Object Owners

By default, only members of the sysadmin, db_owner, and db_ddladmin roles have the permission to create objects in the database. It is recommended that you keep it this way. When members of sysadmin create an object, it is created with dbo as the owner. Members of db_ddladmin and db_owner should specify dbo as the owner, or they will own the object. If an object is owned by dbo, it doesn't need to be referenced by a two-part name, as in dbo.table1. If users other than dbo own objects in the database, then the username must be included with the object name, as in bob.table1. Additional permission checking is also performed each time an object references an object owned by another user.

Changing Object Ownership

If an object is created with an owner other than dbo, then a system-stored procedure, sp_changeobjectowner, can change the owner. The statement to change an owner to dbo is as follows:

```
EXEC sp_changeobjectowner 'tablename' 'dbo'
```

Using Encryption

Managing access to SQL Server and the database objects controls who gets to the data on the server, but what about while it is being sent across the network? For sensitive data, you might have a need to encrypt the data during network transmissions. The Multiprotocol Net-Library supports encryption between the server and client; however, this is provided for backward compatibility only. Windows 2000 has introduced better methods of implementing network security.

Internet Protocol Security, or IPSec, is incorporated into Windows 2000 and allows secure network communication. If SQL Server has been issued a certificate from a Certificate Authority (CA), it can use Secure Sockets Layer (SSL) to encrypt data transmissions. See the Windows 2000 documentation or speak to your network administrators to see which of these options is best for your site.

Summary

This chapter looked at how SQL Server implements security through a combination of logins, users, roles, and permissions. You learned the difference between statement and object permissions and how to apply them using Enterprise Manager and T-SQL. The procedures are fairly straightforward, but careful thought must be taken when implementing a security model to avoid unauthorized access to data. If I can stress one thing about security, it is to always give only the most restrictive access possible. Giving users too high a permission level is often an accident waiting to happen. Remember: As administrator, it is you who will be left behind to clean up the accident scene. If you do run into problems, perhaps the next chapter, "Database Backup and Restore," will come in handy. A thorough understanding of SQL Server's backup and restore procedures are essential to managing your databases.

CHAPTER 16

Database Backup and Restore

by Paul Jensen

IN THIS CHAPTER

One of most important tasks associated with database management is that of performing backups. A **backup** is a full or partial copy of a database, which can be removed from the server environment for safekeeping. A **restore** is the process of applying a backup to return a database to a previous point in time. The restore process can also be used to transfer a database to a different location.

SQL Server 2000 builds on the backup and recovery framework introduced with Version 7.0. Enhancements to SQL Server 2000 backup and recovery include the introduction of **Recovery models**, which simplify balancing data loss against performance, named **log marks** in the transaction log to allow recovery to specific points of work, and the **partial** clause in the restore statement which allows a partial database restore to facilitate recovery of lost or corrupted database objects.

Developing a Backup and Restore Plan

The key to success in backup and recovery is a good backup plan. Take the time to carefully map out the methods you will use to back up, and your procedures for restore. You will be glad you did if disaster strikes. Factors that will affect your backup plan will include:

- The size of the database(s)
- The media to which you backup (Tape or disk? Local or network?)

- Database availability (9 to 5 or 7/24?)
- How data is loaded (Weekly data load or OLTP?)
- Your recovery window (How long will a restore take?)

After you have analyzed your backup needs, you can then implement a backup and recovery plan that is tailored to your environment. For instance, in a data warehouse populated by a weekly bulk load, it would be pointless to do hourly transaction log backups. On the other hand, this might be necessary for an Online Transaction Processing (OLTP) system that processes hundreds of orders an hour. The different backup methods will be discussed in detail in a subsequent section of this chapter.

Document, document, document. I can't emphasize this enough. It does no good for *you* to understand the recovery drill, if you are on vacation in Borneo when the database decides to crash. If you walk out the door right now and get hit by a bus (or perhaps get offered a better job in California) could the new administrator step in and restore your databases if there was a problem? If the answer is no, you don't have sufficient documentation.

Now you have a plan and you have scheduled backups; you're all done, right? Wrong! The plan is not complete until it has been tested. Never assume you will be able to restore data. Initial and ongoing tests of your recoverability are crucial. Find the flaws in your plan before you are in an actual recovery situation. Many companies incorporate scheduled or even surprise data restore exercises. These exercises not only test the recovery plan, but also allow system personnel to get used to the recovery drill without the stress added by an actual database outage.

Why Back Up Your Databases?

If you don't back up your databases, memorize this phrase: "Do you want fries with that?" It will come in handy in your new career.

In this age of reliable, redundant hardware the need for backups is often questioned. Unfortunately, redundant hardware only protects against the failure of that hardware. You can still experience data loss due to user or administrator error (yes, sooner or later even database gurus trash a database), corruption, malicious data destruction, or disasters such as fire. I like a backup plan that passes what I call the Scud Test. If a scud missile were to land in the server room, could you still restore the database? One sure way to answer yes to this question is to have valid backups, *stored offsite*. It is surprising how many mission critical databases do not pass this test. You can substitute fire, theft, flood, or earthquake for the scud missile; pick the one that applies to your locale!

A Typical Backup and Restore Scenario

To illustrate a typical backup and restore scenario, let's look at the fictitious Northwind Trading Company. Northwind is an international company supplying a wide variety of food products to stores across the globe. Because of the different time zones, order personnel staff the phones 24 hours a day, 7 days a week. Grocery retailers call in their orders, they are entered into the database, and then that data is used to fill, ship, and bill the order. As all inventory, orders, and billing information is stored in the database it is considered mission critical. In other words: No database, no Northwind Trading Company. Therefore, a backup plan is in order.

In your analysis of the database, you discover a few key points. The server is configured with two disks. Drive C contains the OS and the SQL Server 2000 installation, and drive D holds the Northwind database and transaction log (not an ideal disk configuration, but you will have to deal with that another day). As the database must be available 24/7, you will perform online backups. You test a backup and discover it takes just under three hours to do a full backup. Querying the order entry staff, you discover that although orders come in around the clock, there is a slow period as the day traverses the Pacific Ocean. This lasts from 1:00 a.m. until 6:00 a.m. local time. With this information, you decide to do a nightly backup at 1:00 a.m. With this plan you can always restore the database to the state it was in at the time the backup completed.

The manager of the order entry department brings to your attention that in this scenario, if the database were to fail at the end of the business day, and the database was restored with the nightly backup, the amount of orders lost would be ruinous to the company. Further questioning reveals that, on average, the amount of orders processed in an hour could be recovered manually by having the data entry people work overtime to call their clients back. Armed with this information, you decide to implement a transaction log backup every hour on the hour. Now you can recover the database up until the time of the last backed up log. Actually, if the current log is not damaged, you could back it up and recover right up until the time of failure!

The following week, at 3:33 p.m. on Tuesday, the database crashes. Your investigation reveals that drive D (remember the one with all the data and transaction logs?) has failed. You replace drive D and restart the system. Because the active transaction log was on this disk, it is unrecoverable, so you will lose all transactions from the time you did the last log backup (3:00 p.m.) and when you crashed (3:33 p.m.). You now proceed to restore the full backup from that morning, and apply all transaction log backups taken since the full backup. When you bring the database on line it is current to 3:00 p.m., and the order entry people get busy calling back clients who placed orders after that time. Some customers understand and reorder; however others are quite irate and vow to deal with Acme Trading Company in the future.

The following morning at the "Post Mortem" meeting, when you finish patting your back for a job well done, the Accounting Manager informs you that one of the customers who went away mad was also your largest customer. He wants to know how you could have done a better recovery. The issue is the loss of the orders between 03:00 p.m. and the time of failure. Had you separated the transaction log file from the data files, by placing it on a separate drive (costing less than $1,000), you could have backed up the current log before you did the restore. This would have given you the ability to recover up until the time of failure. Had the data files and logs been on mirrored drives, the failure would not have affected production at all. The accounting manager approves the purchase of new disks on the spot!

Types of Backups

SQL Server 2000 supports four main types of backups:

- Full Database Backup
- Differential Database Backup
- File and Filegroup Backup
- Transaction Log Backup

Full Database Backup

Full Database Backup creates a consistent image of the database up to the point that the database backup finished. SQL Server 2000 does this by noting the Log Sequence Number (LSN) at the start of a backup. An LSN is a number assigned to each record written to the log, to keep track of changes. It then copies the extents that make up the database (an extent is a block of eight pages—for more information on extents and database storage structures, see Chapter 33, "SQL Server Internals"). As this is a dynamic backup it allows changes to the data while the backup is running. How then would you get a consistent image of the data? Simple. When the extents are all backed up, SQL Server again notes the LSN. It now also backs up the part of the log between the first LSN and the last LSN it recorded. It then appends this "log piece" to the backup. When the backup is restored, the extents are restored, and this log piece is applied, essentially playing back all changes that occurred during the backup. Of course the more changes there are during the backup, the larger this log piece will be. This will affect both backup and restore times, so it is still prudent to schedule backups for periods of low activity.

Differential Database Backup

Differential Database Backup was introduced in Version 7.0. A differential backup backs up all extents that have changed since the last full backup. As only changed extents are backed up, the differential backup is usually substantially smaller than a full backup. This is a major factor in allowing SQL Server to scale to Very Large Databases (VLDB). A full backup must be restored before a differential backup is restored, but only the last differential needs to be restored. Consider a scenario where a full backup is done Saturday night, and a differential is done each subsequent night. If the database fails Friday, you would restore the full backup, and the differential from Thursday night. Apply any log backups done after the differential backup and you're back in business.

File and Filegroup Backup

File and Filegroup Backup is another feature designed with the VLDB in mind. Databases can be backed up file-by-file, or alternatively, filegroup-by-filegroup. Therefore, a 500GB database consisting of five 100GB files could have file1 backed up Monday, file2 Tuesday, and so on. This allows backups to be done in a much smaller window. The restrictions on file and filegroup backups are that if tables and their indexes are stored on separate files or filegroups (this is sometimes done for performance reasons) these must be backed up and restored together, and you must be doing transaction log backups. In both full and differential restore scenarios, the full database had to be restored first. In a file restore, only the damaged file needs to be restored. This can be a huge time saver in a large database. Why restore the entire database when only one file is damaged? Of course the restored file will now be out of sync with the rest of the database. This is why you must have the log backups, including a backup of the log that was active at the time of failure. You restore the file, and then apply all transaction logs taken after the file backup. This brings that file into sync with the rest of the database.

> **NOTE**
>
> You don't have to be doing file or filegroup backups, to take advantage of file level restores. Files and file groups can be restored from full backups as well. Before you rush into a full restore due to media failure, assess what has been damaged. If you have data spread over many disks, but only one disk is damaged, it could be substantially faster to just restore the lost files.

Transaction Log Backup

Transaction Log Backup copies the transactions in the transaction log and then deletes all but the active portion of the log to free up space. As the transaction log is a serial record of all transactions since the last log backup, the log backups can be applied during the restore process to bring the database forward to the point of failure. When you are performing log backups, you can also restore from the log backups to a specific point in time. When a transaction log has been backed up, it is then truncated. This clears the inactive transactions from the log, allowing room for additional transactions. This truncation keeps the log from filling up, or from growing too large if the log is set to automatically grow the file.

Recovery Models

New to SQL Server 2000 are recovery models. You can select a recovery model for each database in SQL Server 2000 to determine how your data is backed up and what your exposure to data loss is. The three types of recovery models available are as follows:

- Full
- Bulk_logged
- Simple

Full Recovery

Full recovery provides the least risk of losing data due to media failure or user or application error. It also provides the most flexibility in restore operations. Full recovery is implemented with a combination of full database backups and transaction log backups. Optionally, differential and file level backups can be performed. Full recovery permits the restoration of a database to a specific point in time. To allow this, all operations are fully logged, including `SELECT INTO`, `BULK INSERT`, `bcp`, and `CREATE INDEX`. The downside to the full recovery model is that this additional logging can cause the transaction log to be much larger.

Bulk_logged Recovery

Bulk_logged recovery also allows for complete restoration of a database and provides improved performance for bulk operations while consuming less log space. In bulk_logged recovery, bulk operations are only minimally logged, providing better performance during the bulk operation. However, point in time recovery is not supported if a transaction log file contains bulk operations. The entire log must be recovered. As mentioned before, the lower logging level might result in less log space being consumed, but if a bulk operation has occurred since the last full or differential backup, the log *backup* can be quite large. This is due to the fact that in the log only *creation* of extents by bulk operations is recorded. When the log is backed up, the actual extents are appended to the log backup to ensure recoverability. The good news is that you can switch back and forth from full to bulk_logged mode. This means you can run in full recovery mode, and switch to bulk_logged to speed up bulk operations.

NOTE

Prior to SQL Server 2000, `SELECT INTO` and bulk copy (minimum logging) could be performed only if the *select into/bulk copy option* was set to true. After a bulk operation had been performed, transaction log backup was disabled. This could cause automated log backup jobs to fail. This is no longer an issue, as SQL Server 2000 supports bulk operations in any mode, as well as supporting transaction log backups in both full and bulk_logged recovery modes.

Simple Recovery

Simple recovery presents the most basic backup and recovery model. In simple recovery the transaction log is regularly truncated, and therefore not available for backup. When in simple recovery mode the backup plan is restricted to full database and differential backups. Recovery to the point of failure, and point in time recovery are not supported. As all data input after the last full or differential backup must be recovered manually, the simple recovery model is not suitable for most production databases. Exceptions are databases that have few updates, and databases where the data is bulk loaded on a scheduled basis. Many decision-support databases fall into this category. If a full backup can be done after each data load, or if the source data remains available, allowing the load to be repeated, simple recovery mode might suffice.

Setting the Recovery Mode

The recovery mode can be set using the `SET` clause of the `ALTER DATABASE` statement, the `sp_dboption` system stored procedure, or Enterprise Manager. To see which mode your database is in you can use Enterprise Manager (Database Properties, Options), or the `DATABASEPROPERTYEX()` property function:

```
SELECT DATABASEPROPERTYEX('<databasename>', 'recovery')
```

> **NOTE**
>
> The simple and bulk_logged recovery modes are intended to replace the SQL 7.0 *`trunc. log on chkpt.`* and *`select into/bulk copy`* options, respectively. However, *`select into/bulk copy`* and *`trunc. log on chkpt.`* can still be set using the *`sp_dboption`* stored procedure, but this will affect the recovery mode. For example, setting *`trunc. log on chkpt.`* to true would set the database into simple recovery mode. If both *`trunc. log on chkpt.`* and *`select into/bulk copy`* options are set, the lower recovery model, simple, takes precedence.

Backup Devices

A backup device is created to provide a storage destination for backups. SQL Server 2000 supports both permanent and temporary backup devices. Permanent backup devices are pre-created, named devices, which can serve as backup devices for multiple backups. Temporary backup devices are specified in the backup statement itself, and are intended for one-time use. Backups are supported to file, tape, and named pipes.

Tape Devices

To state the obvious, tape devices are used to back up to tape. Tape devices must be directly connected to the server, and parallel backups to multiple drives are supported to increase throughput. Tape backups have the advantage of being scalable, portable, and secure. Scalability is important as your database grows. Available disk space often precludes the use of disk backups for large databases. Because tapes are removable media they are easily transported offsite, where they can be secured against theft and damage.

SQL Server supports the Microsoft Tape Format (MTF) for backup devices. This means that SQL Server backups and NT/Windows 2000 backups can share the same tape. This is convenient for small sites with shared use servers and only one tape drive. You can schedule your SQL Server backups and file backups without having to be onsite to change the tape.

Disk Devices

Disk devices consist of a file, generally stored in a folder on a local hard drive. This should not be the same hard drive that your data is stored on! Disk devices have several advantages, including speed and reliability. If you have ever had a backup fail because you forgot to load a tape (come on, admit it), you can appreciate disk backups. On the other hand, if backups are done to a local disk, and the server is destroyed (remember the Scud Test?) you lose your backups as well. Microsoft recognized this issue and SQL Server 2000 allows the use of both mapped network drives and UNC paths in the backup device filename. This allows you to back up to a disk on a remote machine. However, this should be a dedicated or high-speed network connection, and verification of the backup should be done to avoid potential corruption introduced by network error. The time it takes a backup to complete over the network depends on network traffic, so take this into consideration when planning your backups.

NOTE

In a lab test, backing up a 15MB test database to a disk on another server, using a dedicated 10Mbps Ethernet connection, took 47.241 seconds. Compare that to 4.766 seconds backing up to a local disk. This means the database was in backup mode *ten times longer* when backing up over the network.

Disk or Tape?

So which should you use, disk or tape? Traditionally, backups have been done to tape. Although tape is more secure than disk, the main disadvantage of using tape for backups is that it's slower to back up and restore from tape than from disk. Tapes generally require more "hands on" management to load and unload the appropriate tapes for backups or restores.

In the past, the main disadvantage of using disk storage for backups was it was prohibitively expensive, and still might be for many VLDBs. However, the increased availability of inexpensive, fast, reliable, high capacity disks has changed that, and many sites are now adapting a disk backup strategy. But what about the Scud Test? How do you protect the disk backups?

Here's a strategy that leverages the advantages of both disk and tape backups. Schedule your backups, using SQL Server's Backup utility, to back up your databases to disk devices on the local system. If you need high speed or large storage capacity, set up a RAID 0 array to store the backups on. No fault tolerance you say? That's the next step. After your backups have run, the files on the backup device are "cold" files, they have no physical ties to SQL Server, so the database can now go about its business. The backup has been done in the fastest amount of time with the minimum possible disruption. Now, schedule your network file backup utility to back up these files to its remote storage location. Make sure to leave a buffer time between when your SQL Server backups usually complete, and when the network schedule picks them up. When you can verify the network backup was successful, you can delete the local backups to free up storage, if required. You now have fast, scheduled, reliable backups, with offsite redundancy. And that's a good thing.

TIP

You might want to keep the local backup files on disk around until the next backup is performed in the event you need to recover the database. You can restore and have the database online much faster if the backup files are still on disk, rather than having to restore them from tape first.

Named Pipe Devices

Named pipe devices are included in SQL Server 2000 to support third-party backup tools. Named pipe devices are typically used when backing up to remote tape storage systems. See your vendor's documentation for further information.

NOTE

If you decide to use a SQL Server dynamic backup plug-in for your network backup utility instead of a plan such as the one outlined earlier, make sure you test your restores. There are lots of horror stories out there about un-restorable third party backups. Also, the cost of the plug-in is often more than the cost of a few extra disks.

Multiple Devices

To facilitate support for large databases SQL Server supports backing up to multiple devices. This is referred to as a parallel or striped backup. This can significantly reduce your backup and restore times, as the backup is written to multiple devices simultaneously. When backing up to multiple devices all devices must be the same media type and can't be mixed with another type of backup. After a device is used for a parallel backup, that device is considered part of a backup set, and can't be used for other backups unless they, too, stripe across the same set of devices, or the member is reformatted. If you reformat any member of a backup set the data in the remaining members is unusable. Both permanent and temporary backup devices can be part of a backup set. For example, the following syntax could be used to back up to multiple permanent devices:

```
BACKUP DATABASE northwind TO nwback1, nwback2, nwback3
```

Media Sets and Families

When backing up to multiple devices, the terms **media set** and **media family** are used to describe the components of the backup. A media family is all of the media used by a single device. For example, a backup set consists of four tape devices, and each device requires five tapes to be loaded to complete the backup. All five tapes used by tape drive one are considered a backup family. The first tape in the family is referred to as the **initial** media, and the subsequent tapes are referred to as **continuation** media. All of the media families combined are referred to as the **media set**. Therefore, in the preceding example, the media set would consist of 20 tapes. It is recommended to use the `MEDIANAME` parameter of the backup command to specify a name for the media set. This associates the multiple devices as members of the media set. The `MEDIANAME` can then be referenced in future backup operations.

Creating Backup Devices with Transact-SQL

To create permanently defined backup devices in T-SQL, use the system stored procedure `sp_addumpdevice`. The name of this procedure is a throwback to pre–Version 7.0 days, when a backup device was referred to as a dump device, and taking a backup was referred to as taking a dump. I kid you not.

The required syntax is

```
sp_addumpdevice 'devtype', 'logical_name', 'physical_name'
```

Where '`devtype`' is one of '`disk`' '`tape`' or '`pipe`', '`logical_name`' is the name that will be used to refer to this device, and `'physical_name'` is the actual path to the file or tape device.

For example:

To create a disk backup device named NWbackup:

```
USE master
EXEC sp_addumpdevice 'disk', 'NWbackup', 'D:\backups\NWbackup.bak'
```

To create a tape backup device named Nwtapebackup:

```
USE master
EXEC sp_addumpdevice 'tape', ' Nwtapebackup ', '\\.\tape0'
```

Named dump devices are handy for tape backups as it allows you to substitute an easily remembered, logical name for a tape device. For disk backups, unless you plan to reuse the same disk file over and over, you can simply specify a temporary backup device in the `BACKUP` command by specifying the full pathname to the backup file. Here's the syntax for a backup using a temporary device:

```
BACKUP DATABASE northwind TO DISK = 'D:\backups\Nwtemp.bak'
```

> **NOTE**
>
> After you run the sp_addumpdevice stored procedure, don't panic when you go looking for the physical files on disk and can't find them. The files aren't created until the first time you actually use the backup device.
>
> Also, the physical pathname to the dump file is not validated until the first time you use the backup device. If a bad pathname is entered when creating the dump device, you will receive an error message similar to the following when attempting to back up to it:
>
> ```
> Server: Msg 3201, Level 16, State 1, Line 1
> Cannot open backup device 'mydump'. Device error or device off-line.
>  See the SQL Server error log for more details.
> ```

Another advantage of using temporary backup devices when backing up to disk is that you can dynamically build the backup filename. This is often done to include a timestamp in the backup filename to indicate exactly when the backup was initiated, and to keep from overwriting or appending the backup to an existing file. The following stored procedure demonstrates an example of this approach, creating a backup filename in the format of *dbname*_db_*YYMMDDHHMM.bak*:

```
create proc sp_SSU_backup_db (@dbname varchar(30), @backupdir
➥varchar(128) = 'C:\MSSQL2000\BACKUP')
as

set nocount on    -- suppress display of rowcounts
set concat_null_yields_null off  -- prevent concatenating nulls to string
from returning null

exec ('use master')        -- run commands from within master database

declare @starttime datetime,
        @endtime datetime,
        @hours int,
        @minutes int,
        @seconds int,
        @backupdev varchar(4000)

-- First, validate the backup directory
create TABLE #fileexist (file_exists int, file_dir int, parent_dir int)

insert #fileexist exec xp_fileexist @backupdir

if (select file_dir from #fileexist) != 1
```

```
begin
    raiserror ('Invalid backup directory specified', 16, 1)
    return -101
end

print '#########################################################################
➥#######'
print '### Begin backing up ' + @dbname + ' database' + space(48 - datalength
➥(@dbname)) + '###'
select @starttime = getdate()
print '### backup of ' + @dbname + ' started at ' + convert (varchar(30),
➥@starttime, 9)
         + space(25 - datalength(@dbname)) + '###'

select @backupdir = rtrim (@backupdir)

-- trim off the backslash (/) if included as you will be adding it in anyway
if substring(reverse(@backupdir), 1, 1) = '\'
    select @backupdir = substring(@backupdir, 1, datalength(@backupdir) - 1)

--Build backup filename in format of dbname_db_YYYYMMDDHHMM.bak
select @backupdev = @backupdir + '\' + @dbname + '_db_'
      + convert(char(8), getdate(), 112)                        --append YYYYMMDD
      + substring(convert(char(8), getdate(), 108), 1, 2)       --append Hour
      + substring(convert(char(8), getdate(), 108), 4, 2)       --append minutes
      + '.bak'

print '### backing up database ' + @dbname + ' to ' + @backupdev
      + space (50 - datalength(@dbname) - datalength(@backupdev)) + '###'

print '#########################################################################
➥#######'

backup database @dbname to DISK = @backupdev with nounload, init, skip

select @endtime = getdate()
print '#########################################################################
➥#######'
print '### backup of ' + @dbname + ' finished at ' + convert (varchar(30),
➥@endtime, 9)
       + space(24 - datalength(@dbname)) + '###'
print '###
➥     ###'
```

```
select @hours = datediff(ms, @starttime, @endtime)/3600000
select @minutes = (datediff (ms, @starttime, @endtime) / 60000 ) % 60
select @seconds = (datediff (ms, @starttime, @endtime) / 1000 ) % 60
print '### Time to complete: ' + str(@hours, 2, 0) + ' hours, '
      + str(@minutes, 2, 0) + ' minutes, '
      + str(@seconds, 2, 0) + ' seconds                    ###'

print '######################################################################
➥#######'
print ''
print ''

return
```

You can also use the extended stored procedure `xp_sqlmaint` to produce the same results. This stored procedure calls sqlmaint.exe, and is the basis for jobs created by the Database Maintenance Plan Wizard. The following example creates a backup of the Northwind database in the default backup directory with a filename Northwind_db_YYYYMMDDHHMM.BAK:

```
EXEC master.dbo.xp_sqlmaint
'-D Northwind -BkUpMedia DISK -BkUpDB  -UseDefDir  -BkExt "BAK"'
```

16

Creating Backup Devices with SQL Enterprise Manager

For those who prefer to work with the GUI, Enterprise Manager can also be used to create backup devices. Expand the Management node in Enterprise Manager, right-click Backup, and select New Backup Device from the pop-up menu. This invokes the Backup Device Properties – New Device dialog box, which is shown in Figure 16.1.

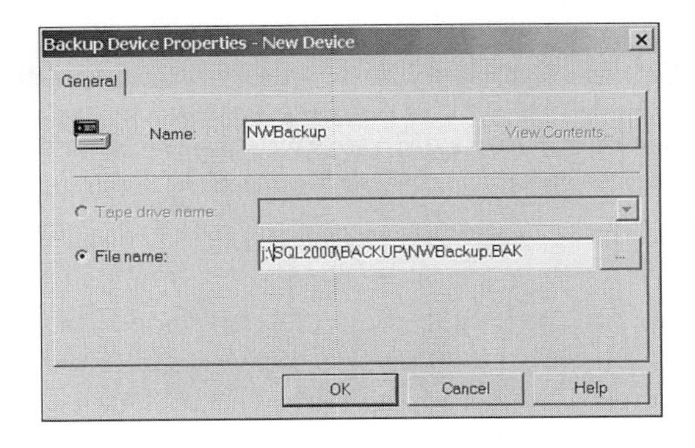

FIGURE 16.1 The new device properties box.

This dialog box allows you to specify a logical name and physical location for the device. Unless you have a valid tape device attached to the server, the tape device name option will be unavailable.

This dialog box is also available from the SQL Server Backup dialog box. Select Backup Database from the tools menu, or right-click a database and select All Tasks, Backup Database. This brings up the SQL Server Backup dialog box. Under destination, click Add, select Backup Device, and choose New Backup Device from the drop-down box.

Backing Up the Database

Having discussed backup types, models, and creating devices, it's time now to look at the actual backup commands. Never has an Enterprise-level Database Management System backup been easier to implement. You can use Transact-SQL commands stored in scripts to do your backups, or Enterprise Manager, which will allow you to set up one-time backups or scheduled backups with just a few clicks. SQL Agent can also be configured to perform backups due to performance conditions and alerts, and there is a Database Maintenance Plan Wizard that steps you through setting up and scheduling your backups.

> **NOTE**
>
> For more information on the SQL Agent and the Maintenance Plan Wizard, see Chapters 17, "Database Maintenance," and 18, "SQL Server Scheduling and Notification."

Backing Up Databases with T-SQL

The `BACKUP DATABASE` command (oddly enough) is used to back up a database. To initiate a full database backup to a permanent backup device the statement would be:

```
BACKUP DATABASE northwind TO nwbackup
```

> **NOTE**
>
> In versions of SQL Server prior to Version 7.0, backups were performed using the `DUMP` command. This command is still supported for backward compatibility purposes, but should be replaced with the `BACKUP` command as the `DUMP` command will likely not be supported in future versions of SQL Server.

Now that I've eased you into the backup command, let's look at the full syntax. Don't worry. It's not as bad as it looks, and I'll provide some examples later with the most commonly used commands. Listing 16.1 shows the `BACKUP DATABASE` syntax.

LISTING 16.1 Complete Syntax for BACKUP DATABASE

```
BACKUP DATABASE { database_name | @database_name_var }
    [< file_or_filegroup > [ ,...n ] ]
TO < backup_device > [ ,...n ]
[ WITH
    [ BLOCKSIZE = { blocksize | @blocksize_variable } ]
    [ [ , ] DESCRIPTION = { 'text' | @text_variable } ]
    [ [ , ] DIFFERENTIAL ]
    [ [ , ] EXPIREDATE = { date | @date_var }
        | RETAINDAYS = { days | @days_var } ]
    [ [ , ] PASSWORD = { password | @password_variable } ]
    [ [ , ] FORMAT | NOFORMAT ]
    [ [ , ] { INIT | NOINIT } ]
    [ [ , ] MEDIADESCRIPTION = { 'text' | @text_variable } ]
    [ [ , ] MEDIANAME = { media_name | @media_name_variable } ]
    [ [ , ] MEDIAPASSWORD = { mediapassword | @mediapassword_variable } ]
    [ [ , ] NAME = { backup_set_name | @backup_set_name_var } ]
    [ [ , ] { NOSKIP | SKIP } ]
    [ [ , ] { NOREWIND | REWIND } ]
    [ [ , ] { NOUNLOAD | UNLOAD } ]
    [ [ , ] RESTART ]
    [ [ , ] STATS [ = percentage ] ]
]
}
< backup_device > ::=
    {
        { logical_backup_device_name | @logical_backup_device_name_var }
        |
        { DISK | TAPE } =
            { 'physical_backup_device_name' | @physical_backup_device_name_var }
    }
< file_or_filegroup > ::=
    {
        FILE = { logical_file_name | @logical_file_name_var }
        |
        FILEGROUP = { logical_filegroup_name | @logical_filegroup_name_var }
    }
```

TABLE 16.1 Detailed Description of Each of the Preceding Parameters

Parameter	Description
BLOCKSIZE	The physical block size specified in bytes. SQL Server will choose a block size that is appropriate to the device if one is not specified.
DESCRIPTION	A text description of the backup set.
DIFFERENTIAL	This indicates that this is to be a differential backup.
EXPIREDATE	Specifies a date, at which time the backup can be overwritten.
RETAINDAYS	Similar to `EXPIREDATE`, the number of days the backup is retained before it can be overwritten.
PASSWORD	Specifies a password for the backup set. If defined, the password must be supplied to perform a restore.
FORMAT I NOFORMAT	`FORMAT` overwrites the backup device and media header. This will render the entire media set unusable, so use caution. `FORMAT` implies skip and init. `NOFORMAT` does not rewrite the media header, and does not rewrite the backup device, unless `INIT` is also specified.
INIT I NOINIT	Specifies whether the backup will be appended (`NOINIT`) to the device or overwrite existing backups (`INIT`).
MEDIADESCRIPTION	A text description of the entire media set.
MEDIANAME	This labels your media set. This name can then be referenced in a restore operation.
MEDIAPASSWORD	Specifies a password for the media set. If defined, the password must be supplied to perform a restore.
NAME	A name for the backup set.
NOSKIP I SKIP	Indicates whether to read (`NOSKIP`) or ignore (`SKIP`) ANSI tape labels. The default is `NOSKIP`.
NOREWIND I REWIND	Indicates whether to rewind the tape.
NOUNLOAD I UNLOAD	Indicates whether to unload the tape.
RESTART	Saves time by restarting an interrupted backup at the point it was interrupted.
STATS	A percentage can be specified to gauge progress of the backup. If not specified, a message is displayed in 10% increments.

As promised, Listings 16.2, 16.3, and 16.4 provide some `BACKUP DATABASE` examples.

LISTING 16.2 Sample Script for a Full Backup

```
-- Backup to a permanent backup device. Don't  unload the tape.
-- Provide a name and description for the backup
USE MASTER
BACKUP DATABASE Northwind TO NWbackup
WITH
NOUNLOAD,
NAME = 'Northwind full database backup',
DESCRIPTION = 'Full backup for Wednesday'
```

LISTING 16.3 Sample Script for a Differential Backup

```
-- Backup to a temporary backup device
-- Perform a differential backup
USE MASTER
BACKUP DATABASE Northwind TO DISK = 'D:\backup\NWtemp.bak'
WITH DIFFERENTIAL
```

LISTING 16.4 Sample Script for a Full Backup to Multiple Devices

```
-- Perform a striped backup to 3 permanent devices.
-- Name the backup and provide a Description.
-- Format the media and name the media set.
USE MASTER
BACKUP DATABASE Northwind
TO NWStripe1, NWStripe2, NWStripe3
WITH
NAME = 'Northwind full backup',
DESCRIPTION = 'Striped to three devices',
FORMAT,  MEDIANAME = 'NWSTRIPE'
```


Transact-SQL provides a powerful command interface to back up SQL Server databases. The T-SQL commands can be saved as scripts to provide easily repeatable backup operations. In the next section you'll look at using Enterprise Manager to perform backups. Enterprise Manager uses a GUI interface to generate and schedule backups.

Backing Up Databases with SQL Enterprise Manager

With Enterprise Manager, Microsoft has made performing backups as easy as a couple of mouse clicks. You're probably thinking if it's that easy, it can't be good. Nothing could be farther from the truth. All the Enterprise Manager does is write the `BACKUP DATABASE` statement for you (without the typos), allows you to run the backup immediately, or saves it as a job and provides a scheduler to run it. After a backup has been saved in this way, you can edit the job at any time to change its parameters.

As with most things in Enterprise Manager there are several ways to perform a backup. If you are using Taskpad View (select View, Taskpad), hovering over the Maintenance arrow provides a drop-down list, from which you can select backup database. This screen is shown in Figure 16.2.

You can also select Backup Database from the Tools menu. Failing that, right-click the Backup icon under management. Or, my personal favorite, right-click the database you want to back up, select All Tasks from the pop-up menu, and then select Backup Database. Any of these actions will bring up the SQL Server Backup dialog box, which is what you are after. This dialog box is illustrated in Figure 16.3.

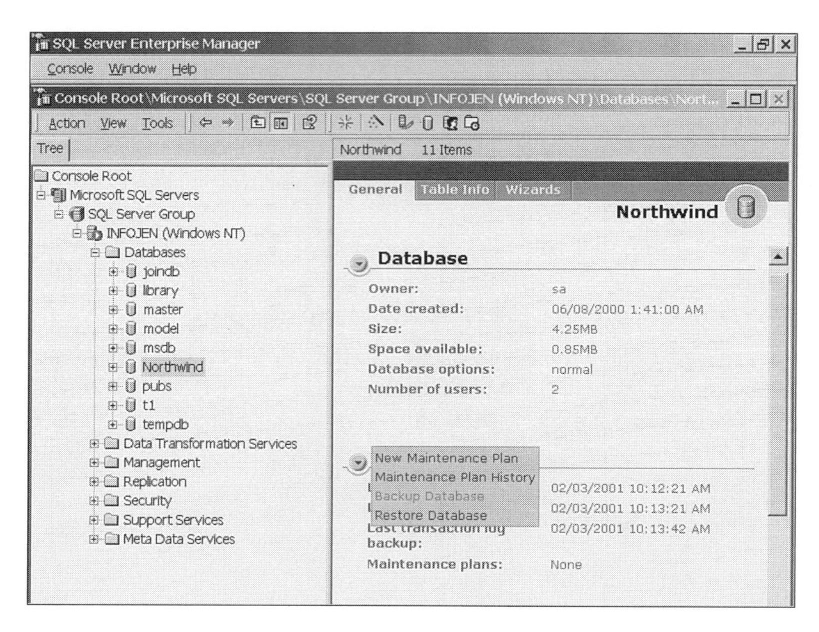

FIGURE 16.2 The Task Pad Maintenance List.

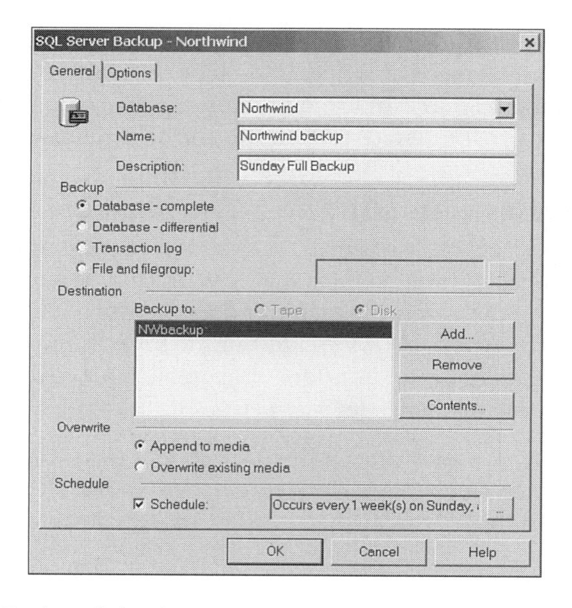

FIGURE 16.3 The Backup dialog box.

From this dialog box, you can back up databases (full and differential), files and filegroups, and transaction logs. You even have the option of creating backup devices if you haven't yet done so. With the exception of the `BLOCKSIZE` parameter, all `BACKUP DATABASE` options are presented. Scheduling backups is as easy as checking the Schedule box, and then selecting the ellipse beside the schedule window. Enter your desired schedule, and when you click OK to exit the dialog box, the backup will be saved as a job under SQL Server Agent. Figure 16.4 shows the location of scheduled backup jobs.

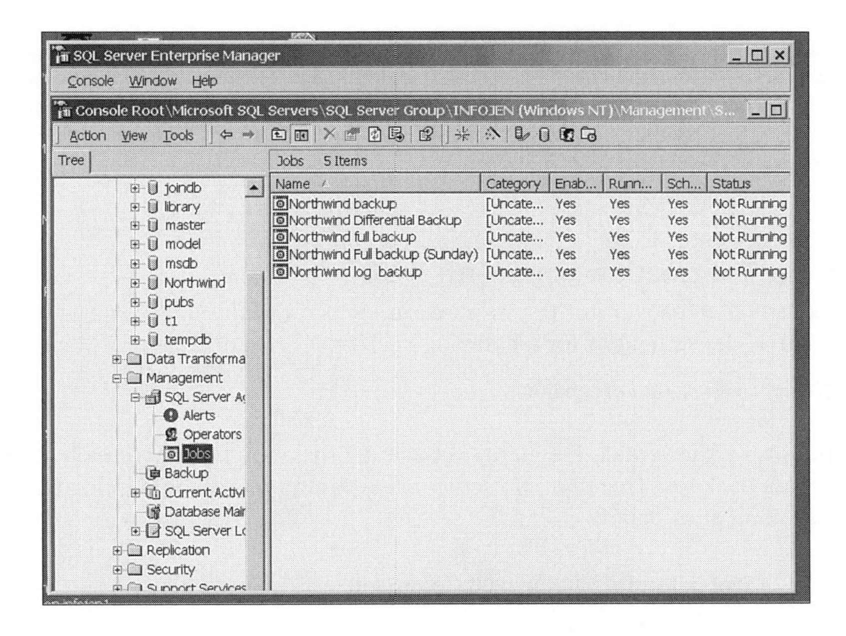

FIGURE 16.4 Scheduled backup jobs.

Double-clicking any of these backup jobs allows you to edit any of the parameters you saved when the job was created. You can even access the `BACKUP DATABASE` script.

I recommend you play a bit with this interface creating various types of backups and examining the scripts each generates. This is a surefire way to quickly become proficient at the syntax for backing up SQL Server databases.

> **NOTE**
>
> If you hate memorizing syntax and need a quick way to write backup scripts (without syntax errors), create a backup job with Enterprise Manager, edit the job it generates, and cut-and-paste the `BACKUP DATABASE` command into your script.

16

Backing Up the Transaction Log

As SQL Server must write all transactions to the transaction log, backing up the log is crucial. Not only does this permit recovery of these transactions, the act of backing up the log also truncates, or clears out, the inactive portion of the log. This allows room for further transactions. The log can be set to auto grow, but this should not be relied on, because if it's unchecked it can fill all available disk space, and can be problematic to shrink back to a reasonable size.

NOTE

In simple recovery mode SQL Server periodically truncates the log without backing it up. Any transactions that are thus purged are unrecoverable. Transaction log backups are not available in this mode.

Backing Up Transaction Logs with T-SQL

The syntax for T-SQL backups of the transaction log is quite similar to that of database backups. Here is the statement for a basic log backup:

```
BACKUP LOG northwind TO Nwlogbackup
```

Listing 16.5 shows the syntax. For clarity, I have removed the options already covered under database backups. There are, however, a few parameters specific to log backups that are worth looking at in detail.

LISTING 16.5 Syntax for the `BACKUP LOG` Command

```
BACKUP LOG { database_name | @database_name_var }

    TO < backup_device > [ ,...n ]
    [ WITH
        [ { NO_LOG | TRUNCATE_ONLY } ]
         [ [ , ] NO_TRUNCATE ]
        [ [ , ] { NORECOVERY | STANDBY = undo_file_name } ]
    ]
}
```

`NO_LOG` and `TRUNCATE_ONLY`

Although part of the `BACKUP LOG` command, `NO_LOG` and `TRUNCATE_ONLY` don't actually back up the log. The two are synonymous so I'll just refer to `NO_LOG` for the sake of simplicity. The purpose of `BACKUP LOG`, when used in conjunction with `NO_LOG`, is to clear, or truncate, the inactive portion of the log. Log truncations actually occur at the *end* of *every* BACKUP LOG command. And therein, as they say, lies the rub. SQL Server 2000 is a **write-ahead** Relational Database Management System (RDBMS), so every transaction must be written first to the transaction log. The bad news is, BACKUP LOG is a transaction and therefore must first be written to the log. If you are trying to back up your log because it is full, the BACKUP LOG command fails, because it can't write to a full log. This would be a catch-22 situation if not for NO_LOG. When you use this option, you are basically telling SQL Server to skip the write to the log, skip backing up the log, and just trash the inactive portion of the log to clear some space. Because the transactions committed in this portion of the log are now unrecoverable, it is strongly suggested that you perform a full database backup after using BACKUP LOG WITH NO_LOG. Mark this page. When your log fills up someday and grinds your database to a halt, you'll be glad you did.

NO_TRUNCATE

The NO_TRUNCATE option is used when the log is available, but the *database* is not. Its function is actually the opposite of NO_LOG and TRUNCATE_ONLY. Under normal circumstances, the BACKUP_LOG command not only writes to the transaction log, but also signals a checkpoint for the database to flush any dirty buffers from memory to the database files. Where this becomes a problem is when the media containing the database is unavailable and you must capture the current contents of a log to a backup file for recovery. If the last time you did a log backup was four hours ago this would mean the loss of all the input since then. If your log is on a separate disk, which is not damaged, you have those four hours of transactions available to you, but BACKUP LOG fails as it can't checkpoint the data files. Run BACKUP LOG with the NO_TRUNCATE option and the log is backed up, but the checkpoint is not run, as the log is not actually cleared. You now have this new log backup to restore as well, enabling recovery to the time of failure. The only transactions lost will be those that were not yet committed.

TIP

Any time you think you might have to do a recovery, the *first* thing you should do is back up the transaction log. If you skip this step and restore the database, you will have unnecessarily lost all the transactions since the last log backup.

NOTE

There was a bug in SQL 7.0 that prevented the NO_TRUNCATE option from working if the primary data file for the database was damaged. Those of you who found this out the hard way will be happy to know it is fixed in SQL Server 2000.

NORECOVERY | STANDBY= *undo_file_name*

The [NORECOVERY | STANDBY= *undo_file_name*] clause for the BACKUP LOG command is new for SQL 2000. This has been part of the RESTORE LOG command since SQL Server 7.0. In the context of the BACKUP LOG command, these options are generally used in conjunction with a Standby Server. When NORECOVERY is specified, the log is backed up, and the database is left in recovery mode. This could be used in a planned switch over to a Standby Server. As the database is in recovery mode, it is ready to have logs applied to it. This avoids having to do a full restore of the Standby Server back to the production server. The logs from the Standby Server are applied back to the production server to bring it up to date. The STANDBY= *undo_file_name* option is similar; however, it leaves the database available in read-only mode. See the section, "Using a Standby Server," later in this chapter, for more information.

BACKUP LOG Examples

Listings 16.6, 16.7, and 16.8 show examples of typical backup scripts.

LISTING 16.6 Sample Script for a Simple Log Backup

```
-- Back up to a permanent backup device. Don't initialize the device.
-- Provide a name for the backup
USE MASTER
BACKUP LOG Northwind TO NWlogback
WITH
NOINIT,
NAME = 'Northwind log  backup',
NOFORMAT
```

LISTING 16.7 Sample Script Clearing a Full Transaction Log

```
-- Clear the transaction log.
USE MASTER
BACKUP LOG Northwind WITH NO_LOG
```

LISTING 16.8 Sample Script for Backing Up the Log When the Database Is Inaccessible

```
-- Back up the log without truncating it.
USE MASTER
BACKUP LOG Northwind TO NWlogback
WITH   NO_TRUNCATE
```

Backing Up Transaction Logs with SQL Enterprise Manager

Backing up transaction logs uses the same dialog box that is used for database backups. Select the Transaction Log radio button, a backup device, and if desired, a schedule. Figure 16.5 illustrates a typical transaction log backup using the GUI. Note that Append to media is selected by default. This is important if you are scheduling a recurring log backup that will reuse a device. You will need all the logs since the last full, differential, or file backup to do a restore, so be careful not to overwrite them by changing this option.

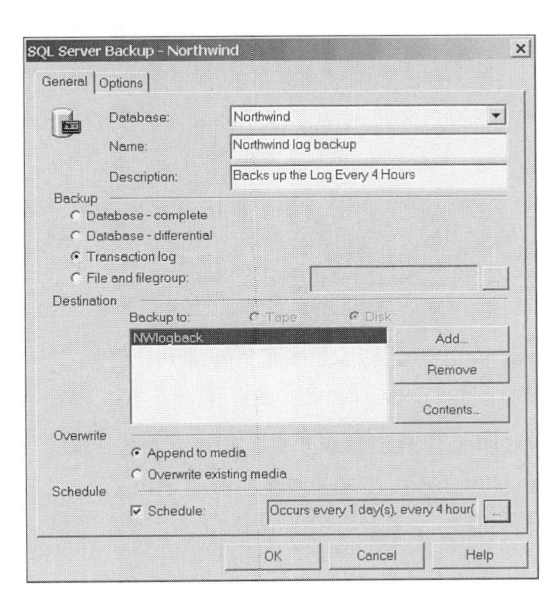

FIGURE 16.5 Selecting a transaction log backup.

You should also take into account the option tab. By default, Remove Inactive Entries from the Transaction Log is selected. Figure 16.6 illustrates this. If you unselect this option, it is the equivalent of using the `NO_TRUNCATE` option.

> **NOTE**
>
> If you try to back up the log and the Transaction Log radio box is unavailable, your database is in Simple recovery mode. You will have to switch (database properties/options) from this mode before transaction log backups are allowed. After switching from Simple recovery mode, perform a full database backup.

16

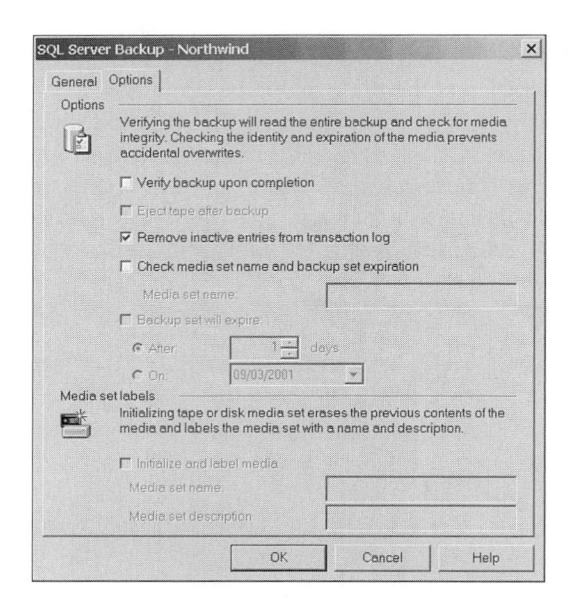

FIGURE 16.6 The Options tab of the Backup dialog box.

Backing Up the System Databases

The system databases, master, msdb, and model, must also be included in your backup plan. There is also a tempdb, but as its name implies, it contains no permanent data. The master and msdb databases are set to Simple recovery mode by default. This is sufficient as they are small, and full backups will suffice. The model database is the basis for any user databases that you create and is set to Full recovery by default. Changing the recovery mode of the model database will change the recovery mode of any subsequently created databases.

As the master database contains information crucial to SQL Server, it should be backed up on a regular basis, and whenever a major system change is implemented. For instance, if you create a new database, the existence of that database is recorded in the master database. It then makes sense to back up not only the new database, but the master as well. The same goes for dropping or altering a database.

The msdb database stores all operations for SQL Server Agent, such as jobs, operators, and alerts. Back it up on a regular basis, and whenever you make major changes to SQL Agent tasks. The model database should be backed up whenever you make modifications to it.

NOTE

If you lose the master database, you will have to rebuild it using the rebuildm.exe command. This will also rebuild the msdb and model databases. All three databases are returned to the state they were in when the SQL Server was installed, and can then be restored from your backups.

Restoring the Database

I hope you have turned to this chapter out of interest, rather than necessity. If you are reading this because you have just lost a database, don't despair. The restore features of SQL Server are as robust and easy to use as the backup features covered in the last section. You *did* read the backup section, didn't you?

Obtaining Information About Your Backups

Before restoring from a backup device, you should ensure that it is valid and that it contains the correct backups. This information can be obtained in Enterprise Manager by double-clicking a backup device and selecting View Contents. Alternately, you can use the following Transact-SQL `RESTORE` options:

- `RESTORE HEADER ONLY`. This returns the header information of a specified backup file or backup set. This header information includes the name and description, the type of media, the backup method, the date and time, the size of the backup, and the sequence number of the backup.
- `RESTORE FILELISTONLY`. This returns information about the original database or transaction log files that are in a backup file.
- `RESTORE LABELONLY`. Use this command to return the label information from the backup media.
- `RESTORE VERIFYONLY`. This command verifies that all files that make up a backup set are complete and that all backups are readable.

Restoring Databases with T-SQL

The T-SQL command `RESTORE DATABASE` is used not only to restore a damaged database, but also to move data and log files, restore a copy of a database with a different name, restore a file or file group, do a partial restore, and to initiate a standby server. Listing 16.9 shows the `RESTORE DATABASE` syntax.

LISTING 16.9 The Syntax for `RESTORE DATABASE`

```
RESTORE DATABASE { database_name | @database_name_var }
    [< file_or_filegroup > [ ,...n ]]
[ FROM < backup_device > [ ,...n ] ]
[ WITH
    [PARTIAL]
    [ RESTRICTED_USER ]
    [ [ , ] FILE = { file_number | @file_number } ]
    [ [ , ] PASSWORD = { password | @password_variable } ]
    [ [ , ] MEDIANAME = { media_name | @media_name_variable } ]
```

LISTING 16.9 Continued

```
    [ [ , ] MEDIAPASSWORD = { mediapassword | @mediapassword_variable } ]
    [ [ , ] MOVE 'logical_file_name' TO 'operating_system_file_name' ]
            [ ,...n ]
    [ [ , ] KEEP_REPLICATION ]
    [ [ , ] { NORECOVERY | RECOVERY | STANDBY = undo_file_name } ]
    [ [ , ] { NOREWIND | REWIND } ]
    [ [ , ] { NOUNLOAD | UNLOAD } ]
    [ [ , ] REPLACE ]
    [ [ , ] RESTART ]
    [ [ , ] STATS [ = percentage ] ]
]
```

The `[< file_or_filegroup > [ ,...n ]]` clause is, as the brackets imply, optional. By specifying a file, filegroup, or a list of files or filegroups, you are instructing SQL Server to restore only those files or filegroups. This allows you to restore only the damaged part of the database, which could vastly decrease your restore time. For more information, see the subsequent section on file and filegroup restore.

The `PARTIAL` option is new to SQL Server 2000. The partial clause is specified in conjunction with a restore from a full backup, a file or filegroup clause, and usually a `MOVE` option. Optionally, you can choose to restore additional differential and or log backups. A partial restore differs from file or filegroup restore in that it restores the primary filegroup and the filegroup specified (if a file is specified, all files in its filegroup are restored). All other filegroups are marked unavailable. For more information, see the subsequent section on partial restore.

The `RESTRICTED_USER` restricts access to the restored database to members of the sysadmin, db_owner, and dbcreator roles. It replaces the `DBO_ONLY` option.

The `FILE` option specifies which backup set to restore from the backup device. A value of 3, for example would restore the third backup set on the device.

The `PASSWORD`, `MEDIANAME`, `MEDIAPASSWORD`, `NOREWIND | REWIND`, `NOUNLOAD | UNLOAD`, `RESTART`, and `STATS` are identical to those in the `BACKUP` command.

The `MOVE` option allows you to restore a file to a new physical location. This is handy when moving a database or log file to a new disk. It is also invaluable, if you lose a disk and must restore the database as quickly as possible; restore the database to an existing disk, and when time permits, replace the defective disk and move the database back to the proper location.

If you have a published database (see the chapter on replication) that is also being backed up to a warm standby server, the `KEEP_REPLICATION` option will preserve your replication settings when you restore to the standby server.

The REPLACE option allows you to restore over an existing database, even if the structure of the database is different than that contained in the backup. SQL Server performs a safety check before a restore, which ensures that it doesn't replace a database if the database exists and the name is different than the name in the backup set, or if the set of files in the database differs from that recorded in the backup set. The REPLACE option cancels this safety check.

NOTE

Conspicuous by its absence here is the syntax for a differential restore. That is because there is none. To perform a differential restore, specify the location of a differential backup in the FROM clause; SQL Server will recognize it as such and act accordingly.

Restoring Transaction Logs with T-SQL

The RESTORE LOG command is used to recover your transaction log backups. More correctly, after you *restore* your database backup you *apply* the associated log backups. The transaction log backups are a continuous record of all the transactions that have transpired on your database. The log records are written serially, so all transaction log backups must be applied in order. You can't restore log1, log2, and log4 because log4 might try to update a record that was created in log3. You can see how this would be a problem. If you have a missing log backup, you can only restore as far as the log backup prior to it. In this case, only log1 and log2 could be recovered.

Listing 16.10 shows the RESTORE LOG syntax. For clarity, I have omitted the options common with the database backup and restore commands.

LISTING 16.10 The RESTORE LOG Syntax

```
RESTORE LOG { database_name | @database_name_var }
[ FROM < backup_device > [ ,...n ] ]
[ WITH
        [ [ , ] { NORECOVERY | RECOVERY | STANDBY = undo_file_name } ]
        [ [ , ] STOPAT = { date_time | @date_time_var }
        | [ , ] STOPATMARK = 'mark_name' [ AFTER datetime ]
        | [ , ] STOPBEFOREMARK = 'mark_name' [ AFTER datetime ]
    ]
]
```

The NORECOVERY | RECOVERY | STANDBY options specify which state to leave the database in after the log is applied. If NORECOVERY is specified SQL Server does not roll back any uncommitted transactions in the log, and it leaves the database in recovery mode. Use this if you still have more logs to apply. The RECOVERY option rolls back any uncommitted transactions and opens the database for use. Use this option only after the last log has been applied. RECOVERY is the default. The STANDBY option is similar to NORECOVERY, but it also leaves the database in read only mode. An undo file must be specified when using STANDBY. See the section "Using a Standby Server" later in this chapter for more information.

The STOPAT option accepts a date and time input to stop recovery at that point in time. New for SQL Server 2000 are STOPATMARK and STOPBEFOREMARK. These options allow recovery to a named 'mark' within a transaction. See the section "Restoring to a Point in Time" later in this chapter for further information.

Transact-SQL Restore Examples

Listings 16.11 through 16.14 show some samples of restoring the database using T-SQL scripts.

LISTING 16.11 Sample Script for a Full Database Recovery

```
--Restore northwind from the first backup on device nwbackup
-- Recover the database
USE MASTER
RESTORE DATABASE Northwind
FROM nwbackup
WITH FILE = 1,
RECOVERY
```

LISTING 16.12 Sample Script for a Full and Log Recovery

```
-- Restore northwind from the first backup on device nwbackup
-- Restore two logs from device nwlogback
-- Recover the database
USE MASTER
RESTORE DATABASE northwind
FROM nwbackup
WITH FILE = 1,
NORECOVERY
GO
RESTORE LOG northwind
FROM nwlogback
WITH FILE = 1,
NORECOVERY
GO
RESTORE LOG northwind
FROM nwlogback
WITH FILE = 2,
RECOVERY
```

LISTING 16.13 Sample Script for a Point in Time Recovery

```
-- Restore northwind from the first backup on device nwbackup
-- Restore two logs from device nwlogback
-- Stop at Jan 15 2001 09:00 AM
-- Recover the database
USE MASTER
RESTORE DATABASE northwind
FROM nwbackup
WITH FILE = 1,
NORECOVERY
GO
RESTORE LOG northwind
FROM nwlogback
WITH FILE = 1,
NORECOVERY
GO
RESTORE LOG northwind
FROM nwlogback
WITH FILE = 2,
RECOVERY,
STOPAT = 'January 15, 2001 09:00 AM'
```


LISTING 16.14 Sample Script for a File Restore

```
-- Restore one file from the northwind database
-- Restore the log from device nwlogback to make the file consistant
-- Recover the database
USE MASTER
RESTORE DATABASE northwind
 FILE = nwdbfile3
FROM nwbackup
WITH
NORECOVERY
GO
RESTORE LOG northwind
FROM nwlogback
WITH FILE = 1,
RECOVERY
```

Performing Restore Operations with Enterprise Manager

When performing restore operations, the last thing you want to do is make a mistake. The consequences of an error at this point could range from a delay in restoring service to your users, to rendering a database unrecoverable. Enterprise Manager helps you avoid costly errors by presenting restore options in an easy-to-use graphic interface.

As with backing up the database, the Restore Database dialog box can be accessed from the Task Pad, the Tools menu, or by right-clicking the database, selecting All Tasks from the pop-up menu, and then selecting Restore Database. The Restore Database dialog box is shown in Figure 16.7.

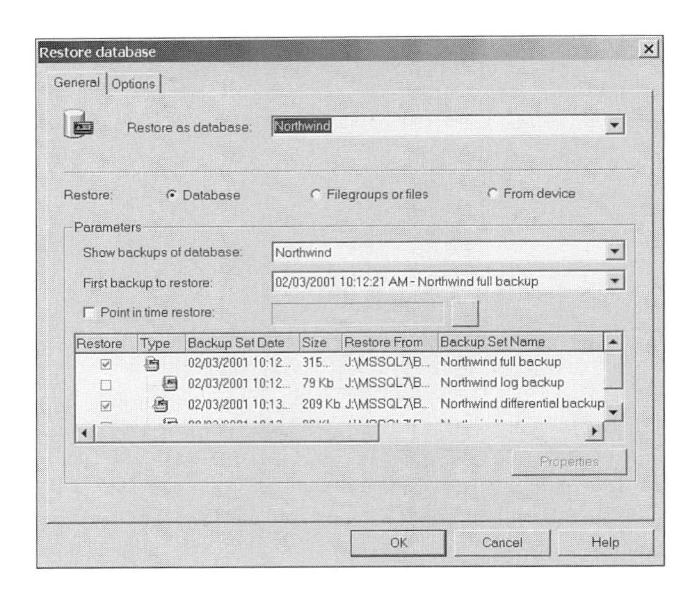

FIGURE 16.7 The Restore Database dialog box.

The Restore as Database window allows you to select an existing database or enter a new database name. Entering a new name automatically creates a new database and restores a copy of the database contained in the backup to it. The default selection is a full database restore, but you can choose a filegroup or file restore, or specify a device to restore from. The parameters section lets you choose which database backups to display and, if there are multiple backups of that database, allows you to choose the First Backup to Restore from a drop-down list. By default the most recent backup is selected. If there are log backups for the database the Point in Time Restore check box is available. From here, you can specify which point in time the database will be restored to. The selection window is tied to the First Backup to Restore drop-down box. As mentioned before, the most recent backup is selected, as this is generally the one you will want to restore. SQL Server takes this one step further. Under the Restore heading, it automatically selects the best restore scenario based on the backups available. You, of course, can override this, but generally won't want to. For example, let's say you have done a full backup, and then three log backups, followed by a differential backup, and then two more log backups. The best full database restore plan for this is to restore the full backup, the differential, and then the two log backups taken after the differential. *This is exactly what Enterprise Manager will have preselected for you.* Click OK and the restore will be performed as selected. Isn't modern technology wonderful?

The Options tab, of the Restore Database dialog box, pictured in Figure 16.8, further extends Enterprise Manager's restore options. The top three check boxes are self-explanatory. The Restore Database Files as window lets you restore files to a new location by typing the path and filename in Restore As column. This is equivalent to the T-SQL `MOVE` option. The three options under Recovery Completion State map to `RECOVERY`, `NORECOVERY`, and `STANDBY`, respectively.

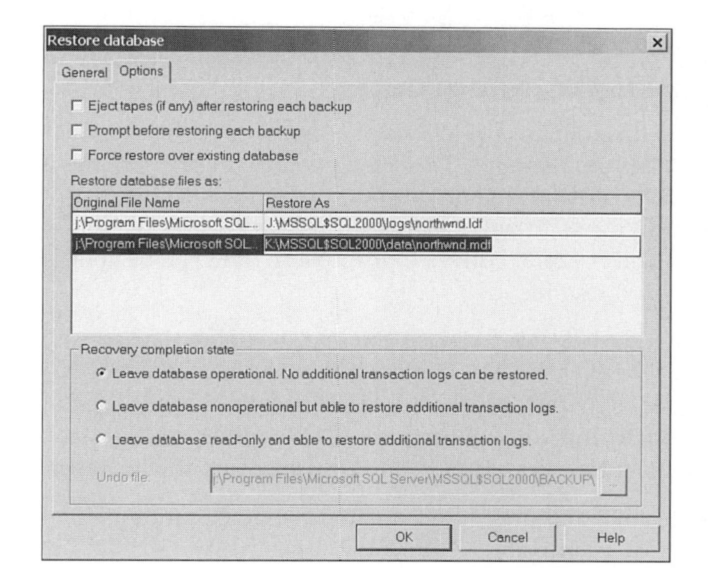

FIGURE 16.8 The Options tab of the Restore Database dialog box.

NOTE

Partial database recovery and recovery to a named mark in the transaction log are advanced recovery options and are not supported through Enterprise Manager. See the sections on T-SQL restore and Restoring to a point in time for further information.

Performing your restore operations with Enterprise Manager will help speed your recovery and reduce the chance of error, without diminishing your ability to override any part of the operation. I highly recommend that you familiarize yourself with the interface, and test its capabilities in practice drills. This will allow you to perform restore operations on your production databases quickly and with confidence.

Restoring to a Different Database

For development and testing purposes it's often desirable to create an exact copy of a database. This is easily done through the Restore Database dialog box. Select the backup of the database you want to restore, and in the Restore as Database window, type the name of the new database. Click OK and the new database will be created. The file structure of the database will be identical to that of the original, but the filenames will be changed to reflect the name of the database you are creating. If you are restoring to a new database on a different server, the servers must have the same character set, sort order, and Unicode collation. In addition, if the location of the database files is in a different directory on the new server, or you want to have the files created in a directory other than where the original database files existed, you will need to adjust the pathnames in the Options tab.

Restoring a File or Filegroup

By specifying a file, filegroup, or list of files or filegroups, you are instructing SQL Server to restore only those files or filegroups. This allows you to restore only the damaged part of the database, which could vastly improve your restore time. Consider a 200GB database spread over ten 20GB drives. If only one drive fails, why restore all 200 gigabytes? Restore only the file or files on the failed drive. Your recovery time will be approximately one-tenth the time of a full restore.

If you want to use file or filegroup restore you *must* be doing transaction log backups. As the restored file will be out of sync with the other files, all transaction log backups from the time the file or filegroup was backed up must be applied to bring it up to date. However, even though all the logs must be read, SQL Server is smart enough to only apply transactions that affect the restored files, and thus speed up the log restoration as well.

If you spread your tables and their associated indexes across multiple files or filegroups, then these must be backed up and restored as a single entity.

TIP

A common misconception is that to do a file or filegroup restore you must be doing file or filegroup backups. It is perfectly acceptable to specify a full database backup as the source of the file or filegroup restore.

Restoring to a Point in Time

SQL Server 2000 permits transaction logs to be restored to a point in time or to a marked transaction in the log. I like to think of point-in-time recovery as time-traveling through the database. Have you ever wished you could take back something you had done? No, this won't help you with that "little episode" in grade 12. But what if you drop a table and need to get it back? You can perform a point-in-time restore to just before you issued the drop-table command and when the restore is finished your table is back. Of course the down side is that all other transactions issued after the point you restored to are lost as well. This is often an acceptable tradeoff, especially if you catch your error quickly. If you want to have your cake and eat it too, see the section on the new Partial Restore option. Restoring to a point in time can be accomplished with the T-SQL `STOPAT` option or in the Restore Dialog Box by selecting Point in Time Restore.

Two new T-SQL options, `STOPATMARK` and `STOPBEFOREMARK` have been added to further enhance point-in-time recoverability. The `BEGIN TRANSACTION` command now includes a `WITH MARK` option. This adds a named mark to that transaction. During recovery `STOPATMARK` and `STOPBEFOREMARK`, as their names suggest, allow you recover to, or just before, the specified mark. Both options also support an `AFTER` clause that accepts a date and time value. As many transactions could be given the same mark "name", the `AFTER` option signifies the first occurrence of the mark after the specified time. This type of recovery is important in related databases where two or more databases must be rolled back to a point where they are logically consistent.

Performing a Partial Database Restore

The `PARTIAL` option is new to SQL Server 2000. The partial clause is specified in conjunction with a restore from a full backup, a file or filegroup clause, and usually a move option. You can also choose to restore additional differential or log backups. A partial restore differs from file or filegroup restore in that it always restores only the primary filegroup and the filegroup specified in the filegroup clause (if a file is specified all files in its filegroup are restored). All other filegroups are marked unavailable. It is for this reason that this restore method is used in conjunction with the `MOVE` option. As only a subset of the database is restored, you generally are not going to want to restore it on top of your existing database.

Why would you want to restore only part of your database? Partial restore is primarily used for object recovery, not media recovery. Picture this scenario: Your database is ticking along just fine, when a developer, testing a new application, drops the customer table. Rather than shut everything down and do a point-in-time recovery to just before the table was dropped, you could do a partial recovery. In the `RESTORE DATABASE` statement, specify a different database name, the name of the filegroup the customer table was on, the `PARTIAL` option, and use the `MOVE` option to restore the files to a new location. Now restore the logs to a point in time when the customer table still existed. Transfer the customer table from this temporary database back to the production database and you are back in business. Now you have only one thing left to do. Go have a word with that developer!

Restoring the System Databases

The system databases have their own special considerations when it comes to recovery. If SQL Server can be started, they can be restored from backup like any other database. However, if the master database is damaged, you will first have to rebuild the system databases. In theory (and according to BOL), to do this, run the rebuildm.exe command prompt utility to re-create the system databases, returning them to the state they were in when SQL Server was installed. Now you start SQL Server in single user mode. You will notice that none of your user databases, SQL Server logins, or SQL Server Agent jobs, alerts, and operators are available. Restore the system databases from a valid backup, and you will be able to access all your databases and objects once again. Well, that's the theory anyway. In reality it is a little more involved than that, so I will outline a step-by-step procedure that will get you back up and running as quickly as possible. Believe me, when your master database is trashed it is not the best time to discover that the restore procedure doesn't work. Don't ask me how I know this!

So, your instance has crashed, and you determine that it is due to a problem with the master database. Of course you have a backup, but you can't restore unless the instance is running, and you can't get the instance running without a valid master database. This is where the rebuildm.exe utility comes in. Before you run the utility, ensure that all SQL Server services are stopped. When you run rebuildm.exe the application prompts you for the server (instance) you are restoring, the location of the source files for the system databases, and the database collation settings, as shown in Figure 16.9.

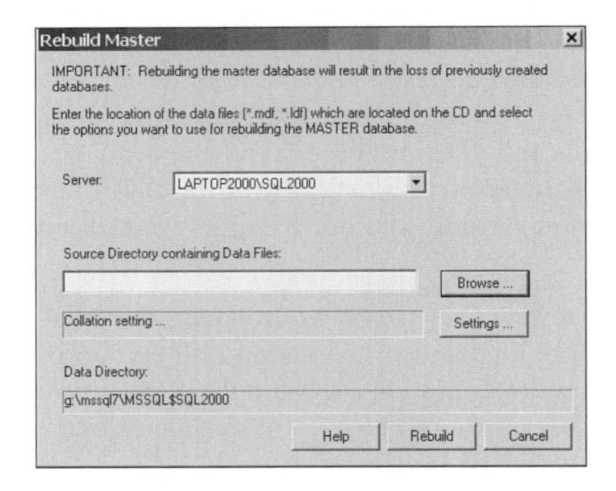

FIGURE 16.9 The Rebuildm.exe interface.

It is here that you can start running into trouble. The location of the source files is defined as the original source of the SQL Server installation, usually the \X86\DATA folder on the installation CD-ROM. The files on the CD are, of course, read only and are copied as such to the data folder where the system databases were installed. After rebuildm.exe copies the files for the system databases to the data directory, it then pops up a Configuring Server screen with a progress bar; this will run forever and never succeed, as you can't modify a read-only database file. If this is the first time you've attempted this (likely) and you don't know how long it takes to run, you can waste an awful lot of time sitting waiting for a process that will never complete. I, for one, am usually hesitant about killing a process that claims to be rebuilding the master database. The fix to get around this is simple. Before you run rebuildm.exe, first copy the DATA folder from the CD to your hard drive. Now right-click the new DATA folder and clear the read-only check box and, when prompted, agree to have the change propagate to all files and subfolders. Now run rebuildm.exe and it will succeed in its reconfiguration of the system databases. This includes running scripts that update the databases to the proper Service Pack level. The process takes only a few minutes.

Now that the original system databases have been restored, you can get the instance started, and restore your backup of the master database. To restore the master database you must start the instance in single user mode. Don't even bother with Enterprise Manager at this point. You will be able to connect and start the instance using EM, however, if you go to the database properties of the master database, you will see that the single user mode option is grayed out. The proper way to start the instance in single user mode is using the -m option from the command prompt or using Control Panel/Services. I recommend using the command prompt, because if you enter a startup option in the services applet, you must remember to go back to it, remove the option, and restart the service or on the next server startup it will revert to single user mode. Here is the next potential pitfall in the restore process; when starting the instance from the command prompt, you must run sqlservr from the Binn folder of the instance you are restoring and specify the –m option for single user mode as well as the –s option to specify the instance name as shown here:

```
G:\MSSQL\SQL2000\Binn\sqlservr -m -s SQL2000
```

Now you are ready to actually restore your master database. The restore process can be run from osql, Query Analyzer, or Enterprise Manager. If you use EM be aware that it will hang when the restore is complete as the restore of master terminates the instance when it finishes. Remember that at this point any backup devices you have previously created won't be available, so you will have to provide the path to the tape or disk where your last valid backup of master is located, as in the following:

```
RESTORE DATABASE MASTER FROM DISK = 'F:\BACKUP\MASTER_BACKUP.BAK'
```

Once the restore is complete, you can restart the instance normally, and you should be back in business. Keep in mind that when you ran rebuildm.exe it rebuilt all the system databases so you will now have to restore msdb, as well as model if you have made any changes to it.

I strongly suggest you run through the preceding procedure on a test server a few times, and create a master database recovery document that is specific to your site. The recovery of the master database is not all that complex once you know the tricks, but you should be comfortable with it before you actually have to perform it on a production server.

After you have rebuilt the system databases, and for some reason (I can't think of a good one) you don't have a valid backup of your master database, all is not lost. You can still gain access to all your user databases without having to restore each and every one of them as well. As long as it is only the master database that was damaged, and the other database files are still intact, you can use the system stored procedure `sp_attach_db` or `sp_attach_single_file_db` to *inform* the master database about your user databases. Think of it as reverse engineering the database information stored in master. The following example "attaches" the Northwind database:

```
USE MASTER
EXEC sp_attach_single_file_db @dbname = 'northwind' @physname =
➥'c:\mssql\data\nwdata.mdf  '
```

This will be much faster (and potentially safer) than restoring the user databases. You will still have to re-create other items such as logins and configuration settings that are stored in the master database.

Additional Backup Considerations

There are three additional backup considerations.

Frequency of Backups

How often you back up your databases will depend on many factors. These will include:

- The size of your databases, and your backup window
- The frequency of changes to the data, and the method by which it is changed
- The acceptable amount of data loss in the event of a failure
- The acceptable recovery time in the event of a failure

First you must establish what your backup window will be. The backup window is the time allocated to you to complete the task of backing up the database. As SQL Server allows dynamic backups, users can still access the database during backup; however, it will impact performance. This means you still must schedule backups for low activity periods, and have them complete in the shortest possible time.

After you have established your backup window, you can determine your backup method and schedule. For example, if it takes four hours for a full backup to complete, and the database is quiescent between midnight and 6:00 a.m., you have time to perform a full backup each night. On the other hand, if a full backup takes 10 hours and you have a two-hour window, you will have to consider monthly or weekly backups perhaps in conjunction with filegroup, differential, and transaction log backups. In many decision support databases that are populated with periodic data loads, it might suffice to back up once, after each data load.

Backup frequency is also directly tied to acceptable data loss. In the event of catastrophic failure, such as a fire in the server room, you can only recover data up to the point of the last backup that was moved offsite. If it is acceptable to lose a day's worth of data entry, nightly backups might suffice. If your acceptable loss is an hour's worth of data, then hourly transaction log backups would have to be added to the schedule.

Your backup frequency will also affect your recovery time. I have worked on sites where transaction log backups complemented weekly full backups every 10 minutes, which was the acceptable data loss factor. A failure a few days after backup meant a full database restore and the application of hundreds of transaction logs. Adding a daily differential backup in this case would vastly improve restore time. The full and differential backups would be restored, and then six logs applied for each hour between the differential and the time of failure.

Using a Standby Server

If the ability to quickly recover from failure is crucial to your operation, you might consider implementing a standby server. Implementing a standby server involves backing up the production server and then restoring it to the standby server, leaving it in recovery mode. As transaction logs are backed up on the production server they are applied to the standby server. If there is a failure on the production server, the standby server can be recovered and used in place of the production server. If the production server is still running, don't forget to back up the current log with the `NO_TRUNCATE` option and restore it to the standby server as well before bringing it online.

NOTE

Another advantage of restoring backups to a standby server is it immediately validates your backups so you can be assured whether they are valid. There is nothing worse than finding out during a recovery process that one of the backup files is damaged or missing.

Prior to SQL Server 7.0, a standby server was often considered prohibitively expensive as it was always in recovery mode and therefore unavailable for anything else. It only came into play in case of failure. As management is rarely as pessimistic as the database administrator, it was a hard sell. A new option `STANDBY =`*`undo_file_name`* changed all that. When the database and subsequent log backups are restored to the standby server with this option, the database is left in recovery mode but is available as a read-only database. Now that the standby database is available for queries, it can actually reduce load on the production database by acting as a decision support system (DSS). Database Consistency Checks (DBCC) can be run on it as well, further reducing load on the production system.

For the database to be available for reads, the data must be in a consistent state. This means that all uncommitted transactions must be rolled back. This is usually taken care of by the `RECOVERY` option during restore. In the case of a standby server, this would cause a problem as you intend to apply more logs, which could, in fact, commit those transactions. This is taken care of by the *`undo_file_name`* clause of the `STANDBY` option. The file specified here holds a copy of all uncommitted transactions rolled back to bring the standby server to a read consistent, read-only state. If those transactions subsequently commit a log restore, this undo information can be used to complete the transaction.

SQL Server 2000 has introduced log shipping, which automates the transfer of logs to the standby server. Log shipping, which is configured with the Database Maintenance Plan Wizard, uses SQL Server Agent jobs on the primary server to back up the transaction log and copy it to a folder on the standby server. SQL Server Agent on the standby server then executes a load job to restore the log. Automating your standby server with log shipping reduces administration and helps to ensure that the standby database is up-to-date. For details on configuring a standby server, Chapter 22, "Data Replication."

Considerations for Very Large Databases

When it comes to backup and recovery, special consideration must be given to Very Large Databases, or VLDBs as they are known. A VLDB will have special requirements for

- Storage—Size might dictate the use of tape backups over network or disk.
- Time—As your backup window grows, the frequency of backups might have to be adjusted.
- Method—How you back up your database will be affected by its size. Differential, or File and Filegroup, backups might have to be implemented.
- Recovery—Partial database recovery, such as restoring a file or filegroup, might be required due to the prohibitive time required to restore the entire database.

When designing a VLDB, your backup plan must be integrated with storage, performance, and availability requirements. Refer to the previous sections in this chapter on File and Filegroup backups, as well as Differential backups. For a complete discussion on large databases, including information specific to backup and recovery, refer to Chapter 21, "Administering Very Large SQL Server Databases."

Summary

Although SQL Server provides excellent tools and models to automate and implement backup and recovery, it is still up to the database administrator to determine the appropriate approach, and to build, document, and test a robust recovery plan. Backup and recovery is a key part of any database project, and should be considered at all stages of development. Periodic reviews of your recovery plan must also be undertaken to make sure it has kept up with the needs of your organization, and the size of the database.

Consideration must be given to data loss prevention as well. By implementing physical security, redundant hardware, and application checks and balances, you can reduce the chances of ever having to recover data. Bear in mind that these measures *complement*, but never replace, your backup plan.

CHAPTER 17

Database Maintenance

by Paul Jensen

IN THIS CHAPTER

- What Needs to Be Maintained
- The Database Maintenance Plan Wizard
- Setting Up Your Own Maintenance Tasks
- The Database Console Commands (DBCC)
- Using `SQLMAINT.EXE` for Database Maintenance

Database administration doesn't stop after the database is created. On the contrary, ongoing maintenance tasks must be performed to maintain data integrity and keep the database performing smoothly. This chapter looks at some of the tasks related to database maintenance, and the tools—in particular the Database Maintenance Wizard—that will help you perform your maintenance chores.

What Needs to Be Maintained

The core tasks related to the maintenance of a SQL Server database are backing up the database and log (including shipping the logs to a standby server), rebuilding indexes, updating statistics, and running integrity checks against the database. These are the ongoing repetitive tasks, which are best run on a scheduled basis and are the backbone of the maintenance plan. Other tasks related to maintenance involve managing access by the users, maintaining data files, and monitoring performance. These tasks are more apt to be performed on an ad hoc basis when the need arises.

The Database Maintenance Plan Wizard

One of the most comprehensive and helpful wizards in SQL Server is the Database Maintenance Plan Wizard. By creating a wizard that steps you through the core maintenance tasks, Microsoft has enabled both novice and experienced administrators to quickly establish a valid maintenance plan. Many administrators discount wizards as simplistic and "beneath" them, and in many cases experienced administrators feel they can perform tasks quicker without them. If you fall into this category, I encourage you to give the Database Maintenance Plan Wizard a chance. The wizard leverages the features of the `SQLMAINT` utility to provide additional functionality such as creating backup files with unique names based on a timestamp. As the functions you define in the wizard are saved as SQL Server jobs, you still maintain control, as the jobs can be edited after they are created.

To access the Database Maintenance Plan Wizard, from the Enterprise Manager toolbar, select Tools, and then Database Maintenance Planner; it can also be accessed from the Magic Wand icon on the toolbar under Management. After you're past the welcome screen, you will be stepped through various screens allowing you to customize your maintenance plan.

Selecting Databases

The first screen allows you to select which databases to back up. The option buttons allow you to select all databases, all system databases, or all user databases, or to build a custom selection of databases. New for SQL Server 2000 is the check box to ship the logs to another server. If this is selected, you will be presented with a new set of screens in the log section of the wizard where you can choose a network share from which to ship the logs, and a remote server and database to act as the standby database. Log shipping is used to keep a standby server up to date. This check box is disabled if the database is in simple recovery mode. Figure 17.1 shows the Select Databases screen.

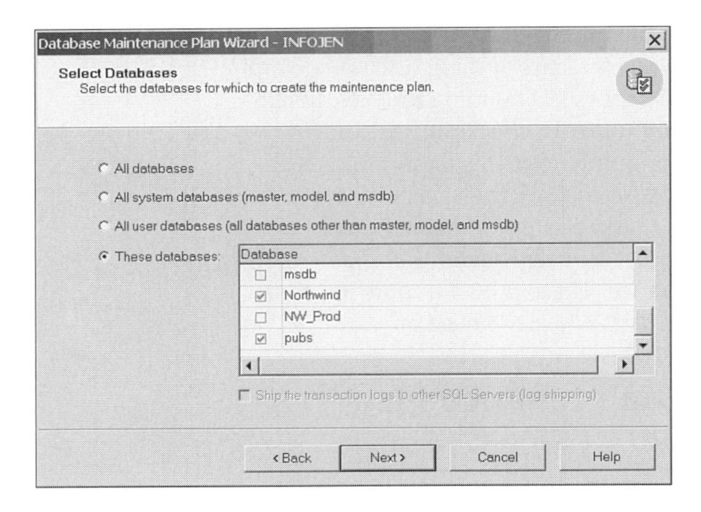

FIGURE 17.1 The Select Databases screen.

Updating Data Optimization Information

The next screen is used to optimize data access and storage. The first option, if selected, specifies that indexes should be dropped and rebuilt, either with the original amount of free space reserved, or a new amount specified as a percentage. The second option allows you to update the statistics used by the query optimizer in building a query plan. A sample percentage tells SQL Server how much of the data to sample. A higher percentage gives more reliable statistics, but takes longer to run. Note that this option is not available if you have chosen to rebuild the indexes, as new stats will be generated when the indexes are created. The next options control file size. You can specify a size at which the database will attempt to remove any free space, and how much free space should be retained in the database to allow for future growth. The schedule window indicates when the operation will run, and the Change button allows you to customize the schedule. Figure 17.2 shows the Update Data Optimization Information screen.

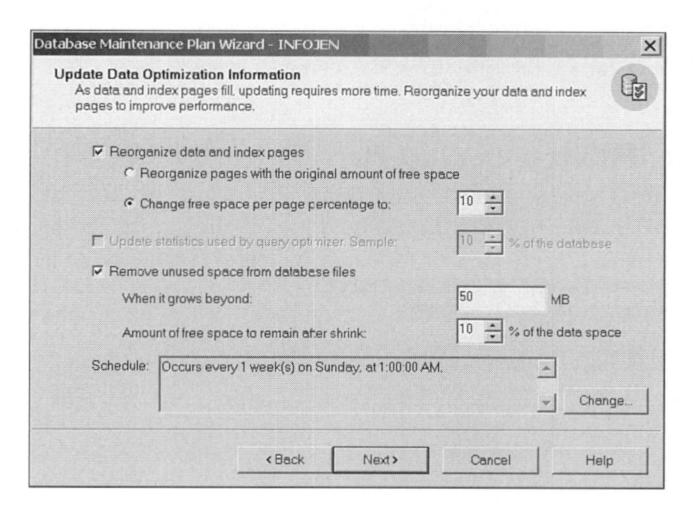

FIGURE 17.2 The Update Data Optimization Information screen.

Checking Database Integrity

The Database Integrity screen allows scheduling of the database consistency check `DBCC CHECKDB`. This checks the data pages for inconsistencies. You are given the option of including the indexes, which is more thorough but time consuming, and also to attempt to repair any minor problems. Note that if problems are found, SQL Server must put the object in Single User Mode before a repair attempt will be made. The repair will not proceed if users are connected to the database. The integrity checks can be made before each backup or on an independent schedule. If you choose to run the check before each backup, and the check fails, the backup doesn't run. Figure 17.3 illustrates the Database Integrity Check screen.

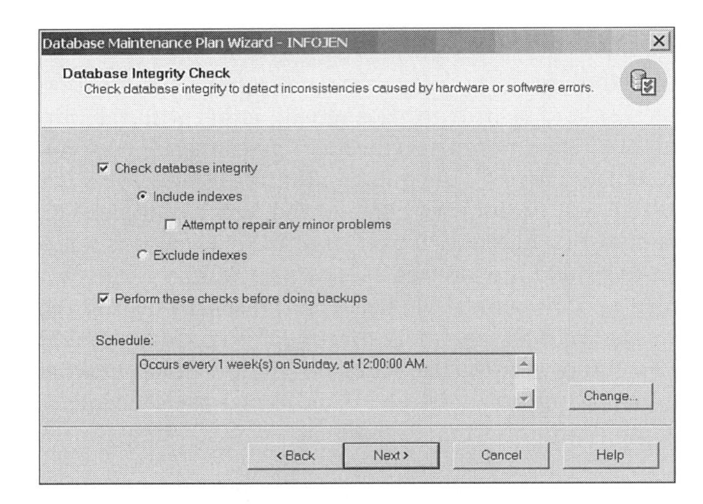

FIGURE 17.3 The Database Integrity Check screen.

Specifying the Database Backup Plan

Moving on to the next screen, you specify whether to include backups as part of the maintenance plan, whether a verification should be done on the completed backup, whether backups should be backed up to disk or tape, and when you would like to schedule the backups. Figure 17.4 shows the Specify the Database Backup Plan screen.

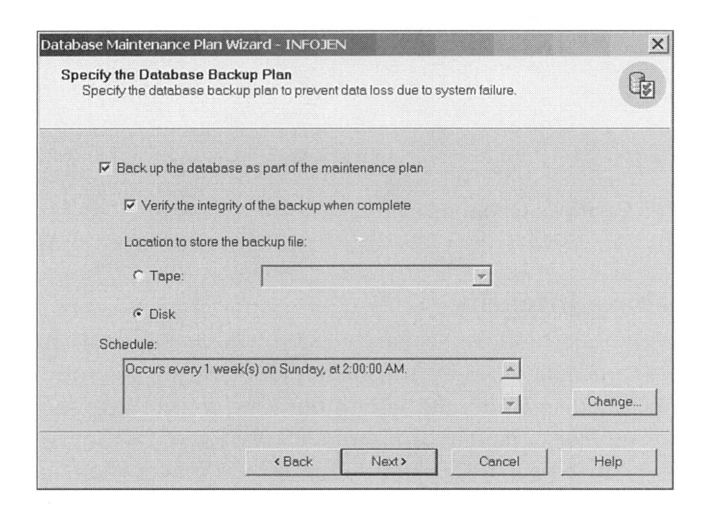

FIGURE 17.4 The Specify the Database Backup Plan screen.

Specifying the Backup Disk Directory

If, in the previous screen, you selected disk as the backup media, the next screen will allow you to customize where the backup files should be located. The first option allows you to choose between the default backup location and a directory that you specify. Next, you can select to create a separate subdirectory in which to store the backups for each database. This will really help keep things organized if you have several databases, or if you keep several backups for each database. This brings you to the next selection where you specify how long to keep each backup. This can be specified in minutes, hours, days, weeks, or months. With this selected, SQL Server will automatically delete backups older than the specified time. This is really handy to maintain a revolving backup schedule, or to clean up disk files if you back up to disk using SQL Server and then back those backup files to disk with your network backup utility. The last option is to specify the file extension for the backup files. Figure 17.5 shows the Specify Backup Disk Directory screen.

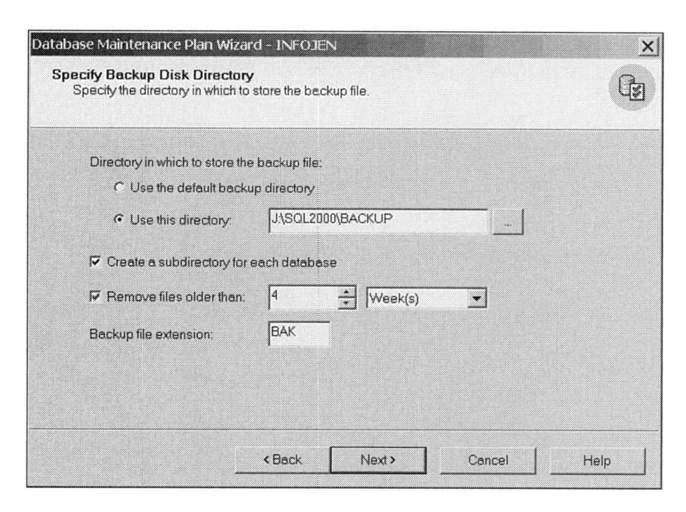

FIGURE 17.5 The Specify Backup Disk Directory screen.

Specifying the Transaction Log Backup Plan

The next screen is the same as the database backup screen, except that here you are specifying whether to include the transaction log in the backup plan. Figure 17.6 shows the Specify the Transaction Log Backup Plan screen.

Specifying the Transaction Log Backup Disk Directory

Next, you come to the Specify the Transaction Log Backup Disk Directory screen, where you are presented with the same options for location and cleanup as you were for the database. See Figure 17.7 for an example of this screen.

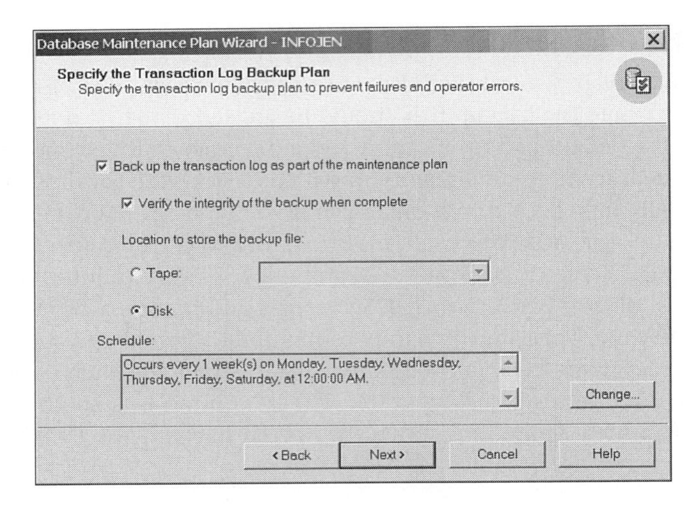

FIGURE 17.6 The Specify the Transaction Log Backup Plan screen.

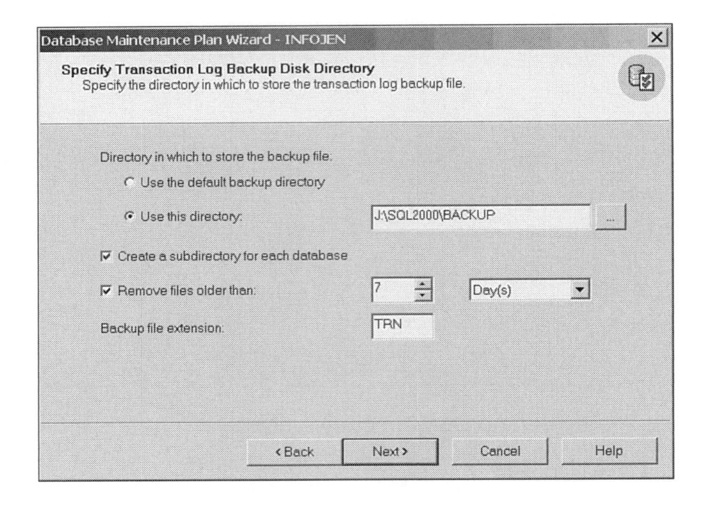

FIGURE 17.7 The Specify the Transaction Log Backup Disk Directory screen.

Generating Reports

Now you can configure how you would like reports of the maintenance plan's activities to be generated. From here, you can choose a directory to which to write the reports, specify how long they should be retained, and even e-mail a report to an operator. This reporting is a great way to keep track of the success or failure of the maintenance plans operations. I especially like the e-mail feature, which enables me to keep track of what is happening even when I am not in the office. Figure 17.8 shows the Reports to Generate screen.

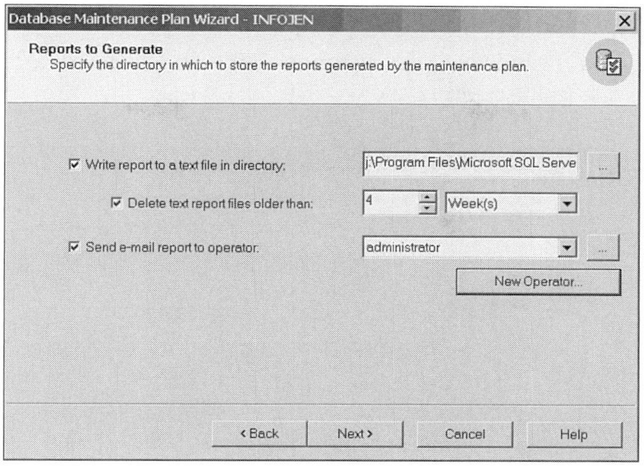

FIGURE 17.8 The Reports to Generate screen.

Maintenance History

The Maintenance Plan History screen has you configure where to store the maintenance plan history, either locally or on a remote server, and specify how many rows of history should be kept before it starts to overwrite. Figure 17.9 shows this screen.

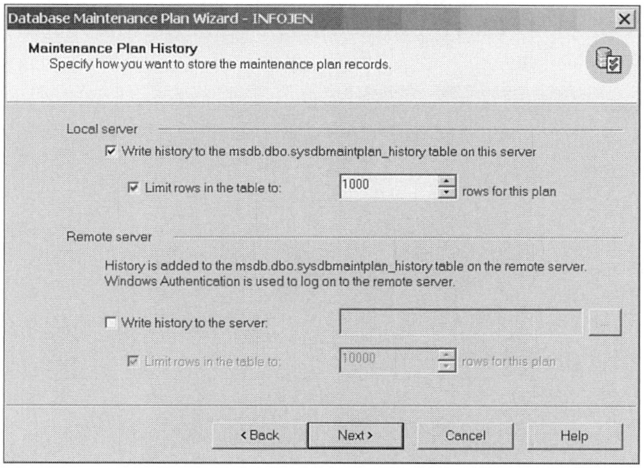

FIGURE 17.9 The Maintenance Plan History screen.

Completing the Database Maintenance Plan Wizard

The last screen lets you review your plan before clicking Finish to create the plan. Figure 17.10 shows the final screen of the wizard.

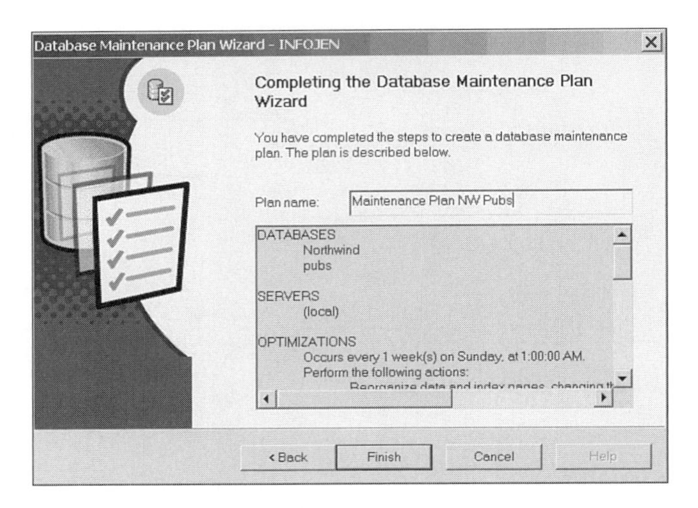

FIGURE 17.10 The Completing the Database Plan Wizard screen.

After a maintenance plan has been created, it can be accessed and revised at any time from the Database Maintenance Plan folder located in the Management folder of Enterprise Manager. Figure 17.11 shows the Properties dialog box for the Maintenance Plan.

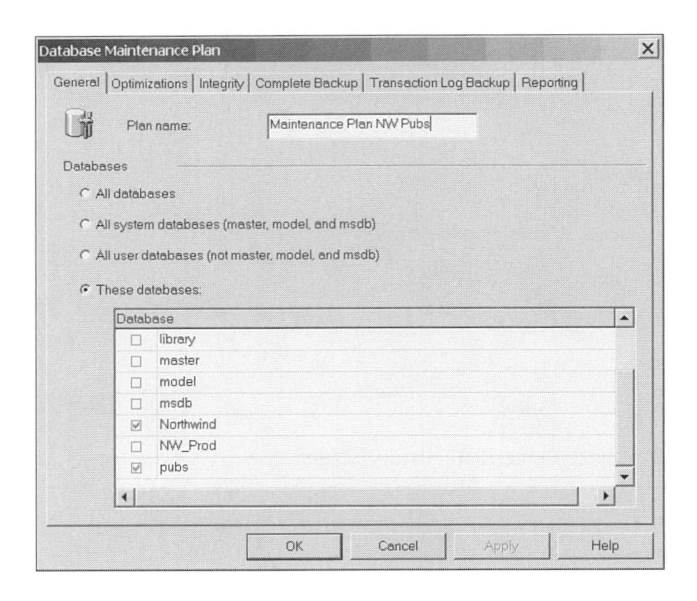

FIGURE 17.11 The Database Maintenance Plan Properties dialog box.

Setting Up Your Own Maintenance Tasks

The Maintenance Plan Wizard makes use of SQL Server jobs to perform its tasks. After the wizard creates these jobs, the jobs can be accessed and modified directly. This is a great way to cut and paste job functions from a Maintenance Plan job into a custom job you have created. Of course, you can create the jobs from scratch using the `BACKUP`, `SQLMAINT` and `DBCC` commands. However, the wizard is so easy to use that I find it easier to build an outline of my maintenance plan with the wizard, and then customize or copy the job steps into other jobs as required. Figure 17.12 shows an example of a backup job created by the wizard. Call me lazy, but I would rather cut, paste, and modify this statement than write it myself! See Chapter 18, "SQL Server Scheduling and Notification," for more details on creating your own custom jobs.

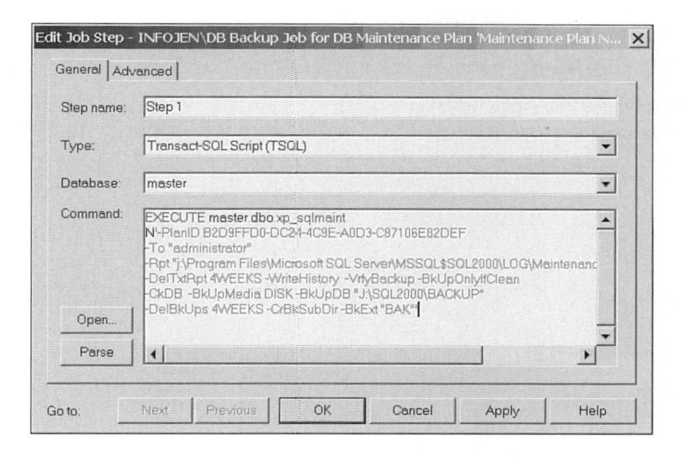

FIGURE 17.12 Viewing a job step created by the Maintenance Plan Wizard.

The Database Console Commands (DBCC)

Those of you familiar with previous versions of SQL Server might know the DBCC statements as the Database Consistency Checker. All documentation now refers to them as the Database Console Commands, probably in deference to the fact that not all of them are used for database consistency checks.

Running DBCC statements are an integral part of database maintenance. Some, such as `DBCC CHECKDB`, can be run on a scheduled basis (this is the one the wizard runs) as a preventative measure, and others, such as `DBCC SHRINKFILE`, you can choose to run when needed. Table 17.1 lists some of the DBCC statements commonly used for database maintenance.

TABLE 17.1 Database Maintenance DBCC Statements

DBCC	Function
`CHECKDB`	Checks allocation and integrity of all DB objects
`CHECKALLOC`	Checks the consistency of disk space allocation
`CHECKTABLE`	Checks the integrity of the specified table and its indexes
`SHRINKDATABASE`	Attempts to shrink all data files in the specified database
`SHRINKFILE`	Attempts to shrink a specified data file
`SHOWCONTIG`	Displays fragmentation information on a table and its indexes
`DBREINDEX`	Rebuilds indexes for a specified table
`INDEXDEFRAG`	Defragments indexes for a specified table or view

Detecting and Resolving Database Corruption

Several of the DBCC statements have the ability to detect and attempt to repair corruption in the database. Power failures or spikes, hardware glitches, or even internal SQL Server errors can cause this corruption. The primary validation DBCCs are the `CHECK` statements listed here:

- `DBCC CHECKDB`
- `DBCC CHECKALLOC`
- `DBCC CHECKCATALOG`
- `DBCC CHECKCONSTRAINTS`
- `DBCC CHECKFILEGROUP`
- `DBCC CHECKIDENT`
- `DBCC CHECKTABLE`

Of these, `DBCC CHECKDB` is the most functional, as it checks all objects in the database. The others, with the exception of `CHECKCATALOG` and `CHECKALLOC`, check specific objects within the database. `CHECKCATALOG` checks for database consistency with the system catalog, and `CHECKALLOC` checks the consistency of disk space structures.

The DBCC statements `CHECKDB`, `CHECKALLOC`, and `CHECKTABLE` have options to attempt to repair any problems they encounter. The `CHECKDB` statement is safest, as it also encompasses all the checks of the other two statements. It is, however, more time- and resource-consuming, so you might opt for using one of the others. For instance, if only allocation errors are being reported, running `CHECKALLOC` might be more efficient. The three repair options are as follows:

- REPAIR_FAST—Attempts minor repairs that can be performed quickly with no chance of data loss.
- REPAIR_REBUILD—Performs all repairs of REPAIR_FAST and also performs index rebuilds. No loss of data will result.
- REPAIR_ALLOW_DATA_LOSS—Encompasses the repairs of the first two options and also includes allocation and deallocation of rows and pages for correcting errors, and deletion of corrupted text objects. This can result in data loss.

To speed up the processing of DBCC statements, The Enterprise and Developer editions of SQL Server can take advantage of multiple processors, and will perform parallel execution of DBCC statements. The DBCC CHECKDB statement performs a serial scan of the database, but parallel scans of multiple objects as it proceeds to the limit of the system "max degree of parallelism" option. This speeds up the operation substantially over previous versions. Another option is to run DBCC CHECKDB or DBCC CHECKTABLE with the NOINDEX option. This speeds the operation of the DBCC statement as it doesn't check the non-clustered indexes on user tables (system table indexes are always checked). Index corruption is not as critical an issue as data corruption, as no data is lost, and the index can always be dropped and re-created if necessary.

Using DBCC to Set Trace Flags

The DBCC statements DBCC TRACEON and DBCC TRACEOFF are used to enable and disable trace flags. Trace flags set various database characteristics and enable detailed reporting of various functions to help in troubleshooting. For example, DBCC TRACEON (1205) displays detailed deadlock information.

Using SQLMAINT.EXE for Database Maintenance

The SQLMAINT utility is used to perform database maintenance activities from the command line. Database backups and certain DBCC statements can be specified to run. The Database Maintenance Plan Wizard actually uses a subset of SQLMAINT options, calling them through the xp_sqlmaint extended-stored procedure.

Why would you want to run T-SQL statements from the command line when SQL Server has its own built-in job and scheduling functions? One advantage of SQLMAINT is its ability to generate a report of its activities and save it to a text or HTML file, or e-mail it to an operator. SQLMAINT can also group several operations into one statement; if this statement is saved as a script, it could then be copied and easily modified to run on other servers. The following shows some examples of the SQLMAINT command.

This example runs DBCC CHECKDB on the Pubs database and creates a report called Pubs.rpt.

```
sqlmaint -S Server1 -U "sa" -P "password"
-D Pubs -CkDB  -Rpt J:\reports\Pubs.rpt
```

Backups can also be run, as in the following example, which backs up the Pubs database to the default backup directory.

```
sqlmaint -S Server1 -U "sa" -P "password"
-D Pubs -BkUpDB -BkUpMedia DISK -UseDefDir
```

Summary

This chapter examined the tools to help you build a maintenance plan, primarily the Database Maintenance Plan Wizard, which can schedule routine maintenance tasks, including backups. This chapter also looked at some of the DBCC commands, which can be used to monitor and repair corruption and fragmentation in the database. The final tool this chapter looked at is the SQLMAINT utility, which allows command-line control of your maintenance tasks.

Just as with your car, performing regular maintenance on your SQL Server databases will help you avoid problems and keep everything running smoothly. With the value placed on data these days and the high cost of downtime, the adage "An once of prevention is worth a pound of cure" still holds true.

The next chapter, "SQL Server Scheduling and Notification," will look at the SQL Server Agent, and how you can utilize it to expand on, and further automate, your database maintenance tasks.

CHAPTER **18**

SQL Server Scheduling and Notification

by Paul Jensen

IN THIS CHAPTER

- SQL Agent Overview
- Configuring SQL Server Agent
- Viewing the SQL Server Agent Error Log
- Operators
- Jobs
- Alerts
- Scripting Jobs and Alerts
- Multiserver Job Management
- Event Forwarding

The ability to easily schedule tasks and send notification regarding the outcome of the task is one of SQL Server's most powerful administrative features. This chapter looks at the "quarterback" of this operation, the SQL Server Agent, and the trinity of jobs, alerts, and operators that work together to automate scheduling and notification.

SQL Agent Overview

The SQL Server Agent is responsible for automation tasks in SQL Server. The Agent, which runs as a Windows service, is responsible for running scheduled tasks, notifying operators of events, and responding with a predefined action to errors and performance conditions. SQL Server Agent performs these functions using alerts, jobs, and operators. Alerts respond to SQL Server or user-defined errors, and can also respond to performance conditions. An alert can be configured to run a job as well as notify an operator. A job is a predefined operation or set of operations, such as transferring data or backing up a transaction log. A job can be scheduled to run on a regular basis, or called to run when an alert is fired. An operator is a user to notify when an alert fires or a job requests notification. The operator can be notified by e-mail, pager, or the `NET SEND` command.

Configuring SQL Server Agent

The SQL Server Agent is accessed through the Management folder of Enterprise Manager. To configure the Agent, right-click SQL Server Agent and select Properties. Figure 18.1 shows the SQL Server Agent Properties dialog box.

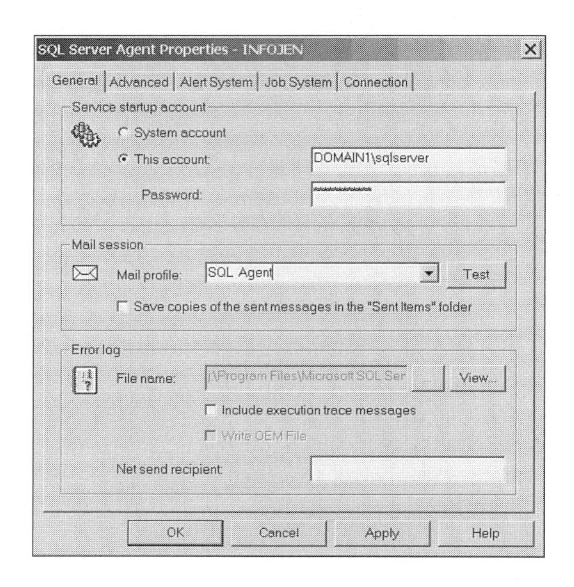

FIGURE 18.1 The Agent Properties dialog box.

The following sections outline some of the key configuration options.

Startup Account

When running SQL Server on Windows NT or 2000, the agent runs as a Windows service. From the General tab of the Agent properties (Figure 18.1), you have the choice of running the Agent under the local system account or with a Windows domain account. The local system account is, as the name suggests, restricted to the local system and has no network access rights. This can be restrictive, particularly if you have multiple servers. The preferred method is to set the Agent to use its own domain user account. This account should have the "logon as a service" user right, and be in the local administrators group. Resist the temptation to use the Administrator account for the Agent; create an account just for the Agent, or use the account under which the MSSQLServer service runs. If you use Administrator, the service will fail on startup the next time you change the Administrator's password.

Mail Profile

A mail profile can also be specified for the SQL Server Agent. This mail account is the one the Agent will use when sending notifications to operators. Create a mail account by logging on to the server with the account the Agent will run under, and set up the mail client as you would any other e-mail user. After the mail profile is configured, you can select it from the Mail Profile drop-down box. The test button checks whether SQL Server can start and stop a MAPI session with the specified profile. If this fails on initial setup, stop and start the SQL Server Agent and retry the test. If you still have problems, log in as the Agent account and ensure you can send and receive e-mail using the mail client.

User Connection

The SQL Server Agent can be configured to use a SQL Server login as opposed to the local system or a domain account, but this is only used in a Windows 98 or Windows CE installation where the Agent runs as an application as opposed to a service. This is configured from the Connection tab, as shown in Figure 18.2, and the account must be in the sysadmin role.

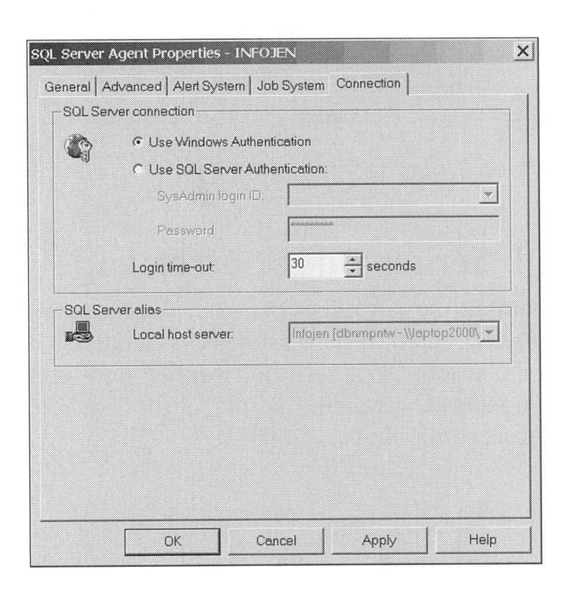

FIGURE 18.2 The Agent Properties Connection tab.

SQL Agent Proxy Account

By default, only users in the Sysadmin role can execute jobs that contain CmdExec (command line) and ActiveScripting job steps. If you choose to allow others this privilege, on the Job System tab of the Properties dialog box, you must unselect the Only Users with Sysadmin Privileges check box. The first time you do this, a pop-up box will appear asking you to specify an account that will be used to execute these tasks. After the account is set up, it can be edited through the Reset buttons. Figure 18.3 shows the SQL Server Agent Job System tab.

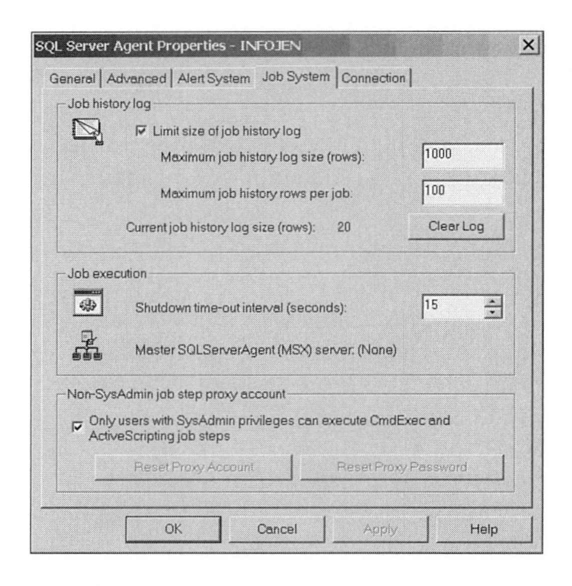

FIGURE 18.3 The Agent Job System tab.

Viewing the SQL Server Agent Error Log

The SQL Server Agent maintains an error log that records information, warnings, and error messages concerning its operation. This error log is useful when debugging Agent-dependent operations, such as jobs. To access the error log, right-click the SQL Server Agent folder in Enterprise Manager and select Display Error Log. You can filter the errors by type and search for errors containing specific text.

Operators

Operators are the accounts that will receive notification when an event occurs, such as the completion of a job or the firing of an alert. Operators are configured from the Operators folder under SQL Server Agent in Enterprise Manager. To create a new operator, right-click the Operators folder and select New Operator. To manage an existing operator, double-click the operator in the Details pane. This will bring up the Properties dialog box for the operator, as shown in Figure 18.4.

From the General tab of the operator properties, you specify a name for the operator and a method of contact. This can be any combination of e-mail, pager e-mail, and Net Send address. Each of the contact methods includes a Test button that sends a test message via the corresponding contact method. If a pager address is supplied, the pager schedule is enabled, allowing you to specify the times that the operator is available to be paged.

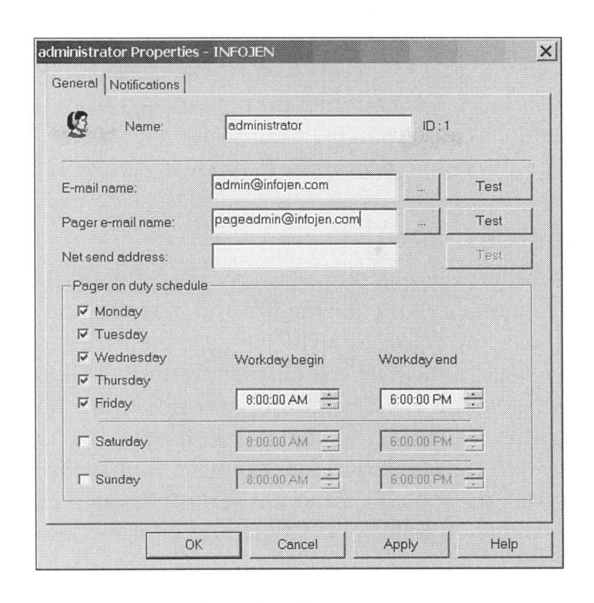

FIGURE 18.4 The Operator Properties dialog box.

The Notifications tab shows for which jobs and alerts the operator is currently receiving notifications. You can disable the operator, send him an e-mail listing the jobs and alerts for which he is receiving notification, send him his pager schedule, and also alert him to a summary of notifications he has received. Figure 18.5 shows the Notifications tab.

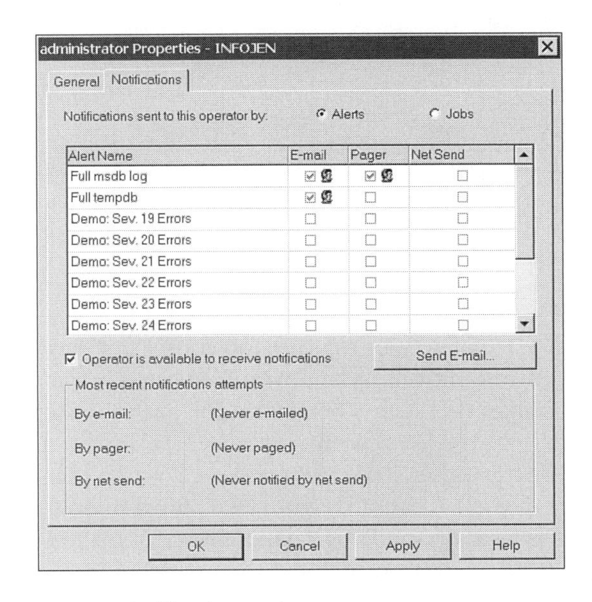

FIGURE 18.5 The Operator Notifications tab.

Jobs

Jobs are the cornerstone of SQL Server automation. Managed from the Jobs folder of the SQL Server Agent folder, jobs can be single or multistep operations, involving any combination of T-SQL, operating system commands, ActiveX scripts, or replication tasks.

Defining Job Properties

Right-clicking the Jobs folder and selecting New Job will bring up the Job Property dialog box. On the General tab, enter a name for the job and make sure the Enabled check box is selected. You can then select a category for the job. Categories are used to organize similar jobs; after you select a category, clicking the Ellipse button (...) beside it will show other jobs in the same category. Next is the Owner drop-down box. By default, this is the ID of the SQL Login creating the job, but if you are the administrator, you can assign the job to someone else. A Description field is also available and, if multiserver jobs are enabled, you can select on which servers the job will run. Multiserver jobs are covered in a following section of this chapter. Figure 18.6 shows the General tab of the Job properties.

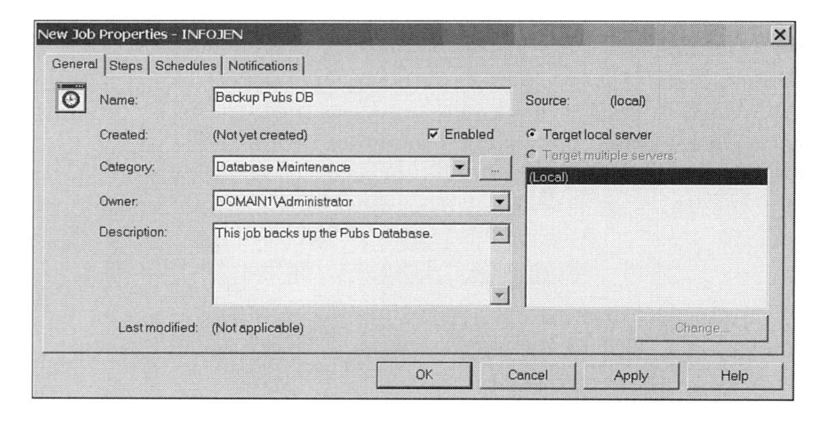

FIGURE 18.6 The Job Properties General tab.

Defining Job Steps

The Steps tab defines the actual actions that the job consists of. From here, job steps can be added, edited, deleted, and moved up or down in the step hierarchy. The division of jobs into steps is what makes this such a powerful tool. Each job step can be defined—on success or on failure—to exit the job reporting failure, exit the job reporting success, go to the next step, or jump to any other step. This creates a go-no-go sequence that is limited only by your ingenuity in what it can do. Figure 18.7 shows a job defined with two steps. The first step attempts to back up the Pubs database to tape. If the first job fails (perhaps you forgot to load the tape), it goes on the next step, which performs a backup to disk.

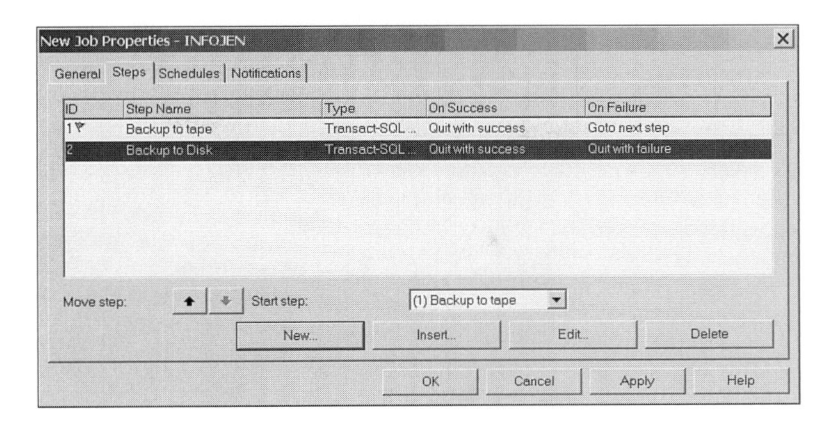

FIGURE 18.7 The Job Properties Steps tab.

When you select New, Insert or Edit, the Edit Job Step dialog box is presented. On the General tab, enter a name for the step, the type of command (T-SQL, CmdExec, and so on), the database, and the actual command to be performed. The Open button allows you to import the command from a file, and parse checks the statement for correct syntax. Figure 18.8 shows the General tab of the Job Step dialog Box.

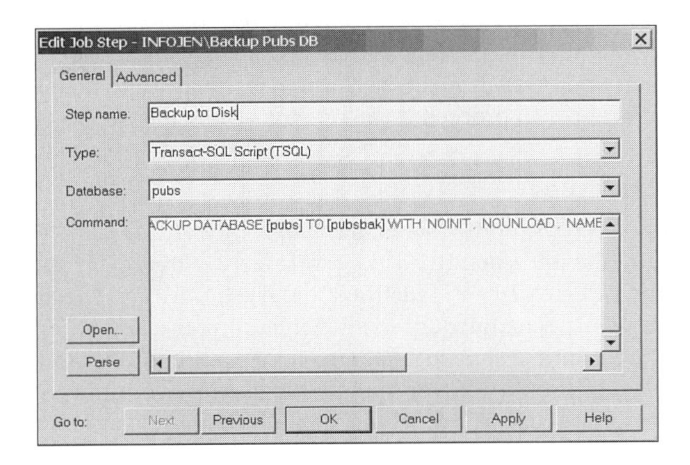

FIGURE 18.8 The General tab of the Job Step dialog box.

The Advanced tab is where you set the action of the step after success or failure, and the number and interval for retry attempts if a failure occurs. From the T-SQL Command Options section, you can also name a file to accept the output of T-SQL or ActiveScript commands, and optionally append the output to the job history. A drop-down box is also provided to select the user under which the command should run. Only a system administrator can choose to run the command as a different user. Figure 18.9 shows the Advanced tab of the Job Step dialog box.

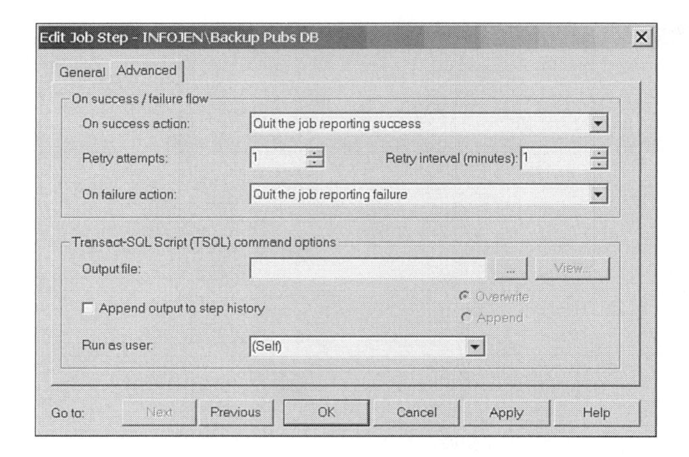

FIGURE 18.9 The Advanced tab of the Job Step dialog box.

Multistep Jobs Versus Multiple Jobs

When do you create a multistep job, as opposed to multiple separate jobs? The idea behind multistep jobs is not so you can perform every task in your database in a single job. The steps in a multistep job should be related or dependent on the other steps in the job. A job that has two steps that each back up a different database should really have been created as two jobs. However, a job that consists of steps that back up the database, import data, and then update a Web page with the new data would be logical, as dependencies could be set on how to proceed if the previous step failed.

Defining Job Schedules

When the job will run is set from the Schedules tab. When creating schedules, you have the option of running the job when the SQL Server Agent starts it (as it would in an alert condition), when the CPU reaches a predefined idle level, once at a specified time, or, as is most common, at regularly scheduled intervals. Scheduling is taken a step further by allowing you to define multiple schedules in any combination of methods. For example, a job could run once a day at 3:00 a.m., or if an alert calls the Agent to run it. The example in Figure 18.10 shows a backup with different schedules for weekdays and the weekend.

Defining Job Notifications

The Notifications tab is where you configure how notifications will be handled. Notifications can be sent by e-mail, pager, or `NET SEND` on job completion, failure, or success. For example, a notification might send an e-mail if the job succeeds, but page someone if it fails. You can also set jobs to report to the Windows Application log. Jobs designed to run only once can be set to be automatically deleted. Figure 18.11 shows the Notifications tab.

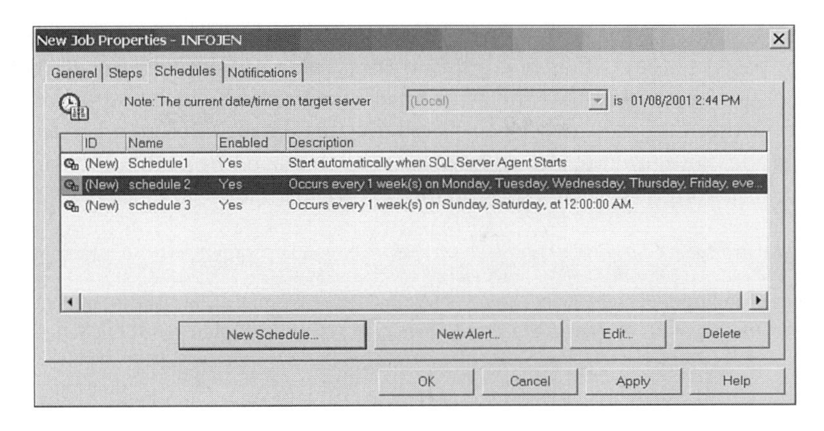

FIGURE 18.10 The Job Properties Schedules tab.

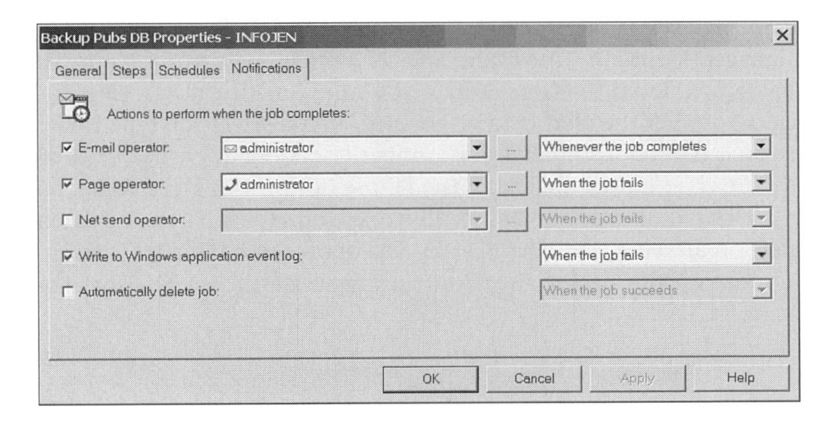

FIGURE 18.11 The Job Properties Notifications tab.

Viewing Job History

To view the history for a job, right-click the job and select View Job History. By default, the SQL Server Agent maintains up to 100 rows of history for each job, to a maximum of 1,000 rows in total. This limit can be configured from the Job System tab of the SQL Server Agent property page. The job history is an excellent tool for troubleshooting problematic jobs.

Alerts

Alerts constitute the "reactive" component of Scheduling and Notification. The SQL Server Agent monitors the Windows Application Log; when an event occurs, the Agent compares that event to its list of alerts. If an alert has been defined on the event, the action defined for that alert is fired. Alerts can be configured to fire on SQL Server or user-defined error messages, or based on performance condition thresholds. When defining alerts to respond to error messages, remember that the error must be set to write to the application log or the alert won't fire. Only severity 19 and higher errors are required to write to the log, but all others can be configured to do so. Errors can be managed from the Enterprise Manager Tools menu, or through the Properties dialog box for the alert.

NOTE

If you are running SQL Server on Windows 98, no Application log is available to which to send the error messages. In this case, the Event Viewer must be substituted by a SQL Server Profiler trace.

Defining Alert Properties

As with jobs and operators, alerts are managed from the SQL Server Agent folder in Enterprise Manager. Right-click the folder and select New Alert to access the Alert Properties dialog box. From the General tab, you can name the alert, select the type of alert, and select whether the alert is to be enabled. If you select the type to be SQL Server Event Alert, you can enter a specific error number or choose a severity level. If you don't know the specific error number, clicking the Ellipse button (...) gives you access to a search tool. The Database drop-down box allows you to pick a particular database or to define the alert on all databases. There is also the option to enter a text string that the error must contain for the alert to fire. Configuring an alert for a SQL Server error is shown in Figure 18.12.

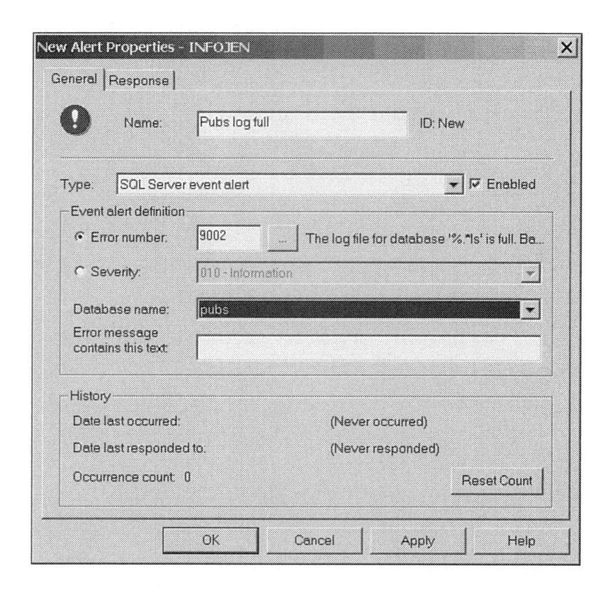

FIGURE 18.12 Configuring an alert for a SQL Server error.

If you choose to create the alert as a type SQL Server Performance Condition Alert, you are presented with a different set of options. Performance condition alerts use the same counters that are used to monitor SQL Server with the Windows Performance Monitor. Select the object to monitor, the specific counter for the object, the instance (database) you want to monitor, and the value for the counter that will fire the alert. The alert can be set to fire if the counter rises above, falls below, or is equal to the value entered. Figure 18.13 shows a performance condition alert that fires when the transaction log of the Pubs database is more than 80% full.

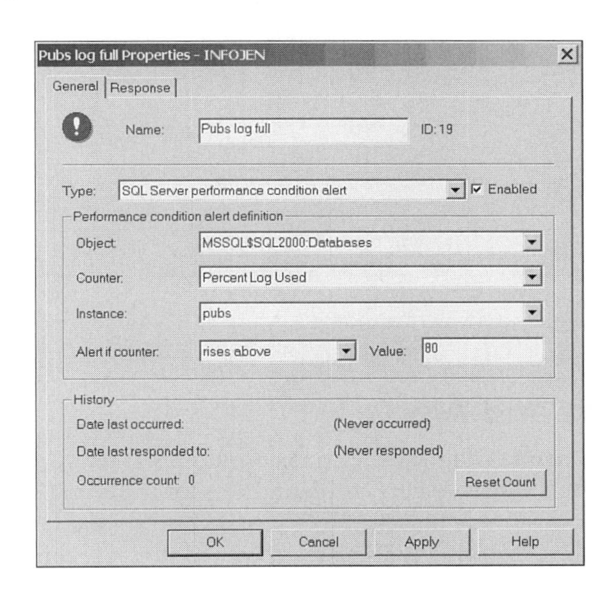

FIGURE 18.13 Configuring an alert for a performance condition.

Defining Alert Responses and Operators

The Response tab enables you to define what to do when the alert fires. You can choose to run a job, as well as define operators to be notified. Notification of an alert is helpful, but the real power of the alert system lies in its ability to run a job. For example, the alert defined in Figure 18.13 fires when the transaction log reaches 80% full. This alert can be defined to run a job that backs up the log. As you saw earlier, the job can contain multiple steps to ensure it completes or notify someone if it doesn't. This allows automated monitoring and correction of potential problems before they reach the critical stage. Figure 18.14 shows the Response tab for just such an alert.

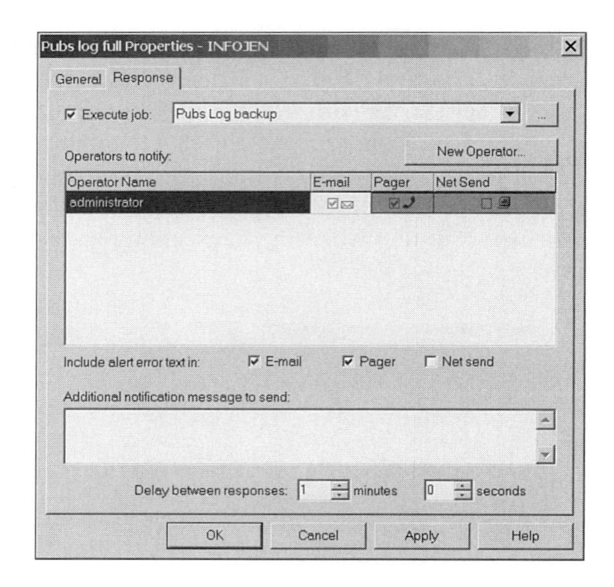

FIGURE 18.14 Configuring an alert response.

Scripting Jobs and Alerts

Alerts and jobs can be quite complex and time consuming to set up and debug. Regular backups of the MSDB database—where the definitions for alerts and jobs are stored—will protect you against loss of these objects; however, it is also a good idea to script at least your most complex jobs. Scripting is also a good way to store versions of a job as it is modified. If the modification doesn't have the desired behavior, the script can be run to restore the previous version. Another use for scripts is to easily transfer jobs or alerts to another server. To generate a script for a job or alert, right-click it and select Generate SQL Script. Provide a name for the file and select the text format and whether the script should generate `DROP` commands (replace) for the object. A Preview button is also available so you can view the script, as shown in Figure 18.15.

Multiserver Job Management

Job management can be centralized on a single SQL Server, with other servers polling this server for the jobs they should run. In this situation, you configure a **master** server and define the jobs on this server. The next step is to enlist **target** servers, which periodically poll the master to see if they have jobs scheduled to run. This works if the servers are identical or similar in configuration. A job set to run on multiple servers to back up the sales database to drive F: will obviously fail if no sales database or drive F: exist on that server! By their nature, multiserver jobs must be generic.

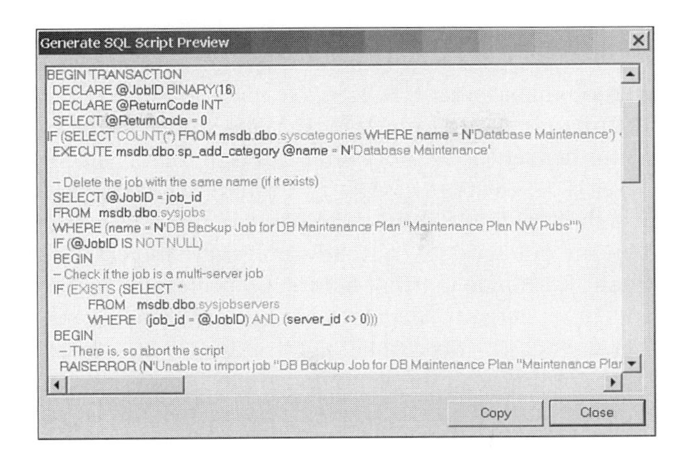

FIGURE 18.15 Previewing SQL script generation.

Creating a Master SQL Server Agent

To create the Master Agent, right-click the SQL Server Agent folder from the server that will be the master. Select Multiserver Administration and then select Make This a Master. This will activate the Make MSX Wizard, which will prompt you for an operator to notify for multiserver jobs and for the servers that should be the target servers. It will also allow you to provide a description for each target server. Click Finish and the master and target servers will be registered.

Enlisting Target Servers

If you want to enlist another target server after a master server has been created, select Make This a Target from the Multiserver Management menu of that server. The wizard will prompt you for the name of the master server and then register the target with the master. This can also be done from the master server by selecting Add Target Servers from the Multiserver Management menu. Remember that a server can be the target of only one master.

Multiserver Jobs

After the master and target servers are set up, jobs are created on the master server and specified as to which target servers they should run on. Periodically, the target servers poll the master server. If any jobs defined for them have been scheduled to run since the last polling interval (which is 5 minutes), the target server downloads the job and runs it. When the job completes, it uploads the job outcome status to the master server.

Event Forwarding

Similar to multiserver job management, SQL Server can also be configured to forward error messages. All or any unhandled event messages that meet or exceed a specified severity level can be sent to another server for processing. For example, you can configure all your servers to forward level 17 or greater messages to an underutilized departmental server. The advantage here is that the alerts, jobs, and operators that respond to the error need to only be configured on the one server. The disadvantages are increased network traffic, and, perhaps most importantly, a single point of failure has been introduced. If the server that is handling the events or its network segment is down, then you are in peril of missing events from the other servers. The downside might outweigh the advantages here. Using Enterprise Manager or scripting, it is simple to create the alerts, jobs, and operators on each server. It's a conundrum really; if I had a few servers, I would let each handle its own affairs. If I had dozens of servers, I wouldn't want one server responsible for all their messaging!

If you want to configure event forwarding, it is done through the Advanced tab of the SQL Server Agent properties. Figure 18.16 illustrates configuring event forwarding.

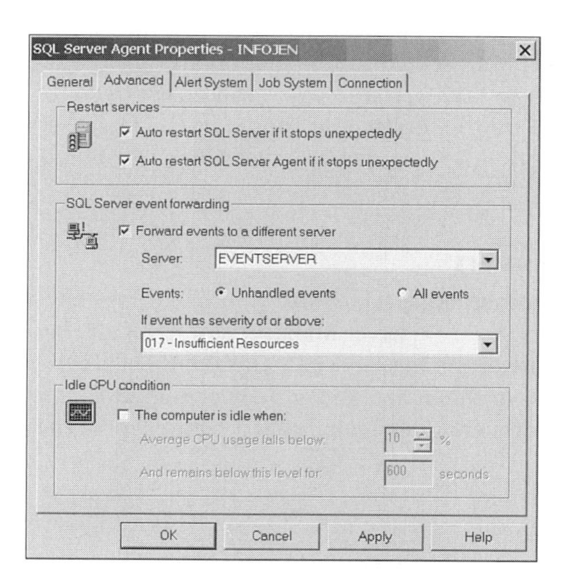

FIGURE 18.16 Configuring event forwarding.

Summary

The SQL Server Agent and its trio of jobs, operators, and alerts provide a flexible and powerful set of tools to manage your servers. Databases thrive on consistency, and one of the best ways to achieve a consistent database environment is through the automation provided by the SQL Server Agent. Schedule regular maintenance, and provide alerts and jobs to correct abnormal conditions. Your databases will love you for it!

If you work with multiple servers, then the next chapter, "Managing Linked and Remote Servers," will be of interest. That chapter will describe how to manage data in a distributed environment.

CHAPTER 19

Managing Linked and Remote Servers

by Ray Rankins and Paul Bertucci

IN THIS CHAPTER

- Remote Servers
- Linked Servers
- Adding, Dropping, and Configuring Linked Servers
- Mapping Local Logins to Logins on Linked Servers
- Obtaining General Information About Linked Servers
- Executing a Stored Procedure Via a Linked Server
- Setting Up Linked Servers Through Enterprise Manager

As your databases grow in size, complexity, or geographic distribution, you might find it necessary to spread out your data across multiple servers. SQL Server has long had the ability to perform server-to-server communication. In versions of SQL Server prior to 7.0, this was done using remote procedure calls (RPCs). A **remote procedure call** is the execution of a stored procedure on a local server that actually resides on a remote server. This capability allows you to retrieve or modify data that resides on a different SQL Server. The main drawback, however, is that you cannot join between tables residing on more than one server using remote procedure calls, nor can you selectively choose the columns of information you want to retrieve from the remote server. You get whatever the stored procedure on the remote server is defined to return.

If you need to join information together across servers, SQL Server 2000 provides the ability to link servers together. In addition to providing the capability to perform remote procedure calls, you can also access remote tables as if they were defined locally. The remote tables can be on another SQL Server or any datasource with an OLE DB provider. You can also define distributed partitioned views that can pull data together from multiple servers into a single view. For your end user queries, it appears as if the data is coming from a single table. For more information on distributed partitioned views, see Chapter 27, "Creating and Managing Views in SQL Server."

This chapter provides an overview of linked servers in SQL Server 2000 along with a brief discussion of remote servers, which are the predecessor to linked servers. Remote servers and remote procedure calls are legacy features that are still supported for backward compatibility. In other words, you can still set up and use remote servers and remote procedure calls, but linked servers are much easier to set up and provide greater functionality.

Remote Servers

By definition, a **remote server** is a server that you access as part of a client process without opening a separate, distinct, direct client connection. SQL Server manages the communication between servers using RPCs. Essentially, the SQL Server to which the client is connected opens up another connection to the remote server and submits the stored procedure request to the remote server. Any results are passed back to the local server, which then passes the results down to the originating client application (see Figure 19.1).

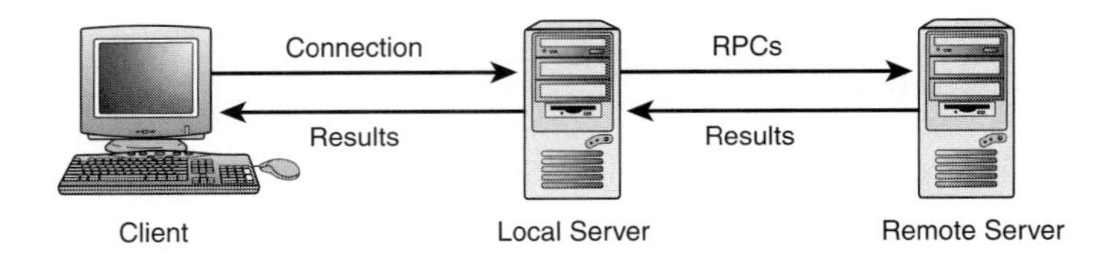

FIGURE 19.1 The remote server is accessed through the local server, and the client maintains only a single connection to the local server.

You call a remote procedure the same way that you call a local procedure; the only difference is that you need to fully qualify the name of the procedure with the name of the server. Following is the syntax:

```
execute remote_server_name.db_name.owner_name.procedure_name
```

Remote servers are more limited in functionality and a bit more time-consuming to set up than linked servers. The following list outlines the steps for setting up remote servers:

1. Define the local and remote servers on both servers.
2. Configure each server for remote access.
3. On the remote server, define the method for mapping logins and users to the server's own logins and users.
4. Set the remote option for password checking.

If you are connecting between multiple SQL Server 2000 or SQL Server 7.0 servers, it is best to set them up as linked servers. However, if you need to execute remote procedure calls on a pre-7.0 SQL Server, you'll need to set up remote servers. Let's take a look at how that is done just in case you might need it.

Remote Server Setup

Assume that the local server is called near_server and the remote server is called far_server. First, you need to use sp_addserver to add the remote server name to the sysservers table in the master database if it's not defined already. You can get a list of the servers defined using sp_helpserver:

```
exec sp_helpserver
go
```

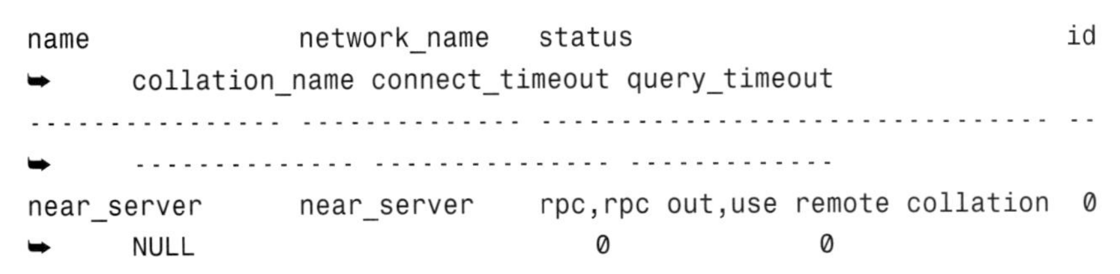

```
name            network_name   status                             id
➥     collation_name connect_timeout query_timeout
--------------- -------------- ---------------------------------- --
➥     -------------- --------------- -------------
near_server     near_server    rpc,rpc out,use remote collation  0
➥     NULL                     0              0
```

Generally, you won't need to execute sp_addserver for the local server name. This is usually taken care of during setup. The local server will have an ID of 0. If you do need to add the definition for the local server, specify the local flag as the second argument:

```
exec sp_addserver near_server, local
```

You will need to execute sp_addserver once for each of the remote servers that you will access from the local server. For example, on the local server (near_server), execute the following command to add far_server:

```
exec sp_addserver far_server
```

If the local server is a 7.0 or later version of SQL Server, you can add the remote servers using sp_addlinkedserver:

```
exec sp_addlinkedserver far_server
```

On the remote server (far_server), you need to define the local server (near_server) that will be connecting to it:

```
exec sp_addserver near_server
```

To add remote servers in Enterprise Manager, open the Security folder, right-click on Remote Servers, and choose the New Remote Server option to bring up the Remote Server Properties dialog box (see Figure 19.2). In this dialog box, you can enter the server name and specify whether it allows the remote server to execute RPCs. You can also establish how logins are mapped when executing RPCs. Login mapping is covered a few paragraphs later in this section.

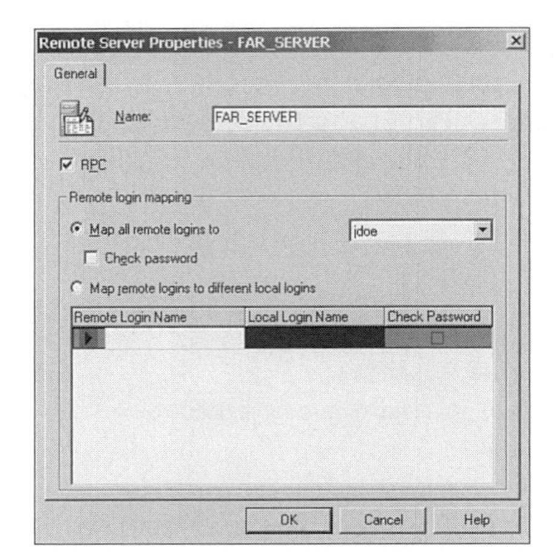

FIGURE 19.2 Adding remote servers in SQL Enterprise Manager.

Next, you need to ensure that each server is configured for remote access. By default, remote access is automatically enabled during setup to support replication. If it has been disabled, you'll need to re-enable it using Enterprise Manager or T-SQL. The syntax to configure each server for remote access is as follows:

```
exec sp_configure 'remote access', 1
reconfigure
```

To enable remote access using Enterprise Manager, right-click the server and choose the Properties option in the pop-up menu. Go to the Connection tab and make sure the check box Allow Other SQL Servers to Connect Remotely to This SQL Server Using RPC is checked (see Figure 19.3). In this dialog box, you can also set the length of time the RPC should wait for query results. The default is `0`, which indicates waiting an infinite amount of time. Click OK to accept any changes.

After enabling remote access, you'll need to shut down and restart each server.

The next step takes place on the remote server. This is where things get a bit tricky.

What you need to do is define how to map the logins from the server making the remote procedure request (`near_server`) to the environment on the server receiving the request (`far_server`). Although you are technically setting things up on the remote server (`far_server`), it is treated as the local server, and the local server (`near_server`) is treated as the remote server. Confused yet? I've always found it easiest to not try to think about it too much and just follow the steps. Following is the syntax:

```
exec sp_addremotelogin remote_server_name [, local_login_name [, remote_login_name]]
```

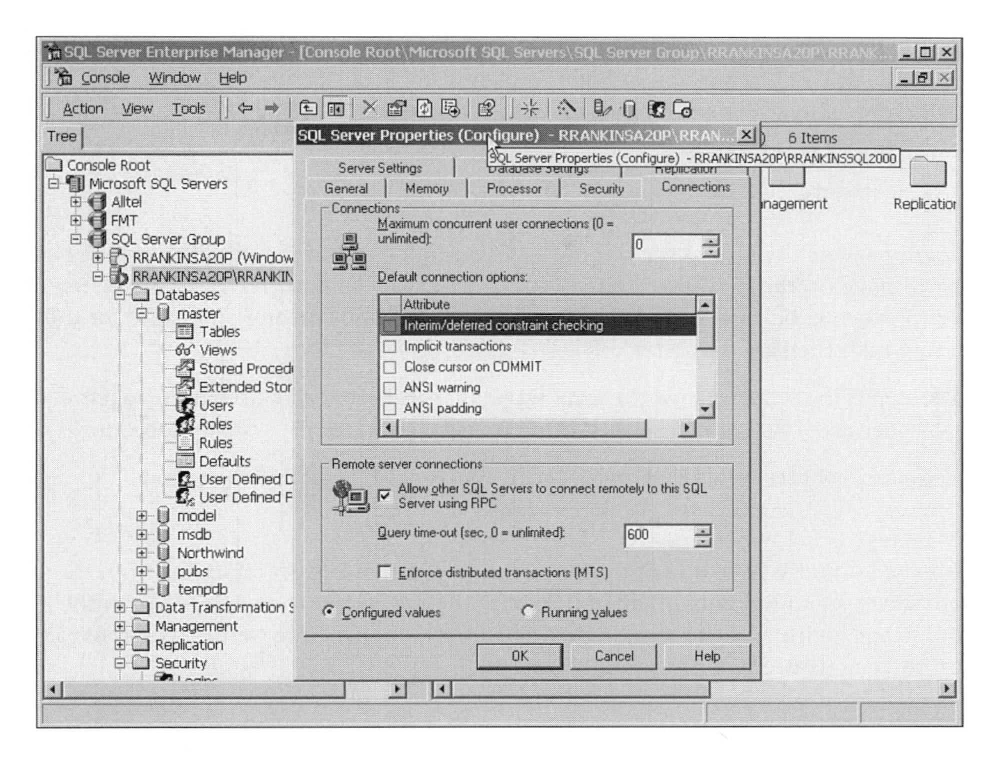

FIGURE 19.3 Enabling remote access in SQL Enterprise Manager.

For example, on the remote server (`far_server`), execute the following command to map each login on `near_server` to the same login on `far_server`:

```
exec sp_addremotelogin near_server
```

This is the simplest mapping method. It presumes that the logins are the same on both servers, and maps login to login.

TIP

If users from the remote server need access on your server, don't forget to add them with `sp_addlogin`.

To map all remote logins from the remote server (`near_server`) to a single local login on the local server (`far_server`), execute the following:

```
exec sp_addremotelogin near_server, far_server_user
```

This is another straightforward mapping method. Any legitimate user on `near_server` will be mapped to the single specified login on `far_server`.

The last login mapping method allows you to map each individual login on the remote server (`near_server`) to a different login name on the local server (`far_server`). In the following example, the login named `mdoe` on `near_server` will be mapped to the login `jdoe` on `far_server`.

```
exec sp_addremotelogin near_server, jdoe, mdoe
```

The login to which you map the remote logins will determine the permissions the remote users will have on the local server. If you want to restrict the procedures that the remote users can execute, be sure to set the appropriate permissions on the procedure for the login to which they are mapping.

The last step is to configure how the local server (`far_server`) validates remote logins coming from `far_server`. This is accomplished using the `sp_remoteoption` system procedure:

```
exec sp_remoteoption remote_server, local_login_name, remote_login_name,
                     option, {true | false}
```

Essentially, you only have one option available—whether to trust all logins from the remote server, or to not trust them and require the passwords to match between the remote server logins and the local logins. This is accomplished by setting the `trusted` option to `true` (trusted) or `false` (not trusted).

NOTE

If the trusted option is not turned on, you need to establish and maintain synchronized passwords between servers. Because you can't specify a separate remote password when executing a remote procedure call, SQL Server validates the passwords by matching the user's password from the originating server with the password for the mapped login ID on the receiving server. If the passwords are not synchronized, remote access will not be granted.

When mapping remote logins to different login IDs or to a single login ID on the receiving server, the `trusted` option is typically used because it would be unfeasible to try and synchronize passwords in these situations. For example, all users on the requesting server executing RPCs would have to have the same password as the login ID to which they are mapped on the receiving server. This would tend to create a bit of a security hole.

For example, on the remote server (`far_server`), execute the following procedure to set up logins without requiring synchronized passwords between servers:

```
sp_remoteoption near_server, near_server_login, null, trusted, true
```

To get information on individual logins mapped for a server and whether they are trusted, use the `sp_helpremotelogin` command:

```
sp_helpremotelogin [remote_server [, remote_name] ]
```

For a list of all remote logins, execute sp_helpremotelogin without a parameter. In the example that follows, three different remote logins are configured for two different remote servers. The sa logins on both remote servers KAYDEROSS and NLCWEST1 map to the local server login repl_subscriber. All other logins from NLCWEST1 map to the remote_login login ID on the local server. All remote logins are trusted so passwords do not have to be synchronized between the servers.

```
sp_helpremotelogin
server                 local_user_name        remote_user_name       options
---------------------- ---------------------- ---------------------- ---------
KAYDEROSS              repl_subscriber        sa                     trusted
NLCWEST1               remote_login           ** mapped locally **   trusted
NLCWEST1               repl_subscriber        sa                     trusted
```

To set up remote logins and the trusted option in Enterprise Manager, open up the Security folder for the server that will be receiving the RPC requests and click Remote Servers to display a list of defined servers. Bring up the Properties dialog box, as shown in Figure 19.2. Within the remote server properties, you can establish the various login mappings and whether passwords need to be checked.

It's easy to see how setting up remote servers can be a confusing and tedious process. You have to perform setup tasks on both the local and remote servers. In addition, the mapping of logins severely limits what types of servers can be accessed. Login mappings are performed at the remote server instead of the local server, which works fine if the remote server is SQL Server, but how do you perform this task in another database environment that doesn't have user mappings? How do you tell an Oracle database to which Oracle user to map a SQL Server user? These are just a few of the problems with remote servers. After you see how linked servers are set up and see the expanded capabilities they provide, you won't want to use remote servers unless you absolutely have to, which should only be when you need to execute RPCs on pre-7.0 SQL Servers.

Linked Servers

Unlike remote servers, linked servers have two simple setup steps:

1. Define the remote server on the local server.
2. Define the method for mapping remote logins on the local server.

Notice that the configuration is performed on the local server. The mapping for the local user to the remote user is stored in the local SQL Server database. In fact, you don't need to configure anything in the remote database. This setup allows SQL Server to use OLE DB to link to datasources other than other SQL Servers.

OLE DB is an API that allows COM applications to work with databases as well as other datasources such as text files and spreadsheets. This lets SQL Server have access to a vast amount of different types of data.

Unlike remote servers, linked servers also allow distributed queries and transactions.

Truly Linked

Keep in mind that when you complete linked servers, SQL Server really keeps these data resources linked in many ways. Most importantly, it keeps the schema definitions linked. In other words, if the schema of a remote table on a linked server changes, any server that has links to it also knows the change. Even when the linked server's schema comes from something such as Excel, if you change the Excel spreadsheet in any way, that change will be automatically reflected back at the local SQL Server. This is extremely significant from a metadata (schema's) integrity point of view. This is what is meant by "completely linked!"

Distributed Queries

Distributed queries access data stored in OLE DB datasources. SQL Server treats these datasources as if they contained SQL Server tables. Due to this treatment, you can view or manipulate this data using the same basic syntax as other SQL Server `SELECT`, `INSERT`, `UPDATE`, or `DELETE` statements. The main difference is the table-naming convention. Distributed queries use this basic syntax when referring to the remote table:

```
linked_server_name.catalog.schema.object_name
```

The following query accesses data from a sales table in an Oracle database, a region table in a Microsoft Access database, and a customer table in a SQL Server database:

```
SELECT s.sales_amount
FROM access_server...region AS r,
oracle_server..sales_owner.sale AS s,
sql_server.customer_db.dbo.customer AS c
where r.region_id=s.region_id
and s.customer_id=c.customer_id
and r.region_name='Southwest'
and c.customer_name='ABC Steel'
```

Distributed Transactions

Distributed transactions are supported if the OLE DB provider has built in the functionality. This means it is possible to manipulate data from several different datasources in a single transaction. For example, suppose two banks decide to merge. The first bank (let's call it OraBank) stores all checking and savings accounts in an Oracle database. The second bank (let's call it SqlBank) stores all checking and savings accounts in a SQL Server 2000 database. A customer has a checking account with OraBank and a savings account with SqlBank. What would happen if a customer wants to transfer $100 from the checking account to the savings account? You can do it simply using the following code while maintaining transactional consistency. The transaction is either committed or rolled back on both databases:

```
BEGIN DISTRIBUTED TRANSACTION
-- One hundred dollars is subtracted from the savings account.
UPDATE oracle_server..savings_owner.savings_table
 SET account_balance = account_balance - 100
WHERE account_number = 12345
-- One hundred dollars is added to the checking account.
UPDATE sql_server.checking_db.dbo.checking_table
 SET account_balance = account_balance + 100
WHERE account_number = 98765
COMMIT TRANSACTION;
```

For more information on distributed transactions, see Chapter 32, "Distributed Transaction Processing."

Adding, Dropping, and Configuring Linked Servers

The next few sections show you how to add, drop, and configure linked servers through system-stored procedures.

sp_addlinkedserver

Before you can access an external datasource through SQL Server, it must be registered inside the database as a linked server. You use the `sp_addlinkedserver` stored procedure for this purpose. Only users with the sysadmin or setupadmin fixed-server roles can run this procedure.

SQL Server 2000 ships with a number of OLE DB providers, including providers for Oracle databases, DB2 databases, Access databases, other SQL Server 6.5/7.0 databases, as well as databases that can be reached through ODBC and JDBC. SQL Server also comes with OLE DB providers for Microsoft Excel spreadsheets and Indexing Service.

Some of the arguments for `sp_addlinkedserver` are needed only for certain OLE DB providers. Because of the number of different options and settings available, refer to the documentation for the OLE DB provider to determine which arguments must be provided and the appropriate strings:

```
sp_addlinkedserver [@server =] 'server'
  [, [@srvproduct =] 'product_name'][, [@provider =] 'provider_name']
  [, [@datasrc =] 'data_source'] [, [@location =] 'location']
  [, [@provstr =] 'provider_string'] [, [@catalog =] 'catalog']
```

The following list describes each element of the syntax:

`server` The name of the linked server that will be added.

`product_name` The product name of the OLE DB provider. If this argument is set to `'SQL Server'`, then only the `@server` argument is required. For all other OLE DB providers delivered with SQL Server, you can ignore this parameter.

`provider_name` The unique programmatic identifier (PROGID). This value must match the PROGID in the Registry for the particular OLE DB provider. The following list shows the OLE DB providers delivered with SQL Server and the corresponding values for this argument:

SQL Server	`SQLOLEDB`
Access/Jet/Excel	`Microsoft.Jet.OLEDB.4.0` Spreadsheets
ODBC	`MSDASQL`
DB2	`DB2OLEDB`
Oracle	`MSDAORA`
File System	`MSIDXS` (Indexing Service)

`data_source` A datasource that points to the particular version of the OLE DB source. For example, for setting up an Access linked server, this argument holds the path to the file. For setting up a SQL Server linked server, this argument holds the machine name of the linked SQL Server. The following list shows the OLE DB providers delivered with SQL Server and the corresponding values for this argument:

SQL Server	Network name of SQL Server
Access/Jet/Excel Spreadsheets	Full pathname to the file
ODBC	System DSN or ODBC connection string
Oracle	SQL*Net alias
File System (Indexing Service)	Indexing Service catalog name

`location` The location string possibly used by the OLE DB provider.

`provider_string` The connection string possibly used by the OLE DB provider.

`catalog` The catalog string possibly used by the OLE DB provider.

Figure 19.4 depicts the overall technical architecture of what is being enabled via linked servers and providers.

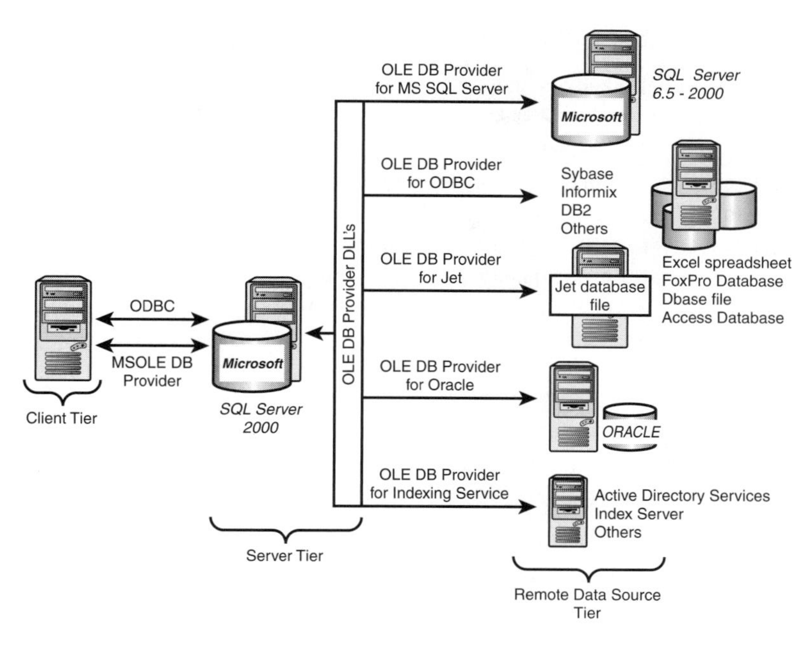

FIGURE 19.4 Linked Servers provider architecture.

This allows datasources to be accessed from within SQL Server 2000 with the highest degree of efficiency possible.

The following example adds an Oracle linked server called `'ORACLE_DATABASE'` that will connect to the database specified by the SQL*Net string `'my_sqlnet_connect_string'`:

```
EXEC sp_addlinkedserver @server='ORACLE_DATABASE',
@srvproduct='Oracle', @provider='MSDAORA',
@datasrc='my_sqlnet_connect_string'
```

The next example adds an Access linked server called `'ACCESS_DATABASE'` that will connect to the database `'Foodmart.mdb'` stored in the C:\temp directory:

```
EXEC sp_addlinkedserver @server='ACCESS_DATABASE',
@srvproduct='Access', @provider='Microsoft.Jet.OLEDB.4.0',
@datasrc='C:\temp\Foodmart.mdb'
```

This example adds a SQL Server linked server that resides on the `'SQL_SERVER_DB'` machine:

```
EXEC sp_addlinkedserver @server='SQL_SERVER_DB',
@srvproduct='SQL Server'
```

This example adds an Excel 8.0 spreadsheet as a linked server:

```
/* Set up of an Excel linked server */
EXEC sp_addlinkedserver
        'ExcelSW',    /* linked server name you want to use*/
        'Jet Excel',   /* product name - can be anything */
        'Microsoft.Jet.OLEDB.4.0', /* OLE provider name */
        'd:\SWCustomers.xls',  /* datasource name */
        NULL,  /* location not needed in this case */
        'Excel 8.0',  /* Provider string if needed */
        NULL    /* catalog name if needed */
go
```

This example adds an ODBC datasource as a linked server called `'ODBC_with_DATA_SOURCE'`. The ODBC connection string must be registered on the local server to use this linked server:

```
EXEC sp_addlinkedserver @server='ODBC_with_DATA_SOURCE',
@srvproduct='ODBC', @provider='MSDASQL',
@datasrc='My_ODBC_connection_string'
```

This example adds an ODBC datasource as a linked server called `'ODBC_with_PROVIDER_STRING'`. Unlike the previous example, an ODBC datasource does not need to exist. The information normally stored as an ODBC datasource is stored in the `provstr` argument:

```
EXEC sp_addlinkedserver @server='ODBC_with_PROVIDER_STRING',
 @srvproduct='ODBC', @provider='MSDASQL',
 @provstr='DRIVER={SQL Server}; SERVER=MyServer; UID=sa;PWD=;'
```

sp_linkedserver

To see the linked servers that have been defined on this SQL Server, simply use `sp_linkedservers`.

```
EXEC sp_linkedservers
Go
```

The `sp_linkedservers` execution provides the list of all linked servers on this SQL Server:

```
SRV_Name          SRV_Provider            SRV_Product SRV_Datasource     ...
----------------- ----------------------- ----------- ------------------ ...
C81124-C\DBARCH01 SQLOLEDB                SQL Server  C81124-C\DBARCH01  ...
ExcelSW           Microsoft.Jet.OLEDB.4.0 Jet Excel   d:\SWCustomers.xls ...
repl_distributor  SQLOLEDB                SQL Server  C81124-C\DBARCH01  ...
```

As you can see, the list now contains the linked server that was just created (ExcelSW). However, you won't be able to use this linked server yet. A linked server login will have to be created for SQL Server to actually get to the datasource. You have essentially established the path to the datasource with `sp_addlinkedserver`.

sp_dropserver

You can unregister linked servers using `sp_dropserver`. Only members of the sysadmin and setupadmin fixed-server roles can execute this stored procedure:

```
sp_dropserver [@server =] 'server' [, [@droplogins =] {'droplogins' | NULL}]
```

The following list describes each element of the syntax:

server	The linked server that will be unregistered.
droplogins	Specifies that the logins associated with the server should be dropped. If this argument is not specified, then the server will only be dropped if logins do not exist for this linked server.

The following example unregisters an Oracle, Access, and SQL Server database:

```
EXEC sp_dropserver @server='ORACLE_DATABASE', @droplogins='droplogins'
EXEC sp_dropserver @server='ACCESS_DATABASE'
EXEC sp_dropserver @server='SQL_SERVER_DB',@droplogins='droplogins'
```

sp_serveroption

You can configure linked servers with `sp_serveroption`. Only users with the sysadmin or setupadmin fixed-server roles can run this procedure:

```
sp_serveroption [[@server =] 'server'] [,[@optname =] 'option_name']
[,[@optvalue =] 'option_value']
```

The following list describes each element of the syntax:

server	The linked server that will be affected by this option.	
option_name	The name of the option to be configured. The valid option names follow:	
	`'collation compatible'`	If the `optvalue` is set to `TRUE`, SQL Server assumes the linked server has the same character set and collation sequence. Only set this option to `true` if you are sure the character sets and collation are identical.

19

'connect timeout'	The length of time, in seconds, to wait before timing out connection attempt to linked server. If `0`, uses `sp_configure` default value.
'data access'	If the `optvalue` is set to `TRUE`, distributed queries will be allowed if the OLE DB provider supports it. If the `optvalue` is set to `FALSE`, distributed queries will be disabled on this linked server.
'dist'	If the `optvalue` is set to `TRUE`, this specifies that the linked server is a distributor (used for replication).
'dpub'	If the `optvalue` is set to `TRUE`, this specifies that the linked server is a remote publisher to this distributor (used for replication).
'lazy schema validation'	If the `optvalue` is set to `TRUE`, skips check the schema of remote tables at the beginning of the query.
'pub'	If the `optvalue` is set to `TRUE`, this specifies that the linked server is a publisher (used for replication).
'query timeout'	Length of time, in seconds, to wait before timing out queries against linked server. If `0`, uses `sp_configure` default value.
'sub'	If the `optvalue` is set to `TRUE`, this specifies that the linked server is a subscriber (used for replication).
'rpc'	If the `optvalue` is set to `TRUE`, this allows RPCs from the linked server.
'rpc out'	If the `optvalue` is set to `TRUE`, this allows RPCs to the linked server.
'system'	For internal use only.
'use remote collation'	If the `optvalue` is set to `TRUE`, will use t he collation of remote columns for SQL Server datasources or the specified `collation name` for non-SQL Server sources. If `FALSE`, will use the local server default collation.

'collation name'	If use remote collation is set to TRUE and the linked server is not a SQL Server, specifies the name of the collation to be used on the linked server. Use this option when the OLE DB datasource has a collation that matches one of the SQL Server collations.

option_value	The value of this option. Valid values are TRUE (or ON) and FALSE (or OFF), a nonnegative integer for the connect timeout and query timeout options, or a collation name for the collation name option.

This example disables distributed queries to the ORACLE_DATABASE linked server:

```
EXEC sp_serveroption @server='ORACLE_DATABASE',
@optname='data access', @optvalue='FALSE'
```

This example enables RPCs to the SQL_SERVER_DB linked server:

```
EXEC sp_serveroption @server='SQL_SERVER_DB',
@optname='rpc out', @optvalue='TRUE'
```

To set the query timeout to 60 seconds for the SQL Server datasource, execute the following command:

```
EXEC sp_serveroption  'SQL_SERVER_DB ', 'query timeout', 60
```

To display the options currently enabled for a linked server, use sp_helpserver, use:

```
EXEC sp_helpserver @server='SQL_SERVER_DB'
GO

name           network_name   status
➥    id   collation_name connect_timeout query_timeout
-------------- -------------- ----------------------------------------------
➥    ---- -------------- --------------- -------------
SQL_SERVER_DB  SQL_SERVER_DB  rpc,rpc out,data access,use remote collation
➥    1    NULL           0               60
```

Mapping Local Logins to Logins on Linked Servers

To gain access to a linked server, the linked server must validate the user for security reasons. The requesting server (that is, the local server) provides a login name and password to the linked server on behalf of the local server user. For this to work, you need to map the local logins with the linked server logins you are going to use.

19

sp_addlinkedsrvlogin

SQL Server provides the sp_addlinkedsrvlogin system stored procedure to map local logins to logins on the linked servers. This stored procedure can be executed by members of the sysadmin and securityadmin fixed-server roles.

```
sp_addlinkedsrvlogin [@rmtsrvname =] 'rmtsrvname'
 [,[@useself =] 'useself'][,[@locallogin =] 'locallogin']
 [,[@rmtuser =] 'rmtuser'] [,[@rmtpassword =] 'rmtpassword']
```

The following list describes each element of the syntax:

rmtsrvname — The linked server that will use this login setting.

useself — The setting that determines whether a user or group of users will use their own usernames and passwords to log in to the linked server. There are two possible settings:

- 'true' — Local server logins use their own usernames and passwords to log in to the linked server. Consequently, the rmtuser and rmtpassword arguments are ignored. For example, the local jdoe user with a password of shrek would attempt to log in to the linked server with the jdoe username and the shrek password.
- 'false' — Local server logins will use the arguments specified in rmtuser and rmtpassword to log in to the linked server. For a linked server that does not require usernames and passwords (such as Microsoft Access), these arguments can be set to NULL.

locallogin — Specifies which local logins are affected by this mapping. You can designate either an individual login or all local logins. To specify that all logins be affected, pass a NULL to this argument.

rmtuser — The username that will be used to connect to the linked server if @useself is set to FALSE.

rmtpassword — The password that will be used to connect to the linked server if @useself is set to FALSE.

By default, after you run sp_addlinkedserver, all local logins will automatically attempt to use their own usernames and passwords to log in to the new linked server. Essentially, SQL Server runs the following statement after sp_addlinkedserver:

```
EXEC sp_addlinkedsrvlogin @rmtsrvname='My_Linked_Server',
@useself='true', @locallogin=NULL
```

You can delete this default mapping with sp_droplinkedsrvlogin, which is described in the next section.

In NT authentication mode, SQL Server will submit the NT username and password to the linked server if the provider supports NT authentication and security account delegation is available on both the client and server.

The following example will connect all users to the 'ORACLE_DATABASE' linked server using the 'guest' username and 'confio' password:

```
EXEC sp_addlinkedsrvlogin @rmtsrvname='ORACLE_DATABASE',
@useself='false', @rmtuser='guest', @rmtpassword='confio'
```

This example will connect all users to the 'SQL_SERVER_DB' linked server using their own local usernames and passwords:

```
EXEC sp_addlinkedsrvlogin @rmtsrvname='SQL_SERVER_DB',
@useself='true'
```

This example will log in the local 'RobinOrdes' user as the remote user 'ROrdes' with the 'new_orleans' password to the 'ORACLE_DATABASE' linked server:

```
EXEC sp_addlinkedsrvlogin @rmtsrvname='ORACLE_DATABASE',
@useself='false', @locallogin='RobinOrdes', @rmtuser='ROrdes',
@rmtpassword='new_orleans'
```

This example will log in the Windows NT user 'Domain1\DonLarson' as the remote user 'DLarson' with the 'five_sons' password:

```
EXEC sp_addlinkedsrvlogin @rmtsrvname='ORACLE_DATABASE',
@useself='false', @locallogin='Domain1\DonLarson',
@rmtuser='DLarson', @rmtpassword='five_sons'
```

This example will connect all users to the 'ACCESS_DATABASE' linked server without providing a username or password:

```
EXEC sp_addlinkedsrvlogin @rmtsrvname='ACCESS_DATABASE',
@useself='false', @rmtuser=NULL, @rmtpassword=NULL
```


sp_droplinkedsrvlogin

You can delete mappings for linked servers using sp_droplinkedsrvlogin. Members of the sysadmin and securityadmin fixed-server roles can execute this stored procedure:

```
sp_droplinkedsrvlogin [@rmtsrvname =] 'rmtsrvname',
[@locallogin =] 'locallogin'
```

The following list describes each element of the syntax:

rmtsrvname	The linked server that will lose this login mapping.
locallogin	The local login that will lose the mapping to the linked server. You can designate either an individual login or all local logins. To specify that all logins should be affected, pass a NULL to this argument.

This first example removes the login mapping for the 'RobinOrdes' user to the 'ORACLE_DATABASE' linked server:

```
EXEC sp_droplinkedsrvlogin @rmtsrvname='ORACLE_DATABASE',
 @locallogin='RobinOrdes'
```

This example removes the default login mapping for all users using the 'SQL_SERVER_DB' linked server:

```
EXEC sp_droplinkedsrvlogin @rmtsrvname='SQL_SERVER_DB',
@locallogin=NULL
```

sp_helplinkedsrvlogin

To determine the current linked server login settings, run the sp_helplinkedsrvlogin procedure:

```
sp_helplinkedsrvlogin [[@rmtsrvname =] 'rmtsrvname',]
 [[@locallogin =] 'locallogin']
```

The following list describes each element of the syntax:

rmtsrvname	The linked server that will have its login settings displayed.
locallogin	The local login mappings that will be displayed.

The first example shows the sp_helplinkedsrvlogin output if no arguments are provided. It displays one line for each linked server login mapping. The first column (Linked Server) shows which linked server owns this mapping. The second column (Local Login) shows which user is affected by this mapping. If set to NULL, this mapping applies to all users who do not have a specific mapping. The third column (Is Self Mapping) displays a 1 if the local username and password will be attempted on the remote server. If it displays a 0, the value in the last column (Remote Login) will be used to log in to the remote server. Note that the remote password is not listed for security reasons:

```
EXEC sp_helplinkedsrvlogin
GO
```

```
Linked Server              Local Login  Is Self Mapping  Remote Login
-------------------------  -----------  ---------------  ------------
ACCESS_DATABASE            NULL         0                NULL
ACCESS_SERVER              NULL         1                NULL
EXCEL_SPREADSHEET          NULL         1                NULL
ODBC_with_DATASOURCE       NULL         1                NULL
ODBC_with_PROVIDER_STRING  NULL         1                NULL
ORACLE_DATABASE            NULL         0                guest
ORACLE_DATABASE            RobinOrdes   0                ROrdes
```

The next example shows the `sp_helplinkedsrvlogin` output if only the `rmtsrvname` argument is provided. The output is identical to the preceding example except only the entries for the specified server are displayed:

```
EXEC sp_helplinkedsrvlogin @rmtsrvname='ORACLE_DATABASE'
GO

Linked Server    Local Login  Is Self Mapping  Remote Login
-------------    -----------  ---------------  ------------
ORACLE_DATABASE  NULL         0                guest
ORACLE_DATABASE  RobinOrdes   0                ROrdes
```

The final example shows the `sp_helplinkedsrvlogin` output if all arguments are provided. Again, the output is identical to the previous examples except that it is limited to the server and is user specified:

```
EXEC sp_helplinkedsrvlogin @rmtsrvname='ORACLE_DATABASE',
 @locallogin='RobinOrdes'
GO

Linked Server     Local Login  Is Self Mapping  Remote Login
----------------- -----------  ---------------  ------------
ORACLE_DATABASE   RobinOrdes   0                ROrdes
```

Obtaining General Information About Linked Servers

You can use both SQL Server Enterprise Manager and the system-stored procedures to gather information about linked servers and the referenced datasources. Following are some of the most-often used system-stored procedures:

- `sp_linkedservers` returns a list of linked servers that are defined on the local server.
- `sp_catalogs` displays a list of catalogs and descriptions for a specified linked server.
- `sp_indexes` shows index information for a specified remote table.

- sp_primarykeys returns the primary key columns for the specified table.
- sp_foreignkeys lists the foreign keys that are defined for the remote table.
- sp_tables_ex displays table information from the linked server.
- sp_columns_ex returns column information for all columns or a specified column for a remote table.
- sp_helplinkedsrvlogin displays the linked server login mappings for each linked server.

For example, during query prototyping time, it is useful to see all of the ways that the linked server objects and columns are being referenced (especially when dealing with other datasources, such as Excel spreadsheets).

First, the exact linked object name is displayed via the sp_tables_ex system-stored procedure. The following is what you would see for the ExcelSW linked server just created:

```
EXEC sp_tables_ex 'ExcelSW'
go
Result set of:
Table_catalog Table_schema Table_Name    Table_Type Remarks
------------- ------------ ------------- ---------- -------
NULL          NULL         SWCustomers$  TABLE      NULL
```

Then you can see all of the table columns of that linked server's datasource by using the sp_columns_ex system-stored procedure. The following command provides the column definitions for the SWCustomers$ table for the linked server 'ExcelSW':

```
EXEC sp_columns_ex 'ExcelSW'
go

Table_catalog Table_schema Table_Name   Column_Name  DataType TypeName ...
------------- ------------ ------------ ------------ -------- -------- ---- ---
NULL          NULL         SWCustomers$ CustomerID   -9       VarChar  255  510
NULL          NULL         SWCustomers$ CompanyName  -9       VarChar  255  510
NULL          NULL         SWCustomers$ ContactName  -9       VarChar  255  510
NULL          NULL         SWCustomers$ ContactTitle -9       VarChar  255  510
NULL          NULL         SWCustomers$ Address      -9       VarChar  255  510
NULL          NULL         SWCustomers$ City         -9       VarChar  255  510
NULL          NULL         SWCustomers$ Region       -9       VarChar  255  510
NULL          NULL         SWCustomers$ PostalCode    6       Double    15    8
NULL          NULL         SWCustomers$ Country      -9       VarChar  255  510
NULL          NULL         SWCustomers$ Phone        -9       VarChar  255  510
NULL          NULL         SWCustomers$ Fax          -9       VarChar  255  510
```

Executing a Stored Procedure Via a Linked Server

It is possible to execute a stored procedure via a linked server. The server that is hosting the client connection will accept the client's request and send it to the linked server. The `EXECUTE` statement must contain the name of the linked server as part of its syntax:

```
EXECUTE servername.dbname.owner.procedure_name
```

This example executes `sp_helpsrvrole` on `SWServer`, which shows a list of available fixed server roles on the `'SWServer'` remote server:

```
EXEC SWServer.master.dbo.sp_helpsrvrole
```

Setting Up Linked Servers Through Enterprise Manager

Although you can set up linked servers and login mappings by directly executing these stored procedures, they can also be set up easily through Enterprise Manager.

To create a linked server, follow these steps:

1. Open Enterprise Manager.
2. Click the plus sign next to the local SQL Server.
3. Click the plus sign next to the Security folder.
4. Right-click Linked Servers and choose New Linked Server (see Figure 19.5).

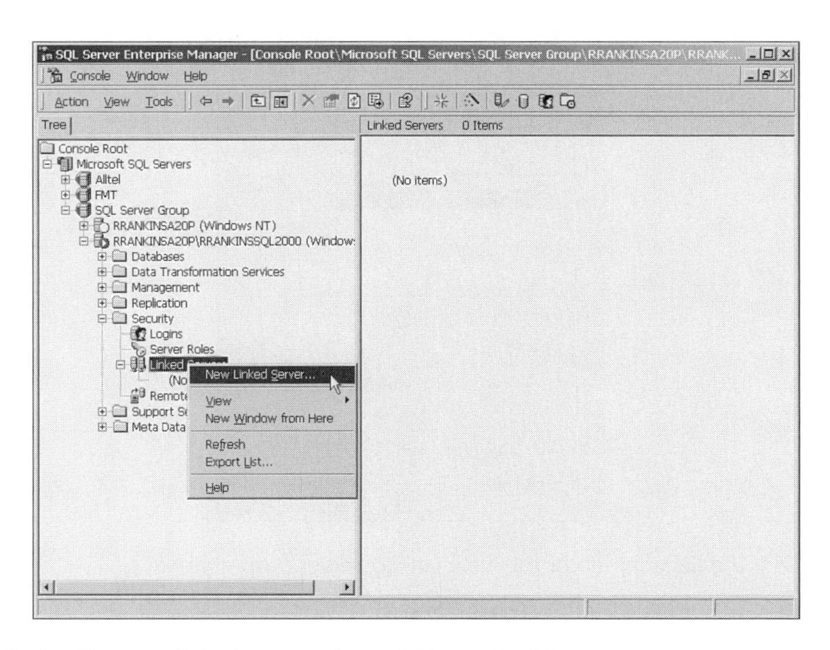

FIGURE 19.5 Creating linked servers through Enterprise Manager.

5. The General tab of the New Linked Server property box is displayed. The fields in the Server Type section are filled in the same way as the corresponding arguments for `sp_addlinkedserver`. The fields in the Server Options section at the bottom of this tab correspond to `sp_serveroption` arguments (see Figure 19.6).

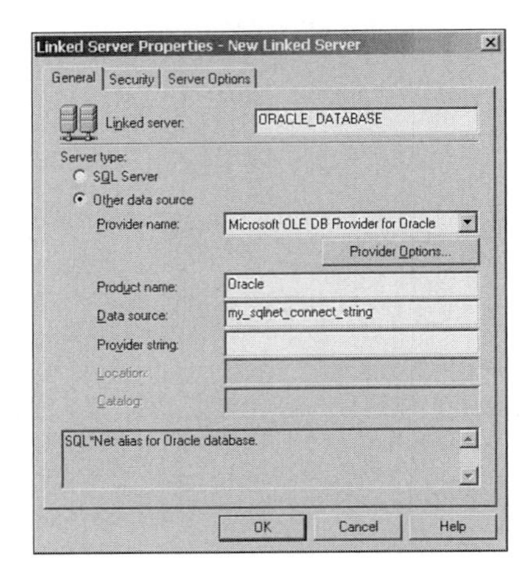

FIGURE 19.6 The General tab of the New Linked Server property box.

6. The Security tab of the New Linked Server property box allows you to map remote logins (see Figure 19.7). The code behind this dialog box actually runs the `sp_addlinkedsrvlogin` and `sp_droplinkedsrvlogin` stored procedures.

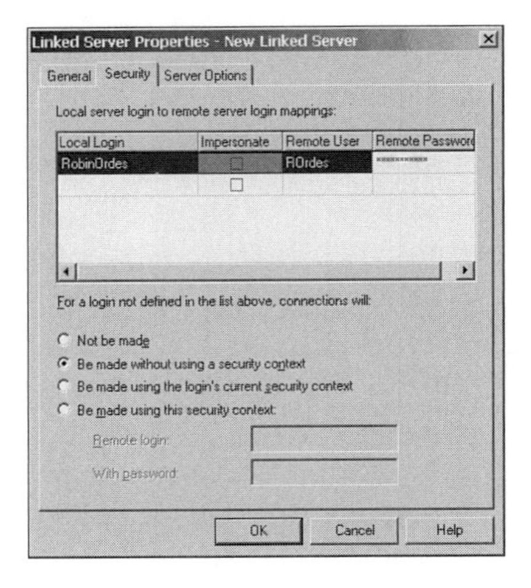

FIGURE 19.7 The Security tab of the New Linked Server property box.

7. The Server Options tab of the New Linked Server property box lets you specify the server options (see Figure 19.8). The code behind this dialog box actually runs the `sp_serveroption` stored procedure.

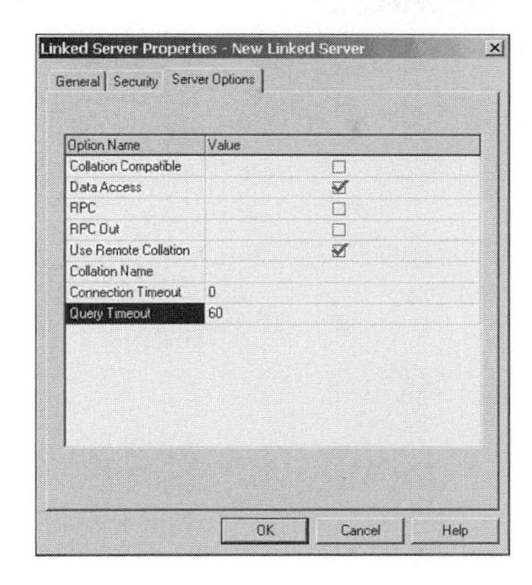

FIGURE 19.8 The Server Options tab of the New Linked Server property box.

TIP

Turns out that when you recycle a server that is involved in a linked or remote server definition, the link gets broken (after all, it is a continuous connection from one server to another). And, it doesn't always re-establish itself. It is a good practice to periodically verify the health of these links to guarantee that they remain intact. It has been on more than one occasion that linked server definitions have had to be removed and readded following a server recycle. Thanks, www.backroads.com, for uncovering this critical issue.

Summary

In this chapter, you saw the difference between the new linked servers and remote servers. You also learned how distributed queries and transactions worked with linked servers. In addition, you learned how to set up, configure, and gather information on linked servers using the system stored procedures, including `sp_addlinkedserver`, `sp_dropserver`, `sp_serveroption`, `sp_linkedserver`, `sp_table_ex`, `sp_column_ex`, `sp_addlinkedsrvlogin`, `sp_droplinkedsrvlogin`, and `sp_helplinkedsrvlogin`. Finally, you learned how to configure linked servers through Enterprise Manager. These foundation skills will be the cornerstone of helping your organization expand its reach to data no matter where it resides.

Although linked servers provide a method to access data in other datasources besides SQL Server, at times, you might need to work with data in a datasource that cannot be linked. In these circumstances, BCP can be used to import data files that have been exported from other datasources into local SQL Server tables or create DTS packages to periodically pull, push, and transform data to other locations. The next chapter, "Importing and Exporting SQL Server Data Using BCP and DTS," discusses how to import and export data as well as how to do complex data transformation processing when called for.

CHAPTER 20

Importing and Exporting SQL Server Data Using BCP and DTS

by Paul Bertucci

IN THIS CHAPTER

The Bulk-Copy Program (BCP) is like an old friend to anyone who needs to get data in to (import) SQL Server tables from flat files or get data out of (export) SQL Server tables in to flat files. In fact, it is more like a warm security blanket because of the ease with which large amounts of data can be loaded or unloaded and the extreme reliability of that data movement. The good news with the SQL Server 2000 version of BCP is that it can handle most data types (including Image and Identity data types). In older versions of SQL Server, BCP was much more limited. And BCP can be extremely fast in its execution. This fact alone probably accounts for its continued presence in the MS SQL Server 2000 product.

Taking over the reigns for BCP and extending it into complex data transformations is Microsoft's Data Transformation Services (DTS). This chapter will describe the DTS environment and how DTS is addressing more complex data needs. The focus will be on importing, exporting, and transforming data from one or more datasources to one or more data targets. Other Microsoft solutions exist for importing and exporting data, but DTS can be used for a larger variety of data transformation purposes, and its strength is in direct data access and complex data transformation.

The alternatives to DTS and BCP in the Microsoft SQL Server 2000 environment include Replication, Distributed Queries, `BULK INSERT`, and `SELECT INTO/INSERT`. This chapter will help you determine how and when to use both BCP and DTS. And, more importantly, for what requirements.

Bulk-Copy Program (BCP)

There are three main ways to initiate bulk-copy operations:

- The bulk-copy program (the BCP utility), a command-prompt utility
- The `BULK INSERT` statement used in Transact-SQL batches and stored procedures
- The bulk-copy APIs for OLE DB, ODBC, and DB-Library applications

These are the potential uses of BCP (in any of its forms):

- Exporting data out of SQL Server tables (to flat files) to other applications and environments
- Importing data in to SQL Server tables (from flat files) from other applications and environments
- Changing the code page of the data already in SQL Server tables (via exporting/importing with special options)
- Restructuring data in tables (exporting data using views or the queryout option, then importing this restructured data back into restructured SQL Server tables)
- Resequencing data in tables that use the identity column (via exporting/importing with special options)
- Re-timestamping data in tables that use the timestamp column (again, via exporting/importing with special options)
- Initiating a new constraint or new insert trigger logic on data in tables for data integrity efforts
- Generating initial snapshots for data replication
- Many others

Figure 20.1 illustrates the typical import and export capabilities of BCP.

However, before utilizing BCP at all, you must first decide whether you should be using BCP or some other mechanism within SQL Server 2000 (because there are alternatives such as Data Transformation Services [DTS]). A few answers to a quick test should make it obvious. There will be two separate tests: one for importing and the other for exporting.

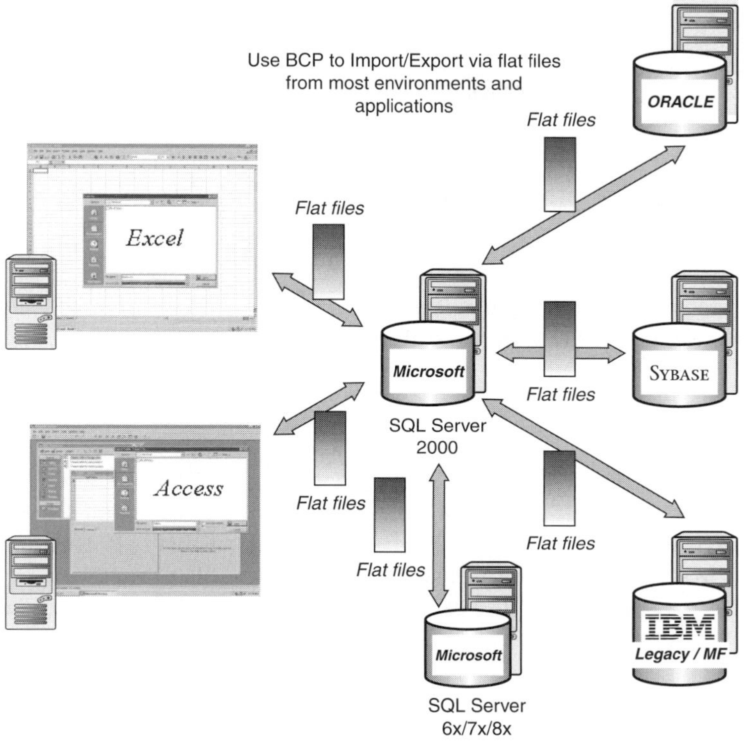

FIGURE 20.1 Using BCP to import and export data with many environments and for many applications.

First consider the "import" direction.

Note: You'll find that deciding to use BCP for exporting is a much simpler decision (fewer questions will need to be answered).

Test: Using BCP to Import Data into SQL Server Tables

1. How often is the source data created? In other words, is it a one-time-only load of data or recurring?

   Assessment:

   If not very frequent, then it is a BCP candidate. BCP is best used in a batch type environment and not as a method of continuous replication (high frequency).

   If it is a one-time-only load of data, then it is a BCP candidate. The reason this utility was created in the first place was so that you don't have to write a special program every time you need to load data in to a table from an external source.

2. How much data is being imported (loaded) into a table?

   Assessment:

   If greater than 500 rows, then it is a BCP candidate. After all, the "B" in "BCP" stands for Bulk. However, even if you are loading one row, BCP could be utilized (to prevent you from having to write a program or doing an insert directly to the table).

3. In what physical form is the source data? (Flat files? SQL tables? Other?)

   Assessment:

   If a flat file is the source, then it is a BCP candidate. If it is other SQL Server tables, this is a candidate for DTS or some simple cross database Insert with selects.

4. What does the source data look like, and how is the source data created?

   Assessment:

   If character delimited, or static in format, then it is a BCP candidate. BCP has long been the mechanism of choice for taking data from a flat file and efficiently loading it in to SQL Server tables. It is highly tuned to support this task. In addition, it might be that the source data is an Access DB, a mainframe file or database, or even an Excel spreadsheet. All have the capability to dump their data ("save as" or "export" in some cases) in to a flat file format of some kind (often with character delimiter options).

5. Is the source data incremental data (new data rows that are appended, or inserted, to the existing target table)?

   Assessment:

   If the source data is truly "new" data and will be appended (inserted) to the existing data in the table, then it is a BCP candidate. BCP does not have an Update Existing Row mode, so it cannot be used in an additive/update situation (where existing column values need to be added to new column values).

6. Is the source data a complete refresh of a table's data?

   Assessment:

   If the source data will completely re-create the data in the target table, then it is a BCP candidate. Essentially, this will be truncating the table first, followed by the BCP data load of all new rows.

7. Are there any `image` data type columns in the target table?

   Assessment:

   If any columns in the target table are of data type `image`, special care must be taken to deal with them when using BCP. So, this would be a borderline candidate for BCP.

The important thing to know is that with SQL Server 2000, it is possible to bulk-copy a data file of `image` data in to an instance of SQL Server. It just isn't that easy and a better mechanism might be available in SQL Server 2000.

By this time, it should be apparent that you have a situation BCP can handle (or not handle) for importing data in to your SQL Server tables. To drive this home, a small example should help. for importing data in to your SQL Server tables. To drive this home, a small example should help.

Company X Sales Force Automation Requirement—Part 1

There's a need to import new order detail data from a Sales Force Automation application's Access database. As you can see in Figure 20.2, each week, each salesperson will dump his or her *new* orders directly to a comma-delimited flat file and then e-mail them to corporate headquarters. There are 75 salespeople spread throughout the country. This flat file corresponds exactly to the target tables on the main SQL Server 2000 tables. There are no image or identity data types in the target tables. New unique order numbers are automatically assigned by the Access database application. On average, there will be 1,000 new orders per salesperson.

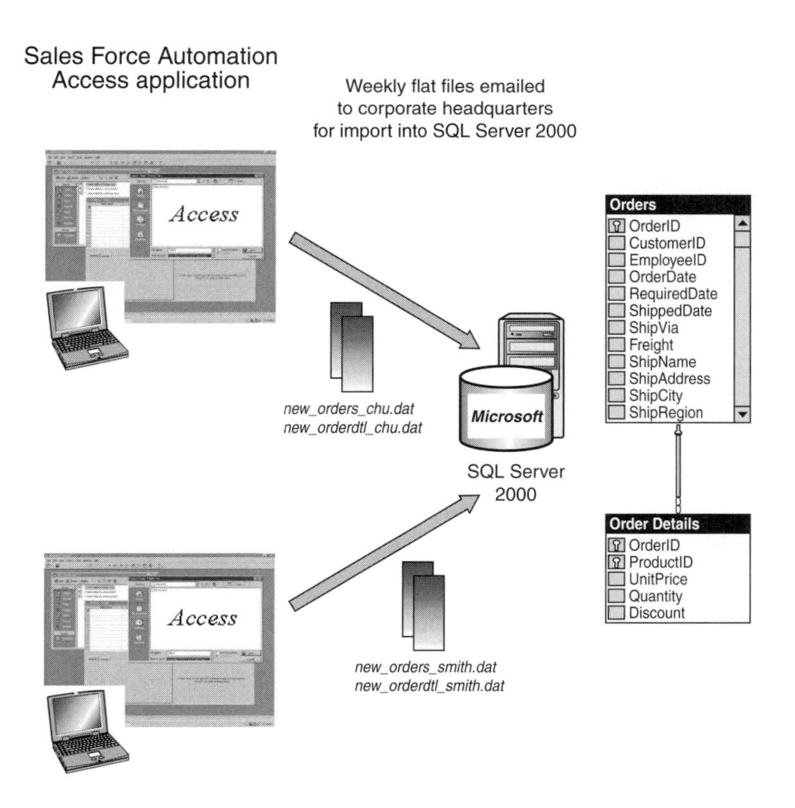

FIGURE 20.2 Sales Force Automation: Access data to SQL Server 2000.

The results of the "import using BCP test" are as listed here: (1) weekly (recurring) source data files, (2) 1,000 new rows per salesperson (75 salespeople), (3) flat files, (4) comma-delimited flat files (that correspond exactly to the SQL Server 2000 target tables, (5) new data only (no updates), (6) not a refresh, and (7) no special data types to be concerned with.

Final Assessment: BCP each new file in to the target tables on the weekend as part of batch processing.

Now let's consider the "export" direction:

Test: Using BCP to Export Data out of SQL Server Tables

1. How often is the data to be exported? In other words, is it a one-time-only export of data or recurring?

   Assessment:

   If not very frequent, then it is a BCP candidate. Again, BCP is best used in a batch type environment and not as a method of continuous replication (high frequency).

   If it is a one-time-only export of data, then it is a high BCP candidate. This could possibly eliminate the need for any special program to be written to do this task.

2. How much data is being exported out of the table?

   Assessment:

   If greater than 500 rows, then it is a BCP candidate.

3. What physical format should the exported data have? (Flat files that are tab or comma delimited? SQL tables? Other?)

   Assessment:

   If a flat file is the target and this file should be in some standard structure (such as tab or comma delimited), then it is a BCP candidate. If it is another SQL Server table, then this is a candidate for DTS.

   In addition, it might be that the exported data is to be pulled in to an Access DB, a mainframe file or database, or even an Excel spreadsheet. All have the capability to load data from a flat file format of some kind (often with character delimiter options).

4. Are there any `image` data type columns in the table to be exported?

   Assessment:

   If any data columns in the table are of data type `image`, special care must be taken to deal with them when using BCP. So, this would be a borderline candidate for BCP. The important thing to know is that with SQL Server 2000, it is possible to bulk-copy a data file of `image` data out of an instance of SQL Server. You must also ask whether the target (receiver) of these files can handle data of this data type.

Again, it should be very apparent that you have a situation BCP can handle (or not handle) for exporting data out of your SQL Server tables. Another small example should help here.

Company X Sales Force Automation Requirement—Part 2

There's a need to export complete customer and product data to each salesperson's Sales Force Automation application's Access database (which they have on their laptops) from the central SQL Server 2000 tables. As seen in Figure 20.3, a single set of flat files for the customer data and product data will need to be created as a comma-delimited flat file and e-mailed to each salesperson over the weekend. In turn, each salesperson will need to pull these flat files in to their Access database. There are 75 salespeople spread throughout the country. These flat files correspond exactly to the customer and product tables on the main SQL Server 2000 tables and in the Access database. There are no image or identity data types in the tables. On average, there will be 3,000 customers and 5,000 products.

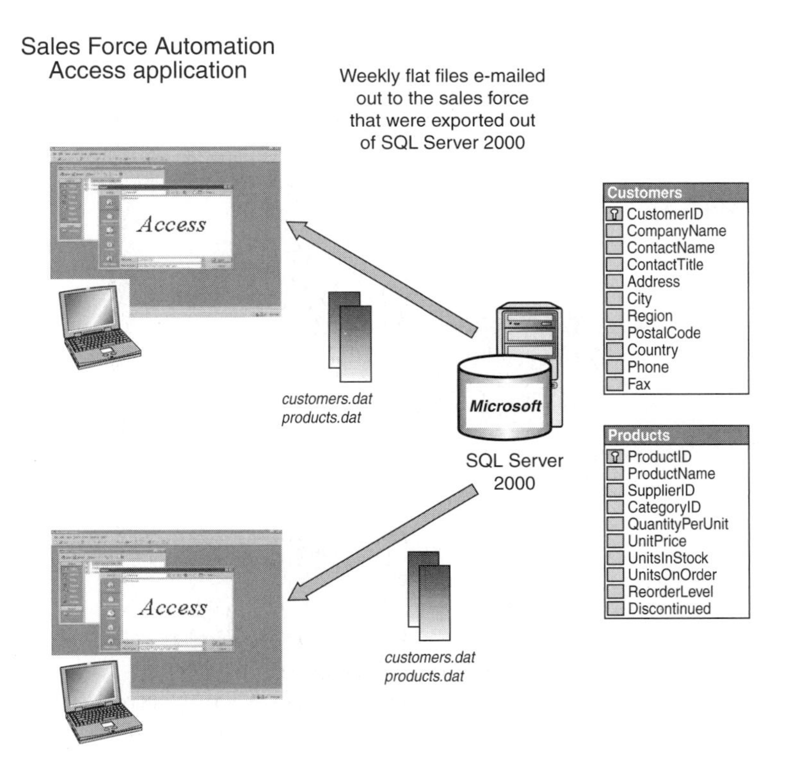

FIGURE 20.3 Sales Force Automation: Pushing data back out to Access databases from SQL Server 2000.

The results of the "export using BCP test" are as listed here: (1) weekly (recurring) data files, (2) 3,000 customer table rows and 5,000 product table rows, (3) comma-delimited flat files (that correspond exactly to the Access DB), (4) no special data types to be concerned with.

Final Assessment: BCP the entire customer and product tables out to comma-delimited flat file, and e-mail them to each salesperson as part of the weekend batch processing.

After it has been decided to use BCP, as mentioned before, there are three main ways to initiate bulk-copy operations:

- The bulk-copy program (the BCP utility), a command-prompt utility
- The `BULK INSERT` statement used in Transact-SQL batches and stored procedures
- The bulk-copy APIs for OLE DB, ODBC, and DB-Library applications

NOTE

To be able to do any BCP operations, you must first set the `SELECT INTO/BULK COPY` option to `true` for the database. There are some issues with this because logging and recovery are affected. It is very common to set this option to `true` in your batch BCP script and reset it to `false` after the BCP operations are done.

The following sections outline the primary initiation methods of BCP, BCP's many switches, the format file, and ways to improve performance when using BCP. By the end of these sections, the reader will be able to optimally execute BCP successfully for several common production scenarios.

Let's first look at the BCP utility from the command prompt. Later in this chapter, the other initiation methods are discussed.

First, do you have the right version of BCP?

A quick check of your version of BCP guarantees that you won't run in to any limitations from older versions of BCP that might be left on your servers. You can do this by executing BCP at the command prompt with the `-v` option and no other parameters. (Note that all BCP switch options are case sensitive; for example, `-v` and `-V` are two very different switches.) Here's an example:

```
C:> bcp -v
BCP - Bulk Copy Program for Microsoft SQL Server.
Copyright (c) 1991-1998, Microsoft Corp. All Rights Reserved.
Version: 8.00.194
```

Yes, this is version 8.0 that is distributed with MS SQL Server 2000 (SQL Server 8.0). If a version other than 8.x is present, you must reinstall BCP immediately.

At any time, you can see the proper usage and BCP switch options that are available by executing BCP at the command prompt with a question mark (?) only:

```
C:> bcp ?
usage: bcp {dbtable | query} {in | out | queryout | format} datafile
[-m maxerrors]            [-f formatfile]          [-e errfile]
. . .
```

The Bulk-Copy Program

The proper usage of BCP is

```
bcp {dbtable | query} {in | out | queryout | format} datafile
```

followed by one or more switches.

In this syntax,

dbtable

is the *database_name* + *owner* + *table_name*|*view_name* (for example, Northwind.dbo.customers or "Northwind.dbo.customers"):

database_name

is the name of the database in which the specified table or view resides. If not specified, this is the default database for the user.

owner

is the name of the owner of the table or view.

table_name | *view_name*

is the name of the destination table or view when copying data in to SQL Server (`in`), and the source table when copying data from SQL Server (`out`).

`query`

is a Transact-SQL query that returns a resultset. `queryout` must also be specified when bulk-copying data from a query.

`in | out | queryout | format`

Specifies the direction of the bulk copy (`in` copies from a file in to the database table or view, `out` copies from the database table or view to a file). `queryout` must be specified when bulk-copying data from a query. `format` creates a format file based on the switch specified (-n, -c, -w, -V, or -N) and the table or view delimiters. If format is used, the -f option must be specified as well.

data_file

is the data file used when bulk-copying a table or view in to or out of SQL Server.

All available Bulk-Copy Program switches are listed in Table 20.1.

TABLE 20.1 BCP Switches

Switch	Description
-m	The maximum errors to allow before stopping the transfer. The default is 10. [-m *max_errors*]
-f	The format file used to customize the load or unload data in a specific style. [-f *format_file*]
-e	The file to write error messages to. [-e *err_file*]
-F	The first row in the data file to start copying from when importing. The default is 1. [-F *first_row*]
-L	The last row in the data file to end copying with when importing. The default is 0, which indicates the last row in the file. [-L *last_row*]
-b	The number of rows to include in each committed batch. By default, all data rows in a file are copied in one batch. [-b *batch_size*]
-n	Native (database) data type formats are to be used for the data. [-n]
-c	Character data type format is to be used for the data. In addition, \t (tab character) is used as the field separator, and \n (newline character) is used as the row terminator. [-c]
-w	Unicode data type format is to be used for the data. In addition, \t (tab character) is used as the field separator, and \n (newline character) is used as the row terminator. [-w]
-N	Use Unicode for character data and native format for all others. This can be used as an alternative to the –w switch. [-N]
-V	Use data type formats from earlier versions of SQL Server. [-V (60 | 65 | 70)]
-6	Don't use this anymore. Use -V instead.
-q	Tells BCP to use quoted identifiers when dealing with table and column names. [-q]
-C	If you are loading extended characters, this switch allows you to specify the code page of the data in the data file. [-C *code_page*]
-t	The terminating character(s) for fields. The default is the \t (tab character). [-t field_term]
-r	The terminating character(s) for rows. The default is the \n (newline character). [-r *row_term*]
-i	A file for redirecting input into BCP (the response file containing the responses to the command prompts). [-i *input_file*]
-o	The file for receiving redirected output from BCP. [-o *output_file*]

TABLE 20.1 Continued

Switch	Description
`-a`	The network packet size (in bytes) used to send to or receive from SQL Server. Can be between 4096 and 65535 bytes. The default size is 4096. `[-a packet_size]`
`-S`	The SQL Server name to connect to. *Local* is the default. `[-S server_name | server_name\instance_name]`
`-U`	The user account to log in as; this account must have sufficient privileges to carry out either a read or a write of the table. `[-U login_id]`
`-P`	The password associated with the user account. `[-P password]`
`-T`	Make a trusted connection to the SQL Server using the network user/security credentials instead of the *login_id/password*. `[-T]`
`-v`	Display the BCP version information. `[-v]`
`-R`	Use the regional format for currency, date, and time data as defined by the locale settings of the client computer. `[-R]`
`-k`	Override a column's default and enforce `NULL` values being loaded into the columns as part of the BCP operation. `[-k]`
`-E`	Use the identity values in the import file rather than generating new ones. `[-E]`
`-h`	Special "hints" to be used during the BCP operation. These include specifying the following: the sort order of the data file, the number of rows of data per batch, the number of kilobytes of data per batch, to acquire a table-level lock, to check constraints, and to fire insert triggers. `[-h hint_type,..]`

Fundamentals of Exporting and Importing Data

One of the great things about BCP is its ease of use. In this section, the full export and import of data using BCP will be done for Company X's Sales Force Automation requirements specified earlier. The minimum number of options and switches needed to fulfill these requirements will be described and execution examples illustrated. All tables being used here can be found in the "Northwind" sample database supplied by Microsoft in SQL Server 2000. Let's first look at the exporting requirement.

As you might recall, the customers and products tables need to be exported once per week and sent to each salesperson (via e-mail). In turn, these files will be pulled in to the salesperson's Access application. The flat files will also need to be comma delimited. From BCP's point of view, the following things must be specified:

- Full table name (*database+owner+table_name*)

  ```
  northwind..customers
  ```

  ```
  northwind..products
  ```

- Direction of BCP (`OUT` in this case because it is exporting data out)

- Data filename (to hold the exported data)

  `customers.dat`

  `products.dat`
- Server name `C814\DBARCH01` for this example (`-S C814\DBARCH01`)
- Username `SFA-Admin`, the Sales Force Automation Admin ID (`-U SFA-Admin`)
- Password; none in this case (`-P `)
- Column terminator (delimiter) of comma (`-t ","`)
- Indication that this should be exported in character data format (`-c`)

That's it. So at the command prompt you would see this:

```
C:> BCP northwind..customers OUT customers.dat -S C814\DBARCH01 -U SFA-Admin
-P -t "," -c
Starting copy...

91 rows copied.
Network packet size (bytes): 4096
Clock Time (ms.):  total       30
```

Here's a sample of the data in the `customers.dat` file:

```
ALFKI,Alfreds Futterkiste,Maria Anders,Sales Representative,Obere Str. 57,
        Berlin,,12209,Germany,030-0074321,030-0076545
ANATR,Ana Trujillo Emparedados y helados,Ana Trujillo,Owner,Avda. de la
        Constitucion 2222,Mexico D.F.,,05021,Mexico,(5) 555-4729,(5) 555-3745
ANTON,Antonio Moreno Taqueria,Antonio Moreno,Owner,Mataderos  2312,
        Mexico D.F.,,05023,Mexico,(5) 555-3932
. . .
```

This would be followed by the export of products:

```
C:> BCP northwind..products OUT products.dat -S C814\DBARCH01
         -U SFA-Admin -P -t "," -c
Starting copy...

77 rows copied.
Network packet size (bytes): 4096
Clock Time (ms.):  total       21
```

The data in `products.dat` file would be this:

```
1,Chai,1,1,10 boxes x 20 bags,18.0000,39,0,10,0
2,Chang,1,1,24 - 12 oz bottles,19.0000,17,40,25,0
3,Aniseed Syrup,1,2,12 - 550 ml bottles,10.0000,13,70,25,0
. . .
```

Now, let's look at importing data into SQL Server 2000.

Each salesperson is providing two flat files containing new orders and order details to be imported in to SQL Server 2000 every week. As part of the weekend batch processing, all of these flat files will be merged (concatenated) into consolidated files (`new_orders.dat` and `new_orddtl.dat`). This is what will be imported into the orders and order details tables in the Northwind database. Remember, the new orders keys are assigned by the Access DB application and must be the keys that get loaded in to the orders table (the `OrderID` in the orders table is an identity column key). The flat files will also be comma delimited. From BCP's point of view, the following things must be specified:

- Full table name (*`database+owner+table_name`*)

  `northwind..orders`

  `northwind..order_details`

- Direction of BCP (`IN` in this case because it is importing data)
- Data filenames (that contain the import data)

  `new_orders.dat`

  `new_orddtl.dat`

  Here's a sample of the input data file (`new_orders.dat`):

  ```
  12010,ERNSH,4,1998-05-05 00:00:00.000,1998-06-02 00:00:00.000,,2,258.6400,
        Ernst Handel,Kirchgasse 6,Graz,,8010,Austria
  12011,PERIC,2,1998-05-05 00:00:00.000,1998-06-02 00:00:00.000,,2,24.9500,
        Pericles Comidas clasicas,Calle Dr. Jorge Cash 321,Mexico
  D.F.,,05033,Mexico
  . . .
  ```

- Server name `C814\DBARCH01` for this example (`-S C814\DBARCH01`)
- Username `SFAAdmin`, the Sales Force Automation Admin ID (`-U SFAAdmin`)
- Password none in this case (`-P`)
- Column terminator (delimiter) of comma (`-t ","`)
- Indication that this should be imported in character data format (`-c`)

- The additional issue with the orders table is that of allowing the keys from the data files to be used instead of the normal identity values being assigned (the primary key OrderID is defined as an identity column); simply use the -E option for this (-E)

That's it. So at the command prompt you would see this:

```
C:> BCP northwind..orders IN new_orders.dat -S C814\DBARCH01
        -U SFAAdmin -P -t "," -c -E
Starting copy...

989 rows copied.
Network packet size (bytes): 4096
Clock Time (ms.): total     13550
```

A quick `SELECT *` from the orders table shows the success of this operation:

```
12018    SIMOB    7    1998-05-06 00:00:00.000    1998-06-03 00:00:00.000    NULL
        2    18.4400    Simons bistro    Vinb[ae]ltet 34    Kobenhavn    NULL
        1734    Denmark
12019    RICSU    8    1998-05-06 00:00:00.000    1998-06-03 00:00:00.000    NULL
        2    6.1900    Richter Supermarkt    Starenweg 5    Genève    NULL
        1204    Switzerland
12020    RATTC    1    1998-05-06 00:00:00.000    1998-06-03 00:00:00.000    NULL
        2    8.5300    Rattlesnake Canyon Grocery    2817 Milton Dr.    Albuquerque
        NM    87110    USA
. . .
```

In addition, a quick check of the current identity value of this table reassures you that all is well (using OSQL/ISQL/SQL Analyzer):

```
Use northwind
go
DBCC CHECKIDENT ('orders', NORESEED)
Go
```

This yields the following:

```
Checking identity information: current identity value '12020', current column
        value '12020'.
DBCC execution completed. If DBCC printed error messages, contact your
         system administrator.
```

You can now do the import into the order details table.

Note: The -E switch is not needed for this table because no columns in the order details table are defined as identity columns. In addition, the order details table contains a space in its name and must be enclosed in brackets ([]) for BCP.

At the command prompt you would have the following:

```
C:> BCP northwind..[order details] IN new_orddtl.dat -S C814\DBARCH01
         -U SFAAdmin -P -t "," -c
Starting copy...
1000 rows sent to SQL Server. Total sent: 1000
1000 rows sent to SQL Server. Total sent: 2000
1000 rows sent to SQL Server. Total sent: 3000

3243 rows copied.
Network packet size (bytes): 4096
Clock Time (ms.): total      5163
```

Again, a quick SELECT * from the order details table shows the successful imports:

```
12020    64    33.2500    2    2.9999999E-2
12020    66    17.0000    1    0.0
12020    73    15.0000    2    9.9999998E-3
12020    75     7.7500    4    0.0
12020    77    13.0000    2    0.0
. . .
```

Great! The Sales Force Automation requirements have been successfully implemented quickly and accurately. That's the beauty and power of using BCP.

The next sections take a look at how BCP can work with basic data representations (character, native, or unicode), the use of format file, and a few other extended BCP capabilities.

File Datatypes

BCP can handle data in one of three forms: character (ASCII), native, or Unicode. You have the choice of which character format is used, depending on the source or destination of the data file.

- The character format (-c) is the most commonly used of the three datatypes because it reads or writes using ASCII characters and carries out the appropriate datatype conversion for the SQL Server representations. The CHAR datatype is the default storage type; it uses tabs as field separators and the newline character as the row terminator.

- The native format (-n) is used for copying data between SQL Servers. This format allows BCP to read and write using the same datatypes used by SQL Server, leading to a performance gain. This format does, however, render the data file unreadable by any other means.
- The Unicode option (-w) uses Unicode characters rather than ASCII characters. The NCHAR datatype is the default storage type; it uses tabs as field separators and the newline character as the row terminator.

The Format File

By using a format file, you can customize the data file created by BCP or specify complex field layouts for data loads. There are two ways to create this format file: interactive BCP and the format switch.

Customizing a Format File Using Interactive BCP

If you do not specify one of the -n, -c, or -w datatype format switches, BCP (in or out) prompts you for the following information for each column in the data set:

- File storage type
- Prefix length
- Field length
- Field terminator

BCP offers a default for each of these prompts that you can accept. If you accept all the defaults, you wind up with the same format file you would have by specifying the native format (with the -n switch). The prompts look like this:

```
Enter the file storage type of field au_id [char]:
Enter prefix length of field au_id [0]:
Enter length of field au_id [11]:
Enter field terminator [none]:
```

or

```
Enter the file storage type of field OrderID [int]:
Enter prefix length of field OrderID [0]:
Enter field terminator [none]:
```

By pressing the Enter key at the prompt, you take the default. Alternatively, you can type your own value at the prompt if you know the new value and it is different from the default.

Creating a Format File Using a Switch

By using the `format` option, you can create a format file without actually transferring any data. Here is an example of creating a format file for the orders table in the Northwind database:

```
C:> BCP "northwind..orders" format orders.dat -S C814\DBARCH01
        -U SFAAdmin -P -f orders.fmt -c
```

The format file created looks like this:

```
8.0
14
1       SQLCHAR   0       12      "\t"     1     OrderID             ""
2       SQLCHAR   0       10      "\t"     2     CustomerID     SQL_Latin1_General_
        CP1_CI_AS
3       SQLCHAR   0       12      "\t"     3     EmployeeID          ""
4       SQLCHAR   0       24      "\t"     4     OrderDate           ""
5       SQLCHAR   0       24      "\t"     5     RequiredDate        ""
6       SQLCHAR   0       24      "\t"     6     ShippedDate         ""
7       SQLCHAR   0       12      "\t"     7     ShipVia             ""
8       SQLCHAR   0       30      "\t"     8     Freight             ""
9       SQLCHAR   0       80      "\t"     9     ShipName       SQL_Latin1_General_
        CP1_CI_AS
10      SQLCHAR   0       120     "\t"     10    ShipAddress    SQL_Latin1_General_
        CP1_CI_AS
11      SQLCHAR   0       30      "\t"     11    ShipCity       SQL_Latin1_General_
        CP1_CI_AS
12      SQLCHAR   0       30      "\t"     12    ShipRegion     SQL_Latin1_General_
        CP1_CI_AS
13      SQLCHAR   0       20      "\t"     13    ShipPostalCode SQL_Latin1_General_
        CP1_CI_AS
14      SQLCHAR   0       30      "\r\n"   14    ShipCountry     SQL_Latin1_General_
        CP1_CI_AS
```

Table 20.2 provides a description of the lines and columns in the preceding format file example.

TABLE 20.2 The Contents of the Format File

Line or Column	Description
1st line	Version of BCP
2nd line	Number of columns
3rd line-1st column	Data field position
3rd line-2nd column	Datatype
3rd line-3rd column	Prefix

TABLE 20.2 Continued

Line or Column	Description
3rd line-4th column	Data file field length
3rd line-5th column	Field or row terminator
3rd line-6th column	Column position
3rd line-7th column	Column name
3rd line-8th column	Column collation

You get different format files depending on your table and whether you chose character, native, or Unicode as your data type. As you can see in the preceding example, only the last two columns in the format file relate to the actual table; the remaining columns specify properties of the data file.

File Storage Type

The storage type is the description of how the data is stored in the data file. Table 20.3 lists the definitions used during Interactive BCP and what appears in the format file. The storage type allows data to be copied as its base type (native format), as implicitly converted between types (`tinyint` to `smallint`), or as a string (in character or Unicode format).

TABLE 20.3 Storage Datatypes

File Storage Type	Interactive Prompt	Host File Datatype
`char`	`c[har]`	`SQLCHAR`
`varchar`	`c[har]`	`SQLCHAR`
`nchar`	`w`	`SQLNCHAR`
`nvarchar`	`w`	`SQLNCHAR`
`text`	`T[ext]`	`SQLCHAR`
`ntext`	`W`	`SQLNCHAR`
`binary`	`x`	`SQLBINARY`
`varbinary`	`x`	`SQLBINARY`
`image`	`I[mage]`	`SQLBINARY`
`datetime`	`d[ate]`	`SQLDATETIME`
`smalldatetime`	`D`	`SQLDATETIM4`
`decimal`	`n`	`SQLDECIMAL`
`numeric`	`n`	`SQLNUMERIC`
`float`	`f[loat]`	`SQLFLT8`
`real`	`r`	`SQLFLT4`
`int`	`i[nt]`	`SQLINT`
`smallint`	`s[mallint]`	`SQLSMALLINT`
`tinyint`	`t[inyint]`	`SQLTINYINT`
`money`	`m[oney]`	`SQLMONEY`
`smallmoney`	`M`	`SQLMONEY4`

TABLE 20.3 Continued

File Storage Type	Interactive Prompt	Host File Datatype
bit	b[it]	SQLBIT
uniqueidentifier	u	SQLUNIQUEID
timestamp	x	SQLBINARY

Note: If the table makes use of user-defined data types, these customized data types appear in the format file as their base data type.

If you are having problems loading certain fields in to your table, you can try the following tricks:

- Copy the data in as `CHAR` data types and force SQL Server to do the conversion for you.
- Duplicate the table and replace all the SQL Server data types with `CHAR` or `VARCHAR` of a length sufficient to hold the value. This trick allows you to further manipulate the data after it is loaded using Transact-SQL.

Prefix Length

For reasons of compactness in native data files, BCP precedes each field with a prefix length that indicates the length of the data stored. The space for storing this information is specified in characters and is called the **prefix length**.

Table 20.4 indicates the value to specify for prefix length for each of the datatypes.

TABLE 20.4 Prefix Length Values

Prefix Length	Use
0	Non-null data of type `bit` or numerics (`int`, `real`, and so on). Use this value when no prefix characters are wanted. This value causes the field to be padded with spaces to the size indicated for the field length.
1	Non-null data of type `binary` or `varbinary`, or null data with the exception of `text`, `ntext`, and `image`. Use this value for any data (except `bit`, `binary`, `varbinary`, `text`, `ntext`, and `image`) that you want stored using a character-based datatype.
2	When storing the datatypes `binary` or `varbinary` as character-based datatypes. Two bytes of `char` file storage and four bytes of `nchar` file storage are required for each byte of `binary` table data.
4	Use this value for the datatypes `text`, `ntext`, and `image`.

Prefix lengths are likely to exist only within data files created using BCP. It is unlikely that you will encounter a reason to change the defaults BCP has chosen for you.

Field Length

When using either the native or the character data format, you must specify the maximum length of each field. When converting data types to strings, BCP suggests lengths large enough to store the entire range of values for each particular data type. Table 20.5 lists the default values for each of the data formats.

TABLE 20.5 Default Field Lengths for Data Formats

Datatype	Length (/c)	Length (/n)
bit	1	1
binary	Column length×2	Column length
datetime	24	8
smalldatetime	24	4
float	30	8
real	30	4
int	12	4
smallint	7	2
tinyint	5	1
money	30	8
smallmoney	30	4
decimal	41	up to 17
numeric	41	up to 17
uniqueidentifier	37	16

NOTE

You must specify a field length that is long enough for the data being stored. BCP error messages regarding overflows indicate that the data value has been truncated in at least one of the fields. If the operation is a load, an overflow error usually results in BCP terminating. However, if you are dumping the data to a file, the data will be truncated without error messages.

The field length value is used *only* when the prefix length is `0` and you have specified no terminators. In essence, you are doing a fixed-length data copy. BCP uses the exact amount of space stated by the field length for each field; unused space within the field is padded out.

NOTE

Preexisting spaces in the data are not distinguished from added padding.

Field Terminator

If you are not making use of fixed-width fields or length prefixes, you must use a field terminator to indicate the character(s) that separate fields; for the last field in the data row, you must also indicate which character(s) ends the line.

BCP recognizes the following indicators for special characters:

Terminator	Escape Code
Tab	`\t`
Backslash	`\\`
Null terminator	`\0`
Newline	`\n`
Carriage return	`\r`

You cannot use spaces as terminators, but you can use any other printable character. Choose field and row terminators that make sense for your data. Obviously, you should not use any character you are trying to load. You must combine the `\r` and `\n` characters to get your data into an ASCII data file with each row on its own line.

TIP

By specifying the `-t` and `-r` switches, you can override the defaults that appear for the prompts during Interactive BCP.

NOTE

You can specify terminators for data copied in native format. You should be careful if you decide to go this route; the accepted approach is to use length prefixes.

The prefix length, field length, and terminator values interact. In the following examples, `T` indicates the terminator character(s), `P` indicates the prefix length, and `S` indicates space padding.

For data of type `char`, the data file has the following repeating pattern:

	Prefix Length=0	Prefix Length=1,2,4
No terminator	*string*S*string*S	P*string*SP*string*S
Terminator	*string*ST*string*ST	P*string*STP*string*ST

For data of other types converted to char, the data file has the following repeating pattern:

	Prefix Length=0	Prefix Length=1,2,4
No terminator	*string*S*string*S	P*string*P*string*
Terminator	*string*T*string*T	P*string*TP*string*T

The next few sections examine how to load data into tables when there are differences in column number and layout.

Different Numbers of Columns in File and Table

If you have fewer fields in the data file than exist in the table, you have to "dummy up" an extra line in your format file.

Suppose that you want to load a data file that is missing most of the address information for each customer. By using the format file you created in the section "The Format File," you can still load the data file. Suppose that the data file looks like this:

```
WELLI    Wellington Importadora    Jane Graham    Sales (14)555-8122
        (14)555-8111
WHITC    White Clover Markets    Donald Bertucci    Owner (206)555-4112
        (206)555-4113
```

To introduce a dummy value for the missing ones, you must make the following changes to the format file: Make the prefix and data lengths 0 and set the field terminator to nothing ("").

The modified format file will look like this (custwoaddr.fmt):

```
8.0
11
1       SQLCHAR 0    10    "\t"   1    CustomerID      SQL_Latin1_General_
        CP1_CI_AS
2       SQLCHAR 0    80    "\t"   2    CompanyName     SQL_Latin1_General_
        CP1_CI_AS
3       SQLCHAR 0    60    "\t"   3    ContactName     SQL_Latin1_General_
        CP1_CI_AS
4       SQLCHAR 0    60    "\t"   4    ContactTitle    SQL_Latin1_General_
        CP1_CI_AS
5       SQLCHAR 0    0      ""    5    Address         SQL_Latin1_General_
        CP1_CI_AS
6       SQLCHAR 0    0      ""    6    City            SQL_Latin1_General_
        CP1_CI_AS
7       SQLCHAR 0    0      ""    7    Region          SQL_Latin1_General_
        CP1_CI_AS
8       SQLCHAR 0    0      ""    8    PostalCode      SQL_Latin1_General_
        CP1_CI_AS
```

```
9       SQLCHAR 0    0       ""    9    Country          SQL_Latin1_General_
        CP1_CI_AS
10      SQLCHAR 0    48     "\t"   10   Phone            SQL_Latin1_General_
        CP1_CI_AS
11      SQLCHAR 0    48   "\r\n"   11   Fax              SQL_Latin1_General_
        CP1_CI_AS
```

Now BCP can load the data file by using this new format file, with the Address, City, Region, PostalCode, and Country columns containing NULLs for the new rows.

For data files that have more fields than the table has columns, you change the format file to add additional lines of information. Suppose that the Customer data file contains an additional CreditStatus value at the end:

```
WELLI    Wellington Importadora    Jack McElreath    Sales Manager    Rua do Mer-
cado,
        12    Resende    SP    08737-363    Brazil    (14) 555-8122    NULL 1
WHITC    White Clover Markets    Scott Smith    Owner    305 - 14th Ave. S.
        Suite 3B    Seattle    WA    98128    USA    (206) 555-4112    (206) 555-
➥4115 2
```

Starting with the same format file as before, you modify it in two important areas: Change the second line to reflect the actual number of values, and add new lines for the extra column in the file that is not in the table. Notice that the column position has a value of 0 to indicate the absence of a column in the table.

Thus the modified format file will look like this (custwcrdt.fmt):

```
8.0
12
1       SQLCHAR 0    10     "\t"   1    CustomerID       SQL_Latin1_General_
        CP1_CI_AS
2       SQLCHAR 0    80     "\t"   2    CompanyName      SQL_Latin1_General_
        CP1_CI_AS
3       SQLCHAR 0    60     "\t"   3    ContactName      SQL_Latin1_General_
        CP1_CI_AS
4       SQLCHAR 0    60     "\t"   4    ContactTitle     SQL_Latin1_General_
        CP1_CI_AS
5       SQLCHAR 0   120     "\t"   5    Address          SQL_Latin1_General_
        CP1_CI_AS
6       SQLCHAR 0    30     "\t"   6    City             SQL_Latin1_General_
        CP1_CI_AS
7       SQLCHAR 0    30     "\t"   7    Region           SQL_Latin1_General_
        CP1_CI_AS
8       SQLCHAR 0    20     "\t"   8    PostalCode       SQL_Latin1_General_
        CP1_CI_AS
```

```
9       SQLCHAR 0     30     "\t"    9    Country          SQL_Latin1_General_
        CP1_CI_AS
10      SQLCHAR 0     48     "\t"   10    Phone            SQL_Latin1_General_
        CP1_CI_AS
11      SQLCHAR 0     48     "\t"   11    Fax              SQL_Latin1_General_
        CP1_CI_AS
12      SQLCHAR 0      1   "\r\n"    0    CreditStatus     SQL_Latin1_General_
        CP1_CI_AS
```

The ***bold italic*** in the preceding format file indicates the changes made.

These two examples show you the possibilities that the format file offers for customizing the loading and unloading of data.

Renumbering Columns

Using the techniques described previously, you can also handle data file fields that are in different orders than the target tables. All that needs to be done is to change the column order number to reflect the desired sequence of the columns in the table. The fields will then be automatically mapped to the corresponding columns in the table.

For example, suppose that a customer data file that you got from another source system came with the following layout (the fields are in this order):

1. Address
2. City
3. Country
4. PostalCode
5. Region
6. CompanyName
7. ContactName
8. ContactTitle
9. Fax
10. Phone
11. CustomerID

The SQL Server table itself has columns in a different order. To load your data file into this table, you modify the format file to look like this (`custreord.fmt`):

```
8.0
11
1       SQLCHAR 0     10     "\t"   11    CustomerID       SQL_Latin1_General_
        CP1_CI_AS
```

```
2       SQLCHAR 0    80    "\t"    6    CompanyName      SQL_Latin1_General_
        CP1_CI_AS
3       SQLCHAR 0    60    "\t"    7    ContactName      SQL_Latin1_General_
        CP1_CI_AS
4       SQLCHAR 0    60    "\t"    8    ContactTitle     SQL_Latin1_General_
        CP1_CI_AS
5       SQLCHAR 0   120    "\t"    1    Address          SQL_Latin1_General_
        CP1_CI_AS
6       SQLCHAR 0    30    "\t"    2    City             SQL_Latin1_General_
        CP1_CI_AS
7       SQLCHAR 0    30    "\t"    5    Region           SQL_Latin1_General_
        CP1_CI_AS
8       SQLCHAR 0    20    "\t"    4    PostalCode       SQL_Latin1_General_
        CP1_CI_AS
9       SQLCHAR 0    30    "\t"    3    Country          SQL_Latin1_General_
        CP1_CI_AS
10      SQLCHAR 0    48    "\t"    10   Phone            SQL_Latin1_General_
        CP1_CI_AS
11      SQLCHAR 0    48  "\r\n"    9    Fax              SQL_Latin1_General_
        CP1_CI_AS
```

The ***bold italic*** in the preceding format file indicates the changes made. The principal thing to remember with the format file is that all but the last three columns deal with the data file. The last three columns deal with the database table.

Using Views

BCP can also use views to export data from the database. What this means is that an export of data can be a resultset of data from multiple tables (and with distributed queries, even multiple servers).

You can also use a view with BCP to load data back in to tables. However, as is the case with normal Transact-SQL inserts, you can load into only one of the underlying tables at a time.

Loading Image Data

It is actually fairly easy for BCP to load image data into SQL Server. For example, the command to load the data file `custlogo.doc` (a word document) into the `pub_info` table in the pubs database using the bcp utility is this:

```
C:> bcp pubs..pub_info in c:\temp\custlogo.doc -Usa
        -Ppassword -Sservername
```

```
bcp prompts:

Enter the file storage type of field pub_id [char]:
Enter the prefix length of field pub_id [0]:
Enter length of field pub_id [4]:
Enter the field terminator [none]:

Enter the file storage type of field logo [image]:
Enter the prefix length of field logo [4]: 0
Enter length of field logo [4096]: 5578
Enter the field terminator [none]:
```

In this example, the data file `custlogo.doc` will be loaded into column logo, and `5578` is the length of the data file.

Using the `BULK INSERT` statement, a format file needs to be created first and then used to provide the format information. To create the `format` file, use the bcp utility format option:

```
C:> bcp "pubs..pub_info" format xxx.dat -S servername -Usa
-P -f pub_info.fmt
```

The bcp utility prompts for the file storage type, prefix length, field length, and field terminator of each column of `pub_info`. The values for the logo column are the same as previously. This yields the following format file (`pub_info.fmt`):

```
8.0
3
1       SQLCHAR     0    4      ""   1    pub_id   SQL_Latin1_General_
        CP1_CI_AS
2       SQLIMAGE    0    5578   ""   2    logo         ""
3       SQLCHAR     4    0      ""   3    pr_info  SQL_Latin1_General_
        CP1_CI_AS
```

Now the `BULK INSERT` can be executed:

```
BULK INSERT "pubs..pub_info" FROM 'c:\temp\custlogo.doc'
WITH (
   FORMATFILE = 'c:\pub_info.fmt'
)
```

More information on `BULK INSERT` will be given later.

NOTE

There is now some sample code (named Bii) that is a standalone console application that mimics the BCP utility that ships with Microsoft SQL Server 2000. Unlike the BCP utility, the bii utility detects when an image field is the destination database field and the input is a filename that can be located in the file system. In this case, instead of loading the filename string in to the image field, the program opens the file, loads the data, and inserts the file contents in the image data type field.

Logged and Non-Logged Operations

There are two modes in which bulk-copy operations can occur: logged and non-logged (also known as slow and fast BCP, respectively). The ideal situation is to operate in non-logged mode because this arrangement dramatically decreases the load time and the consumption of other system resources such as memory, processor use, and disk access. However, the default runs the load in logged mode, which causes the log to grow rapidly for large volumes of data.

To achieve a non-logged operation, the target table must not be replicated (the replication log reader needs the log records to relay the changes made). The database holding the target table must also have its `SELECT INTO/BULK COPY` option set, and finally, the `TABLOCK` hint must be specified.

NOTE

Remember that setting the `SELECT INTO/BULK COPY` option disables the capability to back up the transaction log until a full database backup has been performed. Transaction log dumps are disabled because if the database had to be restored, the transaction log would not contain a record of the new data.

Although you can still perform fast loads against tables that have indexes, it is advisable to drop and re-create the indexes after the data transfer operation is complete. In other words, the total load time includes the loading of the data and the index creation time. If there is existing data in the table, the operation will be logged; you achieve a non-logged operation only if the table is initially empty. Generally, you get at least a 50 percent drop in transfer speed if the table has an index. The more indexes, the greater the performance degradation. This is due to the logging factor; more log records are being generated, and index pages are being loaded into the cache and modified. This can also cause the log to grow, possibly filling it (depending on your log file settings).

NOTE

Even the so-called non-logged operation logs some things. In the case of indexes, index page changes and allocations are logged, but the main area of logging is of extent allocations every time the table is extended for additional storage space for the new rows.

Batches

By default, BCP puts all the rows that are inserted into the target table into a single transaction (as seen in Figure 20.4). BCP calls this a "batch." This arrangement reduces the amount of work that the log must deal with; however, it locks down the transaction log by keeping a large part of it active, which can make truncating or backing up the transaction log impossible or unproductive.

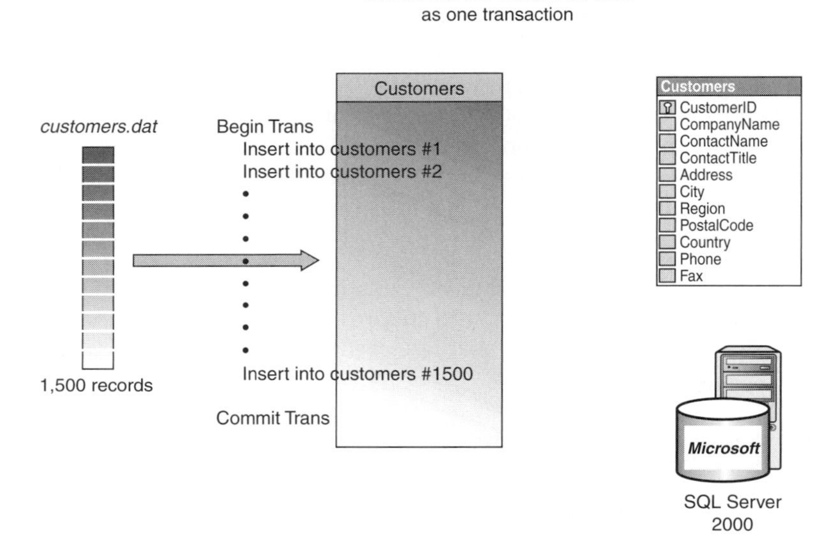

FIGURE 20.4 Default transaction behavior of BCP.

By using the BCP batch (`-b`) switch, you can control the number of rows in each batch (or effectively, each transaction). This switch controls the frequency of commits; although it can increase the activity in the log, it enables you to trim the size of the transaction log. You should tune the batch size in relation to the size of the data rows, transaction log size, and total number of rows to be loaded. The value you use for one load might not necessarily be the right value for all other loads.

As you can see in Figure 20.5, a batch switch of 500 is specified for the customer table load. This creates committed milestones during the load at the end of each 500 rows inserted.

Note that if the third batch fails, the first and second batches *are* committed, and those rows are now part of the table. However, any rows copied up to the point of failure in the third batch are rolled back.

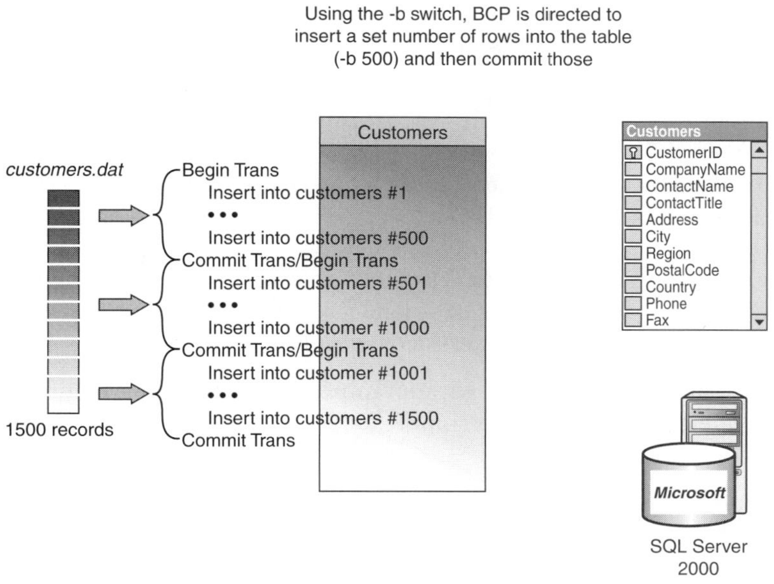

FIGURE 20.5 Changing the Transaction behavior of BCP with the `-b` switch.

Parallel Loading

A great enhancement of BCP is that of being able to do parallel loads of tables. To take advantage of this feature, the following must be true:

- The bulk-copy operation must be non-logged; all requirements specified in the previous discussion on non-logged operations must be met.
- There must be no indexes on the target table.

Only applications using the ODBC or SQL OLE DB–based APIs can perform parallel data loads into a single table.

The procedure is straightforward. After you have ascertained that the target table has no indexes (which could involve dropping primary or unique constraints) and is not being replicated, you must set the database option `SELECT INTO/BULK COPY` to `true`. The requirement to drop all indexes comes from the locking that has to occur to load the data. Although the table itself can have a shared lock, the index pages are an area of contention that prevents parallel access.

Now all that is required is to set up the parallel BCP loads to load the data into the table. You can use the `-F` and `-L` switches to specify the range of the data you want each parallel BCP to load into the table if you are using the same data file. These switches remove the need to manually break up the file. Here is an example of the command switches involved for a parallel load with BCP for the customers table:

```
bcp "northwind..customers"in customers.dat -T -S servername -c -F 1
       -L 10000 -h "TABLOCK"

bcp "northwind..customers"in customers.dat -T -S servername -c -F 10001
       -L 20000 -h "TABLOCK"
```

The `TABLOCK` hint (`-h` switch) provides better performance by removing contention from other users while the load takes place. If you do not use the hint, the load will take place using row-level locks, which will be considerably slower.

SQL Server 2000 allows parallel loads without impacting performance by making each BCP connection create extents in non-overlapping ranges. The ranges are then linked into the table's page chain.

After the table is loaded, it is also possible to create multiple nonclustered indexes in parallel. If there is a clustered index, do this one first, followed by the parallel nonclustered index created.

Supplying Hints to BCP

The SQL Server 2000 version of BCP comes with the capability to further control the speed of data loading and to invoke constraints and have insert triggers fired during loads by using something called hint switches (`-h`). One or more hints can be specified at a time:

```
-h "hint [, hint]"
```

This option cannot be used when bulk-copying data into versions of SQL Server before version 7.0 because, starting with SQL Server 7.0, BCP works in conjunction with the query processor. The query processor optimizes data loads and unloads for OLE database rowsets that the latest versions of BCP and `BULK INSERT` can generate.

The `ROWS_PER_BATCH` Hint

The `ROWS_PER_BATCH` hint is used to tell SQL Server the total number of rows in the data file. This hint helps SQL Server to optimize the entire load operation. This hint and the `-b` switch heavily influence the logging operations that occur with the data inserts. If you specify both this hint and the `-b` switch, they must have the same values or you will get an error message.

When you use the `ROWS_PER_BATCH` hint, you copy the entire resultset as a single transaction. SQL Server automagically optimizes the load operation using the batch size you specify. The value you specify does *not* have to be accurate, but you should be aware of what the practical limit will be, based on the database's transaction log.

TIP

Do not be confused by the name of the hint. You are specifying the *total file size* and *not* the batch size (as is the case with the `-b` switch).

The `CHECK_CONSTRAINTS` Hint

The `CHECK_CONSTRAINTS` hint controls whether check constraints are executed as part of the BCP operation. With BCP, the default is that check constraints are not executed. This hint option allows you to turn the feature on (to have check constraint be executed for each insert). If you do not use this option, you either should be very sure of your data or should rerun the same logic as the check constraints you deferred after the data has been loaded.

The `FIRE_TRIGGER` Hint

The `FIRE_TRIGGER` hint controls whether the insert trigger on the target table will be executed as part of the BCP operation. With BCP, the default is that no triggers are executed. This hint option allows you to turn the feature on (to have insert triggers be executed for each insert). As you can imagine, when this option is used, it slows down the BCP load operation. However, the business reasons to have the insert trigger fired might outweigh the slower load.

The `ORDER` Hint

If the data you want to load is already in the same sequence as the clustered index on the receiving table, you can use the `ORDER` hint. The syntax for this hint is shown here:

```
ORDER( {column [ASC | DESC] [,...n]})
```

There *must* be a clustered index on the same columns, in the same key sequence as you specify in the `ORDER` hint. Using a sorted data file (in the same order as the clustering index) helps SQL Server place the data into the table with minimal overhead.

The `KILOBYTES_PER_BATCH` Hint

The `KILOBYTES_PER_BATCH` hint gives the size, in kilobytes, of the data in each batch. This is an estimate and is used internally by SQL Server to optimize the data load and logging areas of the BCP operation.

The `TABLOCK` Hint

The `TABLOCK` hint is used to place a table-level lock for the BCP load duration. This hint gives you increased performance at a loss of concurrency as described in "Parallel Loading," earlier in this chapter.

The BULK INSERT Statement (Transact-SQL)

BULK INSERT allows the bulk load of data into a database table via transact-SQL. The main difference between this statement and BCP is that BULK INSERT is for loads only (and is SQL code), whereas BCP is a bidirectional, command-line–based utility.

The syntax for the BULK INSERT statement is shown here:

```
BULK INSERT [ [ 'database_name'.][ 'owner' ].] { 'table_name'
FROM 'data_file' }
[ WITH
(
[ BATCHSIZE [ = batch_size ] ]
[ [ , ] CHECK_CONSTRAINTS ]
[ [ , ] CODEPAGE [ = 'ACP' | 'OEM' | 'RAW' | 'code_page' ] ]
[ [ , ] DATAFILETYPE [ =
{ 'char' | 'native'| 'widechar' | 'widenative' } ] ]
[ [ , ] FIELDTERMINATOR [ = 'field_terminator' ] ]
[ [ , ] FIRSTROW [ = first_row ] ]
[ [ , ] FIRE_TRIGGERS ]
[ [ , ] FORMATFILE = 'format_file_path' ]
[ [ , ] KEEPIDENTITY ]
[ [ , ] KEEPNULLS ]
[ [ , ] KILOBYTES_PER_BATCH [ = kilobytes_per_batch ] ]
[ [ , ] LASTROW [ = last_row ] ]
[ [ , ] MAXERRORS [ = max_errors ] ]
[ [ , ] ORDER ( { column [ ASC | DESC ] } [ ,...n ] ) ]
[ [ , ] ROWS_PER_BATCH [ = rows_per_batch ] ]
[ [ , ] ROWTERMINATOR [ = 'row_terminator' ] ]
[ [ , ] TABLOCK ]
)
]
```

As you can see, most of the options for this statement are the same as (or similar to) the switches for the BCP utility. So you can think of BULK INSERT as the SQL code version of BCP IN.

The CODEPAGE option is used when you need to load extended characters (values greater than 127); this option allows you to specify one of the following values for char, varchar, and text datatypes:

ACP	Convert from the ANSI/Microsoft Windows code page (ISO 1252) to the SQL Server code page.
OEM	Convert from the system OEM code page to the SQL Server code page. This is the default.

RAW — No conversion, which makes this the fastest option.

<value> — Specific code page number (for example, 850 for the 4.2x default code page). For a list of the available code pages, look under the "Code Pages and Sort Orders" entry in the SQL Server Books Online.

The DATAFILETYPE option allows the specification of the data character set:

char — Data is in ASCII format.

native — Data is in SQL Server native format.

widechar — Data is in Unicode format.

widenative — Data is native, except for the char, varchar, and text columns, which are stored as Unicode.

This last option, widenative, is used when you need to transfer extended characters but want the performance offered by native data files.

You can easily use isql or Query Analyzer to execute the following sample statement. This example loads customer data from the file c:\temp\customer.dat into the customers table in the Northwind Database:

```
BULK INSERT northwind..customers
FROM 'd:\customers.dat'
WITH ( FORMATFILE = 'd:\customers.fmt'  )
```

Improving Load Performance

Here are the performance guidelines for BCP operation:

- You can improve load performance by two or more times by dropping indexes from the target table.
- If you have clean, verified data, you should determine the tradeoffs between ignoring check constraints using the BCP hint, and allowing the check to take place as part of the load operation.
- If you have business reasons that override the performance slowdown of firing insert triggers, this option can be used. But they better be good reasons.
- When you're importing/exporting from one SQL Server to another, use native mode; it is a bit faster than the other modes.
- If you have a recurring load, take the time to determine the best batch size for it. Otherwise, start with a batch size value on the order of a quarter to a half of the number of rows in the file, unless the number of rows is small (less than a few thousand).

- Consider the possibility of performing parallel data loads if you are loading large data files.
- Specify a large batch size for the `ROWS_PER_BATCH` hint. Ideally, the batch size should represent the total size of the file.
- Create ordered data files that match the clustered index, and utilize the `ORDER` hint.
- Lock the table to allow uninterrupted access during parallel loads.
- Perform non-logged operations whenever possible.
- Microsoft recommends that you use the `BULK INSERT` statement instead of the BCP utility when you want to bulk-copy data into SQL Server. The `BULK INSERT` statement is faster than BCP.

BCP Extras

Here are two stored procedures that can automate the entire exporting and importing of tables in a database. They are especially useful when you need to move entire databases around but don't want to use dump/load database operations (such as when creating many test databases for programmers' unit testing, or restructuring physical file locations). Execute this using OSQL/ISQL/SQL Query Analyzer.

The first stored procedure is for BCPing `OUT` all tables in a database. It is named `BCP_out_AllTables`.

```
if exists(select name from sysobjects where name = 'BCP_out_AllTables')
  begin
    drop procedure BCP_out_AllTables
  end
GO
CREATE PROCEDURE BCP_out_AllTables
    @dbname          varchar(30),
    @path             varchar(50) = "C:\Temp"
AS

SET NOCOUNT ON

DECLARE @tablename      varchar(30)
DECLARE @srvname        varchar(30)
DECLARE @cmdline        varchar(125)
DECLARE @ssql           varchar(255)
DECLARE @tabcount        smallint

SELECT @tabcount = 0
select @srvname=@@servername
```

```
EXEC ('USE ' + @dbname)

create table #dumptables ([name] varchar(255))
set @ssql = 'insert into #dumptables SELECT [name] from ' + @dbname + '..sysobjects
 where type = ''U'''
exec (@ssql)

DECLARE cnames     CURSOR FOR
select [name] from #dumptables

OPEN cnames

FETCH NEXT FROM cnames INTO @tablename
WHILE (@@fetch_status <> -1)
BEGIN
    IF (@@fetch_status = -2)
    BEGIN
        FETCH NEXT FROM cnames INTO @tablename
        CONTINUE
    END
    PRINT 'Exporting table: ' + @tablename
    /* build commandline */
    /* '-T' is used for trusted connection,  */
    /*  or '-U and -P switches for sql connections */

SELECT @cmdline = 'bcp "' + @dbname + '..[' + @tablename + ']" out "' +
         @path + '\' + @tablename + '.dat" -c  -Usa -P -S ' + @srvname
    PRINT 'Executing: ' + @cmdline
    EXEC master..xp_cmdshell @cmdline--, NO_OUTPUT
    SELECT @tabcount = @tabcount + 1
    FETCH NEXT FROM cnames INTO @tablename
END
DEALLOCATE cnames
/* Print usermessage */
SELECT CONVERT(varchar(10),@tabcount) + ' tables from database '+ @dbname
        + ' exported to ' + @path
GO
sp_help "BCP_out_AllTables"
GO
```


After the stored procedure is defined, it can be executed easily:

```
exec BCP_out_AllTables "Northwind", "D:\Temp"
```

This yields the following:

```
Exporting table: Orders
```

```
Executing: bcp "northwind..[Orders]" out "D:\Temp\Orders.dat" -c
       -Usa -P -S C814\DBARCH01
Exporting table: Products
Executing: bcp "northwind..[Products]" out "D:\Temp\Products.dat" -c
       -Usa -P -S C814\DBARCH01
. . .
15 tables from database northwind exported to D:\Temp
```

The next stored procedure is for BCPing `IN` all tables in a database. It is named `BCP_in_AllTables`.

```
if exists(select name from sysobjects where name = 'BCP_in_AllTables')
  begin
    drop procedure BCP_in_AllTables
  end
GO
CREATE PROCEDURE BCP_in_AllTables
    @dbname         varchar(30),
    @path            varchar(50) = "C:\Temp"
AS
SET NOCOUNT ON
DECLARE @tablename         varchar(30)
DECLARE @srvname          varchar(30)
DECLARE @cmdline         varchar(125)
DECLARE @ssql               varchar(255)
DECLARE @tabcount         smallint
SELECT @tabcount = 0
SELECT @srvname = @@servername
EXEC ('USE ' + @dbname)
create table #dumptables ([name] varchar(255))
set @ssql = 'insert into #dumptables SELECT [name] from ' + @dbname
        + '..sysobjects where type = ''U'''
exec (@ssql)
DECLARE cnames     CURSOR FOR
select [name] from #dumptables
OPEN cnames
FETCH NEXT FROM cnames INTO @tablename
WHILE (@@fetch_status <> -1)
BEGIN
    IF (@@fetch_status = -2)
    BEGIN
        FETCH NEXT FROM cnames INTO @tablename
        CONTINUE
    END
    PRINT 'Importing table: ' + @tablename
    /* build commandline */
```

```
    /* '-T' is used for trusted connection, */
    /*  or '-U and -P switches for sql connections */
SELECT @cmdline = 'bcp "' + @dbname + '..[' + @tablename + ']" in "'
       + @path + '\' + @tablename + '.dat" -c  -Usa -P -S ' + @srvname
    PRINT 'Executing: ' + @cmdline
    EXEC master..xp_cmdshell @cmdline--, NO_OUTPUT
    SELECT @tabcount = @tabcount + 1
    FETCH NEXT FROM cnames INTO @tablename
END
DEALLOCATE cnames
/* Print usermessage */
PRINT CONVERT(varchar(10),@tabcount) + ' files imported into database '
       + @dbname + '  from ' + @path
GO
sp_help "BCP_in_AllTables"
GO
```

After the stored procedure is defined, it can be executed easily:

```
exec BCP_in_AllTables "Northwind", "D:\Temp"
```

This yields the following:

```
Importing table: Orders
Executing: bcp "northwind..[Orders]" in "D:\Temp\Orders.dat" -c
       -Usa -P -S C814\DBARCH01
Importing table: Products
Executing: bcp "northwind..[Products]" in "D:\Temp\Products.dat" -c
       -Usa -P -S C814\DBARCH01
. . .
15 files imported into database northwind from D:\Temp
```

Data Transformation Services (DTS)

As the world becomes ever more data oriented, a much larger emphasis is being placed on getting data from one place to another. To complicate matters, the data can be stored in many different formats, contexts, file systems, and locations. In addition, the data often requires significant transformation and conversion processing as it is being moved around. Whether you are trying to move data from Excel to SQL Server, create a data mart (or data warehouse), or distribute data to heterogeneous databases, you are essentially enabling someone with data.

This section will describe Microsoft's Data Transformation Services (DTS) environment and how it is addressing these needs. As mentioned earlier, the focus will be on importing, exporting, and transforming data from one or more datasources to one or more data targets.

Common requirements of DTS might include the following:

- Exporting data out of SQL Server tables to other applications and environments (ODBC or OLE DB datasources, or via flat files)
- Importing data into SQL Server tables from other applications and environments (ODBC or OLE DB datasources, or via flat files)
- Initializing data in some data replication situations, such as initial snapshots
- Aggregating data (data transformation) for distribution to/from data marts or data warehouses
- Changing the data's context or format before importing or exporting it (data conversion)

Some typical business scenarios might include the following:

- Enabling data marts to receive data from a master data warehouse through periodic updates (see Figure 20.6)

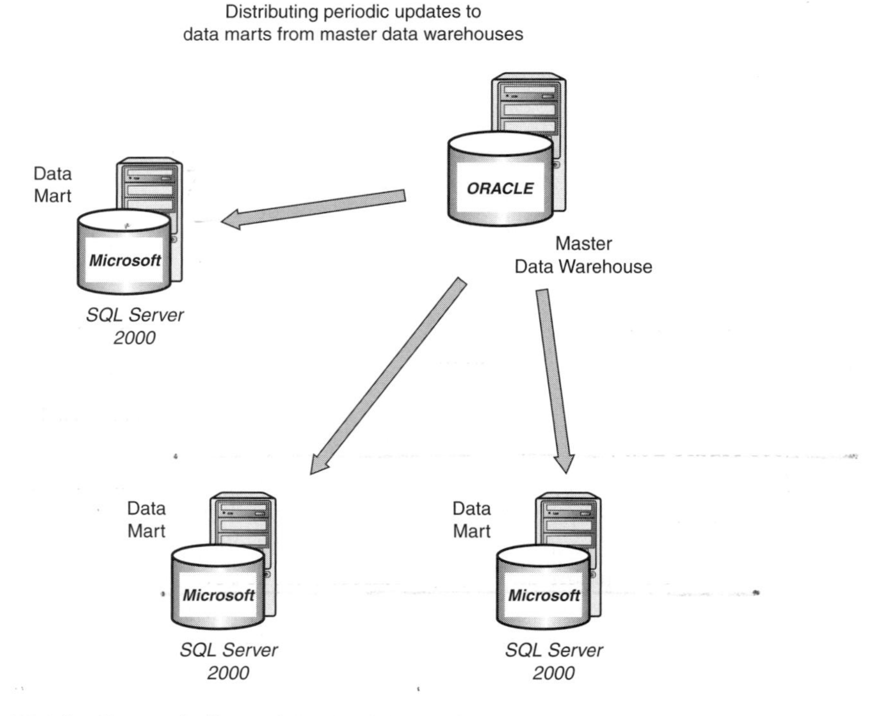

FIGURE 20.6 Distributing periodic updates to data marts.

- Populating a master data warehouse from legacy systems (see Figure 20.7)

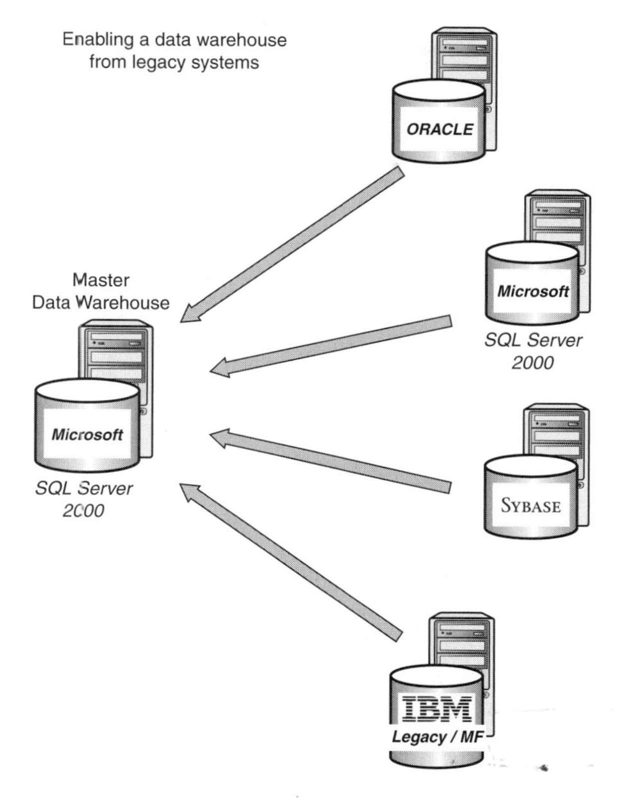

FIGURE 20.7 Populating a data warehouse.

- Initializing heterogeneous replication subscriber tables on Oracle from a SQL Server 2000 Publisher (see Figure 20.8)
- Pulling sales data directly into SQL Server 2000 from an Access or Excel application (see Figure 20.9)
- Exporting static time-reporting data files (flat files) for distribution to your remote consultants
- Importing new orders directly or indirectly from your sales force or distributed sales systems

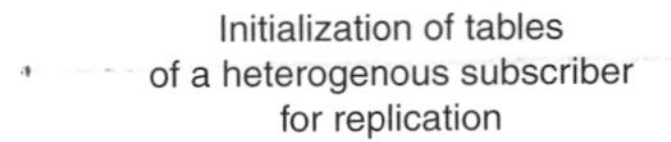

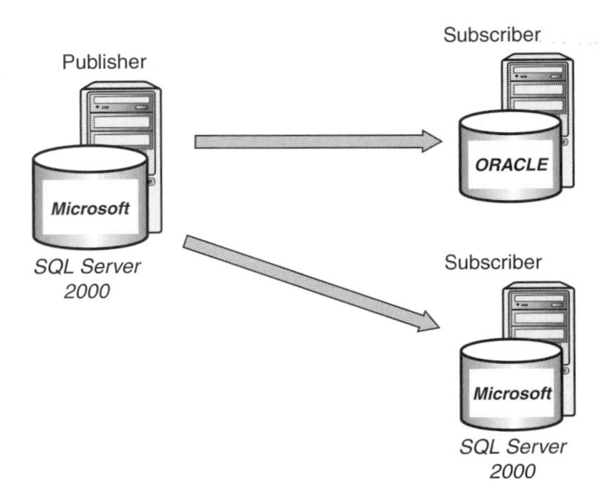

FIGURE 20.8 Initializing heterogeneous replication subscribers.

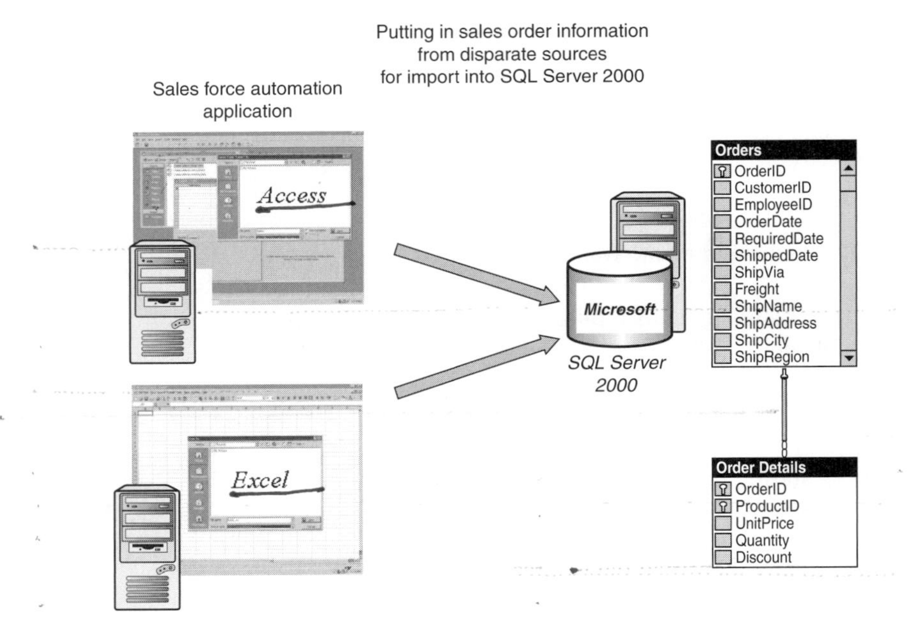

FIGURE 20.9 Pulling data from other applications.

You might be thinking at this point that DTS is what you might need for something you are trying to build. In general, DTS is what you will need if any of the following conditions exist:

- You need to import data directly into SQL Server from one or more ODBC datasources, OLE DB datasources, or via flat files.
- You need to export data directly out of SQL Server to one or more ODBC datasources, OLE DB datasources, or via flat files.
- You need to perform data conversions, transformations, or aggregations on data from one or more datasources for distribution to one or more data targets. You also need to access the data directly via any ODBC datasource, OLE DB datasource, or via flat files.
- Your bulk data movement doesn't have to be faster than the speed of light. Unfortunately, DTS must utilize conventional connection techniques to these datasources. It also must create intermediate buffers to hold data during the transformation steps. This usually disqualifies DTS on the high performance side of requirements (for large, bulk data movements with any type of data transformations defined at least). Alternative importing/exporting facilities like BCP offer better performance but lack the flexibility of DTS.

DTS Architecture and Concepts

You can think of DTS as a Data Import/Export/Transformation layer in the overall system architecture that you are deploying for at least most of your Microsoft-based applications and a few non-Microsoft applications (see Figure 20.10). DTS will allow you to "data enable" almost all of the individual applications or systems that are part of your overall implementation, such as OLTP databases, multidimensional cubes, OLAP data warehouses, Excel files, Access databases, flat files, and other heterogeneous database sources.

Microsoft uses DTS Packages to capture the specific requirements of a data movement/transformation. DTS Packages contain a collection of connections, tasks, transformations, and even workflow constraints needed to fully implement a data movement/transformation requirement. DTS Packages contain one or more steps that are either executed sequentially or in parallel at package execution time. In a nutshell, when a DTS Package is executed, it will do the following:

- Connect to any identified datasource
- Copy data (and database objects if needed)
- Transform data
- Disconnect from the datasources
- Notify users, processes, or even other packages of events (such as sending an e-mail when something is done or has errors)

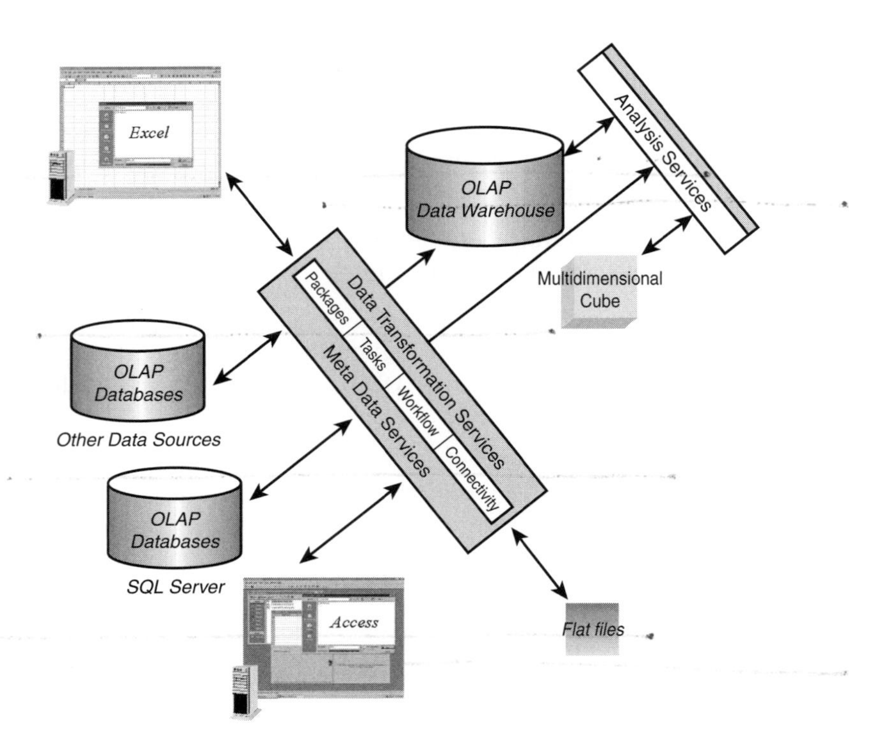

FIGURE 20.10 DTS architecture.

Defined within a DTS Package are the following:

- DTS Tasks—A discrete set of functionality, executed as a single step in a package. Tasks are the actions to be taken to accomplish the desired data transformation and movement. A task can execute any SQL statement, send mail, bulk insert data, execute an ActiveX script, or launch an external program.
- DTS Transformations—One or more functions or operations applied against a piece of data before the data arrives at the destination.
- DTS Package Workflow—Definable precedence constraints that allow you to link two tasks based on whether the first task executes, executes successfully, or executes unsuccessfully. Steps are the workflow wrappers for the tasks and are the means for the flow of control. A task step can run alone, parallel to another task step, or sequentially, according to precedence constraints. Precedence constraints are of three types:

- Unconditional—It does not matter whether the preceding step failed or succeeded.
- On success—The preceding step must have been successful for the execution of the next step.
- On failure—Return appropriate error.

A task without an associated step will not execute. DTS Designer creates a step for the task by default. However, if you write an external program using the DTS COM interface, you can easily miss the step, and the task will not run.

In addition, DTS Workflows have a number of advanced features. For instance, you can add a step to a transaction, commit or roll back a transaction at this step after success or failure, close the connection on completion of this step (saving resources), use an ActiveX script for the step execution, or expose the resultset as a datasource object (DSO) rowset provider. Exposing the resultset as a DSO rowset provider lets you use the result at this step in another package, either with the `OPENROWSET` statement or by setting up the package as a linked server. However, after you set this option, the step does not complete, so use it only for a package that is intended to be queried from external sources.

- DTS Connectivity—Based on OLE DB architecture. It allows you to get to data from a large variety of datasources.
- Metadata—The capability to save the DTS Package metadata and data lineage information to Microsoft's Metadata Services. This allows Packages and anything else stored in Metadata Services to be utilized from throughout the Microsoft and external environment.

DTS Tools

Data Transformation Services includes several tools that simplify package creation, execution, and management:

- The DTS Import/Export Wizard can easily be used to build packages to import, export, and transform data, or to copy database objects (see Figure 20.11).
- DTS Designer (which is available through Enterprise Manager) is a GUI that lets you construct/manipulate packages containing complex workflows, multiple connections to heterogeneous datasources, and even event-driven logic (see Figure 20.12).

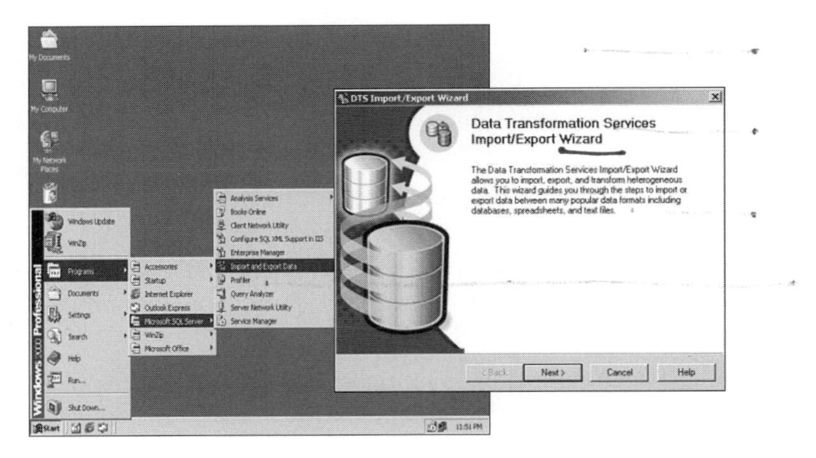

FIGURE 20.11 Invoking DTS from the Windows program group.

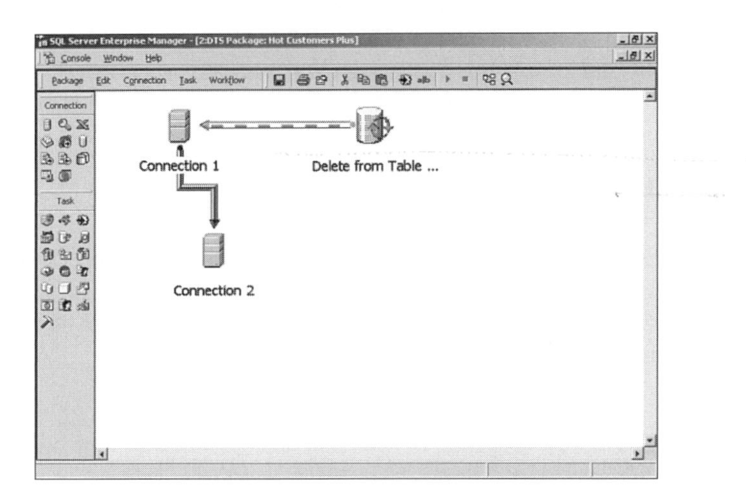

FIGURE 20.12 DTS Designer workbench.

- The Data Transformation Services entry in the SQL Server Enterprise Manager console tree, which is used to view, create, load, and execute DTS packages; to control DTS Designer settings; and to manage execution logs (see Figure 20.13).

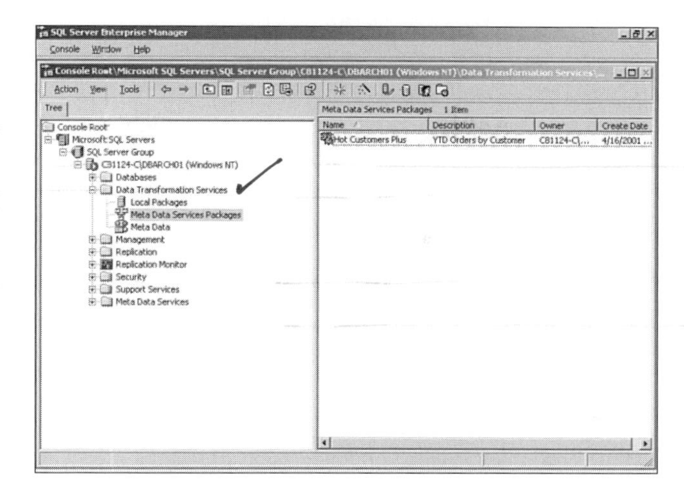

FIGURE 20.13 Enterprise Manager Console with DTS.

Package Execution Utilities

The dtswiz utility starts the DTS Import/Export Wizard by using command prompt options. It's great for initiating the wizard from within other tools.

The dtsrun utility runs a DTS Package from a command prompt.

Usage: dtsrun /option [value] [/option [value]] ...

Options ('/?' shows the complete option list; '-' May be substituted for '/'):

The package retrieval options include the following:

/~S	Server name
/~U	Username
/~P	Password
/~E	Use trusted connection instead of /U /P
/~ /~M	Package password
/~G	Package Guid string
/~V	Package version Guid string
/~F	Structured storage UNC filename (overwritten if /S is also specified)
/~R	Repository database name (uses default if blank; loads package from repository database)

The package operation options that override stored package settings include the following:

/~A	Global variable name:typeid=Value (may quote entire string [including name:typeid])
/~L	Log filename
/~W	Write completion status to Windows Event Log (True or False)

Following is the DTSRun action to perform (the default is to execute the package):

/!X	Do not execute; retrieves package to /F filename
/!D	Do not execute; drop package from SQL Server (cannot drop from storage file)
/!Y	Do not execute; output encrypted command line
/!C	Copies command line to Windows Clipboard (can be used with /!Y and /!X)

Additional DTSRun notes include the following:

~ is optional; if present, the parameter is hex text of encrypted value (0x313233...)

Whitespace between command switch and value is optional

Embedded whitespace in values must be embedded in double quotes

If an option is specified multiple times, the last one wins (except multiple /A)

The DTS Run GUI utility (dtsrunui) allows you to run a DTS Package using a standalone GUI. Just execute dtsrunui from the command prompt and it starts the UI. This facility also has the option to fully manipulate scheduling for the package (see Figure 20.14).

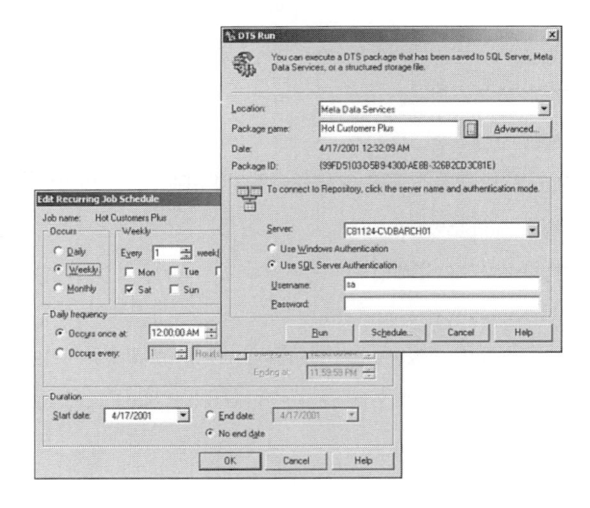

FIGURE 20.14 DTS Run Package execution and scheduling.

DTS Query Designer is the embedded GUI functionality within DTS Designer that makes it easy to build up queries in a visual manner (see Figure 20.15).

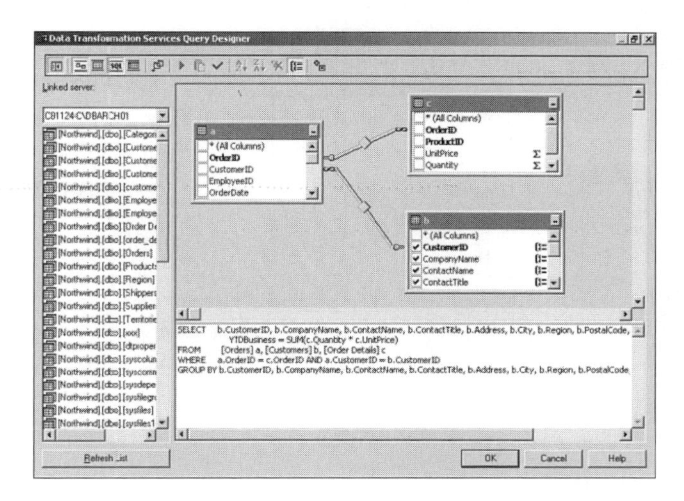

FIGURE 20.15 DTS Query Designer workbench.

Now, you will look at an actual live data export requirement that is best served by using DTS (as described earlier in this chapter). This is because both ends (source and target) of the data export will be SQL Server 2000 tables and there will be a bit of data transformation along the way.

The requirement is for a small business intelligence data mart (on SQL Server 2000) to be spun off each week from the main OLTP database (also on SQL Server 2000) that addresses a product sales manager's need to see the total year-to-date business that a customer has generated. This requirement has been named "Hot Customers Plus" to indicate the emphasis on customers that are generating ample business for the company. Of course, the data mart is on a separate machine from the critical OLTP system for all of the right reasons. The need will be to spin off this data to the data mart in a total "refresh" scenario after all OLTP processing has concluded on the weekends (see Figure 20.16).

Essentially, order data from the OLTP database (contained in Customers, Orders, and Order Details tables) must be aggregated (summed) for every order for each customer. In addition, the total amount to be stored in the YTDBusiness column in the data mart will have to be extended out to reflect the UnitPrice times (*) Quantity calculation during the data transformation. After the data mart is repopulated on the weekend, an e-mail notification must be sent to the primary business user. Although the requirements are many, DTS should be able to handle all of them with no problem.

For the reader to get a good feel for the two main DTS tool capabilities, you will generate the solution to this requirement using the DTS Wizard first, followed by the same solution being generated using DTS Designer.

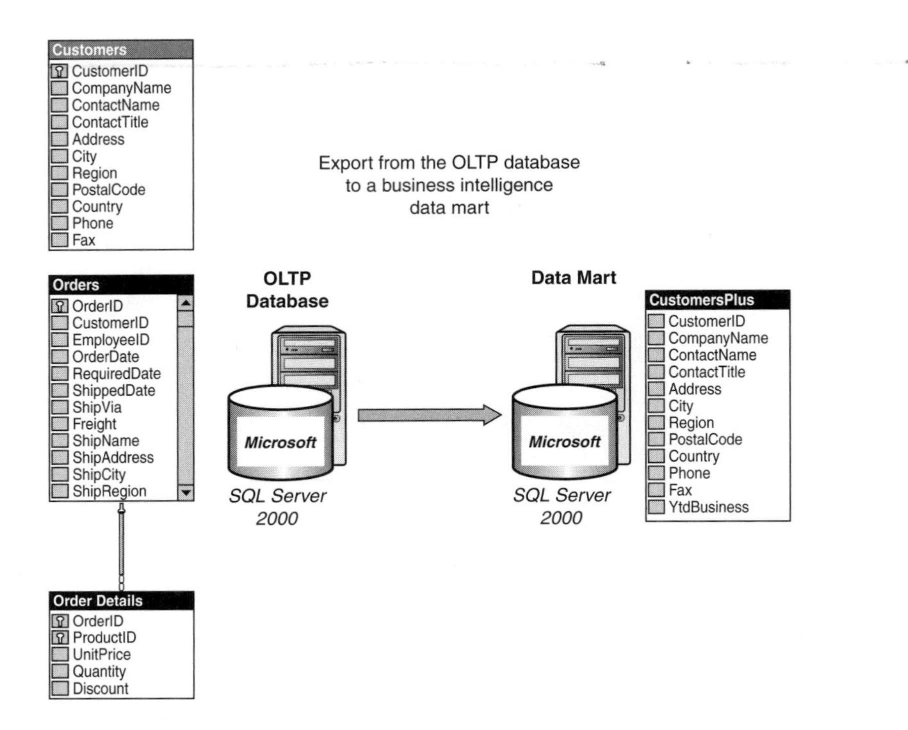

FIGURE 20.16 Populating a data mart.

Running the DTS Wizard

The DTS Wizard is a streamlined interface solely to generate DTS packages for importing or exporting of data. However, you will find that it is really quite powerful and provides an easy but sophisticated way to move data from or to any OLE DB, ODBC, or text source to another OLE DB, ODBC, or text source. You can also define simple or complex data transformations using the many options provided by the wizard or, for more complex transformations, using an ActiveX script written in VBScript or JScript from within the wizard. You can also copy database schema, but the transfer of all other database objects, such as indexes, constraints, users, permissions, stored procedures, and so on, is only supported between SQL Server 7.0 and above SQL Servers.

The DTS Wizard (whether an Export or Import is selected) takes the user through five basic steps:

1. Select/identify the datasource.
2. Select/identify the destination (target).

3. Select the data copy and transformation type. The options are to copy data with or without the schema, to move data based on a query, or to transfer objects and data between SQL 7.0 (or above) servers.
4. Define any data transformations, if required.
5. Save, schedule, and execute the package.

Now follow along with the DTS Wizard steps.

1. Fire up the DTS Wizard from the Microsoft SQL Server Program Group or from within Enterprise Manager, Tools (see Figure 20.17).

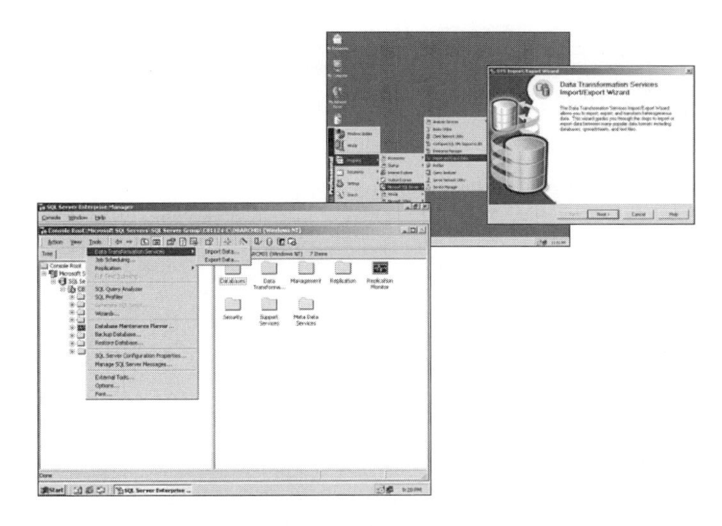

FIGURE 20.17 Two methods of invoking DTS Wizard.

2. After the DTS Wizard has been initiated, it will walk you through the steps previously outlined. The initial step is identifying the source and target (destination) data connections. In addition, there is also the capability to set any advanced connection options that are needed by a specific connection requirement (see Figure 20.18).
3. Next is the data and transformation type. For this, you will specify that a SQL Query will be needed to do the aggregations that you need (using SQL) at a transformation and movement (see Figure 20.19).

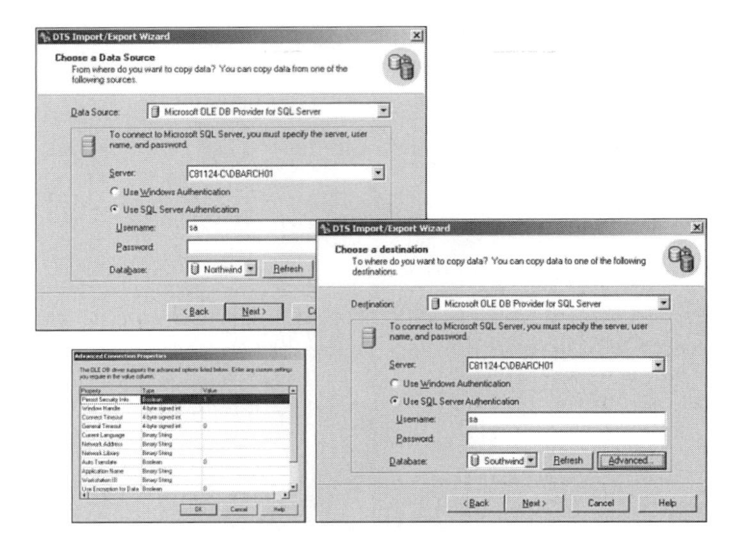

FIGURE 20.18 DTS Wizard connection options.

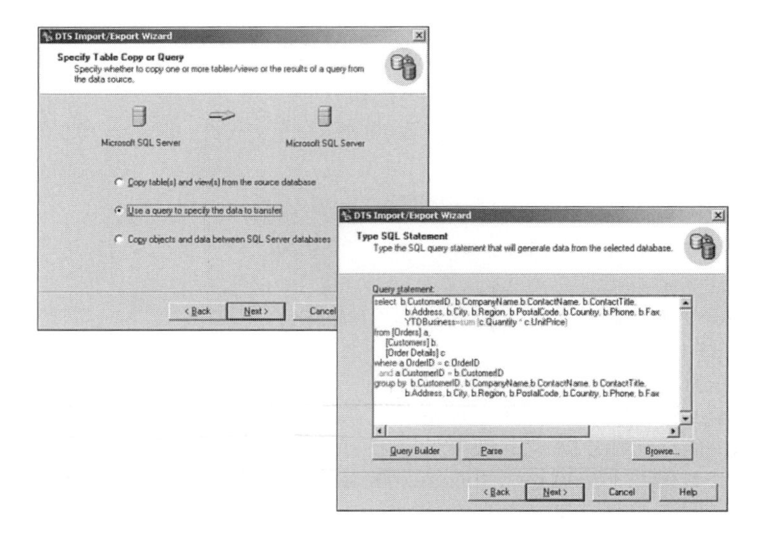

FIGURE 20.19 Table Query specification.

4. You will be prompted to identify the destination information (the target table in this case) and also have a chance to preview the data that will be generated from the Query execution (see Figure 20.20).

   Hint: When initially setting up your packages, make sure they point to a valid test environment (not production!). The connection information can be updated to point to the right place after you have completely debugged the DTS package.

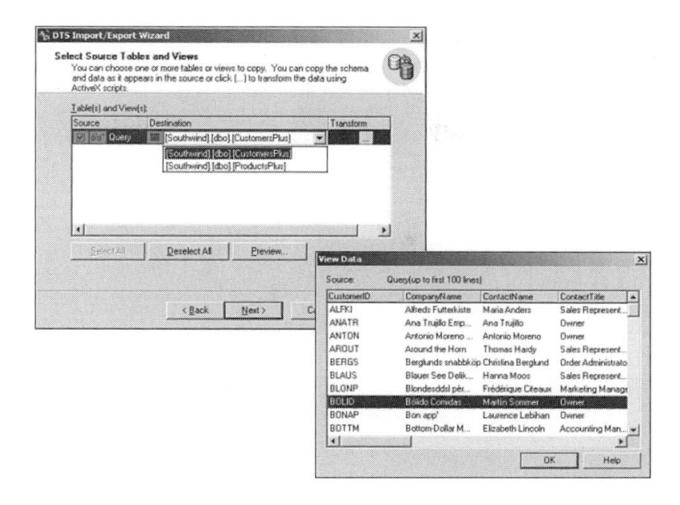

FIGURE 20.20 Source tables and Data view.

5. The next couple of wizard prompts take you through the Column selection process for the destination (target). You will also be prompted for the additional things you might need to do on the destination table side (that is, delete the rows first, create the destination table, or just append rows in the destination table). You can now see the column mappings from source to destination (see Figure 20.21).

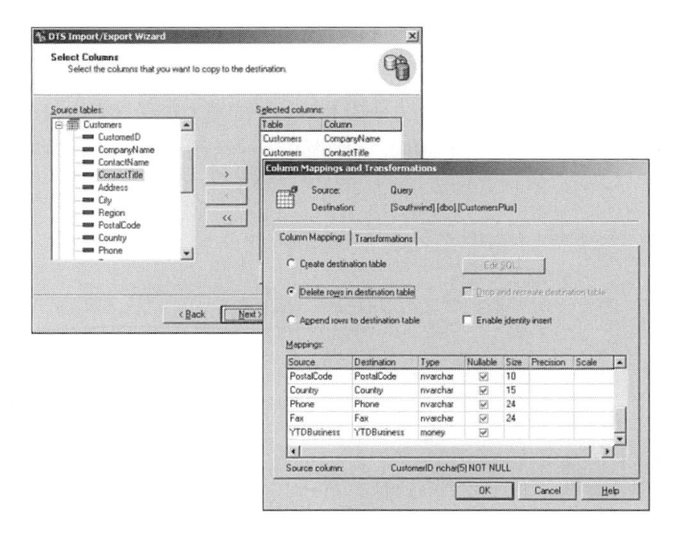

FIGURE 20.21 Column selection and mappings.

6. Figure 20.22 indicates that you are now ready to save the DTS Package (which can be password protected) and asks what you would like to do next:

- Run immediately.
- Schedule DTS package for later execution.
- Save DTS package. You can save it in a SQL Server (MSDB), SQL Server Metadata Services (recommended), in a structured storage file, or in a Visual Basic file (see Figure 20.22).

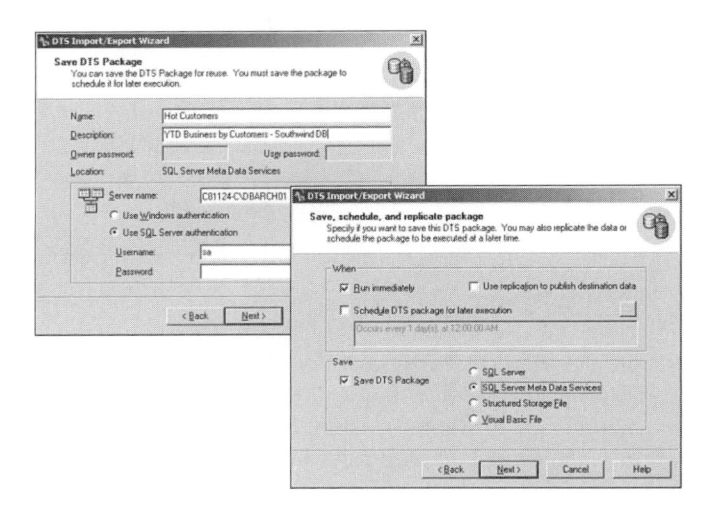

FIGURE 20.22 Naming and saving DTS Packages.

7. Last, the DTS Wizard will display its summary dialog box and ask you to finish. After you select Finish, the DTS Package will be executed because Run Immediately was selected. You will see the Executing Package dialog box with each major task listed along with the progress and status of each task (see Figure 20.23).

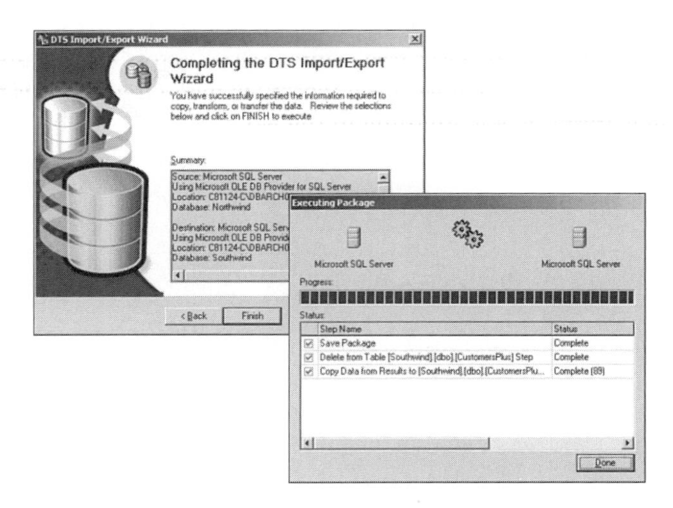

FIGURE 20.23 DTS Wizard summary and execution.

Next, you will look at the DTS Designer GUI and its visual manipulation capabilities.

DTS Designer

DTS Designer is extremely easy to use and allows a user the flexibility of editing and manipulating any of the package properties in any order that is needed, as opposed to the strict sequential order of the DTS Wizard. You will find that after you have mastered all of the package concepts, you will be spending most of your time using DTS Designer instead of the wizard.

Because you have already created a DTS Package using the wizard, you will just open this package with DTS Designer to demonstrate its capabilities (see Figure 20.24).

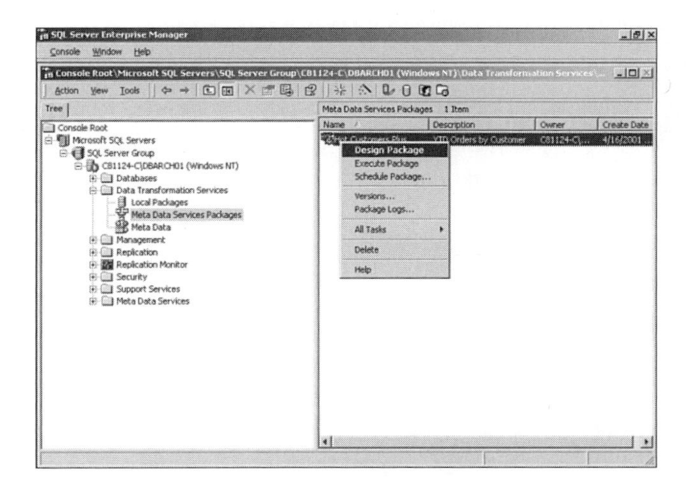

FIGURE 20.24 DTS Package—Design package option.

As you can see with DTS Designer, a main workspace pane and a palette of icons are to the left of Connection Properties and of Tasks (see Figure 20.25). Across the top are many of the same pull-down menu items along with the Workflow menu item. This is truly a point, click, and drag workspace. For anything in the workspace, you simply click on the icon, such as Connection 1 or Connection 2, to see its properties, or click on the solid line between Connection 1 and Connection 2 to see the transformation that is defined between them. The Delete from Table icon shows that a delete of rows for the destination table will be initiated after the connections are established.

Figure 20.26 shows the properties of Connections and of Workflows.

When you click on the Transformation line between Connection 1 and Connection 2, you see some familiar properties that were originally set up with the DTS Wizard. Specifically, you can see the Source SQL Query that is pulling data out of the source Connection 1.

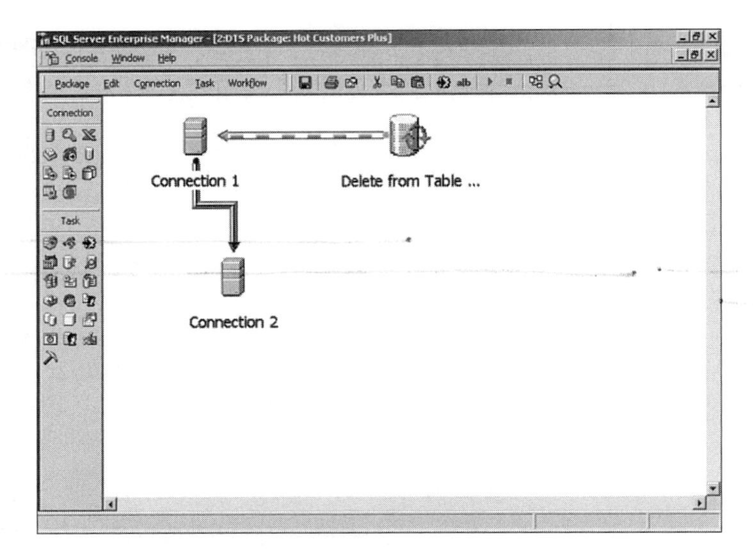

FIGURE 20.25 DTS Designer workbench.

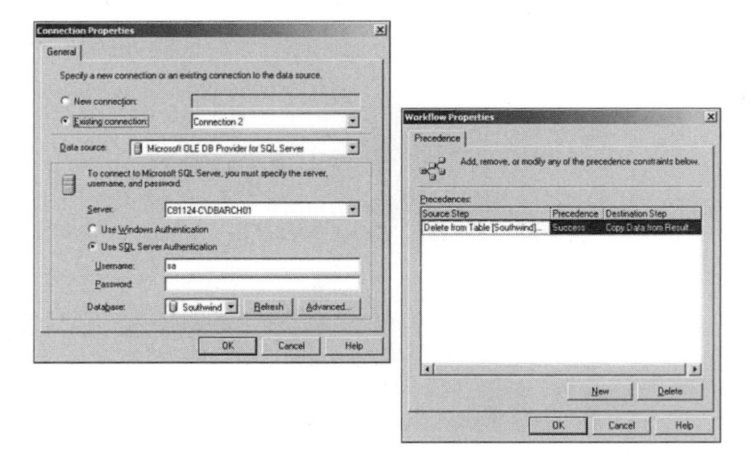

FIGURE 20.26 Connection and Workflow properties.

Because you are doing a transformation, the package cannot be saved without first defining this transformation with an ActiveX script. This is easy to do with DTS Designer and the ActiveX scripting capabilities. As you can see in Figure 20.27, you can simply name the ActiveX script in creating it for the first time or edit the one you need. It will be based on the source/destination picture on the lower portion of this dialog box.

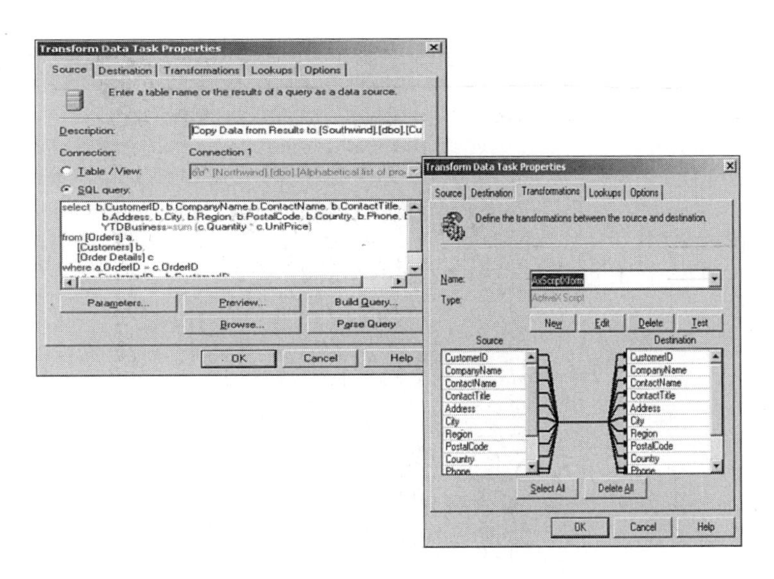

FIGURE 20.27 SQL Query and Transformation Data Task properties.

The following ActiveX script depicts the source to destination copying for the transformation. All you do is specify your preference of what the script should be written in, and the script will be generated for you. It is now possible to modify the script as you see fit.

```
'**************** VBcustomermap.txt ********************************
'  Visual Basic Transformation Script
'  Copy each source column to the
'  destination column
'*******************************************************************
Function Main()
       DTSDestination("CustomerID") = DTSSource("CustomerID")
       DTSDestination("CompanyName") = DTSSource("CompanyName")
       DTSDestination("ContactName") = DTSSource("ContactName")
       DTSDestination("ContactTitle") = DTSSource("ContactTitle")
       DTSDestination("Address") = DTSSource("Address")
       DTSDestination("City") = DTSSource("City")
       DTSDestination("Region") = DTSSource("Region")
       DTSDestination("PostalCode") = DTSSource("PostalCode")
       DTSDestination("Country") = DTSSource("Country")
       DTSDestination("Phone") = DTSSource("Phone")
       DTSDestination("Fax") = DTSSource("Fax")
       DTSDestination("YTDBusiness") = DTSSource("YTDBusiness")
       Main = DTSTransformStat_OK
End Function
```

When you are at the Source tab of the Transform Data Task Properties, you can see that you can choose from several options with the SQL Query option. You can have DTS parse the query to make sure it has the correct syntax, you can preview its execution like you saw with DTS Wizard, or you can invoke the Build Query (Query Designer) option. Figure 20.28 shows you the graphical representation of the query that has been defined. You will find that this is a great facility to build up and visualize the SQL queries that you will be using in complex transformations. It is dynamic, in that when you make a change to the graphics or the SQL code, each is changed automatically.

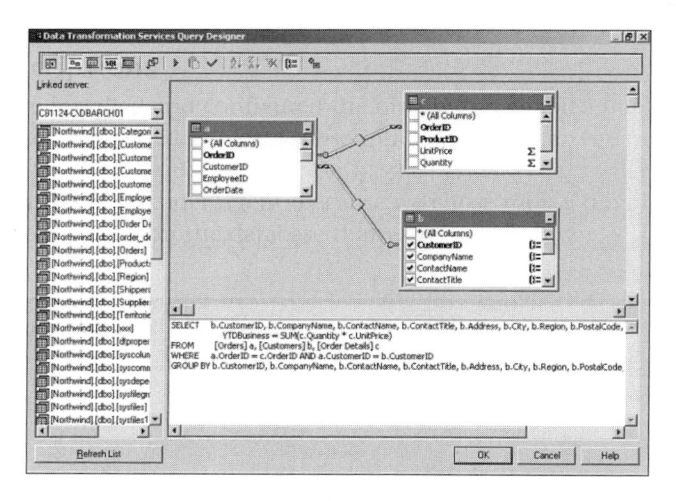

FIGURE 20.28 DTS Query Designer.

Figure 20.29 shows the final version of DTS Package: Hot Customers Plus that has been saved into the SQL Server Metadata Services. A Send Mail task was added on successful completion, following the Transformation execution to complete the business requirement. Then it was executed as a test. The Send Mail Task had an error on it because the mail profile was not completed yet; however, you can see that the prior tasks of deleting from the destination table first, and then copying the result rows to the destination table, executed successfully. Mission accomplished!

The choice of saving this Package in the Metadata Services automatically makes it available to more than just SQL Server. As you can see from Figure 20.30, the package is now part of the overall Data Warehousing Framework/Contents portion of the Metadata Services. Most of the Package properties can be edited directly though Enterprise Manager now.

Saving to the Metadata Repository also allows you to audit all data transformations, including the user information and any errors in package execution. This auditing, referred to as data lineage, provides a powerful tool for monitoring data loads. The Metadata Services Repository provides the most versatile long-term method of storing DTS packages.

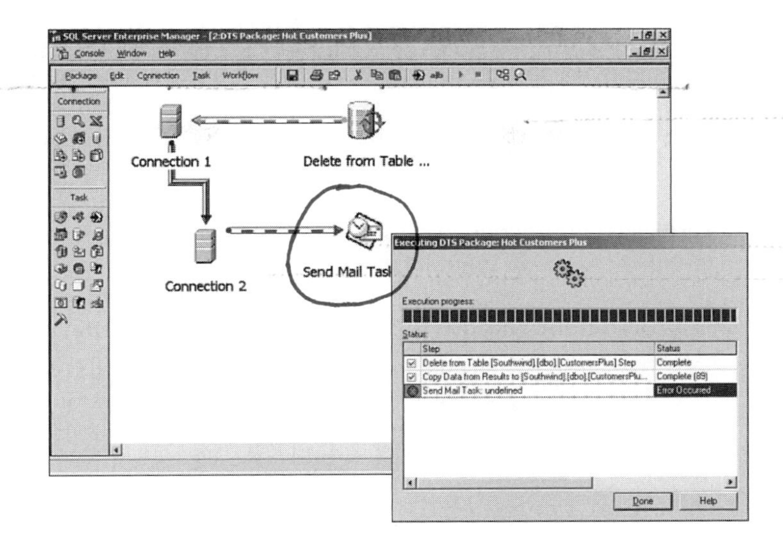

FIGURE 20.29 DTS Designer and Package execution.

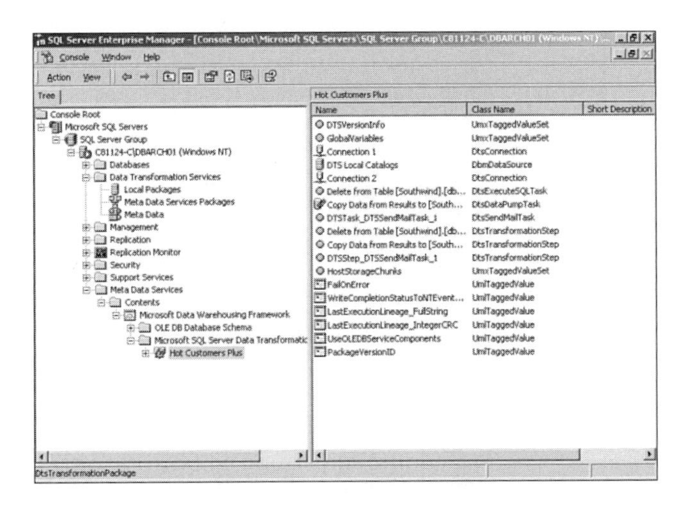

FIGURE 20.30 Metadata Services storage of packages.

The Data Pump

The DTS data pump is an OLE DB provider that provides the interfaces and methods to import, export, and transform data from an OLE DB datasource to an OLE DB destination. The DTS data pump is the engine of the Transform Data task, Data Driven Query task, and the Parallel Data Pump task. The data pump's main goal is to move and transform data from one source to another.

You can use the DTS Designer to create a simple transformation using the data pump. In DTS Designer, you create two connection objects, select them both, and choose Add Transform from the Workflow menu. You can see the additional data pump phases depicted in the Transformations tab of the Transform Data Task Properties dialog box (see Figure 20.31). This is called Multiphase Data Pump Functionality. Advanced users can add the programs that customize the data pump at various phases of its operation. By this customization, a vast range of functionality can be added to a package. This is essentially giving the user a detailed chance to manipulate the process during the data transformation step.

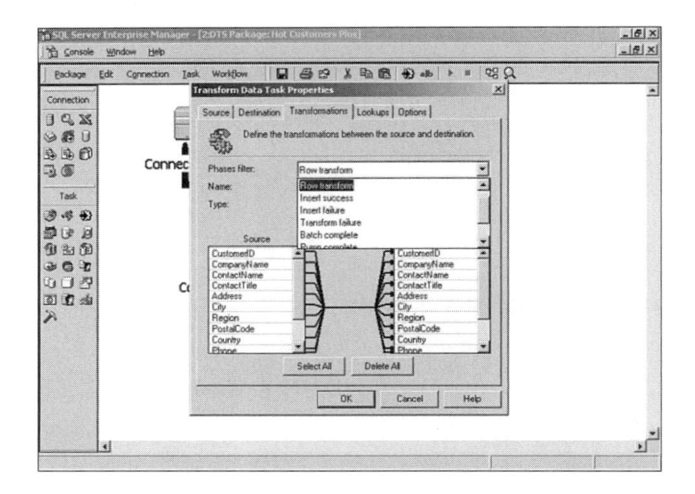

FIGURE 20.31 Transform Data Task Properties.

Data-Driven Queries

In real life, loading things like data warehouse tables tends to be more complex than selecting data, transforming it, and then inserting it into the tables. Data-driven queries (DDQs) provide more flexibility than the Transform task but are row-based, whereas an insert-based data pump task is implemented as one insert statement or as a bulk copy. A DDQ loops through a resultset, taking actions as determined by conditions defined in an ActiveX script. DDQs can have up to four queries defined. These are defined as one insert query, one delete query, one update query, and one user query. One query is executed per row in the resultset, depending on the ActiveX script associated with the DDQ.

NOTE

Although the queries are named insert, update, delete, and user, these queries are not required. You can use any SQL statement. It is preferable to perform inserts with the insert query, but you could actually have three user-defined queries called from the ActiveX script as update, delete, or user-defined queries.

When you need more complex business logic to transform data, a DDQ is also a good candidate. In addition to the four queries that can be executed from the ActiveX script, you can write the row to an error log, skip the row in the insert, or abort the entire task. The action taken for the row by the data pump is determined by the DTSTransform_Stat constant.

A Bit More on Metadata

Metadata is defined as "data about data," and the Microsoft Metadata Services Repository contains the metadata for the server database objects, including packages.

You can use the Metadata or Metadata Services Packages view in the DTS section of Enterprise Manager to view database schema and to view the versioning and data lineage of a DTS package. Data lineage determines the source of a piece of data, and you can use DTS packages stored in the Metadata Services Repository to perform this auditing. You can then use the Metadata view to browse the lineage for a package execution, which will show the system name, account name, and date for every execution of a package that has lineage enabled. You enable data lineage in the Advanced options of the Package Properties page.

Summary

As you have seen in this chapter, it is fairly easy to create and implement a typical data export or data import from one datasource to another using either BCP or DTS. We have shown you how to bulk load data into and out of SQL Server using the BCP utility and just bulk load data into SQL Server using the `BULK INSERT` statement. The multitude of switches BCP offers is very comprehensive and addresses most, if not all, importing and exporting situations. More important, with the advent of some additional switches like `ORDER` (within hints), `TABLOCK` (within hints), batches (`-b`), network packet sizes (`-a`), and others, it is significantly easier to increase the performance of BCP in a big way. BCP has been around for a long time, and it will continue to be the work-horse of bulk data loading and unloading.

For those who need to do complex data transformations, DTS provides a great place for building up and executing any transformations/imports/exports without having to venture into the world of programming. This is a big win for the data enablers of the world. However, in the future, you can expect to see more performance enhancements to DTS because that is still where DTS suffers the most.

The next chapter, "Administering Very Large SQL Server Databases," discusses issues related to large databases, including maintenance, backups and restores, indexes, and partitioning.

CHAPTER 21

Administering Very Large SQL Server Databases

IN THIS CHAPTER

- Do I Have a Very Large Database (VLDB)?
- VLDB Maintenance Issues
- Partitioning Data

by Paul Jensen

The realm of the very large database was once reserved for the mainframe environment and mega-corporations, but with the advent of fast, affordable processors and disks and database management software such as SQL Server 2000, large databases have proliferated as companies store huge amounts of data to assist in business analysis.

SQL Server 2000 was designed with the Very Large Database (VLDB) in mind, effectively scaling to support databases into the terabyte range.

Do I Have a Very Large Database (VLDB)?

What constitutes a VLDB? These days, with databases scaling into hundreds of gigabytes and even terabytes, what constitutes a VLDB is hard to define. However, a database can be said to be a VLDB if it is too large to be maintained within the window of opportunity. The window of opportunity is the time when the database is quiet, the time you have allocated to perform maintenance tasks such as backing up the database. For example, if this window of opportunity is only one hour, then a database could be said to be a VLDB if its backup time exceeds that period. On the other hand, a database 10 times that size, with a 12-hour backup window, might not be considered a VLDB.

VLDB Maintenance Issues

The maintenance plan for your VLDB must be carefully considered. As with all databases, maintenance should be planned with the least impact on users. When a database reaches a point in which maintenance tasks can no longer run in their allotted window, adjustments must be made to the scheduling of tasks, perhaps running them weekly or monthly rather than daily, or to the methods used to perform tasks, such as adjusting the backup methodology.

Backing Up and Restoring Databases

The key to SQL Server's support for the VLDB is its ability to back it up. As the length of time to back up a database is proportional to its size, this can be a major issue with large databases. It wouldn't do to run a daily full backup if the backup ran for 25 hours! Fortunately, other options are available. A full backup can be scheduled less frequently on a VLDB by combining it with log, differential, and file or filegroup backups. When considering which combination of backup methods to use, don't forget to consider restore time as well; if quick recovery is imperative, designing your database so you can leverage file or filegroup restores can vastly improve your time to recover. For example, if a database has 80GB of data spread over four disks in 20GB files, and one of the disks fails, you can restore only the file that is on the disk that failed, which should take roughly one quarter of the time that it would take to restore the entire database. In addition to this, SQL Server, when restoring the logs to bring the file up-to-date, will only process transactions from the log, which recorded data on the affected file, thus speeding the log file restores to a similar degree.

Another time saver for VLDB backups is to back up to multiple devices. Using multiple devices can help improve backup time by almost the reciprocal of the number of devices used; simply put, a backup to three devices could be complete in one third the time it takes to a single device. Results will vary, of course, and they are dependent on hardware limitations such as disk, tape, and bus configuration. You will also see diminishing returns as the number of devices are increased. If three devices are three times as fast, it doesn't always follow that ten devices will be proportionately faster. You will have to test the configuration to find the optimal balance between cost and performance.

All the SQL Server backup methods are dynamic, so the database can be accessed during backup; however, there will be a performance hit during the backup operation. To service the needs of high availability databases with no tolerance for backup-associated performance loss, SQL Server 2000 provides support for snapshot backups as well.

Snapshot backups are implemented in conjunction with independent hardware and software vendors to provide almost instantaneous backups. This is done by implementing a third-party Virtual Device Interface (VDI) that supports split mirror or copy on write operations. Through the VDI, Microsoft has allowed third-party vendors to fully leverage SQL Server 2000's native backup utilities. This means that the vendor can leverage advanced hardware and software backup solutions while still retaining full SQL Server recovery functionality. For example, a vendor could implement a three-way mirror data storage solution. In this solution, as the name implies, three mirror images of the data are maintained. When the backup application performs a backup, it issues commands to SQL Server through the VDI to prepare the database(s) or datafile(s)for backup and issues the backup database with snapshot command. At this point the database or files being backed up are momentarily frozen, so a consistent image of the data can be preserved. What is actually being backed up is not the data, but metadata containing information about the current state of the data. Once this is recorded, the backup application can "split off" one of the mirrored copies containing the actual data files, and the database or files are unfrozen. As the only data that is being backed up is a small amount of metadata, the backup time is reduced to seconds or minutes, rather than hours. Once complete the data is still protected by a two-way mirror, and the third copy that was split off is available to be backed up in a conventional manner such as to tape, used as a snapshot to initiate replication or create a warm standby, or brought online as a copy of the database, perhaps for development purposes. Once the process is complete the third disk can be resynced with the mirror set, and the process is ready to start over.

The specification for the VDI can be downloaded from Microsoft at `http://www.microsoft.com/SQL/downloads/virtualbackup.asp`; however, this spec is really intended for independent software vendors who are developing SQL Server backup solutions. Microsoft recommends you contact your backup or storage solution provider if you are interested in implementing snapshot backups.

Performing Consistency Checks on Databases

Consistency checks on data are performed with the Database Consistency Checker, or DBCC. Running DBCCs is both disk and memory intensive, as each data page to be checked must be read into memory if it is not already there. Therefore, adding more memory will speed the DBCC, as data is more likely to be found in cache. This solution is not always feasible in VLDBs in which the ratio of data to memory is high. In this case, running DBCCs causes spooling to tempdb, which resides on disk and causes an I/O bottleneck, slowing the DBCC process. By placing tempdb on a separate disk system, preferably RAID 0, you can optimize the tempdb throughput and speed up your DBCC.

The Enterprise and Developer editions of SQL Server can take advantage of multiple processors, and will perform parallel execution of DBCC statements. The `DBCC CHECKDB` statement performs a serial scan of the database, but parallel scans of multiple objects as it proceeds to the limit of the system "max degree of parallelism" option. This speeds up the operation substantially over previous versions, but in the case of extremely large tables, it may still be advantageous to schedule `DBCC CHECKTABLE` commands against individual tables or groups of tables on a rotating basis, if `DBCC CHECKDB` doesn't complete in your allotted time frame.

Another option is to run DBCC CHECKDB or DBCC CHECKTABLE with the NOINDEX option. This speeds the operation of the DBCC statement as it doesn't check the non-clustered indexes on user tables (system table indexes are always checked). Index corruption is not as critical an issue as data corruption, as no data is lost, and the index can always be dropped and re-created if necessary.

Another method would be to not perform DBCCs on your production database. If you are running a standby server, the DBCCs can be run against the standby database. The theory here is that if the consistency checks run okay on the standby database, the production database should be okay as it is the source of the standby. If the standby database reports corruption, then DBCCs or other tests for corruption can be run against the production database.

Updating Statistics

Statistics are used by SQL Server to determine the optimum way to access data. By default, SQL Server maintains statistics automatically, using samples of the data to estimate statistics. The frequency at which statistics are updated is based on the amount of data in the column or index and the amount of changes to the data. SQL Server optimizes the statistics updates to run with the least amount of overhead possible, so unless you find your statistics aren't correctly populated by the automatic update or you can't afford the overhead it incurs, it is not recommended that you disable the automatic updates.

If you opt to manually update statistics for your VLDB, you must plan how to optimize the operation. As updating statistics can cause excessive overhead, you should determine whether statistics actually need to be updated, rather than arbitrarily scheduling updates. For example, in a large data warehouse populated with monthly data loads, the statistics updates should be scheduled after the completion of the data load. The DBCC SHOW_STATISTICS, as well as Query Analyzer and SQL Profiler, are all useful in determining statistics usage. When updating statistics, if your data is evenly distributed, you might also find that you can get away with running UPDATE STATISTICS and specifying a percentage to sample rather than all the rows.

Rebuilding Indexes

Rebuilding indexes on large tables can be extremely time-consuming and I/O intensive. Consideration must be taken for all indexes on the table, as, in the case of a clustered index, dropping and re-creating the index would cause all non-clustered indexes to be rebuilt as well. Fortunately, SQL Server provides options to avoid such a situation. If you are rebuilding an index to reduce fragmentation, use DBCC INDEXDEFRAG instead, as this will compact the pages of the index, removing any empty pages it creates without having to drop and rebuild the full index. DBCC INDEXDEFRAG is fully logged, doesn't hold locks for extended periods, and doesn't block running queries or updates.

The CREATE INDEX statement now has a DROP EXISTING clause that allows the rebuilding of existing indexes without dropping and re-creating them. This can save time on VLDBs, as it accelerates the rebuild by eliminating the sorting process. If you are rebuilding a clustered index, the non-clustered indexes are not dropped and re-created provided the index is rebuilt on the original column(s). Normally, because non-clustered indexes contain the clustered keys, the non-clustered indexes are rebuilt when the clustered index is dropped via DROP INDEX, and then rebuilt again when the clustered index is re-created.

The DBCC DBREINDEX is still available as well, but it doesn't provide as much functionality as DROP EXISTING; its only advantage is the ability to rebuild multiple indexes on a single table simultaneously.

Another option to consider when creating or rebuilding indexes is to specify WITH SORT_IN_TEMPDB in the statement. By default, when indexes are created or rebuilt, they are sorted in the destination filegroup for the index. If tempdb is on a separate file system (a dedicated RAID 0 array for example), SORT_IN_TEMPDB forces the index build to occur in tempdb, and when it is complete, it is then written to its destination file group. This is an often overlooked option that can provide huge reductions in index build times.

Purging and Archiving Data

One of the most important aspects of managing a VLDB is knowing when to let go of your pack-rat instincts and purge unneeded data. Examine your legal and business requirements to store data, and purge data that falls outside these requirements. For example, I once managed a database for a utility company. The data was monitored for 30- and 90-day service commitments, and we were required to keep records for a year. By daily purging completed records into storage as history, the number of active records was reduced, and query time was improved. History records older than 30 days required storage of only a subset of data, so these reduced records were transferred to 90-day storage. This sped up queries against the 30-day history and reduced storage requirements drastically as only about 10% of the original data was still required at this point. Once a week, the data that had aged past 90 days was backed up to tape and deleted from the database. The tape backups were kept for one year. Performed religiously on a daily, weekly, monthly, or yearly basis, these types of purge operations can keep your VLDB from growing into a problematic monster.

Partitioning Data

Partitioning the data across multiple files within a database, or even across multiple databases on multiple servers, can alleviate many of the woes associated with VLDBs. By breaking the database up into smaller, more manageable "chunks," the time and performance constraints of the VLDB are reduced.

When multiple servers are used to partition data, they are referred to as *federated servers*. Partitioning data across multiple servers adds a high degree of administrative overhead and should really only be considered when your performance or storage needs absolutely exceed that of a single server. With SQL Server 2000 on Windows 2000 Datacenter supporting 32 processors and 64GB of RAM, only a small percentage of installations will need the added capacity of federated servers.

Vertical Partitioning

Vertical partitioning is used to split a "wide" table with many or large columns into two or more tables joined by a common key, or to separate multiple tables for performance or manageability. Splitting a wide table is useful with tables containing text or image data, or a subset of rarely accessed columns. This could be considered denormalizing the table, which is acceptable if it improves performance. In truth, however, partitioning is often done to compensate for data that wasn't properly normalized in the first place.

When vertically partitioning multiple tables, filegroups can be leveraged to spread the tables over multiple disks to improve I/O and allow backup by filegroup. When vertically partitioning across filegroups, planning the location of data is critical. Tables should be located to optimize I/O. Consider a database with four tables: orders, items, products, and suppliers. If orders and items are frequently joined in queries, and the same is true for products and suppliers, placing orders and products on one filegroup and items and suppliers on the other should improve performance. Remember to consider how this placement will affect your backup plan.

By using vertical partitioning across multiple servers, you can scale your database for high performance and high storage capacity. In this case, rather than the tables residing in multiple filegroups within a database, they are spread over two or more servers. These servers are generally configured as linked servers, and the data is queried using the fully qualified four-part object name. The following statement joins the local products table with the suppliers table on a linked server:

```
SELECT ProductName, CompanyName
FROM Products p JOIN
RemoteServer.Northwind2.dbo.Suppliers s
ON p.supplierid= s.supplierid
```

When modifying data on linked servers, you must perform a distributed transaction. This can be referenced through the API functions of a client application or by executing the `BEGIN DISTRIBUTED TRANSACTION` statement. This ensures that data on both the local and linked server is updated or rolled back as a unit.

Horizontal Partitioning

When data is partitioned horizontally, the data in a table is split across multiple tables based on values within the data. The division here is to break up long, as opposed to wide tables. For example, a single table containing customer data for the year could split into 12 tables, each containing rows that correspond to a particular month. Check constraints on each table ensure that only data for the correct month is inserted into each table; the check constraint is also referenced by the query optimizer, allowing it to build an execution plan that uses only the appropriate tables. As with vertical partitioning, these tables can be spread among multiple filegroups, databases, or servers, depending on the degree to which you must scale. A view can be created that accesses all the tables (known as **member tables**) using the `UNION` operator, providing access to the data that is transparent to the application. Views that access tables on the local server are referred to as **Local Partitioned Views** and views that reference member tables on remote servers are referred to as **Distributed Partitioned Views**.

Using Distributed Partitioned Views

When distributing data using partitioned views, distribute the data by a value that spreads the data evenly over all servers, or by a value, such as region, that distributes the data with a logical association with the server location. This will minimize the need for distributed queries. SQL Server 2000 introduces support for updateable distributed partitioned views. Data modifications are performed against the view, allowing true transparency. The view is accessed as if it were a base table, with the user or application unaware of the actual location of the data. If configured properly, SQL Server will determine via the `where` clause specified in the update query which partition defined in the view must be updated rather than updating all tables in the join. For more information on defining distributed partitioned views, see Chapter 27, "Creating and Managing Views in SQL Server."

Summary

As you saw in this chapter, careful design of the VLDB is crucial to the success of your installation. The VLDB needs to be designed not only for performance, as is often the case, but with recovery in mind as well. With each design step, you must ask yourself, "How will this affect my ability to back up and recover data?" and "Could this adversely affect performance?" It is comforting to know that many of the steps taken to accommodate VLDBs, such as the use of multiple filegroups, if planned correctly, can solve both performance and backup issues.

As well as the considerations for VLDBs, another aspect of the administrator's job in large or geographically dispersed environments is transferring data. The following chapter, "Data Replication," deals with SQL Server's replication feature, a powerful tool for transferring and updating data on remote servers.

CHAPTER 22

Data Replication

by Paul Bertucci

IN THIS CHAPTER

Nothing is typical anymore. Companies now have to support numerous hardware and software configurations in multitiered, distributed environments. These diverse configurations and applications (and users of the applications) come in all sizes and shapes. And, of course, you need a way to deal with varied data access requirements for these different physical locations, these remote or mobile users over a local area network, any dial-up connection users, and any needs over the Internet. Microsoft's Data Replication facility allows for a great breadth of capability to deal with many of these demands. However, to build a proper data replication implementation that meets many of these user requirements, you must have a thorough understanding of the business requirements and of the technical capabilities of data replication. This chapter does the following:

- Aides you in understanding what data replication is
- Shows you how to look at the users' requirements of data
- Allows you to choose which replication configuration best meets these requirements (if any)
- Demonstrates how to implement this configuration
- Describes how to administer and monitor a data replication implementation

What Is Replication?

Long before you ever start setting up and using SQL Server data replication, you need to have a solid grasp of what data replication is and how it can be used to meet your company's needs. In its classic definition, data replication is based on the "store and forward" data distribution model, as shown in Figure 22.1. In other words, data that is stored in one location (inserted) is automatically "forwarded" to one or more distributed locations.

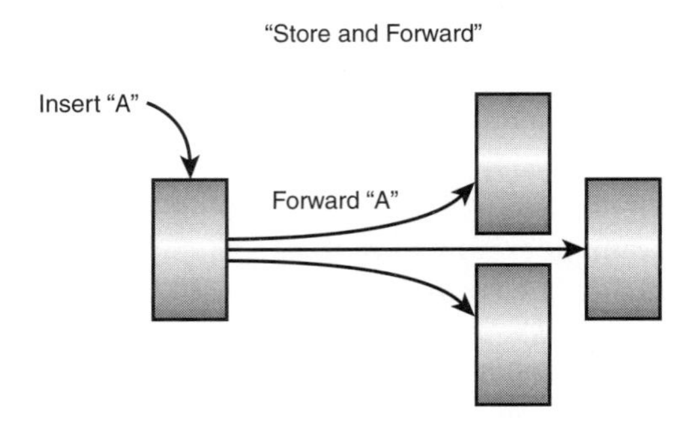

FIGURE 22.1 Store and Forward distribution model.

Of course, the more complete data distribution model addresses updates, deletes, data latency, autonomy, and so on. It is this data distribution model that Microsoft's data replication facility serves to implement. It has come a long way since the early days of Microsoft SQL Server replication (earlier than 6.5) and is now easily categorized as "production worthy." I have personal experience in implementing several worldwide data replication scenarios for some of the biggest companies in Silicon Valley without a hitch. These scenarios have fallen into three typical areas. The first is when you need to deliver data to different locations to eliminate network traffic and unnecessary loads on a single server. Another is when you need to move data off a single server onto several other servers to provide for high availability and decentralization of data (or partitioning of data). Finally, you could be replicating all data on a server to another server so that if the primary server crashes, users can switch to this other server quickly and continue to work with little downtime or data loss (fail-over server). Figure 22.2 illustrates the topology of some of these replication variations.

You can use data replication for many reasons. A few of these will be discussed later in this chapter. First, however, you need to understand some of the common terms and metaphors used by Microsoft in data replication.

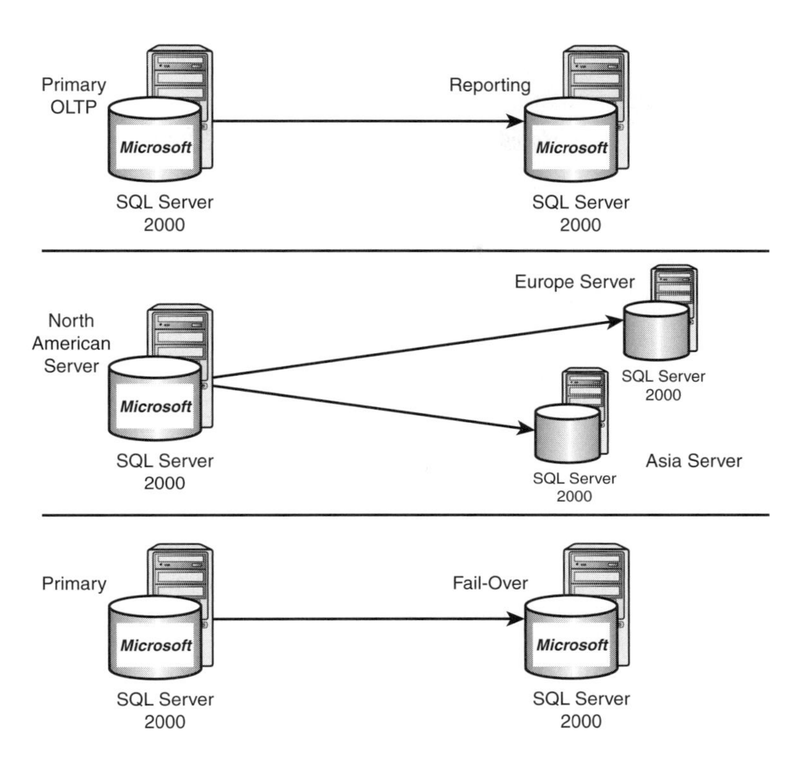

FIGURE 22.2 Data replication example scenarios.

The Publisher, Distributor, and Subscriber Metaphor

Any SQL Server can play up to three distinct roles in a data replication environment, as represented in Figure 22.3:

- Being a publication server (the publisher of data)
- Being a distribution server (the distributor of data)
- Being a subscription server (the subscriber to the data being published)

The **publication server** contains the database or databases that are going to be published. This is the source of the data that is to be replicated to other servers. In Figure 22.3, the Customers table in the Northwind database is the data to be published. To publish data, the database that contains the data that is going to be published must first be enabled for publishing. Full publishing configuration requirements will be discussed later in this chapter in the "Setting Up Replication" section.

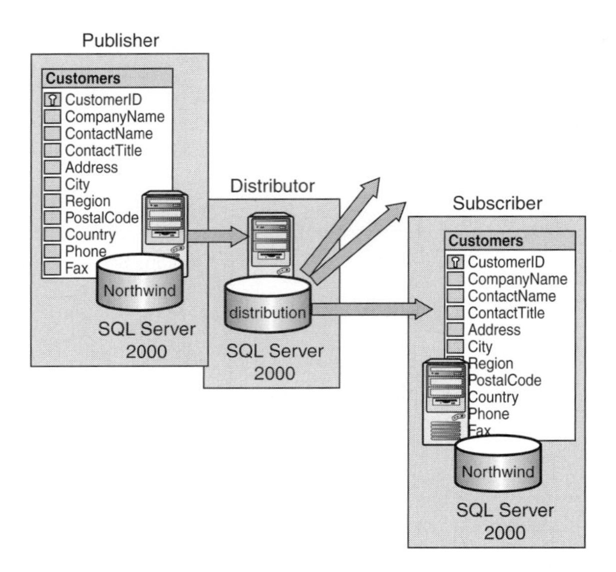

FIGURE 22.3 The publisher, distributor and subscriber.

The **distribution server** (distributor) can either be on the same server as the publication server or on a different server—in this case, a remote distribution server. This server will contain the distribution database. This database, also called the store-and-forward database, holds all the data changes that are to be forwarded from the published database to any subscription servers that subscribe to the data. A single distribution server can support several publication servers. The distribution server is truly the workhorse of data replication.

The **subscription server** contains a copy of the database or portions of the database that are being published, like the Customers table in the Northwind database. The distribution server sends any changes made to the published database via the subscription server's copy of the Customers table. This is known as store-and-forward. In previous versions of SQL Server, many data replication approaches would only send the data to the subscription server and then the data was treated as read-only. In SQL Server 7.0 and 2000, subscribers can make updates, which are returned to the publisher, known as the updating subscriber. It is important to note that an updating subscriber is not the same as a publisher. This chapter will cover more on updating subscribers in the "Publishing Subscriber" section.

Along with these distinct server roles, Microsoft utilizes a few more metaphors. These are publications and articles. A **publication** is a group of one or more articles, and is the basic unit of data replication. An article is simply a pointer to a single table, or a subset of rows or columns out of a table, that will be made available for replication.

Publications and Articles

A single database can contain more than one publication. You can publish data from tables, database objects, the execution of stored procedures, and even schema objects, such as referential integrity constraints, clustered indexes, non-clustered indexes, user triggers, extended properties, and collation. Regardless of what you plan to replicate, all articles in a publication are synchronized at the same time. Figure 22.4 depicts a typical publication with two articles. You can choose to replicate whole tables, or just parts of tables via filtering.

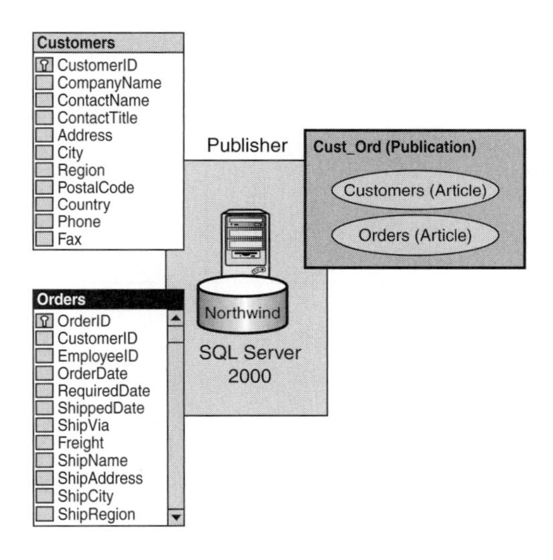

FIGURE 22.4 Cust_Ord publication (Northwind DB).

Filtering Articles

You can create articles on SQL Server in several different ways. The basic way to create an article is to publish all of the columns and rows that are contained in a table. Although this is the easiest way to create articles, your business needs might require that you publish only certain columns or rows out of a table. This is referred to as filtering vertically or horizontally. Vertical filtering filters only specific columns, whereas horizontal filtering filters only specific rows. In addition, SQL Server 2000 provides the added functionality of join filters and dynamic filters.

As an example, you might only need to replicate a customer's customer ID, company name, and phone number to various subscribing servers around your company. For this application, the Address data is restricted information and should not be replicated. You can create an article for data replication which contains a subset of the Customers table that will be replicated to these other locations (see Figure 22.5).

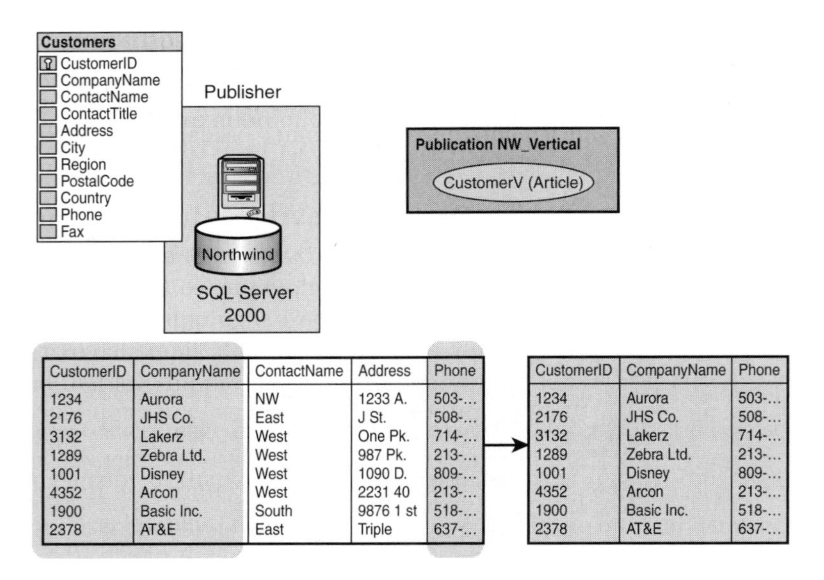

FIGURE 22.5 Vertical filtering is the process of creating a subset of columns from a table to be replicated to subscribers.

In another example, you might need to publish only the Customers table data that is in a specific region, requiring you to geographically partition the data. This process, as shown in Figure 22.6, is known as horizontal filtering.

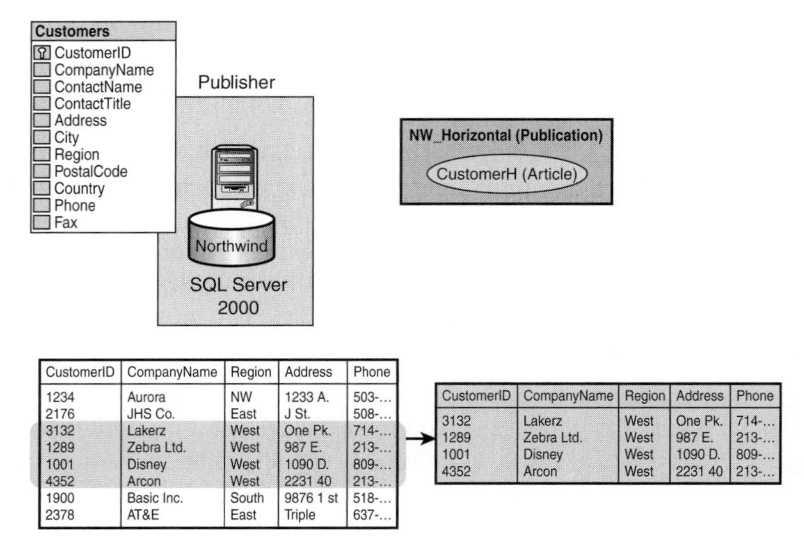

FIGURE 22.6 Horizontal filtering is the process of creating a subset of rows from a table to be replicated to subscribers.

It is possible for you to combine both horizontal and vertical filtering, as shown in Figure 22.7. This allows you to pare out unneeded columns and rows that aren't required for replication. In our example, we might only need the "west" Region data and only require CustomerID and CompanyName data to be published.

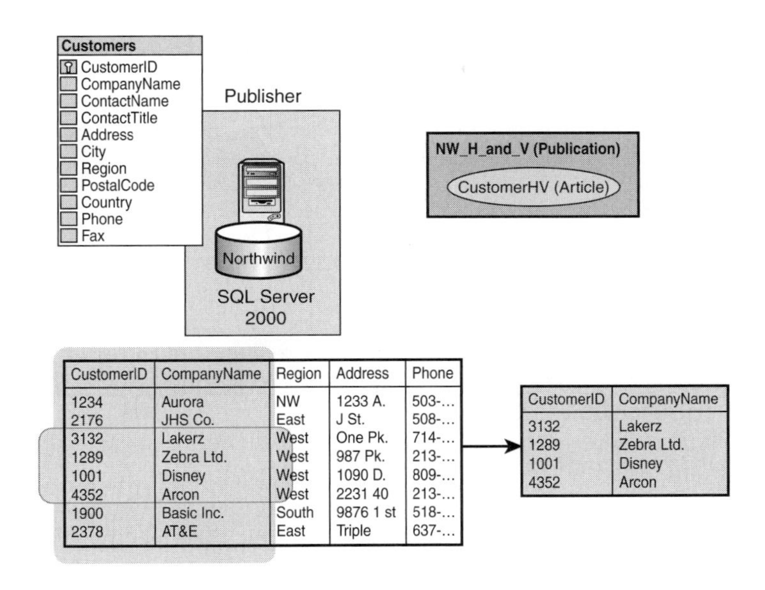

FIGURE 22.7 Combining horizontal and vertical filtering allows you to pare down the information in an article to only the important information.

As mentioned earlier, it is now possible for you to have join filters. Join filters enable you to go one step further for a particular filter created on a table to another. In other words, if you are publishing the Customers table data based on the Region (west), you can extend filtering to the related Orders and Order Details tables for these west region customers, as shown in Figure 22.8. This way, you will only be replicating orders for customers in the west to a location that only needs to see west data in all related tables. This can be efficient if it is done well.

You also can publish "stored procedure executions" as articles, along with their parameters. This can be either a standard procedure execution article or a serializable procedure execution article. The difference is that the latter is executed as a serializable transaction, and the other is not. What this stored procedure execution approach buys you is the major reduction of mass SQL statements being replicated across your network.

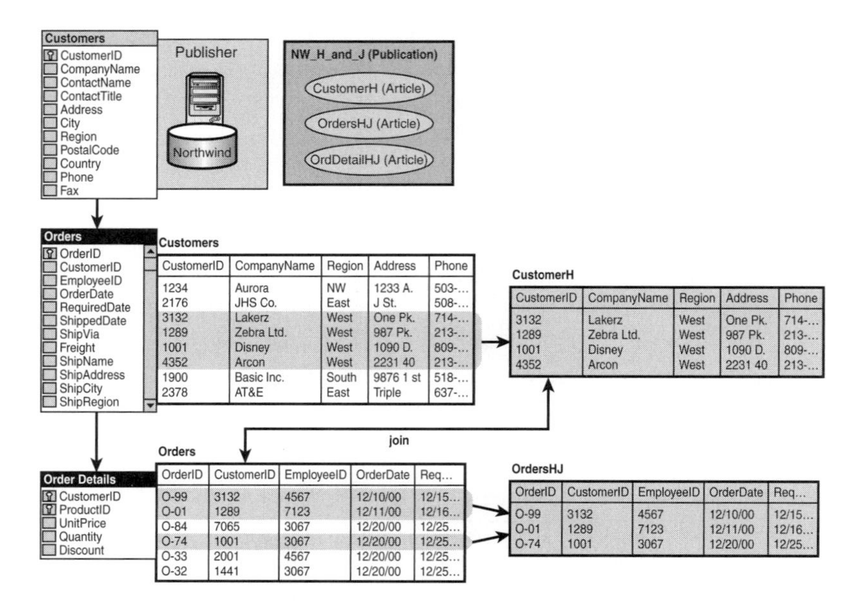

FIGURE 22.8 Horizontal and join publication.

For instance, if you wanted to update the Customers table for every customer, the resulting Customers table updates also would be replicated as a large multistep transaction involving 5,000 steps at minimum. This would significantly bog down your network. However, with stored procedure execution articles, only the execution of the stored procedure is replicated to the subscription server, and the stored procedure is executed on that subscription server. Figure 22.9 illustrates the difference in execution described earlier. Some subtleties when utilizing this type of data replication processing can't be overlooked, such as making sure that the published stored procedure behaves the same on the subscribing server side.

Many more data replication terms will be presented in this chapter, but it is essential first to learn about the different types of replication scenarios that can be built, and the reasons why any one of these would be desired over the other. It also is worth noting that Microsoft SQL Server 2000 supports replication to and from many different "heterogeneous" data sources. In other words, OLE DB or ODBC data sources can subscribe to SQL Server publications, as well as receive data replicated from a number of data sources, including Microsoft Exchange, Microsoft Access, Oracle, and DB2.

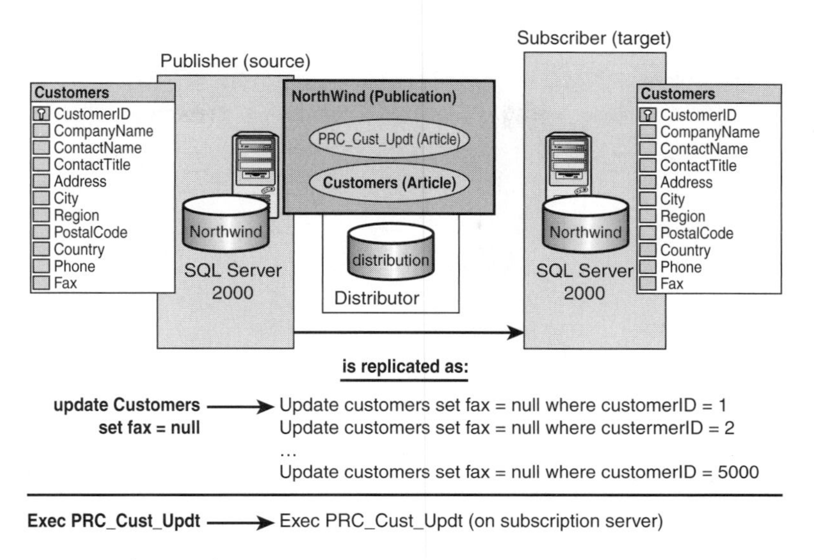

FIGURE 22.9 Stored procedure execution comparison.

Replication Scenarios

In general, depending on your business requirements, one of several different data replication scenario models can be implemented. These include the following:

- Central publisher
- Central publisher with a remote distributor
- Publishing subscriber
- Central subscriber
- Multiple publishers or multiple subscribers
- Updating subscribers

Central Publisher

The central publisher replication model, as shown in Figure 22.10, is Microsoft's default scenario. In this scenario, one SQL Server performs the function of both publisher and distributor. The publisher/distributor can have any number of subscribers. These subscribers can come in many different varieties, such as SQL Server 2000, SQL Server 7.0, and Oracle.

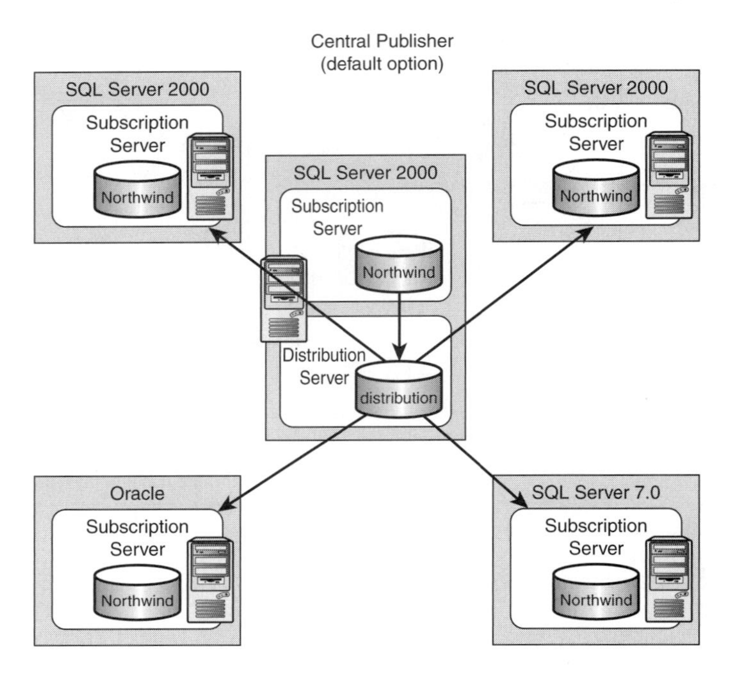

FIGURE 22.10 The central publisher scenario is a simple and often used scenario.

The central publisher scenario can be used in the following situations:

- Creation of a copy of a database for ad hoc queries and report generation (classic use)
- Publication of master lists to remote locations, such as master customer lists or master price lists
- Maintenance of a remote copy of an online transaction processing database (OLTP) that could be used by the remote sites during communication outages
- Maintenance of a "spare" copy of an online transaction processing database (OLTP) that could be used as a "hot spare" in case of server failure

However, it's important to consider the following for this scenario:

- If your OLTP server's activity is substantial and affects greater than 10 percent of your total data per day, then this scenario is not for you. Other scenarios will better fit your need.
- If your OLTP server is maximized on CPU, memory, and disk utilization, you also should consider another data replication scenario. This one is not for you either.

Central Publisher with Remote Distributor

The central publisher with remote distributor scenario, as shown in Figure 22.11, is similar to the central publisher scenario and would be used in the same general situations. The major difference in the two is that a second server is used to perform the role of distributor. This is highly desirable when you need to free the publishing server from having to perform the distribution task from a CPU, disk, and memory point of view. This also offers the best scenario from which to expand the number of publishers and subscribers. Also remember that a single distribution server can distribute changes for several publishers. The publisher and distributor must be connected to each other via a reliable, high-speed data link. This remote distributor scenario is proving to be one of the best data replication approaches due to minimal impact on the publication server and maximum distribution capability to any number of subscribers.

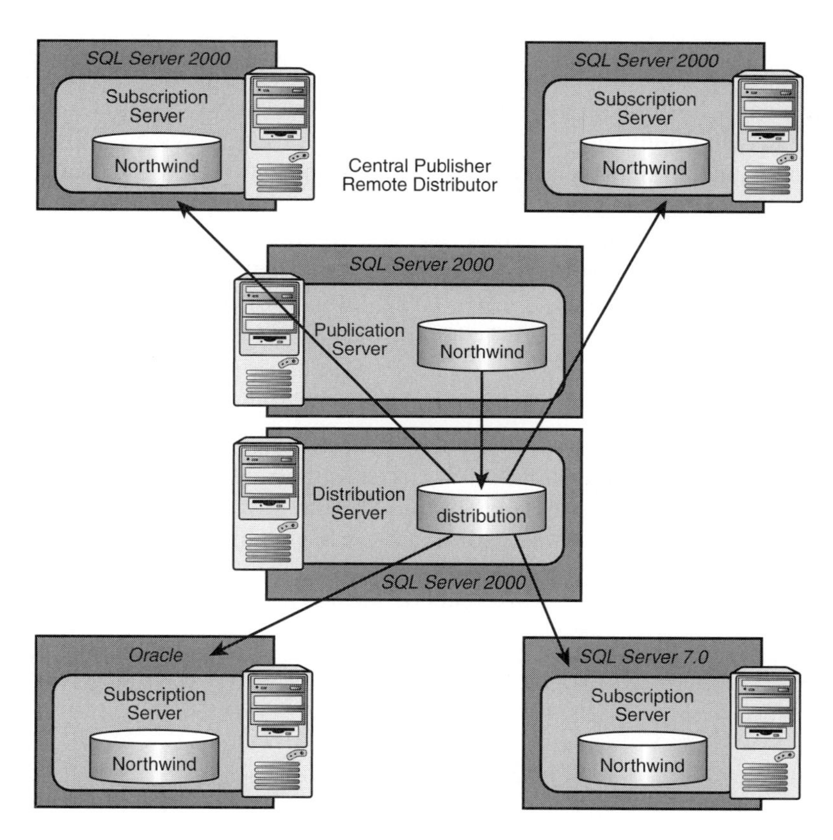

FIGURE 22.11 The central publisher with remote distributor is used when the role of distributor must be removed from the publishing server.

As mentioned previously, the central publisher remote distributor approach can be used for all of the same purposes as the central publisher scenario, but it also provides the added benefit of having minimal resource impact on your publication servers. If your OLTP server's activity affects greater than 10 percent of your total data per day, this scenario can usually handle it without much issue. If your OLTP server has overburdened its CPU, memory, and disk utilization, you easily have solved this issue as well.

Publishing Subscriber

In the publishing subscriber scenario, as shown in Figure 22.12, the publication server also will have to act as a distribution server to one subscriber. This subscriber, in turn, will immediately publish this data to any number of other subscribers. The configuration depicted here is not using a remote distribution configuration option, but is serving the same distribution model purpose. This scenario is best used when a slow or expensive network link exists between the original publishing server and all of the other potential subscribers. This will allow the initial (critical) publication of the data to be distributed from the original publishing server to that single subscriber across that slow, unpredictable, or expensive network line. Then, each of the many other subscribers can subscribe to the data using faster, more predictable, "local" network lines that they will have with the publishing subscriber server. A classic example of this would be that of a company whose main office is in San Francisco and has several branch offices in Europe. Instead of replicating changes to all the branch offices in Europe, the updates are replicated to a single publishing subscriber server in Paris. This publishing subscriber server in Paris then replicates the updates to all other subscriber servers around Europe. Voila!

Central Subscriber

In the central subscriber scenario, as shown in Figure 22.13, several publishers replicate data to a single, central subscriber. Basically, this is supporting the concept of consolidating data at a central site. An example of this might be that of consolidating all new orders from regional sales offices to company headquarters. Remember, you now will have several publishers of the Orders table; you need to take some form of precaution, such as filtering by region. This would guarantee that no one publisher could be updating another region's orders.

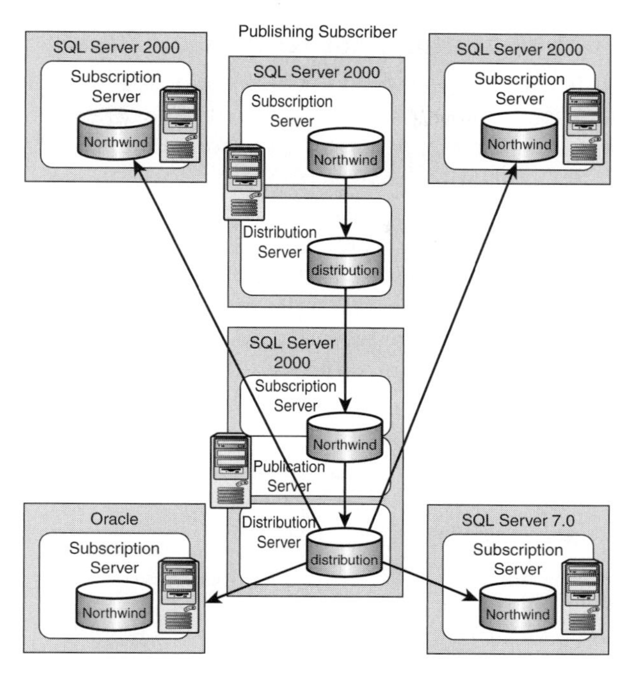

FIGURE 22.12 The publishing subscriber scenario works well when having to deal with slow, unpredictable, or expensive network links in diverse geographic situations.

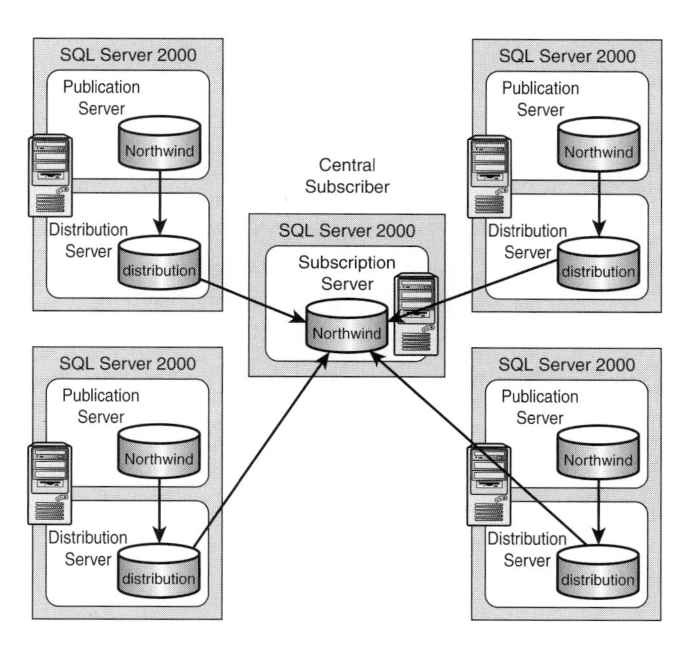

FIGURE 22.13 When using the central subscriber scenario, several publishers send data to a single, central subscriber.

Multiple Publishers or Multiple Subscribers

In the multiple publishers or multiple subscribers scenario, as shown in Figure 22.14, a common table (like the Customers table) is maintained on every server participating in the scenario. Each server publishes a particular set of rows that pertain to it—usually via filtering on something that identifies that site to the data rows it owns—and subscribes to the rows that all the other servers are publishing. The result is that each server has all the data at all times, and can make changes to their data only. You must be careful when implementing this scenario to ensure that all sites remain synchronized. The most frequently used applications of this system are regional order processing systems and reservation tracking systems. When setting up this system, make sure that only local users update local data. This check can be implemented through the use of stored procedures, restrictive views, or a check constraint.

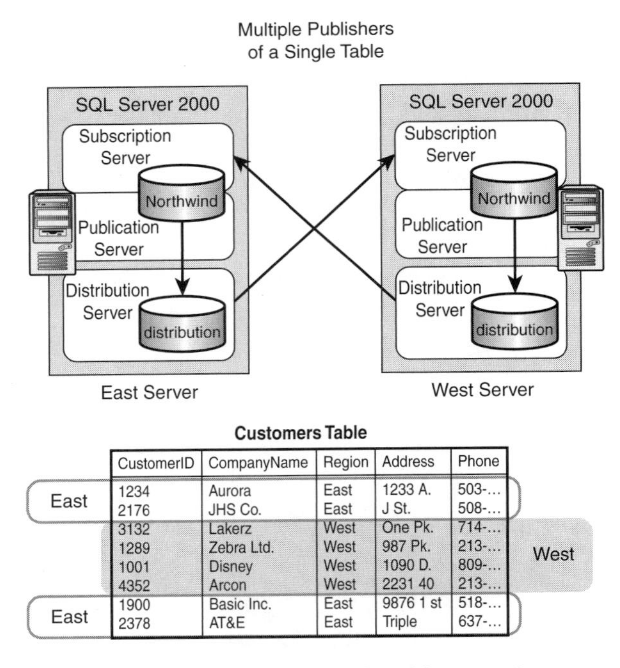

CustomerID	CompanyName	Region	Address	Phone
1234	Aurora	East	1233 A.	503-...
2176	JHS Co.	East	J St.	508-...
3132	Lakerz	West	One Pk.	714-...
1289	Zebra Ltd.	West	987 Pk.	213-...
1001	Disney	West	1090 D.	809-...
4352	Arcon	West	2231 40	213-...
1900	Basic Inc.	East	9876 1 st	518-...
2378	AT&E	East	Triple	637-...

FIGURE 22.14 In the multiple publishers of a single table scenario, every server in the scenario maintains a common table.

Updating Subscribers

SQL Server 2000 has built-in functionality that allows the subscriber to update data in a table to which it subscribes, and have those updates automatically made back to the publisher through either immediate or queued updates. This model, called "updating subscribers," utilizes a two-phase commit process to update the publishing server as the changes are made on the subscribing server. These updates then are replicated to any other subscribers, but not to the subscriber that made the update.

Immediate updating allows subscribers to update data only if the publisher will accept them immediately. If the changes are accepted at the publisher, they will be propagated to the other subscribers. The subscribers must be continuously and reliably connected to the publisher to make changes at the subscriber.

Queued updating allows subscribers to update data and then store those updates in a queue while disconnected from the publisher. When the subscriber reconnects to the publisher, the updates are propagated to the publisher. This functionality utilizes SQL Server 2000 queue and the Queue Reader Agent or Microsoft Message Queuing.

A combination of immediate updating with queued updating allows the subscriber to use immediate updating, but switch to queued updating if a connection cannot be maintained between the publisher and subscribers. After switching to queued updating, reconnecting to the publisher, and emptying the queue, the subscriber can switch back to immediate updating mode. An updating subscriber is shown in Figure 22.15.

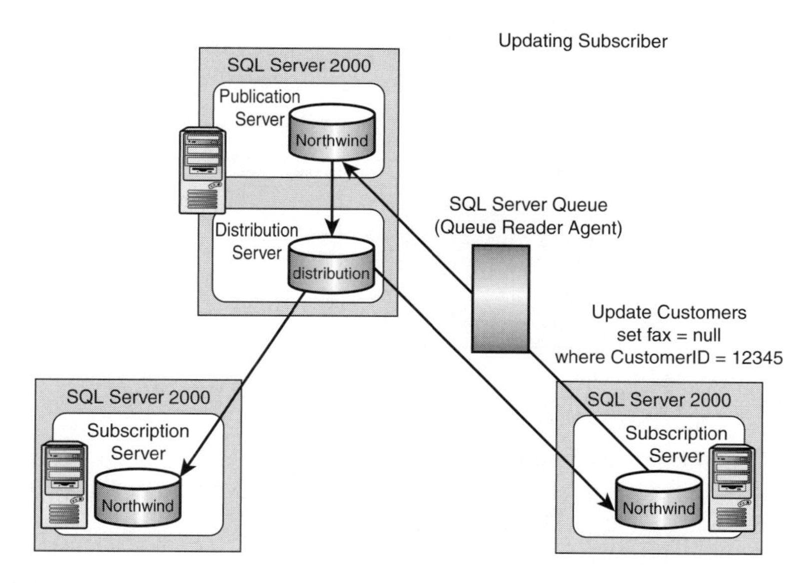

FIGURE 22.15 Updating subscriber.

Subscriptions

A subscription is essentially a formal request and registration of that request for data that is being published. By definition, you will subscribe to all articles of a publication.

When this formal request (the subscription) is being set up, you will have the option of either having the data pushed to the subscriber server, or the option of pulling the data to the subscription server when it is needed. This is referred to as either a *push subscription* or a *pull subscription*.

As depicted in Figure 22.16, a pull subscription is set up and managed by the subscription server. The biggest advantage here is that pull subscriptions allow the system administrators of the subscription servers to choose what publications they will receive and when they receive it. With pull subscriptions, publishing and subscribing are separate acts and are not necessarily performed by the same user. In general, pull subscriptions are best when the publication does not require high security, or if subscribing is done intermittently when the subscriber's data needs to be periodically brought up to date.

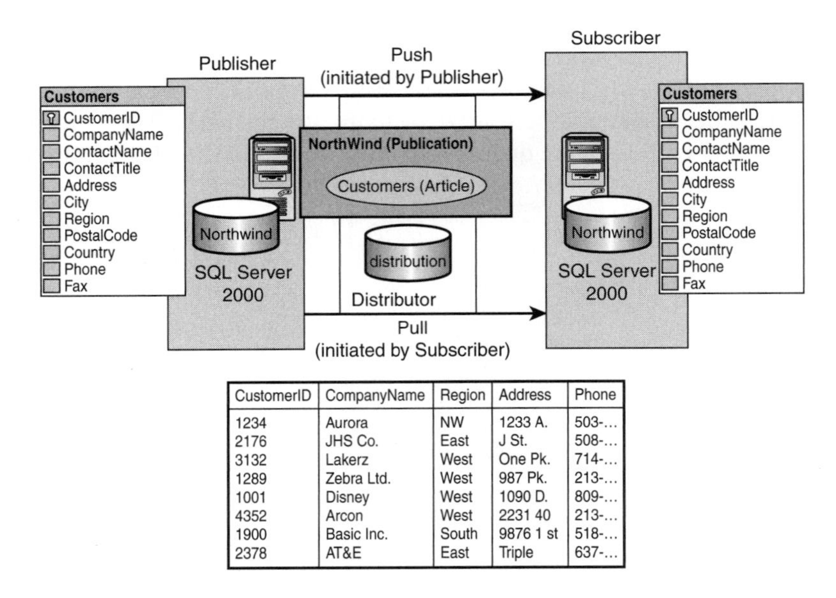

CustomerID	CompanyName	Region	Address	Phone
1234	Aurora	NW	1233 A.	503-...
2176	JHS Co.	East	J St.	508-...
3132	Lakerz	West	One Pk.	714-...
1289	Zebra Ltd.	West	987 Pk.	213-...
1001	Disney	West	1090 D.	809-...
4352	Arcon	West	2231 40	213-...
1900	Basic Inc.	South	9876 1 st	518-...
2378	AT&E	East	Triple	637-...

FIGURE 22.16 Push and pull.

A push subscription is created and managed by the publication server. In effect, the publication server is pushing the publication to the subscription server. The advantage of using push subscriptions is that all of the administration takes place in a central location. In addition, publishing and subscribing happen at the same time, and many subscribers can be set up at once. This also is recommended when dealing with heterogeneous subscribers because of the lack of pull capability on the subscription server side.

Anonymous Subscriptions (Pull Subscriptions)

It is also possible to have what is called "anonymous" subscriptions. An anonymous subscription is a special type of pull subscription that can be used in the following circumstances:

- You are publishing data to the Internet
- You have a huge number of subscribers

- You don't want the overhead of maintaining extra information at the publisher or distributor
- All the rules of your pull subscriptions apply to all of your anonymous subscribers

Normally, information about all of the subscribers, including performance data, is stored on the distribution server. Therefore, if you have a large number of subscribers, or you do not want to track detailed information about the subscribers, you might want to allow anonymous subscriptions to a publication. Then little is kept at the distribution server, but it then becomes the responsibility of the subscriber to initiate the subscription and to keep synchronized.

The Distribution Database

The distribution database is a special type of database installed on the distribution server. This database is known as a store-and-forward database and holds all transactions waiting to be distributed to any subscribers. This database receives transactions from any published databases that have designated it as their distributor. The transactions will be held here until they are sent to the subscribers successfully. After a period of time, these transactions will be purged from the distribution database. In some special situations, the transactions might not be purged for a longer period, enabling anonymous subscribers ample time in which to synchronize. The distribution database is the "heart" of the data replication facility. As you can see in Figure 22.17, the distribution database has several "MS" tables, such as MSarticles. These tables contain all necessary information for the distribution server to fulfill the distribution role. These tables include the following:

- All the different publishers who will use it, such as MSpublisher_databases and MSpublication_access
- The publications and articles that it will distribute, such as MSpublications, MSarticles
- The complete information for all the agents to perform their tasks, such as MSdistribution_agents
- The complete information of the executions of these agents, such as MSdistribution_history
- The subscribers, such as MSsubscriber_info, MSsubscriptions, and so on
- Any errors that occur during replication and synchronization states, such as MSrepl_errors, MSsync_state, and so on
- The commands and transactions that are to be replicated, such as MSrepl_commands and MSrepl_transactions

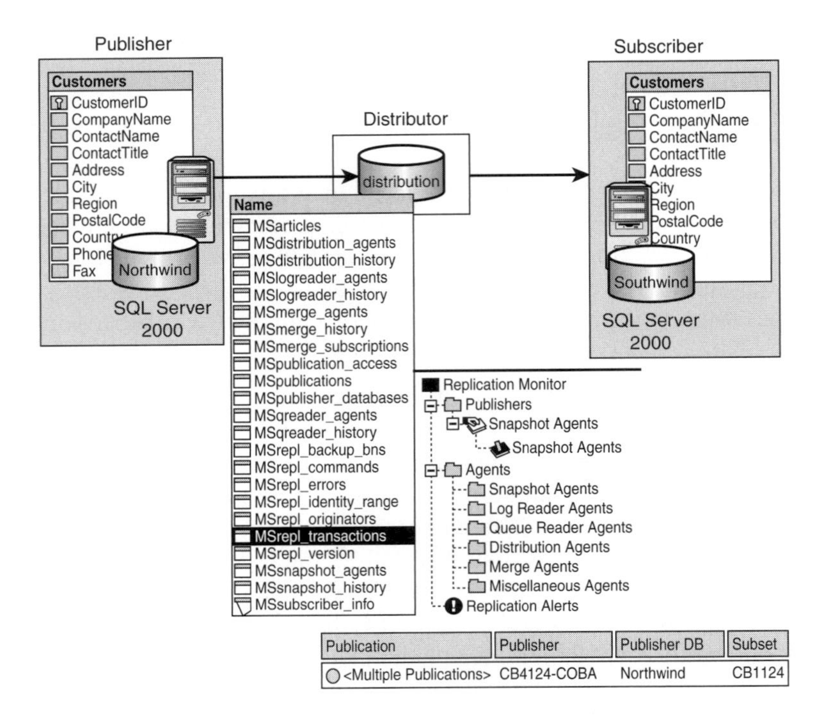

FIGURE 22.17 Tables of the distribution database.

Replication Agents

SQL Server utilizes replication agents to do different tasks during the replication process. These agents are constantly waking up at some frequency and fulfilling specific jobs. As you can see in Figure 22.18, several replication agent categories are listed under the Replication Monitor branch. Let's look at the main ones.

The Snapshot Agent

The snapshot agent is responsible for preparing the schema and initial data files of published tables and stored procedures, storing the snapshot on the distribution server and recording information about the synchronization status in the distribution database. Each publication will have its own snapshot agent that runs on the distribution server. It will take on the name of the publication within the publishing database, within the machine on which it executes ([Machine][Publishing database][Publication Name]).

Figure 22.18 shows what this snapshot agent looks like under the SQL Server Agent (Management > SQL Server Agent > Jobs) branch in Enterprise Manager. In addition, it also can be referenced from the Replication Monitor option (within the Replication Monitor > Agents > Snapshot Agents branch). You probably most often will use the Replication Monitor path to these agents!

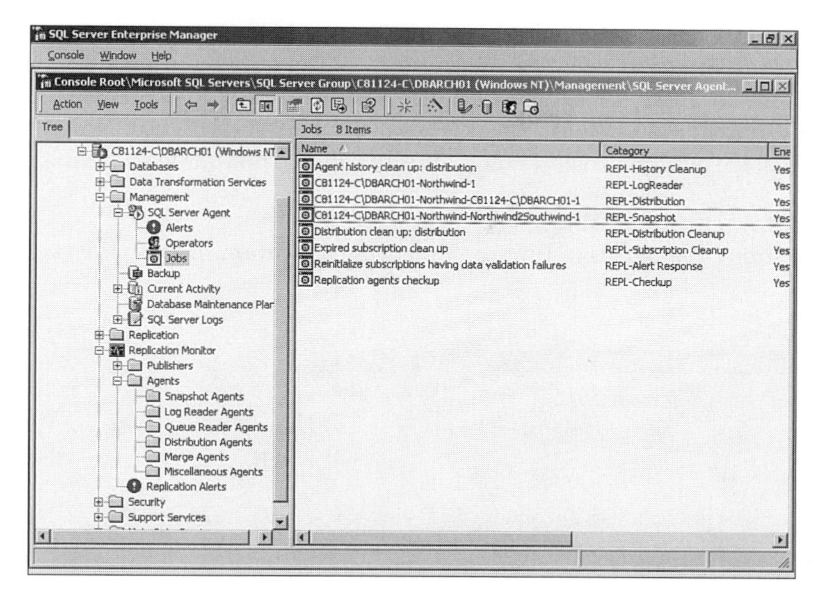

FIGURE 22.18 Various agent jobs.

It's worth noting that the snapshot agent might not even be used if the initialization of the subscriber's schema and data is done manually.

The Snapshot Agent

The snapshot agent is the process that ensures that both databases start on an even playing field. This process is known as **synchronization**. The synchronization process is performed whenever a publication has a new subscriber. Synchronization happens only one time for each new subscriber and ensures that database schema and data are exact replicas on both servers. After the initial synchronization, all updates are made via replication.

When a new server subscribes to a publication, synchronization is performed. When synchronization begins, a copy of the table schema is copied to a file with an .SCH extension. This file contains all the information necessary to create the table and any indexes on the tables, if they are requested. Next, a copy is made of the data in the table to be synchronized and written to a file with a .BCP extension. The data file is a BCP, or bulk copy file. Both files are stored in the temporary working directory on the distribution server.

After the synchronization process has started and the data files have been created, any inserts, updates, and deletes are stored in the distribution database. These changes will not be replicated to the subscription database until the synchronization process is complete.

When the synchronization process starts, only new subscribers are affected. Any subscriber that has been synchronized already and has been receiving modifications is unaffected. The synchronization set is applied to all servers that are waiting for initial synchronization. After the schema and data have been re-created, all transactions that have been stored in the distribution server are sent to the subscriber.

When you set up a subscription, it is possible to manually load the initial snapshot onto the server. This is known as manual synchronization. For extremely large databases, it is frequently easier to dump the database to tape and then reload the database on the subscription server. If you load the snapshot this way, SQL Server will assume that the databases already are synchronized and automatically will begin sending data modifications.

The Snapshot Agent Processing

Figure 22.19 shows the details of the snapshot agent execution for a typical push subscription.

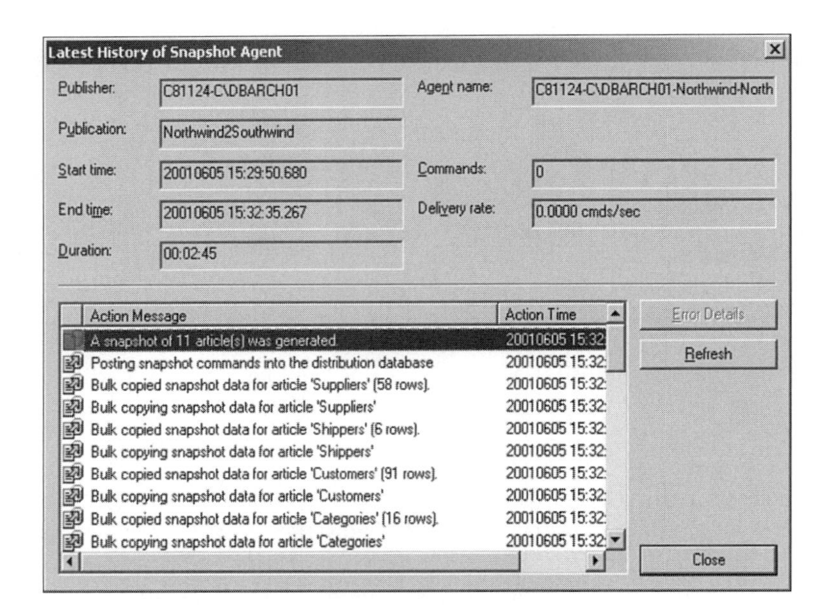

FIGURE 22.19 Snapshot agent execution.

Following is the sequence of tasks that are carried out by the snapshot agent:

1. The snapshot agent is initialized. This initialization can be immediate or at a designated time in your company's nightly processing window.
2. The agent will then connect to the publisher.
3. The agent then generates schema files with an .SCH file extension for each article in the publication. These schema files are written to a temporary working directory on the Distribution Server. These are the Create Table statements, and such, that will be used to create all objects needed on the subscription server side. They will only exist for the duration of the snapshot processing!
4. All the tables in the publication are then locked (held). The lock is required to ensure that no data modifications are made during the snapshot process.

5. The agent extracts a copy of the data in the publication and writes it into the temporary working directory on the distribution server. If all the subscribers are SQL Servers, then the data will be written using a SQL Server native format with a .BCP file extension. If you are replicating to databases other than SQL Server, the data will be stored in standard text files with the .TXT file extension. The .SCH file and the .TXT files/.BMP files are known as a synchronization set. Every table or article will have a synchronization set.

CAUTION

Please make sure that you have enough disk space on the drive that contains the temporary working directory. The snapshot data files will potentially be huge, which might be the most common reason for snapshot failure.

6. The agent will then execute the object creations and Bulk Copy Processing at the subscription server side in the order that they were generated (or skip the object creation part if the objects have already been created on the subscription server side and you have indicated this during setup). This will take a while. For this reason, it is best to do this in an off time so as not to impact the normal processing day. Network connectivity is critical here. Snapshots often fail at this point.
7. The snapshot agent will then post the fact that a snapshot has occurred and what articles/publications were part of the snapshot to the distribution database. This will be the only thing that is sent to the distribution database.
8. When all the synchronization sets have finished being executed, the agent releases the locks on all of the tables of this publication. The snapshot is now considered finished.

The Log Reader Agent

The log reader agent is responsible for moving transactions marked for replication from the transaction log of the published database to the distribution database. Each database published using transactional replication has its own log reader agent that runs on the distribution server. It will be easy to find because it takes on the name of the publishing database whose transaction log it is reading [Machine name][Publishing DB name] and REPL-LogReader category. Figure 22.18 also shows a Log Reader agent for the Northwind database.

After initial synchronization has taken place, the log reader agent begins to move transactions from the publication server to the distribution server. All actions that modify data in a database are logged to the transaction log in that database. Not only is this log used in the automatic recovery process, but it also is used in the replication process. When an article is created for publication and the subscription is activated, all entries about that article are marked in the transaction log. For each publication in a database, a log reader agent reads the transaction log and looks for any marked transactions. When the log reader agent finds a change in the log, it reads the changes and converts them to SQL statements that correspond to the action that was taken in the article. The SQL statements then are stored in a table on the distribution server waiting to be distributed to subscribers.

Because replication is based on the transaction log, several changes are made in the way the transaction log works. During normal processing, any transaction that has either been successfully completed or rolled back, is marked inactive. When you are performing replication, completed transactions are not marked inactive until the log reader process has read them and sent them to the distribution server.

It should be noted that truncating and fast bulk-copying into a table are non-logged processes. In tables marked for publication, you will not be able to perform non-logged operations unless you, temporarily, turn off replication on that table.

> One of the major changes in the transaction log comes when you have the Truncate Log on Checkpoint database option turned on. When the Truncate Log on Checkpoint option is on, SQL Server truncates the transaction log every time a checkpoint is performed, which can be as often as every several seconds. The inactive portion of the log will not be truncated until the log reader process has read the transaction.

The Distribution Agent

A distribution agent moves transactions and snapshot jobs held in the distribution database out to the subscribers. This agent won't be created until a push subscription is defined. This distribution agent will take on the name of what the publication database is along with the subscriber information [machine name][publication DB name][subscriber machine name]. Figure 22.18 also shows a distribution agent for the Northwind database.

Those not set up for immediate synchronization share a distribution agent that runs on the distribution server. Pull subscriptions, to either snapshot or transactional publications, have a distribution agent that runs on the subscriber. Merge publications do not have a distribution agent at all. Rather, they rely on the merge agent, discussed next.

In transactional replication, the transactions have been moved into the distribution database, and the distribution agent either pushes out the changes to the subscribers or pulls them from the distributor, depending on how the servers were set up. All actions that change data on the publishing server are applied to the subscribing servers in the same order they were incurred. Figure 22.20 shows the latest history of the distribution agent and the successful delivery of a transaction.

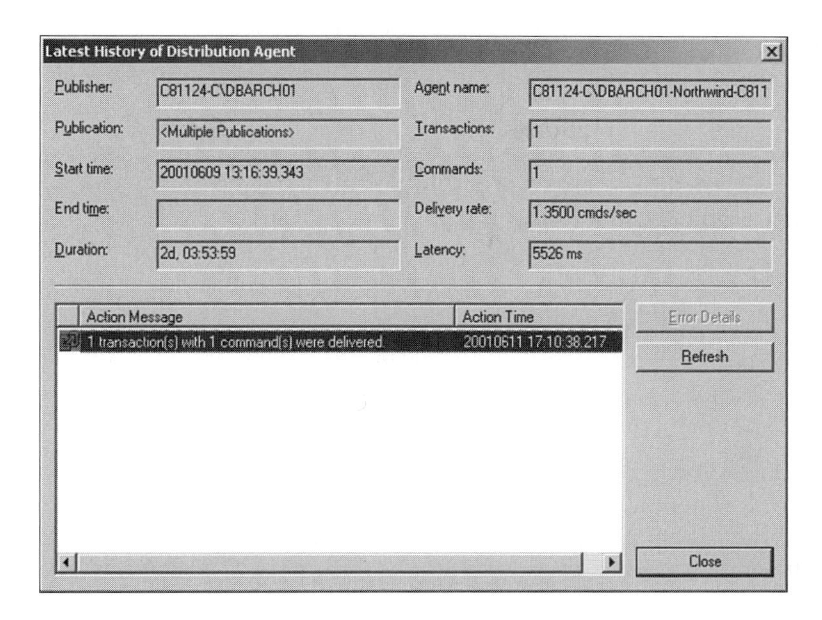

FIGURE 22.20 Distribution agent activity.

The Merge Agent

When dealing with merge publications, the merge agent moves and reconciles incremental data changes that occurred after the initial snapshot was created. Each merge publication has a merge agent that connects to the publishing server, and the subscribing server and updates both as changes are made. In a full merge scenario, the agent first uploads all changes from the subscriber where the generation is 0, or the generation is greater than the last generation sent to the publisher. The agent gathers the rows in which changes were made, and those rows without conflicts are applied to the publishing database.

A "conflict" can arise when changes are made at both the publishing server and the subscription server to a particular row(s) of data. A conflict resolver handles these conflicts. Conflict resolvers are associated with an article in the publication definition. These conflict resolvers are sets of rules or custom scripts that can handle any complex conflict situation that might occur. The agent then reverses the process by downloading any changes from the publisher to the subscriber. Push subscriptions have merge agents that run on the publication server, whereas pull subscriptions have merge agents that run on the subscription server. Snapshot and transactional publications do not use merge agents.

The Miscellaneous Agents

In Figure 22.21, you can see that several miscellaneous agents have been set up to do house cleaning around the replication configuration. These agents include the following:

- Agent History Clean Up: distribution—Clears out agent history from the distribution database every 10 minutes (by default). Depending on the size of the distribution, you might want to vary the frequency of this agent.
- Distribution Clean Up: distribution—Clears out replicated transactions from the distribution database every 72 hours by default. This agent is used for snapshot and transactional publications only. If the volume of transactions is high, the frequency of this agent will want to be adjusted downward so you don't have too large of a distribution database. However, the frequency of synchronization with subscribers drives this frequency adjustment.
- Expired Subscription Clean Up—Detects and removes expired subscriptions from the published databases. As part of the subscription setup, an expiration date will be set. This agent usually runs once per day by default. You won't need to change this.
- Reinitialize Subscriptions Having Data Validation Failures—This agent is manually invoked. It is not on a schedule, but it could be. It automatically will detect the subscriptions that failed data validation and mark them for reinitialization. This can then potentially lead to a new snapshot being applied to a subscriber that had data validation failures.
- Replication Agents Checkup—Detects replication agents that are not actively logging history. This is critical because debugging replication errors is often dependent on an agent's history that has been logged.

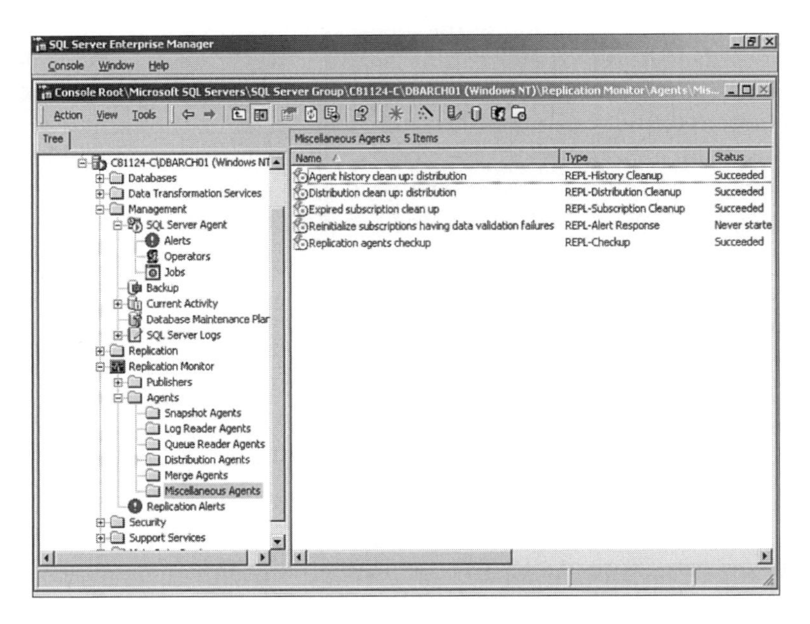

FIGURE 22.21 Miscellaneous agents.

Planning for SQL Server Data Replication

You must consider many factors when choosing a method to distribute data. Your business requirements will determine which is the right method for you. In general, you will need to understand the timing and latency of your data, its independence at each site, and your specific need to filter or partition the data.

Autonomy, Timing, and Latency of Data

Distributed data implementations can be accomplished using a few different facilities in Microsoft. These are Data Transformation Services (DTS), Distributed Transaction Coordinator (DTC), and Data Replication. The trick is to match the right facility to the type of data distribution that you need to get done.

In some applications, such as online transaction processing and inventory control systems, data must be synchronized at all times. This requirement, called **immediate transactional consistency**, was known as tight consistency in previous versions of SQL Server.

SQL Server implements immediate transactional consistency data distribution in the form of two-phase commit processing. A **two-phase commit**, sometimes known as **2PC**, ensures that transactions are committed on all servers, or the transaction is rolled back on all servers. This ensures that all data on all servers is 100 percent in sync at all times. One of the main drawbacks of immediate transactional consistency is that it requires a high-speed LAN to work. This type of solution might not be feasible for large environments with many servers because occasional network outages can occur. These types of implementations can be built with DTC and DTS.

In other applications, such as decision support and report generation systems, 100 percent data synchronization all of the time is not as important. This requirement, called **latent transactional consistency**, was known as loose consistency in previous versions of SQL Server.

Latent transactional consistency is implemented in SQL Server via data replication. Replication allows data to be updated on all servers, but the process is not a simultaneous one. The result is "real-enough time" data. This is known as real-enough time data, or latent transactional consistency, because a lag exists between the data updated on the main server and the replicated data. In this scenario, if you could stop all data modifications from occurring on all servers, then all of the servers would eventually have the same data. Unlike the two-phase consistency model, replication works over both LANs and WANs, as well as slow or fast links.

When planning a distributed application, you must consider the effect of one site's operation on another. This is known as **site autonomy**. A site with complete autonomy can continue to function without being connected to any other site. A site with no autonomy cannot function without being connected to all other sites. For example, applications that utilize two-phase commits, or 2PC, rely on all other sites being able to immediately accept changes that are sent to it. In the event that any one site is unavailable, no transactions on any server can be committed. In contrast, sites using merge replication can be completely disconnected from all other sites and continue to work effectively, not guaranteeing data consistency. Luckily, some solutions combine both high data consistency and site autonomy.

Methods of Data Distribution

After you have determined the amount of transactional latency and site autonomy based on your business requirements, it is important to select the data distribution method that corresponds. Each different type of data distribution has a different amount of site autonomy and latency. With these distributed data systems, you can choose from several methods:

- Distributed transactions—Distributed transactions ensure that all sites have the same data at all times. This method requires a certain amount of overhead cost to maintain this consistency. We will not be discussing this non-data replication method here.
- Transactional replication with updating subscribers—Users can change data at the local location, and those changes are applied to the source database at the same time. The changes are then eventually replicated to other sites. This type of data distribution combines replication and distributed transactions because data is changed at both the local site and source database.
- Transactional replication—With transactional replication, data is changed only at the source location and is sent out to the subscribers. Because data is only changed at a single location, conflicts cannot occur.
- Snapshot replication with updating subscribers—This method is much like transactional replication with updating subscribers; users can change data at the local location, and those changes are applied to the source database at the same time. The entire changed publication is then replicated to all subscribers. This type of replication provides a higher autonomy than transactional replication.
- Snapshot replication—A complete copy of the publication is sent out to all subscribers. This includes both changed and unchanged data.
- Merge replication—All sites make changes to local data independently and then update the publisher. It is possible for conflicts to occur, but they will be resolved.

SQL Server Replication Types

Microsoft has narrowed the field to three major types of data replication approaches within SQL Server: snapshot, transactional, and merge. Each replication type applies only to a single publication. However, it is possible to have multiple types of replication per database.

Snapshot Replication

Snapshot replication makes an image of all the tables in a publication at a single moment in time, and then moves that entire image to the subscribers. Little overhead on the server is incurred because snapshot replication does not track data modifications like the other forms of replication do. It is possible, however, for snapshot replication to require large amounts of network bandwidth, especially if the articles being replicated are large. Snapshot replication is the easiest form of replication to set up and is used primarily with smaller tables for which subscribers do not have to perform updates. An example of this might be a phone list that is to be replicated to many subscribers. This phone list is not considered to be critical data, and the frequency of it being refreshed is more than enough to satisfy all its users.

AGENTS USED: Snapshot Agent and the Distribution Agent primarily.

The snapshot agent creates files that contain the schema of the publication and the data. The files are temporarily stored in the snapshot folder of the distribution server, and then the distribution jobs are recorded in the distribution database.

The distribution agent is responsible for moving the schema and data from the distributor to the subscribers.

A few other agents also are used that deal with other needed tasks for replication, such as cleanup of files and history. In snapshot replication, after the snapshot has been delivered to all the subscribers, these agents will delete the associated .BCP and .SCH files from the distributor's working directory.

Transactional Replication

Transactional replication is the process of capturing transactions from the transaction log of the published database and applying them to the subscription databases. With SQL Server transactional replication, you can publish all or part of a table, views, or one or more stored procedures as an article. All data updates are then stored in the distribution database and sent and applied to any number of subscribing servers. Obtaining these updates from the publishing database's transaction log is extremely efficient. No direct reading of tables is required except during initial snapshot, and only the minimal amount of traffic is generated over the network. This has made transactional replication the most often used method.

As data changes are made, they are propagated to the other sites at nearly real time—you determine the frequency of this propagation. Because changes are usually made only at the publishing server, data conflicts are avoided for the most part. As an example, Push subscribers usually receive updates from the publisher in a minute or less, depending on the speed and availability of the network. Subscribers also can be set up for pull subscriptions. This is useful for disconnected users who are not connected to the network at all times.

AGENTS USED: Snapshot Agent, Log Agent, and the Distribution Agent primarily.

The snapshot agent creates files that contain the schema of the publication and the data. The files are stored in the snapshot folder of the distribution server, and then the distribution jobs are recorded in the distribution database.

The log reader agent monitors the transaction log of the database that it is set up to service. Each database published has its own log reader agent set up for replication and it will copy the transactions from the transaction log of that published database into the distribution database.

The distribution agent is responsible for moving the schema and data from the distributor to the subscribers for the initial synchronization and then moving all of the subsequent transactions from the published database to each subscriber as they come in. These transactions are stored in the distribution database for a certain length of time and eventually purged.

As always, a few other agents are used that deal with the other housekeeping issues surrounding data replication, such as schema files cleanup, history cleanup, and transaction cleanup.

Merge Replication

Merge replication involves getting the publisher and all subscribers initialized and then allowing data to be changed at all sites involved in the merge replication at the publisher and at all subscribers. All these changes to the data are subsequently merged at certain intervals so that again, all copies of the database have identical data.

Occasionally, data conflicts will have to be resolved. The publisher will not always win in a conflict resolution. Instead, the winner is determined by whatever criteria you establish.

AGENTS USED: Snapshot Agent and the Merge Agent primarily.

The snapshot agent creates files that contain the schema of the publication and the data. The files are stored in the snapshot folder of the distribution server, and then, the distribution jobs are recorded in the distribution database. This is essentially the same behavior as all other types of replication methods.

The merge agent takes the initial snapshot and applies it to all of the subscribers. It then reconciles all changes made on all the servers based on the rules that you configure.

Preparing for Merge Replication

When you set up a table for merge replication, SQL Server performs three schema changes to your database. First, SQL Server must either identify or create a unique column for every row that is going to be replicated. This column is used to identify the different rows across all of the different copies of the table. If the table already contains a column with the `ROWGUIDCOL` property, SQL Server will automatically use that column for the row identifier. If not, SQL Server will add a column called rowguid to the table. SQL Server also will place an index on this rowguid column.

Next, SQL Server adds triggers to the table to track changes that occur to the data in the table and record them in the merge system tables. The triggers can track changes at either the row or the column level, depending on how you set it up. SQL Server will support multiple triggers of the same type on a table, so merge triggers will not interfere with user-defined triggers on the table.

Last, SQL Server adds new system tables to the database that contains the replicated tables. The MSMerge_contents and MSMerge_tombstone tables track the updates, inserts, and deletes. These tables rely on the rowguid to track which rows have actually been changed.

The merge agent is responsible for moving changed data from the site where it was changed to all other sites in the replication scenario. When a row is updated, the triggers that were added by SQL Server fire off and update the new system tables, setting the generation column equal to 0 for the corresponding rowguid. When the merge agent runs, it collects the data from the rows where the generation column is 0, and then resets the generation values to values higher than the previous generation numbers. This allows the merge agent to look for data that has already been shared with other sites without having to look through all the data. The merge agent then sends the changed data to the other sites.

When the data reaches the other sites, the data is merged with existing data according to rules that you have defined. These rules are flexible and highly extensible. The merge agent evaluates existing and new data and resolves conflicts based on priorities or which data was changed first. Another available option is that you can create custom resolution strategies using the Component Object Model (COM) and custom stored procedures. After conflicts have been handled, synchronization occurs to ensure that all sites have the same data.

The merge agent identifies conflicts using the MSMerge_contents table. In this table, a column called lineage is used to track the history of changes to a row. The agent updates the lineage value whenever a user makes changes to the data in a row. The entry into this column is a combination of a site identifier and the last version of the row created at the site. As the merge agent is merging all the changes that have occurred, it examines each site's information to see whether a conflict has occurred. If a conflict has occurred, the agent initiates conflict resolution based on the criteria mentioned earlier.

User Requirements Drive the Replication Design

As mentioned before, it is really the business requirements that will drive your replication configuration and method. You also will find that nailing down all the details to the business requirement is the hardest part of a data replication design process. After you have completed the requirements gathering, the replication design usually just falls out from it easily. The requirements gathering is highly recommended to get a prototype up and running as quickly as possible to measure the effectiveness of one approach over the other. You must understand several key aspects to make the right design decisions. These include the following:

1. What is the number of sites and site autonomy in the scope [location]?
2. Which ones have the "master" data [data ownership]?
3. What is the data latency requirement [by site]?
4. What type of data accesses are being made [by site]?
    - Reads
    - Writes

- Updates
- Deletes

This needs to include exactly what data and data subsets that drive filtering are needed for the data accesses [by site].

5. What is the volume of activity/transactions, including the number of users [by site]?
6. How many machines do you have to work with [by site]?
7. What is the available processing power (CPU & Memory), and disk space on each of these machines [by site]?
8. What is the stability, speed, and saturation level of the network connections between machines [by site]?
9. What is the dial-in, Internet, or other access mechanism requirement for the data?
10. What are the potential subscriber or publisher database engines involved?

Figure 22.22 depicts the factors that contribute to replication designs and the possible data replication configuration that would best be used. It is only a partial table because of the numerous factors and the many replication configuration options that are available. However, it will give you a good idea of the general design approach described here. Perhaps 95 percent of user requirements can be classified fairly easily. It is those last 5 percent that might take some imagination in determining the best overall solution. Depending on the requirements that need to be supported, you might even end up with a solution using something like log shipping. We will discuss this limited alternative in a later section.

Data Access	Latency	Autonomy	Sites (locations)	Frequency	Network	Machines	Owner	Other	REPLICATION
Read Only Reporting	short	high	many	high	fast/ stable	1 server/site	1 OLTP site	Each site only needs regional data	Central Publisher Transactional repl filter by region
Read Only Reporting	long	high	many	low	fast/ stable	1 server/site	1 OLTP site	Each site only needs regional data	Central Publisher Snapshot repl filter by region
Read mostly A few updates	short	high	<10	medium	fast/ stable	1 server/site	1 OLTP site	Regional updates on one table	Central Publisher Transactional repl Updating Subs
Read mostly A few updates	medium	high	<10	medium	slow/ unreliab	1 server/site	All update	Regional updates on all tables	Central Publisher Merge repl
...									
Inserts (new orders)	short	high	many	high	fast/ stable	1 server/site	1 report site	Each site only needs regional data	Central Subscriber Transactional repl

FIGURE 22.22 Replication design factors.

Data Characteristics

Additionally, you need to analyze the underlying data types and characteristics thoroughly. Issues such as collation or character set and data sorting come into play. You must be aware of what these are set to on all nodes of your replication configuration. MS SQL Server 2000 does not convert the replicated data and might even mistranslate the data as it is replicated because it is impossible to map all characters between character sets. It is best to look up the character set "mapping chart" for MS SQL Server replication to all other data target environments. Most are covered well, but problems arise with certain data types such as image, timestamp, and identity. Sometimes, using the Unicode data types at all sites is best for consistency. Following is a general list of things to watch out for in this regard:

- Collation consistency across all nodes of replication.
- Timestamp column data in replication. It might not be what you think.
- Identity, Uniqueidentifier, and GUID column behavior with data replication.
- Text or Image data types to heterogeneous subscribers.
- Missing or nonsupported data types because of prior versions of SQL Server or Heterogeneous Subscribers as part of the replication configuration.
- Maximum row size limitations between merge replication and transactional replication (6000 bytes versus 8000 bytes, respectively).

If you have triggers on your tables and you want them to be replicated along with your table, you might want to revisit them and add a line of code reading `NOT FOR REPLICATION` so that the trigger code isn't executed redundantly on the subscriber side.

Setting Up Replication

In general, SQL Server 2000 data replication is exceptionally easy to set up via Enterprise Manager/Wizards. However, please be warned: If you use the wizards, be sure to generate SQL scripts for every phase of replication configuration. In a production environment, you most likely will rely heavily on scripts and will not have the luxury of much time to set up and break down production replication configurations via wizards.

You always will have to define any data replication configuration in the following order:

1. Create or enable a distributor to enable publishing.
2. Enable publishing. (A distributor must be designated for a publisher.)
3. Create a publication and define articles within the publication.
4. Define subscribers and subscribe to a publication.

In Figure 22.23, you can see a shot of Enterprise Manager without data replication configuration defined yet. This picture will change dramatically as we build up a typical data replication configuration and allow it to begin replicating data.

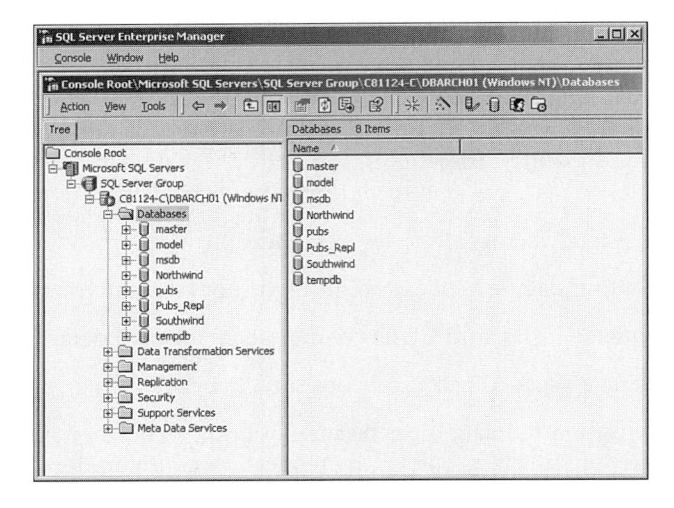

FIGURE 22.23 Enterprise Manager.

Enable Publishing

Before setting up a publisher, you will have to designate a distribution server to be used by that publisher. As has already been discussed, you can either configure the local server as the distribution server, or choose a remote server as the distributor. You can create a distributor in one of two ways. You can configure the server as a distributor and publisher at the same time, or you can configure the server as a dedicated distributor. You can do this using the Configure Publishing, Subscribers, and Distribution Wizard. After the distributor has been set up, you can finish enabling publishing.

You must be a member of the sysadmin server role to use this wizard. Use the following steps to configure a server as a distributor:

1. From Enterprise Monitor, choose the Tools, Replication, Configure Publishing, Subscribers, and Distribution selection. This will start you through the wizard to accomplish three tasks:
   - Specify and create a distributor
   - Configure the properties of the distribution server
   - Configure the properties of a publisher that will use that distributor

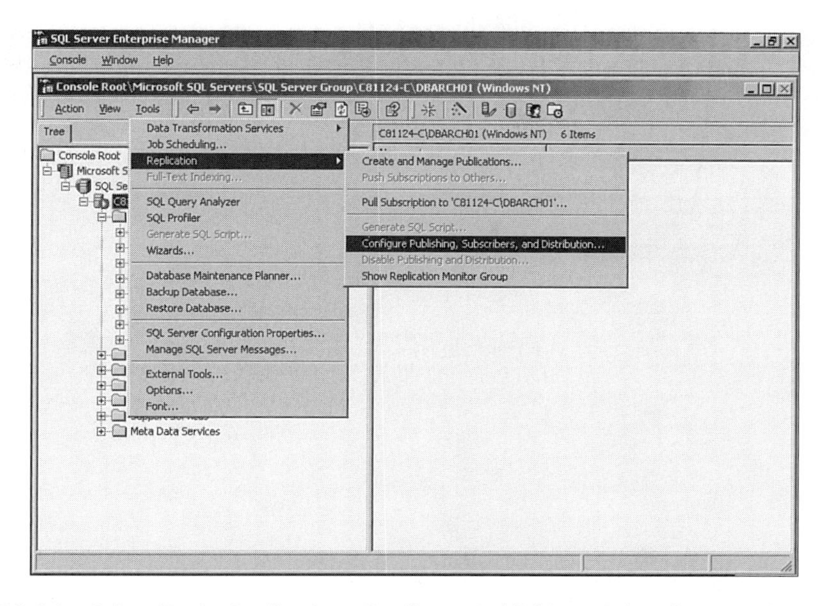

FIGURE 22.24 Select Tools, Replication, Configure Publishing, Subscribers, and Distribution.

2. You must either select or install a distributor for this publisher to use. We will choose to have the distributor on the same machine as the publisher.

3. You'll be asked to specify a snapshot folder. Give it the proper network full pathname. Remember: Much data will be coming here, and it should be on a drive that can support the snapshot concept without filling up the drive.

4. You are then asked to configure the distribution database. The default settings will cover most of your needs. Figure 22.25 shows all of the things that will be configured using this default setting option.

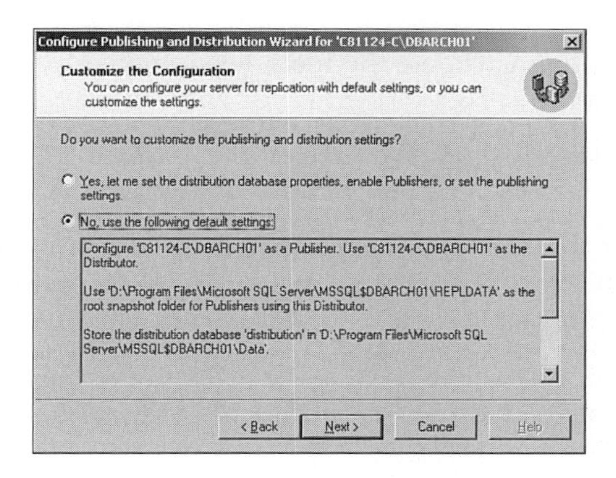

FIGURE 22.25 Summary of default settings.

5. The end result will yield a distribution database being created, the distribution server set up, Replication Monitor being added to Enterprise Manager, and Publishing enabled. In fact, if you look a bit closer at Figure 22.26, you will see some replication agents being set up as well.

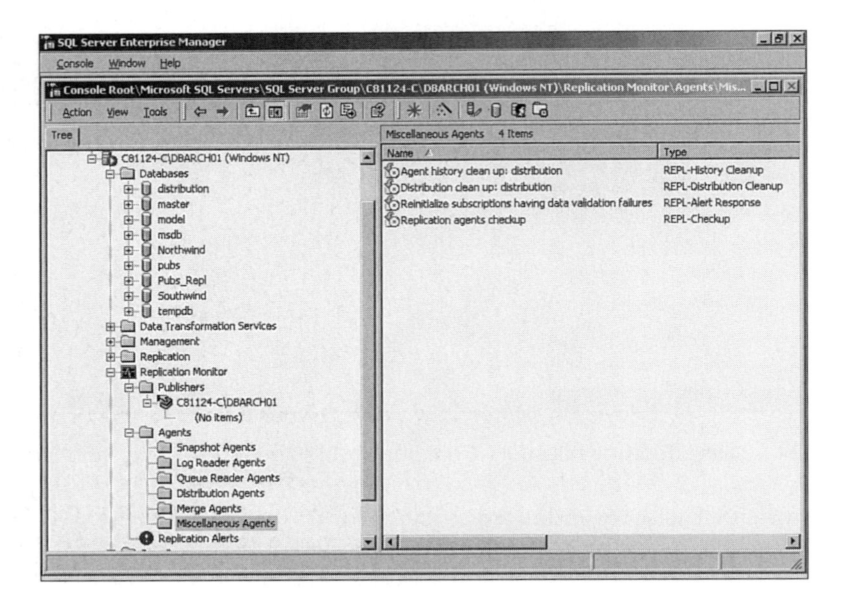

FIGURE 22.26 Replication agents are set up.

Creating a Publication

Now that the distribution database has been created and publishing has been enabled on the server, you can create and configure a publication. Again, select the Replication option from the Tools menu:

1. From Enterprise Monitor, choose the Tools, Replication, Create and Manage Publications selection.

2. You will be immediately prompted to select the database on which you are going to set up a publication. We chose the Northwind database.

3. You must now choose the type of replication method for this publication. This will be Snapshot replication, Transactional replication, or Merge replication. We have selected Transactional replication.

4. In the next screen, you will be asked to select the Updatable Subscriptions method you want to use. If you have not decided to allow this, just skip this screen by clicking the Next button.

5. In addition, you now can choose to utilize Data Transformation Services (DTS) as part of this publication if you have extremely complex data transformations that you want to be part of this process. Otherwise, just click No.

6. Now, you must indicate what the possible subscribers are going to be. Will they be MS SQL Server 2000 servers, MS SQL Server 7.0, or Heterogeneous data sources (Oracle, Access, or earlier versions of MS SQL Server 6.5 and below)?

7. From the Specify Articles screen, you are prompted to create articles in your publication (see Figure 22.27). You must include at least one article in your publication. These can be tables, views, or stored procedures. After you select an article, a button with an ellipsis (...) appears after the article name. If you click this button, you are able to select options for your article. For snapshot and transactional replication, you can determine how the snapshot portion of the replication will occur. If you have selected Merge replication, you will be able to select the conflict resolver that you are going to use. You can either select the default SQL Server resolver or create your own stored procedure or COM objects.

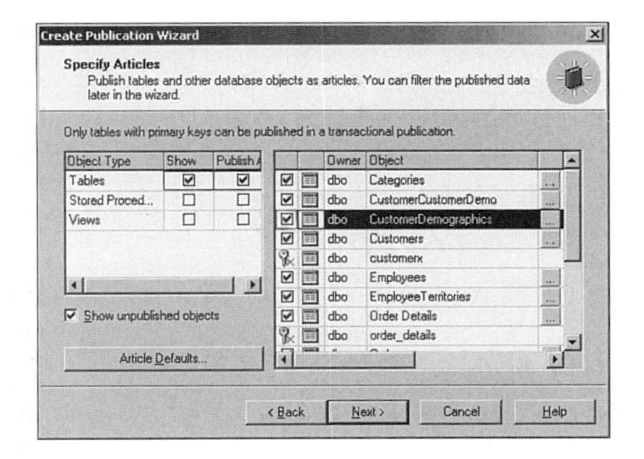

FIGURE 22.27 The Specify Articles screen allows you to choose which tables you are going to publish.

8. If article issues exist, they will be presented to you here. Identity columns might be an issue because of the way they will be treated in replication.

9. You can now name your publication something meaningful.

10. You are given a chance to customize the properties of the publication. This includes adding data filters and allowing anonymous subscribers. If you select that you do want to create anonymous subscribers, SQL Server will allow any server to connect to and receive data from your publication.

11. As you finish this wizard, it displays what it is doing in a nice dialog box, as shown in Figure 22.28. When this finishes, you will have a valid publication that simply needs to be subscribed to.

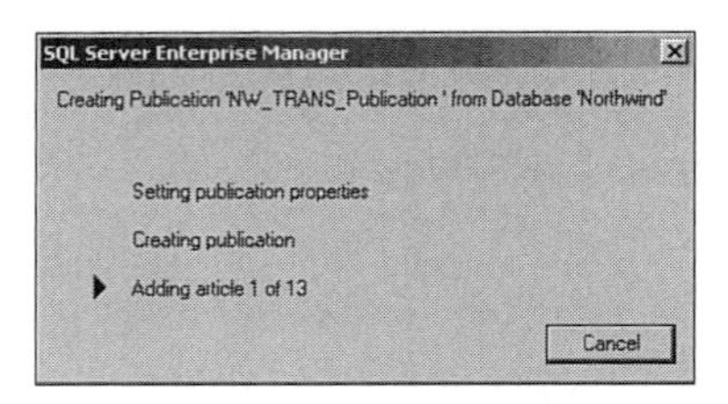

FIGURE 22.28 Wizard summary.

Creating Subscriptions

Now that you have installed and configured the distributor, enabled publishing, and created a publication, you need to create subscriptions. As you can see from Enterprise Manager in Figure 22.29, after the publication has been defined, the snapshot agent is created along with the Log Reader Agent (because we chose transactional replication). Also notice that a shared hand is on the database that we are publishing.

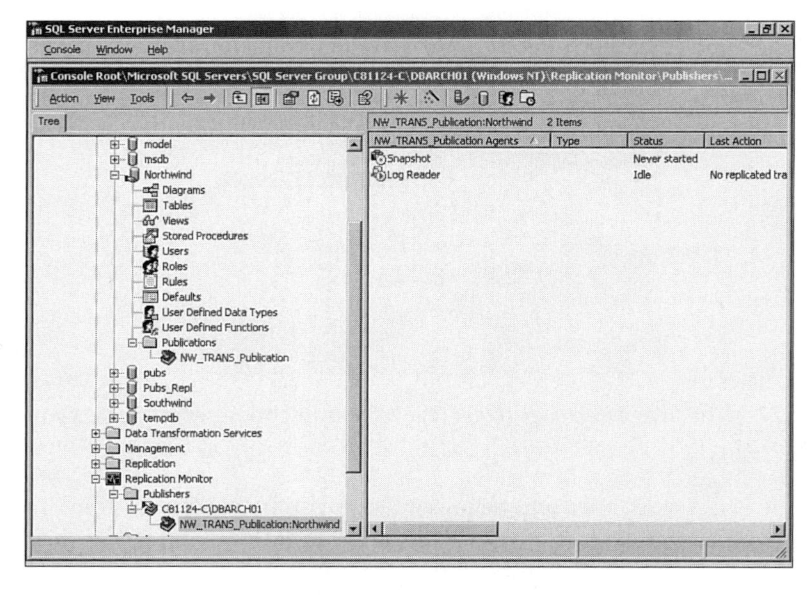

FIGURE 22.29 Enterprise Manager with publication agents.

Remember that two types of subscriptions can be created: push and pull. Pull subscriptions allow remote sites to subscribe to any publication that they are allowed to, but you must be confident that the administrators at the other sites have properly configured the subscriptions at their sites. Push subscriptions are easier to create because all of the subscription processes are performed and administered from one machine. This also makes them the most common approach taken. Following are the steps to create a push subscription:

1. From Enterprise Manager, choose the Tools, Replication, Create and Manage Publications selection. You will now see, in Figure 22.30, the Push New Subscription option active. This will allow you to do the following:

    - Select one or more subscribers
    - Specify where the data is to be replicated into for each subscriber
    - Set/configure the initialization and synchronization process schedule so that they happen when they need to

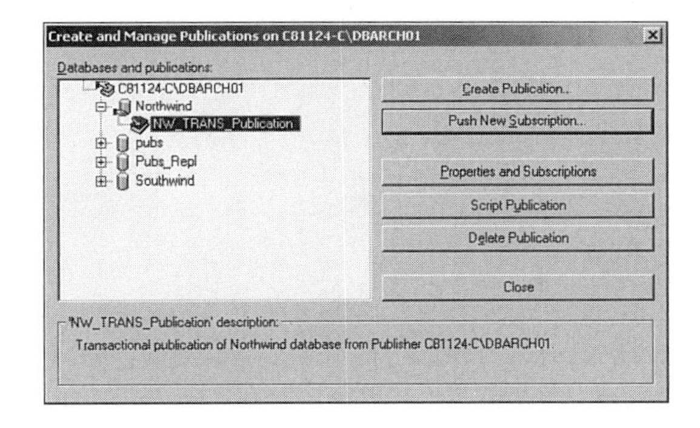

FIGURE 22.30 Create and manage publications.

2. Specify the subscriber from the list that has been registered to SQL Server and has been enabled for subscribing.

3. From the Choose Destination Database screen, you are prompted to choose to which database you will publish. If you click the Browse Database button, you can see a list of all the databases on the destination server (see Figure 22.31). If you want to create a new database on the destination server, click the Create New button.

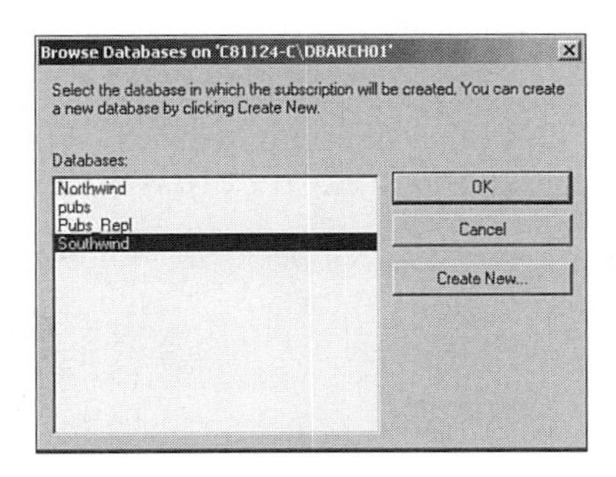

FIGURE 22.31 The Choose Destination Database screen.

4. Next, we will configure how the distribution agent will run. If you want to provide the shortest latency, select the Run Continuously option. Otherwise, configure the distribution agent to run at specific times during the day. By default, the distribution agent runs once an hour every day.
5. You then are prompted to set the initialization of the database schema and data. You will have an option to create the schema and data at the subscriber (and also to do it immediately) or to skip this initialization altogether because you have already created the schema and loaded the data manually.
6. The next part of the process, the Start Required Services dialog box, checks whether the required services are running on the server.
7. The last screen, shown in Figure 22.32, is a summary screen that outlines the options you selected and the steps SQL Server will perform to create the subscription. After you click the Finish button, SQL Server will create the subscription according to your specification.

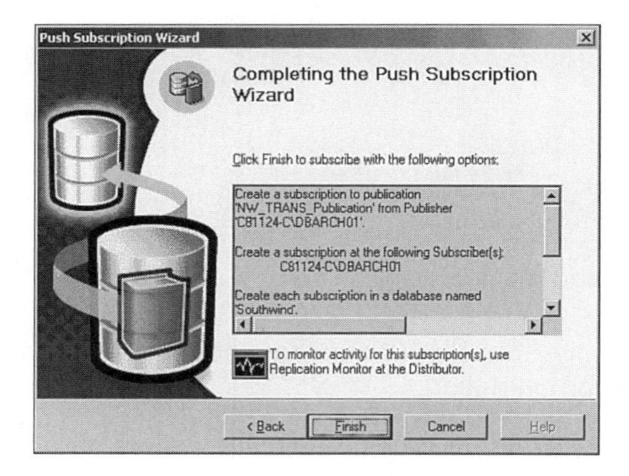

FIGURE 22.32 Push Subscription Wizard summary.

Now that replication is set up, the only thing left to do is wait. If you have specified that the schema and data be created immediately, things will start happening quickly.

You will first see the snapshot agent start up and begin creating schema files (.SCHs), extracting the data into .BCP files (.BCPs), and putting everything in the snapshot folder on the distribution server. Figure 22.33 shows the last part of the snapshot tasks in its log.

In addition, in Figure 22.34, we took a quick peek, via Windows Explorer, at the contents of the snapshot working directory to see all of our .SCHs and .BCPs being created. This is often where trouble is encountered because of the lack of space on the disk drive.

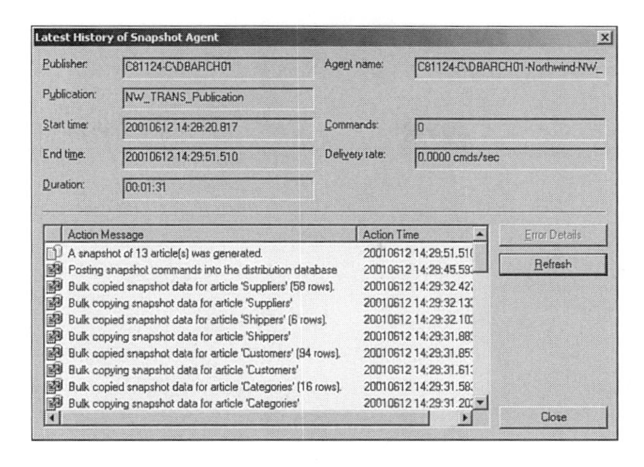

FIGURE 22.33 Snapshot task details.

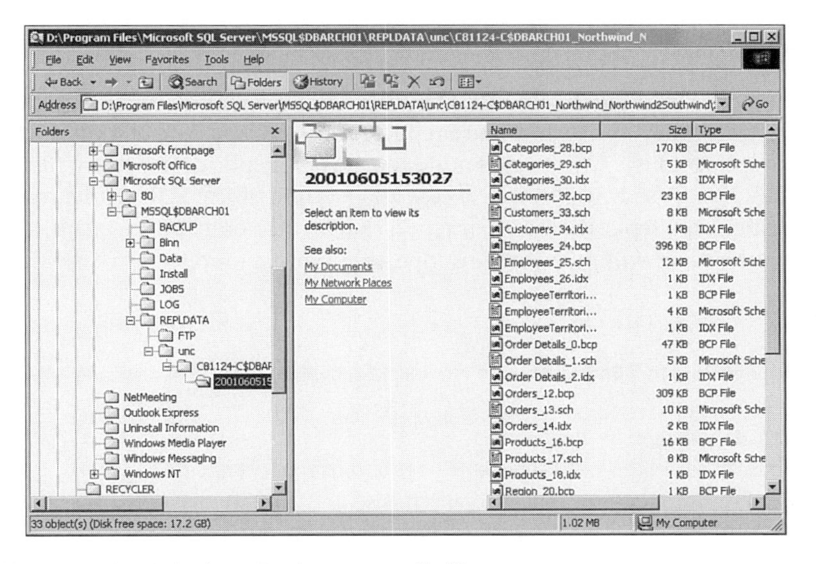

FIGURE 22.34 Using Windows Explorer to verify files.

Now that the snapshot agent is essentially finished with its tasks, the distribution agent finishes the job. As you can see from Figure 22.35, the distribution agent is applying the schemas to the subscriber. The bulk copying of the data into the tables on the subscriber side will follow accordingly. After this bulk copying is done, the initialization step is completed and active replication begins.

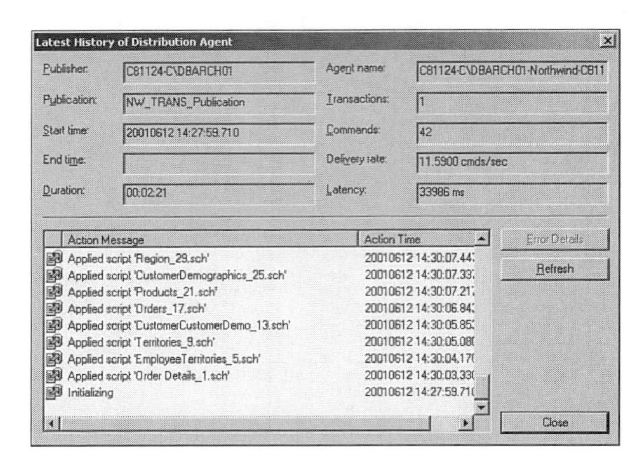

FIGURE 22.35 Applying schemas to the subscriber.

Scripting Replication

Earlier, it was suggested to generate SQL Scripts for all that you do because going through wizards every time you have to configure replication is no way to run a production environment. An option in the Configure and Manage Data Replication screen allows you to generate SQL scripts. Use this option! Next is an example of the SQL scripts needed to generate the same data replication configuration that we just built with wizards. These scripts minimize the errors we will make while supporting our data replication environments.

```
use master
GO
exec sp_adddistributor  @distributor = 'C81124-C\DBARCH01', @password =''
GO
-- Adding the distribution database
exec sp_adddistributiondb  @database = 'distribution', @data_folder =
   'd:\MSSQL2000\data',
@data_file ='distribution.MDF', @data_file_size = 3, @log_folder =
   'd:\MSSQL2000\data',
@log_file = 'distribution.LDF', @log_file_size = 1, @min_distretention = 0,
@max_distretention = 72, @history_retention = 48, @security_mode = 1
GO
-- Adding the distribution publisher
exec sp_adddistpublisher  @publisher = 'C81124-C\DBARCH01',
   @distribution_db = 'distribution',
@security_mode = 1, @working_directory = 'd:\MSSQL2000\ReplData',
   @trusted = 'true',
@thirdparty_flag = 0
```

```
GO
-- Enabling the replication database
use master
go
exec sp_replicationdboption @dbname = 'Northwind', @optname = 'publish',
    @value = 'true'
go
use [Northwind]
GO
-- Adding the transactional publication
exec sp_addpublication @publication = 'NW_TRANS_Publication',
   @restricted = 'false',
@sync_method = 'native', @repl_freq = 'continuous',
@description='Transactional publication of Northwind database from Publisher
   C81124-C\DBARCH01.',
@status = 'active', @allow_push = 'true', @allow_pull = 'true', @allow_
   anonymous = 'false',
@enabled_for_internet = 'false', @independent_agent = 'false', @immediate_
   sync = 'false',
@allow_sync_tran = 'false', @autogen_sync_procs = 'false', @retention = 336,
@allow_queued_tran = 'false',@snapshot_in_defaultfolder = 'true', @compress_
   snapshot='false',
@ftp_port = 21, @ftp_login = 'anonymous',@allow_dts ='false',@allow_
   subscription_copy='false',
@add_to_active_directory = 'false',@logreader_job_name =
   'C81124-C\DBARCH01-Northwind-1'

exec sp_addpublication_snapshot @publication = 'NW_TRANS_Publication',
   @frequency_type = 4,
@frequency_interval = 1, @frequency_relative_interval = 0, @frequency_
   recurrence_factor = 1,
@frequency_subday = 1, @frequency_subday_interval = 0, @active_
   start_date = 0,
@active_end_date = 0, @active_start_time_of_day = 224300, @active_end_
   time_of_day = 0,
@snapshot_job_name = 'C81124-C\DBARCH01-Northwind-NW_TRANS_Publication-1'
GO
-- Granting access to the publication
exec sp_grant_publication_access @publication = 'NW_TRANS_Publication',
@login = 'BUILTIN\Administrators'
GO
```

```
exec sp_grant_publication_access @publication = 'NW_TRANS_Publication',
@login = 'distributor_admin'
GO
exec sp_grant_publication_access @publication = 'NW_TRANS_
   Publication', @login = 'sa'
GO
-- Adding the transactional articles
exec sp_addarticle @publication = 'NW_TRANS_Publication',
   @article = 'Categories',
@source_owner = 'dbo', @source_object = 'Categories', @destination_
   table = 'Categories',
@type = 'logbased', @creation_script = null, @description = null,
   @pre_creation_cmd = 'drop',
@schema_option = 0x00000000000000F3, @status = 16, @vertical_
   partition = 'false',
@ins_cmd = 'SQL', @del_cmd = 'SQL', @upd_cmd = 'SQL', @filter = null,
   @sync_object = null,
@auto_identity_range = 'false'
GO
exec sp_addarticle /* etc. for all 13 tables to be published */
go
exec sp_addsubscriber @subscriber = 'C81124-C\DBARCH01',
   @type = 1, @login = '',
@password = '', @security_mode = 0, @frequency_type = 64,
   @frequency_interval = 1,
@frequency_relative_interval = 2, @frequency_recurrence_factor = 0,
   @frequency_subday = 8, @frequency_subday_interval = 1, @active_
   start_date = 0, @active_end_date = 0,
@active_start_time_of_day = 0, @active_end_time_of_day = 235900,
   @description = ''
GO
-- Adding the transactional subscription
exec sp_addsubscription @publication = 'NW_TRANS_Publication',
   @article = 'all',
@subscriber = 'C81124-C\DBARCH01', @destination_db = 'Southwind',
   @sync_type = 'none',
@update_mode = 'read only'
GO
```

You also need to monitor the appropriate replication stored procedures and break down the configuration.

Monitoring Replication

After replication is up and running, it is important for you to monitor the replication and see how things are running. You can do this in several ways, including SQL statements, SQL Enterprise Monitor, and Windows NT Performance Monitor. You are interested in the agent's successes and failures, the speed at which replication is done, and the synchronization state of tables involved in replication. Other things to be watched are the sizes of the distribution database, the growth of the subscriber databases, and the available space on the distribution server's snapshot working directory.

SQL Statements

One way to look at the replication configuration and do things like validate row counts is to use various replication stored procedures.

These include the following:

- `sp_helppublication`—Info on the publication server
- `sp_helparticle`—Article definition information
- `sp_helpdistributor`—Distributor information
- `sp_helpsubscriberinfo`—Subscriber server information
- `sp_helpsubscription`—The subscription information

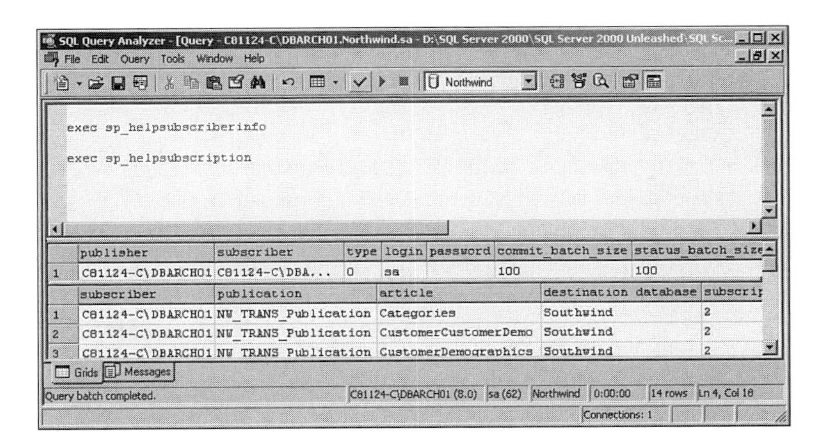

FIGURE 22.36 Replication stored procedure results.

These are all extremely useful for verifying exactly at what the replication configuration is really configured.

Also

- sp_replcounters—Shows the activity of this replication session. You can see the volume of traffic and the throughput here.

```
exec sp_replcounters
go
```

Yields

```
database repl_trans rate trans/sec latency (sec) etc.
Northwind 110    71.428574        2.1830001
```

For actual row count validation:

- sp_publication_validation—Goes through and checks the row counts of the publication and subscribers.

```
exec sp_publication_validation @publication = 'NW_TRANS_Publication'
go
```

Yields

```
Generated expected rowcount value of 53 for Territories.
Generated expected rowcount value of 58 for Suppliers.
Generated expected rowcount value of 6 for Shippers.
Generated expected rowcount value of 4 for Region.
Generated expected rowcount value of 154 for Products.
Generated expected rowcount value of 1690 for Orders.
Generated expected rowcount value of 2155 for Order Details.
Generated expected rowcount value of 49 for EmployeeTerritories.
Generated expected rowcount value of 18 for Employees.
Generated expected rowcount value of 95 for Customers.
Generated expected rowcount value of 0 for CustomerDemographics.
Generated expected rowcount value of 0 for CustomerCustomerDemo.
Generated expected rowcount value of 16 for Categories.
```

Another way to monitor replication is to look at the actual data that is being replicated. To do this, first run a `SELECT count (*) FROM tblname` statement against the table where data is being replicated. Then verify directly if the most current data available is in the database. If you make a change to the data in the published table, do the changes show up in the replicated tables? If not, you might need to investigate how replication was configured on the server.

If you are allowing updatable subscriptions, the replication queue comes into play. You'll need to learn all about the queueread utility. This utility configures and begins the Queue Reader Agent, which reads messages stored in the SQL Server queue, or a Microsoft message queue, and applies those messages to the publisher. queueread is a command prompt utility.

SQL Enterprise Manager

As you can imagine, Enterprise Manager provides considerable information about the status of replication. Most of this is available via the Replication Monitor branch. In Replication Monitor, you can see the activity for publishers, agents, and the ability to configure alerts:

- Publishers—This folder contains information about publishers on the machine. By selecting any publisher on the machine, you can view information about any computers that have subscribed to the publication. This will tell you the current status and the last action taken by the subscriber.
- Agents—The Agents folder contains information about the different agents on the machine. By choosing any Agents folder, you can see the current status of that agent. Selecting an agent and double-clicking it will display the history of that agent.
- Replication Alerts—The Replication Alerts folder allows you to configure alerts to fire in response to events that occur during replication. These can activate when errors occur, or in response to success messages.

As you can see from Figure 22.37, it appears that this transactional replication scenario is operating successfully.

If you drill down even more, you will see the execution history. Figure 22.38 shows a healthy Log Reader history.

Through Enterprise Manager and Replication Monitor, you also can invoke the validate subscriptions processing to see if replication is in sync. Under the Publication branch of Replication Monitor, simply right-click on the publication you wish to validate. You will see the menu option to Validate Subscriptions. You can validate all subscriptions or just a particular one. After invoked, the results can be viewed via the distribution agent history as depicted in Figure 22.39.

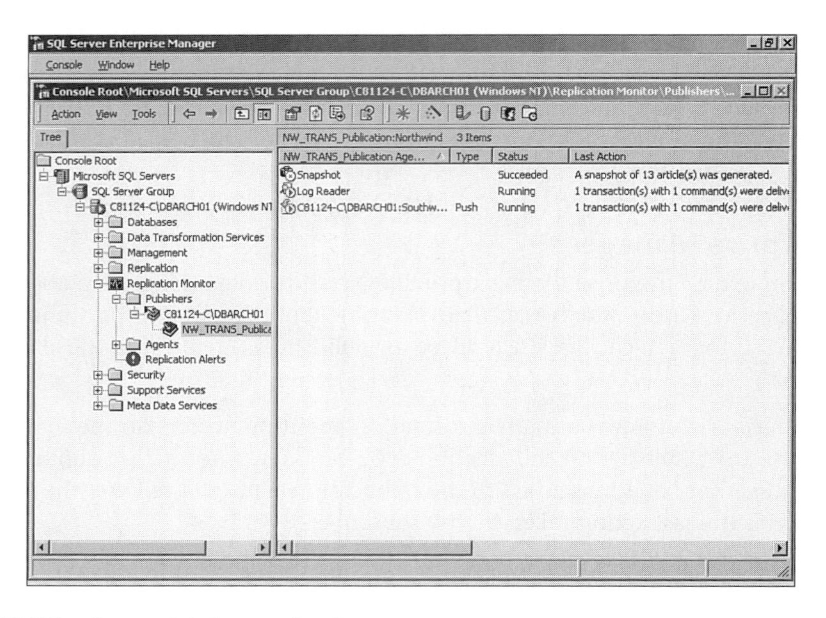

FIGURE 22.37 Successful data replication.

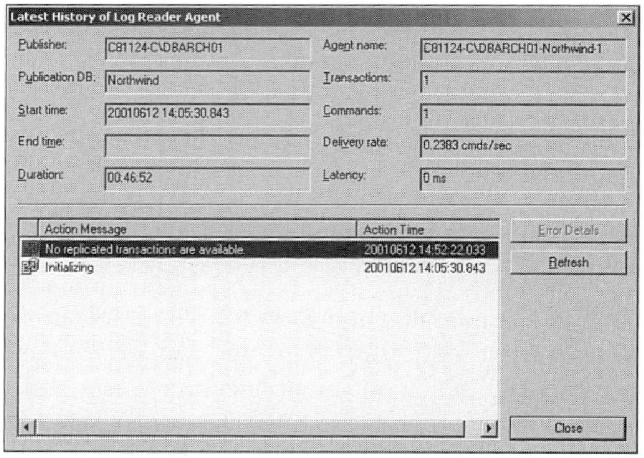

Latest History of Log Reader Agent

Publisher:	C81124-C\DBARCH01	Agent name:	C81124-C\DBARCH01-Northwind-1
Publication DB:	Northwind	Transactions:	1
Start time:	20010612 14:05:30.843	Commands:	1
End time:		Delivery rate:	0.2383 cmds/sec
Duration:	00:46:52	Latency:	0 ms

Action Message	Action Time
No replicated transactions are available.	20010612 14:52:22.033
Initializing	20010612 14:05:30.843

Error Details
Refresh
Close

FIGURE 22.38 Execution history.

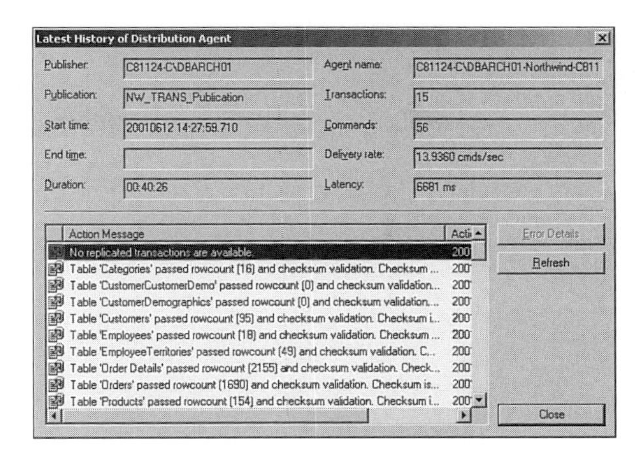

FIGURE 22.39 Distribution agent—validated subscription details.

Troubleshooting Replication Failures

Configuring replication and monitoring for successful replication are pretty easy. The fun begins when failures start arising. Using Replication Monitor starts paying for itself in big dividends quickly. Red flags begin appearing to indicate agent failures. Depending on how you have the Alerts defined, you are probably also getting considerable e-mails or pages.

The following are the most common issues you will find with data replication:

- Data row count inconsistencies, as we looked at in the prior section
- Subscriber/publisher schema change failures
- Connection failures
- Agent failures

For the conventional replication situations, if the problem is with the validation of subscriptions processing, it is usually best to resync the subscription by dropping it and resubscribing.

Another common issue is that of the SQL Server Agent service not starting. Manually attempting to restart this service usually shakes things loose.

Sometimes an object on the subscriber will become messed up and result in an error like that in Figure 22.40. The solution is usually to create that object again and reload its data via BCP or DTS. Then resync the subscription. The subscription included this object originally, but it has become invalid in some way.

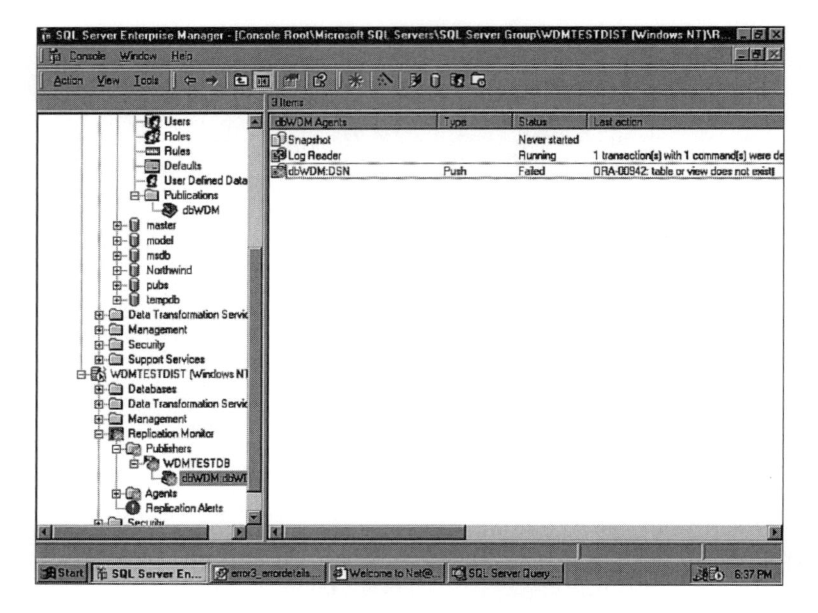

FIGURE 22.40 Replication error—object existence issue.

With a heterogeneous subscriber, you often see connection errors due to invalid login IDs used in the ODBC connection. Figure 22.41 illustrates just such a failure. The quick fix is usually to just redefine the ODBC data source connection information.

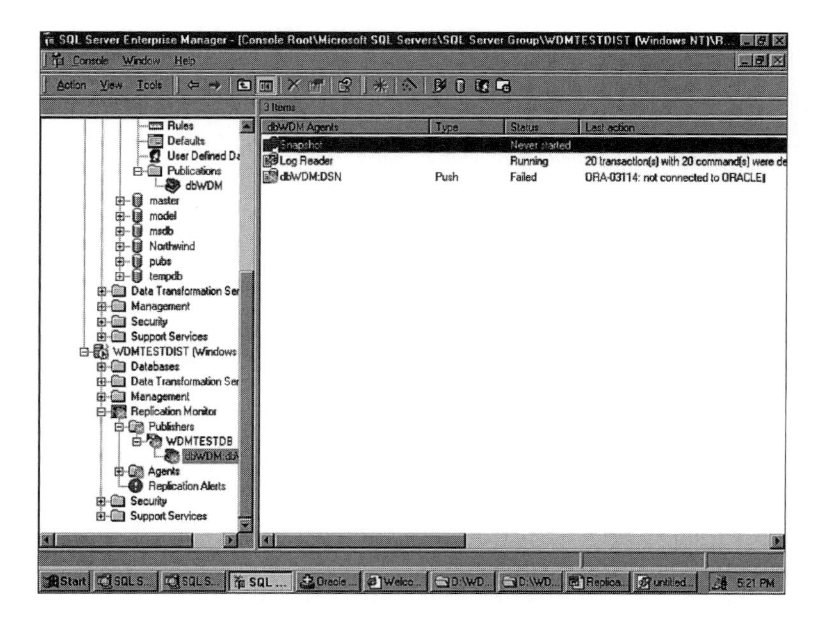

FIGURE 22.41 Replication error—connectivity issue.

A much more complex failure can arise when the replication queue is stopped due to some type of SQL language failure in the command being replicated. This is extremely serious because it stops all replication from continuing and the distribution database starts growing rapidly. Replication keeps trying to execute this, failing each time. This situation is essentially a permanent road block.

Figure 22.42 shows such a failure. The solution is to locate the exact transaction in the distribution database, and delete it physically from the transaction queue. This is highly unusual, but necessary when the circumstance presents itself.

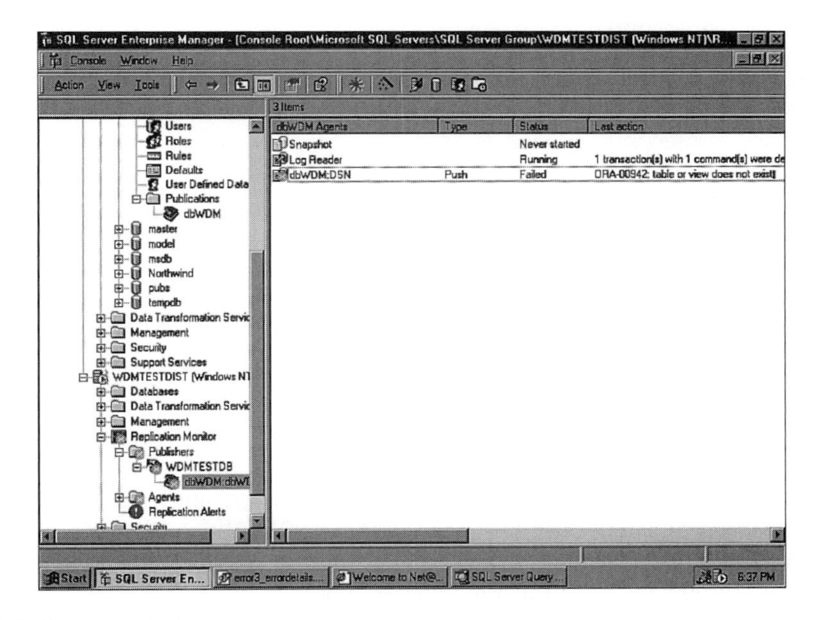

FIGURE 22.42 Push failure.

First, by looking at the error detail information in the Distribution Agent History dialog box, you will be able to isolate the SQL statement on which it is choking. You now have to find this in the distribution database. Start by executing the sp_browsereplcmds stored procedure. This gives you all the replication transactions (xact_seqno's) along with the associated SQL command. You will have to pump this to a text file for searching. You then must search this data for the matching SQL command. When you locate it, look for its associated transaction number (xact_seqno). Use this xact_seqno value to delete it from the Msrepl_commands table in the distribution database. This will free up the road block. You will see this type of issue about once every six months.

The Performance Monitor

You also can use Windows NT Performance Monitor to monitor the health of your replication scenario. Installing SQL Server adds several new objects and counters to Performance Monitor:

- SQLServer:Replication Agents—This object contains counters used to monitor the status of all replication agents, including the total number running.
- SQLServer:Replication Dist—This object contains counters used to monitor the status of the distribution agents, including the latency and the number of transactions transferred per second.
- SQLServer:Replication Logreader—This object contains counters used to monitor the status of the log reader agent, including the latency and the number of transactions transferred per second.
- SQLServer:Replication Merge—This object contains counters used to monitor the status of the merge agents, including the number of transactions and the number of conflicts per second.
- SQLServer:Replication Snapshot—This object contains counters used to monitor the status of the snapshot agents, including the number of transactions per second.

Replication in Heterogeneous Environments

SQL Server 2000 allows for transactional and snapshot replication of data into and out of environments other than SQL Server. This is termed **heterogeneous** replication. The easiest way to set up this replication is to use ODBC or OLE DB, and create a push subscription to the subscriber. This is much easier to make work than you would imagine. SQL Server can publish to the following database types:

- Microsoft Access
- Oracle
- Sybase
- IBM DB2/AS400
- IBM DB2/MVS

SQL Server can replicate data to any other type of database, providing that the ODBC driver supports the following:

- The driver must be ODBC Level-1 compliant.
- The driver must be 32-bit, thread-safe, and designed for the processor architecture on which the distribution process runs.

- The driver must support transactions.
- The driver and underlying database must support Data Definition Language (DDL).
- The underlying database cannot be read-only.

Replicating to Internet Subscribers

With SQL Server 2000, you easily can replicate data to Internet subscribers. The first requirement for this feature is that your publication allows pull and anonymous subscriptions. You must take three steps to configure an Internet subscription:

1. Configure the publisher or distributor to listen on TCP/IP.
2. Configure a publication to use FTP.
3. Configure a subscription to use FTP.

Configuring a Publisher or Distributor to Listen on TCP/IP

Before you can set up replication to Internet subscribers, you must configure SQL Server to communicate on TCP/IP or the multiprotocol network library. You can configure this area using the SQL Server Network Utility. You also must have Internet Information Server set up on the distribution server because Internet replication relies on the FTP service to transfer the snapshots from the distribution server to the subscribers. You have to set up the FTP home directory to the snapshot folder and configure the FTP home directory as an FTP site.

Configuring a Publication to Use FTP

After you have configured the server to use FTP, the next step is to set up the publication to allow for Internet replication. You can do this using SQL Enterprise Manager. After it is configured, the distribution or merge agents will use FTP to download the snapshot files to the subscriber server. After the snapshot files are copied to the subscriber, the agent applies the files to the tables at the subscriber. The following steps walk you through setting up an existing database to use the Internet:

1. Connect to the publishing server in SQL Enterprise Manager. From the Tools menu, choose Create and Modify Publications. This will open the Create and Manage Publication dialog box.
2. From the dialog box, choose the publication that you want to edit and click the Properties & Subscriptions button. This will open the publication's Properties box.
3. From the Subscription Options tab, put a check in the Allow Subscriptions to Be Downloaded Using FTP check box.

Configuring a Subscription to Use FTP

After the publication has been configured to use FTP, you must create a pull or anonymous subscription to the database. These subscriptions are created the same way that you would create any other subscription. The difference is that you need to configure the FTP options. The following steps walk you through setting up Internet-enabled subscriptions:

1. Connect to the publishing server in SQL Enterprise Manager. From the Tools menu, choose Pull Subscriptions. This will open the Pull Subscriptions dialog box.

2. From the dialog box, choose the publication that you want to edit and click the Properties button. This will open the publication's properties box.

3. From the Pull Subscriptions Properties screen, choose the Snapshot Delivery tab. Put a check in the Use the File Transfer Protocol When Downloading Snapshot Files from the Distributor check box. Enter the options in the FTP Parameters section.

Backup and Recovery in a Replication Configuration

Something that will reap major benefits for you after you have implemented a data replication configuration is a replication-oriented backup strategy. You must realize that the scope of data and what you must back up together has changed. In addition, you must be aware of what the recovery timeframe is and plan your backup/recovery strategy for this. You might not have multiple hours available to you to recover an entire replication topology. You now have databases that are conceptually joined, and you might need to back them up together as one synchronized backup. Figure 22.43 depicts an overall backup strategy for the most common recovery needs.

Recovery Need	Backup Strategy
100% data, All sites, Small Recovery Window	Coordinated DB backups at all sites involved in the replication configuration (publisher, distributor & all subscribers). Somewhat complex to do.
100% data, All sites, Medium Recovery Window	Backup Publication DB and Distribution DB together. Replication can be recovered from this point very easily without reconfiguring anything. Just have to re-initialize the subscribers. This is the most common approach being used.
100% data, All sites, Big Recovery Window	Backup of Publication DB only. Can then reconfigure replication via scripts and reinitialize distribution, and all subscribers fairly easily.

FIGURE 22.43 Common backup strategy for different recovery needs.

When backing up environments, back up the following at each site:

- Publisher (published db, msdb, and master)
- Distributor (distribution db, msdb, and master)
- Subscribers (subscriber db, optionally msdb and master when pull subscriptions are being done)

Always make copies of your replication scripts and keep them handy. At a very minimum, keep copies at the publisher and distributor and one more location, such as at one of your subscribers. You will end up using these for recovery someday.

Don't forget to back up master and msdb when any new replication object is created, updated, or deleted.

If you have allowed updating subscribers using queued updates, you will have to expand your backup capability to include these queues.

In general, you will find that even when you walk up and pull the plug on your distribution server, publication server, or any subscribers, automatic recovery works well to get you back online and replicating quickly without human intervention.

Some Performance Thoughts

From a performance point of view, you will find that the replication configuration defaults err toward the optimal throughput side. That's the good news. The bad news is that everybody is different in some way, in which case you will have to consider a bit of tuning of your replication configuration. In general, you can get your replication configuration working well by doing the following:

- Keeping the amount of data to be replicated at any one point small by running agents continuously, instead of at long, scheduled intervals.
- Setting a minimum amount of memory allocated to SQL Server using the Min Server Memory option to guarantee ample memory across the board.
- Using good disk drive physical separation rules, such as keeping translog on a separate disk drive from the data portion. Your transaction log will be much more heavily used when you have opted for transactional replication.
- Putting your snapshot working directory on a separate disk drive to minimize disk drive arm contention. Make sure you use separate snapshot folders for each publication.
- Publishing only what you need. By selectively publishing only the minimum amount of data that your requirements need, you will, by definition, be implementing a much more efficient replication configuration, which is faster overall.

- Trying to run snapshots in nonpeak times so your network and production environments won't be bogged down.
- Minimizing transformation of data involved with replication.

Log Shipping: An Alternative to Data Replication

If you have a small need to create a read-only (ad hoc query/reporting) database environment that can tolerate a certain high degree of data latency, you might be a candidate to use log shipping. Log shipping is a new feature for SQL Server 2000. Using log shipping as an alternative to data replication has been referred to as "the poor man's data replication." Keep in mind that log shipping has three primary purposes:

- Making an exact image copy of a database on one server from a database dump
- Creating a copy of that database on one or more other servers from that dump
- Continuously applying transaction log dumps from the original database to the copy

In other words, log shipping is effectively replicating the data of one server to one or more other servers via transaction logs. This is a great solution when you have to create one or more fail-over servers. It turns out that, to some degree, log shipping fits the requirement of creating a read-only subscriber as well.

You need to consider some important issues associated with log shipping, however:

- The user IDs and the permissions associated with them will be copied as part of this scenario. They will be the same at all servers, which might or might not be what you want.
- Log shipping has no filtering.
- Log shipping has no data transformation.
- Data latency exists because of the frequency of transaction log dumps being performed at the source and when they can be applied to the destination copies.
- Sources and destinations must be the same SQL Server version.
- All tables must be copied.
- Indexes cannot be tuned in the copies to support the read-only reporting requirements.
- Data is read-only.

Some of these restrictions might quickly disqualify log shipping as an alternative to using data replication. However, log shipping might be adequate for certain situations.

In Figure 22.44, you can see the start of the Database Maintenance Plan Wizard that includes the setup for log shipping if you are using the Enterprise Edition.

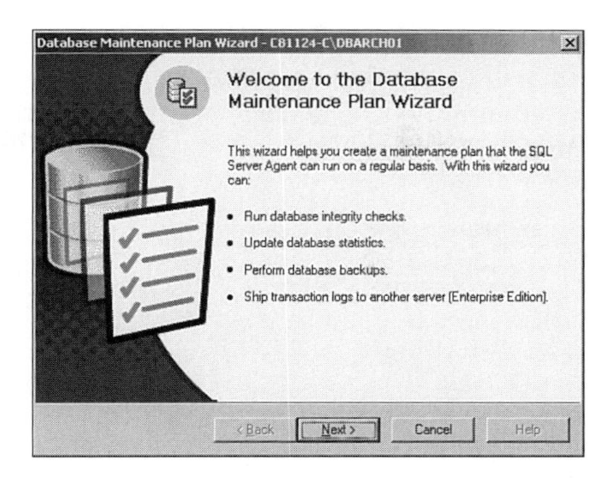

FIGURE 22.44 Log shipping.

You will simply specify what your source database is at this point and check the box that indicates you will be log shipping. When this box is checked, you are taken through a series of log shipping–specific dialog box screens. You will specify the database backup plan, the location where backups are stored (on a shared drive for log shipping), and the backup schedule. For the log shipping part, the next step is to identify the destination database. You can either have the destination be created automatically, or start from a database that was manually created. Figure 22.45 indicates that a new database should be created.

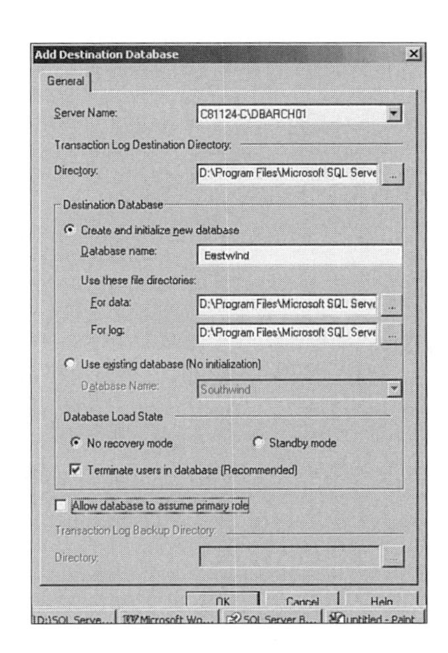

FIGURE 22.45 Log shipping—new destination database creation.

After a destination database has been specified, you can set up as many other destination databases as you want. You will go through a series of steps that further define the log shipping details. Figure 22.46 indicates the detailed log shipping schedule information (copy/load, delay, and retention information).

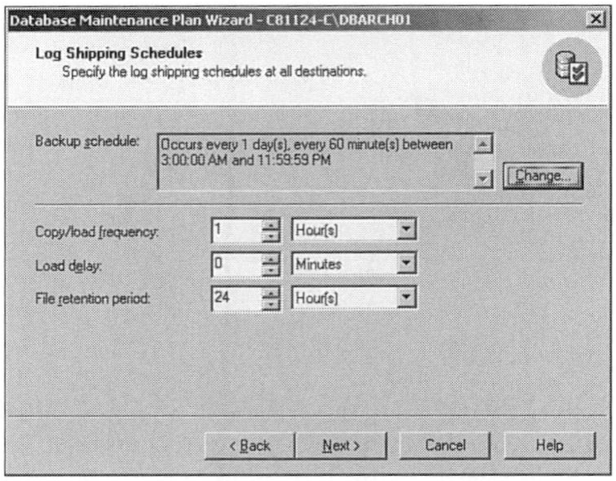

FIGURE 22.46 Log shipping schedule.

After the scheduling has been set up, a series of jobs dedicated to the log shipping processes will be set up along with the database maintenance job for the backups. Figure 22.47 shows the end results of this setup. Also, you can see that a log shipping Monitor branch has been added to the Maintenance branch for you to manage these tasks.

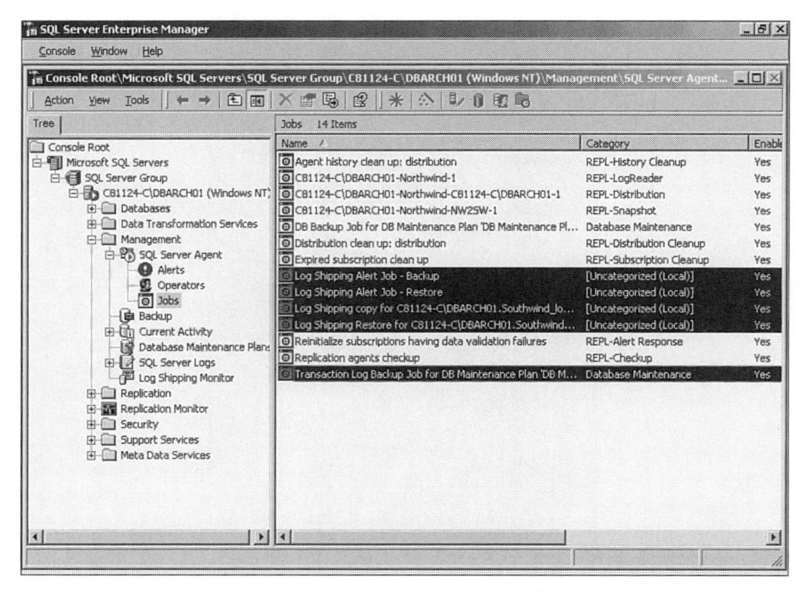

FIGURE 22.47 Log shipping agents.

Finally, if you right-click on the log shipping task and choose Properties, you will be able to view and edit the properties of this source/destination log shipping pair.

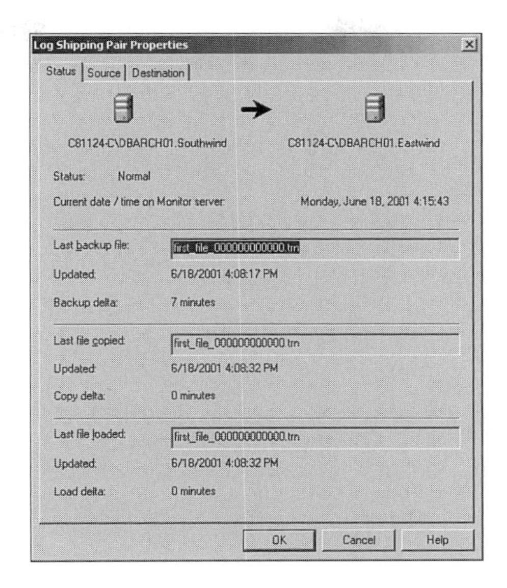

FIGURE 22.48 Log shipping pair properties.

Summary

Replication is a powerful feature of SQL Server that can be used in many business situations. Companies can use replication for anything from roll-up reporting to relieving the main server from ad hoc queries and reporting. It is critical to let your company's requirements drive the exact type of replication technique to use. Determining the replication option and configuration to use is difficult, whereas actually setting it up is pretty easy. Microsoft has come a long way in this regard. Unfortunately, a few minor bugs are still present in this version; however, you should not be afraid to use this facility. It is more than production-worthy, and the flexibility it offers and the overall performance is just short of incredible, incredible, incredible (replication humor for you).

In the next chapter, you will be taken into the realm of SQL Mail and see how to integrate this capability into your applications.

CHAPTER 23

SQL Mail

by Ray Rankins

IN THIS CHAPTER

- Setting Up an E-Mail Client/Profile
- Configuring SQL Mail
- Configuring SQLAgentMail
- SQL Mail Stored Procedures

One of the unique features of SQL Server 2000 is its ability to integrate with the existing server architecture of an established network. This integration provides SQL Server the functionality to send and receive messages and send query results to mail recipients via a configured mail provider.

SQL Server uses two separate mail sessions: one for SQL Server and one for SQL Server Agent. The MSSQLServer service uses a mail session that is referred to as SQL Mail. SQL Server uses the SQL Mail session when database applications execute the `xp_sendmail` extended stored procedure to send a message or query result set to a recipient. SQL Server Agent uses the SQLAgentMail mail session that is exclusive to SQL Server Agent activities to send messages related to job status or when an alert is triggered.

To send e-mail from SQL Server or SQL Server Agent, you must first set up a mail profile for the account(s) that SQL Server and SQL Server Agent run under and then associate the profile with SQL Server and SQL Server Agent. After that is completed, you can set up jobs, operators, and alerts for SQL Server Agent, which can be configured to notify the intended recipient by sending an e-mail or pager message through the SQL Agent mail system. You can also use the mail stored procedures provided with SQL Server to send messages or result sets to e-mail recipients.

Setting Up an E-Mail Client/Profile

Before you can use SQL Mail or SQLAgentMail, a MAPI-enabled e-mail client must be installed on the same server as SQL Server 2000. Although this can be any MAPI-enabled mail provider, it is recommended that you install Outlook 2000. Next, you must have an e-mail account on an available mail server (either a Microsoft Exchange or Internet mail server) that is linked to the domain user account under which SQL Server is running.

The following are the steps to follow for setting up an e-mail profile to support SQL Mail or SQLAgentMail:

1. Install a MAPI-compliant mail client that can connect to your mail host. Outlook 2000 is recommended because it can connect to either Exchange servers or Internet Mail providers.

2. Make sure that the SQL Server and SQL Agent services are configured to run under a user account that has access to the e-mail system rather than the default local System Account. This account, whether a domain user ID or local user ID, will need to have administrative rights on the SQL Server machine. For more information on setting up SQL Server and SQL Agent to run under a user account, see Chapter 8, "Installing and Upgrading SQL Server."

3. Make sure an e-mail account is set up on your mail server for the SQL Server user account. Details on how to set up these accounts for Exchange Server, Internet Mail servers, and Lotus Notes are covered later in this section.

4. Log into the server on which SQL Server is running using the user account specified as the startup account for SQL Server and SQL Agent.

5. After you are logged in, open the Mail Control Panel and click on the Add button to create a mail profile for the SQL Server user account (see Figure 23.1). Choose a profile name that will be meaningful to the recipients of the e-mail messages. Configure an e-mail account for the mail profile that SQL Mail and SQLAgentMail will use for sending e-mail. This can be an account for an Exchange Server, a POP3 server, an IMAP server, an HTTP server, or another installed mail provider such as Lotus Notes. If any of your mail servers require a password for sending e-mail, be sure to save the password for the e-mail account in the mail profile when you set up the account as SQL Mail and SQLAgentMail. Do not prompt for a password when sending e-mail from SQL Server.

6. After the mail profile has been set up, start up your mail client using the newly created profile and test it. Send a test message addressed to the e-mail account set up in the profile to ensure that the mail client, mail profile, and e-mail provider are working properly. If your e-mail message does not appear right away, the e-mail client might not be configured to deliver mail immediately when it is sent. If you are using Outlook 2000, go to the Tools menu and choose the Options menu option. On the Mail Setup tab, make sure that the Send Immediately When Connected option is checked.

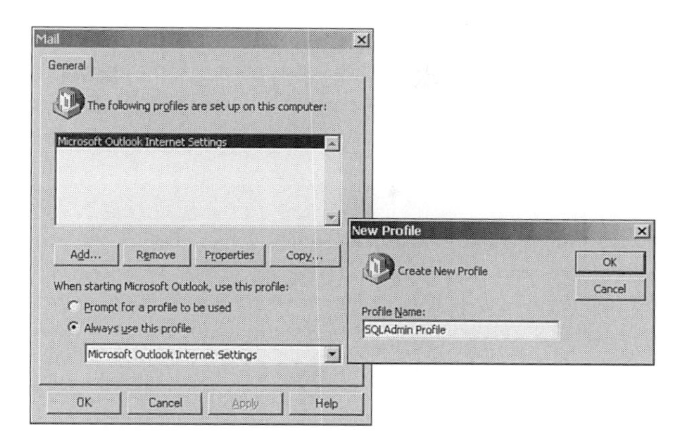

FIGURE 23.1 Use the Mail Control Panel to create a new mail profile for SQL Mail and SQLAgentMail.

How to Set Up SQL Mail with Exchange

The following steps describe the process for setting up an e-mail account on Exchange Server to use with SQL Mail:

1. On the Microsoft Exchange Server, create a mailbox that is associated with the user account that is used as the startup account for SQL Server and SQL Server Agent. This account must be a domain account with administrative rights on the SQL Server server. The mailbox created has to be mapped to the domain user ID so that NT authentication can be used to validate the user when sending e-mail messages. SQL Server cannot send mail using SQL Mail if a login ID and password have to be manually entered to connect to the Exchange Server.

2. On the SQL Server machine, log on using the same user account that is to be used as the startup account for SQL Server and SQL Server Agent.

3. Install an Exchange client on the SQL Server machine. This can be the Exchange client that ships with Microsoft Exchange Server, Microsoft Outlook 98, or preferably, Microsoft Outlook 2000.

4. Start the mail client and configure it to connect to the Microsoft Exchange Server. Verify that you can send and receive mail interactively using the mail client.

5. Open the Mail Control Panel and click Show Profiles to find the name of the profile that was created when you set up the mail client. If the profile name is longer than 32 characters or contains unusual characters (periods, hyphens, pound signs, and so forth), change the profile name to be less than 32 characters and remove the unusual characters. (Spaces are okay.)

6. Configure SQL Mail and SQLAgentMail to use this mail profile name. More details on setting up SQLMail and SQLAgentMail are presented later in this chapter in the "Configuring SQL Mail" and "Configuring SQLAgentMail" sections.

NOTE

If no profiles appear in the drop-down list box for SQL Server 2000 or the profile name you type is not recognized, you probably have started SQL Server or SQL Server Agent under the Local System account. Change the service to start under the domain account associated with the mail profile, stop and restart SQL Server or SQL Server Agent, and then try to configure the mail profile again.

How to Set Up SQL Mail with an Internet Mail Server

The steps for setting up SQL Mail with an Internet Mail server (POP3/SMTP) are not too different from setting up SQL Mail for an Exchange Server:

1. Create a mailbox on the POP3 server for incoming e-mail for the user account that will be used by SQL Mail. You will also need to set up a mailbox for outgoing mail on the SMTP server if it is different from the POP3 server.
2. On the SQL Server machine, log on using the same user account that is to be used as the startup account for SQL Server and SQL Server Agent.
3. Install an Internet Mail client on the SQL Server computer that is supported by SQL Mail such as Microsoft Windows Messaging (which ships with Windows NT 4.0), Microsoft Outlook 97, Microsoft Outlook 98, or Microsoft Outlook 2000 (recommended). Microsoft Outlook Express cannot be used because it is a simple MAPI client and does not create a mail profile, which SQL Mail needs.
4. Start the Internet Mail client and configure a profile to use the Internet Mail service and to connect to the POP3 (incoming) and SMTP (outgoing) servers. Specify the account name and password of the account set up in step 1 for access to the POP3/SMTP servers (the user ID and password are not necessarily the same as the user ID and password of the domain user account used to start SQL Server). Verify that you can send and receive mail interactively using the mail client.

TIP

If you are using Outlook 2000, you have the option when you set up your initial mail profile whether you want to set it up for Internet Only or for Corporate or Workgroup. Even though you might be setting it up to connect only to an Internet Mail server, choose the Corporate or Workgroup mode. You don't have to add an Exchange Server mail account. However, your mail profile will behave differently. In Corporate or Workgroup mode, SQL Mail will send e-mail messages immediately when they are generated, whether or not the Outlook client is running. For some reason, when configured for Internet Only mode, the mail messages go into limbo and are not sent unless the Outlook 2000 client is running, is online to the mail server, and is configured to automatically send and receive mail on a schedule (for example, every 2 minutes). I have found similar behavior using the Outlook XP mail client when it is configured with only Internet mail accounts.

NOTE

To verify that SQL Mail will be able to successfully establish a connection to a POP3 mail server, you must be able to repeatedly connect and send mail, using the following steps:

1. Start the mail client.
2. Send an e-mail message through the configured POP3 mail server, specifying a recipient's e-mail address and message.
3. Exit the mail client.
4. Repeat steps 1–3 several times to simulate expected e-mail traffic from SQL Mail.

If at any point while you are testing the e-mail client any dialog boxes appear that require a response, such as clicking OK to log on or a password prompt, then the e-mail user profile will not work with SQL Mail. For an Internet mail connection to work with SQL Mail, you must have 100% connectivity without user input. The reason for this is that SQL Mail cannot prompt for information and does not provide for retries when accessing a POP3 account. If SQL Mail cannot connect to the POP3 server on the first attempt, the Internet Mail connector normally opens a dialog box that prompts you to click OK to retry. If that should occur, SQL Mail, which is running as part of the SQL Server service, cannot see the dialog box and stops responding. You might have to use Task Manager to stop the Mapisp32.exe application or even restart the server to clear the problem.

---

5. Open the Mail Control Panel and click Show Profiles to find the name of the profile that was created when you set up the mail client. If the profile name is longer than 32 characters or contains unusual characters (periods, hyphens, pound signs, and so forth), change the profile name to be less than 32 characters and remove the unusual characters. (Spaces are okay.)
6. Configure SQL Mail and SQLAgentMail to use this mail profile name. More details on setting up SQLMail and SQLAgentMail are presented in the "Configuring SQL Mail" and "Configuring SQLAgentMail" sections later in this chapter.

   As with setting up SQL Mail with Exchange, if no profiles appear in the drop-down list box, SQL Server or SQL Server Agent was probably started under the Local System account.

NOTE

Using SQL Mail with a Lotus Notes server is not a configuration that Microsoft currently supports. However, I realize that many of you might be working in an environment where Lotus Notes is the default mail system. You might not have an Exchange Server or POP3 Server available, but you would still like to send e-mail notifications from SQL Server Agent.

I have been able to successfully configure Outlook 2000 with a Lotus Notes transport provider at one of my client sites that appears to be working successfully. However, because this is not a supported configuration, I cannot make guarantees that it will work successfully for everyone. I'm no Lotus Notes expert, but I was able to get it to work simply through trial and error. I'm providing the solution that worked for me here in the hopes that some of you might be able to make it work as well.

To set up SQL Mail with a Lotus Notes Server, do the following:

1. Create an account in Lotus Notes for the user account that will be used by SQL Mail.
2. On the SQL Server machine, log on using the same user account that is to be used as the startup account for SQL Server and SQL Server Agent.
3. Install the Outlook 2000 e-mail client.
4. Install the Lotus Notes client software. (Note: If you choose to use integrated security between Notes and Windows NT/2000, be sure you set up your Notes password to be the same as the domain user password.)
5. Configure the Lotus Notes client to connect to the Notes server. Verify that it works to send and receive mail from the Lotus Notes server.
6. Open the Mail Control Panel and click Show Profiles. Create a new e-mail profile and add a new e-mail account specifying Lotus Notes Mail as the server type. Provide a name for this profile that is 32 characters or less and contains no unusual characters (periods, hyphens, pound signs, and so forth).
7. Start up the Outlook 2000 mail client.
8. Set up contacts in the Contacts folder by creating e-mail usernames that map to Lotus Notes e-mail addresses. (SQL Mail cannot handle a Lotus Notes address directly, but it can send to an entry in the Outlook Address Book.) To be able to use the Contact names that you set up, right-click on the Contacts folder and choose Properties to bring up the Properties dialog. On the Outlook Address Book tab, make sure the Show This Folder as an E-Mail Address Book option is checked. When it comes time to specify an e-mail name for an operator (this is covered in the "Configuring SQL Mail" section later in this chapter), choose a name from the Outlook Contacts Address book, not from the Lotus Notes Address book. (It can help to set up Outlook to use the Contacts address list first so it shows up in the list first instead of the Lotus Notes address book.)

9. Verify that you can send e-mail messages to the Lotus Notes recipients you have set up in Outlook 2000. The easiest way to test is to send an e-mail to the user account that you have set up for SQL Mail to use to send and receive Lotus Notes mail.

   If you are prompted at any point for a password to connect to the Lotus Notes server, then you likely installed and configured to the Notes client without using integrated security. This is fine, but SQL Mail will not work if it is prompted for a password. I have found that it seems to work okay if you start up the Outlook 2000 client first and get it connected to the Lotus Notes server and enter the password when prompted. If you leave the Outlook 2000 client running, it appears to keep the connection to Lotus Notes open and no additional password is required for SQL Mail to connect.

10. Configure SQL Mail and SQLAgentMail to use the mail profile name you have set up in the preceding steps. (More details on setting up SQLMail and SQLAgentMail are presented later in this chapter.)

What's Next

After you have set up the mail profile and tested and confirmed that it works properly, the next phase is to set up SQL Server and SQL Agent to use the new mail profile.

Configuring SQL Mail

SQL Mail is the vehicle by which special stored procedures within SQL Server can interact with MAPI systems. For these procedures to run correctly, you must link a mail profile set up for SQL Mail with the SQL Mail service. This is done by opening the Support Services folder under the server in Enterprise Manager, right-clicking on the SQL Mail item, and choosing the Properties option. This brings up the SQL Mail Properties dialog box where you can choose the mail profile you want SQL Mail to use (see Figure 23.2). This list should include the mail profile setup for the SQL Server user account, as described in the previous section.

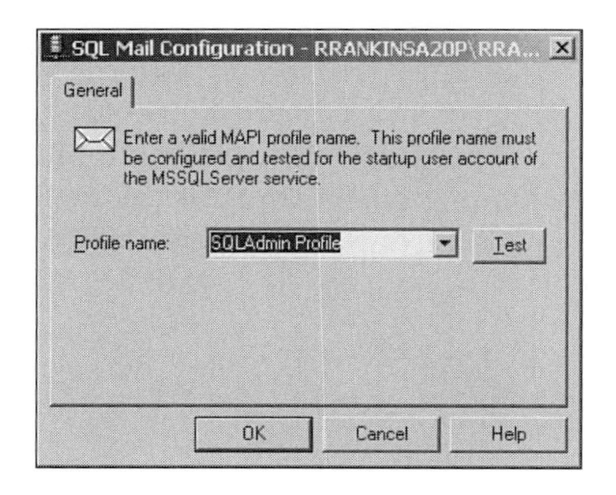

FIGURE 23.2 Choosing the mail profile for SQL Mail in the SQL Mail Properties dialog box.

Alternatively, you can set up the mail profile for SQL Mail on the Server Settings tab of the Server Properties dialog box, as shown in Figure 23.3.

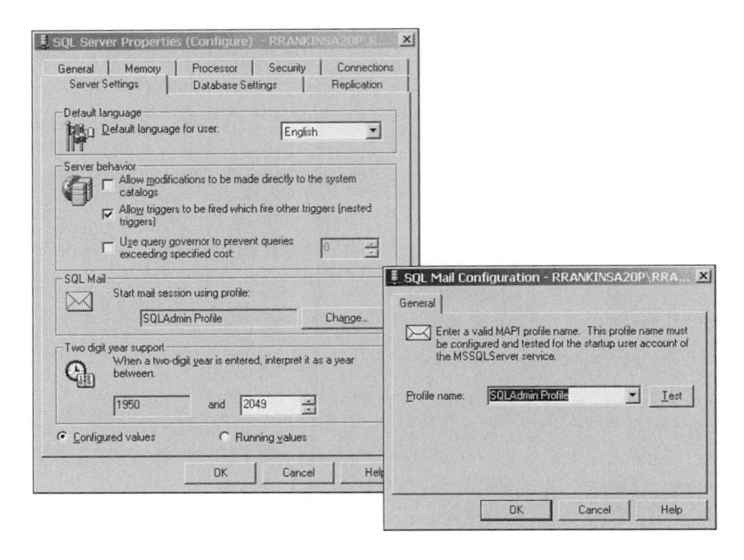

FIGURE 23.3 Invoking the SQL Mail Properties dialog box from the Server Settings tab of the Server Properties dialog box.

After choosing the appropriate mail profile, it is helpful to click on the Test button to ensure that SQL Server can initiate a mail session using the supplied mail profile.

Autostarting SQL Mail

In previous versions of SQL Server, an option on the SQL Mail Service Configuration dialog box was available to autostart SQL Mail on SQL Server startup. That option has disappeared in SQL Server 2000 because SQL Mail will automatically start when you execute the `xp_sendmail` stored procedure. Use of the `xp_sendmail` stored procedure is covered later in this chapter in the "SQL Mail Stored Procedures" section.

If you have problems with SQL Mail not starting automatically, or you prefer to have SQL Mail start during SQL Server startup, you have to create a startup stored procedure that invokes the `xp_startmail` stored procedure. (For more information on creating startup procedures, see Chapter 28, "Creating and Managing Stored Procedures in SQL Server.") Listing 23.1 provides a sample startup procedure to start SQL Mail automatically.

LISTING 23.1 Sample Startup Procedure to Start SQL Mail Automatically on SQL Server Startup

```
use master
go

create proc sp_SSU_startmail
as
declare @rval int
exec @rval = xp_startmail
if @rval = 1
   print 'Unable to start SQL Mail'
else
   print 'SQL Mail started'
go

-- set the procedure option to run at SQL Server startup
exec sp_procoption sp_SSU_startmail, 'startup', 'true'
```


NOTE

In versions of SQL Server 2000 prior to Service Pack 2, there were some SQL Mail issues related to MAPI profile handling that resulted in overall performance, thread safety, and memory leak issues. At times, the MAPI application would hang, sometimes requiring a reboot of the machine to clear the problem and allow SQLMail to resume sending messages. According to Microsoft Knowledge Base Article Q300414, these bugs have been identified and addressed in Service Pack 2.

If you are using a version of SQL Server 2000 prior to Service Pack 2, you can minimize some of the memory leaks by starting SQL Mail once using the xp_startmail procedure and leave it running for the life of the SQL Server process, rather than stopping and starting SQL Mail repeatedly. Stopping and starting SQL Mail causes the connect and disconnect code for MAPI to run repeatedly, increasing the chances of a memory leak and stability problems.

If you are unable to upgrade SQL Server 2000 to Service Pack 2, you might want to implement the startup procedure shown in Listing 23.1 as a work-around until you are able to apply the SP2 fix.

Configuring SQLAgentMail

Another way to allow e-mail messaging and alerts is through SQL Server Agent. SQL Server Agent allows you to set up alerts to notify users or operators via e-mail, pager, or a Net Send message when certain events are triggered, or it can send messages to report job or job step status. The mail profile used for SQL Agent will typically be the same mail profile used for SQL Mail, but it could be a different mail profile if a different e-mail configuration was needed.

You can set up different mail profiles for SQL Server and SQL Server Agent in two ways. You can either set up separate domain user accounts for each service and configure a mail profile for each user account, or you can use the same domain account for each service and create two different mail profiles.

To specify the mail profile to be used by SQLAgentMail, open up the Management folder in SQL Enterprise Manager, right-click on SQL Server Agent, and choose the Properties option. In the Mail Session section of the General tab, specify the mail profile you want SQL Server Agent to use (see Figure 23.4). After the profile is chosen, click on the Test button to ensure that SQL Server Agent can initial a mail session using the specified mail profile. In addition, you might want to check the option to have SQLAgentMail record all messages sent in the Sent folder of the e-mail client so you'll have a record of e-mail messages sent by SQL Server Agent.

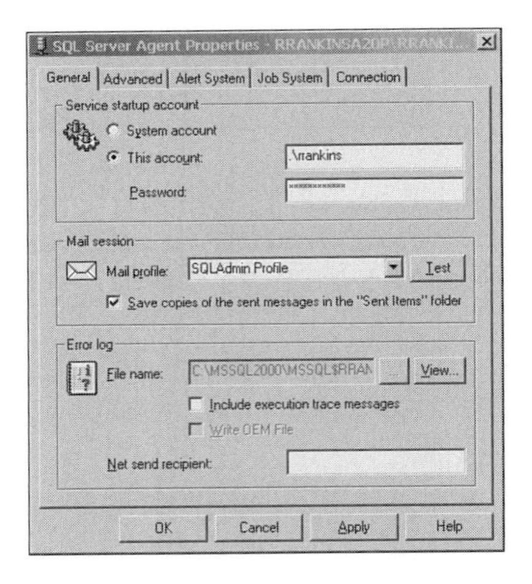

FIGURE 23.4 Specifying the mail profile to be used by SQLAgentMail in the SQL Server Agent Properties dialog box.

Setting Up Mail Notification for Operators in SQL Server Agent

You can configure SQL Server Agent to send e-mail notifications for either of the following events:

- When an alert is triggered
- When you want to report completion status of a job

Before you can send an e-mail for either of these events, you need to set up the e-mail account(s) for the operators you will be notifying. Click on the Operators item in the SQL Server Agent folder in SQL Enterprise Manager to bring up a list of the configured operators.

(For more information on defining SQL Server Agent operators, see Chapter 18, "SQL Server Scheduling and Notification.") In the Operators dialog box, you can enter the e-mail information for the operator, as shown in Figure 23.5.

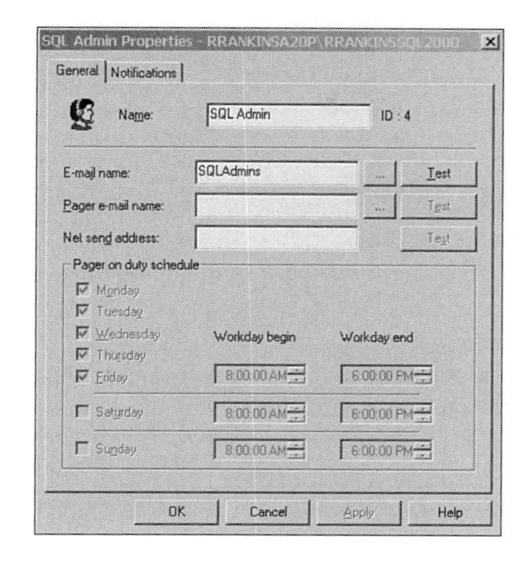

FIGURE 23.5 Specifying the e-mail addresses for an operator in the Operator Properties dialog box.

You can choose to notify the operator via standard e-mail, pager notification, or Network Send message. You can enter the e-mail address directly or, if you've set up e-mail addresses in the e-mail client address book, you can click on the Ellipsis button (...) to bring up the e-mail client address book and choose the recipient e-mail address, as shown in Figure 23.6.

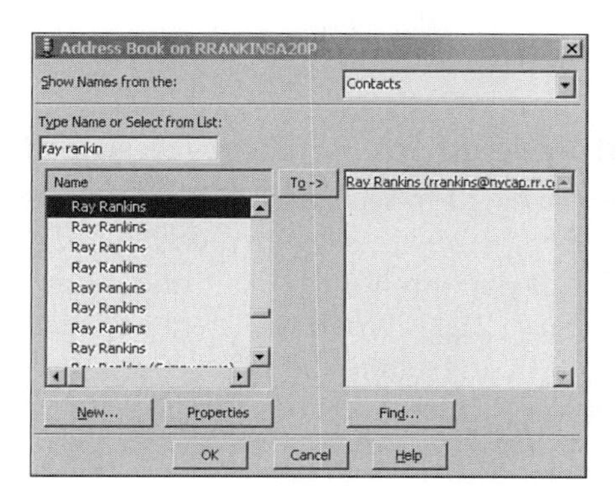

FIGURE 23.6 Choosing the e-mail addresses for an operator from the Outlook 2000 Address Book.

NOTE

If you are running Enterprise Manager from a client workstation and not the server where SQL Server is running, the address book displayed will be the local address book on the client workstation. SQL Server will not be able to send e-mail to entries from the local client's address book. Do not choose recipient addresses from an address book unless you are configuring SQL Mail on the server machine.

TIP

The e-mail address you choose can be an individual's e-mail address or a distribution list. Using a distribution list makes it easier to send e-mails to multiple operators or to multiple e-mail addresses for a single operator. You can create a single operator in SQL Server Agent and link it to a distribution list. To change the operators to be notified, you only need to change the members of the distribution list; you do not have to add or remove and configure individual e-mail addresses for operators in SQL Server Agent.

If your e-mail server software supports sending messages to a pager, you can enter the e-mail address for pager notification in the Pager e-mail name box. Typically, you will need to install a pager transport provider for your e-mail server so that it has the ability to dial a pager directly when an e-mail is sent to a pager e-mail address.

If you are using a POP3 server to send e-mails, you might still be able to send pager notifications. Many pager vendors today support sending pages by sending an e-mail to an Internet address. The pager vendor's e-mail system will receive the e-mail and forward it to the associated pager. The e-mail address usually includes the pager number and the domain name of the pager vendor. For example, for many pager vendors, the e-mail address is of the format *pagernumber@pagerdomain.net*. Check with your pager vendor for the specific e-mail address format, the message type (alphanumeric or numeric only), and size it supports.

Setting Up Mail Notification for SQL Server Agent Alerts

You can configure SQL Server Agent to send e-mail messages to specified SQL Server operators when specific alert events are generated. When configuring alerts, you have the opportunity to select a type of response for this alert under the Response tab of the Alert Properties dialog box (see Figure 23.7). When this alert is triggered, a message is sent to the designated operator(s), with any additional instructions or messages specified in the Additional Notification Message to Send text box.

If you have to set up a number of alert notifications for a new operator, it can be tedious to go through each alert individually to add the notification for the operator. Fortunately, an easier method exists. You can bring up the Properties dialog box for the operator and click on the Notifications tab. Doing so brings up a dialog box that lists all defined alerts and lets you check off which ones you want to have send an e-mail, pager, or Net Send notification to the operator (see Figure 23.8).

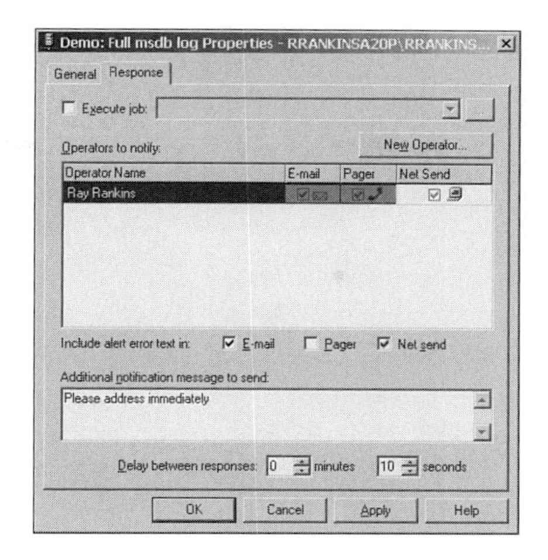

FIGURE 23.7 Setting up operator notification for an alert in the Alert Properties dialog box.

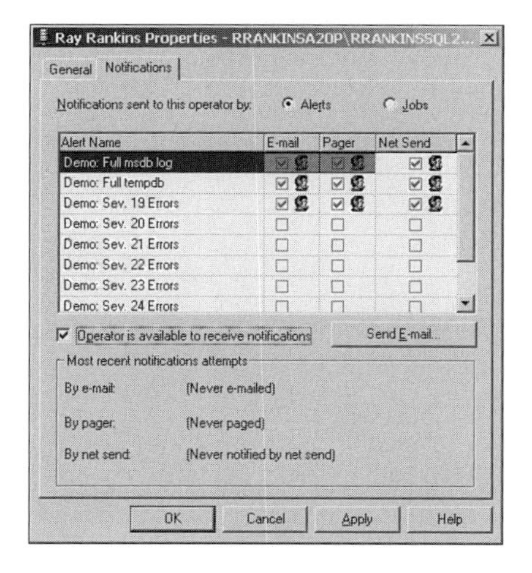

FIGURE 23.8 Specifying which alerts send notification to an operator in the Operator Properties dialog box.

In this dialog box, you can also turn off notification of the operator temporarily by unchecking the Operator Is Available to Receive Notifications check box. This option lets you suspend sending of notifications without having to clear out all the notification selections. You can also click on the Send E-mail button to send an e-mail message to the operator to inform him of what types of events he will be notified and what the pager notification schedule is. A sample of the text of this message is shown in Listing 23.2.

LISTING 23.2 Sample SQL Server Alert and Job Notifications Message

```
The following alerts have been assigned to operator 'Ray Rankins':

[Via E-mail]  Demo: Full msdb log
[Via E-mail]  Demo: Full tempdb
[Via E-mail]  Demo: Sev. 19 Errors
[Via Pager]  Demo: Full msdb log
[Via Pager]  Demo: Full tempdb
[Via Pager]  Demo: Sev. 19 Errors
[Via Net Send]  Demo: Full msdb log
[Via Net Send]  Demo: Full tempdb
[Via Net Send]  Demo: Sev. 19 Errors

The pager schedule for operator 'Ray Rankins' is as follows:

Monday  -  08:00  to  18:00
Tuesday  -  08:00  to  18:00
Wednesday  -  08:00  to  18:00
Thursday  -  08:00  to  18:00
Friday  -  08:00  to  18:00
Saturday  -  08:00  to  18:00
Sunday  -  08:00  to  18:00


Jobs that send notifications to this operator:

DB Backup Job for DB Maintenance Plan 'DB Maintenance Plan1'
 - By e-mail (Upon failure)
Optimizations Job for DB Maintenance Plan 'DB Maintenance Plan1'
 - By e-mail (Upon failure)
```

Setting Up Mail Notification for SQL Server Agent Jobs

SQL Server Agent jobs can specify e-mail notifications as well on job completion. You can specify whether to send the notification on job success, failure, or simply on job completion regardless of success or failure.

To set up notification for a job, right-click a predefined job, select Properties, and then select the Notifications tab (see Figure 23.9).

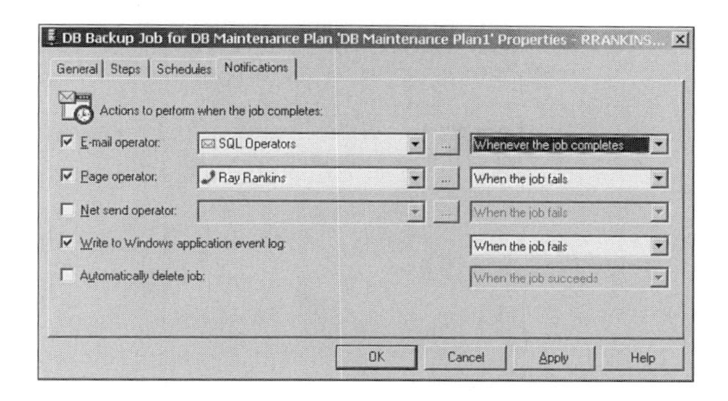

FIGURE 23.9 Specifying job notification settings in the Job Properties dialog box.

In this example, the job will send an e-mail to the SQL Operators operator on job completion, and send a page to the operator Ray Rankins on job failure. Both of these are previously defined operators with valid e-mail addresses.

NOTE

Actually, the e-mail address for the SQL Operators operator in the previous example is a distribution group rather than an individual e-mail message. The current SQL Server job architecture does not provide the ability to send e-mail notification to more than one operator on job completion. The only way to notify multiple operators is to set up a generic operator whose e-mail address is a distribution group that contains all the persons who need to be notified of job success or failure.

In the Operator Properties dialog box, you can also see which jobs an operator is configured to receive notifications for by clicking on the Notifications tab and then clicking on the Jobs option (see Figure 23.10). However, you cannot configure the job notification settings through this dialog box—that can only be done in the Notifications tab of the Job Properties dialog box. If you need to change the operator to be notified for a number of jobs, you have to manually edit each job individually to change the notification information.

SQL Mail Stored Procedures

SQL Server 2000 provides built-in stored procedures and extended stored procedures that you can use to process e-mail messages received in a predefined SQL Mail account mailbox or to send e-mail messages from within your own SQL code. The following sections describe the stored procedures (with their corresponding syntax) that can be run individually or executed within the instructions of another stored procedure.

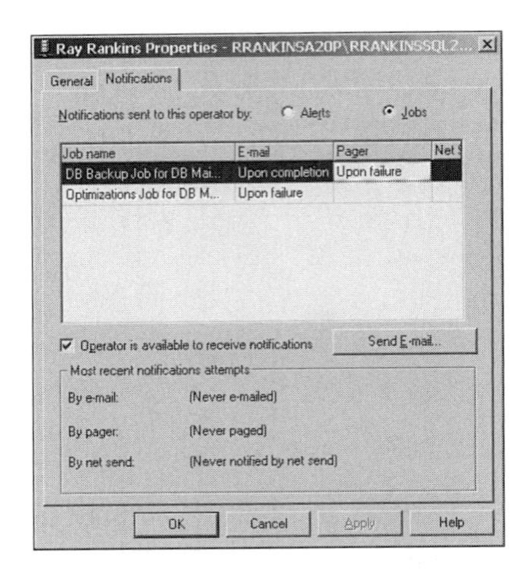

FIGURE 23.10 Viewing job notification settings for an operator in the Operator Properties dialog box.

xp_startmail

You use the `xp_startmail` procedure to start a mail client session. This procedure should be executed first to ensure that a SQL Mail session is running. The syntax for `xp_startmail` is as follows:

```
xp_startmail [@user = 'username'], [@password = 'password']
```

'username' is optional; when it's specified, the SQL Server attempts to log on to the MAPI provider using this name.

'password' is optional; when specified, it's used as the password for the *'username'*.

'username' and *'password'* are both optional parameters defined with the sysname datatype and no default value. If these arguments are not provided, SQL Server will use the default mail profile associated with SQL Mail.

> **NOTE**
>
> `sysname` is a SQL Server-supplied, user-defined datatype. It is used for table columns, variables, and stored procedure parameters that store object names.

Permission to execute `xp_startmail` defaults to members of the `sysadmin` fixed server role, but can be granted to any SQL Server user. Only one mail session can be active at a time; however, after a SQL Mail session is started, all users can use the same mail session. If an existing mail session is already active, `xp_startmail` will not start a new one and will return a message indicating that it is already running, as shown in the following example:

```
declare @rval int
exec @rval = xp_startmail --'Outlook'
select @rval as rval
go

SQL Mail session is already started.
rval
-----------
          1
```

You can use xp_stopmail to stop the current mail session.

xp_stopmail

You use the xp_stopmail procedure to stop the current mail client session. The syntax is simple:

```
xp_stopmail
```

Permission to execute xp_stopmail defaults to members of the sysadmin fixed server role, but can be granted to any SQL Server user.

xp_sendmail

The xp_sendmail stored procedure is used to send messages or query result sets to specified mail recipients. When invoking xp_sendmail, only the @recipients parameter is required; all other parameters are optional. To specify subsequent parameters, you will have to specify the parameters by name if you want to skip any. The full syntax for xp_sendmail is as follows:

```
xp_sendmail @recipients = 'recipients [;...n]'
,[@message = 'message']
,[@query = 'query']
,[@attachments = attachments]
,[@copy_recipients = 'copy_recipients [;...n]]'
,[@blind_copy_recipients = 'blind_copy_recipients [;...n]]'
,[@subject = 'subject']
,[@type = type]
,[@attach_results = 'attach_value']
,[@no_output = 'output_value']
,[@no_header = 'header_value']
,[@width = width]
,[@separator = separator]
,[@echo_error = 'echo_value']
,[@set_user = user]
,[@dbuse = database]
```

Table 23.1 describes each element of the syntax.

TABLE 23.1 `xp_sendmail` Parameters

Parameter Name	Description
`@recipients = 'recipients [;...n]'`	This is the list of e-mail recipients separated by semicolons.
`[@message = 'message']`	This is the message to be sent, which can be up to 8000 bytes in size.
`[@query = 'query']`	This will send the specified T-SQL query result set, up to 8000 bytes. The result set of the query will be sent in the mail body. Because the query is being submitted by an external program and not the connection that issues the `xp_sendmail` command, bound connections are used to prevent blocking from occurring between the `xp_sendmail` DLL and the client that issued the `xp_sendmail` command.
`[@attachments = attachments]`	This specifies the filename for an attachment. The file, which can reside on a local or network share, must be accessible to the user account under which SQL Server is running.
`[@copy_recipients = 'copy_recipients[;...n]]'`	This is the list of "copy to" recipients, separated by semi-colons. This is what would appear in the Cc: box of a mail message dialog box.
`[@blind_copy_recipients = 'blind_copy_recipients [;...n]]'`	This is a list of recipients, separated by semicolons, who are to receive a blind copy. This list would appear in the Bcc: section of a mail message dialog box.
`[@subject = 'subject']`	This is where you provide a subject line for the message.
`[@type = type]`	This is the input message type. The default is `NULL`. This is a fairly esoteric setting that for most uses is left `NULL`. For more information, investigate SQL Mail in the Windows NT Resource Kit.
`[@attach_results = 'attach_value']`	The default setting for this is `False`, which will cause a query result set to be included in the message body. A `True` value will cause the query result to be sent as an attachment.
`[@no_output = 'output_value']`	If set to `True`, this option will send the mail but not out-put anything to the client session. The default is `False`.
`[@no_header = 'header_value']`	If set to `True`, this option does not send the column header information with the query result set; it sends only the data rows. The default is `False`.
`[@width = width]`	This parameter is the same as the `/w` parameter in the ISQL utility. It indicates the output width for a query result set. The default is 80 characters—anything longer than 80 characters will wrap to the next line. Use a larger width to send a wide result set without line breaks inside the output lines.

TABLE 23.1 Continued

Parameter Name	Description
`[@separator = separator]`	Here, you specify a configurable column separator for the result set. Tabs are the default separator, but using a comma here with the `@attach_results` option will produce a comma-delimited file.
`[@echo_error = 'echo_value']`	Setting this option to `True` will cause server messages and d-Library errors to be appended to the message rather than written to the SQL Server error log. In addition, a count of the rows affected by the query is appended to the mail message. Setting this option to `True` causes the `xp_sendmail` stored procedure to always return a success status (`0`) if the mail is successfully sent, regardless of any errors encountered by the query.
`[@set_user = user]`	This is the security context for the query. This allows a query to be run under a different security context from the session initiating the `xp_sendmail` command. The default user context is that of the user executing `xp_sendmail`.
`[@dbuse = database]`	This is the database name from which the query should be run. If it is not specified, the database context will be the user's default database.

Only one user at a time can send an e-mail through the active SQL Mail session. Other users who are sending mail messages at the same time will wait in a queue until the previous user's mail message has been sent.

Permission to execute `xp_sendmail` defaults to members of the `sysadmin` fixed server role, but can be granted to any SQL Server user.

The following example sends an e-mail message to the SQL Operators distribution list with the output from `sp_who2` as an attachment, setting the width of the query output to 255 bytes:

```
exec master..xp_sendmail 'SQL Operators',
    'The attached file shows all current user activity on the server',
    'exec sp_who2',
    @subject = 'Current User Activity',
    @width = 255,
    @attach_results = 'True'
```

NOTE

While the SQL Mail stored procedures can be used to provide useful e-mail capabilities within your database applications and SQL code (for example, `xp_sendmail` can be used to automatically send the results of a report to a recipient list), a new feature is available for SQL Server 2000 to provide a means of forwarding messages and information to end users. This feature is called SQL Server Notification Services. SQL Server Notification Services is a platform for the development and deployment of notification applications. Notification applications send messages to users based upon subscriptions made to the notification application. Depending on how the subscriptions are configured, messages can be sent to the subscriber immediately or on a predetermined schedule.

For more information on setting up and using SQL Server Notification Services, see Chapter 45, "SQL Server Notification Services."

xp_findnextmsg

The `xp_findnextmsg` procedure is used to find the next message to be read from the mail profile's Inbox. It returns the message ID as an output parameter or a result row. The syntax is as follows:

```
xp_findnextmsg [@msg_id = 'message_number' [OUTPUT]]
,[@type = type]
,[@unread_only = 'unread_value']
```

The following paragraphs describe the elements of the syntax:

```
[@msg_id = 'message_number' [OUTPUT]]
```

This is the number of the message, returned as a `varchar(255)`. When the `OUTPUT` clause is used, the message number is placed in this parameter. Otherwise, it is returned as a result set.

```
[@type = type]
```

This is the MAPI mail type. The default is `NULL`.

```
[@unread_only = 'unread_value']
```

When this is set to `True`, only unread messages are processed by the stored procedure. The default is `False`.

The following is an example that returns the message ID of the next unread message in the Inbox:

```
exec xp_findnextmsg @unread_only = 'true'
go
```

```
Message ID
-----------------------------------------------------------------------------
0xE4D12200
```

xp_readmail

The xp_readmail procedure reads a mail message from the SQL Server Inbox. You can use xp_readmail to return the contents of the Inbox as a result set to the client or to read a single message from the Inbox. The syntax for xp_readmail is as follows:

```
xp_readmail [@msg_id = 'message_number']
,[ @type = 'type' [OUTPUT]]
,[@peek = 'peek']
,[@suppress_attach = 'suppress_attach']
,[@originator = 'sender' OUTPUT]
,[@subject = 'subject' OUTPUT]
,[@message = 'message' OUTPUT]
,[@recipients = 'recipients [;...n]' OUTPUT]
,[@cc_list = 'copy_recipients [;...n]' OUTPUT]
,[@bcc_list = 'blind_copy_recipients [;...n]' OUTPUT]
,[@date_received = 'date' OUTPUT]
,[@unread = 'unread_value' OUTPUT]
,[@attachments = 'attachments [;...n]' OUTPUT]
,[@skip_bytes = bytes_to_skip OUTPUT]
,[@msg_length = length_in_bytes OUTPUT]
,[@originator_address = 'sender_address' OUTPUT]
```

When the OUTPUT keyword is specified for one or more of the xp_readmail parameters, the resulting value is returned to this parameter.

Table 23.2 describe each element of the syntax:

TABLE 23.2 xp_readmail Parameters

Parameter Name	Description
[@msg_id = '*message_number*']	This is a varchar (255) string indicating the message number to be read.
[@type = '*type*' [OUTPUT]]	This is a message type; the default is NULL. This is a fairly esoteric setting that for most uses is left NULL. For more information, investigate SQL Mail in the Windows NT Resource Kit.
[@peek = '*peek*']	This parameter, when set to False, causes the message to be marked as read in the mail Inbox. A True value causes the message to remain marked as unread.

TABLE 23.2 Continued

Parameter Name	Description
[@suppress_attach = '*suppress_attach*']	If this parameter is set to True, message attachments are suppressed, and no temporary files are created.
[@originator = '*sender*' OUTPUT]	This returns the mail address of the message sender as a varchar(255).
[@subject = '*subject*' OUTPUT]	This returns the subject of the message as a varchar(255).
[@message = '*message*' OUTPUT]	This returns the actual text of the message as a text parameter.
[@recipients = '*recipients* [;...*n*]' OUTPUT]	This returns a list of recipients separated by semicolons as a varchar(255).
[@cc_list = 'copy_recipients [;...n]' OUTPUT]	This returns a list of copied recipients separated by semicolons as a varchar(255).
[@bcc_list = 'blind_copy_recipients [;...n]' OUTPUT]	This returns a list of blind-copied recipients separated by semicolons as a varchar(255).
[@date_received = '*date*' OUTPUT]	This returns the date the mail message was received.
[@unread = '*unread_value*' OUTPUT]	This returns True if the message was previously unread.
[@attachments = '*attachments* [;...*n*]' OUTPUT]	This returns a semicolon-separated list of the tempo rary paths of the attachments as a varchar(255).
[@skip_bytes = *bytes_to_skip* OUTPUT]	This parameter indicates the number of bytes to skip before reading the next 255 bytes of a message. It returns the next starting point within the message as an int.
[@msg_length = *length_in_bytes* OUTPUT]	This returns the total length, in bytes, of the message. Using this parameter with the bytes_to_skip output parameter in a stored procedure allows a message to be read in chunks of 255 bytes.
[@originator_address = '*sender_address*' OUTPUT]	This returns the resolved mail address of the message sender as a varchar(255).

To return the entire contents of the Inbox as a result set to the client, either set message_number to NULL or do not include the message_number parameter. If you want to limit the messages returned, the @msg_id can be used to read specific messages. You can also specify the @peek and @suppress_attach as input parameters to control how the message is read.

If using xp_readmail without specifying @msg_id to return the Inbox contents, xp_readmail returns a result set containing the mail messages (older messages appear first) with the columns, as shown in Table 23.3.

TABLE 23.3 `xp_readmail` Result Columns

Column Name	Description
Originator	The sender of the e-mail message
Date Received	The date the e-mail message was received
Recipients	The people to whom the message was sent
Cc List	The people on the Cc line of the e-mail message
Bcc List	The people on the Bcc line of the e-mail message
Subject	The subject line of the e-mail message
Message	The message body (text)
Unread	The read/unread status of the message
Attachments	Any attachments for the message
Message ID	The message ID
Type	The message type

To read a single message from the Inbox, you need to supply a valid message number as an input parameter to `xp_readmail`. You can obtain the message number using the `xp_findnextmsg` procedure. When reading a single message, you can use the output parameters to return the specified information about the message into local variables, as shown in the following example:

```
declare @msg varchar(8000),
        @msgid varchar(255),
        @subject varchar(255),
        @sender varchar(255)
exec xp_findnextmsg @unread_only = 'true', @msg_id = @msgid output
if @msgid is NOT NULL -- make sure we have a message to read
begin
    exec xp_readmail @msgid, @peek = 'True',
                     @subject = @subject output,
                     @originator = @sender output,
                     @message = @msg output
    print 'Subject:  ' + @subject
    print 'Sent By:  ' + @sender
    print '-----------------------------'
    print 'Message:  ' + @msg
end
go

Subject:  Microsoft SQL Server Alert System Test
Sent By:  Ray Rankins
-----------------------------
Message:  Microsoft SQLServerAgent test notification - please ignore.
```

xp_deletemail

The xp_deletemail procedure deletes the specified message from the SQL Server Inbox. The syntax is as follows:

```
xp_deletemail 'message_number'
```

'message_number' is the number, specified as varchar(255), of the message that is to be deleted.

sp_processmail

The sp_processmail procedure invokes the extended-stored procedures xp_findnextmsg, xp_readmail, and xp_deletemail to read and process incoming mail messages that are expected to contain a SQL query. The messages are read from the Inbox of the mail profile configured for SQL Server. Any result sets generated by the queries processed are sent back to the message sender using xp_sendmail. Typically, you will set up sp_processmail in a regularly scheduled job to periodically check for mail received in the SQL Mail Inbox.

The syntax is as follows:

```
sp_processmail [@subject = 'subject'],
        [@filetype = 'filetype'],
        [@separator = 'separator'],
        [@set_user = 'user'],
        [@dbuse = 'dbname']
```

Table 23.4 describes the parameters for the sp_processmail procedure.

TABLE 23.4 sp_processmail Parameters

[@subject =] *'subject'*	If you enter a subject line in this parameter, only messages with that subject line are processed. The default value of NULL indicates that all messages should be processed.
[@filetype = *'filetype'*]	This is the file extension, as a varchar(3) parameter, that will be used for the file attachment sent back containing the result set. The default is txt.
[@separator = *'separator'*]	This is the column separator to be used between each column in the result set. This is a varchar(3) parameter. The default separator is the tab character.
[@set_user = *'user'*]	This is the user context under which the query will be run. If not specified, the query will run in the current user context.
[@dbuse = *'dbname'*]	This specifies the name of the database where the query should be run. If not specified, the query will run in the current database context.

The following example uses one session to send an e-mail containing a query to the e-mail account used by SQL Mail, and the next session uses `sp_processmail` to read the e-mail, execute the query, and return the result set as an e-mail attachment to the originating e-mail account:

```
xp_sendmail 'SQLAdmin', 'exec sp_who2', @subject = 'Run This Query'
go

exec sp_processmail @subject = 'Run This Query'
go

Mail sent.
Queries processed: 1.
```


Summary

SQL Mail and the SQL Server Agent are tools that allow SQL users to integrate SQL Server with an existing mail service. One of the benefits of this integration is automatic notification of the status of certain jobs and alerts generated in SQL Server via e-mail, pager, or a Net Send message. By not having to monitor the system constantly to identify when scheduled jobs have failed or the system has run out of resources, administrators can devote more time to their users' needs. These tools, along with the other tools available in SQL Server 2000, help administrators maintain an efficient and dependable database system.

In addition, the mail stored procedures can be used to provide useful e-mail capabilities within your SQL code. For example, `xp_sendmail` can be used to automatically send the results of a report to a recipient list without having to save the results to a file manually and then manually insert or attach the file to an e-mail. For a more robust and customizable means of sending information or data to users, you may want to consider using SQL Server Notification Services, which is discussed in Chapter 45.

Admittedly, getting SQL Mail working can be troublesome at times. With the information presented in this chapter, you should be able to successfully configure SQL Mail and take advantage of the benefits it provides.

CHAPTER 24

SQL Server Clustering

by Paul Bertucci

IN THIS CHAPTER

- From Windows NT Enterprise Edition to Windows 2000 Advanced Server
- Cluster Services
- SQL Clustering and Fail-Over Support
- Network Load Balancing

You might be facing the need to gear up your environment into a truly enterprise-class computing platform. The question is whether Microsoft can support your needs. Windows 2000 Advanced Server (AS) has taken over the reigns from Windows NT 4.0 Enterprise Edition (NTSEE). Microsoft has also spun off other versions, such as Windows 2000 Datacenter that also leverages off of the former Windows NT 4.0 Enterprise Edition features.

When using Windows 2000 AS, you will be able to build SQL Server clustering within this architecture. This should launch you into a rigorous fault-tolerant and nonstop SQL computing environment.

Before you get into SQL clustering, you will need to understand what clustering is from the operating system point of view and then how SQL Server clustering works within this. The two are different, but heavily related.

Enterprise computing defines the entire set of technologies required to develop the mission-critical business applications of today's organizations. These technologies include the network operating systems, the application development environments, the database management systems, the servers, the desktops, and everything in between. When you think of enterprise development, you probably think of n-tier, distributed, and Web-based application development. Although these are certainly types of enterprise development, they are just pieces of a larger puzzle.

The following are the primary characteristics of an enterprise:

- Scalability—As organizations grow, so does the need for more computing power. The systems in place must enable an organization to leverage existing hardware and to quickly and easily add computing power as needs demand.
- Availability—As organizations rely more on information, it is more critical that the information is available at all times and under all circumstances. Downtime is not acceptable.
- Interoperability—As organizations grow and evolve, so do their information systems. It is impractical to think that an organization will not have many heterogeneous sources of information. The ability for applications to get to all the information, regardless of its location, is becoming increasingly important.
- Reliability—An organization is only as good as its data and information. It is critical that the systems that provide that information are bulletproof.

From Windows NT Enterprise Edition to Windows 2000 Advanced Server

You are probably familiar with the Windows NT Server family and now the Windows 2000 Server family. Just out is the new and improved Windows 2000 Advanced Server. Of course, Windows NT 4.0 Enterprise Edition is at the core of this new offering. It has been renamed, improved, and repackaged. You will likely experience an easy and painless migration into the Windows 2000 Server family offerings. These will form many of today's organizational computing infrastructures. In years past, many large organizations relied solely on Unix or on mainframe-based operating systems to provide their mission-critical application services. This was due in large part to the inherent scalability and reliability in both of those operating environments. Microsoft has recognized the need to provide the same level of performance, reliability, and scalability in its Windows 2000 Advanced Server product.

Both Windows 2000 AS and Windows 2000 Datacenter are based on the original Windows NT 4.0 Server Enterprise Edition engine with several enhancements and bundled services to provide the high availability, enhanced performance, and comprehensive services required in the largest enterprises. A couple significant performance features along with enhancements to server clusters and load balancing top the list:

- 8GB RAM main memory on Intel PAE systems—This enhancement enables Windows 2000 AS to address up to 8GB of RAM. The standard NT Server can only address up to 2GB of RAM per process. This addition can provide a major performance boost for applications' large databases on machines with more than 2GB of physical RAM.
- Eight-processor symmetric multiprocessor (SMP) support—Windows 2000 AS is licensed for use on up to eight-processor SMP servers.

- Enhanced two-node server clusters—These enable you to more affectively create and manage fault-tolerant/fail-over environments.
- Network (TCP/IP) load balancing—This provides another avenue for improving scalability.

In addition to these performance-enhancing features, Windows 2000 AS is bundled with several other services that are designed to enhance your ability to develop the large-scale distributed applications that are necessary within your enterprise. These other services are described in the following section.

Transaction Server

One of the primary characteristics of enterprise computing is scalability. This implies not only scalable computing power, but also scalable application development. As an organization grows, its need for rapid development and easy modification of mission-critical applications intensifies.

This need has resulted in an explosion of component-based distributed application development. This type of application development is commonly referred to as **n-tier application development**. It is characterized by the separation of business logic from presentation and data logic. By creating a set of independent, reusable components that can encapsulate an organization's business logic, you can create a scalable application development architecture. This type of architecture enables you to quickly bring new applications online and to change business logic without having to recompile and redistribute client applications. Chapter 43, "Microsoft Transaction Server," covers MTS and the features that make it the architecture of choice for developers.

Message Queue Server

Two other important characteristics of enterprise computing are availability and interoperability. An enterprise usually consists of many heterogeneous entities that must function together as a logical whole. For example, your enterprise might have both a Windows NT Server network and a legacy mainframe system. Likewise, you might have remote or disconnected users who need access to enterprise application resources. In any event, the enterprise systems must be available and interoperable.

The Message Queue Server (MSMQ) enables availability and interoperability by allowing applications to easily communicate with one another. You might be thinking, "Applications communicate with each other all the time, so why do I need MSMQ?" The answer is that MSMQ allows applications to communicate with one another asynchronously. In other words, an application can send a request to a receiving application and continue with another task even if the receiving application is unusable or disconnected from the network.

The MSMQ is based on a store-and-forward model. Applications send messages to MSMQ, and those messages are stored in queues. Each application involved in the communication sends messages to MSMQ and receives messages from MSMQ. MSMQ is effective in situations in which sending and receiving applications run at different times, or in which the cost of message loss or interruption is extremely high.

Cluster Services

Probably the most important feature of Windows 2000 AS—the one that truly makes it an enterprise-class operating system—is Microsoft Cluster Services (MSCS). This is the feature that provides the availability and reliability that your enterprise will demand.

Reliability and availability are two of the characteristics that are inherent in enterprise computing. When your systems are reliable and available, you are able to minimize downtime. It has been estimated that system downtime costs U.S. businesses as much as $4 billion annually. Clustering minimizes system downtime by allowing you to create systems that continue to run, even in the event of a system failure.

MSCS allows you to create a cluster of two computers, referred to as nodes, each running Windows 2000 AS and MSCS. These two computers will function as one logical server. All the client applications that access a clustered server see only one entity.

MSCS is capable of detecting hardware or software failures and automatically shifting control of the server to the healthy node. Not only do clusters provide the capability to fail-over due to hardware or software failure, but you can also manually switch control from one node to the other to perform routine maintenance or even replacement. Because the users are only aware of one server, they will never notice that a failure has occurred. Their applications will continue to be serviced without interruption. Figure 24.1 illustrates a typical two-node cluster configuration that share a disk (or a typical fiber channel alternate configuration). All devices must be SCSI devices or fiber channel and a separate domain user account must be set up prior to configuration to provide the access required by each node with each other.

If you choose to use fiber channel to connect to your cluster storage, you must be sure that the fiber channel adapter is on the Hardware Compatibility list. Microsoft is very picky here. Windows 2000 AS will be able to manage your fiber channel disks just like any other disk connection to a SCSI bus. In addition, the fiber channel controller ID is preconfigured with a unique ID which simplifies setup (you do not need to manually configure each cluster node with a separate ID). Fiber channel solutions also don't have bus termination issues that you might see in other shared SCSI clusters. The device bus between the switch/hub may be fiber or SCSI.

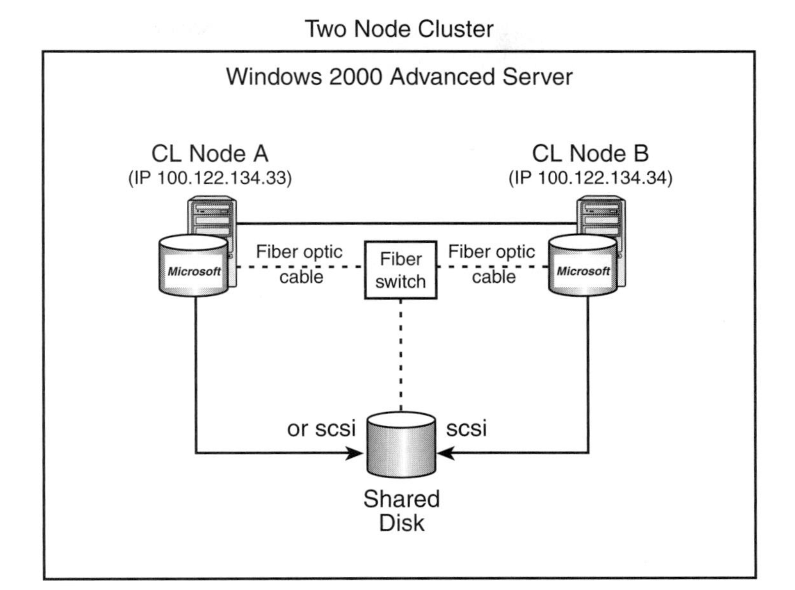

FIGURE 24.1 Two-node fail-over cluster.

Clustering should not be confused with fault tolerance. In a fault-tolerant solution, one server is generally kept idle and contains a mirror image of the primary server. The backup server is only utilized in case of a failure. In a clustering solution, both systems are active, meaning that each processor can service clients. When one node fails, the other node simply picks up the slack. Later, you will see how SQL Server 2000 can use a clustered server configuration to provide highly available and reliable database service to the enterprise. Figure 24.2 shows the Cluster Server Setup Wizard and a request to form a new cluster.

After the cluster has been set up and a domain user has been identified for access, the cluster disks that are to be shared must be identified to the cluster. Figure 24.3 shows multiple shared cluster disks.

It's important to understand the building blocks of the cluster before you add on the extra layer of SQL Server clustering.

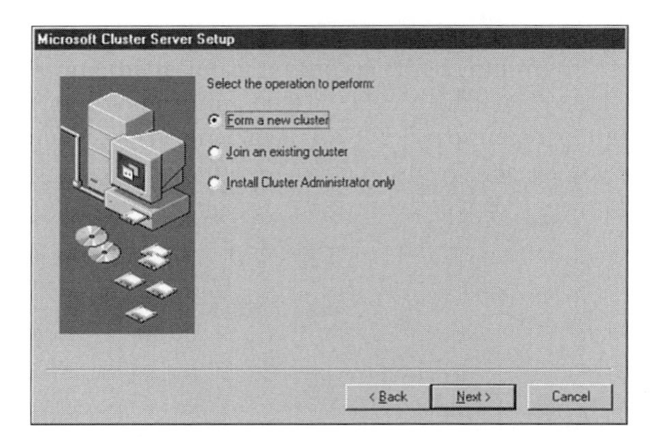

FIGURE 24.2 Cluster Setup Wizard: Form a new cluster.

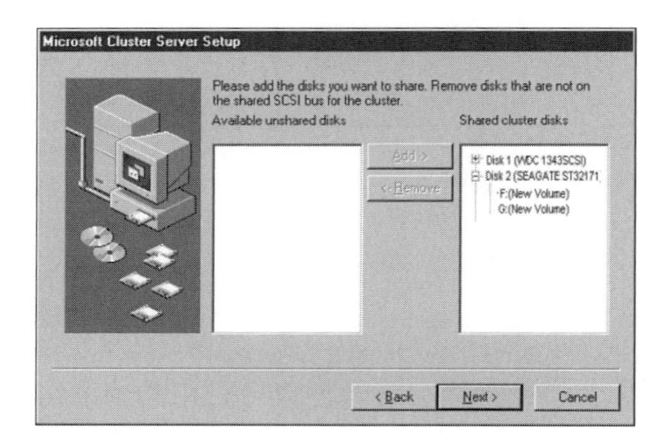

FIGURE 24.3 Shared cluster disks.

SQL Clustering and Fail-Over Support

By taking advantage of the clustering capabilities of Windows 2000 Advanced Server, SQL Server 2000 provides the high availability and reliability required of an enterprise class database management system. You can install up to 16 instances of Microsoft SQL Server 2000 in a Microsoft cluster service.

As alluded to before, SQL Server 2000 implements fail-over clustering based on the clustering features of the Microsoft Clustering Service in Windows NT 4.0 EE and Windows 2000 Advanced Server. The type of MSCS fail-over cluster used by SQL Server consists of multiple server computers. Windows 2000 would normally handle up to two servers, whereas Windows 2000 Datacenter can handle up to four servers. The fail-over cluster shares a common set of cluster resources (or cluster groups), such as clustered disk drives. You can install SQL Server on as many nodes as you want. This is only limited by the operating system limitations. Each server in the cluster is called a **node**. Each node must be connected to the network and be able to communicate with each other. In addition, each node must be running the same version of MSCS. Figure 24.4 shows a typical SQL Server clustering con-figuration for a two-node cluster. The cluster nodes are named CL Node A and CL Node B.

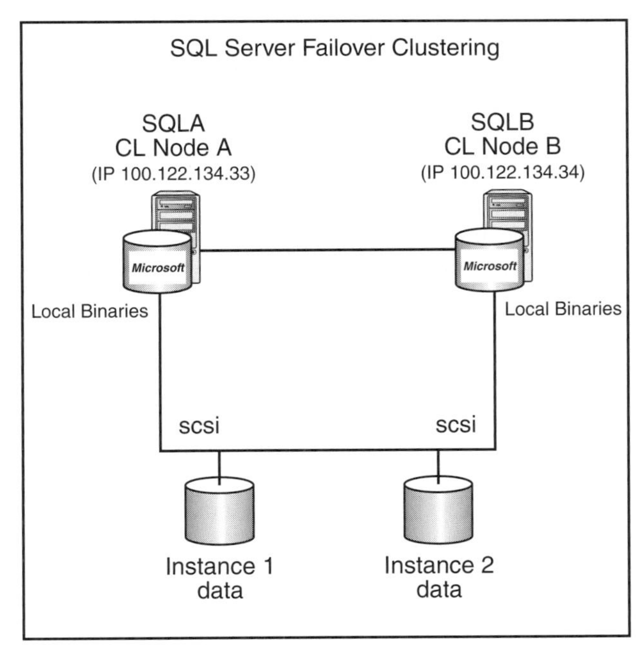

FIGURE 24.4 SQL Server fail-over clustering.

When you install SQL Server on a clustered server using SQL Server Setup, you create it as a virtual server. Figure 24.5 shows the SQL Server Setup dialog box where you will be able to specify the creation of a virtual server. You must first install it from one of the cluster servers (CL Node A, in this example). Figure 24.5 shows the virtual server option grayed-out because MSCS hasn't been installed properly on the server yet. Therefore, the first step in creating a SQL Server clustering configuration entails installing the MSCS feature. After MSCS has been installed and a cluster has been configured (as explained earlier), you can create a virtual server such as one named SQL A.

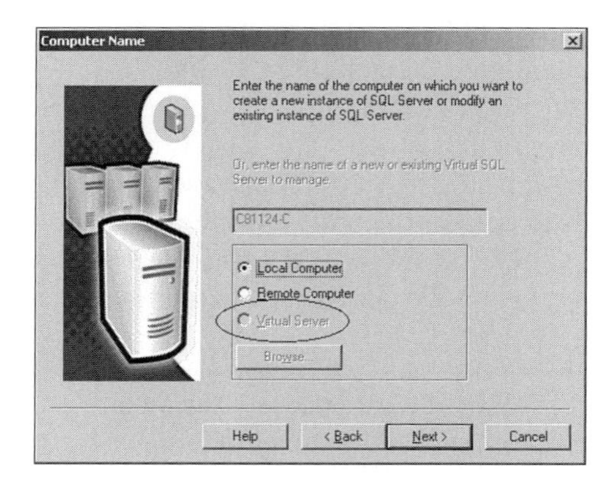

FIGURE 24.5 SQL Server Setup Wizard for virtual servers.

It is this virtual server that the client applications will see and to which they will connect. When an application attempts to connect to an instance of SQL Server 2000 that is running on a fail-over cluster, the application must specify both the virtual server name and the instance name, such as SQL B\Instance 1. The application does not have to specify an instance name if the instance associated with the virtual server is a default instance because it has no name. Additionally, you cannot access the SQL Server by specifying the machine name and instance name because the SQL Server is not listening on the IP address of the local server. It is listening on the clustered IP addresses created during the setup of a virtual server.

As part of the SQL Server setup, you will identify the nodes available to run this SQL Server. As shown in Figure 24.4, the nodes CL Node A and CL Node B will be able to run SQLA virtual server. This allows either of these nodes to take over in the event of a hardware or network failure. You will now create another virtual server from the other cluster server node of CL Node B named SQLB. SQLB will also be identified to run on both CL Node A and CL Node B.

This configuration yields two virtual servers running in the MSCS cluster consisting of CL Node A and CL Node B. Each virtual server resides in a different MSCS cluster group, and each has a different set of IP addresses, a distinct network name, and data files that reside on separate sets of shared cluster disks. In this example, these resources are identified as Instance 1 data and Instance 2 data.

Now, if a failure does occur, the MSCS automatically handles the fail-over process. In the event of a fail-over, any transactions in process at the time of the fail-over are rolled back, and the clients must reconnect to SQL Server.

Don't confuse fail-over support in a clustering scenario with a standby server. SQL Server 2000 supports the concept of a standby server using techniques, such as data replication or log shipping, which are covered in other chapters.

Heading Off Issues

Many potential issues can arise during setup and configuration. Following are some things for you to watch out for:

1. SQL Server service accounts and passwords should be kept the same on all nodes or the node will not be able to restart a SQL Server service.
2. Drive letters for the cluster disks must be the same on both node servers. Otherwise, you might not be able to access a clustered disk.
3. You must use Cluster Administrator in MSCS to automatically start a fail-over cluster.
4. You might have to create an alternative method to connect to SQL Server if the network name is offline and you cannot connect using TCP/IP. The method is to use Named Pipes specified as `\\.\pipe\$$\SQLA\sql\query`.
5. Very often, you will run into trouble getting MSCS to install due to hardware incompatibility. Be sure to check Microsoft's hardware compatibility list *before* you venture into this install.

Recovery Steps Example

Using the SQL Server clustering example in Figure 24.4, if failure is caused by hardware failure in CL Node A like a bad SCSI card, then the following summarized events occur:

1. After CL Node A fails, the SQL Server 2000 fail-over cluster fails over to CL Node B.
2. Run SQL Server Setup and remove CL Node A.
3. Evict CL Node A from MSCS.

4. Install new hardware to replace the failed hardware in CL Node A.
5. Install/reconfigure the operating systems on CL Node A.
6. Install MSCS and join the existing cluster.
7. Run the SQL Server Setup on CL Node B and add CL Node A back to the fail-over cluster.

Network Load Balancing

Now the picture grows a bit more to include network load balancing (NLB) so that you can truly enter into the realm of high availability and reliability at the enterprise level.

Network load balancing serves to balance incoming IP traffic among multinode clusters. If done correctly, this load balancing will provide ample scalability and high availability to enterprise-wide TCP/IP services such as Web, Terminal Services, Proxy, Virtual Private Networks (VPNs), and streaming media services.

NLB sits between the TCP/IP protocol layer and the Network Adapter drivers. Figure 24.6 shows this positioning as an intermediate driver in the Windows 2000 network stack.

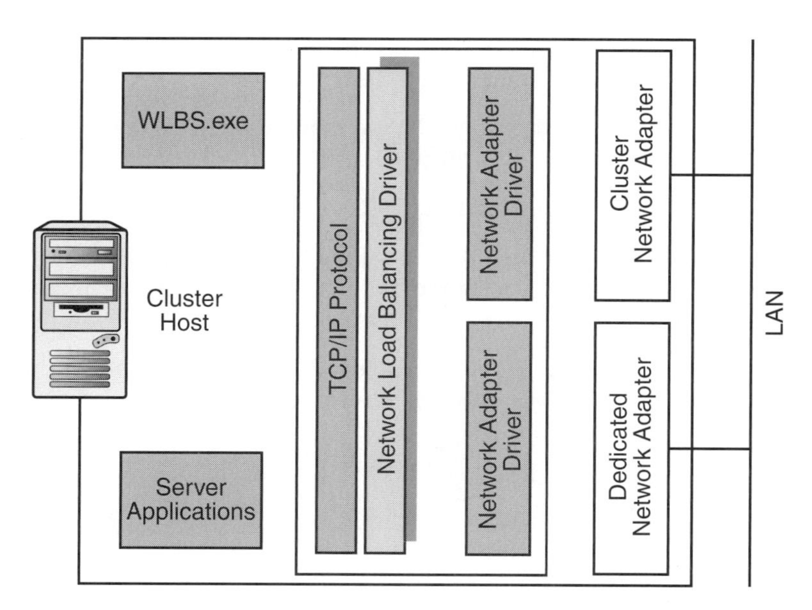

FIGURE 24.6 Network load balancing internals positioning.

Identical copies of the NLB drivers run in parallel on each cluster host. By this means, incoming client requests are partitioned and load balanced among the cluster hosts. Figure 24.7 illustrates a four-host NLM cluster architecture acting as a virtual server to handle the network traffic. Each NLM host works together among the four hosts distributing the work efficiently.

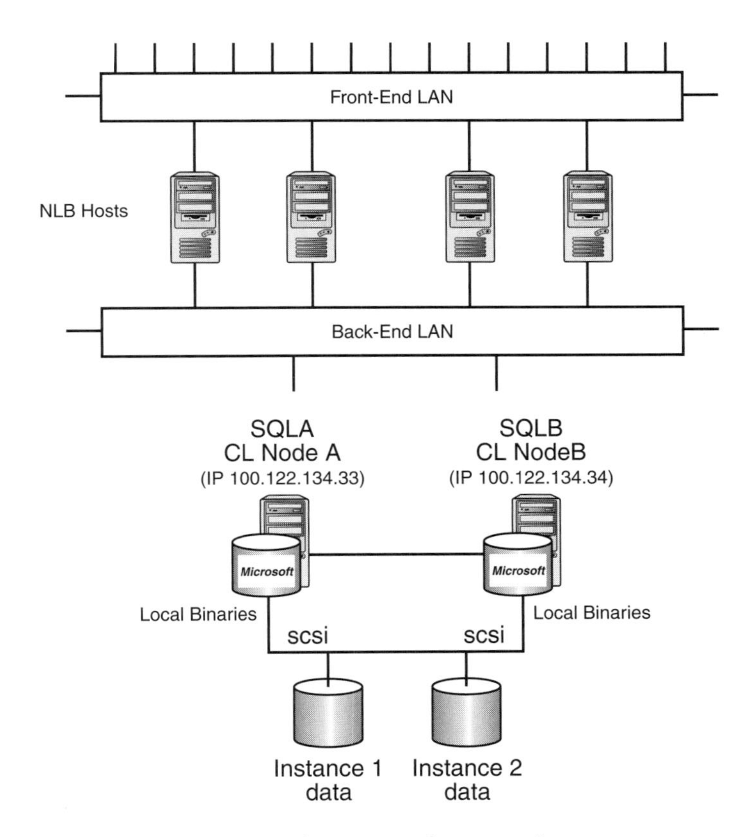

FIGURE 24.7 An NLM host cluster with a two-node server cluster.

Up to 32 NLB servers, called hosts, can be in any one host cluster. Each NLB server distributes its client requests across multiple servers within the cluster. As traffic increases, additional NLB servers can be added to handle this increase.

In addition, NLB can automatically detect the failure of a server and repartition client traffic among the remaining servers.

Summary

As you have seen, the Microsoft Windows 2000 Advanced Server includes two clustering technologies designed to provide fail-over support for critical line-of-business applications—such as databases, messaging systems, and file/print services—and to balance incoming IP traffic among multinode clusters. Building on top of these technologies is the SQL Server clustering capability that places your SQL computing environment in a high availability and reliability level that cannot be achieved on any other Windows operating system.

CHAPTER 25

Defining System Administration and Naming Standards

by Ray Rankins

IN THIS CHAPTER

- The SQL Server Environment Approach
- SQL Server Naming Standards

As the number of applications that you deploy on SQL Server increases, you will need to develop standards that enable you to administer your servers in a consistent manner. Most companies that successfully implement SQL Server applications have good standards in place. Standards are defined to provide a foundation for administrative tasks, and often result in the establishment of an infrastructure which allows for easier creation of procedures and scripts to automate database activities.

What if you don't have standards in place? The cost of application development without standards is usually very high. The price is paid in effort and delay, as well as credibility. Client/server is really no different from any other application environment. Success comes from the right mix of discipline and creativity. Thoughtful standards provide the discipline within which creativity can thrive.

This chapter focuses on those core standards that are needed to enable you to further develop procedures within your environment. It looks at two core activities: the management and maintenance of SQL Server environment standards for the different phases of the software development life cycle and the naming standards used in these environments. After you decide on names, directory structure, and how you are going to approach development, you can start building those site-specific procedures and scripts to automate activities in your organization.

The SQL Server Environment Approach

It is important to attempt to maintain a separate SQL Server environment for each phase in the development, quality control, implementation, and maintenance of a SQL Server implementation.

Depending on the organization's resources, the number of different environments might differ, but there should be at least a development environment, a quality control or test environment, and a production environment with clear boundaries between each. An organization might choose to add stress testing, user-acceptance, pre-production, and other environments, which can be considered subsets of the test environment. This chapter focuses primarily on the development, test, and production environments.

In an ideal configuration, each environment should be on a separate SQL Server, preferably on separate physical machines. As a minimum, the production environment must be on a separate server from the development and test environments. If the development and test environments are on the same server machine, they should at least be running under separate instances of SQL Server.

The least desirable environment is a single SQL Server with only separate databases for development, testing, and production—the needs of each environment conflict with the other environments. The development environment might require the SQL Server to be rebooted often, but the production environment is likely to have continuous up-time as an important business requirement. The testing environment often is constructed to be able to gather performance statistics. The activity of the development and production environments, however, might skew these performance statistics, and testing might affect performance for production. This is why it is *strongly recommended* that development, testing, and production activities take place on separate SQL Servers.

The Development Environment

A development environment is by definition volatile and unstable and should be flexible enough to allow developers to modify database objects and data as needed, as well as start and stop the server as needed. For this reason, the development environment should be on a dedicated SQL Server apart from the production environment.

The development environment is the area in which developers first attempt to create new modules of an application. Development is an iterative process. Multiple revisions of code are normally created in the process of correctly satisfying design requirements. Consequently, the code might have unexpected results on tables. During the refinement of a module, database activities such as `DELETE`, `INSERT`, or `UPDATE` might need several modifications before they are deemed to work correctly. This requires the developer to create test conditions to test individual pieces of functionality. Additionally, new requirements might necessitate the addition or deletion of columns from tables to test the new pieces of code. These changes might become permanent modifications to the existing structures, validated by the iterative testing of an application. The development environment needs to be structured to minimize contention and conflict between developer changes while at the same time maximizing developer flexibility.

Although flexibility is at a maximum for the developer, so is developer responsibility. A developer has much more responsibility for administrative activities. Developers often create their own objects (tables, indexes, procedures, triggers, and so forth) in the pursuit of satisfying a business problem. Developers often are responsible for managing their own test data. Those responsible for database administration (the DBA group) still have some responsibilities, however. A DBA might create a base set of objects or manage a core set of data. As always, DBAs still get calls about any problems that a developer cannot handle (killing processes, adding space, and so forth).

Occasionally, a single logical database is physically implemented as several SQL Server databases in production. The distribution of tables to databases in the development environment should match the production model. Remember that referencing tables from two different databases requires that at least one of the table names be qualified by the database name. If the development environment does not have the same database structure, the SQL has to be modified before production implementation, which is likely to introduce new bugs. Your development environment should look *exactly* like the production environment in the base structure (databases, tables, and objects).

If other projects share the development server, create a document to provide information about all groups. It should contain information such as project name, manager, contact name, phone, and specific instructions. Development environments are volatile. You might need to reboot the server to continue development. Because a reboot affects all users on the system, you should contact user representatives to prepare them for this situation.

Due to the nature of development, it is assumed that the development environment will use a SQL Server separate from the test and production environments. Based on that assumption, you can then determine an approach to constructing the development environment at the database and object level. Development in a SQL Server environment can be approached in three ways. The differences between the approaches are based on whether the developers share a database and whether they have their own copies of objects and data. The rest of this section covers three possible scenarios for the development environment:

- Shared database/shared objects and data
- Individual database/individual objects and data
- Shared database/individual objects and data

Shared Database/Shared Objects and Data

In this approach, all developers share the same objects and data. This works well for small development teams with good communication channels and for maintenance projects.

Advantages Advantages of this approach include:

- Because all objects are shared, changes are immediately available to all developers, avoiding the often difficult process of merging different definitions together.
- This approach is simple to manage because it involves maintaining fewer objects and databases.
- Storage requirements are reduced because only one copy of the database and one copy of objects and data exist.
- If your tables are spread across multiple databases, and the development environment runs in a separate instance from the test and production environments, the names used for databases can be *identical* between development, test, and production environments. Therefore, code that is developed that uses fully qualified object names does not have to be modified to be promoted to the next level.

Disadvantages Disadvantages of this approach include:

- The natural volatility of the development process causes contention for data. Developer 1 might be testing a delete activity on the same row that Developer 2 is using to test an update activity. Development will be impeded as confusion results from "unexpected" changes to data.
- The same can be true of contention for database objects, although this should be less of a problem because architectural changes are normally modeled and are part of a much larger process of impact analysis and change control. The developer's freedom to change the underlying structure to support a hypothesis or test condition is decreased significantly.
- Development flexibility is somewhat reduced.

Individual Database(s)/Individual Objects and Data

In the individual database(s)/individual objects and data environment, each of the developers is assigned a separate database, or in some cases, their own dedicated SQL Server instance. Because SQL Server 2000 can be installed on a Windows NT or Windows 2000 workstation, as well as on Windows 95/98 or Windows Me, these environments can be completely controlled by the individual developer. The developers are the database owners, with complete control over the database structures and data, which they can change at will.

Advantages Advantages of this approach include:

- No developer is dependent on another; therefore, no contention or conflict occurs over data or database structures, providing maximum flexibility.
- Because object and database names are identical in each of the environments, no changes are necessary to the SQL code as it is promoted to the next level in the development process.

Disadvantages Disadvantages of this approach include:

- This approach requires much more space because each developer requires a separate copy of the database(s). Some organizations might not be able to support this approach.
- As the number of servers or the number of databases in a server increases, administrative tasks are complicated. A greater number of servers and/or databases need to be backed up and managed.
- Any changes to the database structures must, at some time, be integrated into the other developer's environments. This task can be time-consuming and generally requires good communication and process control.
- If the application architecture requires that tables be spread across multiple databases and the development environment consists of a single SQL Server instance, using this development approach is likely to require code changes to promote code to production. In a single database approach, code is consistent from development to production because you never need to *qualify* the name of a table with the database name. In a multiple database scenario, if a query is executed that refers to tables in different databases, at least one of the tables has to be qualified with the database name.

  Consider an example with five developers with their own copies of each of the databases. The first developer writes code against `customerdb_1` and `purchasedb_1`, the second developer writes code against `customerdb_2` and `purchasedb_2`, and so on. The following is an example of SQL access across databases:

  ```
  select *
  from customerdb_1..customer c, purchasedb_1..purchase p
  where c.cust_id = p.cust_id
  ```

  Migrating this code into the test or production environments requires changes because these environments likely would contain different database names (`customerdb`, `purchasedb`). You have to modify the code to arrive at the following statement:

  ```
  select *
  from customerdb..customer c, purchasedb..purchase p
  where c.cust_id = p.cust_id
  ```

Migrating code from one environment to the next is much more difficult, and for this reason, the private database approach for multi-database implementations is not recommended unless each developer can be provided with their own private SQL Server instance. Database names can be the same within each of the SQL Server development instances.

Shared Database/Individual Objects and Data

In the shared database/individual objects and data environment, developers use the same database, but they maintain separate objects and data by creating their own objects in the database under their own database usernames rather than under the `dbo` user name. The new database roles of `db_owner`, `db_ddladmin`, `db_datawriter`, and `db_datareader` are applied to the developer username, and any new objects will have the username as object owner.

As long as the owner name is not explicitly specified in the SQL code, the SQL will execute within the current user context. As a developer the SQL will execute against the developer's own objects in development. As an end user, the SQL will execute against the production objects owned by `dbo` in the production environment.

This approach is similar to the individual database/individual objects and data approach, but it requires less maintenance for the database administrator because only one set of databases must be administered.

Advantages Advantages of this approach include:

- Each developer has an individual set of data. A developer has complete freedom to update, delete, and insert data without affecting other developers.
- Migration from the development environment to the production environment is eased. All developers work with the same database and object names. This ensures that any SQL created is identical in all environments. No code changes that are due to different database or object names are necessary.
- Systems spanning multiple databases do not require modifications to the SQL to promote it to production (unlike the Private Database development approach) because the development environment database structure is identical to the production database structure.

Disadvantages Disadvantages of this approach include:

- The number of tables in a single database can be large. A system with 100 tables and 10 developers could have 1,000 tables in the development database.
- Storage requirements are magnified by the number of developers as compared to the shared object approach.

- If a developer needs to reference an object created by another developer, that object will have to be fully qualified with the owner name. The SQL code referencing the object will need to be changed when the code is promoted to the next level where all objects will likely be owned by the `dbo` user account.
- Any differences between the database objects must, at some time, be integrated into each developer's copy of the structures. This task can be time-consuming and generally requires good communication and process control. Eventually, when the code is promoted to the next level, all changes must be integrated together and the objects re-created under the `dbo` user account.

The Test Environment

The test environment can consist of a number of different testing scenarios, including functional, integration, user-acceptance, performance, preproduction, and production-fix.

The Functional Testing Environment

Functional testing ensures that all code functions as expected, and it is usually the first formal quality assurance (QA) test performed by a QA team.

A functional test environment should always be in a separate SQL Server instance from both the development and production environments. The hardware in which the SQL Server is running might or might not be dedicated. The functional test environment could be a separate SQL Server instance. Dedicated hardware is preferred, but not required because you are testing functionality and usability across modules, not performance. The test machine also does not need to be configured exactly as the production machine for this same reason.

On a test machine, the database administrator generally creates all objects under the `dbo` user account. Development logins can be added to enable developers to add specific system test data or to assist in the creation of a core set of data. Developers *should not*, however, have the capability to change the structure of tables or add, drop, or modify other existing objects. Database administrators should run all DDL from a central source control location that contains the DDL and installation scripts. Developers need to understand that the DDL for the objects is considered source code and must be under source code control, completely unit tested, and delivered to the QA team.

A core set of data should be used that is representative of production data. The amount of data does not need to represent production volumes, because it will be used to support feature, integration, and system testing, not performance testing.

Although developers might have access to tables to add or modify data, testing should be conducted using the logins of users with database permissions that are representative of production users. This enforces the testing of the system in the same manner as it would be used by the actual production users. By simulating real users, potential problems, such as improper permissions, can be identified.

Functional testing tests not only the stored procedures and data in the system, but also the scripts used to install them.

The User-Acceptance Testing Environment

The user-acceptance testing environment should be treated like a production environment. Developers can be given read-only access to help identify problems, but should not be able to modify the data or objects in any way. The environment should be created by database administrators using the same scripts that will be used to install the production system.

A user-acceptance test machine should, at a minimum, be in a separate SQL Server instance from any other test, development, or production environment. The hardware in which the SQL Server is running might or might not be dedicated. The test environment should be configured as closely to the production environment as possible.

The user-acceptance test environment should be populated with a core set of data that is representative of production data. The amount of data does not need to represent production volumes. It is best if full production database volumes can be used to help catch possible performance and query response time issues during testing.

The user-acceptance test environment should be backed up after it is created so that it can be re-created easily to provide a baseline environment for repeat testing.

The Performance Testing Environment/Pre-Production Testing Environment

The performance testing and pre-production testing environment should exactly reflect the production environment, including data and logins. Although an organization with limited resources can select to use only a subset of data, this is not recommended because this testing phase is considered the dry run for the final implementation, and all possible problems need to be flushed out at this time. Often, performance issues, locking contention, and other unanticipated problems might not surface until this point. Although some of these problems should appear at an earlier point in the development and testing process, the performance testing phase might be the only time that the server environment is identical to the production environment, so in practice, a number of issues tend to arise here.

The hardware used for the performance testing environment should be configured identically to the production hardware so that statistics gathered can be considered representative of production performance. This environment is used to validate the system's capability of handling production loads. This should be a dedicated machine so that activity in other databases or environments does not affect the performance statistics being gathered.

The performance/pre-production testing server should be populated regularly with data from the production server to ensure that all data and objects are up-to-date. Developers can be given read-only access to help resolve problems, but they should not be able to modify the data or objects in any way. Logins and database user permissions should be representative of production users, and all modifications to database structures should be conducted only by database administrators.

At this stage, you not only implement performance, multiuser, blocking, and other tests, but you also test the installation of all the database objects and data. This is called *pre-production testing,* and it is the last chance to verify an installation before it is released to production.

The Production-Fix Testing Environment

The production-fix testing environment should be an exact copy of the current production environment. This environment is used for applying hot-fixes or patches to the production system to correct critical production problems. Due to the urgency of these fixes, they usually do not go through the full software development life cycle. It is the database administrator's responsibility to ensure that the changes made in the production-fix environment are migrated back to the current development and testing environments using the same DDL scripts used to implement the changes in production.

Although the production-fix testing environment should be treated like a production environment, developers might need to be given limited access to help identify and fix problems.

A production-fix test machine should be, at a minimum, a separate SQL Server instance. It should be configured as identically to the production environment as possible.

TIP

Regularly restoring backups to the production fix environment also serves to ensure that your production environment can be successfully restored from backups. The worst time for finding out that your backup and recovery strategy doesn't work is during a system disaster!

The Production Environment

A production environment should be completely separate from the development and test environments, on a separate server, and maintained only by administrators.

CAUTION

A developer would probably never need to change or have access to a production server as an administrator. Once a system is in production, it is under the care and responsibility of the database administrators. Security standards and procedures should be in place and strongly enforced.

The SQL Server and database hardware that are used for production should be dedicated. A dedicated SQL Server machine is preferred because it greatly simplifies analysis of performance statistics that are captured at the SQL Server or hardware level. It is not recommended that multiple SQL Server instances be installed on the production machine. Most production implementations use dedicated hardware for the production SQL Server.

An initial load of data might be required. Database administration normally is responsible for loading the core supporting data (for example, code lookup tables), as well as any other baseline production data needed to support production use of the application.

Production servers hold an organization's data and should be regularly maintained and guarded as the valuable assets that they are. For more information on backing up and maintaining SQL Server environments, see Chapter 16, "Database Backup and Restore" and Chapter 17, "Database Maintenance."

Using Source Code Control

Source code control software has been used for a number of years in the development of software to manage changes to application code (COBOL, C, Visual Basic, and so forth). Source code control software also can be used to manage changes to your DDL. Source code control software can act as a logbook, enabling only one person to check out a file at a time. Checking in a file normally requires entering information to indicate why the file was checked out. The version number of the file is incremented each time a file is checked in. Some development teams cross-reference the check-in statement with a database change request document.

Source code control software also provides the capability to "cut a version" or label a group of related files. For example, 20 different source code files (each having its own revision number based on the number of times it was changed) can be used to create a C application. Cutting a version relates these 20 files together and logically groups them. Database changes happen for a reason. These changes usually parallel application changes that can be listed as part of the check-in comment.

Source code control gives DBAs a mechanism to manage distinct versions of the database effectively. Through use of this tool, a DBA can identify what versions of DDL files to load to re-create a specific version of a database, object, or stored procedure. This can help to keep track of the proper DDL to use to rebuild a specific test environment.

CAUTION

Although some third-party SQL development tools can integrate with source code control software, such as Microsoft Visual SourceSafe, it is still possible to edit and change a stored procedure without going through the source code control software to check out the stored procedure code first. Any DBA or developer with the appropriate rights can use Enterprise Manager or Query Analyzer to extract the source code from the database directly and modify the stored procedure. If they do not remember to save the source code to a file and check the changes back into the source code control system, the changes will be lost when the next build is generated.

If you are using source code control for your DDL, it is essential that all developers and DBAs follow proper protocol. They must check out the DDL from the source code control system first, make changes to the source code file directly, create and test the modified code in the database, and then save the changes back to the file and check the file back in.

SQL Server Naming Standards

What's in a name? The answer to this simple question often takes organizations months—or years—to define. Names should be chosen in a consistent manner across all SQL Server systems in your organization; for example, a word should not be abbreviated two different ways in two different places. Consistency with names is one of the building blocks of an infrastructure to which employees and users can become accustomed. Consistent naming enables employees to move from system to system (or software to software) and have basic expectations regarding names. This can help in the transition when learning a new environment.

NOTE

Naming standards are like filing standards. You have to think about the person who is storing the information and the person who will retrieve it. For the person defining the name, the choice should be automatic. For the person retrieving or accessing an object, the name should completely define its content without ambiguity.

Naming standards can be broken into two areas: SQL Server names and operating system names. SQL Server names are the names that you specify in the SQL Server environment (databases, objects, and so forth). Operating system names are the names that you specify for files and directories.

SQL Server Names

In SQL Server, you are responsible for naming the server, each user database, each object in the database (tables and columns, indexes, views, stored procedures, and functions), and any integrity constraints (rules, defaults, user datatypes, triggers, and declarative constraints).

Capitalization standards must be defined for each type of name. (Should names be in all capital letters, all lowercase letters, or mixed case?) This decision can be different for different groups of names (for example, server names could be in all capital letters and object names could be in mixed case).

Consider also whether to use an indicator of the item being named. For example, does the word database or the abbreviation DB get included in a database name? In the end, your standard should identify whether a customer database will be named `Customer`, `CUSTOMER`, `CustomerDB`, or `CUSTOMERDB`. For most database objects, the structure of names is the personal preference of the person writing the standard.

NOTE

A naming convention that is often debated within many shops is whether to use the underscore (_) character between descriptive words or indicators (for example, `sales_detail`) or mixed case (for example, `SalesDetail`). I prefer to use underscores, because that method is, in my opinion, more readable and easier to type. Others tend to prefer the latter because it saves one character per word, which can help to keep names shorter and within any standard enforced size limitations without having to abbreviate as often. It also saves them from having to search for the underscore key on their keyboards. (If only computer manufacturers would design a standard keyboard with an underscore character that doesn't requiring using the Shift key to type, life would be near bliss!)

The method that you choose to use is entirely up to you or your organization's preference. Throughout this chapter, I will attempt to alternate between both alternatives in the examples provided to avoid alienating either camp in this ongoing battle, and provide you the opportunity to see both methods and decide for yourself which you prefer.

Object Type Indicators

An indicator is a string of characters that is embedded in a name to indicate something about the object. In SQL Server, these characters are often used to indicate an object type. For example, `CurrDate_Def` could be used as a name for a default setting a column to the current date and time. There are two schools of thought on the use of indicators:

- An indicator is not needed because the type of object can be retrieved from the system tables (the `type` column in the `sysobjects` table) or is indicated by the table from which you are selecting (`sysdatabases`, `sysservers`). Including an indicator in the name is redundant and a waste of valuable characters. Although names in SQL Server can be up to 128 characters long, naming conventions might often limit them further to be compatible with existing guidelines or other systems (for example, object names within a DB2 environment are limited to 18 characters). An indicator can easily take four or five characters (`_tbl` or `_view`, for example), which limits the number of available characters in an object name. Indicators can also propagate through to dependent objects (`Customer_Tbl_CIdx`), further reducing the number of available characters. When users need to use a name frequently, indicators also mean extra typing. If you decide to put an indicator in a name, it is best to make that indicator as short as possible.

- An indicator is needed because it simplifies reporting. A DBA can tell the type of object from just a listing of object names. Application designers are cognizant of what type of objects they are accessing (for example, the name tells them whether they are selecting from a table or view). Indicators also enable you to use similar, meaningful names for two objects, once with each indicator (for example, `price_check` and `price_default`).

NOTE

All object names within a database must be unique for the owner. In other words, the `dbo` can own only one object of any name. If you have a rule named `price_check`, you cannot create a constraint named `price_check`. This restriction applies to tables and views, as well as rules, defaults, constraints, procedures, and triggers. To avoid being constrained by these names, consider using indicators, especially for objects with which users do not interact and whose names users will never type (rules, defaults, constraints, and triggers).

Table 25.1 lists the most common indicators used by SQL Server installations throughout the world. Consider that many sites choose no indicators at all for referenced objects such as tables, views, and stored procedures, and use them only for internal objects such as indexes, triggers, and constraints.

TABLE 25.1 Common SQL Server Indicators

Item	Possible Indicators	Preferred
Database	`Database, DATABASE, DB`	`DB`
Table	`Table, TABLE, T, TBL, tbl, t`	None
Clustered index	`ClusIdx, Cidx, clus, C, CI`	`CI`
Non-clustered index	`Idx[#],NCIdx[#], NCI[#], I[#]`	`NCI[#]`
View	`V, View, VIEW`	None
Rule	`Rul, rul, RUL, rule, RULE, R`	`Rul`
Default	`Def, def, DEF, default, DEFAULT, D, DF`	`DF`
User-defined datatype	`TYPE, Type, type, TYP, Typ,`	`type`
Stored procedure	`Proc, PROC, Pr, PR, pr, p, P`	`pr`
Trigger	`InsertTrigger, InsTrig, ITrg, Itrg, TR, TR_I`	`TR_I`
Check constraint	`Check, CK, Chk, CkCon,`	`CK`
Primary key constraint	`PK, Pk, Pk`	`PK`
Unique constraint (alternate key)	`Unique, Uniq, UN, UQ, AK`	`AK`
Foreign key constraint	`FK, RI`	`FK`

NOTE

It is probably not a good idea to use indicators in the names of tables or views. Many sites use the table name in the name of other objects. The inclusion of `_tbl` increases the number of redundant characters in the dependent object name (trigger, index, and so forth). In addition, views exist to give users the feeling that their queries are acting against a real table, although they actually are accessing a view. Therefore, table and view names should be identical in format, and should not contain anything that would distinguish one from the other (`_tbl` or `_view`, for example).

Your standards likely will be different, but the important thing is to be consistent in your implementation of names. Knowing the standards up front can save you days or weeks of costly name conversion changes (with SQL code, administration activities, and so forth).

Prefix Versus Suffix

As with most standards, there are differing schools of thought as to where the indicators should go in the name: at the beginning or at the end.

One argument for using indicators as prefixes is that it makes it easier to identify the type of object when its name begins with the indicator. It's easier to scan the beginning of the names to see the type indicator than the end of the name. Also, if you are listing out all the objects in the database, sorting by name also results in sorting by type, as shown in the following example.

```
select name, type from sysobjects
and type != 'S'
order by name
go

name                          type
----------------------------- ----
CK_titles_type                C
FK_titles_publishers          F
PK_publishers                 K
PK_titles                     K
pr_publishers_delete          P
pr_publishers_update          P
pr_titles_select              P
pr_titles_update              P
publishers                    U
titles                        U
TR_DU_publishers              TR
TR_IU_titles                  TR
```

The main argument for using indicators as suffixes is that if the dependent objects for a table (indexes, triggers, stored procedures) begin with the table name, then the table and its dependent objects will be grouped together in an alphabetical listing of database objects, as in the following example:

```
select name, type from sysobjects
and type != 'S'
order by name
go

name                          type
----------------------------- ----
publishers                    U
publishers_delete_proc        P
publishers_PK                 K
publishers_TR_DU              TR
publishers_update_proc        P
titles                        U
titles_PK                     K
titles_publishers_FK          F
titles_select_proc            P
titles_TR_IU                  TR
titles_type_ck                C
titles_update_proc            P
```

Again, the method you choose is a matter of personal preference. No matter which method you choose, you can always list your objects by type in your SQL:

```
select name, type
   from sysobjects
   order by type
```

Naming Servers

In versions of SQL Server prior to SQL Server 2000, naming the SQL Server was easy. Because only one SQL Server could be running on the server machine, SQL Server for Windows NT took its name from the NT Server name by default. Changing this required editing registry values. Because hacking the registry can be dangerous, and a SQL Server with a different name from the NT Server name would probably lead to confusion, the SQL Server name was generally never modified. You simply hoped that the NT Server machine was named as you would want the SQL Server named. For example, you would much rather have a server named `DEVELOPMENT` than one named `RSR8_AB100`.

TIP

Some companies like to name their servers according to cartoons or movies. There are Snow White servers (`DOPEY`, `GRUMPY`, `DOC`, and so forth), Batman servers (`BATMAN`, `ROBIN`, `JOKER`, `PENGUIN`), and Mickey Mouse servers (`MICKEY`, `MINNIE`, `GOOFY`, `DONALD`). Although these names are fun, they should be used only for development or general server names, because they don't convey information as to the purpose of the server. Servers intended to support applications should be named in a consistent manner across *all* applications.

With SQL Server 2000's support for multiple named instances on a single server machine, meaningful names will need to be applied to the different named instances. Although the base of the named instance will still be the name of the server on which SQL Server is running, you can control what the instance name will be. The actual server name becomes less important.

If the instance supports a single application, the instance name should indicate both the system and environment name. The following is a good format:

```
\\SERVERNAME\SYSTEMNAME_ENVIRONMENTNAME
```

For the development of a customer service system, you might use instance names such as `CUST_DEVEL`, `CUST_TEST`, and `CUST_PROD`.

If the SQL Server instance supports multiple application databases, the instance name should be more generic, but still include an environment name if applicable. The first part of the instance name could reflect the company name, department name, or another meaningful designation. The following is a possible solution:

```
\\SERVERNAME\DEPARTMENTNAME_ENVIRONMENTNAME
```

For the marketing department's server, you might use instance names, such as `MARKETING_DEVEL`, `MARKETING_TEST`, and `MARKETING_PROD`.

Although the case of server names does not matter for client connectivity, server names are generally specified in uppercase.

Naming Databases

Databases should be named according to their contents—for example, the type of data (customer or product) or activity (security or administration). A database that contains security tables could be named `SecurityDB`, and a database that contains customer data could be called `CustomerDB`. The name selected should be intuitive. If documentation is required to relate a database's name to its contents, it probably is not intuitive. Would you rather have a database named `B123` or `ProductDB`? Avoid nondescriptive database names!

Table and View Names

Table and view names should be unambiguous and representative of the underlying data. A customer table could be called `Customer`; a view of the California customers could be called `CaliforniaCustomer`. Some organizations like to use nondescriptive table names (`TBL0001`). *Again, avoid nondescriptive table and view names.* If names are not intuitive, a decode document might be required to relate the table name to its contents. This delays development and makes it harder to write SQL statements. Column names should indicate the data in the column. Name a column containing the age of a customer either `Age` or `CustomerAge`.

Although names should not be too long, it is best to avoid abbreviations, except for the indicators already discussed. If an abbreviation is required, one commonly accepted method of abbreviation is to simply remove the vowels.

CAUTION

Be careful not to use generic nouns for objects' names (such as page, time, share, country, and item). Although they are concise and might not be reserved keywords at this time, they might become reserved words in the future.

Column Names

Column names should clearly indicate the domain of a column (such as `FirstName` or `CustomerFirstName` and `SupplierFirstname`). There are two schools of thought again on whether the column name should include the table name as well. Some people feel that including the table name is redundant—if the FirstName column is in the Customer table, would it not be the customer's first name? On the other hand, if you have to join between the two tables and display FirstName from both tables, how do you easily distinguish in the result set which is which? Both would have the same column heading of FirstName unless different column aliases were specified. It is recommended that for common attributes (name, ID, address), the object descriptor be used in the column name.

It can also be helpful to standardize suffixes for your columns to indicate the type of data that the columns contain. For example, for numeric and character keys, you could use the suffix `ID` consistently to indicate a numeric key and the suffix `Code` to indicate a character key (as in `SupplierID` and `CountryCode`). Additional suffixes can be used to indicate whether the column contains a name (`CompanyName`), a date (`LastModifiedByDate`), a user (`LastModifiedByUserID` or `ChangedByUserName`), an amount (`LoanAmount`), a flag (`active_flag`), and so on.

If you use descriptive suffixes, you might want to abbreviate them to save space, following a set of standards for abbreviation.

Column Abbreviation Standards Because your naming standards might limit the length of column names and database object names, it might be necessary to abbreviate descriptive components of column and object names. It is recommended that abbreviation standards be included in your standards definitions so that all users and developers are using a consistent method of abbreviation to avoid confusion.

Some guidelines for applying abbreviations and keeping names shorter yet descriptive are as follows:

- Avoid the use of prepositions in the name (for example, `BIRTH_DT` instead of `Date_of_Birth`).
- Drop the least informative descriptors and abbreviate those that lend themselves most naturally to abbreviation (for example, `social_security_number` abbreviated as `ssn`, or `document` abbreviated as `doc`).
- Remove all vowels from a word, similar to what you see on some vanity license plates (for example, `customer` would become `cstmr`).
- Use abbreviations consistently for common identifiers as defined by a master list of common abbreviations, similar to the example provided in Table 25.2.

TABLE 25.2 Common Abbreviations

Base Word	Abbreviation
NAME	NM
NUMBER	NUM
CODE	CD
COUNT	CNT
AMOUNT	AMT
DATE	DT
TEXT	TXT
ADDRESS	ADDR
FLAG	FL

TABLE 25.2 Continued

Base Word	Abbreviation
PERCENT	PCT
TIMESTAMP	TS
IDENTIFIER	ID

NOTE

In some cases, you might debate whether certain abbreviations really save you anything. I've seen some shops where code and date were abbreviated as cde and dte, respectively. Not only did these abbreviations only save a single letter, but most developers and DBAs (myself included) also found themselves constantly typing out the whole word anyway out of habit. The abbreviations were more frustrating than helpful. As a general rule, unless the abbreviation saves two or more characters, it's not worth abbreviating.

Using Column Datatype Indicators In addition to, or instead of, column type indicators, some organizations require the use of indicators to make the datatype apparent to developers (for example, `mSaleAmount` and `vchAddress`). Others consider it a waste of space, and a well-named column can indicate enough about the datatype. (A column named CustomerFirstName is obviously a character datatype and one called SaleAmount is obviously a numeric type.) The naming philosophy is something that must be determined by the individual organization. Sometimes, the tools most often used within that organization might impact the decision on naming conventions. For example, the way that a commonly used tool organizes and orders objects when displaying them might be a deciding factor. If an indicator is used, make it as short and concise as possible.

Using an indicator for the datatype on column and variable names can prevent errors that occur from datatype mismatches, as well as let you avoid constantly referencing a diagram or other document to determine the datatype. Table 25.3 lists some common indicators that normally preface a column or variable name.

TABLE 25.3 Common Datatype Indicators

Item	Indicator
`Bit`	`b`
`Char`	`ch`
`text`	`tx`
`Datetime`	`dt`
`Integer`	`int`
`Bigint`	`bi`
`Tinyint`	`ti`
`Float`	`f`

TABLE 25.3 Continued

Item	Indicator
Money	m
Smallmoney	sm
Numeric	num
Varchar	vch

Index Names

Generally, index names contain only information about the table and the index type, with no information about what columns are included in the index. Including column names in an index can make the index name overly wordy without providing much value, especially for compound indexes. Some examples are `CustomerCU` (clustered unique index on Customer), `CustomerIDX1`, and `CustomerIDX2` (general non-clustered indexes). However, like with all naming standards, people have differing opinions on index naming. The SQL Server 2000 optimizer has the capability to use multiple indexes for a single table in a query, which means that many administrators might select to create many single-column indexes to support this new feature. In this environment, you might want to include the use of the column name in the index name to make it easier to distinguish them when viewing execution plans or providing index hints.

Constraints

Constraint names vary based on the scope of the constraint. Constraints can be used to check for valid values, add unique or primary keys, and establish relationships between tables (foreign keys).

A check constraint checks for valid values in a single column or multiple columns. Its name should indicate the table, column(s) and possibly the type of check.

Unique and primary key constraints are based on a table and should contain the table name and an indicator of the type of constraint (`PK` or `AK`). If multiple unique keys exist, you can distinguish them with a number or add the column name to the constraint name.

A foreign key constraint implements referential integrity between two tables. Its name should contain the tables or columns involved in the relationship and an indicator (`FK` or `RI`). Table 25.4 shows a sample list of constraint indicators and names for the `Customer` table.

TABLE 25.4 Sample Constraint Indicators and Names

Constraint Type	Indicator	Name Based On	Constraint Name
Check constraint	CK	Table and Column or columns	Customer_Age_CK
Primary key constraint	PK	Table	Customer_PK
Unique key constraint	AK	Table or table and column	Customer_AK
Foreign key constraint	FK	Related tables or columns	Customer_Purchase_FK

TIP

Remember that constraints are objects. For an owner, constraint names must be unique among all objects within the database. Qualifying the constraint name by including the table name helps to ensure uniqueness of the constraint names. (You won't have two primary key constraints that contain the same table name for the same user in a database.)

Table-level constraints can evaluate many columns. Include in your naming standard a method of naming table-level constraints. For example, the constraint that requires an invoice amount to be greater than zero whenever the type is `'SALE'` might look like this:

```
constraint Invoice_AmtType_CK
check ((amt > 0) or (type <> 'SALE'))
```

If you plan to use table names in your constraint names, it helps to keep table and column names fairly short, yet descriptive.

Stored Procedure Names

A stored procedure name should include a standardized verb to indicate the action performed. You should set a standard for where the verb should fall in the name (a prefix or a suffix). Some suffix examples are `CustomerDataUpdate`, `CustomerDelete`, `CustomerSelect`, and `UserValidate`.

SQL Server also allows the definition of customized system stored procedures. System stored procedures must be created in the master database and begin with `sp_`. User-defined system stored procedures, however, should be named in a way to avoid conflict with existing or future Microsoft-supplied system stored procedures. The naming convention used for user-defined system stored procedures should prevent confusion as to whether a system stored procedure was provided with SQL Server or was created by a local administrator. It is recommended that an additional prefix be added to the procedure name after the `sp_` to distinguish it from standard system stored procedures. Often, this prefix is an abbreviation of the company name. For example, a custom system stored procedure to display locking information developed for use within the XYZ Company would be named `sp_XYZ_lockinfo`. The `XYZ` indicator identifies this system procedure as one created by the XYZ Company, and prevents it from conflicting with Microsoft-supplied stored procedures.

Trigger Names

Trigger names should consist of the table name and an indicator of the trigger action (insert, update, delete). A good format is `TableName_TR_[IUD]`:

Object Type	Object Name
Table name	`Customer`
Insert trigger	`Customer_TR_I`
Delete trigger	`Customer_TR_D`
Update trigger	`Customer_TR_U`
Update and delete trigger	`Customer_TR_UD`

With the introduction of INSTEAD OF triggers in SQL Server 2000, you might also want to devise a method to distinguish between INSTEAD OF and AFTER triggers. One approach would be to use a different indicator for INSTEAD OF triggers, such as `ITR`. For example, an INSTEAD OF insert trigger on Customer would be named `Customer_ITR_I`.

User-Defined Functions

Like stored procedures, user-defined function names should include a standardized verb to indicate the action performed. However, because functions are generally more generic than stored procedures and don't necessarily operate on specific tables, the names will usually be more generic as well. Try to use names that are descriptive of the action performed by the function. You might also want to use a prefix indicator, such as `udf_`, to differentiate user-defined functions from system-supplied functions. Some examples are `udf_getdateonly`, `udf_compare_addresses`, and `udf_CheckJobStatus`.

Rules and Defaults

Rules and defaults are implemented at the database level and can be used across tables. Their names should be based on the function that they are providing. A rule that checks for a valid age range could be called `ValidAge_Rul`; a default that places the current date in a field could be called `CurrDate_Def`.

User-Defined Datatypes

Following is an effective format for user-defined types:

```
contents_type
```

Because user-defined datatypes normally are targeted at certain types of columns, the name should contain the type of column for which it is to be used (`ssn`, `price`, `address`) followed by the indicator `_type`.

A SQL Server Naming Standards Example

Table 25.5 outlines a sample naming standard that uses the guidelines presented in this chapter. Note that in this example, prefixes are used for object indicators.

TABLE 25.5 A Sample Naming Standard Summary

Object Type	Object Name	Example
SQL Servers	*DEPARTMENTn*	MORTGAGE1
Databases	*Nnnnnnn[Nnnnnnnn]*	Insurance, Payments
Columns	*Nnnnnnn[Nnnnnnnn]Indicator*	PolicyID, CustomerLastName
Check constraints	*CK_TableName_ColumnName*	CK_Loan_Amount
Default constraints	*DF_TableName_ColumnName*	DF_Loan_Amount
Foreign key constraints	*FK_FkeyTablename_PkeyTablename*	FK_Loan_Customer
Primary key constraints	*PK_TableName*	PK_Loan
Unique constraints	*AK_TableName_ColumnName*	AK_Loan_LoanNo

TABLE 25.5 A Sample Naming Standard Summary

Object Type	Object Name	Example
Indexes—clustered	CI_*TableName*	CI_Customer
Indexes—non-clustered	NC#_*TableName*	NC2_Customer
Stored procedures	*pr_Verb*[*Tablename[Nnnnn]*]	pr_GetCustomerInfo
User Defined Functions	*udf_nnnnnnnnnn*	udf_getdateonly
System stored procedures	sp_SSU_*nnnnnnnnnnnnnnnnnn*	sp_SSU_helplogin
Tables	*nnnnnnnnn*[*Nnnnnnnn...*]	LoanType
Triggers	tr_[d][i][u]_ *Nnnnnnn*[*Nnnnnnnn*]	tr_iu_Loan
Views	*Nnnnnnn*[*Nnnnnnnn*]	NewLoans
Rules	*Nnnnnnn*[*Nnnnnnnn*]_rule	ValidID_rule
Defaults	*Nnnnnnn*[*Nnnnnnnn*]*_dflt*	Country_dflt
User-defined datatypes	*nnnnnnnn*_type	ssn_type

Operating System Naming Standards

You need to establish a naming standard for operating system files and directories. This standard normally is needed to organize DDL files. You need a DDL file for *every* important action and object that exists in SQL Server. This includes configuration changes (`sp_configure`), adding users and logins, creating and altering databases, setting database options, creating objects (tables, views, indexes, and so forth), and granting permissions. Place the files in directories that are organized in a way that enables you to easily re-create an entire environment from scratch.

Sometimes overlooked in standards creation is the criticality of scripting every database object at its lowest level and storing these scripts in a standard directory structure, under source control. This lets you build servers from scratch from tested common scripts, either in their entirety or in pieces. When a table has become corrupt and must be immediately dropped and re-created during production hours, a tested script that can run without editing is critical. Creating object scripts at their lowest levels means that there should be an object creation script and an object drop script that create and drop only that object. Therefore, a table would have a create-table script, a drop-table script, and a grant-permissions script.

Directory Naming Standards

Specifying and organizing directory names should be based on your environment. Create a directory structure that can handle multiple SQL Servers, multiple databases within a SQL Server, and individual creation files for each object within a database. The object scripts should be contained in separate object type directories. Although the hierarchy presented here might seem overly complex, it allows the most flexibility in a production environment.

Base Directory: Server Name All DDL for a server/environment should be stored relative to a base directory named according to the server name. For example, if you have three SQL Servers named CUSTOMER_DEVEL, CUSTOMER_TEST, and CUSTOMER_PROD, the base directories would be \CUSTOMER_DEV, \CUSTOMER_TEST, and \CUSTOMER_PROD, respectively.

The base directory and all subdirectories should contain all necessary DDL statements to re-create the entire SQL Server. Separating the files from different SQL Server environments by directory enables different environments to contain different versions of the same file. This is helpful in regression testing.

The server-level directory would contain scripts or subdirectories for server-level configuration settings, custom error messages, scheduled tasks and operators, SQL Server logins, and user-defined system procedures.

First Level Subdirectory: Database Names

Under the base directory for the server are subdirectories for each of the databases supported by the server. Database-level scripts, such as database option and filegroup definition scripts, would be stored at this level.

Second Level Subdirectory: Database Object Types

Under the database subdirectory should be a directory for each object type. (If you have modified the model database, it should have a directory as well.) The actual scripts to drop and create the database objects would be stored in the appropriate subdirectories.

Figure 25.1 shows a sample directory hierarchy for storing DDL script files.

Object Files and File Extensions

Usually, the operating system filename should be the same as the object name. It is common in some organizations to name a file with an extension that indicates the type of object or activity (such as .trg for trigger scripts, .viw for view scripts, and .tbl for table scripts). The philosophy is similar to using indicators in SQL Server names.

Table 25.6 lists examples of extensions for the various object types. (Note that these extensions correspond with those generated by Enterprise Manager.)

TABLE 25.6 Sample Filenames and Extensions

Object	Extension
Database	.dbs
Tables and indexes	.tbl
View	.viw
Rule	.rul
Default	.def
User-defined datatypes	.udt
Triggers	.trg

TABLE 25.6 Continued

Object	Extension
Stored procedures	`.prc`
User-defined functions	`.udf`
User-defined error messages	`.err`
Logins	`.lgn`
Users	`.usr`

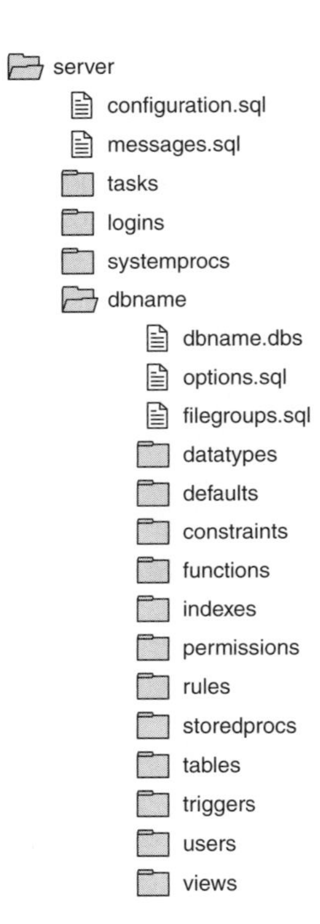

FIGURE 25.1 Suggested server and database object directory hierarchy.

SQL Server Enterprise Manager uses these indicator extensions when it scripts database objects because all of the scripts are generally saved to one directory, requiring a distinguishing extension. However, if you maintain a standard object directory structure, you don't need object type filename extensions because the directory name identifies the object type. In addition to the redundancy of being in the subdirectory for the object type, the extension might also be redundant because the object name might contain a type indicator. For example, a rule called `ValidPrice_Rul` would have a filename of `ValidPriceRul.rul`. Notice the triple redundancy. The rule script would be created in the `rules` subdirectory with a filename of `ValidPrice_Rul` and a file extension of `.rul`.

If you are using an object-level database hierarchy, like the one recommended in Figure 25.1, you might find it more useful to use a filename extension of `.sql`. This is because most query or script management tools out there, Query Analyzer included, look for and save files with a `.sql` extension by default. Although you can set up associations between the other script file extensions and your query/script management tool of choice, it is a bit tedious to do so.

Summary

Although you can choose among many schemes, it is well worth the initial effort and time to develop standards. Standards lower development costs and mistakes and provide an infrastructure and framework for future development.

There are a number of SQL Server names that need to be defined in your environment. Too many SQL Server customers approach development without established standards. This is likely to result in costly rework to bring an existing system up to standard after the standards are defined. Sometimes, customers decide not to change the database because of the cost of conversion. This results in a nonstandard SQL Server implementation in their environment.

It is important to define naming standards as early as possible and stick with them. Naming standards apply to the operating system as well as to SQL Server. With a consistent approach to naming, you can build upon the underlying structure. Scripts can be written to automate activities on the server, decreasing the overall workload.

You should apply standards to many other areas that were not covered in this chapter: testing standards, documentation and commenting standards, and application standards. These areas are critical to a professional information-systems organization and should also be a part of a cohesive approach to database system development and maintenance.

PART IV

Transact-SQL

IN THIS PART

CHAPTER 26

Using Transact-SQL in SQL Server 2000

by Ray Rankins

IN THIS CHAPTER

The intent of this chapter is to provide an overview of the elements of the Transact-SQL (T-SQL) language. The focus is primarily on the Data Manipulation Language (DML) commands and the programming constructs built into T-SQL. The various Data Definition Language (DDL) commands are covered in other chapters, primarily Chapters 11–14 and 27–30. This chapter is not intended as a learning tool for the general SQL language. Several such books are on the market, from beginning to advanced levels; some describe the standard ANSI SQL syntax and some specialize in T-SQL. Look for the *Sams Teach Yourself* line of books on SQL and Transact-SQL, *SQL Unleashed*, and *Microsoft SQL Server Programming Unleashed* from Sams Publishing for more specific information on each of these.

T-SQL and ANSI/ISO SQL

The ANSI SQL standard has evolved over the years and provides standards for commands for data definition, data access, and data manipulation. Each new iteration of the ANSI SQL standard incorporates more features and capabilities than the previous standards. The most recent version of the ANSI SQL standard is SQL-99. ANSI SQL-92 was the last major ANSI SQL standard released. Three levels of compliance are defined for the ANSI SQL standards: entry level, intermediate, and full.

SQL Server 2000 is entry-level compliant with the ANSI SQL-92 standard. What this means is that SQL Server provides all of the core features defined in the ANSI SQL-92 standard to achieve any level of compliance. In addition, SQL Server already provides some features defined in the ANSI-99 standard, such as user-defined roles.

Like any vendor that develops a product that conforms to a standard, Microsoft incorporates additional features into SQL Server to extend the capabilities of the SQL language. Examples of such features include the following:

- Operating-system–dependent statements, such as defining physical database storage.
- Legacy syntax and commands—Even if the current version supports the ANSI way of expressing a command, backward compatibility is still necessary.
- Extensions to the ANSI standards—All vendors strive to implement competitive features. Microsoft is no exception.

Some of the extensions that Microsoft provides in T-SQL to provide it with a competitive advantage include the following:

- Server-resident programs such as user-defined functions, stored procedures, and triggers
- Control of flow statements
- Additional datatypes, including user-defined datatypes
- Various types of built-in integrity, such as rules, defaults, and triggers
- Additional built-in functions

Some of the commands in SQL Server 2000 existed before a SQL standard existed for them, or the SQL standard has been modified over the years and has redefined the way certain commands are supposed to function. For some of these commands, SQL Server supports both the old style syntax and behavior while also supporting the new ANSI style syntax and behavior. Providing this sort of backward compatibility helps to ease the process of upgrading database and applications from previous versions of SQL Server. However, in certain instances, the default behavior of some commands is now the ANSI behavior—to have the T-SQL command mimic the old-style behavior might require setting a session level option.

For example, in versions of SQL Server prior to 7.0, when you concatenated a `NULL` value with a character string, the query returned the character string. The ANSI standard states it should return a `NULL`, so the default behavior in SQL Server 7.0 was modified to return `NULL`. Needless to say, this wreaked havoc with SQL code that was expecting the old behavior. To get 7.0 or SQL Server 2000 to mimic the old behavior, you need to set the database compatibility level to version 6.5 with the `sp_dbcmptlevel` *`dbname`*`, 65` statement, or turn the new behavior off with the `SET CONCAT_NULL_YIELDS_NULL OFF` command.

Although the various SET options and sp_dbcmptlevel help ease the migration process from earlier versions of SQL Server, it is strongly encouraged that you become familiar with and begin using the newer ANSI standard features in SQL Server. This is a good idea for two primary reasons:

- It allows your application code to take advantage of new capabilities available only with some of the ANSI SQL commands.
- Support for the older style syntax and behavior might no longer be supported in future releases of SQL Server.

What's New for T-SQL in SQL Server 2000

SQL Server 7.0 was a significant upgrade from SQL Server 6.5 in terms of the new features available in Transact-SQL. SQL Server 2000 doesn't really provide many new Transact-SQL features over what was available in 7.0. It has a few new datatypes, the ability to create user-defined functions, and the ability to create indexed views.

New Datatypes

SQL Server 2000 introduces three new datatypes:

- bigint
- sql_variant
- table

The bigint Datatype

The bigint datatype is an 8-byte integer that holds integer (whole number) values from -2^{63} (–9,223,372,036,854,775,808) through 2^{63-1} (9,223,372,036,854,775,807). The bigint datatype is intended for use when integer values would exceed the range of the int datatype and can be used in all syntax locations where the int datatype is allowed. Although SQL Server will sometimes promote tinyint or smallint values to the int datatype, it will not automatically promote tinyint, smallint, or int to bigint. For example, certain functions (for example, SUM()) might accept a tinyint or smallint value and return an int as the resulting expression. These aggregate functions will not return a bigint unless the parameter expression is of type bigint.

SQL Server 2000 provides two new functions specifically for use with bigint values:

- COUNT_BIG()—Similar to COUNT, but returns a bigint result. Use this function when the count of a number of items in a resultset would exceed the range supported by the int datatype.

- ROWCOUNT_BIG()—Similar to @@ROWCOUNT, but returns the number of rows affected by the previous command as a bigint result. Use when the number of rows affected would exceed the range supported by the int datatype.

If you find a need to deal with integer values even greater than the range of the bigint datatype, you need to use the numeric datatype and specify a precision between 20–38 with a scale of 0.

Be aware that by default, a constant expression that exceeds the range of the int datatype will implicitly be interpreted as numeric datatypes with a scale of 0. To return a bigint expression, you will need to use the CAST or CONVERT function to convert the numeric result to a bigint.

The sql_variant Datatype

The sql_variant datatype stores values of various SQL Server–supported datatypes, except for text, ntext, image, timestamp, and sql_variant. The sql_variant datatype is similar to the variant datatype used in Microsoft Visual Basic or the DBTYPE_VARIANT datatype used in OLE DB. You can use the sql_variant datatype in column definitions, variables, parameters, and the return values of user-defined functions. When used in a column, the sql_variant datatype allows you to store values of different datatypes in different rows. For example, one row could contain an integer value, another row could contain a float value, and another could contain a character string.

The maximum size of a sql_variant is 8016 bytes; however, you do not specify a specific size for sql_variant. The size is determined by the actual data value stored in the sql_variant variable or column. You can determine the size of data in a sql_variant datatype with the DATALENGTH function. The DATALENGTH function returns only the size of the data and doesn't include the size of the metadata contained in the sql_variant.

Before a sql_variant can be used in any arithmetic or character operations or be assigned to a column or variable of a different datatype, it must first be explicitly converted to its base datatype using CAST or CONVERT.

Columns defined with a sql_variant datatype can be used in indexes and unique keys, as long as the total length of the data in the key columns does not exceed 900 bytes. The total size of the sql_variant is the number of bytes to store the data plus the size of the metadata. sql_variant columns can also be used in primary or foreign keys. A sql_variant column cannot be used in a computed column, however.

When comparing sql_variant datatypes, they adhere to the following rules based on the datatype hierarchy for datatype families, as shown in Table 26.1.

- When comparing sql_variant expressions that have different base datatypes and the base datatypes are in different datatype families, the expression whose datatype family is higher in the hierarchy chart is considered the greater of the two expressions.

- When comparing sql_variant expressions that have different base datatypes but are in the same datatype family, the expression whose base datatype is lower in the hierarchy chart is implicitly converted to the other datatype before the comparison is made.
- When comparing sql_variant expressions of char, varchar, nchar, or varchar, they are evaluated based on additional criteria, including the locale code ID (LCID), the LCID version, the comparison flags used for the column's collation, and the sort ID. In other words, they are compared just like character expressions.

TABLE 26.1 Datatype Hierarchy and Associated Datatype Families for Comparison of sql_variant Expressions

Datatype Hierarchy	Datatype Family
sql_variant	sql_variant
datetime	datetime
smalldatetime	datetime
float	approximate numeric
real	approximate numeric
decimal	exact numeric
money	exact numeric
smallmoney	exact numeric
bigint	exact numeric
int	exact numeric
smallint	exact numeric
tinyint	exact numeric
bit	exact numeric
nvarchar	Unicode
nchar	Unicode
varchar	Unicode
char	Unicode
varbinary	binary
binary	binary
uniqueidentifier	uniqueidentifier

In the following example, you are comparing a sql_variant variable containing a float value with sql_variant containing an integer value.

```
declare @variant1 sql_variant,
        @variant2 sql_variant

set @variant1 = convert(float, 100.0)
set @variant2 = 123
```

```
select case when @variant1 > @variant2 then 'Variant1 is bigger'
            when @variant2 > @variant1 then 'Variant2 is bigger'
            else 'They are equal'
            end
go
------------------
Variant1 is bigger
```

Notice that even though the value of the integer is greater than the value of the float, SQL Server reports `@variant1` as being greater because the two datatypes are in different datatype families and the `float` datatype is higher in the datatype hierarchy.

In the next example, you are comparing two datatype values that are in the same datatype family—`money` and `int`.

```
declare @variant1 sql_variant,
        @variant2 sql_variant

set @variant1 = $100.0
set @variant2 = 123

select case when @variant1 > @variant2 then 'Variant1 is bigger'
            when @variant2 > @variant1 then 'Variant2 is bigger'
            else 'They are equal'
            end
go

------------------
Variant2 is bigger
```

Notice that in this example, SQL Server reports `@variant2` as being greater because the two datatypes are in the same datatype family. SQL Server converts the integer expression to `money` (which is higher in the datatype hierarchy) and then compares the two values both as `money` datatypes.

The `sql_variant` datatype cannot be used in `LIKE` expressions or in full-text indexes.

To obtain information about the data stored in a `sql_variant` expression, you can use the `sql_variant_property()` function:

```
sql_variant_property(variant_expression, property)
```

This function returns a `sql_variant` result for the property specified. The property options that can be specified are as follows:

- BaseType—The underlying SQL Server datatype for the sql_variant value
- Precision—The maximum number of digits to the left of the decimal point for any type of numeric data value
- Scale—The maximum number of digits to the right of the decimal point for any type of numeric data value
- TotalBytes—The total number of bytes required to hold the data value and the metadata
- Collation—The collation sequence of the sql_variant
- MaxLength—The length of the datatype of the value contained in the sql_variant

TIP

If you are assigning a string containing a datetime value to a sql_variant expression, use the convert or cast function to explicitly convert the string to a datetime first, or it will be stored simply as a character string in the sql_variant.

```
DECLARE @VARIANT1 SQL_VARIANT,
    @VARIANT2 SQL_VARIANT

SET @VARIANT1 = 'April 23, 2001'
SET @VARIANT2 = convert(datetime, 'April 23, 2001')


select convert(char(10),
               SQL_VARIANT_PROPERTY(@VARIANT1, 'BASETYPE')) AS Datatype,
       convert(int,
               SQL_VARIANT_PROPERTY(@VARIANT1, 'MaxLength')) as MaxLength,
       convert(int,
               SQL_VARIANT_PROPERTY(@VARIANT1, 'TotalBytes')) as TotalBytes

select convert(char(10),
               SQL_VARIANT_PROPERTY(@VARIANT2, 'BASETYPE')) AS Datatype,
       convert(int,
               SQL_VARIANT_PROPERTY(@VARIANT2, 'MaxLength')) as MaxLength,
       convert(int,
               SQL_VARIANT_PROPERTY(@VARIANT2, 'TotalBytes')) as TotalBytes
GO

Datatype   MaxLength   TotalBytes
---------- ----------- -----------
varchar             14          22
```

```
Datatype   MaxLength   TotalBytes
---------- ----------- -----------
datetime           8           10
```

The `table` Datatype

In addition to `sql_variant`, SQL Server 2000 introduces another new datatype—the `table` datatype. `table` datatypes can be used for local variables in user-defined functions, stored procedures, and batches, or as the return value of a user-defined function. Columns in a table cannot be defined with the `table` datatype, nor can `table` variables be used as stored procedure or user-defined function parameters.

The syntax to define a variable using the `table` datatype is similar to the `CREATE TABLE` syntax except it's done in a `DECLARE` statement and the name of the variable comes before the `TABLE` keyword:

```
DECLARE @variable TABLE ( column definition | table_constraint [, ...] )
```

Notice that constraints are allowed in `table` variables, but the only constraint types allowed are primary key, unique key, check, or default constraints. Column properties can be `NULL`, `NOT NULL`, or `IDENTITY`. Foreign key constraints are not allowed.

`table` variables, like other kinds of local variables discussed in the "Programming Constructs" section later in this chapter, have a well-defined scope, which is limited to the procedure, function, or batch in which they are declared. The following is a simple example of using a `table` variable in a batch:

```
declare @title_info TABLE (title_id varchar(6),
                           title varchar(80),
                           pubdate datetime,
                           price money null)
insert @title_info select title_id, title, pubdate, price from titles
select count(*) from @title_info
go

-----------
         18
```

The following example shows what happens if you try to access the `table` variable in a subsequent batch:

```
-- now try to access variable in a new batch
select * from @title_info
go

Server: Msg 137, Level 15, State 2, Line 2
Must declare the variable '@title_info'.
```

table variables can be treated like any other table. Any SELECT, INSERT, UPDATE, or DELETE statement can be performed on the rows in a table variable, with two exceptions:

- SELECT INTO cannot be used to add data to a table variable because the table variable must first be created using DECLARE, and SELECT INTO creates a table.
- You cannot specify the resultset of a stored procedure when inserting into a table variable, as in the following example:

```
INSERT INTO table_variable EXEC stored_procedure
```

In addition, table variables cannot participate in transactions. A ROLLBACK TRANSACTION command will not affect data added to, modified in, or deleted from a table variable. You also cannot create indexes on table variables using the CREATE INDEX command.

For more detailed examples of using the table datatype in stored procedures and user-defined functions, see Chapter 28, "Creating and Managing Stored Procedures in SQL Server," and Chapter 30, "User-Defined Functions."

User-Defined Functions

SQL Server has always had a number of built-in functions that extended the capabilities of T-SQL, but these were hard coded into SQL Server and could not be modified. They still cannot be modified, but SQL Server 2000 now supports the creation of user-defined functions.

User-defined functions are defined using the CREATE FUNCTION statement, modified using the ALTER FUNCTION statement, and removed using the DROP FUNCTION statement. The user-defined function name must be unique for each user in the database.

User-defined functions take 0–1,024 arguments and can return either a scalar value or a table. User-defined functions that return a scalar value can be used anywhere a constant expression can be used in your queries, just like many of the built-in functions. User-defined functions that return a table datatype can be used in queries in which a table expression can be specified.

For more information and examples on how to define and use user-defined functions, see Chapter 30.

Indexed Views

Normal views are essentially nothing more than a virtual table. The resultset returned by the view is not stored in the database as a distinct object, but is stored in and retrieved from the actual underlying table(s). A normal view is just a SELECT statement. Whenever a query references a view, the resultset is generated from existing data in the underlying table(s). For a normal view, the overhead involved to dynamically build the resultset each time the view is referenced can be substantial if the views involve complex processing against tables with many rows, such as aggregating large amounts of data or joining many rows.

To solve this problem, SQL Server 2000 provides the ability to create indexes on views. You can improve performance on complex views by creating a unique clustered index on the view. Unlike normal views, when you create a unique clustered index on a view, the view is executed and the resultset for the view is physically stored and indexed in the database, in much the same way a table with a clustered index would be stored. (See Chapter 34, "Indexes and Performance," for more information on index structures and how they are stored.)

Although an indexed view stores a resultset for the data as it existed at the time the index was created, an indexed view will automatically reflect any modifications made to the data in the underlying base tables, similar to the way an index created on a base table does. As modifications are made to the data in the base tables, they are also reflected in the data stored in the indexed view.

Indexed views can significantly improve the performance of applications where queries frequently perform certain joins or aggregations on large tables. If the applications already make use of views, they do not need to be modified to reap the performance benefits provided by indexing the views. For more information on how and when to define indexed views, see Chapter 27, "Creating and Managing Views in SQL Server."

In Case You Missed It: New Stuff Introduced in SQL Server 7.0

In case you are making the leap directly from SQL Server 6.x or earlier to SQL Server 2000, following is a brief summary of many of the new T-SQL features/changes introduced in SQL Server 7.0:

- Support for new unicode datatypes: `nchar`, `nvarchar`, and `ntext`.
- Addition of the `TOP` *n* `[PERCENT]` extension to the `SELECT` statement syntax to limit the number of rows returned for that `SELECT` statement only (unlike the `SET ROWCOUNT` *N* command, which set the row limit for all queries in a session).
- Improved cursor support via the definition of local cursors and the ability to define cursor variables and return cursors as parameters from stored procedures.
- Identifiers from 30 characters up to 128 characters. Also, the left square bracket ([) and right square bracket (]) can be used to delimit identifiers in addition to using the SQL-92 standard double quotation mark (").
- Increased the maximum size of the `char`, `varchar`, `binary`, and `varbinary` datatypes from 255 bytes to 8000 bytes.
- Ability to use the `SUBSTRING` function on text and image columns.
- Modification to the handling of `NULL`s and empty strings to conform to the ANSI-92 SQL standard.

NOTE

This change is one of the primary causes of some of the compatibility problems when upgrading SQL code from pre-7.0 databases. For example, concatenating a NULL with a string now returns NULL by default unless the CONCAT_NULL_YIELDS_NULL option is turned off. For more information on upgrade compatibility issues, please see the "Upgrading from Previous Versions" section in Chapter 8, "Installing and Upgrading SQL Server."

- Addition of the uniqueidentifier datatype for storing a globally unique identifier (GUID).
- Additional functionality to the ALTER TABLE command to allow you to add non-nullable columns, change a column datatype, or drop columns from the table without having to export and reimport the data. For more details, see Chapter 12, "Creating and Managing Tables in SQL Server."
- Addition of the ALTER PROCEDURE, ALTER TRIGGER, and ALTER VIEW commands, which allows you to modify the definition of a procedure, trigger, or view without having to drop them first and lose permissions or dependencies.
- Deferred name resolution in stored procedures, triggers, and SQL batches. Table and other object names are not resolved at compile time but at runtime. This allows you to create a procedure that references a table that does not exist when the procedure is created, providing greater flexibility to applications that create tables at runtime.

NOTE

This feature also allows you to think you created a procedure successfully only to have it generate an error at runtime because you mistyped a table name or created it in the wrong database!

- Ability to define multiple triggers for the same action on a single table. For example, a single table can now have multiple triggers for update, insert, or delete. This enhancement provides the ability to put different business rules into different triggers. For more information on defining triggers, see Chapter 29, "Creating and Managing Triggers."

SELECT, INSERT, UPDATE, and DELETE

Four basic SQL statements allow you to retrieve and modify data in tables. SELECT retrieves data from one or more tables, INSERT inserts rows into one table, UPDATE modifies rows in one table, and DELETE removes rows from one table.

NOTE

If you are already familiar with these statements, you might want to just skim this section.

You could easily fill a book with examples and explanations of these statements (in fact, many authors already have). This section covers the major parts of syntax and shows some basic examples.

The SELECT Statement

The SELECT statement has the following basic syntax:

```
SELECT [DISTINCT] [TOP N [PERCENT]] column1 [AS column_heading]
       [, column2 [AS column_heading], ...]
 [INTO new_table_name]
 FROM table1 [ [AS] table_alias ]
 [ [INNER | { LEFT | RIGHT | FULL} [OUTER] ] JOIN table2 [ [AS] table_alias2 ]
       on ( join_conditions )] [...]
 [WHERE search_conditions]
 [GROUP BY aggregate_free_expression]
 [HAVING search_condition]
 [ORDER BY order_expression [ASC | DESC]]
 [ compute row_aggregate(column_name) [, ... ]
      [ by column_name [ , column_name ] ... ] ]
```

To return all the Utah authors' first and last names from the authors table and rename the column heading in your result, you would execute the following:

```
SELECT au_lname AS 'First', au_fname AS 'Last'
   FROM authors
   WHERE STATE = 'UT'
```

By default, SELECT returns all the rows that meet the search conditions. If you specify SELECT DISTINCT, any duplicate rows will be removed. Be careful not to use DISTINCT unnecessarily because it can slow query performance having to put the resultset into a work table to remove duplicates before returning the final resultset.

The WHERE Clause

The columns that you base your search condition on do not have to be returned in the resultset. You can filter rows in several ways with the WHERE clause. The following expressions are available for the WHERE clause:

Operators: =, <> (not equals), <, >, >=, and >=.

BETWEEN *expression1* AND *expression2*. Between is inclusive.

IN(*element1*, *element2*, ...). Returns all rows whose values are equal to the elements specified in the list.

LIKE *string_expression*. Used for pattern matching. Table 26.2 lists the available wildcard characters.

TABLE 26.2 Wildcards and LIKE

Wildcard	Meaning
%	Any number of characters
_	Any single character
[]	Any character listed in the bracket

Logical OR and AND are used to connect multiple search arguments. AND takes precedence over OR, so use parentheses to provide the proper logical grouping. For example, you might want to write a query to return all the business books for which the price is less than $10 or ytd_sales greater than $10,000. If you don't use parentheses, notice what happens when you run the following query:

```
SELECT substring(title, 1, 30) as title, type, price, ytd_sales
   from titles
   where type = 'business'
     and price < $10 or ytd_sales > 10000
go

title                          type         price     ytd_sales
------------------------------ ------------ --------- ---------
You Can Combat Computer Stress business     2.9900    18722
The Gourmet Microwave          mod_cook     2.9900    22246
Fifty Years in Buckingham Pala trad_cook    11.9500   15096
```

You didn't get what you wanted. You only got business books with a price less than $20 and all books with ytd_sales greater than $10,000. Using parentheses, you get the result you want:

```
SELECT substring(title, 1, 30) as title, type, price, ytd_sales
   from titles
   where type = 'business'
     and (price < $10 or ytd_sales > 10000)
go

title                          type       price    ytd_sales
------------------------------ ---------- -------- ---------
You Can Combat Computer Stress business   2.9900   18722
```

26

The ORDER BY Clause

The ORDER BY clause sorts the resultset by the specified column or columns. Ascending sorting is the default, but you can use ORDER BY column_name DESC to specify descending ordering. You should always specify ORDER BY if you require a certain order for your results. No specific ordering of resultsets are guaranteed otherwise, even when using DISTINCT or GROUP BY. The following is an example of a query using the ORDER BY clause to sort the resultset by au_lname:

```
SELECT au_lname, au_fname, state
   FROM authors
   WHERE state IN('CA', 'KS')
     AND au_lname LIKE 'S%'
   ORDER BY au_lname
```

As an alternative to specifying the column expression in the ORDER BY clause, you can specify the positional number of the expression in the select list or the column heading:

```
SELECT au_lname AS 'Last', au_fname As 'First', state
   FROM authors
   WHERE state IN('CA', 'KS')
     AND au_lname LIKE 'S%'
   ORDER BY 1, First DESC
```

The TOP Keyword

You can use the TOP keyword to restrict the number of rows returned. You can specify a fixed number of rows or a percentage of the number of rows in the resultset. The query shown in Listing 26.1 uses TOP along with ORDER BY to retrieve the title and price for the five most expensive books.

LISTING 26.1 Using TOP to Restrict the Number of Rows Returned

```
SELECT TOP 5 price, title
   FROM titles
   ORDER BY price DESC
go

price                 title
--------------------- --------------------------------------
22.9500               But Is It User Friendly?
21.5900               Computer Phobic AND Non-Phobic Indi...
20.9500               Onions, Leeks, and Garlic: Cooking ...
20.0000               Secrets of Silicon Valley
19.9900               The Busy Executive's Database Guide
```

> **NOTE**
>
> Be aware that the TOP keyword will not speed up a query if the query also contains an ORDER BY clause. This is because the entire resultset is selected into a work table and sorted before the top *N* rows in the ordered resultset are returned.

When using the TOP keyword, you can add the WITH TIES option to specify that additional rows should be returned from the resultset if duplicates are on the last values returned that are specified in an ORDER BY clause. The WITH TIES option can only be specified if an ORDER BY clause is specified. In Listing 26.2, you add WITH TIES so that all books that match the last price of the top five are returned.

LISTING 26.2 Using TOP WITH TIES

```
SELECT TOP 5 WITH TIES price, title
   FROM titles
   ORDER BY price DESC
go

price         title
------------- --------------------------------------------------------------
22.9500       But Is It User Friendly?
21.5900       Computer Phobic AND Non-Phobic Individuals: Behavior Variations
20.9500       Onions, Leeks, and Garlic: Cooking Secrets of the Mediterranean
20.0000       Secrets of Silicon Valley
19.9900       Prolonged Data Deprivation: Four Case Studies
19.9900       Silicon Valley Gastronomic Treats
19.9900       The Busy Executive's Database Guide
19.9900       Straight Talk About Computers
```

If you don't use ORDER BY with TOP, the rows that will be returned cannot be predicted—it is based on the execution plan chosen by the optimizer. You can also specify TOP *n* PERCENT to restrict the number of rows based on a percentage of the number of rows in the final resultset instead of specifying an absolute value.

> **NOTE**
>
> The TOP keyword was introduced in version 7.0. To get similar functionality, SET ROWCOUNT *n* was often used in previous versions. The optimizer recognizes when TOP is used in a query and may choose to optimize the query differently. This can result in better query performance than when using ROWCOUNT. Another difference between the two is that SET ROWCOUNT *n* specifies the number of rows to be affected by all commands. The TOP keyword applies only to the SELECT statement in which it is specified.

SELECT INTO

You can create a table and store the resultset into it by using `SELECT` *`column(s)`* `INTO` *`table_name`* `....` The table specified will be created with the same columns and datatypes as columns in the resultset. Most `SELECT` options (aggregates, `GROUP BY`, `ORDER BY`) are allowed except for the `COMPUTE` clause. If a column is a calculated expression such as an aggregate function or string concatenation, you will need to provide a column heading that can be used as a column name. (The column heading will have to conform to the rules for SQL Server identifiers.)

If you precede the table name with one or two hash signs (#), a temporary table is created in tempdb. If you want to create a permanent table with `SELECT...INTO`, you must have create table permission in the destination database, and the database option `select into/bulkcopy` must be set to `TRUE`.

The following example selects the type column and the average price from the titles table into a temporary table with the resultsets ordered in descending order by average price:

```
select type, avg(price) AS avg_price
   into #type_avg_prices
   from titles
   group by type
   order by avg_price DESC
```

UNION

When you use the `UNION` keyword, a logical union between two or more resultsets is returned. Each select list must have the same number of columns, and the corresponding columns must be of the same datatype or must allow implicit datatype conversions. The column headings specified in the first select list will be the column headings used for the entire resultset.

This query returns the city and state of each author and publisher as a single resultset:

```
SELECT city, state FROM authors
UNION ALL
SELECT city, state FROM publishers
```

By default, SQL Server removes all the duplicate rows in a `UNION`. You can add the keyword `ALL` if you do not want the duplicates to be removed. Using the `ALL` keyword will speed up the return of the resultset because a work table is not required to remove the duplicate rows—the results are simply appended to the previous resultset.

To sort the resultset for a `UNION`, specify an `ORDER BY` clause in the last select statement in the union. The column names specified in the `ORDER BY` clause must match those in the first select statement in the union, or you can specify the column number.

GROUP BY and HAVING

GROUP BY and HAVING are used with aggregate functions (which are described in the section "SQL Server Functions," later in this chapter). GROUP BY allows you to calculate aggregates for groups within your tables. The following example calculates the average price for each book category in the titles table:

```
SELECT type, AVG(price)
   FROM titles
   GROUP BY type
go

type
--------------- ----------
business         13.7300
mod_cook         11.4900
popular_comp     21.4750
psychology       13.5040
trad_cook        15.9633
UNDECIDED        NULL
```

If a WHERE clause is used, it is applied before the grouping takes place. The following query calculates the average price per book category for books published by the publisher with the ID 1389:

```
SELECT type, AVG(price)
   FROM titles
   WHERE pub_id = 1389
   GROUP BY type
go

type
--------------- ----------
business         17.3100
popular_comp     21.4750
```

The HAVING lets you restrict the number of rows returned by filtering on the aggregate values calculated. The clause is applied after the grouping is applied and the aggregate values are determined. Perhaps you want to return the average price for book categories, but only the categories with an average that is higher than $14:

```
SELECT type, AVG(price)
   FROM titles
   GROUP BY type
   HAVING AVG(price) > $14
```

```
go

type
---------------- -----------
popular_comp     21.4750
trad_cook        15.9633
```

CUBE, ROLLUP, and GROUPING

CUBE, ROLLUP, and GROUPING are used in conjunction with GROUP BY.

ROLLUP

The ROLLUP operator provides aggregates and super-aggregates for elements within a GROUP BY statement. The ROLLUP operator can be used to extract running aggregates as well as cumulative aggregates within a resultset. The ROLLUP operator creates groupings from right to left, along the list of columns in the GROUP BY clause, applying the aggregate function to each grouping superset. A rollup value for a level displays NULL for that column, as shown in Listing 26.3.

LISTING 26.3 Using ROLLUP to Calculate Super-Aggregates

```
select pub_id, type, t.title_id, sum(qty) as total_qty
   from titles t, sales s
   where t.title_id = s.title_id
     and type in ('business', 'popular_comp')
   group by pub_id, type, t.title_id
   with rollup
go

pub_id type         title_id total_qty
------ ------------ -------- -----------
0736   business     BU2075   35
0736   business     NULL     35
0736   NULL         NULL     35
1389   business     BU1032   15
1389   business     BU1111   25
1389   business     BU7832   15
1389   business     NULL     55
1389   popular_comp PC1035   30
1389   popular_comp PC8888   50
1389   popular_comp NULL     80
1389   NULL         NULL     135
NULL   NULL         NULL     170
```

Notice that you first get the aggregates rolled up by pub_id, type, and title_id, then by pub_id and type, then by pub_id, and finally a rollup for the entire resultset.

CUBE

The CUBE operator is used with GROUP BY to generate a cross-referenced superset of groups to generate aggregates and super-aggregates. Unlike ROLLUP, which rolls up super-aggregate values from right to left, CUBE rolls up super-aggregates for every possible combination of the columns or expressions in the GROUP BY clause. The number of non-aggregate columns in the select list determines the number of groups in the resultset. If *n* columns or expressions exist, 2 (*n*) - 1 possible super-aggregate combinations will be present.

If you add CUBE to the query that returns the average price for book categories, you get an extra row with the average price of all books, as shown in Listing 26.4.

LISTING 26.4 Using CUBE to Calculate Super-Aggregates

```
SELECT type, AVG(price) AS average
   FROM titles
   GROUP BY type
   WITH CUBE
go

type         average
------------ ---------
business     13.7300
mod_cook     11.4900
popular_comp 21.4750
psychology   13.5040
trad_cook    15.9633
UNDECIDED    NULL
NULL         14.7662
```

The book type is returned as NULL for the extra row.

CUBE is more useful if you group over several columns. In Listing 26.5, you want to return the average price grouped by book type and publisher.

LISTING 26.5 Grouping Over Several Columns

```
SELECT type, pub_id, AVG(price) AS average
   FROM titles
   GROUP BY type, pub_id
go
```

LISTING 26.5 Continued

```
type         pub_id average
------------ ------ --------
business     0736   2.9900
psychology   0736   11.4825
mod_cook     0877   11.4900
psychology   0877   21.5900
trad_cook    0877   15.9633
UNDECIDED    0877   NULL
business     1389   17.3100
popular_comp 1389   21.4750
```

In Listing 26.6, you add `WITH CUBE`, which provides the total average, the average for each book type, and the average for each publisher.

LISTING 26.6 Grouping Over Several Columns with `CUBE`

```
SELECT type, pub_id, AVG(price) AS average
   FROM titles
   GROUP BY type, pub_id
   WITH CUBE
go

type         pub_id    average
------------ --------- --------
business     0736      2.9900
business     1389      17.3100
business     NULL      13.7300
mod_cook     0877      11.4900
mod_cook     NULL      11.4900
popular_comp 1389      21.4750
popular_comp NULL      21.4750
psychology   0736      11.4825
psychology   0877      21.5900
psychology   NULL      13.5040
trad_cook    0877      15.9633
trad_cook    NULL      15.9633
UNDECIDED    0877      NULL
UNDECIDED    NULL      NULL
NULL         NULL      14.7662
NULL         0736      9.7840
NULL         0877      15.4100
NULL         1389      18.9760
```

The GROUPING Function

When working with the CUBE or ROLLUP operator, you can use the GROUPING function to distinguish between real null values and null values that represent a rollup of all values for a column in the resultset.

The GROUPING function returns 1 when the value is grouped, and 0 when the column contains a null value.

In Listing 26.7, you use the GROUPING function to replace null values for the rolled up columns with ALL.

LISTING 26.7 Using the GROUPING Function

```
SELECT CASE when GROUPING(type) = 1 then 'ALL'
            else isnull(type, 'Other')
            END AS type,
       CASE when (grouping(pub_id) = 1) then 'ALL'
            else isnull(pub_id, 'Unknown')
            END as pub_id,
       AVG(price) AS average
   FROM titles
   GROUP BY type, pub_id
   WITH CUBE
go

type         pub_id average
------------ ------ ------------
business     0736   2.9900
business     1389   17.3100
business     ALL    13.7300
mod_cook     0877   11.4900
mod_cook     ALL    11.4900
popular_comp 1389   21.4750
popular_comp ALL    21.4750
psychology   0736   11.4825
psychology   0877   21.5900
psychology   ALL    13.5040
trad_cook    0877   15.9633
trad_cook    ALL    15.9633
UNDECIDED    0877   NULL
UNDECIDED    ALL    NULL
ALL          ALL    14.7662
ALL          0736   9.7840
ALL          0877   15.4100
ALL          1389   18.9760
```

You can also use the GROUPING function to order the resultsets to move all the rollups toward the bottom, as shown in Listing 26.8.

LISTING 26.8 Using the GROUPING Function to Order the Resultset

```
SELECT CASE when GROUPING(type) = 1 then 'ALL'
            else isnull(type, 'Unknown')
            END AS type,
       CASE when (grouping(pub_id) = 1) then 'ALL'
            else isnull(pub_id, 'Unknown')
            END as pub_id,
       AVG(price) AS average
   FROM titles
   GROUP BY type, pub_id
   WITH CUBE
   ORDER by GROUPING(type), GROUPING(pub_id)
go

type         pub_id average
------------ ------ ----------
business     0736   2.9900
business     1389   17.3100
mod_cook     0877   11.4900
popular_comp 1389   21.4750
psychology   0736   11.4825
psychology   0877   21.5900
trad_cook    0877   15.9633
UNDECIDED    0877   NULL
UNDECIDED    ALL    NULL
trad_cook    ALL    15.9633
psychology   ALL    13.5040
popular_comp ALL    21.4750
mod_cook     ALL    11.4900
business     ALL    13.7300
ALL          0736   9.7840
ALL          0877   15.4100
ALL          1389   18.9760
ALL          ALL    14.7662
```

Joining Tables

Transact-SQL allows you to correlate data between two or more tables by performing a join. Generally, you connect the tables using a common column, which is most often a column for which a foreign key and primary key relationship has been specified.

You can specify a join in two ways. First, you can specify the join condition in the WHERE clause. This is an older way of specifying a join, but it is still supported. Those of you who have been using SQL for a while are probably more familiar with this method.

You can also specify the join condition in the FROM clause. This method complies with the ANSI-92 standard.

NOTE

The ANSI-92 join syntax (or ANSI join for short) was introduced in version 6.5 and is now the preferred method of expressing joins.

One advantage with the ANSI join syntax is that the actual join operation performed is easier to identify because it is explicitly stated in the FROM clause. However, it can be harder to identify the list of tables involved in the query because you now have to wade through all the join verbiage to identify the tables involved. The old style syntax specified a more easily readable list of tables in the FROM clause.

The ANSI JOIN syntax has a few advantages over the old syntax:

- The new join syntax supports double outer joins, which the old style syntax does not.
- The new style syntax allows you to specify optimizer hints for how to join the tables in a query, which you cannot provide using the old style syntax.
- It is harder to create a Cartesian product by leaving out a join condition because the lack of an ON statement in the JOIN clause leads to a syntax error.
- Microsoft has stated that the old style join syntax might not be supported in future releases. Because Microsoft encourages use of the new join syntax, you can probably safely assume that Microsoft will be more willing to fix problems regarding ANSI joins than those of the older T-SQL join syntax.

The following example shows both ways of expressing a join. Both statements return the same resultset:

```
SELECT title, qty
   FROM titles t, sales s
   WHERE t.title_id = s.title_id

SELECT title, qty
   FROM titles t INNER JOIN sales s ON t.title_id = s.title_id
```

A table alias was also introduced in the example. The titles table was aliased to the name t and sales to s. Aliasing is useful when you have to refer to a table in several places in the query; you don't have to type the entire table name each time. Although defined in the FROM clause, a table alias can be used anywhere in the query that you have to qualify the column name.

The different types of joins are INNER, OUTER, and CROSS. An INNER join is based on equality between the column values. Only rows with matching values on the join columns between the two tables will be returned in the resultset. The following example lists all authors and the average royalty paid to them for all matching records between authors and titleauthor:

```
select au_lname, au_fname, avg(royaltyper) AS avg_royalty
   from authors a join titleauthor ta on a.au_id = ta.au_id
   group by au_lname, au_fname
   order by 3
go
```

```
au_lname                                 au_fname             avg_royalty
---------------------------------------- -------------------- -----------
Gringlesby                               Burt                 30
O'Leary                                  Michael              35
Ringer                                   Anne                 37
Yokomoto                                 Akiko                40
MacFeather                               Stearns              42
Hunter                                   Sheryl               50
Dull                                     Ann                  50
Bennet                                   Abraham              60
Green                                    Marjorie             70
DeFrance                                 Michel               75
Karsen                                   Livia                75
Ringer                                   Albert               75
Panteley                                 Sylvia               100
Locksley                                 Charlene             100
Carson                                   Cheryl               100
Blotchet-Halls                           Reginald             100
del Castillo                             Innes                100
Straight                                 Dean                 100
White                                    Johnson              100
```

The OUTER join returns all the rows from the specified outer table (specified with LEFT OUTER, RIGHT OUTER, or FULL OUTER), even if the other table has no match. Rows returned from the outer table that have no corresponding match in the inner table will display the NULL symbol for any columns retrieved from the inner table. For example, you might want to display the names of all authors along with the average royalty paid if available:

```
select au_lname, au_fname, avg(royaltyper)
   from authors a left outer join titleauthor ta on a.au_id = ta.au_id
   group by au_lname, au_fname
   order by 3
go
```

```
au_lname                                 au_fname             avg_royalty
---------------------------------------- -------------------- -----------
Greene                                   Morningstar          NULL
Greenfield                               Tom                  NULL
McBadden                                 Heather              NULL
Smith                                    Meander              NULL
Stringer                                 Dirk                 NULL
Gringlesby                               Burt                 30
O'Leary                                  Michael              35
Ringer                                   Anne                 37
Yokomoto                                 Akiko                40
MacFeather                               Stearns              42
Hunter                                   Sheryl               50
Dull                                     Ann                  50
Bennet                                   Abraham              60
Green                                    Marjorie             70
DeFrance                                 Michel               75
Karsen                                   Livia                75
Ringer                                   Albert               75
Panteley                                 Sylvia               100
White                                    Johnson              100
Straight                                 Dean                 100
Locksley                                 Charlene             100
Carson                                   Cheryl               100
Blotchet-Halls                           Reginald             100
del Castillo                             Innes                100
```

26

Note that no real difference exists between a left or right outer join except for specifying which table on which side of the join condition is to be the controlling, or outer table. For example, the previous query would provide the same result if you reversed tables in the join clause and made it a right outer join:

```
select au_lname, au_fname, avg(royaltyper)
   from titleauthor ta right outer join authors a on ta.au_id = a.au_id
   group by au_lname, au_fname
   order by 3
```

A full outer join will return all matching rows from both tables along with all rows from each table without a corresponding match in the other table.

A `CROSS` join returns all possible combinations of rows, also called a **Cartesian product**. Essentially, you are joining each row from one table with *all* the rows from another table. The total number of rows returned is the product of the number of rows in each table. Be careful using cross joins because the resultsets can become quite large, even for relatively small tables. For example, a cross join between a table with 1,000 rows and a table with 5,000 rows would return 1,000 * 5,000, or 5,000,000 rows.

With the ANSI syntax, you specify the join type explicitly in the `FROM` clause, but the join type in the older join syntax is specified in the `WHERE` clause. The old style syntax allowed you to specify only a left outer join or a right outer join using the *= or =* operators, respectively. For example, the preceding outer join would be written as follows using the old style syntax:

```
select au_lname, au_fname, avg(royaltyper)
   from authors a, titleauthor ta
   where a.au_id *= ta.au_id
   group by au_lname, au_fname
   order by 3
```

Subqueries

A subquery is essentially a query contained in another query. You can use a subquery in place of an expression. Depending on the context of the subquery, there might be restrictions on the data a subquery can return. Subqueries can only return a single column of data, and in some cases, they can only return a single row.

If the subquery returns only one row and one column, it can be used in place of any expression. This example returns all books published by Binnet & Hardley:

```
SELECT title FROM titles
   WHERE pub_id =
        (SELECT pub_id FROM publishers
            WHERE pub_name = 'Binnet & Hardley')
```

An error message is returned if the subquery would have returned several rows.

A subquery must always appear in parentheses.

NOTE

You will often find that you can achieve the same result with a subquery or a join. A join is often more efficient than a subquery (with the exception of when you want to remove duplicates, in which a subquery with `NOT EXISTS` is more efficient).

You can use a subquery that returns one column and several rows with the `IN` predicate. The following example returns all publishers of business books:

```
SELECT pub_name FROM publishers
   WHERE pub_id IN
        (SELECT pub_id FROM titles
            WHERE type = 'business')
```

You can also use a subquery that returns several rows with the EXISTS keyword. The following example returns the same resultset as the preceding example:

```
SELECT pub_name FROM publishers p
   WHERE EXISTS
        (SELECT * FROM titles t
            WHERE p.pub_id = t.pub_id
              AND type = 'business')
```

Although the subquery specifies the * in the SELECT list, the subquery actually returns no column data. When the EXISTS keyword is used, the subquery returns a true or false condition depending on whether a matching record was found.

This type of subquery is a **correlated subquery**. The inner query refers to a table in the outer query in the WHERE clause of the subquery (WHERE p.pub_id = t.pub_id). SQL Server executes the inner query for each row in the outer query, testing for a match on pub_id. After a match is found, SQL Server stops looking for additional matching rows and returns a true condition, adding the outer row to the resultset.

Although this query could be represented as well with an IN predicate, you would have to use a correlated subquery like this when checking for the existence of matching rows between two tables where the common key is made up of more than one column. The IN predicate can only match against a single column in the subquery.

A subquery can also be used in a column expression in query. For example, the following query substitutes the average price in place of price for any rows where price is null:

```
select title, type, isnull(price, (select avg(price) from titles))
   from titles
```

26

Subqueries Versus Joins

SQL Server treats the subquery with the IN predicate or an EXISTS subquery in much the same way as a join, with one major exception. For example, following is a query using a join condition to return a resultset:

```
select pub_name
   from publishers p, titles t
   where p.pub_id = t.pub_id
     and type = "business"
go

pub_name
----------------------------------------
New Age Books
Algodata Infosystems
Algodata Infosystems
Algodata Infosystems
```

Notice that duplicate rows are in the resultset. This is because the nature of a join is to find *all matching rows*. To remove the duplicates, you would need to specify the DISTINCT clause, which adds overhead of putting the rows into a work table to sort and remove the duplicate rows. With a large resultset, this could be expensive to do. The second method is to use the exists keyword to find only rows matching the condition, and to stop looking for results after the first match is found for a particular value. Following is the same query with an exists clause:

```
select pub_name
from publishers p
where exists
    (select *
     from titles t
     where p.pub_id = t.pub_id
     and type = "business")
go

pub_name
----------------------------------------
New Age Books
Algodata Infosystems
```

TIP

Always consider using exists rather than joining tables and using distinct. The performance benefits can be dramatic.

However, if you must include columns from both tables in the resultset, the query will have to be written as a join.

not exists **and** not in

Certain results can be defined only with a subquery; for example, non-membership and non-existence can be expressed only in that way. For example, which publishers *do not* publish business books? This query cannot be expressed with a join, but it can be expressed using not exists or not in:

```
select pub_name
   from publishers p
   where not exists
            (select *
                from titles t
                where t.pub_id = p.pub_id
                  and type = 'business')
```

```
select pub_name
   from publishers
   where pub_id not in
            (select pub_id
                from titles
                where type = 'business')
```

TIP

In most cases, `not in` and `not exists` are identical in their behavior. However, by using `not exists`, you can compare tables in which the join condition consists of multiple columns. You can't use `not in` to compare more than a single column.

Subqueries with Aggregates in `where` Clauses

One specific case in which a subquery is required appears when you want to use an aggregate function in a `where` clause. The next example returns the type and price of all books whose price is below the average price. This condition in a `where` clause would be illegal:

```
where price < avg(price)
```

The server requires that the average price be derived in a subquery, as follows:

```
select type, price
   from titles
   where price <
         (select avg(price)
             from titles)
```

Subqueries as Derived Tables

SQL Server provides the ability to use derived tables in your queries. A derived table is a subquery contained in a `FROM` clause that can be referred to by an alias and used as a table in the query. A derived table can be thought of as sort of a dynamic view that exists only for the duration of the query. Derived tables are handy if you don't need to use a resultset in a temp table more than once.

One benefit of using a subquery as a derived table is that unlike a normal subquery, the derived table can return multiple columns that can be referenced by the outer query like normal table columns in the select list, `where` clause, and so on. The subquery can contain aggregates, group by, `UNION`, and so on if needed.

For example, perhaps you need to write a query to return the average, by publisher, of the largest sale for each book. SQL Server doesn't allow an aggregate within an aggregate, so a query like the following wouldn't work:

```
select pub_name, sum(max(qty)) as top_sales
   from sales s
   join titles t on s.title_id = t.title_id
   join publishers p on t.pub_id = p.pub_id
   group by title_id, pub_name
```

You could break it up into two queries, putting intermediate results of the max(qty) from the titles and sales table into a temporary table, and then run a query against the temp table to calculate the avg of the max(qty). You could also write a more elegant solution using a derived table:

```
select pub_name, avg(top_sales) as avg_top_sales
   from publishers p
   join titles t on p.pub_id = t.pub_id
   join (select title_id, max(qty) as top_sales
            from sales
            group by title_id) as tot_sales
     on t.title_id = tot_sales.title_id
   group by pub_name
```

Adding Rows with INSERT

You use the INSERT statement to add rows to a table. The following example adds one row to the authors table:

```
INSERT authors (au_id, au_lname, au_fname, phone, contract)
   VALUES('123-65-7635', 'Johnson', 'Lisa', '408 342 7845', 1)
```

The number of values in the VALUES list must match the number in the column list. You can omit the column list only if you are providing values for all columns in the table, except for any identity column that might exist on the table. It is strongly recommended that you always provide a column list in your insert statement so that the mapping of values to columns is explicitly defined. Without a column list, your INSERT statement depends on the column order not changing or no columns being added or removed form the table. If the number of columns in the table no longer matches the number of values specified, the INSERT will fail with the following error message:

```
Server: Msg 213, Level 16, State 4, Line 1
Insert Error: Column name or number of supplied values does not match table
definition.
```

If you want to omit table columns in your insert statement, you must provide a column list. In addition, you can only omit column(s) from the insert statement if the columns allow NULL, have a default value associated with them, are of the timestamp datatype, or have the identity property defined for them.

You cannot insert more than one row at a time using the VALUES clause. If you need to add multiple rows, you will need to specify a separate insert statement for each row. The only time an insert statement can insert more than one row is when the INSERT uses a SELECT statement in place of the values clause. The following query creates a table called authors_archive and inserts all authors from California into it:

```
if object_id('authors_archive') is null  -- create the archive table
    create table authors_archive
                         (au_id id NOT NULL ,
                          au_lname varchar 40) NOT NULL ,
                          au_fname varchar(20) NOT NULL ,
                          phone char(12) NOT NULL,
                          address varchar(40) NULL ,
                          city varchar(20) NULL ,
                          state char(2) NULL ,
                          zip char(5) NULL)
go

INSERT authors_archive
   (au_id, au_lname, au_fname, phone, city, state, zip)
   SELECT au_id, au_lname, au_fname, phone, city, state, zip
      FROM authors
      WHERE state = 'CA'
go
```


Another useful feature is the ability to insert data from the resultset(s) of a stored procedure, user-defined function, or dynamic query. This can be done as long as the stored procedure, user-defined function, or dynamic query returns one or more resultsets that are compatible with the destination table structure. To be compatible, the resultset(s) must contain the same number of columns as the destination table, and the datatypes of the resultset columns must be compatible with the corresponding datatype columns.

Listing 26.9 creates a table to hold information from DBCC SQLPERF(logspace) and inserts the resultset returned by that command into the table.

LISTING 26.9 Using INSERT with the Resultset from a Dynamic Query

```
CREATE TABLE log_space
(cap_date DATETIME DEFAULT GETDATE(),
 db sysname,
 log_size FLOAT,
 space_used FLOAT,
 status BIT)
```

LISTING 26.9 Continued

```
INSERT log_space(db, log_size, space_used, status)
   EXEC ('DBCC SQLPERF(logspace)')

select * from log_space
go

cap_date                db        log_size  space_used        status
----------------------- --------- --------- ----------------- ------
2002-08-24 18:13:37.010 master    3.3671875 29.698375701904297 0
2002-08-24 18:13:37.010 tempdb    0.4921875 39.186508178710938 0
2002-08-24 18:13:37.010 model     0.4921875 48.809524536132813 0
2002-08-24 18:13:37.010 msdb      2.2421875 32.186412811279297 0
2002-08-24 18:13:37.010 pubs      0.7421875 62.105262756347656 0
2002-08-24 18:13:37.010 Northwind 0.9921875 48.868110656738281 0
2002-08-24 18:13:37.010 bigpubs   0.484375  43.850807189941406 0
```

Modifying Rows with UPDATE

The update statement is straightforward. You specify the table to be updated, the columns to modify, the new values, and the rows to be updated. The following statement changes the royalty to 15% and price to $25 for a book with a `title_id` of `'BU1032'`:

```
UPDATE titles
   SET royalty = 15, price = $25
   WHERE title_id = 'BU1032'
```

If you omit the `WHERE` clause, all rows will be updated.

You can use a join in an `UPDATE` statement (this is a T-SQL extension) to qualify the rows in a table to be modified:

```
/* increase prices by 5 times
** where the author's last name is Smythe */
update titles
   set price = price * 5
   from authors a
   join titleauthor ta on (a.au_id = ta.au_id )
   join  titles t  on (t.title_id = ta.title_id )
   where au_lname = 'White'
```

Notice that the `titles` table is specified twice in the update statement, both in the `UPDATE` and `FROM` clauses. The table name is required in the `UPDATE` statement to specify which table is to be modified, and again in the `FROM` clause to specify the join.

A subquery can provide a similar result as a join:

```
update titles
   set advance = advance * 1.5
        where pub_id in (select pub_id from publishers
                            where state = 'CA')
```

You can also use a correlated subquery in an update. The following type of query is common for generating/refreshing a rollup quantity in a separate table:

```
update titles
   set ytd_sales = (select sum(qty)
                     from sales s
                     where titles.title_id = s.title_id
                     and datediff(yy, ord_date, getdate()) = 0)
```

Removing Rows with DELETE

To remove rows from a table, use the DELETE statement. To remove the rows with an author last name of "Smith", type the following:

```
DELETE authors WHERE au_lname = 'Smith'
```

If you omit the WHERE clause, all rows are removed.

If you really want to remove all rows, it is much more efficient to use the TRUNCATE TABLE statement, which does not log each deleted row to the transaction log.

T-SQL also allows for a join to be used in a delete statement to qualify the rows in a table to be deleted:

```
/* remove titleauthor where author last name
** is 'White' */

delete titleauthor
   from titleauthor t join authors a on ( a.au_id = t.au_id)
   where au_lname = 'White'
```

A subquery will work similar to a join:

```
/* delete titleauthor records for authors with last name "Ringer" */
delete titleauthor
   where au_id  in (select au_id from authors where au_lname = 'Ringer')
```

SQL Server Functions

With version 7.0, Microsoft added more than 30 functions to an already large number of functions. More were added in SQL Server 2000 as well to support new features or capabilities, or to provide additional functionality.

Some of the SQL Server functions provide shortcuts to obtain information that could be retrieved in other ways. For instance, one function will obtain an object ID (`OBJECT_ID()`) if you know the object's name, but looking it up in the `sysobjects` table could also work.

Other functions, such as some of the mathematical functions, are more essential. (Okay, it could be argued that you can calculate the square root, for instance, using T-SQL code, but it is not efficient.)

Most functions have the following structure:

```
FUNCTION_NAME([parameter1 [, parameter2 [, ...]])
```

The parameters might be an expression (such as a column name or another function), a constant, or a special code (such as a formatting code).

A function returns a value. The datatype for the value depends on the function you are using. Take a look at the available functions grouped by category.

String Functions

The string functions allow you to perform concatenation, parsing manipulation, and so on with strings.

> **TIP**
>
> Excessive use of string functions against a column might indicate that the column should be split into several columns. For example, if you find yourself frequently parsing out first name and last name from a name column, perhaps you should split the name into two columns.

Table 26.3 lists the available string functions. They can be used against any string expression.

TABLE 26.3 String Functions

Function Name	Returns
`ASCII(`*`char`*`)`	The ASCII code for the leftmost character in *`char`*.
`CHAR(`*`int`*`)`	The ASCII character represented by *`int`* (an ASCII code).
`CHARINDEX(`*`char_pattern`*`, `*`char`*`, [`*`int_start`*`])`	Starting location of *`char_pattern`* within *`char`*, optionally starting search at *`int_start`*.
`DIFFERENCE(`*`char1`*`, `*`char2`*`)`	The difference between the two character expressions. Used for a phonetic match.

TABLE 26.3 Continued

Function Name	Returns
`LEFT(char, int)`	*int* characters from left of *char*.
`LEN(char)`	Number of characters in *char*, excluding trailing blanks.
`LOWER(char)`	*char* in lowercase.
`LTRIM(char)`	*char* without leading spaces.
`NCHAR(int)`	The character for a given Unicode value.
`PATINDEX(char_pattern, char)`	Starting position of *char_pattern* in *char*, or `0` if the pattern is not found.
`REPLACE(char1, char2, char3)`	String with all occurrences of *char2* replaced with *char3* in *char1*.
`QUOTENAME(char, [char_quote])`	*char* as a valid quoted identifier. Adds the characters `[` and `]` at the beginning and end of *char* (this default can be changed to `'` or `"`, specified as *char_quote*). Returns a Unicode string.
`REPLICATE(char, int)`	Repeat of *char* expression *int* number of times.
`REVERSE(char)`	Reverse of *char*.
`RIGHT(char, int)`	*int* characters from right of *char*.
`RTRIM(char)`	*char* without trailing spaces.
`SOUNDEX(char)`	A four-character string used for comparison of a phonetic match.
`SPACE(int)`	A string of *int* spaces.
`STR(float, [length, [decimal]])`	*float* as a character string, with length of *length* and *decimal* numbers of decimals. Default *length* is 10 and default number of decimals is 0.
`STUFF(char1, start, length, char2)`	A string with *length* number of characters from *char1* replaced with *char2*, starting at *start*.
`SUBSTRING(char, start, length)`	A string of *length* number of characters from *char*, from *start* position.
`UNICODE(char)`	The Unicode code for the leftmost character in *char*.
`UPPER(char)`	*char* in uppercase.

You can use the operator + to concatenate strings.

The following example uses `SUBSTRING` and string concatenation to present each author's first letter of the first name and then the last name:

```
SELECT SUBSTRING(au_fname,1,1) + '. ' + au_lname FROM authors
```

Mathematical Functions

The mathematical functions in Table 26.4 perform calculations based on the input values and return a numeric value. No new mathematical functions were introduced in version 7.0.

TABLE 26.4 Mathematical Functions

Function Name	Returns
ABS(numeric)	The absolute (positive) value of numeric.
ACOS(*float*)	The arc cosine for *float*.
ASIN(float)	The arc sine for *float*.
ATAN(*float*)	The arc tangent for *float*.
ATAN2(*float1*, *float2*)	The arc tangent whose tangent is between *float1* and *float2*.
CEILING(*numeric*)	The smallest integer value that is higher than or equal to *numeric*.
COS(*float*)	The trigonometric cosine of *float*.
COT(*float*)	The trigonometric cotangent of *float*.
DEGREES(*numeric*)	The number of degrees for a given angle, *numeric*, given in radians.
EXP(*float*)	The exponential value of *float*.
FLOOR(*numeric*)	The largest integer value that is lower than or equal to *numeric*.
LOG(*float*)	The natural logarithm of *float*.
LOG10(float)	The base-10 logarithm of *float*.
PI()	The constant pi.
POWER(*numeric1*, *numeric2*)	The value of *numeric1* to the specified power, given in *numeric2*.
RADIANS(*numeric*)	Radians of *numeric*, given in degrees.
RAND([*seed*])	A random value between 0 and 1. *seed* can be specified as the starting value.
ROUND(*numeric*, *length*, *func*)	Number rounded to the specified *numeric* to specified *length*. If *func* is specified and not 0, *numeric* is rounded down to *length*.
SIGN(*numeric*)	1 if *numeric* is positive, 0 if *numeric* is 0, and –1 if *numeric* is negative.
SIN(*float*)	The trigonometric sine of *float*.
SQUARE(*float*)	The square of *float*.
SQRT(*float*)	The square root of *float*.
TAN(*float*)	The trigonometric tangent of *float*.

The operators +, -, *, /, and % (modulo) are also available for numeric expressions.

Date Functions

The date functions perform operations such as formatting and subtracting. The expression given is a datetime datatype.

Some of the functions take a **datepart** as argument. The datepart specifies on what part of the datetime datatype you want to operate. Table 26.5 provides the codes for the datepart.

TABLE 26.5 Available Codes for Datepart

Datepart	Abbreviation	Possible Values
year	yy	1753–9999
quarter	qq	1–4
month	mm	1–12
day of year	dy	1–366
day	dd	1–31
week	wk	1–53
weekday	dw	1–7
hour	hh	0–23
minute	mi	0–59
second	ss	0–59
millisecond	ms	0–999

The date- and time-related functions are listed in Table 26.6.

TABLE 26.6 Date- and Time-Related Functions

Function Name	Returns	New in SQL Server 2000
DATEADD(*datepart*, *int*, *date*)	Date expression as a result of adding *int* *dateparts* to date.	
DATEDIFF(*datepart*, *date1*, *date2*)	The number of *dateparts* between *date 1* and *date2*.	
DATENAME(*datepart*, *date*)	The *datepart* of *date* returned as a character string. For month and day of week, the actual name is returned.	
DATEPART(*datepart*, *date*)	The *datepart* of *date* returned as an integer.	
DAY(*date*)	The day-of-month part as an integer.	
GETDATE()	The current date and time.	
GETUTCDATE()	The current date and time as Universal Time Coordinate Time (Greenwich Mean Time).	Yes
MONTH(*date*)	The month as an integer.	
YEAR(*date*)	The year as an integer.	

You can use the operators + and - directly on datetime expressions in version 7.0 and later. The implied datepart is days. In this example, you use the + operator to add one day to the current date:

```
SELECT GETDATE(), GETDATE() + 1
go

---------------------- ----------------------
1998-03-28 16:08:33     1998-03-29 16:08:33
```

Metadata Functions

The metadata functions, listed in Table 26.7, are useful for retrieving information such as column names, table names, index keys, and so on. Basically, many of the functions are shortcuts for querying the system tables.

TIP

It is better to use the system functions than to directly query the system tables. If the system tables change in forthcoming releases of SQL Server (as they did with version 7.0), your applications and scripts will still work if you use the system functions. You can also use the information schema views for retrieving system-table–related information. The views are ANSI standard and are independent of the system tables, and all have the object owner `INFORMATION_SCHEMA`.

TABLE 26.7 Metadata Functions

Function Name	Returns	New in SQL Server 2000
COL_LENGTH(*table*, *column*)	The length of *column* in *table*.	
COL_NAME(*table_id*, *column_id*)	The name of *column_id* in *table_id*.	
COLUMNPROPERTY(*id*, *column*, *property*)	Information about a *column* in a table, given the table *id*. Returns information for a parameter, given in *column*, for a stored procedure. The *property* parameter defines the type of information to be returned.	
DATABASEPROPERTY (*database_name*, *property*)	Setting of specified *property* for *database_name*. Included for backward compatibility, use DATABASEPROPERTYEX instead.	
DATABASEPROPERTYEX (*database_name*, *property*)	Current setting of specified *property* for *database_name* as a sql_variant.	Yes
DB_ID([*db_name*])	The database ID of *db_name* or the current database.	
DB_NAME([*db_id*])	The database name of *db_id* or the name of the current database.	
FILE_ID(*filename*)	The ID for *filename*.	
FILE_NAME(*file_id*)	The filename for *file_id*.	
FILEGROUP_ID(*filegroupname*)	The ID for *filegroupname*.	
FILEGROUP_NAME(*filegroup_id*)	The filegroup name for *filegroup_id*.	
FILEGROUPPROPERTY (*filegroup_name*,*property*)	The value of *property* for *filegroup_name*.	
FILEPROPERTY (*filename*, *property*)	The value of *property* for *filename*.	
FULLTEXTCATALOGPROPERTY (*catalog_name*, *property*)	The value of *property* for full-text catalog *catalog_name*.	
FULLTEXTSERVICEPROPERTY (*property*)	Information about *property* for full-text service-level.	

TABLE 26.7 Continued

Function Name	Returns	New in SQL Server 2000
INDEX_COL(*table*, *index_id*,*key_id*)	The column name for the specified *table*, *index_id*, and *key_id*.	
INDEXKEY_PROPERTY (*table_ID* , *index_ID* , *key_ID* , *property*)	The *property* information about index key *key_ID* for *index_ID* on *table_ID*.	Yes
INDEXPROPERTY (*table_ID* , *index* , *property*)	The *property* info for index *index* on *table_ID*.	
OBJECT_ID(*object_name*)	The ID for *object_name*.	
OBJECT_NAME(*object_id*)	The database object name for *object_id*.	
OBJECTPROPERTY (*object_id*, *property*)	Information for *object_id*. *property* defines the type of information to be returned.	
SQL_VARIANT_PROPERTY (*expression*,*property*)	The *property* information about sql_variant *expression*, such as base datatype, as a sql_variant.	Yes
TYPEPROPERTY(*datatype*, *property*)	Information defined in *property* for *datatype*.	

System Functions

The system functions, listed in Table 26.8, are useful for retrieving information about values, options, and settings within the SQL Server.

TABLE 26.8 System Functions

Function Name	Returns	New in SQL Server 2000
APP_NAME()	The name of the application that executes the function.	
CAST(*expression* AS *datatype*)	The CAST function is a synonym for the CONVERT function and converts *expression* to *datatype*.	
COALESCE(*expr1*, [*expr2*,,,])	The first non-null expression in the list.	
COLLATIONPROPERTY (*collation_name*, *property*)	The specified *property* of the *collation_name*. *property* can be CodePAgeLCID, ComparisonStyle.	Yes
CONVERT(*datatype[(length)]*, *expression*, *style*)	Converts *expression* to *datatype*. For conversion of datetime or float expressions, *style* defines the formatting.	
DATALENGTH(*expression*)	The storage area of *expression*, including trailing blanks for character information.	
GETANSINULL([*db_name*])	The default nullability option of *db_name* for the current database.	
GETCHECKSUM(*col_name*)	A checksum value for the values in *col_name*.	
HOST_ID()	The process ID of the client application's process.	

TABLE 26.8 Continued

Function Name	Returns	New in SQL Server 2000
`HOST_NAME()`	The client's workstation name.	
`IDENT_CURRENT('`*`tablename`*`')`	The last identity value generated for *tablename* by any session and within any scope.	Yes
`IDENT_INCR(`*`table`*`)`	The identity increment for the identity column in *`table`*.	
`IDENT_SEED(`*`table`*`)`	The identity seed for the identity column in *`table`*.	
`IDENTITY(`*`datatype`*`[,`*`seed`*`, `*`increment`*`]) AS `*`column_name`*	Used only in `SELECT INTO` to create identity column in new table.	
`ISDATE(`*`char`*`)`	1 if *`char`* is in a valid datetime format; otherwise, 0.	
`ISNULL(`*`expression`*`, `*`value`*`)`	*`value`* if *`expression`* is `NULL`.	
`ISNUMERIC(`*`char`*`)`	1 if *`char`* can be converted to a numeric value; otherwise, 0.	
`NEWID()`	A generated global unique identifier.	
`NULLIF(`*`expr1`*`, `*`expr2`*`)`	Null if *`expr1`* equals *`expr2`*.	
`PARSENAME(`*`object_name`*`, `*`object_part`*`)`	Name of *`object_part`* (specified as an int) of *`object_name`*.	
`PERMISSIONS(`*`object_id`*`[,`*`column`*`])`	A bitmap indicating permissions on *`object_id`* and optionally *`column`*.	
`ROWCOUNT_BIG()`	Number of rows affected by previous statement executed in session as a `bigint`.	Yes
`SCOPE_IDENTITY()`	The last identity value inserted into an `IDENTITY` column within current scope (for example, stored procedure, trigger, function, or batch).	Yes
`SERVER_PROPERTY('`*`property`*`')`	The *property* information about the server as a sql_variant.	Yes
`SESSIONPROPERTY(`*`option`*`)`	The `SET` options of a session as a sql_variant.	Yes
`STATS_DATE(`*`table_id`*`, `*`index_id`*`)`	Date when the distribution page was updated for *`index_id`* on *`table_id`*.	
`TRIGGER_NESTLEVEL ([`*`tr_object_id`*`])`	Nesting level of specified or current trigger.	

The following example returns the title ID and price for all books. If the price is not set (`NULL`), it returns a price of 0:

```
SELECT title_id, ISNULL(price, 0) FROM titles
```

Let us expand the example. You want to display the string `'Not Priced'` for those that contain `NULL` values. You have to convert the price to a character value before replacing `NULL` with your text string:

```
SELECT title_id, ISNULL(CONVERT(CHAR(10),price), 'Not Priced')
FROM titles
```

Security Functions

The security functions, listed in Table 26.9, are useful for retrieving information about users and roles.

TABLE 26.9 Security Functions

Function Name	Returns	New in SQL Server 2000
HAS_DBACCESS(*database*)	Information about whether current user has access to *database*.	Yes
IS_MEMBER(*group* | *role*]	1 if the user is a member of specified NT *group* or SQL Server *role*; otherwise, 0.	
IS_SRVROLEMEMBER (*role* [, *login*])	1 if the user's login ID is a member of the specified server *role*; otherwise, 0. An explicit *login* name can be specified.	
SUSER_ID(*login_name*)	The loginid of the specified *login_name*. Included for backward compatibility; use SUSER_SID instead.	
SUSER_NAME([*login_id*])	The login name of *login_id*. Included for backward compatibility; use SUSER_SNAME instead.	
SUSER_SID([*login*])	Security identification number (SID) for *login*.	
SUSER_SNAME([*login_id*])	The login name of *login_id*.	
USER_ID([*username*])	The user ID for *username*.	
USER_NAME([*user_id*])	The username for current user or *user_id*.	

The following example returns the current user's database username, login name, and whether the user is a member of the db_owner role:

```
select substring (user_name(), 1, 20) AS 'user_name',
       substring (suser_sname(),1, 30) AS 'login_name',
       case IS_MEMBER('db_owner')
          when 1 then 'Yes'
          else 'No'
          end AS 'Is_dbOwner'
go

user_name            login_name                     Is_dbOwner
-------------------- ------------------------------ ----------
dbo                  RRANKINSA20P\rrankins          Yes
```

Text and Image Functions

These scalar functions, listed in Table 26.10, perform an operation on a text or image input value or column and return information about the value.

TABLE 26.10 Text and Image Functions

Function Name	Returns
TEXTPTR (*column_name*)	The text-pointer for a text or image column as a varbinary(16) value. Pointer can be used in READTEXT, WRITETEXT, and UPDATETEXT statements.
TEXTVALID('*table.column*', *ptr*)	1 if text or image pointer *ptr* is valid for *table.column*, 0 if pointer is invalid.

The following example shows how to use the TEXTPTR function to retrieve a text pointer and use it in the READTEXT command:

```
USE pubs
GO
DECLARE @ptr varbinary(16)
SELECT @ptr = TEXTPTR(pr_info)
   FROM pub_info
   WHERE pub_id = '0877'
READTEXT pub_info.pr_info @ptr 0 65
GO

pr_info
-----------------------------------------------------------------
This is sample text data for Binnet & Hardley, publisher 0877 in
```

Rowset Functions

The rowset functions listed in Table 26.11 return an object that can be used in place of a table reference in a Transact-SQL statement.

TABLE 26.11 Rowset Functions

Function Name	Returns	New in SQL Server 2000
CONTAINSTABLE (*table*, *column* | * } , '*contains_ conditions*' [,*top_n_by_rank*])	A table of 0 or more rows for columns containing string data using precise or fuzzy matches to a single word or phrases, the proximity of words to one another, or weighted matches, as specified in *contains_conditions*. Result can be limited to the top *n* matching rows ordered by rank.	
FREETEXTTABLE (*table*, { *column* | * } , '*freetext_ string*' [, *top_n_by_rank*])	A table of 0 or more rows that match the meaning of the text in *freetext_string*. *table* is a table marked for full-text querying. *column* must be columns that contain string data. Result can be limited to the top *n* matching rows ordered by rank.	

TABLE 26.11 Continued

Function Name	Returns	New in SQL Server 2000
OPENDATASOURCE (*provider_name*, *init_string*)	The connection information used as the first part (*servername*) of a four-part fully qualified object name. Can be used in place of a linked server name. Should only reference OLE DB data sources.	Yes
OPENQUERY (*linked_server*, '*query*')	Resultset from specified pass-through *query* on *linked_server*.	
OPENROWSET (*provider_name*, {'*datasource*';'*user_id*'; '*password*'|'*provider_string*'} , {[*catalog*.][*schema*.]*object* | '*query*'})	Remote data result from specified connection to OLE DB data source.	
OPENXML(*docid*, *rowpattern*, *flag*) [WITH (*schemaDeclaration* | *tablename*)]	Resultset from an XML document specified with *docid*. Data is returned in edge table format unless *SchemaDeclaration* or *TableName* is specified.	Yes

The following example uses the OPENROWSET function and the Microsoft OLE DB Provider for SQL Server to titles records from the titles table in the pubs database on a remote server named RRANKINSA20P. Notice how the result from the function can be used just like a table, even in a JOIN clause:

```
select p.pub_id, t.title
   from publishers p
   join OPENROWSET('SQLOLEDB','RRANKINSA20P';'sa';'',
                  'SELECT * FROM pubs.dbo.titles ORDER BY pub_id') AS t
     on p.pub_id = t.pub_id
go

pub_id title
------ ------------------------------------------------------------------------
0736   You Can Combat Computer Stress!
0736   Is Anger the Enemy?
0736   Life Without Fear
0736   Prolonged Data Deprivation: Four Case Studies
0736   Emotional Security: A New Algorithm
0877   Silicon Valley Gastronomic Treats
0877   The Gourmet Microwave
0877   The Psychology of Computer Cooking
```

```
0877   Computer Phobic AND Non-Phobic Individuals: Behavior Variations
0877   Onions, Leeks, and Garlic: Cooking Secrets of the Mediterranean
0877   Fifty Years in Buckingham Palace Kitchens
0877   Sushi, Anyone?
1389   The Busy Executive's Database Guide
1389   Cooking with Computers: Surreptitious Balance Sheets
1389   Straight Talk About Computers
1389   But Is It User Friendly?
1389   Secrets of Silicon Valley
1389   Net Etiquette
```

To learn more about the CONTAINSTABLE and FREETEXTTABLE functions, see Chapter 44, "SQL Server Full-Text Search Services." For more information on using XML documents and the OPENXML function, see Chapter 41, "Using XML in SQL Server 2000."

Niladic Functions

The niladic group of functions, listed in Table 26.12, is basically a set of system functions. The reason for grouping them separately is that they are used without parentheses after the function name. They are defined in the ANSI SQL-92 standard.

You often find niladic functions used as defaults in CREATE TABLE and ALTER TABLE.

NOTE

Niladic functions are basically aliases to SQL Server system functions. If you use them for default values in tables and run sp_help for the table, edit the table, or script the table in Enterprise Manager, you will notice that they are translated to the corresponding system function.

TABLE 26.12 Niladic Functions

Function Name	Returns	Corresponding System Function
CURRENT_TIMESTAMP	Current date and time	GETDATE()
CURRENT_USER	The user's username	USER_NAME()
SESSION_USER	The user's username	USER_NAME()
SYSTEM_USER	The user's login name	SUSER_NAME()
USER	The user's username	USER_NAME()

In Listing 26.10, you create a table with three columns with defaults for the current date-time, the user's login name, and the username. The INSERT statement inserts default values for all columns, and the SELECT statements retrieve the row inserted.

LISTING 26.10 Using Niladic Functions with the INSERT Statement

```
CREATE TABLE my_defaults
   (the_datetime DATETIME DEFAULT CURRENT_TIMESTAMP,
    users_login CHAR(128) DEFAULT SYSTEM_USER,
    users_name CHAR(128) DEFAULT CURRENT_USER,)

INSERT my_defaults DEFAULT VALUES

SELECT * FROM my_defaults
go

the_datetime                users_login         users_name
--------------------------- ------------------- -----------------
1998-03-29 19:09:52.377     sa                  dbo
```

Aggregate Functions

The aggregate functions differ from those in the other groups. Aggregate functions perform an aggregation for a column over a set of rows.

Table 26.13 lists the aggregate functions available in SQL Server.

TABLE 26.13 Aggregate Functions

Function Name	Returns	New in SQL Server 2000
AVG([ALL | DISTINCT] *expression*)	The average of all values given in *expression*.	
BINARY_CHECKSUM (* | *expression* [,...*n*]	The binary checksum computed over a row or the list of *expressions*. Can be used to detect changes to a row.	Yes
CHECKSUM(* | *expression* [,...*n*]	The checksum value computed over a row or the list of *expressions*. Intended for use in building hash indices.	Yes
CHECKSUM_AGG [ALL | DISTINCT] *expression*)	The checksum of the values in a group *expression*, ignoring nulls.	Yes
COUNT([ALL | DISTINCT] *expression* | *)	The number of non-NULL values in *expression*. NULLs are counted if * is specified.	
COUNT_BIG([ALL | DISTINCT] *expression* | *)	The number of non- NULL values in *expression* as a bigint. NULLs are counted if * is specified.	Yes
GROUPING (*column_name*)	1 when a row is added to GROUP BY resultset by CUBE or ROLLUP operator. 0 when not.	
MAX([ALL | DISTINCT] *expression*)	The maximum value in *expression*.	

TABLE 26.13 Continued

Function Name	Returns	New in SQL Server 2000
VARP(*expression*)	The statistical variance for the population for all values in the given *expression*.	
STDEVP(*expression*)	The statistical standard deviation for the population for all values in the given *expression*.	
MIN([ALL | DISTINCT] *expression*)	The minimum value in *expression*.	
SUM([ALL | DISTINCT] *expression*)	The sum of all values in *expression*.	
VAR(*expression*)	The statistical variance of all values in the given *expression*.	
STDEV(*expression*)	The statistical standard deviation of all values in the given *expression*.	

If you add the keyword DISTINCT, only distinct values will be aggregated. The default is ALL. You should note that NULL values are not included in the aggregates, except for COUNT(*), which counts the number of rows returned from the relational expression.

Perhaps you want to count the number of rows, prices, and distinct prices in the title table:

```
SELECT COUNT(*) AS Total, COUNT(price) AS Prices,
       COUNT(DISTINCT price) AS "Distinct prices"
   FROM titles
go

Total       Prices      Distinct prices
----------- ----------- ---------------
18          16          11
```

Apparently, two books are not priced yet, or the price is not known (NULL), and there are a total of five duplicate prices.

Now, you want to perform some real aggregation over the prices:

```
SELECT MAX(price) AS 'Max', MIN(price) AS 'Min', AVG(price) AS 'Average'
   FROM titles
go

Max                   Min                   Average
--------------------- --------------------- ---------------------
22.9500               2.9900                14.7662

Warning: Null value is eliminated by an aggregate or other SET operation.
```

Note that even though NULL usually sorts low, the minimum price is 2.99 because NULL is excluded from the aggregate. (The warning message displayed indicates that NULL values were encountered and excluded from the aggregate result.) The average price also does not include the nulls and is calculated only on the 16 rows that contain NULL. To include the rows containing NULL values, use the ISNULL() function to substitute a value for NULL and notice the difference in the average price:

```
SELECT MAX(price) AS 'Max', MIN(price) AS 'Min', AVG(isnull(price, $0)) AS 'Average'
   FROM titles
go

Max                  Min                  Average
-------------------- -------------------- --------------------
22.9500              2.9900               13.1255

Warning: Null value is eliminated by an aggregate or other SET operation.
```

Aggregate functions are often used in conjunction with GROUP BY. The following example retrieves the average price for each book category:

```
SELECT type, AVG(price) AS Average
   FROM titles
   GROUP BY type
go

type         Average
------------ ----------
business     13.7300
mod_cook     11.4900
popular_comp 21.4750
psychology   13.5040
trad_cook    15.9633
UNDECIDED    NULL
```

The following example shows the use of CHECKSUM_AGG to detect changes in the publishers table:

```
select checksum_agg(binary_checksum(*)) as old_checksum
   from publishers

update publishers set state = 'MA'
   where state = 'CA'
```

```
select checksum_agg(binary_checksum(*)) as new_checksum
   from publishers
go

old_checksum
-----------
 -1096815739

new_checksum
-----------
 -1096873083
```

Using COMPUTE and COMPUTE BY

The COMPUTE and COMPUTE BY keywords enable you to return both detail and summary information in a single SELECT statement.

The compute clause reports overall aggregate values for a resultset, as shown in the following example:

```
/*list titles and prices, show overall max price*/
select title, price
   from titles
   compute max(price)
go

title                                                           price
--------------------------------------------------------------- ------------
The Busy Executive's Database Guide                             19.9900
Cooking with Computers: Surreptitious Balance Sheets            11.9500
You Can Combat Computer Stress!                                 2.9900
Straight Talk About Computers                                   19.9900
Silicon Valley Gastronomic Treats                               19.9900
The Gourmet Microwave                                           2.9900
The Psychology of Computer Cooking                              NULL
But Is It User Friendly?                                        22.9500
Secrets of Silicon Valley                                       20.0000
Net Etiquette                                                   NULL
Computer Phobic AND Non-Phobic Individuals: Behavior Variations 21.5900
Is Anger the Enemy?                                             10.9500
Life Without Fear                                               7.0000
Prolonged Data Deprivation: Four Case Studies                   19.9900
Emotional Security: A New Algorithm                             7.9900
```

```
Onions, Leeks, and Garlic: Cooking Secrets of the Mediterranean  20.9500
Fifty Years in Buckingham Palace Kitchens                        11.9500
Sushi, Anyone?                                                   14.9900

                                                                 max
                                                                 =============
                                                                 22.9500
```

> **NOTE**
>
> The way the computed aggregate is displayed is dependent on the query tool you are using. Query Analyzer will line up the computed aggregate under the column that is being aggregated, with a header indicating the type of aggregate. Not all query tools format the result from the COMPUTE clause as nicely.

The COMPUTE BY clause can be used in conjunction with an ORDER BY displaying subtotals within a resultset. You can also include the COMPUTE clause to display a grand total as well, as shown in the following example:

```
/* display type, title and price,
** and show the maximum price for each type */
select type, title, price
   from titles
   order by type
   compute max(price) by type
   compute max(price)
go

type         title                                                 price
------------ ----------------------------------------------------- ----------
business     The Busy Executive's Database Guide                   19.9900
business     Cooking with Computers: Surreptitious Balance Sheets  11.9500
business     You Can Combat Computer Stress!                       2.9900
business     Straight Talk About Computers                         19.9900

                                                                   max
                                                                   ==========
                                                                   19.9900
```

```
type         title                                                    price
------------ -------------------------------------------------------- ----------
mod_cook     Silicon Valley Gastronomic Treats                        19.9900
mod_cook     The Gourmet Microwave                                    2.9900

                                                                      max
                                                                      ==========
                                                                      19.9900


type         title                                                    price
------------ -------------------------------------------------------- ----------
popular_comp But Is It User Friendly?                                 22.9500
popular_comp Secrets of Silicon Valley                                20.0000
popular_comp Net Etiquette                                            NULL

                                                                      max
                                                                      ==========
                                                                      22.9500


type         title                                                    price
------------ -------------------------------------------------------- ----------
psychology   Computer Phobic AND Non-Phobic Individuals               21.5900
psychology   Is Anger the Enemy?                                      10.9500
psychology   Life Without Fear                                        7.0000
psychology   Prolonged Data Deprivation: Four Case Studies            19.9900
psychology   Emotional Security: A New Algorithm                      7.9900

                                                                      max
                                                                      ==========
                                                                      21.5900


type         title                                                    price
------------ -------------------------------------------------------- ----------
trad_cook    Onions, Leeks, and Garlic                                20.9500
trad_cook    Fifty Years in Buckingham Palace Kitchens                11.9500
trad_cook    Sushi, Anyone?                                           14.9900

                                                                      max
                                                                      ==========
                                                                      20.9500
```

```
type        title                                                 price
----------- ----------------------------------------------------- -----------
UNDECIDED   The Psychology of Computer Cooking                    NULL

                                                                  max
                                                                  ==========


                                                                  max
                                                                  ==========
                                                                  22.9500
```

Important point: `compute by` columns must match, *in order,* the columns specified in the `order by` clause. You can specify only a subset of the `order by` columns. Consider a query containing this `order by` clause:

```
order by a, b, c
```

The only allowed `compute by` clauses are the following:

- `compute by a, b, c`
- `compute by a, b`
- `compute by a`

Expressions in a `compute` or `compute by` clause must match exactly the corresponding expression in the `select` list:

```
select type, price, price*2 as 'double price'
   from titles
   where type = 'business'
   compute sum(price), sum(price*2)
go

type        price                double price
----------- -------------------- --------------------
business    19.9900              39.9800
business    11.9500              23.9000
business    2.9900               5.9800
business    19.9900              39.9800

            sum
            ====================
            54.9200
```

```
sum
=====================
109.8400
```

NOTE

Many organizations do not use `compute` for a variety of reasons. First, because it is not ANSI-standard SQL, organizations avoid writing important queries that might need to be modified dramatically to be ported to other database environments. Second, any decent reporting tool will provide all of the totaling and subtotaling directly within the report definition, with much more flexibility about the actual handling of the computed values. Third, not all database APIs or middle-tier database solutions can handle compute results properly.

If you plan to use `compute`, make sure you have spent the necessary time testing how your application reads and presents computed values.

Programming Constructs

The languages that interface to database management systems are sometimes divided into three categories:

- DML, Data Manipulation Language—This includes the ability to read and manipulate the data. Examples are `SELECT`, `INSERT`, `DELETE`, and `UPDATE`.
- DDL, Data Definition Language—Creating and altering the storage structures; an example is `CREATE TABLE`.
- DCL, Data Control Language—Defining permissions for data access; examples are `GRANT`, `REVOKE`, and `DENY`.

T-SQL includes other statements that can be useful, for instance, in tying together the DML statements in a stored procedure, such as `IF`, `ELSE`, and `WHILE`.

The `IF` Statement

The `IF` statement takes one argument: *`boolean_expression`*, which is an expression that can evaluate to `TRUE` or `FALSE`. The code to be conditionally executed is a statement block:

```
IF boolean_expression
    statement_block
ELSE
    statement_block
```

You define a statement block with the statements `BEGIN` and `END`. If no statement block is defined, only the first statement following the `IF` statement is executed when the *`boolean_expression`* is true.

In Listing 26.11, a script checks for the existence of a table, prints a message if the table exists, and, if it does, drops the table.

LISTING 26.11 Using the `IF` Statement to Perform Conditional Processing

```
IF OBJECTPROPERTY(OBJECT_ID('orders'), 'istable') = 1
BEGIN
    PRINT "Dropping orders Table"
    DROP TABLE orders
END
ELSE
    PRINT "Table orders does not exist"
```

WHILE, BREAK, and CONTINUE

The `WHILE` statement allows you to loop while an expression evaluates to true. The syntax for `WHILE` is as follows:

```
WHILE boolean_expression
   statement_block
```

The statement block contains the `BREAK` or the `CONTINUE` statements. `BREAK` exits the `WHILE` loop, and `CONTINUE` skips any remaining statements in the statement block and evaluates the *`boolean_expression`* again. Listing 26.12 demonstrates a simple example of using a `WHILE` loop to repeatedly update the titles table until the average price of all books exceeds $25.

LISTING 26.12 Using the `WHILE` Loop for Iterative Processing

```
/* loop until average price equals or exceeds $25*/
while (select avg (price) from titles) < $25
begin
    update titles set price = price * 1.05
    /* if more than 10 books are less than
    ** $15, continue processing */
    if (select count(*) from titles
           where price < $15) > 1
        continue
    /* If maximum price of any book exceeds
    ** $50, exit loop */
    if (select max(price) from titles) > $50
        break
end
```

CASE Expression

The CASE expression is an ANSI SQL-92 construct that allows for expressions that can evaluate a number of conditions and return a single result. CASE expressions are allowed wherever constant expressions are allowed, such as the SELECT list, the WHERE clause, GROUP BY, and ORDER BY. The CASE expression has two forms of syntax. The simple CASE expression compares an expression to a set of values to determine the result:

```
case expression
     when value1 then result1
     [when value2 then result2]
     [...]
     [else resultN]
     END
```

The searched CASE expression evaluates a set of Boolean conditions to determine the result:

```
case
    when Boolean_expression1 then expression1
    [[when Boolean_expression2 then expression2] [...]]
    [else expressionN]
    END
```

CASE expressions are an excellent tool to replace data values in columns (for example, code columns) with more meaningful values within your resultset, as shown in Listing 26.13.

LISTING 26.13 Using the CASE Expression to Substitute for Column Values

```
select substring (title, 1, 20) as Title,
       case type
          when 'popular_comp' then ' Computer book'
          when 'mod_cook'  then ' Cookbook'
          when 'trad_cook'  then ' Cookbook'
          else 'Other book'
       end as Type,
       'Sales are ' +
       case
          when ytd_sales < 5000 then 'Poor'
          when ytd_sales between 5001 and 10000 then 'Good'
          when ytd_sales > 10000 then 'Awesome'
          else 'Unknown'
       end as Sales
   from titles
go
```

LISTING 26.13 Continued

```
Title                Type            Sales
-------------------- --------------- -------------------
The Busy Executive's Other book      Sales are Poor
Cooking with Compute Other book      Sales are Poor
You Can Combat Compu Other book      Sales are Awesome
Straight Talk About  Other book      Sales are Poor
Silicon Valley Gastr Cookbook        Sales are Poor
The Gourmet Microwav Cookbook        Sales are Awesome
The Psychology of    Other book      Sales are unknown
But Is It User Frien Computer book   Sales are Good
Secrets of Silicon   Computer book   Sales are Poor
Net Etiquette        Computer book   Sales are unknown
Computer Phobic AND  Other book      Sales are Poor
Is Anger the Enemy?  Other book      Sales are Poor
Life Without Fear    Other book      Sales are Poor
Prolonged Data Depri Other book      Sales are Poor
Emotional Security:  Other book      Sales are Poor
Onions, Leeks, and   Cookbook        Sales are Poor
Fifty Years in Bucki Cookbook        Sales are Awesome
Sushi, Anyone?       Cookbook        Sales are Poor
```


The CASE expression can even be used in the SET clause of an UPDATE statement to conditionally set a value based on column values within the row, avoiding the need to use a cursor:

```
update titles
   set price = case when ytd_sales < 500 then price *.75
                    when price > $15 then price * .90
                    else price * 1.15
               end
```

RETURN

RETURN is used to stop execution of a batch, stored procedure, or trigger. When used in a stored procedure, RETURN can take an integer as an argument. The value 0 indicates successful execution. The values -1 to -99 are reserved by Microsoft (currently, -1 to -14 are in use), so you should use values outside that range.

> **TIP**
>
> You might want to set up some standard return values for your stored procedures. One option is to have different return values for the type of statement that caused the error return, such as 1 when a SELECT statement fails, 2 when an UPDATE statement fails, 3 when a DELETE statement fails, 4 when an INSERT statement fails, and so on.

Another approach is to have a different return value for each statement in the procedure that can lead to a return. For example, the first statement would return -101 on failure, the second statement would return -102 on failure, the third statement would return -103 on failure, and so on. The benefit of this approach is that if you capture the return status from the stored procedure, you can identify exactly which statement caused the error that led to the return.

GOTO

GOTO (yes, there is a GOTO statement in T-SQL) branches to a defined label. GOTO can be useful for error handling in stored procedures, for example. The following is a code fragment from a stored procedure that checks for errors after each statement and exits the procedure with a return code if an error occurs:

```
BEGIN TRAN
INSERT orders(customer_number) VALUES(1)
 IF @@ERROR <> 0 GOTO err_handle
RETURN 0
/* ... */
err_handle:
RAISERROR ('An error occurred in the stored procedure.
➥ The transaction has been rolled back', 12, 1)
ROLLBACK TRANSACTION
RETURN -101
```

WAITFOR

You can use WAITFOR to suspend execution for a specified delay (WAITFOR DELAY) or until a specified time (WAITFOR TIME). Say, for example, you want to generate a deadlock. (For instance, you might have defined an alert for a deadlock error and you want to test it.) You must be able to start execution of both batches more or less simultaneously for the deadlock to occur. This is hard to do in real time, so you can introduce a wait for 10 seconds in the first transaction to give you time to initiate the second transaction.

To try this out yourself, open up two separate connections to the same SQL Server in Query Analyzer. In one connection, execute the following code to initiate one transaction:

```
use pubs
go
BEGIN TRAN
UPDATE authors SET au_lname = au_lname
WAITFOR DELAY '00:00:10'
UPDATE titles SET title = title
ROLLBACK TRAN
```

Quickly switch to the other connection, and execute the following code to initiate another transaction:

```
use pubs
go
BEGIN TRAN
UPDATE titles SET title = title
UPDATE authors SET au_lname = au_lname
ROLLBACK TRAN
```

If you time it correctly, this should lead to a deadlock once the WAITFOR DELAY expires in the first connection and the second update statement is executed.

EXECUTE

The EXEC (or EXECUTE) command is used as a keyword for executing stored procedures. Introduced in version 6.0, EXEC also gives you the ability to execute strings and variables containing strings, which can be useful.

Perhaps you want to write a procedure to perform UPDATE STATISTICS for all tables in the database without having to hardcode the table names; that way, if you add or remove tables from the database, you don't have to edit the procedure. Unfortunately, the UPDATE STATISTICS command does not accept a variable as an argument. However, you can build the command dynamically and execute the command using the EXEC statement, as shown in Listing 26.14.

LISTING 26.14 Dynamic SQL Execution Using the EXEC Statement

```
DECLARE c1 cursor
   for select table_name from information_schema.tables
    where TABLE_TYPE = 'Base Table'
declare @tbl_name NVARCHAR(128)
open c1
fetch c1 into @tbl_name
while @@fetch_status = 0
begin
    EXEC('UPDATE STATISTICS ' + @tbl_name)
    fetch c1 into @tbl_name
end
close c1
deallocate c1
```

Another example is if you want to write a stored procedure that will SELECT rows from a table name passed to it as an argument. SQL Server does not accept variables for table names, column names, and so on, so the following syntax will produce an error message:

```
SELECT * FROM @tbl_name
```

To dynamically retrieve data from a table name passed in as a parameter, you can build a dynamic query to be executed by the EXEC command:

```
CREATE PROC general_select @tbl_name NVARCHAR(128) AS
    EXEC('SELECT * FROM ' + @tbl_name)
GO
EXEC general_select authors
GO
```

For more information on executing dynamic SQL within stored procedures, see Chapter 28.

Batches

A batch is simply a set of commands sent to SQL Server for execution. Do not confuse the batch term as used here with traditional batch processing, in which mass modifications are performed, often at low-activity periods.

Basically, SQL Server receives a string (containing T-SQL commands) from the client application. SQL Server parses this string as a unit, searching for keywords. If a syntax error is found, none of the statements in the batch are executed, and an error message is returned to the client application.

In Query Analyzer, ISQL, and OSQL, the string GO is used to separate batches. When the tool finds the string GO, it takes all text up to the preceding GO and submits it to SQL Server for execution.

Some restrictions for batches concern what commands can be combined with other commands within a batch. Some examples follow:

- You cannot combine certain commands within a batch. Most CREATE commands must be executed in a single batch. The exceptions are CREATE TABLE, CREATE INDEX, and CREATE DATABASE.
- When calling a stored procedure, you must precede the procedure name with EXECUTE if it's not the first statement in a batch. If SQL Server doesn't recognize the first statement in a batch, it simply assumes that the string is a call to a stored procedure.

A related concept is the SQL script. A SQL script is a text file containing one or more batches. Scripts are often used with Query Analyzer, ISQL, and OSQL. You do not have to specify GO after the last command in a script file; the tools will automatically generate an end-of-batch signal.

Listing 26.15 creates a table and a view. Note that the CREATE commands are separated by GO.

LISTING 26.15 Creating a Table and a View That Only Display Recent Orders

```
CREATE TABLE orders
   (order_number UNIQUEIDENTIFIER DEFAULT NEWID()  PRIMARY KEY NOT NULL,
    stor_id char(4) REFERENCES stores(stor_id),
    order_date DATETIME DEFAULT CONVERT(CHAR(8), GETDATE(), 112))
GO
CREATE VIEW recent_orders AS
   SELECT order_number, stor_id, order_date
      FROM orders
      WHERE order_date > GETDATE() - 14
GO
```

Comments

Anyone who has ever had to review or change some code recognizes the importance of comments. Even if it seems obvious what the code does when you're writing it, the meaning will most certainly not be as obvious later, especially if someone else other than the original author is looking at it.

When SQL Server finds a comment, it does not execute anything until the end of the comment. The Query Analyzer's syntax coloring indicates commented text with a green color by default. SQL Server supports two types of comment markers:

```
/* Comments */
```

These comment markers are useful for commenting several lines. None of the text between the comment markers is parsed, compiled, or executed. For shorter comments, you can use

```
-- Comments
```

SQL Server will not execute any of the text following the markers up to the end-of-line. The -- comment markers are defined in ANSI SQL-92.

Following is an example of a batch with an opening comment block that describes what the batch performs and a comment line later in the code that can be altered for debugging purposes:

```
/* Retrieves all orders that have been submitted the last day.
The SELECT COUNT is only for debugging purposes */
SELECT order_number, stor_id, order_date
   FROM orders
```

```
   WHERE order_date > GETDATE() -1
--SELECT 'Number of orders returned':, @@ROWCOUNT
```

Both types of comments can be nested within a /*...*/ comment block. Comment blocks are local to a batch and cannot span across multiple batches—in other words, you cannot specify the end-of-batch (GO) separator within a /*...*/ comment block. The example in Listing 26.16 attempts to use a comment block to comment out the GO command. Notice the error messages generated.

LISTING 26.16 Attempting to Comment Out the GO Command

```
/* this is a comment
select * from titles
go
select * from publishers
*/
go

Server: Msg 113, Level 15, State 1, Line 1
Missing end comment mark '*/'.
Server: Msg 170, Level 15, State 1, Line 2
Line 2: Incorrect syntax near '*'.
```

Local Variables

Local variables allow you to store values temporarily. The variable is always declared as a certain datatype with the DECLARE statement. The datatype can either be system supplied or user defined. The variable's name always begins with the @ sign and can be up to 128 characters in length.

Local variables initially are set to NULL. The variable is assigned a value with the SELECT statement or the SET statement. The SET statement can only set one variable at a time. A SELECT statement can assign values to one or more variables at a time and it is more efficient to perform multiple assignments in single select rather than performing multiple SELECT or SET statements. Also, a SELECT statement used to assign values to one or more local variables, referred to as an **assignment select**, cannot also return result rows.

Listing 26.17 prints the number of distinct book types in the titles table. You declare a local variable, assign it a value, and then print the contents of the variable.

LISTING 26.17 Assigning a Value to a Local Variable and Printing Its Contents

```
DECLARE @user_msg VARCHAR(255)
SELECT @user_msg = 'There are ' + CONVERT(VARCHAR(3),
       (SELECT COUNT(DISTINCT type) FROM titles))
        + ' book types in the titles table.'
PRINT @user_msg
go

There are 6 book types in the titles table.
```

> **NOTE**
>
> The life span of a local variable is the batch, trigger, or stored procedure in which it is declared. After any one of these has completed processing, the variable ceases to exist. The scope of a local variable is limited to the batch, trigger, or stored procedure in which it is declared. In other words, a local variable declared in one procedure cannot be accessed by a procedure called within that procedure unless it is passed as a parameter.
>
> If you want to store a value that persists between batches in T-SQL, or is accessible by a called procedure, you must create a temporary table in which to store the value.

Local variables, except for table variables, are scalar variables and can only hold a single value at a time. If an assignment select statement returns multiple rows, the local variable will contain the value from the last row returned. If the assignment select returns no rows, the local variable is not set to `NULL`, but it retains the value it had prior to the assignment select.

Local variables are often used in stored procedures.

Functions That Used to Be Called Global Variables

A certain set of functions used to be called **global variables** in earlier releases of SQL Server. The name **global** was apparently confusing to some, implying that the scope of the variable was beyond that of a local variable. Global variables were apparently mistaken by some as variables that a user could declare and the scope of the variable would extend across batches, which is not the case. You can name a variable starting with two or more at signs (`@@`), but it will still behave as a local variable.

These global variables, now called **functions**, contain information that SQL Server maintains. They exist so that an application can check things such as the error code for the last executed command. Microsoft online books categorizes functions in the various categories of the SQL Server functions. However, the documentation somewhat blurs the lines between session-level and server-level functions the way that Microsoft groups them. For this reason, this chapter categorizes them as connection-specific, monitoring-related, and general functions.

These functions are useful because some of them contain information that cannot be found elsewhere or would be difficult to obtain with other means.

For the connection-specific functions outlined in Table 26.14, SQL Server maintains separate values for each connection.

TABLE 26.14 Connection-Specific Functions

Function Name	Returned Value
@@CURSOR_ROWS	Number of rows populated in the last opened cursor within the connection.
@@DATEFIRST	The first day of the week. (7 is Sunday, 1 is Monday, and so on. Set with SET DATEFIRST.)
@@ERROR	The error number generated by the last executed command within the session. This is valuable for error checking in stored procedures, batches, and triggers.
@@FETCH_STATUS	Indication of whether the last fetch operation from a cursor within the session was successful.
@@IDENTITY	The identity value generated by the last insert statement within the session. The @@IDENTITY value is unaffected by other connections' inserts. To obtain information about the last identity value inserted by any session, use the IDENT_CURRENT('*tablename*') function described previously in this chapter.
@@LOCK_TIMEOUT	The lock wait timeout value in milliseconds (set with SET LOCK_TIMEOUT).
@@LANGID	The connection's language ID in use.
@@LANGUAGE	The connection's language in use; a character string. Set by SET LANGUAGE.
@@NESTLEVEL	The current nesting level for a stored procedure or trigger. This is important to check in recursive procedures to ensure the nesting level doesn't exceed the maximum of 32.
@@PROCID	The ID of the currently executing stored procedure.
@@REMSERVER	The name of the remote SQL Server from which a remote procedure call was invoked.
@@ROWCOUNT	The number of rows affected (modified or read) by the last command executed within a session.
@@SPID	The current connection ID.
@@TEXTSIZE	The maximum number of bytes returned by a SELECT statement when reading text and image data (set by SET TEXTSIZE). Note that this can be further limited by the client application.
@@TRANCOUNT	The current transaction nesting level. See Chapter 31, "Transaction Management and the Transaction Log" to learn more about this function.
@@ERROR	The error number of the previously executed command within a session. Useful for error handling in stored procedures and triggers.

The following code fragment demonstrates using the @@ERROR function to check for errors after each statement and branching to an error-handling routine if an error occurs:

```
BEGIN TRAN
INSERT orders(customer_number) VALUES(1)
 IF @@ERROR <> 0 GOTO err_handle
RETURN 0
/* ... */
err_handle:
RAISERROR ('An error occurred in the stored procedure.
The transaction has been rolled back', 12, 1)
ROLLBACK TRANSACTION
RETURN -101
```

Listing 26.18 demonstrates using the `@@IDENTITY` function. In this example you need to find out the identity value generated by the insert into `customers` so it can be used in the insert into the `orders` table. You can use the `@@IDENTITY` function to capture this. Note that you need to save the value returned from `@@IDENTITY` into a local variable if you need access to it after any subsequent `INSERT` statements. All `INSERT` statements update `@@IDENTITY`, even those that insert into a table without an identity column (if there is no identity column on the table, the insert will set `@@IDENTITY` to `NULL`). You do not have to worry about other connections' inserts affecting the `@@IDENTITY` value because `@@IDENTITY` is maintained per connection.

LISTING 26.18 Using the `@@IDENTITY` Function to Get the Last Generated Identity Value

```
CREATE TABLE customers
  (customer_id INT IDENTITY PRIMARY KEY NOT NULL,
   customer_name NVARCHAR(100) NOT NULL,
   customer_comments NVARCHAR(1000) NULL)
Go

CREATE TABLE orders
  (order_number UNIQUEIDENTIFIER DEFAULT NEWID() PRIMARY KEY NOT NULL,
   customer_number INT REFERENCES customers(customer_id),
   order_date DATETIME DEFAULT CONVERT(CHAR(8), GETDATE(), 112))
GO

DECLARE @cust_id INT
INSERT customers (customer_name, customer_comments)
    VALUES ('Hardware Suppliers AB', 'Stephanie is contact.')
SELECT @cust_id = @@IDENTITY
INSERT orders (customer_number)
    VALUES (@cust_id)
go
```

TIP

Be careful if an insert trigger exists on a table and the insert trigger performs an insert into another table that also has an identity column defined on it. The `@@IDENTITY` value returned will be from the table inserted into by the trigger, not the original insert. You can use the `scope_identity()` function instead of `@@IDENTITY` to return the identity value generated by the original `insert` statement.

The monitoring-related functions are listed in Table 26.15. These functions are rarely used and are included here for completeness. Typically, `DBCC SQLPERF` and SQL Performance Monitor give similar information in a more useful fashion.

TABLE 26.15 Monitoring-Related Functions

Function Name	Returned Value
`@@CONNECTIONS`	The number of login attempts since the last restart of SQL Server.
`@@CPU_BUSY`	The number of time ticks (currently 1/100 second) that the machine's CPU has been performing SQL Server work since the last restart of SQL Server.
`@@IDLE`	The number of time ticks (currently 1/100 second) that the machine's SQL Server has been idle since the last restart of SQL Server.
`@@IO_BUSY`	The number of time ticks (currently 1/100 second) that SQL Server has been performing I/O operations since the last restart of SQL Server.
`@@PACK_RECEIVED`	The number of packets received by SQL Server since the last restart of SQL Server.
`@@PACK_SENT`	The number of packets sent by SQL Server since the last restart of SQL Server.
`@@PACKET_ERRORS`	The number of times that an error occurred while sending a packet since the last restart of SQL Server.
`@@TOTAL_ERRORS`	The number of times that an error occurred while reading or writing since the last restart of SQL Server.
`@@TOTAL_READ`	The total number of physical reads since the last restart of SQL Server.
`@@TOTAL_WRITE`	The total number of physical writes since the last restart of SQL Server.

Outlined in Table 26.16, the configuration functions provide information about the current configuration option settings, which are useful for administrative purposes. The most useful one is `@@VERSION`, which returns the version number and the service pack level.

TABLE 26.16 Configuration Functions

Function Name	Returned Value
`@@DBTS`	The current database's last-used timestamp value. A new timestamp value is generated whenever a row with a timestamp column is updated or inserted.
`@@MAX_CONNECTIONS`	The maximum number of user connections that the installation can support. `@@MAX_CONNECTIONS` does not reflect the currently configured value of user connections.

TABLE 26.16 Continued

Function Name	Returned Value
`@@MAX_PRECISION`	The maximum precision value for decimal and numeric datatypes.
`@@MICROSOFTVERSION`	A Microsoft internal version number. This should not be used for version checking and handling. Use `@@VERSION` instead.
`@@PROCID`	The ID of the currently executing stored procedure.
`@@SERVERNAME`	The name of the SQL Server. This should match the machine name; if it doesn't, you might want to drop the old (wrong name) with `sp_dropserver` and add the new (correct name) with `sp_addserver`.
`@@SERVICENAME`	The registry key name that SQL Server is running under. Returns `MSSQLServer` if the current instance is the default; otherwise, the instance name of the current instance is a named instance.
`@@TIMETICKS`	The number of microseconds per time tick.
`@@VERSION`	The SQL Server version number.

Listing 26.19 shows how you can use `@@VERSION` to check the version number of the SQL Server. The `@@VERSION` function provides the SQL Server version along with the build number and code freeze date of the currently running SQL Server executable. The last three digits after the second decimal point tell the build number, which indicates which service pack you are running. Unfortunately, no standard associates build numbers with service packs. (The service pack number listed on the last line is the service pack of the operating system you are running.) The only way to know which service pack of SQL Server you are running is to check the ReadMe file that comes with the service packs. The following are the current build numbers for SQL Server 2000:

- 194—Initial Release version of SQL Server 2000
- 384—Service Pack 1
- 534—Service Pack 2

LISTING 26.19 Using the `@@VERSION` Function to Determine the Version of SQL Server

```
SELECT @@VERSION
go

Microsoft SQL Server  2000 - 8.00.534 (Intel X86)
        Nov 19 2001 13:23:50
        Copyright (c) 1988-2000 Microsoft Corporation
        Developer Edition on Windows NT 5.1 (Build 2600: )
```

Another way of determining the version of SQL Server is to use the new SERVERPROPERTY() system function and check the productversion or productlevel server properties:

```
select cast (serverproperty('productversion') as varchar(20)) AS 'Product Version'
select cast (serverproperty('productlevel') as varchar(10)) AS 'Product Level'
go

Product Version
--------------------
8.00.534

Product Level
-------------
SP2
```

The advantage of using the new SERVERPROPERTY() system function is obvious—no more looking up the build number in the ReadMe file to determine the service pack applied!

Returning Messages from T-SQL

SQL Server provides two methods of returning messages from within Transact-SQL code: PRINT and RAISERROR. The way that messages are handled and displayed by a client application is determined by the database API that the application uses. For example, DB-Library registers two callback handlers: an error handler and a message handler. The message handler is called when messages are sent via the PRINT statement. The error handler is called when messages are sent via the RAISERROR command. For ODBC applications, the SQLError function handles the results of PRINT and RAISERROR.

PRINT

The PRINT statement is used to pass a message string to the client program. The message string can be a fixed string, local variable or function, or any string expression up to 8,000 characters in length. Anything beyond 8,000 characters is truncated. The syntax is as follows:

```
print {'character_string' | @local_variable | @@function | string_expr}
```

The following example displays the current time from SQL Server:

```
print 'The current time is: ' + convert(char(8), getdate(), 108)
```

Messages returned by the PRINT command return a severity of 0. PRINT is commonly used in SQL script files to print information to the output file.

RAISERROR

Although SQL Server generates most error messages automatically, sometimes you will need to communicate to a client that some type of error has occurred within a SQL batch, trigger, or stored procedure. You can generate a message with the RAISERROR command. The RAISERROR command has the following syntax:

```
RAISERROR([err_no]|[err_string], severity, state [, argument[, ...]])
          [WITH option[, ...]]
```

If you supply an error string, the error number will always be 50,000. If you supply an error number, that error number and corresponding message must be defined in the sysmessages table in the master database.

The *severity* level indicates the type of problem encountered. Typically, the higher the severity level, the more serious the error. Severity levels higher than 19 are considered fatal errors and cause the process to terminate its connection to SQL Server. Only system administrators can raise a severity level of 19 or higher and they must specify the WITH LOG option. Typically, user-generated error messages will use only levels 10 or 16.

NOTE

If you specify a severity of 10 or less, RAISERROR returns the message string similar to the way a print statement is returned. No error number is associated with it and some APIs will not treat it as an error message. For example, examine the difference between the following two error messages, one with severity 16 and one with severity 10:

```
RAISERROR ('Help, I've fallen and I can't get up', 16, 1)
select @@error as 'Error Number'
RAISERROR ('Hello world', 10, 1)
select @@error as 'Error Number'
Server: Msg 50000, Level 16, State 1, Line 1
Help, I've fallen and I can't get up
go

Error Number
------------
       50000


Hello world
Error Number
------------
           0
```

26

Table 26.17 presents the severity levels currently defined in SQL Server.

TABLE 26.17 Descriptions of Severity Levels

Severity Level	Description
0 or 10	Informational status messages
11–16	Non-fatal, user-correctable errors (for example, invalid object name)
17	Insufficient resources; for example, out of locks or disk space
18	Internal errors, non-fatal
19	Resource problems, fatal
20	Fatal error in current process
21	Fatal error in database process
22	Fatal error, table integrity suspect
23	Fatal error, database integrity suspect
24	Fatal error, hardware error

The *state* parameter can be any value from 1–127. For SQL Server–generated error messages, the value of `state` indicates where in the SQL Server code the error came from. This information might be useful for Microsoft Product Support. For user-defined error messages, the *state* really has no meaning. You could use *state* to indicate the line in the SQL code that generated the error. Another situation in which you might find the *state* parameter useful is when you execute a script using ISQL or OSQL. If you execute the `RAISERROR` with a state of 127, the processing of the script file terminates. Suppose you have a simple batch file that executes the following:

```
ISQL /Usa /P /iMyBatch.SQL /n
```

and the script file (MyBatch.SQL) contains the code in Listing 26.20.

LISTING 26.20 Using State 127 to Terminate a Batch Processed with ISQL or OSQL

```
-- Exit if users connected to database.
IF (SELECT COUNT(*) FROM master..sysprocesses
    WHERE dbid = DB_ID('pubs')) > 0
RAISERROR ('Cannot proceed with batch, users connected to database.', 16, 127)
GO
-- If not, continue with whatever you want to do
SELECT au_fname, au_lname FROM pubs..authors
go
```

If the `IF` statement evaluates to true, the `RAISERROR` statement will terminate the processing of the script file. This is not the same result that you get from issuing a `RETURN` statement. The `RETURN` statement would have terminated the batch but executed the remaining batches in the script file.

The *arguments* are used to insert data (table name or other information stored in local variables) into the message string. A maximum of 20 arguments can be specified. In the message string, you need to specify placeholders where the arguments are to be substituted. The placeholders are similar to the ones used in the C language `printf` command and are listed in Table 26.18.

TABLE 26.18 Placeholder Arguments for `RAISERROR`

Argument	Datatype
d or I	Signed integer
o	Unsigned octal
p	Pointer
s	String
u	Unsigned integer
x or X	Unsigned hexadecimal

The following is an example of using `RAISERROR` with arguments:

```
declare @count int,
        @table varchar(128)
select @table = 'titles', @count = count(*) from titles
RAISERROR ('There are %d row(s) in the %s table', 10, 1, @count, @table)
go

There are 18 row(s) in the titles table
```

The available *options* for `RAISERROR` include the following:

`LOG`—The message is sent to SQL Server's error log and NT's event log. Only a system administrator can specify this option.

`NOWAIT`—The message is sent directly to the client. This is useful for long-running operations to return information without waiting until the batch completes, such as to allow an application to display a status indicator.

`SETERROR`—The message forces the actual error number to be returned to the function `@@ERROR`. This is useful when the severity is lower than 11.

TIP

To reduce network traffic, SQL Server typically waits until either the end of a batch or the connection output buffer fills up before returning results or messages to a client application. At times, if you have a long-running SQL batch that possibly contains a loop and you want to return messages or resultsets as they are generated, use the `RAISERROR` command with the `NOWAIT` option. The `NOWAIT` option will cause the current contents of the output buffer to be immediately flushed back to the client application. Any severity less than 11 will be treated similarly to a `print` statement.

Managing SQL Server Error Messages

SQL Server error messages are stored in the sysmessages table in the master database. Table 26.19 describes the columns in the sysmessages table.

TABLE 26.19 Columns in the sysmessages Table

Column Name	Description
error	The error number. Every error message has a unique error number.
severity	The severity level. A higher severity level generally indicates a more severe problem. SQL Server will terminate the connection and perform a rollback (if a transaction was started) for severity levels greater than 19.
dlevel	For internal use.
description	The message string with placeholders.
mslangid	System message group ID.

User-defined error messages must have an error number that is greater than 50,000. The maximum value for an error number is 2,147,483,647.

You can also add your own error messages, which can be useful for centralizing error reporting from your application. Chapter 18, "SQL Server Scheduling and Notification," describes how to add messages in Enterprise Manager. You can also manage messages with the stored procedures sp_addmessage, sp_dropmessage, and sp_altermessage. The error number must be greater than 50,000. For more information on these commands, refer to Chapter 18.

Listing 26.21 adds a user-defined message and calls it from T-SQL code.

LISTING 26.21 Adding an Error Message to SQL Server and Generating the Error

```
sp_addmessage 50001, 16, 'The row(s) from table %s could not
➥ be deleted. There are rows in table %s that refer to this row.
➥ Delete those rows first.'
go

RAISERROR (50001, 16, 1, 'Titles', 'Titleauthor')
go

Server: Msg 50001, Level 16, State 42000
The row(s) from table Titles could not be deleted. There are
➥ rows in table Titleauthor that refer to this row.
➥ Delete those rows first.
```

FORMATMESSAGE

The FORMATMESSAGE function can be used to return a message from the sysmessages table. Its typical use is to substitute arguments into the message string and construct the message as it would be returned by RAISERROR. Unlike RAISERROR, which prints the message immediately, FORMATMESSAGE returns the constructed message for further processing.

The syntax for FORMATMESSAGE is as follows:

```
FORMATMESSAGE ( msg_number , argument [ ,...n ] )
```

The following example uses FORMATMESSAGE with the error number 50001 defined previously:

```
declare @msg varchar(8000)
select @msg = formatmessage(50001, 'Titles', 'Titleauthor')
print @msg

The row(s) from table Titles could not be deleted. There are rows in table
➥Titleauthor that refer to this row. Delete those rows first.
```

SET Options

You can use the SET command to alter a connection's behavior. Options set with the SET command stay active until the connection terminates. For most options, when they are set within a stored procedure, the option is set back to its connection level setting when the procedure returns.

Most SET commands take values of ON or OFF as arguments, whereas some take a specific value. Some of the SET statements do not take effect until the next batch, whereas others will be set at parsing or execution time.

The tuning-related SET parameters are generally used when analyzing and optimizing queries. They can give you information about how SQL Server executes a query and also, to some extent, control how a query is executed. The default option settings are noted by asterisks (*) in Table 26.20.

TABLE 26.20 Tuning-Related SET Parameters

Parameter	Arguments	Description
FORCEPLAN	ON|OFF*	SQL Server will process a JOIN in the same order as specified in the FROM clause.
NOEXEC	ON|OFF*	SQL Server will optimize the query but not execute it. NOEXEC was often used in conjunction with SHOWPLAN in releases of SQL Server prior to 7.0 and is not needed with SHOWPLAN_TEXT or SHOWPLAN_ALL. Note that no other commands will execute for a session until NOEXEC is set back off.

TABLE 26.20 Continued

Parameter	Arguments	Description
PARSEONLY	ON|OFF*	SQL Server will parse the query but not optimize or execute it. It is useful to check the syntax of a SQL batch before executing it. Note that no other commands will execute for a session until PARSEONLY is set back off.
QUERY_GOVERNOR_ COST_LIMIT	*value*	Overrides the server-level configuration setting for query governor cost limit. Permission to execute this setting is limited to members of the sysadmin role.
SHOWPLAN_ALL	ON|OFF*	Displays the query plan that SQL Server uses to execute the query, but it does not execute the query. This is intended for programs that parse the output, such as the Query Analyzer. For textual output, use SHOWPLAN_TEXT instead.
SHOWPLAN_TEXT	ON|OFF*	Displays the query plan that SQL Server uses to execute the query, but it does not execute the query.
STATISTICS_IO	ON|OFF*	Displays information regarding I/O activity for each query.
STATISTICS_TIME	ON|OFF*	Displays information regarding execution time for each query.
STATISTICS_ PROFILE	ON|OFF*	Executes the query and displays the query plan that SQL Server uses to execute the query.

In Listing 26.22, you turn on SHOWPLAN_TEXT so that the execution plan is returned to the client.

LISTING 26.22 Using SHOWPLAN_TEXT

```
SET SHOWPLAN_TEXT ON
GO
SELECT title, au_fname, au_lname
 FROM titles t
   JOIN titleauthor ta ON t.title_id = ta.title_id
   JOIN authors a ON ta.au_id = a.au_id
go

StmtText
------------------------------------------------------------------------------
SELECT title, au_fname, au_lname
 FROM titles t
   JOIN titleauthor ta ON t.title_id = ta.title_id
   JOIN authors a ON ta.au_id = a.au_id

(1 row(s) affected)
```

LISTING 26.22 Continued

```
StmtText
---------------------------------------------------------------------------
  |--Nested Loops(Inner Join, OUTER REFERENCES:([ta].[au_id]))
       |--Nested Loops(Inner Join, OUTER REFERENCES:([t].[title_id]))
       |    |--Index Scan(OBJECT:([pubs].[dbo].[titles].[titleind] AS [t]))
       |    |--Index Seek(OBJECT:([pubs].[dbo].[titleauthor].[titleidind] AS
[ta]), SEEK:([ta].[title_id]=[t].[title_id]) ORDERED FORWARD)
       |--Clustered Index Seek(OBJECT:([pubs].[dbo].[authors].[UPKCL_auidind]
AS [a]), SEEK:([a].[au_id]=[ta].[au_id]) ORDERED FORWARD)
```

For information on how to interpret the SHOWPLAN_TEXT or STATISTICS PROFILE information, see Chapter 36, "Query Analysis."

With the transaction-handling–related SET parameters, you can override SQL Server's default transaction-handling behavior. In Table 26.21, the default option settings are noted by asterisks (*).

TABLE 26.21 Transaction-Handling–Related SET Parameters

Parameter	Argument	Description
CURSOR_CLOSE_ON_COMMIT	ON|OFF*	Controls whether cursors should be automatically closed when a COMMIT TRAN statement is executed.
IMPLICIT_TRANSACTIONS	ON|OFF*	An implicit BEGIN TRANSACTION is triggered for most DML statements when IMPLICIT_TRANSACTIONS is turned on. Transactions are only ended when an explicit COMMIT or ROLLBACK is issued.
LOCK_TIMOUT	*milliseconds*	Specifies the number of milliseconds a process will wait for a lock to be released before returning a locking error. The default value is -1, which indicates no timeout period.
REMOTE_PROC_TRANSACTIONS	ON|OFF*	When enabled, a distributed transaction is started when a remote procedure call is executed within a local transaction.
TRANSACTION_ISOLATION_LEVEL	READ_ COMMITTED* |READ_ UNCOMMITTED| REPEATABLE_ READ| SERIALIZABLE	Specifies the degree of isolation between concurrent transactions.
XACT_ABORT	ON|OFF*	When this option is turned on, SQL Server will roll back the current transaction if a runtime error occurs.

In Listing 26.23, you turn on IMPLICIT_TRANSACTIONS, issue two DELETE statements, print the nesting level, and perform a ROLLBACK.

LISTING 26.23 Setting IMPLICIT_TRANSACTIONS to Get an Implicit BEGIN TRANSACTION

```
SET IMPLICIT_TRANSACTIONS ON
GO
DELETE FROM titleauthor WHERE title_id = 'BU1032'
DELETE FROM titles WHERE title_id = 'BU1032'
print 'Transaction nesting level is: ' + CAST(@@TRANCOUNT AS VARCHAR(5))
ROLLBACK TRAN
print 'Transaction nesting level is now: ' + CAST(@@TRANCOUNT AS VARCHAR(5))
go

Server: Msg 547, Level 16, State 1, Line 1
DELETE statement conflicted with COLUMN REFERENCE constraint
 'FK__sales__title_id__0BC6C43E'. The conflict occurred in database 'pubs', table
'sales',
column 'title_id'.
The statement has been terminated.
Transaction nesting level is: 1
Transaction nesting level is now: 0
```

With the formatting-related SET parameters, you can specify how input and output values are formatted. For instance, you can specify the order in which day, month, and year parts are specified when entering data. In Table 26.22, asterisks note the default options (*). The default specified applies for the U.S. English language.

TABLE 26.22 SET Parameters That Control Data Formatting

Parameter	Argument	Description
DATEFIRST	*number*	Specifies which day is the last weekday. The default is 7 (Saturday).
DATEFORMAT	*mdy*	Specifies how SQL Server will interpret the date, month, and year parts when inserting datetime data. Valid formats include mdy, dmy, ymd, ydm, myd, and dym. The U.S. English default is dmy.
FMTONLY	ON|OFF*	Only returns metadata to the client when turned on. The query is processed and result column information is returned, but no result rows are returned.
IDENTITY_INSERT	*tblname* ON|OFF*	Allows you to insert an explicit value for an identity column when turned on.
LANGUAGE	*language_name*	Controls in which language error messages should be returned. The language must be available on the server. It also controls the language used when returning the weekday and month with the DATENAME function.

TABLE 26.22 Continued

Parameter	Argument	Description
NOCOUNT	ON|OFF*	Controls whether the number of rows affected by the last command should be returned to the client application. Even if turned off, the count is still available in the @@ROWCOUNT global variable.
OFFSETS	ON|OFF*	Controls whether the offset for certain T-SQL keywords should be returned to DB-Library applications. Can only be used in DB-Library applications.
ROWCOUNT	*number*	Causes SQL Server to stop processing the query after the specified number of rows are processed. Note that this also applies to data modification statements. Use the TOP keyword if you want to control how many rows to return from a specific SELECT statement.
TEXTSIZE	*number*	Controls how many bytes a SELECT statement returns from text and ntext columns. Note that ntext uses two bytes per character.

In Listing 26.24, you want to return the weekday and month that a book is published in the Swedish language (assuming that the Swedish language is already installed).

LISTING 26.24 Setting the Language to Display SQL Server Messages

```
SET LANGUAGE Swedish

SELECT '"' + RTRIM(title) + '" is published on a '
       + DATENAME(dw, pubdate) + ' in ' + DATENAME(mm, pubdate) + '.'
 FROM titles
WHERE title_id = 'PC1035'
go

Changed language setting to Svenska.

---------------------------------------------------------------
"But Is It User Friendly?" is published on a söndag in juni.
```

Listing 26.25 sets the date format for specifying datetime data. Note that the SELECT statement uses three possible formats to specify datetime data.

LISTING 26.25 Using SET DATEFORMAT to Specify Order of DateParts When Entering Datetime Data

```
SET DATEFORMAT ymd
GO
SELECT CONVERT(smalldatetime, '1999.12.31') as 'Numeric',
 CONVERT(smalldatetime, '19991231') as 'Unseparated',
 CONVERT(smalldatetime, 'Dec 1999 31') as 'Alphabetic'
go

Numeric              Unseparated          Alphabetic
-------------------- -------------------- --------------------
1999-12-31 00:00:00  1999-12-31 00:00:00  1999-12-31 00:00:00
```

The ANSI-related and miscellaneous SET parameters control behavior for comparison to NULL, division with 0, and so on. In Table 26.23, asterisks note the default options (*).

TABLE 26.23 ANSI and Miscellaneous SET Parameters

Parameter	Argument	Description
ARITHABORT	ON|OFF*	Terminates a query if overflow or divide-by-zero occurs when turned on. Note that rows can be returned before the abort occurs.
ARITHIGNORE	ON|OFF*	Returns NULL if overflow or divide-by-zero errors occur when turned on. No warning message is sent to the client. Default behavior is that NULL and a warning message are returned.
NUMERIC_ROUNDABORT	ON|OFF*	Specifies whether an error message should be returned when a loss of precision occurs due to rounding the result value.
ANSI_NULL_DFLT_OFF	ON|OFF*	Set this to ON if you do not want a column to allow NULL when you create a table and do not specify the NULL or NOT NULL column property. Use when the database option for ANSI NULL Default is set to true.
ANSI_NULL_DFLT_ON	ON|OFF*	Set this to ON if you want a column to allow NULL when you create a table and do not specify the NULL or NOT NULL column property. Use when the database option for ANSI NULL Default is set to false.
ANSI_NULLS	ON|OFF*	Controls how comparison to NULL should be handled. By default, it allows a NULL = NULL comparison to evaluate to TRUE. Setting this option to ON will follow the SQL-92–compliant behavior that any comparison to NULL evaluates to UNKNOWN.
CONCAT_NULL_ YIELDS_NULL	ON*|OFF	Determines whether a string concatenated with NULL returns NULL or the string. The default setting is ON, which returns NULL.

TABLE 26.23 Continued

Parameter	Argument	Description
CONTEXT_INFO	*binary_data*	Provides the ability to programmatically associate up to 128 bytes of binary information with the current session or connection. This option allows you to set the context information stored in the context_info column in the master.dbo.sysprocesses table.
ANSI_PADDING	ON|OFF*	Specifies whether char, varchar, binary, and varbinary columns should be padded with blanks or zeroes. By default, char and binary columns, whether defined to allow NULLs or not, will be padded out to the defined length with spaces or zeroes, respectively. For varchar and varbinary, values are not padded, but trailing spaces or zeroes inserted are not trimmed. The column behavior is determined by the ANSI_PADDING setting in effect at the time the table is created.
ANSI_WARNINGS	ON|OFF	Generates a warning if an aggregate function is applied over rows that contain NULL and if INSERT or UPDATE specifies data with a length that exceeds the column definitions for character, Unicode, or binary data. A division by 0 or overflow results in the rollback of the statement if this option is set. This option is set to ON automatically when using ODBC or OLE DB.
ANSI_DEFAULTS	ON|OFF	Controls a group of MS SQL Server settings that set behavior to SQL-92 standards. If set to ON, the following options will set on: ANSI_NULLS, ANSI_NULL_DFLT_ON, ANSI_PADDING, ANSI_WARNINGS, CURSOR_CLOSE_ON_COMMIT, IMPLICIT_TRANSACTIONS, and QUOTED_IDENTIFIER. This option is set to ON automatically when connecting via ODBC or OLE DB.
DEADLOCK_PRIORITY	NORMAL*|LOW	If LOW, this connection will be the preferred victim if a deadlock occurs. If your application handles deadlock gracefully, set this to LOW to increase the chance that an application that does not handle deadlock can continue processing in the event of a deadlock situation.
FIPS_FLAGGER	OFF*|ENTRY|INTERMEDIATE|FULL	Specifies whether SQL Server will generate a warning if a statement does not comply with the specified level of the FIPS 127-2 standard, which is based on the SQL-92 standard.
QUOTED_IDENTIFIER	ON|OFF*	Specifies whether identifiers are delimited by double quotation marks. When set to OFF, identifiers cannot be quoted and strings can use double or single quotation marks. When set to ON, double quotation marks are used to delimit identifiers, and literals must use single quotation marks.

Listing 26.26 explores the differences when checking for the NULL symbol, depending on how ANSI_NULLS is set. The preferred way of checking for the NULL symbol is to use IS NULL and IS NOT NULL, which is consistent regardless of how ANSI_NULLS is set.

LISTING 26.26 Checking for NULL

```
SET ANSI_NULLS OFF
GO
--Note that both statements will return two rows.
SELECT title_id, price FROM titles WHERE price = NULL
SELECT title_id, price FROM titles WHERE price IS NULL
go

title_id price
-------- ---------
MC3026   NULL
PC9999   NULL

title_id price
-------- ---------
MC3026   NULL
PC9999   NULL



SET ANSI_NULLS ON
GO
--Note that the first statement will return zero rows.
SELECT title_id, price FROM titles WHERE price = NULL
SELECT title_id, price FROM titles WHERE price IS NULL
go

title_id price
-------- ---------

title_id price
-------- ---------
MC3026   NULL
PC9999   NULL
```

Checking Session Options

At times, you might find it necessary to identify which session-level options are in effect. For example, you might need to know if `IMPLICIT_TRANSACTIONS` is enabled so you know whether to issue a `BEGIN TRAN` statement in your code. You might need to know whether `QUOTED_IDENTIFIER` or `CONCAT_NULL_YIELDS_NULL` is enabled.

One way to find out what options are set is to use the @@OPTIONS function:

```
select  @@OPTIONS
go

-----------
       5240
```

The @@OPTIONS function returns an integer representation of the bitmap indicating which options are set for the current session. Table 26.24 lists the options and the bitmap value.

TABLE 26.24 @@OPTIONS Bitmap Values and the Corresponding Session Options

Value	Session Option
1	DISABLE_DEF_CNST_CHK
2	IMPLICIT_TRANSACTIONS
4	CURSOR_CLOSE_ON_COMMIT
8	ANSI_WARNINGS
16	ANSI_PADDING
32	ANSI_NULLS
64	ARITHABORT
128	ARITHIGNORE
256	QUOTED_IDENTIFIER
512	NOCOUNT
1024	ANSI_NULL_DFLT_ON
2048	ANSI_NULL_DFLT_OFF
4096	CONCAT_NULL_YIELDS_NULL
8192	NUMERIC_ROUNDABORT
16384	XACT_ABORT

The previous example returned a value of 5240 from @@OPTIONS. If you add up the appropriate bitmap values, you can determine which settings are enabled:

5240 = 4096 + 1024 + 32 + 64 + 16 + 8

Using the values in Table 22.24, this indicates that the following options are set:

- arithabort
- ansi_null_dflt_on
- ansi_warnings
- ansi_padding
- ansi_nulls
- concat_null_yields_null

Wasn't that fun? It's not the most intuitive way to determine what options are set. Fortunately, another command is available to use—DBCC USEROPTIONS:

```
dbcc useroptions
go

Set Option                                                    Value
------------------------------------------------------------- ----------
textsize                                                      64512
language                                                      us_english
dateformat                                                    mdy
datefirst                                                     7
arithabort                                                    SET
ansi_null_dflt_on                                             SET
ansi_warnings                                                 SET
ansi_padding                                                  SET
ansi_nulls                                                    SET
concat_null_yields_null                                       SET
```

This information is helpful from a user perspective, but doesn't help you much in your T-SQL code because it is a DBCC command result and not a select statement; therefore, you can't really interrogate the results. Fortunately, you can use the SESSIONPROPERTY() function to determine whether specific settings are enabled. The SESSIONPROPERTY() function returns 1 if the specified option is set, or 0 if not. The following example checks to see if CONCAT_NULL_YIELDS_NULL and QUOTED_IDENTIFIER are enabled:

```
select case SESSIONPROPERTY('CONCAT_NULL_YIELDS_NULL')
         when 1 then 'Concat_null_yields_null is on'
         else 'Concat_null_yields_null is off'
         end,
       case SESSIONPROPERTY('QUOTED_IDENTIFIER')
          when 1 then 'Quoted Identifier is on'
          else 'Quoted Identifier is off'
          end
go

------------------------------ ------------------------
Concat_null_yields_null is on  Quoted Identifier is off
```

The following are the currently valid arguments for the SESSIONPROPERTY() function. Any other value passed to the function will return NULL:

- ANSI_NULLS
- ANSI_PADDING

- ANSI_WARNINGS
- ARITHABORT
- CONCAT_NULL_YIELDS_NULL
- NUMERIC_ROUNDABORT
- QUOTED_IDENTIFIER

To avoid having to set substantial options every time a user connects to SQL Server, a member of the sysadmin role can configure the default user options for all connections via the `user options` setting for `sp_configure`. To set the user options you want enabled, specify an integer representation of a bitmap using the same bitmap values shown previously in Table 28.24. For example, if you wanted all connections to have the `CONCAT_NULL_YIELDS_NULL`, `QUOTED_IDENTIFIER`, `ANSI_NULLS` settings enabled automatically, you could execute the following command:

```
exec sp_configure 'user options', 4384 -- 4096 + 256 + 32
reconfigure
```

To set no default session options, set `user options` to zero (0). You can also use `sp_configure` without the second parameter to view the current default user options:

```
exec sp_configure 'user options'
go

name                             minimum   maximum   config_value run_value
-------------------------------- --------- --------- ------------ ---------
user options                     0         32767     4384         4384
```


Using `CONTEXT_INFO`

No user-defined global variables exist, and local variables do not retain values between batches or stored procedures. The `CONTEXT_INFO` setting allows you to store information in the `context_info` column in the `sysprocesses` table in the `master` database. A row in `sysprocesses` exists for every connection to SQL Server, so the data will remain there until you disconnect from SQL Server.

The `context_info` column is a binary (128) column. You can store any data value into it with the `SET CONTEXT_INFO` command, but will have to deal with hexadecimal data when retrieving it. If you are handy at manipulating hexadecimal data, you can store multiple values in the `context_info` column. The following example stored the `avg(price)` from the titles table into the `context_info` column:

```
declare @avg_price money
select @avg_price = avg(price) from titles
set context_info @avg_price
```

You can retrieve the value stored in context_info using a SELECT statement. You will need to convert the binary data back to money when you retrieve it. Because the average price is the only value stored in context_info, you can retrieve it by performing a substring on the first 8 bytes of the context_info column (the money datatype is 8 bytes in size). Because SQL Server assigns a unique server process ID (spid), you will use the @@SPID function to retrieve the information for the current connection:

```
select convert(money, substring(context_info, 1, 8)) as AVG_PRICE
from master..sysprocesses
where spid = @@spid
go

AVG_PRICE
--------------------
14.7662
```

If you hadn't used substring to specify only the first 8 bytes of the context_info column, SQL Server would have assumed the money data was stored in the last 8 bytes and would have returned a result of 0:

```
select convert(money, context_info) as AVG_PRICE
from master..sysprocesses
where spid = @@spid
go

AVG_PRICE
--------------------
.0000
```

Because money can be implicitly converted to binary, you don't need to convert it when setting context_info. For some other datatypes, like char or datetime, you need to explicitly convert the data to binary because implicit conversions from those datatypes to binary is not supported. In the next example, you are appending a datetime value to the average price value already stored in context_info. You explicitly convert the datetime value to binary and append it to the 8 bytes you have already stored in context_info:

```
declare @max_date datetime,
        @context_info binary(128)
select @max_date = max(pubdate) from titles
select @context_info = substring(context_info, 1, 8)
                        + convert(binary(8), @max_date)
   from master..sysprocesses
   where spid = @@spid
set context_info @context_info
```

You now have two values stored in context_info. Using the appropriate substring, you can retrieve either the average price or the maximum pubdate from context_info (note that the binary data converts implicitly to money and datetime):

```
declare @avg_price money,
        @max_pubdate datetime
select @avg_price = substring(context_info, 1, 8),
       @max_pubdate = substring(context_info, 9, 8)
   from master..sysprocesses
   where spid = @@spid

select @avg_price as 'Avg Price', @max_pubdate as 'Max PubDate'
go

Avg Price             Max PubDate
--------------------- ------------------------------------------------------
14.7662               2000-08-06 01:33:54.140
```

Cursors

In contrast to most programming languages, SQL is a set-based processing language. You retrieve sets of rows, update sets of rows, and delete sets of rows. The set of rows affected is determined by the search conditions specified in the query. Unfortunately, most programmers are used to doing record-oriented operations on data and often want to apply the same technique to SQL Server data. Admittedly, at times, processing rows as a single resultset with a single query can seem difficult or impossible.

For example, perhaps you want to update the prices of books in the titles table. For books priced less than $15, you want to increase the price by 15 percent. For books priced $15 or more, you want to decrease the price by 10 percent. For books with ytd_sales less than 500, you want to decrease the price by 25 percent.

To perform this update using set-oriented processing, you need to use three separate updates:

```
update titles
   set price = price * 1.15
   where price < $15
update titles
   set price = price * .9
   where price >= $15
update titles
   set price = price * .25
   where ytd_sales < 500
```

26

Immediately, you can see a potential problem here. If you have a book priced at $14.95, the first update will increase the price by 15 percent. Because the new price will now be $17.19, the second update will subsequently decrease the price by 10 percent. This is not the intended result.

Assuming you don't know about the CASE expression, how do you solve this problem using set-oriented processing?

NOTE

Cursors are one of the common causes of performance problems in SQL Server applications and should almost always be avoided unless no better solution is available. Later in this section, ways to avoid using cursors, as well as instances when cursors might be the best solution, will be discussed.

One approach would be to select the different rows into three temporary tables and update the rows in the titles table by joining between the temporary tables and the titles table. This solution is not ideal because you would have to execute three selects against the titles table to get the data into the temp tables. You would incur the overhead to insert the data into the temporary tables, and then another three lookups against the titles table to update the prices. You could minimize the overhead of the temporary tables by using table variables, but you would still have to make six passes of the titles table, which would be inefficient.

Another approach would be to add an `update_flag` bit column to the titles table. As you process each update, you would set the `update_flag` for the rows you update to 1. The next update would update the qualifying rows matching the search criteria where the update flag is still 0. This prevents rows from being modified more than once. However, you would still have to make three separate passes against the table, and then a fourth to clear the update flags.

However, it might be easier to write a query using cursors, examining each row individually to see whether it fits any of the criteria, and applying the appropriate update. With a cursor, you can make a single pass of the table, looping through each row, saving the relevant column information in local variables, and performing the appropriate calculations and updates as you go.

NOTE

You might be thinking at this point that you could just use the `CASE` expression instead of a cursor and still perform the update in a single pass of the table. You would be right; however, this chapter will continue to look at a cursor solution. Later in this chapter you'll learn why you might or might not want to use a `CASE` expression instead.

Cursor Example and Some Syntax

In Listing 26.27, you find the code for performing the update using a cursor. Take a look at the complete code for now; the different components will be explained in detail later.

LISTING 26.27 Updating the `titles` Table Using a Cursor

```
/* This is a SQL script to update book prices dependent on current price and
ytd_sales */

/*declare cursor*/
declare titles_curs cursor for
  select ytd_sales, price from titles
  for update of price

declare @ytd_sales int, @price money
open titles_curs
fetch next from titles_curs into @ytd_sales, @price

if (@@fetch_status = -1)
begin
    print "No books found"
    close titles_curs
    deallocate titles_curs
    return
end
while (@@fetch_status = 0)
begin
    if @ytd_sales < 500
       update titles set price = @price * .75
          where current of titles_curs
    else
       if @price > $15
           update titles set price = @price * .9
              where current of titles_curs
       else
           update titles set price = @price * 1.15
              where current of titles_curs
       fetch next from titles_curs into @ytd_sales, @price
end
if (@@fetch_status = -2)
    raiserror ('Attempt to fetch a row failed', 16, 1)
close titles_curs
deallocate titles_curs
```

Declaring Cursors

A cursor is declared for a SELECT statement. The ANSI defines the following syntax to declare a cursor:

```
DECLARE cursor_name [INSENSITIVE] [SCROLL] CURSOR
   FOR select_statement
   [FOR {READ ONLY | UPDATE [OF column_list]}]
```

SQL Server Version 7.0 introduced an alternative way of declaring a cursor to give it the same capabilities as an API-based cursor. API cursors are discussed later in this chapter.

NOTE

The different cursor types, API and T-SQL cursors, actually use the same code when executing in SQL Server, so it makes sense that you have the ability to use the same features with T-SQL level cursors that you have at the API level.

The syntax for Transact-SQL cursors is as follows:

```
DECLARE cursor_name CURSOR
     [LOCAL | GLOBAL]
     [FORWARD_ONLY | SCROLL]
     [STATIC | KEYSET | DYNAMIC]
     [READ_ONLY | SCROLL_LOCKS | OPTIMISTIC]
   FOR select_statement
   [FOR {READ ONLY | UPDATE [OF column_list]}]
```

You cannot use COMPUTE, COMPUTE BY, FOR BROWSE, or INTO in the *select_statement*.

Let's use your example to discuss the DECLARE statement:

```
declare titles_curs cursor for
   select ytd_sales, price from titles
   for update of price
```

The cursor declares a SELECT statement that reads from a single table. As for all queries, it is a good idea to limit the number of rows that the cursor will process through a WHERE clause. Don't use the cursor to filter out rows you don't want to process. Also, if SQL Server can use an index to find the rows, it's even better.

Because you are going to be updating the data based on the cursor position, you explicitly declare the cursor for UPDATE. Updateable cursors are the default, but it's best to explicitly specify the purpose of the query. If you are not going to be modifying rows in the cursor resultset, be sure to declare it as READ ONLY so SQL Server uses the appropriate locking strategy. Specifying the specific column(s) that will be updated helps SQL Server identify a unique index on the table to use that does not contain a column that will be modified within the cursor. If you do not specify a *column_list*, all columns are updateable.

Cursors that use the DISTINCT keyword, computed values, or aggregates can only be declared as READ ONLY because the cursor resultset is based on the contents of a work table and does not reflect actual data rows in a table.

The cursor name must follow the general rules for identifiers.

Local and Global Cursors

A new feature introduced in version 7.0 enables you to specify whether the cursor should be local or global.

Global cursors remain defined for a connection until they are explicitly deallocated, or until they are implicitly deallocated at termination of the connection.

A local cursor's scope is limited to the batch, stored procedure, or trigger in which it is defined. The cursor is implicitly deallocated when the batch, stored procedure, or trigger terminates unless a reference to it is passed to a calling stored procedure, batch, and so on via a cursor variable. The cursor will then go out of scope when the last variable referring to it goes out of scope (for more information on cursor variables, see the section "Using CURSOR Variables" later in this chapter).

If neither GLOBAL nor LOCAL is specified when the cursor is declared, the default is determined by the setting of the database option default to local cursor. In SQL Server 2000, this option defaults to FALSE to match versions of SQL Server prior to 7.0, in which all cursors were global. It's possible that the default of this option will change in future versions of SQL Server, so it is a good idea to always specify explicitly whether the cursor should be local or global.

If you are writing a recursive stored procedure that uses cursors, you might need to declare the cursor as local to prevent SQL Server from generating an error message when the subprocedure tries to declare the cursor again with the same name. For an example of using a cursor in a recursive stored procedure, see the "Recursive Stored Procedures" section in Chapter 28.

STATIC and INSENSITIVE Cursors

STATIC and INSENSITIVE cursors are pretty much the same thing. STATIC is the T-SQL style syntax, and INSENSITIVE is the ANSI-style syntax. Both are populated with a snapshot of the data at the time the cursor is opened. The data is stored in a work table in tempdb. Any inserts, updates, or deletions to the table(s) from which the data originated do not affect the rows in the cursor. The rows in the cursor are not affected by any inserts, updates, or deletes to the table(s) the data came from. STATIC and INSENSITIVE cursors are read-only and cannot be updated. A static or insensitive cursor is useful if you do not want to be disturbed by changes to the underlying data while you process the cursor data.

The only real difference between STATIC and INSENSITIVE cursors is that fetches are Forward Only by default for INSENSITIVE cursors unless the SCROLL option is specified. STATIC cursors are scrollable by default.

KEYSET Cursors

For KEYSET cursors, a list of the key values for the rows meeting the SELECT statement criteria are put into a work table in tempdb instead of the entire resultset. The membership of a KEYSET cursor is still static; however, you will be able to see changes to any of the rows to which the KEYSET cursor points, even if the row is modified to no longer meet the original SELECT statement criteria. Only if a row is deleted will it disappear from the resultset. KEYSET cursors are scrollable. To build a keyset, KEYSET cursors require that a unique index exists on the underlying table(s).

> **NOTE**
>
> If a clustered index exists on a table, it is treated internally as a unique index even if it is not explicitly defined as such. Any table that has a clustered index on it can be accessed with a KEYSET cursor. If no unique or clustered index is available on a table, and KEYSET is specified, SQL Server will create the cursor as STATIC instead.

DYNAMIC Cursors

With DYNAMIC cursors, the membership is not fixed, and rows that didn't exist when the cursor was opened can qualify for a subsequent fetch. Likewise, any qualifying rows that have been deleted will disappear from the resultset. Because the rows in the cursor have not been locked, the cursor will see changes made to the data rows.

If a DYNAMIC cursor contains an ORDER BY clause, and no index exists to retrieve the data in the order specified by the ORDER BY clause, the cursor will be opened as a KEYSET or STATIC cursor, depending on whether a unique index exists on the table. This is because when an ORDER BY is specified and an index is not available to retrieve the data rows in sorted order, a work table is needed to sort the resultset. If a work table is needed to sort the resultset or to remove duplicate rows (as for an ORDER BY, UNION, or DISTINCT), the cursor is operating from a work table and not the underlying base table.

FORWARD_ONLY Cursors

If no specific cursor type options are specified, FORWARD ONLY is the default. A FORWARD ONLY cursor is a dynamic cursor that can only fetch the next row in forward order. Rows cannot be revisited. FORWARD ONLY cursors are typically the fastest type of cursor, but they are still slower than a normal SELECT statement.

Opening Cursors

When you open a cursor, the SELECT statement is initiated to begin populating the cursor. For cursors declared with the INSENSITIVE or STATIC option, OPEN creates and populates a work table in tempdb with the cursor resultset. For KEYSET cursors, a work table in tempdb is populated with the unique keys for each row in the cursor resultset. When you specify the OPEN command, the cursor will be positioned above the first row:

```
OPEN lead_cur
```

You can check how many rows the resultset contains with the function @@CURSOR_ROWS. If the value is –1, the cursor is being populated asynchronously, as for a dynamic cursor or forward-only cursor.

If you close a cursor and open it again, the SELECT statement is re-executed and the cursor starts over at the beginning of the resultset. For FORWARD-ONLY cursors, this is the only way to return to a previous row in the cursor.

Declaring Variables

How do you process the values returned from the cursor?

You could simply display each row to the user as a one-row resultset, but that does not make much sense. It would be much simpler to issue an ordinary SELECT statement and display the rows to the user as you need to read them from the input buffer.

What you really want to do is store the values for some of the columns into local variables and perform some processing based on those values.

Note that you have chosen the same variable names as those returned from the SELECT statement. This makes it easier to remember the variable names when processing the cursor, and it makes it easier to maintain the code:

```
declare @ytd_sales int, @price money
```

Fetching Rows

After the cursor is opened, it is time to start reading rows from your cursor, which you do with the FETCH command:

```
fetch from titles_curs into @ytd_sales, @price
```

The default for FETCH is to get the next row from the cursor. Scrolling capabilities for FETCH are discussed in the next section. If the number of variables specified in the FETCH statement does not match the number of columns in the cursor SELECT statement, you will get a runtime error. You will also get a runtime error if the variable datatype does not match the column datatype and SQL Server cannot perform an implicit datatype conversion.

Scrollable Cursors

If you declare the cursor with the SCROLL keyword, you can navigate as you want within the resultset. For a scrollable cursor, you use the FETCH statement to navigate forward, backward, or to an absolute row in the resultset. For example, following is a scrollable version of a cursor:

```
declare leads_curs scroll cursor for
   select cust_id, est_sale, close_date, prob, sales_id, descr
      from leads
   for read only
```

```
open leads_curs
```

The following is the complete syntax for the FETCH command:

```
FETCH [[NEXT|PRIOR|FIRST|LAST|ABSOLUTE n|RELATIVE n] FROM cursor_name
    [INTO @variable_name1, @variable_name2, ...]
```

The default if you don't specify a navigational option is to fetch the next row. The keyword NEXT is optional.

To fetch the previous row in the resultset, execute the following:

```
fetch prior from leads_curs
    into @cust_id, @est_sale, @close_date, @prob, @sales_id, @descr
```

In this case, the cursor moves back one row. If the cursor is already on the first row of the set, the value of @@fetch_status is set to -1 to indicate that the fetch exceeded the cursor set.

This example retrieves the first row in the set:

```
fetch first from leads_curs
    into @cust_id, @est_sale, @close_date, @prob, @sales_id, @descr
```

Use last to fetch the last row in the set.

You also can retrieve a row in an absolute position in the set. For example, to retrieve the tenth row in the cursor, use this:

```
fetch absolute 10 from leads_curs
    into @cust_id, @est_sale, @close_date, @prob, @sales_id, @descr
```

Again, your program should check the value of @@fetch_status to be certain that the absolute position is valid. The value to the ABSOLUTE option can be a variable so your SQL code can dynamically specify the absolute row to fetch.

Scrollable cursors are most useful as API cursors, where a user, for instance, can move up and down a list box and choose some entry based on a cursor value.

The last fetch operator uses relative row scrolling:

```
fetch relative -5 from leads_curs
    into @cust_id, @est_sale, @close_date, @prob, @sales_id, @descr
```

Relative scrolling can be forward (positive values) or backward (negative values). This example scrolls back five rows in the set. Again, always check @@fetch_status after each relative scroll to make sure the new row position is still valid.

The Main Loop

The main loop is where the real processing occurs. The loop looks like this:

```
while (@@fetch_status = 0)
begin
    if @ytd_sales < 500
    begin
        update titles set price = @price * .75
           where current of titles_curs
    end
    else
    begin
        if @price > $15
        begin
            update titles set price = @price * .9
               where current of titles_curs
        end
        else
        begin
            update titles set price = @price * 1.15
               where current of titles_curs
        end
    end
    fetch next from titles_curs into @ytd_sales, @price
end
```


You loop while `@@FETCH_STATUS = 0`. A value of –1 means that you have fetched beyond the last row or first row of the cursor. A value of –2 means that the row that you are trying to fetch has been deleted. When the `@@FETCH_STATUS` is a value other than 0, all columns returned will be `NULL`.

Modifying Cursor Rows

To `update` or `delete` the currently fetched row in a cursor resultset, SQL Server provides the `WHERE CURRENT OF` *cursor_name* clause, which you can use in `UPDATE` and `DELETE` statements:

```
UPDATE table_name
   SET column = expression [, column = expression[, ...]]
   WHERE CURRENT OF cursor_name

DELETE table_name
   WHERE CURRENT OF cursor_name
```

To update or delete rows using the WHERE CURRENT OF clause, you need to declare the cursor as updateable.

If the cursor definition includes a join and you plan to update only one table in the cursor, but need to access information in another, the cursor should be declared FOR UPDATE. You can use the SHARED keyword to indicate which tables you will only be reading from and which will be modified. In the following example, you need to access the publishers table to increase prices on titles published in Massachusetts, but no modifications will be made to the publishers table:

```
declare tp cursor for
   select title_id, type, price
      from titles t, publishers p shared
      where t.pub_id = p.pub_id
        and state = "MA"
   for update of price
```

In addition to limiting updates to the price column of the titles table, this cursor also maintains only shared locks on the publishers table, improving multiuser operations.

Closing the Cursor

Close the cursor as soon as you don't need it anymore. Open cursors hold locks on the underlying tables and use valuable resources.

```
close titles_curs
```

You can reopen the cursor after it has been closed. The SELECT statement is executed again and the cursor is repopulated.

Deallocating Cursors

When you are finished with the cursor definition, you deallocate it. You cannot declare a GLOBAL cursor, or LOCAL cursor within the same scope with the same name until you have deallocated the previous cursor:

```
DEALLOCATE titles_curs
```

It is a good idea to deallocate a cursor when you no longer need it. The query plan is released from memory at that time, and it makes the structure of your code clearer.

Using CURSOR Variables

SQL Server Version 7.0 introduced the cursor datatype that you can use to define cursor variables. To assign a cursor to a cursor variable, you have to use the SET statement. You cannot set a cursor variable with an assignment select statement. You can use cursor variables in OPEN, FETCH, CLOSE, and DEALLOCATE commands as well as input or output parameters for stored procedures.

The following example demonstrates declaring a cursor and assigning it to a cursor variable:

```
declare leads_curs scroll cursor for
   select cust_id, est_sale, close_date, prob, sales_id, descr
      from leads
   for read only
declare @curs_var CURSOR
SET @curs_var = leads_crus
```

You can also declare and set a cursor variable in a `SET` statement alone:

```
declare @curs_var CURSOR
SET @curs_var = cursor scroll for
   select cust_id, est_sale, close_date, prob, sales_id, descr
      from leads
   for read only
```

Listing 26.28 demonstrates a general stored procedure that returns the names of all tables in a database as a cursor output parameter. Then, you can use the returned cursor for performing certain maintenance routines against your tables, such as running `UPDATE STATISTICS`, rebuilding indexes, and so on.

LISTING 26.28 Creating a Stored Procedure That Returns a Cursor That Can Be Used to Operate Against Each Table in a Database

```
CREATE PROC cur_tbl_names @tbl_cur CURSOR VARYING OUTPUT
AS
SET @tbl_cur = CURSOR LOCAL FORWARD_ONLY FOR
   SELECT TABLE_NAME FROM INFORMATION_SCHEMA.TABLES
      WHERE TABLE_TYPE = 'BASE TABLE'
OPEN @tbl_cur
```


First, you can see that the parameter `@tbl_cur` is defined as `CURSOR VARYING OUTPUT`. The `VARYING` keyword is required if you want to return a reference to the cursor from the procedure. If cursor is declared as a local cursor within the stored procedure, it can still be passed back in an output parameter to a cursor variable, but it will only be accessible through the cursor variable, and not by name.

You now have a stored procedure that defines a cursor and returns it as an output parameter. You can write several batches (or stored procedures) that use the same cursor, and if you want to exclude tables, you modify the code only once in the `cur_tbl_names` stored procedure.

Listing 26.29 contains the code that calls your procedure and uses the cursor output parameter.

LISTING 26.29 Calling the Procedure Defined in Listing 26.28

```
DECLARE @tbls CURSOR
DECLARE @table_name sysname
EXEC cur_tbl_names @tbl_cur = @tbls OUTPUT
FETCH NEXT FROM @tbls INTO @table_name
WHILE @@FETCH_STATUS = 0
BEGIN
    EXEC('DBCC DBREINDEX( ' + @table_name + ')')
    FETCH NEXT FROM @tbls INTO @table_name
END
CLOSE @tbls
DEALLOCATE @tbls
```

The cursor can be closed using either the cursor variable or the declared cursor name. After the cursor is closed, you cannot fetch more rows from it until it is reopened, as shown in Listing 26.30.

LISTING 26.30 Attempting to Fetch Rows from a Closed Cursor

```
create proc cursor_proc @cursor CURSOR varying output
as
declare c1 cursor for select title, pubdate from titles
set @cursor = c1
open c1

GO

declare @curs CURSOR
exec cursor_proc @cursor = @curs output
fetch c1
fetch @curs
close c1
fetch @curs
go
deallocate c1
go

title                                                   pubdate
------------------------------------------------------- -----------------------
The Busy Executive's Database Guide                     1991-06-12 00:00:00.000
```

LISTING 26.30 Continued

```
title                                                    pubdate
-------------------------------------------------------- -----------------------
Cooking with Computers: Surreptitious Balance Sheets     1991-06-09 00:00:00.000

Server: Msg 16917, Level 16, State 2, Line 9
Cursor is not open.
```

If a cursor has been declared in one instance and also assigned to a cursor variable, the cursor will exist until it is deallocated via the last remaining reference to the cursor. If the cursor has been closed, it can still be reopened using the remaining cursor reference(s), as shown in Listing 26.31. If the cursor has not been closed, the last deallocation of the cursor will automatically close it.

LISTING 26.31 Deallocating a Cursor by Cursor Name and Cursor Variable

```
declare @curs CURSOR
exec cursor_proc @cursor = @curs output

fetch c1
fetch @curs

close c1          -- close via initial reference
deallocate c1     -- deallocate via initial reference

fetch @curs       -- cursor is not open at this point

open @curs        -- reopen the cursor via the remaining reference

fetch @curs       -- This fetch will work since cursor is now open again

close @curs       -- close last reference to cursor
deallocate @curs  -- deallocate last reference to cursor
open @curs        -- cursor no longer exists
go

title                                                    pubdate
-------------------------------------------------------- -----------------------
The Busy Executive's Database Guide                      1991-06-12 00:00:00.000

title                                                    pubdate
-------------------------------------------------------- -----------------------
Cooking with Computers: Surreptitious Balance Sheets     1991-06-09 00:00:00.000
```

LISTING 26.31 Continued

```
Server: Msg 16917, Level 16, State 2, Line 10
Cursor is not open.

title                                                   pubdate
------------------------------------------------------- -----------------------
The Busy Executive's Database Guide                     1991-06-12 00:00:00.000

Server: Msg 16950, Level 16, State 2, Line 18
The variable '@curs' does not currently have a cursor allocated to it.
```

For more information on using cursors and cursor variables in stored procedures, see Chapter 28.

Getting Information About Cursors

SQL Server 2000 provides some system functions and stored procedures to get information about cursors defined in a session.

The CURSOR_STATUS Function

The CURSOR_STATUS function returns the current state of a cursor or cursor variable. The syntax is as follows:

```
CURSOR_STATUS('local',
              'cursor_name' | 'global', 'cursor_name' | 'variable',
              'cursor_variable')
```

Table 26.25 lists the values returned by this function and what they mean.

TABLE 26.25 CURSOR_STATUS Return Values

Return Value	Cursor Name	Cursor Variable
1	The resultset has at least one row or is a dynamic cursor.	Cursor assigned to the variable is open and has at least one row or is a dynamic cursor.
0	Cursor resultset is empty.	Cursor assigned to the variable is empty.
-1	Cursor is closed.	Cursor assigned to the variable is closed.
-2	N/A.	No valid cursor is assigned to the variable.
-3	Cursor does not exist.	Cursor variable doesn't exist or has not had a cursor assigned to it.

Dynamic cursors never return a value of 0 for CURSOR_STATUS because it is not known how many rows are in the cursor resultset until the rows are fetched.

Cursor Stored Procedures

SQL Server provides a set of system procedures you can use to get detailed information about cursors or cursor variables. Each of these stored procedures returns information as a cursor output parameter. The cursor procedures are listed in Table 26.26.

TABLE 26.26 Cursor System Procedures

<table>
<tr><th>Cursor Procedure</th><th>Information Returned</th></tr>
<tr><td><code>sp_describe_cursor @cursor_var OUTPUT,
'local' | 'global' | 'variable',
cursor_name | cursor_variable</code></td><td>Returns attributes about the specified cursor.</td></tr>
<tr><td><code>sp_cursor_list @cursor_var OUTPUT,
1| 2 | 3</code></td><td>Returns attributes of all cursors open within specified scope. 1 = local, 2 = global, 3 = both. Essentially returns same information as <code>sp_describe_cursor</code>.</td></tr>
<tr><td><code>sp_describe_cursor_tables
@cursor_var OUTPUT,
'local' | 'global' | 'variable',
cursor_name | cursor_variable</code></td><td>Returns information on the base tables referenced by a cursor.</td></tr>
<tr><td><code>sp_describe_cursor_columns
@cursor_var OUTPUT,
'local' | 'global' | 'variable',
cursor_name | cursor_variable</code></td><td>Returns information on the columns in the cursor resultset.</td></tr>
</table>

When you use these system procedures, you'll typically return the output parameter into a local cursor variable and then fetch the results from the cursor variable.

The `sp_describe_cursor` procedure is probably the one you'll find most useful. Listing 26.32 demonstrates using the various cursor procedures to get information about the titles cursor you've been using throughout the chapter.

LISTING 26.32 Using Cursor Stored Procedures

```
declare titles_curs cursor for
   select ytd_sales, price from titles
   for update of price

declare @ytd_sales int, @price money, @blah int
open titles_curs
go

-- check to see if cursor is open
print case cursor_status('global','titles_curs') when 1 then 'It's open'
           else 'Sorry'
           end
go
It's open
```

LISTING 26.32 Continued

```
/* get information about the titles_curs */

declare @curslist CURSOR
exec sp_describe_cursor @curslist output, 'global', 'titles_curs'
if cursor_status('variable','@curslist') = 1
  -- make sure you have a valid cursor from the proc
begin
    fetch Next from @curslist
    while @@fetch_Status = 0
    begin
        fetch Next from @curslist
    end
end
close @curslist
deallocate @curslist
go

reference_name                                                          cursor_name
cursor_scope status      model concurrency scrollable open_status cursor_rows
fetch_status column_count row_count    last_operation cursor_handle
------------------------------------------------------------------------------
-------------------------------------------------- ---------------------------
-----------------------------------------------------------------------------
------------------------ ------------ -------- ----- ----------- ----------
 ----------- ------------ ------------ ------------ ------------ ------------
-- -------------
titles_curs
  titles_curs
                        2           1     3           3          0           1
-1
  -9             2            0              1     180150029

reference_name
         cursor_name
 cursor_scope status      model concurrency scrollable open_status cursor_rows
fetch_status column_count row_count    last_operation cursor_handle
--------------------------------------------------------------------------------
------------------------------------------------ -----------------------------
------------------------------------------------------------------------------
--------------------- ------------ ----------- ----- ----------- ---------- ---
-------- ------------ ------------ ------------ ------------ -------------- --
```

LISTING 26.32 Continued

```
/* Get the same information for all open cursors */
declare @curslist CURSOR
exec sp_cursor_list @curslist output, 3
if cursor_status('variable','@curslist') = 1
  -- make sure you have a valid cursor from the proc
begin
    fetch Next from @curslist
    while @@fetch_Status = 0
    begin
        fetch Next from @curslist
    end
end
close @curslist
deallocate @curslist
go

reference_name
cursor_name
cursor_scope status      model concurrency scrollable open_status cursor_rows
fetch_status column_count row_count    last_operation cursor_handle
-----------------------------------------------------------------------------
---------------------------------------------------- -----------------------
-----------------------------------------------------------------------------
----------------------------- ------------- ----------- ------ ----------- ---
------- ----------- ------------ ------------ ------------ ------------ ---
---------- ------------
titles_curs
        titles_curs
                           2           1     3            3          0            1
-1
  -9             2             0              1      180150029

reference_name
cursor_name
cursor_scope status      model concurrency scrollable open_status cursor_rows
fetch_status column_count row_count    last_operation cursor_handle
------------------------------------------------------------------------------
--------------------------------------------------- ------------------------
-----------------------------------------------------------------------------
---------------------------- ------------ ----------- ------ ----------- ----
------ ----------- ------------ ------------ ------------ ------------ -----
-------- ------------
```

LISTING 26.32 Continued

```
/* Get information about the tables referenced by the titles_curs cursor */
declare @curslist CURSOR
exec sp_describe_cursor_tables @curslist output, 'global', 'titles_curs'
if cursor_status('variable','@curslist') = 1
  -- make sure you have a valid cursor from the proc
begin
    fetch Next from @curslist
    while @@fetch_Status = 0
    begin
        fetch Next from @curslist
    end
end
close @curslist
deallocate @curslist
go

table_owner
table_name
optimizer_hint lock_type server_name
objectid    dbid        dbname
-----------------------------------------------------------------
-----------------------------------------------------------------
 ----------------------------------------------------------------
-----------------------------------------------------------------
- -------------- --------- --------------------------------------
------------------------------------------------------------------
-------------------------- ----------- ----------- -------------
------------------------------------------------------------------
---------------------------------------------------
dbo
titles
                                                   0         0
RRANKINSA20P\RRANKINSSQL2000
 1781581385            8 bigpubs2000

table_owner
table_name
optimizer_hint lock_type server_name
objectid    dbid        dbname
------------------------------------------------------------------------
---------------------------------------------------------- -------------
------------------------------------------------------------------------
```

LISTING 26.32 Continued

```
------------------------------------------ -------------- --------- ---
-----------------------------------------------------------------------
------------------------------------------------------ ----------- ----
------- ----------------------------------------------------------------
----------------------------------------------------------------


/** Get information about the columns returned by the specified cursor **/
declare @curslist CURSOR
exec sp_describe_cursor_columns @curslist output, 'global', 'titles_curs'
if cursor_status('variable','@curslist') = 1
  -- make sure you have a valid cursor from the proc
begin
    fetch Next from @curslist
    while @@fetch_Status = 0
    begin
        fetch Next from @curslist
    end
end
close @curslist
deallocate @curslist
go

column_name
ordinal_position column_characteristics_flags column_size data_type_
sql column_precision column_scale order_position order_direction hidden_
column columnid    objectid    dbid        dbname
--------------------------------------------------------------------------
------------------------------------------------------ ---------------- --
-------------------------- ----------- ------------- ---------------- ----
-------- -------------- --------------- ------------- ----------- --------
--- ----------- ----------------------------------------------------------
----------------------------------------------------------------------
ytd_sales
0                             6           4            56                10
         0               0 NULL                        0           8
1781581385          8 bigpubs2000

column_name
ordinal_position column_characteristics_flags column_size data_type_
sql column_precision column_scale order_position order_direction hidden_
column columnid    objectid    dbid        dbname
```

LISTING 26.32 Continued

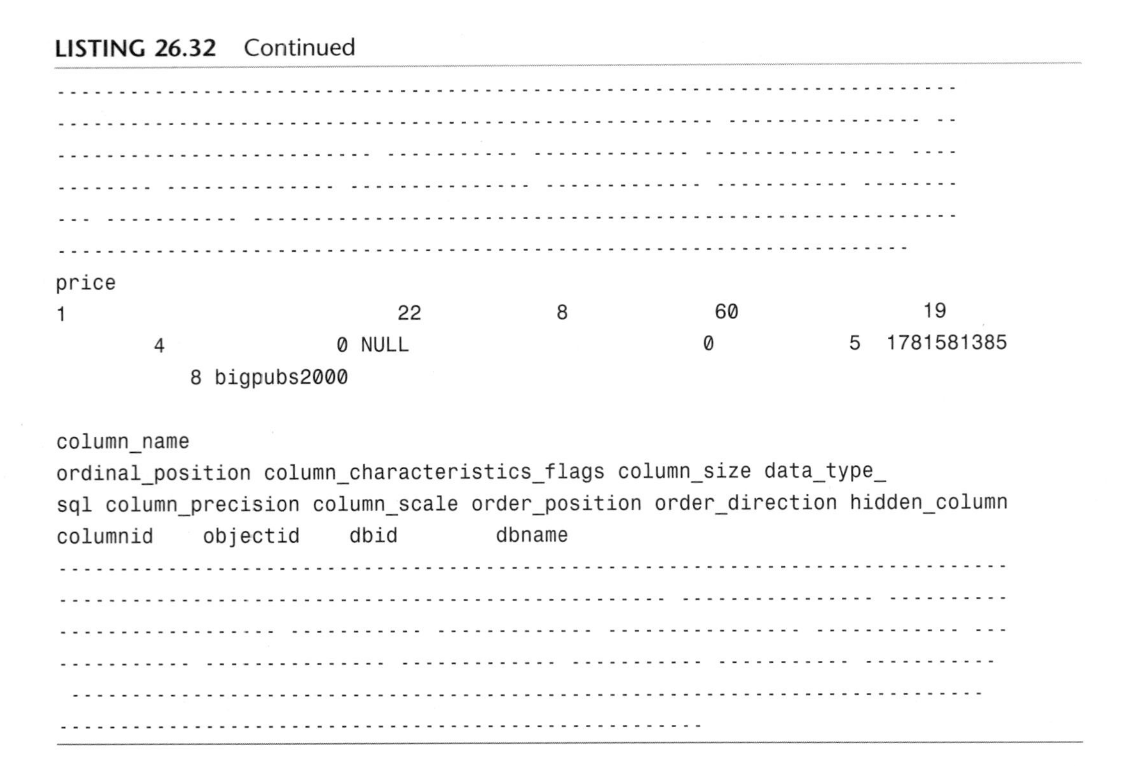

```
--------------------------------------------------------------------------
-------------------------------------------------- --------------- --
------------------------- ---------- ------------ --------------- ----
-------- ------------ -------------- ------------ ----------- --------
--- ---------- -------------------------------------------------------
----------------------------------------------------------------------
price
1                           22          8           60                19
        4               0 NULL                     0           5  1781581385
           8 bigpubs2000

column_name
ordinal_position column_characteristics_flags column_size data_type_
sql column_precision column_scale order_position order_direction hidden_column
columnid    objectid    dbid        dbname
------------------------------------------------------------------------------
------------------------------------------------- --------------- ---------
----------------- ---------- ------------ --------------- ----------- ---
----------- -------------- ------------ ----------- ----------- ----------
 ------------------------------------------------------------------------
----------------------------------------------------
```

Because the results from each of these procedures is a cursor resultset, you could fetch the results into local variables if you needed to use the cursor name or other information returned in your SQL code. For example, you could check to see what cursor is open and conditionally branch to the SQL code or a stored procedure that is set up to fetch data from that cursor. Or, you might want to know what columns are coming back from the cursor so you know what values you will be fetching.

API Cursors

So far, this chapter has examined how you can use cursors through T-SQL. The most common use of cursors, however, is through an application programming interface (API). Each API has calls or methods for defining cursor capabilities.

In fact, you could say that all results from SQL Server are returned through a cursor. The simplest case is that the client retrieves rows one at a time, scrolling forward (reading from the input buffer) through the resultset. This is called a **default resultset**.

If you need more advanced scrolling capabilities, part of the resultset must be cached somewhere, so you can use a key when searching for the previous row. This caching can occur at the client or at the server.

Client cursors are implemented at the client side. ODBC or OLE-DB caches the necessary information. No cursor calls are sent to SQL Server. Client cursors are useful if any of the following conditions exists:

- You have a slow network connection to the SQL Server.
- The resultset doesn't have many rows, or you will navigate through a major part of the resultset.
- You will allow the user to interact rapidly through the cached resultset.

A Web-based application is a good example of where client cursors can be valuable. For example, a SQL statement is sent to SQL Server to retrieve a number of customer names. This resultset is buffered at the client side. When the user chooses a customer, another SQL statement is executed, and customer details are presented in the Web browser.

By default, server-side cursors are used in the programming APIs, but the programmer can choose to use client cursors instead.

You can also choose the number of rows to be returned with each fetch operation sent to SQL Server (**fat** cursors) to minimize network traffic. This is not possible with Transact-SQL cursors; it would not make sense anyway because all processing is done at the server.

API server cursors are implemented through the API cursor support in SQL Server. SQL Server has a number of `sp_cursor` extended-stored procedures used by ODBC and OLE-DB, which implements API server cursors. The following is a list of the cursor procedures used by API cursor libraries:

- `sp_cursoropen`—Defines the SQL statement to be associated with the cursor and the cursor options, and then populates the cursor.
- `sp_cursorfetch`—Fetches a row or block of rows from the cursor.
- `sp_cursorclose`—Closes and deallocates the cursor.
- `sp_cursoroption`—Sets various cursor options.
- `sp_cursor`—Requests positioned updates.
- `sp_cursorprepare`—Generates an execution plan for the cursor but does not create the cursor.
- `sp_cursorexecute`—Creates and populates a cursor from the execution plan created by `sp_cursorprepare`.
- `sp_cursorunprepare`—Discards the execution plan from `sp_cursorprepare`.

Specifying the procedures directly in an application is not supported. I've included them here so you'll know what they are if you see them show up in a SQL Profile trace.

Your application cannot use API server cursors when executing the following statements:

- Batches or stored procedures that return multiple resultsets
- SELECT statements that contain COMPUTE, COMPUTE BY, or INTO clauses
- An EXECUTE statement that references a remote stored procedure

When to Use Cursors

Application performance can sometimes be slow due to the improper use of cursors. Always try to write your T-SQL code so SQL Server can perform what it is good at: set-based operations. It makes little sense to have an advanced RDBMS and only use it for one-row-at-a-time retrievals.

The cursor example discussed earlier in this section can be performed with a single UPDATE statement using the CASE expression as shown in Listing 26.33.

LISTING 26.33 The titles Cursor Example Performed with One UPDATE Statement Instead

```
update titles
   set price = case when ytd_sales < 500 then price *.75
                    when price > $15 then price * .90
                    else price * 1.15
               end
```

The advantage with this approach is a significant performance improvement, not to mention much cleaner and simpler code. I tested the performance of the single update versus the cursor on a Pentium III 700Mhz machine with 256MB of memory using the bigpubs database available on the CD. The titles table contains 537 rows. The single update statement completed in 80 milliseconds (ms). The cursor required 413ms. Although both of these completed in subsecond response time, consider that the cursor took five times longer to complete than the single update. Factor that out over hundreds of thousands or millions of rows, and you are talking a significant performance difference.

Why is the cursor so much slower? Well for one thing, a table scan performed by an UPDATE, DELETE, or SELECT uses internal, compiled C code to loop through the resultset. A cursor uses interpreted SQL code. In addition, with a cursor, you are performing multiple lines of code per row retrieved. The titles cursor example is a relatively simple one, only performing one or two conditional checks and a single update per row, but it is still five times slower. Adding just a single assignment select into the cursor loop added an average of 10ms to the time it took for the cursor to complete. Because of the overhead required to process cursors, set-oriented operations will typically run much faster, even if multiple passes of the table are required.

Although set-oriented operations are almost always faster than cursor operations, the one possible disadvantage of using a single update is locking concurrency. Even though a single update runs faster than a cursor, while it is running, the single update might end up locking the entire table for an extended period of time. This would prevent other users from accessing the table during the update. If concurrent access to the table is more important than the time it takes for the update to complete, you might want to use a cursor. A cursor only locks the data a row at a time instead of locking the entire table (as long as each row is committed individually and the entire cursor is not in a transaction).

Another situation in which you might want to consider using cursors is for scrolling applications when the resultsets can be quite large. Consider a customer service application. The customer representative might need to pull up a list of cases and case contacts associated with a customer. If the resultsets are small, you can just pull the entire resultset down into a list box and let the user scroll through them and not need to use a cursor. However, if thousands of rows of information are likely, you might want to pull back only a block or rows at a time, especially if the user only needs to look at a few of the rows to get the information he needs. It probably wouldn't be worth pulling back all that data across the network just for a few rows.

For this type of situation, you might want to use a scrollable API server cursor. This way, you can retrieve the appropriate number of rows to populate the list box and then use the available scrolling options to quickly fetch to the bottom of the list using the `LAST` or `ABSOLUTE` *n* options, or go backward or forward using the `RELATIVE` option.

NOTE

Be careful using this approach in a multitier environment. Many multitier architectures include a middle data layer that often uses connection sharing for multiple clients, and the users will typically be assigned any available connection when they need to access SQL Server. Users do not necessarily use the same connection each time. Therefore, if a user created a cursor in one connection, the next time the user submitted a fetch through the data layer, he might get a different connection and the cursor will not be available.

One solution for this problem is to go back to retrieving the entire resultset down to the client application. Another possible solution is to use a global temp table as a type of homemade insensitive cursor to hold the resultset and grab the data from the global temp table in chunks as you need it. For the temp table approach, make sure a sequential key is on the table so you can quickly grab the block of rows that you need. Be aware of the potential impact on tempdb performance and the size requirements of tempdb if the resultsets are large and you have many concurrent users.

As a general rule, use cursors only as a last resort when no set-oriented solution is feasible. If you have decided that a cursor is the appropriate solution, try to make it as efficient as possible by limiting the number of commands to be executed within the cursor loop as much as possible. Also, try to keep the cursor processing on the server side within stored procedures. If you will be performing multiple fetches over the network (such as to support a scrolling application), use an API server cursor. Avoid using client-side cursors that will be performing many cursor operations in the client application. You will find your application making excessive requests to the server and the volume of network roundtrips will make for a sloth-like application.

Summary

SQL is a powerful data-access and data-modification language. SQL Server's enhanced version of SQL, Transact-SQL, further expands the powers and capabilities of your SQL queries by providing features such as functions, variables, and commands to control execution flow. The Transact-SQL commands also are the basic building blocks for creating even more powerful SQL Server database components such as views, stored procedures, triggers, and user-defined functions.

The next four chapters, "Creating and Managing Views in SQL Server," "Creating and Managing Stored Procedures in SQL Server," "Creating and Managing Triggers," and "User-Defined Functions" describe how to create these objects using Transact-SQL. Chapter 31 shows you how to group your Transact-SQL statements so multiple actions can be treated as single logical units of work, or transactions, and how the data changes made within your T-SQL statements are managed and recorded in the SQL Server Transaction log.

CHAPTER 27

Creating and Managing Views in SQL Server

by Paul Jensen and Ray Rankins

IN THIS CHAPTER

- Definition of Views
- Using Views to Simplify Retrieval of Data
- Using Views to Hide Underlying Table Structures
- Using Views as a Security Mechanism
- Data Modifications and Views
- Creating Views
- Altering and Dropping Views
- Partitioned Views
- Indexed Views
- Views and Query Performance

Recently, while teaching a database class, one of the students described a view as a window on the data; it could be a picture window, clearly exposing a wide expanse of data, or a mere slit, offering only a peek. This chapter will pull back the curtains on this "window," exposing what a view is and isn't, and how you can leverage this powerful tool in your database design and applications.

Definition of Views

A view is simply a query stored as an object in the database. Essentially, a view behaves like a virtual table. Therefore, a view, with a few exceptions, can be referenced in Transact-SQL statements in the same manner as actual tables. A view can be defined to return a subset of data—namely selected columns and/or rows from a table—or a superset of data, in which two or more tables are combined using a `JOIN` or `UNION` operator to look like a single table. Views are also often used for returning summary values.

Because views are implemented as stored `SELECT` statements, they have virtually no overhead because they don't actually store data. This is a key point in understanding views. It is a common misconception that views have storage requirements that are commensurate with the data they return; this causes some database developers to avoid views. With the exception of indexed views, the only real overhead in a view is creating it and then applying the appropriate user permissions.

There are many uses for views, the most common of which include:

- Simplifying data retrieval for complex queries
- Hiding the underlying table structures
- Controlling access to data at the row or column level

Using Views to Simplify Retrieval of Data

When querying data, it is often required that complex joins, aggregates, functions, and so on, be written in to the SELECT statement to produce the desired results. To mask this complexity, the SELECT statement can be created as a view, and then future queries can be performed against the view. The information_schema views provided by Microsoft are a prime example of this use of a view. Because the system tables used to store metadata are quite complex, developing queries to retrieve information about SQL Server can be a daunting task. By querying the information_schema views instead of the system tables, you can simplify your SELECT statements. Following is a simple SELECT statement to query the information_schema.table_privileges view:

```
SELECT * from Information_schema.table_privileges
```

This query will obtain information about permissions in the database.

In Listing 27.1, you see the actual SELECT statement with which the table_privileges view is defined. Both statements return the same data, so it's up to you to decide which you would rather type!

LISTING 27.1 SELECT Statement Defining the information_schema.table_privileges View

```
select
        user_name(p.grantor)  as GRANTOR
       ,user_name(p.uid)            as GRANTEE
       ,db_name()                           as TABLE_CATALOG
       ,user_name(o.uid)            as TABLE_SCHEMA
       ,o.name                                    as TABLE_NAME
       ,case p.action
              when 26  then 'REFERENCES'
              when 193 then 'SELECT'
              when 195 then 'INSERT'
              when 196 then 'DELETE'
              when 197 then 'UPDATE'
        end                                        as PRIVILEGE_TYPE
       ,case
              when p.protecttype = 205 then 'NO'
              else 'YES'
```

LISTING 27.1 Continued

```
        end                                          as IS_GRANTABLE
 from
        sysprotects p,
        sysobjects o
where
        (is_member(user_name(p.uid)) = 1
        or
               p.grantor = user_id())
   and (p.protecttype = 204 or  /*grant exists without same grant with grant */
   (p.protecttype = 205
               and not exists(select * from sysprotects p2
                              where p2.id = p.id and
                              p2.uid = p.uid and
                              p2.action = p.action and
                              p2.columns = p.columns and
                              p2.grantor = p.grantor and
                              p2.protecttype = 204)))
       and p.action in (26,193,195,196,197)
       and p.id = o.id
       and o.xtype in ('U', 'V')
       and 0 != (permissions(o.id) &
               case p.action
          when 26  then  4              /*REFERENCES basebit on all columns */
          when 193 then  1              /*SELECT basebit on all columns     */
          when 195 then  8              /*INSERT basebit */
          when 196 then  16             /*DELETE basebit */
          when 197 then  2              /*UPDATE basebit on all columns     */
              end)
```

Using Views to Hide Underlying Table Structures

Another benefit to using views to access data is that they act as an additional layer between the application and the actual tables. This allows the view to be used to hide any changes that might be made to the underlying tables. The view shown in Listing 27.1 retrieves data from several columns in the sysprotects and sysobjects tables. If an application uses queries that access these tables directly, any changes made to the tables in future releases of SQL Server could break the application. If the application accesses the data through the view, however, only the view needs to be altered to accommodate the changes in the base tables. As long as the view returns the expected data, the structure of the underlying base tables and columns is irrelevant to the application.

A common scenario that results in changes to tables in a production database is when the data grows so large that it has to be partitioned into multiple tables, usually for performance or maintenance reasons. For example, old data might need to be archived off to an archive table. In order to retrieve data from both the production table and the archive table, the application or end users need to execute multiple `SELECT` statements and combine the results together. Because SQL Server supports the use of the `UNION` statement in views, a view could be defined that makes the partitioned tables appear as a single table. These are referred to as partitioned views and are covered in more detail in a separate section later in this chapter.

Using Views as a Security Mechanism

Views also can be used to limit access to data and simplify permission management. One advantage of using views as a security mechanism is that if the view and its underlying base tables are owned by the same user, no permissions need be granted on the underlying base tables themselves. All permissions can be granted or denied at the view level. The theory here is that if you own the tables or other views that a view accesses, and you grant permissions on the view, you must have wanted to give access to the data stored in the base tables. Therefore, no further permission checking is done. If, however, you have various owners for the objects that a view references, permissions must be checked at each level. If access is denied at any level, access to the view is denied. This is referred to as a broken ownership chain, and it can be a nightmare to administer and keep all permissions configured properly. This can easily be avoided by ensuring that all views and tables are created with the `dbo` user as the owner.

Views can be used to implement column-level security or row-level security.

Views for Column-Level Security

If users need to access certain columns in a table but should be restricted from accessing columns containing sensitive data, a view can be defined on only the required columns. Listing 27.2 shows a statement that creates a view called `contactview`, which returns only the required contact information from the customers table. It then grants `SELECT` permission on the view to the `sales` role, and revokes `SELECT` permission on the `Customer` table from the `sales` role. Users assigned the `sales` role would now only be able to view these five columns of data from the `Customers` table by using the view.

LISTING 27.2 Creating a View to Limit Column Access

```
CREATE VIEW dbo.contactview
AS
SELECT CustomerID, CompanyName, ContactName, ContactTitle, Phone
   FROM  dbo.Customers
Go
GRANT SELECT ON contactview TO sales
REVOKE SELECT on Customers FROM sales
Go
```

TIP

If the table you want to restrict column access to is often used in joins with other tables, be sure to include the table's primary and foreign key fields so that the view can be used in those joins. For example, because the `contactview` view shown in Listing 27.2 contains the `CustomerID` column, users would still be able to use the view in joins with other tables in the database such as the `Orders` table.

The alternative to using views to limit column access would be to define column-level permissions on the table, granting permissions on the individual columns that the users should be able to access. This can be an administrative nightmare because you are managing permissions at a far more granular level. Performance may suffer because permission checking would now be done at the column level as well as at the table level. In addition, users without permissions on all columns would no longer be able to issue a `SELECT *` statement against the table and would have to explicitly list the columns they have access to in their queries.

Views for Row-Level Security

Views can also be used to limit access to specific *rows* in a base table. In SQL Server 2000, this is currently the only method of implementing any form of row-level security. You can enforce row-level security by including a `WHERE` clause in the view, which limits the rows that are to be returned by the view. Listing 27.3 provides an example of a view called `USA_contactview`, which returns only the required contact information from the customers table where the customer's country is 'USA'. It then grants `SELECT` permission on the view to the `usa_sales` role, and revokes `SELECT` permission on the `Customer` table from the `usa_sales` role. Users assigned the `usa_sales` role are now only able to view data rows from the `Customers` table, via the `USA_contactview` view, where the country is `USA`.

LISTING 27.3 Creating a View to Limit Row Access

```
/* create view that allows access to only USA Customers */
CREATE VIEW dbo.USA_contactview
AS
SELECT CustomerID, CompanyName, ContactName, ContactTitle, Phone, Country
   FROM  dbo.Customers
   WHERE Country = 'USA'
Go
GRANT SELECT ON dbo.USA_contactview TO usa_sales
REVOKE SELECT on dbo.Customers FROM usa_sales
GRANT UPDATE ON dbo.USA_contactview TO usa_sales
REVOKE UPDATE on dbo.Customers FROM usa_sales
GRANT INSERT ON dbo.USA_contactview TO usa_sales
REVOKE INSERT on dbo.Customers FROM usa_sales
Go
```

If you used the approach presented in Listing 27.3 to implement row-level security, you would need a separate view for each country or group of countries you wanted to restrict access to. You can implement a more dynamic solution using views if your database provides information on the users and which data they should have access to. For example, in the Northwind database, the Employees table stores the country for each employee. This information can be used to determine which data each employee is allowed to see in the Customers table. Assuming the last name is also the user's SQL Server login name, the view shown in Listing 27.4 uses the user's login name along with a join to the Employee table to dynamically restrict which customers a user can see through the view.

LISTING 27.4 Creating a Dynamic View to Limit Row Access

```
/* create view that restricts the columns and rows users are
   allowed to access in Customers */
if object_id('dbo.contactview') is not null
   and objectproperty (object_id('dbo.contactview'), 'IsView') = 1
    DROP VIEW dbo.contactview
Go
CREATE VIEW dbo.contactview
AS
SELECT CustomerID, CompanyName, ContactName, ContactTitle, Phone, c.Country
   FROM dbo.Customers c
   JOIN dbo.Employees e
     on c.Country = e.country
   WHERE e.LastName = suser_sname()  --login name of the current user
Go
GRANT SELECT ON contactview TO sales
REVOKE SELECT on Customers FROM sales
GRANT UPDATE ON contactview TO sales
REVOKE UPDATE on Customers FROM sales
GRANT INSERT ON contactview TO sales
REVOKE INSERT on Customers FROM sales
Go
```

CAUTION

Be careful when using views in joins to provide row-level security. What looks like a simple join between a couple of views might actually resolve to a complex multitable query. One time, I was at a customer site trying to identify query performance problems with their database. They had implemented row-level security across their database using views with joins. Each view contained at least a three-table join. A simple query joining three views together was actually resulting in a nine- or ten-table query when the execution plan was generated. Needless to say, joins of nine to ten tables typically do not provide good performance! At the very least, when implementing this solution, you'll want to make sure that the columns specified in the join clauses are indexed.

Data Modifications and Views

So far, we have concentrated on using views to query data. Data can also be modified through a view, with a few restrictions. The following points outline the general rules for modifying data through views.

- Modifications to data through views must meet all restrictions that apply to the underlying tables. Modifying data through the view will not circumvent nullibility, rules, constraints, and so on.
- An insert or update through a multitable view cannot affect more than one underlying base table.
- A delete cannot be executed against multitable views.
- Columns consisting of aggregates, computed values, or built-in functions cannot be modified through a view.
- Data cannot be modified through the view if the SELECT statement for the view contains a GROUP BY, DISTINCT, TOP, OR UNION clause. Tables referenced in a view defined with the UNION ALL clause can be modified and will be discussed later in the section, "Partitioned Views."
- Modifications through a view might cause errors if they affect columns not referenced in the view. If you attempt to insert a row through the view and the columns not referenced in the view do not allow NULLS, or do not have default values defined, the insert will fail.
- If a view has been defined with the WITH CHECK OPTION setting specified you cannot perform modifications through the view to the underlying data that would result in that data no longer being accessible through the view.
- The READTEXT or WRITETEXT statements cannot be used with image, text, and ntext columns through a view.

Bearing in mind the preceding restrictions, modifying data through a view uses the same INSERT, UPDATE, and DELETE syntax used when data modifications are performed directly on a table. The following query demonstrates changing the contact name in the view contactview.

```
UPDATE contactview
       SET ContactName = 'Maria Anderson'
       WHERE ContactName = 'Maria Anders'
```

NOTE

The restrictions on modifying data through a view are fairly logical, and some can even be circumvented by defining INSTEAD OF triggers on the view. INSTEAD OF triggers, as their name implies, perform an alternative action than the modification the trigger is defined for. For example, if you are inserting into more than one table of a multitable view, an INSTEAD OF trigger on the view could split the single insert into two separate inserts into the underlying base tables. INSTEAD OF triggers are discussed in further detail in Chapter 29, "Creating and Managing Triggers."

Creating Views

Views can be created using Transact-SQL statements or through Enterprise Manager. Enterprise Manager also provides a Create View Wizard that will step you through the creation of a view. The Create View Wizard can be accessed via the Wizards option in the Tools menu.

This section will first present some guidelines and restrictions for creating views which are applicable no matter which tool you choose.

Guidelines for Creating Views

When creating a view, consider using an intuitive name that identifies it as a view, such as dbo.emp_list_view. The owner name is optional, but it should be specified as dbo to avoid broken ownership chains (assuming the referenced objects are also owned by dbo). When the view is created, the existence of objects referenced in the SELECT statement is verified, and you must have SELECT permission on the objects if the owner differs from that of the view. If the columns referenced in the view are derived (for example, the column contains an arithmetic expression or aggregate function), or if columns from multiple tables have the same name, column names must be specified for the view columns. Column names also can be specified to hide the column names of the base tables, or perhaps to simply make them more user friendly.

Before you create the view, test the SELECT statement to make sure it returns the desired results. This also might be a good time to consider whether additional indexes might be required on columns referenced by the view, especially any columns specified in search arguments or join columns.

Restrictions on Creating a View

Be aware of the following restrictions when creating a view:

- A CREATE VIEW statement cannot contain the INTO keyword or the COMPUTE or COMPUTE BY clauses.
- The ORDER BY clause can only be specified in a view in conjunction with the TOP keyword.

- The CREATE VIEW command cannot be combined with other T-SQL statements in a batch.
- A view cannot reference more than 1,024 columns, nor can it reference temporary tables or table variables.
- Views must be created in the current database. The CREATE VIEW statement does not allow you to specify a database name. However, the view can reference tables or views that exist in other databases, or even other servers when using distributed queries.

Creating Views Using T-SQL

Views are created, surprisingly enough, with the CREATE VIEW statement. The syntax for creating views is as follows:

```
CREATE VIEW owner.view_name [(column[,...n])]
[WITH {ENCRYPTION¦SCHEMABINDING¦VIEW_METADATA}[,...n]]
AS
select_statement
[WITH CHECK OPTION]
```

The CREATE VIEW options are outlined in the next few sections.

WITH ENCRYPTION

When a view is created, its definition is stored in the text column of the syscomments table. If WITH ENCRYPTION is specified when the view is created or altered, the definition is stored encrypted. If you are encrypting a view, make sure you save the original script in case it is required to re-create or alter the view in the future. Encrypting the view also prevents it from being published with replication.

27

> **NOTE**
>
> If you must hide the definition of a view, use the WITH ENCRYPTION option. Do not attempt to remove the view definition by deleting it from the syscomments table. This will prevent you from using the view, and also prevent SQL Server from being able to re-create the view during the next upgrade.

WITH SCHEMABINDING

The WITH SCHEMABINDING option binds the view to the underlying object schemas. Use of the WITH SCHEMABINDING option requires that two-part (owner.object) names be specified for all referenced objects. This option prevents referenced objects from being dropped or modified in a way that would affect the view, without the view first being dropped or modified to remove the schema binding.

WITH VIEW_METADATA
When this option is specified, SQL Server returns information about the view, as opposed to the base tables, when browse-mode metadata is requested for a query that references the view via a database API. Browse-mode metadata is additional information returned by SQL Server to client-side DBLIB, ODBC, and OLE DB APIs, which allows them to implement client-side updateable cursors.

WITH CHECK OPTION
By default, when a view contains a WHERE clause that restricts which rows can be seen through the view, it does not prevent the user from modifying or inserting a row into the view that cannot subsequently be seen through the view. For example, the definition of USA_contactview shown in Listing 27.3 would not prevent the following insert and update statements from being executed, even though the user would not be able to see the rows generated by these statements:

```
update USA_contactview set country = 'Canada'
   where CustomerID = 'WHITC'
insert USA_contactview (CustomerID, CompanyName, ContactName,
                        ContactTitle, Phone, Country)
   values ('GOTHX', 'Gotham Consulting Services', 'Ray Rankins',
           'President', '(518) 555-5555', 'UK')
```

From a user perspective, the effect of modifying a row through a view such that it could no longer be queried through the view would be that of having deleted the row. To prevent this situation, you need to create the view with the WITH CHECK OPTION property specified. The following version of the USA_contactview would prevent the previous insert and update statements from occurring:

```
/* create view that allows access to only USA Customers */
CREATE VIEW dbo.USA_contactview
AS
SELECT CustomerID, CompanyName, ContactName, ContactTitle, Phone, Country
   FROM  dbo.Customers
   WHERE Country = 'USA'
WITH CHECK OPTION
Go
```

Attempting to perform either of those statements would result in the following error message:

```
Server: Msg 550, Level 16, State 1, Line 1
The attempted insert or update failed because the target view either specifies
 WITH CHECK OPTION or spans a view that specifies WITH CHECK OPTION and one or
 more rows resulting from the operation did not qualify under the CHECK OPTION
 constraint.
The statement has been terminated.
```

CREATE VIEW Examples

The following examples illustrate the use of the CREATE VIEW statement.

Listing 27.5 creates a view on the employee table using the WITH CHECK OPTION.

LISTING 27.5 Creating a View Using WITH CHECK OPTION

```
CREATE VIEW Uk_emp_view
AS
SELECT * FROM employees WHERE country = 'UK'
WITH CHECK OPTION
GO
```

A view is often created to retrieve data from multiple tables. Listing 27.6 illustrates this. This view also uses WITH ENCRYPTION to hide the view definition and SCHEMABINDING to prevent changes to underlying tables unless the view is dropped or altered first.

LISTING 27.6 Returning Data from Multiple Tables in a View

```
CREATE VIEW High_Sales_View
WITH ENCRYPTION, SCHEMABINDING
AS
SELECT o.orderid, o.customerid, od.quantity, od.productid
   FROM dbo.orders o
   JOIN dbo.[order details] od
     ON o.orderid = od.orderid
   WHERE od.quantity > 20
GO
```


Creating Views Using the View Designer

If you prefer to create views through the Enterprise Manager, you can access the View Designer by right-clicking the Views icon in the appropriate database and selecting New View. The View Designer is actually based on the Query Designer; however, when you select Save, you are prompted for a name for the view and the query you have built is stored as the view definition. Figure 27.1 shows the View Designer.

After you are in View Designer, you can click on the Add Table icon (it's the one to the far right) in the toolbar, or right-click in the Design pane and click Add Table in the pop-up menu to add tables, views, and table-valued user-defined functions to your query. Selecting the check boxes for the appropriate columns adds them to the SELECT statement that will be saved as your view definition. Figure 27.2 illustrates a join on the Orders and Order Details tables being saved as a view.

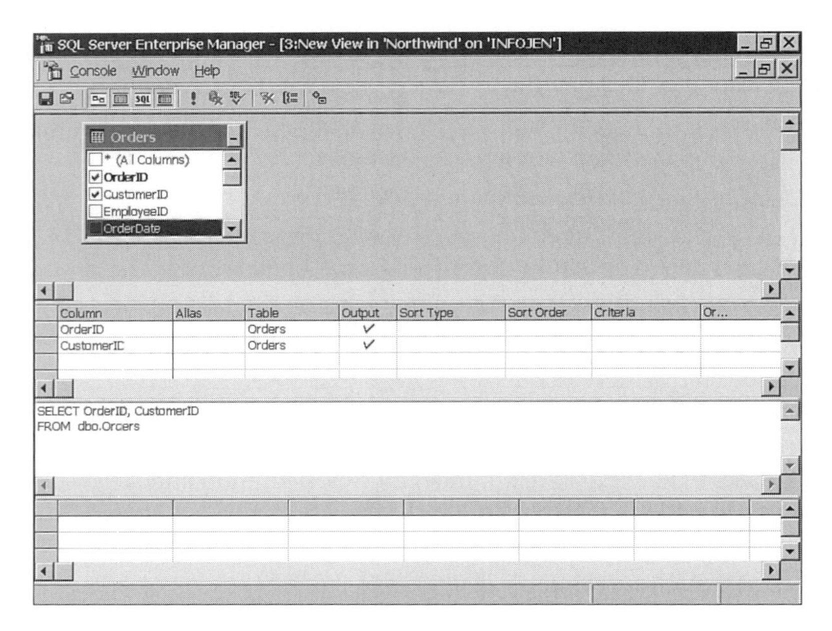

FIGURE 27.1 The View Designer window.

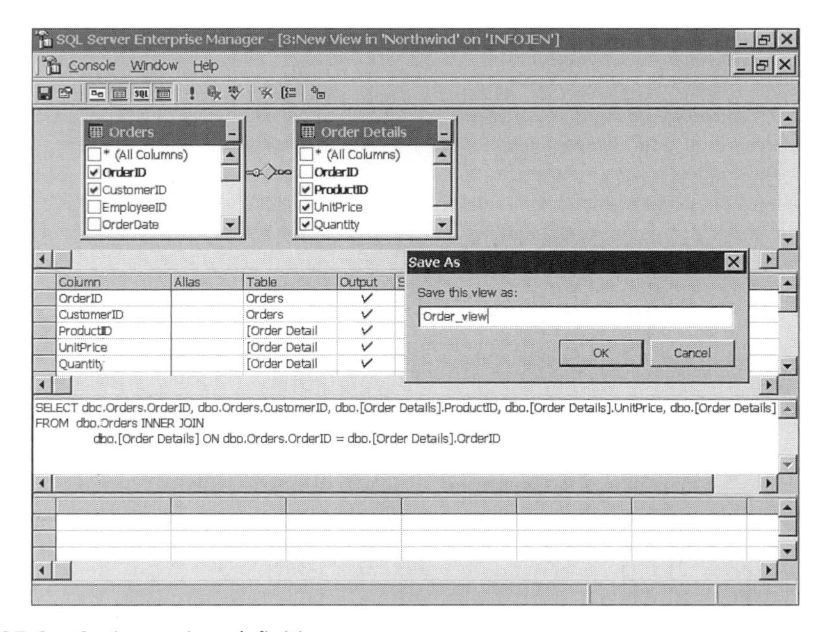

FIGURE 27.2 Saving a view definition.

If you want to add view options such as the `WITH CHECK OPTION` property, select the Properties icon or right-click in the window and choose Properties to bring up the view's Properties page. Figure 27.3 shows the Properties page.

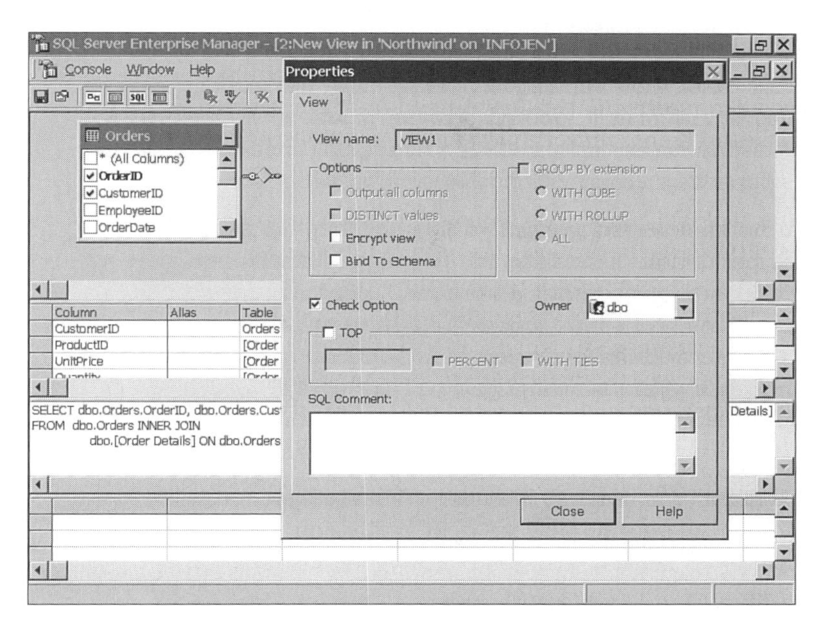

FIGURE 27.3 Defining options for a view.

TIP

When using tools, such as the View Designer, hover over the taskbar icons and a pop-up will describe their function. Context-sensitive help also is available for most functions. To access context-sensitive help, click the Help button on the appropriate page or window, or simply press F1.

Altering and Dropping Views

If you want to change the definition of a view, you can do so using the `ALTER VIEW` statement, or by dropping and re-creating the view. Views can be dropped using the `DROP VIEW` statement.

Altering Views

It is better to alter a view to change its definition than to drop and re-create the view; when you alter the view, the permissions that have been assigned are retained, and dependent objects such as `INSTEAD OF` triggers and stored procedures aren't affected. The `ALTER VIEW` statement accepts the same parameters and options as `CREATE VIEW`. The `ALTER VIEW` syntax is as follows:

```
ALTER VIEW owner.view_name [(column[,n])]
[WITH {ENCRYPTION|SCHEMABINDING|VIEW_METADATA}[,n]]
AS
select_statement
[WITH CHECK OPTION]
```

Since the ALTER VIEW statement re-creates the view definition, any options specified in the original view that you want to retain also must be specified in the ALTER VIEW statement. Alternatively, any options that you want to add can be specified when you alter the view. Listing 27.7 alters the contactview view to add the ENCRYPTION option.

LISTING 27.7 Altering a View

```
ALTER VIEW dbo.contactview
WITH ENCRYPTION
AS
SELECT CompanyName, ContactName, ContactTitle, Phone
FROM  dbo.Customers
Go
```

NOTE

If you define a view with the SELECT * statement, and then subsequently add columns to the table, the new columns will not appear in the view. Use the ALTER VIEW command to redefine the view to get the new columns to appear.

In addition, if columns are dropped from the table, queries against a view defined with SELECT * will fail until the view is altered or dropped and re-created.

You can prevent these problems by creating the view with the WITH SCHEMABINDING option, which will not allow these types of changes to be made to the table until the view is dropped first.

Dropping Views

You can drop a view that is no longer needed with the DROP VIEW command, or you can select and delete it in Enterprise Manager. The following is an example of the DROP VIEW command to drop the view contactview:

```
DROP VIEW dbo.contactview
```

Bear in mind that if a dropped view must be re-created, you need to reassign all permissions. If any other views reference the dropped view, then users querying those views will receive an error message. Before dropping an object such as a view, run sp_depends 'viewname' or right-click the view in Enterprise Manager and select All Tasks, Display Dependencies to determine whether dependent objects exist.

Partitioned Views

Partitioned views are used to access data that has been horizontally split, or **partitioned**, across multiple tables. These tables can be in the same or different databases, or even spread across multiple servers. Partitioning of tables is used to spread the I/O and processing load of large tables across multiple disks or servers. Partitioned views allow access to the tables as if they were one. For example, a multinational company could have an order table with millions of rows. To speed access to the data, the table could be partitioned into multiple tables, with identical column definitions, each with a check constraint specifying a specific country code. Listing 27.8 shows a sample `CREATE TABLE` command to create the tables.

LISTING 27.8 Creating the Base Tables for a Partitioned View

```
CREATE TABLE UK_Order (
   Ord_No     INT,
   Country    Char(2) CHECK (Country = 'UK'),
   Cust_id    INT
   PRIMARY KEY (Ord_no, Country)
   )
go
CREATE TABLE US_Order (
   Ord_No     INT,
   Country    Char(2) CHECK (Country = 'US'),
   Cust_id    INT
   PRIMARY KEY (Ord_no, Country)
   )
go
CREATE TABLE CA_Order (
   Ord_No     INT,
   Country    Char(2) CHECK (Country = 'CA'),
   Cust_id    INT
   PRIMARY KEY (Ord_no, Country)
   )
go
```


Creating a Partitioned View

To create a partitioned view to access the tables, the view definition combines data from multiple tables using the `UNION ALL` operator. If all the tables are on the same server, it is referred to as a local partitioned view; if the tables span multiple servers, it is considered a distributed partitioned view. Listing 27.9 shows the `CREATE VIEW` statement to create a local partitioned view on the tables in the preceding listing.

LISTING 27.9 Creating a Local Partitioned View

```
CREATE VIEW World_Sales
AS
SELECT *
FROM UK_Order
```

LISTING 27.9 Continued

```
       UNION ALL
SELECT *
FROM US_Order
       UNION ALL
SELECT *
FROM CA_Order
```

When designing your partitioning scheme, it should be clear what data belongs to which table. This can be accomplished by defining a check constraint on the column(s) that holds the data used to partition the tables, as shown in Listing 27.8.

A view containing `UNION ALL` statements is not technically considered a partitioned view unless the view definition meets the requirements for partitioned views. A view that doesn't meet the requirements can still be created and queries run against it, but no updates are allowed and queries against the view cannot take advantage of the optimization enhancements provided by partitioned views. The following restrictions must be met to create views that SQL Server can recognize as partitioned views and optimize them effectively:

- A `CHECK` constraint must exist on the partitioning column that specifies the data that resides in each of the table partitions. There cannot be any overlap between the key ranges of the `CHECK` constraints.
- Tables cannot be referenced more than once in the view.
- Tables in the view cannot have any indexes created on computed columns.
- The `PRIMARY KEY` constraints must be defined on the same number of columns for each table in the view and the partitioning columns must be a part of the primary key of the table.
- All columns must be specified for each table in the view and the columns cannot be referenced more than once in the select list. Using `SELECT *` in the view definition is the easiest way to ensure these column requirements are met.
- The columns for each table must be in the same ordinal position in the select list and must be of the same type (including data type, precision, scale, and collation).
- The column used to define the partitioning scheme cannot be an identity, default, timestamp, or computed column and cannot allow NULL values.
- There can be only one constraint defined on the partitioning column.

Queries against partitioned views that meet all of these rules will be optimized using the partitioned view optimizations that are supported by the SQL Server 2000 query optimizer.

When the `CHECK` constraint specifies the range of values each partition holds, the constraint can be used by the query optimizer to determine which table(s) to access if the partitioning column is specified in a search argument. If no `CHECK` constraint exists on the partitioning column, the query optimizer cannot make any assumptions about the values stored in different tables and will search all the underlying base tables.

Modifying Data Through Partitioned Views

Data can be modified through a partitioned view as long as it meets all the requirements specified in the previous section to be considered a truly partitioned view, and also meets the standard requirements for inserts, updates, and deletes against partitioned views. In addition, the following restrictions apply:

- All columns must be specified for `INSERT` statements, even if the columns allow NULL values or have `DEFAULT` constraints defined.
- The `DEFAULT` keyword cannot be specified in the `VALUES` clause of an insert or the `SET` clause of an update.
- Inserts are not allowed if any of the participating tables contain identity columns.
- Inserts and updates are not allowed if any of the participating tables columns contain a timestamp column.
- The view cannot contain any self-joins with the same view or any of the participating tables.

> **NOTE**
>
> Data can be modified through partitioned views only in the Enterprise and Developer Editions of SQL Server 2000.

If a partitioned view is not updatable, you can circumvent the update restrictions by creating an `INSTEAD OF` trigger on the view. The `INSTEAD OF` trigger can be designed to determine which underlying table(s) to modify and submit the appropriate SQL statements to the underlying tables. Be sure to include appropriate error handling into the trigger to ensure no duplicate rows are inserted. For more information on creating `INSTEAD OF` triggers, see Chapter 29.

Distributed Partitioned Views

A distributed partitioned view is defined just like a partitioned view, but one or more of the base tables resides on a different server. You can create distributed partitioned views by first adding linked server definitions for each server containing tables that participate in the partitioned view and referencing the tables using the full four-part name (*server.database.owner.table*) or using an `OPENDATASOURCE-` or `OPENROWSET`-based name. If using the

OPENDATASOURCE or OPENROWSET function, the function must specify a table name rather than a pass-through query. (For more information on configuring and using linked servers, see Chapter 19, "Managing Linked and Remote Servers.")

To help optimize performance of distributed partitioned views, set the lazy schema validation option using the sp_serveroption system procedure. This helps ensure the query processor does not request metadata for any of the linked tables until data is actually needed from the remote table partition. Listing 27.10 displays an example of a distributed partitioned view.

LISTING 27.10 Creating a Distributed Partitioned View

```
CREATE VIEW World_Sales
AS
-- Get data from remote table on UKServer
SELECT *
  FROM UKServer.Northwind.dbo.Order
UNION ALL
  SELECT *
    FROM Northwind.dbo.Order
UNION ALL
-- Get data from remote table on CAServer
  SELECT *
    FROM CAServer.Northwind.dbo.Order
```

Typically, each server participating in the distributed view would have a copy of the World_Sales view created on it, with fully qualified names referencing the tables on the other servers. Therefore, each of three servers in this scenario would contain one table (the local data) and a World_Sales view to access data from the other countries.

If properly defined, SQL Server 2000 will attempt to optimize the performance of distributed partitioned views by minimizing the amount of data transferred between member servers. The query processor uses OLE DB to retrieve the CHECK constraint definitions from each member table. This allows the query processor to map the specified search arguments to the appropriate table(s). The query execution plan then accesses only the necessary tables and retrieves only those remote rows needed to complete the SQL statement.

SQL Server 2000 introduces support for updateable distributed partitioned views. Data modifications are performed against the view, allowing true transparency. The view is accessed as if it were a base table, with the user or application unaware of the actual location of the data. If configured properly, SQL Server will determine via the WHERE clause specified in the update query which partition defined in the view must be updated rather than updating all tables in the join.

> **NOTE**
>
> Data can be modified through distributed partitioned views only in the Enterprise and Developer Editions of SQL Server 2000.

Indexed Views

As stated earlier in this chapter, views are simply stored `SELECT` statements, and as such, have no data storage requirements and incur little if any overhead in the database. However, just when you thought it was safe to come out of the server room, SQL Server 2000 introduces the concept of the indexed view. Just as it sounds, an indexed view is one on which you create an index. To be more precise, an indexed view is one on which there exists a unique clustered index. When a unique clustered index is defined on a view, the resultset generated by the view is materialized and stored in the leaf level of the index as if the clustered index were defined on a table. When the data in the underlying base table(s) changes, the data in the indexed view is updated to reflect the changes, in much the same way that changes to a table are reflected in its indexes. Gone with the indexed view is the concept of the view as a virtual table because it now has associated data storage.

Creating Indexed Views

The syntax to create an indexed view is the same as creating a normal view. However, there are a number of requirements that must be met in order to create an index on a view:

- The `ANSI_NULLS` and `QUOTED_IDENTIFIER` options must be enabled when the view is created, and `ANSI_NULLS` must have been enabled when the tables referenced by the view were created.
- The view can only reference tables and not any other views, and all tables must be in the same database as the view and be owned by the same user creating the view.
- The `SCHEMABINDING` option must be specified when the view is created.
- Only two part names (*`owner.objectname`*) can be specified for all tables and user-defined functions referenced in the view.
- Any functions referenced in the view must be deterministic. A deterministic function is one that returns the same result every time it is called with the same set of input parameters (for information on which functions in SQL Server are nondeterministic, see Chapter 26, "Using Transact-SQL in SQL Server 2000").
- All column names must be explicitly specified in the view (`SELECT *` is not allowed), and cannot be specified more than once.
- The view cannot contain any text, ntext, or image columns.
- The view cannot include data from a derived table, a rowset function, a `UNION`, a subquery, an outer join, or a self join.

- The select statement in the view cannot contain the TOP, ORDER BY, DISTINCT, COMPUTE, COMPUTE BY, HAVING, CUBE, or ROLLUP clauses.
- The select statement in the view can only contain aggregate functions if the GROUP BY clause is specified, and cannot contain the complex aggregate functions: avg(), min(), max(), stdev(), stdevp(), var(), or varp().
- The COUNT(*) function cannot be used, but COUNT_BIG(*) can.

This is a rather extensive list of criteria that must be met for an index to be created on a view. Fortunately, SQL Server provides the OBJECTPROPERTY function to help determine if a view can be indexed. The IsIndexable property can be queried to verify whether index creation would be successful for a view. The following statement checks whether an index can be created on the view high_sales_view; a value of 1 is returned if the index creation will be allowed:

```
SELECT OBJECTPROPERTY (object_id ('high_sales_view'),'IsIndexable')
```

If a value of 0 is returned, then the view doesn't meet the criteria for indexing. Check your view definition against the indexed view requirements, and use ALTER VIEW to adjust the view definition.

Creating an index on a view is just like creating an index on a table, except you specify the view name instead of a table name. The first index on an indexed view must be a unique clustered index. In addition to the unique clustered index, you can create additional nonclustered indexes on indexed views to provide additional query performance. Additional indexes on views might provide more options for the query optimizer to choose from during the optimization process.

The user creating the index must be the owner of the view and the following SET option settings must be in effect when the index is created:

```
SET ARITHABORT ON
SET CONCAT_NULL_YIELDS_NULL ON
SET QUOTED_IDENTIFIER ON
SET ANSI_NULLS ON
SET ANSI_PADDING ON
SET ANSI_WARNINGS ON
SET NUMERIC_ROUNDABORT OFF
```

The following example creates an indexed view on the high_sales_view table:

```
create unique clustered index high_sales_UCI
    on High_Sales_View (orderid, customerid, productid)
```

Advantages of the Indexed View

There must be some method in this madness of saddling a perfectly good view with data storage, and indeed there is.

The question commonly asked about indexed views is, "If indexes are required, why not just create them on the base table columns?" The answer to this question lies in the types of views on which you might create indexes.

When you create an index on a table, an index entry exists for every row. That applies to a view as well. However, if the view were to contain grouped aggregate values, its resultset could be many times smaller than the actual number of rows in the base tables. When the view's index is used to satisfy a query, not only are there fewer rows to be processed, but the aggregate values are already stored in the index ready to be returned without further calculation. This also applies to views containing a `WHERE` clause that reduces the number of rows returned.

Queries against views that join multiple tables also can benefit from an index. Rather than costly join operations being performed for each query, the data is already "joined" and stored in the index. Without the indexed view, even if the referenced base table columns were all indexed, the join operation would still have to be performed.

Another advantage is that the view doesn't have to be referenced in the `FROM` clause for the index to be used by the query optimizer. In the Developer and Enterprise editions of SQL Server, queries referencing the base tables can take advantage of the view's indexes. For example, if a query against a table requests a `SUM` for a particular column, and that column already has a `SUM` stored in an indexed view, the query analyzer is smart enough to consider using the value from the indexed view, rather than compute a new value from the table data.

NOTE

Indexed views can be created in any edition of SQL Server 2000, but they will only be considered for query optimization in the Developer and Enterprise editions of SQL Server 2000. In other editions of SQL Server 2000, the optimizer will only consider the indexed view when it is explicitly referenced in the query and the `NOEXPAND` optimizer hint is specified. For example, to force the optimizer to consider using the `sales_Qty_Rollup` indexed view in the Standard Edition of SQL Server 2000, you need to execute the query as follows:

```
select * from sales_Qty_Rollup WITH (NOEXPAND)
   where stor_id between 'B914' and 'B999'
```

For more information on how indexed views are used by the query optimizer, see Chapter 35, "Understanding Query Optimization."

Disadvantages of the Indexed View

The prime disadvantage of the indexed view is the same disadvantage inherent in all indexes; data is stored and modified in more than one location. This can be even more of a drawback for the indexed view because, as explained earlier, one of the indexed view's great advantages is in storing grouped aggregate data. When data is updated in the base tables from which the aggregate is drawn, the value must be recalculated and stored in the indexed view. Also, the scope of a view's index can be larger than that of any single table's index, especially if the view is defined on several large tables.

Therefore, indexed views may be inappropriate for tables in which the data is frequently updated. Because of this additional maintenance overhead, consider creating indexes only on those views where the advantage provided by the improved speed in retrieving the results outweighs the increased maintenance overhead. Also, if the grouped aggregate value of the view has a high cardinality, meaning it does not reduce the row set significantly as opposed to the table, its drawbacks might outweigh its benefits.

With the exception of indexed views on frequently joined, rarely updated tables, the indexed view is usually more appropriate for Decision Support Systems (DSS) than it is for Online Transaction Processing (OLTP).

Views and Query Performance

Views typically do not add any additional overhead to query performance. A `SELECT` statement against a view is just as fast as the underlying query used to define the view. When a view is combined with other search arguments or join conditions in a query, the query optimizer combines the source of the view and the SQL statement into a single execution plan. Since it doesn't generate separate query plans for the view and the SQL statement, the view result doesn't have to be materialized first before it can resolve the rest of the query. Consider the first query shown in Listing 27.11 that references the `High_Sales_View` view, which was defined in Listing 27.6. The query referencing the view generates the same execution plan as the second query shown in Listing 27.11, which contains a three table join.

LISTING 27.11 Queries That Generate the Same Execution Plan

```
-- Query that references the High_Sales_View
SELECT v.orderid, v.customerid, v.quantity, v.productid
   FROM High_Sales_View v
   JOIN Customers c
     ON v.customerID = c.customerID
   WHERE c.city = 'London'
go
```

LISTING 27.11 Continued

```
-- Query that references the actual tables
SELECT o.orderid, o.customerid, od.quantity, od.productid
   FROM orders o
   JOIN [order details] od
     ON o.orderid = od.orderid
   JOIN Customers c
     ON o.customerID = c.customerID
   WHERE c.city = 'London'
```

One exception to this optimization strategy is when the view contains an aggregate function and the query contains a search argument against the aggregate column. Because the resultset for the view is essentially the contents of a worktable, the view must be materialized first to generate this worktable before a search can be performed on the aggregate column, or before it can be joined with other tables outside of the view definition. Listing 27.12 presents a view that calculates a grouped `SUM` aggregate. The first query that references the `total_customer_sales` view generates a different execution plan than the second query, which references the base tables only. The execution plan for the query using the view is less efficient than the three-table join as it first calculates the sum of the quantity field for all orders before joining that resultset with the Customers tables and evaluating whether the Customer city is "London." The second query first finds the orders for the customers from London and then calculates the sum of quantity for only those orders.

LISTING 27.12 Queries That Generate Different Execution Plans Due to Aggregation in View Definition

```
CREATE VIEW total_customer_sales
AS
SELECT o.customerid, sum(od.quantity) as total_sales
   FROM orders o
   JOIN [order details] od
     ON o.orderid = od.orderid
   group by o.customerid
go

-- Query that references the High_Sales_View
SELECT v.customerid, v.total_sales
   FROM total_customer_sales v
   JOIN Customers c
     ON v.customerID = c.customerID
   WHERE c.city = 'London'
     and v.total_sales > 100
go
```

LISTING 27.12 Continued

```
-- Query that references the actual tables
SELECT o.customerid, sum(od.quantity) as total_sales
   FROM orders o
   JOIN [order details] od
     ON o.orderid = od.orderid
   JOIN Customers c
     ON o.customerID = c.customerID
   WHERE c.city = 'London'
   group by o.customerid
   having sum(od.quantity) > 100
```

For more information on Query Optimization, see Chapter 35.

Summary

Views are a powerful database tool that in their simplest form can be used as a low-overhead way to simplify queries or provide column-level or row-level security. They also can be leveraged to mask schema or layout changes in existing applications, and for this reason should be considered during all phases of database design.

Partitioned views can provide a unified view of a table that has been partitioned, or split, to improve performance or accommodate geographically distributed data. The indexed view, new to SQL Server 2000, may have some drawbacks, but can improve performance for certain types of queries.

The next chapter, "Creating and Managing Stored Procedures in SQL Server," discusses one of the most powerful features of SQL Server. Stored procedures allow you to store your T-SQL statements as executable objects in SQL Server, providing administrative and performance benefits including another method of controlling access to data and hiding changes to underlying data structures.

CHAPTER 28

Creating and Managing Stored Procedures in SQL Server

by Ray Rankins

IN THIS CHAPTER

A **stored procedure** is one or more SQL commands stored in a database as an executable object. Stored procedures can be called interactively, from within client application code, from within other stored procedures, and from within triggers. Parameters can be passed to and returned from stored procedures to increase their usefulness and flexibility. A stored procedure can also return a number of resultsets and a status code.

Advantages of Stored Procedures

Using stored procedures provides many advantages over executing large and complex SQL batches from client applications:

- Modular programming—Subroutines and functions are often used in ordinary 3GL and 4GL languages (such as C, C++, and Microsoft Visual Basic) to break up code into smaller, more manageable pieces. The same advantages are achieved when using stored procedures, with the difference that the stored procedure is stored in SQL Server and can be called by any client application.
- Restricted, function-based access to tables—Someone can have access to execute a stored procedure without having permissions to operate directly on the underlying tables.

- Reduced network traffic—Stored procedures can consist of many individual SQL statements but can be executed with a single statement. This allows you to reduce the number and size of calls from the client to the server.
- Faster execution—Stored procedures query plans are kept in memory after the first execution. The code doesn't have to be reparsed and reoptimized on subsequent executions.
- Enforced consistency—If users modify data only through stored procedures, problems resulting from ad hoc modifications are eliminated.
- Reduced operator and programmer errors—Because less information is being passed, complex tasks can be executed more easily with less likelihood of SQL errors.
- Automated complex or sensitive transactions—If all modifications of certain tables take place in stored procedures, you can guarantee integrity on those tables.

Some of the disadvantages of using stored procedures follow (depending on environment):

- Less powerful programming language—T-SQL is not the most powerful or structured programming language.
- Less integration with programming environment—Many of the larger software development projects use tools for version handling, debugging, reuse, and so on. Those tools might not support code stored within stored procedures.
- Less portability—Although the ANSI-99 SQL standard provides a standard for stored procedures in database management systems, the format and structure is different from SQL Server–stored procedures. Also, few DBMS vendors currently support the new standard.

The question is, "Should you use stored procedures?" The answer is (as it often is), "It depends."

If you are working in a two-tier environment, stored procedures are often advantageous. The trend is shifting to three- (or more) tier environments. In this case, business logic is often handled in some middle tier (possibly ActiveX objects managed by Microsoft Transaction Server). If that is your environment, you might want to restrict the stored procedures to performing basic data-related tasks, such as retrievals, inserts, updates, and deletions.

NOTE

I personally am a big fan of using stored procedures to make the database sort of a "black box" as far as the developers and the application code are concerned. If all database access is managed through stored procedures, the applications are shielded from possible changes to the database structures.

For example, at one of my client sites recently, they found the need to split one database across multiple databases. By simply modifying the existing stored procedures and using distributed partitioned views, we were able to make this change with no changes required to the front-end application.

Creating and Executing Stored Procedures

To create a stored procedure, you need to give the procedure a unique name and then write the sequence of SQL statements to be included in the procedure. The following is the basic syntax for creating stored procedures:

```
create proc [owner.]procedure_name[; number]
[[(]@parm_name datatype = default_value [output]
  [, ... ] [)]]
[with {recompile | encryption}]
as
SQL Statements
[return [integer_status_value]]
```

It is good programming practice to always end a procedure with the `RETURN` statement and to specify a return status other than 0 when an error condition occurs. Listing 28.1 shows a simple stored procedure.

LISTING 28.1 A Stored Procedure That Returns Book Titles and the Names of the Authors Who Wrote Them

```
CREATE PROCEDURE dbo.title_authors
AS
   SELECT a.au_lname, a.au_fname, t.title
      FROM titles t INNER JOIN
           titleauthor ta ON t.title_id = ta.title_id RIGHT OUTER JOIN
           authors a ON ta.au_id = a.au_id
RETURN
```


NOTE

Any user who is a member of the sysadmin fixed server role will map to the special user in each database, called dbo. dbo will own any procedure created by a member of the sysadmin fixed server role.

However, if the user is not a member of the sysadmin fixed server role, but is a member of the fixed database role db_owner, the user will own stored procedures in the database. The exception is if the dbo owner name is explicitly specified when the procedure is created.

For example, a user, joe_developer, uses Windows authentication to connect to SQL Server. He has been granted access to the Pubs database and is assigned the db_owner role. He has not been assigned to the sysadmin fixed server role. If he were to create a procedure in the Pubs database called myproc, myproc would be owned by joe_developer, not dbo. To access this object, you would have to qualify the procedure name as joe_developer.myproc.

Needless to say, this can be quite confusing if developers are creating stored procedures as members of the db_owner database role but are not members of the sysadmin group. It can lead to multiple copies of a stored procedure being created with the same name but owned by different users. Managing the security on objects owned by different users can be quite a chore as well (see Chapter 15, "Security and User Administration").

Fortunately, there is an easy workaround for this problem. Just make sure the procedure name is fully qualified with the dbo user ID when it is created, as shown in the following example:

```
create proc dbo.myproc
as
select * from titles
```

This procedure will now be owned by dbo.

To execute a stored procedure, simply invoke it by its name (the same way you probably have already executed system stored procedures, such as sp_help). If the procedure isn't the first statement in a batch, precede the procedure name with the EXEC keyword. See Chapter 26, "Using Transact-SQL in SQL Server 2000," for more information on batches. The following is the basic syntax for executing stored procedures:

```
[exec[ute]] [@status =] [owner.]procedure_name[; number]
  [[@parm_name =] expression [output][, ... ]]
[with recompile]
```

NOTE

The reason for the EXEC keyword rule is quite simple. SQL Server breaks down the commands sent to it in a batch by searching for keywords. Stored procedure names aren't keywords. If SQL Server finds a procedure name among statements, chances are that SQL Server will return an error message because it tries to treat it as part of the preceding command. Sometimes the execution is successful, but SQL Server doesn't execute what you want:

```
SELECT * FROM titles
sp_help
```

The SELECT statement runs fine, but the procedure is not executed. The reason is that sp_help ends up being used as a table alias for the titles table in the SELECT statement.

If you precede the procedure name with EXEC, you will get the expected behavior:

```
SELECT * FROM titles
EXEC sp_help
```

Why don't you have to put EXEC in front of the procedure name if the procedure is the first statement in a batch? If SQL Server doesn't recognize the first string in a batch, it simply assumes that it is a name of a stored procedure. Execute the following string and notice the error message:

```
Dsfdskgkghk
Server: Msg 2812, Level 16, State 62
Could not find stored procedure 'dsfdskgkghk'.
```

As good programming practice, it is best to always precede stored procedures with the EXEC keyword—this way, it will always work as expected whether it's the first statement in a batch or not.

Stored Procedure Groups

If you create a procedure with a name that already exists, you receive an error message that might not be expected. Let's try to create a procedure with the same name as a procedure that already exists, `title_authors`:

```
CREATE PROCEDURE title_authors AS
SELECT a.au_lname, a.au_fname, t.title
FROM titles t INNER JOIN
 titleauthor ta ON t.title_id = ta.title_id RIGHT OUTER JOIN
 authors a ON ta.au_id = a.au_id
 WHERE a.state = 'CA'
RETURN
Server: Msg 2714, Level 16, State 5, Procedure title_authors, Line 7
There is already an object named 'title_authors' in the database.
```

SQL Server does provide the capability of having multiple procedures created under the same name, but with different group numbers. To create a procedure with a different group number, add a semicolon (;) and an integer as shown in Listing 28.2.

LISTING 28.2 Creating a Stored Procedure with a Group Number

```
CREATE PROCEDURE title_authors;2 AS
SELECT a.au_lname, a.au_fname, t.title
FROM titles t INNER JOIN
 titleauthor ta ON t.title_id = ta.title_id RIGHT OUTER JOIN
 authors a ON ta.au_id = a.au_id
 WHERE a.state = 'CA'
RETURN
GO
EXEC title_authors;2
```

The first procedure created will automatically get an implicit group number of 1. If no group number is specified when executing a stored procedure, SQL Server will execute the stored procedure with group number 1 by default.

Stored procedure groups are an odd feature in SQL Server, and they have limited usefulness. While you can drop all procedures within a group by excluding the group number with the `DROP PROCEDURE` statement, you cannot drop a single procedure within a group. One potential use of grouping functionality is for version handling. For each new version of the procedure, you could add to the grouping number rather than creating a new procedure with a different name. The original stored procedure will still be available for clients that have not yet been modified to use the newer version of the stored procedure. Updated clients can execute the new version of the stored procedure by including the new group number.

Deferred Name Resolution

In SQL Server 2000, the object names that a stored procedure references do not have to exist at the time the procedure is created. Versions of SQL Server prior to 7.0 would return an error message and fail to create if a procedure referenced an object, other than another stored procedure, that didn't exist at the time the stored procedure was created. Stored procedures in SQL Server 7.0 and 2000 check for the existence of database objects at the time the stored procedure is executed and return an error message at runtime if the referenced object doesn't exist. The only exception is when a stored procedure references another stored procedure that doesn't exist. In that case, a warning message will be issued, but the stored procedure will still be created (see Listing 28.3).

LISTING 28.3 Procedure Name Resolution During Stored Procedure Creation

```
create proc p2
as
exec p3
go

Cannot add rows to sysdepends for the current stored procedure because it depends on
the missing object 'p3'. The stored procedure will still be created.
```

In SQL Server 2000, when an object does exist at procedure creation time, the column names in the referenced table will be validated. If a column is mistyped or doesn't exist, the procedure will not be created (see Listing 28.4).

LISTING 28.4 Column Name Validation in Stored Procedures

```
create proc get_authors_and_titles
as

select a.au_lname, au_fname, title, isbn_number
   from authors a join titleauthor ta on a.au_id = ta.au_id
   join titles t on t.title_id = ta.title_id
return
go

Server: Msg 207, Level 16, State 3, Procedure get_authors_and_titles, Line 4
Invalid column name 'isbn_number'.
```

One advantage of delayed (or deferred) name resolution is the increased flexibility when creating stored procedures; the order of creating procedures and the tables they reference does not need to be exact. It is an especially useful feature when a stored procedure references a temporary table that isn't created within that stored procedure. However, at other times, it can be frustrating for a stored procedure to create successfully only to have it fail when it runs due to a missing table, as shown in Listing 28.5.

LISTING 28.5 Runtime Failure of a Stored Procedure with Invalid Object Reference

```
create proc get_authors_and_titles
as

select a.au_lname, au_fname, title, pub_date
   from authors a join titleauthor ta on a.au_id = ta.au_id
   join books t on t.title_id = ta.title_id

go

exec get_authors_and_titles
go

Server: Msg 208, Level 16, State 1, Procedure get_authors_and_titles, Line 4
Invalid object name 'books'.
```

Another issue to be careful of with deferred name resolution is that you can no longer rename objects referenced by stored procedures and have the stored procedure continue to work. In versions of SQL Server prior to 7.0, after the stored procedure was created, object references within the stored procedure were made via the object ID rather than the object name. This allowed stored procedures to continue to function properly if a referenced object were renamed. However, now that object names are resolved at execution time, the procedure will fail at the statement referencing the renamed object. For the stored procedure to execute successfully, it needs to be altered to specify the new object name.

Identifying Objects Referenced in Stored Procedures

Because changing the name of a table can cause stored procedures to no longer work, you might want to identify which stored procedures reference a specific table so you'll know which stored procedures will be affected. SQL Server keeps track of the dependencies between database objects in the `sysdepends` system catalog table. All you'll see if you query the `sysdepends` table is a bunch of numbers; `sysdepends` stores just the IDs of the objects that have a dependency relationship along with some additional status information.

The better way to display a list of stored procedures that reference a specific table or view, or to display a list of objects referenced by a stored procedure, is to use the `sp_depends` system procedure:

```
exec sp_depends {table_name | procedure_name}
```

To display the stored procedures and triggers that reference the titles table, execute the following:

```
exec sp_depends titles
go

In the current database, the specified object is referenced by the following:
name                                                           type
--------------------------------------------------------------------------------
dbo.encr_proc                                                  stored procedure
dbo.group_proc                                                 stored procedure
dbo.reptq1                                                     stored procedure
dbo.reptq2                                                     stored procedure
dbo.reptq3                                                     stored procedure
dbo.title_authors                                              stored procedure
dbo.titles_for_an_author                                       stored procedure
dbo.titleview                                                  view
```

To display the objects referenced by the `title_authors` stored procedure, execute the following:

```
exec sp_depends title_authors
go
```

```
In the current database, the specified object references the following:
name                   type         updated selected column
---------------------- ------------ ------- -------- ---------------
dbo.titles             user table   no      no       title
dbo.authors            user table   no      no       au_lname
dbo.authors            user table   no      no       au_fname
dbo.titles             user table   no      no       title_id
dbo.titleauthor        user table   no      no       au_id
dbo.titleauthor        user table   no      no       title_id
dbo.authors            user table   no      no       au_id
```

Dependency information can also be displayed in Query Analyzer by clicking on the Dependencies folder for an object, or in Enterprise Manager by right-clicking on an object and choosing the Display Dependencies option in the All Tasks submenu.

NOTE

Unfortunately, the dependency information is built only when a stored procedure is created. If a table is dropped and re-created with the same name, the stored procedure will continue to work, but the dependency information will be deleted when the table is dropped. Another way to identify any stored procedures or other objects that reference a table is to search the text of the stored procedure with a query similar to the following. (Replace *tablename* with the name of the object or other text for which you want to search.)

```
select distinct object_name(id)
    from syscomments
    where text like '%tablename%'
```

This method is not foolproof either. If a stored procedure is larger than 4000 bytes, the tablename could be split across rows in the `syscomments` table and wouldn't match the search argument. The `syscomments` table is covered in more detail in the next section.

Viewing and Modifying Stored Procedures

SQL Server 2000 maintains the source code for stored procedures in the system catalog table `syscomments`. You can view this information directly by querying the `text` column of the `syscomments` table, or by using the system procedure `sp_helptext` (see Listing 28.6). Note that in SQL Server 2000, the `text` column is a computed column. The real source code for the proc is stored in a binary format in the `ctext` column.

LISTING 28.6 Viewing Code for a Stored Procedure with `sp_helptext`

```
exec sp_helptext title_authors
go

Text
--------------------------------------------------------------
CREATE PROCEDURE title_authors AS
SELECT a.au_lname, a.au_fname, t.title
FROM titles t INNER JOIN
 titleauthor ta ON t.title_id = ta.title_id RIGHT OUTER JOIN
 authors a ON ta.au_id = a.au_id
RETURN
```

By default, all users have permission to execute `sp_helptext` to view the SQL code for the stored procedures in a database. If you want to protect the source code of your stored procedures and keep its contents from prying eyes, you can create a procedure using the `WITH ENCRYPTION` option. When this option is specified, the source code stored in the `syscomments` table is encrypted.

In versions of SQL Server prior to 6.0, when a developer wanted to prevent users from viewing the source code for stored procedures, he simply set the text field in the `syscomments` table for the stored procedure to null. This worked fine until a DBA tried to run the SQL Server 6.0 upgrade facility, which needed to extract the source code from `syscomments` to re-create the procedures under the new version. Without the source code in the database, the procedures were not migrated and the developers had to dig out the original source code to re-create the procedures. Recognizing this problem, Microsoft implemented the ability to encrypt stored procedures in version 6.0. This allows programmers to protect source code, while keeping it in the database so the upgrade process can re-create the stored procedures from the encrypted code.

NOTE

If you use encryption when creating your stored procedures, be aware that while SQL Server can internally decrypt the source code, no mechanisms exist for the user or for any of the end user tools to decrypt the stored procedure text for display or editing. With this in mind, make sure that you store a copy of the source code for those procedures in a file in case you need to edit or re-create them.

Also, if you use the `WITH ENCRYPTION` option, you can no longer use the Transact-SQL Debugger on the encrypted stored procedure. Don't use the `WITH ENCRYPTION` option unless you have a good reason to hide the stored procedure code.

You can also view the text of a stored procedure using the ANSI INFORMATION_SCHEMA view routines (INFORMATION_SCHEMA views are discussed in more detail later in this chapter). The routines view is an ANSI standard view that is partially based on the syscomments table and provides the source code for the stored procedure in the routine_description column. The following example uses the INFORMATION_SCHEMA.routines view to display the source code for the title_authors stored procedure:

```
select routine_definition
from INFORMATION_SCHEMA.routines
where routine_name = 'title_authors'
go

routine_definition
------------------------------------------------------------------------
CREATE PROCEDURE title_authors AS
SELECT a.au_lname, a.au_fname, t.title
   FROM titles t
   INNER JOIN titleauthor ta ON t.title_id = ta.title_id
   RIGHT OUTER JOIN authors a ON ta.au_id = a.au_id
RETURN
```

You can modify the text of a stored procedure using the ALTER PROCEDURE statement. The syntax for ALTER PROCEDURE is the same as for CREATE PROCEDURE (see Listing 28.7). This new feature, introduced in version 7.0, has a couple of advantages over dropping and re-creating the procedure to modify it. The main advantage is that you don't have to drop the procedure first to make the change. The second advantage is that because you don't have to drop the procedure, you don't have to worry about reassigning permissions to it.

LISTING 28.7 Modifying a Stored Procedure Using ALTER PROCEDURE

```
ALTER PROCEDURE title_authors @state char(2) = '%'
AS
SELECT a.au_lname, a.au_fname, t.title, t.pubdate
   FROM titles t
   INNER JOIN titleauthor ta ON t.title_id = ta.title_id
   RIGHT OUTER JOIN authors a ON ta.au_id = a.au_id
   where state like @state
RETURN
```

The main disadvantage of using ALTER PROCEDURE instead of dropping and re-creating the stored procedures is that the date of the procedure change is not recorded in the database catalogs. As a DBA, it is difficult to tell which procedures have been modified since they were created, and you cannot selectively extract the code for only the stored procedures that have been updated.

In addition to sp_helptext, SQL Server 2000 provides two GUI-based applications for creating, viewing, and modifying stored procedures: Enterprise Manager and Query Analyzer.

To edit a stored procedure in Enterprise Manager, right-click on the procedure name and select the Properties option (see Figure 28.1).

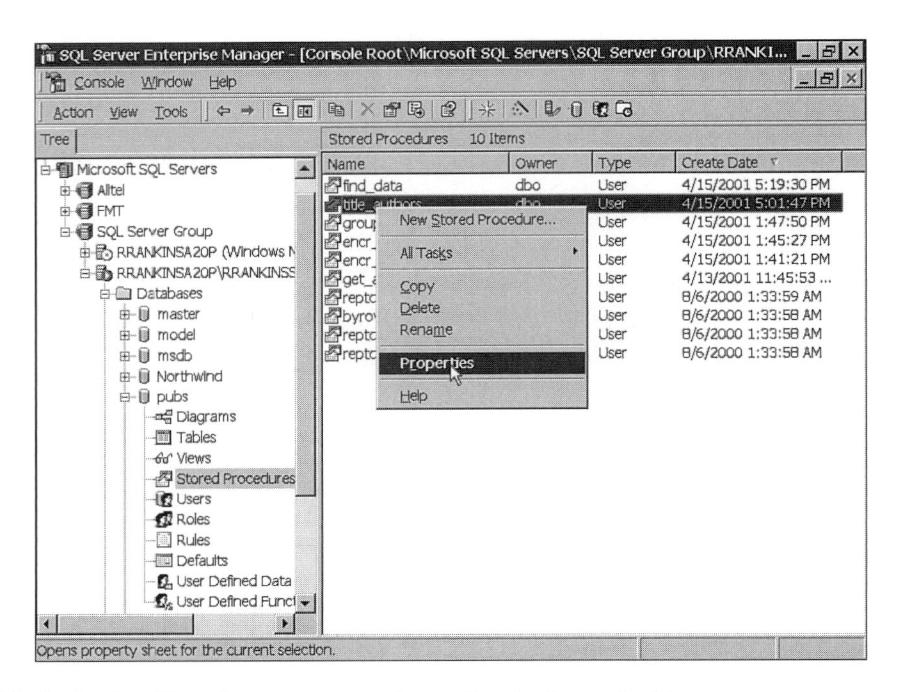

FIGURE 28.1 Invoking the stored procedure editor in Enterprise Manager.

As you'll see, the editor in Enterprise Manager is not very elegant. It lacks a search and replace function and has no ability to save the stored procedure code to a file. The one nice feature is the ability to check the stored procedure syntax before applying changes (see Figure 28.2).

Changes will be applied when clicking on the Apply or OK button at the bottom of the Stored Procedures Properties window. Enterprise Manager applies changes to the stored procedure by using ALTER PROCEDURE. The creation date will not be updated. If you want to modify the stored procedure by dropping and re-creating it, use Query Analyzer. Besides having a full-featured editor as well as a built-in SQL Debugger (see Chapter 6, "SQL Server Query Analyzer and SQL Debugger"), Query Analyzer provides options for extracting the stored procedure source code to modify and apply changes. It will generate code to create, alter, or drop the selected stored procedure. You can script the stored procedure source code to a new window, to a file, or to the Windows Clipboard by right-clicking on the stored procedure name in the Object Browser and choosing the appropriate option (see Figure 28.3).

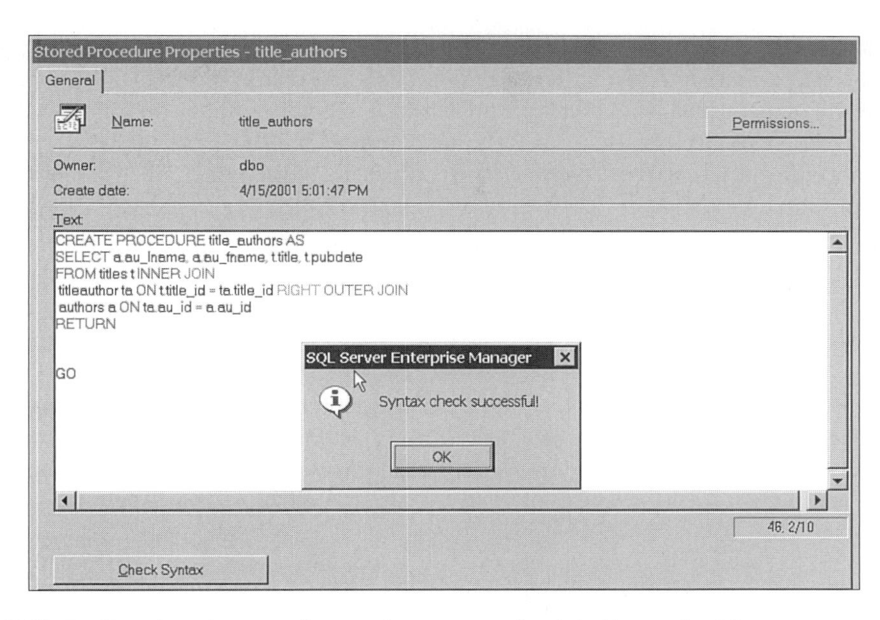

FIGURE 28.2 Running the stored procedure syntax check in Enterprise Manager.

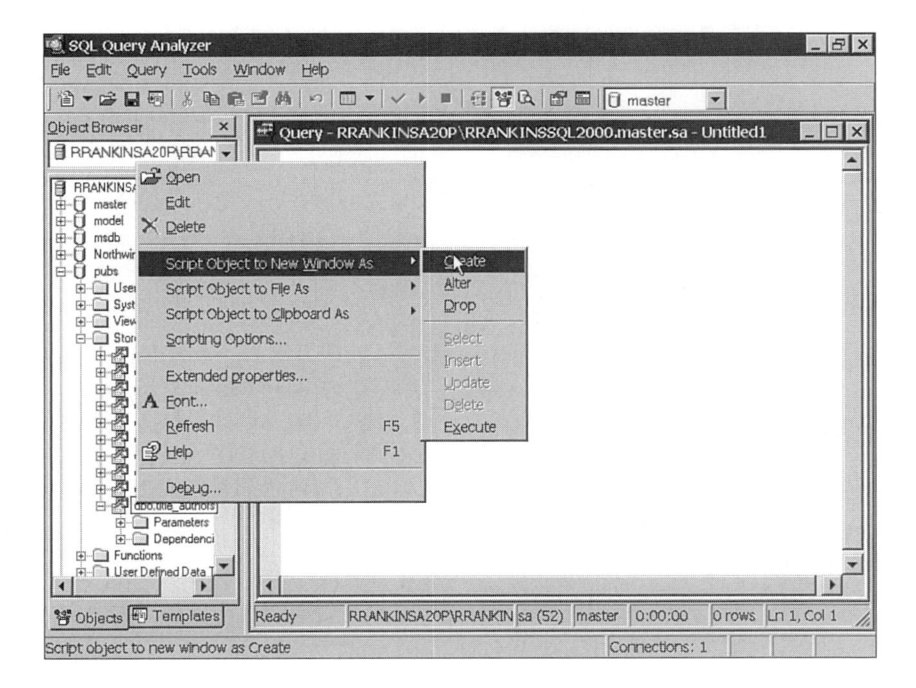

FIGURE 28.3 Extracting stored procedure source code to an editor window.

Query Analyzer provides a number of options for extracting the stored procedure source code. The script generated can automatically include the command to check for the existence of the object and automatically drop it before executing the `CREATE PROCEDURE` command. You can also choose to include the commands to reset permissions when the stored procedure is re-created. To ensure these features are included, make sure the following options are checked:

- Generate Transact-SQL to remove referenced component. Script tests for existence before attempting to remove component.
- Script object-level permissions.

You can set the scripting options by choosing the Script tab in the Options dialog box. Invoke the Options dialog box by selecting Tools, Options; by pressing Ctrl+Shift+O; or by right-clicking on the procedure name in the Object Browser and choosing the Scripting Options menu option (see Figure 28.4).

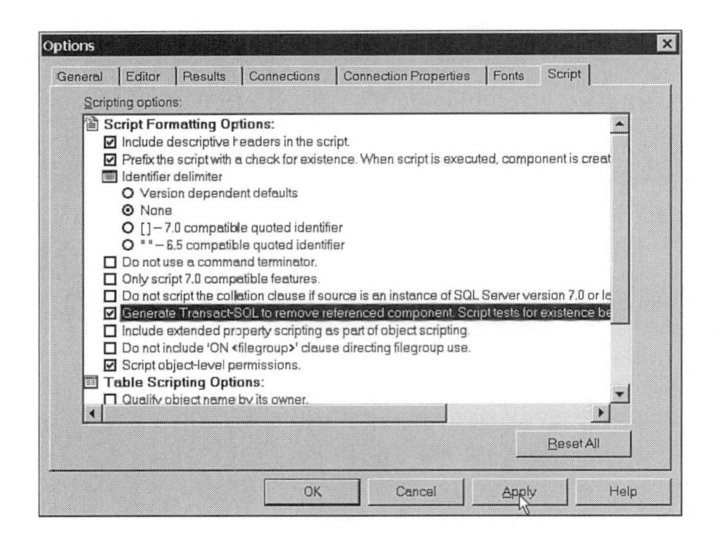

FIGURE 28.4 Setting scripting options in Query Analyzer.

Listing 28.8 shows an example of the script generated by Query Analyzer when the options selected in Figure 28.4 are in effect. The changes can be applied by simply executing the SQL script in Query Analyzer.

LISTING 28.8 Example of Stored Procedure-Creation Script Generated by Query Analyzer

```
SET QUOTED_IDENTIFIER OFF
GO
SET ANSI_NULLS ON
GO

/****** Object:  Stored Procedure dbo.title_authors    Script Date: 4/15/2001
➥ 8:14:15 PM ******/
if exists (select * from sysobjects where id = object_id('dbo.title_authors')
                                    and sysstat & 0xf = 4)
       drop procedure dbo.title_authors
GO

CREATE PROCEDURE title_authors @state char(2) = '%'
AS
SELECT a.au_lname, a.au_fname, t.title
   FROM titles t
   INNER JOIN  titleauthor ta ON t.title_id = ta.title_id
   RIGHT OUTER JOIN  authors a ON ta.au_id = a.au_id
   where state like @state
RETURN



GO

SET QUOTED_IDENTIFIER OFF
GO
SET ANSI_NULLS ON
GO

GRANT EXECUTE ON dbo.title_authors TO public
GO
```

28

TIP

When creating a new stored procedure in Query Analyzer, the procedure will not show up in the Stored Procedures folder in the Object Browser unless you right-click on the Procedures Folder and choose the Refresh option.

Using Input Parameters

To increase stored procedure flexibility and perform more complex processing, you can pass parameters to the procedures. The parameters can be used anywhere that local variables can be used within the procedure. For more information on how to use local variables, refer to Chapter 26.

Following is an example of a stored procedure that requires three parameters:

```
CREATE PROC myproc
 @parm1 int, @parm2 int, @parm3 int
AS
-- Processing goes here
RETURN
```

To help identify the data values for which the parameters are defined, it is recommended that you give your parameters meaningful names. Parameter names, such as local variables, can be up to 128 characters in length including the @ sign, and they must follow SQL Server rules for identifiers. Up to 2,100 parameters can be defined for a stored procedure.

When you execute the procedure, you can pass the parameters by position or by name:

```
--Passing parameters by position
EXEC myproc 1, 2, 3
--Passing parameters by name
EXEC myproc @parm2 = 2, @parm2 = 1, @parm3 =3
--Passing parameters by position and name
EXEC myproc 1, @parm3 =3, @parm2 = 2
```

After you start passing a parameter by name, you cannot pass subsequent parameters by position. All remaining parameters must be passed by name as well. If you want to skip parameters that are not the last parameter(s) in the procedure and have them take default values, you will also need to pass parameters by name.

TIP

When embedding calls to stored procedures in client applications and script files, it is advisable to pass parameters by name. Reviewing and debugging the code becomes easier that way. I once spent half a day debugging a set of nested stored procedures only to find the problem was due to a missed parameter; everything shifted over one and the wrong values ended up in the wrong parameters, resulting in the queries not finding any matching values. That was a lesson learned the hard way!

Input parameter values passed in can only be explicit constant values or local variables or parameters. You cannot specify a function or other expression as an input parameter value. You would have to store the function or expression value in a local variable and pass the variable as the input parameter. Likewise, you cannot use a function or other expression as a default value for a parameter.

Setting Default Values for Parameters

You can assign a default value to a parameter by specifying a value in the definition of the parameter, as shown in Listing 28.9.

LISTING 28.9 Assigning a Default Value for a Parameter in a Stored Procedure

```
CREATE PROCEDURE title_authors @state char(2) = '%'
AS
SELECT a.au_lname, a.au_fname, t.title
   FROM titles t
   INNER JOIN titleauthor ta ON t.title_id = ta.title_id
   RIGHT OUTER JOIN authors a ON ta.au_id = a.au_id
    WHERE a.state like @state
RETURN
GO
```

You can have SQL Server apply the default value for a parameter during execution by not specifying a value or by specifying the `DEFAULT` keyword in the execution of the parameter, as shown in Listing 28.10.

LISTING 28.10 Applying a Default Value for a Parameter When Executing a Stored Procedure

```
EXEC title_authors
EXEC title_authors DEFAULT
EXEC title_authors @state = DEFAULT
```


TIP

If you are involved in creating stored procedures that other people will use, you probably want to make the stored procedures as easy to use as possible.

If you leave out a parameter that is required, SQL Server presents an error message. The `MyProc` procedure, shown earlier in this section, requires three parameters: `@parm1`, `@parm2`, and `@parm3`:

```
EXEC myproc

Server: Msg 201, Level 16, State 2, Procedure myproc, Line 0
Procedure 'myproc' expects parameter '@parm1', which was not
 supplied.
```

Note that SQL Server only complains about the first missing parameter. The programmer passes the first parameter, only to find out that more parameters are required. This is a good way to annoy a programmer or end user.

When you execute a command-line program, you probably expect that you can use /? to obtain a list of the parameters that the program expects. You can program stored procedures in a similar manner by assigning NULL (or some other special value) as a default value to the parameters and checking for that value inside the procedure. Listing 28.11 shows an outline of a stored procedure that presents the user with information about the parameters expected if the user doesn't pass parameters.

You can develop a standard for the way that the message is presented to the user, but what is important is that the information is passed.

LISTING 28.11 Presenting Information to the User About Missing Parameters for a Stored Procedure

```
CREATE PROC MyProc2
 @parm1 int = NULL, @parm2 int = 32, @parm3 int = NULL
AS
IF (@parm1 IS NULL or @parm1 NOT BETWEEN 1 and 10) OR
   @parm3 IS NULL
PRINT 'Usage:
 EXEC MyProc2
 @parm1 int,   (Required: Can be between 1 and 10)
 @parm2 = 32,  (Optional: Default value of 32)
 @parm3 int,   (Required: Any number within range)'
-- Processing goes here
RETURN
GO

EXEC MyProc2
GO

Usage:
 EXEC MyProc2
 @parm1 int,   (Required: Can be between 1 and 10)
 @parm2 = 32,  (Optional: Default value of 32)
 @parm3 int,   (Required: Any number within range)
```

To display the parameters defined for a stored procedure, you can view them in the Query Analyzer Object Browser (see Figure 28.5) or by executing the sp_help stored procedure as shown in Listing 28.12. (Note that the output has been edited to fit the page.)

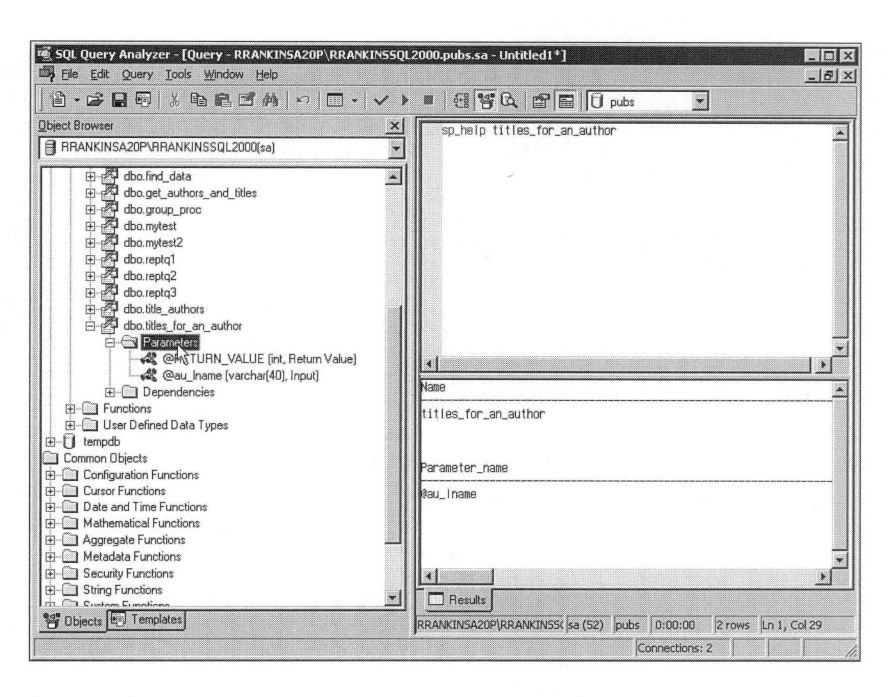

FIGURE 28.5 Displaying stored procedure parameters in Query Analyzer.

LISTING 28.12 Displaying Stored Procedure Parameters Using `sp_help`

```
exec sp_help title_authors
Name              Owner      Type              Created_datetime
----------------- ---------- ----------------- ------------------------------
title_authors     dbo        stored procedure  2001-04-15 21:15:06.540



Parameter_name Type  Length Prec Scale Param_order Collation
-------------- ----- ------ ---- ----- ----------- ----------------------------
@state         char  2      2    NULL            1 SQL_Latin1_General_CP1_CI_AS
```

You can also display the stored procedure parameters by running a query against the `INFORMATION_SCHEMA` view `parameters`:

```
select substring(Parameter_NAME,1, 30) as Parameter_name,
       substring (DATA_TYPE, 1, 20) as Data_Type,
       CHARACTER_MAXIMUM_LENGTH as Length,
       ordinal_position as param_order,
       Collation_name
```

```
from INFORMATION_SCHEMA.parameters
where specific_name = 'title_authors'
order by ordinal_position

go

Parameter_name   Data_Type     Length  param_order Collation_name
---------------- ------------- ------- ----------- ----------------------------
@state           char                2           1 SQL_Latin1_General_CP1_CI_AS
```

Passing Object Names As Parameters

You cannot pass object names as parameters to be used in place of an object name in a stored procedure unless the object name is used as an argument in a where clause or in a dynamically built query using the `EXEC` statement. For example, the code in Listing 28.13 generates an odd error message when you try to create the stored procedure.

LISTING 28.13 Attempting to Create a Stored Procedure Using a Parameter to Pass in a Table Name

```
CREATE  proc find_data @table varchar(128)
as

select * from @table

GO

Server: Msg 137, Level 15, State 2, Procedure find_data, Line 6
Must declare the variable '@table'.
```

This error seems odd because the variable `@table` is declared as a parameter. However, SQL Server is expecting the variable to be defined as a `table` variable. (Using table variables in stored procedures is discussed later in this chapter.) Listing 28.14 shows a possible approach to this problem using the `EXEC()` command.

LISTING 28.14 Passing a Table as a Parameter to a Stored Procedure for Dynamic Query Execution

```
CREATE  proc find_data @table varchar(128)
as

exec ('select * from ' + @table)
return
go
```

LISTING 28.14 Continued

```
exec find_data @table = 'publishers'
go

pub_id pub_name                  city           state country
------ ------------------------- -------------- ----- ---------
0736   New Moon Books            Boston         MA    USA
0877   Binnet & Hardley          Washington     DC    USA
1389   Algodata Infosystems      Berkeley       CA    USA
1622   Five Lakes Publishing     Chicago        IL    USA
1756   Ramona Publishers         Dallas         TX    USA
9901   GGG&G                     München        NULL  Germany
9952   Scootney Books            New York       NY    USA
9999   Lucerne Publishing        Paris          NULL  France
```

Using Wildcards in Parameters

Wildcards can be passed as input parameters and used in a `LIKE` clause in a query to perform pattern matching. Define the parameter with the `varchar` datatype. Do not use the `char` datatype because it will pad spaces onto the value passed into the parameter. For example, if you declared a `@lastname` parameter as `char(40)` and passed in `'S%'`, SQL Server would search not for a string starting with `'S'`, but for a string starting with `'S'` and ending with 38 spaces. This would likely not match any data values.

Also, to increase the flexibility of a stored procedure that searches for character strings, you can default the parameter to `'%'`, as in the following example:

```
create proc find_authors @lastname varchar(40) = '%'
as
    select au_id, au_lname, au_fname
        from authors
        where au_lname like @lastname
        order by au_lname, au_fname
```

This procedure, if passed no parameter, will return data for all authors in the authors table. If passed a string containing wildcard characters, this procedure will return data for all authors matching the search pattern specified. If a string containing no wildcards is passed, the query will perform a search for exact matches against the string value.

Unfortunately, wildcard searches can only be performed against character strings. If you want to have similar flexibility searching against a numeric value, such as an integer, you can default the value to `NULL` and when the parameter is `NULL`, compare the column with itself, as shown in the following example:

```
create proc find_titles_by_sales @ytd_sales int = null
as
    select title_id, title, ytd_sales
        from titles
        where ytd_sales = isnull(@ytd_sales, ytd_sales)
```

However, the problem with this approach is that the procedure returns all rows from the titles table except those where ytd_sales contains a NULL value. This is because NULL is never considered equal to NULL; you cannot compare an unknown value with another unknown value. To return all rows including those in which ytd_sales is NULL, you need to implement a dual query solution, as in the following example:

```
create proc find_titles_by_sales @ytd_sales int = null
as
if @ytd_sales is null
    select title_id, title, ytd_sales
        from titles
else
    select title_id, title, ytd_sales
        from titles
        where ytd_sales= @ytd_sales
```

Using Output Parameters

If a calling batch passes a variable as a parameter to a stored procedure, and that parameter is modified inside the procedure, the modifications will not be passed to the calling batch unless you specify the OUTPUT keyword for the parameter when creating and executing the stored procedure.

If you want a procedure to be able to pass parameters out from the procedure, use the keyword OUT[PUT] when creating and calling the procedure. The following example accepts two parameters, one of which is used as an OUTPUT parameter:

```
CREATE PROC ytd_sales
@title varchar(80), @ytd_sales int OUTPUT
AS
SELECT @ytd_sales = ytd_sales
   FROM titles
   WHERE title = @title
RETURN
```

The calling batch (or stored procedure) needs to declare a variable to store the returned value. The execute statement must include the OUTPUT keyword as well, or the modifications won't be reflected in the calling batch's variable:

```
DECLARE @sales_up_to_today  int
EXEC ytd_sales 'Life Without Fear', @sales_up_to_today OUTPUT
PRINT 'Sales this year until today''s date: ' +
      CONVERT(VARCHAR(10), @sales_up_to_today) + '.'

Sales this year until today's date: 111.
```

You can also pass the output parameter by name:

```
DECLARE @sales_up_to_today  int
EXEC ytd_sales 'Life Without Fear',
      @ytd_sales = @sales_up_to_today OUTPUT
PRINT 'Sales this year until today''s date: ' +
      CONVERT(VARCHAR(10), @sales_up_to_today) + '.'
```

Note that when you pass an output parameter by name, the paramater name (`@ytd_sales` in this example) is listed on the left side of the expression, and the local variable (`@sales_up_to_today`), which will be set equal to the value of the output paramater, is on the right side of the expression. An output parameter can also serve as an input parameter.

`OUTPUT` parameters can also be passed back and captured in a client application using ADO, ODBC, OLE DB, and so on.

Returning Procedure Status

Most programming languages have the ability to pass a status code to the caller of a function or a subroutine. A value of `0` generally indicates that the execution was successful. SQL Server is no exception.

SQL Server will automatically generate an integer status value of `0` after successful completion. If SQL Server detects an error, a status value between `-1` and `-99` is returned. You can use the `RETURN` statement to explicitly pass a status value less than `-99` or greater than `0`. The calling batch or procedure can set up a local variable to retrieve and check the return status.

In Listing 28.15, you want to return the year-to-date sales for a given title as a resultset. If the title does not exist, you do not want to return an empty resultset. Therefore, you perform a check inside the procedure and return the status value `-101` if the title does not exist.

In the calling batch or stored procedure, you need to create a variable to hold the return value. The variable name is passed after the `EXECUTE` statement.

LISTING 28.15 Returning a Status Code from a Stored Procedure

```
--Create the procedure
CREATE PROC ytd_sales2 @title varchar(80)
AS
IF NOT EXISTS (SELECT * FROM titles WHERE title = @title)
    RETURN -101
SELECT ytd_sales
   FROM titles
   WHERE title = @title
RETURN
GO

-- Execute the procedure
DECLARE @status int
EXEC @status = ytd_sales2 'Life without Fear'
IF @status = -101
    PRINT 'No title with that name found.'
```

RETURN values can also be passed back and captured by the client application through ADO, ODBC, OLE DB, and so on.

SQL Server Internal Status Codes

If a stored procedure terminates unexpectedly, SQL Server returns a status code. The values -1 to -99 are reserved by SQL Server, and -1 to -14 are currently in use. Table 28.1 lists the return codes currently in use by SQL Server and their meanings.

TABLE 28.1 SQL Server Return Codes

Status Code	Meaning
0	Successful execution
-1	Object missing
-2	Datatype error occurred
-3	Process chosen as a deadlock victim
-4	Permission error occurred
-5	Syntax error occurred
-6	Miscellaneous user error occurred
-7	Resource error occurred, such as out of space
-8	Nonfatal internal problem encountered
-9	System limit reached
-10	Fatal internal inconsistency occurred
-11	Fatal internal inconsistency occurred
-12	Table or index corrupted
-13	Database is corrupt
-14	Hardware error

Cursors in Stored Procedures

Cursors in SQL Server 2000 can be declared as local or global. A global cursor defined in a stored procedure is available until deallocated or when the connection closes. A local cursor goes out of scope when the stored procedure that declared it terminates. Only stored procedures called from within the procedure that declared the cursor can reference a higher-level local cursor. If neither the `GLOBAL` nor `LOCAL` option is specified when the cursor is declared in a stored procedure, the default cursor type is determined by the current setting of the database level option, `default to local cursor`. In SQL Server 2000, the default value for this database option is `FALSE`, meaning all cursors will be global by default.

TIP

The default setting in SQL Server 2000 for all cursors to be global if neither `GLOBAL` or `LOCAL` is specified provides backward compatibility for versions of SQL Server prior to 7.0, in which all cursors were global. The default setting might change in future versions, so it is recommended that you explicitly specify the local or global option when declaring your cursors so your code will not be affected by changes to the default setting.

As Figure 28.6 illustrates, if stored procedures are nested, they can access cursors declared in higher-level stored procedures in the call tree, whether the cursors are declared as global or local.

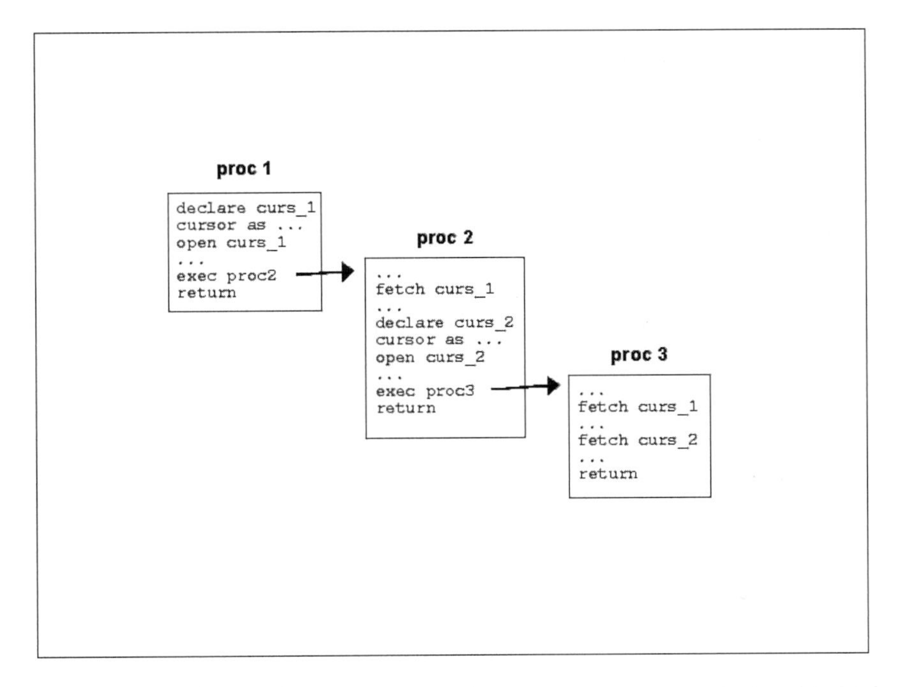

FIGURE 28.6 If stored procedures are nested, they can access cursors declared in higher-level stored procedures in the call tree.

Using CURSOR Variables in Stored Procedures

SQL Server 2000 allows you to declare variables or parameters with a cursor datatype. You must use the SET command to assign a value to a cursor variable because an assignment select is not allowed. Cursor datatypes can be the source or the target in a SET statement. A stored procedure can pass a cursor variable as an output parameter only—cursor variables cannot be passed as input parameters. Cursor variables can be referenced in any of the cursor management statements: OPEN, FETCH, CLOSE, and DEALLOCATE. When defining a CURSOR output parameter, the VARYING keyword must also be specified.

The following stored procedure declares a cursor, opens it, and passes it back as an output parameter:

```
create proc cursor_proc @cursor CURSOR VARYING OUTPUT
as
declare curs1 cursor for select title, pubdate from titles
set @cursor = curs1
open curs1
```

A cursor variable and the declared cursor name can be used interchangeably. You can use either the variable name or the declared name to open, fetch, close, and deallocate the cursor. Fetching using either the cursor name or the cursor variable will fetch the next row in the cursor resultset. Listing 28.16 illustrates how each fetch gets the next row in the resultset.

LISTING 28.16 Fetching Cursor Rows Using the Declared Cursor Name and a Cursor Variable

```
set nocount on
declare @curs CURSOR
exec cursor_proc @cursor = @curs output

fetch curs1
fetch @curs
fetch curs1
fetch @curs
go

title                                                   pubdate
------------------------------------------------------- ------------------------
The Busy Executive's Database Guide                     1991-06-12 00:00:00.000

title                                                   pubdate
------------------------------------------------------- -------------------------
Cooking with Computers: Surreptitious Balance Sheets    1991-06-09 00:00:00.000
```

LISTING 28.16 Continued

```
title                                                   pubdate
------------------------------------------------------- -----------------------
You Can Combat Computer Stress!                         1991-06-30 00:00:00.000

title                                                   pubdate
------------------------------------------------------- -----------------------
Straight Talk About Computers                           1991-06-22 00:00:00.000
```

If the cursor is closed using either the cursor variable or the declared cursor name, you cannot fetch more rows from the cursor until it is reopened:

```
declare @curs CURSOR
exec cursor_proc @cursor = @curs output
fetch curs1
fetch @curs
close curs1
fetch @curs
go

title                                                   pubdate
-------------------------------------------------------------------------------
The Busy Executive's Database Guide                     1991-06-12 00:00:00.000

title                                                   pubdate
------------------------------------------------------- -----------------------
Cooking with Computers: Surreptitious Balance Sheets    1991-06-09 00:00:00.000

Server: Msg 16917, Level 16, State 2, Line 9
Cursor is not open.
```


However, if the cursor is deallocated using either the cursor variable or the cursor name, the cursor definition still exists until it is deallocated via the last remaining reference to the cursor. The cursor can be reopened, but only by using the remaining cursor reference(s) as shown in Listing 28.17. If the cursor has not been closed, only the last deallocation of the cursor closes it.

LISTING 28.17 Deallocating a Cursor by Cursor Name and Cursor Variable

```
declare @curs CURSOR
exec cursor_proc @cursor = @curs output

print 'FETCH VIA NAME:'
fetch curs1
```

LISTING 28.17 Continued

```
print 'FETCH VIA VARIABLE:'
fetch @curs

print 'CLOSE BY NAME'
close curs1
print 'DEALLOCATE BY NAME'
deallocate curs1

print 'ATTEMPT FETCH VIA VARABLE (CURSOR SHOULD BE CLOSED):'
fetch @curs

print 'ATTEMPT TO OPEN VIA VARIABLE (CURSOR SHOULD OPEN, NOT DEALLOCATED YET)'
open @curs

print 'ATTEMPT FETCH VIA VARIABLE (SHOULD START FROM BEGINNING AGAIN):'
fetch @curs

print 'CLOSE AND DEALLOCATE VIA VARIABLE'
close @curs
deallocate @curs

print 'ATTEMPT TO OPEN VIA VARIABLE (SHOULD FAIL, SINCE NOW FULLY DEALLOCATED):'
open @curs
go

FETCH VIA NAME:
title                                               pubdate
--------------------------------------------------- -----------------------
The Busy Executive's Database Guide                 1991-06-12 00:00:00.000

FETCH VIA VARABLE:
title                                               pubdate
--------------------------------------------------- -----------------------
Cooking with Computers: Surreptitious Balance Sheets 1991-06-09 00:00:00.000

CLOSE BY NAME

DEALLOCATE BY NAME

ATTEMPT FETCH VIA VARIABLE (CURSOR SHOULD BE CLOSED):
Server: Msg 16917, Level 16, State 2, Line 15
Cursor is not open.
```

LISTING 28.17 Continued

```
ATTEMPT TO OPEN VIA VARIABLE (CURSOR SHOULD OPEN, NOT DEALLOCATED YET)

ATTEMPT FETCH VIA VARIABLE (SHOULD START FROM BEGINNING AGAIN):
title                                                    pubdate
-------------------------------------------------------- -----------------------
The Busy Executive's Database Guide                      1991-06-12 00:00:00.000

CLOSE AND DEALLOCATE VIA VARIABLE

ATTEMPT TO OPEN VIA VARIABLE (SHOULD FAIL, SINCE NOW FULLY DEALLOCATED):
Server: Msg 16950, Level 16, State 2, Line 28
The variable '@curs' does not currently have a cursor allocated to it.
```

If the cursor is declared as a local cursor within a stored procedure, it can still be passed back in an output variable to a cursor variable, but it will only be accessible through the cursor variable, as shown in Listing 28.18.

LISTING 28.18 Assigning a Local Cursor to a Cursor Output Parameter

```
create proc cursor_proc2 @cursor CURSOR varying output
as
declare curs1 cursor local for select title, pubdate from titles
set @cursor = curs1
open curs1
go
declare @curs CURSOR
exec cursor_proc2 @cursor = @curs output

print 'ATTEMPT FETCH VIA NAME:'
fetch next from curs1
print 'ATTEMPT FETCH VIA VARIABLE:'
fetch next from @curs
go

ATTEMPT FETCH VIA NAME:
Server: Msg 16916, Level 16, State 1, Line 5
A cursor with the name 'curs1' does not exist.
ATTEMPT FETCH VIA VARIABLE:
title                                                    pubdate
-------------------------------------------------------- -----------------------
The Busy Executive's Database Guide                      1991-06-12 00:00:00.000
```

Nested Stored Procedures

Stored procedures can call other stored procedures, and any of those procedures can call other procedures up to a maximum nesting level of 32 levels deep. If you exceed the 32-level limit, an error message will be raised, the batch will be aborted, and any open transaction in the session will be rolled back. The nesting level limit prevents a recursive procedure from calling itself repeatedly in an infinite loop until a stack overflow occurs. To check the depth that a procedure is nested, use the system function @@NESTLEVEL (see Listing 28.19).

LISTING 28.19 Checking @@NESTLEVEL in Nested Stored Procedures

```
create proc main_proc
as
print 'Nesting Level in main_proc before sub_proc1 = ' + str(@@NESTLEVEL, 1)
exec sub_proc1
print 'Nesting Level in main_proce after sub_proc1 = ' + str(@@NESTLEVEL, 1)
exec sub_proc2
print 'Nesting Level in main_proc after sub_proc2 = ' + str(@@NESTLEVEL, 1)
return
go

create proc sub_proc1
as
print 'Nesting Level in sub_proc1 before sub_proc2 = ' + str(@@NESTLEVEL, 1)
exec sub_proc2
print 'Nesting Level in sub_proc1 after sub_proc2 = ' + str(@@NESTLEVEL, 1)
return
go

create proc sub_proc2
as
print 'Nesting Level in sub_proc2 = ' + str(@@NESTLEVEL, 1)
return
go

print 'Nesting Level before main_proc = ' + str(@@NESTLEVEL, 1)
exec main_proc
print 'Nesting Level after main_proc = ' + str(@@NESTLEVEL, 1)
go

select @@NESTLEVEL
exec main_proc
select @@NESTLEVEL
go
```

LISTING 28.19 Continued

```
Nesting Level before main_proc = 0
Nesting Level in main_proc before sub_proc1 = 1
Nesting Level in sub_proc1 before sub_proc2 = 2
Nesting Level in sub_proc2 = 3
Nesting Level in sub_proc1 after sub_proc2 = 2
Nesting Level in main_proce after sub_proc1 = 1
Nesting Level in sub_proc2 = 2
Nesting Level in main_proc after sub_proc2 = 1
Nesting Level after main_proc = 0
```

Although a limit exists for the number of levels that procedures can be nested, the number of stored procedures that can be called from within a single procedure is limitless. The main level procedure can call potentially hundreds of other procedures. As long as the other procedures never invoke another procedure, the nesting level will never exceed two.

Any stored procedure that is called from within another procedure should always return a status code if an error condition occurs. Depending on the severity of the error, failure within a nested procedure will not always cause the calling procedure or batch to be aborted. Checking the error condition from a nested procedure will allow you to conditionally determine whether to continue processing.

Recursive Stored Procedures

A stored procedure can call itself up to the maximum nesting level of 32. This is referred to as recursion. Be aware that when you create a recursive procedure, it will generate the following warning message:

```
Cannot add rows to sysdepends for the current stored procedure because it
depends on the missing object 'procname'. The stored procedure will still
be created.
```

This is simply because it is trying to add the dependency to itself, which it cannot do because it doesn't exist yet. This does not affect the functionality of the stored procedure in any way; it will correctly resolve the reference to itself at runtime, and the warning can be ignored.

When might you want a stored procedure to be recursive? One common example is when you need to expand a tree relationship. Although a self-join can expand a tree relationship, it shows the entire tree relationship (see Listing 28.20). With this type of query, it is difficult to expand the tree at a specific level or to show the tree in a specific hierarchy order when the rows or ID values are not in a logical order in the table.

LISTING 28.20 Using a Self-Join to Expand a Tree Relationship

```
SELECT child.partid, child.partname, parent.partid, parent.partname
   FROM PARTS child left outer join Parts parent
   on child.parentpartid = parent.partid
  order by parent.partid

partid      partname                     partid         partname
----------- ---------------------------- -------------- --------
22          Car                          NULL           NULL
2           Engine                       1              DriveTrain
3           Transmission                 1              DriveTrain
4           Axle                         1              DriveTrain
12          Drive Shaft                  1              DriveTrain
13          Piston                       2              Engine
14          Crankshaft                   2              Engine
5           Radiator                     2              Engine
6           Intake Manifold              2              Engine
7           Exhaust Manifold             2              Engine
8           Carburetor                   2              Engine
16          Gear Box                     3              Transmission
9           Flywheel                     3              Transmission
10          Clutch                       3              Transmission
11          Float Valve                  8              Carburetor
21          Piston Rings                 13             Piston
17          First Gear                   16             Gear Box
18          Second Gear                  16             Gear Box
19          Third Gear                   16             Gear Box
20          Fourth Gear                  16             Gear Box
15          Reverse Gear                 16             Gear Box
1           DriveTrain                   22             Car
23          Body                         22             Car
24          Frame                        22             Car
```

A recursive procedure provides an elegant solution to expand a tree relationship from any level in the tree. This solution also lets you format the output so the child parts are indented within the parent part. An example is shown in Listing 28.21.

LISTING 28.21 Expanding a Tree Relationship Using a Recursive Procedure

```
CREATE PROC SHOW_PARTS_LIST @partid varchar(50)
as
set nocount on
```

LISTING 28.21 Continued

```
declare @treelevel int,
        @partname varchar(50),
        @childpartid int,
        @parentpartid int

select @treelevel = @@NESTLEVEL -- keep track of nesting level for indenting

if @@nestlevel = 1  -- this is the top of the tree
begin
    select @partname = PArtName from Parts where Partid = @partid
    print 'Expanded parts list for ' + @partname
end

if @@NESTLEVEL < 32  -- Make sure we don't exceed the maximum nesting level
begin
    -- set up cursor to find all child parts for the current part
    declare c1 cursor local for
        select PartId, PartName from Parts
           where parentpartid = @partid
    open c1
    fetch c1 into @childpartid, @partname
    while @@fetch_Status = 0
    begin
        -- use the current tree level to set the indenting when
        --  we print out this record
        print replicate('-', @treelevel * 3) + '> '
               + @partname + ', Part Number: ' + ltrim(str(@childpartid))
        -- Now, call the procedure again to find all the child parts
        --  for the current part
        exec show_parts_list @childpartid
        fetch c1 into @childpartid, @partname
    end
    close c1
    deallocate c1
end
else
begin
    -- We are at maximum nesting level, print out message to indicate this
    print 'Nesting level at 32. Cannot expand tree further.'
end
return
go
```

LISTING 28.21 Continued

```
-- show the whole parts tree
declare @car_partid int
select @car_partid = partid from Parts where PartName = 'Car'
exec show_parts_list @partid = @car_partid
go

Expanded parts list for Car
---> DriveTrain, Part Number: 1
------> Engine, Part Number: 2
---------> Radiator, Part Number: 5
---------> Intake Manifold, Part Number: 6
---------> Exhaust Manifold, Part Number: 7
---------> Carburetor, Part Number: 8
------------> Float Valve, Part Number: 11
---------> Piston, Part Number: 13
------------> Piston Rings, Part Number: 21
---------> Crankshaft, Part Number: 14
------> Transmission, Part Number: 3
---------> Flywheel, Part Number: 9
---------> Clutch, Part Number: 10
---------> Gear Box, Part Number: 16
------------> Reverse Gear, Part Number: 15
------------> First Gear, Part Number: 17
------------> Second Gear, Part Number: 18
------------> Third Gear, Part Number: 19
------------> Fourth Gear, Part Number: 20
------> Axle, Part Number: 4
------> Drive Shaft, Part Number: 12
---> Body, Part Number: 23
---> Frame, Part Number: 24


-- show the parts tree for 'Engine'
exec show_parts_list @partid = 2
go

Expanded parts list for Engine
---> Radiator, Part Number: 5
---> Intake Manifold, Part Number: 6
---> Exhaust Manifold, Part Number: 7
---> Carburetor, Part Number: 8
```

LISTING 28.21 Continued

```
------> Float Valve, Part Number: 11
---> Piston, Part Number: 13
------> Piston Rings, Part Number: 21
---> Crankshaft, Part Number: 14
```

Using Temporary Tables in Stored Procedures

Temporary tables are commonly used in stored procedures when you need to store intermediate results in a work table for additional or more advanced processing. You need to keep a few things in mind when using temporary tables in stored procedures.

In versions of SQL Server prior to 7.0, if a subprocedure referenced a temporary table created externally, a temporary table with the same name and structure had to exist at the time the stored procedure was created. This is no longer the case now that SQL Server performs deferred name resolution. The existence of the temporary table is not checked until the stored procedure is executed.

Local temporary tables created in a stored procedure are automatically dropped when the stored procedure exits. Global temporary tables created in a stored procedure will still exist after the stored procedure exits until they are explicitly dropped (see Listing 28.22) or the user session in which they were created disconnects from SQL Server.

LISTING 28.22 Using Local and Global Temporary Tables in Stored Procedures

```
create proc temp_test2
as
select * into ##temp
from publishers
select * into #temp
from publishers
go

exec temp_test2
go

select * from ##temp
go

pub_id pub_name                  city          state country
------ ------------------------- ------------- ----- -----------
0736   New Moon Books            Boston        MA    USA
0877   Binnet & Hardley          Washington    DC    USA
1389   Algodata Infosystems      Berkeley      CA    USA
```

LISTING 28.22 Continued

```
1622    Five Lakes Publishing       Chicago       IL     USA
1756    Ramona Publishers           Dallas        TX     USA
9901    GGG&G                       München       NULL   Germany
9952    Scootney Books              New York      NY     USA
9999    Lucerne Publishing          Paris         NULL   France

select * from #temp
go

Server: Msg 208, Level 16, State 1, Line 1
Invalid object name '#temp'.
```

Note what happens if you try to run the stored procedure again:

```
exec temp_test2
go
Server: Msg 2714, Level 16, State 6, Procedure temp_test2, Line 3
There is already an object named '##temp' in the database.
```

TIP

Personally, I don't find much use for global temporary tables in stored procedures. The typical reason for using temporary tables in stored procedures is that you need a work area within the stored procedure only. You normally wouldn't want it sticking around after the procedure finishes. Creating a global temporary table in a stored procedure requires an explicit drop of the table before the procedure exits if you no longer need it. If that's the case, what's the benefit of using a global temporary table? Any subprocedures will be able to see and reference a local temporary table created in the calling procedure, so global temporary tables are not needed in that case.

Only if you need to create and populate a worktable and have it available after the procedure exits should you consider using a global temporary table. However, you would have to remember to explicitly drop it at some point before attempting to run the procedure again. However, if an error occurs that aborts processing of the stored procedure, the explicit drop might not be executed.

You might want to include a check for the global temporary table in your stored procedure and drop it automatically before attempting to create it again, as in the following code snippet:

```
create proc myproc
as
if exists (select 1 from tempdb..sysobjects where name = '##global_temp'
                                             and type = 'U')
    drop table ##global_Temp

select * into  ##global_temp from ...
```

Temporary Table Performance Tips

All users within SQL Server share the same `tempdb` database for work tables and temporary tables, regardless of the database in which they are working. This makes `tempdb` a potential bottleneck in any multiuser system. The primary bottleneck in `tempdb` is disk I/O, but locking contention can also exist between processes on the `tempdb` system tables.

SQL Server 2000 solves the disk I/O problem a bit by logging just enough information to allow rollback of transactions without logging all the additional information that would be necessary to recover those transactions. The recovery information is needed only when recovering a database at system startup or when restoring from a backup. Because tempdb is rebuilt during SQL Server startup (and no one in their right mind would restore tempdb from a backup), it's unnecessary to keep this recovery information. By reducing the logging in tempdb, data modification operations on tables in tempdb can be up to four times faster than the same operations in other databases.

On the other hand, locking in tempdb is still a potential performance bottleneck. If you create a table in tempdb within a transaction, locks are held on rows in the system tables `sysobjects`, `syscolumns`, and `sysindexes` related to the table created, as shown in Listing 28.23.

LISTING 28.23 Locks Held on System Tables in `tempdb` When Creating a Temporary Table

```
begin tran
select * into #temptab from titles

exec sp_lock
go

spid   dbid   ObjId       IndId  Type Resource         Mode     Status
------ ------ ----------- ------ ---- ---------------- -------- ------
    51      2           0      0 DB   [BULK-OP-LOG]    NULL     GRANT
    51      5           0      0 DB                    S        GRANT
    51      2           0      0 DB   [BULK-OP-DB]     NULL     GRANT
    51      2           1      0 TAB                   IX       GRANT
    51      2           3      0 TAB                   IX       GRANT
    51      2           2      0 TAB                   IX       GRANT
    51      2           3      2 KEY  (bd018d280de1)   X        GRANT
    51      2           3      2 KEY  (b101e50ba351)   X        GRANT
    51      2           3      1 KEY  (080056b1859e)   X        GRANT
    51      2           3      1 KEY  (0900b81e308c)   X        GRANT
    51      2           3      1 KEY  (0e008aeeeebb)   X        GRANT
    51      2           3      1 KEY  (0b0064415ba9)   X        GRANT
    51      2           3      1 KEY  (0f00dcfe8de3)   X        GRANT
    51      2           0      0 PAG  1:78             X        GRANT
    51      2           0      0 PAG  1:77             X        GRANT
```

LISTING 28.23 Continued

```
51      2          0     0 PAG  1:94            X       GRANT
51      2          0     0 PAG  1:95            X       GRANT
51      2          0     0 PAG  1:92            X       GRANT
51      2          0     0 PAG  1:93            X       GRANT
51      2          0     0 PAG  1:90            X       GRANT
51      2          0     0 PAG  1:91            X       GRANT
51      2          0     0 PAG  1:89            X       GRANT
51      2          0     0 EXT  1:104           X       GRANT
51      2          0     0 PAG  1:102           X       GRANT
51      2          0     0 PAG  1:103           X       GRANT
51      2          0     0 PAG  1:100           X       GRANT
51      2          0     0 PAG  1:101           X       GRANT
51      2          0     0 PAG  1:98            X       GRANT
51      2          0     0 PAG  1:99            X       GRANT
51      2          0     0 PAG  1:96            X       GRANT
51      2          0     0 PAG  1:97            X       GRANT
51      2          0     0 PAG  1:110           X       GRANT
51      2          0     0 EXT  1:96            X       GRANT
51      2          0     0 PAG  1:111           X       GRANT
51      2          0     0 PAG  1:108           X       GRANT
51      2          0     0 PAG  1:109           X       GRANT
51      2          0     0 PAG  1:106           X       GRANT
51      2          0     0 PAG  1:107           X       GRANT
51      2          0     0 PAG  1:104           X       GRANT
51      2          0     0 PAG  1:105           X       GRANT
51      2          0     0 PAG  1:118           X       GRANT
51      2          0     0 PAG  1:119           X       GRANT
51      2          0     0 PAG  1:116           X       GRANT
51      2          0     0 PAG  1:117           X       GRANT
51      2          0     0 PAG  1:114           X       GRANT
51      2          0     0 PAG  1:115           X       GRANT
51      2          0     0 PAG  1:112           X       GRANT
51      2          0     0 PAG  1:113           X       GRANT
51      2          0     0 EXT  1:112           X       GRANT
51      2          1     2 KEY  (8516877f1c72)  X       GRANT
51      2          0     0 IDX  IDX: 2:469576711 X      GRANT
51      2  469576711     0 TAB                  Sch-M   GRANT
51      2          3     2 KEY  (54016b2ccfff)  X       GRANT
51      2          1     3 KEY  (0700b7f12a1d)  X       GRANT
51      2          3     2 KEY  (4201380b1b46)  X       GRANT
51      1   85575343     0 TAB                  IS      GRANT
```

LISTING 28.23 Continued

```
51      2          3       2 KEY   (5c013a008346)   X         GRANT
51      2          3       2 KEY   (9f01b84495cc)   X         GRANT
51      2          3       1 KEY   (110057368449)   X         GRANT
51      2          3       1 KEY   (1000b999315b)   X         GRANT
51      2          3       2 KEY   (eb002ad7df7e)   X         GRANT
51      2          3       1 KEY   (0a00dd798c34)   X         GRANT
51      2          3       1 KEY   (0d00ef895203)   X         GRANT
51      2          3       2 KEY   (36027a4d788e)   X         GRANT
51      2          3       1 KEY   (0c000126e711)   X         GRANT
51      2          1       1 KEY   (0700c2f14c59)   X         GRANT
51      2          2       1 KEY   (07000a2e7633)   X         GRANT
51      2          3       2 KEY   (450124fb6f35)   X         GRANT
51      2          3       2 KEY   (d7016cf8d9e5)   X         GRANT
52      5          0       0 DB                     S         GRANT
53      5          0       0 DB                     S         GRANT
```

The `tempdb` database has a `dbid` of 2, and the `sysobjects` table has an object ID of 1; `sysindexes` is object ID 2, and `syscolumns` is object ID 3. These locks being held on the system tables could lead to locking contention with other processes trying to read or update the `tempdb` system catalogs.

To minimize the potential for locking contention on the system tables in `tempdb`, consider creating your temp tables before starting the transaction so that locks are released immediately and not held on the system catalogs until the end of the transaction. If the table must be created in a transaction, commit your transaction as soon as possible.

Also, be aware that even if it's not in a transaction, creating a temporary table using `SELECT INTO` will hold locks on the system catalogs in `tempdb` until the `SELECT INTO` completes. If locking contention in `tempdb` becomes a problem, consider replacing `SELECT INTO` with `CREATE TABLE` followed by an `INSERT` using a `SELECT` statement. Although this might run a bit more slowly than `SELECT INTO`, the system table locks are held only for the brief moment it takes for `CREATE TABLE` to complete.

Another way to speed up temp table creation/population is to keep temporary tables as small as possible so they create more quickly. Select only the required columns, rather than `SELECT *`, and only retrieve the rows that you need. The smaller the temporary table, the faster it will be to create the table as well as to access the table.

If the temp table is of sufficient size and is going to be accessed multiple times within a stored procedure, it might be cost effective to create an index on it on the column(s) that will be referenced in the search arguments of queries against the temp table. The deciding factor of whether to create an index on a temporary table is if the time it takes to create the index plus the time the queries take to run using the index is less than the sum total of the time it takes the queries against the temporary table to run without the index.

The following example demonstrates the creation of an index on a temporary table:

```
use bigpubs2000
go
create proc p1 WITH RECOMPILE
as
select title_id, type, pub_id, ytd_sales
   into #temp_titles
   from titles

create index tmp on #temp_titles(pub_id)

select sum(ytd_sales)
   from #temp_titles
   where pub_id = '0736'
select min(ytd_sales)
   from #temp_titles
   where pub_id = '0736'

return
go
```

Some other final tips when using temporary tables in stored procedures:

- Don't use temp tables to combine resultsets together when a `UNION` or `UNION ALL` will suffice. `UNION ALL` will be the fastest because no work table in `tempdb` is required to merge the resultsets.
- Drop temporary tables as soon as possible to free up space in `tempdb`.
- Consider using the `table` datatype to avoid `tempdb` usage altogether.

Using the `table` Datatype

SQL Server 2000 introduces a new datatype—the `table` datatype. Table variables are defined similarly to regular tables except they are defined in a `DECLARE` statement, rather than using `CREATE TABLE`:

```
DECLARE @table_variable  TABLE ({ column_definition | table_constraint }
                                  [ ,...n ])
```

The following is a simple example showing the use of a table variable in a stored procedure:

```
-- proc to get year-to-date sales for all books published since specified date
-- with ytd_sales greater than specified threshold
```

```
create proc tab_var_test @pubdate datetime = null,
                         @sales_minimum int = 0
as

declare @ytd_sales_tab TABLE (title_id char(6),
                              title varchar(80),
                              ytd_sales int)

if @pubdate is null
    -- if no date is specified, set date to last year
    set @pubdate = dateadd(month, -12, getdate())

insert @ytd_sales_tab
    select title_id, title, ytd_sales
      from titles
      where pubdate > @pubdate
        and ytd_sales > @sales_minimum
select * from @ytd_sales_tab
return
go

exec tab_var_test '6/1/1991', 10000
go
title_id title                                         ytd_sales
-------- ------------------------------------------- ---------
BU2075   You Can Combat Computer Stress!                  18722
MC3021   The Gourmet Microwave                            22246
TC4203   Fifty Years in Buckingham Palace Kitchens        15096
```

Table variables can be used in functions, stored procedures, and batches. Consider using table variables instead of temporary tables whenever possible because they provide the following benefits:

- Table variables are memory resident and require no space in tempdb.
- When table variables are used in stored procedures, fewer recompilations of the stored procedures occur than when temporary tables are used.
- Transactions involving table variables last only for the duration of an update on the table variable. Thus, table variables require less locking and logging resources.
- A table variable behaves like a local variable, and its scope is limited to the stored procedure in which it is declared. It is cleaned up automatically at the end of the function, stored procedure, or batch in which it is defined.

A table variable can be used like a regular table in SELECT, INSERT, UPDATE, and DELETE statements. However, a table variable cannot be used in the following statements:

- INSERT INTO *table_variable* EXEC *stored_procedure*
- SELECT select_list INTO table_variable ...

You need to keep a couple of other limitations in mind when considering using table variables in stored procedures. First, table variables cannot be used as stored procedure parameters. You cannot pass a table variable as an input or output parameter for a stored procedure, nor can you access a table variable declared outside the currently executing stored procedure. If you need to share resultsets between stored procedures, you have to use temporary tables. Second, you cannot create indexes on table variables using the CREATE INDEX command. You can, however, define a primary or unique key on the table variable when it is declared.

TIP

One solution to the inability of stored procedures to pass table variables as output parameters is to convert the stored procedure to a user-defined function if possible. User-defined functions can return a table resultset that can be referenced in a SELECT statement just like a regular table. Thus, you can include it in an insert ... select ... statement and insert the results into a local variable (something you cannot do with a resultset from a stored procedure). For example, I will take the previous tab_var_test stored procedure and convert it to a user-defined function.

```
-- function to get year to date sales for all books published since specified
-- date with ytd_sales greater than specified threshold
create function tab_function (@pubdate datetime ,
                              @sales_minimum int = 0)
returns @ytd_sales_tab TABLE (title_id char(6),
                              title varchar(80),
                              ytd_sales int)
as
begin

insert @ytd_sales_tab
    select title_id, title, ytd_sales
      from titles
      where pubdate > @pubdate
        and ytd_sales > @sales_minimum
return
end
go
```

```
declare @local_tab table (title_id char(6), title varchar(80), ytd_sales int)
insert @local_tab select * from tab_function('6/1/1991', 10000)
select * from @local_tab
go

title_id title                                                      ytd_sales
-------- ---------------------------------------------------------- ---------
BU2075   You Can Combat Computer Stress!                                18722
MC3021   The Gourmet Microwave                                          22246
TC4203   Fifty Years in Buckingham Palace Kitchens                      15096
```

You cannot use the getdate() function inside a user-defined function, so it has to be removed to convert the stored procedure to a function. For more information on defining and using user-defined functions, see Chapter 30, "User-Defined Functions."

Remote Stored Procedures

You can execute a stored procedure residing on another server by using a four-part naming scheme:

```
EXEC server_name.db_name.owner_name.proc_name
```

This concept is called **remote stored procedures** (RPCs). The name implies that the procedure called on the other server is a special type of stored procedure, but it is not. Any stored procedure can be called from another server as long as the remote server has been configured and the appropriate login mapping has been done. The method used to set up servers to allow remote procedure calls is described in Chapter 19, "Managing Linked and Remote Servers."

The processing done by the remote stored procedure is, by default, not done in the local transaction context. If the local transaction rolls back, modifications performed by the remote stored procedure are not undone. You *can* get the remote stored procedures to execute within the local transaction context using distributed transactions, as in the following example:

```
BEGIN DISTRIBUTED TRANSACTION
EXEC purge_old_customers  --A local procedure
EXEC LONDON.customers.dbo.purge_old_customers
COMMIT TRANSACTION
```

Distributed transactions and the Microsoft Distributed Transaction Coordinator (DTC) service are discussed in Chapter 32, "Distributed Transaction Processing."

Debugging Stored Procedures with Query Analyzer

One of the great new tools available with SQL Server 2000 is the SQL Debugger built into Query Analyzer. You invoke the SQL Debugger by right-clicking on a stored procedure in the Object Browser and choosing the Debug option (see Figure 28.7).

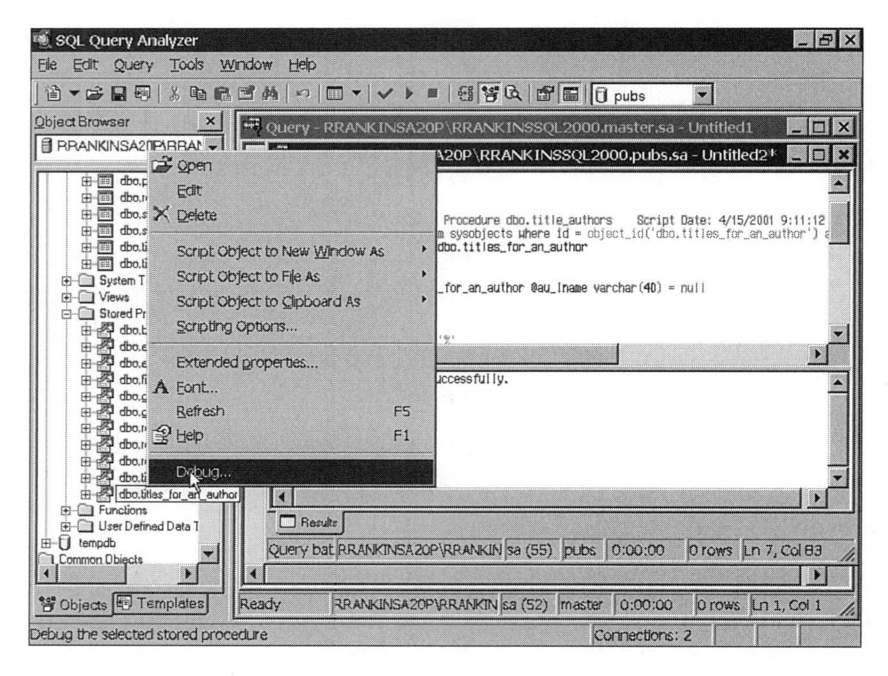

FIGURE 28.7 Invoking the SQL Debugger in Query Analyzer.

If the stored procedure has input parameters, you will be prompted to enter values or provide a null value for the parameter (see Figure 28.8).

The SQL debugger is similar to the debuggers that Microsoft provides with its other programming languages, such as Visual Basic or Visual C++ (see Figure 28.9).

The SQL Debugger has all the features you would expect to find in a debugger:

- Ability to set and clear break points
- Ability to step over/into next statement
- Ability to run to end or next breakpoint
- Ability to view contents of local and global variables
- Ability to display messages/results generated within stored procedure

For a more detailed discussion on using the SQL Debugger, see Chapter 6.

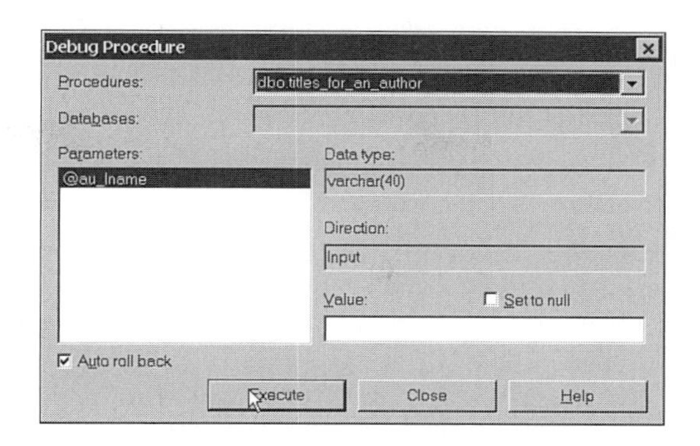

FIGURE 28.8 Providing input parameter values to the SQL Debugger in Query Analyzer.

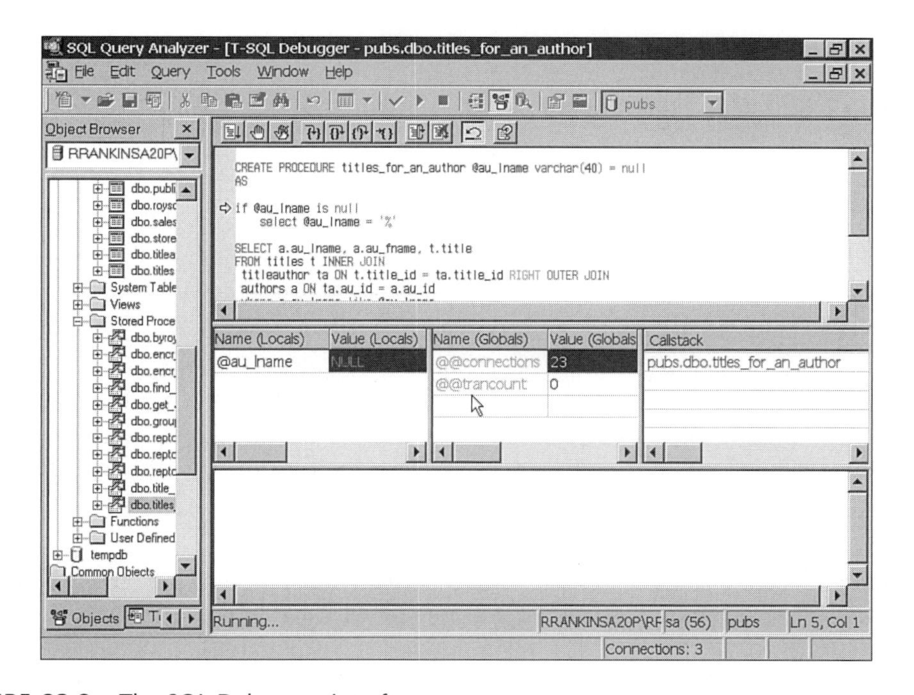

FIGURE 28.9 The SQL Debugger interface.

Debugging with Microsoft Visual Studio and Visual Basic

In addition to the debugger provided with SQL Server Query Analyzer, a T-SQL debugger is provided with the Visual Studio development suite.

If you don't find SQL Server Debugging in the Control Panel, Add/Remove Programs dialog box, you have to add the software. Run the Visual Studio setup program, choose Server Applications and Tools, Launch BackOffice Installation Wizard, Install, Custom, and install SQL Server Debugging.

NOTE

You must have Visual Studio Version 6.0 to debug stored procedures. The T-SQL debugger in Visual Basic 5.0 or Visual Studio 97 does not support SQL Server 2000.

The enterprise edition of Visual Studio (Visual InterDev, Visual J++, and Visual C++) includes a debugger for the Visual Studio developer environment. The project you are working in needs to include a database project.

Open a stored procedure to open the context menu (by right-clicking within your code) and set breakpoints. When you choose Debug from the context, a dialog box asks for the parameters that the procedure expects. As you step through the code, you can inspect the values of variables in the Locals window.

The T-SQL debugger in Visual Basic is similar. Open your Visual Basic project, choose the Add-In Manager, and load the T-SQL debugger. Within the debugger, you define the connection attributes and choose which procedures you want to debug.

System Stored Procedures

A **system stored procedure** is a stored procedure with some special characteristics. These procedures, created when SQL Server is installed or upgraded, are generally used to administer SQL Server. They shield the DBA from accessing the system tables directly. Some are used to present information from the system tables, whereas others modify system tables. Information about login IDs, for instance, can be viewed with the `sp_helplogins` procedure and modified with `sp_addlogin`, `sp_droplogin`, and so on.

The earliest versions of SQL Server had no GUI-based administration tools, so a DBA had to have knowledge of the system stored procedures. With version 4.2 of SQL Server, Microsoft shipped two graphical administration tools, and SQL Enterprise Manager was introduced in version 6. The stored procedure is not an absolute must to administer SQL Server, but it is always a good idea to be familiar with the basic system stored procedures. Nearly 500 documented system stored procedures exist in SQL Server 2000, so it would be a tough job to learn the names and syntax for all of them. The total number of system stored procedures is about 995. Some of the undocumented stored procedures are called by other procedures, whereas others are called from SQL Enterprise Manager or other SQL Server tools and utility programs.

The following attributes characterize a system stored procedure:

- The stored procedure name begins with sp_.
- The procedure is stored in the master database.
- The procedure is owned by dbo (that is, created by sa).

These attributes make the procedure *global*. You can execute the procedure from any database without qualifying the database name. The procedure executes in the current database context regarding system tables.

If a stored procedure resides in the master database but does not begin with sp_ (for instance, xp_logininfo), the procedure has to be fully qualified with the name of the master database when executed from a different database context, as shown in the following example:

```
USE pubs
go

exec xp_logininfo
go
Server: Msg 2812, Level 16, State 62, Line 1
Could not find stored procedure 'xp_logininfo'.

EXEC master..xp_logininfo
go

account name           type   privilege mapped login name      permission path
---------------------- ------ --------- ---------------------- ---------------
BUILTIN\Administrators group  admin     BUILTIN\Administrators NULL
GOTHAM\SQLAdmin        user   admin     GOTHAM\SQLAdmin        NULL
```


Although listed as a system procedure in Enterprise Manager and Query Analyzer, without sp_ at the beginning of the name, the xp_logininfo stored procedure is treated as a local stored procedure that resides in master, not as a system procedure. If your current database context is not the master database, you must fully qualify it with the master database name.

Although system stored procedures reside in master, they will run in any database context when fully qualified with a database name, regardless of your current database context. For instance, sp_helpfile shows information about the files configured for the current database. In the following example, when not qualified, sp_helpfile returns file information for the master database, and when qualified with pubs.., it returns file information for the Pubs database:

```
exec sp_helpfile
go

name    fileid filename                 filegroup size     maxsize   growth
------- ------ ------------------------ --------- -------- --------- ------
master       1 e:\MSSQL\data\master.mdf  PRIMARY   14272 KB Unlimited 10%
mastlog      2 e:\MSSQL\data\mastlog.ldf NULL      3456 KB  Unlimited 10%

exec pubs..sp_helpfile
go

name    fileid filename                 filegroup size     maxsize   growth
------- ------ ------------------------ --------- -------- --------- ------
pubs         1 e:\MSSQL\data\pubs.mdf    PRIMARY   9920 KB  Unlimited 10%
pubs_log     2 e:\MSSQL\data\pubs_log.ldf NULL     11200 KB Unlimited 10%
```

The context of system procedures is global only for references to the database system catalog tables. If a procedure refers to a user table, it will not be global even if a table with the same name and attributes exists in the current local database context.

In Listing 28.24, a `global_example` table is created both in the master and Pubs databases. A system stored procedure is also created in master that returns data from the `global_example` table. When you execute the `sp_global_example` procedure, you will see that it operates on the table in the master database only, regardless of the database from which it is executed. This is because the `global_example` table is not a system table.

LISTING 28.24 System Stored Procedures, Which Are Global Only for System Tables, Not User Tables

```
USE master
GO
CREATE TABLE global_example (a_string VARCHAR(50))
INSERT global_example
 VALUES ('This is in the master database')
GO
USE pubs
GO
CREATE TABLE global_example (a_string VARCHAR(50))
INSERT global_example
 VALUES ('This is in the pubs database')
GO
USE master
GO
CREATE PROC sp_global_example AS
```

LISTING 28.24 Continued

```
 SELECT * FROM global_example
GO

EXEC sp_global_example
go

a_string
--------------------------------------------------
This is in the master database

USE pubs
GO

EXEC sp_global_example
go

a_string
--------------------------------------------------
This is in the master database
```

Table 28.2 describes the eight categories of system stored procedures.

TABLE 28.2 System Stored Procedure Categories

Category	Description
System procedures	Used for general administration of SQL Server.
Security procedures	Used to manage login IDs, usernames, and so on.
Distributed queries procedures	Used to link remote servers and manage distributed queries.
Cursor procedures	Reports information about cursors.
Web Assistant procedures	Sets up and manages Web tasks (used by SQL Server Web Assistant).
Catalog procedures	Provides information about the system tables (used by ODBC).
SQL Server Agent procedures	Used by SQL Server Agent, provides access to the system tables in msdb. These are stored in msdb, so they are not global.
Replication procedures	Used to manage replication.

Some of the more useful system stored procedures are listed in Table 28.3.

TABLE 28.3 Continued

Procedure Name	Description
`sp_who` and `sp_who2`	Returns information about current connections to SQL Server.
`sp_lock`	Returns information about currently held locks.
`sp_help [object_name]`	Lists the objects in a database or returns information about a specified object.
`sp_helpdb [db_name]`	Returns a list of databases or information about a specified database.
`sp_helptext [object_name]`	Returns the `CREATE` statement for stored procedures, views, and so on.
`sp_configure`	Lists or changes configuration settings.

Rolling Your Own System Stored Procedures

SQL Server system administrators can create their own system procedures. All you need to do is create the procedure in the master database with the first three characters of the procedure name being `sp_`. If you write your own system stored procedures, remember to grant execute permission in the master database on the system stored procedure to the appropriate users, groups, or roles that will need to be able to use the stored procedure.

TIP

If you want to create your own system stored procedures, one of the best places to start is to review the Microsoft-supplied system stored procedures and see how it does things. The source code for the system procedures is in the `syscomments` table in the master database and is not encrypted or hidden in any way. Looking at the system procedure source code will also help you learn more about the system catalog tables, learn what is stored in them and how it is stored, and learn how to retrieve the information in a meaningful way. I often "borrow" snippets of the system procedures when creating my own system procedures or queries that access the system catalog tables.

If the procedure needs to modify system tables, the `allow updates` configuration option must be set on when the procedure is *created*. If this option is on when the procedure is created, it remains in effect for the life of the stored procedure. The stored procedure will still be able to modify the system tables when it is executed, regardless of whether the option is on or off at the time of execution.

TIP

I often find that many of the Microsoft-supplied system procedures don't provide all of the information I want to see, or in a format that I want to see it. For example, with the increase in the size of object names from 30 characters to 128 characters, the output from `sp_help` no longer fits on one screen in Query Analyzer and is difficult to read. When scrolling over to see a column datatype, the column name is no longer visible on the screen. This is why one of the first things I do at a new installation is to create my own versions of `sp_help`, `sp_helpindex`, and `sp_helpconstraint`.

Copies of these procedures can be found on the CD under the filenames `sp_SSU_help.sql`, `sp_SSU_helpindex.sql`, and `sp_SSU_helpconstraint.sql`.

When creating your own system stored procedures, I recommend using a procedure name that will not conflict with any of the Microsoft-supplied system procedures. If you replace the Microsoft-supplied system procedures, you might break compatibility with existing applications. Also, if you install a Service Pack or run an upgrade, your versions of the system procedures might be replaced. I usually use my initials or the company's initials after `sp_` to designate it as a custom system procedure. It also makes it easier to locate any custom system procedures when browsing the stored procedures in the master database.

CAUTION

Be careful if you implement custom system stored procedures that update the system catalog tables. It is easy to corrupt a database or the server if any of the records in the system catalogs are modified incorrectly.

A Caution on Querying System Tables Directly

Whenever possible, avoid embedding queries against the SQL Server system tables in your applications or stored procedures.

One of the areas that will involve the most work when porting an application to version 2000 is handling queries to the system tables (if any exist). The engineers at Microsoft have done a good job of providing a high level of backward compatibility with earlier versions of SQL Server. Nevertheless, some of the information in the system tables does not correspond between the versions.

A better approach than querying the system tables is to use the information schema views or system functions to retrieve metadata information.

System Information Schema Views

ANSI SQL-92 defined a set of views that provides information about system data. These views are available in SQL Server 2000. The advantage of using the views instead of querying the system tables directly is that the application is less dependent on the database management system or its particular version and potential changes to the system catalog tables.

Both SQL-92 and SQL Server use a three-part naming scheme for objects. Even though they use different names for each part, the names map quite nicely to each other (see Table 28.4).

TABLE 28.4 Three-Part Naming Scheme for SQL Server and SQL-92

SQL Server Name	SQL-92 Name
Database	Catalog
Owner	Schema
Object	Object

A user-defined datatype is called a domain in the ANSI SQL-92 standard.

SQL Server ANSI-Compliant Views

The information schema views are owned by the user `INFORMATION_SCHEMA`. The user is created by the installation script that creates the views. Queries against these views must qualify the object name with `INFORMATION_SCHEMA`, as in the following example:

```
SELECT TABLE_NAME, TABLE_TYPE
   FROM INFORMATION_SCHEMA.TABLES
```

The information schema views display information applicable for the user who queries them (for instance, the tables that the user has permissions to use). Note that the names are in uppercase.

Table 28.5 lists the information schema views.

TABLE 28.5 Information Schema Views

Name	Description
`CHECK_CONSTRAINTS`	Information about check constraints
`COLUMN_DOMAIN_USAGE`	Information about which column uses user-defined datatypes
`COLUMN_PRIVILEGES`	Permissions at the column level
`COLUMNS`	Information about columns in the database
`CONSTRAINT_COLUMN_USAGE`	Table, column, and constraint name for each column that has a constraint defined
`CONSTRAINT_TABLE_USAGE`	Table, column, and constraint name for each table that has a constraint defined
`DOMAIN_CONSTRAINTS`	Information about user-defined datatypes that has rules bound to it
`DOMAINS`	One row for each user-defined datatype
`KEY_COLUMN_USAGE`	Information about which columns are defined as `PRIMARY KEY` or `UNIQUE`
`REFERENTIAL_CONSTRAINTS`	One row for each `FOREIGN_KEY` constraint
`SCHEMATA`	Returns character set information for each database (always the same in SQL Server)
`TABLE_CONSTRAINTS`	One row for each table constraint defined in the database
`TABLE_PRIVILEGES`	Permissions at the table level
`TABLES`	One row for each table in the database for which the user has permissions
`VIEW_COLUMN_USAGE`	Columns used in views
`VIEW_TABLE_USAGE`	Tables used in views
`VIEWS`	One row for each view in the database for which the user has permissions

Stored-Procedure Performance

As stated at the beginning of this chapter, using stored procedures can provide a number of benefits to your SQL Server applications. One performance benefit is reduced network traffic by minimizing the number of round trips between client applications and SQL Server. Stored procedures can consist of many individual SQL statements but can be executed with a single statement. This allows you to reduce the number and size of calls from the client to the server. If you have to take different actions based on your data values, you can make these decisions directly in the procedure, avoiding the need to send data back to the application to determine what to do with the data values.

By default, SQL Server sends a message back to the client application after each statement is completed within the stored procedure to indicate the number of rows affected by the statement. To further reduce the amount of "chatter" between the client and server, and as a result, to further improve stored procedure performance, these `DONE_IN_PROC` messages can be eliminated by issuing the `set nocount on` command at the beginning of the stored procedure. Be aware that if you turn this option on, the number of rows affected by the commands in the procedure will not be available to the ODBC `SQLRowCount` function or its OLE DB equivalent. You can still issue the `select @@rowcount` after a statement executes to determine the number of rows affected.

Another performance benefit of using stored procedures is potentially faster execution due to the caching of stored procedure query plans. Stored procedure query plans are kept in cache memory after the first execution. The code doesn't have to be reparsed and reoptimized on subsequent executions.

Query Plan Caching

When a batch of SQL statements is submitted to SQL Server, SQL Server performs a number of steps before the data can be returned to the client. These steps include the following:

1. Parsing the SQL statements and building a query tree (the internal format on which SQL Server operates)
2. Optimizing the SQL statements and generating an execution plan
3. Checking for permissions for access to the underlying objects
4. Executing the execution plan for the SQL statements

The first time that a stored procedure executes, SQL Server loads the SQL code for the stored procedure from the syscomments table into the procedure code and optimizes and compiles an execution plan. The first step, parsing, is skipped on the first execution because the SQL was already parsed and the query tree built when the stored procedure was created.

The optimization of SQL statements is based on the parameters passed, the index distribution statistics, the number of rows in each table, and other information available at the time of the first execution. The compiled plan is then saved in cache memory. For subsequent executions, all SQL Server has to do is find the plan in cache and execute it, essentially skipping steps 1 and 2. Parsing and compilation always add some overhead, and depending on the complexity of the stored procedure code, they can sometimes be as expensive as the actual execution. Just by skipping these two steps, you can achieve a performance gain by using stored procedures.

Procedure Cache

In versions of SQL Server prior to 7.0, a separate memory area was reserved for the procedure cache. As you set aside more memory for the procedure cache, less memory was available for the data cache. Tuning the size of the procedure cache appropriately was an inexact science and often required a bit of trial and error before it was tuned properly. Often, the procedure cache was left at the default value (30 percent of available cache memory), which in many large memory configurations was unnecessarily high.

In version 7.0, the data and procedure cache were unified. SQL Server now uses the same cache area for storing data and index pages as well as procedure query plans. Also, SQL Server Versions 7.0 and later have the ability to keep query plans in cache for ad hoc queries as well. This means that even dynamic SQL queries might be able to reuse a cached execution plan and skip recompilation.

If an ad hoc query is cheap to compile, SQL Server will typically not keep the query plan in memory—it is cheaper to recompile the plan than to keep it around and waste valuable cache memory when it might never be needed again. Also, the query plans for ad hoc queries have the lowest priority in the procedure cache. If cache space is needed, they are the first to go.

With the ability to keep query plans for ad hoc queries in memory, it is not as critical in SQL Server 2000 for applications to use stored procedures to achieve performance benefits of using precompiled plans. However, when and how the plans are stored and reused for ad hoc queries is not nearly as predictable as with stored procedures. The query plans for stored procedures will remain in cache memory more persistently. In addition, you have little explicit control over the recompilation of ad hoc queries.

TIP

You can get a summary of the amount of memory used by the procedure cache with the `DBCC PROCCACHE` commands. `DBCC PROCCACHE` returns the current size of the procedure cache. (SQL Server grows and shrinks this size automatically.)

```
num proc buffs num proc buffs used num proc buffs active proc cache size
➥ proc cache used proc cache active
```

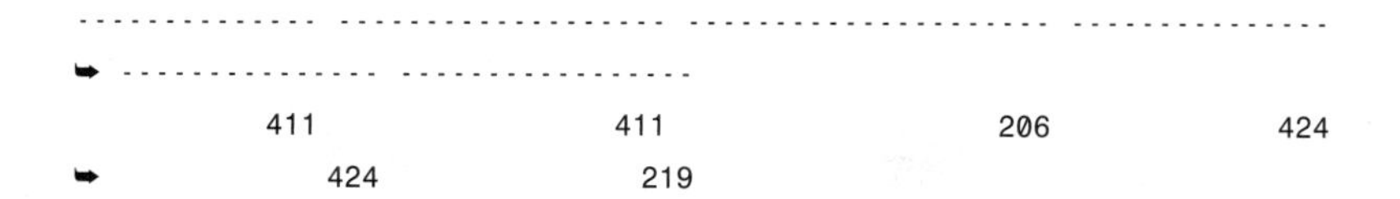

```
-------------- ------------------ -------------------- --------------
➥ --------------- ----------------
           411                411                  206              424
➥              424                 219
```

The information in the DBCC PROCCACHE output is as follows:

num_proc_buffs value is the total number of query plans that could be in the procedure cache.

num proc buffs used is the number of cache slots currently holding query plans.

num proc buffs active is the number of cache slots holding query plans that are currently executing.

proc cache size is the total size of the procedure cache in number of pages.

proc cache used is the amount of memory, in number of pages, used in the procedure cache to hold query plans.

proc cache active is the amount of memory, in number of pages, being used in the procedure cache for currently executing query plans.

You can also get more detailed information about what is currently in procedure cache via the syscacheobjects table. The syscacheobjects table is a memory-resident table that exists in the master database, but is materialized only when a query is executed against it.

Shared-Query Plans

Procedure plans were not re-entrant in versions of SQL Server prior to 7.0. If two users executed a procedure at the same time, two execution plans were created and stored in procedure cache memory. This sometimes led to multiple copies of a query plan for a stored procedure residing in memory. This resulted in suboptimal usage of the cache area, an environment that was harder to tune, and unpredictable execution times (because two plans could have different access strategies).

Because query plans in SQL Server 2000 are re-entrant, it's typical that no more than one copy of an execution plan for a stored procedure is in cache memory. However, sometimes multiple query plans can be created and exist in procedure cache at the same time. One of the more likely causes is when users run the same procedure with different settings for specific session options. The following list shows the options that will result in different query plans if set differently from the settings for a query plan already in memory:

- ANSI_NULL
- ANSI_PADDING
- ANSI_NULL_DFLT_ON
- ANSI_NULL_DFLT_OFF
- CONCAT_NULL_YIELDS_NULL

- QUOTED_IDENTIFIER
- ANSI_WARNINGS
- FORCEPLAN
- DATEFORMAT
- LANGUAGE

In addition, if the owner name is not specified for a table in a query and SQL Server has to implicitly resolve the owner name, other users cannot reuse the plan. This is because depending on who the user is at the time of execution, the table being referenced could be different. For example, if Joe owns a titles table in addition to one owned by the dbo, when he runs `select * from titles`, it references his version of the titles table. If Tom executes the same query, it references the dbo's version of the table. To avoid ambiguity when referencing an object and to help ensure reuse of the query plan, fully qualify the table with the owner name as follows:

```
select * from dbo.titles
```

How does SQL Server know what plans are currently in memory and what settings were in effect when they were created? This information is contained in the syscacheobjects table in the master database. syscacheobjects keeps track of all the currently compiled plans in the procedure cache. The key columns to focus on when evaluating stored procedure recompilation are as follows:

- objtype—The type of object being cached. For stored procedures, the type is proc.
- dbid—ID of database in which the procedure was compiled.
- objid—The object ID of the stored procedure as stored in sysobjects.
- langid—Language ID of the connection that created the query plan.
- dateformat—Used by the connection that created the object.
- setopts—A bitmap field of the options in effect at the time the query plan was compiled.
- sql—The stored procedure name, or the first 128 characters of the batch submitted.

For each procedure, you'll typically see a Compiled Plan and at least one Executable Plan listed in the cacheobjtype column. The compiled plan is the actual plan generated and used that can be shared by sessions running the same procedure. The executable plan will be generated for each concurrent execution of a compiled plan. It keeps track of the execution environment in which the plan was run. Each executable plan must be associated with a compiled plan, but not all compiled plans will have an associated executable plan.

If you see multiple compiled plans in cache for a stored procedure (sort the results by `dbid` and `objid` or by `sql` to have them listed together), look at the other columns to determine the reason. Look for differences in the `langid` or `dateformat` columns, which would indicate that the session was running under a different language or using a different date format. If the `bitmap` values for setopts are different, one of the key session options described previously in this section was set differently.

TIP

A large number of entries can exist in the `syscacheobjects` table. To clear the procedure cache buffers, and subsequently, the `syscacheobjects` table, you can issue the `DBCC FREEPROCCACHE` procedure, which removes all cached plans from memory. Alternatively, you can use the undocumented command, `DBCC FLUSHPROCINDB(`*`dbid`*`)`, to flush all procedure query plans for the specified database from memory. Needless to say, you shouldn't execute these commands in a production environment because they can impact the performance of the production applications running at the time.

For more information on the syscacheobjects table and how query plans are cached and used in SQL Server, see Chapter 36, "Query Analysis."

Automatic Query Plan Recompilation

Reusing execution plans for stored procedures provides a performance advantage over ad hoc SQL commands. However, stored procedures will recompile new query plans in the following circumstances:

- Whenever there is a change to the schema of a referenced table
- When an index for a referenced table is dropped
- When SQL Server activity is heavy enough to cause query plans to be flushed from cache memory
- When running `sp_recompile` on a table referenced by a stored procedure
- When specifying the `WITH RECOMPILE` option in the `CREATE PROCEDURE` or `EXEC` command
- When restoring a database containing the stored procedure or an object referenced by the stored procedure
- When shutting down and restarting SQL Server, because this flushes all query plans from memory

In addition to these reasons, SQL Server Versions 7.0 and later introduced other events that can cause stored procedures to recompile new query plans:

- When the statistics in a table have been updated
- When a sufficient amount of data changes in a table that is referenced by the stored procedure
- When a procedure interleaves DDL and DML commands
- When a procedure involves certain operations on temporary tables, such as the creation of temporary table within an `IF... ELSE` construct

Monitoring Stored Procedure Recompilation

You can monitor when stored procedures are automatically recompiled using SQL Profiler. The two events you want to monitor are located in the Stored Procedure category and are called `SP:StmtStarting` and `SP:Recompile` (see Figure 28.10).

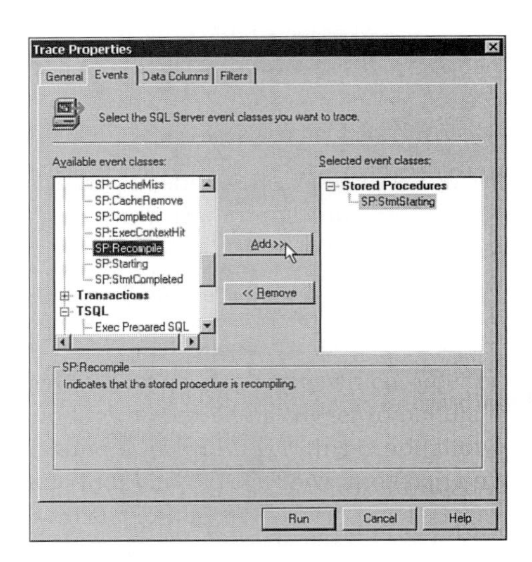

FIGURE 28.10 Adding events in SQL Profiler to monitor stored procedure recompilation.

If a stored procedure is automatically recompiled during execution, SQL Profiler will display a `SP:Recompile` event and an `SP:StmtStarting` event because the statement that caused the recompile will be displayed before and after the recompile event. For example, you can create the following stored procedure to create and populate a temporary table:

```
create proc recomp_test
as
create table #titles (title_id varchar(6), title varchar(80), pubdate datetime)
insert #titles select title_id, title, pubdate from titles
select * from #titles where pubdate > '10/1/1991'
```

If you turn on SQL Profiler and then execute the procedure, you will capture the events as shown in Figure 28.11.

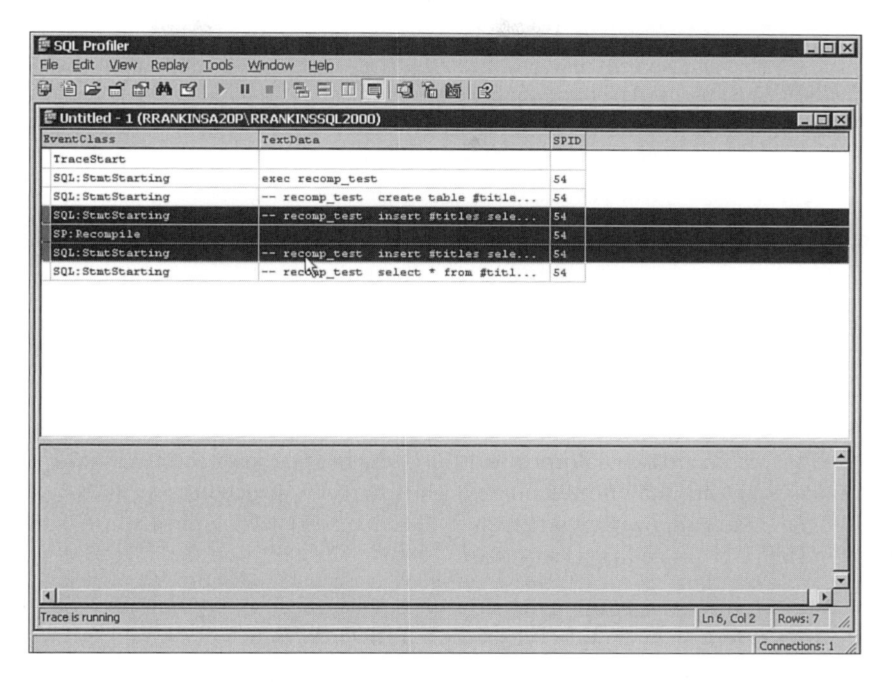

FIGURE 28.11 Recompile event captured for a stored procedure in SQL Profiler.

The key statement that causes the recompile is the insertion of rows into the temporary table. You can see this because SQL Profiler displays the statement starting event followed by a recompile event and the insert statement starting again. These statements are listed in Table 28.6.

TABLE 28.6 SQL Profiler Events for an Automatic Recompile

EventClass	TextData	SPID
SQL:StmtStarting	exec recomp_test	54
SQL:StmtStarting	-- recomp_test create table #titles (title_id varchar(6), title varchar (80), pubdate datetime)	54
SQL:StmtStarting	-- recomp_test insert #titles select title_id, title, pubdate from titles	54
SP:Recompile		54
SQL:StmtStarting	-- recomp_test insert #titles select title_id, title, pubdate from titles	54

TABLE 28.6 Continued

EventClass	TextData	SPID
SQL:StmtStarting	-- recomp_test select * from #titles where pubdate > '10/1/1991'	54

For more information on using SQL Profiler to monitor SQL Server performance, see Chapter 7, "Using the SQL Server Profiler."

Minimizing Stored Procedure Recompilation

Repeated recompiles during stored procedure execution can lead to less than optimal performance of stored procedures as a result of the overhead of the recompiles. To minimize recompiles due to row modifications in a table, write your stored procedures to meet the following guidelines:

- Execute the statement using `sp_executesql` (covered later in the "Using Dynamic SQL in Stored Procedures" section in this chapter). Statements executed in `sp_executesql` are not compiled as part of the stored procedure, so SQL Server is free to choose an existing plan for the query or create a new one at runtime without recompiling the procedure query plan.
- Execute the statement using dynamic SQL with `EXEC`. This approach will have the same effect as `sp_executesql`, but it is less efficient because it doesn't allow parameterization of the query.
- Move the statements that cause the recompilations into subprocedures. They will still cause recompilation, but they will recompile only the small subprocedure rather than the larger calling procedure.

If recompiles are occurring because of interleaved DDL and DML commands, rewrite the stored procedure to move all DML commands to the top of the procedure. When DDL operations (create table, create index, and so on) are performed in a stored procedure, a recompile will occur when the first DML statement (select, insert, update, or delete) is encountered on the table affected by the DDL.

For example, rewrite the previous stored procedure as follows:

```
create proc recomp_test
as
create table #titles (title_id varchar(6), title varchar(80), pubdate datetime)
insert #titles select title_id, title, pubdate from titles
create index idx1 on #titles (pubdate)
select * from #titles where pubdate > '10/1/1991'
return
```

Table 28.7 shows the events captured by SQL Profiler, showing two recompiles for the procedure.

TABLE 28.7 SQL Profiler Events for an Automatic Recompile

EventClass	TextData	SPID
SQL:StmtStarting	exec recomp_test	54
SQL:StmtStarting	-- recomp_test create table #titles (title_id varchar(6), title varchar(80), pubdate datetime)	54
SQL:StmtStarting	-- recomp_test insert #titles select title_id, title, pubdate from titles	54
SP:Recompile		54
SQL:StmtStarting	-- recomp_test insert #titles select title_id, title, pubdate from titles	54
SQL:StmtStarting	-- recomp_test create index idx1 on #titles (pubdate)	54 54
SQL:StmtStarting	insert [#titles____________________000100000023] select *, %%bmk%% from [#titles_____________________________000100000023]	54
SQL:StmtStarting	-- recomp_test select * from #titles where pubdate > '10/1/1991'	54
SP:Recompile		54
SQL:StmtStarting	-- recomp_test select * from #titles where pubdate > '10/1/1991'	54

These recompiles occur on every execution of the stored procedure. To minimize the recompiles, perform all DDL statements at the beginning of the procedure, if possible, before performing any DML on the affected tables, as shown in the following example:

```
create proc recomp_test
as
create table #titles (title_id varchar(6), title varchar(80), pubdate datetime)
create index idx1 on #titles (pubdate)
insert #titles select title_id, title, pubdate from titles
select * from #titles where pubdate > '10/1/1991'
return
```

The first execution of this version of the stored procedure will recompile the insert and select, but the execution plan will be reused for subsequent executions.

To minimize the recompiles due to usage of temporary tables in stored procedures, follow these guidelines:

- Make sure all statements that contain temporary table names reference temporary tables created in the same procedure and not in a calling or called procedure or created by an `EXEC` statement or `sp_executesql`.
- Ensure that all statements referencing a temporary table occur syntactically after the creation of the temporary table in the stored procedure.
- Ensure that all references to any temporary table occur prior to any `DROP TABLE` references to the temporary table in the stored procedure. Because temporary tables created in a stored procedure are automatically dropped when the procedure returns, the `DROP TABLE` command is not really necessary.
- Avoid `DECLARE CURSOR` statements that reference a temporary table.
- Don't put statements that create temporary tables within any control-of-flow commands (`IF... ELSE` or `WHILE`).

By default, SQL Server will generate new query plans for a stored procedure whenever a referenced temporary table created in the stored procedure is modified more than six times. In the event that a temporary table is modified frequently, but not in a significant manner that would affect the query plan chosen, consider using the `KEEP PLAN` option in `SELECT` statements that reference the temp table to reduce the number of recompilations. This will not prevent recompilation completely, but it will follow a more relaxed recompilation strategy similar to recompilations that occur on regular tables due to row modifications.

Forcing Recompilation of Query Plans

In some situations, a stored procedure might generate different query plans depending on the parameters passed in. At times, depending on the type of query and the parameter values passed in, it can be difficult to predict the best query plan for all executions. Consider the following stored procedure:

```
create proc advance_range
    (@low money, @high money)
as
select * from dbo.titles
  where advance between @low and @high
return
```

Assume that a nonclustered index exists on the advance column in the titles table. A search where the advance is between 1,000 and 2,000 might be highly selective, and the index statistics might indicate that less than 5 percent of the rows fall within that range, and thus an index would be the best way to find the rows. If those were the values passed on the first execution, the cached query plan would indicate that the index should be used.

Suppose, however, that if on a subsequent execution, search values of 5,000 and 10,0000 were specified. These values match against 90 percent of the rows in the table, and if optimized normally, SQL Server would likely use a table scan because it would have to visit almost all rows in the table anyway. Without recompiling, however, it would use the index as specified in the cached query plan, which would be a suboptimal query plan because it would likely be accessing more pages using the index than a table scan would.

When a lot of variance exists in the distribution of data values in a table or in the range of values passed as parameters, you might want to force the stored procedure to recompile and build a new query plan during execution and not use a previously cached plan. Although you will incur the overhead of compiling a new query plan for each execution, it typically will be much less expensive than executing the wrong query plan.

You can force recompiling the query plan for a stored procedure by specifying the `WITH RECOMPILE` option when creating or executing a stored procedure. Including the `WITH RECOMPILE` option in the `create procedure` command will cause the procedure to generate a new query plan for each execution.

```
create proc advance_range
    (@low money, @high money)
    WITH RECOMPILE
as
select * from dbo.titles
  where advance between @low and @high
return
```

If the procedure is not created with the `WITH RECOMPILE` option, you can generate a new query plan for a specific execution by including the `WITH RECOMPILE` option in the `EXEC` statement:

```
exec advance_range 5000, 10000 WITH RECOMPILE
```

Because of the performance overhead of recompiling query plans, try to avoid using `WITH RECOMPILE` whenever possible. One approach is to create different subprocedures and execute the appropriate one based on the passed-in parameters. For example, have a subprocedure to handle small range retrievals that would benefit from an index, and a different subprocedure to handle large range retrievals. The queries in each procedure are identical—the only difference is in the parameters passed to them. This is controlled in the top level procedure. An example of this approach is demonstrated in Listing 28.25.

LISTING 28.25 Using Multiple Stored Procedures As an Alternative to Using `WITH RECOMPILE`

```
create proc get_orders_smallrange
   (@lowdate datetime, @highdate datetime)
as
```

LISTING 28.25 Continued

```
select * from orders
  where saledate between @lowdate and @highdate
return
go
create proc get_orders_bigrange
   (@lowdate datetime, @highdate datetime)
as
select * from orders
  where saledate between @lowdate and @highdate
return
go
create proc range_value
   (@lowdate datetime, @highdate datetime)
as
if datediff(hh, @highdate, @lowdate) >= 12
-- if the date range is 12 hours or more, execute the bigrange procedure
     exec get_orders_bigrange @lowdate, @highdate
else
-- execute the small range procedure
     exec get_orders_smallrange @lowdate, @highdate
```

Obviously, this solution would require substantial knowledge of the distribution of data in the table and where the threshold is on the range of search values that results in different query plans. Another approach that is simpler to implement is to execute the query dynamically in an `EXEC` statement or by using `sp_executesql`. The specific query will recompile for each execution, but the main procedure containing the query will likely not need to be recompiled.

Another type of stored procedure that can sometimes generate different query plans based on initial parameters is the multipurpose procedure, usually performing different actions based on conditional branching, as in the following example:

```
create proc get_order_data (@flag tinyint, @value int)
as
if @flag = 1
     select * from orders where price = @value
else
     select * from orders where qty = @value
```

At query compile time, the optimizer doesn't know which branch will be followed because the `if ... else` construct isn't evaluated until runtime. On the first execution of the procedure, the optimizer generates a query plan for all `select` statements in the stored procedure, regardless of the conditional branching, based on the parameters passed in on the first execution. A value passed into the parameter intended to be used for searches against a specific table or column (in this example, `price` versus `qty`) might not be representative of normal values to search against another table or column.

Again, a better approach would be to break the different `select` statements into separate subprocedures and execute the appropriate stored procedure for the type of query to be executed:

```
create proc get_order_data_by_price (@value int)
as
     select * from orders where price = @value

create proc get_order_data_by_qty (@value int)
as
     select * from orders where qty = @value

create proc get_order_data (@flag tinyint, @value int)
as
if @flag = 1
     exec get_order_data_by_price @value
else
     exec get_order_data_by_qty @value
```

Using `sp_recompile`

In versions of SQL Server prior to 7.0, you used the `sp_recompile` system stored procedure when you wanted to force all stored procedures that referenced a specific table to generate a new query plan upon the next execution. This was necessary if you had added new indexes to a table or had run `UPDATE STATISTICS` on the table. However, the usefulness of this command in SQL Server 2000 is questionable because new query plans are generated automatically whenever new indexes are created or statistics are updated on a referenced table. It appears that `sp_recompile` is available primarily for backward compatibility or for those times when you want the recompilations to occur explicitly for all procedures referencing a specific table.

Using Dynamic SQL in Stored Procedures

SQL Server allows the use of the `EXEC` statement in stored procedures to execute a string dynamically. This capability allows you to do things like pass in object names as parameters and dynamically execute a query against the table name passed in, as in the following example:

```
create proc get_order_data
 (@table varchar(30), @column varchar(30), @value int)
as
declare @query varchar(255)
```

```
select @query = 'select * from ' + @table
          + ' where ' + @column
          + ' = ' + convert(varchar(10), @value)

EXEC (@query)

return
```

This feature is especially useful when you have to pass a variable list of values into a stored procedure. The string would contain a comma separated list of numeric values or character strings just as they would appear inside the parentheses of an `IN` clause. If you are passing character strings, be sure to put single quotes around the values, as shown in Listing 28.26.

LISTING 28.26 Passing a Variable List of Values into a Stored Procedure

```
create proc find_books_by_type @typelist varchar(8000)
as

exec ('select title_id, title = substring(title, 1, 40), type, price
         from titles where type in ('
       + @typelist + ') order by type, title_id')
go

set quoted_identifier off
exec find_books_by_type "'business', 'mod_cook', 'trad_cook'"
go

title_id title                                    type         price
-------- ---------------------------------------- ------------ --------
BU1032   The Busy Executive's Database Guide      business      19.9900
BU1111   Cooking with Computers: Surreptitious Ba business      11.9500
BU2075   You Can Combat Computer Stress!          business      2.9900
BU7832   Straight Talk About Computers            business      19.9900
MC2222   Silicon Valley Gastronomic Treats        mod_cook      19.9900
MC3021   The Gourmet Microwave                    mod_cook      2.9900
TC3218   Onions, Leeks, and Garlic: Cooking Secre trad_cook     20.9500
TC4203   Fifty Years in Buckingham Palace Kitchen trad_cook     11.9500
TC7777   Sushi, Anyone?                           trad_cook     14.9900
```

When using dynamic SQL in stored procedures, you need to be aware of a few issues:

- The query plan for the dynamic SQL statement is not saved in cache memory as a stored procedure query plan normally would be. The query plan will have to be generated each time the procedure is executed.

- Any local variables that are declared and assigned a value in the constructed string within an EXEC statement will not be available to the stored procedure outside of the EXEC command. The lifespan of a local variable is limited to the context in which it is declared, and the context of the EXEC command ends when it completes. For a solution to passing values back out from a dynamic query, see the section "Using OUTPUT Parameters with sp_executesql" later in this chapter.
- Any local variables declared and assigned a value in the stored procedure can be used to build the dynamic query statement, but the local variables cannot be referenced by any statements within the EXEC string. The commands in the EXEC statement run in a different context from the stored procedure, and you cannot reference local variables declared outside the current context.
- Commands executed in an EXEC string execute within the security context of the user executing the procedure, not the user who created the procedure. Typically, if a user has permission to execute a stored procedure, that user will also have implied permission to access all objects referenced in the stored procedure that are owned by the same person who created the stored procedure. However, if a user has permission to execute the procedure, but hasn't explicitly been granted the permissions necessary to perform all the actions specified in the EXEC string, a permission violation will occur at runtime.
- If you issue a USE command to change the database context in an EXEC statement, it is in effect only during the EXEC string execution. It will not change the database context for the stored procedure (see Listing 28.27).

LISTING 28.27 Changing Database Context in an EXEC Statement

```
use pubs
go
create proc db_context as
print db_name()
exec ('USE Northwind print db_name()')
print db_name()
go

exec db_context
go

pubs
Northwind
pubs
```

Using sp_executesql

If you want to have the flexibility of dynamic SQL, but the persistence of a stored query plan, consider using sp_executesql in your stored procedures instead of EXEC. The syntax for sp_executesql is as follows:

```
sp_executesql @SQL_commands, @parameter_definitions, param1,...paramN
```

sp_executesql operates just as the EXEC statement with regard to the scope of names, permissions, and database context. However, sp_executesql is more efficient when executing the same SQL commands repeatedly, and the only change is the values of the parameters. Because the SQL statement remains constant and only the parameters change, SQL Server is more likely to reuse the execution plan generated for the first execution and simply substitute the new parameter values. This saves the overhead from having to compile a new execution plan each time.

Listing 28.28 provides an example of a stored procedure that takes up to three parameters and uses sp_executesql to invoke the dynamic queries.

LISTING 28.28 Invoking Dynamic Queries in a Procedure Using sp_executesql

```
create proc find_books_by_type2 @type1 char(12),
                                @type2 char(12) = null,
                                @type3 char(12) = null
as

exec sp_executesql N'select title_id, title = substring(title, 1, 40),
      type, price from pubs.dbo.titles where type = @type',
      N'@type char(12)',
      @type = @type1
if @type2 is not null
    exec sp_executesql N'select title_id, title = substring(title, 1, 40),
          type, price from pubs.dbo.titles where type = @type',
          N'@type char(12)',
          @type = @type2
if @type3 is not null
    exec sp_executesql N'select title_id, title = substring(title, 1, 40),
          type, price from pubs.dbo.titles where type = @type',
          N'@type char(12)',
          @type = @type3
go

set quoted_identifier off
exec find_books_by_type2 'business', 'mod_cook', 'trad_cook'
go
```

LISTING 28.28 Continued

```
title_id title                                   type         price
-------- ---------------------------------------- ------------ -------
BU1032   The Busy Executive's Database Guide      business     19.9900
BU1111   Cooking with Computers: Surreptitious Ba business     11.9500
BU2075   You Can Combat Computer Stress!          business      2.9900
BU7832   Straight Talk About Computers            business     19.9900

title_id title                                   type         price
-------- ---------------------------------------- ------------ -------
MC2222   Silicon Valley Gastronomic Treats        mod_cook     19.9900
MC3021   The Gourmet Microwave                    mod_cook      2.9900

title_id title                                   type         price
-------- ---------------------------------------- ------------ -------
TC3218   Onions, Leeks, and Garlic: Cooking Secre trad_cook    20.9500
TC4203   Fifty Years in Buckingham Palace Kitchen trad_cook    11.9500
TC7777   Sushi, Anyone?                           trad_cook    14.9900
```

Note that the SQL command and parameter definition parameters to `sp_executesql` must be of type `nchar`, `nvarchar`, or `ntext`. Also, for the query plans to be reused, the object names must be fully qualified in the SQL command.

Using `OUTPUT` Parameters with `sp_executesql`

The important concept to remember about dynamic SQL is that it runs in a separate scope from the stored procedure that invokes it. This is similar to when a stored procedure executes another stored procedure. Because local variables are available only within the current scope, you cannot access a local variable declared in a calling procedure from within a nested procedure. Similarly, you cannot access a local variable declared outside the scope of a dynamic SQL statement. With stored procedures, you can work around this limitation by using input and output parameters to pass values into and out of a nested stored procedure.

If you use `sp_executesql` to execute dynamic SQL, you can use local variables to pass values both into and out of the dynamic SQL query. As described in the previous section, the second parameter to `sp_executesql` is a comma-separated list that defines the parameters you will be using within the dynamic SQL statement. Just like parameter definitions for a stored procedure, some of these parameters can be defined as output parameters. To get the values back out, define the parameter as an output parameter in the parameter list, and then specify the output keyword when passing the variable in the corresponding argument list for `sp_executesql`.

Listing 28.29 shows an example of a stored procedure that uses sp_executesql to execute a dynamic SQL query and return a value via an output parameter. You can use the parameters inside the dynamic SQL-like parameters inside a stored procedure. Any values assigned to output parameters within the dynamic SQL query will be passed back to the local variable in the calling procedure.

LISTING 28.29 Using Output Parameters in sp_executesql

```
create proc get_avg_price @dbname sysname,
                          @type varchar(12) = '%'
as

declare @dsql nvarchar(500),
        @avgval float

/**********************************************************
** build the dynamic query using the @avg and @type as
** variables, which will be passed in via sp_executesql
**********************************************************/
select @dsql = 'select @avg = avg(isnull(price, 0)) from '
               + @dbname+ '..titles '
               + 'where type like @type'

--print @dsql

/**************************************************************
** submit the dynamic query using sp_executesql, passing type
**  as an input parameter, and @avgval as an output parameter
**  The value of @avg in the dynamic query will be passed
**  back into @avgval
**************************************************************/
exec sp_executesql @dsql, N'@avg float OUT, @type varchar(12)',
                   @avgval OUT, @type
print 'The avg value of price for the titles table'
      + ' where type is like ''' + @type
      + ''' in the ' + @dbname + ' database'
      + ' is ' + ltrim(str(@avgval, 9,4))

go

exec get_avg_price @dbname = 'pubs',
                   @type = 'business'
go
```

LISTING 28.29 Continued

```
The avg value of price for the titles table where type is like 'business' in
 the pubs database is 13.7300

exec get_avg_price @dbname = 'pubs',
                   @type = DEFAULT
go
The avg value of price for the titles table where type is like '%' in the pubs
 database is 11.8130

exec get_avg_price @dbname = 'bigpubs2000',
                   @type = 'business'
go
The avg value of price for the titles table where type is like 'business' in
 the bigpubs2000 database is 15.0988
```

Autostart Procedures

A SQL Server administrator can create procedures called autostart stored procedures, which are normal stored procedures that are flagged to be executed automatically when SQL Server starts. Autostart procedures are useful to perform housekeeping type tasks or start up a background process when SQL Server starts. Some possible uses for autostart procedures include the following:

- Automatically setting permissions in `tempdb`.
- Creating a global temporary table and keeping the procedure in an indefinite `WAITFOR` loop to keep the global temp table permanently available.
- Enabling "Black Box" recording for SQL Profiler (for more information on "black box" trace files, see Chapter 7.
- Automatically starting other external processes on the SQL Server machine using `xp_cmdshell`. (Using `xp_cmdshell` is discussed in the "Extended Stored Procedures" section later in this chapter.)
- "Priming" the data cache with the contents of your critical, frequently used tables.
- "Priming" the procedure cache by executing procedures or functions you want to have compiled and cached before applications start using them.

To create an autostart procedure, log in as a system administrator and create the procedure in the `master` database. Then set the procedure startup option to true using `sp_procoption`:

```
sp_procoption procedure_name, startup, true
```

If you no longer want the procedure to run at startup, remove the *startup* option by executing the same procedure and changing the value to FALSE.

You can also set the autostart option within Enterprise Manager for stored procedures that reside in the master database. Right-click on a stored procedure in the master database and choose the Properties option to bring up the Properties dialog box. Put a checkmark in the Execute Whenever SQL Server Starts check box, and click OK or Apply to save the changes to the procedure (see Figure 28.12).

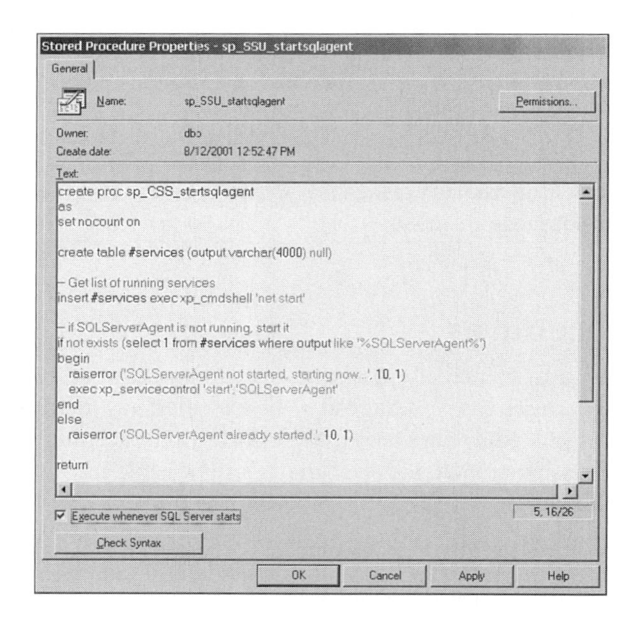

FIGURE 28.12 Using Enterprise Manager to set the autostart option for a stored procedure.

An autostart procedure will run in the context of a system administrator account, but it can use SETUSER to impersonate another account if necessary. If you need to reference objects in other databases from within the startup procedure, you'll need to fully qualify the object with the appropriate database and owner names.

Startup procedures are launched asynchronously; that is, SQL Server doesn't wait for them to complete before continuing with additional startup tasks. This allows a startup procedure to execute in a loop for the duration of the SQL Server process, or allows several startup procedures to be launched simultaneously. While a startup procedure is running, it runs as a separate active user connection.

If you need to execute a series of stored procedures in sequence during startup, nest the stored procedure calls within a single startup procedure. Nested startup procedures consume only a single user connection.

Any error messages or print statements generated by a startup procedure will be written to the SQL Server error log. For example, consider the following whimsical, but utterly useles startup procedure:

```
use master
go
create procedure good_morning
as
print "Good morning, Dave"
return
go
sp_procoption good_morning, startup, true
go
```

When SQL Server is restarted, the following entries would be displayed in the error log:

```
2001-04-21 01:30:56.03 spid3     Launched startup procedure 'good_morning'
2001-04-21 01:30:56.07 spid51    [autoexec] Good morning, Dave
```

Any resultsets generated by a startup procedure vanish into the infamous bit bucket. If you need to return resultsets from a startup procedure, write the procedure to insert the results into a table. The table needs to be a permanent table and not a temporary table because a temporary table would be automatically dropped when the startup procedure finishes executing.

The following startup procedure is an example of a procedure that could preload all tables within the Pubs database into data cache memory on SQL Server startup:

```
use master
go
create procedure prime_cache
as
declare @tablename varchar(128)

declare c1 cursor for select name from pubs.dbo.sysobjects where type = 'U'
open c1
fetch c1 into @tablename
while @@fetch_status = 0
begin
    print 'Loading ''' + @tablename + ''' into data cache'
    exec ('select * from pubs.dbo.' + @tablename)
    fetch c1 into @tablename
end
close c1
deallocate c1
return
go
```

```
sp_procoption prime_cache, startup, true
go
```

The errorlog output from this startup procedure would be as follows:

```
2001-04-21 01:44:28.93 spid3  Launched startup procedure 'good_morning'
2001-04-21 01:44:28.93 spid3  Launched startup procedure 'prime_cache'
2001-04-21 01:44:28.98 spid52 [autoexec] Good morning, Dave
2001-04-21 01:44:29.16 spid51 [autoexec] Loading 'titleauthor' into data cache
2001-04-21 01:44:29.19 spid51 [autoexec] Loading 'stores' into data cache
2001-04-21 01:44:29.19 spid51 [autoexec] Loading 'sales' into data cache
2001-04-21 01:44:29.19 spid51 [autoexec] Loading 'roysched' into data cache
2001-04-21 01:44:29.20 spid51 [autoexec] Loading 'discounts' into data cache
2001-04-21 01:44:29.20 spid51 [autoexec] Loading 'jobs' into data cache
2001-04-21 01:44:29.23 spid51 [autoexec] Loading 'pub_info' into data cache
2001-04-21 01:44:29.28 spid51 [autoexec] Loading 'employee' into data cache
2001-04-21 01:44:29.30 spid51 [autoexec] Loading 'test' into data cache
2001-04-21 01:44:29.30 spid51 [autoexec] Loading 'authors' into data cache
2001-04-21 01:44:29.32 spid51 [autoexec] Loading 'publishers' into data cache
2001-04-21 01:44:29.33 spid51 [autoexec] Loading 'titles' into data cache
```

If a startup procedure is creating problems on startup, or if you simply want to prevent startup procedures from executing, start the server using trace flag 4022. You can set the trace flag in Enterprise Manager by using the SQL Server Properties dialog box. Just right-click on the name of your server and choose Properties to bring up the SQL Server Properties dialog box. Click on the Startup Parameters button, enter the **-T4022** trace flag in the Parameter text box, and click the Add button (see Figure 28.13).

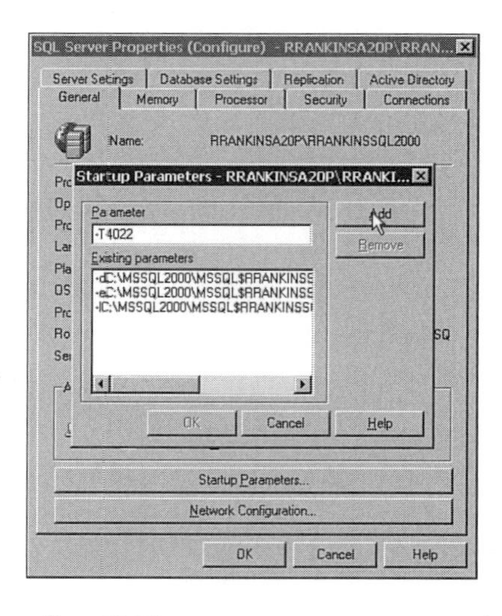

FIGURE 28.13 Setting trace flag 4022 to prevent startup procedures from executing.

Extended Stored Procedures

Open Data Services (ODS) is a server-based application programming interface (API) that you can use to create an application that is accessed just like SQL Server. Another useful application of the ODS library is creating extended stored procedures. You have probably come across stored procedures with names that begin with `xp_`. These are extended stored procedures and are not built with T-SQL commands; instead, they map to a function stored in a DLL. Extended stored procedures provide a way to extend SQL Server functionality through external functions written in C or C++ that can return resultsets and output parameters from a variety of external datasources.

Extended stored procedures are invoked and managed similarly to regular stored procedures. You can grant and revoke permissions on extended stored procedures as you do for normal stored procedures. The main difference is that extended stored procedures are created only in the master database. Unlike system procedures, however, when extended procedures are invoked from a database other than master, the procedure name has to be fully qualified with the master database name, as in the following example:

```
use pubs
go
exec master..xp_fixeddrives
```

Creating Extended Stored Procedures

Extended stored procedures are typically written in Microsoft C or Visual C++. When compiling your extended stored procedure DLLs, you need to include the srv.h header file and the Opends60.lib library file.

To create an extended stored procedure DLL in Visual C++, follow these steps:

1. Create a new Win32 Dynamic Link Library project.
2. Select the Options item on the Tools menu. In the Options dialog box, click the Directories tab and set the directory for include files and library files. Set the include files directory to C:\Program Files\Microsoft SQL Server\80\Tools\DevTools\Include and the library directory to C:\Program Files\Microsoft SQL Server\80\Tools\DevTools\Lib.
3. From the Project menu, choose the Settings option and in the Project Settings dialog box, click the Link tab. Choose the General category, and type **`opends60.lib`** in the Object/Library Modules text box.
4. Add your source files containing your custom extended procedure code to your project.
5. Compile and link your project.

NOTE

There's not enough room here to go into detail on writing C++ code. For more information on creating DLLs, refer to your development environment documentation and the Microsoft Win32 SDK documentation. The "Extended Stored Procedure Programming" section in SQL Server Books Online provides helpful examples of extended stored procedure code, as well as a reference to the extended stored procedure API calls.

CAUTION

Because the extended stored procedure DLL and SQL Server share the same address space, poorly written extended procedure code can adversely affect SQL Server functioning. Any memory access violations or exceptions thrown by an extended stored procedure could possibly damage SQL Server data areas. Extended procedures should be thoroughly tested and verified before they are installed.

Adding Extended Stored Procedures to SQL Server

To add an extended stored procedure to SQL Server for which you have created a DLL, use the sp_addextendedproc system stored procedure. Only SQL Server system administrators can add extended stored procedures to SQL Server. The syntax is as follows:

```
sp_addextendedproc [ @functname = ] 'procedure' ,  [ @dllname = ] 'dll'
```

Extended stored procedures are added only in the master database. sp_addextended procedure will add an entry for the extended stored procedure to the sysobjects and syscomments tables in the master database and register the DLL with SQL Server. To remove an extended procedure from SQL Server, use sp_dropextendedproc:

```
sp_dropextendedproc [ @functname = ] 'procedure'
```

Obtaining Information on Extended Stored Procedures

To obtain information on the extended stored procedures in SQL Server, use sp_helpextendedproc as follows:

```
sp_helpextendedproc [ [@funcname = ] 'procedure' ]
```

If the procedure name is specified, sp_helpextendedproc lists the procedure name along with the DLL that is invoked when the extended stored procedure is executed. If no procedure name is passed in, sp_helpextendedproc lists all extended stored procedures that are defined in SQL Server and their associated DLLs.

Extended Stored Procedures Provided with SQL Server

Most of the extended stored procedures that ship with SQL Server are undocumented. All extended stored procedures (or rather, the references to them) are stored in the master database. A folder in SQL Enterprise Manager under the master database lists the extended stored procedures.

If you plan to use an undocumented extended stored procedure, be careful. First, you have to find out what it does and what parameters it takes. You should also be aware that Microsoft does not support the use of undocumented extended stored procedures. Moreover, the procedure might not be included in a later version of SQL Server, or if it is included, it might behave differently.

Table 28.8 lists the categories of extended stored procedures.

TABLE 28.8 Extended Stored Procedures Categories

Category	Description
General extended procedures	General functionality. Perhaps the most useful is `xp_cmdshell`, which executes external programs and returns the output from them as a resultset.
SQL Mail extended procedures	Used to perform e-mail operations from within SQL Server.
SQL Server Profiler extended procedures	Used by SQL Server Profiler. These can also be used directly, for instance, to create a trace queue and start the trace from within a stored procedure.
OLE automation procedures	Allows SQL Server to create and use OLE automation objects.
API system stored procedures	Undocumented extended stored procedures used by the API libraries. The server cursor functionality, for instance, is implemented as a set of extended stored procedures.

Using `xp_cmdshell`

One of the most useful extended stored procedures is `xp_cmdshell`. `xp_cmdshell` can execute any operating system command or program (as long as it is a console program that doesn't require user input). The following example uses `xp_cmdshell` to list the files in a directory on the SQL Server computer's hard disk:

```
EXEC xp_cmdshell 'DIR c:\*.*'
```

`xp_cmdshell` returns a resultset of one `nvarchar(255)` column. A common use of `xp_cmdshell` is to dynamically execute a series of BCP commands to export data from a database rather than having to create a script file. (For an example, see the `BCP_out_AllTables` stored procedure in Chapter 20, "Importing and Exporting SQL Server Data Using BCP and DTS.")

`xp_cmdshell` runs synchronously. Control is not returned to the SQL Server user session until the shell command completes. This is why you have to ensure that the shell command does not prompt for user input (for example, running the bcp command and not providing a password on the command line, requiring a prompt for it).

CAUTION

After SQL Server passes off the `xp_cmdshell` command to the operating system, SQL Server cannot interact with the command. The process will wait indefinitely and it usually doesn't go away without a fight. Killing the process in SQL Server usually just leaves it in a `KILLED/ROLLBACK` state. Closing the session that invoked the `xp_cmdshell` statement won't help either. Usually, you need to stop and restart SQL Server for it to finally go away.

If `xp_cmdshell` is invoked from another database, it has to be fully qualified as `master..xp_cmdshell`. Unlike system procedures, SQL Server doesn't automatically look for extended stored procedures in the master database.

By default, permission to execute `xp_cmdshell` is granted only to users with the `sysadmin` server role. For these users, `xp_cmdshell` runs under the account that the SQL Server service is running under, with all of the rights granted to this account. At a minimum, this account has administrative rights on the machine on which SQL Server is running. If you need to access shared resources on the network via `xp_cmdshell`, the account that SQL Server is running under will also need to be a domain user account afforded the appropriate rights necessary to access those shared resources.

Permission to execute `xp_cmdshell` can be granted to other users who are not members of the sysadmin role. However, for these users, `xp_cmdshell` does not run under the SQL Server service account, but under a special account: the SQL Server Agent proxy account.

In SQL Server 6.5, if non-sysadmin users were granted permission to execute `xp_cmdshell`, by default `xp_cmdshell` commands ran under the account the SQL Server service ran under. Because this was typically an administrative account, that meant that any users with permission to run `xp_cmdshell` could invoke administrative level commands that could be potentially dangerous to the system. SQL Server administrators could close this gaping hole by setting a SQL Server option to restrict non-SA execution of `xp_cmdshell` commands to run under a special account, `SQLExecutiveCmdExec`. This was a local account whose password was known only internally to SQL Server. As a local, and not a domain account, it had no rights to access shared resources on other servers in the domain.

Microsoft recognized this potential security hole and patched it in version 7.0. Unfortunately, for many shops, the patch was too big. Non-sysadmin users could only run `xp_cmdshell` under the local account `SQLAgentCmdExec`. This account could be granted rights on the local SQL Server machine, but because it was only a local account, it could not be granted access rights in the NT Domain. Therefore, non-sysadmin users couldn't access shared directories on other servers via `xp_cmdshell`. Although this fixed a potential security hole, the net effect was that it often ended up resulting in a bigger one. For those applications that needed access to shared network resources via xp_cmdshell, some shops would change their user applications to run under a SQL Server sysadmin account!

Fortunately in SQL Server 2000, they fixed the "fix" by allowing a proxy account to be associated with SQL Server Agent instead of using a fixed account. A proxy account is a Windows account that a system administrator defines and sets a security context for within the Windows environment. When xp_cmdshell is run by a member of the sysadmin group, it still runs within the security context of the account under which the SQL Server service is running. However, when a user who is not a member of the sysadmin group runs xp_cmdshell, the commands are run within the security context of the SQL Server Agent proxy account. If no proxy account has been defined, xp_cmdshell will fail.

A proxy account is configured using the xp_sqlagent_proxy account extended stored procedure:

```
xp_sqlagent_proxy_account {'GET' | 'SET'}, 'agent_domain_name',
                          'agent_username', 'agent_password'
```

A Windows or network administrator needs to first set up a Windows or a domain account and configure it with the appropriate permissions necessary to access the resources needed by xp_cmdshell when xp_cmdshell is executed by a non-sysadmin user. Assume the network administrator sets up an account called SQLProxy with a password of "unleashed" in the SMALLWORLD domain. This account is then granted rights to a shared directory on the network that xp_cmdshell needs to access for BCP export files. To set the SQL Agent proxy account to this account, execute the following:

```
xp_sqlagent_proxy_account 'SET', 'SMALLWORLD', 'SQLProxy', 'unleashed'
```

NOTE

Setting a SQL Agent proxy account will only work in Windows NT or Windows 2000. Under Windows 9.x and Windows Me, xp_cmdshell always runs under the security context of the user account that started SQL Server. No proxy account can be set for Windows 9.x or Windows Me.

To configure the SQLAgent proxy account in SQL Enterprise Manager, right-click on SQL Server Agent and choose the Properties option. Click on the Job Systems tab. Unchecking the Only Users with SysAdmin Privileges Can Execute CmdExec and ActiveScripting Job Steps check box will bring up the SQL Agent Proxy Account dialog box, as shown in Figure 28.14. Enter the username, password, and domain name and click OK to save the changes. This same dialog box is presented if you need to modify the SQLAgent proxy account information. You can bring it up by clicking the Rest Proxy Account button in the Job Systems tab of the SQL Server Agent Properties dialog box.

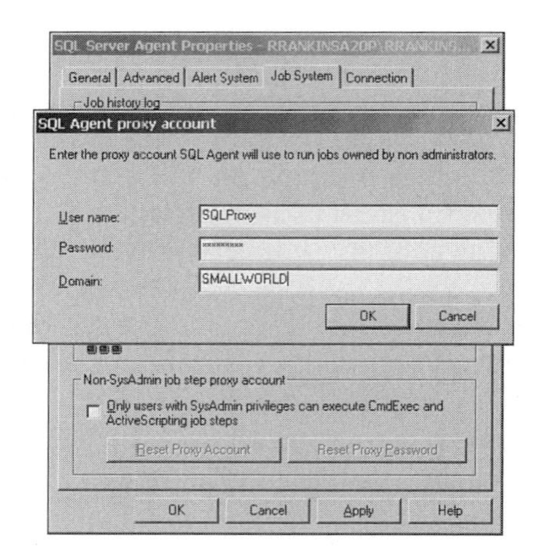

FIGURE 28.14 Setting the SQLAgent proxy account in SQL Enterprise Manager.

Stored Procedure Coding Guidelines and Limitations

Stored procedures should be treated just like reusable application code. Follow these suggested guidelines to ensure your stored procedures are solid and robust:

- Check all parameters for validity and return an error message if a problem exists.
- Be sure that the parameter datatypes match the column datatypes they are compared against to avoid datatype mismatches and poor query optimization.
- Check the `@@error` system function after each SQL statement, especially `insert`, `update`, and `delete`, to verify that the statements executed successfully. Return a status code other than 0 if a failure occurs.
- Be sure to comment your code so that when you or others have to maintain it, the code is self-documenting.
- Consider using a source code management system, such as Microsoft Visual Studio SourceSafe or PVCS, to maintain versions of your stored procedure source code.

Avoid using "`select * ...`" in your stored procedure queries. In the event someone adds columns to, or removes columns from a table, the stored procedure will generate a different resultset, which could potentially break application code.

Whenever using `INSERT` statements in stored procedures, always provide the column list associated with the values being inserted. This will allow the procedure to continue to work if the table is ever rebuilt with a different column order or additional columns are added to the table. Listing 28.30 demonstrates what happens if the column list is not provided and a column is added to the referenced table.

LISTING 28.30 Lack of Column List in Insert Statement Causes Procedure to Fail If Column Is Added to Table

```
create proc insert_publishers @pub_id char(4),
                              @pub_name varchar(40),
                              @city varchar(20),
                              @state char(2),
                              @country varchar(30)
as
INSERT INTO pubs.dbo.publishers
VALUES(@pub_id, @pub_name, @city, @state, @country)
if @@error = 0
    print 'New Publisher added'
go

exec insert_publishers '9911', 'Sams Publishing', 'Indianapolis', 'IN', 'USA'
go
New Publisher added

alter table publishers add street varchar(80) null
go

exec insert_publishers '9912', 'Pearson Education', 'Indianapolis', 'IN', 'USA'
go
Server: Msg 213, Level 16, State 4, Procedure insert_publishers, Line 3
Insert Error: Column name or number of supplied values does not match table
 definition.
```

A stored procedure cannot directly create views, triggers, defaults, rules, or other stored procedures. You can, however, execute a dynamic SQL string that creates the object:

```
CREATE PROC create_other_proc AS
  EXEC ('CREATE PROC get_au_lname AS
        SELECT au_lname from authors
        RETURN')
```

You can create tables in stored procedures. Generally, only temporary tables are created in stored procedures. Temporary tables created in stored procedures are dropped automatically when the procedure terminates. Global temporary tables, however, exist until the connection that created them terminates.

You cannot drop a table and re-create another table with the same name within the procedure unless you use dynamic SQL to execute a string that creates the table.

A stored procedure cannot issue the `USE` statement to change the database context in which it is running; the database context for execution is limited to a single database. If you need to reference an object in another database, qualify the object name with the database name in your procedure code.

Calling Stored Procedures from Transactions

Stored procedures can be called from within a transaction as well as initiate a transaction. SQL Server notes the transaction nesting level, which is available from the `@@trancount` function, before calling a stored procedure. If the transaction nesting level when the procedure returns is different from the level when it is executed, SQL Server displays the following message: `Transaction count after EXECUTE indicates that a COMMIT or ROLLBACK TRAN is missing`. This message indicates that transaction nesting is out of balance. Because a stored procedure does not abort the batch on a `rollback transaction`, a `rollback transaction` inside the procedure could result in a loss of data integrity if subsequent statements are executed and committed.

A `rollback transaction` statement rolls back all statements to the outermost transaction, including any work performed inside nested stored procedures that have not been fully committed. A `commit tran` within the stored procedure decreases the `@@trancount` by only one. Because the transaction is not fully committed until `@@trancount` returns to 0, the work can be completely rolled back at any time prior to that.

You need to develop a consistent error-handling strategy for failed transactions or other errors that occur within transactions within your stored procedures and implement this strategy consistently across all procedures and applications. Within stored procedures that might be nested, you need to check whether the procedure is already being called from within a transaction before issuing another `begin tran` statement. If a transaction is already active, issue a `save tran` statement so that the procedure can roll back only the work that it has performed and allow the calling proc that initiated the transaction determine whether to continue or abort the overall transaction.

To maintain transaction integrity when calling procedures that involve transactions, follow these guidelines:

- Make no net change to `@@trancount` within your stored procedures.
- Issue a `begin tran` only if no transaction is already active.
- Set a savepoint if a transaction is already active so that a partial rollback can be performed within the stored procedure.
- Implement appropriate error handling and return an error status code if something goes wrong and a rollback occurs.
- Issue a `commit tran` only if the stored procedure issued the `begin tran` statement.

Listing 28.31 provides a template for a stored procedure that can provide transactional integrity whether it is run as part of an ongoing transaction or run independently.

LISTING 28.31 Template Code for a Stored Procedure That Can Run as Part of a Transaction or Run As Its Own Transaction

```
/* proc to demonstrate no net change to @@trancount
** but rolls back changes within the proc
** VERY IMPORTANT: return an error code
** to tell the calling procedure rollback occurred */

create proc p1
as
declare @trncnt int

select @trncnt = @@trancount  -- save @@trancount value

if @trncnt = 0    -- transaction has not begun
  begin tran p1   -- begin tran increments nest level to 1

else              -- already in a transaction
  save tran p1    -- save tran doesn't increment nest level

/* do some processing */

if (@@error != 0) -- check for error condition
begin
    rollback tran p1  -- rollback to savepoint, or begin tran
    return 25           -- return error code indicating rollback
end

/* more processing if required */

if @trncnt = 0      -- this proc issued begin tran
  commit tran p1    -- commit tran, decrement @@trancount to 0
                    -- commit not required with save tran

return 0 /* successful return */
```

Listing 28.32 provides a template for the calling batch that might execute the stored procedure shown in Listing 28.31. The main problem you need to solve is handling return codes properly and responding with the correct transaction handling.

LISTING 28.32 Template Code for a Calling Batch or Stored Procedure That Might Execute a Stored Procedure Built with the Template in Listing 28.31

```
/* Retrieve status code to determine if proc was successful */

declare @status_val int, @trncnt int

select @trncnt = @@trancount  -- save @@trancount value

if @trncnt = 0    -- transaction has not begun
  begin tran t1   -- begin tran increments nest level to 1
else              -- otherwise, already in a transaction
  save tran t1    -- save tran doesn't increment nest level

/* do some processing if required */

if (@@error != 0) -- or other error condition
begin
    rollback tran t1   -- rollback to savepoint,or begin tran
    return             -- and exit batch/procedure
end

execute @status_val = p1 --exec procedure, begin nesting

if @status_val = 25 -- if proc performed rollback
begin         -- determine whether to rollback or continue
    rollback tran t1
    return
end

/* more processing if required */

if @trncnt = 0    -- this proc/batch issued begin tran
  commit tran t1  -- commit tran, decrement @@trancount to 0
return            -- commit not required with save tran
```

Summary

Stored procedures are one of the premier features of Microsoft SQL Server. They provide a number of benefits over using ad hoc SQL, including faster performance, restricted, function-based access to tables, protection of your application code from database changes, and the ability to simplify complex tasks into a simple stored procedure call.

It is important, however, to understand the various capabilities and limitations of stored procedures before writing much stored procedure code. Poorly written procedures will make the server appear to run sluggishly and inefficiently. Well-written procedures will run efficiently and solidly. Following the guidelines and tips presented in this chapter should help you write efficient and solid stored procedures.

If you have additional SQL code that must be executed every time a table is modified, you can put that code in stored procedures and require all applications to use the stored procedures to perform the modifications. However, this doesn't prevent a dbo or system administrator from accessing the table directly and modifying its contents without using the stored procedure. This can lead to data integrity problems. To ensure that the code is executed every time the data is modified, you can use triggers. Triggers are essentially a special type of stored procedure that is executed automatically when data modifications are performed on the table. For more information on defining and using triggers in SQL Server, you might want to read the next chapter now.

CHAPTER 29

Creating and Managing Triggers

by Chris Gallelli

IN THIS CHAPTER

- Benefits and Uses of Triggers
- Creating Triggers
- AFTER Triggers
- inserted and deleted Tables
- Checking for Column Updates
- Nested Triggers
- Recursive Triggers
- Enforcing Referential Integrity with Triggers
- INSTEAD OF Triggers

A **trigger** is a special type of stored procedure that is executed automatically as part of a data modification. A trigger is created on a table and associated with one or more actions linked with a data modification (INSERT, UPDATE, or DELETE). When one of the actions for which the trigger is defined occurs, the trigger fires automatically. The trigger executes within the same transaction space as the data modification statement, so the trigger becomes a part of it.

Benefits and Uses of Triggers

Triggers are powerful objects for maintaining database integrity because the triggers can evaluate data before it has been committed to the database. While the triggers are executing, they can perform a myriad of actions, including the following:

- Compare before and after versions of data
- Roll back invalid modifications
- Read from other tables including those in other databases
- Modify other tables including those in other databases
- Execute local and remote stored procedures

Declarative referential integrity (DRI) was introduced in version 6.0 of SQL Server. DRI is established via foreign keys that are declared as part of the table definition. These foreign keys specify columns in one table that are automatically validated against primary keys or unique index values in another table. This validation is referred to as **referential integrity (RI)**, which ensures that proper relationships between tables are enforced.

In previous releases, RI had to be performed by the client application through stored procedures or triggers. No declarative mechanism such as foreign keys was available, but triggers could provide the same type of functionality. Because of this, the vast majority of triggers written over the years were written to perform referential integrity checks.

Because DRI is available now, triggers generally handle more complex integrity concepts, restrictions that cannot be handled through datatypes, constraints, defaults, or rules. Following are some examples of trigger uses:

- Maintenance of duplicate and derived data—A denormalized database generally introduces data duplications (redundancy). Instead of exposing this redundancy to end users and programmers, you can keep the data in sync through triggers. If the derived data is allowed to be out of sync, you might want to consider handling the refresh through batch processing or some other method instead.
- Complex column constraints—If a column constraint depends on other rows within the same table or rows in other tables, a trigger is the best method for that column constraint.
- Cascading referential integrity—You can use triggers to implement actions that maintain referential integrity. This includes cascading actions and the like.
- Complex defaults—You can use a trigger to generate default values based on data in other columns, rows, or tables.
- Inter-database referential integrity—When related tables are found in two different databases, triggers can be used to ensure referential integrity across the databases.

You can use stored procedures for all of these tasks, but the advantage of using triggers is that they can fire on all data modifications. Stored procedure code or SQL in application code is only executed when it makes the data modifications. With triggers, all data modifications are subject to the trigger code, except for bulk copy and a few other non-logged actions. Even if a user utilizes an ad hoc tool, such as Query Analyzer, the integrity rules cannot be bypassed after the trigger is in place.

NOTE

Triggers and stored procedures are not mutually exclusive. You can have both a trigger and stored procedures that perform modifications and validation on that same table. If desired, you can perform some of the aforementioned tasks via triggers and other tasks via stored procedures.

Creating Triggers

You can create and manage triggers in SQL Enterprise Manager. Right-click the table for which you want to manage triggers and choose All Tasks, Manage Triggers from the pop-up menu (see Figure 29.1).

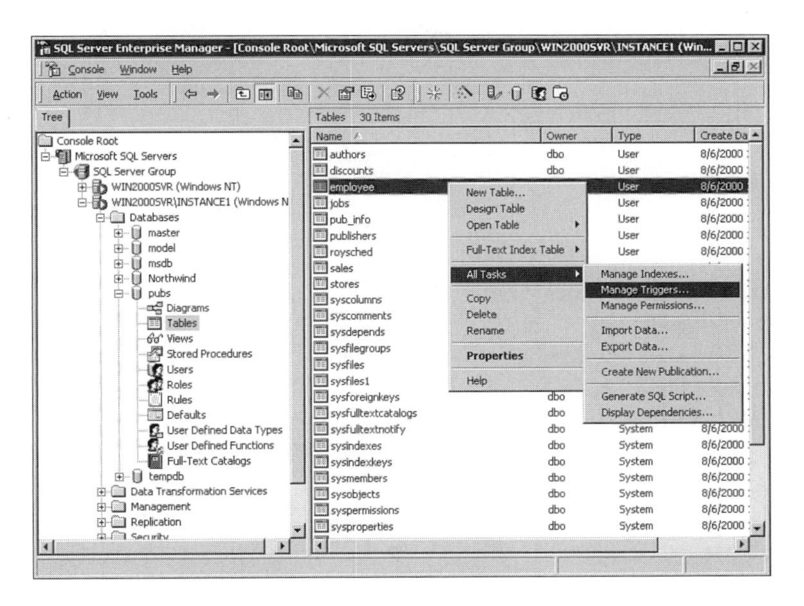

FIGURE 29.1 Managing triggers for the current table in SQL Enterprise Manager.

Figure 29.2 displays the Trigger Properties window that is displayed after you select a table for which you want to manage a trigger. It provides a basic template from which you can code your trigger.

TIP

The best way to use the Trigger Properties window is to check for a table with existing triggers and retrieve the source code for it. The code can be copied from the Properties window and pasted into Query Analyzer, which is a more powerful editing tool.

Note that if you make changes in the Trigger Properties window and click OK, SQL Enterprise Manager executes an `ALTER TRIGGER` command. If you copy and paste the source code into SQL Query Analyzer, make sure that you change `CREATE` to `ALTER` or add a drop trigger statement before the create statement.

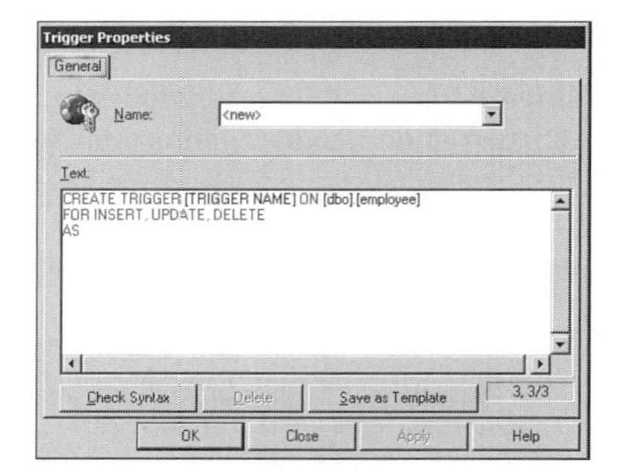

FIGURE 29.2 The Trigger Properties window.

Another alternative for managing triggers is Query Analyzer. With SQL Server 2000, a couple of new tools have been added to the Query Analyzer to facilitate the creation or modification of triggers. The first addition is the Object Browser that allows you to manage database objects, including triggers. Figure 29.3 shows the Edit menu option for triggers in the Object Browser. It also shows the resulting trigger text (shown in the background) that was generated after the Edit option was chosen for an existing trigger on the `employee` table in the Pubs database.

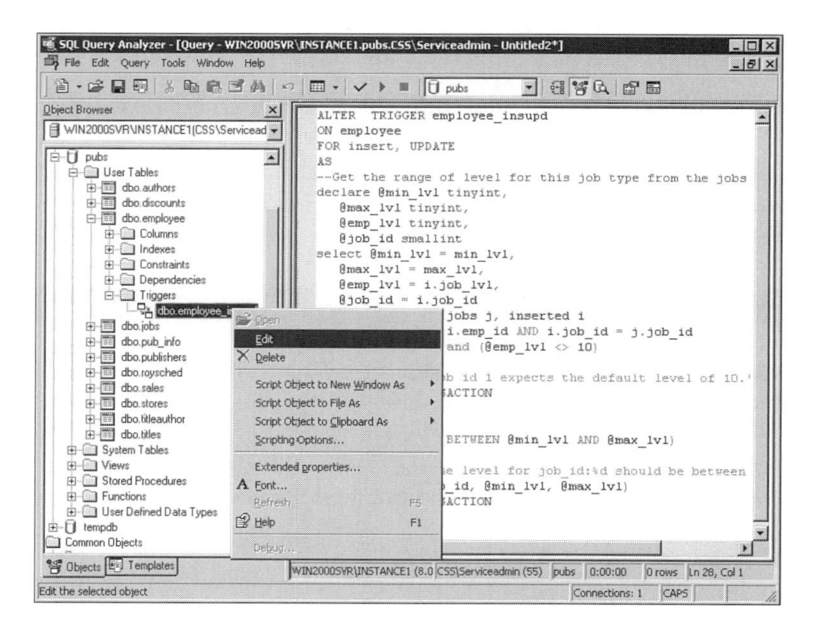

FIGURE 29.3 Managing triggers with the Query Analyzer Object Browser.

The other new Query Analyzer feature for managing triggers is a template. Templates are the basic building blocks for commonly added database objects. SQL Server 2000 added this new feature to streamline the creation of common database objects, including triggers. Figure 29.4 displays the Template tab of Query Analyzer and the available templates for trigger creation. The template text for the creation of a basic trigger is displayed in the right pane of Query Analyzer.

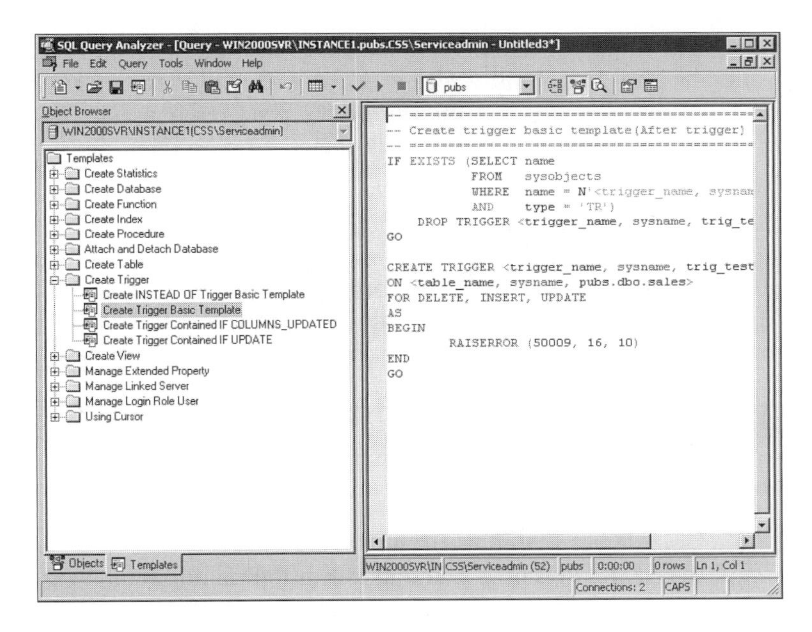

FIGURE 29.4 Query Analyzer Trigger Templates.

The template variables, such as <trigger name>, can be changed manually or replaced using the Replace Template Parameters option available on the Edit menu of Query Analyzer.

After you have your basic trigger template, you can code the trigger with limited restrictions. Almost every Transact-SQL statement that you would use in a SQL batch or stored procedure is also available for use in the trigger code. The commands that *cannot* be used in a trigger are found in the following list:

- `ALTER DATABASE`
- `CREATE DATABASE`
- `DISK INIT`
- `DISK RESIZE`
- `DROP DATABASE`

- LOAD DATABASE / LOAD LOG
- RECONFIGURE
- RESTORE DATABASE / RESTORE LOG

AFTER Triggers

An AFTER trigger is the original mechanism that SQL Server created to provide an automated response to data modifications. Prior to the release of SQL Server 2000, the AFTER trigger was the only type of trigger, and the word *AFTER* was rarely used in its name. Any trigger written for prior versions of SQL Server or documentation referring to these triggers is for AFTER triggers.

SQL Server 2000 has a new type of trigger called an INSTEAD OF trigger. This trigger will be discussed in a later section in this chapter (see the later section titled "INSTEAD OF Triggers"). The introduction of this new trigger and the inclusion of the word *AFTER* in the name of the old trigger has helped accentuate the behavior of the AFTER trigger—namely the fact that the AFTER trigger executes *after* a data modification has taken place.

> **NOTE**
>
> For the rest of this chapter, if the trigger type is not specified, you can assume that it is a reference to an AFTER trigger.

The fact that an AFTER trigger fires *after* a data modification might seem like a simple concept, but it is critical to understanding how it works. What this means is that the AFTER trigger fires after the data modification statement completes, but before the statement's work is committed to the databases. The statement's work is captured in the transaction log, but not committed to the database until the trigger has executed and performed its actions.

The trigger has the ability to roll back its actions as well as the actions of the modification statement that invoked it. This is possible because an implicit transaction exists that includes both the modification statement and the trigger it fires. If the trigger does not issue a rollback, then an implicit COMMIT of all the work is issued when the trigger completes.

Now take a look at a simple example before delving deeper into the features of the AFTER trigger:

The basic syntax for creating an AFTER trigger is as follows:

```
CREATE TRIGGER trigger_name
ON table_name
AFTER { INSERT | UPDATE | DELETE }
AS
SQL statements
```

The AFTER trigger is the default type of trigger, so the AFTER keyword is optional.

In Listing 29.1, you will create a trigger in the Pubs database that prints a message stating the number of rows updated by an UPDATE statement. You will then execute a couple of UPDATE statements to see whether the trigger works.

LISTING 29.1 A Simple AFTER Trigger

```
CREATE TRIGGER tr_au_upd ON authors
AFTER UPDATE
AS
PRINT 'TRIGGER OUTPUT: ' +CONVERT(VARCHAR(5), @@ROWCOUNT)
+ ' rows were updated.'
GO

UPDATE authors
SET au_fname = au_fname
WHERE state = 'UT'
GO
TRIGGER OUTPUT: 2 rows were updated.

UPDATE authors
SET au_fname = au_fname
WHERE state = 'CA'
GO
TRIGGER OUTPUT: 15 rows were updated.
```

Even though you did not actually change the contents of the au_fname column (setting it to itself), the trigger fired anyway. This is not a typical use of a trigger, but it gives you some insight into how and when a trigger fires. The fact that the trigger fires regardless of what is updated causes many developers to test the @@rowcount value at the beginning of the trigger code. If the @@rowcount is equal to zero, then the trigger can return without executing the remainder of the trigger code. This is a good tactic for optimizing the performance of your triggers.

NOTE

Triggers are meant to guarantee the integrity of data. Although you can return resultsets and messages in triggers, it is not recommended. The programmers who write applications that perform modifications on your table are probably not prepared to get resultsets or messages when they submit data modification statements.

The exception is returning an error with the RAISERROR command. If a trigger performs ROLLBACK TRAN, it should also execute RAISERROR to communicate the failure to the application.

Execution

You know that the AFTER trigger fires when a data modification (such as INSERT, UPDATE, or DELETE) takes place. What about the trigger's execution in relation to other events, including the execution of constraints? The following list shows those events that take place before an AFTER trigger executes:

- Constraint processing—This includes check constraints, unique constraints, and primary key constraints.
- Declarative referential actions—These are the actions defined by Foreign Key constraints that ensure the proper relationships between tables.
- Triggering action—This is the data modification that caused the trigger to fire. The action occurs before the trigger fires, but the results are not committed to the database until the trigger completes.

You need to consider this execution carefully when you design your triggers. For example, if you have a constraint and a trigger defined on the same column, any violations to the constraint will abort the statement and the trigger execution won't occur.

Firing Order

With SQL Server 2000 and SQL Server 7.0, you can specify more than one trigger for each data modification action. In other words, you can have multiple triggers responding to an INSERT, UPDATE, or DELETE. This can be useful in certain situations, but can also generate confusion because you might not know the order in which these triggers fire for the particular action.

SQL Server 2000 has alleviated some of the confusion by allowing you to specify the first and last trigger that fires for a particular action. If you have four triggers responding to updates on a given table, you can set the order for two of the triggers (first and last), but the order of the remaining two triggers will remain unknown.

The sp_settriggerorder procedure is the tool that you use to set the order. This procedure has the trigger name, order value (FIRST, LAST, or NONE), and action (INSERT, UPDATE, or DELETE) as parameters. For example, the following syntax can be used to set the firing order on the trigger used in this chapter's simple example:

```
sp_settriggerorder tr_au_upd, FIRST, 'UPDATE'
```

The execution of this command will set the tr_au_upd trigger as the first trigger to fire when an update happens to the table on which this trigger has been placed.

NOTE

It is recommended that you avoid defining multiple triggers for the same event on the same table when possible. Oftentimes, it is possible to include all of the logic in one trigger defined for the action. This can simplify your database and avoid the uncertainty of the firing order.

Special Considerations

Following are a few other points that are good to know about AFTER triggers:

- AFTER triggers can be used on tables that also have cascading referential integrity constraints. The cascading feature, which is new to SQL Server 2000, allows you to define cascading actions when a user updates or deletes a key to which a foreign key points. This new feature is discussed in more detail in Chapter 12, "Creating and Managing Tables in SQL Server."
- WRITETEXT and TRUNCATE TABLE do not fire triggers. BCP by default does not fire triggers either, but the FIRE_TRIGGERS bulk copy hint can be specified to cause both AFTER and INSTEAD OF triggers to execute.
- Triggers are objects, so they must have unique names within the database. If you try to add a trigger that already exists, an error message is returned. You can, however, ALTER an existing trigger.

AFTER Trigger Restrictions

The following restrictions apply to AFTER triggers:

- AFTER triggers can be placed only on tables, not on views.
- An AFTER trigger cannot be placed on more than one table.
- The text, ntext and image columns cannot be referenced in the AFTER trigger logic.

inserted and deleted Tables

In most trigger situations, you need to know what changes were made as part of the data modification. You can find this information in the inserted and deleted tables. For the AFTER trigger, these tables are actually views of the rows in the transaction log that were modified by the statement. With the new INSTEAD OF trigger, the inserted and deleted tables are actually temporary tables that are created on-the-fly.

The tables have identical column structures and names as the tables that were modified. Consider the following statement that you can run against the Pubs database:

```
UPDATE titles
 SET price = $15.05
 WHERE type LIKE '%cook%'
```

When this statement is executed, a copy of the rows to be modified is recorded along with a copy of the rows after the modification. These copies are available to the trigger in the `deleted` and `inserted` tables.

TIP

If you want to be able to see the contents of these tables for testing purposes, create a copy of the table, and then create a trigger on that copy (see Listing 29.2).

You can perform data modification statements and view the contents of these tables without the modification actually taking place.

LISTING 29.2 Viewing the Contents of the `inserted` and `deleted` Tables

```
--Create a copy of the titles table in the Pubs database
SELECT *
 INTO titles_copy
 FROM titles
GO
--add an AFTER trigger to this table for testing purposes
CREATE TRIGGER tc_tr ON titles_copy
 FOR INSERT, UPDATE, DELETE
 AS
 PRINT 'Inserted:'
 SELECT title_id, type, price FROM inserted
 PRINT 'Deleted:'
 SELECT title_id, type, price FROM deleted
 ROLLBACK TRANSACTION
```

The `inserted` and `deleted` tables are available within the trigger after `INSERT`, `UPDATE`, and `DELETE`. In Listing 29.3, you can see the contents of `inserted` and `deleted`, as reported by the trigger when executing the preceding `UPDATE` statement.

LISTING 29.3 Viewing the Contents of the `inserted` and `deleted` Tables When Updating the `titles_copy` Table

```
UPDATE titles_copy
 SET price = $15.05
 WHERE type LIKE '%cook%'
```

LISTING 29.3 Continued

```
Inserted:
title_id type        price
-------- ----------- --------------------
MC2222   mod_cook    15.0500
MC3021   mod_cook    15.0500
TC3218   trad_cook   15.0500
TC4203   trad_cook   15.0500
TC7777   trad_cook   15.0500

Deleted:
title_id type        price
-------- ----------- --------------------
MC2222   mod_cook    19.9900
MC3021   mod_cook    2.9900
TC3218   trad_cook   20.9500
TC4203   trad_cook   11.9500
TC7777   trad_cook   14.9900
```

When a trigger executes after more than one data modification statement (INSERT, UPDATE, or DELETE), you can identify which statement initiated the trigger by examining the contents of the inserted and deleted tables, as shown in Table 29.1.

TABLE 29.1 Determine the Action That Fired the Trigger

Statement	Contents of inserted	Contents of deleted
INSERT	Rows added	Empty
UPDATE	New rows	Old rows
DELETE	Empty	Rows deleted

NOTE

Triggers do not fire on a row-by-row basis. One common mistake is to assume that only one row is modified when coding your trigger. Triggers are set based. If a single statement affects multiple rows in the table, then the trigger will need to handle the processing of all of the rows that were affected, not just one row at a time.

One common approach to dealing with the multiple rows in the trigger is to place the rows in a cursor and then process each row that was affected one at a time. This will work, but it can have an adverse affect on the performance of the trigger. Try to use rowset-based logic instead of cursors in your triggers when possible. This will keep your trigger execution fast.

Checking for Column Updates

The UPDATE() function is available inside INSERT and UPDATE triggers. UPDATE() allows a trigger to determine whether a column was affected by the INSERT or UPDATE statement that fired the trigger. By testing whether a column was actually updated, you can avoid performing unnecessary work.

For example, perhaps a rule mandates that you cannot change the city for an author (a silly rule, I agree, but it will demonstrate a few key concepts). Listing 29.4 creates a trigger for both INSERT and UPDATE on the authors table in the Pubs database.

LISTING 29.4 Using the UPDATE() Function in a Trigger

```
CREATE TRIGGER tr_au_ins_upd ON authors
FOR INSERT, UPDATE
AS
IF UPDATE(city)
 BEGIN
 RAISERROR ('You cannot change the city.', 15, 1)
 ROLLBACK TRAN
 END
GO
UPDATE authors
SET city = city
WHERE au_id = '172-32-1176'

Server: Msg 50000, Level 15, State 1, Procedure
 tr_au_ins_upd, Line 5
You cannot change the city.
```

This is how you generally write triggers that verify the integrity of data. If the modification violates an integrity rule, an error message is returned to the client application and the modification is rolled back.

The UPDATE() function evaluates to TRUE if you reference the column in the UPDATE statement. You did not actually change the value for city, (setting it to itself), but you referenced the column in the query.

NOTE

If you created the tr_au_upd trigger on the authors table as part of the AFTER trigger example earlier in this chapter, then you might have also seen the TRIGGER OUTPUT: 1 rows were updated message. This trigger was set to be the first trigger to fire and executes in addition to the new ins_upd trigger that was added in the example from this section.

Now try a couple of INSERTs on the authors table:

```
INSERT authors (au_id, au_lname, au_fname, city, contract)
VALUES('111-11-1111', 'White', 'Johnson','Menlo Park', 1)

Server: Msg 50000, Level 15, State 1
You cannot change the city.
```

The UPDATE() function evaluated to TRUE and displayed the error message. This is expected because the trigger was created for INSERT as well, and the IF UPDATE is evaluated for both inserts and updates.

Now change the INSERT statement so that it does not include the city column in the INSERT and see what happens:

```
INSERT authors (au_id, au_lname, au_fname, contract)
VALUES('111-11-2222', 'White', 'Johnson', 1)

Server: Msg 50000, Level 15, State 1
You cannot change the city.
```

The error message is still displayed even though the INSERT was performed without the city column. This might seem counter-intuitive, but the IF UPDATE condition will always return a TRUE value for INSERT actions. This is because the columns have either explicit default values or implicit (NULL) values inserted even if they are not specified. The IF UPDATE conditions see this as a change and evaluate to TRUE.

If you change the tr_au_ins_upd trigger to be for UPDATE only (not INSERT and UPDATE), then the inserts can take place without error.

Nested Triggers

Triggers can be nested up to 32 levels. If a trigger changes a table on which another trigger exists, the second trigger is fired and can then fire a third trigger, and so on.

If any trigger in the chain sets off an infinite loop, the nesting level is exceeded, the trigger is canceled, and the transaction is rolled back.

The following error message is returned if the nesting level is exceeded:

```
Server: Msg 217, Level 16, State 1, Procedure ttt2, Line 2
Maximum stored procedure nesting level exceeded (limit 32).
```

You can disable nested triggers by setting the `nested triggers` option of `sp_configure` to `0` (off):

```
EXEC sp_configure 'nested triggers', 0
GO
RECONFIGURE WITH OVERRIDE
GO
```

After the `nested triggers` option has been turned off, the only trigger (or triggers) to fire are those that are part of the original data modification: the top-level trigger(s). If updates to other tables are made via the top-level trigger(s), then those updates will be completed but the triggers on those tables will not fire. For example, perhaps you have an `UPDATE` trigger on the `jobs` table in the Pubs database and an `UPDATE` trigger on the `employee` table as well. The trigger on the `jobs` table updates the `employee` table. If an update is made to the `jobs` table, then the `jobs` trigger will fire and complete the updates on the `employee` table. However, the trigger on the `employee` table will not fire.

The default configuration allows nested triggers.

Recursive Triggers

The recursive triggers were introduced in version 7.0. If a trigger modifies the same table where the trigger was created, the trigger will not fire again unless recursive triggers is turned on. Recursive triggers is a database option, which is off by default.

The first command of the following example checks the setting of `recursive triggers` for the Pubs database, and the second sets `recursive triggers` to `TRUE`:

```
EXEC sp_dboption pubs, 'recursive triggers'
EXEC sp_dboption pubs, 'recursive triggers', TRUE
```

If you turn off nested triggers, recursive triggers is automatically disabled, regardless of how the database option is set. The maximum nesting level for recursive triggers is the same as for nested triggers: 32 levels.

Recursive triggers should be used with care. It is easy to create an endless loop, as shown in Listing 29.5, which creates a recursive trigger on a new test table in the Pubs database.

LISTING 29.5 Error Message Returned for an Endless Loop with Recursive Triggers

```
EXEC sp_configure 'nested triggers', 1
RECONFIGURE WITH OVERRIDE
EXEC sp_dboption pubs, 'recursive triggers', TRUE
CREATE TABLE rk_tr_test (id int IDENTITY)
GO
CREATE TRIGGER rk_tr ON rk_tr_test FOR INSERT
```

LISTING 29.5 Continued

```
AS INSERT rk_tr_test DEFAULT VALUES
GO
INSERT rk_tr_test DEFAULT VALUES

Server: Msg 217, Level 16, State 1, Procedure rk_tr, Line 2
Maximum stored procedure nesting level exceeded (limit 32).
```

The recursion described thus far is known, more explicitly, as **direct recursion**. Another type of recursion exists as well, and it is known as indirect recursion. With **indirect recursion**, a table with a trigger fires an update to another table, and this table, in turn, causes an update to happen to the original table on which the trigger fired. This causes the trigger on the original table to fire again.

With indirect recursion, setting the `recursive triggers` database setting to false does not prevent the recursion from happening. The only way to prevent this type of recursion is to set the `nested triggers` setting to false, which, in turn, prevents all recursion.

Enforcing Referential Integrity with Triggers

Several options are available to enforce RI, but the trigger is still a viable alternative. The trigger provides a great deal of flexibility and allows you to customize your RI solution to fit your needs. Some of the other alternatives do not provide the same degree of customization.

TIP

If you are in a database environment in which multiple databases are used with related data, then the trigger can be invaluable for enforcing referential integrity. The trigger has the ability to span databases, and it can ensure that data rows that are inserted into a table in one database are valid based on rows in another database.

In Listing 29.6, you will re-create and populate the `customers` and `orders` tables in the sample Pubs database.

LISTING 29.6 Creating and Populating the `customers` and `orders` Tables

```
if exists (select * from sysobjects
   where id = object_id('orders') and sysstat & 0xf = 3)
       drop table orders
GO
if exists (select * from sysobjects
   where id = object_id('customers') and sysstat & 0xf = 3)
       drop table customers
GO
```

LISTING 29.6 Continued

```
CREATE TABLE customers
(customer_id INT PRIMARY KEY NOT NULL,
customer_name NVARCHAR(25) NOT NULL,
customer_comments NVARCHAR(22) NULL)
CREATE TABLE orders
(order_id INT  PRIMARY KEY NOT NULL,
customer_id INT,
order_date DATETIME,
CONSTRAINT FK_orders_customers
       FOREIGN KEY (customer_id) REFERENCES customers (customer_id))

INSERT customers (customer_id, customer_name, customer_comments)
VALUES(1, 'Hardware Suppliers AB','Stephanie is contact.')
INSERT customers (customer_id, customer_name, customer_comments)
VALUES(2, 'Software Suppliers AB','Elisabeth is contact.')
INSERT customers (customer_id, customer_name, customer_comments)
VALUES(3, 'Firmware Suppliers AB','Mike is contact.')

INSERT orders (order_id, customer_id, order_date)
VALUES(100, 1, GETDATE())
INSERT orders (order_id, customer_id, order_date)
VALUES(101, 1, GETDATE())
INSERT orders (order_id, customer_id, order_date)
VALUES(102, 1, GETDATE())

SELECT * FROM customers
SELECT * FROM orders
customer_id customer_name            customer_comments
----------- ------------------------ ---------------------
1           Hardware Suppliers AB    Stephanie is contact.
2           Software Suppliers AB    Elisabeth is contact.
3           Firmware Suppliers AB    Mike is contact.

order_id    customer_id order_date
----------- ----------- --------------------------
100         1           1998-09-17 18:29:46.943
101         1           1998-09-17 18:29:46.973
102         1           1998-09-17 18:29:46.973
```

The foreign key constraint prohibits the following:

- Inserting rows into the orders table for customer numbers that don't exist in the customers table
- Updating the orders table, changing the customer number to values that don't exist in the customers table
- Deleting rows in the customers table for which orders exist
- Updating the customers table, changing the customer number for which orders exist

You might want a cascading action instead of a restriction for the previous two actions. This would include automatically cascading the DELETE or UPDATE statement executed on the customers table to the orders table. You can do this with triggers.

Cascading Deletes

TIP

SQL Server 2000 has added a new feature that allows you to define cascading actions on your foreign key constraint. When defining the constraints on a table, you can use the ON UPDATE CASCADE or the ON DELETE CASCADE clauses, which cause changes to the primary key of a table to cascade to the related foreign key tables. Refer to Chapter 12 for further information on this option.

A cascading delete is relatively simple to create. Listing 29.7 shows a cascading delete trigger for the customers table.

LISTING 29.7 Cascading Delete for the customers Table

```
CREATE TRIGGER cust_del_orders ON customers
FOR DELETE
AS
IF @@ROWCOUNT = 0
 RETURN
DELETE orders
 FROM orders o , deleted d
 WHERE o.customer_id = d.customer_id
IF @@ERROR <> 0
 BEGIN
  RAISERROR ('ERROR encountered in cascading trigger.', 16, 1)
  ROLLBACK TRAN
  RETURN
 END
```

The following DELETE statement deletes the row for customer 1, so all three rows for that customer in the orders table should be deleted by the trigger:

```
DELETE customers WHERE customer_id = 1

Server: Msg 547, Level 16, State 1
DELETE statement conflicted with COLUMN REFERENCE
constraint 'FK_orders_customers'.
The conflict occurred in database 'pubs',
table 'orders', column 'customer_id'.
The statement has been aborted.
```

This might not be what you expected. The foreign key constraint restricted the `DELETE` statement, so the trigger never fired. The trigger in this example is an `AFTER` trigger. Therefore, the trigger never fired, and the cascading action never took place.

You have several options to get around this:

- Remove the foreign key constraint from orders to customers.
- Disable the foreign key constraint from orders to customers.
- Keep the foreign key constraint and perform all cascading in stored procedures.
- Keep the foreign key constraint and perform all cascading in the application.
- Use an `INSTEAD OF` trigger in place of the `AFTER` trigger.
- Use the new cascading referential integrity constraints.

The second option will be exploited, as shown in Listing 29.8.

LISTING 29.8 Disabling the Foreign Key Constraint to the `customers` Table So That Cascading Delete Can Occur

```
ALTER TABLE orders
 NOCHECK CONSTRAINT FK_orders_customers
GO

GO
DELETE customers WHERE customer_id = 1
SELECT * FROM customers
SELECT * FROM orders
customer_id customer_name            customer_comments
----------- ------------------------ ---------------------
2           Software Suppliers AB    Elisabeth is contact.
3           Firmware Suppliers AB    Mike is contact.

order_id    customer_id order_date
----------- ----------- --------------------------
```

The cascading took place and the foreign key constraint was disabled. A trigger for cascading updates is more complex and not so common. That will be discussed in the next section.

If you disable the constraint, you have a potential integrity problem. If rows are inserted or updated in the orders table, no verification ensures that the customer number exists in the customer table. You can take care of that with an INSERT and UPDATE trigger on the orders table (see Listing 29.9).

LISTING 29.9 Handling a Restriction with a Trigger on the orders Table

```
if exists (select * from sysobjects where id = object_id('dbo.ord_ins_upd_cust')
        and sysstat & 0xf = 8)
        drop trigger dbo.ord_ins_upd_cust
GO

CREATE TRIGGER ord_ins_upd_cust ON orders
FOR INSERT, UPDATE
AS
IF EXISTS (SELECT * FROM inserted
           WHERE customer_id NOT IN
          (SELECT customer_id FROM customers))
 BEGIN
  RAISERROR('No customer with such customer number', 16, 1)
  ROLLBACK TRAN
  RETURN
 END
```

Cascading Updates

The cascading update is tricky to achieve. Modifying a primary key, per definition, is really deleting a row and inserting a new row. That is the problem. You lose the connection between the old and the new row in the customers table. How do you know which changes to cascade to which rows?

It's simpler if you can restrict the changes to one row (see Listing 29.10) because you have only one row in the deleted and the inserted tables. You know the customer number before and after the modification.

LISTING 29.10 Cascading UPDATE in a Trigger

```
if exists (select * from sysobjects where id = object_id('dbo.cust_upd_orders')
        and sysstat & 0xf = 8)
        drop trigger dbo.cust_upd_orders
GO
```

LISTING 29.10 Continued

```
CREATE TRIGGER cust_upd_orders ON customers
FOR UPDATE
AS
DECLARE @rows_affected int, @c_id_before int, @c_id_after int
SELECT @rows_affected = @@ROWCOUNT
IF @rows_affected = 0
 RETURN -- No rows changed, exit trigger
IF UPDATE(customer_id)
BEGIN
 IF @rows_affected = 1
 BEGIN
   SELECT @c_id_before = customer_id FROM deleted
   SELECT @c_id_after = customer_id FROM inserted
   UPDATE orders
    SET customer_id = @c_id_after
    WHERE customer_id = @c_id_before
 END
ELSE
  BEGIN
     RAISERROR ('Cannot update more than 1 row.', 16, 1)
     ROLLBACK TRAN
     RETURN
  END
END
```

If several rows were updated, it's not easy to know which order belongs to which customer. You can easily modify the preceding trigger to handle the situation, where several rows change to the same value; however, this is not allowed because of the primary key on the `customers` table. Modifying several rows and changing the primary key value is rare, and you are not likely to encounter it.

NOTE

SQL Server 2000's new cascading foreign key constraints are an excellent alternative to triggers, and they are efficient. If you choose not to use the cascading feature, I still like the simplicity of constraints. That leaves handling cascading actions in stored procedures or in client applications.

Stored procedures are often a good choice because they essentially give application developers a function-based interface for modifications. If the implementation details (table structure or rules) change, client applications can be isolated from the changes, as long as the interfaces to the stored procedures stay the same. The question of how to handle a cascade is a matter of personal preference, however.

A note on cascading updates handled in a client application or stored procedure: This is a chicken-and-the-egg situation. You cannot change the primary key table first because other tables reference it. You also cannot change the referencing table because no row exists in the primary key table with a corresponding value.

The solution is to insert a new row in the referenced table with the new primary key value, change the referencing rows, and then delete the old row in the referenced table.

INSTEAD OF Triggers

SQL Server 2000 introduced a new type of trigger called an INSTEAD OF trigger. This new trigger extends SQL Server's trigger capabilities and provides an alternative to the AFTER trigger that was heavily utilized in prior versions of SQL Server.

The name of the trigger gives you some insight into how this new trigger operates. The INSTEAD OF prefix is relevant because this particular trigger performs its actions *instead of* the action that fired it. This is much different from the AFTER trigger that will perform its actions *after* the statement that caused it to fire has completed. This means that you can have an INSTEAD OF UPDATE trigger on a table that successfully completes but does not include the actual update to the table. Take a look at the following example.

The basic syntax for creating an INSTEAD OF trigger is this:

```
CREATE TRIGGER trigger_name
ON table_name
INSTEAD OF { INSERT | UPDATE | DELETE }
AS
SQL statements
```

In Listing 29.11, you will create a trigger that prints a message stating the number of rows updated by an UPDATE statement. You will then execute an UPDATE against the table that has the trigger on it. Finally, you will select the rows from the table for review.

LISTING 29.11 A Simple INSTEAD OF Trigger

```
if exists (select * from sysobjects where id = object_id('dbo.cust_upd_orders')
        and sysstat & 0xf = 8)
        drop trigger dbo.cust_upd_orders
GO
CREATE TRIGGER trI_au_upd ON authors
INSTEAD OF UPDATE
AS
PRINT 'TRIGGER OUTPUT: '
+CONVERT(VARCHAR(5), @@ROWCOUNT) + ' rows were updated.'
GO
```

LISTING 29.11 Continued

```
UPDATE authors
SET au_fname = 'Rachael'
WHERE state = 'UT'
GO
TRIGGER OUTPUT: 2 rows were updated.

SELECT au_fname, au_lname FROM authors
WHERE state = 'UT'
GO
au_fname             au_lname
-------------------- ----------------------------------------
Anne                 Ringer
Albert               Ringer
```

As you can see from the results of the SELECT statement, the first name (au_fname) column was not updated to 'Rachael'. The update statement is correct, but the INSTEAD OF trigger did not apply the update from the statement as part of its INSTEAD OF action. The only action that the trigger did is to print its message.

The important point to realize is that after you define an INSTEAD OF trigger on a table, you need to include all of the logic in the trigger to perform the actual modification as well as any other actions that the trigger might need to carry out.

Execution

To gain a complete understanding of the INSTEAD OF trigger, you must also understand its execution in relation to the other events that are happening. The following list details the key event execution relative to the INSTEAD OF trigger firing:

- Triggering Action—The INSTEAD OF trigger fires *instead of* the triggering action. As shown earlier, the actions of the INSTEAD OF trigger replace the actions of the original data modification that fired the trigger.
- Constraint Processing—This action happens *after* the INSTEAD OF trigger fires. This includes check constraints, unique constraints, and primary key constraints.

To demonstrate the trigger execution order, refer to the following trigger in Listing 29.12.

LISTING 29.12 INSTEAD OF Trigger Execution

```
CREATE TRIGGER employee_insInstead
ON employee
INSTEAD OF insert
AS
```

LISTING 29.12 Continued

```
DECLARE @job_id smallint

--Insert the jobs record for the employee if it does not already exist
IF NOT EXISTS
(SELECT 1
   FROM jobs j, inserted i
  WHERE i.job_id = j.job_id)
BEGIN
   INSERT jobs
       (job_desc, min_lvl, max_lvl)
      SELECT 'Automatic Job Add', i.job_lvl, i.job_lvl
       FROM inserted i

--Capture the identify value for the job just inserted
--This will be used for the employee insert later
   SELECT @job_id = @@identity

   PRINT 'NEW job_id ADDED FOR NEW EMPLOYEE:' + convert(char(3),@job_id)

END

--Execute the original insert action with the newly added job_id
INSERT employee
       (emp_id, fname, minit, lname, job_id, job_lvl, pub_id, hire_date)
   SELECT emp_id, fname, minit, lname, @job_id, job_lvl, pub_id, hire_date
     FROM Inserted

GO
```

This trigger can be created in the Pubs database that ships with SQL Server 2000. The key feature of this `INSTEAD OF` trigger is that it can satisfy a referential integrity constraint that was not satisfied before the `INSERT` was executed. Note the foreign key constraint on the `employee` table that references the `job_id` on the `jobs` table. The trigger first checks to see whether the `jobs` record associated with the `job_id` of the employee being inserted exists. If the `jobs` record does not exist for the inserted employee's `job_id`, then the trigger inserts a new `jobs` record and uses it for the insertion of the employee record.

If you execute the following `INSERT` statement, which has a `job_id` that does not exist, it will succeed:

```
INSERT EMPLOYEE
       (emp_id, fname, minit, lname, job_id, job_lvl, pub_id, hire_date)
   VALUES ('KNN33333F', 'Kayla', 'N', 'Nicole', 20, 100, 9952, getdate())
Go
```

That statement succeeds because the constraint processing happens after the `INSTEAD OF` trigger completes its actions. Conversely, if you were to create the same trigger as an `AFTER` trigger, the foreign key constraint would execute before the `AFTER` trigger and the following error message would be displayed:

```
INSERT statement conflicted with COLUMN FOREIGN KEY constraint
'FK__employee__job_id__1BFD2C07'. The
conflict occurred in database 'pubs', table 'jobs', column 'job_id'.
-->The statement has been terminated.
```

Notice also, with the previous `INSTEAD OF` trigger example, that the last action that the trigger performs is the actual insertion of the `employee` record. The trigger was created to fire when an employee was inserted, so the trigger must perform the actual `INSERT`. This `INSERT` occurs in addition to any other actions that justify the trigger's creation.

`AFTER` Versus `INSTEAD OF` Triggers

Now that you have seen some of the key differences between the two types of triggers, you need to decide which trigger to use. In the previous example, the `INSTEAD OF` trigger was your only option for this kind of functionality. But, often, either trigger type can be used to attain the same result.

Something you should consider when making your choice is the efficiency of the overall modification. For example, if you have a modification that will cause a trigger to fire and often reject the modification, you might want to consider using the `INSTEAD OF` trigger. The rationale is that the `INSTEAD OF` trigger will not perform the actual modification until after the trigger completes. You will not need to undo the modification. If you were to use an `AFTER` trigger in the same scenario, any modifications that were rejected need to be rolled back because they have already been written to the transaction log by the time the `AFTER` trigger fires.

Conversely, if you have a situation in which the vast majority of the updates are not rejected, then the `AFTER` trigger might be your best choice. The particular situation will dictate the preferred type, but keep in mind that the `INSTEAD OF` triggers tend to be more involved. This is driven by the fact that you can only have one `INSTEAD OF` trigger on a table, and that trigger must perform the actual data modification that fired it.

AFTER and INSTEAD OF Triggers

One other consideration when coding INSTEAD OF triggers is that they can exist on the same table as an AFTER trigger. INSTEAD OF triggers can also execute based on the same data modifications.

Take, for example, the previous INSTEAD OF trigger that was placed on the employee table in the Pubs database that ships with SQL Server 2000. An AFTER trigger exists on the employee table by default (see Listing 29.13).

LISTING 29.13 AFTER Trigger Placed on the Same Table as an INSTEAD OF Trigger

```
if exists (select * from sysobjects where id = object_id('dbo.employee_insupd')
        and sysstat & 0xf = 8)
        drop trigger dbo.employee_insupd
GO

CREATE TRIGGER employee_insupd
ON employee
FOR INSERT, UPDATE
AS
--Get the range of level for this job type from the jobs table.
declare @min_lvl tinyint,
   @max_lvl tinyint,
   @emp_lvl tinyint,
   @job_id smallint
select @min_lvl = min_lvl,
   @max_lvl = max_lvl,
   @emp_lvl = i.job_lvl,
   @job_id = i.job_id
from employee e, jobs j, inserted i
where e.emp_id = i.emp_id AND i.job_id = j.job_id
IF (@job_id = 1) and (@emp_lvl <> 10)
begin
   raiserror ('Job id 1 expects the default level of 10.',16,1)
   ROLLBACK TRANSACTION
end
ELSE
IF NOT (@emp_lvl BETWEEN @min_lvl AND @max_lvl)
begin
   raiserror ('The level for job_id:%d should be between %d and %d.',
      16, 1, @job_id, @min_lvl, @max_lvl)
   ROLLBACK TRANSACTION
End
go
```

This AFTER trigger checks whether the job level assigned to the employee falls within a valid range for the job_id that the employee was assigned. It is fired for both inserts and updates, and it can exist on the same table as the employee_insInstead INSTEAD OF trigger that was described earlier. The combined effect on an employee INSERT (with both the triggers on the employee table) is to have the following actions happen in the order listed:

1. The INSERT data modification is executed.
2. The INSTEAD OF trigger fires, completes its validation, and ultimately does the employee INSERT that is written to the transaction log.
3. Constraint Processing completes.
4. The AFTER trigger fires performing its actions on the employee record that was inserted by the INSTEAD OF trigger.
5. The AFTER trigger completes and commits the transaction to the database.

One of the key points in this example is that the AFTER trigger performs its actions on the row inserted by the INSTEAD OF trigger. It does not use the record from the original INSERT that started the trigger execution. Therefore, in this chapter's example, where the INSTEAD OF trigger generates a new job_id, the new job_id value is used in the AFTER trigger, not the job_id that was originally inserted.

Rollback and recovery need to be considered in this scenario as well, but it is beyond the scope of this discussion. This example simply shows you that these two types of triggers can be combined, and that the order of execution needs to be considered when designing your trigger solution.

Views with INSTEAD OF Triggers

One of the most powerful applications of an INSTEAD OF trigger is to a View. The INSTEAD OF trigger, unlike the AFTER trigger, can be applied to a View and triggered based on modifications to it. For more information on Views, see Chapter 27, "Creating and Managing Views in SQL Server."

The reason that this is so important is because data modifications have many restrictions when made via a View. The list is extensive, but following are a few examples:

- You cannot use data modification statements that apply to more than one table in the View in a single statement.
- All columns defined as NOT NULL in the underlying tables that are being updated must have the column values specified in the modification statement.
- If the View was defined with the WITH CHECK OPTION clause, then rows cannot be modified in a way that will cause them to disappear from the View.

The INSTEAD OF trigger is a mechanism that can be used to overcome some of these restrictions. In particular, the first restriction (related to a single table modification) can be addressed with the INSTEAD OF trigger. The INSTEAD OF trigger fires before the actual modification takes place so it can resolve the modifications to the underlying tables associated with the View. It can then execute the modification directly against those base tables. This capability is demonstrated in the following example:

```
Use PUBS
go
CREATE VIEW employeeJobs
AS
select j.min_lvl, j.max_lvl, j.job_id, j.job_desc, e.job_lvl, e.emp_id
 from employee e, jobs j
where e.job_id = j.job_id
GO
```

This creates a View in the Pubs database that joins data from the employee and jobs tables. It retrieves the job types and the associated levels, the employees assigned to the job types, and the employee's current job level. A sample set of rows from the view are shown next:

```
min_lvl max_lvl job_id job_desc                             job_lvl emp_id
------- ------- ------ ------------------------------------ ------- ---------
25      100     14     Designer                             35      ENL44273F
25      100     14     Designer                             89      PSA89086M
25      100     14     Designer                             100     KFJ64308F
25      100     12     Editor                               32      Y-L77953M
25      100     12     Editor                               35      H-B39728F
25      100     12     Editor                               100     HAS54740M
```

Perhaps you want to change the minimum job level (min_lvl) for the Designer job to 40 and at the same time set the job level (job_lvl) for any employees who have this job to 40 as well. If you execute the following update—without an INSTEAD OF trigger—against the View, you get the message shown:

```
UPDATE employeeJobs
   SET min_lvl = 40,
       job_lvl = 40
 WHERE job_id = 12
GO
View or function 'employeeJobs' is not updateable
because the modification affects multiple base tables.
```

29

To get around this problem, you can use an INSTEAD OF trigger. The trigger can decipher the update to the View and apply the updates to the base table without receiving the error. This functionality is demonstrated in the INSTEAD OF trigger found in Listing 29.14.

LISTING 29.14 Basic View with an INSTEAD OF Trigger

```
CREATE TRIGGER employeeJobs_updInstead
ON employeeJobs
INSTEAD OF UPDATE
AS
IF @@ROWCOUNT = 0 RETURN
--update the data related to the jobs table
UPDATE jobs
   SET jobs.min_lvl = i.min_lvl,
       jobs.max_lvl = i.max_lvl,
       jobs.job_desc = i.job_desc
  FROM inserted i
 WHERE jobs.job_id = i.job_id
   AND (jobs.min_lvl <> i.min_lvl
       OR jobs.max_lvl <> i.max_lvl
       OR jobs.job_desc <> i.job_desc)

--update the data related to the jobs table
UPDATE employee
   SET employee.job_lvl = i.min_lvl
  FROM inserted i
 WHERE employee.emp_id = i.emp_id
GO
```

This example has a section that checks the fields related to the jobs table and updates the base table if any of the values have changed. It also has a section that updates the employee table for the employee fields that have been changed in the View.

> **NOTE**
>
> This trigger could be enhanced to include logic to check for specific updates or to update only those employees who are assigned to the job and have a job level below the new minimum. These enhancements were not added to keep the example simple.

If you now execute the same update statement, you don't get an error message. You get the results shown here:

```
UPDATE employeeJobs
   SET min_lvl = 40,
```

```
       job_lvl = 40
 WHERE job_id = 12
GO

min_lvl max_lvl job_id job_desc                                  job_lvl emp_id
------- ------- ------ ----------------------------------------  ------- ---------
25      100     14     Designer                                  35      ENL44273F
25      100     14     Designer                                  89      PSA89086M
25      100     14     Designer                                  100     KFJ64308F
25      100     13     Sales Representative                      35      PMA42628M
25      100     13     Sales Representative                      64      CGS88322F
25      100     13     Sales Representative                      100     TPO55093M
40      100     12     Editor                                    40      Y-L77953M
40      100     12     Editor                                    40      H-B39728F
40      100     12     Editor                                    40      HAS54740M
```

Notice that the Editor job now has a minimum level (`min_lvl`) equal to 40, and that all of the employees who have that job level (`job_lvl`) are also set to 40.

You can see the added flexibility that you get by using the `INSTEAD OF` trigger on a basic View. This flexibility is also applicable to a more sophisticated View called a Distributed Partitioned View. With this type of View, data for the View can be partitioned across different servers. This gives you the ability to scale your database solution and still have a single view of the data that appears as one table.

You can make data modifications via a Distributed Partitioned View, but some restrictions exist. In the case in which the requirements are not met for updating the View, the `INSTEAD OF` trigger can be used to bypass these restrictions; this is similar to the previous example.

For a more in-depth discussion of Distributed Partitioned Views, see Chapter 21, "Administering Very Large SQL Server Databases."

`INSTEAD OF` Trigger Restrictions

You have seen many of the capabilities of `INSTEAD OF` triggers, but they also have limitations. The following list shows you some of them:

- `INSTEAD OF` triggers do not support recursion. This means that they cannot call themselves regardless of the setting of the Recursive Triggers database option. For example, if an `INSERT` is executed on a table that has an `INSTEAD OF` trigger and the `INSTEAD OF` trigger performs an `INSERT` on this same table, then the `INSTEAD OF` trigger for this `INSERT` will not fire for a second time. Any `AFTER` triggers defined on the same table for `INSERT` will fire based on the INSTEAD OF trigger `INSERT`.

- You can define only one `INSTEAD OF` trigger for each action on a given table. Therefore, you can have a maximum of three `INSTEAD OF` triggers for each table: one for `INSERT`, one for `UPDATE`, and one for `DELETE`.
- A table cannot have an `INSTEAD OF` trigger and a foreign key constraint with `CASCADE` defined for the same action. For example, you cannot have an `INSTEAD OF` trigger defined for delete on a given table as well as a foreign key with a `CASCADE DELETE` definition. You will receive an error if you attempt to do this. In this situation, you could have `INSTEAD OF` triggers defined on `INSERT` and `UPDATE` without receiving an error.

Summary

Triggers are one of the most powerful tools for ensuring the quality of the data in your database. The range of commands that can be executed from within them and their ability to automatically fire give them a distinct role in defining a sound database solution.

The next chapter, "User-Defined Functions," covers a new set of subroutines that allow users to expand upon the built-in functions that are defined as part of the Transact-SQL language.

CHAPTER 30

User-Defined Functions

by Ray Rankins

IN THIS CHAPTER

- Why Use User-Defined Functions?
- Types of Functions
- Creating and Managing Functions
- System-Wide Table Valued Functions
- Rewriting Stored Procedures as Functions

SQL Server provides a number of predefined functions built in to Transact-SQL. (These functions are covered in more depth in Chapter 26, "Using Transact-SQL in SQL Server 2000.") The supplied functions help extend the capabilities of Transact-SQL, providing the ability to perform string manipulation, mathematical calculations, datatype conversions, and so on, within your T-SQL code. Although SQL Server provides a pretty extensive set of functions, there are always times when you wish you had a function that is not provided. You could always create a stored procedure to do custom processing, but you can't use the result of a stored procedure in a where clause or as a column in a select list. If only you could create your own functions.

In SQL Server 2000 you can, with the ability to create user-defined functions. User-defined functions can return a single scalar value like the built-in functions, or can return a result set as a table variable. (For more information on table variables, see Chapter 26.)

This chapter takes a look at how to create and use user-defined functions as well as when you might want to rewrite stored procedures as functions.

Why Use User-Defined Functions?

The main benefit of user-defined functions is that you are no longer limited to just the functions that SQL Server provides. For example, the `getdate()` function returns both a date component and a time component, with a time down to the milliseconds. What if you wanted it to return just the date with the time always set to midnight? In that case, you would have to pass the result from getdate() through some other functions to zero out the time component. The following is a possible solution:

```
select convert(datetime, convert(char(10), getdate(), 110))
```

Any time you want just the date with the time always set to midnight, you have to perform the same conversion operation. Alternatively, you can create a user-defined function that performs the operations on a date value and returns the date with a time value of midnight. You could then use that function in your select lists, set clauses of update statements, values clauses for inserts, as default values, and so on, instead of having to perform the more complex conversion each time. For example, the following query uses a user-defined function, getdateonly(), to return the current date with a time of midnight:

```
select dbo.getdateonly(getdate())
```

The following examples show how you can use the function in other statements:

```
CREATE TABLE Orders (
       OrderID int IDENTITY (1, 1) NOT NULL Primary Key,
       CustomerID nchar (5) COLLATE SQL_Latin1_General_CP1_CI_AS NULL ,
       EmployeeID int NULL ,
       OrderDate datetime NULL default dbo.getdateonly(getdate()),
       RequiredDate datetime NULL ,
       ShippedDate datetime NULL
)
go

insert Orders (CustomerID, EmployeeID, RequiredDate)
    values ('BERGS', 3, dbo.getdateonly(getdate() + 7))
go

update Orders
     set ShippedDate = dbo.getdateonly(getdate())
     where OrderID = 1
go

select OrderDate,
       RequiredDate,
       ShippedDate
    from Orders
  where OrderDate = dbo.getdateonly(getdate())
go

OrderDate                 RequiredDate              ShippedDate
------------------------- ------------------------- -------------------------
2001-05-23 00:00:00.000   2001-05-30 00:00:00.000   2001-05-23 00:00:00.000
```

If you use the new getdateonly() function consistently, it makes it easier to search against datetime values because you don't have to concern yourself with the time component. Without the getdateonly() function, you might have to write the previous query as follows to make sure you find all records for a particular day:

```
select OrderDate,
       RequiredDate,
       ShippedDate
    from Orders
  where OrderDate >= convert(varchar(10), getdate(), 110)
    and OrderDate < convert(varchar(10), getdate() + 1, 110)
```

See how much easier the user-defined function makes things?

User-defined functions can accept 0–1024 input parameters, but can return only a single result: either a scalar value or a table result. Functions that return a table can be used in queries anywhere a table can be used, including joins, subqueries, and so on. The following are a couple examples of using a table-valued function that returns a list of valid book types:

```
select * from dbo.valid_book_types()
go
insert titles
select * from newtitles
where type in (select * from dbo.valid_book_types())
```

Essentially, you have reduced a query to a simple function that you can now use anywhere a table can be referenced.

With a few restrictions, which will be covered later in this chapter in the "Creating Functions" section, you can write all types of functions in SQL Server to perform various calculations or routines. For example, you could write a more robust soundex() function, a function to return the factorial of a number, an address comparison function, a function that returns a valid list of code values, a function to determine the number of days that items are backordered, a function to return the average price of all books, and so on. The possibilities are nearly endless, and user-defined functions significantly increase the capabilities and flexibility of Transact-SQL.

Types of Functions

Officially, SQL Server supports three types of user-defined functions:

- Scalar functions
- Inline table-valued functions
- Multistatement table-valued functions

The next few sections take an in-depth look at the differences between the function types and how and where you can use them.

Scalar Functions

Scalar functions are like the built-in functions provided with SQL Server. They return a single scalar value that can be used anywhere a constant expression can be used in a query, as you saw in the previous example of the `getdateonly()` function.

Scalar functions typically take one or more arguments and return a value of a specified datatype. All functions must return a result using the `RETURN` statement. The value to be returned can be contained in a local variable defined within the function, or the value can be computed in the return statement. The following two functions are variations of a function that returns the average price for a specified type of book from the titles table:

```
CREATE FUNCTION AverageBookPrice(@booktype varchar(12) = '%')
RETURNS money
AS
BEGIN
    DECLARE @avg money
    SELECT @avg = avg(price)
    FROM titles
    WHERE type like @booktype

    RETURN @avg
END
go


CREATE FUNCTION AverageBookPrice2(@booktype varchar(12) = '%')
RETURNS money
AS
BEGIN

    RETURN ( SELECT avg(price)
             FROM titles
             WHERE type like @booktype)
END
```

As mentioned earlier in this chapter, the scalar functions can be used anywhere a constant expression can be used. For example, SQL Server doesn't allow aggregate functions in a `WHERE` clause unless they are contained in a subquery. The `AvgBookPrice()` function lets you compare against the average price without having to use a subquery:

```
select title_id, type, price from titles
where price > dbo.AverageBookPrice('popular_comp')
go

title_id type         price
-------- ------------ --------------------
PC1035   popular_comp              22.9500
PS1372   psychology                21.5900
```

When invoking a user-defined scalar function, you must include the owner name. The owner name is typically the name of the user that created the function. If you omit the owner name, you will see the following error, even if the function is owned by dbo and is the only instance of such a function in the database:

```
select AverageBookPrice('popular_comp')
go

Server: Msg 195, Level 15, State 10, Line 1
'AverageBookPrice' is not a recognized function name.
```

You can return the value from a user-defined scalar function into a local variable in two ways. You can assign the result to a local variable using the SET statement or an assignment select, or you can use the EXEC statement. The following commands are functionally equivalent:

```
declare @avg1 money,
        @avg2 money,
        @avg3 money
select @avg1 = dbo.AverageBookPrice('popular_comp')
set @avg2 = dbo.AverageBookPrice('popular_comp')
exec @avg3 = dbo.AverageBookPrice 'popular_comp'
select @avg1 as avg1, @avg2 as avg2, @avg3 as avg3
go

Warning: Null value is eliminated by an aggregate or other SET operation.
avg1                 avg2                 avg3
-------------------- -------------------- --------------------
             21.4750              21.4750              21.4750
```

Notice, however, that when using a function in an EXEC statement, it is invoked similarly to a stored procedure and no parentheses are used around the function parameters. Also, when invoked in the EXEC statement, the function generated the warning message `Warning: Null value is eliminated by an aggregate or other SET operation.` This warning wasn't generated when invoked in the SET or SELECT statement. To avoid confusion, stick to using the EXEC statement for stored procedures and invoke scalar functions as you would normally invoke a SQL Server built-in function.

Table-Valued Functions

Table-valued user-defined functions return a rowset instead of a single scalar value. You can invoke a table-valued function in the FROM clause of a SELECT statement, just as you would a table or view. In some situations, a table-valued function can almost be thought of as a view that accepts parameters so the result set is determined dynamically. A table-valued function specifies the keyword TABLE in its RETURNS clause. Table-valued functions are of two types: inline and multistatement. What the two types return and the way they are invoked are the same. The only real difference is the way the function is written to return the rowset. The next couple of sections look at each of these types of table-valued functions.

Inline Table-Valued Functions

An inline table-valued function specifies only the TABLE keyword in the RETURNS clause without table definition information. The code inside the function is a single RETURN statement that invokes a SELECT statement.

For example, you could create an inline table-valued function that returns a rowset of all book types and the average price for each type where the average price exceeds the value passed into the function:

```
CREATE FUNCTION AveragePricebyType (@price money = 0.0)
RETURNS table
AS

    RETURN ( SELECT type, avg(price) as avg_price
             FROM titles
             group by type
             having avg(price) > @price)
```

You can invoke the function by referencing it in a FROM clause as you would for a table or view:

```
select * from AveragePricebyType (15.00)
go

type         avg_price
------------ ---------------------
popular_comp              21.4750
trad_cook                 15.9633
```

Notice that when you invoke a table-valued function, the owner name does not have to be specified as it does with a user-defined scalar function.

Multistatement Table-Valued Functions

Multistatement table-valued functions differ from inline functions in two major ways:

- The RETURNS clause specifies a table variable and its definition.
- The body of the function contains multiple statements, at least one of which populates the table variable with data values.

Before getting into an example of a multistatement table-valued function, this chapter will briefly discuss table variables. (For more information on table variables, see Chapter 26.)

The table datatype is defined in the RETURNS clause. The syntax to define the table variable is similar to the CREATE TABLE syntax. Note that the name of the variable comes before the TABLE keyword:

```
RETURNS @variable TABLE ( column definition | table_constraint [, ...] )
```

The scope of the table variable is limited to the function in which it is defined. While the contents of the table variable are returned as the function result, the table variable itself cannot be accessed or referenced outside the function itself.

Within the function, table variables can be treated like a regular table. Any SELECT, INSERT, UPDATE, or DELETE statement can be performed on the rows in a table variable, except for SELECT INTO and an INSERT where the result set to be inserted is from a stored procedure, as in the following example:

```
INSERT INTO table_variable EXEC stored_procedure
```

The following example defines the inline table-valued function AveragePricebyType() as a multistatement table-valued function:

```
CREATE FUNCTION AveragePricebyType2 (@price money = 0.0)
RETURNS @table table (type varchar(12) null, avg_price money null)
AS
begin
    insert @table
       SELECT type, avg(price) as avg_price
             FROM titles
             group by type
             having avg(price) > @price
    return
end
```

Notice the main differences between this version and the inline version. In the multistatement version, you had to define the structure of the table rowset you are returning and also had to include the BEGIN and END statements as wrappers around the multiple statements that the function can contain. Other than that, both functions are invoked the same way and return the same rowset:

```
select * from AveragePricebyType2 (15.00)
go

type         avg_price
------------ --------------------
popular_comp              21.4750
trad_cook                 15.9633
```

Why use multistatement table-valued functions instead of inline table-valued functions? The main reason is if you need to perform further inserts, updates, or deletes on the contents of the table variable before returning a result set, or if you need to perform additional processing on the input parameters to the function before invoking the query to populate the table variable.

Creating and Managing Functions

The preceding sections of this chapter have already shown examples of creating functions. In this section, we'll discuss in more detail the CREATE FUNCTION syntax and what types of operations are allowed in functions. This section will also show you how to create and manage functions using SQL Enterprise Manager and SQL Query Analyzer.

Creating Functions

Functions are created using Transact-SQL. The Transact-SQL code can be entered in isql, osql, Query Analyzer, or any other third-party query tool that allows you to enter ad hoc T-SQL code. This section first looks at the basic syntax for creating functions, and then looks at how you can create functions using the features of Enterprise Manager and Query Analyzer.

T-SQL

The syntax for the create function command for scalar functions is as follows:

```
CREATE FUNCTION [ owner_name. ] function_name
    ( [ { @parameter_name scalar_datatype [ = default ] } [ ,...n ] ] )
RETURNS scalar_datatype
[ WITH {ENCRYPTION , SCHEMABINDING}
[ AS ]
BEGIN
    SQL_Statements
    RETURN scalar_expression
END
```

The syntax for the create function command for inline table-valued functions is as follows:

```
CREATE FUNCTION [ owner_name. ] function_name
    ( [ { @parameter_name scalar_datatype [ = default ] } [ ,...n ] ] )
RETURNS TABLE
[ WITH {ENCRYPTION , SCHEMABINDING}
[ AS ]
RETURN [ ( ] select-stmt [ ) ]
```

The syntax for the create function command for multistatement table-valued functions is as follows:

```
CREATE FUNCTION [ owner_name. ] function_name
    ( [ { @parameter_name scalar_datatype [ = default ] } [ ,...n ] ] )
RETURNS @table_variable TABLE ( { column_definition | table_constraint } [ ,...n ] )
[ WITH {ENCRYPTION , SCHEMABINDING}
[ AS ]
BEGIN
    SQL_Statments
    RETURN
END
```

The types of SQL statements that are allowed in a function include:

- `DECLARE` statements to define variables and cursors that are local to the function.
- Assignments of values to variables local to the function using the `SET` command or an assignment select.
- Cursor operations on local cursors that are declared, opened, closed, and deallocated within the function. `FETCH` statements must assign values to local variables using the `INTO` clause.
- Control-of-flow statements such as `IF`, `ELSE`, `WHILE`, `GOTO`, and so on.
- `UPDATE`, `INSERT`, and `DELETE` statements modifying table variables that are defined within the function.
- `EXECUTE` statements that call an extended stored procedure. (Any results returned by the extended stored procedure are discarded.)

If you specify the `ENCRYPTION` option, the SQL statements used to define the function will be stored encrypted in the `syscomments` table. This prevents anyone from viewing the function source code in the database.

NOTE

If you choose to encrypt the function code, be sure to save a copy of the script used to create the function to a file outside the database in case you ever need to modify the function or re-create it. After the source code for the function is encrypted, you cannot extract the original unencrypted source code from the database.

If a function is created with the SCHEMABINDING option, then the database objects that the function references cannot be altered or dropped unless the function is dropped first, or the function is altered and the SCHEMABINDING option is not specified. A CREATE FUNCTION statement with the SCHEMABINDING option specified will fail unless all of the following conditions are met:

- Any user-defined functions and views referenced within the function are also schema-bound.
- Any objects referenced by the function must be referenced using a two-part name (*owner.object_name*).
- The function and the objects it references must belong to the same database.
- The user executing the CREATE FUNCTION statement has REFERENCES permission on all database objects that the function references.

The following example creates a function with the SCHEMABINDING option specified:

```
CREATE FUNCTION AveragePricebyType2 (@price money = 0.0)
RETURNS @table table (type varchar(12) null, avg_price money null)
with schemabinding
AS
begin
    insert @table
       SELECT type, avg(price) as avg_price
             FROM dbo.titles
             group by type
             having avg(price) > @price
    return
end
```

The following example shows what happens if you try to modify a column in the titles table that is referenced by the function:

```
alter table titles alter column price smallmoney null
go

Server: Msg 5074, Level 16, State 3, Line 1
The object 'AveragePricebyType2' is dependent on column 'price'.
```

```
Server: Msg 4922, Level 16, State 1, Line 1
ALTER TABLE ALTER COLUMN price failed because one or more objects access this column.
```

The SQL statements within a function cannot generate side effects; that is, the function cannot generate permanent changes to any resource whose scope extends beyond the function. For example, a function cannot modify data in a table, operate on cursors that are not local to the function, create or drop database objects, issue transaction control statements, or generate a result set that is returned to the user. The only changes that can be made by the SQL statements in a function are to the objects that are local to the function, such as local cursors or variables.

In addition, user-defined functions cannot invoke built-in functions that can return different data values on each call. These are referred to as nondeterministic functions. For example, the `GETDATE()` function is considered nondeterministic because even though it is always invoked with the same argument, it returns a different value each time it is executed. Nondeterministic built-in functions that are not allowed in user-defined functions include the following:

- @@CONNECTIONS
- @@CPU_BUSY
- @@ERROR
- @@IDLE
- @@IO_BUSY
- @@MAX_CONNECTIONS
- @@PACK_RECEIVED
- @@PACK_SENT
- @@PACKET_ERRORS
- @@TIMETICKS
- @@TOTAL_ERRORS
- @@TOTAL_READ
- @@TOTAL_WRITE
- GETDATE()
- GetUTCDate()
- NEWID()
- RAND()
- TEXTPTR()

This is why the `getdateonly()` function created earlier in this chapter must be passed the date value and cannot invoke the `getdate()` function directly. This limitation actually helps to extend the functionality of the `getdateonly()` function because it now can be used to strip the time component off of any date expression instead of just returning the current date.

Creating Functions in Enterprise Manager

To create a function in Enterprise Manager, right-click the database in which you want to create the function, move the cursor to the New menu option, and then choose the New User-Defined Function option from the menu list. Alternatively, you can open the database folder, right-click the User-Defined Functions folder, and choose the New User-Defined Function option. Either approach will bring up the User-Defined Function Properties window shown in Figure 30.1.

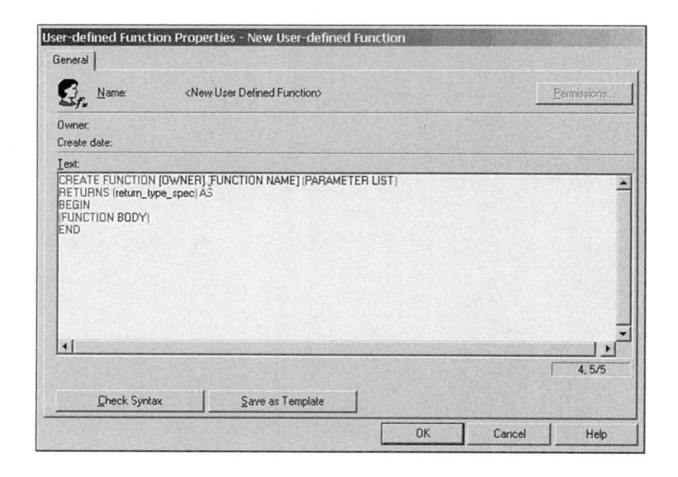

FIGURE 30.1 The New User-Defined Function Properties window.

The Properties window presents you with a basic template for creating a function. You simply fill in the function name and return type spec and function body, coding it just as you would in Transact-SQL. When the information is complete, you can check the syntax before creating the function by clicking the Check Syntax button. Click OK when you are ready to create the function.

Creating Functions in Query Analyzer

You can also create user-defined functions from predefined function templates using Query Analyzer. To open a function template, select File, New from the menu. This will bring up a dialog box with a list of folders of templates. Double-click the Create Function Folder to bring up a list of function templates from which to choose. Currently, SQL Server has three templates:

- Create Inline Function
- Create Scalar Function
- Create Table Function

Double-click the template for the type of function you want to create, or select the template and click the OK button and you will be presented with a Query Analyzer window with the appropriate template code, as shown in Figure 30.2.

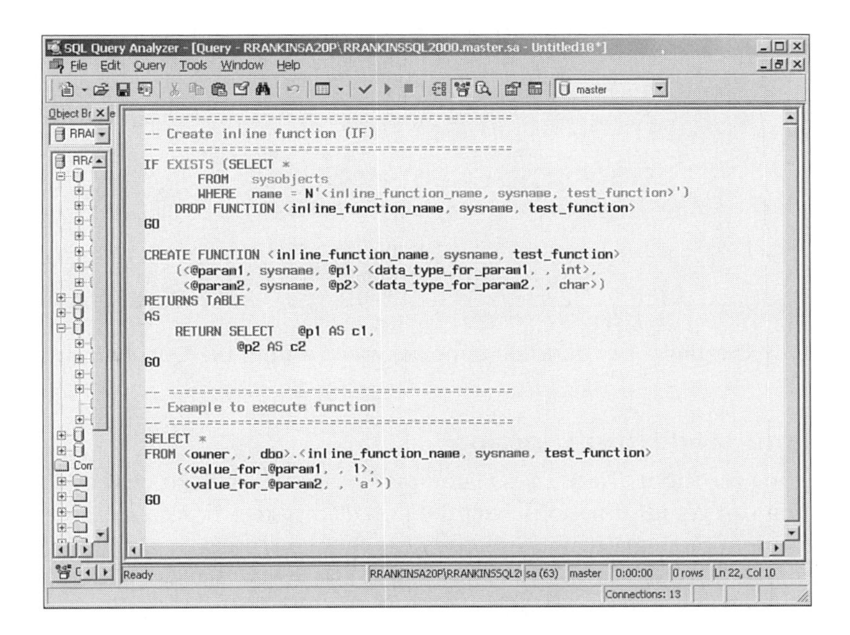

FIGURE 30.2 A Query Analyzer window populated with template code for a function.

Modify the template code as necessary to name the function and to specify the parameters, return value, and function body. When you are finished, execute the contents of the window to create the function. Note that the template also contains template code for executing or testing the created function. You will need to edit, delete, or comment this code out before creating the function to avoid having it generate a syntax error when SQL Server attempts to execute it after creating the function. When you have created the function successfully, it is recommended that you save the source code to a file by choosing the Save or Save As option from the File menu. This way, you can re-create the function from the file if it is accidently dropped from the database.

A quicker way to bring up a function template is to click the drop-down arrow on the New Document icon in the Query Analyzer toolbar and scroll down to the Create Function option, which brings up a menu of function templates from which to choose (see Figure 30.3).

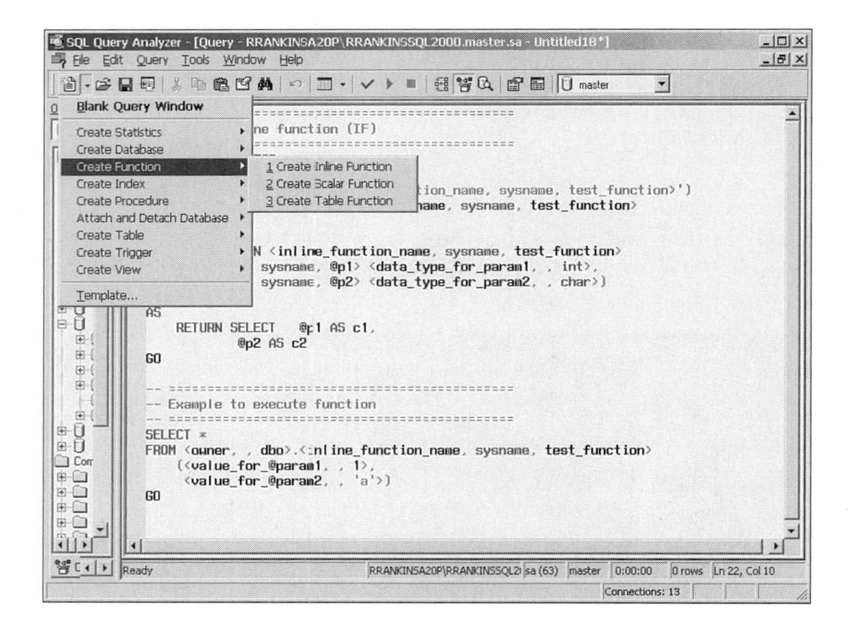

FIGURE 30.3 Creating a new function template window from the Query Analyzer toolbar.

Viewing and Modifying Functions

Besides creating functions, Transact-SQL commands are also used to view and modify functions. You can get information using the provided system procedures and queries against the system catalog. This section describes these methods.

Viewing Functions with Transact-SQL

To view the source code for a user-defined function, you can use the `sp_helptext` procedure:

```
exec sp_helptext getdateonly
go

Text
------------------------------------------------------------------------
create function dbo.getdateonly(@datetime datetime)
returns datetime
as
begin
declare @date datetime
set @date = convert(datetime, convert(char(10), @datetime, 110))
return @date
end
```

In addition to sp_helptext, you can write queries against the INFORMATION_SCHEMA view routines to display the source code for a function:

```
select routine_definition
from INFORMATION_SCHEMA.routines
where routine_name = 'getdateonly'
go

routine_definition
-----------------------------------------------------------------------------
create function dbo.getdateonly(@datetime datetime)
returns datetime
as
begin
declare @date datetime
set @date = convert(datetime, convert(char(10), @datetime, 110))
return @date
end
```

If you want to display information about the input parameters for a function, use the INFORMATION_SCHEMA view PARAMETERS. For scalar functions, the view will also display information for the return parameter, which will have an ordinal position of 0 and no parameter name:

```
select substring(parameter_name,1,30) as parameter_name,
       substring(datatype, 1, 30) as datatype,
       Parameter_mode,
       ordinal_position
from INFORMATION_SCHEMA.parameters
where specific_name = 'getdateonly'
order by ordinal_position
go

parameter_name       datatype      Parameter_mode ordinal_position
-------------------- ------------- -------------- ----------------
                     datetime      OUT                           0
@datetime            datetime      IN                            1
```

If you want to display information about the result columns returned by a table-valued function, use the INFORMATION_SCHEMA view ROUTINE_COLUMNS:

```
select substring(column_name, 1, 30) as column_name,
       substring (datatype, 1, 20)
            + case when character_maximum_length is not null
                then '(' + cast(character_maximum_length as varchar(4)) + ')'
```

30

```
                    else ''
                    end
                as datatype,
        numeric_precision,
        numeric_scale,
        ordinal_position
from INFORMATION_SCHEMA.routine_columns
where table_name = 'AveragePricebyType'
order by ordinal_position
go

column_name      datatype    numeric_precision numeric_scale ordinal_position
---------------- ----------- ----------------- ------------ ----------------
type             char(12)                    0 NULL                       1
avg_price        money                      19            4               2
```

Additionally, SQL Server provides the OBJECTPROPERTY function, which you can use to get information about your functions. One of the things you can find out is whether the function is a multistatement table function, an inline function, or a scalar function. The OBJECTPROPERTY function accepts an object ID and an object property parameter and returns the value of 1 if the property is TRUE, 0 if it is FALSE, or NULL if an invalid function ID or property parameter is specified. The following is a list of the property parameters appropriate for functions:

- IsTableFunction—Returns 1 if function is a table-valued function but not an inline function
- IsInlineFunction—Returns 1 if function is an inline table-valued function
- IsScalarFunction—Returns 1 if function is a scalar function
- IsSchemaBound—Returns 1 if function was created with SCHEMABINDING option
- IsDeterministic—Returns 1 if function is deterministic; that is, it always returns the same result each time it is called with a specific set of input values

The following example demonstrates a possible use of the OBJECTPROPERTY function with the INFORMATION_SCHEMA.routines view:

```
select convert(varchar(30), specific_name) as 'function',
  case objectproperty(object_id(specific_name), 'IsScalarFunction')
      when 1 then 'Yes' else 'No' end as IsScalar,
  case objectproperty(object_id(specific_name), 'IsTableFunction')
      when 1 then 'Yes' else 'No' end as IsTable,
  case objectproperty(object_id(specific_name), 'IsInlineFunction')
      when 1 then 'Yes' else 'No' end as IsInline,
```

```
  case objectproperty(object_id(specific_name), 'IsSchemaBound')
     when 1 then 'Yes' else 'No' end as IsSchemaBound,
  case objectproperty(object_id(specific_name), 'IsDeterministic')
     when 1 then 'Yes' else 'No' end as IsDeterministic
from information_Schema.routines
where routine_type = 'FUNCTION'
order by specific_name
go

function             IsScalar IsTable IsInline IsSchemaBound IsDeterministic
-------------------- -------- ------- -------- ------------- ---------------
AverageBookPrice     Yes      No      No       No            No
AveragePricebyType   No       No      Yes      No            No
AveragePricebyType2  No       Yes     No       Yes           No
valid_book_types     No       No      Yes      No            No
```

Modifying Functions with Transact-SQL

You can use the ALTER FUNCTION command to change the function's definition without having to drop and re-create it. The syntax for the ALTER FUNCTION command is identical to the CREATE FUNCTION syntax except for replacing the CREATE keyword with the ALTER keyword. The following example modifies the AveragePricebyType2 function:

```
ALTER FUNCTION AveragePricebyType2 (@price money = 0.0)
RETURNS @table table (type varchar(12) null, avg_price money null)
with schemabinding
AS
begin
    insert @table
       SELECT type, avg(price) as avg_price
             FROM dbo.titles
             group by type
             having avg(price) > @price
        order by avg(price) desc
    return
end
```

The ALTER FUNCTION command has a couple of advantages over dropping and re-creating the function to modify it. The main advantage is that you don't have to drop the function first to make the change. The second advantage is that because you don't have to drop the function, you don't have to worry about reassigning permissions to the function.

The main disadvantage of using ALTER FUNCTION instead of dropping and re-creating the function is that the date of the function modification is not recorded in the database catalogs. As a DBA, it is not possible to tell which functions have been modified since they were created, making it difficult to selectively extract the code for only the functions that have been modified.

Also, you cannot use `ALTER FUNCTION` to change a table-valued function to a scalar function or to change an inline function to a multistatement function. You'll have to drop and re-create it.

You can also view and modify functions in Enterprise Manager and Query Analyzer.

Viewing and Modifying Functions in Enterprise Manager

To view and edit a function in Enterprise Manager, browse to the User-Defined Functions folder within the appropriate database folder, and then either double-click the function name or right-click the function name and select the Properties option (see Figure 30.4) to bring up the function editor.

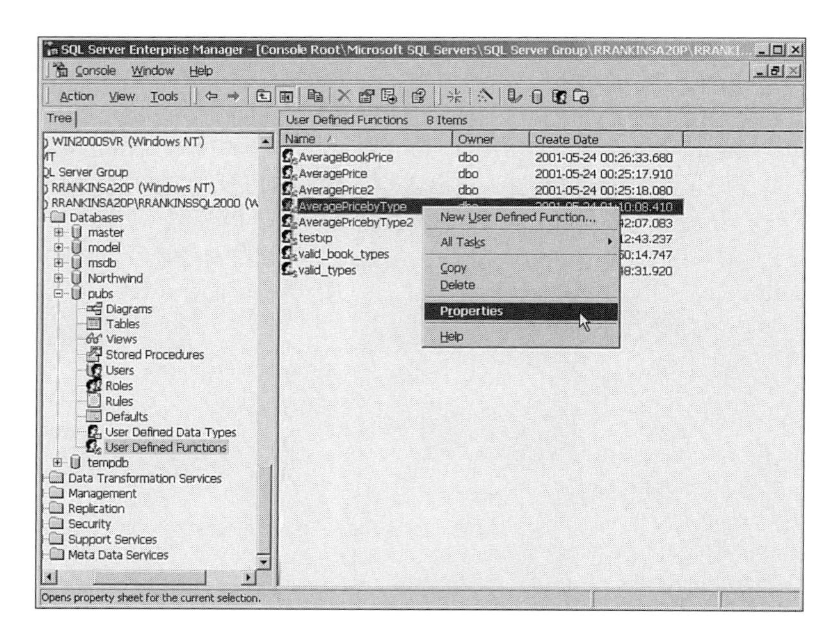

FIGURE 30.4 Invoking the function editor in Enterprise Manager.

This is the same editor you used to create a function in Enterprise Manager (refer to Figure 30.2), except that now it contains the actual function source code instead of template code.

The function editor in Enterprise Manager is not elegant. It lacks any sort of search and replace capability as well as the ability to save the function code to a file. One nice feature, however, is the ability to check the function syntax before applying changes by clicking the Check Syntax button. The actual changes to the function will be applied when clicking the Apply or OK button.

Enterprise Manager applies changes to the stored procedure by using the `ALTER FUNCTION`. The creation date of the function will not be updated.

Viewing and Modifying Functions in Query Analyzer

If you want to modify a function by dropping and re-creating it, Query Analyzer is the better tool to use. Besides having a full-featured editor, Query Analyzer provides options for how to extract the function source code to modify and apply changes. It will generate code to create, alter, or drop the selected function. You can choose to script the function source code to a new window, to a file, or to the Windows Clipboard by right-clicking the function name in the Object Browser and choosing the appropriate option (see Figure 30.5).

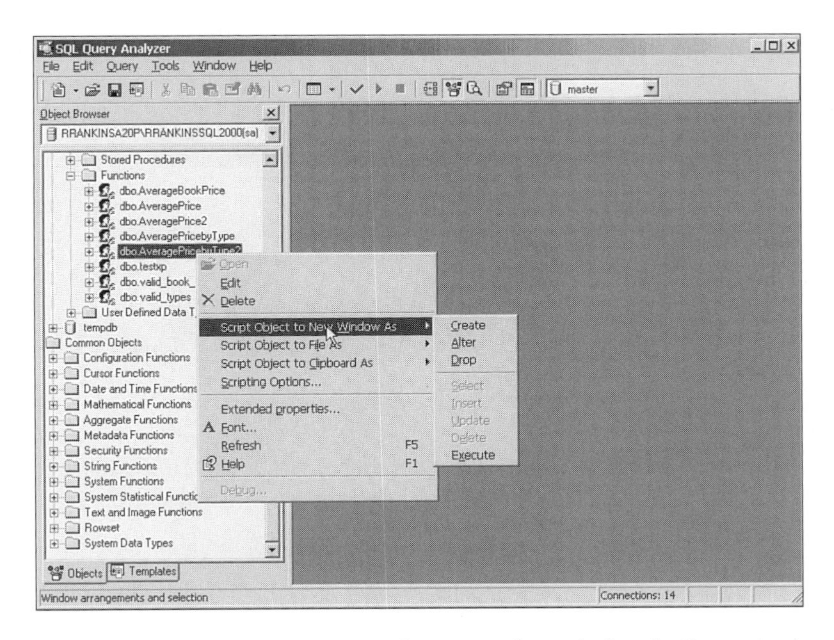

FIGURE 30.5 Extracting function source code to an editor window in Query Analyzer.

Query Analyzer provides a number of options for how to extract the stored procedure source code. The script generated can automatically include the command to check for the existence of the object and automatically drop it before executing the `CREATE FUNCTION` command. You can also choose to include the commands to reset permissions when the function is re-created. To ensure these features are included, make sure the following options are set within Query Analyzer:

- Generate Transact-SQL to remove referenced component. Script tests for existence before attempting to remove component.
- Script object-level permissions.

You can set the scripting options by selecting the Script tab in the Options dialog box. The Options dialog box can be invoked by selecting it from the Tools menu, by pressing Ctrl+Shift+O, or by right-clicking the function name in the Object Browser and choosing the Scripting Options menu option. This will bring up the Scripting Options dialog box, as shown in Figure 30.6.

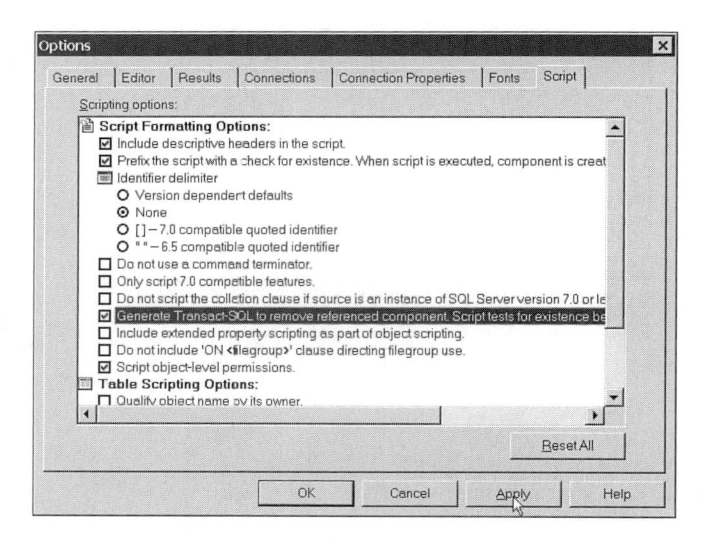

FIGURE 30.6 Setting scripting options in Query Analyzer.

Listing 30.1 shows an example of the script generated by Query Analyzer when the options selected are in effect. The changes can be implemented by simply executing the SQL script in Query Analyzer.

LISTING 30.1 Example of Function Creation Script Generated by Query Analyzer

```
SET QUOTED_IDENTIFIER OFF
GO
SET ANSI_NULLS OFF
GO

/****** Object:  User Defined Function dbo.AveragePricebyType2
        Script Date: 5/25/2001 3:08:53 AM ******/
if exists (select * from dbo.sysobjects
   where id = object_id('dbo.AveragePricebyType2')
     and xtype in ('FN', 'IF', 'TF'))
drop function dbo.AveragePricebyType2
GO
```

LISTING 30.1 Continued

```
CREATE FUNCTION AveragePricebyType2 (@price money = 0.0)
RETURNS @table table (type varchar(12) null, avg_price money null)
--with schemabinding
AS
begin
    insert @table
       SELECT type, avg(price) as avg_price
             FROM dbo.titles
             group by type
             having avg(price) > @price
    return
end

GO

SET QUOTED_IDENTIFIER OFF
GO
SET ANSI_NULLS ON
GO
```

Managing User-Defined Function Permissions

When a function is initially created, the only user who has permission to execute the function is the user who created it. To allow other users to execute a scalar function, you need to grant `EXECUTE` permission on the function to the appropriate user(s), group(s), or role(s). For a table-valued function, you need to grant `SELECT` permission to the user(s), group(s), or role(s) that will need to reference it. In the following example, you are granting `EXECUTE` permission on the `getdateonly()` function to everyone and `SELECT` permission on the `AveragePriceByType` function to the database user `fred`:

```
grant execute on dbo.getdateonly to public
grant select on AveragePricebyType to fred
```

For more detailed information on granting and revoking permissions, see Chapter 15, "Security and User Administration."

System-Wide Table Valued Functions

In addition to the built-in scalar functions, SQL Server 2000 now provides a set of system-wide table-valued functions that can be invoked from any database. Usually, when you invoke a user-defined table-valued function that is not local to the current database context, you have to fully qualify the function name with the database name. This is not required for system-wide table-valued functions. A special syntax is used to invoke system-wide table-valued funcions. You must precede the function name with two colons (::), as shown in the following example:

```
SELECT * FROM ::fn_virtualfilestats(5, 1)
go

DbId FileId TimeStamp NumberReads NumberWrites BytesRead BytesWritten IoStallMS
---- ------ --------- ----------- ------------ --------- ------------ ---------
   5      1  88725180          36            2    294912        16384       460
```

The `fn_virtualfilestats` function returns IO statistics for a database file. It is passed the database ID and a file ID as parameters. The previous example returned the IO stats for the datafile of the pubs database.

SQL Server 2000 provides a number of documented and undocumented table-valued functions. The following is a list of the documented functions:

- `fn_helpcollations()`—Lists all collations supported by SQL Server 2000.
- `fn_listextendedproperty(`*`propertyname,level0objecttype, level0objectname, level1objecttype, level1objectname, level2objecttype, level2objectname`*`)`—Lists extended property values for a database or objects stored in a database.
- `fn_servershareddrives()`—Returns the names of shared drives used by a clustered server.
- `fn_trace_geteventinfo(`*`traceID`*`)`—Returns information about the events being traced for the trace specified.
- `fn_trace_getfilterinfo(`*`traceID`*`)`—Returns information about the filters applied to the trace specified.
- `fn_trace_getinfo(`*`traceID`*`)`—Returns information about the specified trace.
- `fn_trace_gettable(`*`filename, numfiles`*`)`—Returns trace file information from the specified file in table format.

- `fn_virtualfilestats(dbid, fileid)`—Returns file I/O information for the file of the specified database.
- `fn_virtualservernodes()`—Returns a list of nodes on which a virtual server can run. This information is useful in failover clustering environments.

The trace-related functions perform actions that previously could only be performed via extended stored procedures. These functions will be discussed in more detail in Chapter 7, "Using the SQL Server Profiler."

The majority of the undocumented system-wide table-valued functions are used within SQL Server replication and are not intended for end-user execution.

Rewriting Stored Procedures as Functions

In previous releases of SQL Server, if you wanted to do custom processing, you had to create stored procedures to do things that would have worked better as functions. For example, you couldn't use the result set of a stored procedure in a where clause or a return value as a column in a select list. Using a stored procedure to perform calculations on columns in a result set often required using a cursor to step through each row in a result set and pass the column values fetched to the stored procedure, which typically returned the computed value via an output parameter. Another alternative was to retrieve the initial result set into a temporary table and then perform additional queries/updates against the temporary table to modify the column values, which often required multiple passes. Neither of these methods were an efficient means of processing the data, but few other alternatives existed. If you needed to join against the result set of a stored procedure, you had to insert the result set into a temporary table first, and then join against the temporary table, as shown in the following code fragment:

```
...
insert #results exec result_proc
select * from other_Table
   join #results on other_table.pkey = #results.keyfield
...
```

Now that SQL Server 2000 supports user-defined functions, you might want to consider rewriting some of your stored procedures as functions to take advantage of the capabilities of functions and improve the efficiency of your SQL code. The main criteria are situations where you would like to be able to invoke the stored procedure directly from within a query. If the stored procedure returns a result-set, it is a candidate for being written as a table-valued function. If it returns a scalar value, usually via an output parameter, it is a candidate for being written as a scalar function. However, the following criteria should also be considered when deciding whether a procedure is a good candidate for being rewritten as a function:

- The procedure logic is expressible in a single SELECT statement; however, it is written as a stored procedure, rather than a view, because of the need for it to be parameter driven.
- The stored procedure does not perform update operations on tables, except against table variables.
- The need for dynamic SQL statements executed via the `EXECUTE` statement or `sp_executesql` does not exist.
- The stored procedure returns no more than a single result set.
- If the stored procedure returns a result set, its primary purpose is to build an intermediate result that is typically loaded into a temporary table, which is then queried in a SELECT statement.

The `result_proc` stored procedure, referenced earlier in this section, could possibly be rewritten as a table-valued function called fn_result(). The preceding code fragment then could be rewritten as follows:

```
SELECT *
    FROM fn_results() fn
    join other_table o.pkey = fn.keyfield
```

Summary

User-defined functions are one of the more welcome new features in SQL Server 2000. Scalar functions can be used to perform more complex operations than those provided by the built-in scalar functions. Table-valued functions provide a way to create what are essentially parameterized views and allow you to include them inline in your queries just like a table or view. User-defined functions allow you to create reusable routines that can help to make your SQL code more straightforward and efficient. In this chapter, you have seen how to create and modify scalar functions and inline and multistatement table-valued functions and how they can be invoked and used within your queries. If you are considering converting any existing stored procedures to functions, the guidelines and example presented should offer some help.

CHAPTER 31

Transaction Management and the Transaction Log

by Ray Rankins

IN THIS CHAPTER

Transaction management is an important area within database programming. The transactions you construct and issue can have a huge impact on the performance of SQL Server and the consistency of your databases. This chapter takes a look at the methods for defining and managing transactions within SQL Server 2000.

What Is a Transaction?

A **transaction** is one or more SQL statements that must be completed as a whole, or in other words, as a single **Logical Unit of Work** (LUW). Transactions provide a way of collecting and associating multiple actions into a single all-or-nothing multiple operation action. All operations within the transaction must be fully completed or not performed at all.

Consider a bank transaction in which you move $1,000 from your checking to your savings account. This transaction is, in fact, *two* operations: a decrement of your checking account and an increment of your savings account. Consider the impact on your finances if the bank's server went down after completing the first stage and never got to the second! By collecting the two operations together, as a transaction, they either both succeed or both fail as a single, complete unit of work.

A transaction is a logical unit of work that has four special characteristics, known as the ACID properties:

- *A*tomicity—Associated modifications are an all-or-nothing proposition; either all are done or none are done.
- *C*onsistency—After a transaction finishes, all data is in the state it should be, all internal structures are correct, and everything accurately reflects the transaction that has occurred.
- *I*solation—One transaction cannot interfere with the processes of another transaction.
- *D*urability—After the transaction has finished, all changes made are permanent.

The responsibility for enforcing the ACID properties of a transaction is split between T-SQL developers and SQL Server. The developer is responsible for ensuring that the modifications are correctly collected together and that the data is going to be left in a consistent state that corresponds with the actions being taken. SQL Server ensures that the transaction is isolated and durable, undertakes the atomicity requested, and ensures the consistency of the final data structures. The transaction log of each database provides the durability for the transaction. As you will see in this chapter, you have some control over how SQL Server handles some of these properties. For example, you can modify a transaction's isolation by enlisting bound connections.

How SQL Server Manages Transactions

SQL Server uses the database's transaction log to record the modifications occurring within the database. Each log record is labeled with a unique log sequence number (LSN), and all log entries that are part of the same transaction are linked together so they can be easily located if the transaction needs to be undone or redone. The primary responsibility of logging is to ensure transaction durability—either ensuring that the completed changes make it to the physical database files, or ensuring that any unfinished transactions are rolled back should there be an error or a server failure.

What is logged? Obviously, the start and end of a transaction are logged, but also the actual data modification, page allocations and deallocations, and changes to indexes. SQL Server keeps track of a number of pieces of information, all with the aim of ensuring the ACID properties of the transaction.

After a transaction has been committed, it cannot be rolled back. The only way to undo a committed transaction is to write another transaction to reverse the changes made. Before a transaction is committed, it can be rolled back.

SQL Server provides transaction management for all users using the following components:

- Transaction-control statements to define the logical units of work
- A write-ahead transaction log

- An automatic recovery process
- Data-locking mechanisms to ensure consistency and transaction isolation

Defining Transactions

You can carry out transaction processing with Microsoft SQL Server in three ways:

- AutoCommit—Every Transact-SQL statement is its own transaction and automatically commits when it finishes. This is the default mode in which SQL Server operates.
- Explicit—This approach provides programmatic control of the transaction using the `BEGIN TRAN` and `COMMIT/ROLLBACK TRAN/WORK` commands.
- Implicit—SQL Server is placed into a mode of operation in which issuing certain SQL commands automatically starts a transaction. The developer must finish the transaction by explicitly issuing the `COMMIT/ROLLBACK TRAN/WORK` commands.

Each of these methods is discussed in the following sections.

NOTE

The terms for explicit and implicit transactions can be somewhat confusing as to which is which. The way to keep them straight is to think of how a multistatement transaction is initiated, not how it is completed. AutoCommit transactions are in a separate category because they are both implicitly started and committed. Implicit and explicit transactions have to be explicitly ended, but explicit transactions must also be explicitly started with the `BEGIN TRAN` statement, whereas no `BEGIN TRAN` is necessary to start a multistatement transaction when in implicit transaction mode.

AutoCommit Transactions

AutoCommit transactions are the default transaction mode for SQL Server. Each individual Transact-SQL command automatically commits or rolls back its work at the end of its execution. Each SQL statement is considered to be its own transaction, with begin and end control points implied.

```
[implied begin transaction]
UPDATE account
SET balance = balance + 1000
WHERE account_no = "123456789"
[implied commit or rollback transaction]
```

If an error is present within the execution of the statement, the action is undone (rolled back); if no errors occurred, the action is completed and the changes are saved.

Now consider the banking transaction again and write the T-SQL statements to move money from the savings account to the checking account. Assume it was written as follows:

```
declare @checking_account char(10),
        @savings_account char(10)
select @checking_account = '0003456321',
       @savings_account = '0003456322'
update account
   set balance = balance - $1000
   where account_number = @checking_account
update savings_account
   set balance = balance + $1000
   where account_number = @savings_account
```

What would happen if an error occurred updating the savings account? With AutoCommit, each statement is implicitly committed after it completes successfully, so the update for the checking account has already been committed. You would have no way of rolling it back except to write another separate update to add the $1,000 back to the account. If the system crashed during the updates, how would you know which if any completed, and whether you would need to undo any of the changes because the subsequent commands were not executed? You would need some way to group the two commands together as a single logical unit of work so they complete or fail as a whole. SQL Server provides transaction control statements that allow you to create multistatement user-defined transactions.

Explicit User-Defined Transactions

To have complete control of a transaction and define logical units of work that consist of multiple data modifications, you need to write explicit user-defined transactions. Any SQL Server user can make use of the transaction control statements; no special privileges are required.

To start a multistatement transaction, use the `BEGIN TRAN` command, which optionally takes a transaction name:

```
BEGIN TRAN[SACTION] [transaction_name [WITH MARK ['description']]]
```

This name is essentially meaningless as far as transaction management is concerned, and if transactions are nested (which will be discussed later in this chapter), the name is only useful for the outermost `BEGIN TRAN` statement. Rolling back to any other name, besides a savepoint name, will generate an error and not roll back the transaction. The statements can only be rolled back when the outermost transaction is rolled back.

Naming transactions is really only useful when using the `WITH MARK` option. If the `WITH MARK` option is specified, a transaction name must be specified. `WITH MARK` allows for restoring a transaction log backup to a named mark in the transaction log. (For more information on restoring database and log backups, see Chapter 16, "Database Backup and Restore.") This option allows you to restore a database to a known state, or to recover a set of related databases to a consistent state. However, be aware that BEGIN TRAN records are only written to the log if an actual data modification occurs within the transaction.

A transaction is completed successfully by issuing either a COMMIT TRAN or COMMIT [WORK] statement, or can be undone using either ROLLBACK TRAN or ROLLBACK [WORK]. The syntax of these commands is as follows:

```
COMMIT [TRAN[SACTION] [transaction_name]] | [WORK]

ROLLBACK [TRAN[SACTION] [transaction_name | savepointname]] | [WORK]
```

The COMMIT statement marks the successful conclusion of the transaction. This statement can be coded as COMMIT, COMMIT WORK, or COMMIT TRAN. It makes no difference—other than that the first two versions are SQL-92 ANSI compliant.

The ROLLBACK statement unconditionally undoes all work done within the transaction. This statement can also be coded as ROLLBACK, ROLLBACK WORK, or ROLLBACK TRAN. The first two commands are ANSI-92 SQL compliant and do not accept user-defined transaction names. ROLLBACK TRAN is required if you want to roll back to a savepoint within a transaction.

The following is an example of how you could code the previously mentioned banking example as a single transaction in SQL Server:

```
declare @checking_account char(10),
        @savings_account char(10)
select @checking_account = '0003456321',
       @savings_account = '0003456322'
begin tran
update account
   set balance = balance - $1000
   where account_number = @checking_account
if @@error != 0
begin
    rollback tran
    return
end
update savings_account
   set balance = balance + $1000
   where account_number = @savings_account
if @@error != 0
begin
    rollback tran
    return
end
commit tran
```

There are certain commands that cannot be specified within a user-defined transaction, primarily because they cannot be effectively rolled back in the event of a failure. In most cases, because of their long-running nature, you would not want them to be specified within a transaction anyway. Here are the commands you cannot specify in a user-defined transaction:

`ALTER DATABASE`	`CREATE DATABASE`	`DROP DATABASE`
`BACKUP DATABASE`	`RESTORE DATABASE`	`RECONFIGURE`
`BACKUP LOG`	`RESTORE LOG`	`UPDATE STATISTICS`

Savepoints

Savepoints allow you to set a marker in a transaction that you can roll back to undo a portion of the transaction, but commit the remainder of the transaction. The syntax is as follows:

```
SAVE TRAN[SACTION] savepointname
```

Savepoints are not ANSI-SQL 92 compliant, so you must use the SQL Server-specific transaction management commands that allow you to specify a named point within the transaction and then recover back to it.

The following code illustrates the differences between the two types of syntax when using the `SAVE TRAN` command:

SQL-92 Syntax	SQL Server-Specific Syntax
`BEGIN TRAN mywork`	`BEGIN TRAN mywork`
`  UPDATE table1...`	`  UPDATE table1...`
`   SAVE TRAN savepoint1`	`  SAVE TRAN savepoint1`
`      INSERT INTO table2...`	`      INSERT INTO table2...`
`      DELETE table3...`	`      DELETE table3...`
`      IF @@error = -1`	`      IF @@error = -1`
`         ROLLBACK WORK`	`         ROLLBACK TRAN savepoint1`
`COMMIT WORK`	`COMMIT TRAN`

Note the difference between the SQL-92 syntax on the left and the SQL Server–specific syntax on the right. In the SQL-92 syntax, when you reach the `ROLLBACK WORK` command, the *entire* transaction is undone, rather than undoing only to the point marked by the savepoint. You have to use the SQL Server–specific `ROLLBACK TRAN` command and specify the savepoint name to roll back the work to the savepoint and still be able to subsequently roll back or commit the rest of the transaction.

Nested Transactions

By rule, you can't have more than one active transaction per user session within SQL Server. However, consider that you have a SQL batch that issues a `BEGIN TRAN` statement, and then subsequently invokes a stored procedure, which also issues a `BEGIN TRAN` statement. Because you can only have one transaction active, what does the `BEGIN TRAN` inside the stored procedure accomplish? In SQL Server, this leads to an interesting anomaly referred to as **nested transactions**.

To determine whether transactions are open and how deep they are nested within a connection, you can use the global function called `@@trancount`.

If no transaction is active, the transaction nesting level is `0`. As a transaction is initiated, the transaction nesting level is incremented; as a transaction completes, the transaction nesting is decremented. The overall transaction remains open and can be entirely rolled back until the transaction nesting level returns to `0`.

You can use the `@@trancount` to monitor the current status of a transaction. For example, what would SQL Server do when encountering the following transaction (which produces an error because of the reference constraint on the `titles` table)?

```
BEGIN TRAN
   DELETE FROM publishers
   WHERE pub_id = '0736'
```

Is the transaction still active? You can find out using the `@@trancount` function:

```
select @@trancount
go

-----------
          1
```

In this case, `@@trancount` returns a value of `1`, which indicates that the transaction is still open and in progress. This means that you can still issue commands within the transaction and commit the changes, or roll back the transaction. Also, if you were to log out of the user session from SQL Server before the transaction nesting level reached `0`, SQL Server would automatically roll back the transaction.

Although nothing can prevent you from coding a `BEGIN TRAN` within another `BEGIN TRAN`, doing so has no real benefit even though such cases might occur. However, if you nest transactions in this manner, you must execute a `COMMIT` statement for each `BEGIN TRAN` statement issued. This is because SQL Server modifies the `@@trancount` with each transaction statement and considers the transaction finished only when the transaction nesting level returns to `0`. Table 31.1 shows the effects that transaction control statements have on `@@trancount`.

TABLE 31.1 Transaction Statements' Effects on `@@trancount`

Statement	Effect on `@@trancount`
`BEGIN TRAN`	+1
`COMMIT`	-1
`ROLLBACK`	Sets to 0
`SAVE TRAN` *`savepoint`*	No effect
`ROLLBACK TRAN` *`savepoint`*	No effect

Following is a summary of how transactional control relates to the values reported by `@@trancount`:

- When you log in to SQL Server, the value of `@@trancount` for your session is initially `0`.
- Each time you execute `begin transaction`, SQL Server increments `@@trancount`.
- Each time you execute `commit transaction`, SQL Server decrements `@@trancount`.
- Actual work is committed only when `@@trancount` reaches `0` again.
- When you execute `rollback transaction`, the transaction is canceled and `@@trancount` returns to `0`. Notice that `rollback transaction` cuts straight through any number of nested transactions, canceling the overall main transaction. This means that you need to be careful how you write code that contains a `rollback` statement. Be sure to return up through all levels so you don't continue executing data modifications that were meant to be part of the larger overall transaction.
- Setting savepoints and rolling back to a savepoint do not affect `@@trancount` or transaction nesting in any way.
- If a user connection is lost for any reason when `@@trancount` is greater than `0`, any pending work for that connection is automatically rolled back. SQL Server requires that multistatement transactions be explicitly committed.
- Because the `BEGIN TRAN` statement increments `@@trancount`, each `BEGIN TRAN` statement must be paired with a `COMMIT` for the transaction to successfully complete.

Take a look at some sample code to show the values of `@@trancount` as the transaction progresses. This first example is a simple explicit transaction with a nested `BEGIN TRAN`:

SQL Statement	`@@trancount` Value
`SELECT "Starting....."`	0
`BEGIN TRAN`	1
`    DELETE FROM table1`	1
`    BEGIN TRAN`	2

```
        INSERT INTO table2              2
    COMMIT                              1
    UPDATE table3                       1
COMMIT                                  0
```

Nested transactions are *syntactic only*. The only `commit tran` statement that has an impact on real data is the last one, the statement returning `@@trancount` to `0`. That statement fully commits the work done by the initial transaction and the nested transactions. Until that final `COMMIT TRAN` is encountered, all of the work can be rolled back with a `ROLLBACK` statement.

As a general rule, if a transaction is already active, you shouldn't issue another `BEGIN TRAN` statement. Check the value of `@@trancount` to determine if a transaction is already active. If you want to be able to roll back the work performed within a nested transaction without rolling back the entire transaction, set a savepoint instead of issuing a `BEGIN TRAN` statement. Later in this chapter, you will see an example of how to check `@@trancount` within a stored procedure to determine if the stored procedure is being invoked within a transaction and issuing a `BEGIN TRAN` or `SAVE TRAN` as appropriate.

Implicit Transactions

AutoCommit transactions and explicit user-defined transactions in SQL Server are not ANSI-92 SQL compliant. The ANSI-92 SQL standard states that any data retrieval or modification statement issued should implicitly begin a multistatement transaction that remains in effect until an explicit `ROLLBACK` or `COMMIT` statement is issued.

To enable implicit transactions for a connection, you need to turn on the `IMPLICIT_TRANSACTIONS` session setting. The syntax is as follows:

```
SET IMPLICIT_TRANSACTIONS {ON | OFF}
```

After this option is turned on, transactions will be implicitly started, if not already in progress, whenever any of the following commands are executed:

```
ALTER TABLE        CREATE            DELETE
DROP               FETCH             GRANT
INSERT             OPEN              REVOKE
SELECT             TRUNCATE TABLE    UPDATE
```

Note that neither the `ALTER VIEW` nor `ALTER PROCEDURE` statement starts an implicit transaction.

Implicit transactions must be explicitly completed by issuing a COMMIT or ROLLBACK, and a new transaction is started again on the execution of any of the preceding commands. If you plan to use implicit transactions, the main thing to be aware of is that locks are held until you explicitly commit the transaction. This can cause problems with concurrency and the ability of the system to back up the transaction log.

Even when using implicit transactions, you can still issue the BEGIN TRAN statement and create transaction nesting. In this next example, IMPLICIT TRANSACTIONS ON has been turned on to see the effect this has on the value of @@trancount.

SQL Statements	@@trancount Value
SET IMPLICIT_TRANSACTIONS ON	0
go	0
INSERT INTO table1	1
UPDATE table2	1
COMMIT	0
go	
BEGIN TRAN	2
DELETE FROM table1	2
COMMIT	1
go	
DROP TABLE table1	1
COMMIT	0

As you can see in this second example, if a BEGIN TRAN is issued while a transaction is still active, transaction nesting will occur and a second COMMIT is required to finish the transaction. The main difference is that a BEGIN TRAN was *not* required to start the transaction. The first INSERT statement initiated the transaction. When you are running in implicit transaction mode, you don't need to issue a BEGIN TRAN statement; in fact, you should avoid it to prevent transaction nesting and the need for multiple commits.

Look at the previous banking transaction using implicit transactions:

```
set implicit_transactions on
go

declare @checking_account char(10),
        @savings_account char(10)
select @checking_account = '0003456321',
       @savings_account = '0003456322'
update account
   set balance = balance - $1000
```

```
   where account_number = @checking_account
if @@error != 0
begin
    rollback
    return
end
update savings_account
   set balance = balance + $1000
   where account_number = @savings_account
if @@error != 0
begin
    rollback
    return
end
commit
```

This example is nearly identical to the explicit transaction example except for the lack of a BEGIN TRAN statement. In addition, when in implicit transaction mode, you cannot roll back to a named transaction because no name is assigned when the transaction is invoked implicitly. You can, however, still set savepoints and roll back to savepoints to partially roll back work within an implicit transaction.

TIP

If you need to know within your SQL code whether implicit transactions are enabled so you can avoid issuing explicit BEGIN TRAN statements, you can check the @@options function. @@options returns a bitmap indicating which session level options are enabled for the current session. If bit 2 is on, then implicit transactions are enabled. The following code snippet can be used in stored procedures or SQL batches to check this value and decide whether to issue a BEGIN TRAN statement:

```
if @@options & 2 != 2 -- if bit 2 is not turned on
    BEGIN TRAN --a begin tran can be issued since implicit transactions are off
...
```

Implicit Transactions Versus Explicit Transactions

When would you want to use implicit transactions versus explicit transactions? If you are porting an application from another database environment that used an implicit transaction, that application will port over more easily with fewer code changes if you run in implicit transaction mode. Also, if the application you are developing needs to be ANSI-compliant and run across multiple database platforms with minimal code changes, you might want to use implicit transactions.

If you use implicit transactions in your applications, just be sure to issue COMMIT statements as frequently as possible to prevent leaving transactions open and holding locks for an extended period of time, which can have an adverse impact on concurrency and overall system performance.

If your application is only going to be hosted on SQL Server, it is recommended that you use AutoCommit and explicit transactions so that changes are committed as quickly as possible and only those logical units of work that are explicitly defined will contain multiple commands within a transaction.

Transaction Logging and the Recovery Process

Every SQL Server database has its own transaction log that keeps a record of all data modifications in a database (insert, update, delete) in the order in which they occur. This information is stored in one or more log files associated with the database. The information stored in these log files cannot be modified or viewed effectively by any user process.

SQL Server uses a write-ahead log. The buffer manager guarantees that changes are written to the transaction log before the changes are written to the database. The buffer manager also ensures that the log pages are written out in sequence so that transactions can be recovered properly in the event of a system crash.

The following is an overview of the sequence of events that occurs when a transaction modifies data:

1. Write a BEGIN TRAN record to the transaction log in buffer memory.
2. Write data modification information to transaction log pages in buffer memory.
3. Write data modifications to the database in buffer memory.
4. Write a COMMIT TRAN record to the transaction log in buffer memory.
5. Write transaction log records to transaction log file(s) on disk.

Send a COMMIT acknowledgement to the client process.

The end of a typical transaction is indicated by a COMMIT record in the transaction log. The presence of the COMMIT record indicates that the transaction must be reflected in the database or be redone if necessary. A transaction that is aborted during processing by an explicit rollback or a system error will automatically undo the changes made by the transaction.

Notice that the data records are not written to disk when a COMMIT occurs. This is done to minimize disk I/O. All log writes are done synchronously to ensure that the log records are physically written to disk and written in the proper sequence. Because all modifications to the data can be recovered from the transaction log, it is not critical that data changes be written to disk right away. Even in the event of a system crash or power failure, the data can be recovered from the log if it hasn't been written to the database.

SQL Server ensures that the log records are written before the affected data pages by recording the Log Sequence Number (LSN) for the log record making the change on the modified data page(s). Modified, or "dirty," data pages can only be written to disk when the LSN recorded on the data page is less than the LSN of the last log page written to the transaction log.

When and how are the data changes written to disk? Obviously, they must be written out at some time, or it would take forever for SQL Server to start up if it had to redo all transactions in the log. Also, how does SQL Server know during recovery which transactions to reapply, or "roll forward," and which transactions to undo, or "roll back." The following section looks at the mechanisms involved in the recovery process.

The Checkpoint Process

During recovery, SQL Server examines the transaction log for each database and verifies whether the changes reflected in the log are also reflected in the database. In addition, it examines the log to determine if any data changes were written to the data that were caused by a transaction that didn't complete before the system failure.

As discussed earlier, a `COMMIT` writes the log records for a transaction to the transaction log (see Figure 31.1). Dirty data pages are written out either by the Lazy Writer process or the checkpoint process. The Lazy Writer process runs periodically to check whether the number of free buffers has fallen below a certain threshold, reclaims any unused pages, and writes out any dirty pages that haven't been referenced recently. (For more information on the Lazy Writer process and SQL Servers I/O architecture, see Chapter 33, "SQL Server Internals.")

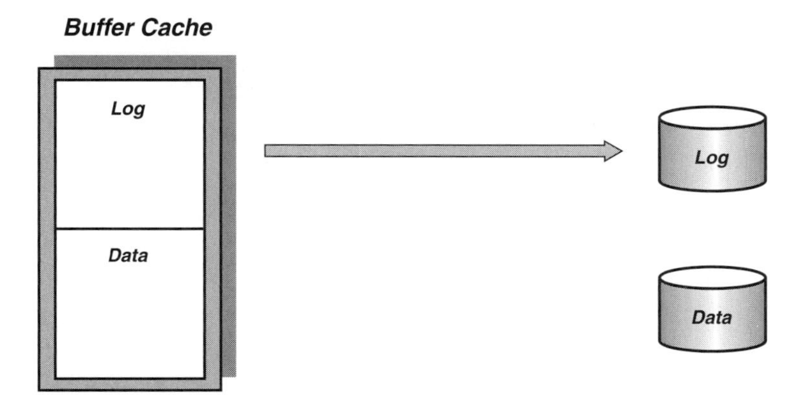

FIGURE 31.1 A commit writes all "dirty" log pages from cache to disk.

The checkpoint process also scans the buffer cache periodically and writes all dirty log pages and dirty data pages to disk (see Figure 31.2). The purpose of the checkpoint is to sync up on disk the data with the changes recorded in the transaction log. Typically, the checkpoint process finds little work to do because most dirty pages have been written out previously by the worker threads or lazywriter process.

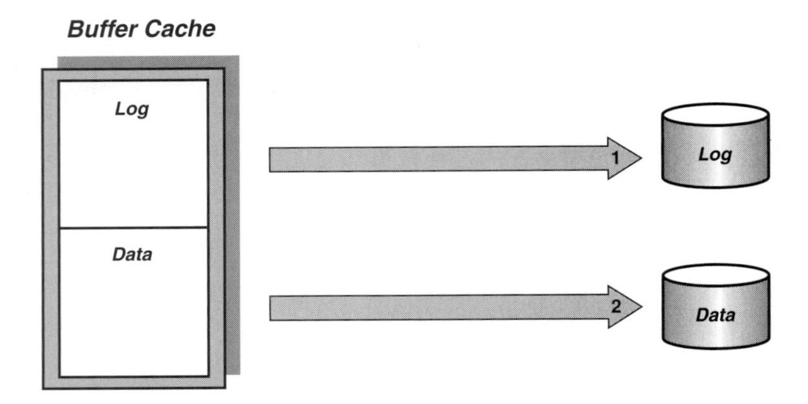

FIGURE 31.2 A checkpoint writes log pages from cache to disk, and then writes all "dirty" data pages.

The following list outlines the steps that SQL Server performs during a checkpoint:

1. Writes a record to the log file to record the start of the checkpoint.
2. Writes the LSN of the start of the checkpoint log records to the database boot page. (This is so SQL Server can find the last checkpoint in the log during recovery.)
3. Records the Minimum Recovery LSN (MinLSN), which is the first log image that must be present for a successful database-wide rollback. The MinLSN is either the LSN of the start of the checkpoint, the LSN of the oldest active transaction, or the LSN of the oldest transaction marked for replication that hasn't yet been replicated to all subscribers.
4. Writes a list of all outstanding, active transactions to the checkpoint records.
5. Writes all modified log pages to the transaction log on disk.
6. Writes all dirty data pages to disk. (Data pages that have not been modified are not written back to disk to save I/O.)
7. Writes a record to the log file indicating the end of the checkpoint.

Figure 31.3 shows a simplified version of the contents of a transaction log after a checkpoint. (For simplicity, the checkpoint records are reflected as a single log entry.)

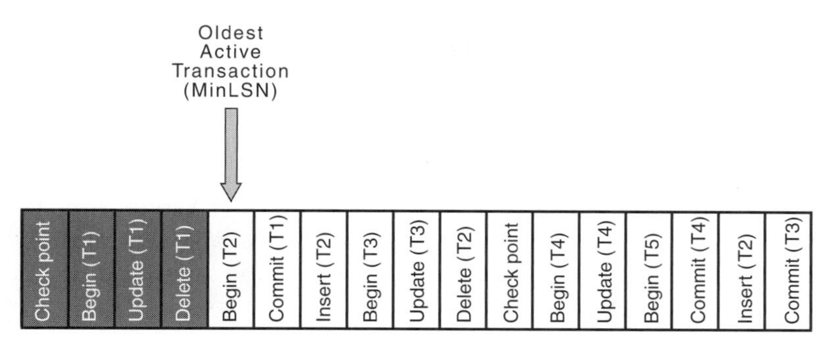

FIGURE 31.3 A simplified view of the end of the transaction log with various completed and active transactions, as well as the last checkpoint.

The primary purpose of a checkpoint is to reduce the amount of work the server needs to do at recovery time to redo or undo database changes. A checkpoint can occur under the following circumstances:

- When a checkpoint statement is executed explicitly for the current database.
- When `ALTER DATABASE` is used to change a database option. `ALTER DATABASE` automatically checkpoints the database when database options are changed.
- When an instance of SQL Server is shut down gracefully by either executing the `SHUTDOWN` statement or by stopping the SQL Server service.
- When SQL Server periodically generates automatic checkpoints in each database to reduce the amount of time the instance would take to recover the database.

Automatic Checkpoints

The frequency of automatic checkpoints is determined by the setting of the recovery interval for SQL Server. However, the decision to perform a checkpoint is based on the number of records in the log, not a period of time. The time interval between the occurrence of automatic checkpoints can be highly variable. If few modifications are made to the database, the time interval between automatic checkpoints could be quite long. Conversely, automatic checkpoints can occur quite frequently if the update activity on a database is high.

The recovery interval does not state how often an automatic checkpoint should occur. It is actually an estimate of the amount of time it would take SQL Server to recover the database by applying the number of transactions recorded since the last checkpoint. By default, the recovery interval is set to `0`, which means SQL Server will determine the appropriate recovery interval for each database. It is recommended that you keep this setting unless you notice that checkpoints are occurring too frequently and are impairing performance. Try increasing the value in small increments until you find one that works well. Just be aware: The higher you set the recovery interval, the fewer checkpoints will occur, but the database will likely take longer to recover following a system crash.

If the database is using either the full or bulk-logged recovery model, an automatic checkpoint occurs whenever the number of log records reaches the number that SQL Server estimates it can process within the time specified by the `recovery interval` option.

If the database is using the simple recovery model or if the truncate log on checkpoint option is enabled, an automatic checkpoint occurs whenever the log becomes 70 percent full or the number of log records reaches the number that SQL Server estimates it can process within the time specified by the `recovery interval` option. If using the simple recovery model, the automatic checkpoint also truncates the unused portion of the transaction log prior to the oldest active transaction.

The Recovery Process

When SQL Server is started, it verifies that completed transactions recorded in the log are reflected in the data, and that incomplete transactions whose changes are reflected in the data are rolled back out of the database. This is the recovery process. Recovery is an automatic process performed on each database during SQL Server startup. Recovery must be completed before the database is made available for use.

The recovery process guarantees that all completed transactions recorded in the transaction log are reflected in the data, and all incomplete transactions reflected in the data are rolled back. During recovery, SQL Server looks for the last checkpoint record in the log. Only the changes that occurred or were still open since the last checkpoint need to be examined to determine the need to be redone (rolled forward) or undone (rolled back). After all the changes are rolled forward or rolled back as necessary, the database is checkpointed and recovery is complete.

The recovery algorithm has three phases that are centered around the last checkpoint record in the transaction log, as shown in Figure 31.4.

A description of these phases is as follows:

1. Analysis Phase—SQL Server reads forward from the last checkpoint record in the transaction log. This pass identifies a list of pages (the dirty page table, or DPT) that might have been dirty at the time of the system crash or when SQL Server was shut down, as well as a list of the uncommitted transactions at the time of the crash.

2. Redo (Roll Forward) Phase—During this phase, SQL Server rolls forward all the committed transactions recorded in the log since the last checkpoint. This phase returns the database to the state it was in at the time of the crash. The starting point for the redo pass is the LSN of the oldest committed transaction within the DPT, so that only changes that were not previously checkpointed (only the committed "dirty" pages) are reapplied.

3. Undo (Roll Back) Phase—This phase moves backward from the end of the log to the oldest active transaction at the time of the system crash or shutdown. All transactions that were not committed at the time of the crash but that had pages written to the database are undone so that none of their changes are actually reflected in the database.

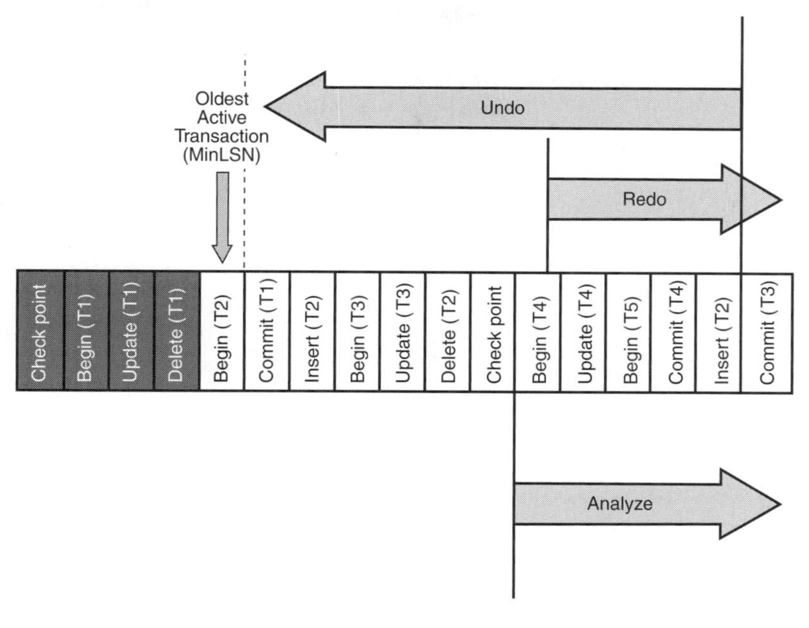

FIGURE 31.4 The phases of the recovery process.

Now examine the transactions in the log in Figure 31.4 and determine how they will be handled during the recovery process:

- Transaction T1 is started and committed prior to the last checkpoint. No recovery is necessary.
- Transaction T2 started before the last checkpoint, but had not completed at the time of the system crash. The changes written out by the checkpoint process for this transaction will have to be rolled back.
- Transaction T3 started before the last checkpoint and committed after the checkpoint prior to the system crash. The changes made to the data after the checkpoint will need to be rolled forward.
- Transaction T4 started and committed after the last checkpoint. This entire transaction will need to be rolled forward.
- Transaction T5 started after the last checkpoint, but no changes to the data were recorded in the log, so no data changes were written to the data. (Remember: Changes must be written to the log before they can be written to the data.) No undo action is required for this transaction.

In a nutshell, this type of analysis is pretty much the same analysis the recovery process would do. To identify the number of transactions rolled forward or rolled back during recovery, you can examine the SQL Server error log and look at the recovery startup messages for each database:

```
2001-06-13 17:07:00.06 spid8      Starting up database 'pubs'.
2001-06-13 17:07:00.07 spid9      Starting up database 'Northwind'.
2001-06-13 17:07:00.07 spid10     Starting up database 'bigpubs2000'.
2001-06-13 17:07:01.85 spid5      Clearing tempdb database.
2001-06-13 17:07:02.07 server     SQL server listening on 10.244.174.172: 1533.
2001-06-13 17:07:02.07 server     SQL server listening on 127.0.0.1: 1533.
2001-06-13 17:07:04.86 spid8      48 transactions rolled forward in database
 'pubs' (5).
2001-06-13 17:07:05.03 spid8      0 transactions rolled back in database
 'pubs' (5).
2001-06-13 17:07:05.33 spid8      Recovery is checkpointing database 'pubs' (5)
2001-06-13 17:07:06.10 spid5      Starting up database 'tempdb'.
2001-06-13 17:07:06.96 spid3      Recovery complete.
```

Transactions and Batches

There is no inherent transactional quality to batches. As you have seen already, unless you provide the syntax to define a single transaction made up of several statements, each individual statement in a batch is its own separate transaction, and each statement will be carried to completion or fail individually. The failure of a transaction within a batch does not cause the batch to stop processing.

In other words, transaction flow does not affect process flow. After a `rollback tran` statement, processing continues with the next statement in the batch or stored procedure. For this reason, you want to be sure to check for error conditions after each data modification within a transaction and exit the batch or stored procedure as appropriate.

Now go back to the banking example again and remove the `RETURN` statements:

```
declare @checking_account char(10),
        @savings_account char(10)
select @checking_account = '0003456321',
       @savings_account = '0003456322'
begin tran
update account
   set balance = balance - $1000
   where account_number = @checking_account
if @@error != 0
    rollback tran
update savings_account
   set balance = balance + $1000
   where account_number = @savings_account
if @@error != 0
    rollback tran
commit tran
```

Assume that a check constraint on the account prevents the balance from being set to a value less than 0. If the checking account had less than $1,000 in it, the first update would fail, and you would catch the error condition and roll back the transaction. At this point, the transaction is no longer active, but the batch still contains additional statements to execute. Without a return after the rollback, SQL Server continues with the next statement in the batch, which is the update to the savings account. However, this will now execute as its own separate transaction and will AutoCommit if it completes successfully. This is not what you want to happen because now that second update is its own separate unit of work; you will have no way to roll it back.

The key concept to keep in mind here is that transaction flow does not affect program flow. In the event of an error within the transaction, you need to make sure you have the proper error checking and a means to exit the transaction in the event of an error. That will prevent the batch from continuing with any remaining modifications that were meant to be a part of the original transaction. As a general rule of thumb, a return statement should almost always follow rollbacks.

Although you can have multiple transactions within a batch, you can also have transactions that span multiple batches. For example, you could write an application that begins a transaction in one batch and then asks for user verification during a second batch. The SQL might look like this:

First Batch:

```
begin transaction
insert publishers (pub_id, pub_name, city, state)
    values ("1111", "Joe and Mary's Books", "Northern Plains", "IA")
if @@error = 0
    print "publishers insert was successful. Please go on."
else
    print "publisher insert failed. Please roll back"
```

Second Batch:

```
update titles
    set pub_id = "1111"
    where pub_id = "1234"
delete authors
    where state = "CA"
commit transaction
```

Writing transactions that span multiple batches is almost always a bad idea. The locking and concurrency problems can become complicated, with awful performance implications. What if the application prompted for user input between batches and the user went out to lunch? Locks would be held until the user got back and continued the transaction. In general, you want to enclose each transaction in a single batch, using conditional programming constructs to handle situations like the preceding example. Following is a better way to write that program:

```
begin transaction
insert publishers (pub_id, pub_name, city, state)
    values ("1111", "Joe and Mary's Books", "Northern Plains", "IA")
if @@error = 0
begin
    print "publishers insert was successful. Continuing."
    update titles
        set pub_id = "1111"
        where pub_id = "1234"
    delete authors
        where state = "CA"
    commit transaction
end
else
begin
    print "publisher insert failed. rolling back transaction"
    rollback transaction
end
```

The important point in this example is that the transaction now takes place within a single batch for better performance and consistency. As you will see in the next section, it is usually best to encode transactions in stored procedures for even better performance and to avoid the possibility of unfinished transactions.

Transactions and Stored Procedures

Because SQL code in stored procedures runs locally on the server, it is recommended that transactions be coded in stored procedures to speed transaction processing. The less network traffic going on within your transactions, the faster they can finish.

Another advantage of using stored procedures for transactions is that it helps avoid the occurrence of partial transactions—that is, transactions that are started but not fully committed. It also avoids the possibility of user interaction within a transaction. The stored procedure keeps the transaction processing completely contained because it starts the transaction, carries out the data modifications, completes the transaction, and returns the status or data to the client.

Stored procedures also provide the additional benefit that if you need to fix, fine tune, or expand the duties of the transaction, you can do it all at one time in one central location. Your applications can share the same stored procedure, providing consistency for the “logical unit of work” across your applications.

Although stored procedures provide a useful solution to managing your transactions, you do need to know how transactions work within stored procedures and code for them appropriately. Consider what happens when one stored procedure calls another, and they both do their own transaction management. Obviously, they now need to work in concert with each other. If the called stored procedure has to roll back its work, how can it do this correctly without causing data-integrity problems?

The issues you need to deal with go back to the earlier topics of transaction nesting and transaction flow versus program flow. Unlike a rollback in a transaction (see the next section), a rollback in a stored procedure does not abort the rest of the batch or the calling procedure.

For each `BEGIN TRAN` encountered in a nested procedure, the transaction nesting level is incremented by 1. For each `COMMIT` encountered, the transaction nesting level is decremented by 1. However, if a rollback other than to a named savepoint occurs in a nested procedure, it rolls back all statements to the outermost `BEGIN TRAN`, including any work performed inside the nested stored procedures that has not been fully committed. It continues processing the remaining commands in the current procedure as well as the calling procedure(s).

To explore the issues involved, you will use the following stored procedure. The procedure takes a single integer argument, which it then attempts to insert into a table (`testable`). All data entry attempts—whether successful or not—are logged to a second table (`auditlog`). The code for the stored procedure is as follows:

```
CREATE PROCEDURE trantest @arg INT
AS
BEGIN TRAN
   IF EXISTS( SELECT * FROM testable WHERE col1 = @arg )
   BEGIN
      RAISERROR ('Value %d already exists!', 16, -1, @arg)
      ROLLBACK TRANSACTION
   END
   ELSE
   BEGIN
      INSERT INTO testable (col1) VALUES (@arg)
      COMMIT TRAN
   END

INSERT INTO auditlog (who, valuentered) VALUES (USER_NAME(), @arg)
return
```

Now explore what happens if you call this stored procedure in the following way and check the values of the two tables:

```
EXEC trantest 1
EXEC trantest 2
SELECT * FROM testable
SELECT valuentered FROM auditlog
go
```

The execution of this code gives the following results:

```
col1
-----------
1
2

valuentered
-----------
1
2
```

These would be the results you would expect because no errors would occur and nothing would be rolled back. Now if you were to run the same code a second time, `Testable` would still only have two rows because the trigger would roll back the attempted insert of the duplicate rows. However, because the procedure and batch are not aborted, the code would continue processing and the rows would still be added to the `auditlog` table. The result would be as follows:

```
Server: Msg 50000, Level 16, State 1, Procedure trantest, Line 6
Value 1 already exists!

Server: Msg 50000, Level 16, State 1, Procedure trantest, Line 6
Value 2 already exists!

col1
-----------
1
2

valuentered
-----------
1
2
1
2
```

Now explore what happens when you execute the stored procedure from within a transaction:

```
BEGIN TRAN
EXEC trantest 3
EXEC trantest 1
EXEC trantest 4
COMMIT TRAN
SELECT * FROM testable
SELECT valuentered FROM auditlog
go
```

The execution of this code gives the following results:

```
Server: Msg 266, Level 16, State 2, Procedure trantest, Line 16
Transaction count after EXECUTE indicates that a COMMIT or ROLLBACK TRANSACTION
 statement is missing. Previous count = 1, current count = 0.
Server: Msg 50000, Level 16, State 1, Procedure trantest, Line 6
Value 1 already exists!
Server: Msg 3902, Level 16, State 1, Line 5
The COMMIT TRANSACTION request has no corresponding BEGIN TRANSACTION.

col1
-----------
          1
          2
          4

valuentered
-----------
          1
          2
          1
          2
          1
          4
```

A number of problems are occurring now. For starters, you get back a message telling you that the transaction nesting level was messed up. More seriously, the results show that the value 4 made it into the table anyway, and that the audit table picked up the inserts of 1 and the 4 but lost the fact that you tried to insert a value of 3. What happened?

Take this one step at a time. First, you start the transaction and insert into `trantest` with the value of 3. The stored procedure starts its own transaction, adds the value to `testable`, commits that, and then adds a row to the `auditlog`. Next, you execute the procedure with the value of 1. This value already exists within the table, so the procedure raises an error and rolls back the transaction. Remember that a ROLLBACK undoes work to the outermost BEGIN TRAN—that means the start of this batch. This rolls back everything, including the insert of 3 into trantest and auditlog. The auditlog entry for the value of 1 *is* inserted and not rolled back because it occurred after the transaction was rolled back and is a standalone, auto-committed statement now.

You then receive the error regarding the change in the transaction nesting level because a transaction should leave the state of a governing transaction in the same way it was entered; it should make no net change to the transaction nesting level. In other words, the value of @@trancount should be the same when the procedure exits as when it was entered. If it is not, the transaction control statements are not properly balanced.

Also, because the batch is not aborted, the value of 4 is inserted into trantest, an operation that completes successfully and is auto-committed. Finally, when you try to commit the transaction, you receive the last error regarding a mismatch between BEGIN TRAN and COMMIT TRAN because no transaction is currently in operation.

The solution to this problem is to write your stored procedures so that transaction nesting doesn't occur and that a stored procedure only rolls back its own work. When a rollback occurs, it should return an error status so that the calling batch or procedure is aware of the error condition and can choose to continue or abort the work at that level. You can manage this by checking the current value of @@trancount and determining what needs to be done. If a transaction is already active, the stored procedure should not issue a BEGIN TRAN and nest the transaction, but rather set a savepoint. This allows the procedure to perform a partial rollback of its work. If no transaction is active, then the procedure can safely begin a new transaction. The following SQL code fragment is an example of using this approach:

```
DECLARE @trancount INT
/* Capture the value of the transaction nesting level at the start */
SELECT @trancount = @@trancount
IF (@trancount = 0)  -- no transaction is current active, start on
   BEGIN TRAN mytran
ELSE                 -- a transaction is active, set a savepoint only
   SAVE TRAN mytran
.
.
/* This is how to trap an error. Roll back either to your
   own BEGIN TRAN or roll back to the savepoint. Return an
   error code to the caller to indicate an internal failure.
   How the caller handles the transaction is up to the caller.*/
IF (@@error <> 0)
BEGIN
   ROLLBACK TRAN mytran
   RETURN -1969
```

```
END
.
.
/* Once you reach the end of the code, you need to pair the BEGIN TRAN,
   if you issued it, with a COMMIT TRAN. If you executed the SAVE TRAN
   instead, you have nothing else to do...end of game! */
IF (@trancount = 0)
  COMMIT TRAN

RETURN 0
```

If these concepts are applied to all stored procedures that need to incorporate transaction processing as well as the code that calls the stored procedures, you should be able to avoid problems with transaction nesting and inconsistency in your transaction processing. Just be sure to check the return value of the stored procedure and determine whether the whole batch should be failed, or whether that one call is of little importance to the overall outcome and the transaction can continue.

For additional examples and discussion on coding guidelines for stored procedures in transactions, see Chapter 28, "Creating and Managing Stored Procedures in SQL Server."

Transactions and Triggers

SQL Server 2000 provides two types of triggers—AFTER triggers and INSTEAD OF triggers. INSTEAD OF triggers perform their actions before and modifications are made to the actual table the trigger is defined on.

Whenever trigger is invoked, it is *always* invoked within another transaction, whether it's a single statement AutoCommit transaction, or a user-defined multistatement transaction. This is true for both AFTER triggers and INSTEAD OF triggers. Even though an INSTEAD OF trigger fires before, or "instead of" the data modification statement itself, if a transaction is not already active, an AutoCommit transaction is still automatically initiated as the data modification statement is invoked. (For more information on AFTER and INSTEAD OF triggers, see Chapter 29, "Creating and Managing Triggers.")

NOTE

While the information presented in this section applies to both AFTER and INSTEAD OF triggers, the primary focus and the examples presented pertain primarily to AFTER triggers.

Because the trigger will already be operating within the context of a transaction, the only transaction control statements you should ever consider using in a trigger are ROLLBACK and SAVE TRAN. You don't need to issue a BEGIN TRAN because a transaction is already active; a BEGIN TRAN would only serve to increase the nesting level, which would only complicate things further.

To demonstrate the relationship between a trigger and the transaction, use the following SQL code to create a trigger on the employee table:

```
use pubs
go
CREATE TRIGGER tD_employee ON employee
FOR DELETE
AS
   DECLARE @msg VARCHAR(255)

   SELECT @msg = 'Trancount in trigger = ' + CONVERT(VARCHAR(2), @@trancount)

   PRINT @msg

   RETURN
go
```

The purpose of this trigger is to simply show the state of the @@trancount within the trigger as the deletion is taking place.

If you now execute code for an implied and an explicit transaction, you can see the values of @@trancount and the behavior of the batch. First, here's the implied transaction:

```
print 'Trancount before delete = ' + CONVERT(VARCHAR(2), @@trancount)
DELETE FROM employee WHERE emp_id = 'PMA42628M'
print 'Trancount after delete = ' + CONVERT( VARCHAR(2), @@trancount)
go
```

The results of this are as follows:

```
Trancount before delete = 0
Trancount in trigger = 1
(1 row(s) affected)
Trancount after delete = 0
```

Because no transaction starts until the DELETE statement executes, the first value of @@trancount indicates this with a value of 0. Within the trigger, the transaction count has a value of 1; you are now inside the implied transaction caused by the DELETE. After the trigger returns, the DELETE is automatically committed and the transaction is finished, and @@trancount returns to 0 to indicate that no transaction is currently active.

Now explore what happens within an explicit transaction:

```
begin tran
print 'Trancount before delete = ' + CONVERT(VARCHAR(2), @@trancount)
DELETE FROM employee WHERE emp_id = 'PMA42628M'
```

```
print 'Trancount after delete = ' + CONVERT( VARCHAR(2), @@trancount)
commit tran
print 'Trancount after commit = ' + CONVERT( VARCHAR(2), @@trancount)
go
```

This code gives the following results:

```
Trancount before delete = 1
Trancount in trigger = 1
(0 row(s) affected)
Trancount after delete = 1
Trancount after commit = 0
```

In this example, a transaction is already active when the `DELETE` is executed. The `BEGIN TRAN` statement initiates the transaction and `@@trancount` is `1` before the `DELETE` is executed. The trigger becomes a part of that transaction, which is not committed until the `COMMIT TRAN` statement is executed.

What would happen, however, if the trigger performed a rollback? Now modify the trigger to perform a rollback as follows:

```
ALTER TRIGGER tD_employee ON employee
FOR DELETE
AS
print 'Trancount in trigger = ' + CONVERT(VARCHAR(2), @@trancount)

ROLLBACK TRAN

return
```

Now rerun the previous batch. The outcome this time is as follows:

```
Trancount before delete = 1
Trancount in trigger = 1
```

Notice in this example that the batch did not complete, as evidenced by the missing output from the last two print statements. When a rollback occurs within a trigger, SQL Server aborts the current transaction, continues processing the commands in the trigger, and after the trigger returns, aborts the rest of the batch. A `ROLLBACK TRAN` in a trigger will roll back all work to the first `BEGIN TRAN` statement. It is not possible to roll back to a specific named transaction, although you can roll back to a named savepoint, as will be discussed later in this section.

Again, the batch and transaction are finished when the trigger rolls back; any subsequent statements in the batch are not executed. The key concept to remember is that the trigger becomes an integral part of the statement that fired it and of the transaction in which that statement occurs.

Now look at another example. First, create a trigger to enforce referential integrity between the titles table and the publishers table:

```
create trigger tr_titles_i on titles for insert as
declare @rows int  -- create variable to hold @@rowcount
select @rows = @@rowcount
if @rows = 0 return
if update(pub_id) and (select count(*)
        from inserted i, publishers p
        where p.pub_id = i.pub_id ) != @rows
  begin
        rollback transaction
        raiserror ('Invalid pub_id inserted', 16, 1)
  end
return
go
```

Next, for the trigger to take care of the referential integrity, you need to disable the foreign key constraint on the titles table:

```
alter table titles nocheck constraint FK__titles__pub_id__014935CB
```

Now, run a multistatement transaction with an invalid `pub_id` provided in the second insert statement:

```
/* transaction inserts rows into a table */
begin tran add_titles
insert titles (title_id, pub_id, title)
       values ('BU1234', '0736', 'Tuning SQL Server')
insert titles (title_id, pub_id, title)
       values ('BU1235', 'abcd', 'Tuning SQL Server')
insert titles (title_id, pub_id, title)
       values ('BU1236', '0877', 'Tuning SQL Server')
commit tran
```

How many rows are inserted if `'abcd'` is an invalid `pub_id`? No rows will be inserted because the `rollback tran` in the trigger rolls back all modifications made by the trigger, including the insert with the bad `pub_id` and all statements preceding in the transaction. After the return statement is encountered in the trigger, it then aborts the rest of the batch. Remember to perform a `return` following a `rollback tran` in a trigger to prevent unwanted results. If the trigger subsequently performs data modifications before the return, they will no longer be part of the transaction and will be auto-committed with no opportunity to roll them back.

Never issue a BEGIN TRAN statement in a transaction because a transaction is already active at the time the trigger is executed. Rolling back to a named transaction is illegal and will generate a runtime error, rolling back the transaction and immediately terminating processing of the trigger and the batch. The only transaction control statements you should include in a trigger are ROLLBACK TRAN or SAVE TRAN.

Using Savepoints in Triggers

You can set a savepoint in a trigger and roll back to the savepoint. This will roll back only the operations within the trigger subsequent to the savepoint. The trigger and the transaction it is a part of will still be active until the transaction is subsequently committed or rolled back. The batch will continue processing.

Savepoints can be used to avoid a trigger arbitrarily rolling back an entire transaction. You can roll back to the named savepoint in the trigger and then issue a raiserror and return immediately to pass the error code back to the calling process. The calling process can then check the error status of the data modification statement and take appropriate action, either rolling back the transaction, rolling back to a savepoint in the transaction, or ignoring the error and committing the data modification.

The following is an example of a trigger using a savepoint:

```
if object_id('tr_titles_i') is not null
    drop trigger tr_titles_i
go
create trigger tr_titles_i on titles for insert as
declare @rows int  -- create variable to hold @@rowcount
select @rows = @@rowcount
if @rows = 0 return
save tran titlestrig
if update(pub_id) and (select count(*)
        from inserted i, publishers p
        where p.pub_id = i.pub_id ) != @rows
  begin
       rollback transaction titlestrig
       raiserror ('Invalid pub_id inserted', 16, 1)
  end
return
```

This trigger will roll back all work since the savepoint and return with an error number of 50000. In the transaction, you can check for the error number and make the decision whether to continue the transaction, roll back the transaction, or if savepoints were set in the transaction, roll back to a savepoint and let the transaction continue. The following example rolls back the entire transaction if either of the first two inserts fail, but only rolls back the third if it fails, allowing the first two to be committed:

```
begin tran add_titles
insert titles (title_id, pub_id, title)
       values ('BU1234', '0736', 'Tuning SQL Server')
if @@error = 50000 -- roll back entire transaction and abort batch
   begin
   rollback tran add_titles
   return
   end
insert titles (title_id, pub_id, title)
       values ('BU1236', '0877', 'Tuning SQL Server')
 if @@error = 50000 -- roll back entire transaction and abort batch
   begin
   rollback tran add_titles
   return
   end
save tran keep_first_two  -- set savepoint for partial rollback
insert titles (title_id, pub_id, title)
       values ('BU1235', 'abcd', 'Tuning SQL Server')
 if @@error = 50000  -- roll back to save point, continue batch
   begin
   rollback tran keep_first_two
   end
commit tran
```

TIP

Important reminder: When using a savepoint inside the trigger, the trigger is not rolling back the transaction. Therefore, the batch will not be automatically aborted. You must explicitly return from the batch after rolling back the transaction to prevent subsequent statements from executing.

NOTE

Don't forget to re-enable the constraint on the `titles` table when you are finished testing:

```
alter table titles check constraint FK__titles__pub_id__014935CB
```

Transactions and Locking

SQL Server issues and holds onto locks for the duration of a transaction to ensure the isolation and consistency of the modifications. Data modifications that occur within a transaction will acquire **exclusive locks**, which are then held until the completion of the transaction. **Shared locks**, or read locks, are held for only as long as the statement needs them; usually, a shared lock is released as soon as data has been read from the resource (row, page, table). The length of time a shared lock is held can be modified by the use of keywords such as `HOLDLOCK` in a query. If this option is specified, shared locks are held onto until the completion of the transaction.

What this means for database application developers is that you should try to hold onto as few locks or as small a lock as possible for as short a time as possible to avoid locking contention between applications and to improve concurrency and application performance. The simple rule when working with transactions is "Keep them short and keep them simple!" In other words, do what you need to do in the most concise manner in the shortest possible time. Keep any extraneous commands that do not need to be part of the logical unit of work—such as select statements, dropping temp tables, setting up local variables, and so on—outside of the transaction.

To modify the manner in which a transaction and its locks can be handled by a `SELECT` statement, you can issue the `SET TRANSACTION ISOLATION LEVEL` statement. This statement allows the query to choose how much it is protected against other transactions modifying the data being used. The `SET TRANSACTION ISOLATION LEVEL` statement has the following mutually exclusive options:

- `READ COMMITTED`—This setting is the default for SQL Server. Modifications made within a transaction are locked exclusively, and the changes cannot be viewed by other user processes until the transaction completes. Commands that read data only hold shared locks on the data for as long as it is reading it. Because other transactions are not blocked from modifying the data after you have read it within your transaction, subsequent reads of the data within the transaction might encounter **non-repeatable reads** or **phantom data**.
- `READ UNCOMMITTED`—With this level of isolation, one transaction can read the modifications made by other transactions prior to being committed. This is, therefore, the least restrictive isolation level, but one that allows the reading of dirty and uncommitted data. This option has the same effect as issuing `NOLOCK` within your `SELECT` statements, but it only has to be set once for your connection. This should never be used in an application in which accuracy of the query results is required.
- `REPEATABLE READ`—When this option is set, as data is read, locks are placed and held on the data for the duration of the transaction. These locks prevent other transactions from modifying the data you have read, so that you can carry out multiple passes across the same information and get the same results each time. This isolation level is obviously more restrictive and can block other transactions. However, although it prevents non-repeatable reads, it does not prevent the addition of new rows or *phantom rows* because only *existing* data is locked.
- `SERIALIZABLE`—This option is the most restrictive isolation level because it places a range lock on the data. This prevents *any* modifications to the data being read from until the end of the transaction. It also avoids phantom reads by preventing rows from being added or removed from the data range set.

For more information on lock types, locking behavior, and performance, see Chapter 38, "Locking and Performance."

Coding Effective Transactions

Poorly written or inefficient transactions can have a detrimental effect on concurrency of access to data and overall application performance. SQL Server can hold locks on a number of resources while the transaction is open; modified rows will acquire exclusive locks, and other locks might also be held depending on the isolation level used. To reduce locking contention for resources, transactions should be kept as short and efficient as possible. During development, you might not even notice that a problem exists; the problem might become noticeable only after the system load is increased and multiple users are executing transactions simultaneously. Following are some guidelines to consider when coding transactions to minimize locking contention and improve application performance:

- Do not return result sets within a transaction. Doing so prolongs the transaction unnecessarily. Perform all data retrieval and analysis outside the transaction.
- *Never* prompt for user input during a transaction. If you do, you lose all control over the duration of the transaction. (I have seen even the best programmers miss this one on occasion.) On the failure of a transaction, be sure to issue the rollback before putting up a message box telling the user that a problem occurred.
- Keep the start and end of a transaction together in the same batch, or better yet, use a stored procedure for the operation.
- Keep the transaction short. Start the transaction at the point you need to do the modifications. Do any preliminary work beforehand.
- Make careful use of different locking schemes and transaction isolation levels.
- If user input is unavoidable between data retrieval and modification, and you need to handle the possibility of another user modifying the data values read, use optimistic locking strategies rather than actual locks by using `HOLDLOCK` or other locking options. Optimistic locking makes use of the `WHERE` clause to update the data rather than holding onto locks. Chapters 26, "Using Transact-SQL in SQL Server 2000," and 38 both cover optimistic locking methods.
- Collect multiple transactions into one transaction, or batch transactions together, if appropriate. This might seem to go against some of the other suggestions, but it reduces the amount of overhead that SQL Server will encounter to start, finish, and log the transactions.

Long-Running Transactions

As you have already seen, transaction information is recorded in each database's transaction log. However, long-running transactions can be a cause of consternation to the system administrator who is attempting to back up and prune the transaction log. Only the inactive portion of the log can be truncated during this operation. The inactive portion of the log is the pages containing log records for all completed transactions prior to the first log record of the oldest still-active transaction (see Figure 31.5). Even if completed transactions follow the first record of the oldest active transaction, they cannot be removed from the log until the oldest active transaction completes. This is because the log is pruned by clearing out entire pages of information prior to the oldest active transaction. Pages after this point cannot be cleared because they might contain records for the active transaction that would be needed in the event of a rollback or database recovery.

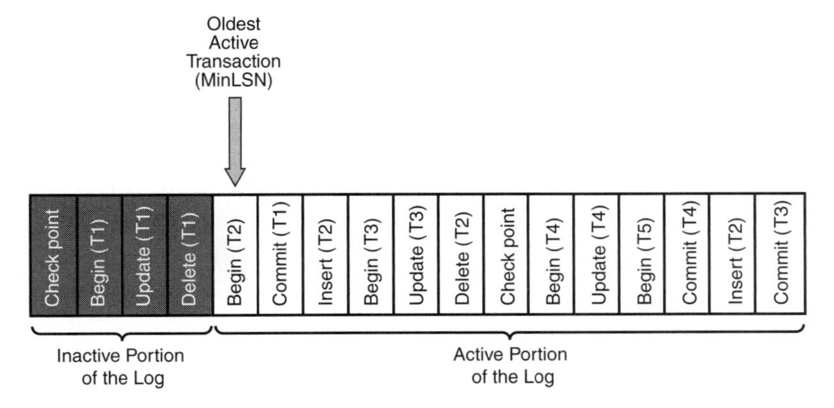

FIGURE 31.5 The inactive portion of the log is the pages in the log prior to the oldest active transaction.

In addition to preventing the log from being pruned, long-running transactions can degrade concurrency by holding locks for an extended period of time, preventing other users from accessing the locked data.

To get information about the oldest active transaction in a database, you can use the `DBCC OPENTRAN` command. The syntax is as follows:

```
DBCC OPENTRAN [('DatabaseName' | DatabaseId)]
[WITH TABLERESULTS [, NO_INFOMSGS]]
```

The following example examines the oldest active transaction for the pubs database:

```
DBCC OPENTRAN (pubs)
go

Transaction information for database 'pubs'.
```

```
Oldest active transaction:
    SPID (server process ID) : 51
    UID (user ID) : 1
    Name          : t1
    LSN           : (62:207:1)
    Start time    : Jun 13 2001 11:58:16:820PM
DBCC execution completed. If DBCC printed error messages, contact your
 system administrator.
```

DBCC OPENTRAN returns the spid of the process that initiated the transaction, the user ID, the name of the transaction (this is when naming transactions are helpful because they might help you identify the SQL code that initiated the transaction), the Log Sequence Number (LSN) of the page containing the initial BEGIN TRAN statement for the transaction, and finally, the time the transaction was started.

If you specify the TABLERESULTS option, this information is returned in two columns that you can load into a table for logging or comparison purposes. The NO_INFOMSGS option suppresses the display of the 'DBCC execution completed...' message. The following example runs DBCC OPENTRAN and inserts the results into a temp table:

```
CREATE TABLE #opentran_results
( result_label VARCHAR(30), result_value VARCHAR(46))

insert #opentran_results exec ('dbcc opentran (pubs) WITH TABLERESULTS,
➥no_infomsgs')

select * from #opentran_results
go

result_label                   result_value
------------------------------ ----------------------------------------------
OLDACT_SPID                    51
OLDACT_UID                     1
OLDACT_NAME                    t1
OLDACT_LSN                     (62:211:11)
OLDACT_STARTTIME               Jun 14 2001 12:50:28:233AM
```

If no open transactions exist for the database, you will receive the following message from DBCC OPENTRAN:

```
No active open transactions.
DBCC execution completed. If DBCC printed error messages, contact your
 system administrator.
```

DBCC OPENTRAN provides a means for you to identify which transactions are potential problems based on their longevity. If you capture the process information at the same time using sp_who, you can identify who or what application is causing the longest-running transaction(s). Using this information, you can terminate the process if necessary, or you can just have a quiet word with the user if the query is *ad hoc* or with the application developers if it is SQL code generated by a custom application.

Bound Connections

During the course of a transaction, the process that initiated the transaction acquires exclusive locks on the data that is modified. These locks prevent other user processes or connections from seeing any of these changes until they are committed. However, it is common for some SQL Server applications to have multiple connections to SQL Server. Even though each connection might be for the same user, SQL Server treats each connection as an entirely separate SQL Server process, and by default, one connection cannot see the uncommitted changes of another, nor modify records locked by the other connection.

Bound connections provide a means of linking multiple connections together to share the same lock space and participate in the same transaction. This can be useful, especially if your application makes use of extended-stored procedures. Extended-stored procedures, although invoked from within a user session, run externally in a separate session. The extended-stored procedure might need to call back into the database to access data. Without bound connections between the original process and the extended-stored procedure, the extended-stored procedure would be blocked by the locks held on the data by the originating process.

Bound connections are of two types: local and distributed. **Local bound connections** are two or more connections within a single server that are bound into a single transaction space. **Distributed bound connections** make use of the Microsoft Distributed Transaction Coordinator (described in more detail in the later section "Distributed Transactions") to share a transaction space across connections from more than one server. This section will discuss how to set up and use local bound connections.

Creating Bound Connections

Binding connections together is actually fairly simple and requires the acquisition of a token by the first process that can be passed to another connection that identifies the lock space to be shared.

A bind token is acquired using the stored procedure sp_getbindtoken. This stored procedure creates a bound connection context and returns the unique identifier for this through an output parameter:

```
sp_getbindtoken @TokenVariable OUTPUT [, @for_xp_flag]
```

The *@TokenVariable* is a variable defined as a varchar(255) and is used to receive the bind token from the stored procedure. If you pass the @for_xp_flag argument a 1, the stored procedure will create a bind token that can be used by extended-stored procedures to call back into SQL Server.

NOTE

Only the owner of a connection can gain the bind token for it.

After you have the bind token, you have to pass it to the intended co-client, who then uses a different stored procedure, sp_bindsession, to participate in your transaction context:

```
sp_bindsession [@TokenVariable | NULL]
```

The *@TokenVariable* is the value created in the previous step. The NULL value is used to unbind a connection from another. You can also unbind a connection by executing sp_bindsession without arguments.

CAUTION

Some users have reported that attempting to unbind from a connection while a transaction is still active might cause all the involved connections to hang. It is recommended that after a connection is bound to another, you should wait until the completion of the transaction before attempting to unbind it.

To illustrate the use of these procedures together, consider the following code:

```
DECLARE @token VARCHAR(255)
EXECUTE sp_getbindtoken @token OUTPUT
```

This results in the following value for @token:

```
NQ9---5---.Q>Z4YC:T>1F:N-1-288TH
```

Each call to sp_getbindtoken results in a different value. Depending on who the intended recipient is, you must find some way to programmatically communicate this value to them, which they then use in the call:

```
EXEC sp_bindsession 'NQ9---5---.Q>Z4YC:T>1F:N-1-288TH'
```

In addition to sharing lock space, bound connections also share the same transaction space. If you execute a ROLLBACK TRAN from a bound connection, it will roll back the transaction initiated in the orginating session. It is recommeded that all transaction control statements be kept in the initial connection. If an error occurs in a bound connection, it should return an error code to the originating session so that it can perform the appropriate rollback.

Binding Multiple Applications

If you bind connections across applications, you have to find a way of communicating the bind token so that it can be used with `sp_bindsession`. SQL Server does not provide a simple solution to this problem; you can consider mechanisms like these:

- Using an IPC such as Remote Procedure Calls (RPC), Dynamic Data Exchange (DDE), or Net-DDE.
- Placing the bind token in a file that is accessible by each application.
- Storing the bind token in a SQL Server table. You might also create a stored procedure to manage the assignment of the token to the requesting applications.
- If the applications are local, you might be able to pass the token through global or shared memory, or directly with a function call.

An important downside exists to using bound connections: sequential processing. Only one connection out of all the connections bound together can actually be doing any work at any given time. This means that during a result set retrieval, the entire result set must be retrieved or the command canceled before any other work can be done by a participating connection. Any attempt to perform an operation while another operation is in process results in an error that should be trapped so that you can resubmit the work after a certain time interval.

Distributed Transactions

Typically, transaction management controls only the data modifications made within a single SQL Server. However, with the increasing interest and implementation of distributed systems is a need to access and modify distributed data within a single unit of work. What if in the banking example the checking accounts reside on one server, and the savings accounts on another? To move money from one account to another would require updates to two separate servers. How do you modify data on two different servers and still treat it as a single unit of work? You need some way to ensure that the distributed transaction retains the same ACID properties as a local transaction.

To provide this capability, SQL Server ships with the Microsoft Distributed Transaction Coordinator (MS DTC) service, which provides the ability to control and manage the integrity of multiserver transactions. MS DTC uses the industry standard two-phase commit protocol to ensure the consistency of all parts of any distributed transaction passing through MS SQL Server and any referenced Linked Servers.

The process for configuring your servers and writing your SQL code to support distributed transactions is covered in the next chapter.

Summary

A transaction is a Logical Unit of Work as well as a unit of recovery. The successful control of transactions is of the utmost importance to the correct modification of related information. In this chapter, you learned how to define and control transactions, examined different transaction-management schemes, learned how the recovery process works, and discovered how to correctly code transactions within triggers and stored procedures. You also learned methods for optimizing transactions to improve application performance and got an overview of locking and distributed transactions. Distributed transactions will be discussed further in the next chapter, "Distributed Transaction Processing," and locking will be covered in more detail in Chapter 38.

CHAPTER 32

Distributed Transaction Processing

by Paul Bertucci

IN THIS CHAPTER

- Distributed Transaction Processing
- Distributed Queries
- Linked Servers
- Distributed Transactions
- MS DTC Architecture

To take advantage of distributed databases (data), you need to understand their capabilities, their management, and the monitoring and tuning considerations that are unique to them.

With the rapid deployment and massive increase of new computers and databases throughout a company's infrastructure, ways to harness this distributed data are becoming one of the top needs (and top problems!). Microsoft's latest version of the Distributed Transaction Coordinator (MS DTC) for SQL Server 2000 has become one of the best and most self-contained distributed transaction managers around. It takes advantages of numerous capabilities that provide a company with an environment to make use of its data no matter where it is. This chapter will outline the main features of MS DTC (within Component Services), identify what you need to look out for with MS DTC, and show how to build up and execute a distributed transaction that is controlled by MS DTC.

Distributed Transaction Processing

A distributed database (data) environment is a connected set of datasources that might or might not need to be accessed together. The Distributed Transaction Processing breadth is illustrated in Figure 32.1.

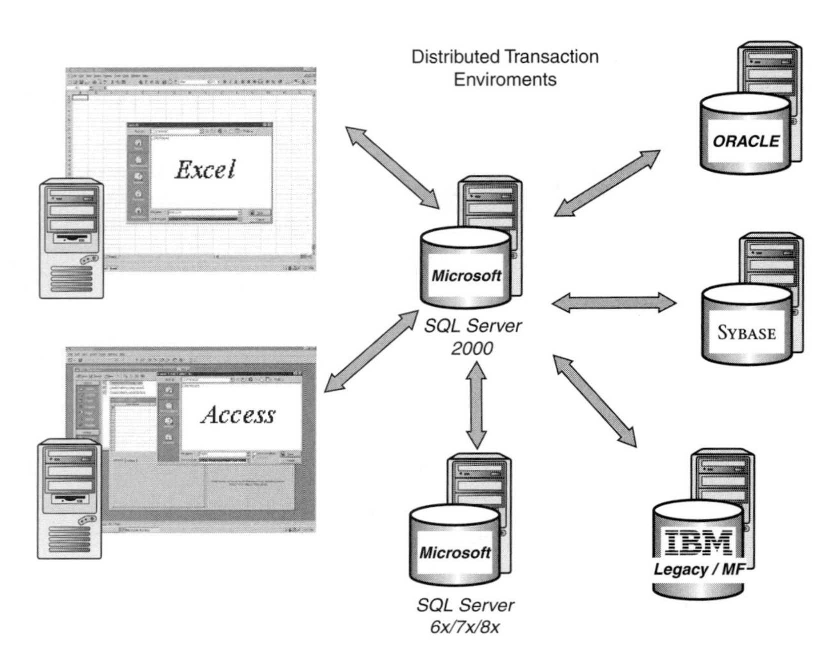

FIGURE 32.1 Distributed Transaction Processing breadth.

That distributed access could be read only (as with Distributed Queries) or contain updates (as with Distributed Transactions). You might have data distributed for a variety of reasons, some of which might include the following:

- Physically partition data within your company (by geographic regions or by business function) for performance and integrity reasons. You can see physically partitioned data sources in Figure 32.2.
- Disparate data containers on numerous separate computer systems within your company (some datasources in Excel, Access, DB2, Oracle, MS SQL Server, and so on) because of operational necessity. This is shown in Figure 32.3.
- Different company datasources due to company merges and acquisitions (parent company datasources versus subsidiary company datasources—these might always remain different). Datasource partitioning is shown in Figure 32.4.

Regardless of the reasons of the distributed data or the types of access required against this data, the Microsoft SQL Server 2000 environment along with the Distributed Transaction Coordinator can readily address most of your needs.

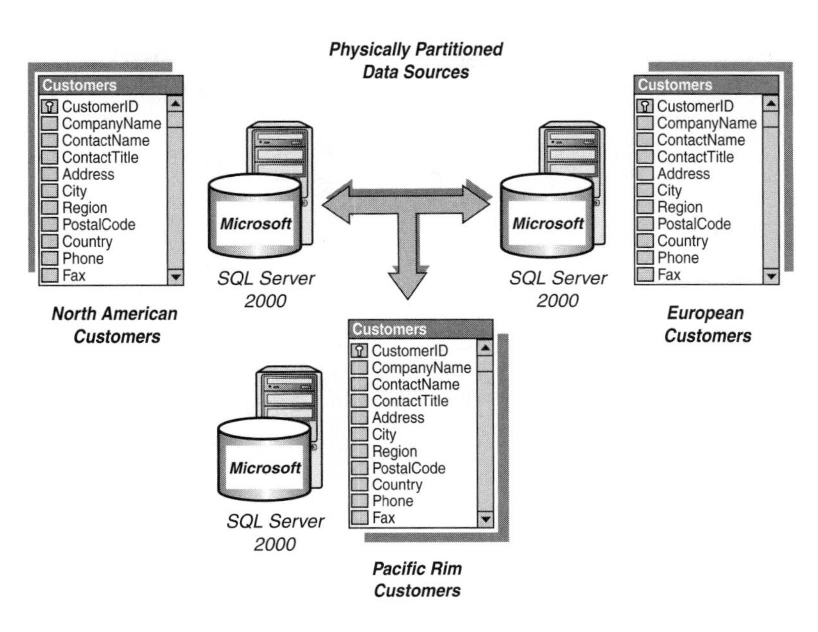

FIGURE 32.2 Physically partitioned data sources.

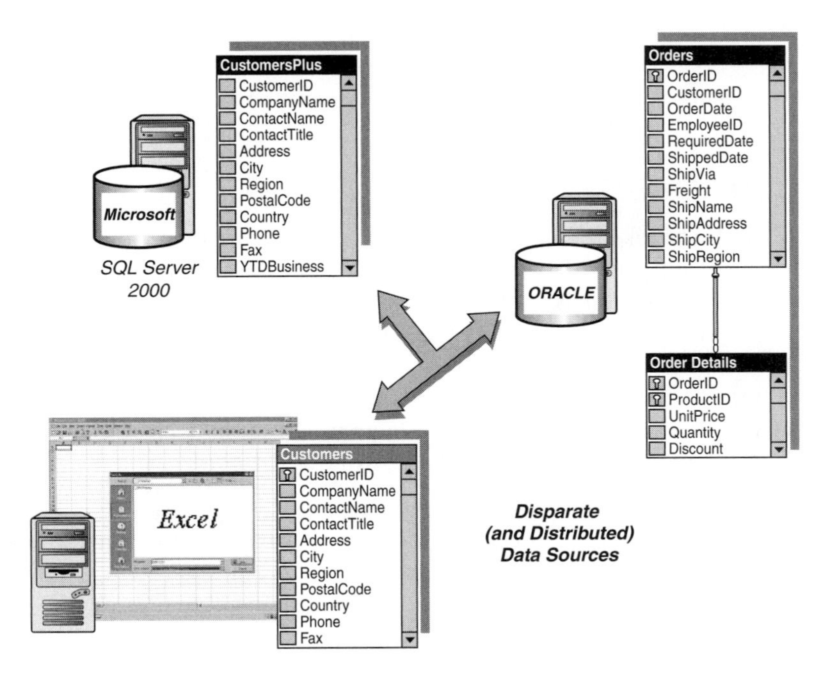

FIGURE 32.3 Disparate and distributed data sources.

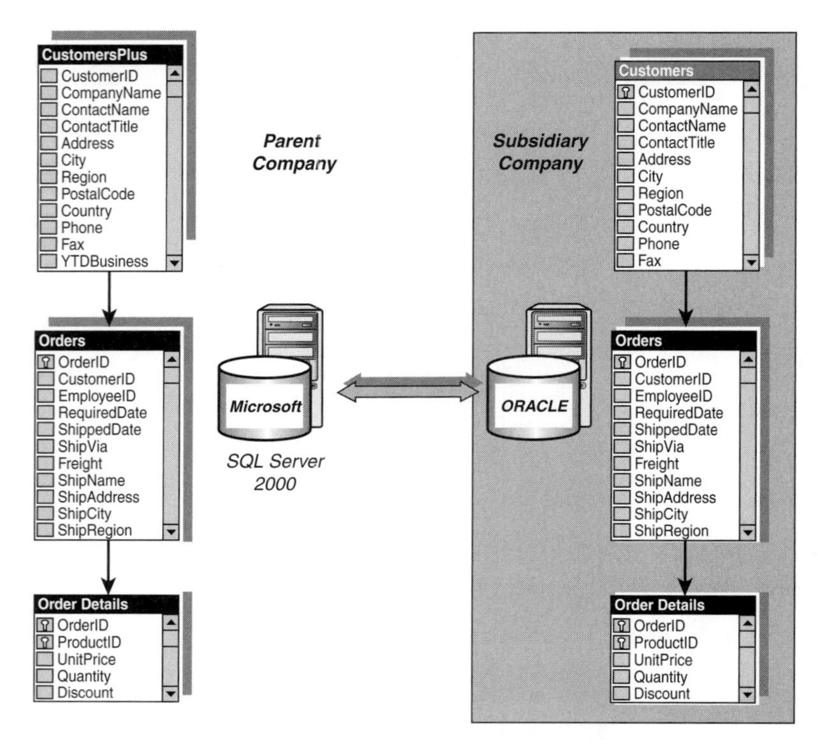

FIGURE 32.4 Parent and Subsidiary Company datasource partitioning.

Distributed Queries

This chapter will first look at what needs to be in place to support a pure read-only, distributed query requirement. For read only, Microsoft offers the most data access power because not as many things need to be coordinated for reads. Distributed queries are easily created for most types of datasources via OLE DB providers and ODBC drivers. This even includes flat files. Basically, any datasource that can provide the ODBC or OLE DB compliance information can serve as a datasource in the Microsoft SQL Server environment. OLE DB providers and ODBC expose their data in tabular objects called rowsets that can be referenced in Transact-SQL statements as if they were a SQL Server table.

One of the previously mentioned distributed data examples was that of a company with disparate (and distributed) datasources (refer to Figure 32.3). Now take this a step further and implement a distributed query that reads across one or more servers. More specifically, the sales director needs to see a weekly report of all customers, their most current addresses, and the "YTD business" (sales) of each of these customers. The Excel spreadsheet is being used for the address information because this spreadsheet (SWCustomers.xls) comes directly from the sales force and is highly accurate.

Unfortunately, the customer information on the SQL Server tables (CustomersPlus table) is not updated very often and has a tendency to become quickly out of date. However, the YTD business sales data on this CustomersPlus table is maintained via triggers and is up to the minute. The report is called Customer Orders Report (CustOrders.rpt). This report can easily be fulfilled via a single distributed query that will join the customer information in Excel with that of the OLTP Customer YTD business data on SQL Server 2000, as seen in Figure 32.5.

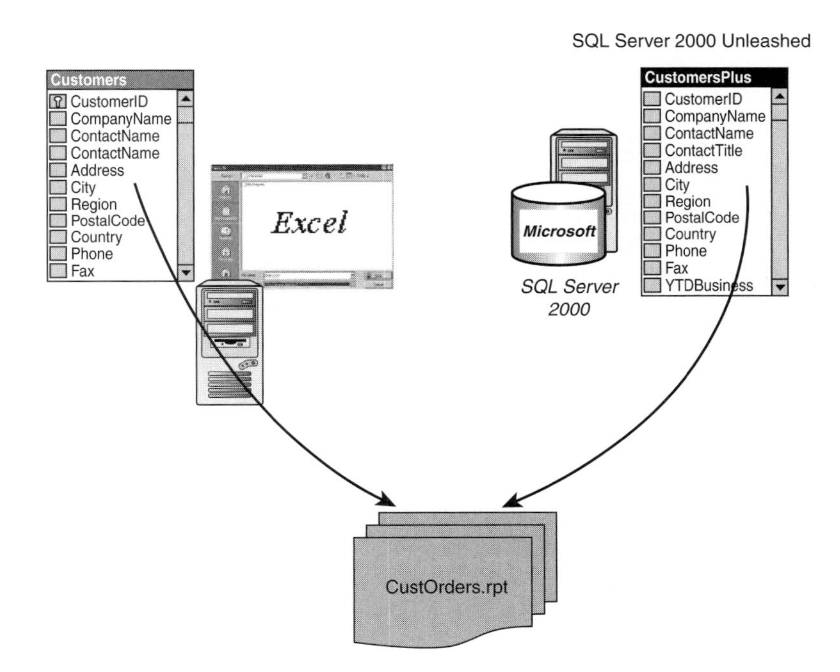

FIGURE 32.5 Cross-system report (distributed query).

In general, you will need to create a SQL Query that joins the CustomerPlus table on SQL Server 2000 in the Southwind database with the Excel spreadsheet on the sales director's machine (SWCustomers.xls).

```
SELECT a.CustomerID, a.CompanyName, b.ContactName, b.Address,
b.City, b.Region, b.PostalCode, b.Country, b.Phone,
b.Fax, a.YTDBusiness
FROM CustomersPlus AS a
INNER JOIN SWCustomers (from the Excel spreadsheet) AS b
ON a.CustomerID = b.CustomerID
```

The previous Transact-SQL statement won't run this way because it is not referencing the tables or Excel spreadsheet correctly yet. A few things will need to be set up on the SQL Server side first, such as defining a linked server and a login. You will also need to modify the `FROM` statement to reflect a distributed datasource location (a linked server location). For this requirement, you will do the following:

- Define a linked server reference that will represent the Excel spreadsheet as if it were a relational table. (This Linked Server reference will be called ExcelSW.)
- Set up a linked server login for SQL Server 2000 to use to access this spreadsheet. This is needed when using the OLE DB provider of Microsoft.Jet.OLEDB.4.0.

Linked Servers

As mentioned before, you must first create a linked server before you can work with data from a remote SQL Server or another OLE DB datasource, such as Excel, Access, or Oracle. A linked server consists of an OLE DB or other datasource that is registered on the local SQL Server. After this is set up, Transact-SQL statements can be sent directly to a remote datasource via this linked server reference as if it were a normal relational table on SQL Server. This will be needed for both distributed queries and distributed transactions. For an extensive description of linked servers, see Chapter 19, "Managing Linked and Remote Servers."

Linked Server Setup to Remote Datasources

To enable you to execute Transact-SQL statements on a remote SQL Server or OLE DB datasource, you must create a link to the server or datasource. You can do so using either Enterprise Manager or the `sp_addlinkedserver` system-stored procedure:

```
 sp_addlinkedserver [@server =] 'server'
[, [@srvproduct =] 'product_name'][, [@provider =] 'provider_name']
[, [@datasrc =] 'data_source'] [, [@location =] 'location']
[, [@provstr =] 'provider_string'] [, [@catalog =] 'catalog']
```

This defines a remote datasource as a linked server (like an Excel spreadsheet) and includes the OLE DB provider.

As you can see in the following code, not all of these parameters are required. You simply provide the ones needed for the particular type of OLE DB provider. Some parameters require less information than others to establish connectivity to that remote datasource. In the Customer Orders report example (Figure 32.5), you will need to set up a linked server called ExcelSW with `sp_addlinkedserver` as follows:

```
/* Set up of an Excel linked server */
EXEC sp_addlinkedserver
'ExcelSW',    /* linked server name you want to use*/
```

```
'Jet Excel',   /* product name - can be anything */
'Microsoft.Jet.OLEDB.4.0', /* OLE provider name */
'd:\SWCustomers.xls',  /* datasource name */
NULL,  /* location not needed in this case */
'Excel 8.0',  /* Provider string if needed */
NULL    /* catalog name if needed */
go
```


To see the linked servers that have been defined on this SQL Server, simply use `sp_linkedservers`.

```
EXEC sp_linkedservers
Go
```

The `sp_linkedservers` execution provides the list of all linked servers on this SQL Server:

```
SRV_Name            SRV_Provider  SRV_Product SRV_Datasource etc..
C81124-C\DBARCH01          SQLOLEDB      SQL Server    C81124-C\DBARCH01
ExcelSW      Microsoft.Jet.OLEDB.4.0    Jet Excel d:\SWCustomers.xls   Excel 8.0
repl_distributor           SQLOLEDB      SQL Server    C81124-C\DBARCH01
```

As you can see, the list now contains the linked server that was just created (ExcelSW). However, you won't be able to use this linked server yet. A linked server login will have to be created for SQL Server to actually get to the datasource. You have essentially established the path to the datasource with `sp_addlinkedserver`.

To do this from Enterprise Manager, it is a simple one-step process from the linked server tree node. Navigate to the Security node and then right-click the Linked Servers Node (or choose the New Linked Server option from the Action menu pull-down list). Just provide the same information as is required for the type of OLE DB provider you want to access. As you can see from Figure 32.6, the General properties tab allows easy entry of a new linked server and a datasource file.

Connecting to a Remote SQL Server

You do not need to specify the *`provider_name`*, *`data_source`*, *`location`*, *`provider_string`*, *or `catalog name`* when you are connecting to a SQL Server 6.5 (or higher) remote datasource. It is a simple process of providing the server name and the product name. As an example, you will create a linked server for another SQL Server named `'NWServer'`.

```
sp_addlinkedserver 'NWServer', 'SQL Server'
```

Establishing Linked Server Security

When a remote/distributed query is executed, the local SQL Server logs into the remote SQL Server or datasource on behalf of the user. Therefore, it might be necessary to establish security between the local and remote datasources. However, if the user's login ID and password exist on both the local and remote SQL servers, the local SQL Server can use the account information of the user to log into the remote SQL Server.

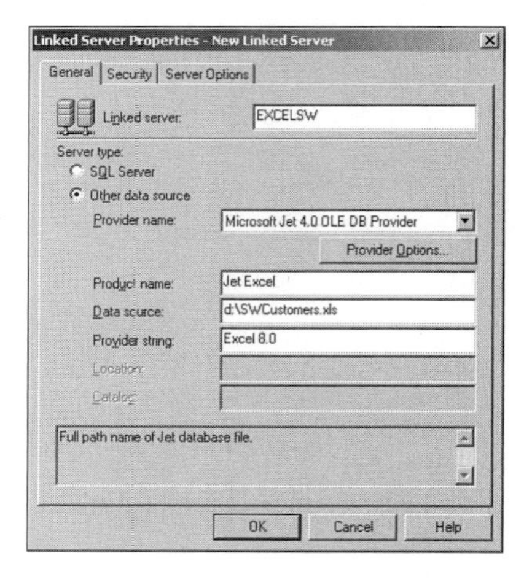

FIGURE 32.6 New Linked Server Properties specification.

To establish login IDs and passwords between local and remote SQL Servers (or data-sources), use the `sp_addlinkedsrvlogin` system-stored procedure.

Keep in mind that `sp_addlinkedsrvlogin` does not create user accounts. It merely maps a login account created on the local server to an account created on the remote server. In some cases, it utilizes a default system login placeholder (like with the Admin account with Excel spreadsheets). Again, for more detailed information on linked servers, refer to Chapter 19.

The syntax for the `sp_addlinkedsrvlogin` system-stored procedure is as follows:

```
sp_addlinkedsrvlogin [ @rmtsrvname = ] 'rmtsrvname'
                          [ , [ @useself = ] 'useself' ]
                          [ , [ @locallogin = ] 'locallogin' ]
                          [ , [ @rmtuser = ] 'rmtuser' ]
                          [ , [ @rmtpassword = ] 'rmtpassword' ]
```

In the next example, you will set up the mapping required to use a SQL Server login ("sa" in this case) to access a linked server that is an Excel spreadsheet. Again, you will be setting up the linked server login for the ExcelSW linked server.

```
EXEC sp_addlinkedsrvlogin
'ExcelSW',     /* remote/linked server name */
'false',              /* don't use user's own info */
'sa',          /* use already created login id */
'Admin',              /* maps to login id (for Excel) */
NULL                  /* no password, in this example */
```

Now the linked server reference is registered to SQL Server and the login/access has been mapped to enable it to be used.

You can also use a system-stored procedure to quickly find out what linked server logins have been defined. Simply execute the procedure without parameters to see all that have been defined on this local SQL Server:

```
EXEC sp_helplinkedsrvlogin
```


The list of linked server logins are easily viewed as follows:

```
Linked Server       Local Login   Is Self Mapping   Remote Login
C81124-C\DBARCH01   NULL          1                 NULL
ExcelNW             NULL          1                 NULL
ExcelNW             sa            0                 Admin
ExcelSW             NULL          1                 NULL
ExcelSW             sa            0                 Admin
NWServer            NULL          1                 NULL
repl_distributor    NULL          0                 distributor_admin
```

If you haven't yet added the login for the linked server that is a valid login at the referenced server, you will probably get the following error message on your first query attempt:

```
Server: Msg 7399, Level 16, State 1, Line 1
OLE DB provider 'Microsoft.Jet.OLEDB.4.0' reported an error.
Authentication failed.
```

SQL Server simply has nothing to map to on the linked/remote server side. You must resolve this by adding a valid user ID with the appropriate permissions for the linked server to use when attempting data access.

Keep in mind that when you complete the linking process, SQL Server really keeps these data resources linked in many ways. Most importantly, it keeps the schema definition linked. In other words, if the schema of a remote table on a linked server changes, any server that has links to it also knows the change. Even when the linked server's schema comes from something such as Excel, if you change the Excel spreadsheet in any way, that change will be automatically reflected back at the local SQL Server. This is extremely significant from a metadata (schema's) integrity point of view. This is what is meant by "completely linked!"

Querying a Linked Server

When you write a distributed query (or a distributed transaction for that matter), you must use a four-part name to refer to the linked objects. The linked server is said to conform to the IDBSchemaRowset interface. (It allows for the schema information to be retrieved from the remote server.) If the linked server doesn't conform to this interface, you will have to do all access using pass-through queries in the `OPENDATASOURCE` or `OPENROWSET` function. However, in most cases, you will be using this four-part name:

```
linked_server_name.catalog.schema.object_name
```

The name can be broken down as follows:

linked_server_name	The unique network-wide name of the linked server `[Servername\instancename|Servername]`
catalog	The catalog or database in the OLE DB that contains the object
schema	The schema or object owner
object_name	The name of the table or data object

For example, if you want to use the CustomersPlus table that is owned by the database owner (dbo) in the Southwind database on the C81124-C\DBARCH01 linked SQL Server, use the following four-part name to reference the CustomersPlus table:

```
[C81124-C\DBARCH01].[Southwind].[dbo].[CustomersPlus]
```

Transact-SQL with Linked Servers

You can use the following Transact-SQL statements with linked servers:

- `SELECT` statement with a `WHERE` clause or a `JOIN` clause
- `INSERT`, `UPDATE`, and `DELETE` statements

> **NOTE**
>
> Restrictions for use of Insert, Update, and Delete exist with certain OLE DB providers. Some OLE DB providers only allow reads, such as with flat files.

You cannot use the following:

- `CREATE`, `ALTER`, or `DROP` statements
- An `ORDER BY` clause in a `SELECT` statement if a large object column from a linked table is in the select list of the `SELECT` statement
- `READTEXT`, `WRITETEXT`, and `UPDATETEXT` statements

Whenever possible, SQL Server pushes relational operations such as joins, restrictions, projections, sorts, and group by operations to the OLE DB datasource. SQL Server does not default to scanning the base table into SQL Server and performing the relational operations itself. SQL Server will actually query the OLE DB provider to determine the level of

SQL grammar it supports, and, based on that information, will push as much as possible to the OLE DB provider.

To execute the original Customer Orders report-distributed query, you can execute the following SQL statement. As you will recall, the statement will need to join the Excel spreadsheet file (SWCustomers.xls) to the SQL Server table named CustomersPlus, resulting in this week's Customer Orders report for the sales director. The linked server and linked server login needed to fulfill this access have been set up. The following query generates the required report:


```
USE Southwind
Go
SELECT a.CustomerID, a.CompanyName, b.ContactName, b.Address,
b.City, b.Region, b.PostalCode, b.Country, b.Phone,
b.Fax, a.YTDBusiness
FROM CustomersPlus AS a
INNER JOIN [ExcelSW]...[SWCustomers$] AS b
ON a.CustomerID = b.CustomerID
go
```

The Customer Orders report now can generate a valid distributed resultset as follows:

```
CustomerID   CompanyName                 ContactName
        Address              City        Region        . . . YTDBusiness
BLAUS                Blauer See Delikatessen    Vilay Sithongkang
        4394 Water Bridge     Concord      CA             3239.8000
CHOPS                Chop-suey Chinese          Martin Sommer
        6 of One Half a St.    Berkeley    CA            12886.3000
PICCO                Piccolo und mehr           Adam Greifer
121 All the way up Ct. Los Angeles CA            26259.9500
```

An alternative method of executing a distributed SQL Query is to use the `OPENQUERY` syntax. Following is an example of a remote/distributed query against the ExcelSW linked server:

```
SELECT CustomerID, Address
FROM OPENQUERY([ExcelSW], 'SELECT CustomerID, Address
  FROM [SWCustomers$]')
Go
```

Executing a Stored Procedure Via a Linked Server

It is possible to execute a stored procedure via a linked server. The server hosting the client connection will accept the client's request and send it to the linked server. The `EXECUTE` statement must contain the name of the linked server as part of its syntax:

```
EXECUTE servername.dbname.owner.procedure_name
```

This example executes sp_helpsrvrole, which shows a list of available fixed server roles on the 'NWServer' remote server:

```
EXEC NWServer.master.dbo.sp_helpsrvrole
```

Distributed Transactions

With the increasing proliferation of distributed systems is a need to access and modify data that is often in separate physical locations and in varying types of datasources. In addition, it is extremely important that these transactions be one logical transaction (one Unit of Work, or UOW). You need a way to ensure that the distributed transaction operates in the same way that a local transaction does, and that it adheres to the same ACID properties of a local transaction, across multiple servers.

Microsoft has implemented its distributed transaction processing capabilities based on the industry standard **two-phase commit protocol**. It utilizes the Distributed Transaction Coordinator service (MS DTC) as the controller of this capability. This ensures the consistency of all parts of any distributed transaction passing through MS SQL Server and any referenced linked servers. The variation on the ACID test is that all sites (servers) depend on one another for completion of an update, and they must give up the site autonomy part of ACID.

After you decide to do distributed transaction processing, you must know and understand the MS DTC architecture thoroughly.

MS DTC Architecture

In general, each Microsoft SQL Server will have an associated distributed transaction coordinator (MS DTC) on the same machine with it.

The MS DTC allows applications to extend transactions across two or more instances of MS SQL Server and participate in transactions managed by transaction managers that comply with the X/Open DTP XA standard.

The MS DTC will act as the primary coordinator for these distributed transactions. The specific job of the MS DTC is to enlist (include) and coordinate SQL Servers and remote servers (linked servers) that are part of a single distributed transaction.

SQL Server will automatically promote a local transaction to a distributed transaction when it encounters the remote server access in combination with an update request, whether or not you have explicitly started a distributed transaction. The MS DTC coordinates the execution of the distributed transaction at each participating datasource and makes sure the distributed transaction completes. It ensures that all updates are made permanent in all datasources (committed), or makes sure that all of the work is undone (rolled back) if it needs to be. At all times, the state of all datasources involved are kept intact. To guarantee that this is taken care of properly, the MS DTC manages each distributed transaction using the two-phase commit protocol.

Two-Phase Commit Protocol

An MS DTC service provides two-phase commit functionality based on its ability to act as a transaction manager across one or more resource managers. A SQL Server or other OLE DB datasource is considered a resource manager of its own data. A distributed transaction is made up of local transactions in each individual resource manager. Each resource manager must be able to commit or roll back its local transaction in coordination with all the other resource managers enlisted in the distributed transaction (as illustrated in Figure 32.7). That is the transaction manager's job (MS DTC in this case). This distributed transaction is referred to as a UOW. In fact, it will appear in the Transaction List portion of DTC and have a status and a unique UOW ID assigned to it.

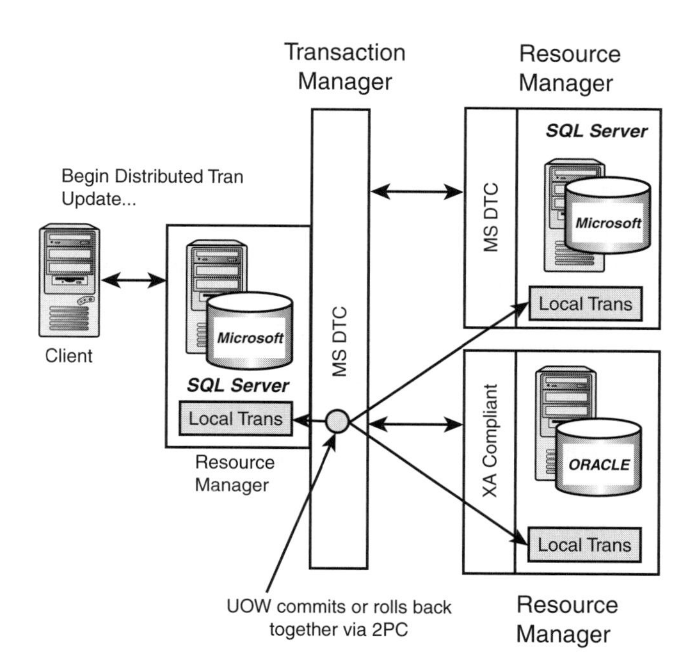

FIGURE 32.7 MS DTC architecture.

A distributed transaction goes through the following steps:

1. The distributed transaction is started and is assigned a unique UOW ID by the controlling distributed transaction coordinator (the transaction manager) for the SQL Server.

2. Data modification statements are issued against any linked/remote servers available to SQL Server (as well as to SQL Server). These become local transactions at each linked/remote server and are controlled by the local resource manager (the DBMS engine in most cases).

3. The transaction server (MS DTC) enlists the appropriate servers into the distributed transaction.

4. Phase One (Prepare): The transaction manager sends a "prepare to commit" request to each resource manager. The resource managers, in turn, perform their local transaction commit processing to the point just before releasing the minimal locks on the affected resources. All of the resource managers communicate back to the transaction manager that they are "ready to commit."

5. Phase Two (Commit): If all the resource managers return an okay to their prepare requests, the transaction manager sends commit transaction commands to each of them. Then, each resource manager can do a final commit for the local transaction and release the locks on the held resources. The distributed transaction is complete. However, if any of the resource managers returns an error to the prepare request, the transaction manager will send rollback commands to each of the resource managers to undo all the local transactions.

If one of the enlisted SQL Servers is unable to communicate with the transaction server, the database involved is marked as suspect. When the transaction server is "visible" again, the affected server should be restarted so that the database and the in-doubt transaction can be recovered.

In general, an application can initiate a distributed transaction from SQL Server by doing the following:

- Starting with a local transaction and then issuing a distributed query. The transaction will automatically be promoted to a distributed transaction that is controlled by MS DTC.
- Issuing a `BEGIN DISTRIBUTED TRANSACTION` statement explicitly.
- Starting with a local transaction and then issuing a remote procedure call (SQL Server option of `REMOTE_PROC_TRANSACTIONS` must be set "on"). Again, this will automatically be promoted to a distributed transaction.
- Allowing a SQL Server connection to participate in a distributed transaction.

Data Transformation Services (DTS) uses functions offered by the MS DTC to include the benefits of distributed transactions to the DTS package developer. This adds significant data integrity to DTS package programming.

If you haven't already done so, start up the MS DTC service. It should be listed as a service under Microsoft SQL Manager, or it can be started via the Control Panel, Services option. Figure 32.8 shows this.

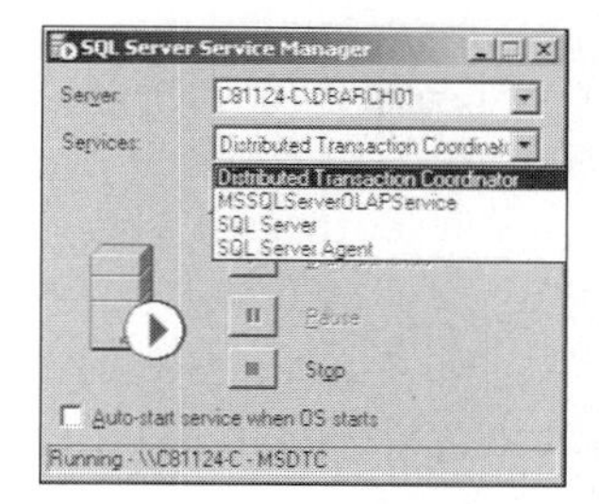

FIGURE 32.8 Starting the MS DTC service.

Another quick way to determine whether your server can communicate with DTC is to open a query window and execute a `BEGIN DISTRIBUTED TRANSACTION` statement:

```
BEGIN DISTRIBUTED TRANSACTION
Go
Server: Msg 8501, Level 16, State 3, Line 1
MSDTC on server 'C81124-C\DBARCH01' is unavailable.
```

The service was probably not started automatically and can be easily done so.

The MS DTC is the transaction manager for distributed transactions. It makes use of a log file to record the outcome of all transactions that have made use of its services.

The Importance of `MSDTC.LOG`

Never modify or delete the `MSDTC.LOG` file. If you delete this file, MS DTC has nowhere to write its activity and ultimately fails.

MSDTC.LOG Location

By default, the DTC log file is installed in the `\System32\DTClog` directory under WIN2000 or WINNT. If you want it somewhere else for performance and backup/recovery purposes, specify this location at install time. It's much easier to change the location at install time than to rewire it later. Plan ahead!

CAUTION

Before you apply service packs or upgrades, make sure that all in-doubt transactions are resolved. Microsoft reserves the right to change the format of the DTC log file between versions.

Executing Distributed Transactions

As a developer, you can change the way you code very slightly by using `BEGIN DISTRIBUTED TRANSACTION` instead of the usual `BEGIN TRANSACTION` (used for local transactions).

Earlier in this chapter, a business requirement of generating a weekly Customer Orders report was described, and the distributed query was coded to fulfill this requirement. You are now ready to turn this into a distributed transaction that will update the address information on SQL Server with the most recent values available from the Excel spreadsheet. You can simply create the distributed transaction as follows:

```
Begin Distributed Transaction
Update CustomersPlus
set Address = b.Address,
City = b.City
FROM CustomersPlus AS a
INNER JOIN [ExcelSW]...[SWCustomers$] AS b
ON a.CustomerID = b.CustomerID
commit transaction
go
```

A quick peek at MS DTC via the MS DTC Client as this distributed transaction is being executed shows its uniquely assigned UOW ID and "active" status. For Windows 2000, this is available through Control Panel, Administrative Tools, Component Services, Transaction List. Figure 32.9 illustrates the active transaction list on a server.

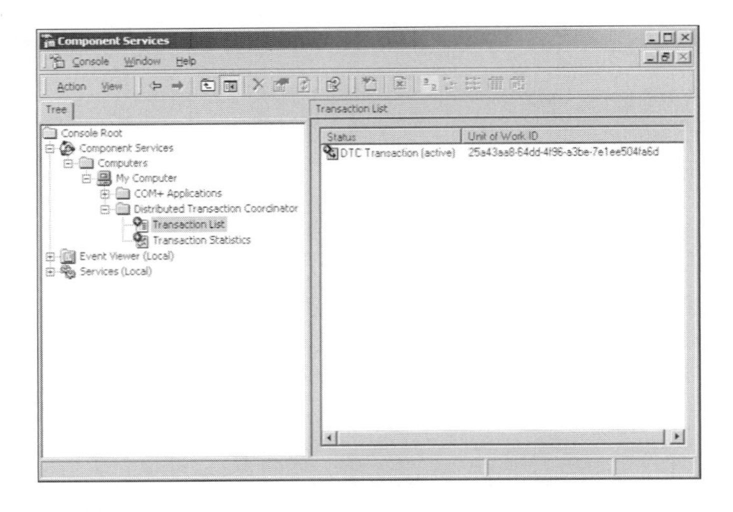

FIGURE 32.9 MS DTC Transaction list.

In general, you will want to try to limit the number of linked/remote servers in a single distributed transaction for performance reasons, locking reasons, and to limit the risk of being hit by a downed network. If you keep the number of linked/remote servers short, they will reward you with great durability.

Performance Monitoring and Troubleshooting

Obviously, because the transaction is more complicated and involves more components (servers, the network, and so on), things are going to go wrong.

The MS DTC Console provides you with a comprehensive set of statistics and information on the DTC service running on the server. It is one of the better ways to monitor some key areas:

- General—Version information, coordinator name, and the ability to start and stop the MS DTC service.
- Transactions—The currently active transactions and their state. From this window, you can also resolve a transaction by forcing a commit, abort, or forget (see Figure 32.10).
- Statistics—The current number of active and in-doubt transactions, together with historical information on the total number committed, aborted, and so on.

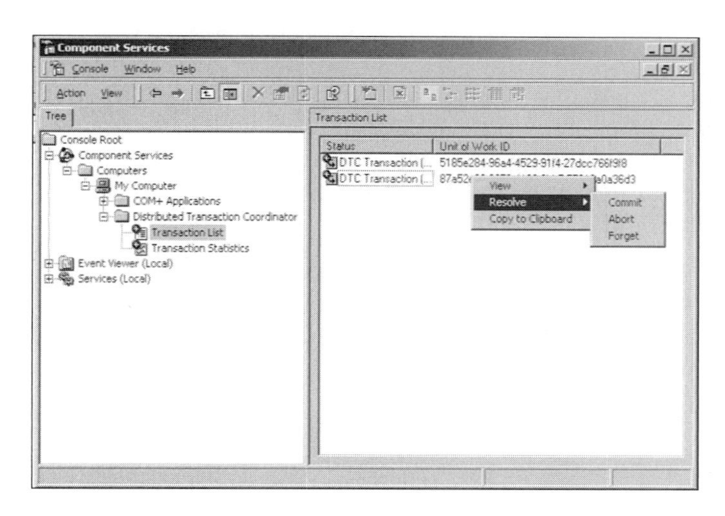

FIGURE 32.10 Resolving a transaction.

You can only resolve a transaction if the transaction status is "in-doubt." The only other way to deal with this is to kill the process `spid`:

```
kill 64      /* the spid id of the initiating transaction */
go
```

If the distributed transaction status is "in-doubt," you can also issue a kill to the UOW and have it rolled back.

```
kill '5185e284-96a4-4529-91f4-27dcc766f9f8' with rollback
go           /* the UOW of the distributed transaction */
```

The Transaction Statistic option is great for seeing current and aggregate distributed transaction quantities. As depicted in Figure 32.11, you can see the workload of the MS DTC and the response times associated with all distributed transactions being handled by this MS DTC.

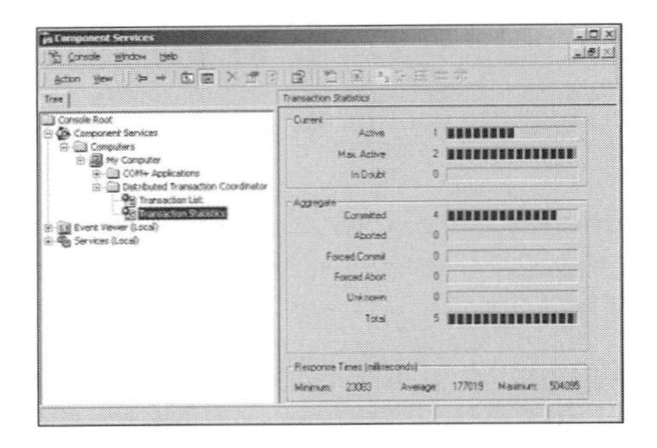

FIGURE 32.11 Transaction statistics.

If you have opened more than one connection to SQL Server (or other linked/remote Server) and submitted asynchronous updates (distributed transactions), one connection can become blocked (locked) by the other. This is said to be a **distributed deadlock**. To avoid this, make sure you have a query time-out for each connection and perhaps a lock time-out for each connection as well. An overall look at the reason for issuing asynchronous updates is in order as well. SQL Server 2000 cannot automatically detect a distributed deadlock. I have had to resort to kills to resolve this situation.

The MS DTC service is also sending application events to the event log. You can start here to investigate the reasons for this service not starting successfully. Figure 32.12 shows the Event Viewer and the MSDTC source information entries.

Event Viewer

Application Log 386 event(s)

Type	Date	Time	Source	Category	Event	User
Information	5/3/2001	3:49:08 PM	MSSQL$DBARCH01	(2)	17055	N/A
Information	5/3/2001	3:39:04 PM	MSDTC	CM	4156	N/A
Information	5/3/2001	3:39:03 PM	MSDTC Client	CM	4156	N/A
Information	5/3/2001	3:03:48 PM	MSDTC Client	CM	4156	N/A
Information	5/3/2001	3:03:47 PM	MSDTC	CM	4156	N/A
Information	5/3/2001	2:11:12 PM	MSDTC Client	CM	4156	N/A
Information	5/3/2001	2:11:12 PM	MSDTC	CM	4156	N/A
Information	5/3/2001	2:07:51 PM	MSDTC Client	CM	4156	N/A
Information	5/3/2001	2:07:51 PM	MSDTC	CM	4156	N/A
Information	5/3/2001	1:45:46 PM	MSSQL$DBARCH01	(2)	17055	SYSTEM
Information	5/3/2001	1:45:42 PM	MSSQL$DBARCH01	(2)	17055	SYSTEM
Information	5/3/2001	1:45:42 PM	MSSQL$DBARCH01	(2)	17055	SYSTEM
Information	5/3/2001	1:45:36 PM	SQLAgent$DBARCH01	Service C...	101	N/A
Information	5/3/2001	1:45:32 PM	MSSQL$DBARCH01	(2)	17055	SYSTEM
Information	5/3/2001	1:45:25 PM	MSDTC	SVC	4097	N/A
Information	5/3/2001	1:45:07 PM	MSSQL$DBARCH01	(2)	17055	N/A
Information	5/3/2001	1:45:07 PM	MSSQL$DBARCH01	(2)	17055	N/A
Warning	5/3/2001	1:45:07 PM	MSSQL$DBARCH01	(8)	19011	N/A
Information	5/3/2001	1:45:06 PM	MSSQL$DBARCH01	(2)	17055	N/A

FIGURE 32.12 Event Viewer and MSDTC source.

Make sure you have enough user connections for all servers involved. The ease and transparency of doing distributed queries/transactions often is overlooked from the remote server's point of view as far as available user connections.

Often overlooked is the bigger picture of distributed transactions and the impact on database backups and recovery. When you enter into supporting distributed transactions, you should also build a well-synchronized set of backup and recovery scripts. Logically related databases that are being updated via distributed transactions should be backed up and recovered together!

SQL Query Analyzer also provides a great picture and details of how a distributed query/transaction is executed. Use it extensively. Following is an example of the execution of the distributed transaction (the "Update statement" from earlier in this chapter). The Execution Plan option, as shown in Figure 32.13, has been chosen to show the cost and method of execution of all pieces of the distributed SQL statement.

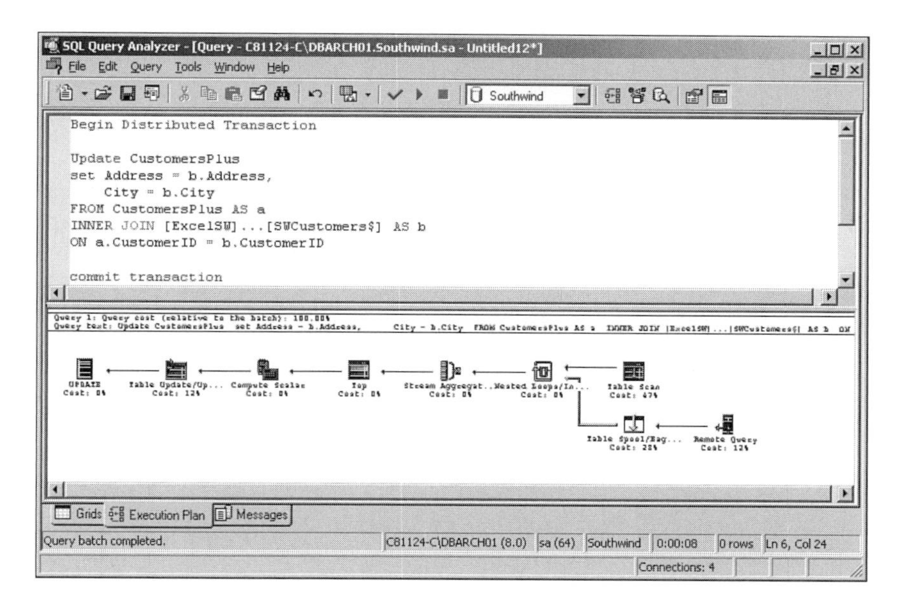

FIGURE 32.13 Execution Plan for a Distributed Query.

In addition, SQL Server 2000 has a mechanism for an OLE DB provider to return data distribution statistics that can be utilized by the query optimizer, increasing the chances of an optimal query plan.

Summary

The breadth of a distributed query/transaction increases the reach of SQL Server to many varied datasources. This power can be extraordinary, but it can be abused if not done properly. It is critical to understand the behavior of a distributed query/transaction so that each affected datasource is kept intact at all times. The MS DTC plays the major role in this capability by controlling the UOW. By implementing a robust two-phase commit protocol environment, Microsoft has provided developers with a safe and fairly simple way to use distributed data regardless of its location in your company. From here, you will head into the world of SQL Server internals and see how SQL Server has been put together to handle concurrent processing, many simultaneous users, large data volumes, and security.

PART V

SQL Server Internals and Performance Tuning

IN THIS PART

CHAPTER 33

SQL Server Internals

by Ray Rankins

IN THIS CHAPTER

If you are migrating to SQL Server 2000 from versions prior to SQL Server 7.0, you will notice that the physical database architecture in SQL Server 2000 is quite different. The new architecture provides increased performance, better scalability, and improved stability. The new architecture also provides a foundation for features that might be introduced in future versions (for example, table partitioning, intertable clustering, and so on).

Why bother learning about the SQL Server internals at all? Although there are fewer settings to tweak and tune and fewer knobs to turn in SQL Server 2000 and 7.0 than in previous versions, you have a better chance of getting the most out of SQL Server if you have a basic knowledge of the internal architecture. This chapter is also meant for those who just like to know this kind of stuff.

This chapter looks at the internal architecture as well as the storage structures in SQL Server and how the storage structures are maintained and managed. This information will help you better understand various issues raised in many of the subsequent chapters.

SQL Server Memory Management

By default, SQL Server 2000 dynamically allocates and deallocates system memory as needed to balance the needs of other applications running on the machine and the needs of its own internal components. As in versions prior to SQL Server 7.0, you do have the option of configuring SQL Server to use a fixed amount of memory; however, unless you have identified a specific problem that requires allocating a fixed amount of memory to SQL Server, it is best to let SQL Server dynamically manage memory.

Regardless of whether the memory is allocated dynamically or is fixed, the total memory space for each SQL Server instance on a system is considered a single unified cache and is managed as a collection of various memory pools. Each memory pool has its own policies and purposes, and memory can be requested by and granted to any of several internal components.

The Buffer Manager and Memory Pools

The main memory component in SQL Server is the buffer pool. Any memory not being used by another memory-related component remains in the buffer pool. The buffer manager handles bringing data and index pages into the buffer pool so that data can be accessed and shared among users. When other components require memory, they request a buffer from the buffer pool. The memory buffers are pages in memory that are the same size (8KB) as a data or index page.

Unlike pre-7.0 versions of SQL Server, there is no fixed, separate procedure cache area. The procedure cache is simply another memory pool in which query trees and plans from stored procedures, triggers, user-defined functions, or ad hoc queries can reside while executing. The size of the procedure cache grows and shrinks as needed (for more information on procedure cache and how it's used, see Chapter 28, "Creating and Managing Stored Procedures in SQL Server," and Chapter 35, "Understanding Query Optimization").

In addition, other pools are used by memory-intensive queries that use sorting or hashing, and by special memory objects that need less than one 8KB page.

The Buffer Manager

Processes in SQL Server can only access data and index pages in memory. Direct access to pages on disk is not allowed. The buffer manager is the process that manages and controls access to the "in memory" versions of the physical disk pages. When a process needs to access a data or index page, the page must first exist in memory in the buffer pool. If the requested page isn't in memory, a physical I/O has to be performed to retrieve the record and then the process can access the in-memory copy of the page. Because physical I/Os are more expensive and time consuming to perform, you want to have a system that performs the fewest physical I/Os as possible. One solution is to provide more memory to SQL Server. The more pages that can reside in memory, and stay there, the more likely a page will be found in memory when requested.

Accessing Memory Buffers

A database appears to a SQL Server process as a simple sequence of numbered pages. The pages in the database are uniquely identified by the database ID, file number, and page number. When a process needs to access a page, it submits a request to the buffer manager, specifying the unique database ID, file number, and page number identifier.

To provide fast access to data in memory and avoid memory scans for data pages, pages in the buffer pool are hashed for fast access. **Hashing** is a technique that uniformly maps a key via a hash function across a set of hash buckets. A **hash bucket** is a structure in memory that contains an array of pointers (implemented as a linked list) to the buffer pages. A linked list chain of hash pages is built when the pointers to buffer pages do not fit on a single hash page. The number of hash buckets used is determined dynamically by SQL Server depending on the total size of the buffer pool.

In SQL Server, the hash values are generated from a combination of the database ID, file number, and page number. The hash function generates the hash key and stores it in a hash bucket. Essentially, the hash bucket serves as an index to the specific page needed. Hashing allows SQL Server to find a specific data page in memory quickly and with only a few memory reads, even in large memory environments. Use of a hashing algorithm also allows SQL Server to quickly determine whether a requested page is not in memory and has to be read in from disk, without having to perform an exhaustive scan of the data cache.

If the requested page is found in memory, the buffer manager returns a pointer to the memory buffer holding the page to the process that requested it. If the page is not in memory, the buffer manager must first initiate a disk I/O request to bring the page into memory. After the page has been read into a memory buffer, the pointer to that buffer is returned to the requesting process.

If the process that requested the page ends up modifying any information on the page, the page is marked as "dirty" and the buffer manager is notified when the process is finished making updates to the page. The buffer manager is then responsible for making sure that the changes to the page are written out to disk in a way that coordinates with logging and transaction management. This is handled by the checkpoint and lazywriter processes.

The Checkpoint Process

Checkpoints help minimize the amount of work that SQL Server must do when databases are recovered during system startup. Checkpoints flush modified data pages from memory out to disk so that those changes don't have to be redone during database recovery (for more details on the checkpoint process and how it affects recovery, see Chapter 31, "Transaction Management and the Transaction Log").

The checkpoint process takes care of performing automated checkpoints that occur based on the setting of the recovery interval. When recovery time is estimated to exceed the configured recovery interval, the checkpoint process issues a checkpoint for the database. The method SQL Server uses to determine whether a checkpoint is necessary is to examine how large the log has grown since the last checkpoint. SQL Server assumes that 10MB of log equates to 1 minute of recovery time. Therefore, if the recovery interval is set to 5 minutes, a checkpoint is triggered when the log grows by 50MB since the last checkpoint. The default recovery interval in SQL Server 2000 is `0`, which means that SQL Server dynamically chooses the appropriate recovery interval depending on the amount of database activity.

SQL Server limits checkpoint operations to a maximum of 100 concurrent write operations in an effort to limit the amount of resources checkpoints consume. Also, to optimize checkpoints and to make sure that checkpoints don't perform more work than necessary, the checkpoint process keeps track of which pages it has written out to disk already by setting the generation flag for each buffer in the cache. Without this flag to help keep track of the pages already written, checkpoint operations could potentially write the same page to disk multiple times. When the checkpoint is initiated, all generation flags are turned off. As the checkpoint process checks a page, it toggles the generation bit to the opposite value. If it happens to revisit a page whose generation bit has already been toggled, SQL Server skips writing that page as the page might have already been written due to its proximity to other pages that were already written. Again, to minimize overhead, SQL Server attempts to gather physically contiguous pages together that need to be written and write them out once to avoid excessive I/O.

If you want to find out how often checkpoints are occurring, and possibly adjust the recovery interval setting, start up SQL Server with trace flag 3502. This trace flag writes information to SQL Server's error log every time a checkpoint occurs.

The Lazywriter Process

Before a requested page can be brought into memory, a free buffer must be available in the buffer pool. If no free buffers are available in the free buffer list, an existing buffer needs to be reused. When an existing buffer has to be reused, many buffer pages might have to be searched simply to locate a buffer to free up for use. If the buffer found is marked as dirty—in other words, it contains changes that haven't been written out to disk first—the buffer manager must first write the changes out before the page can be reused and assigned to the requesting process. The requesting process would have to wait for this process to complete. To provide optimal performance, it is crucial that SQL Server keep a supply of buffers available for immediate use.

The buffer pool is managed by the lazywriter process, which uses a clock algorithm to sweep through the buffer pool looking for pages to be placed in the free buffer pool. The lazywriter thread maintains a pointer into the buffer pool that "sweeps" sequentially through it (like the hand on a clock). As the lazywriter visits each buffer, it determines whether that buffer has been referenced since the last sweep by examining a reference count value stored in the buffer header. If the reference count is greater than 0, the buffer remains in the pool, but its reference count is decremented. If the reference count reaches 0, the buffer is made available for reuse—if the page is still dirty, it is first written out to disk before being removed from the hash lists and put onto the free list.

> **NOTE**
>
> The lazywriter is so named because it is not an aggressive process. It runs as a low-priority process, working only during periods of low disk I/O. This is done to minimize the impact of the lazywriter operations on other SQL Server processes.

To keep frequently referenced pages in memory, SQL Server increments the reference count of a buffer each time the buffer is accessed by any process. For data or index pages, the reference count is incrmented by 1 each time. For objects that are expensive to create, such as stored procedure plans, a higher reference count is set initially that better reflects their "replacement cost."

The lazywriter applies a bit of a weighting factor to pages in memory to keep the more expensive pages in the buffer. When sweeping through checking the reference counts, instead of simply decrementing the reference count by 1, it divides the reference count by 4. This provides a means for the more frequently referenced pages (those with a high reference count) and those with a high replacement cost to remain in cache longer because it takes longer for the reference count to reach 0. This keeps the pages that are likely to be reused often in the buffer pool longer.

SQL Server 2000 dynamically estimates the number of free pages that should be available based on the load on the system and the number of stalls occurring. A stall is what occurs when a process needs a free page, and none are available. The process has to be put into a sleep status until the lazywriter can free up some pages. The minimum size of the buffer free list is computed dynamically as a percentage of the overall buffer pool size but is always between 128KB and 4MB.

The lazywriter process monitors the free buffer list and when the number of pages on the free list falls below its minimum size, it kicks off the process to begin sweeping the buffer cache. If a lot of stalls occur, SQL Server increases the minimum size of the free list. If the load on the system is light and few stalls occur, the minimum free list size can be reduced, and the excess pages can be used for hashing additional data and index pages or query plans. The Performance Monitor has counters that let you examine not only the number of free pages but also the number of stalls occurring (for more information on monitoring SQL Server with Performance Monitor, see Chapter 37, "Monitoring SQL Server Performance").

All user threads in SQL Server also perform a function similar to that of the lazywriter process. This happens when a user process needs to read a page from disk into a buffer. After the read has been initiated, the client process worker thread checks to see whether the free list is too small, and if it is, the user thread itself performs the same function as the lazywriter, searching for buffers that can be freed. Having user worker threads share in the work of the lazywriter helps better distribute the cost across all the CPUs in an SMP environment. In a multiple CPU environment, SQL Server 2000 maintains a separate free list for each CPU. When a user thread needs a free page, it first checks the free list for the

CPU it is currently running on. Only when no pages are available in its own free list will the user thread check the free lists of other CPUs.

Keeping Pages in the Cache Permanently

If you have critical tables you want to keep in memory, such as code lookup tables, you can mark these tables so that their pages are never put on the free list and are therefore kept in memory indefinitely. This process is referred to as **pinning** a table. When a table is **pinned**, none of the pages associated with that table are marked as free, and thus are never reused until the table is unpinned.

You use the `sp_tableoption` stored procedure to pin or unpin a table by specyifying `TRUE` or `FALSE` for the `pintable` option. Be careful not to pin too many tables to the cache as you can end up starving the buffer cache of available pages for other processes. In general, only pin tables after you've carefully tuned your system, when you have plenty of memory available, and you have a good feel for which tables are the heavy hitters.

Remember, if pages are accessed frequently, there might be no need to pin the table. Because only pages that have a reference count of 0 are placed in the free list, pages accessed repeatedly should rarely, if ever, end up on the free list, which is as it should be.

Large Memory Support

One of the first solutions to database performance problems is to throw more memory at the system (primarily because adding memory is much cheaper than replacing the CPU or disk subsystem, or even cheaper than hiring a consultant to come in and tune the system correctly). The reasoning behind adding more memory is, of course, to reduce the need for physical I/O by increasing your cache-hit ratio.

Keep in mind that some systems will not benefit from more memory. For example, if your database is 500MB in size and you already have 1GB of RAM installed, you could cache the entire database and still have memory left over. Additionally, typically only a relatively small portion of most databases is accessed frequently and repeatedly. A memory configuration that's only a small percentage of the entire database size can often still yield a high cache-hit ratio. More memory will not help out for the rarely run report that performs a large, single pass, table scan. Because the data is accessed infrequently, it's not likely to stay in cache, and the first read of a page will still have to come in from disk. Only subsequent queries against the table could experience a benefit.

When running the Enterprise Edition of SQL Server 2000 on either the Windows 2000 Advanced Server or Windows 2000 Datacenter Server platforms, you can allocate more than the default maximum of 4GB of memory by enabling the Windows 2000 Address Windowing Extensions (AWE) API. When this option is enabled, a SQL Server instance can then access up to 8GB of physical memory on Advanced Server and up to 64GB on Datacenter Servers. Although standard 32-bit addressing supports up to only 4GB of physical memory, the AWE API allows the additional memory to be acquired as nonpaged memory. The memory manager can then dynamically map views of the nonpaged memory into the 32-bit address space. You must be careful when using this extension because nonpaged memory cannot be swapped out. SQL Server allocates the entire chunk requested and does not release it back to the operating system until SQL Server is shut down. Other applications or other instances of SQL Server running on the same machine might not be able to get the memory they need.

Enabling AWE for the Enterprise Edition of SQL Server involves three steps. First, you must ensure that the account that starts your SQL Server instance has the Windows policy right to lock pages in memory. The user account that you specify to start the SQL Server service during installation will have the page-locking permission granted to it automatically. However, if you have changed the SQL Server startup account since installation, you need to verify that the page-locking permission has been assigned to that account.

The second step is to set the `AWE-enabled` option to 1 with `sp_configure`:

```
EXEC sp_configure 'awe enabled', '1'
RECONFIGURE
```

Finally, you also have to configure Windows 2000 to address physical memory above 4GB by adding the `/pae` switch to the Windows 2000 startup command in the boot.ini file.

TIP

When using AWE with SQL Server 2000, SQL Server can no longer dynamically allocate RAM. By default, it will grab all available memory, leaving only 128MB available for Windows and other applications. You also need to configure the `max server memory` option to limit the amount of memory that SQL Server allocates. Be sure to leave enough memory for Windows and any other applications running on the server, usually at least 500MB.

The Log Manager

As described in Chapter 31, the buffer manager uses a "write-ahead" strategy when writing changes to the transaction log—log records for a transaction are always written to disk before the modified data pages are written. Write-ahead logging ensures that all databases can be recovered to a consistent state. Because processes must wait for acknowledgment that a transaction has been physicially written to disk in the transaction log before it can consider it committed, all writes to the transaction log are performed synchronously. Writes to data pages can be made asynchronously, without waiting for acknowledgment, because if a failure occurs writing the data, the transactions can still be rolled back or committed from the information in the transaction log.

The log manager in SQL Server 2000 maintains contiguous regions of memory, called **log caches**, that are separate from the buffer pools used to store data and index pages. Within these regions of memory, the log manager formats and manages the log records before they are written out to disk. Two or more of these memory regions are used to help achieve maximum throughput—while one log cache is being written out to disk, the other log cache can still be receiving new records. The log manager also maintains two log queues: a flushQueue, which contains full log caches waiting to be written to disk, and a freeQueue, which contains log caches that have been flushed and can be reused.

All transaction records are first written to an available log cache. When the transaction commits, the log cache is placed into the flushQueue (if it isn't already there), to be written out to disk. The user process then goes into a wait queue and does not perform further processing until its log cache records have been flushed to disk.

The flushQueue is monitored by the **log writer**, a dedicated thread that reads the flushQueue in sequence and flushes the log caches out to disk one at a time. When the flush for a particular log cache is completed, any processes waiting on that log cache are woken up and can resume work.

SQL Server Process Management

The key features required of an enterprise-level database server platform are preemptive scheduling, virtual paged memory management, symmetric multiprocessing, and asynchronous I/O. Unlike some other database platforms, SQL Server relies on the Windows operating system to provide these capabilities and uses them fully. Under Windows NT and Windows 2000, the SQL Server engine runs as a single process and, within that process, uses multiple threads of execution. SQL Server relies on the operating system to schedule each thread to the next available processor.

SQL Server Threads

Unlike some other DBMS platforms that run as multiple processes under Windows NT, SQL Server runs as a single process using multiple operating system threads. SQL Server uses a single-process, multithreaded architecture that uses a single memory address space for the DBMS, eliminating the overhead of having to manage shared memory. The threads are scheduled onto a CPU by a User Mode Scheduler, which gives SQL Server more control over the scheduling of threads and fibers.

SQL Server always uses multiple threads, even on a single-processor system. SQL Server keeps separate thread pools for different operations. One pool of threads handles the Net-Libraries that SQL Server simultaneously supports, another thread handles database checkpoints, another handles the lazywriter process, and another handles the log writer, as well as the thread pool for general database cleanup tasks, such as periodically shrinking a database that is in auto-shrink mode or cleaning up ghost records. Most importantly, for handling user requests and queries, there is pool of threads that handles all user commands, the **worker thread pool**.

Worker Threads

SQL Server establishes a pool of worker threads to handle all user connections instead of using a separate thread for each connection and managing hundreds of separate operating system threads to support hundreds of users. Most often, the worker threads are simply waiting for input from the client applications. Instead of having dedicated threads doing nothing most of the time, SQL Server maintains a pool of worker threads and assigns worker threads to connections as needed.

When a client submits a request, the SQL Server network handler places the request in a **completion queue** (actually, the operating system's IOCompletion port) where it is picked up by the next available worker thread in the pool. If no idle worker thread is available to wait for the next incoming request, SQL Server adds a new thread to the worker thread pool. It does this until the limit set by the `max worker threads` configuration option is reached (the default limit is 255 threads, which is generally sufficient for most installations). When the limit has been reached, the client's request has to wait in the queue for a worker thread to be freed. As the workload decreases, SQL Server gradually eliminates idle threads to improve resource and memory utilization.

NOTE

Because the worker threads are not dedicated to processes, idle processes in SQL Server really have no significant impact on server resources or processing. As a matter of fact, it is more overhead to have processes disconnecting and reconnecting than to leave them sitting idle for extended periods of time.

In SQL Server 2000, complex queries can be broken into component parts that can be executed in parallel on multiple CPUs. This intraquery parallelism occurs only if the number of processors available is greater than the number of connections currently processing.

Under the normal pooling scheme, a worker thread remains assigned to the user request until the request is completed. When a user process requests a resource that is not available, such as a memory page that isn't yet in RAM, only that thread (and therefore, only the associated client connection) is halted until the request can be completed.

By default, SQL Server 2000 requests CPU resources from Windows NT or Windows 2000 to process a thread and the operating system then assigns each thread to a specific CPU. SQL Server lets the operating system distribute threads evenly among the CPUs on a system. At times, Windows NT or Windows 2000 can also move a thread from one CPU with heavy usage to another CPU. The `affinity mask` option in SQL Server 2000 can be used to exclude one or more CPUs from processing SQL Server threads and associate SQL Server threads with specific CPUs, but it is recommended that you leave it up to the operating system to schedule and balance the threads among the available CPUs.

SQL Server Disk I/O

SQL Server 2000 relies on features provided by Windows NT/2000 to perform disk I/O. Windows NT/2000 can perform two typs of I/O: scatter-gather I/O and the more common, asynchronous I/O.

Asynchronous I/O

Asynchronous I/O is an I/O method that many operating systems support to provide better performance for concurrent processing environments. With asynchronous I/O, when a process submits a request for a read or write operation, the operating system immediately returns control back to the application while it goes off to perform the I/O. The application is free to perform additional work and check back periodically to see whether the read or write has completed.

In a synchronous I/O environment, the operating system doesn't return control to the application until the read or write completes, which results in unnecessary idle time and processes single threading operations through the I/O manager. SQL Server can perform multiple concurrent asynchronous I/O operations against each database file and will issue as many asynchronous, concurrent I/O requests as possible. The maximum number of I/O operations for any file is determined by the resources of the system.

Scatter-Gather I/O

Before the advent of scatter-gather I/O in Windows NT, all the data for a disk read or write had to be located in a contiguous area of memory. If a read request wanted to bring in 64KB of data, the read request had to locate and specify the address of a contiguous 64KB area of memory. Scatter-gather I/O is an I/O method supported by Windows 2000 and Windows NT 4 Service Pack 2 and later that allows a read or write to transfer data into or out of discontiguous areas of memory.

For example, if SQL Server 2000 were to read in a 64KB extent (8 pages * 8KB), it's not required to locate a single contiguous 64KB area to copy the individual pages into. It can choose to locate 8 separate buffer pages in SQL Server memory and then do a single scatter-gather I/O that reads the data into the 8 buffer pages. Windows NT/2000 places the 8 pages directly into the SQL Server buffer pages, eliminating the need for SQL Server to do a separate memory copy.

Read Ahead Reads

To minimize the number of I/O requests made when data needs to be brought into the buffer pool, SQL Server supports a mechanism called **read ahead**, whereby the need for data and index pages is anticipated, and pages are brought into the buffer pool before they're actually requested. Read ahead is managed completely internally and dynamically, and no configuration adjustments are necessary to fine-tune or enable it. In addition, read ahead doesn't use separate operating system threads. This ensures that read ahead stays far enough ahead of the scan of the actual data, without going too far ahead and reading too much data that is not going to be needed.

SQL Server performs two kinds of read ahead: one for table scans on heaps and one for scans on index ranges.

When performing table scans on a heap, SQL Server looks up the information stored in the table's allocation structures to read the table pages in disk order. SQL Server reads ahead up to a maximum of 32 extents (32 * 8 pages/extent * 8192 bytes/page = 2MB) at a time. If SQL Server is performing a scatter-gather read, only up to 4 extents (32 pages) at a time are read with a single 256KB scatter read. If the table is spread across multiple files in a file group, SQL Server establishes one read ahead thread per file. In SQL Server Standard Edition, each thread can still read up to 4 extents at a time from a file, and up to 32 files can be processed concurrently. In SQL Server Enterprise Edition, the number of pages it can read ahead is adjusted dynamically depending on the amount of available memory—SQL Server Enterprise Edition can read ahead enough data to fill up to 1 percent of the buffer pool.

When peforming index range searches, the read ahead reader looks at the level just above the leaf level of the index to identify which pages to read ahead. When the index scan starts, the read ahead reader searches the index for the search values, and it can tell from the level one index nodes how many pages have to be examined to satisfy the scan and how to best fetch them.

Merry-Go-Round Scans

SQL Server 2000 Enterprise Edition also includes another I/O optimization to improve the performance of nonordered table scans when multiple nonordered scans of the same table are requested simultaneously by different processes. When a process is scanning the table, if there isn't enough memory to cache the entire table, the pages at the beginning of the scan are flushed out of memory to make room for the additional rows. If another process is performing the same or a similar nonordered scan, it normally has to start at the beginning of the table again. With both processes reading from different parts of the table, and neither reading information the other can use, a lot of excessive disk I/O occurs.

Merry-Go-Round scans can avoid this problem by allowing the second process to start at the same point that the original process has already reached. Both processes can then read the same data with a single read of each page, which is used by both scans. When the first process finishes, the second process can then pick up from the beginning of the table and read the first portion of the data.

SQL Server Storage Structures

A DBA does not see data and storage the same way SQL Server does. A DBA or end user sees a database more logically as the following:

- Databases, physically stored in files
- Tables and indexes, placed in filegroups within databases
- Rows, stored in tables

SQL Server sees these things at a lower, physical level as

- Databases, physically stored in files
- Pages, allocated to tables and indexes
- Information, stored in slots on pages

Database Files and Filegroups

Databases are divided into logical 8KB pages. Within each file allocated to a database, the pages are numbered contiguously from 0 to *n*. The actual number of pages in the database file depends on the size of the file. Pages in a database are uniquely referenced by specifying the database ID, the file ID for the file the page resides in, and the page number within the file. When you expand a database with `ALTER DATABASE`, the new space is added at the end of the file and the page numbers continue incrementing from the previous last page in the file. If you add a completely new file, its first page number will be 0. When you shrink a database, pages are removed from the end of the file only, starting at the highest page in the database and moving toward lower-numbered pages until the database reaches the specified size or a used page that cannot be removed. This ensures that page numbers within a file are always contiguous.

Databases in SQL Server 2000 span at least two, and optionally several, database files. There must always be at least one file for data and one file for the transaction log. These database files are normal operating system files created in a directory within the operating system. These files are created when the database is created or when a database is expanded. The maximum size allowed for a database or log file is 32TB.

Each database file has the following set of properties:

- A logical filename—This is used for internal reference to the file.
- A physical filename—This is the actual physical pathname of the file.
- An initial size—If no size is specified for primary data file, its initial size by default is the minimum size required to hold the contents of the model database.

- An optional maximum size.
- A file growth increment specified in megabytes or as a percentage.

The information and properties about each file for a database are stored in the database system catalog table called `sysfiles`. This table exists in every database and contains information about each of the database files. Table 33.1 lists the columns in the `sysfiles` table.

TABLE 33.1 The `sysfiles` Table

Column Name	Description
`fileid`	The file identification number that is unique within each database.
`groupid`	Identification of the filegroup to which the file belongs.
`size`	Size of the file (in pages).
`maxsize`	The maximum size that the file can auto-grow to. `0` means that the file does not auto-grow beyond its initial size; `-1` means that the file can auto-grow until the disk is full. The auto-grow feature is described in the following section.
`growth`	Auto-growth increment in either pages or a percentage of the file size.
`status`	A bitmap field containing status information about the file. The values are described in Table 33.2.
`perf`	Reserved for future use.
`name`	The logical name of the file.
`filename`	The physical name of the file, including path.

TABLE 33.2 Integer Status Values Contained in Status Field in the `sysfiles` Table

Status Value	Description
2	Disk file.
64	Log device.
128	The file has had information written to it since the last backup of the file or database.
16384	The file was implicitly created when the database was created (that is, no explicit name or size was specified in the `CREATE DATABASE` statement).
32768	The file was created during the database creation.
1048576	The growth value specified is a percentage rather than the number of pages to grow when space is needed.

Every database can have three types of files:

- Primary data file
- Secondary data files
- Log files

Primary Data File

Every database has one and only one primary database file. The location of the primary database file is stored in the `filename` column in the `sysdatabases` table in the `master` database. When SQL Server starts up a database, it looks for this file and then reads from the file header the information on the other files defined for the database.

The primary database file contains the `sysfiles` system table, which stores information on all other database files for the database. The `sysfiles` table is a virtual table (exists in memory only) that gets its information from the primary file header and cannot be updated directly. This table contains the current information and status on the database files. There is also an undocumented system table called `sysfiles1` that is a real table that also stores the logical and physical filename for all database files. This table can be modified (for instance, if you wanted to change the logical filename associated with a database file. Standard disclaimer: Modifying system tables directly is strongly discouraged!).

CAUTION

There is some concern that if you lose the primary data file for a database, you cannot back up the transaction log because SQL Server will not be able to find the transaction log files because the transaction log file information stored in the primary data file is lost.

Fortunately, it appears that Microsoft addresses this issue by storing the database file information in the `sysaltfiles` table in the `master` database. According to Books Online, this table only stores database file information under special circumstances. However, whenever I've examined the contents of this table, it has always contained file information for every database in the server. Conceivably, this information is there so that in the event you do lose your primary data file, SQL Server will be able to determine where the log file resides and be able to back it up so that you don't lose the transactions stored in it.

I have tested the capability of SQL Server to back up the log when the primary data file was no longer accessible, and it was able to still back up the log using the `NO_TRUNCATE` option.

The file extension for the primary database file defaults to `.mdf`. The primary database file always belongs to the default filegroup. It is often sufficient to have only one database file for storing your tables and indexes (the primary database file). The file can, of course, be created on a RAID partition to help spread I/O. However, if you need finer control over placement of your tables across disks or disk arrays, or if you want to have the ability to back up only a portion of your database via filegroups, you can create additional, secondary data files for a database.

Secondary Data Files

A database can have any number of secondary files (well, in reality, the maximum number of files per database is 32,767, but that should be sufficient for most implementations). You can put a secondary file in the default filegroup or in another filegroup defined for the database. Secondary data files have a file extension of `.ndf` by default.

Here are some situations in which the use of secondary database files might be beneficial:

- Disk partition size—Suppose that you have to create a database with a size of 8GB (log excluded). You have two 4GB disks for this purpose. You can create the database with two database files, each 4GB in size.
- Partial backup—A backup can be performed for the entire database or a subset of the database. The subset is specified as a set of files or filegroups (you can no longer back up individual tables in SQL Server). The partial backup feature is useful for large databases, where it is impractical to back up the entire database. When recovering with partial backups, a transaction log backup must also be available. For more information about backups, see Chapter 16, "Database Backup and Restore."
- Control over placement of database objects—When you create a table or index, you can specify the filegroup in which the object is created. This could help you spread I/O by placing your most active tables or indexes on separate filegroups that are defined on separate disks or disk arrays.
- Creating multiple files on a single disk provides no real performance benefit but could help in recovery—If you have a 9GB database in a single file and have to restore it, you need to have enough disk space available to create a new 9GB file. If you don't have 9GB of space available on a single disk, you cannot restore the database. On the other hand, if the database was created with three files each 3GB in size, you more likely will be able to find several 3GB chunks of space available on your server.

The Log File

Each database has at least one log file. The log file contains the transaction log records of all changes made in a database (for more information on what is contained in the transaction log, see Chapter 31). By default, log files have a file extension of `.ldf`.

A database can have several log files, and each log file can have a maximum size of 32TB. A log file cannot be part of a filegroup. No information other than transaction log records can be written to a log file.

Regardless of how many physical files have been defined for the transaction log, SQL Server treats it as one contiguous file. The transaction log for a database is actually managed as a set of virtual log files (VLFs). The size of the VLFs is determined by SQL Server based on the total size of all the log files and the growth increment specified for the log. The log can only grow in units of an entire VLF at a time and can only be shrunk to a VLF boundary (see Figure 33.1).

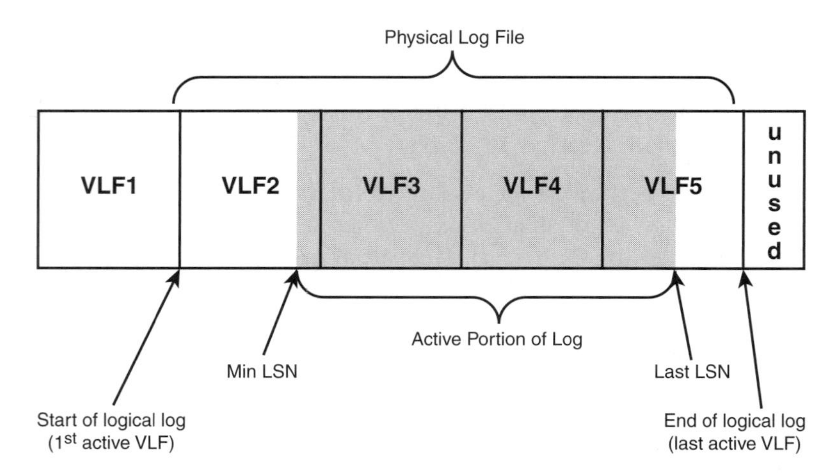

FIGURE 33.1 The structure of a physical log file showing virtual log files (VLF).

When the log file is shrunk, the unused VLFs at the end of the log file after the active portion of the log can be deleted and the size of the log file reduced. The virtual log files will be kept if they meet any of the following conditions:

- If any part of the active portion of the log is contained in the VLF. The active portion of the log is the portion between the minimum Log Sequence Number (LSN) and the end of the log where the last LSN has been written (for more information on transaction logging and LSNs, see Chapter 31). These are considered active VLFs.
- When the VLF contains records prior to the oldest active transaction that haven't been backed up yet and are needed for database recovery.
- When log backups are not being maintained or the log has been backed up, the VLFs prior to the start of the logical log are kept to be reused when the log records reach the current end of the logical log. For example, VLF1 in Figure 33.1 is considered reusable. Figure 33.2 shows an example of the active portion of the log cycling around back to the reusable portion at the beginning of the log file.

In environments where the log is not being maintained, SQL Server recycles the space at the beginning of the log file as soon as it reaches the end of the log file, as long as the records at the beginning of the log are before the start of the oldest active transaction. SQL Server assumes that the log is not being maintained when the log has been truncated, the database is in simple recovery mode (or the `trunc. log on chkpt.` option has been enabled), or you have never performed a full backup of the database.

If you have backed up the database and are keeping log backups, the reusable portion of the log prior to the LSN of the oldest active transaction cannot be overwritten or purged until it has actually been backed up.

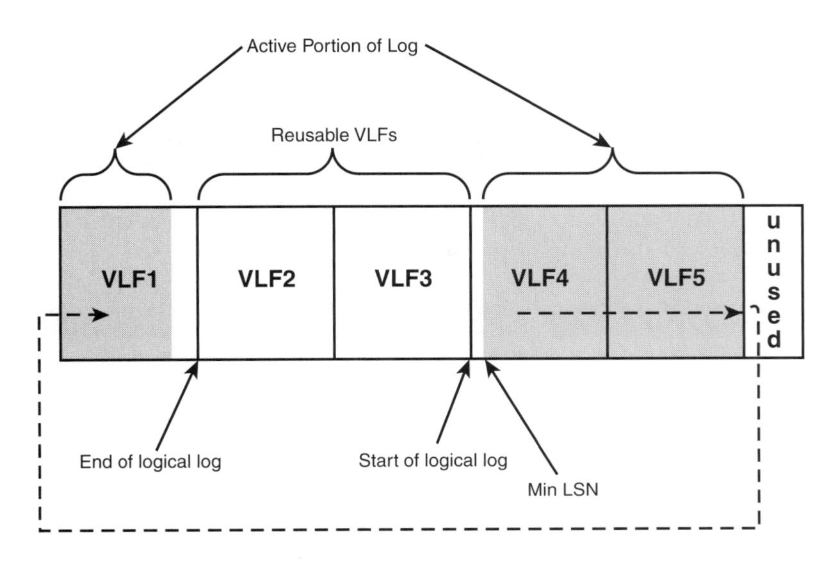

FIGURE 33. Example of active portion of log cycling around to reusable VLF at beginning of log file.

If the log has not been backed up yet preventing the reusable portion from being overwritten, SQL Server grows the log file and adds more VLFs to it (as long as the log file is still configured to grow automatically). After the log has been backed up and the active portion of the log has wrapped around to the first VLF at the beginning of the log file, the VLFs at the end can be deleted and the log file can be shrunk back down.

Shrinking the Log File

Shrinking the log file in SQL Server 7.0 was often an exercise in frustration. Even after backing up or truncating the log, if any part of the active portion of the log was still on the last VLF in the file, the log file could not be shrunk until the active portion moved around to the front of the file. This is because physical shrinking of the log file can only take place from the end of the log file. To shrink the log file, you had to write a routine that would generate a bunch of dummy transactions that would eventually push the active portion of the log back around to the beginning of the file. At that point, you could truncate the log and shrink it to reduce it back down to its original size.

In SQL Server 2000, the log file can still only be shrunk from the end of the log file, but Microsoft addressed the problems that occurred in SQL Server 7.0. When you back up or truncate the log in SQL Server 2000, it automatically issues a series of NO-OP log records to force the active portion of the log back to the beginning of the log file. You can then run the `DBCC SHRINKFILE` or `DBCC SHRINKDATABASE` command to release the unused space in the log file.

If you want to determine how many VLFs are in the log file and which ones are active, you can use an undocumented DBCC command, DBCC LOGINFO. The syntax for DBCC LOGINFO is as follows:

```
DBCC LOGINFO [ ( dbname ) ]
```

Let's walk through an example to see how to use DBCC LOGINFO and at the same time see how log truncation and shrinking of the log file works.

NOTE

The following example, and others in this chapter, make use of the bigpubs2000 database. This database is available on the CD included with this book. Instructions on how to install the bipubs2000 database on your system are presented in the Introduction.

First, create a test database to work with:

```
use master
go
create database logtest
go

The CREATE DATABASE process is allocating 0.63 MB on disk 'logtest'.
The CREATE DATABASE process is allocating 0.49 MB on disk 'logtest_log'.
```

Next, configure the database for full recovery:

```
alter database logtest set recovery full
go
```

Now, examine the log file with DBCC LOGINFO:

```
use logtest
go
DBCC LOGINFO
go

FileId FileSize StartOffset FSeqNo Status Parity CreateLSN
------ -------- ----------- ------ ------ ------ ---------
     2   253952        8192     43      2     64         0
     2   253952      262144      0      0      0         0

(2 row(s) affected)

DBCC execution completed. If DBCC printed error messages,
 contact your system administrator.
```

An active VLF is indicated by a status of 2. You can see at this point that there are two VLFs in the `logtest` database, each 253,952 bytes in size (the log file itself is .49MB), and only one of the VLFs is currently active. Now, create a table and populate it with some rows to generate some log records and examine the log again:

```
select top 10000 * into sales_test
from bigpubs2000..sales
go
dbcc loginfo
go

FileId FileSize    StartOffset FseqNo      Status Parity CreateLSN
------ ----------- ----------- ----------- ------ ------ ----------------
     2      253952        8192          43      2     64                0
     2      253952      262144           0      0      0                0
     2      270336      516096          44      2     64 43000000047100002
     2      262144      786432          45      2     64 44000000044500010

(4 row(s) affected)

DBCC execution completed. If DBCC printed error messages,
 contact your system administrator.
```

You can see now that there are VLFs in the log and three of them are active (`Status = 2`). Now, try to shrink the log and re-examine:

```
dbcc shrinkfile (logtest_log)
dbcc loginfo
go

DbId   FileId CurrentSize MinimumSize UsedPages   EstimatedPages
------ ------ ----------- ----------- ----------- --------------
    13      2          63          63          56             56

(1 row(s) affected)

DBCC execution completed. If DBCC printed error messages, contact your
 system administrator.
FileId FileSize    StartOffset FSeqNo      Status  Parity CreateLSN
------ ----------- ----------- ----------- ------- ------ -----------
     2      253952        8192          47       2     64           0
     2      253952      262144          46       0    128           0

(2 row(s) affected)
```

```
DBCC execution completed. If DBCC printed error messages, contact your
 system administrator.
```

Because you have not backed up the database yet, and there were no active transactions, SQL Server assumes that you do not need to keep the inactive portion of the log, removes it, and shrinks the file back down. Now, back up the database to indicate that you want to maintain the backups:

```
backup database logtest to disk='c:\winnt\temp\logtest.bak'
go
Processed 168 pages for database 'logtest', file 'logtest' on file 5.
Processed 1 pages for database 'logtest', file 'logtest_log' on file 5.
BACKUP DATABASE successfully processed 169 pages in 0.317 seconds
 (4.344MB/sec).
```

Run a command to generate some log records again and re-examine the log:

```
set rowcount 1000
go
begin tran
delete sales_test
rollback
go
set rowcount 0
go
dbcc loginfo
go

FileId FileSize   StartOffset FSeqNo Status Parity CreateLSN
------ ---------- ----------- ------ ------ ------ -------------------
     2     253952        8192     47      2    128                   0
     2     253952      262144     46      0     64                   0
     2     270336      516096     48      2     64   47000000013600531
(4 row(s) affected)

DBCC execution completed. If DBCC printed error messages, contact your
 system administrator.
```

Notice that there are now three VLFs, and two are marked as active (`Status = 2`). Now try to shrink the log:

```
dbcc shrinkfile (logtest_log)
go
```

```
Cannot shrink log file 2 (logtest_log) because all logical log files are in use
DbId   FileId CurrentSize MinimumSize UsedPages   EstimatedPages
------ ------ ----------- ----------- ----------- --------------
    13      2         128          63         128             56

(1 row(s) affected)

DBCC execution completed. If DBCC printed error messages,
 contact your system administrator.
```


It fails because the last VLF in the file is still active, and SQL Server cannot shrink from the end of the file. If we perform another transaction, the log continues to grow:

```
set rowcount 5000
go
begin tran
delete sales_test
rollback
go
set rowcount 0
go
dbcc loginfo
go


(5000 row(s) affected)

FileId FileSize       StartOffset    FSeqNo Status Parity CreateLSN
------ -------------- -------------- ------ ------ ------ -----------------
     2         253952           8192     47      2    128                 0
     2         253952         262144     46      0     64                 0
     2         270336         516096     48      2     64 47000000013600531
     2         262144         786432      0      0      0 48000000013600531
     2         262144        1048576      0      0      0 48000000025600533
     2         262144        1310720     49      2     64 48000000037600533
     2         262144        1572864      0      0      0 49000000001600391
     2         262144        1835008     52      2     64 49000000010400531
     2         262144        2097152     51      2     64 49000000022400533
     2         262144        2359296     50      2     64 49000000034400533

(10 row(s) affected)

DBCC execution completed. If DBCC printed error messages, contact your
 system administrator.
```

The log cannot be shrunk at this point because the VLFs are marked as needed for recovery. The space cannot be reclaimed until the log is backed up or truncated:

```
backup log logtest with truncate_only
dbcc loginfo
go

FileId FileSize        StartOffset      FSeqNo Status Parity CreateLSN
------ --------------- ---------------- ------ ------ ------ ----------------
     2          253952             8192     47      0    128                0
     2          253952           262144     46      0     64                0
     2          270336           516096     48      0     64 47000000013600531
     2          262144           786432      0      0      0 48000000013600531
     2          262144          1048576      0      0      0 48000000025600533
     2          262144          1310720     49      0     64 48000000037600533
     2          262144          1572864      0      0      0 49000000001600391
     2          262144          1835008     52      2     64 49000000010400531
     2          262144          2097152     51      0     64 49000000022400533
     2          262144          2359296     50      0     64 49000000034400533

(10 row(s) affected)

DBCC execution completed. If DBCC printed error messages, contact your
 system administrator.
```

Now that the VLFs have been marked as no longer needed (the log records have either been truncated or backed up to disk), the log file can be shrunk:

```
dbcc shrinkfile(logtest_log)
dbcc loginfo
go

DbId   FileId CurrentSize MinimumSize UsedPages   EstimatedPages
------ ------ ----------- ----------- ----------- --------------
    13      2          63          63          56             56

(1 row(s) affected)

DBCC execution completed. If DBCC printed error messages, contact your
 system administrator.
```

```
FileId FileSize      StartOffset      FSeqNo Status Parity CreateLSN
------ ------------- ---------------- ------ ------ ------ ----------------
     2        253952             8192     54      2     64                0
     2        253952           262144     53      0    128                0

(2 row(s) affected)

DBCC execution completed. If DBCC printed error messages, contact your
 system administrator.
```


SQL Server provides a database option, `autoshrink`, that can be enabled to automatically shrink the log and database files when space is available at the end of the file. If you are regularly backing up or truncating the log, the `autoshrink` option keeps the size of the log file in check. The auto-shrink process runs about every 30 minutes and determines whether the log file can be shrunk. The log manager keeps track of how much log space is used within the 30-minute interval. The auto-shrink process then shrinks the log to the larger of 125 percent of the maximum log space used or the minimum size of the log (the minimum size is the size the log was created with or the size it has been manually increased or decreased to).

CAUTION

The auto-shrink feature has been reported to result in some performance degradation, likely due to the additional monitoring required. It is recommended that instead of using auto-shrink, you should shrink the database manually or create a scheduled task to shrink the database or log file periodically during off-peak times.

Using Filegroups

All databases have a primary filegroup that contains the primary data file. There can be only one primary filegroup. If you don't create any other filegroups or change the default filegroup to a filegroup other than the primary filegroup, all files will be in the primary file group unless specifically placed in another filegroup.

In addition to the primary filegroup, you can add one or more filegroups to the database and a filegroup can contain one or more files. The main purpose of using filegroups is to provide more control over the placement of files and data on your server. When you create a table or index, you can map it a to a specific filegroup, thus controlling the placement of data. A typical SQL Server database installation generally uses a single RAID array to spread I/O across disks and create all files in the primary filegroup; more advanced installations or installations with very large databases spread across multiple array sets can benefit from the finer level of control of file and data placement afforded by additional filegroups.

For example, for a simple database such as pubs, you can create just one primary file that contains all data and objects and a log file that contains the transaction log information. For a larger and more complex database, such as a securities trading system where large data volumes and strict performance criteria are the norm, you might create the database with one primary file and four additional secondary files. You can then set up filegroups so you can place the data and objects within the database across all five files. If you have a table that itself needs to be spread across multiple disk arrays for performance reasons, you can place multiple files in a filegroup, each of which resides on a different disk, and create the table on that filegroup. For example, you can create three files (Data1.ndf, Data2.ndf, and Data3.ndf) on three disk arrays, respectively, and then assign them to the filegroup called spread_group. Your table can then be created specifically on the filegroup spread_group. Queries for data from the table will be spread across the three disk arrays, thereby improving I/O performance.

If a filegroup contains more than one file, when space is allocated to objects stored in that filegroup, the data is stored proportionally across the files. In other words, if you have one file in a filegroup with twice as much free space as another, the first file will have two extents allocated from it for each extent allocated from the second file (extents and space allocation will be discussed in more detail later in this chapter).

Listing 33.1 provides an example of using filegroups in a database to control the file placement of the customer_info table.

LISTING 33.1 Using a Filegroup to Control Placement for a Table

```
CREATE DATABASE Customer
ON ( NAME='Customer_Data',
    FILENAME='D:\SQL_data\Customer_Data1.mdf',
    SIZE=50,
    MAXSIZE=100,
    FILEGROWTH=10)
LOG ON ( NAME='Customer_Log',
    FILENAME='F:\SQL_data\Customer_Log.ldf',
    SIZE=50,
    FILEGROWTH=20%)
GO

ALTER DATABASE Customer
 ADD FILEGROUP Cust_table
GO

ALTER DATABASE Customer
 ADD FILE
   ( NAME='Customer_Data2',
```

LISTING 33.1 Continued

```
    FILENAME='E:\SQL_data\Customer_Data2.ndf',
    SIZE=100,
    FILEGROWTH=20)
 TO FILEGROUP Cust_Table
GO

USE Customer
CREATE TABLE customer_info
(cust_no INT, cust_address NCHAR(200), info NVARCHAR(3000))
 ON Cust_Table
GO
```


The CREATE DATABASE statement in Listing 33.1 creates a database with a primary database file and a log file. The first ALTER DATABASE statement adds a filegroup.

A secondary database file is added with the second ALTER DATABASE command. This file is added to the Cust_Table filegroup.

The CREATE TABLE statement creates a table; the ON Cust_Table clause places the table in the Cust_Table filegroup (the Customer_Data2 file on the E: disk partition).

The sysfilegroups database system table contains information about the database filegroups defined within a database, as shown in Table 33.3.

TABLE 33.3 The sysfilegroups Table

Column Name	Description
groupid	The filegroup identification number. Unique within the database.
allocpolicy	Reserved for future use.
status	0x8 indicates read-only; 0x10 indicates the default filegroup.
groupname	Name of the filegroup.

The following statement returns the filename, size in MB (not including auto-grow), and the name of the filegroup to which each file belongs:

```
SELECT name, size/128, groupname
 FROM sysfiles sf INNER JOIN sysfilegroups sfg
                ON sf.groupid = sfg.groupid
go

name                              groupname
----------------- ----------- ----------------
Customer_Data                  50 PRIMARY
Customer_Data2                100 Cust_table
```

On-Demand Disk Management

In SQL Server 2000, you can specify that a database file should grow automatically as space is needed. SQL Server can also shrink the size of the database if the space is not needed. You can control whether you use this feature along with the increment by which the file is to be expanded. The increment can be specified as a fixed number of megabytes or as a percentage of the current size of the file. You can also set a limit on the maximum size of the file, or allow it to grow until no more space is available on the disk.

Listing 33.2 provides an example of a database being created with a 10MB growth increment for the first database file, 20MB for the second, and 20 percent growth increment for the log file.

LISTING 33.2 Creating a Database with Auto Growth

```
CREATE DATABASE Customer
ON ( NAME='Customer_Data',
    FILENAME='D:\SQL_data\Customer_Data1.mdf',
    SIZE=50,
    MAXSIZE=100,
    FILEGROWTH=10),
   ( NAME='Customer_Data2',
    FILENAME='E:\SQL_data\Customer_Data2.ndf',
    SIZE=100,
    FILEGROWTH=20)
LOG ON ( NAME='Customer_Log',
    FILENAME='F:\SQL_data\Customer_Log.ldf',
    SIZE=50,
    FILEGROWTH=20%)
GO
```

The `Customer_Data` file has an initial size of 50MB, a maximum size of 100MB, and a file increment of 10MB.

The `Customer_Data2` file has an initial size of 100MB, a file growth increment of 20MB, and can grow until the `E:` disk partition is full.

The transaction log has an initial size of 50MB; the file increases by 20 percent with each file growth. The increment is based on the *current* file size, not the size originally specified.

Database Pages

All information in SQL Server is stored at the page level. The **page** is the smallest level of I/O in SQL Server and is the fundamental storage unit. Pages contain the data itself or information about the physical layout of the data. The page size is the same for all page types: 8KB or 8192 bytes (before version 7.0, the page size was 2KB). The pages are arranged in two basic types of storage structures: linked data pages and index trees.

Page Types

There are eight page types in SQL Server, as listed in Table 33.4.

TABLE 33.4 Page Types

Page Type	Stores
Data	The actual rows, found in the tables
Index	Index entries and pointers
Text and Image	Textual and image data
Global Allocation Map	Information about allocated (used) extents
Page Free Space	Information about free space on pages
Index Allocation Map	Information about extents used by a table or an index
Bulk Changed Map	Information about which extents have been used in a minimally logged or bulk-logged operation
Differential Changed Map	Information about which extents have been modified since the last full database backup

33

All pages, regardless of type, have a similar layout. They all have a page header, which is 96 bytes, and a body, which consequently is 8096 bytes. The page layout is shown in Figure 33.3.

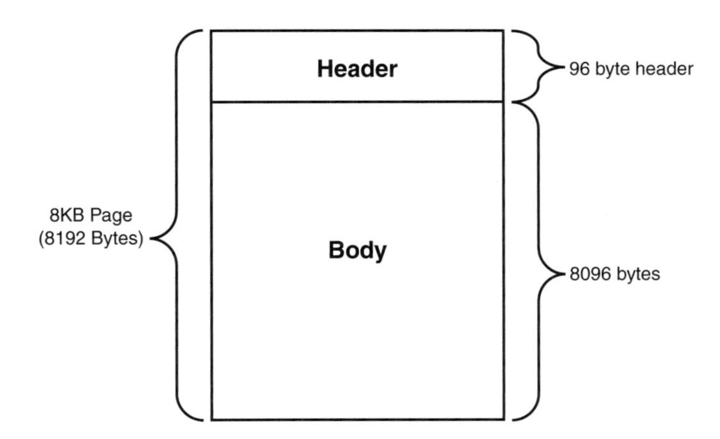

FIGURE 33.3 SQL Server page layout.

Examining Page Content

The information stored in the page header and in the page body depends on the page type. You can examine the raw contents of a page by using the `DBCC PAGE` command. You must be logged in with `sysadmin` privileges to run the `DBCC PAGE` command. The syntax for the `DBCC PAGE` command is as follows:

```
DBCC PAGE (dbid | 'dbname', file_no, page_no [, print_option])
```

The parameters of the DBCC PAGE command are as follows:

- *dbid* or *dbname*—ID or name of the database containing the page to be examined.
- *file_no*—The number of the file in which the page resides. Typically, for a data page, this will be 1, unless the database is created on multiple files. When a command or tool displays a page number—for example, sp_lock—it usually displays the page number in the format of *filenumber:pagenumber* (for example, 1:165). The number to the left of the colon is the file number, the number to the right is the page number.
- *page_no*—The number of the page within the file. Page numbers are unique within a file.
- *print_option*—Optional parameter to specify how you want the page information displayed.

The valid values for the *print_option* are as follows:

- 0—The default option. Displays only the buffer header and page header.
- 1—Displays the buffer header, page header, a hex dump of the contents of the page with each row listed separately, and the contents of the row offset table.
- 2—Displays the buffer and page headers, a hex dump of the page as single block of data, and the contents of the row offset table.
- 3—Displays the buffer header, page header, and a hex dump of each row separately. Each row is followed by a printout of each of the column values in the row.

You must first run DBCC TRACEON (3604) if you want to get the results from DBCC PAGE returned to an application; otherwise, the output will be sent to the SQL Server error log. Listing 33.3 shows an example of using DBCC PAGE.

LISTING 33.3 Sample Execution of DBCC PAGE

```
dbcc traceon(3604)
dbcc page (pubs, 1, 91, 3)
go

PAGE: (1:91)
------------

BUFFER:
-------
```

LISTING 33.3 Continued

```
BUF @0x18F23680
---------------
bpage = 0x1C4F4000          bhash = 0x00000000          bpageno = (1:91)
bdbid = 5                   breferences = 1             bstat = 0x209
bspin = 0                   bnext = 0x00000000

PAGE HEADER:
------------

Page @0x1C4F4000
----------------
m_pageId = (1:91)           m_headerVersion = 1         m_type = 1
m_typeFlagBits = 0x0        m_level = 0                 m_flagBits = 0x8000
m_objId = 2057058364        m_indexId = 0               m_prevPage = (0:0)
m_nextPage = (0:0)          pminlen = 10                m_slotCnt = 8
m_freeCnt = 7699            m_freeData = 477            m_reservedCnt = 0
m_lsn = (3:254:2)           m_xactReserved = 0          m_xdesId = (0:0)
m_ghostRecCnt = 0           m_tornBits = 1

Allocation Status
-----------------
GAM (1:2) = ALLOCATED     SGAM (1:3) = NOT ALLOCATED
PFS (1:1) = 0x60 MIXED_EXT ALLOCATED   0_PCT_FULL   DIFF (1:6) = CHANGED
ML (1:7) = NOT MIN_LOGGED

Slot 0 Offset 0x60
------------------
Record Type = PRIMARY_RECORD
Record Attributes =  NULL_BITMAP VARIABLE_COLUMNS
1C4F4060:  000a0030  36333730  0005414d  23000300 0...0736MA.....#
1C4F4070:  2c002900  77654e00  6f6f4d20  6f42206e .).,.New Moon Bo
1C4F4080:  42736b6f  6f74736f  4153556e           oksBostonUSA
pub_id                           = 0736
pub_name                         = New Moon Books
city                             = Boston
state                            = MA
country                          = USA

Slot 1 Offset 0x8c
------------------
Record Type = PRIMARY_RECORD
Record Attributes =  NULL_BITMAP VARIABLE_COLUMNS
```

LISTING 33.3 Continued

```
1C4F408C:  000a0030  37373830  00054344  25000300 0...0877DC.....%
1C4F409C:  32002f00  6e694200  2074656e  61482026 ./.2.Binnet & Ha
1C4F40AC:  656c6472  73615779  676e6968  556e6f74 rdleyWashingtonU
1C4F40BC:      4153                               SA
pub_id                            = 0877
pub_name                          = Binnet & Hardley
city                              = Washington
state                             = DC
country                           = USA

Slot 2 Offset 0xbe
------------------
Record Type = PRIMARY_RECORD
Record Attributes =  NULL_BITMAP VARIABLE_COLUMNS
1C4F40BE:  000a0030  39383331  00054143  29000300 0...1389CA.....)
1C4F40CE:  34003100  676c4100  7461646f  6e492061 .1.4.Algodata In
1C4F40DE:  79736f66  6d657473  72654273  656c656b fosystemsBerkele
1C4F40EE:  41535579                               yUSA
pub_id                            = 1389
pub_name                          = Algodata Infosystems
city                              = Berkeley
state                             = CA
country                           = USA

Slot 3 Offset 0x120
------------------
Record Type = PRIMARY_RECORD
Record Attributes =  NULL_BITMAP VARIABLE_COLUMNS
1C4F4120:  000a0030  32323631  00054c49  2a000300 0...1622IL.....*
1C4F4130:  34003100  76694600  614c2065  2073656b .1.4.Five Lakes
1C4F4140:  6c627550  69687369  6843676e  67616369 PublishingChicag
1C4F4150:  4153556f                               oUSA
pub_id                            = 1622
pub_name                          = Five Lakes Publishing
city                              = Chicago
state                             = IL
country                           = USA

Slot 4 Offset 0x154
------------------
Record Type = PRIMARY_RECORD
Record Attributes =  NULL_BITMAP VARIABLE_COLUMNS
1C4F4154:  000a0030  36353731  00055854  26000300 0...1756TX.....&
```

LISTING 33.3 Continued

```
1C4F4164:  2f002c00  6d615200  20616e6f  6c627550 .,./.Ramona Publ
1C4F4174:  65687369  61447372  73616c6c    415355 ishersDallasUSA
pub_id                           = 1756
pub_name                         = Ramona Publishers
city                             = Dallas
state                            = TX
country                          = USA

Slot 5 Offset 0x183
-------------------
Record Type = PRIMARY_RECORD
Record Attributes =  NULL_BITMAP VARIABLE_COLUMNS
1C4F4183:  000a0030  31303939  00050000  1a000308 0...9901........
1C4F4193:  28002100  47474700  fc4d4726  6568636e .!.(.GGG&GM.nche
1C4F41A3:  7265476e  796e616d                     nGermany
pub_id                           = 9901
pub_name                         = GGG&G
city                             = München
state                            = [NULL]
country                          = Germany

Slot 6 Offset 0xf2
------------------
Record Type = PRIMARY_RECORD
Record Attributes =  NULL_BITMAP VARIABLE_COLUMNS
1C4F40F2:  000a0030  32353939  0005594e  23000300 0...9952NY.....#
1C4F4102:  2e002b00  6f635300  656e746f  6f422079 .+...Scootney Bo
1C4F4112:  4e736b6f  59207765  556b726f      4153 oksNew YorkUSA
pub_id                           = 9952
pub_name                         = Scootney Books
city                             = New York
state                            = NY
country                          = USA

Slot 7 Offset 0x1ab
-------------------
Record Type = PRIMARY_RECORD
Record Attributes =  NULL_BITMAP VARIABLE_COLUMNS
1C4F41AB:  000a0030  39393939  00050000  27000308 0...9999.......'
1C4F41BB:  32002c00  63754c00  656e7265  62755020 .,.2.Lucerne Pub
1C4F41CB:  6873696c  50676e69  73697261  6e617246 lishingParisFran
1C4F41DB:      6563                               ce
```

LISTING 33.3 Continued

```
pub_id                              = 9999
pub_name                            = Lucerne Publishing
city                                = Paris
state                               = [NULL]
country                             = France

DBCC execution completed. If DBCC printed error messages, contact your
 system administrator.
```

Data Pages

The actual data rows in tables are stored on data pages. Figure 33.4 shows the basic structure of a data page.

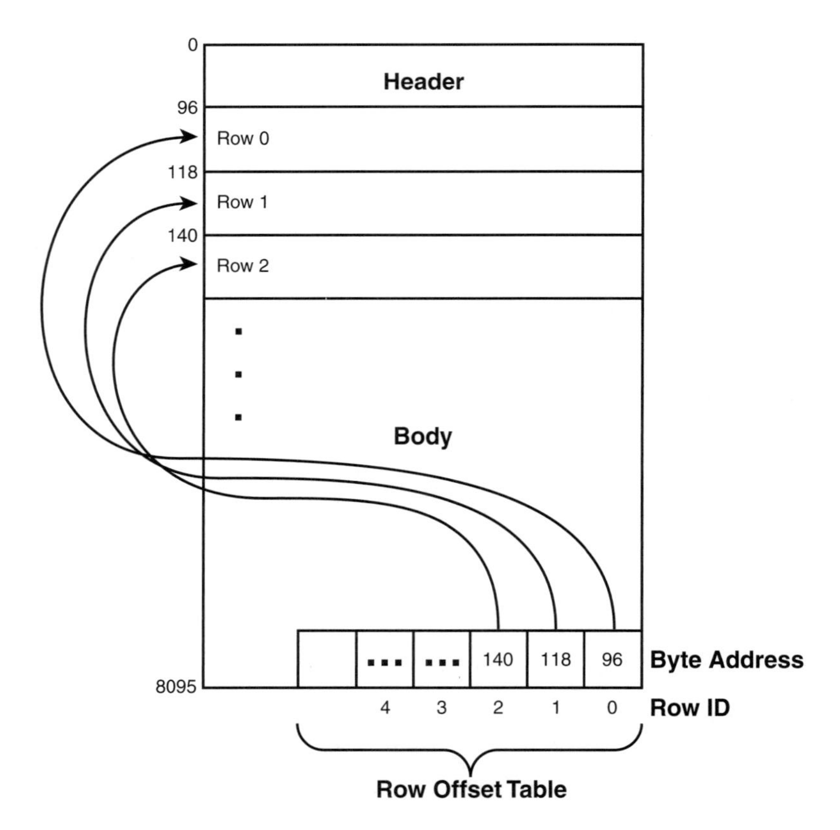

FIGURE 33.4 The structure of a SQL Server data page.

The remainder of this section discusses and examines the contents of the data page.

The Page Header

The **page header** contains control information for the page. Some fields assist when SQL Server checks for consistency among its storage structures, and some fields are used when navigating among the pages that constitute a table. Table 33.5 describes the more useful fields contained in the page header and the corresponding value in the header output of DBCC PAGE.

TABLE 33.5 Useful Fields Contained in the Page Header

Page Header Fields	DBCC PAGE Name	Description
Page ID	m_pageId	Unique identifier for the page. It consists of two parts: the file ID number and the page number.
Next Page in Chain	m_nextPage	Contains the file number and page number of the next page in the chain (0 if the page is the last or only page in the chain or if the page belongs to a heap table).
Previous Page in Chain	m_prevPage	Contains the file number and page number of the previous page in the chain (0 if the page is the first or only page in the chain, or if the page belongs to a heap table).
Object ID	m_objID	ID of the object to which this page belongs.
Log Sequence Number	m_lsn	Log sequence number (LSN) value used for changes and updates to this page.
Number of Rows	m_slotCnt	Total number of rows (slots) used on the page.
Index Level	m_level	The level at which this page resided in an index tree (0 indicates a leaf page or data page).
Index ID	m_indexId	ID of the index this page belongs to. 0 indicates that it is a data page. 1 means that the page is a data page for a clustered table. A value greater than 1 is the ID of a nonclustered index; the value 255 indicates a text or image page.
Free Space Location	m_freeData	The byte offset where the available free space starts on the page.
Minimum Row Length	pminlen	The minimum size of the row. Essentially, this is the number of bytes in the fixed-length portion of the data rows.
Amount of Free Space	m_freeCnt	Number of free bytes available on the page.

The Data Rows

Following the page header, starting at byte 96 on the page, are the actual data rows. Each data row has a unique row number within the page. Data rows in SQL Server cannot cross page boundaries. The maximum available space in a SQL Server page is 8096 bytes (8192 bytes minus the 96 byte header). However, this does not mean that your data rows can be 8096 bytes in size.

When a data row is logged in the transaction log (for an insert, for example), additional logging information is stored on the log page along with the data row. Because log pages are 8192 bytes in size and also have a 96 byte header, a log page has only 8096 bytes of available space. To store the data row and the logging information on a single log page, the data row cannot be more than 8060 bytes in size. This, in effect, limits the maximum data row size for a table in SQL Server 2000 to 8060 bytes as well.

Because each data row also incurs some overhead bytes in addition to the actual data, the maximum amount of actual *data* that can be stored in a single row on a page is slightly less than 8060 bytes. The actual amount of overhead required per row is dependent on whether the table contains any variable length columns. The limit on data row size does not take into account columns of `text`, `ntext`, or `image` datatypes because these data values are stored separately from the data row, as you'll see later in this chapter.

If you attempt to create a table with a minimum row size that exceeds 8060 bytes, you'll receive an error message as in the following example (remember that a multibyte character set datatype such as `nchar` or `nvarchar` requires 2 bytes per character, so an `nchar(4000)` column requires 8000 bytes):

```
CREATE TABLE customer_info
(cust_no INT, cust_address NCHAR(200), info NCHAR(4000))
go

Server: Msg 1701, Level 16, State 2, Line 1
Creation of table 'customer_info' failed because the row size would be 8425,
 including internal overhead.
 This exceeds the maximum allowable table row size, 8060.
```

If the table contains variable length or nullable columns, you can create a table for which the minimum row size is less than 8060 bytes, but the data rows could conceivably exceed 8060 bytes. SQL Server allows the table to be created, but whenever you create or alter such a table, you'll receive the warning message as shown in the following example:

```
CREATE TABLE customer_info
(cust_no INT, cust_address NCHAR(200), info NVARCHAR(4000))

Warning: The table 'customer_info' has been created but its maximum
 row size (8429) exceeds the maximum number of bytes per row (8060).
 INSERT or UPDATE of a row in this table will fail if the resulting row length
 exceeds 8060 bytes.
```

If you then try to insert a row that exceeds 8060 bytes of data and overhead, the insert fails with the following error message:

```
Server: Msg 511, Level 16, State 1, Line 1
Cannot create a row of size 8405 which is greater than the allowable maximum
 of 8060.
The statement has been aborted.
```


The number of rows stored on a page depends on the size of each row. For a table that has all fixed length, non-nullable columns, the number of rows that can be stored on a page will always be the same. If the table has any variable or nullable fields, the number of rows stored on page depends on the size of each row. SQL Server attempts to fit as many rows as possible in a page. Smaller row sizes allow SQL Server to fit more rows on a page, which reduces page I/O and allows more data pages to fit in memory. This helps improve system performance by reducing the number of times SQL Server has to read data in from disk.

The Structure of Data Rows The data for all fixed-length data fields in a table are stored at the beginning of the row. All variable-length data columns are stored after the fixed-length data. Figure 33.5 shows the structure of the data row in SQL Server.

Status Byte A (1 byte)	Status Byte B (1 byte) *not used*	Length of Fixed Length Data (2 bytes)	Fixed Length Data Columns (*n* bytes)	Number of Columns (2 bytes)	Null Bitmap (1 bit for each column)	Number of Variable Length Columns (2 bytes)	Column Offset Array (2 x number of variable columns)	Variable Length Data Columns (*n* bytes)

(Shaded Areas represent data present only when table contains variable length columns)

FIGURE 33.5 The structure of a SQL Server data row.

The total size of each data row is a factor of the sum of the size of the columns plus the row overhead. Seven bytes of overhead is the minimum for any data row:

- 1 byte for status byte A.
- 1 byte for status byte B (in SQL Server 2000, no information is stored in status byte B).
- 2 bytes to store the length of the fixed-length columns.
- 2 bytes to store the number of columns in the row.
- 1 byte for every multiple of 8 columns (`ceiling(numcols / 8)`)in the table for the `NULL` bitmap. A 1 in the bitmap indicates that the column allows nulls.

The values stored in status byte A are as follows:

- Bit 1—Provides version information. In SQL Server 2000, it's always 0.
- Bits 2 through 4—A 3-bit value that indicates the nature of the row. `0` indicates that the row is a primary record, `1` indicates that the row has been forwarded, `2` indicates a forwarded stub, `3` indicates an index record, `4` indicates a blob fragment, `5` indicates a ghost index record, and `6` indicates a ghost data record. (Many of these topics, such as forwarded and ghost records, will be discussed in further detail in the "Data Modification and Performance" section later in this chapter.)
- Bit 5—Indicates that a `NULL` bitmap exists. This is somewhat unnecessary in SQL Server 2000 because a `NULL` bitmap is always present, even if no `NULL`s are allowed in the table.
- Bit 6—Indicates that one or more variable-length columns exists in the row.
- Bits 7 and 8—These bits are not currently used in SQL Server 2000.

If the table contains any variable length columns, the following additional overhead bytes are included in each data row:

- 2 bytes to store the number of variable-length columns in the row.
- 2 bytes times the number of variable-length columns for the offset array. This is essentially a table in the row identifying where each variable-length column can be found within the variable-length column block.

Within each block of fixed-length or variable-length data, the data columns are stored in the column order in which they were defined when the table was created. In other words, all fixed-length fields are stored in column ID order in the fixed-length block, and all nullable or variable-length fields are stored in column ID order in the variable length block.

You can confirm the preceding information using `DBCC PAGE`. First, create a table with all fixed-length rows and add a couple of rows to it (if you use all character columns, you'll be able to read the information in `DBCC PAGE` more easily):

```
use pubs
go
create table withnull (a char(5) default 'aaaaa',
                       b char(5) null default 'bbbbb',
                       c char(5)  default 'ccccc')
go

insert withnull default values
insert withnull values ('abcde', null, 'vwxyz')
go
```

Next, to examine the data page, you need to identify which page it is. Because this is a small table, all data is stored on the first page. You can find out the address of the first page by querying the `first` column in the `sysindexes` table for the table where the index ID is 0 or 1 (the contents of `sysindexes` will be explained in more detail throughout this chapter):

```
select id, indid, first, root from sysindexes
where id = object_id('withnull')
and indid <= 1
go

id          indid  first          root
----------- ------ -------------- --------------
 2009058193      0 0x4F0000000100 0x4F0000000100
```


CAUTION

It is not guaranteed that the `first` column in `sysindexes` will always indicate the first page of a table. In general, it will be a reliable value until you begin to perform deletes and updates on the data in the table.

The values in the `root` and `first` columns represent page numbers within the database. Unfortunately, each is stored in a byte-swapped format as hexadecimal numbers, and `DBCC PAGE` needs the decimal page and file numbers. To convert the file number and page number to decimal values, you must first swap the bytes and then convert the values from hexadecimal to decimal. The last four digits (the 5th and 6th bytes) represent the file number: `0100`. If you reverse the 2 bytes (`01` and `00`), you end up with `0001` to represent the file number. That one is pretty easy to convert to decimal because it's usually a 1 unless the database is on multiple files.

The page number is a little trickier to decipher. You have to reverse the first 4 bytes (the first eight digits) in groups of two. For example, `0x4F000000` becomes `00 00 00 4F`. The page number is then `4F`. Unless you are an assembly programmer, you'll probably need to use the Windows Calculator to convert the hex value to a decimal. A better approach would be to let T-SQL do the conversion for you when you retrieve the data from `sysindexes`. Listing 33.4 provides a stored procedure that contains an example of a query that will do the trick. (You can find the source for this stored procedure on the accompanying CD.)

LISTING 33.4 Stored Procedure to Display Hexadecimal Page Numbers from sysindexes As Decimal

```
use master
go
create proc dbo.sp_SSU_showindexpages @table sysname = null, @indid int = null
as
if @table is not null and object_id(@table) is null
begin
    print 'Invalid table name: ''' + @table + ''''
    return
end
if @indid is not null
  and not exists (select 1 from sysindexes where id = object_id(@table)
                                              and indid = @indid)
begin
    print 'No index with id of ' + cast (@indid as varchar(3))
          + ' exists on table ''' + @table + ''''
    return
end
select convert(char(30), object_name(id)) 'tablename',
    id,
    indid,
    convert(char(30),name) 'indexname',
    convert(varchar(2), (convert(int, substring(root, 6, 1)) * power(2, 8))
            + (convert(int, substring(root, 5, 1))))
        + ':'
        + convert(varchar(11),
           (convert(int, substring(root, 4, 1)) * power(2, 24)) +
           (convert(int, substring(root, 3, 1)) * power(2, 16)) +
           (convert(int, substring(root, 2, 1)) * power(2, 8)) +
           (convert(int, substring(root, 1, 1))))  as 'root',
    convert(varchar(2), (convert(int, substring(first, 6, 1)) * power(2, 8))
            + (convert(int, substring(first, 5, 1))))
        + ':'
        + convert(varchar(11),
           (convert(int, substring(first, 4, 1)) * power(2, 24)) +
           (convert(int, substring(first, 3, 1)) * power(2, 16)) +
           (convert(int, substring(first, 2, 1)) * power(2, 8)) +
           (convert(int, substring(first, 1, 1))))  as 'first',
    convert(varchar(2), (convert(int, substring(firstiam, 6, 1)) * power(2, 8))
            + (convert(int, substring(firstiam, 5, 1))))
        + ':'
        + convert(varchar(11),
```

LISTING 33.4 Continued

```
            (convert(int, substring(firstiam, 4, 1)) * power(2, 24)) +
            (convert(int, substring(firstiam, 3, 1)) * power(2, 16)) +
            (convert(int, substring(firstiam, 2, 1)) * power(2, 8)) +
            (convert(int, substring(firstiam, 1, 1))))  as 'firstiam'
   from sysindexes
   where  1 = case when @table is null then 1
                   when id = object_id(@table) then 1
              end
   and 1 = case when @indid is null then 1
                when @indid = 0 and indid <= 1 then 1
                when @indid = 1 and indid = 1 then 1
                when @indid > 1 and indid = @indid then 1
           end
   and isnull(indexproperty(id, name, 'IsAutoStatistics'), 0) = 0
   order by 1, 3
return
go

use pubs
go

exec sp_SSU_showindexpages withnull
go

tablename      id          indid  indexname    root    first    firstiam
-------------- ---------- ------ ------------ ------- -------- --------
withnull       1061578820      0 withnull     1:79    1:79     1:80
```

Okay, so now you know that the first page number is 79 for this example. You can now use `DBCC PAGE` to look at the page contents:

```
dbcc page (pubs, 1, 79, 3)
go

PAGE: (1:79)
------------

BUFFER:
-------
```

```
BUF @0x18EC48C0
---------------
bpage = 0x19586000          bhash = 0x00000000          bpageno = (1:79)
bdbid = 14                  breferences = 4             bstat = 0xb
bspin = 0                   bnext = 0x00000000

PAGE HEADER:
------------

Page @0x19586000
----------------
m_pageId = (1:79)           m_headerVersion = 1         m_type = 1
m_typeFlagBits = 0x0        m_level = 0                 m_flagBits = 0x8000
m_objId = 2009058193        m_indexId = 0               m_prevPage = (0:0)
m_nextPage = (0:0)          pminlen = 19                m_slotCnt = 2
m_freeCnt = 8048            m_freeData = 140            m_reservedCnt = 0
m_lsn = (43:62:2)           m_xactReserved = 0          m_xdesId = (0:0)
m_ghostRecCnt = 0           m_tornBits = 0

Allocation Status
-----------------
GAM (1:2) = ALLOCATED     SGAM (1:3) = ALLOCATED
PFS (1:1) = 0x61 MIXED_EXT ALLOCATED  50_PCT_FULL   DIFF (1:6) = CHANGED
ML (1:7) = NOT MIN_LOGGED

Slot 0 Offset 0x60
------------------
Record Type = PRIMARY_RECORD
Record Attributes =  NULL_BITMAP
19586060:  00130010  61616161  62626261  63636262 ....aaaaabbbbbcc
19586070:  03636363      0000                     ccc...
a                                = aaaaa
b                                = bbbbb
c                                = ccccc

Slot 1 Offset 0x76
------------------
Record Type = PRIMARY_RECORD
Record Attributes =  NULL_BITMAP
19586076:  00130010  64636261  00000065  77760000 ....abcde.....vw
19586086:  037a7978      0200                     xyz...
a                                = abcde
b                                = [NULL]
c                                = vwxyz
```

```
DBCC execution completed. If DBCC printed error messages,  contact your
 system administrator.
```

Let's break out the values in the row for the second row in the table. The first 4 bytes are in the string `00130010`. Status byte A is `10`. This value indicates that bit 5 is on, which indicates that a null bitmap exists, which it does for every row. What is more telling is that bit 6 is off, indicating that there are no variable-length columns. Skipping status byte B, which is always 0, we have the value of 0013 for the length of the fixed-length data (for some curious reason, this value is not in reverse byte order). Hex 13 converts to decimal 19, which matches the value displayed in the page header for `pminlen`.

The next 19 bytes are then the fixed-length data: `64636261 00000065 77760000 037a7978`. The first 5 bytes are column `a` (notice that the first four are in the first block, and the fifth character is on the right-hand side of the second block). If you reverse the byte order, you end up with 61 62 63 64 65, which are the ASCII values for the string "abcde". Because column `b` contains a null, it is all zeroes, and column `c` is represented, in reverse byte order, by 76 77 78 79 7a, the ASCII sequence for "vwxyz".

If you reverse the next two of the remaining 3 bytes, you get the value 0003, which is the number of columns in the table (3), and the last byte (`02`) is the Null bitmap. A value of `2` means that the second bit is on (00000010), which correlates with the second column (`b`), which in this row contains a null value. If you notice, the null bitmap in the first row is `0` because column `b` contains a value in that row.

To view the contents of page for a table with variable-length columns, create the following table and insert a row; then determine the page number of the first page:

```
use pubs
go
create table withvariable (a char(5) default 'aaaaa',
                           b char(5) null default 'bbbbb',
                           c varchar(10)  default 'ccccc',
                           d char(5) default 'ddddd',
                           e nvarchar(10) default 'eeeee')
go

insert withvariable default values
go

exec sp_SSU_showindexpages withvariable
go

tablename       id          indid  indexname     root    first     firstiam
--------------- ----------- ------ ------------- ------- --------- --------
withvariable     1125579048      0 withvariable  1:81    1:81      1:82
```

You can see from the resultset that the first page is page 81. Now, use DBCC PAGE to display the contents:

```
dbcc page (pubs, 1, 81, 3)
go

PAGE: (1:81)
------------

BUFFER:
-------

BUF @0x191D26C0
---------------
bpage = 0x31C76000          bhash = 0x00000000          bpageno = (1:81)
bdbid = 14                  breferences = 3             bstat = 0xb
bspin = 0                   bnext = 0x00000000

PAGE HEADER:
------------

Page @0x31C76000
----------------
m_pageId = (1:81)           m_headerVersion = 1         m_type = 1
m_typeFlagBits = 0x0        m_level = 0                 m_flagBits = 0x8000
m_objId = 21575115          m_indexId = 0               m_prevPage = (0:0)
m_nextPage = (0:0)          pminlen = 19                m_slotCnt = 1
m_freeCnt = 8051            m_freeData = 139            m_reservedCnt = 0
m_lsn = (43:104:1)          m_xactReserved = 0          m_xdesId = (0:0)
m_ghostRecCnt = 0           m_tornBits = 0

Allocation Status
-----------------
GAM (1:2) = ALLOCATED     SGAM (1:3) = ALLOCATED
PFS (1:1) = 0x61 MIXED_EXT ALLOCATED  50_PCT_FULL   DIFF (1:6) = CHANGED
ML (1:7) = NOT MIN_LOGGED

Slot 0 Offset 0x60
------------------
Record Type = PRIMARY_RECORD
Record Attributes =  NULL_BITMAP VARIABLE_COLUMNS
31C76060:  00130030  61616161  62626261  64646262 0...aaaaabbbbbdd
31C76070:  05646464  00020000  002b0021  63636363 ddd.....!.+.cccc
31C76080:  65006563  65006500    006500           ce.e.e.e.e.
```

```
a                                = aaaaa
b                                = bbbbb
c                                = ccccc
d                                = ddddd
e                                = eeeee

DBCC execution completed. If DBCC printed error messages, contact your
 system administrator.
```


The value for status byte A in this example is hex 30 (decimal 48). This indicates that in addition to bit 5, bit 6 is on, which indicates that this row contains variable-length data. The fixed-length data is still the same size, 19 bytes (`0013`, `pminlen` = 19). You'll also notice by looking at the data values on the far right, that all the fixed-length columns (`a`, `b`, and `d`) are stored at the beginning of the row. The 15-byte fixed data string (`61616161 62626261 64646262 646464`—remember the reverse byte ordering!), is then followed by 2 bytes for the the number of columns (`0005`) and 1 byte for the null bitmap, which in this example is `00` because none of the columns contain a null.

Following the null bitmap, the values are present only because there are variable-length columns. The next 2 bytes (again, curiously not in reverse byte order) are the number of variable-length columns (`0002`). The next 4 bytes (2 × the number of variable columns) are the column offset array (`002b0021`). These provide the location of the variable-length columns in the row. The first variable-length column, column `c`, is located at offset `0021`, or decimal `33` (again, this value is not in reverse byte order). An offset of `33` indicates that the column ends at position `33`, and if you look at the 33rd byte in the row, you'll find the end of the data value for column `c`. Column `e` is at offset `002b`, which means that it ends at position `43`, which is also the end, or total length, of the row. Notice also, that column `e` was defined as an `nvarchar` column and uses 2 bytes (`0065`) for each character.

Estimating Row and Table Sizes Once you know the structure of a data row, you can estimate the size of a data row. Knowing the expected size of a data row and the corresponding overhead per row helps you determine the number of rows that can be stored per page and the number of pages a table will require. In a nutshell, a greater number of rows stored per page can help query performance by reducing the number of pages that need to be read to satisfy the query. In addition, you'll be able to estimate how much disk space your databases will require before you even insert your first row, so you can get the right size disks ordered before implementation.

If you have only fixed-length fields in your table, it's easy to estimate the row size:

n bytes (total of the fixed-column widths)

+ 1 byte for status byte A

+ 1 byte for status byte B

+ 2 bytes for the fixed-length data length

+ 2 bytes for the number of columns

+ ceiling (number of columns/8) for the null bitmap

= total row size

+ 2 bytes for the row offset table entry

There is a minimum amount of 7 bytes of overhead within each data row, plus 2 additional bytes of overhead for the row offset entry for the row (the row offset table is discussed in the next section of this chapter). For example, consider table `withnull`, described previously, which contains three fixed-length, `char(5)`, columns. The total row size is the following:

(3 * 5) for fixed-column width

+ 6 fixed overhead bytes

+ ceiling (3/8) for null bitmap

= 22 total row size

+ 2 row offset table entry

= 24 bytes per row

If the table contains variable-length fields, the average row width is determined as follows:

n bytes (total of the fixed-column widths)

+ 1 byte for status byte A

+ 1 byte for status byte B

+ 2 bytes for the fixed-length data length

+ 2 bytes for the number of columns

+ ceiling (number of columns/8) for the null bitmap

+ 2 bytes for the number of variable-length columns

+ 2 bytes * the number of variable columns for the column offset array

+ sum of average, or expected, size of variable-length columns

= average row size

+ 2 bytes for the row offset table entry

Each row containing variable-length columns has a minimum of 11 bytes of overhead—the 7 fixed bytes of overhead, plus a minimum of 4 bytes of overhead if the row contains at least one variable-length field. Consider table `withvariable`, which contains three fixed-length, (`char(5)`) columns and two variable-length columns of `varchar(10)` and `nvarchar(10)`. Assume that the average data size for both variable-length columns is half the column size—5 and 10 bytes, respectively. The calculation of the average row size is as follows:

(3 * 5)	for fixed fields
+ 6	for fixed-length overhead
+ ceiling (5/8)	for null bitmap
+ (5 + 10)	for sum of average size of variable fields
+ 2	number of variable fields
+ (2 * 2)	for the column offset array
= 43 bytes	average row size
+ 2	row offset table entry
= 45 bytes	

NOTE

For a listing of SQL Server datatypes and their corresponding sizes, see Chapter 26, "Using Transact-SQL in SQL Server 2000."

After you've estimated the data row size, you can determine the number of rows per page by dividing the average row size into the available space on the data page, 8096 bytes. For example, if your average row size is 45 bytes, the average number of rows per page is the following:

8096/45 = 179 rows per page

Remember to "round down" any fractions because you can't have only a portion of a row on a data page. If the calculation were to work out to something like 179.911 rows per page, it actually requires two pages to store 180 rows because the 180th row won't fit entirely on the first data page. If you are using a fill factor other than the default when you create your clustered index (fill factor is discussed in the "Setting the Fill Factor" section later in this chapter), you need to multiply the number of rows per page times the fill factor percentage as well to determine the actual number of rows that will initially be stored on each page. For now, assume that the default fill factor of 0 is used, which indicates that the data pages will be filled as full as possible.

When you know the average number of rows per page, you can calculate the minimum number of pages required to store the data by dividing the total number of rows in the table by the number of rows per page. To follow the example thus far, if you have 100,000 rows in the table, the number of pages required to store the data is the following:

100,000 rows/179 rows per page = 558.659... pages

In this case, you need to "round up" the value to get the actual number of pages (559) required to store all the data rows. The size of the table in pages is also the cost, in number of logical page I/Os, to perform a table scan. A table scan involves reading the first page of the table and following the page chain until all pages in the table have been read. The table scan, as you will explore in subsequent chapters, is the fallback technique employed by the SQL Server optimizer to find the matching rows for a query when there is no less-expensive alternative, such as a clustered or nonclustered index.

Format of the `sql_variant` Datatype The `sql_variant` datatype is new for SQL Server 2000. The `sql_variant` datatype can contain a value of any column datatype in SQL Server except for `text`, `ntext`, `image`, and `timestamp`. For example, a `sql_variant` in one row could contain character data, in another row an `integer` value, and a `float` value in yet another row. Because they can contain any type of value, `sql_variant` columns are always considered variable length. The format of a `sql_variant` column is as follows:

- Byte 1—Indicates the actual datatype being stored in the `sql_variant`.
- Byte 2—The `sql_variant` version, always `1` in SQL Server 2000.
- The remainder of the `sql_variant` contains the data value and, for some datatypes, information about the data value.

The datatype value in byte 1 corresponds to the values in the `xtype` column in the `systypes` database system table. For example, if the first byte contained a hex 38, that would correspond to the `xtype` value of 56, which is the `int` data type.

Some datatypes stored in a `sql_variant` column require additional information bytes stored at the beginning of the data value (after the `sql_variant` version byte). The datatypes requiring additional information bytes, and the values in these information bytes, are described as follows:

- Numeric and decimal datatypes require 1 byte for the precision and 1 byte for the scale.
- Character strings require 2 bytes to store the maximum length and 4 bytes for the collation ID.
- Binary and varbinary data values require 2 bytes to store the maximum length.

The Row Offset Table

The location of a row within a page is identified by the **row offset table**, which is located at the end of the page. To find a specific row within a page, SQL Server looks up the starting byte address for a given row ID in the row offset table, which contains the offset of the row from the beginning of the page (refer to Figure 33.4). Each entry in the row offset table is 2 bytes in size, so for each row in a table, an additional 2 bytes of space is added in from the end of the page for the row offset entry.

Where a row goes when inserted into a table depends on whether there is a clustered index on the table. Without a clustered index, the table is a heap structure (clustered and heap tables are covered in more detail later in this chapter). When you insert a row into a heap table, the row goes at the end of the page as long as the page fits there. When you insert a row in to a clustered table, the clustering sort order must be maintained so that the row is inserted into its clustered position.

When you delete a row from a heap table, the byte address is set to `0`, indicating that there is a "hole," or some available space, at that address. When you delete a row, the rows are not shuffled to keep the free space at the end of the page, as they were prior to SQL Server 7.0. If you insert data on a page where there is free space, but the free space is fragmented across the page because there have been deletions, the rows are compacted before the row is inserted. Figure 33.6 shows how the free space and the offset table are handled when you insert and delete data on a heap table. (Note that more rows would actually fit on the page than are drawn in Figure 33.6.)

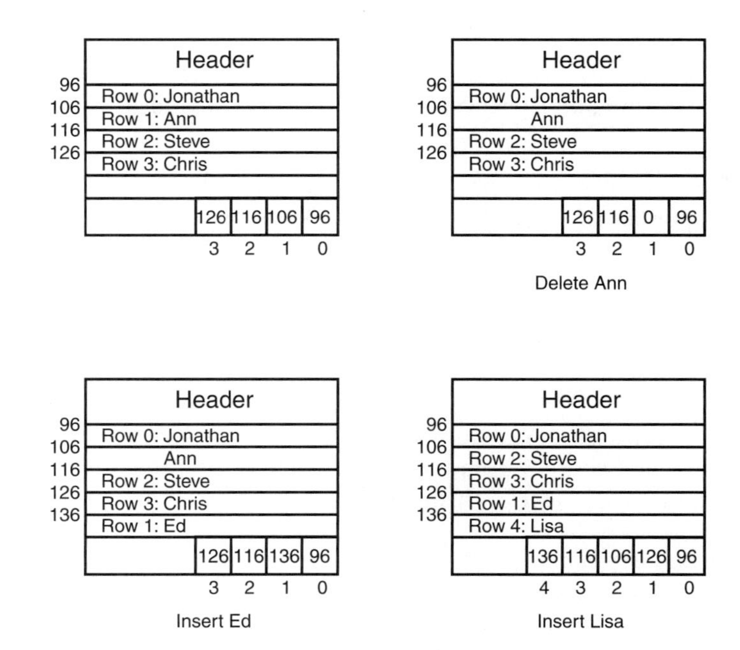

FIGURE 33.6 Inserting and deleting rows on a heap table data page.

33

Note that deleting Ann does not remove the information physically stored on the page; the only modification is that the byte address for Row ID 1 is changed to 0 (unused). Row ID remains at its original offset (116) because the space is not compacted. When Ed is inserted, the row is added at the end of the used space on the page because space is available there. However, when Lisa is to be inserted, no space is available at the end of used space on the page, so the rows are compacted to make space available at the end of the page. Notice that while inserting and deleting rows, the Row IDs do not change for existing rows, so index entries for those rows do not have to be updated, reducing the index overhead for inserts and deletes.

The algorithm for managing the insertion and deletion of rows on a clustered table is similar to that for a heap table. The difference is that when a page is compacted to reclaim free space, the row offset table is adjusted to keep the rows in the clustered key order, by row number.

Index Pages

Index information is stored on index pages. An **index page** has the same layout as a data page. The difference is the type of information stored on the page. Generally, a row in an index page contains the index key and a pointer to the page or row at the next (lower) level.

The actual information stored in an index page depends on the index type and whether it is a leaf level page. A leaf level clustered index page is the data page itself, of which you've already seen the structure. The information stored on other index pages is as follows:

- Clustered indexes, nonleaf pages—Each index row contains the index key and a pointer (the `fileId` and a page address) to a page in the index tree at the next lower level.
- Nonclustered index, nonleaf pages—Each index row contains the index key and a page-down pointer (the file ID and a page address) to a page in the index tree at the next lower level. For nonunique indexes, the nonleaf row also contains the bookmark information for the corresponding data row.
- Nonclustered index, leaf pages—Rows on this level contain an index key and a reference to a data row. For heap tables, this is the Row ID; for clustered tables, this is the clustered key for the corresponding data row.

The actual structure and content of index rows, as well as the structure of the index tree, are discussed in more detail later in this chapter.

Text and Image Data Pages

If you want to store large amounts of text or binary data, you can use the `text`, `ntext`, and `image` datatypes. (For information about how to use these datatypes, see Chapter 12, "Creating and Managing Tables in SQL Server," and Chapter 39, "Database Design and

Performance.") Each column for a row of these datatypes can store up to 2GB (minus 2 bytes) of data. By default, the text and image values are not stored as part of the data row but as a collection of pages on their own. For each text or image column, the data page contains a 16-byte pointer, which points to the location of the initial page of the text or image data. A row with several text and image columns has one pointer for each column.

The pages that hold text and image data are 8KB in size, just like any other page in SQL Server. An individual text/image page can hold text, ntext, or image data for multiple columns and also from multiple rows. A text/image page can even contain a mix of text, ntext, and image data. This helps reduce the storage requirements for the text and image data, especially when smaller amounts of data are stored in these columns. For example, if SQL Server could only store data for a single column for a single row on a single text or image page and the data value consisted of only a single character, it would still use an entire 8KB data page to store it! Definitely not an efficient use of space.

A text or image page can only hold text or image data for a single table, however. A table with a text or image column has a single set of pages to hold all its text and image data. The information on the starting location of this collection of pages is stored in the `sysindexes` system table. The text/image collection always has an index ID (`indid`) of 255.

Text and image information is presented externally (to the user) as a long string of bytes. Internally, however, the information is stored within a set of pages. The pages are not necessarily organized sequentially but are logically organized as a B-tree structure. (B-tree structures will be covered in more detail later in this chapter.) If an operation addresses some information in the middle of the data, SQL Server can navigate through the B-tree to find the data. In previous versions, SQL Server had to follow the entire page chain from the beginning to find the desired information.

If the amount of the data in the text/image field is less than 32KB, then the 16-byte pointer in the data row points to an 84-byte root structure in the text/image B-tree. This root structure points to the pages and the location where the actual text or image data is stored (see Figure 33.7). The data itself can be placed anywhere within the text/image pages for the table. The root structure keeps track of the location of the information in a logical manner. If the data is less than 64 bytes, it is stored in the root structure itself.

If the amount of text or image data exceeds 32KB, SQL Server allocates intermediate B-tree index nodes that point to the text and image pages. In this situation, the intermediate node pages are stored on pages not shared between different occurrences of text or image columns—the intermediate node pages store nodes for only one text or image column in a single data row.

Storing Text and Image Data in the Data Row To further conserve space, and help minimize I/O, SQL Server 2000 supports storing the text or image data in the actual data row. When the text or image data is stored outside the data row pages, at a minimum, SQL Server needs to perform one additional page read per row to get the text of image data.

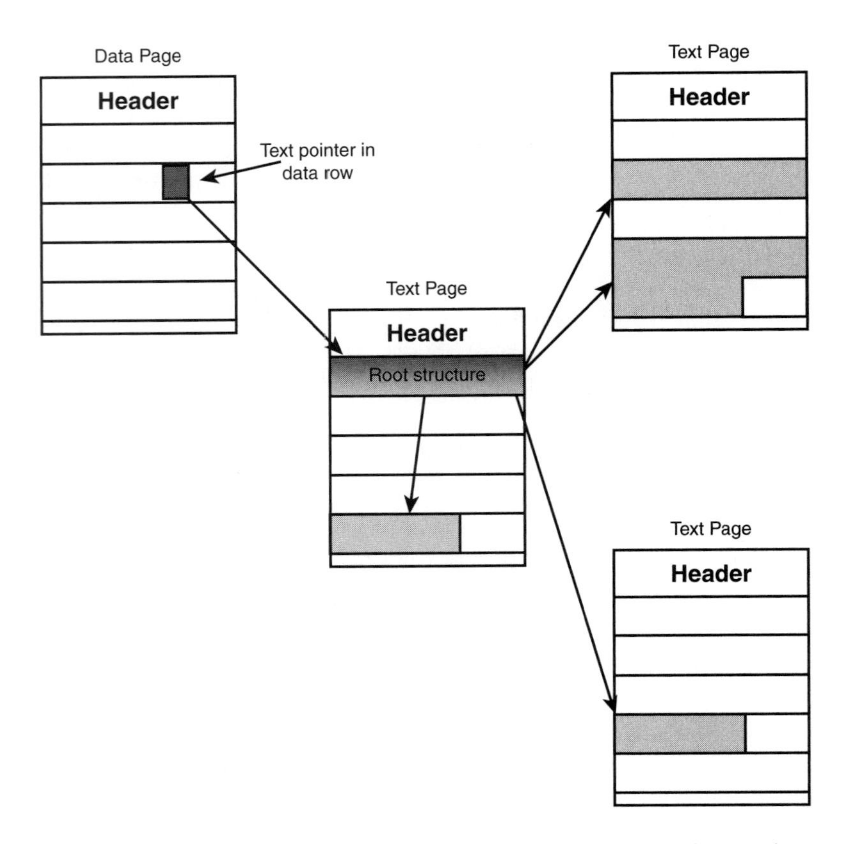

FIGURE 33.7 Text data root structure pointing at the location of text data in the text B-tree.

Why would you want to store text data in the row? Why not just store the data in a `varchar(8000)`? Well, primarily because there is an upper limit of 8KB if the data is stored within the data row (not counting the other columns). Using the `text` datatype, you can store more than 2 *billion* bytes of text. If you know most of your records will be small, but on occasion, some very large values will be stored, the `text in row` option provides optimum performance and better space efficiency for the majority of your text values, while providing the flexibility you need for the occasional large values. It also provides the benefit of keeping the data all in a single column instead of having to split it across multiple columns or rows when the data exceeds the size limit of a single row.

If you want to enable the `text in row` option for a table with a text or image column, use the `sp_tableoption` stored procedure:

```
exec sp_tableoption pub_info, 'text in row', 512
```

This example enables up to 512 bytes of text or image data in the `pub_info` table to be stored in the data row. The maximum amount of text or image data that can be stored in a data row is 7000 bytes. When a text or image value exceeds the specified size, rather than store the 16-byte pointer in the data row as it would normally, SQL Server stores the 24-byte root structure that contains the pointers to the separate chunks of text/image data for the row in the text or image column.

The second parameter to `sp_tableoption` can be just the option of `ON`. If no size is specified, the option is enabled with a default size of 256 bytes. To disable the `text in row` option, set its value to `0` or `'OFF'` with `sp_tableoption`. When the option is turned off, all text and image data stored in the row will be moved off to text/image pages and replaced with the standard 16-byte pointer. This can be a time-consuming process for a large table.

Also, keep in mind that just because this option is enabled doesn't always mean that the text or image data will be stored in the row. All other data columns that are not text or image take priority over text and image data for storage in the data row. If a variable-length column grows and there is not enough space left in the row or page for the text or image data, the text/image data will be moved off the page.

Space Allocation

When a table or index needs more space in a database, SQL Server needs a way to determine where space is available in the database to be allocated. If the table or index is still less than eight pages in size, SQL Server must find a mixed extent with one or more pages available that can be allocated. If the table or index is eight pages or larger in size, SQL Server must find a free uniform extent that can be allocated to the table or index.

Extents

If SQL Server allocated space one page at a time as pages were needed for a table (or an index), SQL Server would be spending a good portion of its time just allocating pages, and the data would likely be scattered noncontiguously throughout the database. Scanning such a table would not be very efficient. For these reasons, pages for each object are grouped together and allocated in **extents**; an extent consists of eight logically contiguous pages.

Earlier versions of SQL Server reserved one extent for a table or index at the time of creation. No other objects could be stored on this extent. Even if the table had no rows in it, it was essentially using 16KB (8 * 2KB) of space in the database that couldn't be used by any other object. In version 7.0, with the increase of page sizes from 2KB to 8KB, this algorithm was changed a bit to more efficiently allocate space to new tables. The concept of the mixed extent was introduced.

When a table or index is created, it is initially allocated a page on a mixed extent. If no mixed extents are available in the database, a new mixed extent is allocated. A mixed extent can be shared by up to eight objects (each page in the extent can be assigned to a different table or index).

As the table grows to at least 8 pages in size, all future allocations to the table are done as **uniform extents**.

Figure 33.8 shows the use of mixed and uniform extents.

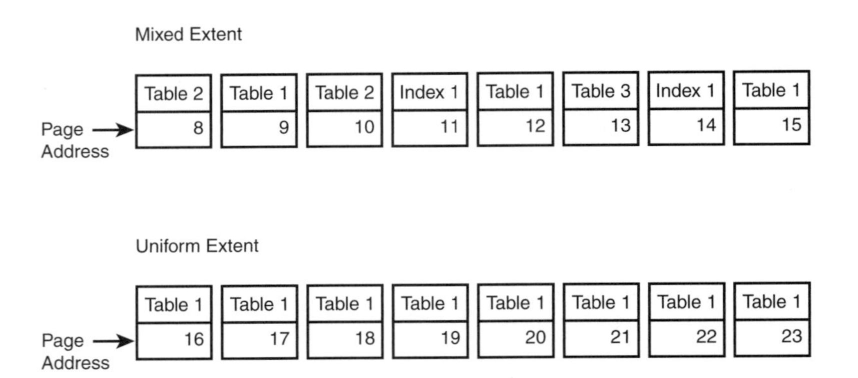

FIGURE 33.8 Mixed and uniform extents.

If SQL Server had to search throughout an entire database file to find free extents, it wouldn't be efficient. Instead, SQL Server uses two special types of pages to record which extents have been allocated to tables or indexes and whether it is a mixed or uniform extent:

- Global Allocation Map Pages (GAMs)
- Shared Global Allocation Map Pages (SGAMs)

Global Allocation Map Pages

The allocation map pages track whether extents have been allocated to objects and indexes and whether the allocation is for mixed extents or uniform extents. There are two types of GAMs:

- Global Allocation Map (GAM)—The GAM keeps track of all allocated extents in a database, regardless of what it's allocated to. The structure of the GAM is straightforward: Each bit in the page outside the page header represents one extent in the file, where `1` means that the extent is not allocated, and `0` means that the extent is allocated. Nearly 8000 bytes (64,000 bits) are available in a GAM page after the header and other overhead bytes are taken into account. Therefore, a single GAM covers approximately 64,000 extents, or 4GB (64,000 * 64KB) of data.
- Shared Global Allocation Map (SGAM)—The SGAM keeps track of mixed extents that have free space available. An SGAM has a structure similar to a GAM, with each bit representing an extent. A value of `1` means that the extent is a mixed extent and there is free space (at least one unused page) available on the extent. A value of `0` means that the extent is not currently allocated, that the extent is a uniform extent, or that the extent is a mixed extent with no free pages.

Table 33.6 summarizes the meaning of the bit in GAMs and SGAMs.

TABLE 33.6 Meaning of the GAM and SGAM Bits

Extent Usage	GAM Bit	SGAM Bit
Free, not used	1	0
Uniform or mixed with no free pages	0	0
Mixed, with free pages available	0	1

When SQL Server needs to allocate a uniform extent, it simply searches the GAM for a bit with a value of 1 and sets it to 0 to indicate it has been allocated. To find a mixed extent with free pages, it searches the SGAM for a bit set to 1. When all pages in a mixed extent are used, its corresponding bit is set to 0. When a mixed extent needs to be allocated, SQL Server searches the GAM for an extent whose bit is set to 1 and sets the bit to 0, and the corresponding SGAM bit is set to 1. There is some more processing involved as well—such as spreading the data evenly across database files—but the allocation algorithms are still relatively simple.

GAM pages are easily located in a database by SQL Server because the first GAM page is located at the third page in the file (page number 2). There is another GAM every 511,230 pages after the first GAM. The fourth page (page number 3) in each database file is the SGAM page, and there is another SGAM each 511,230 pages after the first SGAM.

Page Free Space Pages

A Page Free Space (PFS) page records whether each page is allocated and the amount of free space available on the page. Each PFS covers 8,088 contiguous pages in the file. For each of the 8,088 pages, the PFS has a 1-byte record that contains a bitmap for each page indicating whether the page is empty, 1 to 50 percent full, 51 to 80 percent full, 81 to 95 percent full, or more than 95 percent full. The first PFS page in a file is located at page number 1, the second PFS page is located at page 8088, and each additional PFS page is located every 8,088 pages after that. SQL Server uses PFS pages to find free pages on extents and to find pages with space available on extents when a new row needs to be added to a table or index.

Figure 33.9 shows the layout of GAM, SGAM, and PFS pages in a database file. Note that every file has a single file header located at page 0.

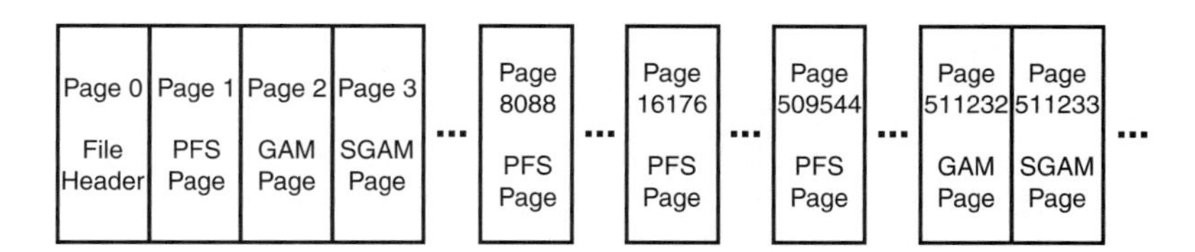

FIGURE 33.9 The layout of GAM, SGAM, and PFS pages in a database file.

If you want to take a peek at the contents of the file header, PFS, GAM, and SGAM pages, DBCC PAGE does a pretty good job when you specify a print_format parameter of 3. The output for the PFS, GAM, and SGAM pages is fairly straightforward to read and shows the pages or range of pages and their allocation status. The following commands show these pages for the pubs database:

```
/* first the file header */
dbcc page (pubs, 1, 0, 3)
/* Next the PFS */
dbcc page (pubs, 1, 1, 3)
/* Here's the GAM */
dbcc page (pubs, 1, 2, 3)
/* Finally, the SGAM */
dbcc page (pubs, 1, 3, 3)
```

Index Allocation Map Pages

Index Allocation Map (IAM) pages keep track of the extents used by a heap or index. Each heap table and index has at least one IAM page for each file that it has extents on. An IAM cannot reference pages in other database files; if the heap or index spreads to a new database file, a new IAM for the heap or index is created in that file. IAM pages are allocated as needed and are spread randomly throughout the database files.

An IAM page contains a small header that has the address of the first extent in the range of pages being mapped by the IAM. It also contains eight page pointers that keep track of index or heap pages that are in mixed extents. These might or might not contain any information, depending on whether any data has been deleted from the tables and the page(s) released. Remember, an index or heap will have no more than eight pages in mixed extents (after eight pages, it begins using uniform extents), so only the first IAM page stores this information. The remainder of the IAM page is for the allocation bitmap. The IAM bitmap works similarly to the GAM, indicating which extents over the range of extents covered by the IAM are used by the heap or index the IAM belongs to. If a bit is on, then the corresponding extent is allocated to the table.

Each IAM covers a possible range of 63,903 extents (511,224 pages). Each bit represents an extent within that range, whether or not the extent is allocated to the object that the IAM belongs to. If the bit is set to 1, then the relative extent in the range is allocated to the index or heap. If the bit is set to 0, the extent is either not allocated or might be allocated to another heap or index.

For example, assume that an IAM page resides at page 649 in the file. If the bit pattern in the first byte of the IAM is `1010 0100`, then the first, third, and sixth extents within the range of the IAM are allocated to the heap or index. The second, fourth, fifth, seventh, and eighth extents are not.

The location of the first IAM page for an index or heap is stored in the `firstiam` column in the `sysindexes` table. All subsequent IAM pages for the object are linked in a chain via the `m_NextPage` and `m_PrevPage` values in the IAM page header. To find the first IAM page for the `sales` table in `bigpubs2000`, you could execute the following:

```
exec bigpubs2000..sp_SSU_showindexpages sales, 1
go

tablename    id          indid  indexname        root    first   firstiam
------------ ----------- ------ ---------------- ------- ------- ---------
sales         1653580929      1 UPKCL_sales      1:124    1:126    1:125
```


This output indicates that the first IAM is at page 125. If you wanted to peek at the contents of the IAM and verify this information, you could use your good friend, `DBCC PAGE`:

```
dbcc page (bigpubs2000, 1, 125, 3)
go

PAGE: (1:125)
-------------

BUFFER:
-------

BUF @0x191CC080
---------------
bpage = 0x31944000          bhash = 0x00000000          bpageno = (1:125)
bdbid = 8                   breferences = 1             bstat = 0x9
bspin = 0                   bnext = 0x00000000

PAGE HEADER:
------------

Page @0x31944000
----------------
m_pageId = (1:125)          m_headerVersion = 1         m_type = 10
m_typeFlagBits = 0x0        m_level = 0                 m_flagBits = 0x0
m_objId = 1653580929        m_indexId = 1               m_prevPage = (0:0)
m_nextPage = (0:0)          pminlen = 90                m_slotCnt = 2
m_freeCnt = 6               m_freeData = 8182           m_reservedCnt = 0
m_lsn = (790:4932:12)       m_xactReserved = 0          m_xdesId = (0:0)
m_ghostRecCnt = 0           m_tornBits = 2
```

```
Allocation Status
-----------------
GAM (1:2) = ALLOCATED     SGAM (1:3) = NOT ALLOCATED
PFS (1:1) = 0x70 IAM_PG MIXED_EXT ALLOCATED   0_PCT_FULL
DIFF (1:6) = CHANGED      ML (1:7) = NOT MIN_LOGGED

IAM: Header @0x31944064 Slot 0, Offset 96
----------------------------------------
sequenceNumber = 0        status = 0x0              objectId = 0
indexId = 0               page_count = 0            start_pg = (1:0)

nIAM: Single Page Allocations @0x3194408E
----------------------------------------
Slot 0 = (1:124)          Slot 1 = (1:13575)        Slot 2 = (1:20648)
Slot 3 = (1:20650)        Slot 4 = (1:20652)        Slot 5 = (1:20653)
Slot 6 = (1:20654)        Slot 7 = (1:20655)


IAM: Extent Alloc Status Slot 1 @0x319440C2
------------------------------------------
(1:0)        - (1:488)      = NOT ALLOCATED
(1:496)      -              =     ALLOCATED
(1:504)      - (1:42280)    = NOT ALLOCATED
(1:42288)    - (1:42296)    =     ALLOCATED
(1:42304)    - (1:42608)    = NOT ALLOCATED
(1:42616)    -              =     ALLOCATED
(1:42624)    - (1:43040)    = NOT ALLOCATED
(1:43048)    - (1:44112)    =     ALLOCATED
(1:44120)    -              = NOT ALLOCATED
(1:44128)    - (1:44856)    =     ALLOCATED

DBCC execution completed. If DBCC printed error messages, contact your
 system administrator.
```

Looking at this output, you can verify that this IAM page belongs to the sales table because the `m_objId` is the same as the object ID of the `sales` table, `1653580929`. Some other things you can see here are that the table is using all eight slots for single page allocations on mixed extents (pages `1:124`, `1:13575`, `1:20648`, `1:20650`, `1:20652`, `1:20653`, `1:20654`, and `1:20655`) and has uniform extents allocated to it within the range of this IAM (for example, the extent at page `1:496` and extents in the range from page `1:42288` to `1:42296`). You can also tell that all space for the `sales` table is within the range of this IAM because no additional IAM pages are linked to it (`m_nextPage = (0:0)`).

NOTE

For a heap table, the data pages and the rows within them are not stored in any specific order. Unlike versions of SQL Server prior to 7.0, the pages in a heap structure are not linked together in a page chain. The only logical connection between data pages is the information recorded in the IAM pages, which are linked together. The structure of heap tables will be examined in more detail a little later in this chapter.

Differential Changed Map Pages

The seventh page (page number 6), and every 511,232nd page thereafter, in the database file is the Differential Changed Map (DCM) page. This page keeps track of which extents in a file have been modified since the last full database backup. When an extent has been modified, its corresponding bit in the DCM is turned on. This information is used when a differential backup is performed on the database. A differential backup copies only the extents changed since the last full backup was made. Using the DCM, SQL Server can quickly tell which extents need to be backed up by examining the bits on the DCM pages for each data file in the database. When a full backup is performed for the database, all the bits are set back to 0.

Bulk Changed Map Pages

The eighth page (page number 7), and every 511,232nd page thereafter, in the database file is the Bulk Changed Map (BCM). SQL Server 2000 introduces the `BULK_LOGGED` recovery model, which allows you to get the best performance and least log space usage for certain bulk operations, such as `BULK INSERT` and `bcp`, while still allowing you to back up and completely restore a database in case of a database or media failure. When the database is configured for `FULL` recovery mode, these bulk operations are fully logged, but in `BULK_LOGGED` recovery mode, they are only minimally logged. In previous versions, when a minimally logged operation was performed, you could not back up the transaction log and had to perform a full backup to provide recoverability.

When you perform a bulk operation in SQL Server 2000 in `BULK_LOGGED` recovery mode, SQL Server only logs the fact that the operation occurred and doesn't log the actual data changes. The operation is still fully recoverable because SQL Server keeps track of what extents were actually modified by the bulk operation in the BCM page. Similar to the DCM page, each bit on a BCM page represents an extent within its range, and if the bit is set to `1`, that indicates that the corresponding extent has been changed by a minimally logged bulk operation since the last full database backup. All the bits on the BCM page are reset to `0` whenever a full database backup or a log backup occurs.

When you initiate a log backup for a database using the `BULK_LOGGED` recovery model, SQL Server scans the BCM pages and backs up all the modified extents along with the contents of the transaction log itself. Be aware that the log file itself might be small, but the backup of the log can be many times larger if a large bulk operation has been performed since the last log backup.

Tables

One cornerstone of the relational database model is that there is only one structure that actually stores information in a relational database: the table.

A table is defined as a set of columns with certain properties, such as the datatype, nullability, constraints, and so on. Information about datatypes, column properties, constraints, and other information related to defining and creating tables can be found in Chapter 12.

Size Limits for Rows and Columns

As discussed earlier in this chapter, the maximum row size for a table is 8060 bytes. The maximum size for character and binary datatypes is 8000 bytes. Note, however, that the new Unicode datatypes require 2 bytes per character and thus require twice the amount of storage space as non-Unicode datatypes. This limits the size of `NCHAR` and `NVARCHAR` columns to 4000 characters. The maximum number of columns per table is 1024.

Heap Tables

A table without a clustered index is a **heap table**. There is no imposed ordering of the data rows for a heap table. Additionally, there is no direct linkage between the pages in a heap table.

In pre-7.0 versions of SQL Server, the data pages were doubly linked in a manner similar to that of a clustered table. To scan the table, SQL Server would look up the first page in the `sysindexes` table and then scan from that point forward, following the page pointers until it reached the last page in the table (`m_nextPage = 0`). Table scanning a linked chain of pages is more efficient when they are contiguous so that it reads the pages in file order, without having to hop around within the file to read the pages in linked page order. Unfortunately, the table could become fragmented over time. As rows were deleted, a whole page could be deallocated and reused, and likely linked into a different part of the page chain. This meant that SQL Server might have to go back and forth within the physical file when scanning the pages in the table sequence.

How, then, does SQL Server find all the data rows when it has to perform a table scan on a heap table? In SQL Server 2000, each heap table has at least one IAM (Index Allocation Map) page. The address of the first IAM page is stored in the `sysindexes` table (`sysindexes.FirstIAM`). The IAM page registers which extents are used by the table. SQL Server can then simply scan the allocated extents referenced by the IAM page, in physical order. This essentially avoids the problem of page chain fragmentation during reads because SQL Server will always be reading full extents in sequential order.

As discussed earlier, each IAM can map a maximum of 63,903 extents for a table. As a table uses extents beyond the range of those 63,903 extents, more IAM pages are created for the heap table as needed. A heap table also has at least one IAM page for each file on which the heap table has extents allocated. Figure 33.10 shows the structure of a heap table and how its contents are traversed using the IAM pages.

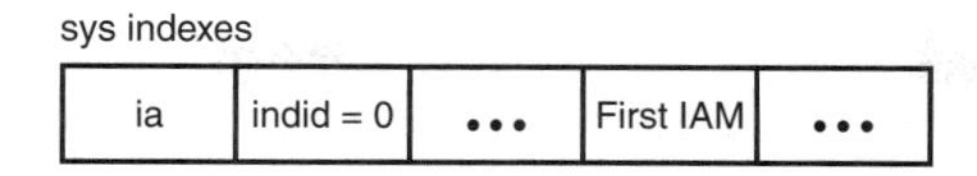

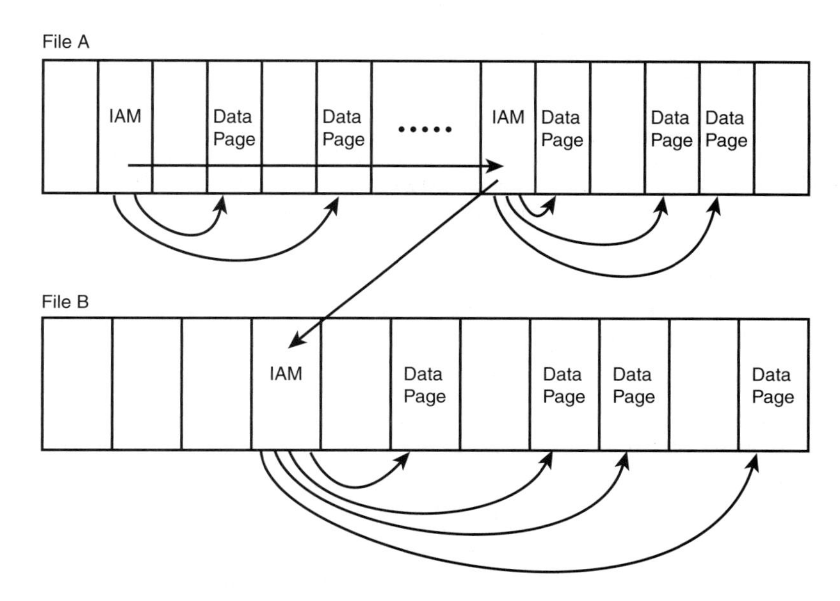

FIGURE 33.10 The structure of a heap table.

Clustered Tables

A **clustered table** is a table that has a clustered index defined on it. When you create a clustered index, the data rows in the table are physically sorted in the order of the columns in the index key. The data pages are chained together in a doubly linked list (each page points to the next page and to the previous page). Normally, data pages are not linked. Only index pages within a level are linked in this manner to allow for ordered scans of the data in an index level. Because the data pages of a clustered table constitute the leaf level of the clustered index, they are chained as well. This allows for an ordered table scan. The page pointers are stored in the page header in the `m_nextPage` and `m_prevPage` fields, as you've seen earlier with `DBCC PAGE`. Figure 33.11 shows an example of a clustered table. (Note that the figure shows only the data pages.)

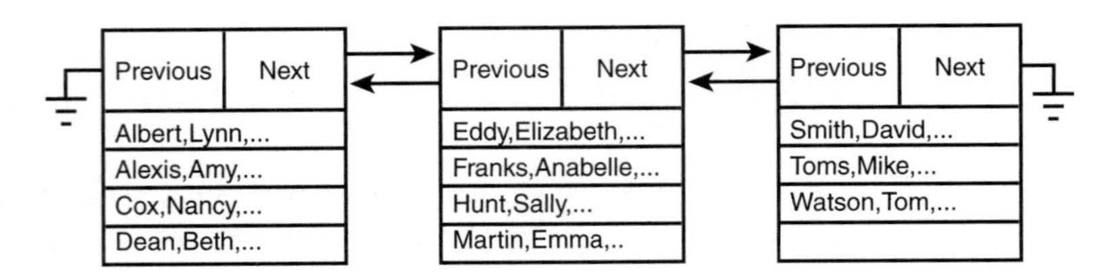

FIGURE 33.11 A clustered table.

Indexes

When running a query against a table with no indexes, SQL Server has to retrieve every page of the table, looking at every row on each page to find out whether the row satisfies the search arguments. SQL Server has to scan all the pages because there's no way of knowing whether any rows found are the only rows that satisfy the search arguments. This search method is referred to as a **table scan**.

For a heap table, a table scan is performed by traversing the IAM pages for the table and reading the pages within the extents allocated to the table in sequential order. For a table scan on a clustered table, SQL Server looks up the location of the root page of the clustered index (found in the `root` column in `sysindexes` where the `indid` is `1`) and then finds its way to either the first or last page of the table, depending on whether it needs to do an ascending or descending scan, respectively. When it is at the first or last page in the table, it then follows the page chain to read the rest of the pages in the table.

Needless to say, a table scan is not an efficient way to retrieve data unless you really need to retrieve all rows. The optimizer in SQL Server always calculates the cost of performing a table scan and uses that as a base line when evaluating other access methods. The various access methods and query plan cost analysis are discussed in more detail in Chapter 35.

Suppose that the table is stored on 10,000 pages; even if only one row is to be returned or modified, all the pages must be searched, resulting in a scan of approximately 80MB of data.

A mechanism is needed to identify and locate specific rows within a table quickly and easily. This functionality is provided through two types of indexes: clustered and nonclustered.

Indexes are structures stored separately from the actual data pages that contain pointers to data pages or rows. Indexes are used to speed up access to the data; they are also the mechanism used to enforce the uniqueness of key values.

Indexes in SQL Server are **balanced trees** (B-trees; see Figure 33.12). There is a single root page at the top of the tree, which branches out into *N* pages at each intermediate level until it reaches the bottom (leaf level) of the index. The leaf level has one row stored for each row in the table. The index tree is traversed by following pointers from the upper-level pages down through the lower-level pages. Each level of the index is linked as a doubly linked list.

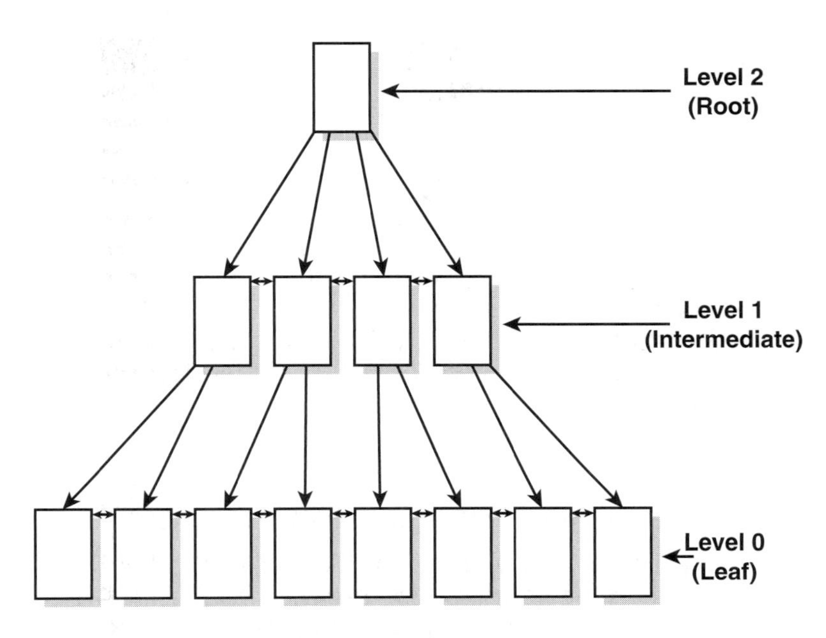

FIGURE 33.12 The basic structure of a B-tree index.

An index can have many intermediate levels depending on the number of rows in the table, the index type, and the index key width. The maximum number of columns in an index is 16; the maximum row width is 900 bytes.

Clustered Indexes

When you create a **clustered index**, all rows in the table are sorted and stored in the clustered index key order. Because the rows are physically sorted by the index key, you can have only one clustered index per table. You can compare the structure of a clustered index to a filing cabinet: The data pages are like folders in a file drawer in alphabetical order, and the data rows are like the records in the file folder, also in sorted order.

You can think of the intermediate levels of the index tree as the file drawers, also in alphabetical order, that assist you in finding the appropriate file folder. Figure 33.13 shows an example of a clustered index.

In Figure 33.13, note that the data page chain is in clustered index order. However, unlike SQL Server versions prior to version 7.0, the rows on each page might not be physically sorted in clustered index order, depending on when rows were inserted or deleted in the page. SQL Server still keeps the proper sort order of the rows via the row IDs and the `rowIDs` are mapped to the appropriate row slot via the row offset table (refer to Figure 33.4). A clustered index is useful for range-retrieval queries or searches against columns with duplicate values because the rows within the range are physically located in the same page or on adjacent pages.

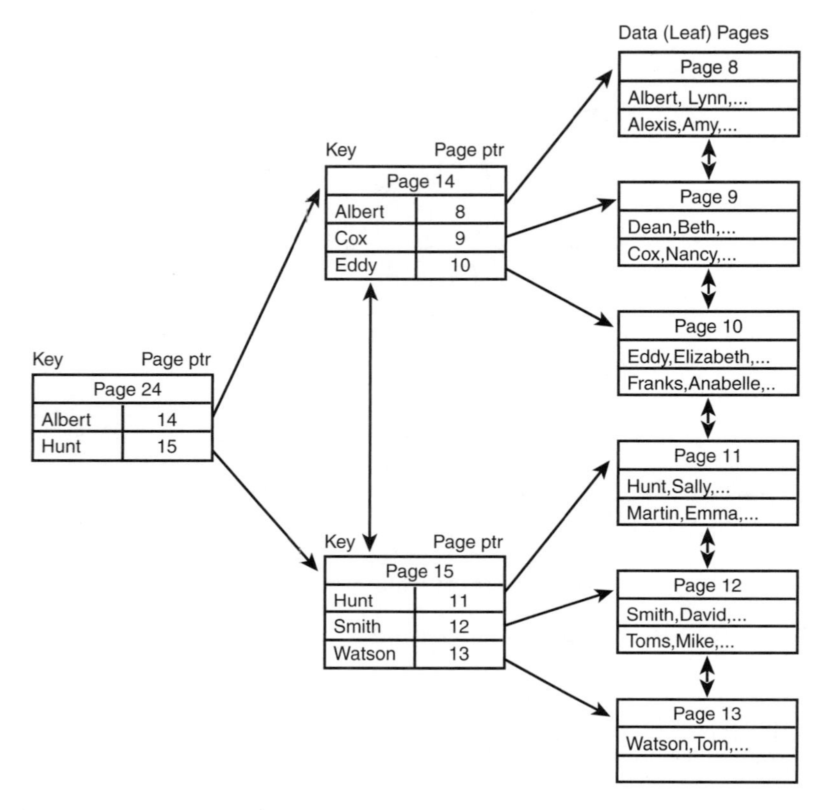

FIGURE 33.13 The structure of a clustered index.

The data pages of the table are also the leaf level of clustered index. To find all clustered index key values, SQL Server must eventually scan all the data pages.

SQL Server performs the following steps when searching for a value using a clustered index:

1. Queries `sysindexes` for the table where `indid = 1`. The `sysindexes.root` column contains the `fileId` and page address for the root page of the index.
2. Compares the search value against the key values stored on the root page.
3. Finds the highest key value on the page where the key value is less than or equal to the search value.
4. Follows the page pointer stored with the key to the appropriate page at the next level down in the index.
5. Continues following page pointers (that is, it repeats steps 3 and 4) until the data page is reached.

6. Searches the rows on the data page to locate any matches for the search value. If no matching row is found on that data page, then the table contains no matching values.

Clustered Index Row Structure

The structure of a clustered index row is similar to the structure of a data row and is detailed in Figure 33.14.

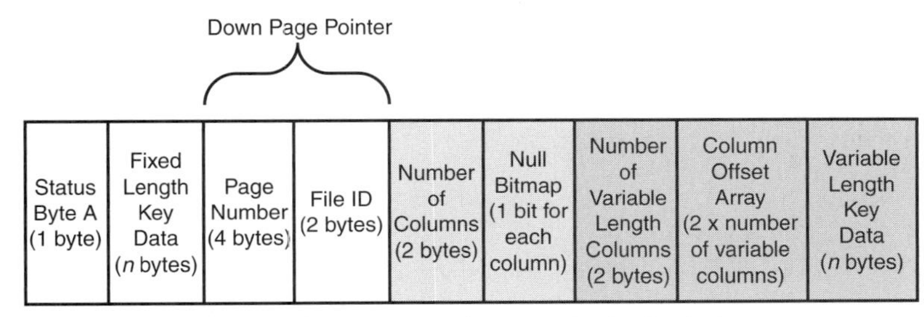

FIGURE 33.14 Clustered index row structure.

Notice that unlike a data row, index rows do not contain the status byte B or the 2 bytes to hold the length of fixed-length data fields. Instead of storing the length of the fixed-length data, which also indicates where the fixed-length portion of a row ends and the variable-length portion begins, the page header `pminlen` value is used to help describe an index row. The `pminlen` value is the minimum length of the index row, which is essentially the sum of the size of all fixed-width fields and overhead. Therefore, if no variable-length or nullable fields are in the index key, then `pminlen` also indicates the width of each index row.

The null bitmap field and the field for the number of columns in the index row are present only when an index key contains nullable columns. The number of columns value is only needed to determine how many bits are needed in the null bitmap, and therefore how many bytes are required to store the null bitmap (1 byte per eight columns). The data contents of a clustered index row include the key values along with a 6-byte down-page pointer (the first 2 bytes are the file ID, and the last 4 bytes are the page number). The down-page pointer is the last value in the fixed-data portion of the row.

To examine the contents of an index page, first create a table with a clustered index:

```
create table index_test ( id int identity,
                          a char(5) not null,
                          b char(10) null,
                          c varchar(10) null)
```

```
go
insert index_test values ('11111', 'b1111', 'cxxxxxx')
insert index_test values ('22222', 'b2222', 'cxxxxxx')
insert index_test values ('33333', 'b3333', 'cxxxxxx')
insert index_test values ('44444', 'b4444', 'cxxxxxx')
insert index_test values ('55555', 'b5555', 'cxxxxxx')
insert index_test values ('66666', 'b6666', 'cxxxxxx')
insert index_test values ('77777', 'b7777', 'cxxxxxx')

go


create clustered index CI_index_test on index_test (a)
go

exec sp_SSU_showindexpages index_test
go

tablename    id          indid  indexname   root       first      firstiam
------------ ----------- ------ ----------- ---------- ---------- ----------
index_test     949578421      1 CI_index_tes 1:162      1:160      1:161
```

Now you can use `DBCC PAGE` to examine the root page of the clustered index. If you specify option `1` to `DBCC PAGE`, it displays the row contents in hex form:

```
DBCC TRACEON(3604)
DBCC PAGE (pubs, 1, 162, 1)
go

PAGE: (1:162)
-------------

BUFFER:
-------

BUF @0x191E3240
---------------
bpage = 0x324D2000          bhash = 0x00000000         bpageno = (1:162)
bdbid = 5                   breferences = 8            bstat = 0x9
bspin = 0                   bnext = 0x00000000

PAGE HEADER:
------------
```

```
Page @0x324D2000
----------------
m_pageId = (1:162)          m_headerVersion = 1         m_type = 2
m_typeFlagBits = 0x0        m_level = 0                 m_flagBits = 0x20
m_objId = 949578421         m_indexId = 1               m_prevPage = (0:0)
m_nextPage = (0:0)          pminlen = 12                m_slotCnt = 1
m_freeCnt = 8082            m_freeData = 108            m_reservedCnt = 0
m_lsn = (5:60:13)           m_xactReserved = 0          m_xdesId = (0:631)
m_ghostRecCnt = 0           m_tornBits = 1

Allocation Status
-----------------
GAM (1:2) = ALLOCATED      SGAM (1:3) = ALLOCATED
PFS (1:1) = 0x60 MIXED_EXT ALLOCATED   0_PCT_FULL   DIFF (1:6) = CHANGED
ML (1:7) = NOT MIN_LOGGED

DATA:
-----

Slot 0, Offset 0x60
-------------------
Record Type = INDEX_RECORD                              Record Attributes =
324D2060:  31313106  00a03131  00010000              .11111......
```

The first byte, 06, is the status A byte (remember the reverse byte order scheme used). Right after that is the actual data in the index key column data, 31 31 31 31 31. After that is the down-page pointer, with the page number as the first 4 bytes (00 00 00 a0) followed by the file number as the last 2 bytes (0001). The page number equates to decimal page number 160, which if you look at the output from sp_SSU_showindexpages is the address of the first data page (because there are so few rows and pages in the table, the index tree consists of only a single page).

If this index has any nullable fields in it, there would be 3 additional bytes after the down-page pointer to hold the number of columns and the null bitmap. If there were any variable-length columns, the overhead columns and data would come after the fixed data or null bitmap in the index row just like they do in a data row.

If you specify option 3 to DBCC PAGE, it displays the index page row contents as index pointers:

```
dbcc traceon(3604)
dbcc page (pubs, 1, 162, 3)
go
```

```
PAGE: (1:162)
-------------

BUFFER:
-------

BUF @0x191E3240
---------------
bpage = 0x324D2000          bhash = 0x00000000          bpageno = (1:162)
bdbid = 5                   breferences = 1             bstat = 0x9
bspin = 0                   bnext = 0x00000000

PAGE HEADER:
------------

Page @0x324D2000
----------------
m_pageId = (1:162)          m_headerVersion = 1         m_type = 2
m_typeFlagBits = 0x0        m_level = 0                 m_flagBits = 0x20
m_objId = 949578421         m_indexId = 1               m_prevPage = (0:0)
m_nextPage = (0:0)          pminlen = 12                m_slotCnt = 1
m_freeCnt = 8082            m_freeData = 108            m_reservedCnt = 0
m_lsn = (5:60:13)           m_xactReserved = 0          m_xdesId = (0:631)
m_ghostRecCnt = 0           m_tornBits = 1

Allocation Status
-----------------
GAM (1:2) = ALLOCATED     SGAM (1:3) = ALLOCATED
PFS (1:1) = 0x60 MIXED_EXT ALLOCATED   0_PCT_FULL   DIFF (1:6) = CHANGED
ML (1:7) = NOT MIN_LOGGED
FileId PageId      Row    Level  ChildFileId ChildPageId a     ?
------ ----------- ------ ------ ----------- ----------- ----- -----------
     1         162      0      0           1         160 NULL  NULL
```

Another undocumented DBCC command to view the contents of an index is DBCC IND. This command displays information about all pages that belong to an index. The syntax for DBCC IND is as follows:

```
DBCC IND ({'dbname' | dbid }, { 'objname' | objid }, { indid | 0 | -1 | -2 })
```

The values for the third parameter are described as follows:

- indid—Displays information for all IAM and index pages for the specified index ID. If the index ID is 1 (meaning the clustered index), the data pages are also displayed.

- 0—Displays the page information for all IAM and data pages only for the specified table.
- -1—Displays the page information for all IAM, data, and index pages for the specified table.
- -2—Displays the page numbers for all IAM pages for the specified table.

Listing 33.5 shows an example of the output of DBCC IND.

LISTING 33.5 Sample Output from DBCC IND

```
DBCC TRACEON(3604)
DBCC IND (pubs, index_test, 0)
go

PageFID PagePID     IAMFID IAMPID      ObjectID    IndexID PageType IndexLevel
➥ NextPageFID NextPagePID PrevPageFID PrevPagePID
------- ----------- ------ ----------- ----------- ------- -------- ----------
➥ ----------- ----------- ----------- -----------
      1         161 NULL   NULL          949578421       1       10          0
➥           0           0           0           0
      1         160      1         161   949578421       0        1          0
➥           0           0           0           0
```

Table 33.7 describes the columns contained in the DBCC IND output.

TABLE 33.7 Description of Columns in DBCC IND

Column	Meaning
PageFID	File ID of this page.
PagePID	Page ID of this page.
IAMFID	File ID of the IAM managing this page.
IAMPID	Page ID of the IAM managing this page.
ObjectID	Object ID of table this page belongs to.
IndexID	Index ID of index this page belongs to.
PageType	Page type: 1 = Data page, 2 = Index page, 10 = IAM page.
IndexLevel	Level of index; 0 is leaf level.
NextPageFID	File ID for next page in page chain.
NextPagePID	Page ID for next page in page chain.
PrevPageFID	File ID for previous page in page chain.
PrevPagePID	Page ID for previous page in page chain.

Nonunique Clustered Indexes

When a clustered index is defined on a table, the clustered index keys are used as bookmarks to identify the data rows being referenced by nonclustered indexes (more on this in the upcoming section on nonclustered indexes). Because the clustered keys are used as unique row pointers, there needs to be a way to uniquely refer to each row in the table. If the clustered index is defined as a unique index, the key itself uniquely identifies every row. If the clustered index was not created as a unique index, SQL Server adds a 4-byte integer field, called a uniqueifier, to the data row to make each key unique when necessary. When is the uniqueifier necessary? SQL Server adds the uniqueifier to a row when the row is added to a table and that new row contains a key that is a duplicate of the key for an already existing row.

The uniqueifier is added to the variable-length data area of the data row, which also results in the addition of the variable-length overhead bytes. Therefore, each duplicate row in a clustered index will have a minimum of 4 bytes of overhead added for the additional uniqueifier. If the row had no variable-length keys previously, then an additional 8 bytes of overhead will be added to the row to store the uniqueifier (4 bytes) plus the overhead bytes required for the variable data (storing the number of variable columns requires 2 bytes, and the column offset array requires 2 bytes).

You can see the behavior of the uniqueifier in the following example:

```
create table dupe_test ( a char(5) not null)
go
insert dupe_test values ('11111')
insert dupe_test values ('22222')

go
create clustered index CI_dupe_test on dupe_test (a)
go
```

Before adding a duplicate row, determine the address of the data page (it will be the first page as stored in `sysindexes`):

```
exec sp_SSU_showindexpages dupe_test
go

tablename    id          indid  indexname    root      first     firstiam
------------ ----------- ------ ------------ --------- --------- ---------
dupe_test     1525580473      1 CI_dupe_test 1:185     1:180     1:181
```

Now, take a look at the page with `DBCC PAGE`:

```
DBCC TRACEON(3604)
DBCC PAGE (pubs, 1, 180, 1)
```

```
go

PAGE: (1:180)
-------------

BUFFER:
-------

BUF @0x18FC0000
---------------
bpage = 0x21340000          bhash = 0x00000000          bpageno = (1:180)
bdbid = 5                   breferences = 1             bstat = 0x9
bspin = 0                   bnext = 0x00000000

PAGE HEADER:
------------

Page @0x21340000
----------------
m_pageId = (1:180)          m_headerVersion = 1         m_type = 1
m_typeFlagBits = 0x0        m_level = 0                 m_flagBits = 0x24
m_objId = 1525580473        m_indexId = 0               m_prevPage = (0:0)
m_nextPage = (0:0)          pminlen = 9                 m_slotCnt = 2
m_freeCnt = 8068            m_freeData = 120            m_reservedCnt = 0
m_lsn = (6:99:11)           m_xactReserved = 0          m_xdesId = (0:885)
m_ghostRecCnt = 0           m_tornBits = 1

Allocation Status
-----------------
GAM (1:2) = ALLOCATED     SGAM (1:3) = ALLOCATED
PFS (1:1) = 0x60 MIXED_EXT ALLOCATED   0_PCT_FULL   DIFF (1:6) = CHANGED
ML (1:7) = NOT MIN_LOGGED

DATA:
-----

Slot 0, Offset 0x60
-------------------
Record Type = PRIMARY_RECORD
Record Attributes =  NULL_BITMAP
21340060:  00090010  31313131  00000131           ....11111...
```

```
Slot 1, Offset 0x6c
-------------------
Record Type = PRIMARY_RECORD
Record Attributes =  NULL_BITMAP
2134006C:  00090010  32323232  00000132          ....22222...

OFFSET TABLE:
-------------
Row - Offset
1 (0x1) - 108 (0x6c)
0 (0x0) - 96 (0x60)

DBCC execution completed. If DBCC printed error messages, contact your
 system administrator.
```

Now, add a duplicate row and examine the page again:

```
insert dupe_test values ('22222')
dbcc page (pubs, 1, 180, 1)
go

PAGE: (1:180)
-------------

BUFFER:
-------

BUF @0x18FC0000
---------------
bpage = 0x21340000          bhash = 0x00000000          bpageno = (1:180)
bdbid = 5                   breferences = 2             bstat = 0xb
bspin = 0                   bnext = 0x00000000

PAGE HEADER:
------------

Page @0x21340000
----------------
m_pageId = (1:180)          m_headerVersion = 1         m_type = 1
m_typeFlagBits = 0x0        m_level = 0                 m_flagBits = 0x8000
m_objId = 1525580473        m_indexId = 0               m_prevPage = (0:0)
m_nextPage = (0:0)          pminlen = 9                 m_slotCnt = 3
m_freeCnt = 8046            m_freeData = 140            m_reservedCnt = 0
m_lsn = (6:109:2)           m_xactReserved = 0          m_xdesId = (0:885)
m_ghostRecCnt = 0           m_tornBits = 1
```

```
Allocation Status
-----------------
GAM (1:2) = ALLOCATED     SGAM (1:3) = ALLOCATED
PFS (1:1) = 0x60 MIXED_EXT ALLOCATED   0_PCT_FULL   DIFF (1:6) = CHANGED
ML (1:7) = NOT MIN_LOGGED

DATA:
-----

Slot 0, Offset 0x60
-------------------
Record Type = PRIMARY_RECORD
Record Attributes =  NULL_BITMAP
21340060:  00090010  31313131  00000131           ....11111...

Slot 1, Offset 0x6c
-------------------
Record Type = PRIMARY_RECORD
Record Attributes =  NULL_BITMAP
2134006C:  00090010  32323232  00000132           ....22222...

Slot 2, Offset 0x78
-------------------
Record Type = PRIMARY_RECORD
Record Attributes =  NULL_BITMAP VARIABLE_COLUMNS
21340078:  00090030  32323232  00000132  00140001 0...22222.......
21340088:  00000001                               ....

OFFSET TABLE:
-------------
Row - Offset
2 (0x2) - 120 (0x78)
1 (0x1) - 108 (0x6c)
0 (0x0) - 96 (0x60)

DBCC execution completed. If DBCC printed error messages, contact your
 system administrator.
```

As you'll see in this example, the third row was added, but with some additional information. The binary string of `00140001` represents the number of variable-length columns (`0001`) and the column offset for the uniqueifier (`0014`), which indicates that the uniqueifier is at byte 20. The string at byte 20 is `00000001`, indicating that this is the first duplicate row. If we added another duplicate, its uniqueifier would be 2.

When calculating the estimated size of a nonunique clustered index, you must remember to include the overhead for the uniquefier for the estimated number of duplicate values.

Estimating Clustered Index Size

Because clustered index rows contain only page pointers, the size and number of levels in a clustered index depends on the width of the index key and the number of pages in the table. The following pseudocode can be used to estimate the size of a clustered index key row:

```
  Sum ( width of fixed-length key fields)
+ 1 byte (for Status Byte A)
+ 6 bytes (to store the down page pointer)
+ sum( avg( width of fixed-length key fields)
+ IF (variable length keys in index) THEN
      2 -- for number of variable length columns
    + 2 * number of variable columns
  END IF
+ if (any index key column allows nulls) THEN
      2 -- for number of columns
    + ceiling ( numcols / 8 ) + 1
+ if ( nonunique index )
    + 4 -- for each duplicate value
```

Assume that you have a unique clustered index on a `char(10)` column that doesn't allow null values. Your index row size would be the following:

10 bytes

\+ 1 byte (for status byte A)

\+ 6 bytes (to store the page pointer)

= 17 bytes per index row

Because the clustered index contains a pointer to each data page in the table, the number of rows at the bottom level of the index is equal to the number of pages in the table.

If a table's data row size is 42 bytes, the total space required for each row is 44 bytes (42 bytes plus 2 bytes for each row's offset table entry). At 44 bytes per row, SQL Server can store a maximum of 184 data rows per data page (8096 bytes divided by 44 bytes per row). If the table has 100,000 rows, that works out to a minimum of 544 pages in the table (100,000 rows divided by 184 rows per page). Therefore, at least 544 rows would be in the lowest nonleaf level of the clustered index. Each index page, like a data page, has 8096 bytes available for storing index row entries. To determine the number of clustered index rows per page, divide the index row size into 8096 bytes and multiply by the fill factor percentage (fill factor is discussed later in this chapter). For this example, assume that the default fill factor is being applied, which leaves one slot available in the index pages, and the data pages are completely filled:

8096/17 = 476.2 rounded down to 476 rows per page – 1 = 475 rows per page

At 475 rows per page, SQL Server would need 544 rows/475 rows per page = 1.15, rounded up to two pages, to store all the rows at the lowest nonleaf level of the index.

The top level of the index must be a single root page. You need to build levels on top of one another in the index until you reach a single root page. To determine the total number of levels in the index, use the following algorithm:

```
N = 0
divide number of data pages by (number of index rows per page - 1)
while number of index pages at level N is > 1
begin
    divide number of pages at level N by (number of rows per page - 1)
    N = N+1
end
```

When the number of pages at level `N` equals `1`, you are at the root page, and `N+1` equals the number of levels in the index. The total number of pages in the clustered index is the sum of all pages at each level.

Applying this algorithm to the example gives the following results:

Level 0: 544/475 = 2 pages

Level 1: 2/475 = 1 page

Thus, the index contains two levels, for a total size of three pages, or 24KB (3 pages times 8KB per page).

The I/O cost of retrieving a single row by using the index is the number of levels in the index plus a single data page read. Contrast this with the cost of a table scan for the example:

Clustered index retrieval = 2 index levels + 1 data page = 3 page I/Os

Table scan = 544 page I/Os

You can easily see the performance advantage that having an index on the table can provide during a `SELECT`. An index is also helpful during data modifications to quickly identify the rows to be updated or deleted.

Nonclustered Indexes

A **nonclustered index** is a separate index structure, independent of the physical sort order of the data rows in the table. You can have up to 249 nonclustered indexes per table.

You can think of a nonclustered index as the index in the back of a book. To find the pages on which a specific subject is discussed, you look up the subject in the index and then go to the pages referenced in the index. This is an efficient method as long as the subject is discussed on only a few pages. If the subject is discussed on many pages, or if you want to read about many subjects, it can be more efficient to read the entire book.

A nonclustered index works similarly to the book index. From the index's perspective, the data rows are randomly spread throughout the table. The nonclustered index tree contains the index key values in sorted order. There is a row at the leaf level for each data row in the table. Each leaf level row contains a "bookmark" to locate the actual data row in the table.

If no clustered index is created for the table, the bookmark for the leaf level of the index is an actual pointer to the data page and the row number within the page where the row is located (see Figure 33.15).

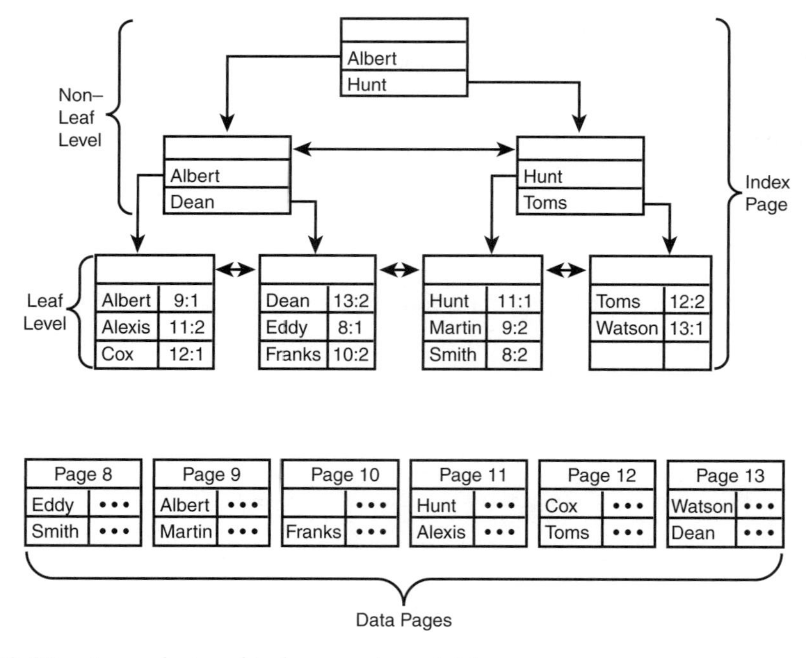

FIGURE 33.15 A nonclustered index on a heap table.

Versions of SQL Server prior to 7.0 stored only the row locators (the `RowId`) in nonclustered indexes to identify the data row that the index key referenced. If the table had a clustered index defined on it and a page split occurred (as a result of an `INSERT` or `UPDATE`), many rows were moved to another page (page splits will be covered in more detail later in this chapter). All corresponding rows in the nonclustered indexes had to be modified to reflect the new row IDs. This made page splits costly. Page splits do not occur with heap tables as all new rows are simply added at the end of the table.

In SQL Server 7.0 and 2000, nonclustered indexes on clustered tables no longer include the data row ID as part of the index. Instead, the bookmark for the nonclustered index is the associated clustered index key value for the record. When SQL Server reaches the leaf level of a nonclustered index, it uses the clustered index key to start searching through the clustered index to find the actual data row (see Figure 33.16). This adds a few I/Os to the search itself, but the benefit is that if a page split occurs in a clustered table, or if a row is moved (for example, as a result of an update), the nonclustered indexes stay the same. As long as the clustered index key is not modified, no row pointers in the index have to be updated.

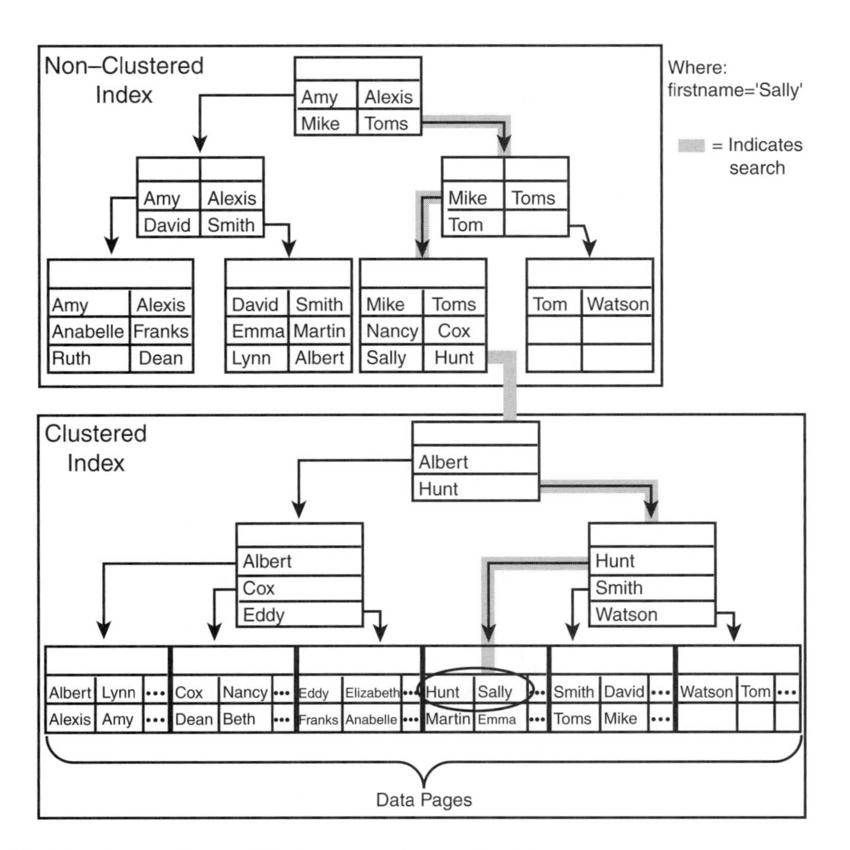

FIGURE 33.16 A nonclustered index on a clustered table.

SQL Server performs the following steps when searching for a value using a nonclustered index:

1. Queries `sysindexes` for the table where `indid > 1` and `indid <= 250`. The `sysindexes.root` column contains the file ID and page address for the root page of the index.
2. Compares the search value against the index key values on the root page.
3. Finds the highest key value on the page where the key value is less than or equal to the search value.
4. Follows the down-page pointer to the next level down in the nonclustered index tree.
5. Continues following page pointers (that is, it repeats steps 3 and 4) until the nonclustered index leaf page is reached.
6. Searches the index key rows on the leaf page to locate any matches for the search value. If no matching row is found on the leaf page, the table contains no matching values.
7. If a match is found on the leaf page, SQL Server follows the bookmark to the data row on the data page.

Nonclustered Index Leaf Row Structures

In nonclustered indexes, if the bookmark is a row ID, it is stored at the end of the fixed-length data portion of the row. The rest of the structure of a nonclustered index leaf row is similar to a clustered index row. Figure 33.17 shows the structure of a nonclustered leaf row for a heap table.

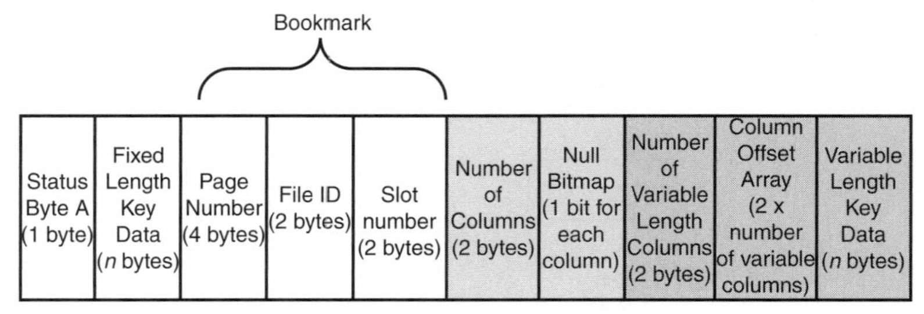

FIGURE 33.17 The structure of a nonclustered index leaf row for a heap table.

If the bookmark is a clustered index key value, the bookmark resides in either the fixed or variable portion of the row, depending on whether the clustered key columns were defined as fixed or variable length. Figure 33.18 shows the structure of a nonclustered leaf row for a clustered table.

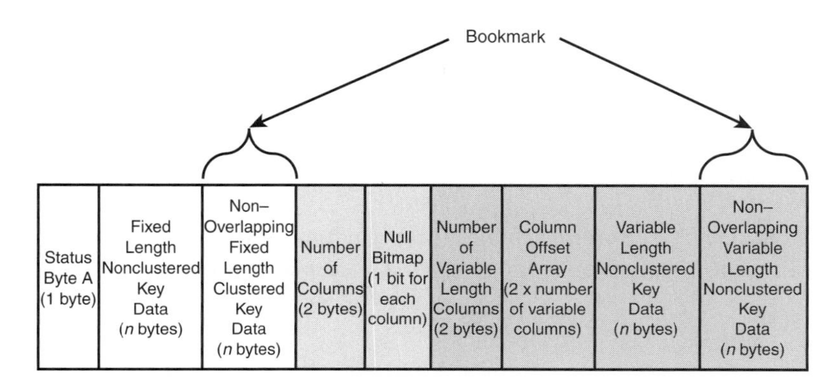

FIGURE 33.18 The structure of a nonclustered index leaf row for a clustered table.

When the bookmark is a clustered key value and the clustered and nonclustered indexes share columns, the data value for the key is stored only once in the nonclustered index row. For example, if your clustered index key is on `lastname` and you have a nonclustered index defined on both `firstname` and `lastname`, the index rows will not store the value of `lastname` twice but only once for both keys.

You can examine the differences in the index row structures using `DBCC PAGE`. First, create the following table and indexes:

```
create table nc_ci_test ( a char(4) not null,
                          b varchar(8) null,
                          c char(4) null,
                          d char(4) not null)
go

insert nc_ci_test values ('aaaa', 'bbbb', 'cccc', 'dddd')
go

create index idx_2col on nc_ci_test (a, b)
create index idx_null on nc_ci_test (c)
go
```

Now, find out the page numbers (because the table is so small, the root page is also the leaf page of the nonclustered index):

```
exec sp_ssu_showindexpages nc_ci_test
go

tablename    id          indid  indexname    root       first      firstiam
------------ ----------- ------ ------------ ---------- ---------- ----------
nc_ci_test    1685581043      0 nc_ci_test   1:196      1:196      1:197
nc_ci_test    1685581043      2 idx_2col     1:198      1:198      1:199
nc_ci_test    1685581043      3 idx_null     1:224      1:224      1:226
```

You can use `DBCC PAGE` to examine the leaf row structure of the `idx_null` index (to save space, only the row information from `DBCC PAGE` is displayed):

```
DATA:
-----

Slot 0, Offset 0x60
------------------
Record Type = INDEX_RECORD
Record Attributes =  NULL_BITMAP
1A8B2060:  63636316  0000c463  00000100  00000300 .cccc...........
```

As you can see, the fixed-length data (`63 63 63 63`) is at the front of the index record, right after status byte A (`16`). After the index key value in the fixed-length portion is the row pointer, consisting of the page ID (`000000c4`, decimal 196), the file ID (`0001`), and the row ID on the page (`0000`, because the first row on a page has a row ID of 0). After that is the information for the null bitmap because column `c` allows nulls. The number of columns (`0003`) represents the three pieces of information stored in the index row—the key data for `c`, the down-page pointer, and the row ID.

Next, you can use `DBCC PAGE` to look at the row information for the `idx_2col` index, which has both fixed- and variable-length columns in it:

```
DATA:
-----

Slot 0, Offset 0x60
------------------
Record Type = INDEX_RECORD
Record Attributes =  VARIABLE_COLUMNS
1A854060:  61616126  0000c461  00000100  15000100 &aaaa...........
1A854070:  62626200        62                     .bbbb
```

You can see the structure is similar for the fixed-length data portion up to byte 13. Because neither column is nullable, there is no null bitmap. The value for column b is stored at the end of the row, after the number of variable-length columns (0001) and the column offset (0015).

Both of these indexes are on a heap table, so the bookmark is the page and row pointer. Now, create a clustered index on the table:

```
create clustered index idx_clust on nc_ci_test(b)
```


With a clustered index on the table, the nonclustered indexes will all be rebuilt and the bookmark changed to the clustered index key. Using DBCC PAGE to examine the index row for the idx_null index shows the following:

```
DATA:
-----

Slot 0, Offset 0x60
-------------------
Record Type = INDEX_RECORD
Record Attributes =  NULL_BITMAP VARIABLE_COLUMNS
1A8B0060:  63636336  00000363  00100001  62626262 6cccc.......bbbb
```

Here you can see that the page and row pointer are no longer in the fixed-length section of the row, and the clustered key value for the row (bbbb) is stored in the variable-length portion of the row because column b is a variable-length key.

Using DBCC PAGE to examine the index row for the idx_2col index, which already contains column b in the nonclustered index, shows the following:

```
DATA:
-----

Slot 0, Offset 0x60
-------------------
Record Type = INDEX_RECORD
Record Attributes =  NULL_BITMAP VARIABLE_COLUMNS
1A8BE060:  61616136  00000361  00100001  62626262 6aaaa.......bbbb
```

Notice from this output how column b is in the index row only once, even though it is part of both the clustered and nonclustered index.

Nonclustered Index Nonleaf Row Structures

The nonclustered index nonleaf rows are similar in structure to clustered index nonleaf rows in that they contain a page-down pointer to a page at the next level down in the index tree. The nonleaf rows don't need to point to data rows; they only need to provide the path to traverse the index tree to a leaf row. If the nonclustered index is defined as unique, the nonleaf index key row contains only the index key value and the page-down pointer. Figure 33.19 shows the structure of a nonleaf index row for a unique nonclustered index.

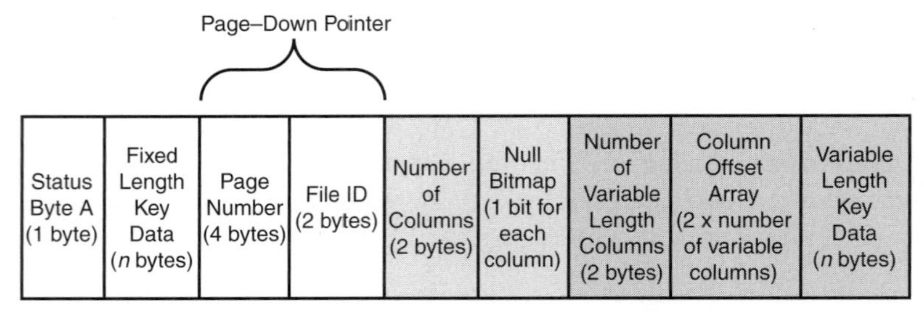

FIGURE 33.19 The structure of a nonclustered nonleaf index row for a unique index.

If the nonclustered index is not defined as a unique index, the nonleaf rows will also contain the bookmark information for the corresponding data row. Storing the bookmark in the nonleaf index row allows any corresponding nonleaf index rows to be located and deleted more easily when the data row is deleted. For a heap table, the bookmark is the corresponding data row's page and row pointer, as shown in Figure 33.20.

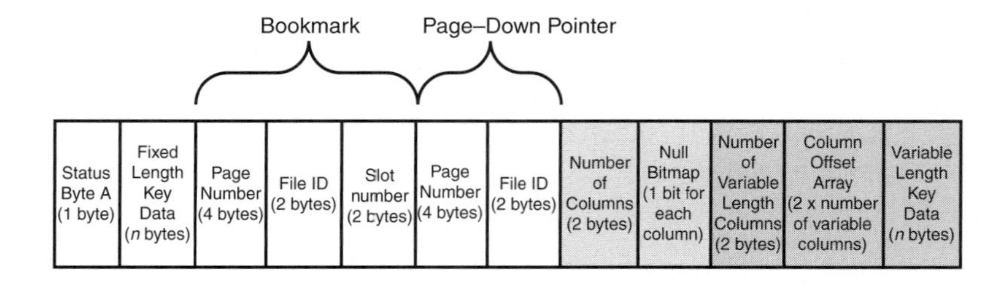

FIGURE 33.20 The structure of a nonclustered nonleaf index row for a nonunique index on a heap table.

If the table is clustered, the clustered key value(s) are stored in the nonleaf index row just as they are in the leaf rows, as shown in Figure 33.21.

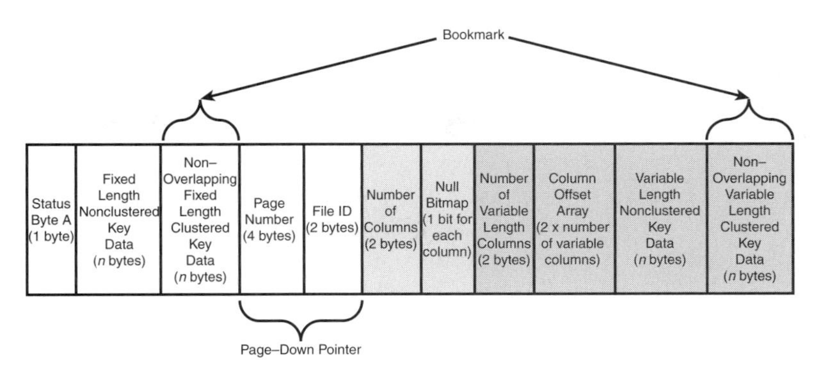

FIGURE 33.21 The structure of a nonclustered nonleaf index row for a nonunique index on a clustered table.

As you can see, it's possible for the index pointers and row overhead to exceed the size of the index key itself. This is why, for I/O and storage reasons, it is always recommended that you keep your index keys as small as possible.

Estimating Nonclustered Index Size

Because nonclustered indexes contain a record for each row in the table, the size and number of levels in a nonclustered index depends on the width of the index key and the number of rows in the table.

Because so many factors influence the structure of the index row (unique or nonunique, clustered table or heap), the formula for determining the width of a nonclustered leaf index row is a bit more complicated. The one constant component is the fixed-length portion. Everything else is dependent on the index definition and whether the table has a clustered index.

The following pseudocode provides the formula for estimating the size of a nonclustered index leaf row:

```
  1   -- for status byte A
+ sum( width of fixed-length index keys)
+ sum ( width of variable length keys in nonclustered index )
+ CASE
    WHEN index on heap
       THEN 8 -- size of bookmark, a page and row pointer
    WHEN index on clustered table
       THEN sum(width of non-overlapping fixed-length clustered keys)
          + sum(avg(width ofnon-overlapping variable length clustered keys))
```

```
        + IF ( nonunique clustered index and duplicate row )
            then 4 -- bytes for uniqueifier
          END IF
  END CASE
+ CASE
    when variable columns in nonclusterd key or clustered key bookmark
      then 2 bytes -- for number of variable columns
         + 2 * number of variable columns -- for column offset array
    ELSE 0
  END CASE
+ CASE
    WHEN nullable column in nonclusterd key or clustered key bookmark
      THEN 2 bytes -- for number of columns in index
         + ceiling ( number of columns / 8) -- for NULL bitmap
    ELSE 0
  END CASE
+
```

Refer back to the `idx_null` index on the `nc_ci_test` table defined earlier. The size of the index before the table had a clustered index on it would be estimated as follows:

1 (for status byte A)

\+ 4 (for size of fixed-width index key)

\+ 8 (for bookmark on a heap)

\+ 2 (for number of columns in index)

\+ 1 (for null bitmap)

= 16 bytes

The size of the `idx_2col` index before the table had a clustered index created on it would be estimated as follows:

1 (for status byte A)

\+ 4 (for size of fixed-width index key on `a`)

\+ 4 (for average size of variable-width key on `b`)

\+ 8 (for bookmark on a heap)

\+ 2 (for number of variable columns)

\+ 2 (for column offset array: 2 * 1 variable column)

= 21 bytes

The size of the `idx_2col` index after the table had a clustered index created on it would be estimated as follows:

  1 (for status byte A)
+ 4 (for size of fixed-width index key on `a`)
+ 4 (for average size of variable-width key on `b`)
+ 0 (for nonoverlapping clustered key on `b`)
+ 2 (for number of variable columns)
+ 2 (for column offset array: 2 * 1 variable column)
+ 2 (for number of columns in index)
+ 1 (for null bitmap)
= 16 bytes

Because the leaf level of a nonclustered index contains a pointer to each data row in the table, the number of rows at the leaf level of the index is equal to the number of rows in the table.

If there are 100,000 rows in the table, there will be 100,000 rows in the leaf level of the nonclustered index. Each nonclustered index page, like a data page, has 8096 bytes available for storing index row entries. To determine the maximum number of nonclustered leaf index rows per page, divide the leaf index row size into 8096 bytes. For this example, assume that a fill factor of 75 percent is used when the index is created so that the leaf pages are 75 percent filled, and the nonleaf pages have one free slot available. The number of rows per page for the leaf level of the `idx_2col` nonclustered index with a 16-byte index row would be calculated as follows:

8096/16 = 506 rows per page × .75 = 379 rows per page

At 379 rows per page, SQL Server would need 100,000/379 = 265.85, rounded up to 266 pages, to store all the rows at the leaf level of the index.

The size of the nonleaf index rows can be calculated according to the following pseudocode:

```
  1 -- for status byte A
+ sum( width of fixed-length index keys)
+ sum ( width of variable length keys in nonclustered index )
+ 6 -- size of page-down pointer
+ IF non-unique index
      then CASE
        when heap table
          then 8 - size of bookmark for heap
```

```
        else sum(width of non-overlapping fixed-length clustered keys)
           + sum(avg(width ofnon-overlapping variable length clustered keys))
           + IF ( nonunique clustered index and duplicate row )
               then 4 -- bytes for uniqueifier
             END IF
  END IF
+ CASE
    when variable columns in nonclusterd key or clustered key bookmark
      then 2 bytes -- for number of variable columns
         + 2 * number of variable columns -- for column offset array
    else 0
  END CASE
+ CASE
    when nullable column in nonclusterd key or clustered key bookmark
      then 2 bytes -- for number of columns in index
         + ceiling ( number of columns / 8)
    else 0
  END CASE
```

For the `idx_2col` index, the size of the nonleaf rows after the clustered index is created would be calculated as

  1 (for status byte A)
+ 4 (for size of fixed-width index key on `a`)
+ 4 (for average size of variable-width key on `b`)
+ 6 (for page-down pointer)
+ 0 (for nonoverlapping clustered key on `b`)
+ 2 (for number of variable columns)
+ 2 (for column offset array: 2 * 1 variable column)
+ 2 (for number of columns in index)
+ 1 (for null bitmap)
= 22 bytes

To determine the number of nonleaf index rows per page for a nonclustered index, divide the nonleaf index row size into 8096 bytes and apply the fill factor. Unless you specify the `PAD_INDEX` along with the `FILL_FACTOR` option when creating an index, SQL Server always leaves one free slot available in the nonleaf pages. Therefore, the number of nonleaf rows for the index in our example would be

8096/22 = 368 rows per page – 1 = 367 nonleaf rows per page

Like the clustered index, the top level of the index must be a single root page. You need to build levels on top of one another in the index until you reach a single root page. To determine the total number of levels in the nonclustered index, use the following algorithm:

```
N = 0
divide number of data rows by number of leaf index rows per page to determine
      the number of leaf level pages
while the number of index pages at level N is > 1
begin
    divide the number of pages at level N
         by (the number of nonleaf rows per page - 1)
    N = N+1
end
```

When the number of pages at level `N` equals `1`, you are at the root page, and `N+1` equals the number of levels in the index. The total size of the nonclustered index in number of pages is the sum of the number of pages at each level.

If you apply this algorithm to the example, you get the following results:

Level 0: 100,000 rows/379 leaf rows per page = 264 pages

Level 1: 264 rows/367 nonleaf rows per page = 1 page

Thus, the nonclustered index contains two levels, for a total size of 265 8KB pages, or 2,120KB. Notice that this is larger than the clustered index, which required only three pages (24KB).

The maximum I/O cost of retrieving a single row by using a nonclustered index on a heap table is the number of levels in the index plus a single data page read. If the table has a clustered index on it (resulting in the clustered key being used as the bookmark in the nonclustered index), the maximum I/O cost is the number of levels in the nonclustered index, plus the number of levels in the clustered index, plus the data page read.

Although nonclustered indexes provide a performance advantage during a `select` and are helpful during data modifications to quickly identify rows to be updated or deleted, they can also add overhead during data modifications, as you'll see in the remainder of this chapter.

Estimated Index Size Versus Actual Size

If you want to confirm the amount of space actually being used by your tables and indexes, you can query the information stored in the `sysindexes` table, or use the supplied `sp_spaceused` system procedure:

```
use bigpubs2000
go
exec sp_spaceused sales_big
go

name         rows      reserved      data          index_size    unused
------------ --------- ------------- ------------- ------------- ---------
sales_big    1687250   476904 KB     273088 KB     50432 KB      153384 KB
```

After a table takes up more than eight pages of space, SQL Server begins allocating uniform extents to the table. As you'll recall from earlier in this chapter, uniform extents can only contain data from a single table. When a uniform extent is allocated to a table, not all of its pages are necessarily going to have data on them right away. However, because no other table can use the rest of the extent, the remaining pages in the extent are "reserved" for use by that table or index. SQL Server always attempts to use free pages in extents already allocated to a table or index before allocating an additional extent.

The `reserved` column therefore represents all the space currently allocated to the table and its indexes, `data` is the amount of the reserved space that contains data rows, and `index_size` is the total size of the allocated pages containing index rows. The `unused` column represents the pages allocated to the table and its indexes that are not yet being used either for data or for index rows.

If you want to determine at a finer level how much space each individual index is using, you can run the following query:

```
select convert(varchar(20), object_name(id)) as 'table',
       convert(varchar(20), name) as 'index',
       indid,
       reserved * 8 as 'reserved',
       dpages * 8 as 'data',
       (reserved - used ) * 8 as 'unused'
from sysindexes
where id = object_id('sales_big')
and isnull(indexproperty(id, name, 'isautostatistics'), 0) = 0
go

table            index            indid  reserved    data        unused
---------------- ---------------- ------ ----------- ----------- -----------
sales_big        ci_sales_big          1      476904      273088      153384
sales_big        idx1                  2       73400       31568       36736
```

When the indid is 0 or 1, the reserved, data, and unused values apply for the entire table and its indexes and are essentially what is displayed by sp_spaceused. However, at the individual index level, the values are for that index only, so you can see just how many pages are allocated and being used by the indexes themselves.

Unfortunately, the information in sysindexes is not always kept up-to-date as data in the table is modified. To update the usage information, execute sp_spaceused and specify true as the value for the second parameter, @updateusage:

```
exec sp_spaceused sales_big, @updateusage = 'true'
go
name        rows       reserved     data          index_size    unused
----------- ---------- ------------ ------------- ------------- ---------
sales_big   1687250    306000 KB    273088 KB     32608 KB      304 KB
```

When the @updateusage option is specified, SQL Server first updates the usage information for the table and its indexes and then reports it. You can also run the DBCC UPDATEUSAGE command directly:

```
DBCC UPDATEUSAGE ( database [, table [. index ]]]
    [ WITH    [ COUNT_ROWS ] [ , NO_INFOMSGS ]
```

When you run this command, it updates the usage information and reports the changes it makes:

```
DBCC UPDATEUSAGE
    (    bigpubs2000, sales_big )
go

DBCC UPDATEUSAGE: sysindexes row updated for table 'sales_big' (index ID 2):
        USED pages: Changed from (4583) to (3960) pages.
        RSVD pages: Changed from (9175) to (3969) pages.
DBCC UPDATEUSAGE: sysindexes row updated for table 'sales_big' (index ID 1):
        USED pages: Changed from (40440) to (38212) pages.
        RSVD pages: Changed from (59613) to (38250) pages.
DBCC execution completed. If DBCC printed error messages, contact your
 system administrator.
```

SQL Server Index Maintenance

SQL Server indexes are self-maintaining, which means that any time a data modification (such as an update, delete, or insert) takes place on a table, the index B-tree is automatically updated to reflect the correct data values and current rows. Generally, you do not have to do any maintenance of the indexes, but indexes and tables can become fragmented over time. There are two types of fragmentation: external fragmentation and internal fragmentation.

External fragmentation is when the logical order of pages does not match the physical order or when the extents in use by the table are not contiguous. These situations occur typically with clustered tables as a result of page splits and pages being allocated and linked into the page chain from other extents. External fragmentation is usually not much of an issue for most queries that are performing small resultset retrievals via an index. It's more of a performance issue for ordered scans of all or part of a table or index. If the table is heavily fragmented and the pages are not contiguous, scanning the page chain will be more expensive.

Internal fragmentation occurs when an index is not using up all space within the pages in the table or index. Fragmentation within an index page can happen for the following reasons:

- As more records are added to a table, space is used on the data page and on the index page. As a result, the page eventually becomes completely full. If another insert takes place on that page and there is no more room for the new row, SQL Server splits the page into two, each page now being about 50 percent full. If the clustered key values being inserted are not evenly distributed throughout the table (as often happens with clustered indexes on sequential keys), this extra free space might not be used.
- Frequent update statements can cause fragmentation in the database at the data and index page level as the updates cause rows to move to other pages. Again, if future clustered key values inserted into the table are not evenly distributed throughout the table, the empty slots left behind might not be used.
- As rows are deleted, space becomes freed up on data and index pages. If no new rows within the range of deleted values on the page are inserted, the page remains sparse.

NOTE

Internal fragmentation is not always a bad thing. Although pages that are not completely full use up more space and require more I/Os during retrieval, free space within a page allows for rows to be added without having to perform an expensive page split. For some environments where the activity is more insert intensive than query intensive, you might want more free space in your pages. This can be accomplished by applying the fill factor when creating the index on the table. Applying the fill factor will be described in more detail in the next section.

Usually in a system, all these factors contribute to the fragmentation of data within the data pages and the index pages. In an environment with a lot of data modification, you might see a lot of fragmentation on the data and index pages over a period of time. These sparse and fragmented pages remain allocated to the table or index even if they have only a single row or two, and the extent containing the page remains allocated to the table or index.

Data fragmentation adversely impacts performance because the data is spread across more pages than necessary. More I/Os will be required to retrieve the data. SQL Server provides a `DBCC` command to monitor the level of fragmentation in the database. The syntax for this command is

```
DBCC SHOWCONTIG({table | view}[,index])
  [ WITH { ALL_INDEXES
        | FAST [ , ALL_INDEXES ]
        | TABLERESULTS [ , { ALL_INDEXES } ]
        [ , { FAST | ALL_LEVELS } ]
      }
  ]
```

33

You can use the `TABLERESULTS` option to receive the output from `DBCC SHOWCONTIG` as a table resultset, which could be inserted into a table for historical or analysis purposes.

The following is an example of a table that has a fair amount of internal fragmentation:

```
DBCC SHOWCONTIG(io_test)
go

DBCC SHOWCONTIG scanning 'io_test' table...
Table: 'io_test' (1845581613); index ID: 1, database ID: 5
TABLE level scan performed.
- Pages Scanned................................: 335
- Extents Scanned..............................: 45
- Extent Switches..............................: 45
- Avg. Pages per Extent........................: 7.4
- Scan Density [Best Count:Actual Count].......: 91.30% [42:46]
- Logical Scan Fragmentation ..................: 8.66%
- Extent Scan Fragmentation ...................: 46.67%
- Avg. Bytes Free per Page.....................: 3906.7
- Avg. Page Density (full).....................: 51.73%
```

Notice that the `Avg. Page Density (full)` is 51.73 percent and the `Avg. Bytes Free per Page` is 3906.7 bytes. This indicates that the majority of pages in the table are only half full. This is wasting space and costing extra I/O when retrieving data. The `Scan Density` is relatively high, so the table is not too externally fragmented yet at this point.

After you determine that data is fragmented, SQL Server provides a couple of different methods for you to reorganize the data on index and data pages so that each page is filled to an optimal level. One method available is the `DBCC INDEXDEFRAG` command:

```
DBCC INDEXDEFRAG ('database', {'table' | 'view'}, index_name)
  [WITH NO_INFOMSGS]
```

`DBCC INDEXDEFRAG` eliminates the internal defragmentation in an index, compacting the index or data rows and removing any completely emptied pages from the index. `DBCC INDEXDEFRAG` can defragment clustered and nonclustered indexes on tables and views. `DBCC INDEXDEFRAG` also defragments the leaf level of an index so that the physical order of the pages matches the logical order of the index leaf nodes, thereby improving index-scanning performance. `DBCC INDEXDEFRAG` does not hold locks long term while it runs and doesn't lock the entire table, so it can be run online and will not block concurrently running queries or updates.

If you were to run `DBCC INDEXDEFRAG` on the `io_test` table in the previous example, it should compact the rows in the clustered index, increasing the number of rows per page, thereby reducing the number of I/Os:

```
DBCC INDEXDEFRAG (pubs, io_test, 1)
go

Pages Scanned Pages Moved Pages Removed
------------- ----------- -------------
          331         164           165
```

You can check the results by running `DBCC SHOWCONTIG` again:

```
DBCC SHOWCONTIG(io_test)
go

DBCC SHOWCONTIG scanning 'io_test' table...
Table: 'io_test' (1845581613); index ID: 1, database ID: 5
TABLE level scan performed.
- Pages Scanned................................: 170
- Extents Scanned..............................: 25
- Extent Switches..............................: 25
- Avg. Pages per Extent........................: 6.8
- Scan Density [Best Count:Actual Count].......: 84.62% [22:26]
- Logical Scan Fragmentation ..................: 0.59%
- Extent Scan Fragmentation ...................: 48.00%
- Avg. Bytes Free per Page.....................: 187.7
- Avg. Page Density (full).....................: 97.68%
```

As you can see, the `Avg. Page Density (full)` is now 97.68 percent, and the `Avg. Bytes Free per Page` is only 187.7 bytes.

Another method that can be used to defragment your data and indexes is to rebuild the indexes. You can do this manually by running a series of `DROP INDEX` and `CREATE INDEX` commands, usually in a T-SQL script file. This can be a tedious process that runs the risk of an index not getting rebuilt if it's missing from the SQL script. Also, if you run out of space while rebuilding an index, the `CREATE INDEX` command fails leaving you without that index on the table. A better way of rebuilding all indexes is to use the `DBCC DBREINDEX` command:

```
DBCC DBREINDEX ([ 'database.owner.table_name' [, index_name[, fillfactor ]]])
  [WITH NO_INFOMSGS]
```

CAUTION

Unlike `DBCC INDEXDEFRAG`, `DBCC DBREINDEX` applies table level locks while rebuilding indexes and should not be run online, as it would block other queries and updates on the table. This should only be run during off-peak hours or during the normal maintenance window.

Using `DBCC DBREINDEX` alleviates you from having to specify all the indexes you want to drop and re-create on a table (if you specify just the table name, it automatically rebuilds all indexes). In addition, if `DBCC DBREINDEX` fails while processing for some reason (out of space, out of locks, and so on), the rebuild is rolled back and the original indexes are left in place.

The following example runs `DBCC DBREINDEX` on `io_test` and reruns `DBCC SHOWCONTIG` to see whether any external fragmentation is eliminated:

```
DBCC DBREINDEX (io_test)
DBCC SHOWCONTIG(io_test)
go

DBCC execution completed. If DBCC printed error messages, contact your
 system administrator.
DBCC SHOWCONTIG scanning 'io_test' table...
Table: 'io_test' (1845581613); index ID: 1, database ID: 5
TABLE level scan performed.
- Pages Scanned................................: 168
- Extents Scanned..............................: 22
- Extent Switches..............................: 21
- Avg. Pages per Extent........................: 7.6
- Scan Density [Best Count:Actual Count].......: 95.45% [21:22]
- Logical Scan Fragmentation ..................: 10.71%
- Extent Scan Fragmentation ...................: 72.73%
- Avg. Bytes Free per Page.....................: 119.8
- Avg. Page Density (full).....................: 98.52%
```

Because the table wasn't overly fragmented, you don't see a dramatic improvement, but the table is more compact than it was originally, using fewer pages and extents.

One of the options to the CREATE INDEX and DBCC DBREINDEX commands is the Fill Factor option. Fill factor allows you to specify the fullness of the pages at the data and leaf index page levels as a percentage.

Setting the Fill Factor

Fill factor is a setting provided when creating an index that specifies, as a percentage, how full you want your data pages or leaf level index pages to be when the index is created. A lower fill factor has the effect of spreading the data and leaf index rows across more pages by leaving more free space in the pages. This reduces page splitting and dynamic reorganization of index and data pages, which can improve performance in environments where there are a lot of inserts and updates to the data. A higher fill factor has the effect of packing more data and index rows per page by leaving less free space in the pages. This is useful in environments where the data is relatively static because it reduces the number of pages required for storing the data and its indexes, and helps improve performance for queries by reducing the number of pages that need to be accessed.

By default, when you create an index on a table, if you don't specify a value for FILLFACTOR, the default value is zero. With a FILLFACTOR setting of 0, or 100, the data pages for a clustered index and the leaf pages for a nonclustered index are created completely full. However, space is left within the nonleaf nodes of the index for one or two more rows. The default fill factor to be used when creating indexes is a server level configuration option. If you want to change the serverwide default for the fill factor, use the sp_configure command:

```
sp_configure 'fill factor',N
```

It is generally recommended that you leave the serverwide default for fill factor as 0 because, typically, you will specify the fill factor to be used for an index within the index creation statement.

You can override the default fill factor value by specifying the FILLFACTOR option for the CREATE INDEX statement:

```
CREATE [UNIQUE] [CLUSTERED | NONCLUSTERED]
    INDEX index_name ON table (column [, ...n])
[WITH
        [[,] FILLFACTOR = fillfactor]
        [PAD_INDEX]
```

The FILLFACTOR option for the CREATE INDEX command allows you to specify, as a percentage, how full the data or leaf level index pages should be when you create an index on a table. The specified percentage can be from 1 to 100. Specifying a value of 80 would mean that each data or leaf page would be filled approximately 80 percent full at the time you create the index. It is important to note that as more data gets modified or added to a table, the fill factor is not maintained at the level specified during the CREATE INDEX command. Over a period of time, you will find that each page has a different percentage of fullness as rows are added and deleted.

TIP

A fill factor setting specified when creating a nonclustered index affects only the nonclustered index pages and doesn't affect the data pages. To apply a fill factor to the data pages in a table, you must provide a fill factor setting when creating a clustered index on the table. Also, it is important to remember that the fill factor is applied only at index creation time and is *not* maintained by the SQL Server. When you begin updating and inserting data, the fill factor eventually is lost. Therefore, specifying a fill factor when creating your indexes is only useful if the table already contains data, or if you simply want to set a default fill factor for the index other than 0 that will be used when indexes are rebuilt by DBCC DBREINDEX.

If you specify only the FILLFACTOR option, only the data or leaf level index pages are affected by the fill factor. To specify the level of fullness for nonleaf pages, use the PAD_INDEX option together with FILLFACTOR. This option allows you to specify how much space to leave open on each node of the index, which can help to reduce page splits within the nonleaf levels of the index. You don't specify a value for PAD_INDEX; it uses the same percentage value that is specified with the FILLFACTOR option. For example, to apply a 50 percent fill factor to the leaf and nonleaf pages in a nonclustered index on title_id in the titles table, execute the following:

```
CREATE INDEX title_id_index on titles (title_id)
        with FILLFACTOR = 50, PAD_INDEX
```

TIP

When you use PAD_INDEX, the value specified by FILLFACTOR cannot be such that the number of rows on each index node falls below two. If you do specify such a value, SQL Server internally overrides it.

Reapplying the Fill Factor

When might you need to re-establish the fill factor for your indexes or data? As data gets modified in a table, the value of FILLFACTOR is not maintained at the level specified during the CREATE INDEX statement. As a result, each page can reach a different level of fullness. Over a period of time, this can lead to heavy fragmentation in the database if insert/delete activity is not evenly spread throughout the table and could impact performance. In addition, if a table becomes very large and then very small, rows could become isolated within data pages. This space will likely not be recovered until the last row on the page is deleted and the page is marked as unused. To either spread rows out or to reclaim space by repacking more rows per page, you need to reapply the fill factor to your clustered and nonclustered indexes.

In environments where insert activity is heavy, reapplying a low fill factor might help performance by spreading out the data and leaving free space on the pages, which helps to minimize page splits and possible page-locking contention during heavy OLTP activity. You can use Performance Monitor to monitor your system and determine whether excessive page splits are occurring (see Chapter 37 for more information on using Performance Monitor).

The DBA must manually reapply the fill factor to improve performance of the system. This can be done using the `DBCC DBREINDEX` command discussed earlier, or by dropping and re-creating the index. `DBCC DBREINDEX` is preferred because, by default, it will apply the original fill factor specified when the index was created, or you can provide a new fill factor to override the default. The original fill factor for an index is stored in `sysindexes` in the `OrigFillFactor` column. Additionally, if you use the `DBCC INDEXDEFRAG` command to defragment your table or index, it attempts to apply the index's original fill factor when it compacts the pages.

TIP

The `DBCC DBREINDEX` command is especially useful if you have indexes created on your table via primary key constraints. To rebuild a primary key index without using `DBCC DBREINDEX` would require you to drop all foreign key constraints that reference the primary key constraint, drop the primary key constraint, re-create the primary key constraint specifying the desired fill factor, and then re-create the foreign key constraints. Obviously, running `DBCC DBREINDEX` to reapply the fill factor for a primary key is a much simpler process.

Data Modification and Performance

Now that you have a better understanding of the storage structures in SQL Server, it's time to take a look at how SQL Server maintains and manages those structures when data modifications are taking place in the database.

Inserting Data

When you add a data row to a heap table, SQL Server adds the row to the heap wherever space is available. SQL Server uses the IAM and PFS pages to identify whether any pages with free space are available in the extents already allocated to the table. If no free pages are found, SQL Server uses the information from the GAM and SGAM pages to locate a free extent and allocate it to the table. With a clustered index on the table, the new data row is inserted to the appropriate location on the appropriate data page relative to the clustered index sort order. If there is no more room on the destination page, SQL Server needs to link a new page in the chain to make room available and add the row. This is called a **page split**.

In addition to modifying the affected data pages when adding rows, all nonclustered indexes need to be updated to add a pointer to the new record. If a page split occurs, this incurs even more overhead as the clustered index needs to be updated to store the pointer for the new page added to the table. Fortunately, because the clustered key is used as the bookmark in nonclustered indexes when a table is clustered, even though the page and row IDs have changed, the bookmarks for rows moved by a page split do not have to be updated as long as the clustered key remains the same.

Page Splits

When a page split occurs, SQL Server looks for an available page to link into the page chain. It first tries to find an available page in the same extent as the pages it will be linked to. If no free pages exist in the same extent, it looks at the IAM to determine whether there are any free pages in any other extents already allocated to the table or index. If no free pages are found, a new extent is allocated to the table.

When a new page is found, the original page is split. Approximately half the rows are moved to the new page, and the rest remain on the original page (see Figure 33.22). Whether the new page goes before or after the original page when the split is made depends on the amount of data to be moved. In an effort to minimize logging, SQL Server moves the smaller rows to the new page. If the smaller rows are at the beginning of the page, SQL Server places the new page before the original page and moves the smaller rows to it. If the larger rows are at the beginning of the page, SQL Server keeps them on the original page and moves the smaller rows to the new page after the original page.

Figure 33.22 illustrates page splitting due to inserts.

After determining where the new row goes between the existing rows and whether the new page is to be added before or after the original page, SQL Server has to move rows to the new page. The simplified algorithm for determining the split point is as follows:

1. Place the first row (with the lowest clustered key value) at the beginning of the first page.
2. Place the last row (with the highest clustered key value) on the second page.
3. Place the row with the next lowest clustered key value on the first page after the existing row(s).
4. Place the next-to-last row (with the second highest clustered key value) on the second page.
5. Continue alternating back and forth until the space between the two pages is balanced or one of the pages is full.

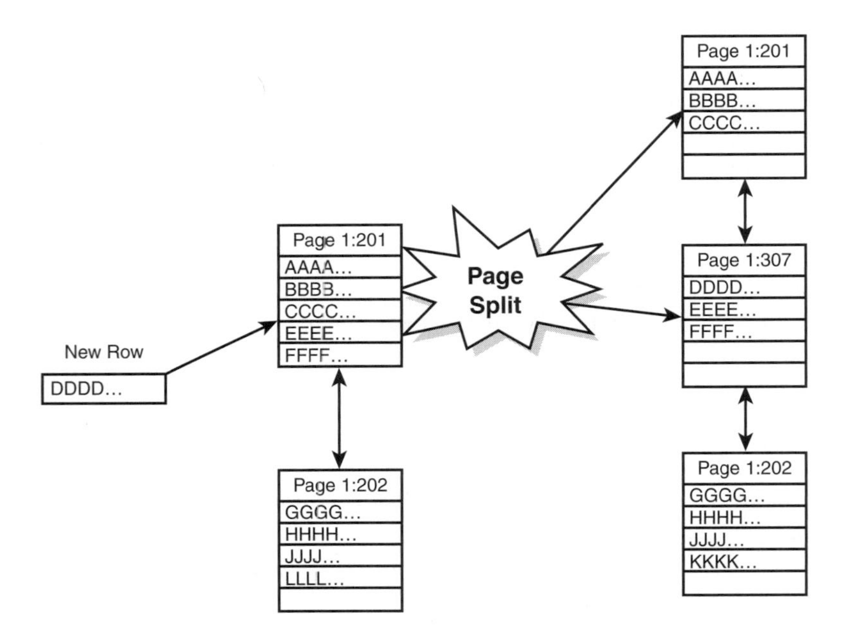

FIGURE 33.22 Page splitting due to inserts.

There are situations where a double split can occur. If the new row has to go between two existing rows on a page, but the new row is too large to fit on either page with any of the existing rows, a new page is added after the original. The new row is added to the new page, a second new page is added after that, and the remaining original rows are inserted into the second new page. An example of a double split is shown in Figure 33.23.

NOTE

Although page splits are expensive when they occur, they do generate free space in the split pages for future inserts into those pages. Page splits also help keep the index tree balanced as rows are added to the table. However, if you monitor the system with Performance Monitor and are seeing hundreds of page splits per second, you might want to consider rebuilding the clustered index on the table and applying a lower fill factor to provide more free space in the existing pages (see `DBCC DBREINDEX` earlier in this chapter). This can help improve system performance until eventually the pages fill up and start splitting again. For this reason, some shops supporting high-volume OLTP environments with a lot of insert activity rebuild the indexes with a lower fill factor on a daily basis.

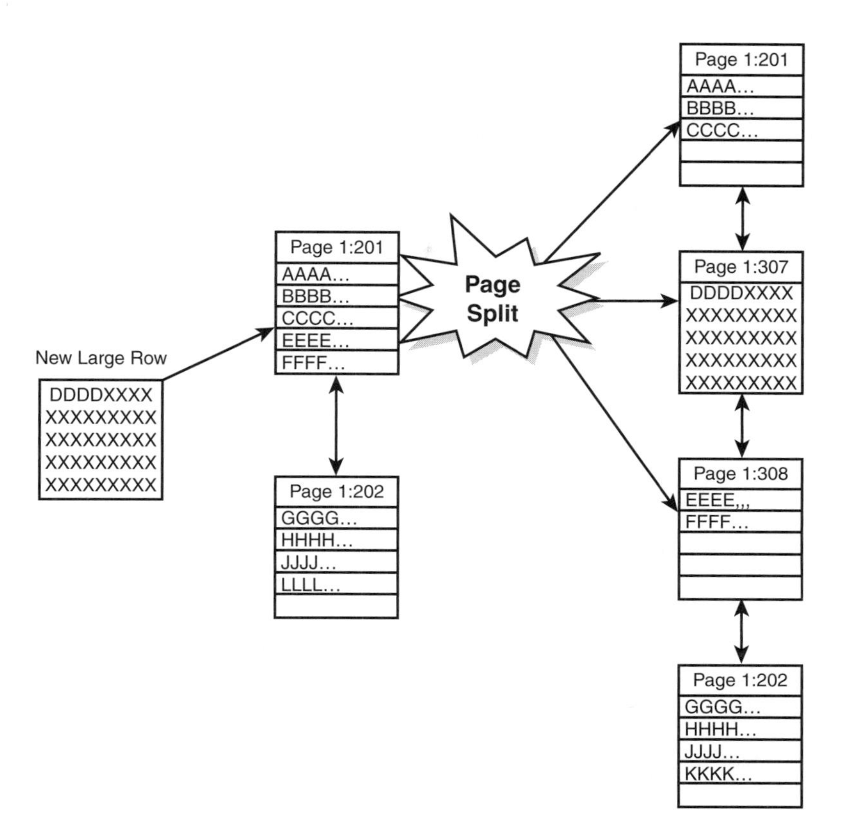

FIGURE 33.23 Double page split due to large row insert.

Deleting Rows

What happens when rows are deleted from a table? How, and when, does SQL Server reclaim the space when data is removed from a table?

Deleting Rows from a Heap

In a heap table, SQL Server does not automatically compress the space on a page when a row is removed—that is, the rows are not all moved up to the beginning of the page to keep all free space at the end, as SQL Server did in versions prior to 7.0. To optimize performance, SQL Server holds off on compacting the rows until the page needs contiguous space for storing a new row. You can see this with a simple example using `DBCC PAGE`. First create a heap table and add some rows to it. Then get the first page of the table:

```
create table heaptable (a char(4))
go
insert heaptable values ('row1')
insert heaptable values ('row2')
```

```
insert heaptable values ('row3')
go
exec sp_SSU_showindexpages heaptable
go

tablename    id          indid  indexname    root       first      firstiam
------------ ----------- ------ ------------ ---------- ---------- ----------
heaptable     1957582012      0 heaptable    1:251      1:251      1:252
go
```

Now examine the row with `DBCC PAGE`. The following displays just the `DATA` and offset table section of `DBCC PAGE`:

```
DBCC PAGE (pubs, 1, 251, 1)
go

DATA:
-----

Slot 0, Offset 0x60
-------------------
Record Type = PRIMARY_RECORD
Record Attributes =  NULL_BITMAP
1A8CC060:  00080010  31776f72    000001            ....row1...

Slot 1, Offset 0x6b
-------------------
Record Type = PRIMARY_RECORD
Record Attributes =  NULL_BITMAP
1A8CC06B:  00080010  32776f72    000001            ....row2...

Slot 2, Offset 0x76
-------------------
Record Type = PRIMARY_RECORD
Record Attributes =  NULL_BITMAP
1A8CC076:  00080010  33776f72    000001            ....row3...

OFFSET TABLE:
-------------
Row - Offset
2 (0x2) - 118 (0x76)
1 (0x1) - 107 (0x6b)
0 (0x0) - 96 (0x60)
```

As you can see at this point, all three rows are contiguous on the page. Take note of the offset of row 3 (`Slot 2, Offset 0x76`). Now, delete row 2 and look at the page again:

```
delete heaptable where a = 'row2'
go

dbcc page (pubs, 1, 251, 1)
go

DATA:
-----

Slot 0, Offset 0x60
-------------------
Record Type = PRIMARY_RECORD
Record Attributes =  NULL_BITMAP
1A8CC060:  00080010  31776f72    000001          ....row1...

Slot 2, Offset 0x76
-------------------
Record Type = PRIMARY_RECORD
Record Attributes =  NULL_BITMAP
1A8CC076:  00080010  33776f72    000001          ....row3...

OFFSET TABLE:
-------------
Row - Offset
2 (0x2) - 118 (0x76)
1 (0x1) - 0 (0x0)
0 (0x0) - 96 (0x60)
```

You can see that row 2 no longer exists in the page, but row 3 remained where it was (`Slot 2, Offset 0x76`). The offset for row 2 (Slot 1) has been set to 0 to indicate there is no row in that slot currently.

Deleting Rows from an Index

Because the data pages of a clustered table are actually the leaf pages of the clustered index, the behavior of data row deletes on a clustered table is the same as row deletions from an index page.

When rows are deleted from the leaf level of an index, they are not actually deleted but marked as ghost records. Keeping the row as a ghost record makes it easier for SQL Server to perform key-range locking (key-range locking is discussed in Chapter 38, "Locking and Performance"). If ghost records were not used, SQL Server would have to lock the entire range surrounding the deleted record. With the ghost record still present and visible internally to SQL Server (it is not visible in query result sets), SQL Server can use the ghost record as an endpoint for the key-range lock to prevent "phantom" records with the same key value from being inserted, while allowing inserts of other values to proceed.

Ghost records do not stay around forever, though. SQL Server has a special internal housekeeping process that periodically examines the leaf level of B-trees for ghost records and removes them. This is the same thread that performs the auto-shrink process for databases.

If you add a clustered index to the heap table in the previous example and then delete a row, you can see the ghost record with `DBCC PAGE`, as shown in Listing 33.6.

LISTING 33.6 Viewing a Ghost Record for a Delete from a Clustered Table

```
create clustered index CI_heaptable on heaptable (a)
go
/* get the new page information
sp_SSU_showindexpages heaptable
go

tablename    id          indid  indexname    root       first      firstiam
----------- ---------- ------ ------------ ---------- ---------- ----------
heaptable     1957582012      1 CI_heaptable 1:256      1:254      1:255

begin tran
delete heaptable where a = 'row1'
/* do not commit the transaction before running DBCC PAGE
** or the ghost record by get cleaned up by the housekeeper
** process first */
dbcc page (pubs, 1, 254, 1)
go

DATA:
-----

Slot 0, Offset 0x60
-------------------
Record Type = GHOST_DATA_RECORD
Record Attributes =  NULL_BITMAP
1A8DC060:  0008001c  31776f72   000001          ....row1...

Slot 1, Offset 0x6b
-------------------
Record Type = PRIMARY_RECORD
Record Attributes =  NULL_BITMAP
1A8DC06B:  00080010  33776f72   000001          ....row3...
```

LISTING 33.6 Continued

```
OFFSET TABLE:
-------------
Row - Offset
1 (0x1) - 107 (0x6b)
0 (0x0) - 96 (0x60)
```

You can see in Listing 33.6 that row1 now has a record type of GHOST_DATA_RECORD. After the transaction is committed, the row can be removed by the housekeeper process. To see the total number of ghost records in a table, you can turn on trace flag 2514 and run DBCC CHECKTABLE, as in the following example:

```
DBCC TRACEON(2514)
DBCC CHECKTABLE (heaptable)
go

DBCC execution completed. If DBCC printed error messages, contact your
 system administrator.
DBCC results for 'heaptable'.
There are 1 rows in 1 pages for object 'heaptable'.
Ghost Record count = 1
DBCC execution completed. If DBCC printed error messages, contact your
 system administrator.
```

Whenever you delete a row, all nonclustered indexes need to be updated to remove the pointers to the deleted row. Nonleaf index rows are not ghosted when deleted. Like heap tables, however, the space is not compressed on the nonleaf index page until needed.

Reclaiming Space

Only when the last row is deleted from a data page is the page deallocated from the table. The only exception is if it is the last page remaining—all tables have to have at least one page allocated, even if it's empty. When a deletion of an index row leaves only one row remaining on the page, the remaining row is moved to a neighboring page, and the now empty index page is deallocated.

If the page to be deallocated is the last remaining used page in a uniform extent allocated to the table, the extent is deallocated from the table as well.

Updating Rows

Versions of SQL Server prior to 7.0 supported **deferred updates**. With deferred updates, the rows to be modified were copied to the transaction log as no-op records. The records were then rescanned in the log and the changes applied back to the actual table. This was a log-intensive and expensive type of update.

SQL Server 2000 does not perform deferred updates. Due to the way SQL Server now maintains clustered indexes, all updates can be done directly without using the transaction log as a holding area.

However, there are two types of direct updates that SQL Server can perform:

- In-place updates
- Not-in-place updates

In-Place Updates

In SQL Server 2000, in-place updates are performed as often as possible to minimize the overhead of an update. An in-place update means that the row is modified where it is on the page and only the affected bytes are changed. In versions of SQL Server prior to 7.0, in-place updates were almost the exception rather than the norm.

When an in-place update is performed, in addition to the reduced overhead in the table itself, only a single modify record is written to the log. However, if the table has a trigger on it or is marked for replication, the update is still done in place but is recorded in the log as a delete followed by an insert (this provides the before-and-after image for the trigger that is referenced in the `inserted` and `deleted` tables).

In-place updates are performed whenever a heap is being updated or when a clustered table is updated, but the clustered key itself is not changed. You can get an in-place update if the clustered key changes but the row does not have to move—that is, the sorting of the rows wouldn't change.

Not-In-Place Updates

If the change to a clustered key prevents an in-place update from being performed, or if the modification to a row increases its size such that it can no longer fit on its current page, the update will be performed as a delete followed by an insert—this is referred to as a not-in-place update.

When performing an update that affects multiple index keys, SQL Server keeps a list of the rows that need to be updated in memory, if it's small enough; otherwise, it is stored in `tempdb`. SQL Server then sorts the list by index key and type of operation (delete or insert). This list of operations, called the **input stream**, consists of both the old and new values for every column in the affected rows as well as the unique row identifier for each row.

SQL Server then examines the input stream to determine whether any of the updates conflict or would generate duplicate key values while processing (if they were to generate a duplicate key after processing, the update cannot proceed), and rearranges the operations in the input stream in a manner to prevent any intermediate violations of the unique key.

For example, consider the following update to a table with a unique key on a sequential primary key:

```
update table1 set pkey = pkey + 1
```

Even though all values would still be unique when the update finished, if the update were performed internally one row at a time in sequential order, it would generate duplicates during the intermediate processing as the pkey value was incremented and matched the next pkey value. SQL Server would rearrange and rework the updates in the input stream to process them in a manner that would avoid the duplicates and then process them a row at a time. If possible, deletes and inserts on the same key value in the input stream are collapsed into a single update. In some cases, you might still get some rows that can be updated in place.

Forward Pointers

As mentioned earlier, when page splits on a clustered table occur, the nonclustered indexes do not need to be updated to reflect the new location of the rows because the bookmark to the row is the clustered index key rather than the row pointer. When an update operation on a heap table causes rows to move, the row pointers in the nonclustered index would need to be updated to reflect the new location or the rows. This could be expensive if there were a larger number of nonclustered indexes on the heap.

SQL Server 2000 addresses this performance issue through the use of forward pointers. When a row in a heap moves, it leaves a forward pointer in the original location of the row. The forward pointer avoids having to update the nonclustered index pointer to the row. When SQL Server is searching for the row via the nonclustered index, the index pointer directs it to the original location where the forward pointer redirects it to the new row location.

A row never has more than one forward pointer. If the row moves again from its forwarded location, the forward pointer stored at the original row location is updated to the row's new location. There is never a forward pointer that points to another forward pointer. If the row ever shrinks enough to fit back into its original location, the forward pointer is removed, and the row is put back where it originated.

When a forward pointer is created, it remains unless the row moves back to its original location. The only other circumstance that results in forward pointers being deleted is when the entire database is shrunk. When a database file is shrunk and the data reorganized, all bookmarks are reassigned because the rows are moved to new pages.

To view the forward pointers for a table, you can enable trace flag 2509. When you run DBCC CHECKTABLE, it displays the number of forwarded records in the table.

Summary

In this chapter, you've been provided with an inside look at SQL Server's internal processes including how memory and I/O are managed. You also were provided with an in-depth look at the SQL Server storage structures. You've seen that databases are created on a set of database files, and those files can be configured to grow automatically, if desired. The smallest unit of I/O and the basic storage construct in SQL Server is a page, which is 8KB in size. These pages are allocated in blocks of 8 called extents. Extents can be shared among tables, resulting in less wasted storage for small tables. Using filegroups, you can more finely control your file placement (or set of files) and specify in which filegroup a table or index should be stored.

You should also now have a better understanding of the table, row, and clustered and nonclustered index structures and how they are maintained by SQL Server during data modifications. You also were introduced to some helpful tools (such as `DBCC PAGE`) to examine the internals of SQL Server to help you further understand its inner workings.

An understanding of SQL Server internals is not a requirement for administering or developing applications for SQL Server, but if you really want to understand why SQL Server performs the way it does, or if you need to really get in and troubleshoot performance problems, a solid understanding of the internals of SQL Server will prove invaluable. Much of this information will help you better understand the concepts presented in the remaining performance-related chapters of this book.

CHAPTER **34**

Indexes and Performance

by Ray Rankins

IN THIS CHAPTER

- Index Usage Criteria
- Index Selection
- Evaluating Index Usefulness
- Index Statistics
- Index Design Guidelines
- Indexed Views
- Indexes on Computed Columns
- The Index Tuning Wizard
- Choosing Indexes: Query Versus Update Performance

There can be a number of reasons why SQL Server performance might be less than optimal, but in many cases, it comes down to poor index design, or simply a lack of appropriate indexes. Often, substantial performance gains can be realized in your applications by creating the proper indexes to support the queries and operations being performed in SQL Server. The great benefit here is that your applications will immediately reap the benefits of the indexes without having to rewrite the code in any way.

You need to closely examine the indexes defined on your tables to ensure that the appropriate indexes exist that the optimizer can use to avoid table scans and reduce the I/O costs of resolving queries. You also need to have a good understanding of the criteria SQL Server uses to determine when to use an index.

It's also important to keep in mind that although many indexes on a table can help improve response time for queries and reports, too many indexes can hurt the performance of inserts, updates, and deletes. At other times, your other index design decisions, such as which column(s) to create your clustered index on, might be influenced as much by how the data is inserted and modified and what the possible locking implications might be, as it is by the query response time alone.

Clearly, proper index design is a key issue in achieving optimum SQL Server performance for your applications. In Chapter 33, "SQL Server Internals," you learned about the structure of an index and how indexes are maintained by SQL Server. In this chapter, the focus is on how indexes are evaluated and used by SQL Server to improve query response time.

Using this information, this chapter explores the issues and factors that influence index design.

> **NOTE**
>
> This chapter assumes that you already have an understanding of the different types of indexes, their structures, and how to define them. For more information on index types, how to create indexes, and the underlying structure of indexes, see Chapter 13, "Creating and Managing Indexes," and Chapter 33.

Index Usage Criteria

To effectively determine the appropriate indexes that should be created, you need to determine whether they'll actually be used by the SQL server. If an index isn't being used effectively, it's just wasting space and creating unnecessary overhead during updates.

The main criterion to remember is that SQL Server will not use an index for the more efficient bookmark lookup if at least the first column of the index is not included in a valid search argument (SARG) or join clause. Keep this in mind when choosing the column order for composite indexes. For example, consider the following index on the `stores` table:

```
create index nc1_stores on stores (city, state, zip)
```

Each of the following queries could use the index because they include the first column, `city`, of the index as part of the SARG:

```
select stor_name from stores
   where city = 'Frederick'
     and state = 'MD'
     and zip = '21702'

select stor_name from stores
   where city = 'Frederick'
     and state = 'MD'

select stor_name from stores
   where city = 'Frederick'
     and zip = '21702'
```

However, the following queries will not use the index for a bookmark lookup because they don't specify the `city` column as a SARG:

```
select stor_name from stores
   where state = 'MD'
     and zip = '21702'

select stor_name from stores
   where zip = '21702'
```

For the index nc1_stores to be used for a bookmark lookup in the last query, you'd have to reorder the columns so that zip was first—but then the index wouldn't be useful for any queries specifying only city and/or state. To satisfy all the preceding queries in this case would require additional indexes on the stores table.

NOTE

For the past two preceding queries, if you were to display the execution plan information (how to display execution plans is described in Chapter 36, "Query Analysis"), you might see that the queries actually use the nc1_stores index to retrieve the resultset. However, if you look closely, you'll see the queries are not using the index in the most efficient manner—it is being used to perform an index scan, rather than an index seek.

Not to get too much into query access methods, as this too is covered in more detail in Chapter 35, "Understanding Query Optimization," an index seek is what we are really after.

In an index *seek*, SQL Server searches for the specific SARG by walking the index tree from the root level down to the specific row(s) with matching index key values and then uses the bookmark value stored in the index key to directly retrieve the matching row(s) from the data page(s)(the bookmark is either a specific row identifier, or the clustered key value for the row).

For an index *scan*, SQL Server searches all the rows in the leaf level of the index looking for possible matches. If any are found, it then uses the bookmark to retrieve the data row.

Although both use the index, the index scan is still more expensive in terms of I/O than an index seek but slightly less expensive than a table scan, which is why it is used. However, the goal of this chapter is to learn to design indexes that result in index seeks, and when I talk about queries using an index, index seeks are what I am referring to (except for the section on index covering, but that's a horse of a slightly different color).

You might think that the easy solution to get bookmark lookups on all possible columns is to index all the columns on a table so that any type of search criteria specified for a query can be helped by an index. This strategy might be somewhat appropriate in a read-only DSS environment supporting ad hoc queries, but not likely because many of the indexes probably still wouldn't even be used. As you'll see in the "Index Selection" section in this chapter, just because an index is defined on a column, it doesn't mean that the optimizer is necessarily always going to use it if the search criteria are not selective enough. Also, creating that many indexes on a large table could take up a significant amount of space in the database, increasing the time required to back up and run dbcc checks on the database. As mentioned earlier as well, too many indexes on a table in an online transaction processing (OLTP) environment can generate a significant amount of overhead during inserts, updates, and deletes and have a detrimental impact on performance.

TIP

A common design mistake I come across in my travels is too many indexes defined on tables in OLTP environments. In many cases, some of the indexes are redundant or are never even considered by the SQL Server optimizer to process the queries used by the applications. These indexes end up simply wasting space and adding unnecessary overhead to data updates.

A case in point was one client that had eight indexes defined on a table, four of which had the same column, which was a unique key, as the first column in the index. That column was included in the `WHERE` clauses for all queries and updates performed on the table. Only one of those four indexes was ever used.

Hopefully, by the end of this chapter, you'll understand why all these indexes were unnecessary and be able to recognize and determine which columns will benefit from having indexes defined on them and which indexes to avoid.

Index Selection

Determining which indexes to define on a table involves performing a detailed query analysis. This involves examining the search clauses to see what columns are referenced, knowing the bias of the data to determine the usefulness of the index, and ranking the queries in order of importance and frequency of execution. You have to be careful not to examine individual queries and develop indexes to support one query, without considering the other queries that are executed on the table as well. You need to come up with a set of indexes that works for the best cross-section of your queries.

TIP

A useful tool to help you identify your frequently executed and critical queries is SQL Profiler. I've found SQL Profiler to be invaluable when going into a new client site and having to identify the problem queries that need tuning. SQL Profiler allows you to trace the procedures and queries being executed in SQL Server and capture the runtime, reads and writes, execution plans, and other processing information. This information can help you identify which queries are providing substandard performance, which ones are being executed most often, which indexes are being used by the queries, and so on.

You can analyze this information yourself manually or save a trace to analyze with the Index Tuning Wizard. The features of SQL Profiler are covered in more detail in Chapter 7, "Using the SQL Server Profiler." The Index Tuning Wizard is discussed later in this chapter.

Because it's usually not possible to index for everything, index first for the queries most critical to your applications or those run frequently by many users. If you have a query that's run only once a month, is it worth creating an index to support only that query and having to maintain it throughout the rest of the month? The sum of the additional processing time throughout the month could conceivably exceed the time required to perform a table scan to satisfy that one query.

If, due to processing requirements, you must have the index in place when the query is run, consider creating the index only when you run the query and then drop the index for the remainder of the month. This is a feasible approach as long as the time needed to create the index and run the query that uses the index doesn't exceed the time needed to run the query without the index in place.

Evaluating Index Usefulness

SQL Server provides indexes for two primary reasons: as a method to enforce the uniqueness of the data in the database tables and to provide faster access to data in the tables. Creating the appropriate indexes for a database is one of the most important aspects of your physical database design. Because you can't have an unlimited number of indexes on a table, and it wouldn't be feasible anyway, you'll want to create indexes on columns that have high selectivity so that the index will be used by your queries. The selectivity of an index can be defined as follows:

Selectivity ratio = (Number of unique index values)/ (Total number of rows in the table)

If the selectivity ratio is high—that is, a large number of rows can be uniquely identified by the key—then the index is highly selective and useful to the optimizer. The optimum selectivity would be 1, meaning that there is a unique value for each row. A low selectivity means that there are many duplicate values and the index would be less useful. The SQL Server optimizer decides whether to use any indexes for a query based on the selectivity of the index. The higher the selectivity, the faster and more efficiently SQL Server can retrieve the resultset.

For example, say that you are evaluating useful indexes on the `authors` table. Assume that most of the queries access the table either by the author's last name or by state. Because a large number of concurrent users modify data in this table, you are allowed to choose only one index—author's last name or state. Which one should you choose? Let's perform some analysis to see which one is a more useful, or selective, index. First, determine the selectivity based on the author's last name with a query on the `authors` table in the `pubs` database:

```
select count(distinct au_lname) as '# unique',
   count(*) as '# rows',
   str(count(distinct au_lname) / cast (count(*) as real),4,2) as 'selectivity'
from authors
go

# unique    # rows      selectivity
----------- ----------- -----------
         22          23 0.96
```

The selectivity ratio calculated for the au_lname column on the authors table, 0.96, indicates that an index on au_lname would be highly selective and a good candidate for an index. All rows but one in the table contain a unique value for last name.

Now, look at the selectivity of the state column:

```
select count(distinct state) as '# unique',
    count(*) '# rows',
    str(count(distinct state) / cast (count(*) as real),4,2) as 'selectivity'
from authors
go

# unique    # rows      selectivity
----------- ----------- -----------
          8          23 0.35
```

As you can see, an index on the state column would be much less selective (0.35) than an index on the au_lname column and possibly not as useful.

One of the questions to ask at this point is whether a few values in the state column that have a high number of duplicates are skewing the selectivity, or whether there are just a few unique values in the table. You can determine this with a query similar to the following:

```
select state, count(*)
from authors
group by state
order by 2 desc
go

state
----- -----------
CA             15
UT              2
TN              1
MI              1
OR              1
IN              1
KS              1
MD              1
```

As you can see, the state values are relatively unique, except for one. More than half the rows in the table have the same value of 'CA' for state. Therefore, state is probably not a good candidate for an indexed column, especially if most of the time you are searching for authors from the state of California. SQL Server would generally find it more efficient to scan the whole table rather than search via the index.

Generally, if the selectivity ratio for a key is less than .85 (in other words, the optimizer cannot discard at least 85 percent of the rows based on the key value), then the optimizer generally chooses a table scan to process the query. In such cases, performing a table scan to find all the qualifying rows is more efficient than seeking through the B-tree to locate a large number of data rows.

NOTE

You can relate the concept of selectivity to a somewhat real-world example. What if you had to find every instance of the words "SQL Server" in this book? Would it be easier to do it by using the index and going back and forth from the index to all the pages that contain the words, or would it be easier just to scan each page from beginning to end to locate them? What if you had to find all references to the word "Squonk," if any? Squonk would definitely be easier to find via the index (actually the index would help you determine that it doesn't even exist). Therefore, the selectivity for "Squonk" would be high, and the selectivity for "SQL Server" would be much lower.

How does SQL Server determine whether an index is selective and which index, if it has more than one to choose from, would be the most efficient to use? For example, how would SQL Server know how many rows might be returned by the following query?

```
select * from table
    where key between 1000000 and 2000000
```

If the table contains 10,000,000 rows with values ranging between 0 and 20,000,000, how does the optimizer know whether to use an index or table scan? There could be 10 rows in the range, or 900,000. How does SQL Server estimate how many rows are between 1,000,000 and 2,000,000? The optimizer gets this information from the index statistics, as described in the next section.

Index Statistics

As mentioned earlier, the selectivity of a key is an important factor that determines whether an index will be used for a query. SQL Server stores the selectivity and the histogram of sample values of the key in the `statblob` column on the `sysindexes` system table. Based on the values stored in this column for the index, and the SARGs specified for the query, the query optimizer decides which index to use.

The `statblob` column is an `image` column. To see the statistical information stored in the `statblob` column, use the `DBCC SHOW_STATISTICS` command, which returns the following pieces of information:

- A histogram containing an even sampling of the values for the first column in the index key. SQL Server stores up to 200 sample values in the histogram.
- Index densities for the combination of columns in the index. Index density indicates the uniqueness of the index key(s) and is discussed later in this section.

- The number of rows in the table at the time the statistics were computed.
- The number of rows sampled to generate the statistics.
- The number of sample values (steps) stored in the histogram.
- The average key length.
- The date and time the statistics were computed.

The syntax for DBCC SHOW_STATISTICS is as follows:

```
DBCC SHOW_STATISTICS (tablename, index)
```

Listing 34.1 displays the statistical information for the aunmind nonclustered index on the au_lname and au_fname columns of the authors table.

LISTING 34.1 DBCC SHOW_STATISTICS Output for the aunmind Index on the authors Table

```
dbcc show_statistics (authors, aunmind )
go

Statistics for INDEX 'aunmind'.
Updated              Rows   Rows Sampled Steps Density    Average key length
-------------------- ------ ------------ ----- ---------- ------------------
Aug  6 2001  1:34AM      23           23    22        0.0           24.52174

All density              Average Length           Columns
------------------------ ------------------------ ------------------------
           4.5454547E-2                7.3913045 au_lname
           4.3478262E-2                 13.52174 au_lname, au_fname
           4.3478262E-2                 24.52174 au_lname, au_fname, au_id

(3 row(s) affected)

RANGE_HI_KEY      RANGE_ROWS   EQ_ROWS      DISTINCT_RANGE_ROWS  AVG_RANGE_ROWS
----------------- ------------ ------------ -------------------- --------------
Bennet                     0.0          1.0                    0            0.0
Blotchet-Halls             0.0          1.0                    0            0.0
Carson                     0.0          1.0                    0            0.0
DeFrance                   0.0          1.0                    0            0.0
del Castillo               0.0          1.0                    0            0.0
Dull                       0.0          1.0                    0            0.0
Green                      0.0          1.0                    0            0.0
Greene                     0.0          1.0                    0            0.0
Gringlesby                 0.0          1.0                    0            0.0
```

LISTING 34.1 Continued

```
Hunter                    0.0        1.0              0           0.0
Karsen                    0.0        1.0              0           0.0
Locksley                  0.0        1.0              0           0.0
MacFeather                0.0        1.0              0           0.0
McBadden                  0.0        1.0              0           0.0
O'Leary                   0.0        1.0              0           0.0
Panteley                  0.0        1.0              0           0.0
Ringer                    0.0        2.0              0           0.0
Smith                     0.0        1.0              0           0.0
Straight                  0.0        1.0              0           0.0
Stringer                  0.0        1.0              0           0.0
White                     0.0        1.0              0           0.0
Yokomoto                  0.0        1.0              0           0.0
```


Looking at the output, you can determine that the statistics were last updated on Aug 6, 2001. The table at the time the statistics were generated had 23 rows, and all 23 rows were sampled to generate the statistics. The average key length is 24.52174 bytes. From the density information, you can see that this index is highly selective (a low density means high selectivity—index densitites will be covered shortly). Of the 23 rows in the table, 22 of them are unique values.

After the general information and the index densities, the index histogram is displayed.

The Statistics Histogram

Up to 200 sample values can be stored in the statistics histogram. Each sample value is called a *step*. The sample value stored in each step is the endpoint of a range of values. Three values are stored for each step, described as follows:

- `EQ_ROWS`—This is the number of rows that have the same value as the sample value. In other words, the number of duplicate values for the step.
- `RANGE_ROWS`—This indicates how many other rows are inside the range between the current step and the step prior, not including the step values themselves.
- Range density—This indicates the number of distinct values within the range. The range density information is actually displayed in two separate columns, `DISTINCT_RANGE_ROWS` and `AVG_RANGE_ROWS`.

  `DISTINCT_RANGE_ROWS` is the number of distinct values between the current step and the step prior, not including the step values itself.

  `AVG_RANGE_ROWS` is the average number of rows per distinct value within the range of the step.

In the output in Listing 34.1, all the distinct key values in the first column of the index are stored as the sample values stored in the histogram. Therefore, there are no data values between the sample values in the histogram, and subsequently all the range values are 0. You can see that there is a duplicate in the index key for the last name of `Ringer` (`EQ_ROWS` = 2). For comparison purposes, Listing 34.2 shows a snippet of the `DBCC SHOW_STATISTICS` output for the `sales` table in `bigpubs2000`.

LISTING 34.2 DBCC `SHOW_STATISTICS` Output for the `titleidind` Index on the `sales` Table in the `bigpubs2000` Database

```
Statistics for INDEX 'titleidind'.
Updated              Rows   Rows Sampled Steps Density      Average key length
-------------------- ------ ------------ ----- ------------ ------------------
Aug 21 2001 11:18PM  168725       168725   200 1.8955356E-3          26.405577

(1 row(s) affected)

All density              Average Length           Columns
------------------------ ------------------------ ----------------------------
            1.8621974E-3                      6.0 title_id
             5.997505E-6                     10.0 title_id, stor_id
            5.9268041E-6                26.405577 title_id, stor_id, ord_num

(3 row(s) affected)

RANGE_HI_KEY RANGE_ROWS EQ_ROWS DISTINCT_RANGE_ROWS AVG_RANGE_ROWS
------------ ---------- ------- ------------------- -------------------
BI0194              0.0   314.0                   0                 0.0
BI2184            613.0   343.0                   2               306.5
BI2574            270.0   277.0                   1               270.0
BI3224            618.0   286.0                   2               309.0
BI3976            311.0   293.0                   1               311.0
BI6450            673.0   300.0                   2               336.5
BI9506            947.0   292.0                   3           315.66666
BU1111            296.0   299.0                   1               296.0
BU7832            349.0   334.0                   1               349.0
CH0249           1011.0   311.0                   3               337.0
CH0639            984.0   307.0                   3               328.0

...

TC4203              0.0   321.0                   0                 0.0
TC7777              0.0   297.0                   0                 0.0
(200 row(s) affected)
```

As you can see in this example, there are a greater number of rows per range and a greater number of duplicates for each step value. Also, all 200 rows in the histogram are used, and the 168,725 rows in the table are distributed across those 200 rows. All 168,725 were sampled to generate the statistics.

The histogram steps can be used for SARGs only when a constant expression is compared against an indexed column and the value of the constant expression is known at query compile time. Examples of SARGs where histogram steps can be used include

- `where col_a = getdate()`
- `where cust_id = 12345`
- `where monthly_sales < 10000 / 12`
- `where l_name like "Smith" + "%"`

Some constant expressions cannot be evaluated until query runtime. These include search arguments containing local variables or subqueries and also join clauses such as

- `where price = @avg_price`
- `where total_sales > (select sum(qty) from sales)`
- `where titles.pub_id = publishers.pub_id`

For these types of statements, you need some other way of estimating the number of matching rows. Additionally, because histogram steps are kept only on the first column of the index, SQL Server must use a different method for determining the number of matching rows for SARGs that specify multiple column values for a composite index, such as the following:

```
select * from sales
   where title_id = 'BI3976'
     and stor_id = 'P648'
```

When the histogram is not used, or cannot be used, SQL Server uses the index density values to estimate the number of matching rows.

Index Densities

SQL Server stores the density values of each column in the index for use in queries where the SARG value is not known until runtime, or when the SARG is on multiple columns of the index. For composite keys, SQL Server stores the density for the first column of the composite key; for the first and second columns; for the first, second, and third columns; and so on. This information can be seen in the `All density` section of the `DBCC SHOW_STATISTICS` output in Listing 34.1.

Index density essentially represents the inverse of all unique key values of the key. The density of each key is calculated by the following formula:

Key density = 1.00 / (Count of distinct key values in the table)

Therefore, the density for the `state` column in the `authors` table in the `pubs` database is calculated as follows:

```
Select Density = 1.00/ (select count(distinct state) from authors)
Go
Density
----------------
.1250000000000
```

The density for the combination of the columns `state` and `zip` is as follows:

```
Select Density = 1.00/ (select count(distinct state+zip) from authors)
Go
Density
----------------
.0555555555555
```

Notice that, unlike the selectivity ratio, a *smaller* index density indicates a more selective index. As the density value approaches 1, the index becomes less selective and essentially useless. When the index selectivity is poor, the optimizer might choose to do a table scan, or a leaf level index scan, rather than perform an index seek, because it is more cost effective.

TIP

Watch out for indexes in your databases with poor selectivity. Such indexes are often more of a detriment to the performance of the system. Not only are they usually not used for data retrieval, but they also slow down your data modification statements because of the additional index overhead. Identify such indexes and consider dropping them.

Typically, the density value should become smaller (that is, more selective) as you add more columns to the key. For example, in Listing 34.2, the densities get progressively smaller (and thus, more selective) as additional columns are factored in, as shown in Table 34.1.

TABLE 34.1 Index Densities for `titleidind` Index on Sales Table

Key Column	Index Density
`title_id`	1.8621974E-3
`title_id, stor_id`	5.997505E-6
`title_id, stor_id, ord_num`	5.9268041E-6

Estimating Rows Using the Index Statistics

So how does the optimizer use the index statistics to determine the effectiveness of the index?

SQL Server uses the histogram information when searching for an index key value across a range or when there are duplicate values in the key. Consider a query on the `sales` table in the `bigpubs2000` database:

```
select * from sales
    where title_id = 'BI2184'
```

Because there are duplicates of `title_id` in the table, SQL Server uses the histogram on `title_id` (refer to Listing 34.2) to estimate the number of matching rows. For the value of `BI2184`, it would look at the `EQ_ROWS` value, which is 343.0. This indicates that there are 343 rows in the table with a `title_id` value of `BI2184`.

When an exact match for the search argument is not found as a step in the histogram, SQL Server uses the `AVG_RANGE_ROWS` value for the next step greater than the search value. For example, SQL Server would estimate that for a search value of `'BI2187'`, on average, it would match 270.0 rows.

For a range retrieval, SQL Server sums up the `RANGE_ROWS` and `EQ_ROWS` values between the endpoints of the range retrieval. For example, using the histogram in Listing 34.2, if the search argument was `where title_id <= 'BI2574'`, the row estimate would be 314 + 613 + 343 + 270 + 277, or 1,817.

When the histogram cannot be used, SQL Server uses just the index density to estimate the number of matching rows. The formula is straightforward for an equality search, such as

```
declare @tid varchar(6)
select @tid = 'BI2574'
select count(*) from sales where title_id = @tid
```

The row estimate is the index density (`1.8621974E-3`) for the specified key multiplied by the number of rows in the table:

```
select count(*) * 1.8621974E-3
from sales
go

-------------------
 314.19925631500001
```

34

If a query specifies both the title_id and stor_id as SARGs, and if the SARG for title_id is a constant expression that can be evaluated at optimization time, SQL Server uses both the index density on title_id and stor_id and the histogram on title_id to estimate the number of matching rows (for some data values, the estimated number of matching rows for title_id and stor_id calculated using the index density could be greater than the estimated number of rows that match the specific title_id as determined by the histogram). SQL Server uses whichever is the smaller of the two to calculate the row estimate.

Looking at the index density for title_id, stor_id, you can see that it is nearly unique:

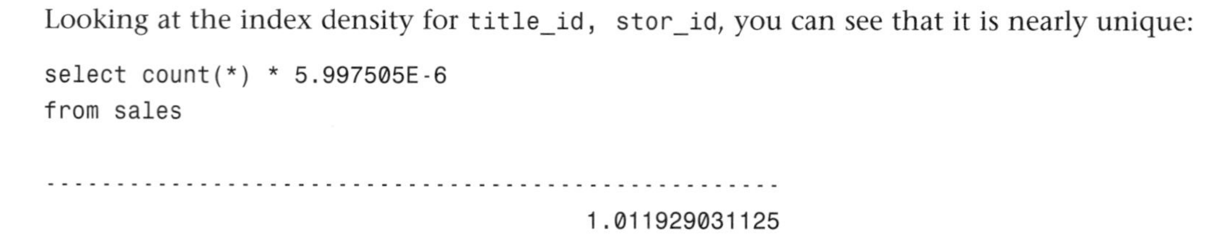

```
select count(*) * 5.997505E-6
from sales

-----------------------------------------------
                                 1.011929031125
```

In this example, SQL Server would use the index density on title_id and stor_id to estimate the number of matching rows. In this case, it is estimated that the query will return one matching row.

Generating and Maintaining Index Statistics

Now, the questions you might ask are "How do the index statistics get created, and how are they maintained?" The index statistics are first created when you create the index on a table or when you run the UPDATE STATISTICS command. In versions of SQL Server prior to version 7.0, index statistics information did not get updated automatically. If you inserted many rows after the index had already been created, the histogram information reflected by the index statistics did not reflect the actual key distribution. As a result, the optimizer sometimes chose an access plan that was inefficient. As part of regular maintenance, DBAs had to create a schedule for running the UPDATE STATISTICS command to keep the index statistics up-to-date with the table data. As of SQL Server 7.0, index statistics are automatically updated by SQL Server. SQL Server constantly monitors the update activity on the indexed key values and updates the statistics through an internal process when appropriate.

Auto-Update Statistics

The AutoStat process monitors the updates to a table to determine when it should run. A column in the sysindexes table called rowmodctr maintains a running total of the number of modifications made to a table that affect the index statistics. The value in this column is incremented under the following circumstances:

- A row is inserted into the table.
- A row is deleted from the table.
- An indexed column is updated.

Whenever the index statistics have been updated for the table, `rowmodctr` is reset to 0. The threshold value for `rowmodctr` that triggers an AutoStat update is governed by the size and the nature of the table. The simple algorithm is as follows:

- If the table contains fewer than six rows and the table is in `tempdb`, statistics are updated for every six modifications to the table.
- If the table has more than six rows, but less than or equal to 500, statistics are updated whenever `rowmodctr` reaches 500.
- If the table has more than 500 rows, update statistics is run whenever `rowmodctr` is equal to 500 plus 20 percent of the number of rows in the table. For example, if a table has 2000 rows, update statistics will run when 500 + (2000 * .20), or 900, modifications have been made to the table.

NOTE

Running `TRUNCATE TABLE` on a table does not cause the `rowmodctr` to be reset. As the table is repopulated, the statistics will be out of sync with the data, and AutoStats might not run right away. You should manually update the statistics after running `TRUNCATE TABLE`.

When AutoStats generates an update of the index statistics, it generates the new statistics based on a sampling of the data values in the table. Sampling helps to minimize the overhead of the AutoStats process. The sampling is random across the data pages, and the values are taken from the table or the smallest nonclustered index on the columns needed to generate the statistics. After a data page containing a sampled row has been read from disk, all the rows on the data page are used to update the statistical information.

CAUTION

Having up-to-date statistics on your tables helps ensure that optimum execution plans are being generated for your queries at all times. In most cases, you would want SQL Server to automatically keep the statistics updated. However, it is possible that Auto-Update Statistics can cause an `update of the index statistics` to run at inappropriate times in a production environment, or in a high-volume environment, to run too often. If this problem is occurring, you might want to turn off the AuotStats feature and set up a scheduled job to update statistics during off-peak periods. Do not forget to update statistics periodically, or the resulting performance problems might end up being much worse than the momentary ones caused by the AutoStats process.

To determine how often the AutoStats process is being run, you can turn on trace flag 8721, which generates output in the errorlog, similar to the following, when an update of the index statistics occurs as a result of `rowmodctr` reaching the threshold for the table:

```
2001-09-04 23:24:31.48 spid53    AUTOSTATS: UPDATED Stats: authors..
➥UPKCL_auidind Dbid = 5 Indid = 1 Rows: 23 Duration: 0ms
2001-09-04 23:24:31.49 spid53    AUTOSTATS: UPDATED Stats: authors..aunmind
➥Dbid = 5 Indid = 2 Rows: 23 Duration: 0ms
2001-09-04 23:24:31.49 spid53    AUTOSTATS: UPDATED Stats: authors.._
➥WA_Sys_state_75D7831F Dbid = 5 Indid = 3 Rows: 23 Duration: 0ms
2001-09-04 23:24:31.49 spid53    AUTOSTATS: UPDATED Stats: authors..st_ind
➥Dbid = 5 Indid = 4 Rows: 23 Duration: 0ms
2001-09-04 23:25:24.21 spid53    AUTOSTATS: UPDATED Stats: authors..
➥UPKCL_auidind Dbid = 5 Indid = 1 Rows: 23 Duration: 16ms
2001-09-04 23:25:24.21 spid53    AUTOSTATS: SUMMARY Tbl: [authors]
➥Objid:1977058079 UpdCount: 1 Rows: 23 Mods: 0 Bound: 500 Duration:
➥ 16ms LStatsSchema: 6
```

You can also use the SQL Profiler to determine when an automatic update of index statistics is occurring by monitoring the `Auto Stats` event in the `Objects` event class (for more information on using SQL Profiler, see Chapter 7).

If necessary, it is possible to turn off the AutoStats behavior by using the `sp_autostats` system stored procedure. This stored procedure allows you to turn the automatic updating of statistics on or off for a specific index or all the indexes of a table. The following command turns off the automatic update of statistics for an index named `aunmind` on the `authors` table:

```
Exec sp_autostats 'authors', 'OFF', 'aunmind'
go

Automatic statistics maintenance turned OFF for 1 indices.
```

When you run `sp_autostats` and simply supply the table name, it displays the current setting for the table, as well as the database. Following are the settings for the `authors` table:

```
Exec sp_autostats 'authors'
Go

Global statistics settings for [pubs]:
  Automatic update statistics: ON
  Automatic create statistics: ON

Settings for table [authors]
```

```
Index Name                AUTOSTATS Last Updated
------------------------- --------- ------------------------
[UPKCL_auidind]           ON        2001-09-04 23:25:24.217
[aunmind]                 OFF       2001-09-04 23:24:31.497
[_WA_Sys_state_75D7831F]  ON        2001-09-04 23:24:31.497
[st_ind]                  ON        2001-09-04 23:24:31.497
```

There are three other ways to disable auto-updating of statistics for an index:

- Specify the `STATISTICS_NORECOMPUTE` clause when creating the index
- Specify the `NORECOMPUTE` option when running the `UPDATE STATISTICS` command
- Specify the `NORECOMPUTE` option when creating statistics with the `CREATE STATISTICS` command (more on this command a bit later in the "Creating Statistics" section)

You can also turn AutoStats on or off for the entire database by setting the database option in Enterprise Manager (bring up the Properties dialog box and click on the Options tab and check or uncheck the Auto Update Statistics option). You can also disable or enable the AutoStats option for a database using the `sp_dboption` procedure:

```
sp_dboption dbname, 'auto update statistics' [, { 'ON' | 'OFF' } ]
```

NOTE

What actually happens when you execute `sp_autostats` or use the `NORECOMPUTE` option in the `UPDATE STATISTICS` command to turn off auto-update statistics for a specific index or a table? SQL Server internally sets a bit in the `status` column of the `sysindexes` table to inform the internal SQL Server process not to update the index statistics for the table or index which has had the option turned off using any of these commands. To turn on auto-update, either run `UPDATE STATISTICS` without the `NORECOMPUTE` option or execute the `sp_autostats` system stored procedure and specify the value of `'ON'` for the second parameter.

Manually Updating Statistics

Whether you've disabled AutoStats or not, you can still manually update index statistics by using the `UPDATE STATISTICS` T-SQL command. In SQL Server 2000, this command was enhanced to support more features. The new syntax of this command is

```
UPDATE STATISTICS {table} [index | (statistics_name [, ...n])
 [WITH [FULLSCAN] | SAMPLE number {PERCENT | ROWS}] | RESAMPLE ]
   ][[,] NORECOMPUTE][[,] [INDEX | COLUMNS | ALL]
```

If neither the `FULLSCAN` nor `SAMPLE` options are specified, the default behavior is to perform a sample scan to calculate the statistics. SQL Server automatically computes the appropriate sample size. For tables less than 8MB in size, the sample will always be the entire table.

The FULLSCAN option forces SQL Server to perform a full scan of the data in the table or index to calculate the statistics. This generates more accurate statistics than using sampling but is also the most time consuming and I/O intensive. When you use the SAMPLE option, you can specify a fixed number of rows or percentage of rows to sample to build or update the index statistics. If the sampling ratio specified ever results in too few rows being sampled, SQL Server automatically corrects the sampling based on the number of existing rows in the table. The RESAMPLE option specifies that the statistics be generated using the previously defined sampling ratio. This RESAMPLE option is useful when you have indexes or column statistics that were created with different sampling values. For example, if the index statistics were created using FULLSCAN, and the column statistics were created using a 50 percent sample, specifying the RESAMPLE option would update the statistics on the indexes using FULLSCAN and using a 50 percent sample for the others.

As previously discussed, SQL Server 2000 automatically updates the index statistics by default. If you specify the NORECOMPUTE option with UPDATE STATISTICS, it disables AutoStats for the table or index.

When the automatic update statistics option is turned off, you should run the UPDATE STATISTICS command periodically when appropriate. To determine the last time statistics were updated, run the following command:

```
select STATS_DATE(tableid, indexid)
```

The following is an example:

```
select STATS_DATE(object_id('authors'), 1)
go

------------------------------------------------------
2001-08-21 23:17:50.510
```

TIP

You can get the *indexid* from sysindexes for each index on a table using the following query:

```
Select indid, name from sysindexes
   Where id = object_id('tablename') and indid > 0
```

Creating Statistics

In addition to statistics on indexes, SQL Server can also store statistics on individual columns that are not part of any indexes. Knowing the likelihood of a particular value being found in a nonindexed column can help the optimizer determine the optimal execution plan, whether or not SQL Server is using an index to actually locate the rows.

For example, consider the following query:

```
select stor_name
   from stores st
   join sales s on (st.stor_id = s.stor_id)
   where s.qty <= 100
```

SQL Server knows the density of the stor_id column in both the sales and stores tables because of indexes on the column in those tables. There is no index on qty. However, if the optimizer were to know how many rows in the sales table had qty less than 100, it would be better able to choose the most efficient query plan for joining between sales and stores. For example, assume that on average, there are approximately 500 sales per store. However, there are only approximately 5 sales per store where the qty is less than 100. With the statistics on qty, SQL Server has the opportunity to determine this and knowing there might be only 5 matching rows in sales versus 500, it might choose a different, more efficient, join strategy between the two tables.

Being able to keep statistics on the qty column without having to add it to an existing index with stor_id, or create a separate index on qty, provides SQL Server with the selectivity information it needs for optimization. By not having to create an index on qty, you avoid incurring the overhead of having to maintain the index key rows for each insert, update, and delete that occurs on the table. Only the index statistics on qty need to be maintained, which is required only after many modifications to the data have occurred.

By default, column statistics are generated automatically in SQL Server when queries are optimized. These statistics are created whenever no column statistics exist and the column is specified in a SARGs or join clause and the optimizer needs to estimate the approximate density or distribution of column values. This rule has two exceptions:

- Statistics will not be created for columns when the cost of creating the statistics exceeds the cost of the query plan itself.
- Statistics will not be created when the SQL Server is too busy (that is, there are currently too many outstanding compilations in progress).

If you want to disable or re-enable the database option to auto-create statistics in the database, use the sp_dboption procedure:

```
sp_dboption dbname, 'auto create statistics' [, { 'ON' | 'OFF' } ]
```

You can also turn the auto-create statistics option on or off for the entire database by setting the database option in Enterprise Manager. Bring up the Properties dialog box for the database. Click on the Options tab and check or uncheck the Auto create statistics option.

Column statistics are stored in the sysindexes table with an ID between 2 and 254. Auto-generated statistics will have a name in the format "_WA_Sys_*colname_systemgeneratednumber*". You can retrieve a list of auto-generated column statistics with a query similar to the following:

```
select cast(object_name(id) as varchar(30)) as 'table',
       name,
       indid
   from sysindexes
   where indexproperty(id, name, 'IsAutoStatistics') = 1
go

table                          name                        indid
------------------------------ --------------------------- ------
authors                        _WA_Sys_state_4AB81AF0      3
sales                          _WA_Sys_ord_num_628FA481    3
stores                         _WA_Sys_state_6477ECF3      3
stores                         _WA_Sys_zip_6477ECF3        4
titles                         _WA_Sys_type_6A30C649       3
```

If you want finer control over how the column statistics are generated, you can use the CREATE STATISTICS command. The syntax is similar to UPDATE STATISTICS with the exception that you specify a column or list of columns instead of an index to create statistics on:

```
CREATE STATISTICS statistics_name ON table (column [,...n])
    [    WITH  [ [ FULLSCAN | SAMPLE number PERCENT ] [,] ]
        [ NORECOMPUTE]     ]
```

You cannot create statistics on computed columns or columns of the ntext, text, or image datatypes.

If you want to create single-column statistics on all eligible columns in a database, you can use the sp_createstats system procedure:

```
sp_createstats [[@indexonly =] 'indexonly']
        [,[@fullscan =] 'fullscan']
        [,[@norecompute =] 'norecompute']
```

The created statistics will have the same name as the column on which they are created. Statistics are not created on columns that already have statistics on them (for example, the first column of an index or a column that already has explicitly created statistics).

To display a list of all column statistics, whether auto-generated or manually created, use a query similar to the previous one, but specify the 'IsStatistics' index option instead of 'IsAutoStatistics':

```
select cast(object_name(id) as varchar(30)) as 'table',
       name,
       indid
from sysindexes
where indexproperty(id, name, 'IsStatistics') = 1
go

table                          name                           indid
------------------------------ ------------------------------ ------
authors                        _WA_Sys_state_4AB81AF0              3
sales                          _WA_Sys_ord_num_628FA481            3
sales                          ord_date                            4
sales                          qty                                 5
sales                          payterms                            6
stores                         _WA_Sys_state_6477ECF3              3
stores                         _WA_Sys_zip_6477ECF3                4
stores                         stor_name                           5
stores                         stor_address                        6
titles                         _WA_Sys_type_6A30C649               3
```


CAUTION

Auto-created statistics again can be useful and help improve performance for your applications by ensuring that the optimizer has the best possible estimates of the selectivity of your SARGs so that it can choose the optimal plan. However, just like auto-update statistics, auto-create statistics can add overhead in a production environment if running frequently or at inappropriate times.

For example, one of my client sites was having a problem every morning with the application generating a query timeout when the users started it up. If one of the users ran the same query from Query Analyzer with query timeout disabled, it eventually finished in about a minute and a half. From that point forward, the user apps worked fine. It turned out that every night, my client dropped and reloaded a very large table. After some sleuthing, it was discovered the first person to run the query in the morning was causing statistics to be created automatically on this table, which took more than a minute to complete. Unfortunately, the application's query timeout was 30 seconds. The problem was solved by disabling auto-update statistics on the database and adding a step to the nightly reload process to create the statistics during the off-peak period.

To remove a collection of statistics on one or more columns for a table in the current database, use the `DROP STATISTICS` command:

```
DROP STATISTICS table.statistics_name
```

Be aware that dropping the column statistics could affect how your queries will be optimized, and less efficient query plans might be chosen. Also, if the auto-create statistics option is enabled for the database, SQL Server will likely automatically create statistics on the columns the next time they are referenced in a SARG or join clause for a query.

Index Design Guidelines

SQL Server indexes are mostly transparent to end users and T-SQL developers. Indexes are typically not specified in queries unless the user uses table hints to force the optimizer to use a particular index (although this is not advised—optimizer table hints will be covered in more detail in Chapter 35). Normally, based on the index key histogram values, the SQL Server cost-based optimizer chooses the index that is least expensive from an I/O standpoint.

Chapter 35 goes into greater detail on how the optimizer estimates I/O and determines the most efficient query plan. In the meantime, this section presents some of the main guidelines to follow to create useful indexes within your environment that the optimizer can use effectively.

Some general guidelines to follow when designing your indexes are as follows:

- For composite indexes, try to keep the more selective columns leftmost in the index. The first element in the index should be the most unique (if possible), and index column order in general should be from most to least unique. However, remember that selectivity doesn't help if the first ordered index column is not specified in your SARGs or join clauses. To ensure that the index is used for the largest number of queries, the first ordered column should be the column used most often in your queries.
- Be sure to index columns used in joins. Joins are processed inefficiently if no index on the column(s) is specified in a join. Remember: A PRIMARY KEY constraint will automatically create an index on a column, but a FOREIGN KEY constraint will not. You will want to create indexes on your foreign key columns if your queries commonly join between the primary key and foreign key tables.
- Tailor your indexes for your most critical queries and transactions. You cannot index for every possible query that might be run against your tables. However, your applications will perform better if you can identify your critical and most frequently executed queries and design indexes to support them. SQL Profiler, which is covered in Chapter 7, is a useful tool for identifying your most frequently executed queries. SQL Profiler can also help identify slow-running queries that might benefit from a better index design.
- Avoid indexes on columns that have poor selectivity. The optimizer will likely not use the indexes and simply take up space and add unnecessary overhead during inserts, updates, and deletes. One possible exception is when the index can be used to cover a query. Index covering is discussed in more detail in the "Index Covering" section later in this chapter.
- Choose your clustered and nonclustered indexes carefully. The next two sections discuss tips and guidelines for choosing between clustered or nonclustered indexes based on the data contained in the columns and the types of queries executed against the columns.

Clustered Index Indications

Searching for rows via a clustered index is almost always faster than searching for rows via a nonclustered index for two reasons. One reason is that a clustered index contains only pointers to pages rather than pointers to individual data rows; therefore, a clustered index is more compact than a nonclustered index. Because a clustered index is smaller and doesn't require an additional bookmark lookup to find the matching rows, the rows can be found with fewer page reads than with a similarly defined nonclustered index. The second reason is that because the data in a table with a clustered index is physically sorted on the clustered key, searching for duplicate values or for a range of clustered key values is faster; the rows are adjacent to each other and SQL Server can simply locate the first qualifying row and then search the rows in sequence until the last qualifying row is found. However, because you are only allowed to create one clustered index per table, you must judiciously choose which column or columns on which to define the clustered index.

If you require only a single index on a table, it's typically advantageous to make it a clustered index; the resulting overhead of maintaining clustered indexes during updates, inserts, and deletes can be considerably less than the overhead incurred by nonclustered indexes.

By default, the primary key on a table is defined as a clustered unique index. In most applications, the primary-key column on a table is almost always retrieved in single-row lookups. For single-row lookups, a nonclustered index usually costs you only a few I/Os more than a similar clustered index. Are you or the users really going to notice a difference between three page reads to retrieve a single data row versus four to six page reads to retrieve a single data row? Not at all. However, if you have to perform a range retrieval, such as a lookup on last name, will you notice a difference between scanning 10 percent of the table versus having to find the rows using a full table scan? Most definitely.

With this in mind, you might want to consider creating your primary key as a unique nonclustered index and choosing another candidate for your clustered index. The following are guidelines to consider for other potential candidates for the clustered index:

- Columns with a number of duplicate values that are searched frequently, for example, `WHERE last_name = 'Smith'`.

  Because the data is physically sorted, all the duplicate values are kept together. Any query that tries to fetch records against such keys will find all the values using a minimum number of I/Os. SQL Server locates the first row that matches the SARG and then scans the data rows in order until it finds the last row matching the SARG.

- Columns that are often specified in the `ORDER BY` clause.

  Because the data is already sorted, SQL Server can avoid having to re-sort the data if the `ORDER BY` is on the clustered index key and the data is retrieved in clustered key order. Remember: Even for a table scan, the data will be retrieved in clustered key order because the data in the table is in clustered key order. The only exception is if a parallel query operation is used to retrieve the data rows—the results will need to be re-sorted when the resultsets from each parallel thread are merged. (For more information on parallel query strategies, see Chapter 35.)

- Columns that are often searched for within a range of values, for example, `WHERE price between $10 and $20`.

  The clustered index can be used to locate the first qualifying row in the range of values. Because the rows in the table are in sorted order, SQL Server can simply scan the data pages in order until it finds the last qualifying row within the range. When the resultset within the range of values is large, a clustered index scan is significantly more efficient in terms of total logical I/Os performed than repeated bookmark lookups via a nonclustered index.

- Columns, other than the primary key, that are frequently used in join clauses.

  Clustered indexes tend to be smaller than nonclustered indexes; the number of page I/Os required per lookup will generally be less than for a nonclustered index (see Chapter 33 for a detailed discussion of index structures and sizes). This can be a significant difference when joining many records. An extra page read or two might not seem like much for a single-row retrieval, but add those additional page reads to 100,000 join iterations, and you're looking at a total of 100,000 to 200,000 additional page reads.

When you consider columns for a clustered index, you might want to try to keep your clustered indexes on relatively static columns to minimize the re-sorting of data rows when an indexed column is updated. Any time a clustered index key value changes, all nonclustered indexes using the clustered key as the bookmark to that row also need to be updated.

Try to avoid creating clustered indexes on sequential key fields that are inserted monotonically, such as on an identity column. This can create a "hot spot" at the end of the table that results in possible locking contention and deadlocks at the end of the table and the index. Additionally, the clustered index will not be reusing available space on preceding data pages because all new rows sort to the end of the table. This situation results in wasted space and your table growing larger than anticipated. The general recommendation is that you try to cluster on a data value that's somewhat randomly distributed throughout your table. Try to choose a clustered key that spreads the insert and update activity across the table but also benefits your other queries as well. Some candidates for clustered index keys to randomize your data include the following:

- Date of birth
- Last name, first name
- ZIP Code
- A random hash key (usually used only when no other actual data columns are good clustered index candidates)

Spreading your data throughout the table helps to minimize page contention, as well as provide more efficient space utilization. If the sequential key is your primary key, you can still use a unique, nonclustered index to provide an access path via the index and maintain the uniqueness of the primary key.

Because you can physically sort the data in a table in only one way, you can have only one clustered index. Any other columns you want to index have to be defined with nonclustered indexes.

Nonclustered Index Indications

SQL Server 2000 allows you to create a maximum of 249 nonclustered indexes on a table. Until tables become extremely large, the actual space taken by a nonclustered index is a minor expense compared to the increased access performance. Always keep in mind, however, that as you add more indexes to the system, database modification statements get slower due to the index maintenance overhead.

Also, when defining nonclustered indexes, you typically want to define indexes on columns that are more selective (that is, columns with low density values) so that they can be used effectively by the optimizer. A high number of duplicate values in a nonclustered index can often make it more expensive (in terms of I/O) to process the query using the nonclustered index than a table scan. Let's look at a hypothetical example:

```
select title from titles
  where price between $5. and $10.
```

Assume that you have 1,000,000 rows within the range; those 1,000,000 rows could be randomly scattered throughout the table. Although the index leaf level has all the index rows in sorted order, reading all data rows one at a time would require a separate bookmark lookup for each row in the worst-case scenario.

Thus, the worst-case I/O estimate for range retrievals using a nonclustered index is as follows:

number of levels in the nonclustered index

+ number of index pages scanned to find all matching rows

+ number of matching rows × the number of pages per bookmark lookup

If you have no clustered index on the table, the bookmark is simply a page and row pointer and requires one data page read to find the matching data row. If 1,000,000 rows are in the range, the worst-case cost estimate to search via the nonclustered index with no clustered index on the table would be as follows:

The number of index page reads to find all the bookmarks

+ 1,000,000 matching rows × 1 data page read

= 1,000,000+ I/Os

If you have a clustered index on the table, the bookmark is a clustered index key for the data row. Using the bookmark to find the matching row requires searching the clustered index tree to locate the data row. Assuming that the clustered index has two non-leaf levels, it would cost three pages to find each qualifying row on a data page. If the range has 1,000,000 rows, the worst-case cost estimate to search via the nonclustered index with a clustered index on the table would be as follows:

The number of index page reads to find all the bookmarks

+ 1,000,000 matching rows × 3 pages per bookmark lookup

= 3,000,000+ I/Os

Contrast each of these scenarios with the cost of a table scan. If the entire table takes up 50,000 pages, a full table scan would cost only 50,000 I/Os. Therefore, in this example, a table scan would actually be more efficient than using the nonclustered index.

The following guidelines help you identify potential candidates for nonclustered indexes for your environment:

- Columns referenced in SARGs or join clauses that have a relatively high selectivity (the density value is low).
- Columns referenced in both the `WHERE` clause and the `ORDER BY` clause.

  When the data rows are retrieved using a nonclustered index, they are retrieved in nonclustered index key order. If the resultset is to be ordered by the nonclustered index key(s) as well, SQL Server can avoid having to re-sort the resultset, resulting in a more efficient query. The following query is an example where SQL Server can avoid the extra step of sorting the resultset if a nonclustered index is on `state` and the index is used to retrieve the matching rows:

```
select * from authors
   where state like "c%"
   order by state
```

In general, nonclustered indexes are useful for single-row lookups, joins, queries on columns that are highly selective, or queries with small range retrievals. Also, when considering your nonclustered index design, don't overlook the benefits of index covering, as described in the following section.

Index Covering

Index covering is a situation where all the information required by the query in the `SELECT` and `WHERE` clauses can be found entirely within the nonclustered index itself. Because the nonclustered index contains a leaf row corresponding to every data row in the table, SQL Server can satisfy the query from the leaf rows of the nonclustered index.

This results in faster retrieval of data because all the information can come directly from the index page, and SQL Server avoids lookups of the data pages.

Because the leaf pages in a nonclustered index are linked together, the leaf level of the index can be scanned just like the data pages in a table. Because the leaf index rows are typically much smaller than the data rows, a nonclustered index that covers a query will be faster than a clustered index on the same columns, due to the fewer number of pages that would need to be read.

In the following example, a nonclustered index on the `au_lname` and `au_fname` columns of the `authors` table would cover the query because the result columns, as well as the SARGs, can all be derived from the index itself:

```
Select au_lname, au_fname
   From authors
   Where au_lname like "M%"
Go
```


Many other queries that use an aggregate function (such as `MIN`, `MAX`, `AVG`, `SUM`, and `COUNT`) or simply check for existence of a criteria also benefit from index covering. The following queries are examples of aggregate queries that can take advantage of index covering:

```
select count(au_lname) from authors where au_lname like 'm%'

select count(*) from authors where au_lname like 'm%'

select count(*) from authors
```

You might be wondering how the last query, which doesn't even specify a SARG, can still use an index. SQL Server knows that by its nature, a nonclustered index contains a row for every data row in the table; it can simply count all the rows in any of the nonclustered indexes instead of scanning the whole table. For the last query, SQL Server chooses the smallest nonclustered index—that is, the one with the fewest number of leaf pages.

Adding columns to nonclustered indexes to get index covering to occur is a common method of improving query response time. Consider the following query:

```
select royalty from titles
   where price between $10 and $20
```

If you create an index on only the `price` column, SQL Server could find the rows in the index where `price` is between \$10 and \$20, but it would have to access the data rows to retrieve `royalty`. With 100 rows in the range, the worst-case I/O cost to retrieve the data rows would be as follows:

The number of index levels

\+ The number of index pages to find the matching rows

\+ 100 × the number of pages per bookmark lookup

If the royalty column were added to the index on the price column, the index could be scanned to retrieve the results instead of having to perform the bookmark lookups against the table, resulting in faster query response. The I/O cost using index covering would be only

The number of index levels

+ The number of index pages to find the matching rows

CAUTION

When considering padding your indexes to take advantage of index covering, beware of making the index too wide. As index row width approaches data row width, the benefits of covering are lost as the number of pages in the leaf level increases. As the number of leaf level index pages approaches the number of pages in the table, the number of index levels also increases, and index scan time begins to approach table scan time.

Also, if you add columns that are updated frequently to an index, any changes to the columns in the data rows cascade into the indexes as well. This increases the index maintenance overhead, which can adversely impact update performance.

As discussed in Chapter 33, when you have a clustered index defined on a table, the clustered key is carried into all the nonclustered indexes to be used as the bookmark to locate the actual data row. The clustered key is the actual columns that make up the clustered index and their data values. This "feature" can sometimes result in index covering when it is not expected.

For example, assume that the authors table has a clustered index on au_lname and au_fname, and a nonclustered primary key defined on au_id. Each row in the nonclustered index on au_id would contain the clustered key values for au_lname and au_fname for its corresponding data row. Because of this, the following query would actually be covered by the nonclustered index on au_id:

```
select au_lname, au_fname
   from authors
   where au_id like '123%'
```

Composite Indexes Versus Multiple Indexes

As your index key gets wider, the selectivity of the key generally becomes higher as well. It might appear as if creating wide indexes should result in better performance. This is not necessarily true. The reason is that the wider the key, the fewer rows SQL Server stores on the index pages, requiring more pages at each level, resulting in a higher number of levels in the index B-tree. To get to specific rows, SQL Server must perform more I/Os.

To get better performance from queries, instead of creating a few wide indexes, consider creating multiple narrower indexes. The advantage here is that with smaller keys, the query optimizer can quickly scan through multiple indexes to create the most efficient access plan. Unlike versions of SQL Server prior to 7.0, SQL Server now has the option of performing multiple index lookups within a single query and merging the resultsets together to generate an intersection of the indexes. Also, with more indexes, the optimizer can choose from a wider variety of query plan alternatives.

If you are considering creating a wide key, check the distribution of values for each member of the composite key individually. If the selectivity on the individual columns is high, you might want to break up the index into multiple indexes. If the selectivity of individual columns is low but is high for combined columns, it makes sense to have wider keys on the table. To get to the right combination, populate your table with real-world data, experiment with creating multiple indexes, and check the distribution of values for each column. Based on the histogram steps and index density, you can make the decisions for an index design that works best for your environment.

Indexed Views

As discussed in Chapter 27, "Creating and Managing Views in SQL Server," SQL Server 2000 allows you to create indexed views. An indexed view is any view that has a clustered index defined on it. When a `CREATE INDEX` statement is executed on a view, the resultset for the view is materialized and stored in the database with the same structure as a table with a clustered index. Changes made to the data in the underlying tables of the view will be automatically reflected in the view the same way any changes to a table are reflected in its indexes. In addition to a clustered index, you can create additional nonclustered indexes on indexed views to provide additional query performance. Additional indexes on views might provide more options for the query optimizer to choose from during the optimization process.

In the Developer and Enterprise Editions of SQL Server 2000, when an indexed view exists on a table and you access the view directly within your query, the optimizer will automatically consider using the index on the view to improve query performance, just as an index on a table is used to improve performance. The query optimizer will also consider using the indexed view even for queries that do not directly name the view in the `FROM` clause. In other words, when a query might benefit from using the indexed view, the query optimizer can use the indexed view to satisfy the query in place of an existing index on the table itself. (For more information on how indexed views are used in query plans, see Chapter 35).

It is important to note that while indexed views can be created in all editions of SQL Server 2000, only the Developer and Enteprise editions will use indexed views automatically to optimize queries. In the other editions, indexed views will not be used to improve query performance unless the view is explicitly specified in the query and the `NOEXPAND` optimizer hint is specified as well. Without the `NOEXPAND` hint, SQL Server will expand the view to its underlying base tables and optimize based upon the table indexes. The following example shows the use of the NOEXPAND option to force SQL Server to use the indexed view specified in the query:

```
select * from sales_Qty_Rollup WITH (NOEXPAND)
   where stor_id between 'B914' and 'B999'SET ARITHABORT ON
```

Indexed views do add overhead and can be more complex for SQL Server to maintain over time than normal indexes. Each time an underlying table of a view is modified, SQL Server has to update the view resultset and potentially the index on that view. The scope of a view's index can be larger than that of any single table's index, especially if the view is defined on several large tables. The overhead associated with maintaining a view and its index during updates can negate any benefit that queries gain from the indexed view. Because of this additional maintenance overhead, create indexes only on those views where the advantage provided by the improved speed in retrieving the results outweighs the increased maintenance overhead.

Guidelines for Indexed Views

Consider these guidelines when you design indexed views:

- Create indexes on views where the underlying table data is relatively static.
- Create indexed views that will be used by several queries.
- Keep the indexes small. Just like with table indexes, a smaller index allows SQL Server to access the data more efficiently.
- Create indexed views that will be significantly smaller than the underlying table(s). An indexed view might not provide significant performance gains if its size is similar to the size of the original table.
- You will need to specify the NOEXPAND hint in editions of SQL Server other than the Developer or Enterprise Editions of SQL Server, or the indexed view will not be used to optimize the query.

Indexes on Computed Columns

SQL Server 2000 allows you to build indexes on computed columns in your tables. Computed columns can participate at any position of an index along with your other table columns, including in a PRIMARY KEY or UNIQUE constraint. To create an index on computed columns, the following SET statements must be set as shown:

```
SET ARITHABORT ON
SET CONCAT_NULL_YIELDS_NULL ON
SET QUOTED_IDENTIFIER ON
SET ANSI_NULLS ON
```

```
SET ANSI_PADDING ON
SET ANSI_WARNINGS ON
SET NUMERIC_ROUNDABORT OFF
```

If any of these seven SET options were not in effect when you created the table, you get the following message when you try to create an index on the computed column:

```
Server: Msg 1934, Level 16, State 1, Line 2
CREATE INDEX failed because the following SET options
 have incorrect settings: '<OPTION NAME>'.
```

Additionally, the functions in the computed column must be deterministic. A **deterministic function** is one that returns the same result every time it is called with the same set of input parameters (for information on which functions in SQL Server are deterministic, see Chapter 26, "Using Transact-SQL in SQL Server 2000").

When you create a clustered index on a computed column, it is no longer a virtual column in the table. The computed value for the column is stored in the data rows of the table. If you create a nonclustered index on a computed column, the computed value is stored in the nonclustered index rows but not in the data rows unless you also have a clustered index on the computed column.

Be aware of the overhead involved with indexes on computed columns. Updates to the columns that the computed columns are based on result in updates to the index on the computed column as well.

Indexes on computed columns can be useful when you need an index on large character fields. As discussed earlier, the smaller an index, the more efficient it is. You could create a computed column on the large character field using the CHECKSUM() function. CHECKSUM() generates a 4-byte integer that is relatively unique for character strings but not absolutely unique (different character strings can generate the same checksum, so when searching against the checksum, you need to include the character string as an additional search argument to ensure that you are matching the right row). The benefit is that you can create an index on the 4-byte integer generated by the CHECKSUM() that can be used to search against the character string, instead of having to create an index on the large character column itself. Listing 34.3 shows an example of applying this solution.

LISTING 34.3 Using an Index on a Computed Checksum Column

```
-- First add the computed column to the table
alter table titles add title_checksum as CHECKSUM(title)
go

-- Next, create an index on the computed column
create index NC_titles_titlechecksum on titles(title_checksum)
go
```

LISTING 34.3 Continued

```
-- In your queries, include both the checksum column and the title column in
--   your search argument
select title_id, ytd_sales
   from titles
   where title_checksum = checksum('Fifty Years in Buckingham Palace Kitchens')
     and title = 'Fifty Years in Buckingham Palace Kitchens'
```

The Index Tuning Wizard

The Index Tuning Wizard is a utility provided by SQL Server that can analyze a set of queries and make recommendations about the right mix of indexes or indexed views that could be defined to improve performance. You can also specify that the Index Tuning Wizard generate a SQL script to implement the index design that it recommends.

The Index Tuning Wizard does a great job of quickly analyzing a database and recommending a basic set of indexing options. Of course, it is not perfect, and it can make mistakes by not recommending an index that it should or by recommending a less than optimal index.

Although the recommended design might not be perfect, the Index Tuning Wizard provides an excellent starting point for any indexing strategy, especially if you are unfamiliar with the T-SQL code or access methods employed by an application. However, you should not rely completely on this tool because there will certainly be some instances in which you know an index should be applied and it is not recommended by the Index Tuning Wizard.

To use the Index Tuning Wizard, first create a workload in a trace file or table generated by SQL Profiler. The workload can then be specified as the input to the Index Tuning Wizard. The Index Tuning Wizard will analyze the workload and make index recommendations to improve query processing performance. If you don't want to go to the trouble of creating a workload using SQL Profiler, you can also choose a selection of one or more T-SQL statements in a Query Analyzer window as an input to the Index Tuning Wizard for index analysis. This is useful for tuning a troublesome query or batch process.

There are a number of ways to start up the Index Tuning Wizard:

- Within SQL Profiler, select the Tools menu. From the Tools menu, select the Index Tuning Wizard menu option.
- Within Enterprise Manager, select the Tools menu. From the Tools menu, select Wizards. In the Wizards dialog box, open up the Management list, click on Index Tuning Wizard, and click OK.
- Within Query Analyzer, select the Query window and choose the Index Tuning Wizard option.

Each of these methods brings up the initial Index Tuning Wizard dialog box. To start using the Index Tuning Wizard, follow these steps:

1. On the Index Tuning Wizard initial dialog box, click Next to continue. The Select Server and Database dialog box appears, as shown in Figure 34.1.

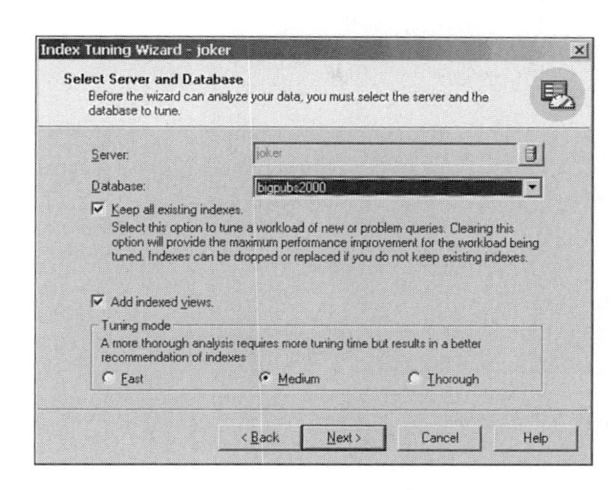

FIGURE 34.1 The Select Server and Database dialog box.

2. In the Select Server and Database dialog box, enter the name of the SQL Server and the database you want to tune. The Index Tuning Wizard considers only one database at a time. Choose the set of options you want the Index Tuning Wizard to apply when performing its analysis. Following are the available options:

   - Keep All Existing Indexes—If you check this option, the Index Tuning Wizard considers adding new indexes only. If you do not check this option, the Index Tuning Wizard considers dropping and redefining inefficient indexes. Allowing the wizard to redefine existing indexes offers the best chance for performance improvement but is also the most risky approach.

   - Add Indexed Views—This option is enabled only when connecting to an Enterprise or Developer Edition of SQL Server 2000. When this option is checked, the Index Tuning Wizard considers creating indexed views in addition to normal indexes. Indexed views will be considered only when specifying the Medium or Thorough tuning mode.

   - Tuning Mode—This option is used to specify how thoroughly you want the Index Tuning Wizard to analyze your database. For large workload files, the runtime could be significant if the thorough mode is specified. The Fast mode takes the least amount of time and generates a quick recommendation based on query analysis and limited interaction with the database. Thorough mode gives the highest quality set of recommendations, but also takes the longest time. The Medium mode balances thoroughness of the analysis with runtime, examining fewer possibilities than Thorough mode but generating a respectable set of recommendations.

Click Next to continue. The Specify Workload dialog box appears, as shown in Figure 34.2.

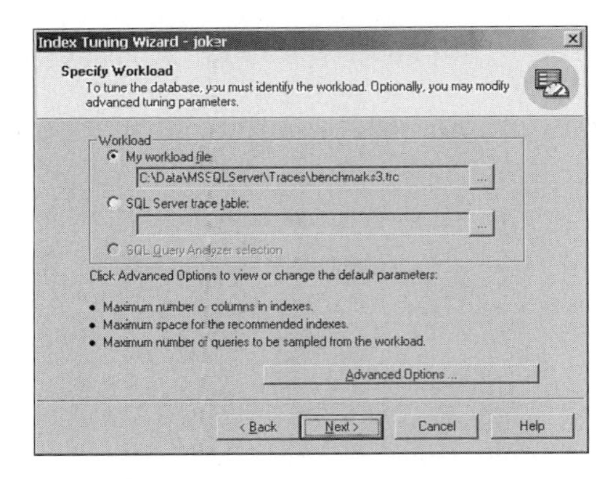

FIGURE 34.2 The Specify Workload dialog box.

3. On the Specify Workload dialog box, you can choose from an existing workload file, a SQL Server trace table, or if you invoked the Index Tuning Wizard from within Query Analyzer, the currently selected SQL in the Query Analyzer window. For a workload file, you can choose from a previously saved SQL Server trace file or a SQL Script file containing queries you want to analyze.

   Also on this screen, the Advanced Options button brings up the index tuning parameters dialog box, as shown in Figure 34.3. This dialog box displays the data size, index size, and available space for the current database. In this screen, you can specify additional control over the tuning parameters to control the number of queries to analyze in the workload file, the maximum amount of space allowed for the recommended indexes, and the maximum number of columns allowed per index.

   If Limit Number of Workload Queries to Sample is unchecked, all queries in the workload file are analyzed. Click OK to save any changes made to the index tuning parameters and then click Next to bring up the Select Tables to Tune dialog box, as shown in Figure 34.4.

4. One of the new features in the Index Tuning Wizard in SQL Server 2000 is the capability to specify a projected number of rows for the tables you choose to analyze. The Index Tuning Wizard takes the projected number of rows into account when recommending indexes and indexed views.

   After you select the tables to analyze and specify any row projections, click Next to continue. Once the index analysis is complete, the Index Recommendations dialog box appears, as shown in Figure 34.5.

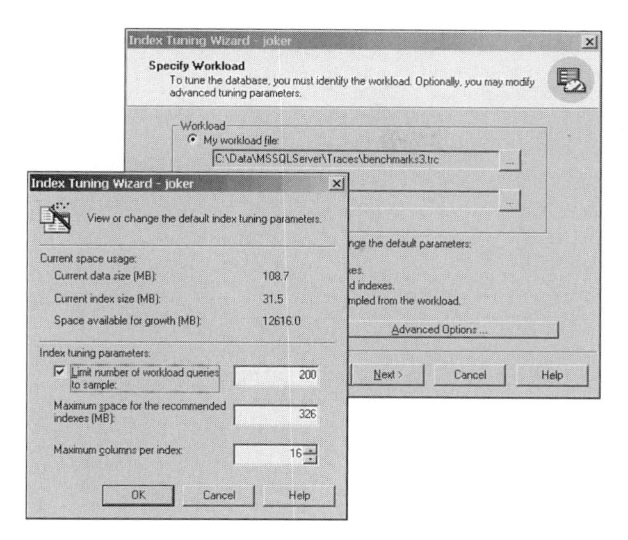

FIGURE 34.3 The Index Tuning Parameters dialog box.

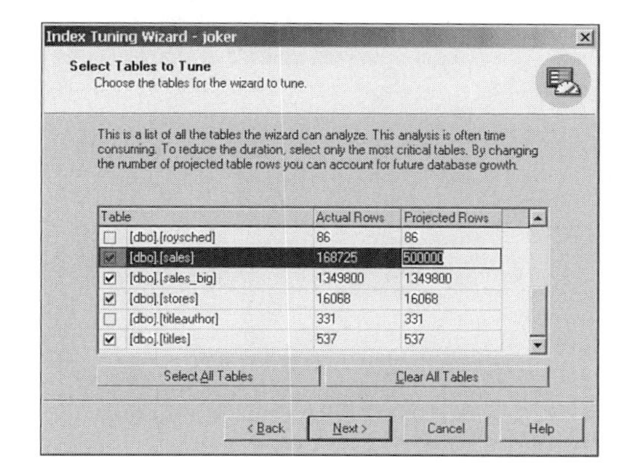

FIGURE 34.4 The Select Tables to Tune dialog box.

5. The Index Recommendations dialog box shows you all the indexes that have been recommended that can potentially improve query performance, as well as the indexes it recommends be dropped, if any. This dialog box shows indexes that it recommends even if they already exist. Remember, if you choose not to keep existing indexes, these indexes will be dropped and re-created when the generated index script is run.

   Clicking on the Analysis button brings up a list of reports generated by the Index Tuning Wizard, as shown in Figure 34.6.

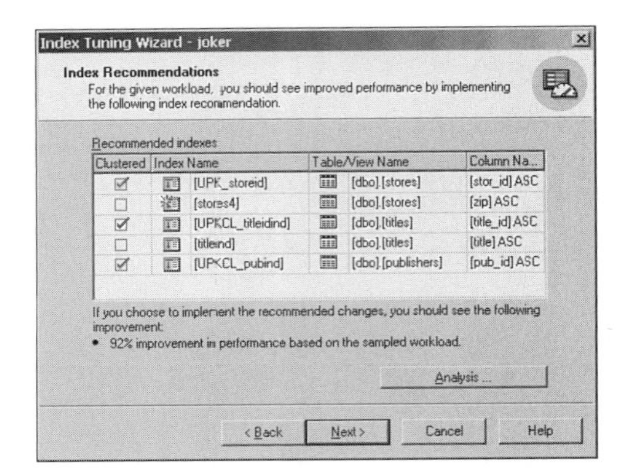

FIGURE 34.5 The Index Recommendations dialog box.

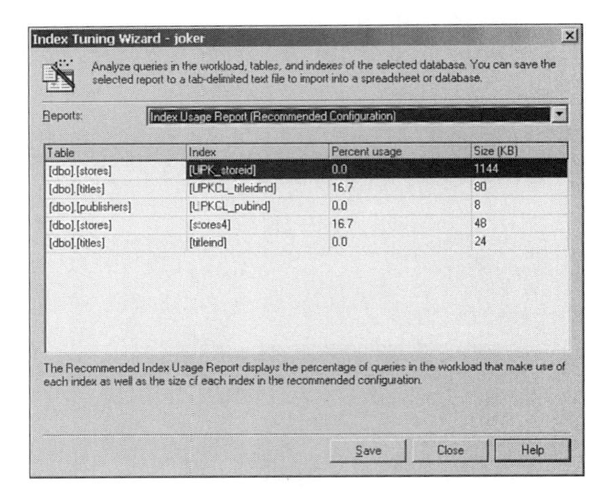

FIGURE 34.6 The Index Tuning Wizard Reports dialog box.

These reports provide further analysis and information regarding the index recommendations. You can analyze the information in these reports to help you decide whether to accept or reject the index recommendations. All reports can be saved to files for easier analysis and historical purposes. The reports generated are summarized in Table 34.2.

TABLE 34.2 Index Tuning Wizard Reports

Report	Description
Index Usage Report (recommended or current)	Provides information about the expected relative usage of the recommended or current indexes by the queries in the workload file and the estimated sizes of the indexes.

TABLE 34.2 Continued

Report	Description
Table Analysis Report	Provides information about the top 100 most heavily used tables in the workload file along with the relative cost of all queries in which the table participates.
View-Table Relations Report	Provides information on the tables referenced by the recommended indexed views.
Query-Index Relations Report (recommended or current)	Reports which indexes are used by which queries in the workload file.
Query Cost Report	Provides the estimated reduction or increase in execution time for the 100 most expensive statements in the workload file.
Workload Analysis Report	Provides information about the frequency of execution of `SELECT`, `INSERT`, `UPDATE`, and `DELETE` queries in the workload file and their relative impact on the total cost of the workload.
Tuning Summary Report	Provides summary information about the analysis performed by the Index Tuning Wizard, including number of tables tuned, number of indexes and indexed views recommended to be created or dropped, number of queries examined, and the total time spent performing the analysis.

When finished analyzing or saving the reports, click the Close button to return to the Index Recommendations dialog box. Click Next to continue. The Schedule Index Update Job dialog box appears, as shown in Figure 34.7.

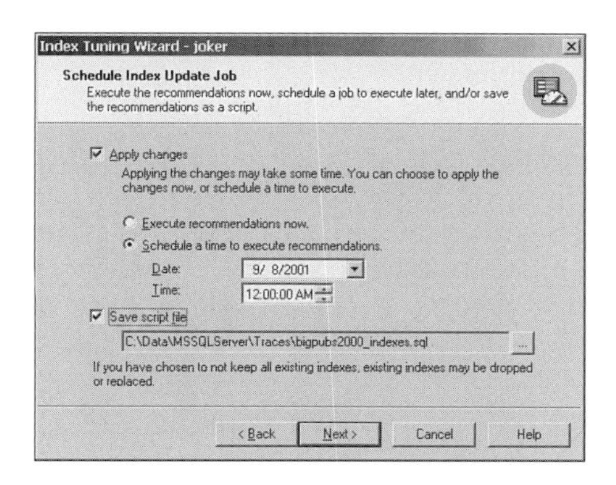

FIGURE 34.7 The Schedule Index Update Job dialog box.

6. The Schedule Index Update Job dialog box allows you to make several choices about when and how to implement the index changes. You can choose to implement the changes immediately, schedule an execution, or create a script file that you can run manually at any later time. Click Next to continue. The Completing the Index Tuning Wizard dialog box appears. Click Finish on the Completing the Index Tuning Wizard dialog box to implement the index changes.

   If you choose to schedule the index creation, the Index Tuning Wizard creates a SQL Server Agent Job. Figure 34.8 shows an example of the T-SQL job step created.

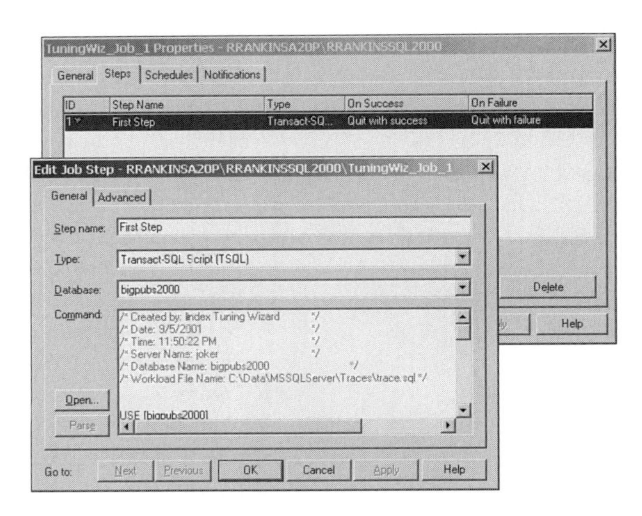

FIGURE 34.8 A T-SQL Job step generated by the Index Tuning Wizard when the Schedule Index Update option is chosen.

   You might prefer not to let the Index Tuning Wizard run or schedule the running of the index script, but save it to a file to run it manually. That way, you can review the script first and see more clearly the indexes and indexed views that the Index Tuning Wizard is recommending. Also, saving the script gives you the ability to apply the changes in multiple environments.

Be aware that the recommendations made by the Index Tuning Wizard depend on the quality of the workload file provided. The most important step in the process is choosing a workload file that is representative of the database systems usage. SQL Profiler provides an excellent means of capturing database activity over a period of time for a production or test environment so that you have a representative sample of actual database activity.

TIP

It is recommended that you run the Index Tuning Wizard on your databases periodically to analyze and re-evaluate your index design. In addition to the changes in data volume and data distribution, it is possible that your users could begin accessing the data differently or use different queries. This is especially true in data warehousing and ad hoc query environments. By continually sampling workload information, you can ensure that you are applying appropriate indexes based on current usage patterns.

Using the `itwiz` Command-Line Utility

If you want to automate and schedule the running of the Index Tuning Wizard instead of running it manually, you can use the `itwiz` command-line utility. You can set up a job in SQL Server Agent to invoke `itwiz` on a scheduled basis, or use an operating system scheduler. (For more information on scheduling jobs using SQL Server Agent, see Chapter 18, "SQL Server Scheduling and Notification.")

The syntax for `itwiz` is as follows:

```
itwiz -D database_name {-i workload_file | -t workload_trace_table_name}
        -o generated_script_file_name
        [-S server_name[\instance]]
        {{-U login_id [-P password]} | -E }
        [-f tuning_feature_set]
        [-K keep_existing_indexes]
        [-M recommendation_quality]
        [-B storage_bound]
        [-n number_of_queries]
        [-C max_columns_in_index]
        [-T table_list_file]
        [-m minimum_improvement_percent]
        [-F][-v]
```

Table 34.3 describes the `itwiz` command-line options.

TABLE 34.3 `itwiz` Command-Line Options

Option	Description
`-D` *`database_name`*	Specifies the name of the database to which to connect and tune the indexes.
`-i` *`workload_file`*	Specifies the path and filename of the workload file. The workload file can be a SQL Profiler trace file or a SQL script file.
`-t [`*`server`*`].[`*`database`*`].[`*`owner`*`].`*`workload_trace_table_name`*	Specifies the location of a trace table that contains the workload trace.
`-o` *`generated_script_file_name`*	Specifies the path and filename of the recommended index script file.
`-S` *`server_name`*`[\`*`instance`*`]`	Specifies the name and optional instance of the SQL Server to which to connect. The default is the local server.
`-U` *`login_id`*	Specifies the SQL Server login ID to use to connect to SQL Server.
`-P` *`password`*	Specifies the password for the SQL Server login ID used to connect to SQL Server.
`-E`	Specifies that a trusted connection is to be used to connect to SQL Server.
`-f` *`tuning_feature_setting`*	Specifies the features to be used when tuning the indexes. The values that can be specified are as follows: `0`—All features (the default) `1`—Indexes only `2`—Indexed views only
`-K` *`keep_existing_indexes`*	Specifies whether the existing indexes can be dropped. The values that can be specified are as follows: `0`—Do not keep existing indexes `1`—Keep all existing indexes (the default)
`-M` *`quality_of recommendation`*	Specifies the runtime versus recommendation quality trade-off. The values that can be specified are as follows: `0`—Fast Mode `1`—Medium Mode (the default) `2`—Thorough Mode
`-B` *`max_index_space`*	Specifies the maximum space to be used for the recommended set of indexes.
`-n` *`number_of_queries`*	Specifies the number of queries to be tuned. The default is 200.
`-C` *`max_columns_in_index`*	Specifies the maximum number of columns allowed in the recommended indexes.

TABLE 34.3 Continued

Option	Description
`-T` *`table_list_file`*	Specifies the path and filename of a file that contains a list of tables to be tuned. You can also specify a row projection for each table. The format of the file is as follows: `[`*`owner`*`.]`*`table`* `[`*`projected_number_of_rows`*`]` `[`*`owner`*`.]`*`table`* `[`*`projected_number_of_rows`*`]` ...
`-m` *`minimum_improvement_percent`*	Specifies the minimum performance improvement percentage for the workload file that must be met for `itwiz` to output an index recommendation.
`-F`	Specifies that `itwiz` can overwrite an existing output file.
`-v`	Enables `itwiz` to output verbose messages to the screen during execution.

The following is a sample execution of the `itwiz` command-line utility:

```
itwiz -D bigpubs2000 -i bigpubs_20010901.trc -M 2 -K 0 -E -o bigpubs_itwiz.sql
```

This example specifies that `itwiz` should perform a thorough analysis, allowing the dropping of existing indexes. It will connect to the local server using a trusted connection and perform the analysis on the `bigpubs2000` database. It uses a SQL Profiler trace file as input and outputs the index recommendation script to a file called `bigpubs_itwiz.sql` in the current directory.

Choosing Indexes: Query Versus Update Performance

I/O is the primary factor in determining query performance. The challenge for the database designer is to build a physical data model that provides efficient data access. Creating indexes on database tables allows SQL Server to access data with a reduced number of I/Os. Defining useful indexes during the logical and physical data modeling step is crucial. The SQL Server optimizer relies heavily on index key distribution and index density to determine which indexes to use for a query. The optimizer in SQL Server can use multiple indexes in a query (through index intersection) to reduce the number of I/Os to retrieve information. In the absence of indexes, the optimizer performs a table scan, which can be costly from an I/O standpoint.

Although indexes provide a means for faster access to data, they slow down data modification statements due to the extra overhead of having to maintain the index during inserts, updates, and deletes (for more information on index maintenance during updates, see Chapter 33).

In a Decision Support System (DSS), defining many indexes can help your queries and does not create much of a performance issue because the data is relatively static and doesn't get updated frequently. You typically load the data, create the indexes, and forget about it until the next data load. As long as you have the necessary indexes to support the user queries, and they're getting decent response time, the penalties of having too many indexes in a DSS environment is the space wasted for indexes that possibly won't be used, the additional time required to create the excessive indexes, and the additional time required to back up and run `DBCC` checks on the data.

In an OLTP environment, on the other hand, too many indexes can lead to significant performance degradation, especially if the number of indexes on a table exceeds four or five. Think about it for a second. Every single-row insert is at least one data page write and one or more index page writes (depending on whether a page split occurs) for every index on the table. With eight nonclustered indexes, that would be a minimum of nine writes to the database for a single-row insert. Therefore, for an OLTP environment, you want as few indexes as possible—typically only the indexes required to support the update and delete operations and your critical queries, and to enforce your uniqueness constraints.

So the natural solution, in a perfect world, would be to create a lot of indexes for a DSS environment and as few indexes as possible in an OLTP environment. Unfortunately, in the real world, you typically have an environment that must support both DSS and OLTP applications. How do you resolve the competing indexing requirements of the two environments? To meet the indexing needs of DSS and OLTP applications requires a bit of a balancing act, with no easy solution. It often involves making hard decisions as to which DSS queries might have to live with table scans, and which updates have to contend with additional overhead.

One solution is to have two separate databases—one for DSS applications and another for OLTP applications. Obviously, this method requires some method of keeping the databases in sync. The method chosen depends on how up-to-date the DSS database has to be. If you can afford some lag time, you could consider using a dump-and-load mechanism, such as Log Shipping or periodic full database restores. If the DSS system requires up-to-the-minute concurrency, you might want to consider using replication (see Chapter 22, "Data Replication").

TIP

Although replication might seem like a slick solution, do not enter into this type of decision lightly—setting up and maintaining a replicated environment can be complex and time consuming. Consider your options fully before you take this approach.

Also, I wouldn't recommend using triggers as a method to keep two databases in sync. I once saw a system in which such a design had been implemented. The performance overhead of the trigger in the OLTP environment was much greater than any overhead caused by having the additional indexes on the tables to support the DSS queries. Replication is a much cleaner, behind-the-scenes approach with minimal impact on query performance in the OLTP database.

Another possible alternative is to have only the required indexes in place during normal processing periods to support the OLTP requirements. At the end of the business day, create the indexes necessary to support the DSS queries and reports, which can run as batch jobs after normal processing hours. When the DSS reports are complete, drop the additional indexes, and you're ready for the next day's processing. Note that this solution assumes that the time required to create the additional indexes is offset by the time saved by the faster running of the DSS queries. If the additional indexes do not result in substantial time savings, they probably are not necessary and need not be created in the first place. The queries need to be more closely examined to select the appropriate indexes that will best support your queries.

It is therefore important to choose indexes carefully to provide a good balance between data search and data modification performance. The application environment usually governs the choice of indexes. For example, if the application is mainly OLTP with transactions requiring fast response time, creating too many indexes might have an adverse impact on performance. On the other hand, the application might be a decision support system (DSS) with few transactions doing data modifications. In that case, it makes sense to create a number of indexes on the columns frequently used in the queries.

Summary

One of the most important aspects to improving SQL Server performance is proper index design. Choosing the appropriate indexes to be used by SQL Server to process queries involves thoroughly understanding the queries and transactions being run against the database, understanding the bias of the data, understanding how SQL Server uses indexes, and staying aware of the performance implications of overindexing tables in an OLTP environment. In general, consider using clustered indexes to support range retrievals or when data needs to be sorted in clustered index order; use nonclustered indexes for single or discrete row retrievals or when you can take advantage of index covering. Use the Index Tuning Wizard to help you identify the appropriate mix of indexes that will optimize performance for your database applications.

To really make good index design choices, it helps to have an understanding of the SQL Server query optimizer to know how it uses indexes and index statistics to develop query plans. This would be a good time to read Chapter 35.

CHAPTER 35

Understanding Query Optimization

by Ray Rankins

IN THIS CHAPTER

- What Is a Query Optimizer?
- Query Compilation and Optimization
- Step 1: Query Analysis
- Step 2: Index Selection
- Step 3: Join Selection
- Step 4: Execution Plan Selection
- Reusing Query Plans
- Other Query Processing Strategies
- Parallel Query Processing
- Data Warehousing and Large Database Query Strategies
- Common Query Optimization Problems
- Managing the Optimizer

Query optimization is the process SQL Server goes through to analyze individual queries and determine the best way to process them. To achieve this end, SQL Server uses a cost-based optimizer. As a **cost-based** optimizer, the optimizer's purpose is to determine the query plan that will access the data with the least amount of processing time in terms of logical and physical I/Os. The query optimizer examines the parsed SQL queries and, based on information about the objects involved (number of pages in the table, types of indexes defined, index statistics, and so on), generates a query plan. The query plan is the set of steps to be carried out to execute the query.

To allow the optimizer to do its job properly, you need to have a good understanding of how the optimizer determines query plans for queries. This will help you to understand what types of queries can be optimized effectively and to learn techniques to help the optimizer choose the best query path. This knowledge will help you write better queries, choose better indexes, and detect potential performance problems.

NOTE

To better understand the concepts presented in this chapter, you should have a reasonable understanding of how SQL Server manages data objects and indexes and how indexes affect performance. If you haven't already read Chapter 33, "SQL Server Internals," and Chapter 34, "Indexes and Performance," I recommend that you review them now.

NOTE

Occasionally throughout this chapter, some graphical execution plans are used to illustrate some of the principles discussed. In the next chapter, "Query Analysis," a more detailed discussion of the graphical showplan output is discussed that describes the various bits of information contained in the execution plans and how to interpret it. In this chapter, the execution plans are provided primarily to give you an idea of what you can expect to see for the different types of queries presented when you are doing your own query analysis.

What Is a Query Optimizer?

For any given SQL statement, the source tables can be accessed in many ways to build the desired resultset. The query optimizer analyzes all the possible ways that the resultset can be built and chooses the most appropriate method. This method is called the query execution plan. SQL Server uses a cost-based optimizer. The optimizer assigns a cost to every possible execution plan in terms of CPU resource usage and disk I/O. The optimizer then chooses the execution plan with the least associated cost.

Thus, the primary goal of the query optimizer is to find the cheapest execution to minimize the total time to process the query. Because I/O is the most significant factor in query processing time, the optimizer analyzes the query and primarily searches for access paths and techniques to minimize the number of logical and physical page accesses as much as possible. The fewer the number of logical and physical I/Os performed, the faster the query should run.

The process of query optimization in SQL Server Versions 7.0 and 2000 is extremely complicated and is based on sophisticated costing models and data-access algorithms. It is beyond the scope of a single chapter to try to explain in detail all the various costing algorithms that the optimizer currently employs. This chapter is intended to help you better understand some of the concepts related to how the query optimizer chooses an execution strategy and provide an overview of the query optimization strategies employed to improve query processing performance.

NOTE

SQL Server 7.0 incorporated a completely revamped and more intelligent query optimizer than in previous versions of SQL Server. Beyond some likely bug fixes and enhancements to the algorithms, no significant changes were made to the query optimizer in SQL Server 2000. The only real enhancements to the optimizer in SQL Server are related to indexed views. In SQL Server 2000, the optimizer can consider using an indexed view to process a query in place of the actual table, if the indexed view exists and contains all the needed data. The indexed view does not have to be explicitly specified in the query. For more information on indexed views, see Chapter 34 and Chapter 27, "Creating and Managing Views in SQL Server."

Query Compilation and Optimization

Query compilation is the complete process from the submission of a query to the actual execution. There are many steps to query compilation—one of which is optimization. All T-SQL statements are compiled, but not all are optimized. Only the standard SQL Data Manipulation Language (DML) statements, `SELECT`, `INSERT`, `UPDATE`, and `DELETE`, require optimization. The other procedural constructs in T-SQL (`IF`, `WHILE`, local variables, and so on) are compiled as procedural logic but do not require optimization. DML statements are set-oriented requests that the optimizer must translate into procedural code that can be executed efficiently to return the desired results.

Compiling DML Statements

When SQL Server compiles an execution plan for a DML statement, it performs the following basic steps:

1. The query is checked for proper syntax and the T-SQL statements parsed into keywords, expressions, operators, and identifiers to generate a **sequence tree**. The sequence tree is an internal format of the query that SQL Server can operate on.
2. The sequence tree is then normalized. During normalization, the tables and columns are verified and the metadata (datatypes, null properties, index statistics, and so on) about them is retrieved. Additionally, any views are resolved to their underlying tables and implicit conversions are performed (for example, an integer compared with a float value).
3. If the statement is a DML statement, SQL Server takes the normalized query and generates a query graph.
4. The query graph is then optimized and a query execution plan is generated.
5. SQL Server executes the query execution plan.

Optimization Steps

When the query graph is passed to the optimizer, the optimizer performs a series of steps to break the query down into its component pieces for analysis in order to generate an optimal execution plan.

1. Query Analysis—The query is analyzed to determine search arguments and join clauses. A search argument is defined as a `WHERE` clause comparing a column to a constant. A join clause is a `WHERE` clause comparing a column from one table to a column in another table.

2. Index Selection—Indexes are selected based on search arguments and join clauses (if any exist). Indexes are evaluated based on their distribution statistics and are assigned a cost.

3. Join Selection—The join order is evaluated to determine the most appropriate order in which to access tables. Additionally, the optimizer evaluates the most appropriate join algorithm to match the data.

4. Execution Plan Selection—Execution costs are evaluated and a query execution plan is created that represents the most efficient solution.

The next four sections of this chapter will examine each of these steps in more detail.

NOTE

Unless stated otherwise, the examples presented in this chapter operate on the tables in the bigpubs2000 database. The pubs and Northwind databases provided with SQL Server generally do not contain enough data to demonstrate many of the query strategies presented in this chapter. A copy of the bigpubs2000 database is available on the CD included with this book. Instructions on how to install the database are presented in the Introduction.

Step 1: Query Analysis

The first step in query optimization is to analyze each table in the query to identify all search arguments (SARGs), `OR` clauses, and join clauses. The SARGs, `OR` clauses, and join clauses will be used in the second step, index selection, to select useful indexes to satisfy a query.

Identifying Search Arguments

A **search argument** (SARG) is defined as a `WHERE` clause comparing a column to a constant. The format of a SARG is as follows:

```
Column operator constant_expression [and...]
```

SARGs provide a way for the optimizer to limit the rows searched to satisfy a query. The general goal is to match a SARG with an index to avoid a table scan. Valid operators for a SARG are any one of =, >, <, >=, and <=, `BETWEEN`, and sometimes `LIKE`. Multiple SARGs can be combined with the `AND` clause (a single index might match some or all of the SARGs `AND`ed together). Following are examples of optimizable search arguments:

- `flag = 7`
- `salary > 100000`
- `city = 'Saratoga' and state = 'NY'`
- `price between $10 and $20` (is the same as `price > = $10 and price <= $20`)
- `100 between lo_val and hi_val` (is the same as `lo_val <= 100 and hi_val >= 100`)
- `au_lname like 'Sm%'` (is the same as `au_lname >= 'Sm' and au_lname < 'Sn'`)

In some cases, the column in a SARG might be compared with a constant expression rather than a single constant value. The constant expression can be an arithmetic operation, a built-in function, a string concatenation, a local variable, or a subquery result. As long as the left side of the SARG contains a column alone, it's still a SARGable expression.

The `LIKE` clause will be treated as a SARG only if the first character in the string is a constant. The following statement wouldn't be treated as a SARG:

```
au_lname like '%son'
```

A `LIKE` clause with a wildcard as the first character is not considered a SARGable expression because it doesn't limit the search. In other words, every row would have to be examined to determine if it were a match. The inequality operator (`!=` or <>) isn't a valid operator for a SARG for this same reason—an index can only help you find matches for a specific value, not everything that doesn't match. Additionally, if any operation is performed on the column, such as a function, it's not considered SARGable, either. Some examples of nonSARGable expressions are as follows:

- `gender != 'M'`
- `lname = fname` (comparison against a column, not a constant expression)
- `upper(city) = 'POULSBO'` (function performed on the column)

TIP

If you have a search clause with a nonSARGable expression, try to rewrite it as a SARG so that it can be optimized by the query optimizer. For example, consider the following query:

```
select title from titles where price != 0
```

If a business rule is enforced on the table to prevent any rows from having a price less than zero, the query could be rewritten as follows:

```
select title from titles where price > 0
```

and still return the same result set. The difference is that the second version contains a SARG that the optimizer will recognize and consider for matching with an index to resolve the query. Although it still might result in a table scan, it at least gives the optimizer the opportunity to consider using an index; it wouldn't have done so with the inequality operator.

Another example of a nonSARG that can be rewritten as a SARGs is as follows:

```
where substring(name, 1, 1) = 'A'
```

can be rewritten as

```
where name like 'A%'
```

TIP

If you cannot avoid using a function on a column in the search expression, consider creating a computed column on the table and indexing it. This will materialize the function result into an additional column on the table, which can be indexed for faster searching because the index statistics can be used on the computed column. An example of using this approach would be for a query that has to find the number of orders placed in a certain month, regardless of the year. The following is a possible solution:

```
select count(*)
   from sales
   where datepart(month, ord_date) = 6
```

This query gets the right resultset but ends up having to do so with a table scan because the function on the `ord_date` column prevents it from using any index that might exist on the `ord_date` column.

If this query is used frequently in the system and quick response time is critical, you could create a computed column on the function and index it as follows:

```
alter table sales add ord_month as datepart(month, ord_date)
create index nc_sales_ordmonth on sales(ord_month)
```

Now, when you run the query on the table again, specify the computed column in the WHERE clause and it can use the index on the computed column to find the rows and avoid a table scan.

```
select count(*)
   from sales
   where ord_month = 6
```

Even if the query still ends up using a table scan, it will now at least have statistics available to know how many rows it can expect to match where the month matches the value specified.

Some expressions involving computations on a column might be treated as SARGs during optimization if SQL Server can simplify the expression into a SARG. For example, the SARG

```
ytd_sales/12 = 1000
```

can be simplified to

```
ytd_sales = 12000.
```

The simplified expression is used only during optimization to determine an estimate of the number of matching rows and the usefulness of the index. During actual execution, the conversion is not done while traversing the index tree as it won't be able to do the repeated division by 12 for each row while searching through the tree. However, doing the conversion during optimization and getting a row estimate from the statistics helps the optimizer decide on other strategies to consider, such as index scanning versus table scanning, or it might help to decide an optimal join order if it's a multitable query.

When tuning performance of your system, keep an eye out for expressions that cannot be treated as SARGs. They're a common cause of poor performance because they prevent an index from being used to resolve the query. Many times, queries containing nonoptimizable SARGs can be rewritten with optimizable SARGs that will return the same resultset faster.

NOTE

The presence of a nonSARGable expression in a query does not guarantee that a table scan will be performed. Other SARGs might be present that will result in an index being used; or, on occasion, an index will cover the query if the index contains all needed columns and the nonSARGable expression can be evaluated by scanning the index instead of the entire table. Index covering is discussed in more detail in Chapter 34.

Identifying OR Clauses

The next statements the optimizer looks for in the query are OR clauses. OR clauses are SARGable expressions combined with an OR statement rather than an AND statement and are treated differently than a standard SARG. The format of an OR clause is as follows:

```
SARG or SARG [or ...]
```

with all columns involved in the OR belonging to the same table.

The following IN statement

```
column in ( constant1, constant2, ...)
```

is also treated as an OR clause, becoming

```
column = constant1 or column = constant2 or ...
```

Some examples of OR clauses are as follows:

```
where au_lname = 'Smith'  or au_fname = 'Fred'
where (type = 'business' and price > $25) or pub_id = "1234"
where au_lname in ('Smith', 'Jones', 'N/A')
```

An OR clause is a disjunction; all rows matching either of the two criteria appear in the resultset. Any row matching both criteria should appear only once.

The main issue is that an OR clause cannot be satisfied by a single index. Consider the first example just presented:

```
where au_lname = 'Smith'  or au_fname = 'Fred'
```

An index on au_lname and au_fname will help us find all the rows where au_lanme = 'Smith' AND au_fname = 'Fred', but searching the index tree will not help us find all the rows where au_fname = 'Fred', but the last name is something other than 'Smith'. Unless an index on au_fname exists as well, the only way to find all rows with au_fname = 'Fred' is to search every row in the table.

An OR clause can be resolved by either a table scan or by using the OR strategy. Using a table scan, SQL Server reads every row in the table and applies each OR criteria to each row. Any row that matches any one of the OR criteria is put into the resultset.

A table scan is an expensive way to process a query, so the optimizer looks for an alternative for resolving an OR. If an index can be matched against all SARGs involved in the OR clause, SQL Server evaluates the possibility of applying the index intersection strategy described later in this chapter in the "Using Multiple Indexes" section.

Identifying Join Clauses

The last type of statement for which the query optimizer looks during the query analysis phase is the **join clause**. A join condition is specified in the `FROM` clause using the `JOIN` keyword as follows:

```
FROM table1 JOIN table2  on table1.column = table2.column
```

Alternatively, join conditions can also be specified in the `WHERE` clause using the old-style join syntax, as shown in the following example:

```
Table1.Column Operator Table2.Column
```

A join clause always involves two tables, except in the case of a self-join, but even in a self-join, you must specify the table twice in the query:

```
select employee = e.LastName + ', ' + e.FirstName,
       manager = m.LastName + ', ' + m.FirstName
    from Northwind..Employees e left outer join Northwind..Employees m
    on e.ReportsTo = m.EmployeeID
   order by 2, 1
```


SQL Server will treat a self-join just like a normal join between two different tables.

Subquery Processing

Depending on how a subquery is written, SQL Server will optimize them differently. For example, SQL Server will attempt to flatten certain subqueries into joins when possible, to allow the optimizer to select the optimal join order rather than be forced to process the query inside out. This section examines the different types of subqueries and how they are optimized by SQL Server.

`IN`, `ANY`, or `EXISTS` Subqueries

In SQL Server, any query containing a subquery introduced with an `IN`, `= ANY`, or `EXISTS` predicate is flattened into an existence join unless the outer query also contains an `OR` clause or unless the subquery is correlated or contains one or more aggregates.

An existence join is optimized the same way as a regular join, with one exception. With an existence join, as soon as a matching row is found in the inner table, the value `TRUE` is returned and SQL Server stops looking for further matches for that row in the outer table and moves on to the next row. A normal join would continue processing to find all matching rows. The following query is an example of a subquery that would be converted to an existence join:

```
select pub_name from publishers
   where pub_id in (select pub_id from titles where type = "business')
```

Materialized Subqueries

If the outer query is comparing a column against the result of a subquery using any of the comparison operators (=, >, <, >=, <=, !=), and the subquery is not correlated, the results of the subquery must be resolved—that is, **materialized**—before comparison against the outer table column. For these types of queries, the optimizer must process them inside out.

An example of this type of query is as follows:

```
select title from titles
   where total_sales = (select max(total_sales) from titles)
```

The subquery must be resolved first to find the value to compare against `total_sales` in the outer query. Although this is an optimizable SARG, the value to be compared with the `total_sales` column will not be known until the query actually runs.

Correlated Subqueries

A **correlated subquery** contains a reference to an outer table in a join clause in the subquery. The following is an example of a correlated subquery:

```
SELECT au_lname, au_fname
FROM authors
WHERE 100 IN
    (SELECT royaltyper
    FROM titleauthor
    WHERE titleauthor.au_ID = authors.au_id)
```

Because correlated subqueries depend on values from the outer query for resolution, they cannot be processed independently. Instead, SQL Server processes correlated subqueries repeatedly, once for each qualifying outer row.

Step 2: Index Selection

When the query analysis phase of optimization is complete and all SARGs, `OR` clauses, and join clauses have been identified, the next step is to determine the selectivity of the expressions (estimated number of matching rows) and to determine the index cost to find the rows. The index costs are measured in terms of logical I/Os. If multiple indexes can be considered, the costs of each are compared with each other and also against the cost of a table scan to determine the least expensive access path.

Indexes are typically considered useful for an expression if the first column in the index is used in the expression and the search argument in the expression provides a means to limit the search. If no useful indexes are found for an expression, typically a table scan will be performed on the table. A table scan is the fall-back tactic for the optimizer to use if no better way exists of resolving a query.

Evaluating SARG and Join Selectivity

To determine selectivity of a SARG, the optimizer uses the index statistics stored for the index or column, if any. If no statistics are available for a column or index, by default, SQL Server will automatically create the statistics.

If no statistics are available for a column or index and the `auto create statistics` and `auto update statistics` options have been disabled for the database or table, SQL Server cannot make an informed estimate of the number of matching rows for a SARG and will have to resort to using some built-in percentages for the number of matching rows for various types of expressions. These percentages are as follows:

Operator	Row Estimate
=	10 percent
between, > and <	10 percent (closed range search)
>, <, >=, <=	30 percent (open range search)

Using these percentages will almost certainly result in inappropriate query execution plans being chosen. Always try to ensure that you have up-to-date statistics available for any columns referenced in your SARGs and join clauses.

When the value of a SARG can be determined at the time of query optimization, the optimizer will use the index statistics histogram to estimate the number of matching rows for the SARG. The histogram contains a sampling of the data values in the column and stores information on the number of matching rows for the sampled values, as well as for values that fall between the sampled values. If the statistics are up-to-date, this is the most accurate estimate of the number of matching rows for a SARG.

If the SARG contains an expression that cannot be evaluated until runtime but is an equality expression (=), the optimizer will use the index density to estimate the number of matching rows. The index density reflects the overall uniqueness of the data values in the column or index. Index density is not as accurate as the histogram because its value is determined across the entire range of values in a column or index keys and can be skewed higher by one or more values that have a high number of duplicates. Expressions that cannot be evaluated until runtime include comparisons against functions, local variables, or other columns.

If the expression cannot be evaluated at the time of optimization, and the SARG is not an equality search but a closed or open range search, the index density cannot be used. The same percentages are used for the row estimates as for when no statistics are available.

As a special case, if a SARG contains the equality (=) operator and there's a unique index matching the SARG, by nature of a unique index, the optimizer knows that one and only one row will match the SARG without having to analyze the index statistics.

If the query contains a join clause, SQL Server determines whether any usable indexes exist that match the column(s) in the join clause. Because the optimizer has no way of determining what value(s) will join between rows in the table at optimization time, it can't use the statistics histogram to estimate the number of matching rows. Instead, it uses the index density as it does for SARGs that are unknown during optimization.

A lower density value indicates a more selective index. As the density approaches 1, the index becomes less selective. If a nonclustered index has a high density value, it will likely be more expensive in terms of I/O than a table scan and will not be used.

NOTE

For a more thorough discussion of index selection and index statistics, see Chapter 34.

Estimating Index Cost

The second phase of index selection is identifying the total cost of various access paths to the data and determining which path results in the lowest cost to return the matching rows for an expression.

The primary cost of an access path, especially for single table queries, is the number of logical I/Os required to retrieve the data. Using the available statistics and the information stored in SQL Server regarding the number of rows per page and the number of pages in the table, the optimizer estimates the number of logical page reads necessary to retrieve the estimated number of rows using the candidate index. It then ranks the candidate indexes to determine which index requires the least amount of logical I/O.

NOTE

A logical I/O occurs every time a page is accessed. If the page is not in cache, a physical I/O is first performed to bring the page into cache memory, and then a logical I/O is performed against the page. The optimizer has no way of knowing whether a page will be in memory when the query actually is executed and does not factor in the physical I/O cost. Physical I/Os are another performance factor that needs to be monitored by watching the overall cache-hit ratio for SQL Server.

TIP

The rest of this section assumes a general understanding of SQL Server storage structures. If you haven't already, now is a good time to read through Chapter 33.

Clustered Index Cost

Clustered indexes are efficient for lookups because the rows matching the SARGs are clustered on the same page or over a range of adjacent pages. SQL Server needs only to find its way to the first page and then read the rows from that page and any subsequent pages in the page chain until no more matching rows are found.

Therefore, the I/O cost estimate for a clustered index is calculated as follows:

```
  the number of index levels in the clustered index
+ the number of pages to scan within the range of values
```

The number of pages to scan is based on the estimated number of matching rows divided by the number of rows per page.

For example, if SQL Server can store 250 rows per page for a table, and 600 rows are within the range of values being searched, SQL Server would estimate that it would require at least three page reads to find the qualifying rows. If the index is three levels deep, the logical I/O cost would be as follows:

```
  3 (index levels to find the first row)
+ 3 (data pages—600 rows divided by 250 rows per page)
= 6 logical page I/Os
```

For a unique clustered index and an equality operator, the logical I/O cost estimate is one data page plus the number of index levels that need to be traversed to access the data page.

When a clustered index is used to retrieve the data rows, you will see a query plan similar to the one shown in Figure 35.1.

Nonclustered Index Cost

When searching for values using a nonclustered index, SQL Server reads the index key values at the leaf level of the index and uses the bookmark to locate and read the data row. SQL Server has no way of knowing if matching search values are going to be on the same data page until it has read the bookmark. It is possible that while retrieving the rows, SQL Server might find all data rows on different data pages, or it might revisit the same data page multiple times. Either way, a separate logical I/O is required each time it visits the data page.

With this in mind, the I/O cost is based on the depth of the index tree, the number of index leaf rows that need to be scanned to find the matching key values, and the number of matching rows. The cost of retrieving each matching row depends on whether the table is clustered or is a heap table. For a heap table, the nonclustered row bookmark is the page and row pointer to the actual data row. A single I/O is required to retrieve the data row. Therefore, the logical I/O cost for a heap table can be estimated as follows:

The number of nonclustered index levels

+ The number of leaf pages to be scanned

+ The number of qualifying rows (each row represents a separate data page read)

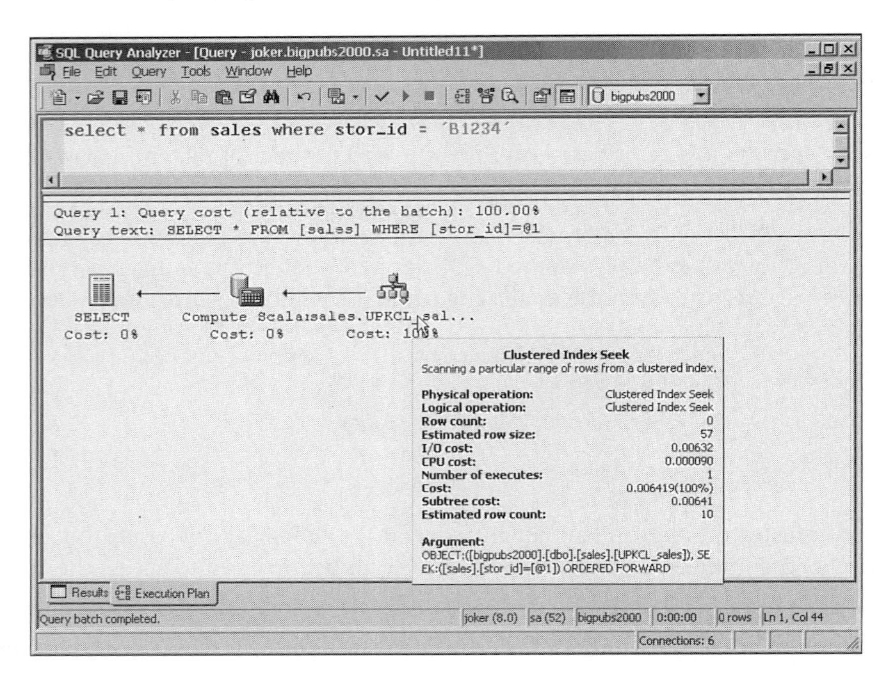

FIGURE 35.1 Execution plan for clustered index seek.

NOTE

This estimate assumes that the data rows have not been forwarded. In a heap table, when a row has been forwarded, the original row location contains a pointer to the new location of the data row; therefore, an additional page read is required to retrieve the actual data row. The actual I/O cost would be one page greater per row than the estimated I/O cost for any rows that have been forwarded.

If the table is clustered, the row bookmark is the clustered key for the data row. The number of I/Os to retrieve the data row depends on the depth of the clustered index tree, as SQL Server has to use the clustered index to find each row. With this in mind, the logical I/O cost of finding a row using the nonclustered index on a clustered table is as follows:

The number of nonclustered index levels

+ The number of leaf pages to be scanned

+ The number of qualifying rows × the number of page reads to find a single row via the clustered index

As an example, consider a heap table with a nonclustered index on last name. Assume the index holds 800 rows per page (they're really big last names!), and 1,700 names are within the range we are looking for. If the index is 3 levels deep, the estimated logical I/O cost for the nonclustered index would be the following:

3 (index levels)

+ 3 (leaf pages—1,700 leaf rows/800 rows per page)

+ 1,700 (data page reads)

= 1,706 total logical I/Os

Now, assume that the table has a clustered index on it, and the size of the nonclustered index is the same. If the clustered index is 3 levels deep, including the data page, the estimated logical I/O cost of using the nonclustered index would be the following:

3 (nonclustered index levels)

+ 3 (leaf pages—1,700 leaf rows/800 rows per page)

+ 5,100 (1,700 rows × 3 clustered page reads per row)

= 5,106 total logical I/Os

NOTE

Although the I/O cost is greater for bookmark lookups in a nonclustered index when a clustered index exists on the table, the cost savings during row inserts, updates, and deletes using the clustered index as the bookmark are substantial, whereas the couple extra logical I/Os per row during retrieval does not substantially impact query performance.

For a unique nonclustered index using an equality operator, the I/O cost is estimated as the number of index levels traversed to access the bookmark plus the number of I/Os required to access the data page via the bookmark.

When a nonclustered index is used to retrieve the data rows, you will see a query plan similar to the one shown in Figure 35.2. Notice the additional bookmark lookup with a nonclustered index seek that was not present in the clustered index seek.

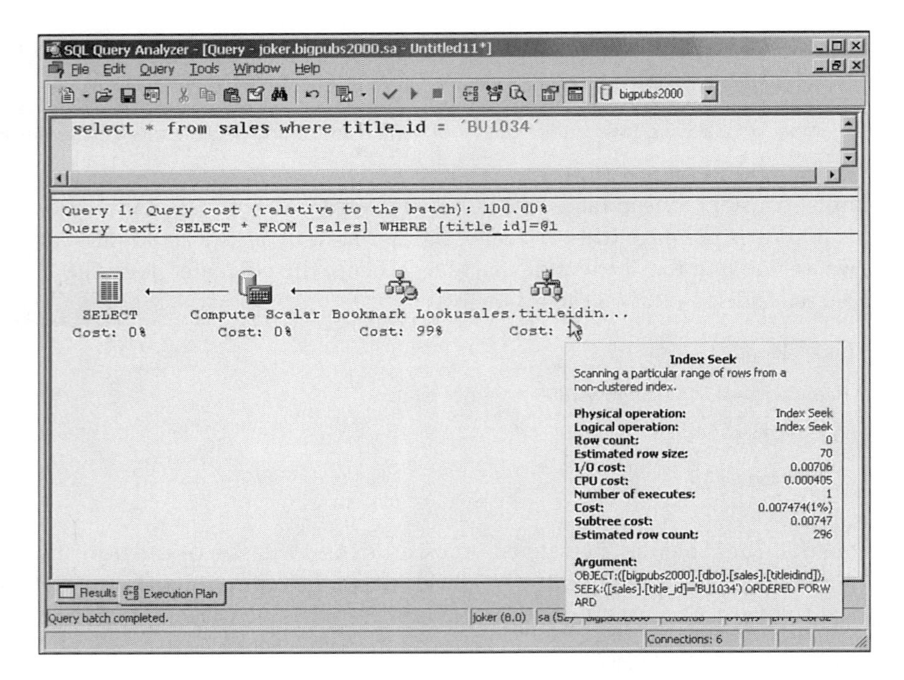

FIGURE 35.2 Execution plan for nonclustered index seek.

Covering Nonclustered Index Cost

When analyzing a query, the optimizer also considers any possibility to take advantage of index covering. **Index covering** is a method of using the leaf level of a nonclustered index to resolve a query when all the columns referenced in the query (in both the select list and `WHERE` clause, as well as any `GROUP BY` columns) are part of the index key.

This can save a significant amount of I/O because the query doesn't have to access the data page. In most cases, a nonclustered index that covers a query is faster than a similarly defined clustered index on the table.

If index covering can take place in a query, the optimizer considers it and estimates the I/O cost of using the nonclustered index to cover the query. The estimated I/O cost of index covering is as follows:

```
  The number of index levels
+ The number of leaf index pages to scan
```

The number of leaf pages to scan is based on the estimated number of matching rows divided by the number of leaf index rows per page.

For example, if index covering could be used on the nonclustered index on last name for the query in the previous example, the I/O cost would be the following:

  3 (nonclustered index levels)

+ 3 (leaf pages—1,700 leaf rows/800 rows per page)

= 6 total logical I/Os

TIP

For more information on index covering and when it can take place, see Chapter 34.

When an index covering is used to retrieve the data rows, you might see a query plan similar to the one shown in Figure 35.3. If the entire leaf level of the index is searched, it will display as an index scan, as shown in this example.

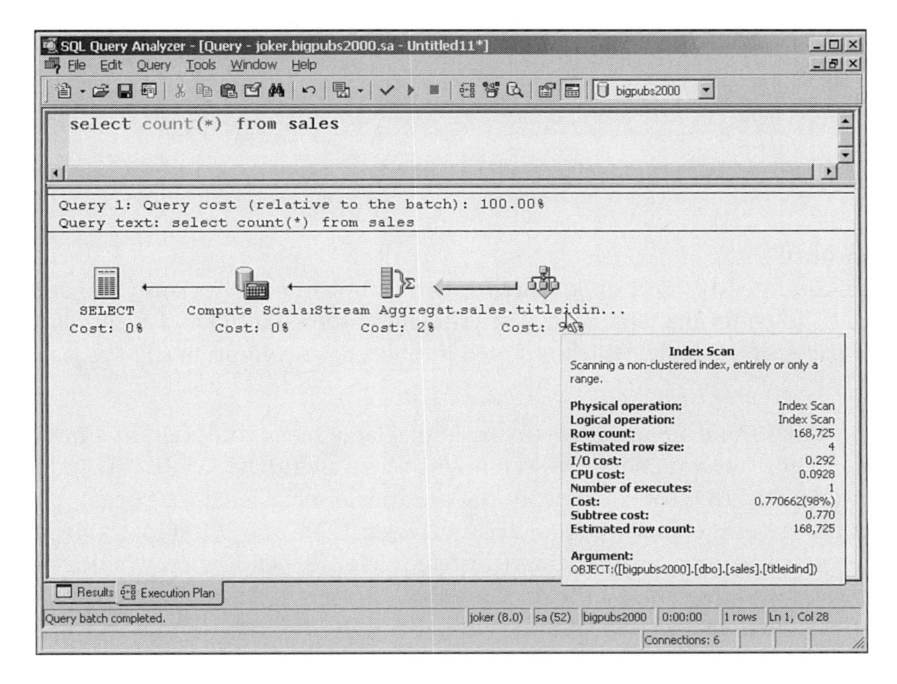

FIGURE 35.3 Execution plan for covered index scan without limits on the search.

Other times, if the index keys can be searched to limit the range, you might see an index seek used as shown in Figure 35.4. Note that the difference here from a normal index lookup is the lack of the bookmark lookup because SQL Server does not need to go to the data row to find the needed information.

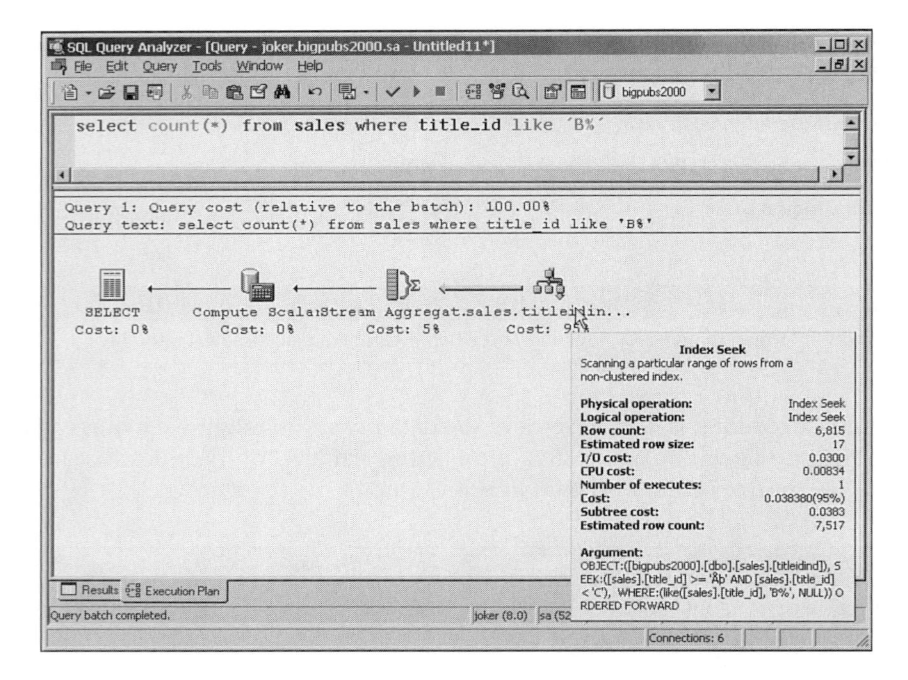

FIGURE 35.4 Execution plan for covered index seek with limits on the search.

Table Scan Cost

If no usable index exists that can be matched with a SARG or a join clause, the optimizer's only option is to perform a table scan. The estimate of the total I/O cost is simply the number of pages in the table, which is stored in the `dpages` column in the `sysindexes` table.

Keep in mind that there are instances (for example, large range retrievals on a nonclustered index column) in which a table scan might be cheaper than a candidate index in terms of total logical I/O. For example, in the previous nonclustered index example, if the index does not cover the query, it would cost between 1,706 and 5,106 logical I/Os to retrieve the matching rows using the nonclustered index, depending on whether a clustered index exists on the table. If the total number of pages in the table is less than either of these values, then a table scan would be more efficient in terms of total logical I/Os than using a nonclustered index.

When a table scan is used to retrieve the data rows from a heap table, you will see a query plan similar to the one shown in Figure 35.5.

When a table scan is used to retrieve the data rows from a clustered table, you will see a query plan similar to the one shown in Figure 35.6. Notice that it displays as a clustered index scan because the table is the leaf level of the clustered index.

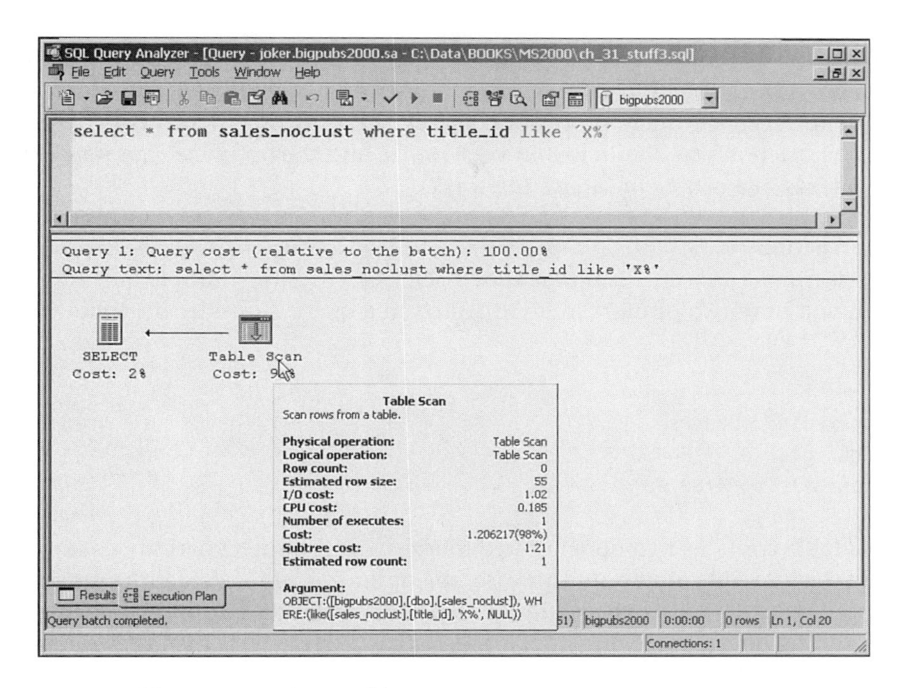

FIGURE 35.5 Table scan on a heap table.

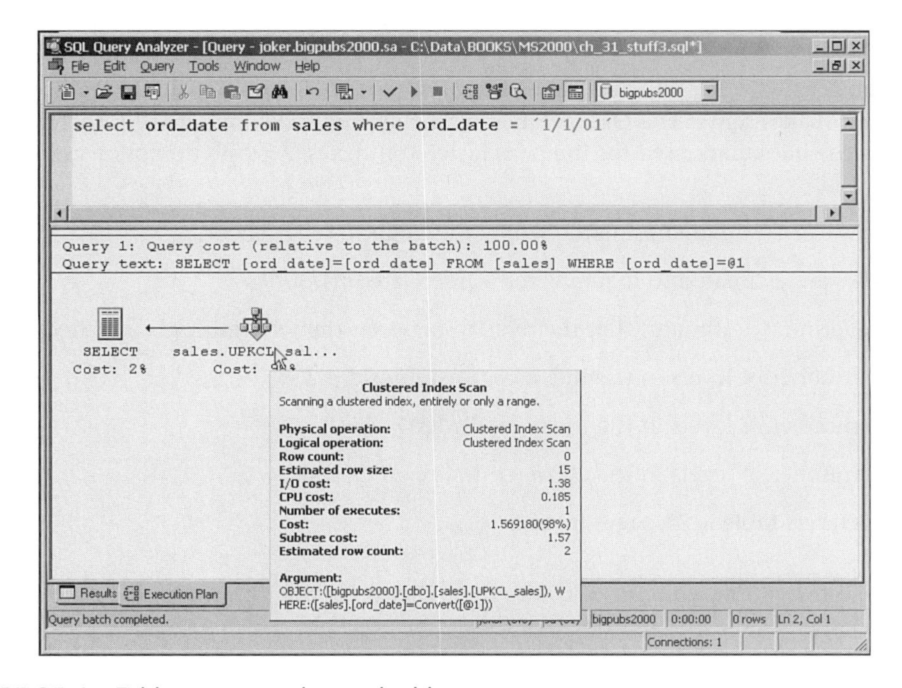

FIGURE 35.6 Table scan on a clustered table.

Using Multiple Indexes

You have always been able to create multiple indexes on a table in SQL Server. Prior to version 7.0, however, the query processor could exploit only one index per table per query. That restriction was eliminated in version 7.0, and the optimizer can now exploit multiple indexes in a couple of interesting ways.

Index Intersection

Index intersection is a mechanism that allows SQL Server to use multiple indexes on a table when you have two or more indexed SARGs in a query. Consider the following example:

```
SELECT *
   FROM northwind..Orders
   where customerid = 'HUNGO'
   and orderdate = '4/30/98'
```

The Orders table contains two nonclustered indexes: one on the OrderDate column and one on the CustomerId column. In this case, the optimizer will consider the option of searching the index leaf rows of each index to find the rows that meet the search conditions and joining on the matching bookmarks for each resultset. It then uses the overlapping bookmarks to retrieve the actual data rows. This strategy will be applied only when the logical I/O cost of retrieving the bookmarks for both indexes and then retrieving the data rows is less than retrieving the qualifying data rows using only one of the indexes or using a table scan.

You can go through the same analysis as the optimizer to determine whether an index intersection makes sense. The Orders table has a clustered index on OrderId; therefore, OrderId is the bookmark used for the nonclustered indexes. Assume the following statistics:

- 19 rows are estimated to match where CustomerId = ‘HUNGO’.
- 4 rows are estimated to match where OrderDate = ‘4/30/98’.
- The optimizer estimates that the overlap between the two resultsets is 1 row.
- The number of levels in the index on CustomerId = 2.
- The number of levels in the index on OrderDate = 2.
- The number of levels in the clustered index on OrderId = 1.
- The Orders table is 21 pages in size.

Using this information, you can calculate the I/O cost for the different strategies the optimizer can consider.

A table scan would cost 21 pages.

A standard data row retrieval via the nonclustered index on CustomerID would cost

2 nonclustered index page reads (root and leaf)

+ 38 (19 rows × 2 pages per bookmark lookup via the clustered index)

= 40 pages

A standard data row retrieval via the nonclustered index on OrderDate would cost

2 nonclustered index page reads (root and leaf)

+ 8 (4 rows × 2 pages per bookmark lookup via clustered index)

= 10 pages

The index intersection is estimated to cost

2 pages (1 root page plus the 1 leaf page to find all the bookmarks for the 19 matching index rows on CustomerID)

+ 2 pages (1 root page plus the 1 leaf page to find all the bookmarks for the 4 matching index rows on OrderDate)

+ 2 page reads to find the 1 estimated overlap between the two indexes

= 6 pages

As you can see from these examples, the index intersection strategy is definitely the cheapest approach. If at any point the estimated intersection cost reached 10 pages, SQL Server would just use the single index on OrderDate and check both search criteria against the four matching rows for OrderId. If the estimated cost of using an index in any way ever reached 21 pages, a table scan would be performed and the criteria checked against all rows.

When an index intersection is used to retrieve the data rows from a table, you will see a query plan similar to the one shown in Figure 35.7.

`OR` Strategy

You will see a strategy similar to an index intersection applied when you have an `OR` condition between your SARGs, as shown in the following example:

```
SELECT *
   FROM Northwind..Orders
   WHERE OrderDate between '1/1/1997' and '1/2/1997'
   OR ShippedDate between '1/8/1997' and '1/9/1997'
```

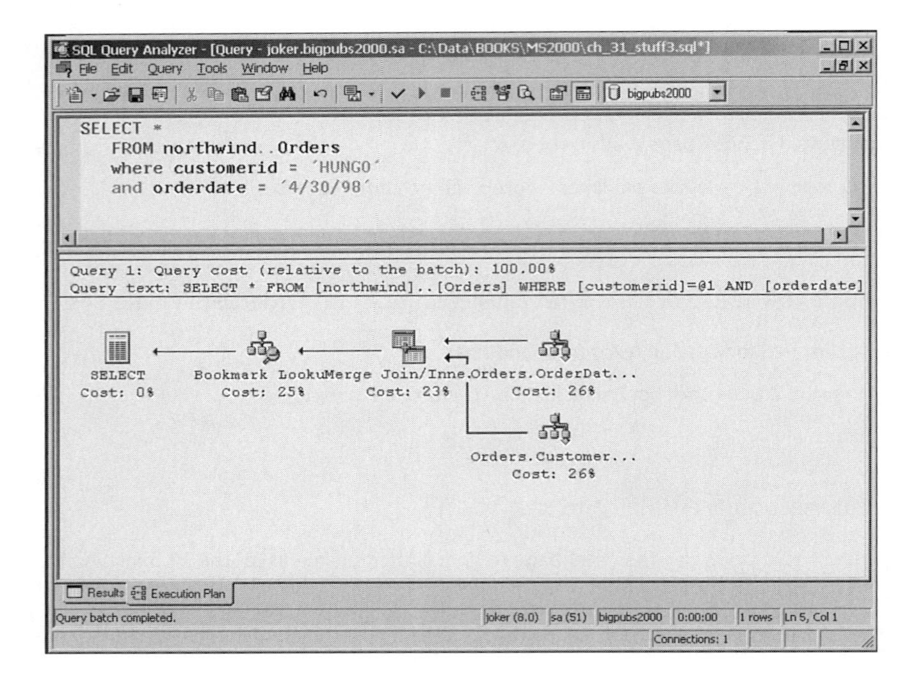

FIGURE 35.7 Execution plan for index intersection.

The `OR` strategy is essentially the same as an index intersection with one slight difference. Using the `OR` strategy, SQL Server executes each part separately using the index that matches the SARG, but instead of merging the results, it has to concatenate the bookmarks in a worktable to sort the bookmarks and remove any duplicates. It then uses the unique bookmarks to retrieve the result rows from the base table.

When the `OR` strategy is used to retrieve the bookmarks from each of the indexes and concatenate them to build a list of bookmarks for retrieving the resulting data rows, you will see a query plan similar to the one shown in Figure 35.8. Notice the concatenation step, which differentiates it from a normal index intersection.

The following steps describe how SQL Server would handle the following query if useful indexes exist on both `au_lname` and `state`:

```
select * from authors
   where au_lname = "Smith"
      or state = "NY"
```

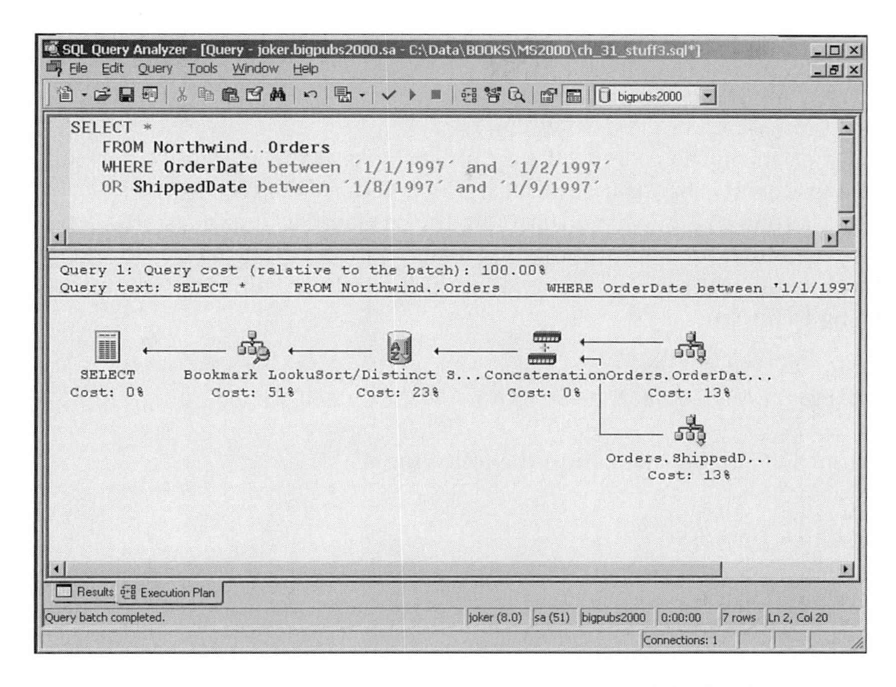

FIGURE 35.8 Execution plan for `OR` clause with concatenation of the bookmarks.

1. Estimate the cost of a table scan and the cost of using the `OR` strategy.
2. If the cost of the `OR` strategy exceeds the cost of a table scan, stop here and simply perform a table scan. Otherwise, continue with the succeeding steps to perform the `OR` strategy.
3. Break the query into multiple parts; for example:

```
select * from authors where au_lname = "Smith"
select * from authros where state = "NY"
```

4. Match each part with an available index.
5. Execute each piece and get the row bookmarks into a worktable.
6. Sort the bookmarks and remove any duplicates.
7. Use the bookmarks to retrieve all qualifying rows from the base table.

If any one of the `OR` clauses needs to be resolved via a table scan for any reason, SQL Server will simply use a table scan to resolve the whole query rather than applying the `OR` strategy.

If the OR involves only a single column

```
where au_lname = 'Smith' or au_lname = 'Varney'
```

and an index exists on the column, the optimizer looks at the alternative of resolving it as a BETWEEN clause rather than using the OR strategy. Because the data in the index is sorted, the optimizer knows that all values satisfying the OR clause in the index are "between" the two values. Therefore, it could find the first matching row for the OR clause and simply scan the succeeding leaf pages of the index until the last matching row is found. Consider the following example:

```
select title_id from titles
   where title_id in ("BU1032", "BU1111", "BU2075", "BU7832")
```

The OR clause could be translated into the following:

```
where title_id = 'BU1032'
   or title_id = 'BU1111'
   or title_id = 'BU2075'
   or title_id = 'BU7832'
```

To process this using the standard OR strategy would involve using four separate lookups on the titles table to get the matching row bookmarks into a worktable. As an alternative, SQL Server might internally translate the OR clause into a range retrieval similar to the following:

```
where title_id between "BU1032" and "BU7832"
   and (title title_id = 'BU1032'
       or title_id = 'BU1111'
       or title_id = 'BU2075'
       or title_id = 'BU7832')
```

The optimizer now has the option of using the index to perform a range retrieval and scan all rows in the range, applying the search criteria to each row in a single pass to find all the matching result rows, ignoring any nonmatching rows in the range. Figure 35.9 shows an example of this approach being applied for an OR condition.

Index Joins

Another way of using multiple indexes on a single table is to join two or more indexes to create a covering index. This is similar to an index intersection, except that the final bookmark lookup is not required because the merged index rows contain all the necessary information. Consider the following example:

```
SELECT orderid, customerid, orderdate
   FROM Northwind..Orders where customerid = 'HUNGO'
   and orderdate = '4/30/98'
```

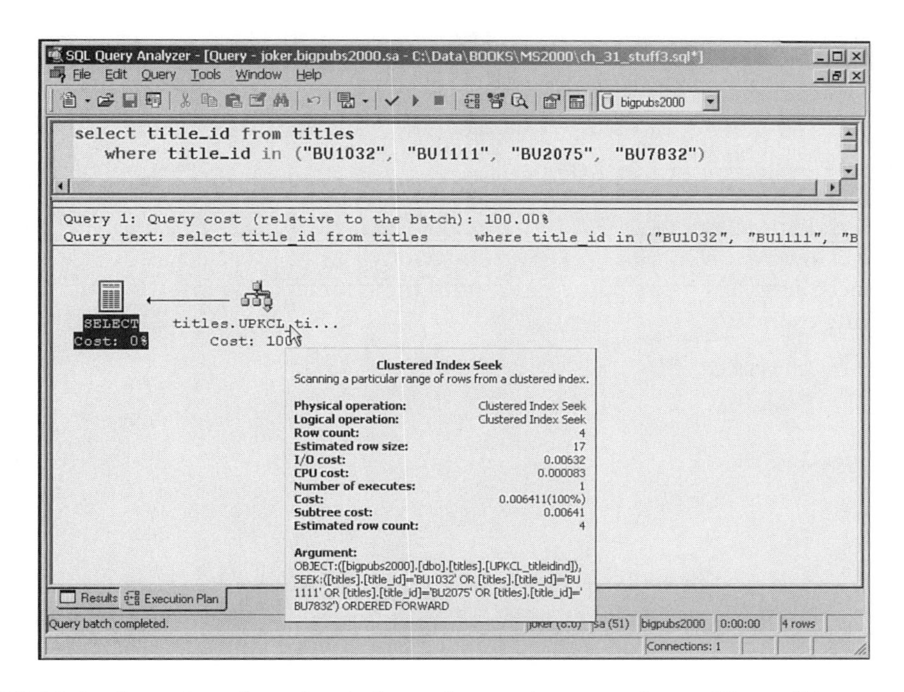

FIGURE 35.9 Execution plan using index seek to retrieve rows for an *OR* condition on a single column.

Again, the Orders table contains indexes on both the CustomerID and OrderDate columns. Each of these indexes contains the clustered key on OrderID as a bookmark. In this instance, when the optimizer merges the two indexes using a merge join, joining them on the matching OrderIDs, the index rows in the merge set have all the information we need because OrderID is part of the nonclustered indexes. There is no need to perform a bookmark lookup on the data page. By joining the two index resultsets, SQL Server created the same effect as having one covering index on CustomerId, OrderDate, and OrderID on the table. Using the same numbers as in the Index Intersection section presented earlier, the cost of the index join would be as follows:

2 pages (1 root page plus the 1 leaf page to find all the CustomerIDs and OrderIDs for the 19 matching index rows on CustomerID)

+ 2 pages (1 root page plus the 1 leaf page to find all the OrderDates and OrderIDs for the 4 matching index rows on OrderDate)

= 4 total page reads

Figure 35.10 shows an example of the execution plan for an index join. Notice that it does not include the bookmark lookup present in the index intersection execution plan, as shown earlier in Figure 35.7.

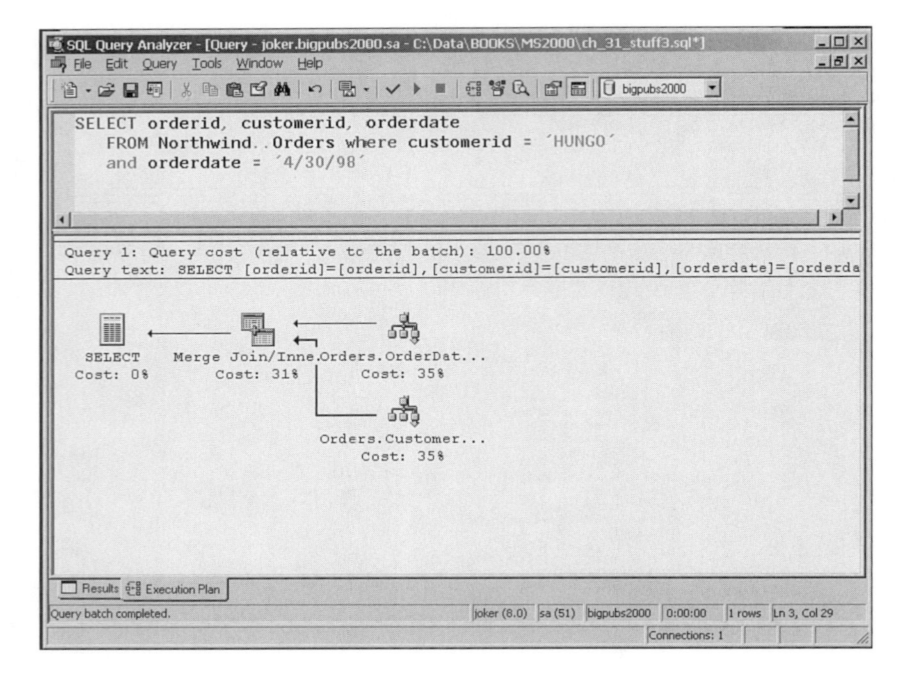

FIGURE 35.10 Execution plan for index join.

Optimizing with Indexed Views

A new feature in SQL Server 2000 is indexed views. When you create a unique clustered index on a view, the resultset for the view is materialized and stored in the database with the same structure as a table that has a clustered index. Changes made to the data in the underlying tables of the view will be automatically reflected in a view the same way as changes to a table are reflected in its indexes. In the Developer and Enterprise editions of SQL Server 2000, the query optimizer will automatically consider using the index on the view to speed up access for queries run directly against the view. The query optimizer in the Developer and Enterprise editions of SQL Server 2000 will also look at and consider using the indexed view for searches against the underlying base table when appropriate.

NOTE

While indexed views can be created in any edition of SQL Server 2000, they will only be considered for query optimization in the Developer and Enterprise editions of SQL Server 2000. In other editions of SQL Server 2000, indexed views will not be used to optimize the query unless the view is explicitly referenced in the query and the `NOEXPAND` optimizer hint is specified. For example, to force the optimizer to consider using the `sales_Qty_Rollup` indexed view in the Standard Edition of SQL Server 2000, execute the query as follows:

```
select * from sales_Qty_Rollup WITH (NOEXPAND)
   where stor_id between 'B914' and 'B999'SET ARITHABORT ON
```

The NOEXPAND hint is only allowed in SELECT statements and the indexed view must be referenced directly in the query (only the Developer and Enterprise editions will consider using an indexed view that is not directly referenced in the query). As always, use optimizer hints with care. Once the NOEXPAND hint is included in the query, the optimizer will not be able to consider any other alternatives for optimizing the query.

Consider the following example that creates an indexed view on the sales table containing the stor_id and sum(qty) grouped by stor_id:

```
set quoted_identifier on
go

create view sales_qty_rollup
with schemabinding
as
   select stor_id, sum(qty) as total_qty, count_big(*) as id
      from dbo.sales
      group by stor_id
go

create unique clustered index idx1 on sales_Qty_Rollup (stor_id)
go
```

The creation of the clustered index on the view essentially creates a clustered table in the database with the three columns stor_id, total_qty, and id. As you would expect, the following query on the view itself will use the clustered index on the view to retrieve the result rows from the view instead of having to scan or search the sales table itself:

```
select * from sales_Qty_Rollup
   where stor_id between 'B914' and 'B999'
```

However, the following query on the sales table itself ends up using the indexed view, sales_qty_rollup, to retrieve the result set as well.

```
select stor_id,  sum(qty)
   from sales
   where stor_id between 'B914' and 'B999'
   group by stor_id
```

Essentially, the optimizer recognizes the indexed view as an index on the sales table that covers the query. The execution plan shown in Figure 35.11 shows the indexed view being searched in place of the table.

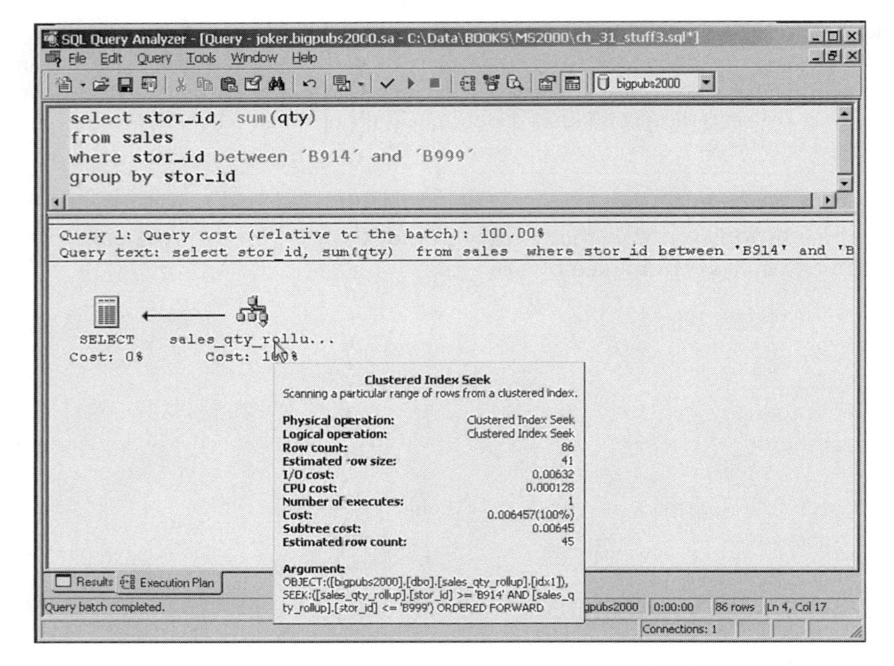

FIGURE 35.11 Execution plan showing indexed view being searched to satisfy query on base table.

NOTE

In addition to the seven required SET options being set accordingly when the indexed view is created, they must also be set the same way for a session to be able to use the indexed view in queries. The required SET option settings are as follows:

```
SET ARITHABORT ON
SET CONCAT_NULL_YIELDS_NULL ON
SET QUOTED_IDENTIFIER ON
SET ANSI_NULLS ON
SET ANSI_PADDING ON
SET ANSI_WARNINGS ON
SET NUMERIC_ROUNDABORT OFF
```

If these SET options are not enabled for the session running a query that could make use of an indexed view, the indexed view will not be used and the table itself is searched instead.

For more information on indexed views, see Chapter 27.

On rare occasions, you might find situations where using the indexed view in the Enterprise or Developer editions of SQL Server 2000 leads to poor query performance, and you might want to avoid having the optimizer use the indexed view. To force the optimizer to ignore the indexed view(s) and optimize the query using the indexes on the underlying base tables, specify the `EXPAND VIEWS` query option as follows:

```
select * from sales_Qty_Rollup
   where stor_id between 'B914' and 'B999'
   OPTION (EXPAND VIEWS)
```

Step 3: Join Selection

The job of the query optimizer is incredibly complex. The optimizer can consider literally thousands of options when determining the optimal execution plan. The statistics are simply one of the tools that the optimizer can use to help in the decision-making process.

In addition to examining the statistics to determine the appropriate use of indexes, the optimizer must consider the optimum order in which to access the tables, the appropriate join algorithms to use, the appropriate sorting algorithms, and many other details that are too many to list here. The goal of the optimizer during join selection is to determine the lowest cost join strategy in terms of logical I/Os and the amount of memory required.

As mentioned at the beginning of this chapter, delving into the detailed specifics of the various join strategies and their costing algorithms is beyond the scope of a single chapter on optimization. In addition, some of these costing algorithms are proprietary and not publicly available.

The goal of this section then is to present an overview of the more common query processing algorithms that the optimizer uses to determine an appropriate execution plan.

Join Processing Strategies

If you are familiar with SQL, you are probably very familiar with using joins between tables in creating SQL queries. As far as the SQL Server query processor is concerned, a join occurs anytime it has to compare two inputs to determine an output. The join can occur between one table and another table, between an index and a table, or between an index and another index (as you've seen previously in the section on index intersection).

The SQL Server query processor uses three basic types of join strategies when it must compare two inputs: nested loops join; merge join; and hash join. The optimizer must consider each one of these algorithms to determine the most appropriate and efficient algorithm for a given situation.

Each of the three supported join algorithms could be used for any join operation. The query optimizer examines all the possible alternatives, assigns costs to each, and chooses the least expensive join algorithm for a given situation. The addition of the merge and hash joins in SQL Server 7.0 has greatly improved the query processing performance of SQL Server in the data warehousing and very large database environment. In previous versions that supported only nested loops join strategies, SQL Server was not as effective at handling large data requests.

Nested Loops Join

The nested loops join algorithm is by far the simplest of the three supported algorithms. The nested loops join uses one input as the "outer" loop and the other input as the "inner" loop. As you might expect, SQL Server processes the outer input one row at a time. For each row in the outer input, the inner input is searched for matching rows.

Figure 35.12 illustrates a query that uses a nested loops join.

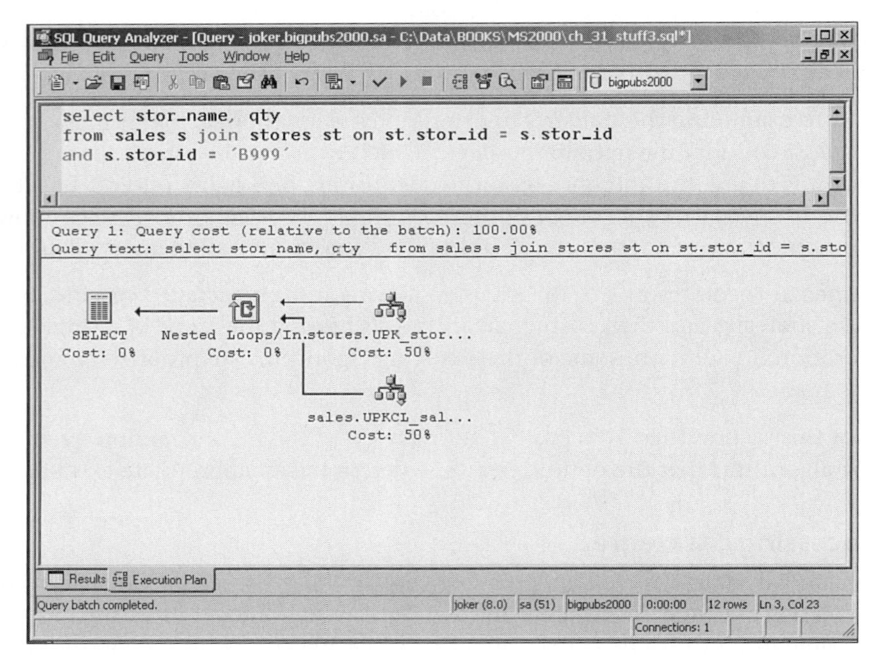

FIGURE 35.12 Execution plan for a nested loops join.

Note that in the graphical showplan, the outer loop is represented as the top input table and the inner loop is represented as the bottom input table. In most instances, the optimizer will choose the input table with the fewest number of qualifying rows to be the outer loop.

The nested loops join is efficient for queries that typically affect only a small number of rows. As the number of rows in the outer loop increases, the effectiveness of the nested loops join strategy diminishes. This is because of the increased number of logical I/Os required as the loops get larger.

The nested loop join is the easiest join strategy to estimate the cost for. The cost of the nested loop join is calculated as follows:

number of pages to read in outer input

+ number of matching rows × number of pages per lookup on inner input

= total logical I/O cost for query

Merge Join

The merge join algorithm is much more effective than the nested loops join when dealing with large data volumes. The merge join works by retrieving one row from each input and comparing them. Figure 35.13 illustrates a query that will use a merge join.

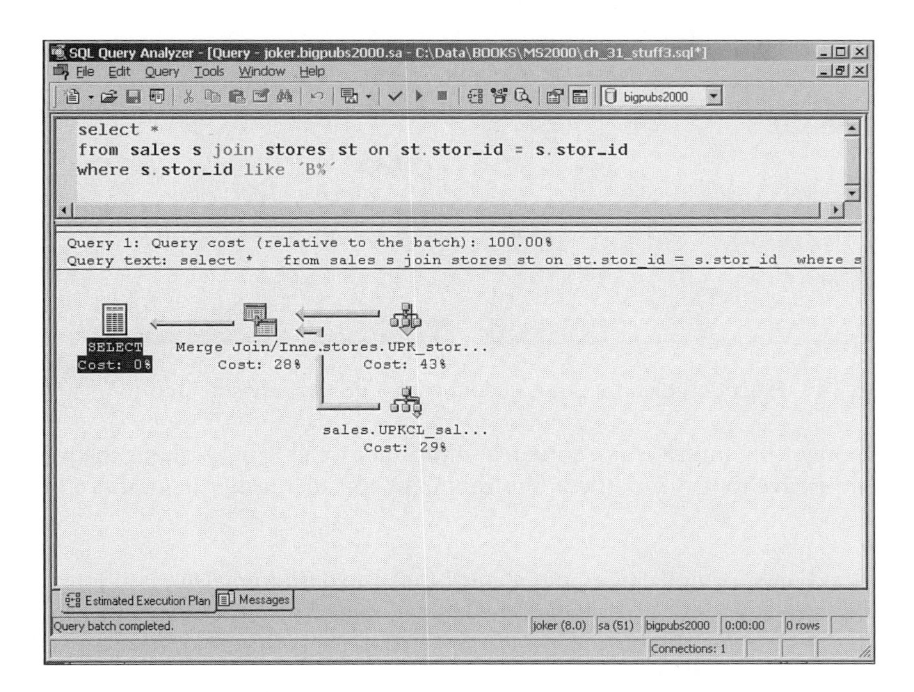

FIGURE 35.13 Execution plan for a merge join.

The merge join requires that both inputs be sorted on the merge columns. The merge join does not work if both inputs are not sorted. In the query shown in Figure 35.13, both tables have a clustered index on stor_id, so the merge column (stor_id) is already sorted for each table.

Usually, the optimizer will choose a merge join strategy, as it did in this example, when the data volume is large and both columns are contained in an existing presorted index, such as a primary key. If either of the inputs is not already sorted, the optimizer has to perform an explicit sort before the join. An example of a sort being performed before the merge join is performed is shown in Figure 35.14.

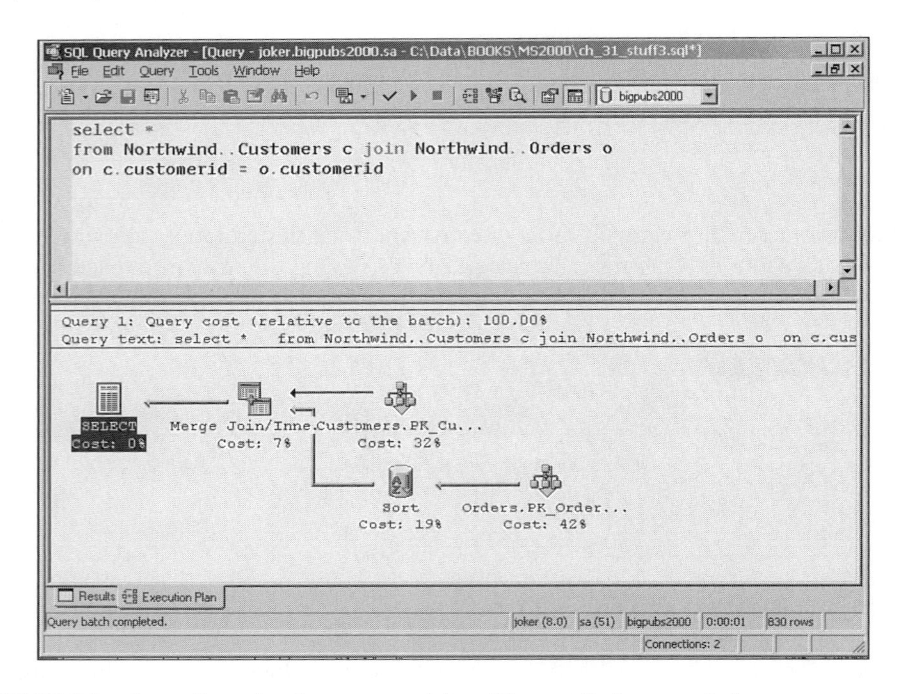

FIGURE 35.14 Execution plan for a merge join with a preliminary sort step.

If one or more of the inputs is not sorted, and the additional sorting causes the merge join to be too expensive to perform, the optimizer might consider using the hash join strategy.

Hash Join

The final—and most complicated—join algorithm is the hash join. The hash join is an effective join strategy for dealing with large data volumes where the inputs might not be sorted and when no useful indexes exist on your tables for performing the join. Figure 35.15 illustrates a query that uses a hash join.

The basic hash join algorithm involves separating the two inputs into a "build" input and a "probe" input. The optimizer will always attempt to assign the smaller input as the build input. The hash join scans the build input and creates a hash table. Each row from the build input is inserted into the hash table based on a hash key value, which is computed. The probe input is then scanned one row at a time. A hash key value is computed for each row in the probe, and the hash table is scanned for matches. The hash join is an effective join strategy when dealing with large data volumes and unsorted data inputs.

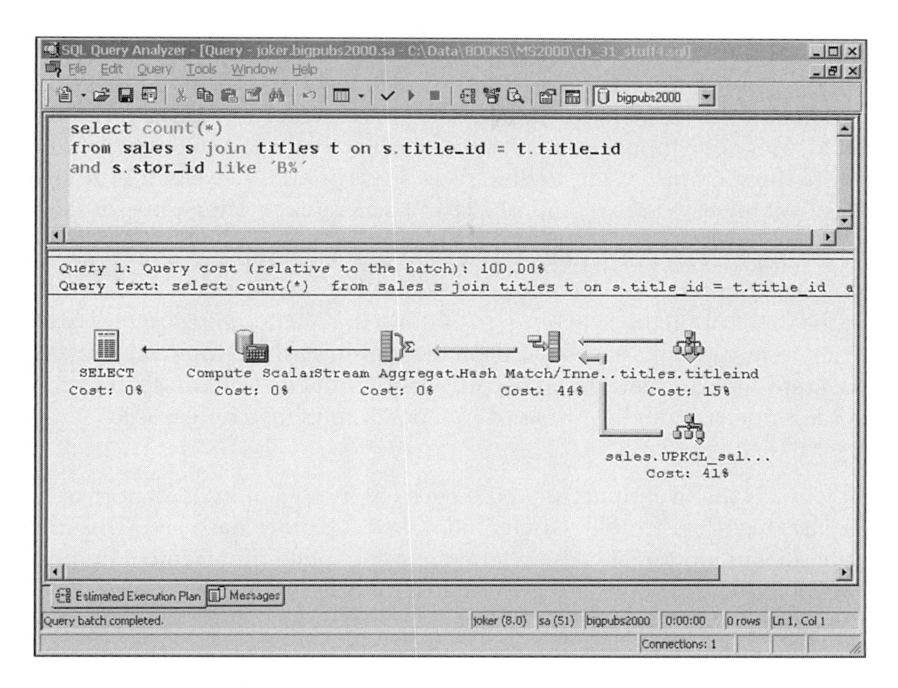

FIGURE 35.15 Execution plan for a hash join.

In a hash join, the keys that are common between the two tables are hashed into a hash bucket using the same hash function. This bucket will usually start out in memory and then move to disk as needed. The type of hashing that occurs depends on the amount of memory required. Hashing is commonly used for inner and outer joins, intersections, unions, and differences. The optimizer often uses hashing for intermediate processing.

Pseudocode for a simple hash join might look like this:

```
create an empty hash table
for each row in the input table
    read the row
    hash the key value
    insert the hashed key into the hash bucket
for each row in the larger table
    read the row
    hash the key value
    if hashed key value is found in the hash bucket
        output hash key and both row identifiers
drop the hash table
```

Although hashing is useful when no useful indexes are on the tables for a join, the query optimizer still might not choose it as the join strategy if it has a high cost in terms of memory required. If the entire hash table doesn't fit in memory, SQL Server has to split both the build and probe inputs into partitions, each containing a different set of hash keys, and write those partitions out to disk. As each partition is needed, it is brought into memory. This will increase the amount of I/O and general processing time for the query.

To use the hashing strategy efficiently, it is best if the smaller input is used as the build input. If, during execution, SQL Server discovers that the build input is actually larger than the probe input, it might switch the roles of the build and probe input midstream. The optimizer usually doesn't have a problem determining which input is smaller if the statistics are up-to-date on the columns involved in the query. Column-level statistics can help the optimzer determine the estimated number of rows matching a SARG, even if no actual index will be used.

Grace Hash Join If the two inputs are too large to fit into memory for a normal hash join, SQL Server might use a modified method, called the **grace hash join**. This method partitions the smaller input table (also referred to as the build input) into a number of buckets. The total number of buckets is calculated by determining the bucket size that will fit in memory and dividing it into the number of rows in the table. The larger table (also referred to as the **probe input**) is then also partitioned into the same number of buckets. Each bucket from each input can then be read into memory and the matches made. A hybrid join is a join method that uses elements of both a simple in-memory hash and a grace hash.

> **NOTE**
>
> Hash and merge join strategies can be applied only when the join is an equijoin; that is, when the join condition compares columns from two inputs with the equality (=) operator. If the join is not based on an equality, for example—using a `BETWEEN` clause, nested loop joins are the only strategy that can be employed.

Step 4: Execution Plan Selection

At this point in the query optimization process, the optimizer has examined the entire query and estimated the costs of all possible indexes to be used and of the various query-processing strategies. It now needs to choose which plan to pass on to SQL Server for execution.

For a single table query, choosing the best query plan involves choosing the index and query processing strategy that results in the fewest number of logical I/Os performed to process the query on that table.

For a multitable query, choosing the best plan involves not only determining the cheapest index and query processing strategy for each table individually, but also determining the best index strategy in conjunction with the optimal join strategy that results in the lowest estimated I/O time, as discussed in the previous section on join selection.

Additionally, if any `ORDER BY`, `GROUP BY`, or `DISTINCT` clauses are present, the optimizer chooses the most efficient method to process them.

For all its options, the overriding factor in selecting a plan is total I/O. The optimizer is committed to selecting a query plan that results in the least amount of I/O processing. After the plan is selected, it's passed to the SQL Server for execution.

NOTE

As you have seen in examples throughout this chapter, you can examine the query plan chosen by the optimizer with the graphical execution plan feature of Query Analyzer. You can also display a text representation of the execution plan by enabling the `SHOWPLAN_TEXT` option or the `STATISTICS PROFILE` option in a user session. How to interpret the output from these tools is covered in the next chapter, "Query Analysis," along with a discussion of other tools available for examining the query plan selection process.

You also have the capability to influence or override the query plan selection process using the methods discussed later in this chapter in the section, "Managing the Optimizer."

The optimizer can choose from many possible execution plans, especially when a large number of tables are involved in the query—and an even greater number of permutations of join strategies and index usage is possible. The number of permutations grows exponentially as the number of tables involved in the query grows. To manage the number of permutations without spending all its time optimizing queries rather than running them, the query optimizer might go through multiple optimization passes before choosing the execution plan to run. Each pass considers a larger set of the possible plans. On each pass, it keeps track of the best plan thus far and uses a cost estimate to reduce the search in succeeding passes.

Initally, SQL Server tries to determine if only one viable plan for a query exists. For simple queries, this can save the optimizer a lot of work. An example of a trivial query plan is a single table `SELECT` statement with a SARG on a unique key. Another example is an `INSERT` statement using a `VALUES` clause—there is only one way to insert this record. For both of these examples, the query plans are fairly obvious plans that are typically very inexpensive, so the optimizer generates the plan without trying to find something better. If the optimizer tried to consider every possible plan, the optimization cost could actually exceed the query processing time, outweighing any benefit provided by well-optimized queries.

If a trivial plan is not available, SQL Server will begin a more thorough optimization process. To avoid just running through all the possibilities that would cause the optimization process to take a long time, the optimization is broken up into phases. After each phase, SQL Server applies a set of rules to evaluate the cost of any resulting plan. If according to these rules, the plan is cheap enough, it chooses and submits that plan for execution. If according to the rules, no plan is still cheap enough, the optimizer continues on to the next phase, with its own set of rules to apply. In the vast majority of cases, SQL Server finds a good plan in the preliminary phases.

If the optimizer has gone through all the preliminary optimization phases and still hasn't found, according to the rules, what is considered to be a cheap plan, it determines the cost of the best plan it has thus far. If the cost of the best plan found is still above a particular threshold, and the system has more than one CPU available to SQL Server, the optimizer enters its full optimization phase that considers using parallel query processing strategies. You can configure this threshold using the `cost threshold for parallelism` configuration option. If the cost of the best plan found so far is still below the parallelism threshold, the full optimization phase continues using a brute-force method to find a serial plan, checking every possible combination of indexes and processing strategies.

Eventually, an execution plan is determined to be the most efficient. After this is determined, the execution plan is passed on to the SQL Server query processor to be executed.

Reusing Query Plans

In versions of SQL Server prior to SQL Server 7.0, only query plans for compiled objects, such as stored procedures and triggers, were kept in the procedure cache. Ad hoc query plans were immediately discarded. In SQL Server 7.0 and 2000, ad hoc query plans might remain in cache as well, if the cost to compile them is high and the query is reused frequently.

In SQL Server 2000, when SQL Server begins processing a query, it first determines if the query is an ad hoc query and if it is inexpensive to compile. If so, SQL Server doesn't bother caching the query plan in memory in order to avoid flooding the cache with query plans that probably won't be reused very often and that are cheaper simply to recompile if needed again. If an ad hoc query is not considered cheap to compile, SQL Server will allocate space in the buffer cache to store the query plan.

Plans are saved in cache along with a cost factor that reflects the cost of actually creating the plan by compiling the query. For ad hoc query plans, SQL Server sets its cost to 0, which indicates that the plan can be kicked out of the procedure cache immediately if space is needed for other plans. Until space is needed, the plan can remain in cache. When another query comes along, SQL Server checks the procedure cache to see if a query plan exists that it can reuse. If an ad hoc plan exists in memory and the query can reuse that plan, SQL Server will increment the query plan cost factor by 1. This allows ad hoc query plans that are constantly being reused to remain in the cache for a little while longer; as their cost factor increases, they are not first in the list to be removed from cache when space is needed. If the plan is reused often, for example, if the same user or other users keep resubmitting the same SQL query, the query plan will likely remain in cache.

This feature can help improve performance for complex queries that are executed frequently, because SQL Server can avoid having to compile a query plan every time it's executed if the query plan is found in memory first.

Multiple Plans in Cache

SQL Server will reuse existing query plans in cache whenever possible. Because plans are re-entrant, the same query plan can be used by multiple connections at the same time, reducing the amount of memory needed to cache the reusable query plans. However, some situations will result in multiple query plans for the same query or procedure to reside in cache. The most common cause is differences in certain SET options, database options, or configuration options that affect the way queries are processed. For example, a query might optimize differently for one session if the ANSI_NULLS option is turned on than it would for a session where it is turned off. The following list of SET options must match for a query plan to be reused by a session:

- ANSI_PADDING
- FORCEPLAN
- CONCAT_NULL_YIELDS_NULL
- ANSI_WARNINGS
- ANSI_NULLS
- QUOTED_IDENTIFIER
- ANSI_NULL_DFLT_ON
- ANSI_NULL_DFLT_OFF

If any one of these setting values does not match with the setting options for a cached plan, the session will generate a new query plan. Likewise, if the session is using a different language or DATEFORMAT setting than a cached plan, it will need to generate a new one.

Another issue that can affect whether a query plan can be reused is whether the table and view names in a query are fully qualified with a username. If the owner name must be resolved implicitly, then a plan cannot be reused. This is because a different table might be referenced based on the current user context. For example, if the user tom executes the following query

```
select * from titles
```

then SQL Server will first try to resolve the titles table reference by determining if the current user owns a table named titles. If no table named titles is owned by the current user, then SQL Server will look for a titles table owned by the dbo user ID. If one user owns a table called titles, his query plan will be resolved differently from a user who does not own a titles table. Because of this ambiguity, the query plan for this query cannot be reused. To avoid this ambiguity and increase the likelihood of the query being reused, fully qualify the table owner, as in the following:

```
select * from dbo.titles
```

Examining the Plan Cache

You can view the query plans currently in memory by executing a query against the syscacheobjects table. This table is actually a pseudotable that resides only in the master database. As a pseudotable, it takes up no space on disk and is materialized in memory only when a query is executed against it. Table 35.1 describes some of the more useful columns in the syscacheobjects table.

TABLE 35.1 Description of Useful Columns in the syscacheobjects Table

Column Name	Description
bucketid	The internal hash key for this plan in an internal hash table in cache, which helps SQL Server locate the plan more quickly.
cacheobjtype	The type of plan in cache.
objtype	The type of object or query for which the plan is cached.
objid	One of the main keys used for looking up a plan in the cache. This is the object ID stored in sysobjects for database objects (procedures, views, triggers, and so on). For cache objects such as ad hoc or prepared SQL, objid is an internally generated value.
dbid	The ID of the database in which the cached plan was compiled.
uid	The user ID of the creator of the plan (for ad hoc query plans and prepared plans).
refcounts	The number of other cached objects that reference this cached plan (if refcount is 1, it is the base object).
usecounts	The number of times this cached plan has been used since it was initially cached.
pagesused	The number of memory pages required to store the cached plan in cache memory.
setopts	A bitmap representing the SET option settings that affect a compiled plan. This is compared with the current session settings to determine if the plan can be reused.
langid	The ID of the language in effect for the session that created the cached plan. This is compared with the current session settings to determine if the plan can be reused.

TABLE 35.1 Continued

Column Name	Description
dateformat	The date format in effect for the session that created the cached plan. This is compared with the current session settings to determine if the plan can be reused.
sql	The name of the stored procedure or the first 128 characters of the batch submitted that generated the cached plan.

The types of plans stored in the `cacheobjtype` can be one of the following:

- `Compiled Plan`—The actual compiled plan generated that can be shared by sessions running the same procedure or query if the `setopts`, `langid`, and `dateformat` values match.
- `Executable Plan`—The actual execution plan and the environment settings for the session that ran the compiled plan. Caching the environment settings for an execution plan makes subsequent executions more efficient. Each concurrent execution of the same compiled plan will have its own executable plan. All executable plans will be associated with a compiled plan having the same `bucketid`, but not all compiled plans have an associated executable plan.
- `Parse Tree`—The internal parsed form of a query generated before compilation and optimization.
- `Cursor Parse Tree`—The parse tree generated for a cursor query.
- `Extended Proc`—The cached information for an extended stored procedure.

The type of object or query for which a plan is cached is stored in the `objtype` column. This column can contain one of the following values:

- `Proc`—The cached plan is for a stored procedure or inline function.
- `Prepared`—The cached plan is for queries submitted using `sp_executesql` or for queries using the prepare and execute method.
- `Ad hoc query`—The cached plan is for queries that don't fall into any other category.
- `ReplProc`—The cached plan is for replication agents.
- `Trigger`—The cached plan is for a trigger.
- `View`—The cached plan is for a view or a non-inline function. You typically will only see a parse tree for a view or non-inline function, not a compiled plan. The view or function typically does not have its own separate plan because it is expanded as part of another query.

- `Table`—The cached plan is for a user or system table that has computed columns. This will typically be only a parse tree.
- `Default`, `Check`, or `Rule`—The cached plan is simply a parse tree for these types of objects because they are expanded as part of another query in which they are applied.

To determine if plans are being reused, you can examine the `usecounts` columns. The `usecounts` value is incremented each time the cached plan is looked up and reused.

TIP

If SQL Server has been running for a while with a lot of activity, the number of rows in the `syscacheobjects` table can become quite large. If you want to run your own tests to determine which queries get cached and when query plans are reused, you will want to clear out the cache occasionally. You can use the `DBCC FREEPROCCACHE` command to clear all cached plans from memory. If you want to clear only the cached plans for objects or queries in a specific database, execute the following command:

```
DBCC FLUSHPROCINDB (dbid)
```

You should not execute these commands in your production servers because that could impact the performance of the currently running applications.

Other Query Processing Strategies

In addition to the optimization strategies covered so far, SQL Server also has some additional strategies it can apply for special types of queries. These strategies are employed to help further reduce the cost of executing various types of queries.

Predicate Transitivity

You might be familiar with the transitive property from algebra. The transitive property simply states that if A=B and B=C then A=C. SQL Server supports the transitive property in its query predicates. Predicate transitivity enables SQL Server to infer a join equality from two given equalities. Consider the following example:

```
SELECT *
   FROM table1 t1
   join table2 t2 on t1.column1 = t2.column1
   join table3 t3 on t2.column1 = t3.column1
```

Using the principle of predicate transitivity, SQL Server is able to infer that `t1.column1` is also equal to `t3.column1`. This provides the optimizer with another join strategy to consider when optimizing this query. This might result in a much cheaper execution plan.

The transitive property can also be applied to SARGs used on join columns. Consider the following query:

```
select *
   from sales s
   join stores st on s.stor_id = st.stor_id
   and s.stor_id = 'B199'
```

Again, using transitive closure, we know that `st.stor_id` is also equal to `'B199'`. SQL Server will also recognize this and be able to apply the constant against the indexes on both tables to more accurately estimate the number of matching rows from each table.

GROUP BY Optimization

Prior to SQL Server 7.0, GROUP BY was always processed in one way—SQL Server retrieved the data matching the SARGs into a worktable where the rows were sorted and the groups formed. In SQL Server 2000, the query optimizer might choose to use hashing to organize the data into groups and then compute the aggregates.

The hash aggregation strategy uses the same basic method for grouping and calculating aggregates as for a hash join. At the point where the probe input row is checked to determine whether it already exists in the hash bucket, the aggregate is computed if a hash match is found. The following pseudocode summarizes the hash aggregation strategy:

```
create a hash table
for each row in the input table
    read the row
    hash the key value
    search the hash table for matches
    if match found
        aggregate the value into the old record
    else
        insert the hashed key into the hash bucket
scan and output the hash table contents
drop the hash table
```

For some join queries that contain a GROUP BY clause, SQL Server might perform the grouping operation before processing the join. This could reduce the size of the input table to the join and lower the overall cost of executing the query.

NOTE

One important point to keep in mind with both of these special strategies is that the rows might not come back in sorted order by the grouping column(s) as they did in earlier releases. If the results must be returned in a specific sort order, you will need to use the ORDER BY clause with the GROUP BY to ensure ordered results. You might want to get into the habit of doing this regularly.

If the compatibility level for a database is set to 60 or 65, SQL Server will automatically include an ORDER BY in a GROUP BY query to order the results because they would be older SQL Server versions.

Queries with DISTINCT

Similar to GROUP BY queries, in versions of SQL Server prior to 7.0, the resultset had to be generated first and then sorted in a worktable to remove duplicates. In SQL Server 2000, the optimizer can employ a hashing strategy similar to that used with GROUP BY to return only the distinct rows before the final resultset is determined.

Queries with UNION

When you specify a UNION in a query, SQL Server merges the resultsets, applying one of the merge or concatenation strings with sorting strategies to remove any duplicate rows. Figure 35.16 shows an example very similar to the OR strategy where the rows are concatenated and then sorted to remove any duplicates.

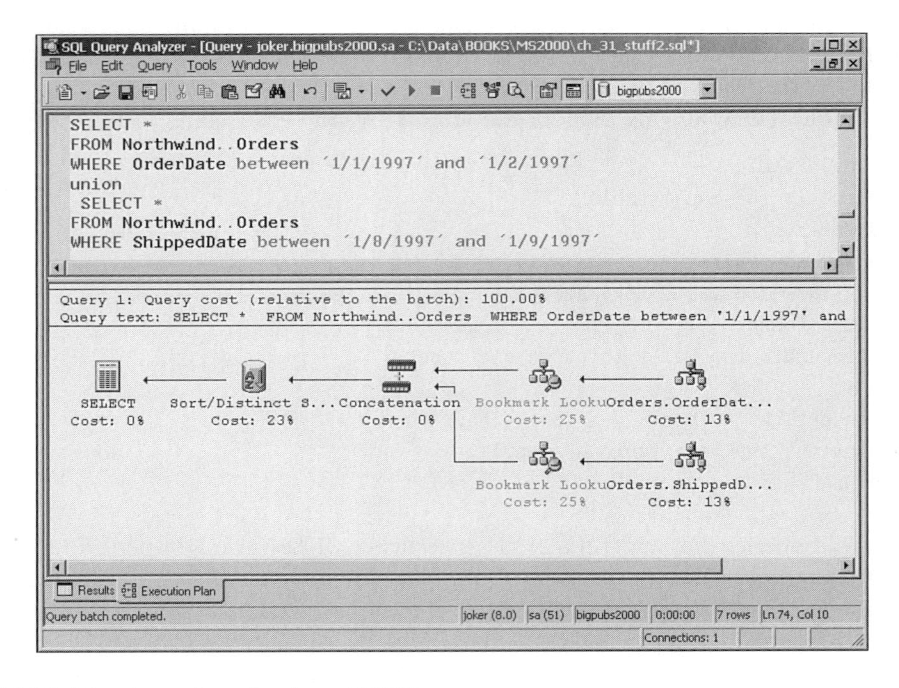

FIGURE 35.16 Execution plan for a UNION.

If you specify UNION ALL in your query, SQL Server simply appends the resultsets together. No intermediate sorting or merge step is needed to remove duplicates. Figure 35.17 shows the same query as in Figure 35.16, except that a UNION ALL is specified.

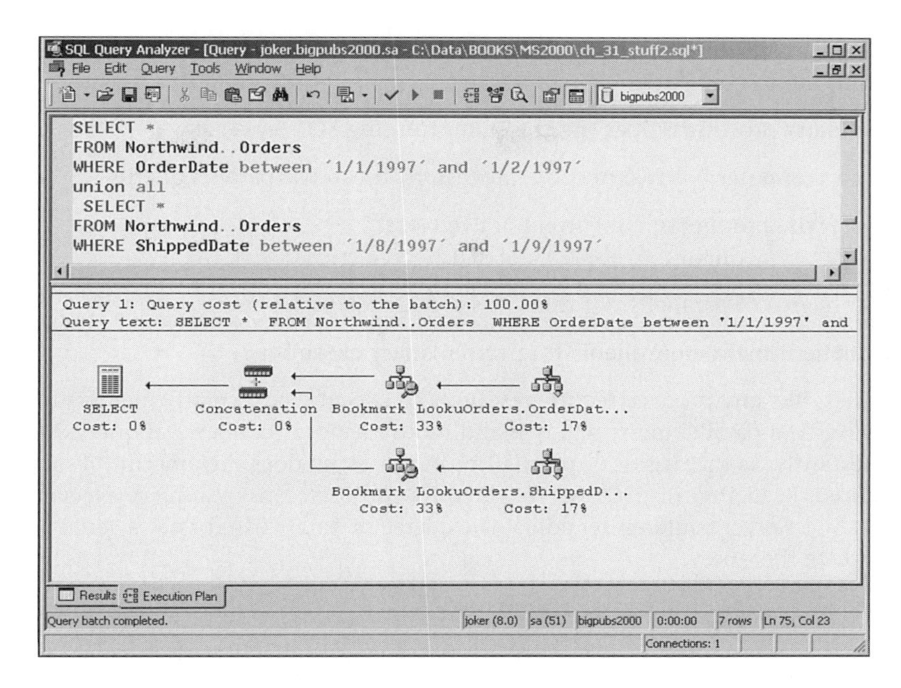

FIGURE 35.17 Execution plan for a `UNION ALL`.

When you know that you do not need to worry about duplicate rows in a `UNION` resultset, always specify `UNION ALL` to eliminate the extra overhead required for sorting.

Parallel Query Processing

The query processor in SQL Server 7.0 and 2000 includes parallel query processing—a new execution strategy that can improve the performance of complex queries on computers with more than one processor.

SQL Server inserts exchange operators into each parallel query to build and manage the query execution plan. The exchange operator is responsible for providing process management, data redistribution, and flow control. It is possible that a parallel query execution plan can use more than one thread, whereas a serial execution plan, used by a nonparallel query, uses only a single thread for its execution. Prior to query execution time, SQL Server determines whether the current system state and configuration allow for parallel query execution. If parallel query execution is justified, SQL Server determines the optimal number of threads, called the degree of parallelism, and distributes the query workload execution across those threads. The parallel query uses the same number of threads until the query completes. SQL Server re-examines the optimal degree of parallelism each time a query execution plan is retrieved from the procedure cache. Individual instances of the same query could be assigned a different degree of parallelism.

SQL Server calculates the degree of parallelism for each instance of a parallel query execution using the following criteria:

- How many processors does the computer running SQL Server have?

  If your computer has two or more processors, it can use parallel queries.

- What is the number of concurrent active users?

  The degree of parallelism is inversely related to CPU usage. SQL Server assigns a lower degree of parallelism if the CPUs are already busy.

- Is sufficient memory available for parallel query execution?

  Queries, like any process, require resources to execute, particularly memory. Obviously, a parallel query will demand more memory than a serial query. More importantly, as the degree of parallelism increases, so does the amount of memory required. Realizing this, SQL Server carefully considers this in a query execution plan. SQL Server could either adjust the degree of parallelism or use a serial plan to complete the query.

- What is the type of query being executed?

  Queries that use several CPU cycles justify using a parallel execution plan. Some examples are joins of large tables, substantial aggregations, and sorting large resultsets. SQL Server determines whether to use a parallel or serial plan by checking the value of the cost threshold for parallelism.

- Are a sufficient number of rows processed in the given stream?

  If the optimizer determines that the number of rows in a stream is too low, it does not execute a parallel plan. This prevents scenarios where the costs exceed the benefits of executing a parallel plan.

Two server configuration options—the maximum degree of parallelism and cost threshold for parallelism—affect the consideration for a parallel query. Although it is not recommended, you can change the default settings for each.

The `maximum degree of parallelism` option limits the number of threads to use in a parallel plan execution. The range of possible values is 0 to 32. This value is automatically configured to `0`, which uses the actual number of CPUs. If you want to suppress parallel processing, set the value to `1`.

You can affect the query optimizer's choice to use a parallel execution plan by changing the values for the `maximum degree of parallelism` and the cost threshold for parallelism server configuration options using either the `sp_configure` system stored procedure or the Enterprise Manager program. It is strongly recommended that you do not change this value on symmetric multiprocessor (SMP) computers. For single processor machines, these values are ignored.

To set the maximum degree of parallelism option, you can use the following:

- The sp_configure system stored procedure

```
USE master
sp_configure 'show advanced options', 1
GO
RECONFIGURE
GO
sp_configure 'max degree of parallelism', 1
GO
RECONFIGURE
GO
```

- The Enterprise Manager

1. Right-click a server, and then click Properties.
2. Click the Processor tab. The Processor settings dialog box appears (see Figure 35.18).

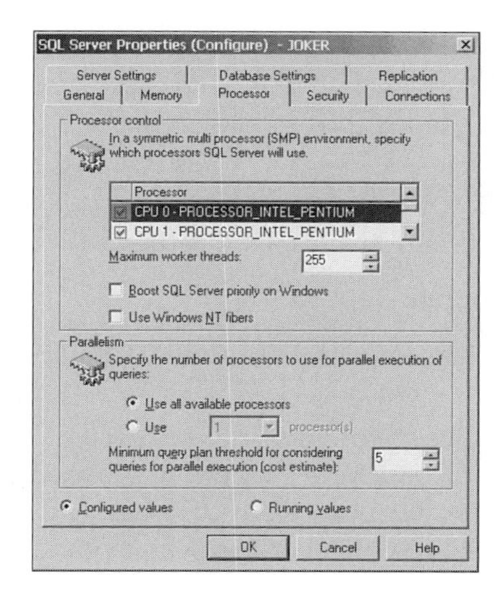

FIGURE 35.18 SQL Server Properties—the Processor settings tab.

3. Under Parallelism, select the number of processors to execute queries in parallel.

The `cost threshold for parallelism` option establishes a ceiling value the query optimizer uses to consider parallel query execution plans. If the calculated value to execute a serial plan is greater than the value set for the cost threshold for parallelism, a parallel plan is generated. This value is defined by the estimated time in seconds to execute the serial plan. The range of values for this setting is 0 to 32767. The default value is `5`. If the maximum degree of parallelism is set to `1`, or the computer has a single processor, the cost threshold for parallelism value is ignored.

You can configure this option using either the `sp_configure` system stored procedure or the Enterprise Manager:

- The `sp_configure` system stored procedure

```
USE master
sp_configure 'show advanced options', 1
GO
RECONFIGURE
GO
sp_configure 'cost threshold for parallelism', 15
GO
RECONFIGURE
GO
```

- The Enterprise Manager

  1. Expand a server group.
  2. Right-click a server, and then click Properties.
  3. Click the Processor tab.
  4. In the Parallelism box, enter a value from 0 through 32,627.

You can identify when a parallel execution plan is being chosen using the SQL Server Query Analyzer. Two formats are available for viewing the execution plan: graphical and tabular. The graphical execution plan uses icons to represent the execution of specific statements and queries in SQL Server. The tabular representation is produced by the `SET SHOWPLAN_ALL` or `SET SHOWPLAN_TEXT` statements. The showplan output for every parallel query will have at least one of these three logical operators:

- Distribute Streams—Receives a single input stream of records and distributes multiple output streams. The contents and form of the record are unchanged. All records enter through the same single input stream and appear in one of the output streams, preserving the relative order.
- Gather Streams—Assembles multiple input streams of records and yields a single output stream. The relative order of the records, contents, and form are maintained.

- Repartition Streams—Accepts multiple input streams and produces multiple streams of records. The record contents and format are unchanged.

Figure 35.19 provides an example of a query plan using parallel query techniques—both repartition streams and gather streams.

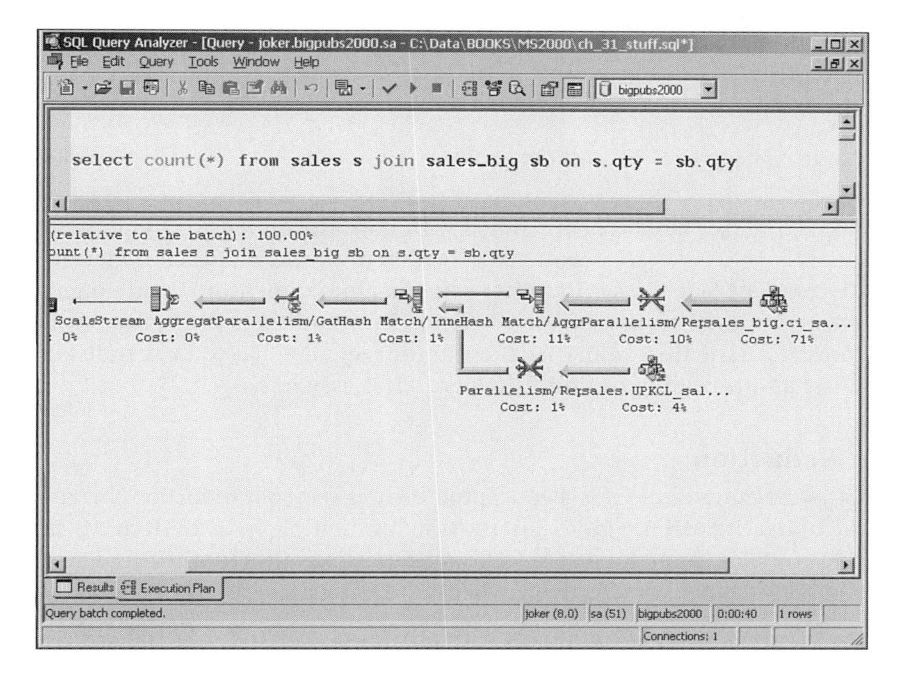

FIGURE 35.19 Graphical execution plan of a query using parallel query techniques.

Data Warehousing and Large Database Query Strategies

In a data warehousing environment, your data is more than likely contained in a star or snowflake schema. These schemas are characterized by having a few fact tables with many rows that contain your detailed transactional data. Several smaller dimension tables might exist that are related to the fact table via foreign keys. The dimension tables often have few rows.

SQL Server has introduced several optimizer enhancements to improve query performance in a star or snowflake schema environment.

Cartesian Product of Dimension Tables

One way in which the SQL Server query optimizer has been enhanced is to support performing a cross join on dimension tables (creating a Cartesian product) before joining to the fact table. This means that the fact table has to participate in fewer joins, which will reduce the overall cost of the operation. This might sound strange, but it makes sense.

Consider the following example:

```
SELECT count(*)
   FROM fact f, dimension1 d1, dinension2 d2
   WHERE f.key1 = d1.key1
   AND f.key2 = d2.key2
```

In this example, the fact table is being joined with both the dimension1 and dimension2 tables. Assume that the fact table contains 1,000,000 rows and that each dimension table contains 10 rows. The SQL Server optimizer will cross join dimension1 and dimension2 first. This creates a Cartesian product of 100 rows. This resultset is then joined with the fact table to produce the final result. As a result, the fact table has to be scanned only once. The logic and reasoning behind this approach is easy to see.

Semijoin Reduction

Another optimizer enhancement is a concept known as **semijoin reduction**. In this scenario, the optimizer will use index intersection on multiple indexes from the fact table. The fact table contains many foreign keys. If indexes exist on each of the foreign keys, SQL Server uses those indexes effectively when processing a query.

The optimizer joins each dimension table with an appropriate index of the fact table. Next, the optimizer intersects the results of those joins. Finally, the optimizer fetches rows from the fact table. By doing this, the optimizer avoids performing any full row fetch of the fact table until it is absolutely necessary.

Common Query Optimization Problems

So you've written the query and examined the query plan, and performance isn't what you expected. It might appear that SQL Server isn't choosing the appropriate query plan that you expect. Is something wrong with the query or with the optimizer? Before we delve into a detailed discussion about how to debug and analyze query plans (covered in detail in the next chapter), this section takes a look at some of the more common problems and SQL-coding issues that can lead to poor query plan selection.

Out-of-Date or Unavailable Statistics

Admittedly, this is not as big a problem as it was in SQL Server releases prior to 7.0. Back in those days, the first question asked when someone was complaining of poor performance was, "When did you last update statistics?" If the answer was "Huh?" we usually found the culprit.

With the Statistics Auto-Update and Auto-Create features in SQL Server 2000, this problem is not as prevalent as it used to be. If a query detects that statistics are out of date or missing, it will cause them to be updated or created and then optimize the query plan based on the new statistics.

NOTE

If statistics are missing or out of date, the first query to run that detects this condition might run a bit more slowly as it updates or creates the statistics first, especially if the table is relatively large, and also if it has been configured for `FULLSCAN` when indexes are updated.

However, do not assume that you always have up-to-date statistics. One suggestion floating around the newsgroups is that having these options on degrades performance in online transaction processing (OLTP) environments, and many DBAs are disabling these options and running update statistics periodically via scheduled jobs (or at least you hope they are). I don't recommend turning these options off arbitrarily; use SQL Profiler or the trace flags described in Chapter 34 to confirm that these options are causing a performance problem before turning them off and doing performance testing to see if performance improves. AutoStats was implemented to ensure that you have up-to-date statistics all the time and does serve a useful purpose.

Another case where you could have bad statistics is if the sample used when the statistics were generated wasn't large enough. Depending on the nature of your data and the size of the table, the statistics might not accurately reflect the actual data distribution and cardinality. If you suspect this is the case, update statistics specifying the `FULLSCAN` option or a larger sample size so it examines more records to derive the statistics.

Poor Index Design

Poor index design is another reason—often a primary reason—why your queries might not optimize as you expect them to. If no supporting indexes exist for the query, or the query contains non-optimizable SARGs that can't use any available indexes, SQL Server will end up either performing a table scan, an index scan, or another hash or merge join strategy that is less efficient. If this appears to be the problem, you need to re-evaluate your indexing decisions or rewrite the query so it can take advantage of an available index. For more information on designing useful indexes, see Chapter 34.

Search Argument Problems

It's the curse of SQL that there are a number of different ways to write a query and get the same resultset. Some queries, however, might not be as efficient as others. A good understanding of the query optimizer can help you avoid writing search arguments that SQL Server can't optimize effectively. This section highlights some of the common "gotchas" encountered in SQL Server SARGs that can lead to poor or unexpected query performance.

Using NonSARGable Expressions

As mentioned previously in the section "Identifying Search Arguments," the query optimizer uses search arguments to help it narrow down the set of rows to evaluate. The search argument is in the form of a `WHERE` clause that equates a column to a constant, as shown in the following example:

```
SELECT column1
   FROM table1
   WHERE column1 = 123
```

The query optimizer can use the search argument to examine an index to find the qualifying rows, avoiding having to perform a full table scan. The following is an example of a nonSARGable expression to watch out for, as it cannot be optimized with an index:

```
SELECT column1
   FROM table1
   WHERE column1 / 10 = 123
```

No SARGs

Watch out for queries in which the SARG might have been left out inadvertently, such as this:

```
select title_id from titles
```

A SQL query with no search argument (that is, no `WHERE` clause) always performs a table scan unless a nonclustered index can be used to cover the query (see Chapter 34 for a discussion of index covering). If you don't want the query to affect the entire table, be sure to specify a valid SARG that matches an index on the table to avoid table scans.

Negative Logic

Any **negative logic** (for example, `!=`, `<>`, `not in`) nearly always results in a table scan being performed, unless index covering can be applied (that is, all columns and information referenced in the query can be found within the leaf level of a nonclustered index).

Operations on a Column in `WHERE` Clauses

Any operation on the column side of a `WHERE` clause causes it to be treated as a nonSARGable expression by SQL Server. Therefore, the optimizer can't match the SARG with an index; typically, a table scan will be performed to satisfy the query unless an index covers the query.

Unknown Values in `WHERE` Clauses

Watch out for expressions where the value cannot be known until runtime. These are expressions that contain local variables or subqueries that can be materialized to a single value. The SQL Server treats these expressions as SARGs but can't use the statistics histogram to estimate the number of matching rows because it doesn't have a value to compare against the histogram values during query optimization. The values for the expressions won't be known until the query is actually executed. What the optimizer does in this situation is use the **index density** information. The optimizer generally is able to better estimate the number of rows affected by a query when it can compare a known value against the statistics histogram than when it has to use the index density to estimate the average number of rows that match an unknown value. This is especially true if the data in a table isn't distributed evenly. When you can, try to avoid using constant expressions that can't be evaluated until runtime, so that the statistics histogram can be used rather than the density value.

To avoid using constant expressions that can't be evaluated until runtime in `WHERE` clauses, consider putting the queries into stored procedures and passing in the constant expression as a parameter. Because the optimizer evaluates the value of a parameter prior to optimization, SQL Server evaluates the expression prior to optimizing the stored procedure.

So for best results when writing queries inside stored procedures, use stored procedure parameters rather than local variables in your SARGs whenever possible. This strategy allows the optimizer to optimize the query by using the statistics histogram, comparing the parameter value against the statistics histogram to estimate the number of matching rows. If you use local variables as SARGs in stored procedures, the optimizer is restricted to using index density, even if the local variable is assigned the value of a parameter.

Datatype Mismatches

Another common problem is datatype mismatches. If you attempt to join tables on columns of different datatypes, the query optimizer might not be able to effectively use indexes to compute the join. This can result in a less-efficient join strategy because the SQL Server will have to convert all values first before it can process the query. Avoid this situation by maintaining datatype consistency across your join key columns in your database.

Triggers

If you are using triggers on `INSERT`, `UPDATE`, or `DELETE`, it is possible that your triggers can cause performance problems. You might think that the `INSERT`, `UPDATE`, or `DELETE` is performing poorly when actually it is the trigger that needs to be tuned. Additionally, you might have triggers that fire other triggers. If you suspect you are having performance problems with the triggers, you can monitor the SQL they are executing and the response time, as well as execution plans generated for statements within triggers using SQL Profiler. For more information on monitoring performance with SQL Profiler, see Chapter 7, "Using the SQL Server Profiler."

Managing the Optimizer

Because the optimizer might sometimes make poor decisions as to how to best process a query, you need to know how and when to override the optimizer and force SQL Server to process a query in a specific manner.

How often does SQL Server require manual intervention to execute a query optimally? Considering the overwhelming number of query types and circumstances in which those queries are run, SQL Server does a surprisingly effective job of query optimization in most instances. For all but the most grueling, complex query operations, my own testing and experience has shown that SQL Server's optimizer is quite clever—and very, very good at wringing the best performance out of any hardware platform. For this reason, you should treat the material covered in this chapter as a collection of techniques to be used only where other methods of getting optimal query performance have already failed.

Before indiscriminately applying the techniques discussed in this section, remember one very important point: Use of these features can effectively hide serious fundamental design or coding flaws in your database, application, or queries. In fact, if you're tempted to use these features (with a few more moderate exceptions), it should serve as an indicator that problems might lie elsewhere in your application.

If you are satisfied that no such flaws exist and that SQL Server is choosing the wrong plan to optimize your query, you can use the methods discussed in this section to override two of the three most important decisions the optimizer makes:

- Choosing which index, if any, to resolve the query
- Choosing the join strategy to apply in a multitable query

The other decision made by the optimizer is the locking strategy to apply. Using table hints to override locking strategies is discussed in Chapter 38, "Locking and Performance."

Throughout this section, one point must remain clear in the reader's mind: These options should be used only in *exception cases* to cope with specific optimization problems in specific queries in specific applications. As such, there are no standard or global rules to follow because the application of these features by definition means that normal SQL Server behavior isn't taking place.

The practical result of this idea is that you should test every option in *your* environment, with *your* data and *your* queries, and use the techniques and methods discussed in this chapter and the other performance-related chapters to optimize and fine-tune the performance of your queries. The fastest-performing query wins, so don't be afraid to experiment with different options—but don't think that these statements and features are globally applicable or fit general categories of problems, either! There are, in fact, only three rules: *test*, *test*, and *test*!

TIP

Personally, I make it a rule to use optimizer and table hints only as a last resort when all other methods to get the optimizer to generate a more efficient query plan have failed. I always try to find other ways to rewrite the queries to encourage the optimizer to choose a better plan. This includes adding additional SARGs, substituting unknown values for known values in SARGS or trying to replace unknown values with known values, breaking up queries, converting subqueries to joins or joins to subqueries, and so on. Essentially, I'll try other variations on the query to get the same result in a different way and try to see if one of the variations ends up using the more efficient query plan that I expect it to.

In reality, about the only time I use these hints is when I'm testing the performance of a query and I want to see if the optimizer is actually choosing the best execution plan. You can enable the various query analysis options, such as `STATISTICS PROFILE` and `STATISTICS IO`, and then see how the query plan and statistics change as you apply various hints to the query. Examine the output to determine whether the IO cost improves or gets worse if you force one index over another, or if you force a specific join strategy or join order.

The problem with hard-coding table and optimizer hints into your application queries is that the hints prevent the optimizer from modifying the query plan as the data in your tables changes over time. Also, if subsequent service packs or releases of SQL Server incorporate improved optimization algorithms or strategies, the queries with hard-coded hints will not be able to take advantage of them.

If you find that you must incorporate any of these hints to solve query performance problems, be sure to document which queries and stored procedures contain optimizer and table hints. Periodically, go back and test the queries to determine whether the hints are still appropriate. You might find that over time, as the data values in the table have changed, the query plan generated because of the hints is no longer the most efficient query plan, and the optimizer now generates a more efficient query plan on its own.

Optimizer Hints

You can specify three types of hints in a query to override the decisions made by the optimizer:

- Table hints
- Join hints
- Query hints

The remainder of this section will examine and describe each type of table hints.

Forcing Index Selection with Table Hints

In addition to locking hints that can be specified for each table in a query, SQL Server 2000 allows you to provide table-level hints that enable you to specify the index SQL Server should use for accessing the table. The syntax for specifying an index hint is as follows:

```
SELECT column_list FROM talename WITH (INDEX (indid | index_name [, ...]) )
```

The old style syntax `INDEX = index_name` is still supported for backward compatibility only.

The new syntax, introduced in SQL Server 7.0, allows you to specify multiple indexes. You can specify the index by name or by ID. It is recommended that you specify indexes by name as the IDs for nonclustered indexes could change if they are dropped and re-created in a different order than they were originally. Specify an index ID of 0 to force a table scan.

When you specify multiple indexes in the hint list, all the indexes listed are used to retrieve the rows from the table, forcing an index intersection or index covering via an index join. If the collection of indexes listed does not cover the query, a regular row fetch is performed after retrieving all the indexed columns.

To get a list of indexes on a table, you can use `sp_helpindex`. However, the stored procedure doesn't display the index ID. To get a list of all user-defined tables and the names of the indexes defined on them, you can execute a query against the `sysindexes` table similar to the following, which was run in the `pubs` database:

```
select 'Table name' = object_name(id), 'Index name' = name, 'Index ID' = indid
   from sysindexes where id > 99 /* only system tables have id less than 99 */
   and indid between 1 and 254   /* do not include rows for text columns
                                    or tables without a clustered index*/
    /* do not include auto statistics */
    and indexproperty(id, name, 'IsAutoStatistics') = 0
    order by 1, 3

Table name                     Index name                     Index ID
------------------------------ ------------------------------ --------
authors                        UPKCL_auidind                         1
authors                        aunmind                               2
Clustered_Dupes                Cl_dupes_col1                         1
clustered_nodupes              idxCL                                 1
dtproperties                   pk_dtproperties                       1
employee                       employee_ind                          1
employee                       PK_emp_id                             2
employee                       emp_tel_idx                           3
jobs                           PK__jobs__117F9D94                    1
nc_heap_nodupes                idxNC_heap                            2
pub_info                       UPKCL_pubinfo                         1
publishers                     UPKCL_pubind                          1
recomp_tab                     idx1                                  2
recomp_tab                     idx2                                  3
roysched                       titleidind                            2
sales                          UPKCL_sales                           1
sales                          titleidind                            2
stores                         UPK_storeid                           1
titleauthor                    UPKCL_taind                           1
titleauthor                    auidind                               2
```

```
titleauthor                  titleidind                  3
titles                       UPKCL_titleidind            1
titles                       titleind                    2
```

An index ID of 1 is for the clustered index, and index IDs 2–254 are the nonclustered indexes. An index ID of 0 indicates a table with no clustered index, and an index ID of 255 is used if the table has any text or image columns. Remember that every table will have either a 0 or a 1—but not both. After you have the index names and IDs, you can use them to specify the index to be used by the query.

SQL Server also supports, for backward compatibility, the `FASTFIRSTROW` option as a table hint. This has been replaced with the `FAST n` query processing hint, described in the "Specifying Query Processing Hints" section later in this chapter.

Forcing Join Strategies with Join Hints

Join hints let you force the type of join that should be used between two tables. The join hints correspond with the three types of join strategies, as follows:

- `LOOP`
- `MERGE`
- `HASH`

Join hints can be specified only when you use the ANSI-style join syntax—that is, when you actually use the keyword `JOIN` in the query. The hint is specified between the type of join and the keyword `JOIN`, which means you can't leave out the keyword `INNER` for an inner join (if you are doing an outer join, the `OUTER` keyword always has to be specified). Thus, the syntax for the `FROM` clause when using join hints is as follows:

```
FROM table1 {INNER | OUTER} [LOOP | MERGE | HASH} JOIN table2
```

The following is an example of forcing SQL Server to use a hash join:

```
select st.stor_name, ord_date, qty
   from stores st INNER HASH JOIN sales s on st.stor_id = s.stor_id
   where st.stor_id between 'B100' and 'B599'
```

Specifying Query Processing Hints

SQL Server 2000 enables you to specify additional query hints to control how your queries are optimized and processed. Query hints are specified at the very end of your query using the `OPTION` keyword. There can be only one `OPTION` clause per query, but you can specify multiple hints in an `OPTION` clause, as shown in the following syntax:

```
OPTION (hint1 [, ...hintn])
```

Query hints are grouped into three categories: `GROUP BY`, `UNION`, and miscellaneous.

GROUP BY Hints The GROUP BY hints specify how GROUP BY or COMPUTE operations should be performed. The GROUP BY hints that can be specified are as follows:

- HASH GROUP—This option forces the optimizer to use a hashing function to perform the GROUP BY operation.
- ORDER GROUP—This option forces the optimizer to use a sorting operation to perform the GROUP BY operation.

Only one GROUP BY hint can be specified at a time.

UNION Hints The UNION hints specify how UNION operations should be performed. The UNION hints that can be specified are as follows:

- MERGE UNION—This option forces the optimizer to use a merge operation to perform the UNION operation.
- HASH UNION—This option forces the optimizer to use a hash operation to perform the UNION operation.
- CONCAT UNION—This option forces the optimizer to use the concatenation method to perform the UNION operation.

Only one UNION hint can be specified at a time and must come after the last query in the UNION. The following is an example of forcing concatention for a UNION:

```
select stor_id from sales where stor_id like 'B19%'
UNION
select title_id from titles where title_id like 'C19%'
OPTION (CONCAT UNION)
```

Miscellaneous Hints The following miscellaneous hints can be used to override various query operations:

- FORCE ORDER—This option tells the optimizer to join the tables in the order they are listed in the FROM clause and not to determine the optimal join order. This option replaces the SET FORCEPLAN option in SQL Server 6.5 and earlier.
- ROBUST PLAN—This option forces the query optimizer to attempt a plan that works for the maximum potential row size, even if it means degrading performance. If you have very wide VARCHAR columns, some types of query plans might create intermediate tables, and if any of the internal operations need to store and process rows in these intermediate tables, some rows might exceed SQL Server's row size limit. If this happens, SQL Server generates an error during query execution. When the ROBUST PLAN hint is specified, the query optimizer will not consider any plans that might encounter this problem.

- `MAXDOP` *`number`*—This hint overrides the server level configuration setting for `max degree of parallelism` for the current query in which the hint is specified.
- `KEEP PLAN`—When this hint is specified, it forces the query optimizer to relax the estimated recompile threshold for a query. In other words, the query is not recompiled as frequently when there are multiple updates to a table. This option is useful primarily for queries whose execution plan stays in memory, such as for stored procedures. An example of when you might want to specify this option is for a stored procedure that does a lot of work with temporary tables, which can lead to frequent recompilations of the execution plan for the stored procedure.
- `KEEPFIXED PLAN`—This query hint tells the optimizer not to recompile the query plan when there are changes in statistics or modifications to indexed columns used by the query via updates, deletes, or inserts. When this option is specified, the query will be recompiled only if the schema of the underlying tables is changed or `sp_recompile` is executed against those tables.
- `EXPAND VIEWS`—The hint tells the query optimizer not to consider any indexed view as a substitute for any part of the query and to force the view to be expanded into its underlying query. This hint essentially prevents direct use of indexed views in the query plan.
- `FAST` *`n`*—This hint instructs SQL Server to optimize the query to return the first rows as quickly as possible, even if the overall throughput is reduced. In other words, it improves response time at the expense of the total query execution time. This option will generally influence the query optimizer to retrieve data using a nonclustered index that matches the `ORDER BY` clause of a query instead of using a different access method that would require a sort operation first to return rows in the specified order. Unlike the `FASTFIRSTROW` option, which this option replaces, after *n* number of rows have been returned, the query continues execution normally to produce its full resultset.

NOTE

Optimizer hints are not always executed. For example, the optimizer will probably ignore a `HASH UNION` hint for a query using the `UNION ALL` statement. Because a `UNION ALL` means to return all rows whether there are duplicates or not, you don't need to hash these values to determine uniqueness and remove duplicates, so the normal concatenation will probably still take place.

Limiting Query Plan Execution with the Query Governor

Another interesting tool available in SQL Server 2000 is the query governor. Because SQL Server uses a cost-based optimizer, the cost of executing a given query is always estimated before the query is actually executed. The query governor enables you to set a cost threshold to prevent certain long-running queries from being executed. This is not so much a tuning tool as it is a performance problem prevention tool.

For example, if you have an application with an English Query front end, you have no way of controlling what the user is going to request from the database and the type of query generated. The query governor will allow you to prevent a runaway query from executing and avoid using up valuable CPU time and memory by processing a poorly formed query.

You can set the query governor cost limit for the current user session by setting the session level property, `QUERY_GOVERNOR_COST_LIMIT`:

```
SET QUERY_GOVERNOR_COST_LIMIT value
```

The value specified is the maximum length of time, in seconds, a query is allowed to run. If the optimizer estimates the query would take longer than the specified value, SQL Server will not execute it.

Although the option is specified in seconds, it is a relative value corresponding to the TotalSubtreeCost estimated by the query optimizer. In other words, if you set the query governor cost limit to 100, it will prevent the execution of any queries whose estimated TotalSubtreeCost is greater than 100 seconds. The TotalSubtreeCost time is based on a generic algorithm in SQL Server and might not map exactly to how long the query takes to run on your own system. The actual runtime depends on a number of factors—CPU speed, IO speed, network speed, the number of rows returned over the network, and so on. You will need to correlate the optimizer runtime estimate to how long the query actually takes to run on your system to set the query governor cost limit to a value related to actual query runtime.

The best way to figure this out is to run your queries with the `STATISTICS PROFILE` and `STATISTICS TIME` session settings enabled (these settings are discussed in more detail in the next chapter, "Query Analysis"). Compare the values in the TotalSubtreeCost column for the first row of the `STATISTICS PROFILE` output with the `elapsed time` displayed by `STATISTICS TIME` for your query. Do this for a number of your queries and you might be able to come up with an average correlation of the actual runtimes with the optimizers' estimated query cost. For example, if the average cost estimate is 30 seconds and the actual runtimes are 15 seconds, you would need to double the setting for query governor cost limit to correspond to the actual execution time threshold—in other words, if you want the threshold to be 60 seconds for this example, you would need to set the query governor threshold to 120.

To configure a query governor threshold for all user connections, you can also set it at the server level. Open Enterprise Manager. Right-click the server and choose Properties from the menu. Next, select the Server Settings tab. In the Server Behavior group box, check the Use Query Governor option and specify a cost threshold (see Figure 35.20). The cost threshold is given in the same TotalSubtreeCost units as specified for the `QUERY_GOVERNOR_COST_LIMIT` session setting.

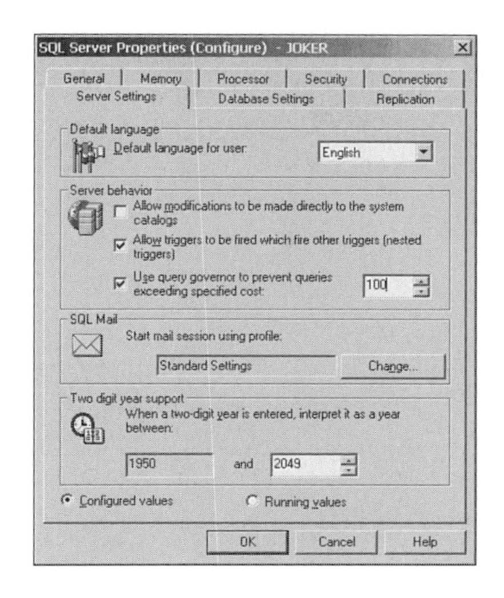

FIGURE 35.20 Configuring the Query Governor settings in the SQL Server Properties dialog box.

Alternatively, you can configure the serverwide setting using sp_configure:

```
sp_configure query governor cost limit, 100
```

Summary

The SQL Server optimizer has continuously improved over the years, taking advantage of new techniques and algorithms to improve its capability to find the most efficient execution plan. Understanding how queries are optimized and what information the optimizer uses to generate and select an execution plan will help you write more efficient queries and choose better indexes. To help the optimizer, you should at least try to avoid the types of nonoptimizable SARGs and other common query optimization problems discussed in this chapter.

The majority of the time, the optimizer chooses the most efficient query plan. When it doesn't, it might be because of problems with the query itself, such as poorly written SARGs and other common query performance problems that were discussed in this chapter. Still, on occasion, the optimizer makes the wrong decision, usually because of inaccurate or incomplete information in the index statistics. When you suspect that the optimizer is making the wrong decision, SQL Server provides table and optimizer hints that you can use to override the optimizer's decisions. However, before arbitrarily applying these hints, you should analyze the queries fully to try to determine why the optimizer is choosing a particular plan. To aid you in this effort, SQL Server provides a number of tools to analyze the query plans generated and determine the source of the problem. These tools are described in the next chapter.

CHAPTER 36

Query Analysis

by Ray Rankins

IN THIS CHAPTER

- Displaying Execution Plans in Query Analyzer
- Query Analyzer Server Trace
- Query Analyzer Client Statistics
- SHOWPLAN_ALL and SHOWPLAN_TEXT
- Statistics
- Query Analysis with SQL Profiler

SQL Server's cost-based query optimizer typically does a good job of determining the best query plan to process a query. At times, however, you might be a little bit skeptical about the plan that the optimizer is generating or want to understand why it is choosing a specific plan. At the least, you will want to know the specifics about the query plans that the optimizer is generating, such as the following:

- Is the optimizer using the indexes that you have defined, or is it performing table or index scans?
- Are worktables being used to process the query?
- What join strategy is being applied?
- What join order is the optimizer using?
- What actual statistics and cost estimates is the optimizer using to make its decisions?
- How do the optimizer's estimates compare to actual I/O costs?

Fortunately, SQL Server provides some tools to help you answer these questions. The primary tool is Query Analyzer. Query Analyzer provides a number of features for monitoring the estimated execution plan as well as viewing the actual runtime statistics for your queries. The following features will be looked at in this chapter:

- Displaying the Graphical Execution Plan
- Displaying the Server Trace

- Displaying client statistics
- Managing indexes and statistics

Although Query Analyzer is a powerful and useful tool for query analysis, SQL Server still provides some text-based query analysis utilities as well. These tools are also described in this chapter, along with tips on how to use them most effectively.

> **NOTE**
>
> Note that the examples presented in this chapter use the bigpubs2000 database. The pubs and Northwind databases provided with SQL Server generally do not contain enough data to demonstrate many interesting query plans. A copy of the bigpubs2000 database is available on the CD included with this book. Instructions on how to install the database are presented in the Introduction.

Displaying Execution Plans in Query Analyzer

The Query Analyzer produces a graphical execution plan that provides analysis information in an intuitive and easy-to-view manner. You can display the execution plan in one of two ways. You can display an estimated execution plan for the entire contents of the Query Panel, or for any highlighted SQL code in the Query Panel, by choosing Display Estimated Execution Plan from the Query menu. You can also invoke it by using the Ctrl+L keyboard shortcut. This feature is useful for displaying and analyzing execution plans for long-running queries or queries with large result sets without having to wait for the results to be returned.

You can also display the actual execution plans for queries as they are executed by selecting the Show Execution Plan option in the Query menu, or by using the Ctrl+K keyboard shortcut. This option is a toggle that remains on until you select it again to disable it. When this option is enabled, your query results will be displayed along with an Execution Plan tab in the results panel. Click on the Execution Plan tab to display the execution plan for the query or queries that are executed. This option is especially useful when you want to execute commands and compare the actual runtime and I/O statistics with the execution plan estimates. (These statistics can be displayed with the SET STATISTICS options described in the "Statistics" section later in this chapter.)

The graphical execution plans display a series of nodes that are connected by lines. Each node is represented by an icon, which indicates the logical and physical operator executed for that node. The execution plan flows from right to left and top to bottom, eventually ending at a statement icon, which indicates the type of query that generated the execution plan. This query might be a `SELECT`, `INSERT`, `UPDATE`, `TABCREATE`, and so on. The arrows between the icons indicate the movement of rows between operators. If the query window contains multiple statements, multiple query execution plans are displayed in the execution plan panel. For each query in the batch that is analyzed and displayed, the relative cost of the query is displayed as a percentage of the total cost of the batch.

To interpret and analyze the execution plan output, start with the farthest icon on the right, and read each ToolTip as you move left and down through the tree. Each icon in the query tree is called a node, and icons displayed under each other participate in the same level of the execution tree.

NOTE

The displayed width of each of the arrowhead lines in the graphical execution plan can indicate the relative cost in estimated number of rows and the row size of the data moving through the query. The smaller the width of the arrow, the smaller the estimated row count or row size. Moving the cursor over the line displays a ToolTip that indicates the estimated row count and row size.

Figure 36.1 shows a sample Query Analyzer graphical execution plan window.

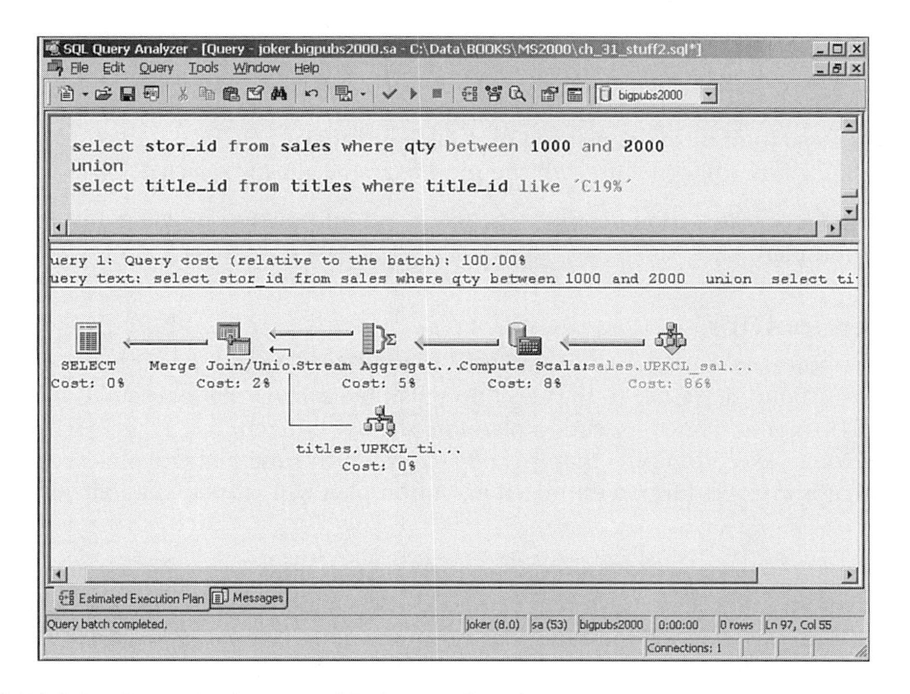

FIGURE 36.1 Query Analyzer graphical execution plan.

The Query Analyzer will indicate tables that are missing statistics by displaying the icon text in red in the graphical execution plan. You can create the missing statistics by right-clicking the icon and selecting the Create Missing Statistics option, which will bring up the dialog box displayed in Figure 36.2.

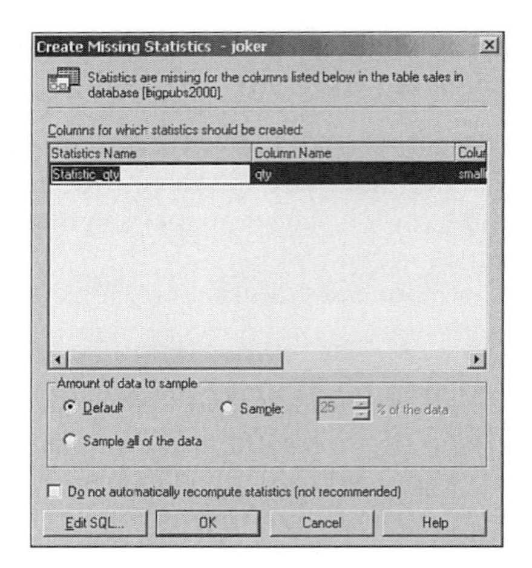

FIGURE 36.2 The Create Missing Statistics dialog box that is invoked from the graphical query plan.

Right-clicking on any icon in the tree presents the Manage Indexes and Manage Statistics options. These options invoke a dialog box from which you can create, edit, or drop indexes, or create, update, or drop statistics, respectively. If you right-click on a node that represents some form of access method on a table or index (table scan, index seek, and so on), the dialog box will come up with the specified table already selected.

The remainder of this section describes the icons and information provided in the graphical execution plan.

Analyzer ToolTips

When a graphical execution plan is presented in the Query Analyzer, you can get more information about each node in the execution plan by moving the mouse cursor over the icon. ToolTips for estimated execution plans are slightly different from the ToolTips displayed for an execution plan that is generated when the query is actually executed. The ToolTip that is displayed for an estimated execution plan will provide the following information:

- Physical operation—The physical operation that is being performed for the node, such as an Index Seek, Hash Join or Nested Loops, and so on. A physical operator that is displayed in red indicates that the query optimizer has issued a warning, such as missing column statistics or missing join predicates. In this case, the query optimizer will suggest action that should be taken, such as creating or updating statistics, or creating an index.

- Logical operation—The logical operation that corresponds with the physical operation, such as the logical operation of a union being physically performed as a merge join. The logical operator, if different from the physical operator, is listed after the physical operator, separated by a forward slash (/), in the icon text and at the top of the ToolTip.

- Estimated row count—The estimated number of rows to be output by the operation and passed on to the parent operation.
- Estimated row size—The estimated row size of the rows output by the operator.
- Estimated I/O cost—The estimated relative I/O cost for the operation. This value should be as low as possible.
- Estimated CPU cost—The estimated relative CPU cost for the operation.
- Estimated number of executes—The estimated number of times the operation will execute during the query.
- Estimated cost—The relative cost to execute this operation as well as a percentage of the total cost of the operation relative to the entire query.
- Estimated subtree cost—The cumulative total cost of this operation and all operations preceding it in the same subtree.
- Argument—The interpreted predicates and parameters used by the operation in the query.

The ToolTips for an execution plan that is generated when the query is actually executed display the same information as the estimated execution plan with two primary differences. The first difference is that the Number of executes displayed represents the actual number of times the operator was executed, rather than an estimate. The second difference is that in addition to the Estimated row count, the ToolTip also displays the actual number of rows (Row count) returned by the operation. This information is useful in determining the effectiveness of the statistics on the column or index by comparing how closely the estimated row count matches the actual row count. If a significant difference exists, (significant being a relative term) then you might need to update the statistics and possibly increase the sample size used when the statistics are updated to generate more accurate statistics.

NOTE

Note that even though the Estimated keyword is dropped from the ToolTip values that are displayed for a runtime execution plan, the values displayed still reflect the row estimates and cost estimates that are generated by the query optimizer. The only actual row estimates and cost estimates displayed are the Row count and Number of executes values.

Figure 36.3 displays a sample ToolTip for one of the operators in an execution plan that is similar to the one shown in Figure 36.1. Notice the difference between the estimated row count (15,185) and the actual row count (9,032). This indicates an obvious issue with missing or out-of-date statistics.

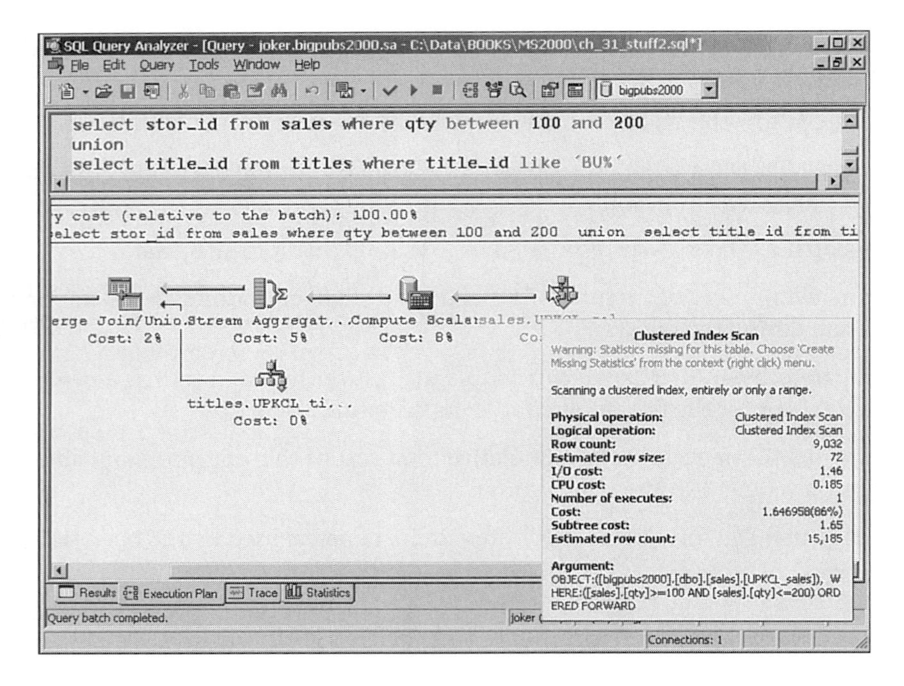

FIGURE 36.3 A ToolTip example.

In this example, the ToolTip displays the information for a Clustered Index Scan physical operation. You will also notice that the lines flowing from this node are much wider than the lines from the other node, reflecting the greater estimated number of rows being returned by this operation (15,185 versus 4).

The I/O cost and CPU cost provide critical information about the relative performance of this query. You want these numbers to be as low as possible.

The Subtree cost will display cumulated costs for this node and any previous nodes that feed into it. This number increases as you move to the left. For the last icon, the statement icon, the ToolTip displays the total Subtree cost for the entire query, as well as the total Row count.

NOTE

The total Subtree cost that is displayed for the statement icon is the cost that is compared against the Query Governor cost threshold setting, if enabled, to determine whether the query will be allowed to run. For more information on configuring the Query Governor, see Chapter 35, "Understanding Query Optimization."

The Cost and Number of executes values provide helpful information about this particular part of the query operation. Merge joins make only one pass through both sets of input data, so the Number of executes for each input to a merge join should be 1. For nested loops, which are iterative, one of the inputs will typically have an estimated Number of Executes that is more than 1, usually equal to the estimated number of rows in the outer input to the nested loop. You can see this for this query by selecting the ToolTips for both of the inputs to a nested loops operation.

The Argument section outlines the predicates and parameters that the query uses. In this case, you can see how the BETWEEN operator is being treated as an `>= AND <=` operation. This information is useful in determining how the optimizer is interpreting your search arguments (SARGs) and if they are being interpreted as optimizable SARGs.

Putting all of the ToolTip information together provides the key to understanding each operation and its potential cost. You can use this information to compare various incarnations of a query to determine whether changes to the query result in improved query plans, and whether the estimated values are consistent with actual values.

Logical and Physical Operator Icons

To better understand the graphical execution plans displayed, it helps to be able to recognize what each of the displayed icons represents. This is especially valuable so that you can quickly locate operations that appear out of place for the type of query being executed. The following sections cover the more common logical and physical operators displayed in the Query Analyzer execution plans.

NOTE

For more examples of graphical execution plans, see Chapter 35. In the sections that discuss the different query strategies are examples of the graphical showplans that correspond to the strategies. Many of these provide varied examples of the operator icons that are discussed in this session.

Assert

Assert is used to verify a condition, such as an RI or check constraint. It sort of acts as a roadblock, allowing a result stream to continue only if the check being performed is satisfied. The argument that is displayed in the Assert ToolTip will spell out each check being performed.

For example, a deletion from the stores table in the bigpubs2000 database has to be verified to ensure that it doesn't violate referential integrity with the discounts and sales tables. The reference constraint needs to check that the stor_id being deleted does not exist in the sales or discount table. If the result of the Assert returns a NULL, the stream continues through the query. Figure 36.4 shows the execution plan and ToolTip of the Assert that appears for a delete on stores. The argument indicates that the reference constraint rejects any case in which the matching foreign key expression that returns from both child tables is NOT NULL. Notice that it returns a different value (0 or 1) depending on which table the foreign key violation occurs so that the appropriate error message can be displayed.

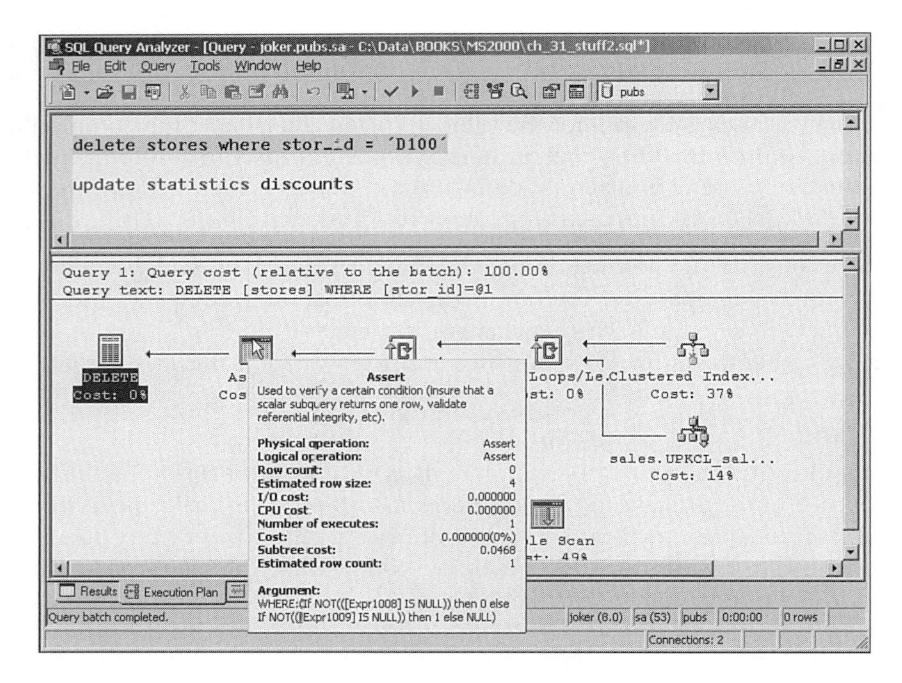

FIGURE 36.4 Assert example.

Bookmark Lookup

The Bookmark Lookup icon in the execution plan indicates that the query processor needed to look up the row in the table or clustered index. One example of when this can happen is when the nonclustered index being used for the operation needs to retrieve information from the data page. (In other words, the index doesn't cover the query.) This situation is an example of when the columns in the `SELECT` clause of the statement can influence the execution plan. The `WITH PREFETCH` clause indicates that the query optimizer will use asynchronous prefetch (read-ahead) on this lookup.

Clustered Index or Index: Delete, Insert, and Update

The Clustered Index or Index physical operators Delete, Insert, and Update indicate that one or more rows in the specified clustered index or nonclustered index are being deleted, inserted, or updated.

Clustered Index or Index: Scan and Seek

Seek is a logical and physical operator that indicates the optimizer is using either a clustered or nonclustered index to find rows via the index pointers. An index scan (also a logical and physical operator) indicates whether the optimizer is scanning all or a subset of the table or index rows.

Figure 36.5 shows a Clustered Index Seek ToolTip. The ToolTip indicates that the seek is being performed against the `UPK_Storeid` index on the stores table. The Argument section indicates that the seek is looking for the value in the parameter, and the optimizer determines that the results need to be output in clustered index order, as indicated by the `ORDERED FORWARD` keyword at the end of the Argument.

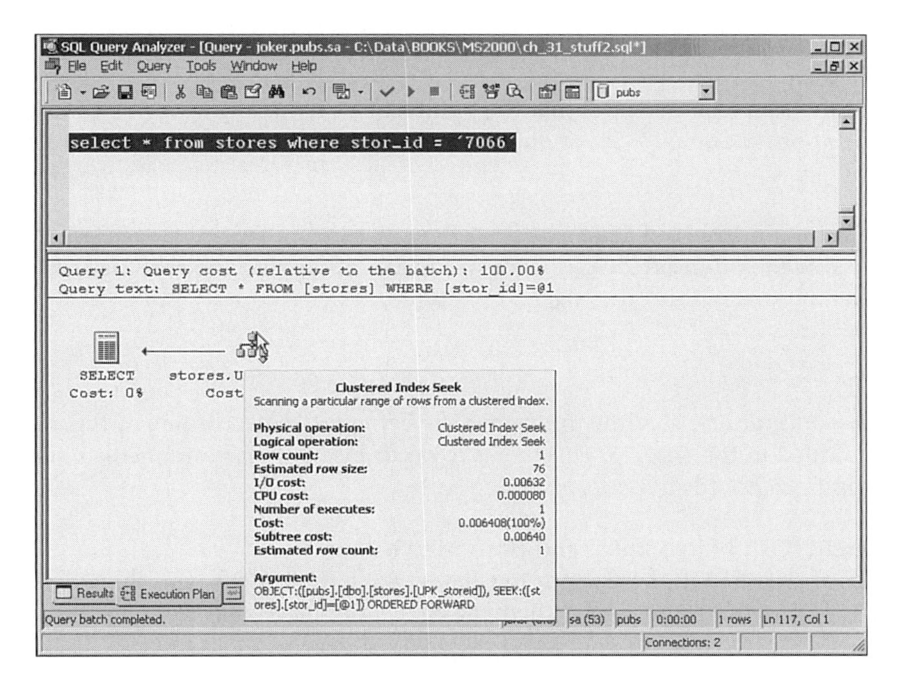

FIGURE 36.5 Clustered Index Seek ToolTip example.

Collapse and Split

A Split physical and logical operator indicates that the query optimizer has decided to break the rows input from the previous update optimization step into a separate delete and insert operation. The Estimated Row Count in the Split icon ToolTips will normally be double the input row count, reflecting this two-step operation. If possible, the optimizer might then choose later in the plan to collapse those rows, grouping by a key value.

Compute Scalar

The optimizer uses the Computer Scalar operator to output a computed scalar value. This is a value that might be returned in the result set, or used as input to another operation in the query, such as a filter predicate. You might see this operator when data values that are feeding an input need to be converted to a different datatype first.

Concatenation

The Concatenation operator indicates that the result sets from two output sources are being concatenated. You often see this when a `UNION ALL` is being used. You can force a concatenation union strategy by using the `OPTION` clause in the query and specifying a `CONCAT UNION`. Optimization of Union queries with examples of the execution plan outputs is covered in Chapter 35.

Constant Scan

The Constant Scan icon indicates that the optimizer is comparing against a constant value in the operation. A Compute Scalar operation often provides the input to the constant scan.

Deleted Scan and Inserted Scan

The Deleted Scan and Inserted Scan icons in the execution plan indicate that a trigger is being fired and that within that trigger, the optimizer needs to scan either the deleted or inserted tables.

Filter

The Filter icon indicates that the input rows are being filtered according to the argument that is indicated in the ToolTip. This seems to occur primarily for intermediate operations that the optimizer needs to perform.

Hash Match, Hash Match Root, and Hash Match Team

Hash joins are covered in more depth in Chapter 35, but to understand these three physical operators, you must understand the basic concept of hash joins to some degree.

In a hash join, the keys that are common between the two tables are hashed into a hash bucket using the same hash function. This bucket will usually start out in memory and then move to disk as needed. The type of hashing that occurs depends on the amount of memory required. Hashing is commonly used for inner and outer joins, intersections, unions, and differences. The optimizer often uses hashing for intermediate processing.

A hash join requires at least one equality clause in the predicate, which includes the clauses used to relate a primary key to a foreign key. Usually, the optimizer will select a hash join when the input tables are unsorted or are different in size, when no appropriate indexes exist, or when specific ordering of the result is not required. Hash joins help provide better query performance for large databases, complex queries, and distributed tables.

A hash match uses the hash join strategy and might also include other criteria to be considered a match. The other criteria is indicated in the `RESIDUAL` clause shown in the Hash Match ToolTip.

A hash match team is a group of operators that share a common hash function and strategy. The hash match root is the operator that coordinates the hash match team and is responsible for outputting the results to the next step in the process.

Index Spool, Row Count Spool, and Table Spool

An Index Spool, Row Count Spool, or Table Spool icon indicates that the rows are being stored in a temporary spooling table in the tempdb database. This is similar to the worktable that was created in SQL Server 6.5. Generally, this spool will be created to support a nested iteration operation because the optimizer might need to use the rows again. Often, you see a spool icon under a Nested Loops icon in the execution plan. A Table Spool ToolTip will not show a predicate because no index is used. An Index Spool ToolTip will show a `SEEK` predicate. A temporary worktable is created for an index spool, and then a temporary index is created on that table. These temporary worktables are local to the connection and live only as long as the query.

Eager or Lazy Spool

The optimizer will select to use either an Eager or Lazy method of filling the spool, depending on the query. The Eager method means that the spool table is built all at once upon the first request. The Lazy method builds the spool table as a row is requested.

Log Row Scan

The Log Row Scan icon indicates that the transaction log is being scanned.

Merge Join

The merge join is a strategy requiring that both the inputs be sorted on the common columns, defined by the predicate. This allows one pass through each input table, matching the merge columns defined in the `WHERE` clause as it steps through each input. A merge join looks similar to a simple nested loop but occurs in only one pass. Occasionally, you might see an additional sort operation prior to the merge join operation when the initial inputs are not sorted properly.

Nested Loops

Nested loop joins are also known as **nested iteration**. Basically, in a nested iteration, every qualifying row in the outer table is compared to every qualifying row within the inner table. This is why you will often see a Spool icon of some sort providing input to a Nested Loop icon. This allows the inner table rows to be reused—or "rewound." When every row in each table is being compared, it is called a **naive nested loops join**. If an index is used to find the qualifying rows, it is referred to as an **index nested loops join**.

The number of comparisons for this method is the calculation of the number of outer rows times the number of inner rows. This can become expensive. Generally, a nested loops join is considered to be most effective when both input tables are small.

Parallelism

The Parallelism icon indicates that parallel query processing is being performed. The associated logical operator displayed will be one of the Distribute Streams, Gather Streams, or Repartition Streams logical operations.

Parallel query processing strategies are covered in more detail in Chapter 35.

Parameter Table Scan

The Parameter Table Scan icon indicates that a table is acting as a parameter in the current query. Typically, this is displayed when INSERT queries exist within a stored procedure.

Remote Delete, Remote Insert, Remote Query, Remote Scan, and Remote Update

The Remote Delete, Remote Query, Remote Scan, and Remote Update operators indicate that the operation is being performed against a remote server.

Sequence

The Sequence operator executes each operation in its child node, moving from top to bottom in sequence, and returns only the end result from the bottom operator. You see this most often in the updates of multiple objects.

Sort

The Sort operator indicates that the input is being sorted. The sort order will be displayed in the ToolTip Argument section.

Stream Aggregate

You will most often see the Stream Aggregate operation when you are aggregating a single input, such as a `distinct` clause, or a `sum`, `count`, `max`, `min`, or `avg` operator.

Table Delete, Table Insert, Table Scan, and Table Update

You will see the Table Delete, Table Insert, Table Scan, and Table Update operators when the indicated operation is being performed against that table as a whole. This does not always mean that a problem exists, although a table scan can be an indicator that you need some indexes to support the query. A table scan can still occur on small tables, especially when they are only a single page in size. A `SELECT INTO` statement that produces a Table Insert might also be an indication that you need a better indexing strategy.

Top

The Top operator indicates a limit that is set, either by number of rows or a percentage, on the number of results to be returned from the input. The Argument column in the ToolTip might contain a list of the columns that are being checked for ties if the `WITH TIES` options has been specified.

Analyzing Stored Procedures

Like other SQL statements, stored procedures are not executed when you choose to display the estimated execution plan in Query Analyzer. Because the stored procedures are not executed when displaying the estimated execution plan, any temporary tables that would be created within the stored procedure during execution will not actually be created. Because the tables are not created, any subsequent references to these tables in the stored procedure will generate an `Invalid object name` error message. This error prevents the estimated execution plan from being displayed for stored procedures that create and reference temporary tables. You will only be able to view actual execution plans for stored procedures that create and reference temporary tables.

TIP

If you use table variables instead of temporary tables in your stored procedures, you will avoid the problem of not being able to display the estimated execution plan. A table variable that is defined and referenced in the same stored procedure does not generate the `Invalid object name` error like the use of a temporary table does, and an estimated execution plan will be displayed for the stored procedure. This is another reason to consider using table variables instead of temporary tables in your stored procedures.

When you are able to display the estimated execution plan for a stored procedure, you will see multiple statement operators as inputs to the Execute statement operator, especially if you have any conditional branching in the stored procedure. One operator will exist for each statement that is defined in the stored procedure. At query optimization time, SQL Server does not know which statements in the stored procedure will actually be executed. An example is shown in Figure 36.6.

When you execute the stored procedure with the Show Execution Plan option enabled, Query Analyzer will display only the execution plans for the path or statements that are actually executed, as shown in Figure 36.7.

In addition, because stored procedures can become quite complex with multiple SQL statements, seeing the graphical execution plan in the Query Analyzer window can be difficult. You might find it easier to break up the stored procedure into smaller batches or individual queries and analyze it a bit at a time.

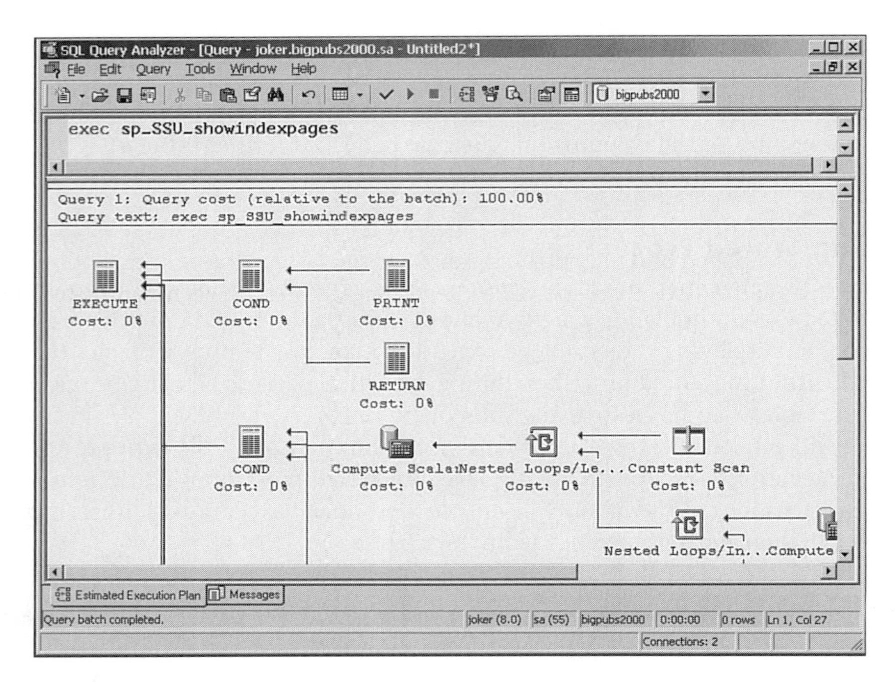

FIGURE 36.6 Estimated execution plan for a stored procedure.

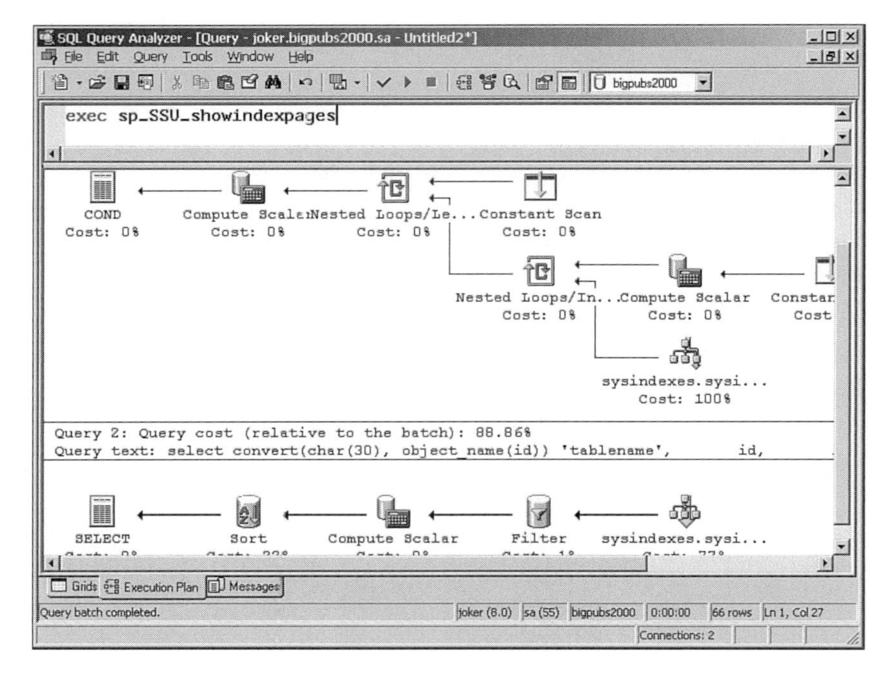

FIGURE 36.7 Actual execution plan used for a stored procedure.

Query Analyzer Server Trace

In addition to the graphical query plan output, Query Analyzer also provides a Show Server Trace option. This option can be toggled on or off in the Query menu. When on, an additional Trace tab is displayed in the results panel. The Server Trace output displays information that is similar to what you would see in SQL Profiler, but only for the SQL being executed in the Query Anlyzer window. The trace output displays information for the SQL:StmtCompleted and SP:StmtCompleted event classes. The columns of information displayed include the Text, Duration, CPU, Reads, and Writes for each completed statement. An example of this output is shown in Figure 36.8.

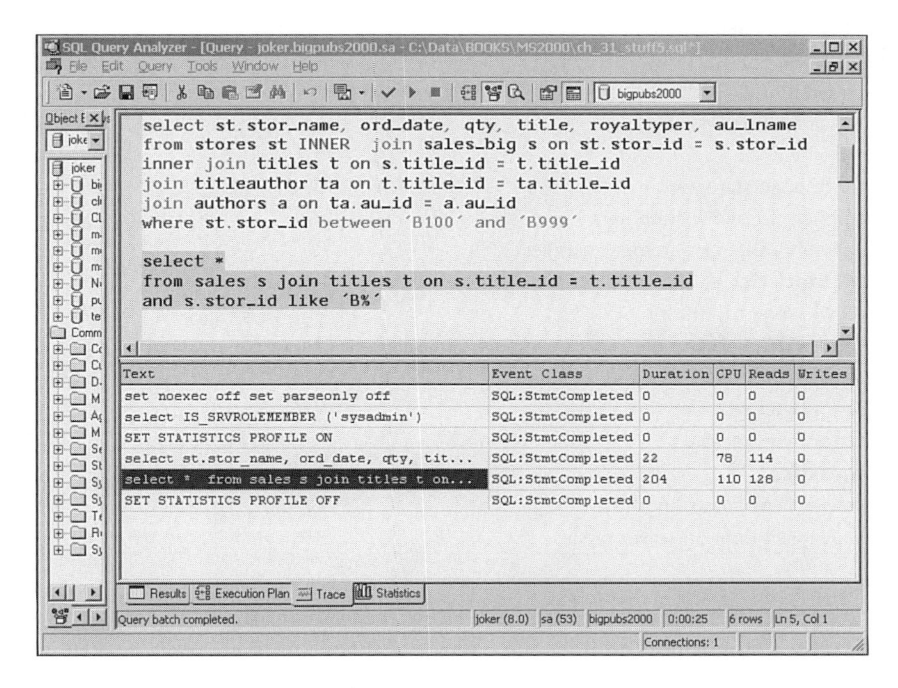

FIGURE 36.8 Query Analyzer server trace output.

The Show Server Trace information is useful for identifying the actual query perfomance statistics, which can be compared to the estimated query cost to see if the optimizer is making accurate query cost estimates.

Query Analyzer Client Statistics

Query Analyzer also provides additional information that is related to the client-side performance of the query by toggling the Show Client Statistics option in the Query menu. When turned on, the Client Statistics tab is added to the results panel. This tab displays useful performance statistics in a tabular format that is related to how much work the client had to do to submit the query and process the results. Table 36.1 displays a representation of the Client Statistics output.

TABLE 36.1 Information Displayed in the Client Statistics Tab

Counter	Value	Average
Application Profile Statistics		
Timer resolution (milliseconds)	0	0
Number of INSERT, UPDATE, DELETE statements	0	0.222222
Rows effected by INSERT, UPDATE, DELETE statements	0	1
Number of SELECT statements	4	2.11111
Rows effected by SELECT statements	57000	4325
Number of user transactions	8	8.27778
Average fetch time	0	0
Cumulative fetch time	0	0
Number of fetches	0	0
Number of open statement handles	0	0
Max number of opened statement handles	0	0
Cumulative number of statement handles	0	0
Network Statistics		
Number of server roundtrips	3	3
Number of TDS packets sent	3	3
Number of TDS packets received	1257	132.278
Number of bytes sent	976	402
Number of bytes received	5.12232e+006	519507
Time Statistics		
Cumulative client processing time	29	18.3889
Cumulative wait time on server replies	138621	4.18096e+006

Some of the more useful pieces of information include the number of rows retrieved, the total client processing time, the time the client spent waiting for results, and the number of bytes sent and received across the network. The time values are specified in number of seconds. The values displayed in the Value column represent the statistics for the most recently run batch. The Average column contains the cumulative average since the Show Client Statistics option was enabled. Turning the option off and back on will reset the averages.

SHOWPLAN_ALL and SHOWPLAN_TEXT

In addition to the graphical query plan available in Query Analyzer, SQL Server provides two versions of SHOWPLAN options to display the execution plan in a text format. These options are SET SHOWPLAN_TEXT and SET SHOWPLAN_ALL. When enabled, SQL Server will return the execution plan that is generated for the query, but no results because the query is not run. This is similar to the pre-7.0 options of SET SHOWPLAN ON and SET NOEXEC ON.

You can turn on the textual output in a couple of ways. You can execute the `SET SHOWPLAN_TEXT ON` or `SET SHOWPLAN_ALL ON` command directly in the Query Analyzer window. These commands must be executed in a separate batch by themselves before running a query. The `SHOWPLAN_TEXT` option can also be enabled by choosing the Options item from the Tools menu, or by choosing the Current Connection Properties item from the Query menu. On the Connection Properties tab within either dialog box, check the "Set showplan_text" option.

TIP

Before enabling `SHOWPLAN_TEXT` or `SHOWPLAN_ALL` options, be sure to disable the Show Execution Plan option; otherwise, the showplan options will have no effect. Also, if you turn on the showplan option by executing the command in the query window, make sure the Show Server Trace option in the Query menu is disabled. Otherwise, you will keep getting an annoying `Access Denied` error message, stating that you need to be a system administrator to proceed.

Typing the following command in a Query Analyzer window will turn on the `SHOWPLAN_TEXT` option:

```
SET SHOWPLAN_TEXT ON
GO
```

Setting this option will cause the textual showplan output to be displayed in the results panel, but not execute the query.

The `SHOWPLAN_TEXT` option displays a textual representation of the query plan. Listing 36.1 shows a sample for a simple inner join query.

LISTING 36.1 Example of the `SHOWPLAN_TEXT` Output

```
set showplan_text on
go
select st.stor_name, ord_date, qty
from stores st join sales_noclust s on st.stor_id = s.stor_id
where st.stor_id between 'B100' and 'B199'
go

StmtText
---------------------------------------------------------------------------------
select st.stor_name, ord_date, qty
from stores st join sales_noclust s on st.stor_id = s.stor_id
where st.stor_id between 'B100' and 'B199'

(1 row(s) affected)
```

36

LISTING 36.1 Continued

```
StmtText
-----------------------------------------------------------------------------
 |--Bookmark Lookup(BOOKMARK:([Bmk1001]), OBJECT:([bigpubs2000].[dbo].
➥[sales_noclust] AS [s]))
   |--Nested Loops(Inner Join, OUTER REFERENCES:([st].[stor_id]))
       |--Clustered Index Seek(OBJECT:([bigpubs2000].[dbo].[stores].
➥[UPK_storeid] AS [st]), SEEK:([st].[stor_id] >= 'B100'
➥ AND [st].[stor_id] <= 'B199') ORDERED FORWARD)
       |--Index Seek(OBJECT:([bigpubs2000].[dbo].[sales_noclust].[idx1] AS [s]),
➥SEEK:([s].[stor_id]=[st].[stor_id]) ORDERED FORWARD)
```

The output is read from right to left, similar to the graphical query plan. Each line represents a physical/logical operator. The text displayed matches the logical and physical operator names displayed in the graphical query plan. If you can read the graphical query plan, you should have no trouble reading the `SHOWPLAN_TEXT` output.

In the example in Listing 36.1, SQL Server is performing a clustered index seek on the stores table using the UPK_storedid index, and a nonclustered index seek on sales_noclust using index idx1. The inputs are being combined using a nested loop join. Finally, a bookmark lookup is being performed to retrieve the ord_date and qty information from the sales_noclust table.

To turn off the textual showplan output, type the following command:

```
SET SHOWPLAN_TEXT OFF
GO
```

The `SHOWPLAN_ALL` option displays the same textual query plan as the `SHOWPLAN_TEXT` option, but also provides additional columns of output for each row of textual output. These columns provide the same information that is viewable in the graphical showplan ToolTips, and the column headings correspond to the ToolTip items listed in the "Analyzer ToolTips" section earlier in this chapter.

> **NOTE**
>
> The `SHOWPLAN_ALL` option is actually what provides the information to the Show Estimated Execution Plan option in Query Analyzer. In essence, you are looking at the same information, just without the pretty pictures.

Statistics

SQL Server 2000 still supports both the `SET STATISTICS IO` option and the `SET STATISTIC TIME` option, which will display the actual logical and physical page reads incurred by a query and the CPU and elapsed time, respectively. These two `SET` options return actual execution statistics, as opposed to the estimates returned by the Query Analyzer and the two showplan options discussed in the previous section. These two tools are invaluable for determining the actual query impact.

The `SET STATISTICS PROFILE` option is also provided to display execution plan information while still allowing the query to run.

STATISTICS PROFILE

The `SET STATISTICS PROFILE` option returns the same textual information that is displayed with the `SET SHOWPLAN_ALL` statement, with the addition of two columns that display actual execution information. This is essentially the same as enabling the Show Execution Plan option in Query Analyzer, but without the graphical display.

The `Rows` column displays the actual number of rows that is returned in the execution step, and the `Executions` column shows the actual number of executions for the step. The `Rows` column can be compared to the `EstimatedRows` column, and the `Execution` column can be compared to the `EstimatedExecution` column to determine the accuracy of the execution plan.

You can set the `STATISTICS PROFILE` option for individual user sessions. In a Query Analyzer window, type the following:

```
SET STATISTICS PROFILE ON
GO
```


STATISTICS IO

You can set the `STATISTICS IO` option for individual user sessions, and you can turn it on in a Query Analyzer window by typing the following:

```
SET STATISTICS IO ON
GO
```

You can also set this option for the user session in Query Analyzer by choosing the Options item in the Tools menu, or the Current Connection Properties item in the Query menu. In the Connection Properties tab in the dialog box displayed, check the Show Statistics IO check box.

The `STATISTICS IO` option displays the scan count (number of iterations), the logical reads (from cached data), the physical reads (from physical storage), and the read-ahead reads.

Listing 36.2 displays the `STATISTICS IO` output for the same query that was executed in Listing 36.1. (Note that the result set has been deleted to save space.)

LISTING 36.2 Example of the STATISTICS IO Output

```
set statistics io on
go
select st.stor_name, ord_date, qty
from stores st join sales_noclust s on st.stor_id = s.stor_id
where st.stor_id between 'B100' and 'B199'
go

-- output deleted


Table 'sales_noclust'. Scan count 100, logical reads 1279, physical reads 0,
 read-ahead reads 0.
Table 'stores'. Scan count 1, logical reads 3, physical reads 0,
 read-ahead reads 0.
```

Logical Reads

The logical reads value indicates the total number of page accesses necessary to process the query. Every page is read from cache memory, even if it first has to be read from disk. Every physical read will always have a corresponding logical read, so the number of physical reads will never exceed the number of logical reads. Because the same page might be accessed multiple times, the number of logical reads for a table could exceed the total number of pages in the table.

Physical Reads

The physical reads value indicates the actual number of pages that were read from disk. The value for physical reads can vary greatly and should decrease, or drop to zero, with subsequent executions of the query because the data will be loaded into the data cache by the first execution. The number of physical reads will also be lowered by pages that were brought into memory by the read-ahead mechanism.

Read-Ahead Reads

The read-ahead reads value indicates the number of pages that were read into cache memory using the read-ahead mechanism while the query was processed. Pages read by the read-ahead mechanism will not necessarily be used by the query. When a page that was read by the read-ahead mechanism is accessed by the query, it counts as a logical read, but not as a physical read.

The read-ahead mechanism can be thought of as an optimistic form of physical I/O, reading the pages into cache memory that it expects the query will need before the query needs them. When scanning a table or index, the table's index allocation map pages (IAMs) are looked at to determine which extents belong to the object. An extent consists of eight data pages. The eight pages in the extent are read with a single read and the extents are read in the order that they are stored on disk. If the table is spread across multiple files, the read-ahead mechanism attempts parallel reads from up to eight files at a time instead of sequentially reading from the files.

Scan Count

The scan count value indicates the number of times that the corresponding table was accessed during query execution. The outer table of a nested loop join will have a scan count of 1. The scan count for the inner tables will typically reflect the number of times that the inner table is searched, usually the same as the number of qualifying rows in the outer table. The number of logical reads for the inner table will be equal to the scan count times the number of pages per lookup for each scan. Note that the scan count for the inner table might sometimes be only 1 for a nested join if SQL Server copies the needed rows from the inner table into a worktable in cache memory and reads from the worktable for subsequent iterations. The scan count for hash joins and merge joins will typically be 1 for both tables involved in the join, but the logical reads for these types of joins will usually be substantially higher.

Analyzing `STATISTICS IO` output

The output shown in Listing 36.2 indicates that the sales_noclust table was scanned 100 times, with all reads coming from cache. (No physical I/Os were performed.) The stores table was scanned once, with all reads coming from cache as well.

You can use the `STATISTICS IO` option to evaluate the effectiveness of the size of the data cache, and to evaluate over time how long a table will stay in cache. The lack of physical reads is a good sign, indicating that memory is sufficient to keep the data in cache. If you keep seeing many physical reads when you are analyzing and testing your queries, you might want to consider adding more memory to the server to improve the cache hit ratio. You can estimate the cache-hit ratio for a query using the following formula:

```
cache hit ratio = (logical reads - physical reads) / logical reads
```

The number of physical reads will also appear lower if pages were preloaded by read-ahead activity. Because read-ahead reads lower the physical read count, they give the indication of a good cache-hit ratio, when in actuality, the data is still being physically read from disk. The system could still benefit from more memory so that the data remains in cache and the number of read-ahead reads is reduced. `STATISTICS IO` is generally more useful for evaluating individual query performance than for evaluating overall cache-hit ratio. The pages that reside and remain in memory for subsequent executions will be determined by the data pages and other queries being executed at the same time, and the number of data pages that are being accessed by the other queries. If no other activity is occurring, you will likely see no physical reads for subsequent executions of the query if the amount of data being accessed fits in the available cache memory. Likewise, if the same data is being accessed by multiple queries, the data will tend to stay in cache and the number of physical reads will be low. However, if other queries executing at the same time are accessing large volumes of data from different tables or ranges of values, the data needed for the query you are testing might end up being flushed from cache, and the physical I/Os will increase. (For more information on how the data cache in SQL Server is managed, see Chapter 33, "SQL Server Internals.") Depending on the other ongoing SQL Server activity, the physical reads you see displayed by `STATSITICS IO` can be inconsistent.

When you are evaluating individual query performance, examining the logical reads value is usually more helpful because the information is consistent across all executions, regardless of other SQL Server activity. Generally speaking, the queries with the fewest logical reads will be the fastest queries. If you want to monitor the overall cache-hit ratio for all SQL Server activity to evaluate the SQL Server memory configuration, use Performance Monitor, which is discussed in Chapter 37, "Monitoring SQL Server Performance."

STATISTICS TIME

You can set the `STATISTICS TIME` option for individual user sessions. In a Query Analyzer window, type the following:

```
SET STATISTICS TIME ON
```

You can also set this option for the user session in Query Analyzer by choosing the Options item in the Tools menu, or the Current Connection Properties item in the Query menu. In the Connection Properties tab in the dialog box displayed, check the Show Statistics Time check box.

The `STATISTICS TIME` option displays the total CPU and elapsed time that it takes to actually execute a query. The `STATISTICS TIME` output for the query in Listing 36.1 returns the output shown in Listing 36.3. (Again, the output has been deleted to save space.)

LISTING 36.3 Example of the `STATISTICS TIME` Output

```
set statistics io on
set statistics time on
go
select st.stor_name, ord_date, qty
   from bigpubs2000.dbo.stores st
   join bigpubs2000.dbo.sales_noclust s
     on st.stor_id = s.stor_id
   where st.stor_id between 'B100' and 'B199'go
go

SQL Server parse and compile time:
   CPU time = 0 ms, elapsed time = 0 ms.
```

LISTING 36.3 Continued

```
--output deleted

Table 'sales_noclust'. Scan count 100, logical reads 1383, physical reads 0,
 read-ahead reads 0.
Table 'stores'. Scan count 1, logical reads 3, physical reads 0,
 read-ahead reads 0.

SQL Server Execution Times:
   CPU time = 15 ms,  elapsed time = 15 ms.
```

Here, you can see that the total execution time, denoted by the elapsed time, was all CPU time. This is due to the lack of any physical reads and the fact that all activity is performed in memory.

NOTE

In some situations, you might notice that there will be two sets of output for parse and compile time for a query. This happens when the query plan is being added to the `syscacheobjects` table for possible reuse. The first set of information output is the actual parse and compile before placing the plan in cache, and the second set of information output appears when SQL Server is retrieving the plan from cache. Subsequent executions will still show the same two sets of output, but the parse and compile time will be 0 when the plan is reused because a query plan is not being compiled.

If elapsed time is much higher than CPU time, the query had to wait for something, either I/O or locks. If you want to see the effect of physical versus logical I/Os on your query performance, you need to flush the pages accessed by the query from memory. You can use the `DBCC DROPCLEANBUFFERS` command to clear all clean buffer pages out of memory. Listing 36.4 shows an example of clearing the pages from cache and rerunning the query with the `STATISTICS IO` and `STATISTICS TIME` options enabled.

TIP

To ensure that none of the table is left in cache, make sure that all pages are marked as clean before running the `DBCC DROPCLEANBUFFERS` command. A buffer is dirty if it contains a data row modification that has either not been committed yet, or has not been written out to disk yet. To clear the greatest number of buffer pages from cache memory, make sure all work is committed, checkpoint the database to force all modified pages to be written out to disk, and then execute the `DBCC DROPCLEANBUFFERS` command.

LISTING 36.4 Example of Clearing the Clean Pages from Cache to Generate Physical I/Os

```
USE bigpubs2000
go
CHECKPOINT
go
DBCC DROPCLEANBUFFERS
go

SET STATISTICS IO ON
SET STATISTICS TIME ON
go
select st.stor_name, ord_date, qty
   from bigpubs2000.dbo.stores st
   join bigpubs2000.dbo.sales_noclust s
     on st.stor_id = s.stor_id
   where st.stor_id between 'B100' and 'B199'go
go

SQL Server parse and compile time:
   CPU time = 0 ms, elapsed time = 0 ms.

--output deleted

Table 'sales_noclust'. Scan count 100, logical reads 1383, physical reads 16,
 read-ahead reads 3.
Table 'stores'. Scan count 1, logical reads 3, physical reads 1,
 read-ahead reads 2.

SQL Server Execution Times:
   CPU time = 15 ms,  elapsed time = 78 ms.
```

Notice that this time around, the CPU time was the same, but the elapsed time was 78 milliseconds (ms), nearly 5 times slower, due to the physical I/Os that had to be performed during this execution.

You can use the `STATISTICS TIME` and `STATISTICS IO` options together in this way as a useful tool for benchmarking and comparing performance.

Using `datediff()` to Measure Runtime

While the `STATISTICS TIME` option works fine for displaying the runtime of a single query, it is not as useful for displaying the total CPU time and elapsed time for a stored procedure. This option will end up generating time statistics for every command run in the stored procedure. This makes it difficult to read the output and determine the total elapsed time for the stored procedure.

Another way to display runtime for a stored procedure is to capture the time right before it starts, capture the time as it completes, and display the difference between the two. Specify the appropriate-sized datepart parameter depending on how long your procedures typically run. For example, if a procedure takes minutes to complete, you probably want to display the difference in seconds or minutes, rather than milliseconds. If the time to complete is in seconds, then you would want to specify a datepart of seconds or milliseconds. Listing 36.5 displays an example of using this approach.

LISTING 36.5 Using `datediff()` to Determine Stored Procedure Runtime

```
declare @start datetime
select @start = getdate()
exec sp_help
select datediff(ms, @start, getdate()) as 'runtime(ms)'
go

-- output deleted

runtime(ms)
-----------
        20
```


NOTE

With all the fancy graphical tools available, why would you want to use the text-based analysis tools? Although the graphical tools are useful for analyzing individual queries one at a time, they can be a bit tedious if you have to perform analysis on a number of queries. As an alternative, you can put all the queries you want to analyze in a script file and set the appropriate options to get the query plan and statistics output you want to see. You can then run the script through a tool such as isql and route the output to a file. You can then quickly scan the file, or use an editor's Find utility, to look for the more obvious potential performance issues, such as table scans or long running queries. Next you can copy the problem queries you identify from the output file into Query Analyzer, where you can perform a more thorough analysis on them.

You could also set up a job to run this SQL script periodically to constantly capture and save performance statistics, providing you with a means to keep a history of the query performance and execution plans over time. This information can be used to compare performance differences as the data volumes and SQL Server activity levels change over time. It is impossible to save the Query Analyzer graphical plan information to a file for historical analysis.

In addition, for very complex queries, the graphical plan tends to get very big and spread out so much that it's difficult to read and follow. The textual output is much more compact and easier to see all at once.

It also helps to become familiar with the query plan textual output because that is what is displayed when you capture execution plan information with SQL Profiler.

Query Analysis with SQL Profiler

With the additions to SQL Profiler in SQL Server 2000, it has become an even more powerful tool for query analysis. When you must monitor a broad range of queries and database activity and analyze the performance, it is difficult to analyze manually. For example, if you have a number of stored procedures to analyze, how would you know which ones to focus on as problem procedures? You would have to identify sample parameters for all of them and execute them to see which ones were running too slowly and then after they were identified, do some query analysis on them.

With SQL Server Profiler, you can simply define a trace to capture performance-related statistics on-the-fly while the system is being used normally. This way, you can capture a representative sample of the type of activity your database will receive and capture statistics for the stored procedures as they are being executed with real data values. Also, to avoid having to look at everything, you can set a filter on the Duration column so that it only displays items with a runtime longer than the specified threshold.

The events that you want to capture to analyze query performance include Performance:Execution Plan, Performance:Show Plan All, Performance:Show Plan Statistics, and Performance:Show Plan Text. The data columns that you want to be sure to include are the TextData, CPU, StartTime, Duration, and Reads and Writes.

Capturing this performance information with SQL Profiler will provide you with all the same information that you can capture with all the other individual tools discussed in this chapter. The trace information can be easily saved to a file or a table for replaying the sequence to test index or configuration changes, or simply for historical analysis.

For more information on using SQL Profiler, see Chapter 7, "Using the SQL Server Profiler."

Summary

Between the features of Query Analyzer and the text-based query-analysis tools, SQL Server provides you with a number of powerful utilities to analyze and understand how your queries will perform, and also to develop a better understanding of how queries in general are processed in SQL Server 2000. Such an understanding can only help ensure that your users' queries become more optimized through experience with the tools.

The tools discussed in this chapter are useful for analyzing individual query performance. If you want to monitor the overall performance for all SQL Server activity to evaluate your SQL Server configuration and identify potential performance bottlenecks, use Performance Monitor, which is discussed in the next chapter, "Monitoring SQL Server Performance."

CHAPTER **37**

Monitoring SQL Server Performance

by Paul Bertucci

IN THIS CHAPTER

- Performance-Monitoring Approach
- Performance Monitor
- Windows Performance Counters
- SQL Server Performance Counters
- SNMP Support
- Using DBCC to Examine Performance
- Other SQL Server Performance Considerations

No SQL Server implementation will be perfect "out of the box." As you build and add SQL Server applications to your server, you will want to start taking an active approach to monitoring performance. You will also need to keep re-evaluating things as more and more load is placed on your servers. This chapter will focus on SQL Server monitoring and leave the other types of servers for those specialists. Other types of servers would include application servers, backup servers, domain controllers, file and print servers, mail/messaging servers, and Web servers.

You can monitor many things on your SQL Server platform, ranging from physical and logical I/O to network packets being handled by the server. To make this monitoring task a little cleaner, this chapter has classified the key monitoring handles into network, processors, memory/cache, and disk systems. Figure 37.1 shows how these key elements interrelate with SQL Server 2000 and Windows. The aspect of utilization will be at the center of most of the discussions in this chapter, whether it is something like CPU utilization, memory utilization, or something else. The important concept to remember will be how to monitor or measure utilization and how to make changes to improve this utilization because you are still not in a perfect world of infinite CPU power, infinite disk space, infinite network load capability, and infinite memory.

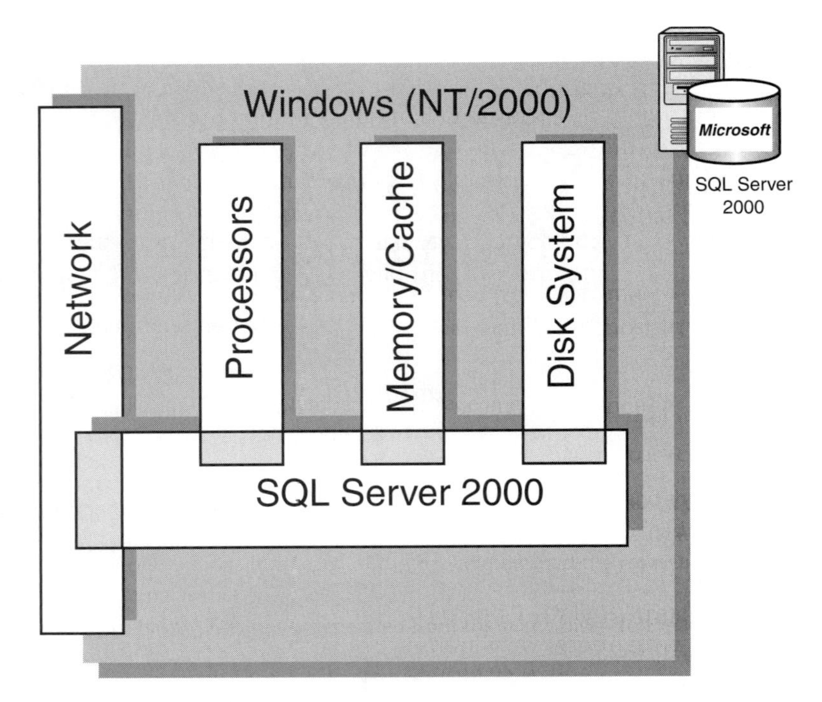

FIGURE 37.1 SQL Server performance-monitoring key elements.

It will also be essential to know which tools you can use to get this valuable information. The tools you can use include Windows NT/2000 Performance Monitor with various counters, SQL Servers DBCC, and even a variety of SQL Server system-stored procedures. Many other third-party products are also available that you might already have in-house.

Performance-Monitoring Approach

Taking a closer look at the performance-monitoring handles depicted in Figure 37.1, you can see that SQL Server spans all of them. SQL Server must process requests submitted to it via the network, service these requests with one or more processors, and rely on accessing a request's data from both memory/cache and the disk system. If you maximize utilization on these resources from the point of view of SQL Server and the operating system, you will end up with a well-tuned database server.

One area of interest is the amount of network traffic that is handled by SQL Server and the size of these network requests. Another area of interest is the ability of the available processors to service the load presented to them by SQL Server without exceeding certain CPU saturation. This chapter will look at the overall memory utilization of what is available on the server and how effective SQL Server is utilizing the disk system.

In general, you will want to start from the bottom with the network and work your way up into the SQL Server-specific elements. This will quickly serve to isolate certain issues that are paramount in performance tuning. In each of these areas, this chapter will provide you with a minimum list of detail performance handles or counters that can be looked at. This approach can be summarized into the following steps:

1. Understand and monitor network request characteristics as they relate to SQL Server and the machine on which SQL Server has been installed. This will mean a complete profile of what is coming into and sent back out over the network from SQL Server.

2. Understand processor utilization. It might be that the processing power is the biggest issue. You need to get a handle on this early.

3. Understand and monitor memory and cache utilization. This is the next detail step into the overall memory usage at the operating system point of view and into the memory that SQL Server is using for such things as data caching, procedure caching, and so on.

4. Understand and monitor disk system utilization. You are often rewarded for a simple disk configuration or data storage approach. You won't know you have a problem unless you look for it. Techniques that are often used include disk stripping, isolation of logs from data, and so on.

To summarize, repeat steps 1 through 4 on a regular basis. Your continued success and salary increases will reflect your diligence here. For each step, certain tools and facilities will be available to you to use that gather all that is needed to identify and monitor performance issues. The Performance Monitor facility of Windows NT/2000 will be explored first.

Performance Monitor

Performance Monitor is a graphical tool supplied as part of the installation of any NT/2000 Server or Workstation that lets you monitor various performance indicators. Hundreds of counters are organized within performance objects. These counters can be monitored on the local machine or over the network and can be set up to monitor any object and counter on multiple systems at once from one session. A small subset of performance information is also available via the Windows Task Manager Performance tab. However, all of this information and more is available using the Performance Monitor facility.

Performance Monitor can be launched from many different points. Figure 37.2 shows how to launch Performance Monitor from SQL Profiler. You can also launch it from the Administrative Tools window in both Windows NT and Windows 2000. In Windows 2000, Performance Monitor has been renamed as System Monitor. However, it looks and feels just like Windows NT Performance Monitor.

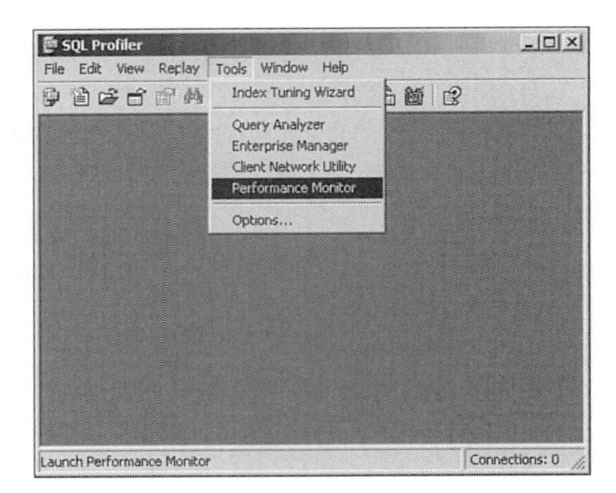

FIGURE 37.2 Launching Performance Monitor from SQL Profiler.

Performance Monitor Views

You can switch the Performance Monitor between any of four views on Windows NT or three views on Windows 2000:

- Chart—(Windows NT and Windows 2000) This is the default view that shows the selected counters as colored lines with the y-axis representing the value and the x-axis representing time.
- Alert— (Windows NT only) In this view, you can set thresholds for counters, and the Performance Monitor will maintain a visual log of when they are reached.
- Log— (Windows NT and Windows 2000) This option allows you to capture counter values with times to a file. This gives you a set of values that you can load back into the Performance Monitor facility at a later time. That way, you can monitor the system after hours and capture statistical data.
- Report— (Windows NT and Windows 2000) In this mode, you see the current values for counters collected under their parent object.

You need to be aware of what counters you will examine, whether you should monitor from another machine, and how the counter values are to be tracked. Figure 37.3 shows the basic graphical user interface for Performance Monitor on Windows 2000 and the Chart view of one of the system counters.

Monitoring Values

When you open the Performance Monitor/System Monitor from the Administrative Tools group, you will have an empty workspace that defaults to the Chart view. You will want to add all counters that you want to appear in the chart (or other views) to reflect what you want to measure. This chapter will explain the right ones for SQL Server in the "SQL Server Performance Counters" section later in this chapter.

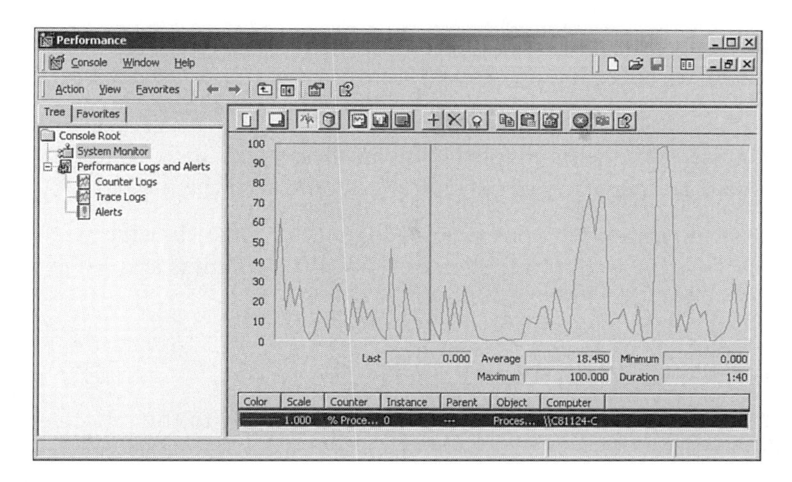

FIGURE 37.3 Performance Monitor Chart view.

You add a counter by clicking the large plus sign toolbar button. The Add Counters dialog box (see Figure 37.4) allows you to select a computer (for monitoring remotely), a performance object, any or selected counters, and an instance of the counter if applicable.

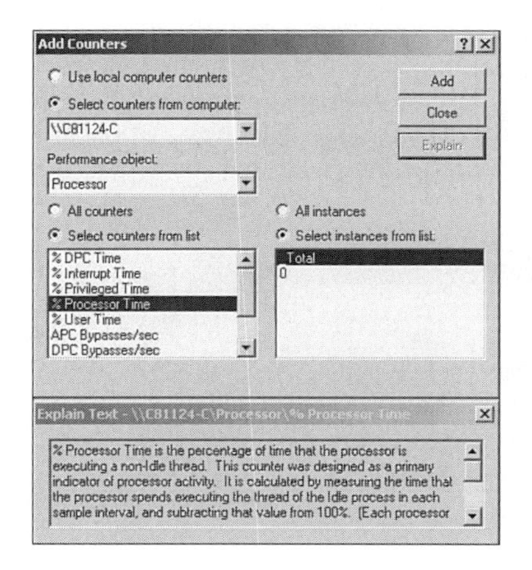

FIGURE 37.4 Adding a counter in the Performance Monitor/System Monitor.

You can customize the look of the line in the chart view by specifying color, width, and style from the System Monitor Properties, Data tab. The default counter that you will be presented with is from the %Processor Time counter from the Processor performance object. This counter indicates the percentage of time that the processor (CPU instance 0) is executing a nonidle thread and is the primary indicator of processor activity.

By clicking the Explain button, you can get a simple explanation of the counter. You can change the scale of a counter's value as well. In this case, you don't need to change the scale because it is a percentage, and the chart y-axis is numbered to 100.

To remove a counter, simply highlight the line in the bottom area of the Chart View window and press the Delete key or click on the X button in the toolbar.

You follow the same process whether you're adding the counter to Chart view, Histogram, or Report view. The next section will discuss some of the counters and when you want to use them.

Windows Performance Counters

You need to be able to tell how NT/Windows 2000 is reacting to the presence of SQL Server running within it: how SQL Server is using memory, the processors, and other important system resources. A large number of objects and counters relate to Windows and the services it is running. The next few sections will look at which objects and counters provide useful information in investigating certain areas of the system and focus on the ones that you need for monitoring SQL Server.

TIP

Some of the network counters are available only if you add the Network Monitor Agent. You can add this software component through the Network icon (Add Network Components) in the Control Panel. This is highly recommended because it will allow you to monitor all activity passing through the installed network card. Figure 37.5 shows the Install Network Component option for both Windows 2000 and Windows NT.

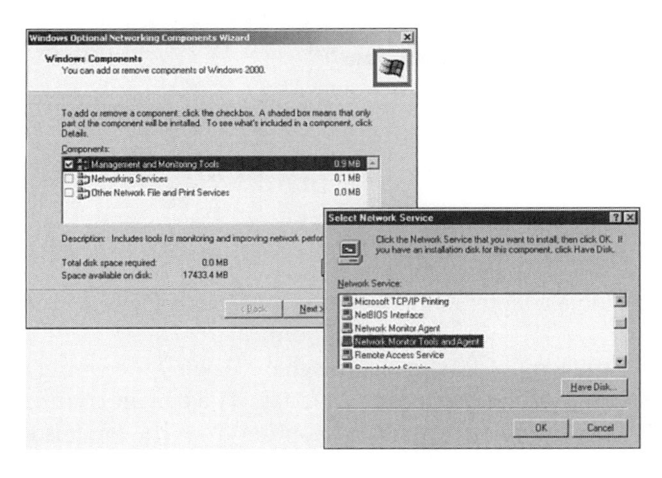

FIGURE 37.5 Windows 2000/NT install network management and monitoring tools.

Monitoring the Network Interface

One area of possible congestion is the network card or network interface; it does not matter how fast the server's work is if it has to queue up to go out through a small pipe.

Remember: Any activity on the server machine might be consuming some of the bandwidth of the network interface/card. You can see the total activity via Performance Monitor. The detail information is good now. Table 37.1 shows the typical network performance object and counters you will want to be using to measure the total network interface activity.

TABLE 37.1 Network Interface Performance Objects and Counters

Performance Monitor Object	Description
Network Inter: Bytes Received	The rate at which bytes are received on the interface.
Network Inter: Bytes Sent	The rate at which bytes are sent on the interface.
Network Inter: Bytes Total	The rate at which all bytes are sent and received on the interface.
Network Inter: Current Bandwidth	The bits per second (bps) of the interface card.
Network Inter: Output Queue Length	The length of the output packet queue (in packets). If this is longer than 2, delays are being experienced and a bottleneck exists.
Network Inter: Packets Received	The rate at which packets are received on the network interface.
Network Inter: Packets Sent	The rate at which packets are sent on the network interface.
Network Inter: Packets	The rate at which packets are sent and received on the network interface.
Server: Bytes Received	The number of bytes the server has received from the network. This is the big picture indicator of how busy the server is.
Server: Bytes Transmitted	The number of bytes the server has sent/transmitted to the network. Again, this is a good overall picture of how busy the server is.

Figure 37.6 illustrates a pretty low usage picture for a particular network interface.

NOTE

Under previous versions of SQL Server (6.5 and earlier), a counter called SQLServer:Network Reads/sec indicated SQL Server's contribution. With SQL Server 2000, you need to use the `DBCC PERFMON` command to find similar information or use sp_monitor.

37

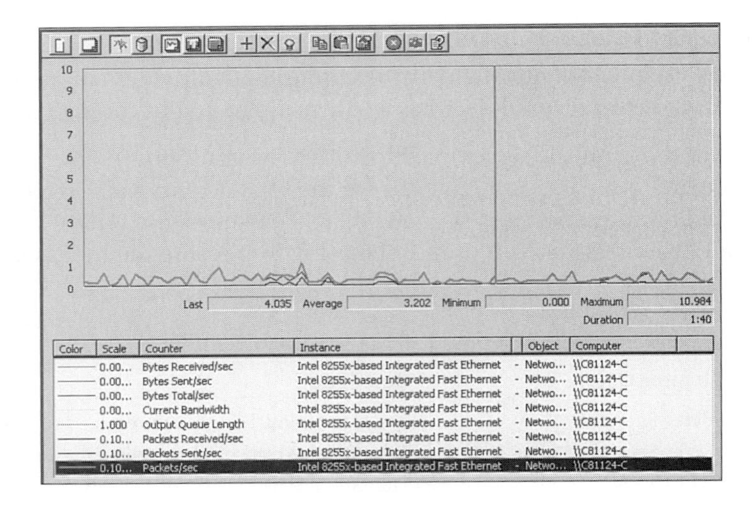

FIGURE 37.6 Network interface's performance object and counters.

In general, if the SQL Server counter is grossly lower than the server's counter, then other activity on the server is occurring that is potentially bogging this server down or not allowing SQL Server to be used optimally. The rule of thumb here is to isolate all other functionality to other servers if you can and let SQL Server be the main application on a machine.

Pay strict attention to how many requests are queuing up, waiting to make use of the network interface. You can see this by using the `DBCC PERFMON` command and looking at the Command Queue Length value. As mentioned earlier, this number should be 0. If it is 2 or more, then the network interface has a bottleneck. Check the bus width of the card. Obviously, a 32-bit PCI card is faster than an 8-bit ISA one. Also, check that you have the latest drivers from the hardware vendor.

When using DBCC PERFMON, the detail information of actual bytes read and written allows you to understand the size of this network activity. A quick calculation of reads/bytes gives you an average size of reads from the network. If this is large, then you might want to question what the application is doing and whether the network as a whole can handle this big of a bandwidth request.

```
DBCC PERFMON
Go

Statistic                        Value
-------------------------------- ------------------------
Network Reads                    39.0
Network Writes                   47.0
Network Bytes Read               4008.0
```

```
Network Bytes Written           70975.0
Command Queue Length            0.0
Max Command Queue Length        0.0
Worker Threads                  0.0
Max Worker Threads              0.0
Network Threads                 0.0
Max Network Threads             0.0

Wait Type         Requests        Wait Time        Signal Wait Time
----------------- --------------- ---------------- ------------------------
NETWORKIO         18.0            40.0             0.0
```

Sp_Monitor as well as several SQL Server system variables can also be used to see much of what is being shown in DBCC PERFMON. DBCC PERFMON:Network Reads corresponds to sp_monitors (or @@pack_received system variable) packets_received and DBCC PERFMON:Network Writes corresponds to sp_monitors (or @@pack_sent system variable) packets_sent.

The following SELECT statement retrieves the current picture of what is being handled by SQL Server from a network packets point of view:

```
SELECT  @@connections as 'Connections',
        @@pack_received as 'Packets Received',
        @@pack_sent as 'Packets Sent',
        getdate() as 'As of datetime'
go
Connections     Packets Received      Packets Sent    As of datetime
39              998                   1799            2001-09-01 14:11:56.660

(1 row(s) affected)
```

Monitoring the Processors

The main processor(s) of your server is doing the majority of all the hard work, executing the operating system code and all applications. This is the next logical point to start looking at the performance of your system. The emphasis here will be to see if the processors that are allocated to the server are busy enough to maximize performance, but not too saturated as to create a bottleneck. The rule of thumb here is to see if your processors are working at between 50–80 percent. If this usage is consistently above 90–95 percent, then you must look at splitting off some of the workload or adding processors. Table 37.2 indicates some of the key performance objects and counters for measuring processor utilization.

TABLE 37.2 Processor-Related Performance Objects and Counters

Performance Monitor Object	Description
Processor: % Processor Time	The rate at which bytes are received on the interface.
System: Processor Queue Length	The number of threads in the processor queue. A sustained processor queue of greater than two threads indicates a processor bottleneck.
System: Threads	The number of threads executing on the machine. A thread is the basic executable entity that can execute instructions in a processor.
System: Context Switches	The rate at which the processor and SQL Server had to change from executing on one thread to executing on another. This costs CPU resources.
Processor: % Interrupt Time	The percentage of time that the processor spends receiving and servicing hardware interrupts.
Processor: Interrupts/sec	The average number of hardware interrupts the processor is receiving and servicing.

The counters System: % Total Processor Time, System: Processor Queue Length and Processor: % Processor Time are the most critical to watch. If the percentages are consistently high (above that 90–95 percent level), then you need to identify which specific processes and threads are consuming so many CPU cycles.

From the SQL Server point of view, you can execute a simple `SELECT` statement that yields the SQL Server processes and their corresponding threads.

```
SELECT spid, lastwaittype, dbid, uid, cpu, physical_io, memusage,status, loginame,
program_name
from master..sysprocesses
ORDER BY cpu desc
Go
```

This will give you the top CPU resource hogs that are active on SQL Server. After you identify which processes are causing a burden on the CPU, check whether they can be either turned off or moved to a different server. If they cannot be turned off or moved, then you might want to consider upgrading the processor.

No one should use the SQL Server box as a workstation because using the processor for client applications can cause SQL Server to starve for processor time. The ideal Windows setup for SQL Server is on a standalone member server to the Windows domain. Do not install SQL Server onto a primary domain Controller (PDC) or backup domain controller (BDC) because they run additional services that consume memory, CPU, and network resources.

Before you upgrade to the latest processor just because the % Processor Time counter is constantly high, you might want to check the load placed on the CPU by your other adapters. By checking Processor: % Interrupt Time and Processor: Interrupts/sec, you can tell whether the CPU is interrupted more than normal by adapters such as disk controllers.

The % Interrupt Time should be as close to 0 as possible; controller cards should handle any processing requirements. The optimum value of Interrupts/Sec varies with the CPU used; DEC Alpha processors generate a nonmaskable interrupt every 10 milliseconds (ms), whereas Intel processors interrupt every 15ms. The lowest absolute values are 100 interrupts per second and 67 interrupts per second, respectively.

The System: Context Switches counter can reveal when excessive context switching occurs, which usually directly affects overall performance. In addition, the System: Threads counter can give a good picture of the excessive demand on the CPU of having to service huge numbers of threads. In general, only look at these counters if processor queuing is happening.

By upgrading inefficient controllers to bus-mastering controllers, you can take some of the load from the CPU and put it back on the adapter. You will also want to keep the controller patched with the latest drivers from the hardware vendor.

Monitoring Memory

Memory, like the processor, is divided into segments for each process running on the server. If memory has too much demand, the operating system has to use virtual memory to supplement the physical memory. Virtual memory is storage allocated on the hard disk; it is named PAGEFILE.SYS under Windows. Table 37.3 reflects the main performance objects and counters that are best utilized to monitor memory for SQL Server.

TABLE 37.3 Memory-Related Performance Objects and Counters

Performance Monitor Object	Description
Process: Working Set|sqlservr	The set of memory pages touched recently by the threads in the process (SQL Server in this case).
MSSQL Buffer Manager: Buffer	The percentage of pages that were found in the cache hit ratio buffer pool without having to incur a read from disk.
MSSQL Buffer Manager: Total Pages	The total number of pages in the buffer pool, including database pages, free pages, and stolen pages.
MSQL Memory Manager: Total Server Memory (KB)	The total amount of dynamic memory the server is currently consuming.
Memory: Pages	The number of pages read from or written to disk to resolve hard page faults. This usually gives a direct indication of memory issues.
Memory: Pages Read	The number of times that the disk was read to resolve hard page faults.

TABLE 37.3 Continued

Performance Monitor Object	Description
Memory: Page Faults	The overall rate at which faulted pages are handled by the processor.
Process: Page Faults|sqlservr	The rate of page faults occurring in the threads associated with a process (SQL Server in this case).

Numerous goals can be achieved related to memory and SQL Server. Figure 37.7 shows a typical monitoring of memory underway.

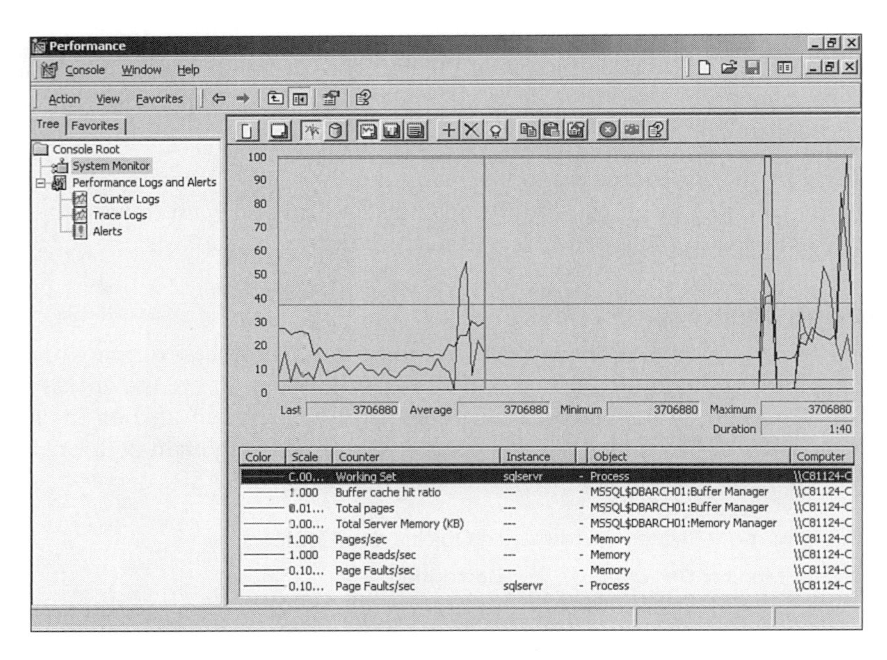

FIGURE 37.7 Memory performance object and counters.

It is important to remember that when the operating system or SQL Server isn't able to use memory to find something and has to use virtual memory stored on the disk, performance will degrade. Therefore, you need to work on minimizing this situation, known as **swapping** or **page faulting**.

To observe the level of the page faulting, you can look at the Memory: Page Faults/sec and Process: Page Faults (for a SQL Server Instance) counters.

Next in line are the MSSQL Buffer Manager: Buffer Cache hit ratio and MSSQL Buffer Manager: Total Pages counters. These directly indicate how well SQL Server is finding data in its controlled memory (cache). You need to achieve a near 90 percent or higher ratio here. DBCC PERFMON also has the Cache Hit Ratio and Cache Size information.

If the Memory: Pages/sec counter is greater than 0 or the Memory: Page Reads counter is greater than 5, the operating system is being forced to use disk to resolve memory references. These are called **hard faults**. The Memory: Page counter is one of the best indicators of the amount of paging that Windows is doing and the adequacy of SQL Server's current memory configuration.

Because the memory used by SQL Server 2000 dynamically grows and shrinks, you might want to track the exact usage using either Process: Working Set: SQLServr or MSSQL: Memory Manager: Total Server Memory (KB). These counters indicate the current size of the memory used by the SQL Server process. If these are consistently high as compared to the amount of physical memory in the machine, then you are probably ready to install more memory on this box. If you see a performance degradation because SQL Server must continually grow and shrink its memory, you should either remove some of the other services or processes running or use the configuration option Use a Fixed Memory Size.

Monitoring the Disk System

By monitoring the portion of the system cache used for the server services (synchronous) and that related to the SQL Server (asynchronous), you can see how much disk access is related to SQL Server. Not all asynchronous disk activity is SQL Server, but on a dedicated box, it should be. You can watch a number of different synchronous and asynchronous counters, depending on the type of activity you want to monitor. The essential performance objects and counters related to monitoring the disk system are indicated in Table 37.4.

TABLE 37.4 Disk Usage–Related Performance Objects and Counters

Performance Monitor Object	Description
Physical Disk: Current Disk Queue Length	The number of outstanding requests (read/write) for a disk.
Physical Disk: Avg. Disk Queue Length	The average number of both read and write requests that were queued for disks.
Physical Disk: Disk Read Bytes	The rate that bytes are transferred from the disk during read operations.
Physical Disk: Disk Write Bytes	The rate that bytes are transferred to the disk during write operations.
Physical Disk: % Disk Time	The percentage of elapsed time that the selected disk drive is busy servicing read or write requests.
Logical Disk: Current Disk Queue Length	The number of outstanding requests (read/write) for a disk.
Logical Disk: Avg. Disk Queue Length	The average number of both read and write requests that were queued for disks.
Logical Disk: Disk Read Bytes	The rate that bytes are transferred from the disk during read operations.

TABLE 37.4 Continued

Performance Monitor Object	Description
Logical Disk: Disk Write Bytes	The rate that bytes are transferred to the disk during write operations.
Logical Disk: % Disk Time	The percentage of elapsed time that the selected disk drive is busy servicing read or write requests.

Before you can get information from some of these counters, you must first turn them on by using `diskperf`. From a command prompt, you need to execute `diskperf -y` and then reboot the computer (see Figure 37.8). This is done this way so that nothing is slowing down disk performance in any way (as the default). If you want to monitor this area, you have to ask for it and take a slight hit on overall performance due to the overhead of these counters.

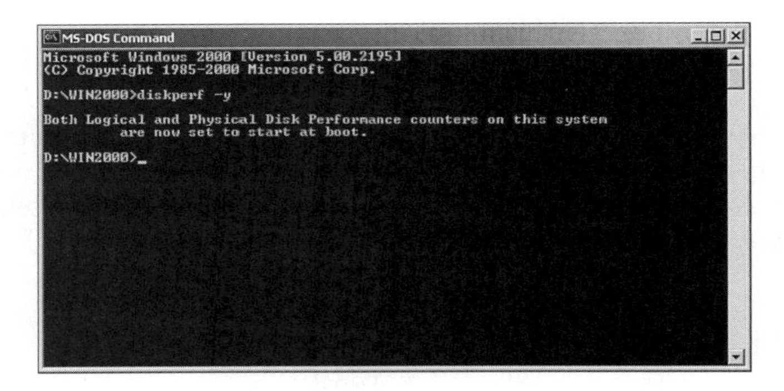

FIGURE 37.8 Setting the `diskperf -y` option on.

Slow disk I/O causes a reduction in the transaction throughput. To identify which disks are receiving all the attention, you should monitor both the Physical Disk and Logical Disk performance objects. You have many more opportunities to tune at the disk level than you do with other components such as processors. This has long been the area that database administrators and system administrators have been able to get better performance.

CAUTION

A critical oversight such as specifying "compression" when configuring a disk drive that will be used to store either the data portion or log portion of a SQL Server database can be fatal. Well, maybe not fatal, but the degradation in performance at the disk-file system level can impact SQL Server between 40 and 50 percent. Here's an example of a situation that was discovered the hard way during a recent production implementation. Queries were taking much longer in production than in test, even with the exact same size databases and same workload. The system admin for the production system discovered this compression error, expanded the disk, and was given a week's vacation in Hawaii. Do yourself a favor and just take a quick glance at the disk management properties of each of your production drives to verify that compression is not being used (NTFS).

The place to start is with looking at the Physical Disk: Current Disk Queue Length and Physical Disk: Avg. Disk Queue Length counters' behavior of all disks or of each particular disk. This will identify where much of the attention is from a disk-usage point of view. Figure 37.9 shows a disk-monitoring session under way that is loaded with long disk queues. In other words, disk operations are being stacked up and there appears to be a major issue here.

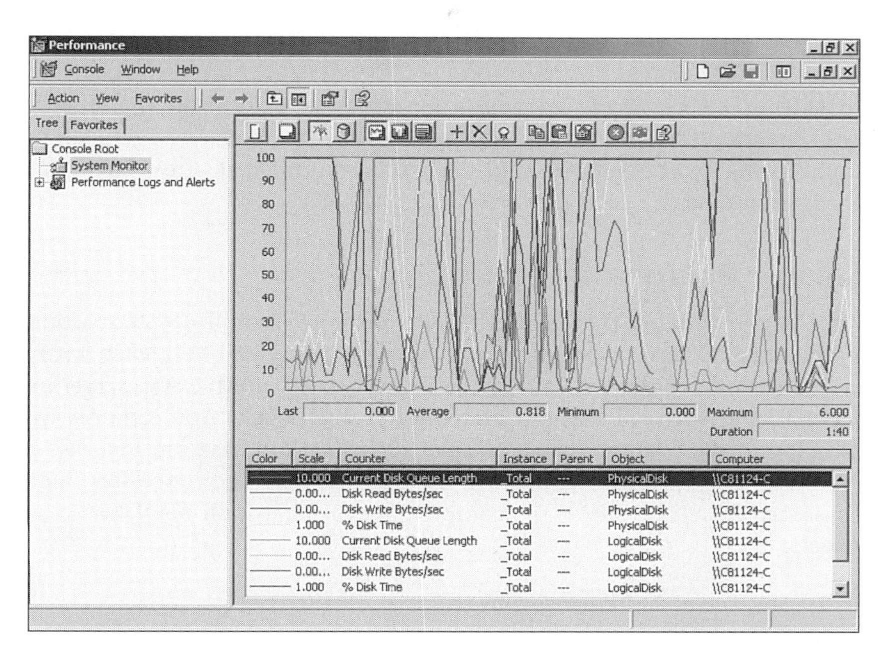

FIGURE 37.9 Disk performance object and counters.

As you monitor each individual disk, you might see that some drives are not as busy as others. You can relocate heavily used resources to minimize these long queue lengths that you have uncovered and spread out the disk activity. Common techniques for this are to relocate indexes away from tables, isolate read-only tables away from volatile tables, and so on.

The Physical Disk: % Disk Time counter for each physical disk drive will show you the percentage of time that the disk is active; a continuously high value could indicate an under-performing disk subsystem.

CAUTION

Remember to turn off the disk-performance counters when you are finished by executing `diskperf -n`. Running your system with these counters on will impact your performance.

Of course, the monitoring up to this point will only show half the picture if drives are partitioned into multiple logical drives. To see the work on each logical drive, you need to examine the logical disk counters; in fact, you can monitor read and write activity separately with Logical Disk: Disk Write Bytes/sec and Logical Disk: Disk Read Bytes/sec.

TIP

If you are running disk striping, you need to turn on the disk counters using `diskperf -y`.

If you use RAID, it is necessary to know how many physical drives are in each RAID array to figure out the monitored values of disk queuing for any one disk. In general, just divide the disk queue value by the number of physical drives in the disk array. This will give you a fairly accurate number for each physical disk's queue length.

SQL Server Performance Counters

For each SQL Server instance that is installed, Performance Monitor/System Monitor will have a number of SQL Server–specific performance objects added to it, each with a number of associated counters. Because you can now have multiple SQL Server instances on a single machine, each will have separate monitoring objects. You certainly wouldn't want to mix monitoring values across multiple instances. You have already seen a few of these as you were monitoring each major component of network, processors, memory, and disk systems. Table 37.5 shows the complete list of the installed SQL Server performance objects.

TABLE 37.5 SQL Server Performance Objects

Performance Monitor Object	Description
MSSQL:Access Methods	Information on searches and allocations of database objects.
MSSQL:Backup Device	Information on throughput of backup devices.
MSSQL:Buffer Manager	Memory buffers used by SQL Server.
MSSQL:Buffer Partition	Buffer Free list page request information.
MSSQL:Cache Manager	Information on any cacheable objects, such as stored procedures, triggers, and query plans.
MSSQL:Databases	Database-specific information, such as the log space usage or active transactions within the database.
MSSQL:General Statistics	Server-wide activity, such as number of logins started per second.
MSSQL:Latches	Information regarding latches on internal resources.
MSSQL:Locks	Individual lock information, such as lock timeouts and number of deadlocks.
MSSQL:Memory Manager	SQL Server's memory usage, including counters such as the connection and lock memory use.
MSSQL:Replication Agents	Information about the SQL Server Replication agents that are currently running.

TABLE 37.5 Continued

Performance Monitor Object	Description
MSSQL:Replication Dist.	Commands and transactions that are read from the distribution database and delivered to the subscriber databases by the distribution agent and latency information.
MSSQL:Replication Logreader	Commands and transactions that are read from the published databases and delivered to the distribution database by the logreader agent.
MSSQL:Replication Merge	Information about merge replication.
MSSQL:Replication Snapshot	Information about snapshot replication.
MSSQL:SQL Statistics	Query statistics, such as the number of batches of SQL received by SQL Server.
MSSQL:User Settable	Counters that return anything you might want to monitor.

The following sections will look at some of the most relevant performance objects and counters.

MSSQL:Cache Manager Object

For finding information about the operation of SQL Server's caches, the MSSQL:Cache Manager object holds a number of useful counters that measure such things as data cache, procedure, and trigger cache operations.

These cache counters allow you to watch how each of the caches is used and what each one's upper limit is. These useful counters help indicate whether additional physical memory would benefit SQL Server:

Cache Pages—The number of pages used by the cache

Cache Object Counts—The number of objects using the cache pages

Cache Use Counts/sec—The object usage

Cache Hit Ratio—The difference between cache hits and lookup

You can display each of these counters for specific cache instances, ranging from ad hoc SQL plans to procedure plans and trigger plans.

A few related cache counters provide more of an overview on the cache operations: MSSQL:Memory Manager:SQL Cache Memory and MSSQL:Memory Manager:Optimizer Memory.

The MSSQL:Buffer Manager object also contains a counter that pertains to the operation of the Read Ahead Manager: Readahead Pages/sec. The information returned by this counter will indicate how much work is done populating the page cache due to sequential scans of data. This might indicate the need to optimize certain queries, add more physical memory, or even consider pinning a table into the cache.

Monitoring SQL Server's Disk Activity

In the section "Monitoring the Disk System" earlier in this chapter, you saw how to monitor disk activity. Here, we will examine what SQL Server's contribution is to all of this disk activity. Disk activity can be categorized into reads and writes.

SQL Server carries out writes to the disk for the following processes:

- Logging records
- Writing dirty cache pages at the end of a transaction
- Freeing space in the page cache

Logging is a constant occurrence in any database that allows modifications, and SQL Server attempts to optimize this process by batching a number of writes together. To watch how much work is done on behalf of the database logs, examine the MSSQL:Databases:Log Bytes Flushed and MSSQL:Databases:Log Flushes/sec counters. The first tells you the quantity of the work, and the second tells you the frequency.

The third kind of write occurs to make space within the page cache. This is carried out by the Lazy Writer process, which we can track with the counter MSSQL:Buffer Manager:Lazy Writes.

It is easy to monitor the amount of reading SQL Server is doing using the counter MSSQL:Buffer Manager:Page Reads. All read and write counter values are combined server-level values.

Locks

One of the necessary areas of performance degradation is locking. However, you need to ensure that the correct types of locks are issued and that the worst kind of lock, a blocking lock, is kept to a minimum. A blocking lock, as its name implies, prevents other users from continuing their own work. An easy way to identify the level of blocking locks is to use the counter MSSQL:Memory Manager:Lock Blocks. If this counter indicates a value greater than 0 on a frequent basis, you need to examine the queries being executed or even revisit the database design.

Users

Even though you cannot always trace performance problems directly to the number of users connected, it is a good idea to occasionally monitor how this number fluctuates. It is fairly easy to trace one particular user that is causing a massive performance problem.

The leverage point here is to see the current number of user connections with MSSQL: General Statistics :User Connections counter in conjunction with other objects and counters. It is easy to say that the disk subsystem is a bottleneck, but how many users is SQL Server supporting at the time?

Procedure Cache

Another area of memory used by SQL Server exclusively is the procedure cache, and corresponding to the procedure cache is a large number of counters that provide insight on its utilization.

The procedure cache maintains pointers to the procedure buffer, which is where the executable from the stored procedures is actually kept. You can separately monitor the amount of memory used by the procedure buffers and cache.

For the procedure buffers, you can track how many are currently in use with MSSQL:Cache Manager:Object Counts:Procedure Plans. SQL Server also maintains a separate set of counters for the parts of the cache that are active as opposed to only in use. You can also track the total size of the procedure cache using the MSSQL:Cache Manager:Cache Pages:Procedure Plans counter, which is in 8KB pages. This counter value will fluctuate with the execution of each new stored procedure and other server activity.

User-Defined Counters

You can extend the range of information that the Performance Monitor displays by creating up to 10 of your own counters. These user-defined counters appear under the MSSQL:User Settable:Query object, which contains the 10 counters as instances, starting with User Counter 1. You define your own counters by calling stored procedures with the names `sp_user_counter1` through `sp_user_counter10`, which are found in the master database.

These counters work differently than they did under previous versions and require you to call the stored procedures to update the information they return to the Performance Monitor. To make any real use of these stored procedures, you now need to call them within a loop or as part of a job that is scheduled on some recurring basis.

37

Using these counters allows you to monitor any information you want, whether it is system, database, or even object specific. The only restriction is that the stored procedure can only take a single integer value argument.

The following sample procedure sets the average connection time for all user connections. Processes that have a kernel ID (`kpid`) of 0 are system ones: checkpoint, Lazy Writer, and so on:

```
DECLARE @value INT

SELECT @value = AVG( DATEDIFF( mi, login_time, GETDATE()))
FROM master..sysprocesses
WHERE kpid > 0

EXEC sp_user_counter1 @value
```

You could further extend this information by creating additional user procedures for returning the minimum and maximum times connected, as well as database usage. Your only limitation is that you can monitor only 10 pieces of information at one time.

SNMP Support

An aid for monitoring the status and performance of SQL Server is the Simple Network Management Protocol (SNMP). This service is widely used across the industry for enterprise-wide management, using its cross-platform capabilities, monitoring, and event-processing features.

Ideally, you will have SNMP support installed for Windows before you install SQL Server. The SQL Setup program will then copy the files MSSQL.MIB and SQLSNMP.DLL. If SNMP is not installed before you install SQL Server, you can turn this feature on after you have installed the service. The SNMP files for SQL Server will already have been copied into the MSSQL\BINN directory, and all you need do is open the Server Network utility and select the Enable SNMP check box at the bottom of the dialog box.

SNMP's architecture can be broken into two main pieces: the SNMP network management machine and the SNMP agent (the system being monitored, which in this case is SQL Server). The SNMP agent responds to requests from the management machine for information, but can also trap and notify when certain critical events occur.

Under Windows, the data being accessed by SNMP is held in the Registry, and the agent service makes this information available in a form readable by SNMP monitors. The events that elicit SNMP traps are not defined in an ad hoc way by users, but rather through a Management Information Base (MIB). The MIB is a data file that has all the details about the objects available to be managed via SNMP. Different services provide different MIBs; for example, Internet Information Server (IIS) has an INETSRV.MIB file that is implemented using the IIS.DLL file.

Security for SNMP is implemented using a shared password (the community name) so that only systems with the correct name can manage associated agents. To further increase the security of your SNMP installation, you can configure an SNMP packet filter so that control packets are accepted only from certain host systems.

When the SNMP service is started on the SQL Server machine, the SQLSNMP.DLL file is loaded. This process contains a trap mechanism for raising SQL Server alerts and is what coordinates SQL Server with the NT-based SNMP service.

On the Windows NT Server Resource Kit CD-ROM, you will find a number of SNMP utilities, one of which will allow you to carry out simple management tasks (`snmputil`). Using other utilities, you can compile new MIBs to allow monitoring of other performance counters.

`snmputil` allows you to easily test your installation, but you will need a full management tool for use in your production environment, such as HP OpenView, Unicenter TNG, SunNet Manager, Advent, or Intraspection. Each of these provides a different variety of graphical tools, add-ons, and foundation objects for developing tools in Visual Basic, Java, and many other development languages.

Using DBCC to Examine Performance

Microsoft might have targeted the `DBCC` command for extinction, but it can still provide useful information on the current state of SQL Server. The next several sections detail the available options. Many of the same commands are used and presented in a more friendly format by the SQL tools; however, you can capture information from these `DBCC` commands into tables for historical statistics. The old DBCC MEMUSAGE is all but a stripped-out skeleton of a command now only returning the Procedure Cache top-20 list now.

SQLPERF

The `DBCC SQLPERF` command has been drastically altered from previous versions and now only reports transaction-log space usage for all databases and active threads on the server. The syntax for the transaction log information is as follows:

```
DBCC SQLPERF( LOGSPACE )
go
```

The results of this command are tabular and can be captured into a database table to maintain historical statistics on log usage on the server. The information returned is as follows:

Data	Description
Database Name	Name of the database
Log Size (MB)	Current size of the log file
Log Space Used (%)	Percentage of the log file currently used
Status	Status of the log file (always contains 0)

For the active threads information, the syntax is as follows:

```
DBCC SQLPERF(THREADS)
go
```

The results of this command are also tabular and can be captured into a database table to maintain historical statistics on the threads used and for what purpose. The information returned is as follows:

Data	Description
Spid	Server process ID
Thread ID	Thread ID at the operating system level
Status	Status of the process (sleeping, background, and so on)
LoginName	SQL Server login associated with the spid
IO	Amount of IO accumulated
CPU	Amount of CPU accumulated
MemUsage	Amount of memory touched

Overall, `DBCC SQLPERF` is great for corresponding SQL Server processes back to the operating system thread information.

PERFMON

Another `DBCC` command useful for finding performance information on SQL Server is `DBCC PERFMON`. This command returns information about the I/O work that SQL Server has been performing, the page cache state and operation, and network statistics. The system-stored procedure equivalent is sp_monitor. PERFMON might be left out of future SQL Server releases, so use caution when embedding its use in your activities.

```
DBCC PERFMON
Go
```

SHOWCONTIG

The `DBCC SHOWCONTIG` command has been discussed in other chapters and is only mentioned here for completeness. The `DBCC SHOWCONTIG` command illustrates the internal state of extents and pages and is helpful in determining how SQL Server is likely to perform when reading data from a table. This can be valuable information when trying to determine the level of fragmentation and the page density of table allocations.

```
USE dbname
Go
DBCC SHOWCONTIG
Go
```

PROCCACHE

The DBCC PROCCACHE command returns the following information on the procedure cache:

Data	Description
num proc buffs	The number of possible cache slots in the cache
num proc buffs used	The number of cache slots in use by procedures
num proc buffs active	The number of cache slots that have currently executing procedures
proc cache size	The total size of the procedure cache
proc cache used	The amount of the procedure cache holding stored procedures
proc cache active	The amount of the procedure cache holding stored procedures that are currently executing

Even though SQL Server 2000 grows and shrinks the procedure cache size as required, you will still want to monitor how much of the memory allocated to SQL Server is in use by the procedure cache. This need makes the DBCC command quite useful. This, combined with DBCC MEMUSAGE, lets you know what the complete picture of procedure cache is. You can also use the DBCC FREEPROCCACHE command to remove all elements from the procedure cache. This will, for example, cause an ad hoc SQL statement to be recompiled rather than reused from the cache.

INPUTBUFFER and OUTPUTBUFFER

You use the DBCC INPUTBUFFER/OUTPUTBUFFER command to examine the statements sent by a client to the SQL Server. The syntax for these commands is as follows:

```
DBCC INPUTBUFFER(spid)
DBCC OUTPUTBUFFER(spid)
```

INPUTBUFFER shows the last statement sent from the specified client, and OUTPUTBUFFER shows the results sent back from the SQL Server.

SQL tools use INPUTBUFFER and OUTPUTBUFFER to display current activity, and you can also use them to examine the commands sent by certain processes that are affecting system performance.

Other SQL Server Performance Considerations

Earlier, it was mentioned that many opportunities exist for SQL Server performance tuning in the area of disk usage. The classic server-level configuration typically will try to separate certain SQL Server items across different hard drives, RAID controllers, and PCI channels. This results in a physical I/O segregation with minimal confusion and maximum value. The main items to try to segregate are transaction logs, Temp DB, databases, certain tables, and even nonclustered indexes.

Transaction logs are easily segregated (isolated) away from the data files simply by specifying this different location during database creation. Don't have transaction logs located on the same physical device as the data files.

Temp DB is a bit harder in that you must use an Alter DB command to change the physical file location of the SQL Server logical filename associated with Temp DB. However, by isolating tempdb away from the data files of your other databases, you will almost achieve minimal disk arm contention for one of the most heavily used databases in SQL Server.

Database partitioning can be accomplished using files and file groups. In general, you can employ a concept of segregating databases with high volatility away from other databases with high volatility by defining the files/file groups on physically separate devices and not sharing a single device.

For tables and nonclustered indexes, you can reference the file groups from within their create statements (the ON statement) to physically segregate these objects away from others. This can be extremely powerful for heavily used tables and indexes.

Summary

Attacking SQL Server performance is, by definition, not a simple task because so many variables are involved. Tuning queries and proper database design are a huge part of this, but dealing with SQL Server as an engine that consumes resources and the physical machine are equally important. This is why it is so critical to take an orderly, methodical approach when undertaking this task. As was pointed out in this chapter, you need to basically peel apart the box on which SQL Server has been installed, one component at a time. This will allow you to explore the individual layer or component in a clear and concise manner. You will also find that within a short amount of time, you will be able to identify the biggest performance offenders and be able to resolve them. In the next chapter, "Locking and Performance," you will get to see how to monitor for locking of resources, isolate locking issues, and understand the effects on performance and throughput.

CHAPTER **38**

Locking and Performance

by Ray Rankins

IN THIS CHAPTER

- The Need for Locking
- Transaction Isolation Levels in SQL Server
- The Lock Manager
- Monitoring Lock Activity in SQL Server
- SQL Server Lock Types
- SQL Server Lock Granularity
- Lock Compatibility
- Locking Contention and Deadlocks
- Table Hints for Locking
- Optimistic Locking

This chapter examines locking and its impact on transactions and performance in SQL Server. You will also review locking hints that can be specified in queries to override SQL Server's default locking behavior.

The Need for Locking

In any multiuser database, there must be a consistent set of rules for making changes to data. For a true transaction-processing database, the database-management system is responsible for resolving potential conflicts between two different processes that are attempting to change the same piece of information at the same time. Such a situation cannot occur because the consistency of a transaction cannot be guaranteed. For example, if two users were to change the same data at approximately the same time, whose change would be propagated? Theoretically, the results would be unpredictable, because the answer is dependent on whose transaction completed last. Because most applications try to avoid "unpredictability" with data wherever possible (imagine your payroll systems returning "unpredictable" results, and you'll get the idea), some method must be available to guarantee sequential and consistent data changes.

Any relational database must support the ACID properties for transactions, which were previously discussed in Chapter 31, "Transaction Management and the Transaction Log." These ACID properties ensure that data changes in a database are correctly collected together and that the data is going to be left in a consistent state that corresponds with the actions being taken. The ACID properties are as follows:

- Atomicity
- Consistency
- Isolation
- Durability

The main role of locking is to provide the isolation that transactions need. Isolation ensures that individual transactions don't interfere with one another, that a given transaction does not read or modify the data being used by another transaction. In addition, the isolation that locking provides helps ensure consistency within transactions. Without locking, consistent transaction processing is impossible. Transactions are logical units of work that rely on a constant state of data, almost a "snapshot in time" of what they are modifying, to guarantee their successful completion. The highest lock isolation level that SQL Server provides allows a transaction in a multiuser system to have access to the data it is reading or modifying as if it were in a single-user system.

Although locking provides isolation for the transactions and helps ensure their integrity, it can also have a significant impact on the performance of the system. To keep your system performing well, it is necessary to keep transactions as short, concise, and non-interfering as possible. In this chapter, you'll explore the locking features of SQL Server that provide transaction isolation to transactions. You'll also come to understand the performance impact of the various levels and types of locks in SQL Server and how to define your transactions to minimize locking performance problems.

Transaction Isolation Levels in SQL Server

Isolation levels determine the proportion to which data being accessed or modified in one transaction is protected from changes to the data by other transactions. In theory, each transaction should be fully isolated from other transactions. However, in practice, for practical and performance reasons, this might not always be the case. In a concurrent environment in the absence of locking and isolation, the following four scenarios can happen:

- Lost update—In this scenario, no isolation is provided to a transaction from other transactions. Multiple transactions can read the same copy of data and modify it. The last transaction to modify the dataset prevails, and the changes by all other transactions are lost.

- Dirty reads—In this scenario, one transaction can read data that is being modified by other transactions. Data read by the first transaction is inconsistent because the other transaction might choose to roll back the changes.

- Nonrepeatable reads—This is somewhat similar to zero isolation. In this scenario, a transaction reads the data twice, but before the second read occurs, another transaction modifies the data; therefore, the values read by the first read will be different from those of the second read. Because the reads are not guaranteed to be repeatable each time, this scenario is called **nonrepeatable reads**.
- Phantom reads—This scenario is similar to nonrepeatable reads. However, instead of the actual rows that were read changing before the transaction is complete, additional rows are added to the table, resulting in a different set of rows being read the second time. Consider a scenario where Transaction A reads rows with key values within the range of 1–5 and returns three rows with key values 1, 3, and 5. Before Transaction A reads the data again within the transaction, Transaction B adds two more rows with the key values 2 and 4 and commits the changes. Assuming that Transaction A and Transaction B both can run independently without blocking each other, when Transaction A runs the query a second time, it is now going to get 5 rows with key values 1, 2, 3, 4, and 5. This phenomenon is called **phantom reads** because in the second pass, you are getting records you did not expect to retrieve.

Ideally, a DBMS must provide levels of isolation to prevent these types of scenarios. Sometimes, because of practical and performance reasons, databases do relax some of the rules. ANSI has defined four transaction isolation levels, each providing a different degree of isolation to cover the previous scenarios. ANSI SQL-92 defines the following four standards for transaction isolation:

- Read Uncommitted (Level 0)
- Read Committed (Level 1)
- Repeatable Read (Level 2)
- Serializable (Level 3)

SQL Server does support all these levels. Each higher level incorporates the isolation provided at the lower levels. You can set these isolation levels for your entire session by using the `SET TRANSACTION ISOLATION LEVEL` T-SQL command, or for individual `SELECT` statements by specifying the isolation level hints within the query. Using table-level hints will be covered later in this chapter in the "Table Hints for Locking" section.

Read Uncommitted

If you set the Read Uncommitted mode for a session, no isolation is provided to the `SELECT` queries in that session. A transaction that is running with this isolation level is not immune to dirty reads, nonrepeatable reads, or phantom reads.

To set the Read Uncommitted mode for a session, run the following statements from the client:

- T-SQL—`SET TRANSACTION ISOLATION LEVEL READ UNCOMMITTED`.
- ODBC—Use the function call `SQLSetConnectAttr` with `Attribute` set to `SQL_ATTR_TXN_ISOLATION` and `ValuePtr` set to `SQL_TXN_READ_UNCOMMITTED`.
- OLE DB—Use the function call `ITransactionLocal::StartTransaction` with the `isoLevel` set to `ISOLATIONLEVEL_READUNCOMMITTED`.
- ADO—Set the `IsolationLevel` property of the Connection object to `adXactReadUncommitted`.

Be careful when running queries at Read Uncommitted isolation; it is possible to read changes that have been made to data that are subsequently rolled back. In essence, the accuracy of the results cannot be guaranteed. You should only use this mode when you need to get information quickly from an OLTP database without impacting or being impacted by the ongoing updates, and when the accuracy of the results is not critical.

Read Committed

The Read Committed mode is the default locking-isolation mode for SQL Server. With Read Committed as the transaction isolation level, read operations can only read pages for transactions that have already been committed. No "dirty reads" are allowed. Locks acquired by update transactions are held for the duration of the transaction. However, in this mode, read requests release locks as soon as the query finishes reading the data. Although this improves concurrent access to the data for updates, it does not prevent nonrepeatable reads or phantom reads. For example, within a transaction, a process could read one set of rows early in the transaction, and then before reading the information again, another process could modify the resultset, resulting in a different resultset being read the second time.

Because Read Committed is the default isolation level for SQL Server, you do not need to do anything to set this mode. If you need to set the isolation level back to Read Committed mode for a session, run the following statements from the client:

- T-SQL—`SET TRANSACTION ISOLATION LEVEL READ COMMITTED`.
- ODBC—Use the function call `SQLSetConnectAttr` with `Attribute` set to `SQL_ATTR_TXN_ISOLATION` and `ValuePtr` set to `SQL_TXN_READ_COMMITTED`.
- OLE DB—Use the function call `ITransactionLocal::StartTransaction` with `isoLevel` set to `ISOLATIONLEVEL_READCOMMITTED`.
- ADO—Set the `IsolationLevel` property of the `Connection` object to `adXactReadcommitted`.

Repeatable Read

In Repeatable Read mode, SQL Server provides the same level of isolation for updates as in Read Committed mode, but it also allows the data to be read many times within the same transaction and guarantees that the same values will be read each time. Repeatable Read isolation mode prevents other users from updating data that has been read within the transaction until the transaction in which it was read is committed or rolled back. This way, the reading transaction will not pick up changes to the rows it read previously within the transaction. However, this isolation mode does not prevent additional rows (phantom reads) from appearing in the subsequent reads.

Although preventing nonrepeatable reads is desirable for certain transactions, it requires holding locks on the data that has been read until the transaction is completed. This reduces concurrent access for multiple update operations and causes performance degradation due to lock waits and locking contention between transactions. It can also potentially lead to deadlocks. (Deadlocking will be discussed in more detail in the "Deadlocks" section later in this chapter.)

To set Repeatable Read mode for a session, run the following statements from the client:

- T-SQL—`SET TRANSACTION ISOLATION LEVEL REPEATABLE READ`.
- ODBC—Use the function call `SQLSetConnectAttr` with `Attribute` set to `SQL_ATTR_TXN_ISOLATION` and `ValuePtr` set to `SQL_TXN_REPEATABLEREAD`.
- OLE DB—Use the function call `ITransactionLocal::StartTransaction` with `isoLevel` set to `ISOLATIONLEVEL_REPEATABLEREAD`.
- ADO—Set the `IsolationLevel` property of the `Connection` object to `adXact REPEATABLEREAD`.

Serializable

Serializable Read mode is similar to repeatable reads but adds to it the restriction that rows cannot be added to a resultset that was read previously within a transaction. This prevents phantom reads. In other words, Serializable Read locks the existing data being read as well as rows that do not yet exist. It accomplishes this by locking the data being read. In addition, SQL Server puts locks on the range of values being read so that additional rows cannot be added to the range.

For example, perhaps you run a query in a transaction that retrieves all records for the Sales table in the Pubs database for a store with the stor_id of 7066. To prevent additional sales records from being added to the sales table for this store, SQL Server locks the range of values with stor_id of 7066. It accomplishes this by using key-range locks, which will be discussed in the "Serialization and Key-Range Locking" section later in this chapter.

Although preventing phantom reads is desirable for certain transactions, Serializable mode, like Repeatable Read, reduces concurrent access for multiple update operations and can cause performance degradation due to lock waits and locking contention between transactions, and potentially lead to deadlocks.

To set the Serializable mode for a session, run the following statements from the client:

- T-SQL—`SET TRANSACTION ISOLATION LEVEL SERIALIZABLE`.
- ODBC—Use the function call `SQLSetConnectAttr` with `Attribute` set to `SQL_ATTR_TXN_ISOLATION` and `ValuePtr` set to `SQL_TXN_SERIALIZABLE`.
- OLE DB—Use the function call `ITransactionLocal::StartTransaction` with `isoLevel` set to `ISOLATIONLEVEL_SERIALIZABLE`.
- ADO—Set the `IsolationLevel` property of the `Connection` object to `adXact SERIALIZABLE`.

NOTE

Only one of the transaction isolation levels can be active at any given time for a user session. The isolation level you set within your application is active for the duration of the connection or until manually reset. To check the current transaction isolation level settings, run the following command:

```
DBCC USEROPTIONS
Go

Set Option                          Value
----------------------------------  -----------
textsize                            64512
language                            us_english
dateformat                          mdy
datefirst                           7
quoted_identifier                   SET
ansi_null_dflt_on                   SET
ansi_defaults                       SET
ansi_warnings                       SET
ansi_padding                        SET
ansi_nulls                          SET
concat_null_yields_null             SET
isolation level                     serializable
```

The Lock Manager

The responsibility for ensuring lock conflict resolution between user processes falls on the SQL Server Lock Manager. SQL Server automatically assigns locks to processes to guarantee that the current user of a resource (a data page, index page, table, index, database, and so on) has a consistent view of that resource from beginning to end of a particular operation. In other words, what you start with will be what you work with throughout your operation. Nobody can change what you are working on in mid-state, thereby ensuring the consistency of your transaction.

The Lock Manager is responsible for deciding the appropriate lock type (shared, exclusive, update, and so on) and the appropriate granularity of locks (row, page, table, and so on) according to the type of operation being performed and the amount of data being affected. Based on the type of transaction, the SQL Server Lock Manager chooses different types of lock resources. For example, a `CREATE INDEX` statement might lock the entire table, whereas an `UPDATE` statement might lock only a specific row.

The Lock Manager also manages compatibility between lock types attempting to access the same resources, resolves deadlocks, and escalates locks to a higher level if necessary.

The Lock Manager manages locks for both shared data and for internal system resources. For shared data, the Lock Manager manages row locks, page locks, and table locks on tables, as well as data pages, text pages, and leaf level index pages. Internally, the Lock Manager uses latches to manage locking on index rows and pages, controlling access to internal data structures, and in some cases, for retrieving individual rows of data. Latches provide better system performance because they are less resource intensive than locks. Latches also provide greater concurrency than locks. Latches are typically used for operations such as page splits, deletion of index rows, movement of rows in an index, and so on. The main difference between a lock and a latch is that a lock is held for the duration of the transaction, and a latch is held only for the duration of the operation for which it is required. Locks are used to ensure the logical consistensy of the data, whereas latches are used to ensure the physyical consistency of the data and the data structures.

The remainder of this chapter will examine how the Lock Manager determines the type and level of lock to assign based on the type of command being executed, the number of rows affected, and the lock isolation level in effect at the time.

Monitoring Lock Activity in SQL Server

To monitor the performance of the system, it is necessary to keep track of locking activity in SQL Server. Following are the more commonly used methods to do so:

- Using the `sp_lock` stored procedure
- Querying the `syslockinfo` table directly
- Viewing locking activity with SQL Enterprise Manager

- Viewing locking activity with SQL Profiler
- Viewing the current quantity of locks with Performance Monitor

As you read through the rest of this chapter, you might want to examine or monitor the locking activity for the examples presented. To assist you in that effort, the remainder of this section describes the methods of examining lock activity in SQL Server 2000.

Using the sp_lock Stored Procedure

The stored procedure sp_lock provides a snapshot of the locks that are currently being held on resources by various commands and transactions in SQL Server. The syntax of sp lock is as follows:

```
Exec sp_lock [SPID1] [,SPID2]
```

Following is the sample output of this command:

```
Exec sp_lock
go

spid   dbid   ObjId       IndId  Type Resource        Mode     Status
------ ------ ----------- ------ ---- --------------- -------- ------
    51      8           0      0 DB                   S        GRANT
    51      1    85575343      0 TAB                  IS       GRANT
    53      8  1685581043      1 PAG  1:5798          IX       GRANT
    53      8           0      0 DB                   S        GRANT
    53      8  1685581043      0 TAB                  IX       GRANT
    54      8  1653580929      1 KEY  (c6028dcecb9e)  RangeS-S GRANT
    54      8  1653580929      1 PAG  1:126           IS       GRANT
    54      8  1653580929      1 KEY  (7601e649921b)  RangeS-S GRANT
    54      8           0      0 DB                   S        GRANT
    54      8  1653580929      1 KEY  (bc023be5404b)  RangeS-S GRANT
    54      8  1653580929      1 KEY  (b3018d0ff0ac)  RangeS-S GRANT
    54      8  1653580929      1 KEY  (c70165b0fdb4)  RangeS-S GRANT
    54      8  1653580929      1 KEY  (020285578a77)  RangeS-S GRANT
    54      8  1653580929      0 TAB                  IS       GRANT
    54      8  1653580929      1 KEY  (c402f8d775ed)  RangeS-S GRANT
    54      8  1653580929      1 KEY  (3803e05ac6f2)  RangeS-S GRANT
    54      8  1653580929      1 KEY  (6e01b3d59a06)  RangeS-S GRANT
    54      8  1653580929      1 KEY  (67018a3bdf5c)  RangeS-S GRANT
    54      8  1653580929      1 KEY  (9e028a40b4ce)  RangeS-S GRANT
```

The columns in the sp_lock output provide the following information:

- The spid is the process ID for a transaction.
- The dbid is the ID of the database on which locks are held.
- The ObjId is the ID of the resource on which table, key, or page locks are held.
- The IndId is the ID for the table index on which locks are held. A value of 0 indicates that the lock is on a data row, data page, table, or database. A value of 1 indicates that the lock is on a clustered index data row, index row, or index page. A value between 2 and 254 indicates that the lock is on a nonclustered index row or page, and a value of 255 indicates that the lock is on a text or image page.
- The Type is the type of lock being held on the resource.
- The Resource is the internal name of the resource on which locks are placed. This information comes from the syslockinfo table in the master database. Information displayed by this column is directly governed by the type of lock held on the resource. An explanation of the values in this column is presented later in this chapter in the "Lock Types and the syslockinfo Table" section.
- The Mode is the type of lock that is requested by the transaction. All the lock types possible will be discussed in the "SQL Server Lock Types" section later in this chapter.
- The Status is the current status of request. The possible values are GRANT, WAIT, and CNVRT.

By default, sp_lock returns locking information for all processes in SQL Server. In a system with a large number of concurrent processes executing, this can generate a substantial amount of output. If you are interested in examining the locks for only one or two processes, you can specify the process ID (spid) for those processes as arguments to sp_lock. sp_lock will then display only the locks that are associated with those spid(s):

```
exec sp_lock 53
spid   dbid   ObjId       IndId  Type Resource         Mode     Status
------ ------ ----------- ------ ---- ---------------- -------- ------
    53      8           0      0 DB                    S        GRANT
    53      8  1685581043      0 TAB                   IX       GRANT
    53      8  1685581043      1 PAG  1:5798           IX       GRANT
```

Additional examples of using sp_lock will be presented in other sections in this chapter where appropriate.

Querying the syslockinfo Table

The information presented by sp_lock is retrieved from the memory resident table syslockinfo, which resides in the master database. The syslockinfo table contains information on all the locks currently granted or waiting to be granted in SQL Server. (The information contained in the syslockinfo table and the meaning of the values is described in more detail later in this chapter in the "Lock Types and the syslockinfo Table" section.) If you would like to see the information more directly, or you don't like the way the information is presented by sp_lock, you can write your own queries against the syslockinfo table to view and monitor the locking behavior.

For example, sp_lock displays the database ID instead of the database name, and displays the object ID instead of the object name, even if run in the same database in which the object exists. It would also be helpful to display the login ID associated with the spid. Listing 38.1 provides an example of a query against the syslockinfo table.

LISTING 38.1 Example of a Query Against the syslockinfo Table

```
select convert(varchar(30), suser_sname(p.sid)) as login,
       convert (smallint, req_spid) As spid,
       convert(varchar(30), db_name(rsc_dbid)) As db_name,
       case rsc_dbid when db_id()
            then convert(varchar(30), object_name(rsc_objid))
            else convert(varchar(30), rsc_objid) end As Object,
       rsc_indid As indid,
       substring (lock_type.name, 1, 4) As Type,
       substring (lock_mode.name, 1, 12) As Mode,
       substring (lock_status.name, 1, 5) As Status,
       substring (rsc_text, 1, 16) as Resource
   from master..syslockinfo s
   join master..spt_values lock_type on s.rsc_type = lock_type.number
   join master..spt_values lock_status on s.req_status = lock_status.number
   join master..spt_values lock_mode on s.req_mode = lock_mode.number -1
   join master..sysprocesses p on s.req_spid = p.spid
   where lock_type.type = 'LR'
     and lock_status.type = 'LS'
     and lock_mode.type = 'L'
     and db_name(rsc_dbid) not in ('master', 'msdb', 'tempdb', 'model')
order by spid, lock_type.number
go

login spid db_name       Object    indid  Type Mode       Status Resource
----- ---- ------------- --------- ------ ---- ---------- ------ --------------
sa      51 bigpubs2000   NULL          0 DB   S          GRANT
sa      53 bigpubs2000   NULL          0 DB   S          GRANT
```

LISTING 38.1 Continued

```
sa       53 bigpubs2000    stores         0 TAB  IX         GRANT
sa       53 bigpubs2000    stores         1 PAG  IX         GRANT  1:5798
sa       54 bigpubs2000    NULL           0 DB   S          GRANT
sa       54 bigpubs2000    sales          0 TAB  IS         GRANT
sa       54 bigpubs2000    sales          1 PAG  IS         GRANT  1:126
sa       54 bigpubs2000    sales          1 KEY  RangeS-S   GRANT  (7601e649921b)
sa       54 bigpubs2000    sales          1 KEY  RangeS-S   GRANT  (c6028dcecb9e)
sa       54 bigpubs2000    sales          1 KEY  RangeS-S   GRANT  (bc023be5404b)
sa       54 bigpubs2000    sales          1 KEY  RangeS-S   GRANT  (b3018d0ff0ac)
sa       54 bigpubs2000    sales          1 KEY  RangeS-S   GRANT  (c402f8d775ed)
sa       54 bigpubs2000    sales          1 KEY  RangeS-S   GRANT  (3803e05ac6f2)
sa       54 bigpubs2000    sales          1 KEY  RangeS-S   GRANT  (c70165b0fdb4)
sa       54 bigpubs2000    sales          1 KEY  RangeS-S   GRANT  (020285578a77)
sa       54 bigpubs2000    sales          1 KEY  RangeS-S   GRANT  (6e01b3d59a06)
sa       54 bigpubs2000    sales          1 KEY  RangeS-S   GRANT  (67018a3bdf5c)
sa       54 bigpubs2000    sales          1 KEY  RangeS-S   GRANT  (9e028a40b4ce)
```

Note that to translate the integer values for the lock type, mode, and status, you need to do lookups against the values stored in the `spt_values` table in the master database. Also, the query contains a `CASE` expression for displaying the object name. If the database ID of the locked resource is the same as the current database context, it returns the object name; otherwise, it returns the object ID because the `object_name()` function operates only in the current database context.

To save yourself the trouble of having to type in the query listed in Listing 38.1, or having to read it in from a file each time you want to run it, you might want to consider creating your own system-stored procedure that invokes this query. You can then use that stored procedure to monitor locks instead of `sp_lock`. (For more information on creating system-stored procedures, see Chapter 28, "Creating and Managing Stored Procedures in SQL Server.")

Viewing Locking Activity with SQL Enterprise Manager

You have seen that the output of `sp_lock` is somewhat unfriendly because it displays the IDs of the database and objects. The custom query against the `syslockinfo` table provides somewhat more user-friendly output. You can also use the SQL Server Enterprise Manager to display the locking information. To see the output from the Enterprise Manager, expand the server items, expand the Management folder, expand the Current Activity item, and click on either Locks/Process ID or Locks/Object to display the locking information in SQL Server.

TIP

To see more information when viewing the lock activity in Enterprise Manager, be sure to go to the EM View menu and choose the Detail option. EM will then display detailed information about the locks beyond just the process ID or object name. The information displayed includes the lock type, lock mode, lock status, and index involved.

The Locks/Process ID item displays in the left windowpane a list of the processes that are currently holding locks in SQL Server. Clicking on one of the processes lists the locks currently being held by that process (see Figure 38.1).

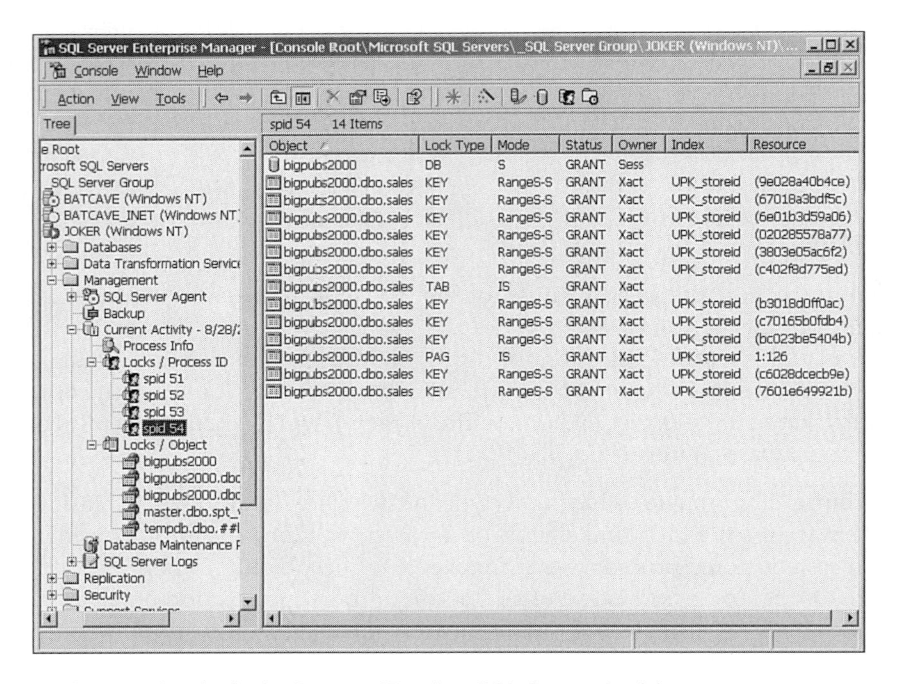

FIGURE 38.1 Viewing locks by Process ID using SQL Enterprise Manager.

The Locks/Object item displays in the left windowpane a list of all the objects that currently have locks held on them. Clicking on one of the objects lists the processes currently holding locks on that object and the locks being held (see Figure 38.2).

To display the command that was last executed by a process associated with a lock, you can double-click on an item in the right windowpane, or right-click on the item and select the Properties menu option. This will bring up a pop-up window containing the SQL text of the last command that was executed by that process.

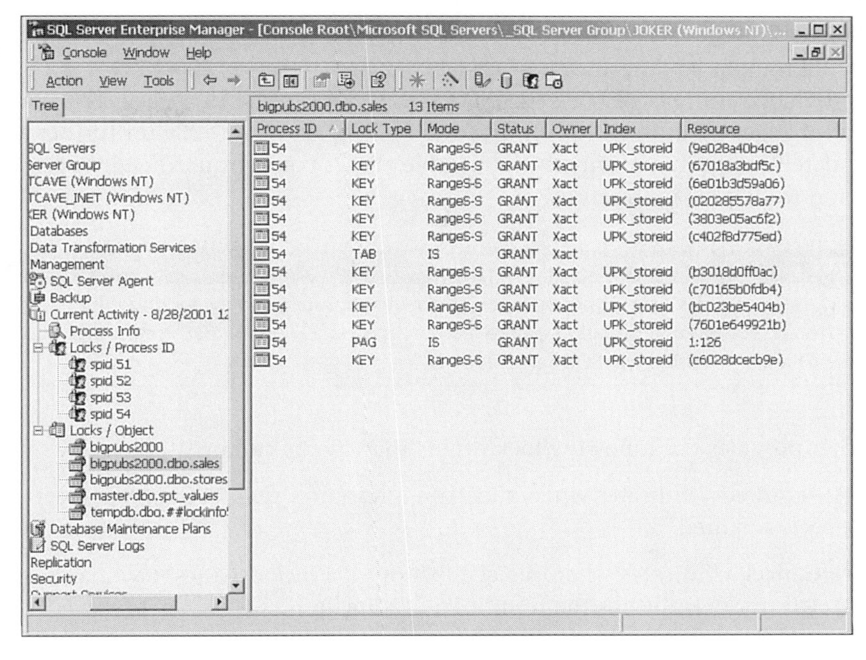

FIGURE 38.2 Viewing locks by Object using SQL Enterprise Manager.

NOTE

Personally, I am not a big fan of Enterprise Manager (EM) as a lock-monitoring tool because it has a number of frustrating shortcomings.

One problem you might run into when using EM to monitor locks is that it uses tempdb to build the results that it displays onscreen. At times, Enterprise Manager might end up being blocked requesting a lock in tempdb, and you are left watching an hourglass mouse cursor. This sort of defeats the purpose of a having a lock-monitoring tool to identify the process that is causing locking contention if the tool ends up being blocked as well, and cannot display the information.

Another shortcoming of lock monitoring in EM is that the lock information can only be displayed for a single process or for a single object. You cannot view all the current locks together in a single window. This makes it difficult to identify conflicting or competing lock requests between multiple processes or multiple objects.

A third, and one of the most annoying, shortcomings of using EM as a method of monitoring locking in SQL Server is that it has no automatic refresh capability for refreshing the lock information. To update the information displayed, you have to right-click on the Current Activity item in the left windowpane and choose the Refresh menu option. Unfortunately, when you do this, EM closes out the Locks/Process and Locks/Object windows and you have to go back and reopen them to get back to what you were looking at before. This can be tedious and cumbersome when you are trying to watch what is going on in real time.

Personally, I find that using Query Analyzer and `sp_lock` or a custom system-stored procedure that retrieves information from `syslockinfo` to be a better method of monitoring locking in SQL Server 2000. It provides more flexibility over what you can display, and a refresh of the results is as simple as clicking on the Execute button.

Viewing Locking Activity with SQL Profiler

Another tool to help you monitor locking activity in SQL Server 2000 is SQL Profiler. SQL Profiler provides a number of Lock events that you can capture in a trace. The trace information can be viewed in real time, or saved to a file or database table for further analysis at a later date. Saving the information to a table allows you to run different reports on the information to help in the analysis.

NOTE

This chapter provides only a brief overview of how to capture and view locking information using SQL Profiler. For more information on the features and capabilities of SQL Profiler and how to use it, see Chapter 7, "Using the SQL Server Profiler."

SQL Profiler provides the following lock events that can be captured in a trace:

- Lock:Acquired—Indicates when a lock on a resource, such as a data page or a row, has been acquired.
- Lock:Cancel—Indicates when the acquisition of a lock on a resource has been canceled (for example, as the result of a deadlock).
- Lock:Deadlock—Indicates when two or more concurrent processes have deadlocked with each other.
- Lock:Deadlock Chain—Provides the information for each of the events leading up to the deadlock. This information is similar to that provided by the 1204 trace flag, which is covered in the "Deadlocks" section later in this chapter.
- Lock:Escalation—Indicates when a lower-level lock has been converted to a higher-level lock (for example, when page-level locks are escalated to a table-level lock).
- Lock:Released—Indicates that a process has released a previously acquired lock on a resource.
- Lock:Timeout—Indicates that a lock request that is waiting on a resource has timed out due to another transaction holding a blocking lock.

Figure 38.3 shows an example of choosing a set of locking events to monitor with SQL Profiler.

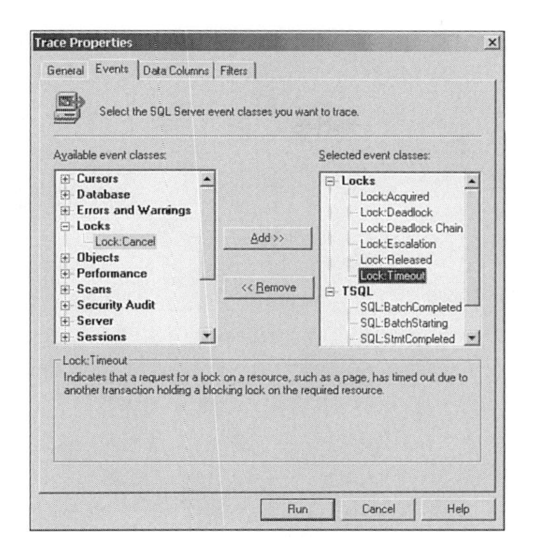

FIGURE 38.3 Choosing lock events in SQL Profiler.

SQL Profiler also provides a number of data values to display for the events being monitored. The following data columns are ones that you might find most useful when monitoring locking activity:

- spid—The process ID of the process that generated the event.
- EventClass—The type of event that is being captured.
- Mode—For lock monitoring, the type of lock that is involved in the captured event.
- ObjectID—The ID of the object that is involved in the locking event—that is, the object that the lock is associated with.
- ObjectName—The name of the object involved in the locking event.
- IndexID—The ID of the index that the lock is associated with.
- TextData—The query that generated the lock event.
- LoginName—The login name associated with the process.
- ApplicationName—The name of the application that is generating the lock event.

Keep in mind that many internal system processes also acquire locks within SQL Server. If you want to filter out those processes and focus on specific processes, users, or applications, use the filters in SQL Profiler to include the information you want to trace or exclude the information you don't want to trace (see Figure 38.4).

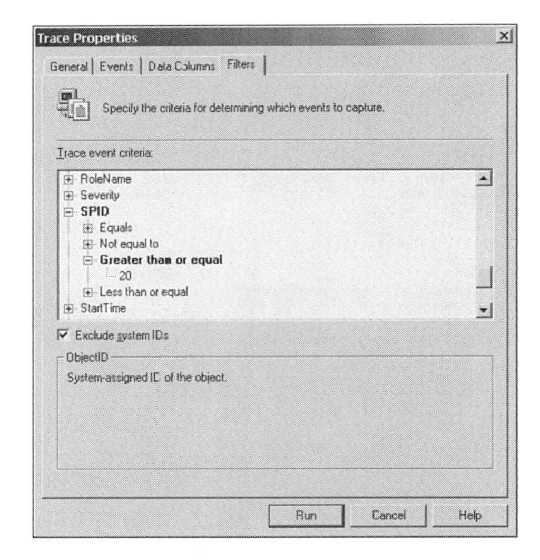

FIGURE 38.4 Filtering out unwanted information in SQL Profiler.

After you have set up your events, data columns, and filters, you can begin the trace. An example of the type of information captured is shown in Figure 38.5.

SQL Profiler

File Edit View Replay Tools Window Help

Locking Activity (joker)

SPID	EventClass	Mode	ObjectID	O	IndexID	TextData	Applicatio
54	Lock:Acquired	Intent-Share	1685581043		1		SQL Query A
54	SQL:StmtCom...					select count(state) from stores hol...	SQL Query A
54	SQL:BatchCo...					begin tran select count(state) fr...	SQL Query A
54	SQL:BatchSt...					delete from stores where stor_id = ...	SQL Query A
54	SQL:StmtSta...					delete from stores where stor_id = ...	SQL Query A
54	Lock:Acquired	Intent-Ex...	1957582012		0		SQL Query A
54	Lock:Acquired	Intent-Ex...	1957582012		0		SQL Query A
54	Lock:Timeout	Share	1685581043		1		SQL Query A
53	SQL:BatchSt...					delete from stores where stor_id = ...	SQL Query A
53	SQL:StmtSta...					delete from stores where stor_id = ...	SQL Query A
53	Lock:Acquired	Intent-Ex...	1957582012		0		SQL Query A
53	Lock:Acquired	Intent-Ex...	1957582012		0		SQL Query A
53	Lock:Timeout	Share	1685581043		1		SQL Query A
54	Lock:Deadlock	Share	1685581043		1		SQL Query A
54	Lock:Released		1685581043		0		SQL Query A
54	Lock:Released		1653580929		1		SQL Query A
54	Lock:Released		1653580929		1		SQL Query A
54	Lock:Released		1653580929		1		SQL Query A

```
delete from stores where stor_id = '7200'
```

Trace is running | Ln 307, Col 2 | Rows: 334

Connections: 1

FIGURE 38.5 Lock information captured in SQL Profiler trace.

Viewing the Current Quantity of Locks with Performance Monitor

Another method of monitoring locking in SQL Server is through the Performance Monitor. The stored procedure `sp_lock` and Enterprise Manager provide a snapshot of the actual locks currently in effect in SQL Server. If you want to monitor the locking activity as a whole on a continuous basis, you can use the NT Performance Monitor and monitor the counters that are available for the SQLServer:Locks performance object (see Figure 38.6).

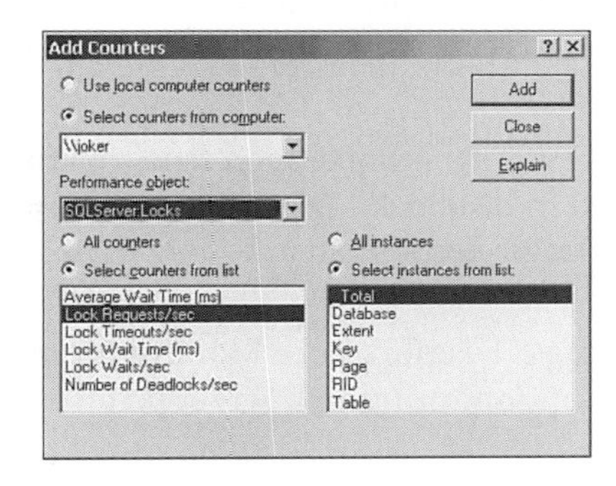

FIGURE 38.6 Choosing counters for the SQLServer:Locks performance object in Performance Monitor.

You can use the SQLServer:Locks object to help detect locking bottlenecks and contention points in the system, as well as to provide a summary of the overall locking activity in SQL Server. You can use the information that Performance Monitor provides to identify whether locking problems are the cause of any performance problems. You can then take appropriate corrective actions to improve concurrency and the overall performance of the system. The counters that belong to the SQLServer:Locks object are as follows:

- Average Wait Time—This counter represents the average wait time (in milliseconds) for each lock request. A high value is an indication of low concurrency of the system.
- Lock Requests/sec—This counter represents the total number of new locks and lock conversion requests made per second. A high value for this counter is not necessarily a cause for alarm; it might simply indicate a system with a high number of concurrent users.
- Lock Timeouts/sec—This counter represents the total number of lock timeouts per second that occur for lock requests on a resource that cannot be granted before the lock timeout interval is exceeded. By default, a blocked process will wait indefinitely unless the application specifies a maximum timeout limit using the `SET LOCK_TIMEOUT` command. A high value for this counter might indicate that the timeout limit is set to a low value in your application, or that you are experiencing excessive locking contention.

- Lock Wait Time—This counter represents the cumulative wait time for each lock request. It is given in milliseconds. A high value here indicates that you might have long-running or inefficient transactions that are causing blocking and locking contention.
- Lock Waits/sec—This counter represents the total number of lock requests generated per second for which a process had to wait before a lock request on a resource was granted. A high value might indicate inefficient or long-running transactions or a poor database design that is causing a large number of transactions to block one another.
- Number of Deadlocks/sec—This number represents the total number of lock requests per second that resulted in deadlocks. Deadlocks and how to avoid them are discussed in the "Deadlocks" section later in this chapter.

For more information on using NT Performance Monitor for monitoring SQL Server performance, see Chapter 37, "Monitoring SQL Server Performance."

SQL Server Lock Types

Locking is handled automatically within SQL Server. The Lock Manager chooses the type of locks based on the type of transaction (such as `select`, `insert`, `update`, and `delete`). The various types of locks used by Lock Manager are as follows:

- Shared
- Update
- Exclusive
- Intent
- Schema Locks
- Bulk Update Locks

As in version 7.0, the Lock Manager in SQL Server 2000 automatically adjusts the granularity of the locks (row, page, table, and so on) based on the nature of the statement that is executed and the number of rows that are affected.

Shared Locks

SQL Server uses shared locks for all read operations. A **shared lock** is, by definition, not exclusive. Theoretically, an unlimited number of shared locks can be held on a resource at any given time. In addition, shared locks are unique in that, by default, a process locks the resource only for the duration of the read on that page. For example, a query such as `select * from authors` would lock the first page in the `authors` table when the query starts. After data on the first page is read, the lock on that page is released, and a lock on the second page is acquired. After the second page is read, its lock is released and a lock on the third page is acquired, and so on. In this fashion, a `select` query allows other data pages that are not being read to be modified during the read operation. This increases concurrent access to the data.

Shared locks are compatible with other shared locks as well as with update locks. In this way, a shared lock does not prevent the acquisition of additional shared locks or an update lock by other processes on a given page. Multiple shared locks can be held at any given time for a number of transactions or processes. These transactions do not affect the consistency of the data. However, shared locks do prevent the acquisition of exclusive locks. Any transaction that is attempting to modify data on a page or a row on which a shared lock is placed will be blocked until all the shared locks are released.

NOTE

It is important to point out that within a transaction running at the default isolation level of Read Committed, shared locks are not held for the duration of the transaction, or even the duration of the statement that acquires the shared locks. Shared lock resources (row, page, table, and so on) are normally released as soon as the read operation on the resource is completed. SQL Server provides the `HOLDLOCK` clause to the `SELECT` statement if you want to continue holding the shared lock for the duration of the transaction. `HOLDLOCK` is explained later in this chapter in the section "Table Hints for Locking." Another way to hold shared locks for the duration of the transaction is to set the isolation level for the session or the query to repeatable reads or higher.

Update Locks

Update locks are used to lock pages that a user process would like to modify. When a transaction tries to update a row, it must first read the row to ensure that it is modifying the appropriate record. If the transaction were to put a shared lock on the resource initially, it would eventually need to get an exclusive lock on the resource to modify the record and prevent any other transaction from modifying the same record. The problem is that this could lead to deadlocks in an environment in which multiple transactions are trying to modify data on the same resource at the same time. Figure 38.7 demonstrates how deadlocks can occur if lock conversion takes place from shared locks to exclusive locks. When both processes attempt to escalate the shared lock they both hold on a resource to an exclusive lock, it results in a deadlock situation.

Update locks in SQL Server are provided to prevent this kind of deadlock scenario. Update locks are partially exclusive in that only one update lock can be acquired at a time on any resource. However, an update lock is compatible with shared locks, in that both can be acquired on the same resource simultaneously. In effect, an update lock signifies that a process wants to change a record, and keeps out other processes that also want to change that record. However, an update lock does allow other processes to acquire shared locks to read the data until the update or delete statement is finished locating the records to be affected. The process then attempts to escalate each update lock to an exclusive lock. At this time, the process will wait until all currently held shared locks on the same records are released. After the shared locks are released, the update lock is escalated to an exclusive lock. The data change is then carried out and the exclusive lock is held for the remainder of the transaction.

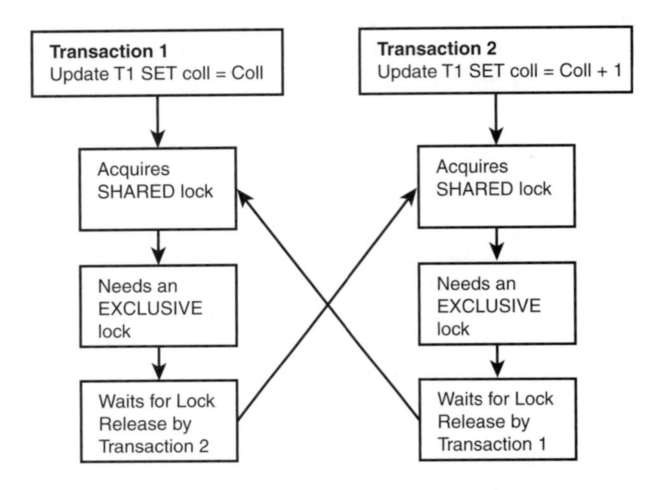

FIGURE 38.7 Deadlock scenario with shared and exclusive locks.

NOTE

Update locks are not used just for update operations. SQL Server uses update locks any time that a search for the data is required prior to performing the actual modification, such as qualified updates and deletes (that is, when a `where` clause is specified). Update locks are also used for inserts into a table with a clustered index because SQL Server must first search the data and the clustered index to identify the correct position at which to insert the new row to maintain the sort order. After SQL Server has found the correct location and begins inserting the record, it escalates the update lock to an exclusive lock.

Exclusive Locks

As mentioned earlier, an exclusive lock is granted to a transaction when it is ready to perform data modification. An exclusive lock on a resource makes sure that no other transaction can interfere with the data locked by the transaction that is holding the exclusive lock. SQL Server releases the exclusive lock at the end of the transaction.

Exclusive locks are incompatible with any other lock type. If an exclusive lock is held on a resource, any other read or data modification requests for the same resource by other processes will be forced to wait until the exclusive lock is released. Likewise, if a resource currently has read locks held on it by other processes, the exclusive lock request is forced to wait in a queue for the resource to become available.

Intent Locks

Intent locks are not really a locking mode, but a mechanism to indicate at a higher level of granularity the type of locks held at a lower level. The types of intent locks mirror the lock types previously discussed: shared intent locks, exclusive intent locks, and update intent locks. SQL Server Lock Manager uses intent locks as a mechanism to indicate that a shared, update, or exclusive lock is held at a lower level. For example, a shared intent lock on a table by a process signifies that the process currently holds a shared lock on a row or page within the table. The presence of the intent lock prevents other transactions from attempting to acquire a lock on the table.

Intent locks improve locking performance by allowing SQL Server to examine locks at the table level to determine the types of locks held on the table, rather than searching through the multiple locks at the page or row level within the table. Intent locks also prevent two transactions that are both holding locks at a lower level on a resource from attempting to escalate those locks to a higher level while the other transaction still holds the intent lock. This prevents deadlocks during lock escalation.

There are three types of intent locks that you will typically see when monitoring locking activity: intent shared (IS) locks, intent exclusive (IX) locks, and shared with intent exclusive (SIX) locks. The IS lock indicates that the process currently holds, or has the intention of holding, shared locks on lower-level resources (row or page). The IX lock indicates that the process currently holds, or has the intention of holding, exclusive locks on lower-level resources. The SIX (pronounced as the letters *S-I-X*, not like the number six) lock occurs under special circumstances when a transaction is holding a shared lock on a resource, and later in the transaction, an IX lock is needed. At that point, the IS lock is converted to an SIX lock.

In the following example, the `SELECT` statement run at the serializable level acquires a shared table lock. It then needs an exclusive lock to update the row in the `sales_big` table.

```
SET TRANSACTION ISOLATION LEVEL serializable
go
BEGIN TRAN
 select sum(qty) FROM sales_big
UPDATE sales_big
    SET qty = 0
    WHERE sales_id = 1001
COMMIT TRAN
```

Because the transaction initially acquired a Shared (S) table lock and then needed an exclusive row lock, which requires an intent exclusive (IX) lock on the table within the same transaction, the S lock is converted to an SIX lock.

> **NOTE**
>
> If only a few rows were in `sales_big`, SQL Server might only acquire individual row or key locks rather than a table-level lock. SQL Server would then have an intent shared (IS) lock on the table rather than a full shared (S) lock. In that instance, the `UPDATE` statement would then acquire a single exclusive lock to apply the update to a single row, and the X lock at the key level would result in the IS locks at the page and table level being converted to an IX lock at the page and table level for the remainder of the transaction.

Schema Locks

SQL Server uses schema locks to maintain structural integrity of SQL Server tables. Unlike other types of locks that provide isolation for the data, schema locks provide isolation for the schema of database objects, such as tables, views, and indexes within a transaction. The Lock Manager uses two types of schema locks:

- Schema stability locks—When a transaction is referencing either an index or a data page, SQL Server places a schema stability lock on the object. This ensures that no other process can modify the schema of an object—such as dropping an index or dropping or altering a stored procedure or table—while other processes are still referencing the object.
- Schema modification locks—When a process needs to modify the structure of an object (alter the table, recompile a stored procedure, and so on), the Lock Manager places a schema modification lock on the object. For the duration of this lock, no other transaction can reference the object until the changes are complete and committed.

Bulk Update Locks

Bulk Update locks are a special type of lock used only when bulk copying data into a table using the `bcp` utility or the `BULK INSERT` command. This special lock is used for these operations only when either the `TABLOCK` hint is specified to `bcp` or the `BULK INSERT` command, or when the `table lock on bulk load` table option has been set for the table. Bulk Update locks allow multiple bulk copy processes to bulk copy data into the same table in parallel, while preventing other processes that are not bulk copying data from accessing the table.

Lock Types and the syslockinfo Table

As stated before, the Lock Manager automatically manages the different types of locks that are placed on SQL Server objects. SQL Server keeps all this information in memory in its internal lock structures. To monitor the current locking activity in SQL Server 2000, you can view the contents of the internal lock structures via the syslockinfo system table. The syslockinfo table, which is defined in the master database, exists in memory only and is populated when queried. This table can be queried directly or via the sp_lock stored procedure to provide a snapshot of the locks currently held in SQL Server.

NOTE

In versions of SQL Server prior to SQL Server 7.0, lock information was contained in the syslocks system table. The syslockinfo table replaced the syslocks table. For backward compatibility with existing applications that might still reference the syslocks table, syslocks is provided in SQL Server 2000 as a view on the syslockinfo table. For future compatibility, all references to syslocks should be replaced with syslockinfo.

Some of the more significant and useful columns in the syslockinfo table are described as follows:

- rsc_dbid—This column contains the ID of the database that is associated with the object on which the lock is held.
- rsc_objid—This is the ID of the table on which the lock is placed.
- rsc_indid—This column contains the index ID of the resource on which the lock is held. This value is NULL if no locks are held on the index pages (or the rows of the index pages).
- rsc_type—This column contains a numeric code that represents the type of resource being locked by a transaction. The possible values for this column are outlined in Table 38.1.

NOTE

The numeric code values in the rsc_type and the req_mode and req_status fields can be translated into more meaningful values by looking them up in the spt_values table. The following query shows an example of retrieving information from syslockinfo and translating the lock request type, lock request mode, and resource type code values into more meaningful names from spt_values.

```
select convert (smallint, req_spid) As spid,
       convert(varchar(30), db_name(rsc_dbid)) As db_name,
       rsc_objid As ObjId,
       rsc_indid As IndId,
       substring (lock_type.name, 1, 4) As Type,
```

```
        substring (lock_mode.name, 1, 8) As Mode,
        substring (lock_status.name, 1, 5) As Status,
        substring (rsc_text, 1, 16) as Resource
    from master..syslockinfo s
    join master..spt_values lock_type on s.rsc_type = lock_type.number
    join master..spt_values lock_status on s.req_status = lock_status.number
    join master..spt_values lock_mode on s.req_mode = lock_mode.number
    where lock_type.type = 'LR'
      and lock_status.type = 'LS'
      and lock_mode.type = 'L'
 order by spid, lock_type.number
```

TABLE 38.1 Resource Type

Column Value	Description	sp_lock **Displayed Value (from** spt_values**)**
1	No resources used	
2	Database	DB
3	File	FIL
4	Index	IDX
5	Table	TAB
6	Page	PAG
7	Key	KEY
8	Extent	EXT
9	Row ID	RID
10	Application	APP

- req_mode—This column contains a numeric code that represents the type of lock being requested by the transaction. The status of the request is kept in another column called req_status. Possible values for the req_mode column are shown in Table 38.2.

TABLE 38.2 Lock Request Mode

Value	Lock Type	Description	sp_lock **Displayed Value (from** spt_values**)**
1	N/A	No access is provided to the requestor	NULL
2	Schema	Schema stability lock	Sch-S
3	Schema	Schema modification lock	Sch-M
4	Shared	Acquisition of a shared lock on the resource	S
5	Update	Acquisition of an update lock on the resource	U
6	Exclusive	Exclusive lock granted on the resource	X
7	Intent	Intent for a shared lock	IS

TABLE 38.2 Continued

Value	Lock Type	Description	`sp_lock` **Displayed Value (from** `spt_values`**)**
8	Intent	Intent for an update lock	IU
9	Intent	Intent for an exclusive lock	IX
10	Intent	Shared lock with intent for an update lock on subordinate resources	SIU
11	Intent	Shared lock with intent for an exclusive lock on subordinate resources	SIX
12	Intent	Update lock with intent for an exclusive lock on subordinate resources	UIX
13	Bulk	`BULK UPDATE` lock used for bulk copy operations	BU
14	Key-Range	Shared lock on the range between keys and shared lock on the key at the end of the range; used for serializable range scan	Range_S_S
15	Key-Range	Shared lock on the range between keys with update lock on the key at the end of the range	Range_S_U
16	Key-Range	Exclusive lock used to prevent inserts into a range between keys	RangeIn-Null
17	Key-Range	Key-Range conversion lock created by overlap of RangeIn-Null and shared (S) lock	RangeIn-S
18	Key-Range	Key-Range conversion lock created by overlap of RangeIn-Null and update (U) lock	RangeIn-U
19	Key-Range	Key-Range conversion lock created by overlap of RangeIn-Null and exclusive (X) lock	RangeIn-X
20	Key-Range	Key-Range conversion lock created by overlap of RangeIn-Null and RangeS_S lock	RangeX-S
21	Key-Range	Key-Range conversion lock created by overlap of RangeIn-Null and RangeS_U lock	RangeX-U
22	Key-Range	Exclusive lock on range between keys with an exclusive lock on the key at the end of the range	RangeX-X

- `req_status`—This column contains a numeric code that represents the status of a lock request. It can have the values as shown in Table 38.3.

TABLE 38.3 Lock Status

Value	Description	`sp_lock` **Displayed Value (from** `spt_values`**)**
1	Request for lock approved (granted)	GRANT
2	Request in the process of converting to approved (converting)	CNVT
3	Waiting to be approved (waiting)	WAIT

- `req_spid`—This column contains the SQL Server process ID of the session that is requesting the lock.
- `rsc_text`—This column contains a textual description of the locked resource. For example, for a lock on a page, the `rsc_text` column contains the file number and page number of the locked page. Table 38.4 describes the contents of the `rsc_text` column depending on the type of lock.

TABLE 38.4 Definition of Values Contained in the `rsc_text` Column

Lock Type	Description of `rsc_text` Value
Table	ObjectId.
Extent	FileNumber:PageNumber of first page in extent.
Page	FileNumber:PageNumber of data or index page.
Row	FileNumber:PageNumber:RowID.
Index Key	A hashed value derived from all the key components and the key locator. For example, for a nonclustered index on a heap table, the hash value would contain contributions from each of the key columns and the row ID.
Key-Range	Same as the index key.
Application	A hash value that is generated from the name given to the lock.

SQL Server Lock Granularity

The values listed earlier in Table 38.1 represent all the various levels, or granularity, of locks from which the SQL Server Lock Manager can choose when processing queries and transactions.

Lock granularity is essentially the minimum amount of data that is locked as part of a query or update to provide complete isolation and serialization for the transaction. The Lock Manager needs to balance the concurrent access to resources versus the overhead of maintaining a large number of lower-level locks. For example, the smaller the lock size, the greater the number of concurrent users who can access the same table at the same time, but the greater the overhead in maintaining those locks. The greater the lock size, the less overhead that is required to manage the locks, but concurrency is also less. Figure 38.8 demonstrates the tradeoffs between lock size and concurrency.

Currently, SQL Server balances performance and concurrency by locking at the row level or higher. Based on a number of factors, such as key distribution, number of rows, row density, search arguments (SARGs), and so on, the query optimizer makes lock granularity decisions internally, and the programmer does not have to worry about such issues. SQL Server 2000 does provide a number of T-SQL extensions that give you better control over query behavior from a locking standpoint. These optimizer overrides are discussed in the "Table Hints for Locking" section later in this chapter.

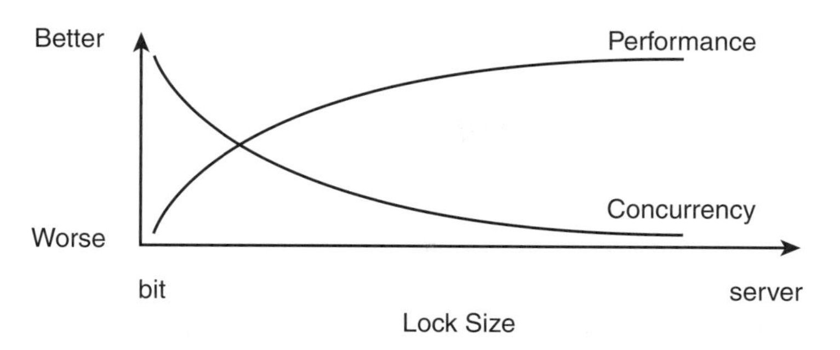

FIGURE 38.8 Tradeoffs between performance and concurrency depending on lock granularity.

The following list describes the locking levels in SQL Server 2000 in more detail:

- Database—Whenever a SQL Server process is using a database other than Master, the Lock Manager grants a DB lock to the process. These are always shared locks, and they are used to keep track of when a database is in use to prevent another process from dropping the database, setting the database offline, and restoring the database. Note that because master and tempdb cannot be dropped or set offline, DB locks are not required on those databases.
- Extent—Extent locks are used for locking extents, usually only during space allocation and deallocation. An extent consists of eight contiguous data or index pages. (See Chapter 33, "SQL Server Internals," for more information on extents.) Extent locks can be shared extent or exclusive extent locks.
- Table—The entire table, inclusive of data and indexes, is locked. Examples of when table-level locks can be acquired include selecting all rows from a large table at the serializable level, performing an unqualified update or delete on a table, or creating a clustered index on a table.
- Page—The entire page, consisting of 8KB of data or index information, is locked (for more information on pages, see Chapter 33). Page-level locks might be acquired when all rows on a page need to be read or when page level maintenance needs to be performed, such as updating page pointers after a page split.
- Row—A single row within a page is locked. Row locks are acquired whenever efficient and possible to do so in an effort to provide maximum concurrent access to the resource.
- Key—SQL Server uses two types of key locks. The one that is used depends on the locking isolation level of the current session. For transactions that run in Read Committed or Repeatable Read isolation modes, SQL Server locks the actual index keys that are associated with the rows being accessed. (If a clustered index is on the table, the data rows are the leaf level of the index. You will see key locks on those

rows instead of row locks.) When in Serialized isolation mode, SQL Server prevents phantom rows by locking a range of key values so that no new rows can be inserted into the range. These are referred to as **key-range locks**. Key-range locks associated with a particular key value lock that key and the previous one in the index to indicate that all values between them are locked. Key-range locks are covered in more detail in the next section.

- Application—SQL Server provides a new type of user-defined lock: the application lock. The application lock allows users to essentially define their own locks by specifying a name for the resource, a lock mode, an owner, and a timeout interval. Using application locks will be discussed in the "Using Application Locks" section.

Serialization and Key-Range Locking

As mentioned in the previous section, SQL Server provides serialization (isolation level 3) through the `SET TRANSACTION ISOLATION SERIALIZABLE` command. One of the isolations that is provided by this isolation level is the prevention against phantom reads. Preventing phantom reads means that the recordset that a query obtains within a transaction must return the same resultset when it is run multiple times within the same transaction. That is, while a transaction is active, another transaction should not be allowed to insert new rows that would appear in the recordset of a query that were not in the original recordset retrieved by the transaction. SQL Server 2000 provides this capability though key-range locking.

As described earlier, key-range locking within SQL Server provides isolation for a transaction from data modifications made by other transactions. This means that a transaction should return the same recordset each time. In this section, you will see how key-range locking works with various lock modes. Key-range locking covers the scenarios of a range search that returns a resultset as well as searches against nonexistent rows.

Key-Range Locking for Range Search

In this scenario, SQL Server places locks on the index pages for the range of data covered in the `WHERE` clause of the query. (For a clustered index, the rows would be the actual data rows in the table.) Because the range is locked, no other transaction will be able to insert new rows that fall within the range. In Figure 38.9, Transaction B tries to insert a row with a key value (`stor_id = 7200`) that falls within the range being used by Transaction A (`stor_id` between `6000` and `7500`).

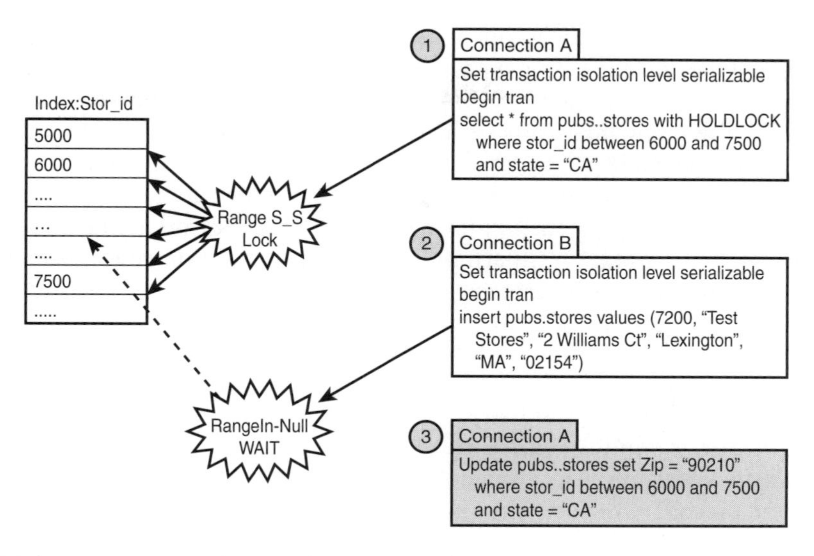

FIGURE 38.9 Key-range locking with range search.

Now take a look at the locks acquired using the `sp_lock` stored procedure (in this sample output, `spid` 52 is executing the `SELECT` statement, and `spid` 54 is attempting the `INSERT`):

```
exec sp_lock
go

spid   dbid   ObjId       IndId  Type Resource         Mode     Status
------ ------ ----------- ------ ---- ---------------- -------- ------
    52      5   117575457      1 KEY  (36000050901c)   RangeS-S GRANT
    52      5   117575457      1 KEY  (3700560a5b33)   RangeS-S GRANT
    52      5   117575457      1 KEY  (ffffffffffff)   RangeS-S GRANT
    52      5   117575457      1 PAG  1:105            IS       GRANT
    52      5   117575457      1 KEY  (3700f04c0158)   RangeS-S GRANT
    52      5           0      0 DB                    S        GRANT
    52      5   117575457      0 TAB                   IS       GRANT
    52      5   117575457      1 KEY  (370087018ad1)   RangeS-S GRANT
    52      5   117575457      1 KEY  (370011318da6)   RangeS-S GRANT
    52      5   117575457      1 KEY  (38004ab7b2bc)   RangeS-S GRANT
    54      5   117575457      0 TAB                   IX       GRANT
    54      5           0      0 DB                    S        GRANT
    54      5   117575457      1 KEY  (3700f04c0158)   RangeIn- WAIT
    54      5   117575457      1 PAG  1:105            IX       GRANT
```

To provide key-range isolation, SQL Server places RangeS-S locks (shared lock on the key range and shared lock on the key at the end of the range) on the index keys for the rows with the matching values. It also places intent share (IS) locks on the page(s) and the table that contain the rows. The insert process acquires intent exclusive (IX) locks on the destination page(s) and the table. In this case, the insert process is waiting for a RangeIn-Null lock on the key range until the RangeS-S locks in the key range are released. As described earlier in this chapter, the RangeIn-Null lock is an exclusive lock on the range between keys with no lock on the key. This is acquired because the insert process is attempting to insert a new store ID that has no associated key value.

Key-Range Locking When Searching Nonexistent Rows

In this scenario, if a transaction is trying to delete or retrieve a row that does not exist in the database, it still should not find any rows at a later stage in the same transaction with the same query. For example, in Figure 38.10, Transaction A is trying to fetch a nonexistent row with the key value `7200`, and another concurrent transaction (Transaction B) is trying to insert a record with the same key value (`stor_id = 7200`).

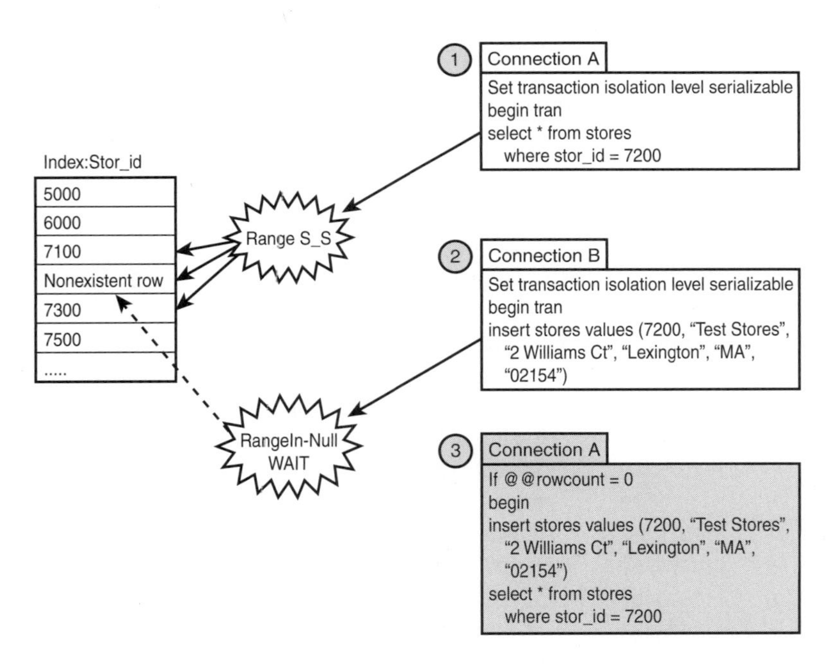

FIGURE 38.10 Key-range locking with a nonexistent dataset.

SQL Server in this mode will prevent Transaction B (`spid 54`) from inserting a new row by using a RangeS-S lock for Transaction A (`spid 52`). This lock is placed on the index key rows for the rows in the range between `MAX(stor_id) < 7200` (key value `7100` in Figure 38.10) and `MIN(stor_id) > 7200` (key value `7300` in Figure 38.10). Transaction B will hold a RangeIn-NULL lock and wait for the RangeS-S lock to be released.

Following is the sample output of the sp_lock command for these two transactions:

```
Exec sp_lock
Go

spid   dbid   ObjId       IndId  Type Resource         Mode     Status
------ ------ ----------- ------ ---- ---------------- -------- ------
    52      5   117575457      1 KEY  (36000050901c)   RangeS-S GRANT
    52      5   117575457      1 KEY  (3700560a5b33)   RangeS-S GRANT
    52      5   117575457      1 KEY  (ffffffffffff)   RangeS-S GRANT
    52      5   117575457      1 PAG  1:105            IS       GRANT
    52      5   117575457      1 KEY  (3700f04c0158)   RangeS-S GRANT
    52      5           0      0 DB                    S        GRANT
    52      5   117575457      0 TAB                   IS       GRANT
    52      5   117575457      1 KEY  (370087018ad1)   RangeS-S GRANT
    52      5   117575457      1 KEY  (370011318da6)   RangeS-S GRANT
    52      5   117575457      1 KEY  (38004ab7b2bc)   RangeS-S GRANT
    54      5   117575457      0 TAB                   IX       GRANT
    54      5           0      0 DB                    S        GRANT
    54      5   117575457      1 KEY  (3700f04c0158)   RangeIn- WAIT
    54      5   117575457      1 PAG  1:105            IX       GRANT
```

Using Application Locks

The SQL Server Lock Manager knows nothing about the object or the structure of the object it is locking. The actual resources are represented only as strings. (This information can be seen in the rsc_text field in syslockinfo.) The Lock Manager simply checks to see if two processes are trying to obtain incompatible locks on the same resource. If so, blocking will occur.

SQL Server 2000 allows you to extend the resources that can be locked beyond the ones automatically provided. You can define your own custom locking resources and let the Lock Manager control the access to those resources as it would for any resource in a database. This essentially allows you to choose to lock anything you want. These user-defined lock resources are called **application locks**. To define an application lock, you use the sp_getapplock stored procedure and specify a name for the resource you are locking, a mode, an optional lock owner, and an optional lock timeout interval. The syntax for sp_getapplock is as follows:

```
sp_getapplock [ @Resource = ] 'resource_name',
    [ @LockMode = ] 'lock_mode'
    [ , [ @LockOwner = ] { 'transaction'  | 'session' } ]
    [ , [ @LockTimeout = ] 'value' ]
```

Two resources are considered to be the same resource and are subject to lock contention if they have the same name and the same lock owner in the same database. The resource name used in these procedures can be any identifier up to 255 characters long. The lock owner can be specified as either `transaction` or `session`. Multiple requests for locks on the same resource can be granted only if the locking modes of the requests are compatible. (See the "Lock Compatibility" section later in this chapter for a lock compatibility matrix.) The possible modes of the lock allowed are Shared, Update, Exclusive, IntentExclusive, and IntentShared.

For what purpose can you use application locks, and how do you use them? Suppose you have a table that contains a queue of items to be processed by the system. You need a way to serialize the retrieval of the next item from the queue so that the multiple concurrent processes do not grab the same item at the same time. In the past, one way this could be accomplished was by forcing an exclusive lock on the table. (The use of table hints to override default locking behavior is covered in the "Table Hints for Locking" section later in this chapter.) Only the first process to acquire the exclusive lock would be able to retrieve the next item from the queue. The other processes would have to wait until the exclusive lock was released. The problem with this approach is that the exclusive lock would also block other processes that might need to simply retrieve data from the table.

You could make use of application locks to avoid having to place an exclusive lock on the entire table. Using `sp_getapplock`, you can define and lock a custom lock resource for a transaction or session. Locks that are owned by the current transaction are released when the transaction commits or rolls back. Locks that are owned by the session are released when the session is closed. Locks can also be explicitly released at any time with the `sp_releaseapplock` stored procedure. The syntax for `sp_releaseapplock` is as follows:

```
sp_releaseapplock [ @Resource = ] 'resource_name'
    [ , [ @LockOwner = ] { 'transaction'  | 'session' }]
```

NOTE

If a process calls `sp_getapplock` multiple times for the same lock resource, `sp_releaseapplock` must be called the same number of times to fully release the lock. In addition, if `sp_getapplock` is called multiple times on the same lock resource, but it specifies different lock modes each time, the resulting lock on the resource is a union of the different lock modes. Generally, the lock mode ends up being promoted to the more restrictive level of the existing lock mode and the newly requested mode. The resulting lock mode is held until the last lock release call is made to fully release the lock. For example, assume a process initially called `sp_getapplock` requested a shared lock. If it subsequently called `sp_getapplock` again and requested an exclusive lock, an exclusive lock would be held on the resource until `sp_releaseapplock` were executed twice.

In the following example, you first request an exclusive lock on an application lock called `'QueueLock'` by using `sp_getapplock`. You then invoke the procedure to get the next item in the queue. After the procedure returns, you call `sp_releaseapplock` to release the application lock called `'QueueLock'` to let another session acquire the application lock:

```
sp_getapplock 'QueueLock', 'Exclusive', 'session'
exec get_next_item_from_queue
sp_releaseapplock 'QueueLock', 'session'
```

As long as all processes that need to retrieve items from the queue execute this same sequence of statements, no other process can execute the `get_next_item_from_queue` process until the application lock is released. The other processes will block attempts to acquire the exclusive lock on the resource `'QueueLock'`. For example, the following output from `sp_lock` shows one process (`spid 55`) holding an exclusive lock on `QueueLock` (the hash value generated internally for `QueueLock` is shown as Queu1e2eefa9 in the Resource field), while another process (`spid 52`) is waiting for an exclusive lock on `QueueLock`:

```
sp_lock
go
spid   dbid   ObjId       IndId  Type Resource        Mode     Status
------ ------ ----------- ------ ---- --------------- -------- ------
    51      4           0      0 DB                   S        GRANT
    52      8           0      0 DB                   S        GRANT
    52      8           0      0 APP  Queu1e2eefa9    X        WAIT
    53      1    85575343      0 TAB                  IS       GRANT
    53      8           0      0 DB                   S        GRANT
    55      8           0      0 DB                   S        GRANT
    55      8           0      0 APP  Queu1e2eefa9    X        GRANT
```

CAUTION

This method of using application locks to control access to the queue will work only as long as all processes that are attempting to retrieve the next item in the queue follow the same protocol. The `get_next_item_from_queue` procedure itself is not actually locked. If another process attempted to execute the `get_next_item_from_queue` process without attempting to acquire the application lock first, the Lock Manager in SQL Server would not prevent the sesssion from executing the stored procedure.

Index Locking

Similar to locks on the data pages, SQL Server manages locks on index pages internally. Compared to data pages, there is the opportunity for greater locking contention in index pages. Contention at the root page of the index is the highest because the root is the starting point for all searches via the index. Contention usually decreases as you move down the various levels of the B-tree, but it is still higher than contention at the data page level due to the typically greater number of index rows per index page than data rows per data page.

If locking contention in the index becomes an issue, SQL Server provides a system-stored procedure called `sp_indexoption` that allows expert users to manage the locking behavior at the index level. The syntax of this stored procedure is as follows:

```
Exec sp_indexoption {[@IndexNamePattern = ] 'index_name'}[,
                     [@OptionName = ] 'option_name'] [,
                     [@OptionValue = ]'value']
```

The following describes the parameter values:

- *`index_name`* is the name of the table or a specific index name on the table.
- *`option_name`* can be one of the following four values:

  `AllowRowLocks`—When set to false, this will prevent any row-level locking on the index pages. Only page- and table-level locks will be applied.

  `AllowPageLocks`—When set to false, this will prevent page-level locks. Only row- or table-level locks will be applied.

  `DisAllowRowLocks`—When set to true, this will prevent any row-level locking on the index pages. Only page- and table-level locks will be applied.

  `DisAllowPageLocks`—When set to true, this will prevent page-level locks. Only row- or table-level locks will be applied.
- *`value`* can be true or false for the specified `option_name` parameter.

SQL Server usually makes good choices for the index locks, but based on the distribution of data and nature of the application, you might want to force a specific locking option on a selective basis. For example, if you are experiencing a high level of locking contention on index pages of an index, you might want to force SQL Server to use row-level locks by turning off page locks. If you turn off both row and page locks, only table-level locks will be acquired.

The following example turns off page-level locking for index pages on an index named `aunmind` for the `authors` table:

```
Exec sp_indexoption 'authors.aunmind', 'AllowPageLocks', false
```

NOTE

Note that these options are available only for indexes. SQL Server provides no mechanism for globally controlling the locking on data pages for a table at the table level. However, if a table has a clustered index, the data pages are essentially the leaf level of the clustered index. The locking methods used on the data pages will be affected by the options set with `sp_indexoption`.

Row-Level Versus Page-Level Locking

For years, it was often debated whether row-level locking was better than page-level locking. That debate still goes on in some circles. Many people will argue that if databases and applications are well designed and tuned, row-level locking is unnecessary. This can be borne out somewhat by the number of large and high-volume applications that were developed when row-level locking wasn't even an option. (Prior to version 7, the smallest unit of data that SQL Server could lock was at the page level.) However, at that time, the page size in SQL Server was only 2K. With page sizes expanded to 8K, a greater number of rows (four times as many) can be contained on a single page. Page-level locks on 8K pages could lead to greater page-level contention because the likelihood of the data rows being requested by different processes residing on the same page is greater. Using row-level locking increases the concurrent access to the data.

On the other hand, row-level locking consumes more resources (memory and CPU) than page-level locks, simply because there are a greater number of rows in a table than pages. If a process needed to access all rows on a page, it would be more efficient to lock the entire page than acquire a lock for each individual row. This would result in a reduction in the number of lock structures in memory that the Lock Manager would have to manage.

Which is better—greater concurrency or lower overhead? As shown earlier in Figure 38.8, it's a tradeoff. As lock size decreases, concurrency improves, but performance degrades due to the extra overhead. As the lock size increases, performance improves due to less overhead, but concurrency degrades. Depending on the application, the database design, and the data, either page-level or row-level locking can be shown to be better than the other in different circumstances.

SQL Server will make the determination at runtime—based on the nature of the query, the size of the table, and the estimated number of rows affected—of whether to initially lock rows, pages, or the entire table. In general, SQL Server attempts to first lock at the row level more often, than the page level, in an effort to provide the best concurrency. With the speed of today's CPUs and the large memory support, the overhead of managing row locks is not as expensive as in the past. However, as the query processes and the actual number resources locked exceed certain thresholds, SQL Server might attempt to escalate locks from a lower level to a higher level as appropriate.

Lock Escalation

When SQL Server detects that the locks acquired by a query are using too much memory and consuming too many system resources for the Lock Manager to manage the locks efficiently, it will automatically escalate row, key, or page locks to table-level locks. For example, as a query on a table continues to acquire row locks and every row in the table eventually will be accessed, it makes more sense for SQL Server to escalate the row locks to a table-level lock. After the table-level lock is acquired, the row-level locks are released. This helps reduce locking overhead and keeps the system from running out of available lock structures. Recall from earlier sections in this chapter that the potential need for lock escalation is reflected in the intent locks that are acquired on the table by the process locking at the row or page level.

NOTE

If another process is also holding locks at the page or row level on the same table (indicated by the presence of that process's intent lock on the table), lock escalation cannot take place if the lock types are not compatible until the lower-level locks by the other processes are released. In this case, SQL Server will continue acquiring locks at the row or page level until the table lock becomes available.

What are the lock escalation thresholds? They are determined dynamically and do not require user configuration. When the number of locks acquired within a transaction exceeds 1,250, or when the number of locks acquired by an index or table scan exceeds 765, the Lock Manager examines how much memory is currently being used by all locks in the system. When more than 40 percent of the available memory is being used for locks, the Lock Manager attempts to escalate multiple page, key, or row locks to table locks. SQL Server attempts to identify all tables that are locking at the row or page level that are capable of escalation (that is, no other processes hold incompatible locks on other pages or rows in the table) for which escalation has not yet been performed. This will continue until all possible lock escalations have taken place, or the total memory used for locks drops to below 40 percent.

At times, SQL Server might choose to do both row and page locking for the same query. For example, if a query returns multiple rows, and enough contiguous keys in a nonclustered index page are selected to satisfy the query, SQL Server might place page locks on the index while using row locks on the data. This reduces the need for lock escalation.

The `locks` Configuration Setting

As mentioned previously, the total number of locks available in SQL Server is dependent on the amount of memory available for the lock structures. This is controlled by the `locks` configuration option for SQL Server. By default, this option is set to 0, which allows SQL Server to allocate and deallocate lock structures dynamically based on ongoing system requirements. Initially, SQL Server allocates 2 percent of the total memory allocated to SQL Server to the lock structure pool. Each lock structure consumes 64 bytes of memory, and each held or waiting lock on the resource requires an additional 32 bytes of memory.

As the pool of locks is exhausted, additional lock structures are allocated up to a maximum of 40 percent of the memory currently allocated to SQL Server. If more memory is required for locks than is currently available to SQL Server, and more server memory is available, SQL Server will allocate additional memory from the operating system dynamically. Doing so will satisfy the request for locks as long as the allocation of the additional memory does not cause paging at the operating system level. If paging were to occur, more lock space would not be allocated, and SQL Server would essentially run out of locks.

In addition, the transaction would be aborted, and the user would see a message like the following:

```
Server: Msg 1204, Level 19, State 1, Line 1
The SQL Server cannot obtain a LOCK resource at this time. Rerun your statement
 when there are fewer active users or ask the system administrator to check the
 SQL Server lock and memory configuration.
```

It is recommended that you leave the `locks` configuration setting at 0 to allow SQL Server to allocate lock structures dynamically. If you repeatedly receive error messages that you have exceeded the number of available locks, you might want to override SQL Server's ability to allocate lock resources dynamically by setting the `locks` configuration option to a value large enough for the number of locks needed. Because each lock structure requires 96 bytes of memory, be aware that setting the `locks` option to a high value might result in an increase in the amount of memory dedicated to the server. For more information on changing SQL Server configuration options, see Chapter 40, "Configuring, Tuning, and Optimizing SQL Server Options."

Lock Compatibility

If a process has already locked a resource, the granting of lock requests by other transactions on the same resource is governed by the lock compatibility matrix within SQL Server. Table 38.5 shows the lock compatibility diagram for the SQL Server Lock Manager, indicating which lock types are compatible and which lock types are incompatible when requested on the same resource.

TABLE 38.5 SQL Server Lock Compatibility Matrix

	Existing Lock Type								
Requested Lock Type	**IS**	**S**	**U**	**IX**	**SIX**	**X**	**Sch-S**	**SCH-M**	**BU**
Intent Shared	Yes	Yes	Yes	Yes	Yes	No	Yes	No	No
Shared	Yes	Yes	Yes	No	No	No	Yes	No	No
Update	Yes	Yes	No	No	No	No	Yes	No	No
Intent Exclusive	Yes	No	No	Yes	No	No	Yes	No	No
Shared with Intent Exclusive	Yes	No	No	No	No	No	Yes	No	No
Exclusive	No	No	No	No	No	No	Yes	No	No
Schema Stability	Yes	Yes	Yes	Yes	Yes	Yes	Yes	No	Yes
Schema Modify	No	No	No	No	No	No	No	No	No
Bulk Update	No	No	No	No	No	No	Yes	No	Yes

For example, if a transaction has acquired a shared lock on a resource, the possible lock types that can be acquired on the resource by other transactions are intent shared, shared, update, and schema stability locks. Intent exclusive, SIX, exclusive, schema modification, and bulk update locks are incompatible with a shared lock and cannot be acquired on the resource until the shared lock is released.

Locking Contention and Deadlocks

In the grand scheme of things, the most likely culprits of SQL Server application performance problems are typically poorly written queries, poor database and index design, and locking contention. Whereas the first two problems will result in poor application performance regardless of the number of users on the system, locking contention becomes more of a performance problem the greater the number of users. It is further compounded by increasingly complex or long-running transactions.

Locking contention occurs when a transaction requests a lock type on a resource that is incompatible with an existing lock type on the resource. By default, the process will wait indefinitely for the lock resource to become available. Locking contention is noticed in the client application by the apparent lack of response from SQL Server.

Figure 38.11 demonstrates an example of locking contention. Process 1 has initiated a transaction and acquired an exclusive lock on page 1:325. Before Process 1 can acquire the lock that it needs on page 1:341 to complete its transaction, Process 2 acquires an exclusive lock on page 1:314. Until Process 2 commits or rolls back its transaction and releases the lock on Page 1:341, the lock will continue to be held. Because this is not a deadlock scenario (which will be covered in the "Deadlocks" subsection later in this section), SQL Server takes no action. Process 1 simply waits indefinitely.

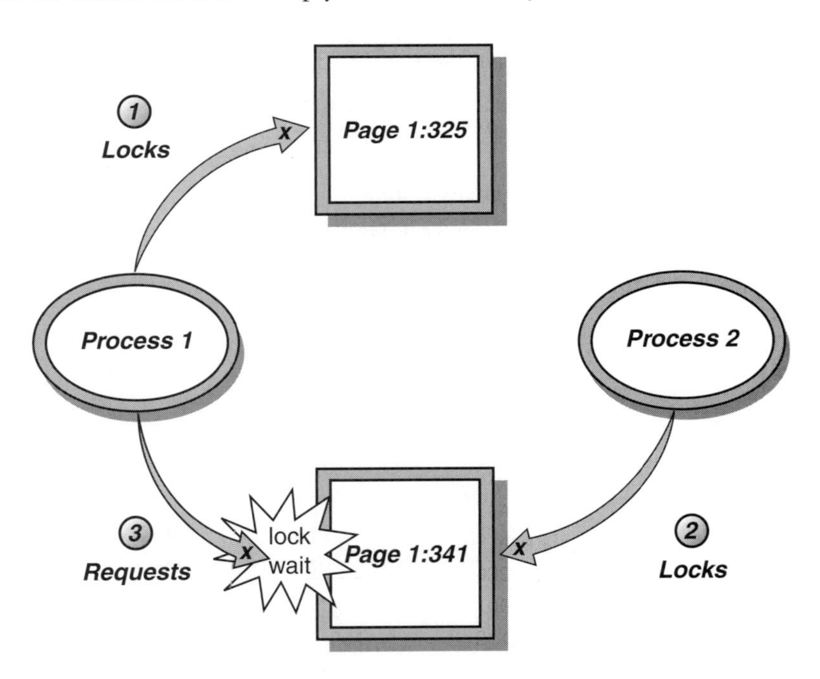

FIGURE 38.11 Locking contention between two processes.

Identifying Locking Contention

When a client application appears to freeze after submitting a query, it often is due to locking contention. To identify locking contention between processes, you can use Enterprise Manager as discussed earlier in this chapter in the "Monitoring Lock Activity in SQL Server" section, or the system-stored procedures sp_who and sp_lock.

TIP

I prefer to use sp_who and sp_lock because they tend to be faster than using Enterprise Manager. Sometimes, because of the additional information that Enterprise Manager is trying to display, it can become blocked by locking activity in tempdb and not display anything. The sp_who and sp_lock system procedures, as well as querying the syslockinfo table directly, will still work. Also, when sp_who and sp_lock are run in Query Analyzer, it is easier and faster to refresh the resultsets than it is to refresh the display in Enterprise Manager. The examples in the rest of this section will use sp_who and sp_lock. The output from these commands can be easily translated to what you would see in EM.

To identify whether a process is being blocked, you can examine the blk column in the output from sp_who:

```
exec sp_who
go
spid ecid   status      loginame hostname    blk dbname      cmd
---- ------ ----------- -------- ----------  --- ------      ---------------
   1      0 sleeping    sa                   0   NULL        LOG WRITER
   2      0 background  sa                   0   NULL        LOCK MONITOR
   3      0 background  sa                   0   NULL        LAZY WRITER
   4      0 background  sa                   0   NULL        SIGNAL HANDLER
   5      0 background  sa                   0   NULL        TASK MANAGER
   6      0 background  sa                   0   NULL        TASK MANAGER
   7      0 sleeping    sa                   0   NULL        CHECKPOINT SLEEP
   8      0 background  sa                   0   NULL        TASK MANAGER
   9      0 background  sa                   0   NULL        TASK MANAGER
  10      0 background  sa                   0   NULL        TASK MANAGER
  11      0 background  sa                   0   NULL        TASK MANAGER
  12      0 background  sa                   0   NULL        TASK MANAGER
  13      0 background  sa                   0   NULL        TASK MANAGER
  52      0 sleeping    sa       RRANKINSA20P 0  bigpubs2000 AWAITING COMMAND
  55      0 sleeping    sa       RRANKINSA20P 52 bigpubs2000 SELECT
```

If the value in the blk column is 0, then no blocking is occurring for that session. If the value is anything non-zero, the session is being blocked and the number in the blk column is the spid of the process that is causing the blocking. In the previous example, you can see process 52 blocking process 55.

To determine what table, page, or rows are involved, and at what level the blocking is occurring, you can use the sp_lock stored procedure:

```
exec sp_lock
go

spid   dbid   ObjId       IndId  Type Resource         Mode     Status
------ ------ ----------- ------ ---- ---------------- -------- ------
    51      4           0      0 DB                    S        GRANT
    52      8           0      0 DB                    S        GRANT
    52      8  1685581043      0 TAB                   IX       GRANT
    52      8  1685581043      1 PAG  1:5798           IX       GRANT
    52      8  1685581043      1 KEY  (37005ad7376d)   X        GRANT
    53      1    85575343      0 TAB                   IS       GRANT
    53      8           0      0 DB                    S        GRANT
    55      8           0      0 DB                    S        GRANT
    55      8  1685581043      1 PAG  1:5798           IS       GRANT
    55      8  1685581043      0 TAB                   IS       GRANT
    55      8  1685581043      1 KEY  (37005ad7376d)   S        WAIT
```

From this output, you can see that process 55 is waiting for a Shared (S) lock on the key for the object whose ID is 1685581043 and whose index ID is 1 (indicating that this is a data or index row in a clustered index). Process 52 has an Exclusive (X) lock granted on the same key resource (Resource = (37005ad7376d)). To identify the name of the table, you can use the object_name() function, running it in the database in which the object resides:

```
select db_name(8)
go

---------------------------------
bigpubs2000

use bigpubs2000
go

select object_name(1685581043)
go

---------------------------------
stores
```

When the IndId in the sp_lock output is 1 and the Type is KEY, it is not clear whether the lock is on a nonleaf index row or a data row. You can determine this by examining the page header for the corresponding page using the DBCC PAGE command and passing it the dbid, the file ID, and the page number. (For more information on using DBCC PAGE, see Chapter 33.)

```
dbcc traceon(3604)
dbcc page (8, 1, 5798)
go

DBCC execution completed. If DBCC printed error messages, contact your system
 administrator.

PAGE: (1:5798)
--------------

BUFFER:
-------

BUF @0x18FA6640
---------------
bpage = 0x20672000          bhash = 0x00000000          bpageno = (1:5798)
bdbid = 8                   breferences = 85            bstat = 0xb
bspin = 0                   bnext = 0x00000000

PAGE HEADER:
------------

Page @0x20672000
----------------
m_pageId = (1:5798)         m_headerVersion = 1         m_type = 1
m_typeFlagBits = 0x0        m_level = 0                 m_flagBits = 0x0
m_objId = 1685581043        m_indexId = 0               m_prevPage = (0:0)
m_nextPage = (1:5797)       pminlen = 15                m_slotCnt = 20
m_freeCnt = 6769            m_freeData = 1383           m_reservedCnt = 0
m_lsn = (555:1135:3)        m_xactReserved = 0          m_xdesId = (0:0)
m_ghostRecCnt = 0           m_tornBits = 0

Allocation Status
-----------------
GAM (1:2) = ALLOCATED     SGAM (1:3) = NOT ALLOCATED
PFS (1:1) = 0x40 ALLOCATED   0_PCT_FULL             DIFF (1:6) = CHANGED
ML (1:7) = NOT MIN_LOGGED

DBCC execution completed. If DBCC printed error messages, contact your system
 administrator.
```

38

If you look at the value for m_indexId, you can determine whether the lock is on an index page or a data page. If m_indexId is 0, then it is a data page. If m_indexId is 1, then the lock is on a nonleaf clustered index page.

Finally, you might also want to know which commands were last executed by the sessions involved in the locking contention. This can be determined by using the DBCC INPUTBUFFER command and passing it the spid for each process involved:

```
dbcc traceon(3604)
dbcc inputbuffer (52)
go

EventType      Parameters EventInfo
-------------- ---------- ------------------------------------------------------
Language Event          0 begin tran

INSERT INTO stores(stor_id, stor_name, stor_address, city, state, zip)
VALUES('7200', 'my store', 'noplace', 'nowhere', 'NW', '00000')

dbcc traceon(3604)
dbcc inputbuffer (55)
go

EventType      Parameters EventInfo
-------------- ---------- ------------------------------------------------
Language Event          0 select * from stores where stor_id = '7200'
```

Setting the Lock Timeout Interval

If you do not want a process to wait indefinitely for a lock to become available, SQL Server allows you to set a lock timeout interval using the SET LOCK_TIMEOUT command. The timeout interval is specified in milliseconds. For example, if you want your processes to wait only 5 seconds (5,000 milliseconds) for a lock to become available, execute the following command in the session:

```
SET LOCKTIMEOUT 5000
```

If your process requests a lock resource that cannot be granted within 5 seconds, the statement will be aborted with the following error message:

```
Server: Msg 1222, Level 16, State 54, Line 1
Lock request time out period exceeded.
```

To examine the current LOCK_TIMEOUT setting, you can query the system function @@LOCK_TIMEOUT:

```
select @@lock_timeout
go

-----------
       5000
```

If you want processes to abort immediately if the lock cannot be granted (in other words, no waiting at all), set the timeout interval to `0`. If you want to set the timeout interval back to infinity, execute the `SET_LOCK_TIMEOUT` command and specify a timeout interval of `-1`.

Minimizing Locking Contention

Although setting the lock timeout prevents a process from waiting indefinitely for a lock request to be granted, it doesn't address the cause of the locking contention. In an effort to maximize concurrency and application performance, you will want to minimize locking contention between processes as much as possible. Some general guidelines to follow to minimize locking contention include the following:

- Keep transactions as short and concise as possible. The shorter the period of time that locks are held, the less chance for lock contention. Keep commands that are not essential to the unit of work being managed by the transaction outside the transaction (such as assignment selects, retrieval of updated or inserted rows, and so on).
- Keep statements that comprise a transaction in a single batch to eliminate unnecessary delays caused by network I/O between the initial `BEGIN TRAN` statement and the subsequent `COMMIT TRAN` commands.
- Consider coding transactions entirely within stored procedures. Stored procedures typically run faster than commands executed from a batch. In addition, because they are server resident, stored procedures reduce the amount of network I/O that occurs during execution of the transaction, resulting in faster completion of the transaction.
- Commit updates in cursors frequently and as soon as possible. Cursor processing is much slower than set-oriented processing and will cause locks to be held longer.

NOTE

Even though cursors might run more slowly than set-oriented processing, cursors can sometimes be used to minimize locking contention for unqualified updates and deletes of a large number or rows from a table, which might result in a table lock being acquired. The update or delete might complete faster; however, it is running with an exclusive lock on the table, and no other process can access the table until it completes. By using a cursor to update a large number of rows one row at a time and committing the changes frequently, the cursor will use page or row-level locks rather than a table-level lock. It might take longer for the cursor to complete the actual update or delete, but while the cursor is running, other processes will still be able to access other rows or pages in the table that the cursor doesn't currently have locked. For more information on using cursors, see Chapter 26, "Using Transact-SQL in SQL Server 2000."

- Use the lowest level of locking isolation required by each process. For example, if dirty reads are acceptable and accurate results are not imperative, consider using transaction isolation level 0. Use level 3, or HOLDLOCK, only if absolutely necessary.
- Consider breaking one large table into multiple tables using a logical horizontal or vertical partitioning scheme. This minimizes the chances for table-level locks being acquired and increases concurrency by allowing multiple users to go against multiple tables rather than contending for access to a single table. (Table partitioning is covered in more detail in Chapter 21, "Administering Very Large SQL Server Databases.")
- Never allow user interaction between a `begin tran` and a `commit tran` because doing so will cause locks to be held for an indefinite period of time. If a process needs to return rows for user interaction and then update one or more rows, consider using optimistic locking in your application. (Optimistic locking is covered in the "Optimistic Locking" section later in this chapter.)
- Minimize "hot spots" in a table. Hot spots occur when the majority of the update activity on a table occurs within a small number of pages. For example, hot spots occur for concurrent inserts to the last page of a heap table or the last pages of a table with a clustered index on a sequential key. Hot spots can often be eliminated by creating a clustered index on a table on a column or columns that would order the rows in the table in such a way that insert and update activity is spread out more evenly across the pages in the table.

Deadlocks

A deadlock is a scenario that occurs when two processes are waiting for a locked resource that the other process currently holds. Neither process can move forward until it receives the requested lock on the resource, and neither process can release the lock it currently is holding until it can receive the requested lock. Essentially, neither process can move forward until the other one completes, and neither one can complete until it can move forward.

Two primary types of deadlocks can occur in SQL Server: cycle deadlocks and conversion deadlocks. A cycle deadlock occurs when two processes acquire locks on different resources, and then need to acquire a lock on the resource that the other process has. Figure 38.12 demonstrates an example of a cycle deadlock.

In Figure 38.12, Process 1 acquires an exclusive lock on page 1:201 in a transaction. At the same time, Process 2 acquires an exclusive lock on page 1:301 in a transaction. Process 1 then attempts to acquire a lock on page 1:301 and begins waiting for the lock to become available. Simultaneously, Process 2 requests an exclusive lock on page 1:201 and a deadlock, or "deadly embrace" occurs.

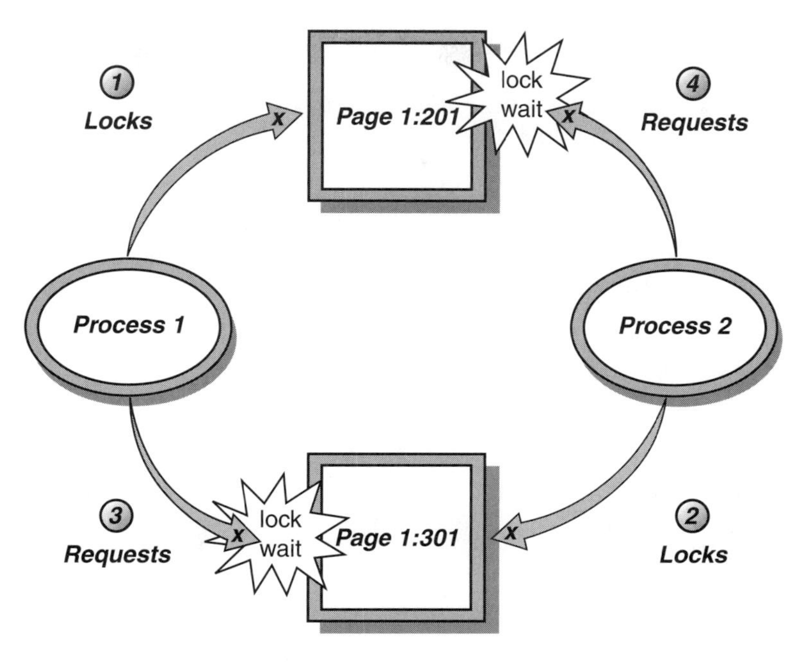

FIGURE 38.12 Example of a cycle deadlock.

A conversion deadlock occurs when two or more processes each hold a shared lock on the same resource within a transaction and each wants to promote the shared lock to an exclusive lock, but neither can do so until the other releases the shared lock. An example of a conversion deadlock is shown in Figure 38.13.

SQL Server automatically detects when a deadlock situation occurs. A separate process in SQL Server, called the LOCK_MONITOR, checks the system for deadlocks roughly every 5 seconds. In the first pass, this process detects all the processes that are waiting on a lock resource. The LOCK_MONITOR thread checks for deadlocks by examining the list of waiting lock requests to see if any circular lock requests exist between the processes that are holding locks and the processes that are waiting for locks. When the LOCK_MONITOR detects a deadlock, SQL Server aborts the transaction of one of the involved processes.

How does SQL Server determine which process to abort? It attempts to choose as the deadlock victim the process that has accumulated the least amount of CPU time since the start of its session. In some cases, certain operations are marked as unkillable and cannot be chosen as the deadlock victim. One such example is a process that involves rolling back a transaction. This process cannot be chosen as a deadlock victim because the changes being rolled back could be left in an indeterminate state, which could lead to data corruption.

You can influence which process will be the deadlock victim by using the `SET DEADLOCK_PRIORITY` statement. If you have lower priority processes that would prefer to be chosen as the deadlock victims, you can set the process's deadlock priority to `LOW`. When this process is detected in a deadlock situation, it will automatically be chosen as the deadlock victim if the other process's deadlock priority is NORMAL. Currently, SQL Server does not have an option to set the deadlock priority to HIGH to specify processes that should always come out as the winner in a deadlock scenario.

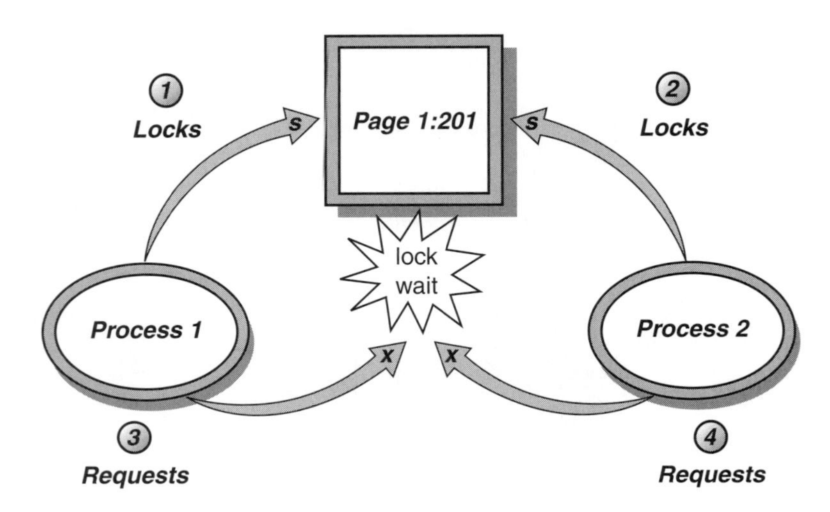

FIGURE 38.13 Example of a conversion deadlock.

It is often assumed that deadlocks happen at the data page or data row level. In fact, deadlocks often occur at the index page level. Figure 38.14 depicts a scenario in which a deadlock occurs due to contention at the index page level.

Avoiding Deadlocks

Although SQL Server automatically detects and handles deadlocks, you will want to try to avoid deadlocks in your applications. When a process is chosen as a deadlock victim, it has to resubmit its work again because it has been rolled back. Frequent deadlocks create performance problems if you have to keep repeating work.

You can follow a number of guidelines to minimize, if not completely eliminate, the number of deadlocks that occur in your application(s). Following the guidelines presented earlier to minimize locking contention and speed up your transactions will also help to eliminate deadlocks. The less time for which a transaction is holding locks, the less likely the transition will be around long enough for a conflicting lock request to be requested at the same time. In addition, you might want to follow this list of additional guidelines when designing your application:

- Be consistent about the order in which you access the data from tables to avoid cycle deadlocks.

- Minimize the use of HOLDLOCK or queries that are running using repeatable reads or serializable lock isolation levels. This helps avoid conversion deadlocks. If possible, perform UPDATEs before SELECTs so that your transaction acquires an update or exclusive lock first. This eliminates the chance of a conversion deadlock. (Later in the "Table Hints for Locking" section in this chapter, you will see how to use table-locking hints to force SELECT statements to use update or exclusive locks as another strategy to avoid conversion deadlocks.)
- Choose the transaction isolation level judiciously. You might be able to reduce deadlocks by choosing lower isolation levels.

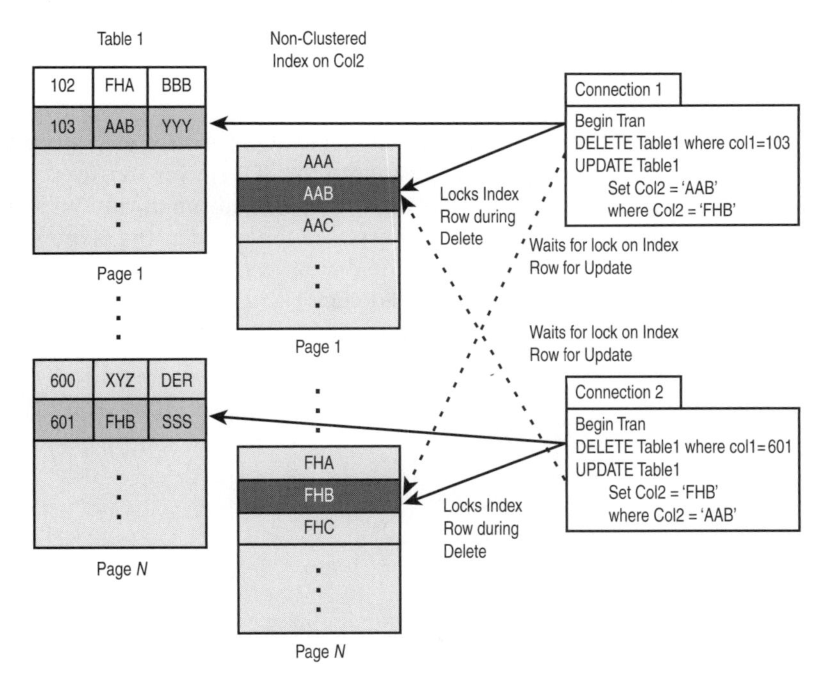

FIGURE 38.14 Deadlocks due to locks on index pages.

Handling and Examining Deadlocks

SQL Server returns an error number 1205 to the client when it aborts a transaction as a result of deadlock. Because a deadlock is not a logical error, but merely a resource contention issue, the client can resubmit the entire transaction. To handle deadlocks in your applications, be sure to trap for message 1205 in your error handler. When a 1205 error occurs, the application can simply resubmit the transaction automatically. It is considered bad form to allow end users of an application to see the deadlock error message returned from SQL Server.

Earlier in this chapter, you learned how to use `sp_lock` and `sp_who` to monitor locking contention between processes. However, when a deadlock occurs, one transaction is rolled back and one is allowed to continue. If you were to examine the output from `sp_lock` and `sp_who` after a deadlock occurs, the information likely would not be useful because the locks on the resources involved have since been released.

Fortunately, SQL Server provides a couple of trace flags to monitor deadlocks within SQL Server. Use the `DBCC TRACEON` command to turn on the trace flags and `DBCC_TRACEOFF` to turn them off. To have SQL Server write the output from the deadlock trace flags to the error log for further analysis, first execute the `DBCC TRACEON(3605)` command. The following is an example of setting the 1204 trace flag:

```
dbcc traceon(3605)
dbcc traceon(1204)
```

Optionally, you can also set the trace flags on whenever SQL Server is started up by adding the `-T` option with the appropriate trace flag value to the SQL Server startup parameters. For example, to have SQL Server turn on the 1204 trace flag automatically on startup, bring up the Server Properties dialog box in Enterprise Manager. On the General tab, click the Startup Parameters button. This brings up the dialog box shown in Figure 38.15. Type `-T1204` in the Parameter box, click Add, and then click OK to save the changes. Do the same to add the 3605 trace flag option as well, or no output from the 1204 trace flag will be sent to the errorlog.

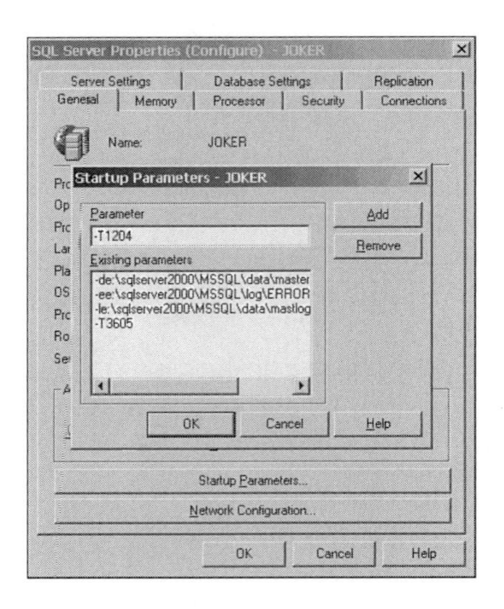

FIGURE 38.15 Setting the 1204 trace flag to be enabled on SQL Server startup.

CAUTION

The 1204, 1205, and 1200 trace flags do incur some additional processing overhead in SQL Server. They should be used only when debugging and tuning SQL Server performance, and should not be left on indefinitely in a production environment. Turn them off after you have diagnosed and fixed the problems.

The 1204 Trace Flag

Trace flag 1204 prints useful information to the SQL Server error log when a deadlock is detected. Listing 38.2 presents a sample of the output from the error log for this trace flag.

LISTING 38.2 Sample Output for the 1204 Trace Flag When a Deadlock Occurs

```
Deadlock encountered .... Printing deadlock information
2001-08-27 05:35:01.40 spid2
2001-08-27 05:35:01.40 spid2     Wait-for graph
2001-08-27 05:35:01.40 spid2
2001-08-27 05:35:01.40 spid2     Node:1
2001-08-27 05:35:01.40 spid2     PAG: 8:1:5798                 CleanCnt:2 Mode:
 S Flags: 0x2
2001-08-27 05:35:01.40 spid2      Grant List::
2001-08-27 05:35:01.40 spid2        Owner:0x2c3cabe0 Mode: S       Flg:0x0
 Ref:0 Life:02000000 SPID:55 ECID:0
2001-08-27 05:35:01.40 spid2       SPID: 55 ECID: 0 Statement Type: DELETE Line
 #: 1
2001-08-27 05:35:01.40 spid2        Input Buf: Language Event: delete from
 stores where stor_id = '7200'

2001-08-27 05:35:01.40 spid2      Requested By:
2001-08-27 05:35:01.40 spid2        ResType:LockOwner Stype:'OR' Mode: IX SPID:
 52 ECID:0 Ec:(0x193a7500) Value:0x2c3cabc0 Cost:(0/0)
2001-08-27 05:35:01.40 spid2
2001-08-27 05:35:01.40 spid2     Node:2
2001-08-27 05:35:01.40 spid2     PAG: 8:1:5798                 CleanCnt:2 Mode:
 S Flags: 0x2
2001-08-27 05:35:01.40 spid2      Grant List::
2001-08-27 05:35:01.40 spid2        Owner:0x2b1b9c00 Mode: S       Flg:0x0
 Ref:0 Life:02000000 SPID:52 ECID:0
2001-08-27 05:35:01.40 spid2       SPID: 52 ECID: 0 Statement Type: DELETE Line
 #: 1
2001-08-27 05:35:01.40 spid2        Input Buf: Language Event: delete from
 stores where stor_id = '7200'
```

LISTING 38.2 Continued

```
2001-08-27 05:35:01.40 spid2      Requested By:
2001-08-27 05:35:01.40 spid2        ResType:LockOwner Stype:'OR' Mode: IX SPID:
 55 ECID:0 Ec:(0x2ac59500) Value:0x265083e0 Cost:(0/0)
2001-08-27 05:35:01.40 spid2     Victim Resource Owner:
2001-08-27 05:35:01.40 spid2      ResType:LockOwner Stype:'OR' Mode: IX SPID:
 55 ECID:0 Ec:(0x2ac59500) Value:0x265083e0 Cost:(0/0)
```

Although the 1204 output is somewhat cryptic, it is not too difficult to read. If you look through the output, you can see where it lists the SPIDs of the processes involved in the deadlock, the type of statement involved (`Statement Type`) and the actual text of the query (`Input Buf`) that each process was executing at the time the deadlock occurred. The output also displays the locks granted to each process (`Grant List`), as well as the lock resources requested by the deadlock victim. The output might also display the page information (`PAG`) on the pages involved. In this case, the output is showing that the deadlock occurred in database ID (8), the file ID (1), and the actual page ID (5798).

The 1205 Trace Flag

The 1205 trace flag provides further insight into the `LOCK_MONITOR` process and how it searches for deadlock situations and displays the information when the deadlock is encountered. Notice how the deadlock search is performed every 5 seconds and only blocking locks are detected until the actual deadlock is encountered. At this point, no blocking locks remain. An example of the output generated by the 1205 trace flag is shown in Listing 38.3.

LISTING 38.3 Sample Output for the 1205 Trace Flag

```
2001-08-27 05:20:46.40 spid2     ---------------------------------
2001-08-27 05:20:46.40 spid2     Starting deadlock search 2682

2001-08-27 05:20:46.40 spid2     Target Resource Owner:
2001-08-27 05:20:46.40 spid2      ResType:LockOwner Stype:'OR' Mode: IX SPID:52
 ECID:0 Ec:(0x193a7500) Value:0x2c3cabe0
2001-08-27 05:20:46.40 spid2      Node:1  ResType:LockOwner Stype:'OR' Mode:
 IX SPID:52 ECID:0 Ec:(0x193a7500) Value:0x2c3cabe0
2001-08-27 05:20:46.40 spid2
2001-08-27 05:20:46.40 spid2     End deadlock search 2682 ... a deadlock was
 not found.
2001-08-27 05:20:46.40 spid2     ---------------------------------

2001-08-27 05:20:51.40 spid2     ---------------------------------
2001-08-27 05:20:51.40 spid2     Starting deadlock search 2683
```

LISTING 38.3 Continued

```
2001-08-27 05:20:51.40 spid2     Target Resource Owner:
2001-08-27 05:20:51.40 spid2      ResType:LockOwner Stype:'OR' Mode: IX SPID:52
 ECID:0 Ec:(0x193a7500) Value:0x2c3cabe0
2001-08-27 05:20:51.40 spid2      Node:1  ResType:LockOwner Stype:'OR' Mode:
 IX SPID:52 ECID:0 Ec:(0x193a7500) Value:0x2c3cabe0
2001-08-27 05:20:51.40 spid2      Node:2  ResType:LockOwner Stype:'OR' Mode:
 IX SPID:55 ECID:0 Ec:(0x2ac59500) Value:0x265083a0
2001-08-27 05:20:51.40 spid2      Cycle:  ResType:LockOwner Stype:'OR' Mode:
 IX SPID:52 ECID:0 Ec:(0x193a7500) Value:0x2c3cabe0
2001-08-27 05:20:51.40 spid2
2001-08-27 05:20:51.40 spid2
2001-08-27 05:20:51.40 spid2     Deadlock cycle was encountered .... verifying
 cycle
2001-08-27 05:20:51.40 spid2      Node:1  ResType:LockOwner Stype:'OR' Mode:
 IX SPID:52 ECID:0 Ec:(0x193a7500) Value:0x2c3cabe0 Cost:(0/0)
2001-08-27 05:20:51.40 spid2      Node:2  ResType:LockOwner Stype:'OR' Mode:
 IX SPID:55 ECID:0 Ec:(0x2ac59500) Value:0x265083a0 Cost:(0/0)
2001-08-27 05:20:51.40 spid2      Cycle:  ResType:LockOwner Stype:'OR' Mode:
 IX SPID:52 ECID:0 Ec:(0x193a7500) Value:0x2c3cabe0 Cost:(0/0)
2001-08-27 05:20:51.40 spid2
2001-08-27 05:20:51.40 spid2
2001-08-27 05:20:51.40 spid2     End deadlock search 2683...a deadlock was found
2001-08-27 05:20:51.40 spid2     ----------------------------------

2001-08-27 05:20:51.40 spid2     ----------------------------------
2001-08-27 05:20:51.40 spid2     Starting deadlock search 2684

2001-08-27 05:20:51.40 spid2     Target Resource Owner:
2001-08-27 05:20:51.40 spid2      ResType:LockOwner Stype:'OR' Mode: IX SPID:55
ECID:0 Ec:(0x2ac59500) Value:0x265083a0
2001-08-27 05:20:51.40 spid2      Node:1        ResType:LockOwner Stype:'OR' Mode:
 IX SPID:55 ECID:0 Ec:(0x2ac59500) Value:0x265083a0
2001-08-27 05:20:51.40 spid2      Node:2        ResType:LockOwner Stype:'OR' Mode:
 IX SPID:52 ECID:0 Ec:(0x193a7500) Value:0x2c3cabe0
2001-08-27 05:20:51.40 spid2
2001-08-27 05:20:51.40 spid2     Previous victim encountered ... aborting search
2001-08-27 05:20:51.40 spid2
2001-08-27 05:20:51.40 spid2     End deadlock search 2684 ... a deadlock was not
 found.
2001-08-27 05:20:51.40 spid2     ----------------------------------
```

This information could be useful to monitor the frequency and duration of blocking locks between processes to help identify the culprits of locking contention. Again, be careful using this trace flag because it can generate copious amounts of output in a system where substantial activity and locking contention is occurring.

Trace Flag 1200

Trace flag 1200 prints all of the lock request/release information back to the client program as it occurs in SQL Server. This information is displayed regardless of whether a deadlock is involved. This trace flag can be expensive in terms of system performance overhead, but it can be useful for analysis to display the acquisition, escalation, and release of locks within your SQL commands.

If you enable trace flag 1200 from a user session, it only applies to the current session unless you specify the optional parameter of `-1` to the `DBCC TRACEON` command to enable the trace setting for all user sessions:

```
DBCC TRACEON(1200, -1)
```

Also, when enabled in this manner, the output comes back only to the client and not to the errorlog. Capturing and analyzing this information for multiple client connections would be difficult.

> **NOTE**
>
> It is possible to capture this information to the errorlog for all user sessions by setting the 1200 and 3605 trace flags as startup parameters for SQL Server, as shown in Figure 38.16. However, because the 1200 trace flag will be capturing lock information for *all* processes, including internal system processes, the amount of output generated to the error log by this trace flag can be considerable. I do not recommend capturing the 1200 trace information in this manner on a high volume system, or even a medium volume system. The errorlog can grow to many megabytes in size very quickly.

The following code displays a sample of the output from the 1200 trace flag:

```
DBCC TRACEON (1200)
go
begin tran
--select count (state) from stores holdlock
delete from stores where stor_id = '7200'
go

Process 52 acquiring IX lock on TAB: 8:1685581043 [] (class bit2000000 ref1)
 result: OK
Process 52 acquiring IS lock on TAB: 8:1957582012 [] (class bit0 ref1) result:
 OK
```

```
Process 52 acquiring IX lock on PAG: 8:1:5798 (class bit2000000 ref1) result:
 OK
Process 52 acquiring Range-X-X lock on KEY: 8:1685581043:1 (3700f04c0158)
 (class bit2000000 ref1) result: OK
Process 52 releasing lock on TAB: 8:1957582012 []go
```

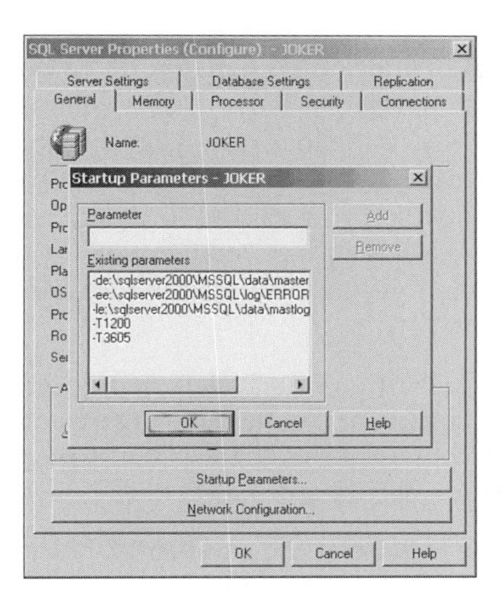

FIGURE 38.16 Setting the 1200 and 3605 trace flags to be enabled on SQL Server startup.

TIP

You can also monitor deadlocks and lock escalation with SQL Profiler, which was discussed in the "Monitoring Lock Activity in SQL Server" section earlier in this chapter. SQL Profiler provides two deadlock events that can be monitored. Under the Locks event list, you can choose to display a simple message that indicates when a deadlock occurs between two processes, as well as the complete deadlock chain. (This information is similar to that provided by the 1205 trace flag.)

Lock acquisition, escalation, and the release of locks is also more easily monitored using SQL Profiler than using trace flag 1200. This is because you can filter the lock information that SQL Server captures to specific processes, and the information captured can easily be saved to a file or a database table for further analysis.

For more information on using SQL Profiler to monitor SQL Server activity, see the "Monitoring Lock Activity in SQL Server" section earlier in this chapter, as well as Chapter 7.

Table Hints for Locking

As mentioned previously in this chapter in the "Transaction Isolation Levels in SQL Server" section, you can set an isolation level for your connection using the `SET TRANSACTION ISOLATION LEVEL` command. This command sets a global isolation level for your entire session, which is useful if you want to provide a consistent isolation level for your application. However, sometimes you will want to specify different isolation levels for different queries in the system, or different isolation levels for different tables within a single query. SQL Server allows you to do this by supporting table hints in the `FROM` clause of `SELECT`, `UPDATE`, and `DELETE` statements. This allows you to override the isolation level that is currently set at the session level.

In this chapter, you have seen that locking is dynamic and automatic in SQL Server. Based on certain factors (such as SARGs, key distribution, data volume, and so on), the query optimizer chooses the granularity of the lock (row, page, or table level) on a resource. Although it is usually best to leave such decisions to the cost-based optimizer, you might encounter certain situations in which you want to force a different lock granularity on a resource than what the optimizer has chosen. SQL Server provides additional table hints that you can use in the query to force lock granularity for various tables that are participating in a join.

SQL Server also automatically determines the lock type (`SHARED`, `UPDATE`, `EXCLUSIVE`) to use on a resource depending on the type of command being executed on the resource. For example, a `SELECT` statement will use a shared lock. SQL Server 2000 also provides additional table hints to override the default lock type.

The table hints to override the lock isolation, granularity, or lock type for a table can be provided in the `FROM` clause of the query by using the `WITH` operator. The following is the syntax of the `FROM` clause when using table hints:

```
FROM table_name [ [AS] table_alias ] WITH ( table_hint [ ,...n ] ) [, ...n]
```

The following sections discuss the various locking hints that can be passed to an optimizer to manage isolation levels and the lock granularity of a query.

NOTE

Although many of the table-locking hints can be combined, you cannot combine more than one hint at a time on a table from the granularity and isolation level hints. Also, the `NOLOCK`, `READUNCOMMITTED`, and `READPAST` hints described in the following sections cannot be used on tables that are the target of `INSERT`, `UPDATE`, or `DELETE` queries.

Transaction Isolation-Level Hints

SQL Server provides a number of hints that you can use in a query to override the default transaction isolation level. These hints are described as follows:

- `HOLDLOCK`—Within a transaction, a shared lock on a resource (row, page, table) is released as soon as the T-SQL statement that is holding the shared lock is finished with the resource. To maintain a shared lock for the duration of the entire statement, or for the entire transaction if the statement is in a transaction, use the HOLDLOCK clause in the statement. The following example demonstrates the usage of the HOLDLOCK statement within a transaction:

```
declare @seqno int
begin transaction
-- get a UNIQUE sequence number from sequence table
SELECT @seqno = isnull(seq#,0) + 1
from sequence WITH (HOLDLOCK)

-- in the absence of HOLDLOCK, shared lock will be released
-- and if some other concurrent transaction ran the same
-- command, both of them could get the same sequence number

UPDATE sequence
set    seq# = @seqno

--now go do something else with this unique sequence number
commit tran
```

NOTE

As discussed earlier in this chapter in the "Deadlocks" section, using HOLDLOCK in this manner leads to potential deadlocks between processes that are executing this transaction at the same time. For this reason, the HOLDLOCK hint, as well as the REPEATABLEREAD and SERIALIZABLE hints, should be used sparingly if at all. In this example, it might be better for the SELECT statement to use an update or exclusive lock on the sequence table using the hints discussed later in the section in the "Lock Type Hints" section. Another option would be to use an application lock as discussed previously in this chapter in the "Using Application Locks" section.

- NOLOCK—You can use this option to specify that no shared lock be placed on the resource and that requests for update or exclusive locks be denied. This option is similar to running a query at isolation level 0 (READUNCOMMITTED), which allows the query to ignore exclusive locks and read uncommitted changes. The NOLOCK option is a useful feature in reporting environments, where the accuracy of the results is not critical.
- READUNCOMMITTED—This is the same as specifying the Read Uncommitted mode when using the SET TRANSACTION ISOLATION LEVEL command, and it is the same as the NOLOCK table hint.
- READCOMMITTED—This is the same as specifying the Read Committed mode when you use the SET TRANSACTION ISOLATION LEVEL command. The query will wait for exclusive locks to be released before reading the data. This is the default locking isolation mode for SQL Server.

- REPEATABLEREAD—This is the same as specifying Repeatable Read mode with the SET TRANSACTION ISOLATION LEVEL command. It prevents nonrepeatable reads within a transaction, and behaves similarly to using the HOLDLOCK hint.
- SERIALIZABLE—This is the same as specifying Serializable mode with the SET TRANSACTION ISOLATION LEVEL command. It prevents phantom reads within a transaction, and behaves similarly to using the HOLDLOCK hint.
- READPAST—This hint applies only to the SELECT statement. By specifying this option, you can skip over the rows that are locked by other transactions, returning the rows that can be read. In the absence of the READPAST option, the SELECT statement will wait (or time out if lock timeout values are set) until the locks are released on the rows by other transactions. A statement that uses the READPAST clause can only read past row locks that are held by transactions running in Read Committed mode. This lock hint is useful when reading information from a SQL Server table used as a work queue.

Lock Granularity Hints

You can use the following optimizer hints to override lock granularity:

- ROWLOCK—You can use this option to force the Lock Manager to place a row-level lock on a resource instead of a page-level or a table-level lock. This can be used in conjunction with the XLOCK lock type hint to force exclusive row locks.
- PAGLOCK—You can use this option to force a page-level lock on a resource instead of a row-level or table-level lock. This can be used in conjunction with the XLOCK lock type hint to force exclusive page locks.
- TABLOCK—You can use this option to force a table-level lock instead of a row-level or a page-level lock. This option can be used in conjunction with the HOLDLOCK table hint to hold the table lock until the end of the transaction.
- TABLOCKX—You can use this option to force a table-level exclusive lock instead of a row-level or a page-level lock. No shared or update locks are granted to other transactions as long as this option is in effect. If you are planning maintenance on a SQL Server table and you don't want interference from other transactions, this is one of the ways to essentially put a table into a single user mode.

Lock Type Hints

You can use the following optimizer hints to override the lock type that SQL Server uses:

- UPDLOCK—This option is similar to HOLDLOCK except that whereas HOLDLOCK uses a shared lock on the resource, UPDLOCK places an update lock on the resource for the duration of the transaction. This allows other processes to read the information, but not acquire update or exclusive locks on the resource. This option provides read repeatability within the transaction while preventing deadlocks that can result when using `HOLDLOCK`.

- `XLOCK`—This option is similar to `HOLDLOCK` except that whereas `HOLDLOCK` uses a shared lock on the resource, `XLOCK` places an exclusive lock on the resource for the duration of the transaction. This prevents other processes from acquiring locks on the resource.

Optimistic Locking

With many applications, clients need to fetch the data to browse through it, make modifications to one or more rows, and then post the changes back to the database in SQL Server. These human-speed operations are slow in comparison to machine-speed operations, and the time lag between the fetch and post might be significant. (Consider the user who goes to lunch after retrieving the data.)

For these applications, you would not want to use normal locking schemes such as `SERIALIZABLE` or `HOLDLOCK` to lock the data so it can't be changed from the time the user retrieves it to the time he applies any updates. This would violate one of the cardinal rules of not allowing user interaction within transactions. You also would lose all control over the duration of the transaction. In a multiuser, OLTP environment, this could significantly affect concurrency and overall application performance due to blocking on locks and locking contention.

So how do you implement such an application? How do you allow users to retrieve information without holding locks on the data and still ensure that when they apply the updates, no other process has modified the information since it was initially retrieved?

Optimistic locking is a technique used in such situations where reading and modifying data processes are widely separated in time. Optimistic locking helps a client avoid overwriting another client's changes to a row without holding locks in the database.

38

Optimistic Locking Using the Timestamp Datatype

SQL Server provides a special datatype called timestamp. A **timestamp** is an eight-byte binary datatype. SQL Server automatically generates the value for a timestamp whenever a row that contains a column of this type is inserted or updated. Other than guaranteeing that the value is unique and monotonically increasing, the value is not meaningful; you cannot look at the individual bytes and make any sense out of them. Despite the name of the datatype, the value has no relation to the time that the record was modified. The purpose of the timestamp datatype is to serve as a version number in optimistic locking schemes.

The following two conditions must be met to utilize optimistic locking:

- The table must have a primary key so that each row can be uniquely identified.
- The table must have a column defined with the timestamp datatype.

In an application that uses optimistic locking, the client reads one or more records from the table, being sure to retrieve the current value of the timestamp column for each row. Any locks are released after the data has been read. At some later time, when the client wants to update a row, it must ensure that no other client has changed the same row in the intervening time. (Because no locks exist, it is the client's responsibility to make sure that the other client's changes are preserved.) The `UPDATE` statement must include a `WHERE` clause that compares the timestamp value held in the client application with the current timestamp value for the record in the database. If the timestamp values match—that is, if the value that was read is the same as the value in the database—then no changes to that row have occurred since it was originally retrieved. As such, the change attempted by the application can proceed. If the timestamp value in the client application *does not* match the value in the database, then that particular row has been changed since the original retrieval of the record. As a result, the state of the row that the application is attempting to modify is not the same as the row that currently exists in the database. As a result, the transaction should not be allowed to take place to avoid the "phantom values" problem.

To ensure that the client application does not overwrite the changes made by another process, the client needs to prepare the T-SQL `UPDATE` statement in a special way, using the timestamp column as a versioning marker. The following pseudo-code represents the general structure of such an update:

```
UPDATE theTable
   SET theChangedColumns = theirNewValues
   WHERE primaryKeyColumns = theirOldValues
     AND timestamp = itsOldValue
```

Because the `WHERE` clause includes the primary key, the `UPDATE` can only apply to exactly one row or to no rows; it cannot apply to more than one row because the primary key is unique. The second part of the `WHERE` clause is what provides the optimistic "locking." If another client has updated the row, the timestamp will no longer have its old value (remember that the server changes the timestamp value automatically with each update), and the `WHERE` clause will not match any rows. The client needs to check to see whether any rows were updated. If the number of rows affected by the update statement is 0, the row has been modified since it was originally retrieved. The application can then choose to reread the data or do whatever recovery it deems appropriate.

This approach has one problem. How does the application know that it didn't match the row because the timestamp was changed, or because the primary key had changed or the row had been deleted altogether?

In SQL Server 2000, the `tsequal()` function is available that can be used in the `WHERE` clause to compare the timestamp value retrieved by the client application with the timestamp value in the database. If the two match, the update will proceed. If not, the update will fail because the where clause cannot be satisfied.

The following pseudo-code illustrates how this works:

1. The client reads a row:

```
select * from data_table where primary_key_field = <value>
```

2. The client prepares an `UPDATE` statement with new data values for this row.

3. The client submits the following `UPDATE` statement with the additional search clause using the `tsequal()` function:

```
update data_table set data_field_1 = foo
   where primary_key_field = <value>
     and tsequal (timestamp, <retrieved timstamp value>)
```

The difference between this approach and the one presented earlier is that rather than simply not matching any rows when the timestamp value is different, the `tsequal` function evaluates to FALSE and causes the update statement to fail with an error message similar to the following:

```
Server: Msg 532, Level 16, State 1, Line 1
The timestamp (changed to 0x00000000000001f7) shows that the row has been
 updated by another user.
The statement has been terminated.
```

At this point, the application will receive the error message and know for sure that the reason the update didn't take place is because the timestamp values didn't match. If no rows were found and updated, then it clearly would be due to the original row having been deleted or the primary key having been changed. If the row is found and the timestamp values match, then `tsequal()` evaluates to TRUE and the update proceeds normally.

NOTE

Curiously enough, even though the `tsequal()` function has been around for as long as I can remember and it still works as it always has, it is not documented in SQL Server Books Online except as a reserved keyword. Although it appears safe to continue to use the `tsequal()` function, it is possible that it is no longer supported or will be dropped in future releases of SQL Server. For this reason, use `tsequal()` with caution because your code might no longer work as expected in future releases.

Summary

Locking is critical in a multiuser environment for providing transaction isolation. SQL Server supports all ANSI-defined transaction isolation levels. The Lock Manager in SQL Server automatically locks data at the row level or higher as necessary to provide the appropriate isolation while balancing the locking overhead with concurrent access to the data. It is important to understand how locking works and what its effect is on application performance to develop efficient queries and applications.

SQL Server provides a number of tools for monitoring and identifying locking problems and behavior. In addition, SQL Server provides a number of table-locking hints that give the developer better control over the default lock types and granularity used for certain queries.

Although following the guidelines to minimize locking contention in your applications is important, another factor that impacts locking behavior and query performance is the actual database design. Chapter 39, "Database Design and Performance," discusses database design and its effect on database performance, and provides guidelines to help ensure that your transactions and T-SQL code run efficiently.

CHAPTER 39

Database Design and Performance

by Bennett McEwan and Ray Rankins

IN THIS CHAPTER

Various factors contribute to the optimal performance of a database application. Some of these factors include logical database design (rules of normalization), physical database design (denormalization, indexes, data placement), choice of hardware (SMP servers), network bandwidth (LAN versus WAN), client and server configuration (memory, CPU), data access techniques (ODBC, ADO, OLEDB), and application architecture (two-tier versus n-tier). This chapter will help you understand some of the key database design issues that will ensure you have a reliable and high-performance application.

NOTE

Index design is often considered part of the physical database design. Because index design guidelines and the impact of indexes on query and update performance are covered in detail in Chapter 34, "Indexes and Performance," this chapter does not discuss index design, focusing instead on other aspects of database design and performance.

Basic Tenets of Designing for Performance

Designing for performance requires making tradeoffs. To get the best write performance out of your database, you must sacrifice read performance. Before tackling database design issues for your application, it is critical to understand your goals. Do you want faster read performance? Write performance? A more understandable design?

Following are some basic truths about physical database design for SQL Server 2000 and their performance implications:

- Keep table row sizes as small as possible. This is not about saving disk space; smaller rows mean more rows will fit on a single 8KB page, which means less physical disk reads are required to read a given quantity of rows.
- Use indexes to speed up read access, *but...*
- The more indexes that a table has, the longer it takes to insert, update, and delete rows from that table.
- Using triggers to perform any kind of work during an insert, update, or delete will exact a performance toll, and decrease concurrency by lengthening transaction duration.
- Implementing declarative referential integrity (primary and foreign keys) helps maintain data integrity, but enforcing foreign key constraints requires extra lookups on the primary key table to ensure existence.
- Using `ON DELETE CASCADE` referential integrity constraints likewise helps maintain data integrity, but requires extra work on the server's part.

Keeping tables as narrow as possible—that is, ensuring that the row size is as small as possible—is one of the most important things you can do to ensure your database performs well. To keep your tables narrow, choose column data types with size in mind. Don't use an `int` datatype if a `tinyint` will do. If you have zero-to-one relationships in your tables, consider vertically partitioning your table. (See "Vertical Data Partitioning" under the "Denormalizing the Database" section later in this chapter for details on this scenario.)

Cascading deletes (and updates) causes extra lookups to be done whenever a delete runs against the parent table. In many cases, the optimizer will use worktables to resolve delete and update queries. Enforcing these constraints manually, from within stored procedures, for example, can give better performance. This is not a wholehearted endorsement against referential integrity constraints. In most cases, the extra performance hit is worth the saved aggravation of coding everything by hand. However, you should be aware of the cost of this convenience.

Logical Database Design Issues

A good database design is fundamental to the success of any application. Logical database design for relational databases follows a set of rules called **rules of normalization**. As a result of normalization, you create a data model that is usually, but not necessarily, translated into a physical data model. A logical database design does not depend on the relational database you intend to use. The same data model can be applied to Oracle, Sybase,

SQL Server, or any other relational database. On the other hand, a physical data model makes extensive use of the features of the underlying database engine to yield optimal performance for the application. Physical models are much less portable.

TIP

If portability is a big concern to you, consider using a third-party data modeling tool, such as ERwin or ERStudio. These tools have features that make it easier to migrate your logical data models to physical data models for different database platforms. Of course, this will just get you started; to get the best performance out of your design, you will need to tweak the physical design for the platform you have chosen.

Normalization Conditions

Any database designer must address two fundamental issues:

- Designing the database in a simple, understandable way that is maintainable and makes sense to its developers and users
- Designing the database such that fetching and saving data with the fastest response time, resulting in high performance

Normalization is a technique used by relational databases to organize data across many tables so that related data is kept together based on certain guidelines. Normalization results in controlled redundancy of data; therefore, it provides a good balance between disk space usage and performance. Normalization helps people understand the relationships between data, and enforces rules that ensure the data is meaningful.

TIP

Normalization rules exist, among other reasons, to make it easier for people to understand the relationships between the data. But a perfectly normalized database sometimes won't perform well under certain circumstances, and it may be difficult to understand. There are good reasons to deviate from a perfectly normalized database.

Normalization Forms

Five normalization forms exist. If you follow the rules for the first rule of normalization, your database can be described as "in first normal form." This is represented by the symbol 1NF for first normal form, 2NF for second normal form, and so on.

Each rule of normalization depends on the previous rule for successful implementation, so to be in second normal form (2NF), your database must also follow the rules for first normal form.

A typical relational database used in a business environment falls somewhere between second and third normal form. It is rare to progress past the third normal form because fourth and fifth normal form are more academic than practical in real-world environments.

Following is a brief description of the first three rules of normalization.

First Normal Form

The first rule of normalization requires removing repeating data values and specifies that no two rows can be identical in a table. This means that each table must have a logical primary key that uniquely identifies a row in the table.

Consider a table that has four columns, PublisherName, Title1, Title2, and Title3 for storing up to three titles for each publisher. This table is not in first normal form due to the repeating Title columns. The main problem with this design is it limits the number of titles associated with a publisher to three.

Removing the repeating columns so there is just a PublisherName column and a single Title column puts the table in first normal form. A separate data row is stored in the table for each title published by each publisher. The combination of PublisherName and Title becomes the primary key that uniquely identifies each row and prevents duplicates.

Second Normal Form

A table is considered to be in second normal form if it conforms to the first normal form and all nonkey attributes of the table are fully dependent on the entire primary key. If the primary key consists of multiple columns, then nonkey columns should depend on the entire key and not just on a part of the key. A table with a single column as the primary key is automatically in second normal form.

Assume you need to add the Publisher address to the database. Adding it to the table with the PublisherName and Title column would violate second normal form. The primary key consists of both PublisherName and Title, but the PublisherAddress attribute is an attribute of the Publisher only. It does not depend on the entire primary key.

To put the database in second normal form requires adding an additional table for storing publisher information. One table consists of the PublisherName column and PublisherAddress. The second table contains the PublisherName and Title columns. To retrieve the PublisherName, Title, and PublisherAddress information in a single result would require a join between the two tables on the PublisherName column.

Third Normal Form

A table is considered to be in third normal form if it already conforms to the first two normal forms and none of the nonkey columns are dependent on any other nonkey columns. All such attributes should be removed from the table.

Following is an example that comes up often during database architecture. Suppose that an employee table has four columns: EmployeeID (the primary key), salary, bonus, and total_salary, where total_salary = salary + bonus. Existence of the total_salary column in the table violates the third normal form because a nonkey column (total_salary) is dependent on two other nonkey columns (salary and bonus). Therefore, to conform to the third rule of normalization, you must remove the total_salary column from the employee table.

Benefits of Normalization

The following are the major advantages of normalization:

- Because information is logically kept together, normalization provides a better overall understanding of the system.
- Because of controlled redundancy of data, normalization can result in fast table scans and searches (less physical data has to be processed).
- Because tables are smaller with normalization, index creation and data sorts are much faster.
- With less redundant data, it is easier to maintain referential integrity for the system.
- Normalization results in narrower tables. Because you can store more rows per page, more rows can be read and cached for each I/O performed on the table. This results in better I/O performance.

Drawbacks of Normalization

One result of normalization is that data is stored in multiple tables. To retrieve or modify information, you usually have to establish joins across multiple tables. Joins are expensive from an I/O standpoint. Multitable joins can have an adverse impact on the performance of the system. The following sections discuss some of the denormalization techniques that you can use to improve the performance of the system.

TIP

A wise, old database architect I knew passed on a wise, old adage to me: "Normalize 'til it hurts, denormalize 'til it works." To put this into use, try to put your database in third normal form initially. After this is done, when you're ready to implement the physical structure, drop back from third normal form where excessive table joins are hurting performance. One of the common mistakes I've seen is when developers make too many assumptions and over-denormalize the database design before even a single line of code has been written to even begin to assess the database performance.

Denormalizing the Database

After a database has been normalized to the third form, database designers intentionally backtrack from normalization to improve the performance of the system. This technique of rolling back from normalization is called **denormalization**. Denormalization allows you to keep redundant data in the system, reducing the number of tables in your schema and reducing the number of joins to retrieve data.

TIP

Duplicate data is more helpful when the data does not change very much, such as in data warehouses. If the data changes often, keeping all "copies" of the data in sync can create significant performance overhead, including long transactions and excessive write operations.

Denormalization Guidelines

When should you denormalize a database? Consider the following points first:

- Be sure you have a good overall understanding of the logical design of the system. This knowledge helps in determining how other parts of the application are going to be affected when you change one part of the system.
- Don't make an attempt to denormalize the entire database at once. Instead, focus on the specific areas and queries that are accessed most frequently and are suffering from performance problems.
- Understand the types of transactions and the volume of data associated with specific areas of the application that is having performance problems. You can resolve many such issues by tuning the queries without denormalizing the tables.
- Determine whether you need virtual (computed) columns. Virtual columns can be computed from other columns of the table. Although this violates third normal form, computed columns can provide a decent compromise because they do not actually store another exact copy of the data in the same table.
- Understand data integrity issues. With more redundant data in the system, maintaining data integrity is more difficult and data modifications are slower.
- Understand storage techniques for the data. Using RAID and SQL Server filegroups may improve performance without denormalization.
- Determine the frequency at which data changes. If the data is changing too often, the cost of maintaining data and referential integrity might outweigh the benefits provided by redundant data.

TIP

If you are experiencing severe performance problems, denormalization should not be the first step you take to rectify the problem. Identify specific issues that are causing performance problems. Usually, you will discover factors such as poorly written queries, poor index design, inefficient application code, or poorly configured hardware. You should try to fix such issues before taking steps to denormalize database tables.

Essential Denormalization Techniques

You can employ various methods to denormalize a database table and achieve desired performance goals. Some of the useful techniques used for denormalization include the following:

- Keeping redundant data and summary data
- Using virtual columns
- Performing horizontal data partitioning
- Performing vertical data partitioning

Redundant Data

Joins are inherently expensive in a relational database from an I/O standpoint. To avoid common joins, add redundancy to the table by keeping exact copies of the data in multiple tables. The following example demonstrates this point. The example shows a three-table join to get the title of a book and the primary authors' name:

```
select c.title,
       a.au_lname,
       a.au_fname
   from   authors a join titleauthor b on a.au_id = b.au_id
   join titles c on b.title_id = c.title_id
   where  b.au_ord = 1
   order by c.title
```

You could improve the query performance for this example by adding the columns for the first and last name of the primary author to the `titles` table itself and storing the information in the titles table directly. This will eliminate the joins altogether. Here is what the revised query would look like if this denormalization technique were implemented:

```
select title,
       au_lname,
       au_fname
   from  titles
   order by title
```

As you can see, the au_lname and au_fname columns are now redundantly stored in two places: the `titles` table and the `authors` table. It is obvious that with more redundant data in the system, maintaining referential integrity and data integrity is more difficult. For example, if the author's last name changed in the authors table, to preserve data integrity, you must also change the corresponding au_lname column value in `titles` table to reflect the correct value. You could use SQL Server triggers to maintain data integrity, but recognize that update performance could suffer dramatically. For this reason, it is best if redundant data is limited to data columns whose values are relatively static and are not modified often. In the example presented, it is highly unlikely that an author's last name for a published book would change.

Computed Columns

A number of queries calculate aggregate values derived from one or more columns of a table. Such computations can sometimes be CPU intensive and can have an adverse impact on performance if they are performed frequently. One of the techniques to handle such situations is to create an additional column that stores the computed value. Such columns are called virtual columns or contrived columns. Starting with SQL Server 7.0, computed columns are natively supported. You can specify such columns during `create table` or `alter table` commands. The following example demonstrates the use of computed columns:

```
create table emp (
        empid int not null primary key,
        salary money not null,
        bonus money not null default 0,
        total_salary as ( salary+bonus )
        )
go
insert emp (empid, salary, bonus) values (100, $150000.00, $15000)
go
select * from emp
go
empid       salary          bonus                total_salary
----------- ------------  -------------------- ---------------
100         150000.0000   15000.0000           165000.0000
```

Virtual columns are not physically stored in SQL Server tables. SQL Server internally maintains a column property `iscomputed` in the system table syscolumns to determine whether a column is computed. The value of the virtual column is calculated at the time the query is run. Computed columns cannot pull data from more than one table, however, so if this is required, you must create a physical column and use stored procedures or triggers to generate and maintain its value.

In SQL 2000, computed columns can participate in joins to other tables, and they can be indexed. Creating an index that contains a computed column creates a physical copy of the computed column in the index tree. Whenever a base column participating in the computed column changes, the index must also be updated, which adds overhead and possibly slows down update performance.

Summary Data

Summary data is most helpful in a decision support environment. To satisfy reporting requirements, calculate sums, row counts, or other summary information and store it in a separate table. You can create summary data in a number of ways:

- Real time—Every time your base data is modified, recalculate the summary data using the base data as a source. This is typically done using stored procedures or triggers.
- Real time incremental—Every time your base data is modified, recalculate the summary data using the old summary value and the new data. This is more complex, but it could save time if the increments are relatively small compared to the entire data set. This too is typically done using stored procedures or triggers.
- Delayed—Use a scheduled job to recalculate summary data on a regular basis. This is the recommended method to use in an OLTP system to keep update performance optimal.

Horizontal Data Partitioning

As tables grow larger, data access time also tends to increase. For queries that need to perform table scans, the query time is proportional to the number of rows in the table. Even when you have proper indexes on such tables, access time slows as the depth of the index trees increase.

The solution is splitting the table into multiple tables such that each table has the same table structure as the original one but stores a different set of data. Figure 39.1 shows a billing table with 90 million records. You can split this table into 12 monthly tables (each with an identical table structure) to store billing records for each month.

You should carefully weigh the options when performing horizontal splitting. Although a query that only needs data from a single month gets much faster, other queries that need a full year's worth of data become more complex. Also, queries that are self-referencing do not benefit much from horizontal partitioning. For example, the business logic might dictate that each time you add a new billing record to the billing table, you need to check any outstanding account balance for previous billing dates. In such cases, before you do an insert in the current monthly billing table, you must check the data for all the other months to find any outstanding balance.

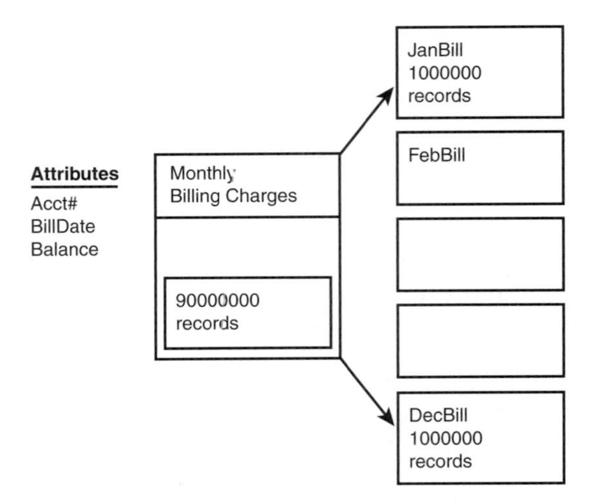

FIGURE 39.1 Horizontal partitioning of data.

TIP

Horizontal splitting of data is useful where a subset of data might see more activity than the rest of the data. For example, in a healthcare provider setting, 98 percent of the patients are inpatients and only 2 percent are outpatients. In spite of the small percentage involved, the system for outpatient records sees a lot of activity. In this scenario, it makes sense to split the patient table into two tables, one for the inpatients and one for the outpatients.

When splitting tables horizontally, you must perform some analysis to determine the optimal way to split the table. Try to find a logical dimension along which to split the data. The best choice will take into account the way your users use your data. In the previous example, date was mentioned as the optimal split candidate. However, if your users often did ad hoc queries against the billing table for a full year's worth of data, they would be unhappy with your choice to split that data among 12 different tables. Perhaps a customer type or other attribute would be more useful.

NOTE

With support for partitioned views in SQL Server 2000, you can hide the horizontal splitting of the tables by defining a partitioned view on the tables. The benefit of partitioned views is that multiple horizontally split tables will appear to the end users and applications as a single large table. When properly defined, the optimizer will automatically determine which tables in the partitioned view need to be accessed and will avoid searching all tables in the view. The query will run as quickly as if it were run only against the necessary tables directly. For more information on defining and using partitioned views, see Chapter 27, "Creating and Managing Views in SQL Server."

Vertical Data Partitioning

As you know, a database in SQL Server consists of 8KB pages, and a row cannot span across multiple pages. Therefore, the total number of rows on a page depends on the width of a table. This means the wider the table, the fewer the number of rows per page. You can achieve significant performance gains increasing the number of rows per page, which in turn reduces the number of I/Os on the table. Vertical splitting is a method of reducing the width of a table by splitting the columns of a table into multiple tables. Usually, all frequently used columns are kept in one table and others are kept in the other table. This way, more records can be accommodated per page, fewer I/Os are generated, and more data can be cached into SQL Server memory. Figure 39.2 illustrates a vertically partitioned table. The frequently accessed columns of the authors table are stored in the `author_primary` table, whereas less frequently used columns are stored in the `author_secondary` table.

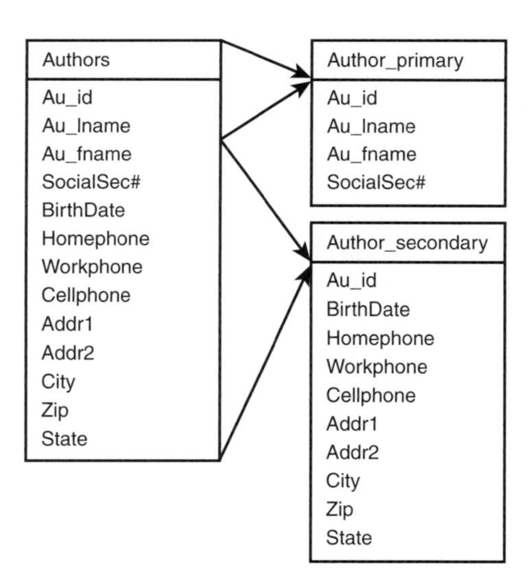

FIGURE 39.2 Vertical partitioning of data.

TIP

Make the decision to split data very carefully, especially when the system is already in production. Changing the data structure might have a system-wide impact on a large number of queries that reference the old definition of the object. In such cases, to minimize risks, SQL Server views can be effective in hiding the vertical partitioning of data. Also, if you find that users and developers are frequently joining between the vertically split tables because they need to pull data together from both tables, you might want to reconsider the split point or the splitting of the table itself. Frequent joins between split tables with smaller rows will require more I/Os to retrieve the same data than if the data resided in a single table with wider rows.

Performance Implications of Zero to One Relationships

Suppose that one of the development managers in your company, Bob, approaches you to discuss some database schema changes. He is one of several managers whose groups all use the central User table in your database. Bob's application makes use of about 5 percent of the users in the User table. Bob has a requirement to track five yes/no/undecided flags associated with those users. He would like you to add five, one-character columns to the user table to track this information. What do you tell Bob?

Bob has a classic zero-to-one problem. He has some data he needs to track, but it applies to only a small subset of the data in the table. You can approach this problem in one of three ways:

- Option one: Add the columns to the User table—95 percent of your users will have NULL values in those columns, and the table will become wider for everybody.
- Option two: Create a new table with a vertical partition of the User table—The new table will contain the User primary key and Bob's five flags. 95 percent of your users still have NULL data in the new table, but the User table is safe from the effects of this. Because other groups don't need to use the new partition table, this is a nice compromise.
- Option three: Create a new vertically partitioned table as in option two, but populate it only with rows that have at least one non-NULL value for the columns in the new partition—This is great for database performance, and searches in the new table will be wonderfully fast. The only drawback to this is that Bob's developers will have to add additional logic to their applications to determine if a row exists during updates. Bob's folks will need to use an outer join to the table to cover the possibility that a row doesn't exist.

Depending on the goals of your project, any one of these options is appropriate. The first option is simple and is the easiest to code for and understand. The second option is a good compromise between performance and simplicity. The third option gives the best performance in certain circumstances, but impacts performance in certain other situations and definitely causes more coding work to be done.

Database Filegroups and Performance

Filegroups allow you to decide where on the disk a particular object will be placed. You can do this by defining a filegroup within your database, extending the database onto a different drive or set of drives, and then placing a database object on the new filegroup.

Filegroups are most often used in high-performance environments to isolate key tables or indexes on their own set of disks, which are in turn typically part of a high-performance RAID array. Assuming that you start with a database with just a PRIMARY file group (the default), this example shows how you would add an index filegroup on a new drive and move some nonclustered indexes over to it. Moving the indexes to a separate RAID array minimizes I/O contention by spreading out the I/O generated by updates to the data that affect data rows and require changes to index rows as well.

NOTE

Because the leaf level of a clustered index is the data page, if you create a clustered index on a file group, the entire table moves from the existing file group to the new file group. If you want to put indexes on a separate file group, reserve this space for nonclustered indexes, only.

```
-- add the file group
alter database Grocer
      add filegroup FG_INDEX

-- Create a new database file and add it to the FG_INDEX filegroup
alter database Grocer
add file(
        NAME = Grocer_Index,
       FILENAME = 'g:\Grocer_Index.ndf',
       SIZE = 2048MB,
       MAXSIZE = 8192MB,
       FILEGROWTH = 10%
) to filegroup FG_INDEX

create nonclustered index xOrderDetail_ScanDT
    on OrderDetail(ScanDT)
    on FG_INDEX
```

With your indexes on a separate filegroup, you get the following advantages:

- Index scans and index page reads come from a separate disk group, so they need not compete with other database processes for disk time.
- Inserts, updates, and deletes on the table are spread across two separate disk arrays. The clustered index, including all the table data, is on a separate array from the nonclustered indexes.
- You can target your budget dollars more precisely because faster disks will improve system performance more if they are given to the index filegroup rather than the database as a whole.

The next section on RAID will give specific recommendations on how to architect a hardware solution based on using separate filegroups for data and indexes.

RAID Technology

Redundant Array of Inexpensive Disks (RAID) is used to configure a disk subsystem to provide better performance and fault tolerance for an application. The basic idea behind using RAID is that you spread data across multiple disk drives so that I/Os are spread across multiple drives. RAID has special significance for database-related applications, where you want to spread random I/Os (data changes) and sequential I/Os (for the transaction log) across different disk subsystems to minimize head movement and maximize I/O performance.

The four significant levels of RAID implementation that are of most interest in database implementations are as follows:

- RAID 0 is data striping with no redundancy or fault tolerance.
- RAID 1 is mirroring, where every disk in the array has a mirror (copy).
- RAID 5 is striping with parity, where parity information for data on one disk is spread across the other disks in the array. The contents of a single disk can be re-created from the parity information stored on the other disks in the array.
- RAID 10, or 0+1, is a combination of RAID 0 and 1. Data is striped across all drives in the array, and each disk has a mirrored duplicate, offering the fault tolerance of RAID 1 with the performance advantages of RAID 0.

RAID Level 0

RAID Level 0 provides the best I/O performance among all other RAID levels. A file has sequential segments striped across each drive in the array. Data is written in a round-robin approach to ensure that data is evenly balanced across all drives in the array. However, if a media failure occurs, no fault tolerance is provided and all data stored in the array is lost. RAID 0 should not be used for a production database where data loss or loss of system availability is not acceptable. RAID 0 is occasionally used for `tempdb` to provide the best possible read and (especially) write performance. RAID 0 is helpful for random read requirements, such as those that occur on `tempdb` and in data segments.

TIP

While the data stored in `tempdb` is temporary and non-critical data, failure of a RAID 0 stripeset containing `tempdb` will result in loss of system availability, as SQL Server requires a functioning `tempdb` to carry out many of its activities. If loss of system availability is not an option, do not put `tempdb` on a RAID 0 array. Use one of the other RAID technologies that provides redundancy.

If momentary loss of system availability is acceptable in exchange for the improved I/O and reduced cost of RAID 0, recovery of `tempdb` is relatively simple. To rebuild a suspect `tempdb` on a RAID 0 array, use the following steps:

1. Restore the disk array to service by either replacing the failed drive or by re-creating the array on surviving disks.
2. Remove the old `tempdb` files—they are useless without all the pieces.
3. Restart SQL Server with `traceflag 3608`, which bypasses recovery of all databases except master.
4. Reset the `tempdb` status with `sp_resetstatus tempdb`.
5. Restart SQL Server. New `tempdb` files will be created during the recovery phase.

RAID 0 is the cheapest of the RAID configurations because 100 percent of the disks in the array are available for data, and none are used to provide fault tolerance. Performance is also the best of the RAID configurations since there is no overhead required to maintain redundant data.

Figure 39.3 depicts a RAID 0 disk array configuration.

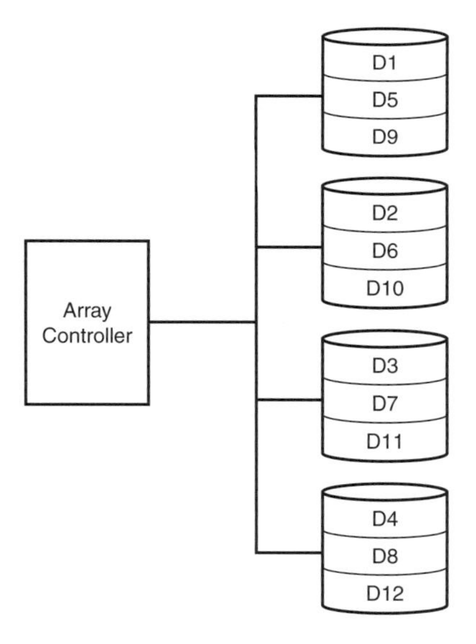

FIGURE 39.3 RAID Level 0.

RAID Level 1

RAID Level 1 is known as disk mirroring. Every write to the primary disk is written to the mirror set. Either member of the set can satisfy a read request. RAID 1 devices provide excellent fault tolerance because in the event of a media failure, either on the primary disk or the mirrored disk, the system can still continue to run. Writes are much faster than RAID 5 arrays as no parity information needs to be calculated first. The data is simply written twice.

RAID 1 arrays are best for transaction logs and for index file groups. RAID 1 provides the best fault tolerance, and the best write performance, which is critical to log and index performance. Since log writes are sequential write operations and not random access operations, they are best supported by a RAID 1 configuration.

RAID 1 arrays are the most expensive RAID configuration because only 50 percent of total disk space is available for actual storage. The rest is used to provide fault tolerance.

Figure 39.4 shows a RAID 1 configuration.

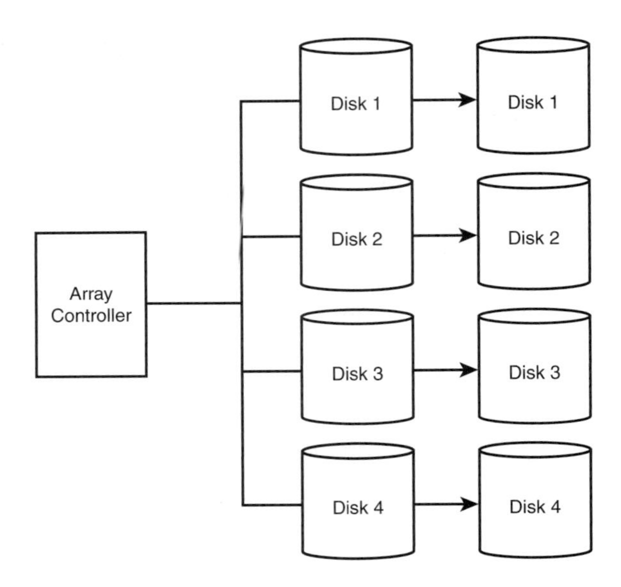

FIGURE 39.4 RAID Level 1.

Because RAID 1 requires the same data be written to two drives at the same time, write performance will be slightly less than writing data to a single drive because the write will not be considered complete until both writes have been done. Using a disk controller with a battery-backed write cache can mitigate this write penalty because the write will be considered complete once it occurs to the battery-backed cache. The actual writes to the disks will occur in the background.

RAID 1 read performance will often be better than a single disk drive as most controllers now support split seeks. Split seeks allow each disk in the mirror set to be read independently of each other, thereby supporting concurrent reads.

RAID Level 10

RAID 10, or RAID 0+1, is a combination of mirroring and striping. If you find that your transaction log or index segment is pegging your RAID 1 array at 100 percent usage, you can implement a RAID 10 array to get better performance. This type of RAID carries with it all the fault tolerance (and cost!) of a RAID 1 array, with all the performance benefits of RAID 0 striping.

RAID Level 5

RAID 5 is most commonly known as striping with parity. In this configuration, data is striped across multiple disks in large blocks. At the same time, parity bits are written across all the disks for a given block. Information is always stored in such a way that any one disk can be lost without losing any information in the array. In the event of a disk failure, the system can still continue to run (at a reduced performance level) without downtime by using the parity information to reconstruct the data that was lost on the missing drive.

Some arrays provide "hot standby" disks. The RAID controller uses the standby disk to rebuild a failed drive automatically using the parity information stored on all the other drives in the array. During the rebuild process, performance is markedly worse.

The fault tolerance of RAID 5 is usually sufficient, but if more than one drive in the array fails, you will lose the entire array. It is recommended that a spare drive be kept on hand in the event of a drive failure, so the failed drive can be replaced quickly before any other drives have a chance to fail.

> **NOTE**
>
> Many of the RAID solutions available today support a "hot spare" drive. A hot spare drive is connected to the array, but doesn't store any data. When the RAID system detects a drive failure, the contents of the failed drive are re-created on the hot spare drive and it is automatically swapped into the array in place of the failed drive. The failed drive can then be manually removed from the array and replaced with a working drive, which will become the new hot spare.

RAID 5 provides excellent read performance, but expensive write performance. A write operation on a RAID 5 array requires two writes: one to the data drive and one to the parity drive. After the writes are complete, the controller will read the data to ensure that the information matches (no hardware failure has occurred). A single write operation will cause four I/Os on a RAID 5 array. For this reason, putting log files or `tempdb` on a RAID 5 array is not recommended. Index filegroups, which suffer worse than data filegroups from bad write performance, are also poor candidates for a RAID 5 array. Data filegroups where more than 10 percent of the I/Os are writes are also not good candidates for RAID 5 arrays.

Note that if write performance is not an issue in your environment—for example, in a DSS/Data Warehousing environment—you should, by all means, use RAID 5 for your data and index segments.

In any environment, avoid putting `tempdb` on a RAID 5 array. `tempdb` typically receives heavy write activity and will perform better on a RAID 1 or RAID 0 array.

RAID 5 is a relatively economical means of providing fault tolerance. No matter how many drives are in the array, only the space equivalent to a single drive is used to support fault tolerance. This method becomes more economical with more drives in the array. You must have at least three drives in a RAID 5 array. Three drives would require that 33 percent of available disk space be used for fault tolerance, four would require 25 percent, five would require 20 percent, and so on.

Figure 39.5 shows a RAID 5 configuration.

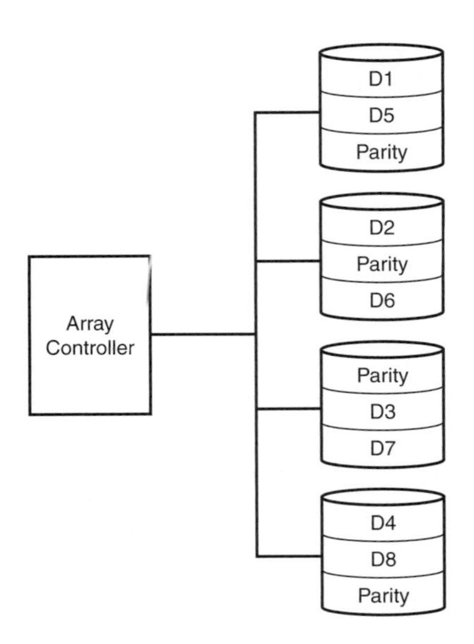

FIGURE 39.5 RAID Level 5.

NOTE

While the recommendations for using the various RAID levels presented here will help ensure that your database performance will be optimal, reality often dictates that your optimum disk configuration might not be available. Often you will be given a server with a single RAID 5 array and told to make it work. While RAID 5 is not optimal for `tempdb` or transaction logs, the write performance can be mitigated using a controller with a battery-backed write cache.

If possible, also try to stripe your database activity across multiple RAID 5 arrays rather than a single large RAID 5 array to avoid overdriving the disks in the array.

Summary

A good database design is the best place to start to ensure a smoothly running system. You can take steps to ensure a solid design. If you inherit a database with an inadequate design, you can take steps to ensure good performance. The primary goals of a database designer should be to index the database effectively and keep table row sizes as narrow as possible. A good database design goes a long way toward ensuring excellent performance.

Using the information you learned in this chapter about designing for performance, the next chapter, "Configuring, Tuning, and Optimizing SQL Server Options," will show you how to take your new database design concepts into production. You will learn how to configure a server for the best performance under different circumstances, and identify and optimize the server when performance is inadequate.

CHAPTER **40**

Configuring, Tuning, and Optimizing SQL Server Options

by Paul Bertucci

IN THIS CHAPTER

As was already discussed in Chapter 37, "Monitoring SQL Server Performance," many components of a system can be monitored and tuned to yield high performance. These addressable components can be server hardware, network configuration, memory allocation, disk systems usage, database design techniques, and so on. This chapter will delve a bit more into what can be done in the SQL Server configurable options—particularly, what can be improved that SQL Server isn't automatically tuning already. By setting the values of several key SQL Server configuration parameters, you can fine-tune SQL Server to provide excellent performance and throughput.

Note that with each release of SQL Server, less needs to be tuned from the SQL Server configuration point of view. With the advent of self tuning or self configuring options, it is only a matter of time before most of your server tuning time will be spent elsewhere, such as with the operating system, disk systems, and network interfaces—and only because SQL Server can't reach there, yet.

SQL Server Instance Architecture

Figure 40.1 illustrates the address space architecture of an instance of SQL Server 2000. When you fire up a SQL Server instance, two main areas are allocated: the code area and the memory pool area. The code area will be mostly static executable code of the SQL Server Kernel, Server Net-library DLLs, Open Data Services code, the Stack Space, and a variable code area that contains distributed query OLE DB providers, OLE Automation objects, and extended-stored procedures as they are needed by user requests.

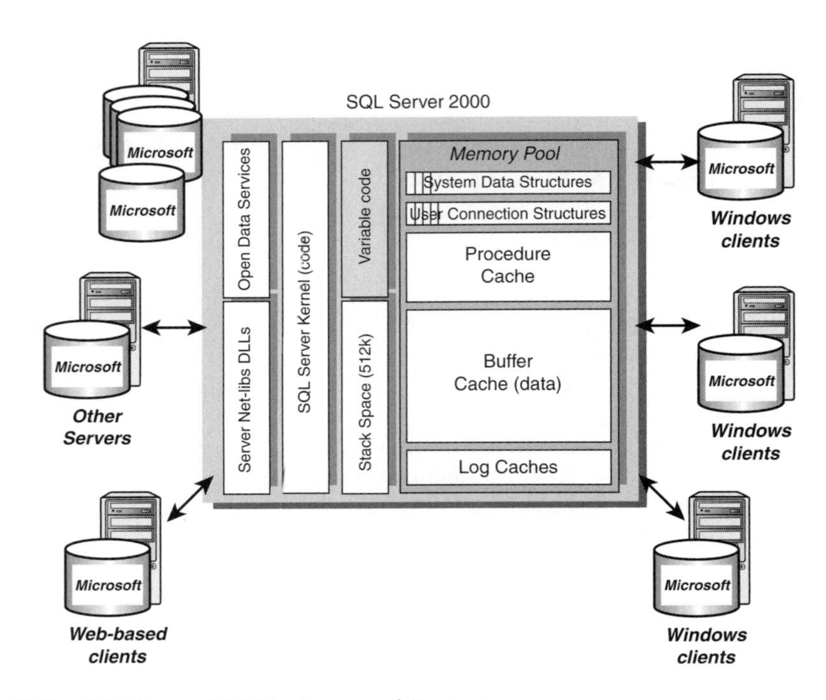

FIGURE 40.1 SQL Server 2000 instance architecture.

The memory pool area of SQL Server is the most dynamically changing part of an instance. Even now, the once-static System Data Structures and User Connection Structures (Connection context) are controlled by user requests and dynamically allocate structures as they are needed.

By default, SQL Server will try to keep the amount of virtual memory allocations on the computer at 4–10 MB less than the physical memory available.

The rest of the memory pool area is divided into Procedure Cache, Data Cache (buffer cache), and Log Cache. SQL Server is actively adjusting these for optimal performance. It wasn't that long ago that the system administrator had to do all of this manually. Many of the configurable options will directly relate to optimizing this address space.

Configuration Options

For SQL Server 2000, this chapter will discuss the configurable options in two distinct categories: basic options and advanced options. The advanced options are a super-set of the basic options. As each option is discussed, it will be noted whether it is self-configuring. Several self-configuring options are available that adjust themselves dynamically according to the needs of the system. In most cases, this eliminates the need for setting the values manually. Sometimes you won't want to rely on certain self-configuring values, depending on how SQL Server is being used.

As you can see in Figure 40.2, SQL Server provides configuration parameters that the system administrator can set to maximize the performance of a system. You can set these parameters either by using the sp_configure system-stored procedure or by using SQL Server Enterprise Manager and the server configuration properties.

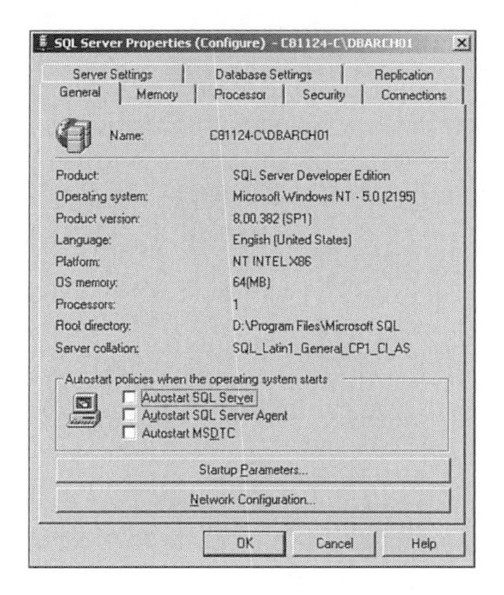

FIGURE 40.2 SQL Server 2000 Configuration Properties dialog box.

Now, the only questions that need to get answered are "What configuration options do I need to set that aren't already fine?" And, "How do I set them?"

To answer the "what" question, you will first determine for what purpose the applications are using SQL Server. This must include understanding variables such as the number of potential connections to support, the amount of resources available on the box, the size of the database, the type of data accesses occurring, and the workload being put on SQL Server. After you know this, it will be easy to determine the configuration option setting to adjust.

Figure 40.3 shows a generalization of the types of applications that you might find in the real world that would be implemented using SQL Server 2000 and the general behavior that they elicit. It is not a complete list, just a generalized list. The four basic categories of application processing are online transaction processing (OLTP), applications, data warehouse/data mart applications, online analytic processing (OLAP) applications, and mixed applications (some OLTP along with some data marts on one SQL Server). Because these configuration options are set at the SQL Server level, it is important to know the combined behavior of all application processing.

Application type	General processing behavior
OLTP	Mix of reads, writes & deletes Large number of users
OLAP	Big loads, then read-only Medium to small number of users
Data Warehouse	Incremental loads, then read-only, big extracts and reporting Medium number of users
Mixed Server	Mix of reads, writes, deletes, big loads, big extracts Large number of users

FIGURE 40.3 General application processing types for SQL Server.

For each SQL Server configuration option that is discussed, you will address the correct setting based on the generalized application processing behaviors that need to be supported.

The "How do I set them?" question will be discussed now. The next few sections describe all of the types of configuration options available on SQL Server 2000. Those sections will show you how to set these configuration options using both Enterprise Manager and sp_configure system-stored procedure. The rule will be that you can certainly set a configuration option using Enterprise Manager, but that you should keep an sp_configure version of that setting change as a backup in case you need to rebuild the entire server configuration from scratch. In addition, keeping an sp_configure version around in a file will provide a great audit trail of what you did and for what reason.

You have already seen, in Figure 40.2, the Enterprise Manager Configuration Properties dialog box. Now, you will look at the sp_configure equivalent. By executing sp_configure without parameters, you will be given the list of options that can be addressed. When you have just installed a SQL Server instance, you will be able to see only the basic configuration options.

Ten basic configuration options are available:

```
sp_configure
go
name                          minimum     maximum     config_value run_value
----------------------------- ----------- ----------- ------------ --------
allow updates                      0           1           0            0
default language                   0           9999        0            0
max text repl size (B)             0           2147483647  65536        65536
nested triggers                    0           1           1            1
remote access                      0           1           1            1
remote login timeout (s)           0           2147483647  20           20
remote proc trans                  0           1           0            0
remote query timeout (s)           0           2147483647  600          600
show advanced options              0           1           0            0
user options                       0           32767       0            0
```

By default, all SQL Server users have permission to run this system-stored procedure, but only users who have sysadmin and serveradmin fixed server roles (such as sa) can actually set the value of a parameter.

The proper syntax of the sp_configure command is as follows:

```
sp_configure  [parameter_name [, parameter_value ]]
```

where *parameter_name* is the name of the configuration parameter you want to set, and *parameter_value* is the value for the parameter. Both of these parameters are optional. Parameters set by `sp_configure` take effect at the server level.

Following is a brief explanation of the output of the `sp_configure` command. As you can see, the output consists of five columns:

- Name—Name of the configurable option.
- Minimum—This is the minimum legal value allowed for this parameter. Passing an illegal value causes SQL Server to return an error.
- Maximum—This is the maximum legal value allowed for this parameter. Passing an illegal value causes SQL Server to return an error.
- Config_value—This column reflects the values that are going to take effect the next time SQL Server is started. If you change static parameters, the new values are listed under this column.
- Run_value—This column reflects the values that SQL Server is currently using. If you change any dynamic parameters, the new values are listed in this column. At the time of SQL Server startup, the `config_value` for all the parameters is copied into `run_value`. Immediately after restart, both columns (`run_value` and `config_value`) should display the same values corresponding to each parameter.

If you specify only the parameter name, SQL Server returns the current configuration value for that particular parameter.

```
sp_configure 'allow updates'
go

name                          minimum     maximum     config_value run_value
----------------------------- ----------- ----------- ------------ --------
allow updates                      0           1           0            0
```

Many more configuration options are available from the total of 36 options. These consist of the original 10 basic options plus 26 advanced options. To see a complete list of all options, you must turn on the Show Advanced Options configuration option with the value 1.

In addition, when using sp_configure to change a setting, use the RECONFIGURE WITH OVERRIDE statement for the change to take effect immediately. You can also choose to use just the RECONFIGURE statement. Depending on the configuration option, it will take effect immediately or not until the server has been restarted.

The following commands will set the Show Advanced Options configuration option and then retrieve the complete list of these options:

```
exec sp_configure 'Show Advanced Options', 1/* Advanced config options */
go
RECONFIGURE WITH OVERRIDE              /* to have it take effect immediately */
go
sp_configure
go

name                          minimum     maximum     config_value run_value
----------------------------- ----------- ----------- ------------ --------
affinity mask                      -2147483648 2147483647  0            0
allow updates                      0           1           0            0
awe enabled                        0           1           0            0
c2 audit mode                      0           1           0            0
cost threshold for parallelism     0           32767       5            5
cursor threshold                   -1          2147483647  -1           -1
default full-text language         0           2147483647  1033         1033
default language                   0           9999        0            0
fill factor (%)                    0           100         0            0
index create memory (KB)           704         2147483647  0            0
lightweight pooling                0           1           0            0
locks                              5000        2147483647  0            0
max degree of parallelism          0           32          0            0
```

```
max server memory (MB)         4          2147483647  2147483647   2147483647
max text repl size (B)              0          2147483647  65536        65536
max worker threads                  32         32767       255          255
media retention                     0          365         0            0
min memory per query (KB)           512        2147483647  1024         1024
min server memory (MB)              0          2147483647  0            0
nested triggers                     0          1           1            1
network packet size (B)             512        65536       4096         4096
open objects                        0          2147483647  0            0
priority boost                      0          1           0            0
query governor cost limit           0          2147483647  0            0
query wait (s)                      -1         2147483647  -1           -1
recovery interval (min)             0          32767       0            0
remote access                       0          1           1            1
remote login timeout (s)            0          2147483647  20           20
remote proc trans                   0          1           0            0
remote query timeout (s)            0          2147483647  600          600
scan for startup procs              0          1           1            1
set working set size                0          1           0            0
show advanced options               0          1           1            1
two digit year cutoff               1753       9999        2049         2049
user connections                    0          32767       0            0
user options                        0          32767       0            0
```

Microsoft suggests that only highly experienced SQL Server administrators change these advanced configuration options. You have been warned!

SQL Server internally maintains two tables: syscurconfigs and sysconfigures. The syscurconfigs table contains the current configuration values of SQL Server parameters. These values are shown under the run_value column of sp_configure. The following is what you might expect to see if you query this table directly:

```
SELECT value, config, substring (comment,1,50),status from master..syscurconfigs
Go

value       config                                                     status
----------- ------ -------------------------------------------------- ------
8           1      Major revision number of config data.              0
0           2      Minor revision number of config data.              0
13          3      Reconfigure revision number of config data         0
2           4      Configuration boot source.                         0
0           101    Maximum recovery interval in minutes               3
0           102    Allow updates to system tables                     1
0           103    Number of user connections allowed                 2
```

```
0          106   Number of locks for all users                          2
0          107   Number of open database objects                        2
0          109   Default fill factor percentage                         2
0          1537  Media retention period in days                         2
1          115   Allow triggers to be invoked within triggers           1
1          117   Allow remote access                                    0
2049       1127  two digit year cutoff                                  3
1033       1126  default full-text language                             3
0          124   default language                                       1
255        503   Maximum worker threads.                                2
0          542   Create DTC Transaction for RPC                         1
10         543   remote connection inactivity timeout                   0
4096       505   network packet size                                    3
0          1505  Memory for index create sorts (kBytes)                 3
0          1517  Priority boost                                         2
1          518   Show advanced options                                  1
20         1519  remote login timeout                                   1
600        1520  remote query timeout                                   1
-1         1531  cursor threshold                                       3
1024       1540  minimum memory per query (kBytes)                      3
-1         1541  query wait (s)                                         3
0          1532  set working set size                                   2
0          1534  user options                                           1
0          1535  affinity mask                                          2
65536      1536  max text repl size                                     1
5          1538  cost threshold for parallelism                         3
0          1539  maximum degree of parallelism                          3
0          1543  Minimum Server Memory size (MB)                        3
2147483647 1544  Maximum Server Memory size (MB)                        3
0          1545  Maximum estimated cost of query allowed to run by      3
0          1546  User mode scheduler uses lightweight pooling           2
1          1547  scan for startup stored procedures                     2
0          544   c2 audit mode                                          2
0          1548  AWE enabled in server                                  2
```

The sysconfigures table stores the new values of the parameters that were changed since the last SQL Server startup. These values are shown in the config_value column of sp_configure.

```
SELECT value, config, substring (comment,1,50),status from master..sysconfigures
Go
```

```
value      config                                                   status
---------- ------ ------------------------------------------------- ------
0          101    Maximum recovery interval in minutes              3
0          102    Allow updates to system tables                    1
0          103    Number of user connections allowed                2
0          106    Number of locks for all users                     2
0          107    Number of open database objects                   2
0          109    Default fill factor percentage                    2
1          115    Allow triggers to be invoked within triggers      1
1          117    Allow remote access                               0
0          124    default language                                  1
255        503    Maximum worker threads                            2
4096       505    Network packet size                               3
1          518    show advanced options                             1
0          542    Create DTC transaction for remote procedures      1
0          544    c2 audit mode                                     2
1033       1126   default full-text language                        3
2049       1127   two digit year cutoff                             3
0          1505   Memory for index create sorts (kBytes)            3
0          1517   Priority boost                                    2
20         1519   remote login timeout                              1
600        1520   remote query timeout                              1
-1         1531   cursor threshold                                  3
0          1532   set working set size                              2
0          1534   user options                                      1
0          1535   affinity mask                                     2
65536      1536   Maximum size of a text field in replication.      1
0          1537   Tape retention period in days                     2
5          1538   cost threshold for parallelism                    3
0          1539   maximum degree of parallelism                     3
1024       1540   minimum memory per query (kBytes)                 3
-1         1541   maximum time to wait for query memory (s)         3
0          1543   Minimum size of server memory (MB)                3
2147483647 1544   Maximum size of server memory (MB)                3
0          1545   Maximum estimated cost allowed by query governor  3
0          1546   User mode scheduler uses lightweight pooling      2
1          1547   scan for startup stored procedures                2
0          1548   AWE enabled in the server                         2
0          1549   affinity64 mask                                   2
```

Dynamic parameters are written to both of these tables. Static parameters are written only to the sysconfigures table. At SQL Server restart, all of the values are copied from the sysconfigures table to the syscurconfigs table.

Fixing an Incorrect Option Setting

Setting a value too high for a parameter might cause SQL Server to crash during startup. For example, if you set the value of the memory option to a value that is higher than the physical memory on the machine, SQL Server will not start. In this case, you start SQL Server with the `-f` option. This causes SQL Server to start with the default parameter values (the same values used by the setup program when you installed SQL Server). After SQL Server is running, change the incorrect value to the correct one and restart SQL Server without the `-f` option.

Setting Configuration Options with SQL Enterprise Manager

As mentioned previously, you can set SQL Server configuration options by using SQL Server Enterprise Manager. Simply invoke Enterprise Manager from the Microsoft SQL Server program group and right-click on the Server folder. Figure 40.4 shows the SQL Server Properties (Configure) dialog box and the different tabs available. Don't be misled: Some of these tab options are not configuration options that correspond to sp_configure, such as the Security tab and some functions under the Database tab. However, as you will see, Microsoft has done a nice job of organizing and presenting the option information. You will also see that several of the configuration options cannot be managed from this interface. The ones not addressed are rarely used options, such as the AWE-enabled option.

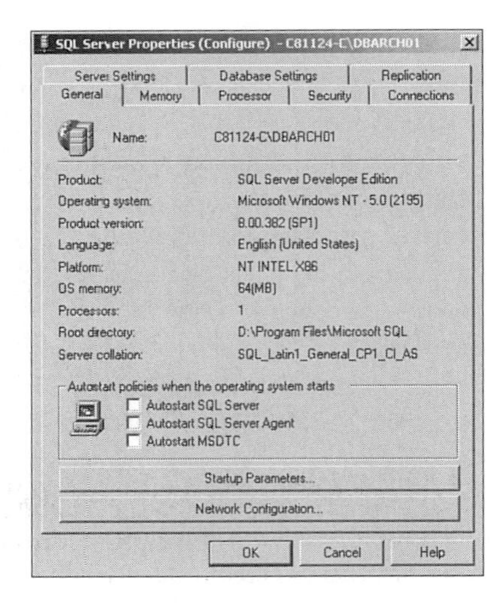

FIGURE 40.4 Enterprise Manager and configuration properties.

Remember: You must have sysadmin and serveradmin fixed server roles to make changes.

Obsolete Configuration Options

Some of the configuration options available in SQL Server 7.0 are obsolete in SQL Server 2000. Some options, such as "time slice," were just introduced in SQL Server 7.0 and then immediately became obsolete.

The following parameters are obsolete in SQL Server 2000:

Obsoleted Configuration Options	
default sortorder id	resource timeout
extended memory size	spin counter
language in cache	time slice
language neutral full-text	unicode comparison style
max async IO	unicode locale id

One of the all-time favorite options in SQL Server 7.0 was max async IO. The reason that option became obsolete is because it has been completely automated with SQL Server 2000. Previously, max async IO was used to specify the number of simultaneous disk I/O requests that SQL Server 7.0 (and earlier versions) could submit to Windows NT and Windows 2000 during a checkpoint operation. It invariably helped overall throughput on systems that used RAID devices that had extensive disk cache mechanisms. Now, SQL Server 2000 adjusts this automatically.

Configuration Options and Performance

This section explains essential information about most of the SQL Server configuration options and their impact on SQL Server performance. Many of the options don't have performance implications, but they will be discussed anyway. As part of each option's explanation, an indication of whether the option is Advanced or Basic will be given along with the option's default value and whether the option is self-configuring or not. Possible values will also be listed depending on the generalized application processing types that were identified earlier.

Affinity Mask

Type—Advanced option

Default value—`0`

SQL Server supports symmetric multiprocessing (SMP). SMP support means that a thread is not tied to a particular processor on the machine. This allows SQL Server to run multiple threads simultaneously, resulting in a high level of load balancing across processors. A value of `0` (the default) allows Windows Scheduling algorithm to set the threads affinity.

This qualifies the affinity mask as self-configuring by the operating system. However, when a server is experiencing a heavy load because of other applications running on the same server, it might be desirable to bind thread affinity to a processor.

The affinity mask is a bitmapped field. Starting from the least significant digit, each bit that is set to 1 represents the processor on which SQL Server will spawn its threads. Processors are numbered from 0 to 7. An example of the bit mask values for the first seven processors of an eight-processor system follows; decimal values are shown in parentheses:

Bit Mask	Processors Used
00000001 (1)	0
00000011 (3)	0,1
00000111 (7)	0,1,2
00001111 (15)	0,1,2,3
00011111 (31)	0,1,2,3,4
00111111 (63)	0,1,2,3,4,5
01111111 (127)	0,1,2,3,4,5,6

You usually leave the eighth processor alone because many system processes—such as domain controllers—default to that processor.

As an example, if you want to create the affinity for one SQL Server instance thread to use four processors of an eight-processor system, you could set this bit mask to be 15 (00001111). The result would be that SQL Server spawns its threads only on those processors, thus reducing overall reloading of the processor cache. This can be especially evident during heavy system loads.

```
sp_configure 'affinity mask', 15
go
RECONFIGURE
Go
```

In general, the default affinity value is able to provide ample load balancing across processors. Based on your particular processing load and application types, you will want to allocate CPUs accordingly. Below is a general recommendation of what to specify based on the different application types you are running:

- OLTP: Use default value of 0.
- Data warehouse: Potentially use 75 percent of available processors to maximize on the huge data loads, large reporting, and number of users.

- OLAP: Use default value of `0`.
- Mixed: Use default value of `0`.

From Enterprise Manager, SQL Server Properties, Processor tab, just select the targeted processors in the Processor Control section.

Allow Update

Type—Basic

Default value—`0`

By default, SQL Server does not allow updates to internal system tables. When you set the allow update value to `1`, any user with proper permissions can update system tables. Sometimes you might want to allow access to system tables.

Following are a couple scenarios:

- In many database applications, business logic is written in stored procedures and triggers. To protect your intellectual property, you might not want anyone to see and modify this logic. One way to accomplish this goal is to delete entries from the syscomments table for the objects you want to protect.
- My database is currently running off a Jaz drive connected to my machine, and sometimes, my Jaz drive is disconnected. In such cases during startup, SQL Server fails to initialize the database file and marks the database corrupt by setting the `status` bit in the sysdatabases table to 256. To bring the database back to life, I connect my Jaz drive, change the `status` bit to the original value, and restart the machine. Then SQL Server recognizes the drive and starts the database normally.

CAUTION

Only highly experienced users of SQL Server should use the Allow Update option. For example, if you create a stored procedure that modifies system tables when the Allow Update option is turned on, the procedure will continue to be able to modify the system table even if you turn off allow update again. Therefore, be very careful when you set this parameter value to `1`.

Even more important is to turn off Allow Update as soon as you are finished with the task of modifying system tables.

From Enterprise Manager, SQL Server Properties, Server Settings tab, select the Allow Modifications box, as shown in Figure 40.5.

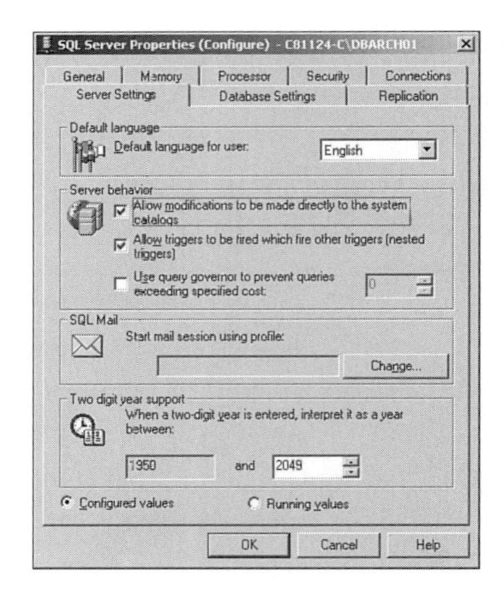

FIGURE 40.5 SQL Server Properties: Server Settings.

AWE Enabled

Type—Advanced

Default value—`0`

SQL Server can use the Advanced Windowing Extensions (AWE) API to support large amounts of physical memory—in fact, as much as 8GB of memory on Windows 2000 Advanced Server and up to 64GB on Windows 2000 Data Center. The default of `0` tells SQL Server to use dynamic memory in standard 32-bit virtual address spaces. By enabling AWE, the SQL Server instance does not dynamically manage the size of the address space. The instance holds all memory acquired at startup until it is shut down, and memory pages come from the Windows nonpageable pool. This means that none of the memory of the instance can be swapped out. You end up with a great deal of all activity occurring in memory only. This is potentially a fast database engine.

AWE enabled is usually used in conjunction with the max server memory option to control how much memory each SQL Server instance will use.

```
sp_configure 'awe enabled', 1
go
RECONFIGURE
Go
```

Setting of this option will vary according to the following application types:

- OLTP: If memory is available, set to 1.
- Data warehouse: Not appropriate for this type.
- OLAP: If memory is available and you are not using OLAP file options, set to 1.
- Mixed: If memory is available, set to 1.

Cost Threshold for Parallelism

Type—Advanced

Default value—5

SQL Server now supports parallel query execution. Before a query is executed, SQL Server's cost-based optimizer estimates the cost of execution for a serial plan, a plan that uses a single thread. The option to set the cost threshold for parallelism allows you to specify a threshold in seconds; if the cost of the serial execution plan (in seconds) is greater than the value specified by this parameter, SQL Server will consider a parallel query execution plan. A query will not become a candidate for parallel query execution simply based on this fact. Because parallel query execution is supported only on an SMP server, this value is ignored for non-SMP hardware. For an application that uses many complex queries, set this value to a lower number so that you can take advantage of the parallel query execution capabilities of SQL Server.

```
sp_configure 'cost threshold for parallelism', 2
go
RECONFIGURE
Go
```

Setting of this option will vary according to the following application types:

- OLTP: Use default value of 5.
- Data warehouse: Many complex queries are candidates for parallelism. Set to low value, perhaps 2 (seconds).
- OLAP: Use default value.
- Mixed: Use default value.

Cursor Threshold

Type—Advanced

Default value—-1

This option allows you to specify when SQL Server should generate a cursor result set asynchronously. If the optimizer estimates that the number of rows returned by the cursor is greater than the value specified by this parameter, it will generate the result set asynchronously. The optimizer makes this decision based on the distribution statistics for each table that is participating in the join in the cursor.

To determine the optimal value for this parameter, make sure that statistics are up to date (by running `update statistics`) for the tables used in the cursors. By default, SQL Server generates a cursor result set synchronously. If you are using a fair amount of cursors that return a large number of result sets, setting this value to a higher value will result in better performance. Setting this value to `0` will force SQL Server to always generate a cursor result set asynchronously.

```
sp_configure 'cursor threshold', 100000
go
RECONFIGURE
go
```

Setting of this option will vary according to the following application types:

- OLTP: Use default value.
- Data warehouse: A data warehousing environment is the largest potential user of this option due to the high volume of result rows returned by applications using data warehouses. Setting this value to 100,000 is a good starting point.
- OLAP: Use default value.
- Mixed: Use default value.

Default Language

Type—Basic

Default value—`0`

This option specifies the language ID currently in use by SQL Server. The default value is `0`, which specifies the U.S. English system. As you add languages on the server, SQL Server assigns a new ID for each language. You can then use these IDs to specify the default language of your choice. You can add languages using the SQL Server setup program. Adding a language allows SQL Server to display error messages and date/time values in the format that is appropriate for that language. Set this option in the Server Settings tab of the SQL Server Properties dialog box.

Fill Factor

Type—Basic, static

Default value—`0`

The Fill Factor option allows you to define the percentage of free space on a data page or an index page when you create an index or a table. The value can range from 1–100. Setting the value to `80` would mean each page would be 80 percent full at the time of the `create index`. SQL Server also allows you to specify the value of fill factor at the server level by providing a `fill factor` parameter.

```
sp_configure 'fill factor', 90
go
RECONFIGURE
Go
```

Setting of this option will vary according to the following application types:

- OLTP: This is a good candidate for leaving space free in pages due to the update, delete, and insert characteristics. Try 90 percent full value first and watch the page split activity.
- Data warehouse: Use default value.
- OLAP: Use default value.
- Mixed: Use default value.

As you can see in Figure 40.6, you set fill factor from the Database Settings tab in the SQL Server Properties dialog box. Just click on the Fixed option and slide the bar until you have the desired fullness of a page.

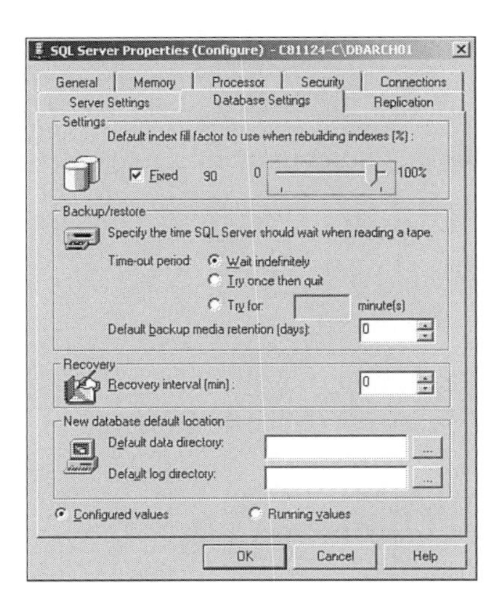

FIGURE 40.6 SQL Server Properties: Database settings.

Index Create Memory (KB)

Type—Advanced, Self-configuring

Default value—0

The index create memory option is used to control the amount of memory used by index creation sorts. It is a self-configuring option and usually doesn't need to be adjusted. However, if you are having problems with the creation of large indexes, you might want to try specifying a KB value here that will contain the sort portion of the index create.

```
sp_configure 'index create memory', 1000
go
RECONFIGURE
go
```

Lightweight Pooling

Type—Advanced

Default value—0

Lightweight pooling is relevant to SMP environments that are having excessive context switching. By flipping this switch, you might get better throughput by performing the context switching inline, thus helping to reduce user/kernel ring transitions. Lightweight pooling causes SQL Server to switch to fiber mode scheduling.

```
sp_configure 'lightweight pooling', 1
go
RECONFIGURE
go
```

Setting of this option will vary according to the following application types:

- OLTP: This is a good candidate for usage if on an SMP environment.
- Data warehouse: This has a good potential for usage if on an SMP environment.
- OLAP: Use default value.
- Mixed: Use default value.

Locks

Type—Advanced, Self-configuring

Default value—0

In earlier versions of SQL Server, the DBA had to specify the number of locks available to SQL Server. If this parameter was set to a low value, a query requiring a large number of locks would fail at runtime. Setting it too high would result in wasting memory that otherwise could be used to cache data. SQL Server 2000 can handle locks dynamically if this parameter is set to the default value (0). SQL Server initially allocates 2 percent of memory available to SQL Server. As lock resource structures are consumed, the lock manager allocates more lock resources to the pool to a maximum of 40 percent of the memory available on SQL Server. Unless you are certain of the overall lock consumption of your application, you probably don't need to change this value.

```
sp_configure 'locks', 10000
go
RECONFIGURE
go
```

Max Degree of Parallelism

Type—Advanced

Default value—0

This option specifies the number of threads to be used for parallel query execution. On a non-SMP server, this value is always ignored. For an SMP server, a default value of 0 signifies that all the CPUs will be used for parallel query execution. If you set this value to 1, all query plans will be serialized. If the affinity mask option is on, parallel query execution will take place only on the CPUs for which the affinity mask bit is turned on. In that way, the two options can be used in conjunction. The application types assessment will be the same as described in the affinity mask option.

This option can be set up using the Processor tab of the SQL Server Configuration dialog box; then, in the Parallelism box, choose the number of processors to use for parallelism from the drop-down list box.

```
sp_configure 'max degree of parallelism', 4
go
RECONFIGURE
go
```

Max Server Memory and Min Server Memory

Type—Advanced, Self-configuring

Default value—2147483647 and 0

Max server memory specifies the maximum amount of memory (in terms of MB) that is available to SQL Server. It is used in conjunction with min server memory and essentially establishes an upper and lower bound for memory allocation. SQL Server uses this memory for user connections, locks, internal data structures, and caching the data. This is the memory pool described earlier. The default value of 2147483647 for the Max Server Memory option means that SQL Server will perform dynamic allocation of memory from the operating system based on available physical memory on the machine. The default value of 0 for the Min Server Memory option means that SQL Server will start allocation memory as it is needed, and then never go below the minimum value after it is reached.

The SQL Server lazywriter process is responsible for making sure that enough memory is available to SQL Server for the optimal number of buffers and Windows so that no excess paging occurs at the operating-system level. The lazywriter process frequently checks physical memory available on the machine. If the memory available is greater than 5MB, lazywriter assigns excess memory to the SQL Server buffer cache.

In addition, watch the Working Set performance counter that shows the amount of memory used by a process (SQL Server in this case). If this number is consistently below the amount of memory for which SQL Server is configured, then SQL Server is configured for more memory than it needs. You can also adjust the Set Working Set Size configuration option.

If SQL Server is the only application running on the machine, you might want to perform static memory allocation. Be careful when you allocate fixed memory to SQL Server. If you allocate more memory to SQL Server than the machine has, SQL Server will fail to start. Use the -f option during startup to bring up SQL Server with the default configuration. Change the value to the correct value, and restart SQL Server.

```
sp_configure 'max server memory', 200
go
RECONFIGURE
Go
sp_configure 'min server memory', 10
go
RECONFIGURE
go
```

For a strict fixed allocation of memory for SQL Server, make the min and max values the desired allocation size the same (like 200MB). A fixed amount of memory will then be allocated for SQL Server.

Figure 40.7 shows two possible settings for these configuration options. One shows the Dynamic Configure option set and a minimum and maximum value are established (other than the defaults). The other one shows the fixed memory specification. This fixed memory setting will result in the minimum and maximum values being set to the same desired value.

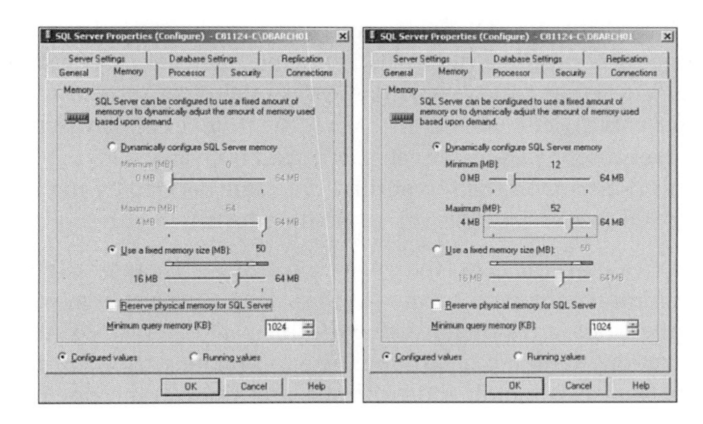

FIGURE 40.7 SQL Server Properties: Memory settings.

Setting of this option will vary according to the following application types:

- OLTP: For those with heavy loads, this is a good candidate for high fixed memory settings.
- Data warehouse: Use default values.
- OLAP: Use default value.
- Mixed: For those with heavy loads, this is a good candidate for high fixed memory settings.

Max Text Repl Size

Type—Basic, dynamic

Default value—65536

This parameter specifies the maximum size of the text and image datatypes for columns that are participating in replication during single `insert`, `update`, `writetext`, and `updatetext` statements. You might need to raise this value if the image sizes with which your application deals are consistently large and the data is part of a replication configuration.

```
sp_configure 'max text repl size', 131072
go
RECONFIGURE
go
```

Max Worker Threads

Type—Basic

Default value—255

SQL Server uses native operating system threads. This parameter specifies the maximum number of threads available for SQL Server processes. One or more threads are used for supporting each network protocol (such as TCP/IP and named pipes). SQL Server is configured to listen. The checkpoint and lazywriter processes also consume threads. A pool of threads is used to handle user connections. When the number of connections is lower than the max worker thread parameter value, a thread is created for each connection. When more connections are on the server than the value defined by the max worker thread parameter, SQL Server provides thread pooling for efficient resource utilization.

More threads can create overhead on the system processors. Therefore, lowering this value might sometimes improve the performance of the system. For a system with a few hundred user connections, a reasonable value for this parameter is 125. You might want to experiment with various values to determine the appropriate setting for this parameter. An SMP environment can easily handle more threads, and you can increase the number of threads accordingly.

```
sp_configure 'max worker threads', 125
go
RECONFIGURE
go
```

Figure 40.8 shows the setting of the Max Worker Threads option from the Processor tab of the SQL Server Properties dialog box. Choose a value between `10–1,024` for this option.

Setting of this option will vary according to the following application types:

- OLTP: For SMP environments, set the value upward because those environments can handle servicing more threads. This will yield performance gains.
- Data warehouse: Use default value.
- OLAP: Use default value.
- Mixed: For SMP environments, set the value upward because those environments can handle servicing more threads. This will yield performance gains.

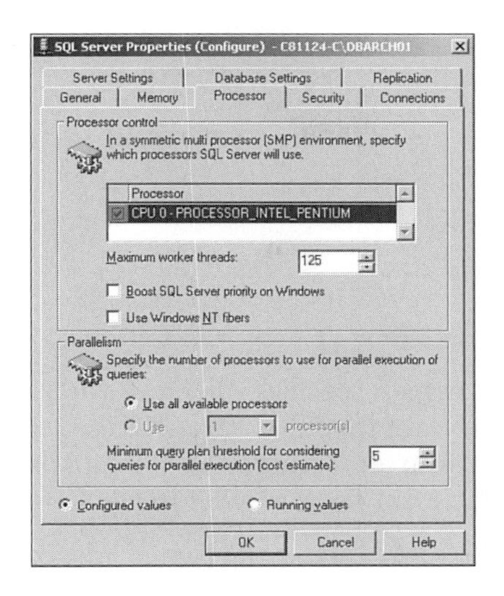

FIGURE 40.8 SQL Server Properties: Processor settings.

Min Memory Per Query

Type—Advanced

Default value—`1024`KB

Min memory per query specifies the minimum amount of memory that will be allocated for the execution of a query. Normally, the SQL Server query processor will attempt to determine the optimal amount of memory for a query. This option allows the sysadmin to specify this value instead. Increasing this value usually improves queries that handle hash and sort operations on a large volume of data. This option replaces the Sort Page option in SQL Server 7.0 and earlier.

```
sp_configure 'min memory per query', 2048
go
RECONFIGURE
go
```

Looking back at Figure 40.7, the Memory tab of the SQL Server Configuration dialog box, you can see the Minimum query memory value option set at 1024 (the default).

Setting of this option will vary according to the following application types:

- OLTP: Use default value.
- Data warehouse: This is a good opportunity to better service numerous canned queries in this environment. Set the value higher than the default.

- OLAP: Use default value.
- Mixed: Use default value.

Nested Triggers

Type—Basic

Default value—1

As the name suggests, nested triggers specifies whether a trigger event on a table will fire another trigger. The nesting level of triggers is 32, and it used to be 16. If you reach this limit of 32, SQL Server will give an error and roll back the transaction. The default value of 1 means that a trigger on a table can cause another trigger to fire.

Take a look again at Figure 40.5; you can see the Nested Trigger option checked under the Server Behavior box.

Network Packet Size

Type—Basic

Default value—4096

This parameter specifies the default network packet size for SQL Server. Setting this value to a higher number (which should be divisible by 512) can improve the performance of applications that involve a large amount of data transfer from the server. Check your network configuration and set an appropriate value for this parameter. In this same regard, you can improve performance by lowering the size value for applications that are small in data transfer size. However, the usual scenario is to increase this size to accommodate large amounts of data transfer, as with Bulk Loads.

```
sp_configure 'network packet size', 8192
go
RECONFIGURE
go
```

TIP

You can also specify the network packet size from the client when you connect to SQL Server (using the -a option for isql, osql, and bcp). Setting the network packet size from a client can be useful when the default network packet size is adequate for general application needs. However, a larger packet size might be needed for some specific operations, such as bulk copy. You can also call OLE DB, ODBC, and DB-Library functions to change the packet size.

Setting of this option will vary according to the following application types:

- OLTP: Possibly decrease this size to 512 if all queries deal with small amounts of data transfer, which is often the case in OLTP or ATM applications.
- Data warehouse: Perhaps increase this to 8192 to handle the consistently large data transfers in this environment.
- OLAP: Use default value.
- Mixed: Use default value.

Open Objects

Type—Advanced, Self-configuring

Default value—0

This option is self-configuring by default (when 0 is the setting). SQL Server will increase or decrease the number of open object descriptors in memory based on the needs of the server. You will rarely have to change from the default.

```
sp_configure 'open objects', 10000
go
RECONFIGURE
Go
```

Priority Boost

Type—Advanced

Default value—0

This option is used to specify the process priority of SQL Server processes on the Windows NT or Windows 2000 operating system. The default value of 0 means that SQL Server should run on the same priority level—a priority base of 7—as other applications on the machine. Priority boost can be turned on if you have plenty of horsepower to deal with all other services on the box, as in an SMP environment. When turning on priority boost, the priority base of SQL Server is elevated to 13.

```
sp_configure 'priority boost', 1
go
RECONFIGURE
go
```

NOTE

Don't set the value of this parameter to 1, except in the case of a dedicated SQL Server with SMP hardware.

From Figure 40.8, you can see the Boost SQL Server Priority on Windows option in the Processor control function. Use care when applying this option.

Query Governor Cost Limit

Type—Advanced

Default value—`0`

Queries are often the cause of major performance problems. SQL Server can handle the queries, but many are poorly written and don't restrict the search criteria enough. This can result in runaway queries that are returning large result sets and can adversely affect the entire server's performance. A method to control this is to cut the query off at the pass by specifying a maximum cost limit to queries. If any query's cost is greater than this maximum value, the query is not allowed to execute. This value is server-wide and cannot be applied to just one query.

```
sp_configure 'query governor cost limit', 300
go
RECONFIGURE
Go
```

Query governor cost limit can be set by going to Server Behavior options, SQL Server Configuration dialog box, Server Settings tab.

Setting of this option will vary according to the following application types:

- OLTP: Use default value.
- Data warehouse: This is a must-have option for this environment. Try setting this value to `300` seconds, and then get ready for the users to scream at you. On the positive side, the server won't get bogged down or freeze again.
- OLAP: For OLAP that use SQL Server storage, set this value to `600` seconds to get started, and then reduce it over time.
- Mixed: Same protection opportunity here. This won't affect the OLTP queries, so it is safe to apply.

Query Wait

Type—Advanced

Default value—-1

Queries that are memory intensive and involve huge sorts might take a long time to execute based on the available memory during execution. SQL Server internally calculates the timeout interval for such queries. Usually, this is quite a large number. You can override this value by specifying a value (in seconds) using the query wait parameter of SQL Server. If you set this value too low, you risk more frequent query timeouts when your system is under a heavy load and a highly concurrent environment.

```
sp_configure 'query wait', 20
go
RECONFIGURE
go
```

Recovery Interval

Type—Advanced, Self-configuring

Default value—0

Recovery interval is used to specify the maximum time (in minutes) that SQL Server would require to recover a database during startup. During startup, SQL Server rolls forward all the changes that were committed during a SQL Server crash and rolls back the changes that were not committed. Based on the value specified by this parameter, SQL Server determines when to issue a checkpoint in every database of SQL Server so that in the event of a crash, SQL Server can recover the databases in a time specified by recovery interval. If the value of the recovery interval parameter is low, SQL Server will issue checkpoints more frequently to allow a recovery to be faster; however, frequent checkpoints can slow down the performance. Setting recovery interval too high will create a longer recovery time for databases in the event of a crash. The default value of 0 leaves this option open to SQL Server to determine the best value.

```
sp_configure 'recovery interval', 10
go
RECONFIGURE
go
```

Figure 40.6 shows the Recovery Interval option setting of 0 within the Recovery section. Values must be between 1 and 32,767.

Setting of this option will vary according to the following application types:

- OLTP: Use default value.
- Data warehouse: This is an opportunity to save on checkpoints and not degrade performance in this mostly read-only environment. Set this value high.
- OLAP: Same performance opportunity here in this read-only environment.
- Mixed: Use default value.

Remote Proc Trans

Type—Basic

Default value—`0`

Remote proc trans allows remote procedures that are taking part in multiserver transactions to use MS-DTC so that transaction integrity is maintained across servers. The default value of `0` means the remote procedure calls will not use MS-DTC. Data modification at the remote server will not be a part of transactions at the local server. If you set this parameter to `1`, SQL Server uses MS-DTC to preserve transaction integrity across servers.

```
sp_configure 'remote proc trans', 1
go
RECONFIGURE
Go
```

Figure 40.9 illustrates the Enforce Distributed Transactions (MTS) option being set in the Remote Server Connections section of the Connections tab. This will primarily be important in OLTP environments.

Setting of this option will vary according to the following application types:

- OLTP: If you are having to support distributed transactions, this option should be set to On.
- Data warehouse: Use default value.
- OLAP: Use default value.
- Mixed: If you are having to support distributed transactions, this option should be set to On.

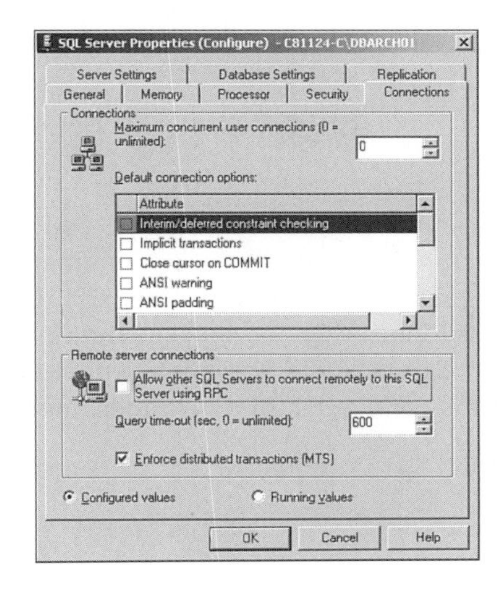

FIGURE 40.9 SQL Server Properties: Connection settings.

Scan for Startup Procs

Type—Advanced

Default value—`0`

When this option is set to `1`, SQL Server will scan for and execute all automatically executed stored procedures on the server on startup. To set a stored procedure to become automatically executed, you use the sp_procoption system-stored procedure. Executing a stored procedure at startup time is typically done when you want to have certain processing occur that creates the proper working environment for all subsequent database processing on the server. Executing at startup can also be done when you want to make sure that certain stored procedures' execution plans (with proper optimizer decisions) are already in procedure cache before anyone else has requested their execution.

```
sp_configure 'scan for startup procs', 1
go
RECONFIGURE
go
```

Set Working Set Size

Type—Advanced

Default value—`0`

When set working set size is set to `1`, SQL Server allocates and locks the requested server fixed memory amount at startup. Min server memory and max server memory options must contain the same value, reflecting a fixed memory size request. This effectively guarantees you the memory for as long as SQL Server is up and running and doesn't ever get pages swapped out when SQL Server is idle. This option has no effect when the memory option is set to `0`; SQL Server is configured for dynamic memory allocation.

```
sp_configure 'set working set size', 1
go
RECONFIGURE
Go
```

Looking at Figure 40.7, you can request that SQL server use a fixed memory size and also reserve physical memory for SQL Server. Set working set size is activated when you check this Reserve Physical Memory for SQL Server box. You cannot use this option when you are allowing SQL Server to dynamically configure memory.

Setting of this option will vary according to the following application types:

- OLTP: For those with heavy loads, this is a good candidate for high fixed memory settings.
- Data Warehouse: Use default values.
- OLAP: Use default value.
- Mixed: For those with heavy loads, this is a good candidate for high fixed memory settings.

Show Advanced Options

Type—Advanced, dynamic

Default value—`0`

By default, you will not see the advanced configuration parameters of SQL Server. By setting show advanced options to `1`, you will be able to see all the SQL Server parameters that can be set by the `sp_configure` command.

User Connections

Type—Advanced, Self-configuring

Default value—`0`

User connections specifies the number of concurrent users that are allowed on SQL Server. When the value is `0`, SQL Server can configure the needed user connections dynamically as they are needed. If you specify a value, you will be limited to this maximum number of user connections until you specify a larger value. If you specify other than a `0` value, the memory allocation for user connections will be allocated at SQL Server startup time and burn up portions of the memory pool. Each connection takes up 40KB of memory space. If you configure SQL Server for 100 connections, SQL Server will pre-allocate 4MB (40KB×100) for user connections. You can see that setting this value too high might eventually impact performance because the extra memory could have been used to cache data. In general, user connections are now best left to be self-configuring.

```
sp_configure 'user connections', 200
go
RECONFIGURE
go
```

Looking back at the SQL Server Properties dialog box and the Connections tab in Figure 40.9, you can set a value for the User Connections option by entering a value in the Maximum Concurrent User Connections box. This value must be between `5` and `32,767`.

User Options

Type—Basic, static

Default value—`0`

User options allows you to specify certain defaults for all the options allowed with the `SET` T-SQL command. Individual users can override these values by using the `SET` command. You are essentially able to establish these options for all users unless the users override them for their own needs. User options is a bit-mask field, and each bit represents a user option. Table 40.1 outlines the values that you can set with this parameter.

TABLE 40.1 Specifying User Options

Bit Mask Value	Description
1	DISABLE_DEF_CNST_CHK controls interim/deferred constraint checking.
2	IMPLICIT_TRANSACTIONS controls whether a transaction is started implicitly when a statement is executed.
4	CURSOR_CLOSE_ON_COMMIT controls the behavior of cursors after a commit has been performed.
8	ANSI_WARNINGS controls truncation and null in aggregate warnings.
16	ANSI_PADDING controls padding of fixed-length variables.
32	ANSI_NULLS controls null handling when using equality operators.
64	ARITHABORT terminates a query when an overflow or divide-by-zero error occurs during query execution.
128	ARITHIGNORE returns NULL when an overflow or divide-by-zero error occurs during a query.
256	QUOTED_IDENTIFIER differentiates between single and double quotation marks when evaluating an expression.
512	NOCOUNT turns off the message returned at the end of each statement that states how many rows were affected by the statement.
1024	ANSI_NULL_DFLT_ON alters the session's behavior to use ANSI compatibility for nullability. New columns that are defined without explicit nullability are defined to allow NULLs.
2048	ANSI_NULL_DFLT_OFF alters the session's behavior to not use ANSI compatibility for nullability. New columns defined without explicit nullability are defined not to allow NULLs.
4096	CONCAT_NULL_YIELDS_NULL will have SQL Server return a NULL when concatenating a NULL value with a string.
8192	NUMERIC_ROUNDABORT will have SQL Server generate an error if loss of precision ever occurs in an expression.
16384	XACT_ABORT will have SQL Server roll back a transaction if a Transact-SQL statment raises a runtime error.

For a given user connection, you can use the @@options global variable to see the values that have been set.

```
sp_configure 'user options', 256
go
RECONFIGURE
Go
```

As you can see from the SQL Server Configuration dialog box and the Connections tab in Figure 40.9, the Default connection options can be checked or unchecked according to what you want to be in effect server-wide for all user connections. Again, a user can override these with his own SET command during a session.

Summary

Dealing with the large number of configurable options in SQL Server is a big undertaking. Not only do you need to know about the internal address space of SQL Server, but you also need to understand what type of applications will be running on the server so that the configuration decision that you make is not counter productive.

Many of the configurable options have a direct effect on the most dynamic part of SQL Server: the memory pool. This is truly where all the action is. Whether you have chosen to let SQL Server help you manage this space dynamically via self-configuring options, or you have decided to manage this yourself, you must constantly monitor the current settings and be prepared to modify them at any time. In general, you will be able to start with the default values given to the server at installation time and then slowly enhance these options over time.

In the next chapter, a detailed explanation of using XML in SQL Server 2000 will be provided that should allow you to start using this feature almost immediately.

PART VI

Additional SQL Server Features

IN THIS PART

CHAPTER 41

Using XML in SQL Server 2000

by Alex T. Silverstein and Paul Bertucci

IN THIS CHAPTER

- Creating a Virtual Directory for Use with SQL Server 2000
- Exploring Extensible Markup Language (XML)
- Retrieving Data Using the `FOR XML` Clause
- Using `FOR XML RAW`
- Using `FOR XML AUTO`
- Using `FOR XML AUTO, ELEMENTS`
- Using `FOR XML EXPLICIT`
- Retrieving XML-Data Schemas
- Retrieving Binary Data in XML
- The Basics of XML Path Language (XPath)
- Using XML in Stored Procedures
- Using OPENXML to Read XML
- Using URL Queries
- Using XML Templates
- Using XML Updategrams

One of SQL Server 2000's major enhancements is the inclusion of native XML support, enabling developers to execute queries that return results as XML-formatted data, rather than standard rowsets. XML is quickly becoming the dominant format for passing data across networks and between diverse code components. With SQL Server 2000, XML can be passed into and returned from stored procedures, passed directly between SQL Server and the Internet, and much more. Developers also will be leveraging XML via ADO.NET, the full impact of which is discussed in Chapter 46, "SQL Server and the Microsoft .NET Framework." All in all, the .NET Framework is now capable of both XML via the ADO.NET layer and native XML support directly with SQL Server 2000. This chapter will introduce XML concepts and usage examples from SQL Server 2000's point of view. We will be using the Web (IIS) for much of the examples so it should be configured for use with SQL Server (if you haven't already done this).

Creating a Virtual Directory for Use with SQL Server 2000

Before you get started, for some of the examples, you will need to create an Internet Information Server (IIS) virtual directory that will enable you to access the SQL Server-provided Northwind database from the Web. All the examples in this chapter use Northwind.

1. First, create a physical directory where you want to store the Web files you create. Create a special subdirectory below this directory called `Template` where the XML templates you create will be saved (templates are covered later in this chapter in the section "Using XML Templates"). `D:\SQL2E\Template` is an example.

   Now, we can create the virtual directory using the IIS Virtual Directory Management for SQL Server tool:

2. From the Start menu, navigate to the Microsoft SQL Server program group and click Configure SQL XML Support in IIS (see Figure 41.1).

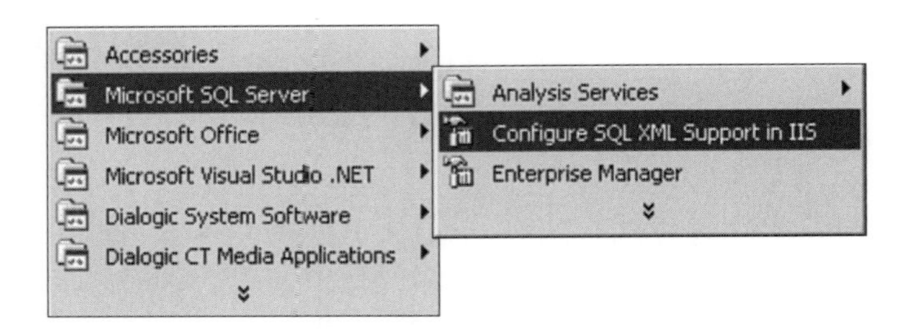

FIGURE 41.1 Configure SQL XML Support in IIS.

3. Select a server and right-click the Web site you will use. (The default Web site usually works if you have it, as you can see in Figure 41.2.) Select New and click Virtual Directory.

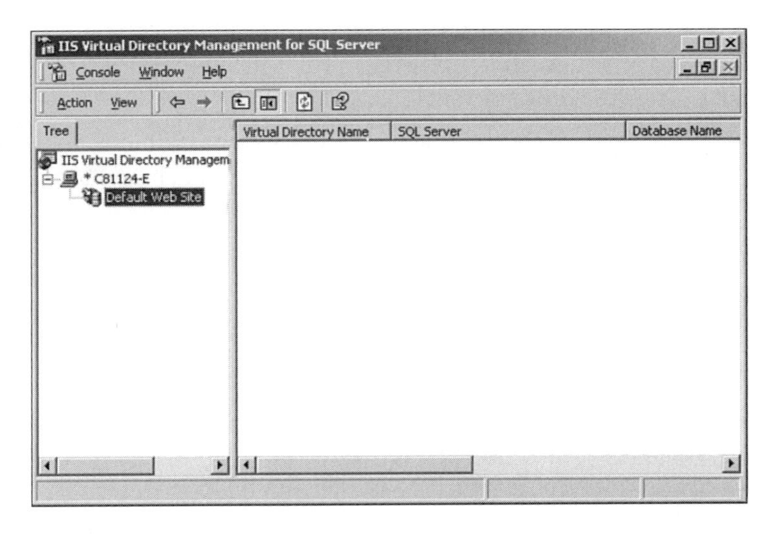

FIGURE 41.2 IIS Virtual Directory Management for SQL Server.

4. On the General Tab (see Figure 41.3) of the New Virtual Directory Properties dialog, type **NorthwindVdir** under Virtual Directory Name. In the Local Path group box, type the name of the physical directory you created (`D:\SQL2E\Template`).

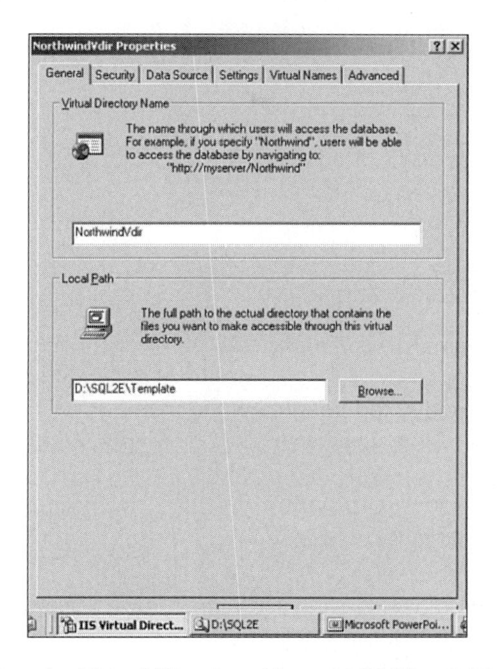

FIGURE 41.3 Specifying the Virtual Directory Name in IIS Virtual Directory Management.

5. On the Security tab, configure a valid SQL Server login (such as sa for these examples).

TIP

Please remember that for a production environment, you will want to specify a login that has very few permissions in its assigned roles. Internet access to SQL Server might open up a new avenue for hackers to exploit. For purposes of this chapter, use a login whose role has at least `SELECT`, `INSERT`, `UPDATE`, and `DELETE` permissions for Northwind.

6. On the Data Source tab, under SQL Server, enter the database server name. (If you use SQL Server instances, use the instance name.) Then under Database type, select Northwind (see Figure 41.4).

7. On the Settings tab, check the Allow URL Queries, Allow Template Queries, Allow XPath, and Allow POST check boxes.

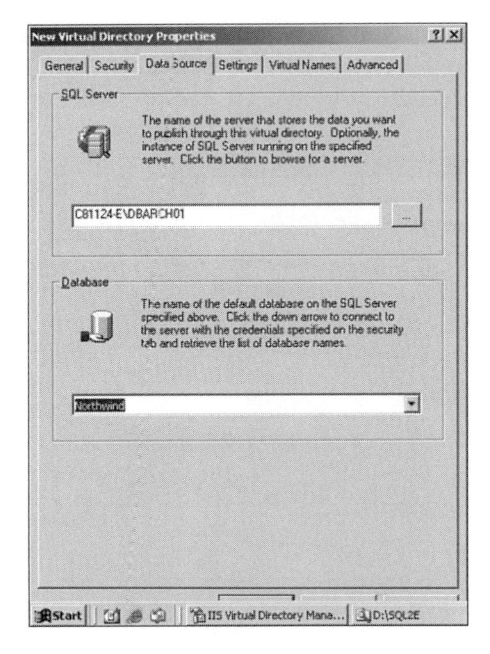

FIGURE 41.4 Specifying a SQL Server data source.

8. On the Virtual Names tab, click New to create a virtual name for the Template subdirectory you created. Name it `Templates`, select the type Template, and enter the path to the Template subdirectory you created (**`D:\SQL2E\Template`**). Click Save.
9. Now, again on the Virtual Names tab, click New to create a virtual name that will be used to access Northwind's intrinsic database objects (tables, rows, fields, and so on). Name this one `dataobjects` and leave the type selection as `dbobject`. Click Save.
10. Click OK in the dialog box to close and save the virtual directory settings.

Barring any unforeseen networking considerations, your NorthwindVdir virtual directory is ready to use. Test it using a URL query (covered later in the section "Using URL Queries") by opening Internet Explorer (IE) and typing the following (substituting your Web server's name for *<myserver>*) in the address box and pressing Enter. (Note: you can probably use *localhost* instead of the server's instance name if you only have one instance of SQL Server up and running):

```
http://<myserver>/NorthwindVdir?sql=SELECT CategoryID FROM Categories
➥FOR XML AUTO&root=testXML
```

The result is shown in Figure 41.5.

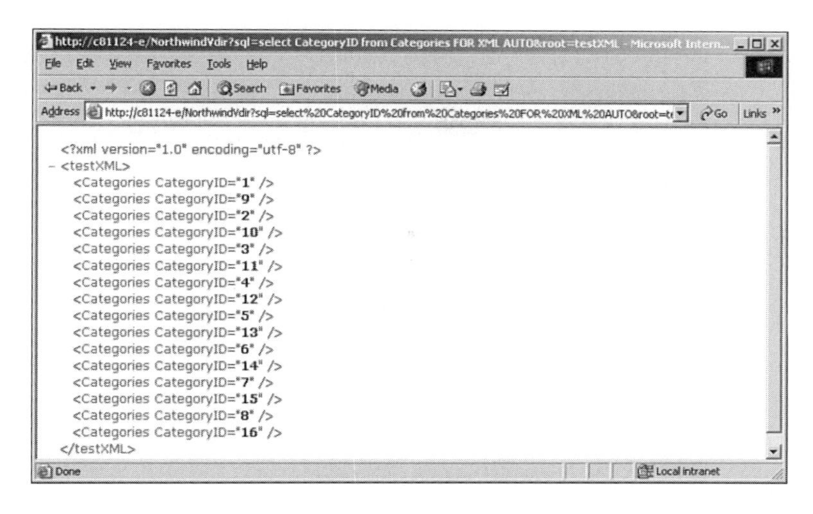

FIGURE 41.5 The URL query `http://<myserver>/NorthwindVdir?sql=SELECT CategoryID FROM Categories FOR XML AUTO&root=testXML`.

Additionally, try the following URL that tests the `dataobjects` virtual name you created (explained in the section "Retrieving Binary Data in XML"):

```
http://<myserver>/NorthwindVdir/dataobjects/Categories[@CategoryID='1']/@Picture
```

This should load an image of some dinner items into the browser (see Figure 41.6).

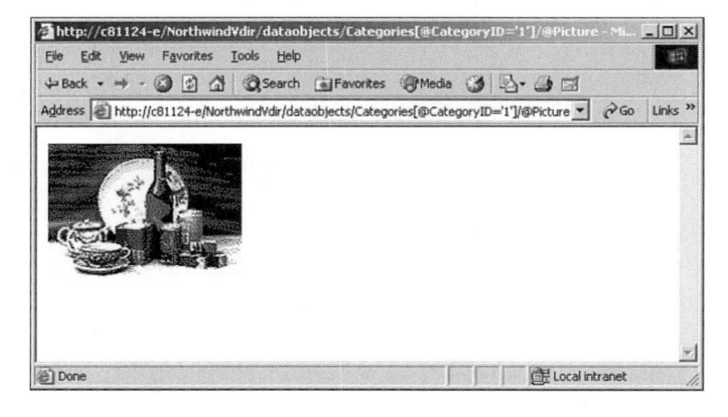

FIGURE 41.6 The URL query `http://<myserver>/NorthwindVdir/dataobjects/Categories[@CategoryID='1']/@Picture`.

The IIS Virtual Directory should now be working and be fully configured to resemble the following (see Figure 41.7):

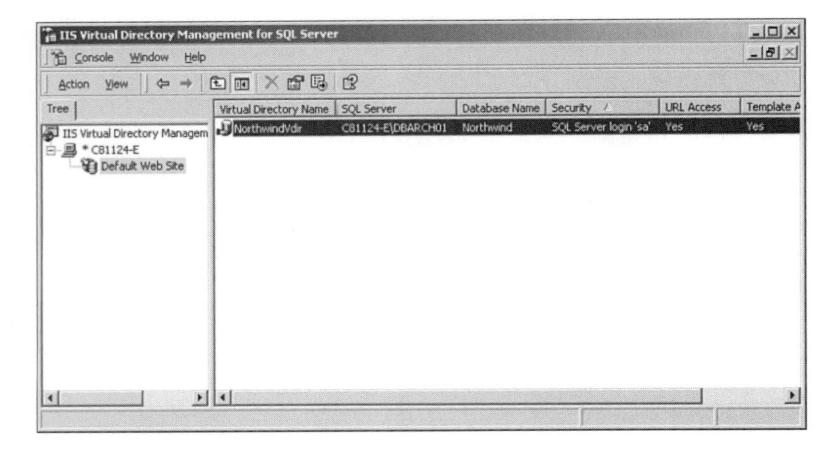

FIGURE 41.7 A fully configured IIS Virtual Directory for SQL Server 2000.

Exploring Extensible Markup Language (XML)

Before delving into the details of this much-awaited feature, you need to learn some basic information about XML (and SQL Server 2000–generated XML in particular).

> **NOTE**
>
> Because most developers will exploit SQL Server 2000's XML capabilities for Web projects, this chapter assumes that you are familiar with the basics of Hypertext Markup Language (HTML). If not, we recommend *Sams Teach Yourself HTML and XHTML in 24 Hours* (0-672-32076-2).

Like HTML, XML is character data consisting of elements—alphanumeric names delimited by < and >—and attributes—name-value pairs of the form name="value"—that reside inside elements, separated from other attributes by whitespace.

The big difference between HTML and XML is that the HTML elements specify display information (how big a font should be for a given element, how bold, and so on), and XML elements do not. XML provides only a specification for how data should be structured and contains no inherent display information. It is up to the object that uses the XML to determine whether and how the data should be displayed.

In XML, elements and attributes both contain only character data. Following is an example of a single element that has an attribute and a value:

```
<element attribute="value">DATA</element>.
```

Unlike HTML, no set list of predefined XML tags exists—the tags can be anything you want, provided that they adhere to a few key rules. For XML documents to be considered **well formed** (that is, suitable for an XML parser to process without error), they must meet the following requirements:

- Every element or tag must have a corresponding end tag. For example: <element>DATA</element> or even <element></element>. If an element has no content (known as having **empty** content), it might also terminate in the following character sequence: />, such as <element/>.

TIP

XML parsers are case sensitive with respect to element and attribute names. When running your XML data through a parser after you get it back from a SQL Server 2000 query, be sure to remember that in the mind of the parser, <Myelement> is not the same as <myelement>, nor is Myattribute the same as myattribute.

- XML documents must have only one root element containing all other elements. Depending on the type of query you design, SQL Server 2000 might return a **document fragment**. These fragments are XML documents that are well formed except that they lack a top-level (or root) element. To illustrate this, test the following URL in IE: http://<myserver>/NorthwindVdir?sql=SELECT TOP 2 CustomerID FROM Customers FOR XML RAW.
- The error message that results is shown in Figure 41.8.

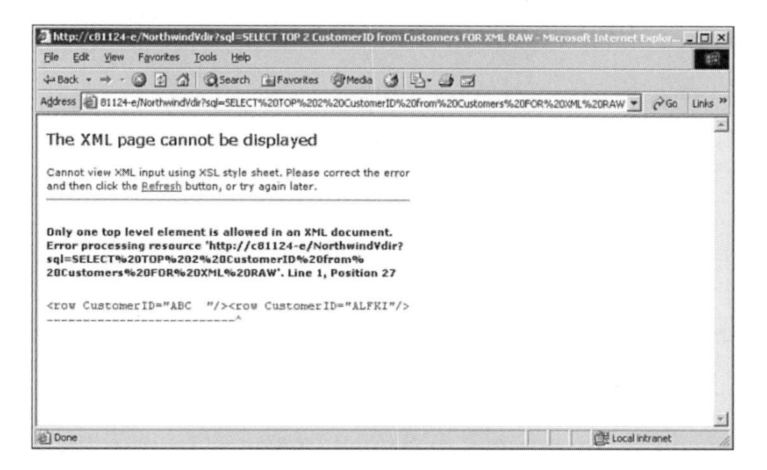

FIGURE 41.8 The URL query http://<myserver>/NorthwindVdir?sql=SELECT TOP 2 CustomerID FROM Customers FOR XML RAW results in a document fragment.

- IE uses an XML parser known as **MSXML** to display XML documents. The error message it displays (`XML document must have a top level element`) tells you that your XML is not well formed. This is because the query results in a document fragment. It has two `<row>` elements but no root element enclosing them both. (If you had selected a single row, however, the results would be well formed.) To render this XML as well formed, add the string `&root=test2XML` to the end of the URL to get a root element called `test2XML` around the resulting rows (see Figure 41.9).

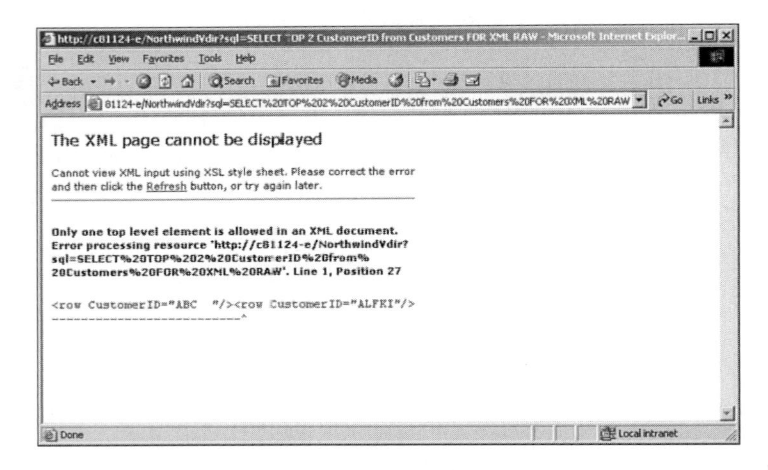

FIGURE 41.9 Specifying a root element via `&root=test2XML`.

- Elements can't overlap. The following is an example of overlapping elements that is legal in HTML but not XML:

  ```
  <h1>This Header <h2>has <h3>overlapping </h2>
  </h3>elements</h1>.
  ```

  The good news: SQL Server will never create XML that looks like this.

- XML has naming conventions for elements and attributes. Most of the time you can opt out of naming the XML elements that are returned from SQL Server—the element and attribute names will match the table and column names being selected.

  Aliasing these names, however, provides an opportunity to change them. The good news, once again: SQL Server will never create XML that violates the following XML naming conventions:

  - Element or attribute names should not contain whitespace, the word *xml*, or a colon (:).
  - Element or attributes must begin with letters or underscores (_), but not digits or any other punctuation.
  - Numbers are permitted in names after the first character, as well as hyphens (-) and periods (.).

TIP

If your table, column names, or aliases do contain unsupported XML characters, you can still retrieve data from them using the FOR XML clause. SQL Server 2000 will permit you to select these objects (Order Details, for example), but it will convert any offending characters (in this case a single space) into a string representation of the hexadecimal equivalent of the character, resulting in element names such as `<Order_x0020_Details>`.

Retrieving Data Using the FOR XML Clause

Now that you have your virtual directory ready, understand the basics of XML, and know a little bit about SQL Server 2000's brand of XML, you're ready to execute queries that return XML.

The `select statement` has been extended to include an optional `FOR XML` clause that produces XML directly from the SQL Server 2000 query engine. This powerful, highly anticipated feature is a major boon to developers who have previously been manually translating the rowsets that queries return into XML documents.

The syntax for retrieving XML using `FOR XML` is as follows:

```
select statement [ FOR XML mode [, XMLDATA] [, ELEMENTS][, BINARY BASE64] ]
```

Mode can be one of the following: `RAW`, `AUTO`, or `EXPLICIT`. It determines the structure of the XML-formatted query results.

NOTE

Multiple XML rowsets might be returned from a single stored procedure having multiple `select statements`, each using a different XML mode. The mode you use applies only to the results of the currently executing `select statement` and not to the results of any subsequent `select statements`.

Using FOR XML RAW

The simplest XML mode to use is `RAW`. In `RAW` mode, each row in the resultset corresponds to an element named "row" in the resulting XML document fragment. Each column in the select list that returns a non-null value generates an attribute of "row" named after the column (or column alias) containing its value. This is known as **attribute-centric** rowset mapping.

Listing 41.1 illustrates the mapping of rows and columns into XML using `RAW` mode. You can try this from your IE browser or from Query Analyzer.

LISTING 41.1 Using FOR XML RAW to Retrieve Customer Data from Northwind

```
SELECT CustomerID CID, CompanyName, ContactName
FROM Customers
WHERE CustomerID = 'ANTON'
FOR XML RAW

go

XML_F52E2B61-18A1-11d1-B105-00805F49916B
---------------------------------------------------------
<row CID="ANTON" CompanyName="Antonio Moreno Taquería"
ContactName="Antonio Moreno"/>
```

As you can see, RAW mode is designed to generate flat (non-hierarchical) XML that structurally mirrors traditional resultsets. Even though you know, for example, that every CustomerID in Customers is tied to zero or more Orders, a row selected from Customers will never contain a row selected from Orders. Listing 41.2 illustrates how adding a join between Orders and Customers on CustomerID to the previous listing results in a separate row created for each unique Customer-Order combination, but no nesting of XML elements. This is true no matter how many tables are involved.

LISTING 41.2 Joining Tables Produces Flat XML in RAW Mode

```
SELECT Cu.CompanyName CO, Cu.ContactName CN, O.OrderID
FROM Customers Cu
JOIN Orders O on O.CustomerID = Cu.CustomerID
WHERE Cu.CustomerID = 'ANTON'
FOR XML RAW

go

XML_F52E2B61-18A1-11d1-B105-00805F49916B
----------------------------------------------------------------------------
<row CO="Antonio Moreno Taquería" CN="Antonio Moreno" OrderID="10365"/>
<row CO="Antonio Moreno Taquería" CN="Antonio Moreno" OrderID="10507"/>
<row CO="Antonio Moreno Taquería" CN="Antonio Moreno" OrderID="10535"/>
<row CO="Antonio Moreno Taquería" CN="Antonio Moreno" OrderID="10573"/>
<row CO="Antonio Moreno Taquería" CN="Antonio Moreno" OrderID="10677"/>
<row CO="Antonio Moreno Taquería" CN="Antonio Moreno" OrderID="10682"/>
<row CO="Antonio Moreno Taquería" CN="Antonio Moreno" OrderID="10856"/>
```

RAW mode will not produce the highly structured view of data that is one of XML's biggest gains over unstructured data. But don't be fooled by its simplicity. It is useful simply because it is generic—you know what to expect. When processing RAW XML using a stylesheet, you can specify rules for transforming row elements produced by a vast number of queries.

Using FOR XML AUTO

For greater control over the names and structure of your XML, use AUTO mode. AUTO mode facilitates the naming of XML elements with something other than "row." Element names correspond to the name or alias of the selected tables.

AUTO mode creates a structured view of data that mirrors the relationships of selected tables by nesting XML elements selected from multiple tables. A nested or **child element** is one that is enclosed by another element, known as its **parent element**. Listing 41.3 shows an example of element nesting.

LISTING 41.3 FOR XML AUTO Enables Nesting of XML Elements Based on Relationships Expressed in a Join

```
SELECT Customer.CustomerID CID, CompanyName CO, ContactName CN, OrderID
FROM Customers Customer
JOIN Orders on Orders.CustomerID = Customer.CustomerID
WHERE Customer.CustomerID = 'ANTON'
FOR XML AUTO

go

XML_F52E2B61-18A1-11d1-B105-00805F49916B
-----------------------------------------------------------------
<Customer CID="ANTON" CO="Antonio Moreno Taquería" CN="Antonio Moreno">
        <Orders OrderID="10365"/><Orders OrderID="10507"/>
        <Orders OrderID="10535"/><Orders OrderID="10573"/>
        <Orders OrderID="10677"/><Orders OrderID="10682"/>
        <Orders OrderID="10856"/>
</Customer>
```

The neat thing about this default behavior is that the XML structure accurately reflects the relationship between the two entities: A Customer places many Orders. This query can be extended to join Employees to Orders, EmployeeTerritories to Employees, and so on, producing a more complex XML document that still accurately reflects the database relationships.

This is only true, however, if you list the selected columns from left to right as if traversing the table hierarchy from parent table to child table. Customers place Orders, for example, so you would list all the columns from Customers before those of the Orders table. Employees are assigned to Orders—list its columns after those of Orders, and so on. What makes `AUTO` mode flexible in its XML results is that you can alter the nesting of XML elements by rearranging the order of columns in the `SELECT` list. If you change the example in Listing 41.3 to specify OrderID first in the `SELECT` list, every Orders element in the results will contain a Customer child element identifying the customer for that order.

Using `FOR XML AUTO, ELEMENTS`

By specifying the syntax `FOR XML AUTO, ELEMENTS`, SQL Server 2000 will render all selected columns as child elements (instead of attributes) of parent elements named after the table to which they belong. This is known as **element-centric** mapping.

In Listing 41.4, every Customers element has three child elements that correspond to the columns selected from Customers, and one Orders child element for every matching row in Orders. Each Orders element in turn has one child element corresponding to OrderID.

LISTING 41.4 `FOR XML AUTO, ELEMENTS` Produces Element-Centric Mapping of Rowsets into XML

```
SELECT Customers.CustomerID CID, CompanyName CO, ContactName CN, OrderID
FROM Customers
JOIN Orders on Orders.CustomerID = Customers.CustomerID
WHERE Customers.CustomerID = 'ALFKI'
AND Orders.OrderID = 10643
FOR XML AUTO, ELEMENTS

go

XML_F52E2B61-18A1-11d1-B105-00805F49916B
----------------------------------------
<Customers>
        <CID>ALFKI</CID>
        <CO>Alfreds Futterkiste</CO>
        <CN>Maria Anders</CN>
        <Orders>
                <OrderID>10643</OrderID>
        </Orders>
</Customers>
```

Using FOR XML EXPLICIT

For still greater control over the structure of your XML results, use EXPLICIT mode. EXPLICIT mode enables you to design the nesting hierarchy of your resulting XML elements in a precise fashion. But be forewarned: EXPLICIT mode adds a bit of complexity to the query.

If you are like me and try to get things coded in the simplest way possible, you probably won't use EXPLICIT mode too often. Sometimes, however, EXPLICIT mode is the best way to do the job. For example, you might want to combine column results from multiple tables into a single XML element without being tied to the flat XML produced by RAW mode or to the select-list-ordered structure produced by AUTO mode. Or you might need a combination of both attribute and element-centric XML.

The first requirement for queries that use EXPLICIT mode is that the select statement needs to be written in such a way as to produce a rowset that is in (what Microsoft calls) **universal table format**. This format makes your table structure XML-friendly by providing columns that indicate parent-child relationships for the selected rows. Listing 41.5 provides an example of a query that returns a rowset in universal table format, and Table 41.1 shows the rowset that was generated by the query in Listing 41.5.

LISTING 41.5 A Query That Generates a Rowset in Universal Table Format

```
SELECT 1           AS Tag,
       NULL          AS Parent,
       C.ContactName AS [Customer!1!CN],
       NULL          AS [Order!2!ID]
FROM Customers C
WHERE C.CustomerID = 'ANTON'

UNION ALL

SELECT 2 AS Tag,
       1 AS Parent,
       NULL,
       O.OrderID
FROM Customers C
JOIN Orders O ON C.CustomerID = O.CustomerID
WHERE C.CustomerID = 'ANTON'
ORDER BY [Order!2!ID]
```

TABLE 41.1 The Rowset Generated by the Query in Listing 41.5

Tag	Parent	Customer!1!CN	Order!2!ID
1	NULL	Antonia Moreno	NULL
2	1	NULL	10365
2	1	NULL	10507
2	1	NULL	10535
2	1	NULL	10573
2	1	NULL	10677
2	1	NULL	10682
2	1	NULL	10856

If you add `FOR XML EXPLICIT` to the query in Listing 41.5, the resulting XML is as follows:

```
<Customer CN="Antonio Moreno">
       <Order ID="10365"/>
       <Order ID="10507"/>
       <Order ID="10535"/>
       <Order ID="10573"/>
       <Order ID="10677"/>
       <Order ID="10682"/>
       <Order ID="10856"/>
</Customer>
```

The three guidelines for `EXPLICIT` queries are as follows:

- Execute at least two `select statements`.
- Join them using `UNION ALL`.
- Order the resulting rows using `ORDER BY`.

The first two columns of every `select statement` in `EXPLICIT` queries must be named Tag and Parent and be of `int` datatype.

The value of Parent in every row must be equal to a value of Tag in a preceding row. This tells the parser which rows produce parent elements and which become child elements.

Only one row can have a Parent field value of `NULL`, indicating that the elements produced by the rows in this `select statement` are top-level elements—they need no Parent element. (Also remember that a row must not have a Tag value equal to its Parent value.)

The universal table has an implied self-referential constraint between Parent and Tag. Every row whose Parent field value is 1 is a child row of the row whose Tag value is 1, and so on. The XML produced reflects this heritage by nesting Tags under their respective Parents.

The first `select statement` of `EXPLICIT` mode queries performs a few important functions. First, it establishes the top-most XML elements because its Parent is `NULL` and its Tag field is 1. All other selected columns that result in a non-null value are mapped as either attributes or child elements (depending on the value of Directive, explained in one of the following bullets) of the elements produced by these rows. Note the special syntax used to alias them:

```
[ElementName!TagNumber!AttributeName!Directive]
```

The parts of syntax in this alias are as follows:

- *ElementName*—Defines the name of the produced element. The column `C.ContactName`, for example, is going to be either an attribute or subelement of Customer elements because its alias is `Customer!1!CN`.
- *TagNumber*—Indicates that the value of the attribute or subelement of the element named in *ElementName* must get its value from a column in the select statement where Tag is equal to *TagNumber*. The alias `Customer!1!CN` thus indicates that `Customer` elements, for example, will have an attribute `CN` whose value is populated in select statement number one, where Tag is 1, indicated by the value (1) of *TagNumber*.
- *AttributeName*—Provides a place for you to name the attributes or subelements of *ElementName*, such as `CN`.
- *Directive*—If *Directive* is equal to "hide," the attribute specified in *AttributeName* is not displayed in the elements named *ElementName*. If *Directive* is equal to "element," the attribute becomes a child element of *ElementName*, working in an element-centric fashion similar to `FOR XML AUTO, ELEMENTS`. (A few other possible values for *Directive* are available that are fairly technical with respect to XML data encoding and will not be specified here. For more information, consult SQL Server Books Online.)

In the first select statement in Listing 41.5, the fourth column `NULL AS [Order!2!ID]` establishes that an element at Tag level 2 named Orders will have an attribute `ID` that must be populated in the fourth column of the select statement where Tag is 2.

Columns in the second (and any subsequent) select statement do not use the special aliasing syntax. Here, only the values needed to populate columns aliased with *TagNumber* 2 (or greater, in any subsequent select statements) are selected.

Note how the selected null values correspond to the non-null columns selected in the first statement, and vice-versa. This will help you remember which select statement needs to produce which attributes.

Take, for example, the third column (`NULL`) in the second select statement. It indicates that rows produced here must leave this space empty because the third column in the first select already has a non-null value (produced by `C.CustomerName`). You can see how these select statements work in parallel, leaving empty columns in their rows where values are to be produced by parent or child rows.

Looking at the null values in the universal table, you can see that this is true. Remembering this will also help you be sure you select the same number of columns in all your statements, and that the union will succeed.

The final line specifies the ordering of the produced elements. The best way to understand how the `ORDER BY` clause works is to remove the `FOR XML EXPLICIT` clause and look at the resultset. Remember: Parent elements (rows) must precede child elements (rows). Order your rows by the value of *TagNumber* with this in mind.

Retrieving XML-Data Schemas

An important feature of SQL Server 2000 is the ability to retrieve XML-formatted metadata that defines the content model (what elements will be present, their nesting structure, and what types of data they contain) of an XML document.

This metadata comes in the form of a well-formed XML document known as an XML-Data schema. It can be returned in queries that use any of the three `FOR XML` modes, and to get it, you specify the `XMLDATA` option, as exemplified in Listing 41.6.

LISTING 41.6 Using the `XMLDATA` Option with `FOR XML AUTO` to Return an XML-Data Schema

```
SELECT TOP 2 OrderID, OrderDate, CustomerID
FROM Orders
FOR XML AUTO, XMLDATA

go

<Schema name="Schema1" xmlns="urn:schemas-microsoft-com:xml-data"
xmlns:dt="urn:schemas-microsoft-com:datatypes">
        <ElementType name="Orders" content="empty" model="closed">
               <AttributeType name="OrderID" dt:type="i4"/>
               <AttributeType name="OrderDate" dt:type="dateTime"/>
               <AttributeType name="CustomerID" dt:type="string"/>
               <attribute type="OrderID"/>
               <attribute type="OrderDate"/>
               <attribute type="CustomerID"/>
        </ElementType>
</Schema>
<Orders xmlns="x-schema:#Schema1" OrderID="10248"
        OrderDate="1996-07-04T00:00:00" CustomerID="VINET"/>
<Orders xmlns="x-schema:#Schema1" OrderID="10249"
        OrderDate="1996-07-05T00:00:00" CustomerID="TOMSP"/>
```

First note that the schema is always output directly on top of your XML results. `Schema` is always its root element, and its `name` attribute has a special function: It declares the document as a **namespace**. When a namespace is used, elements in other XML documents might contain the elements defined in this schema by specifying the name of the schema as the value of their `xmlns` (XML Namespace) attribute.

Orders elements, for example, are linked to Schema1 by way of their `xmlns` attribute. The value of `xmlns` (preceded by "x-schema:") points back to the schema as a way of indicating that the metadata in the schema applies to Orders elements. The # sign indicates that the schema is **inline** (it works just like the # sign does in HTML links) or contained within the XML document it describes. (Note also that schemas themselves refer to a Microsoft namespace in their `xmlns` attribute.)

The `name` attribute will always have a value of Schema followed by an integer. This integer is incremented automatically by SQL Server after every query generated during the same session to prevent what is known as a **namespace collision**—when two XML documents declare the same namespace. It's necessary to rename the schema in this way because it differentiates one schema from any other that might have been produced by a query executed during the same SQL Server session.

The structure of the schema provides useful information about the XML. The values of its elements and attributes will differ depending on the mode and options you specify in the `FOR XML` clause. The elements that will be present (as of this writing—please note that the specification for XML Schemas is a work in progress) are as follows:

- ElementType—For every XML element, an ElementType element that defines it is produced. It has the following attributes:

  ```
  <ElementType content="{empty | textOnly | eltOnly | mixed}" dt:type="data
  type" model="{open | closed}" name="idref" order="{one | seq | many}">
  ```

  The most useful attribute of ElementType is `dt:type`. It tells any code you use to process the schema what kind of data the element named in its name attribute contains. When you convert the schema using an XML stylesheet, for example, it is far easier to generically parse XML elements based on the value of `dt:type` than by testing the element's value.

  The value of `dt:type` is a string representation of the XML datatype to which the SQL Server datatype of the selected column corresponds. The most common are `dateTime`—corresponding to `datetime`, `i4`—a four-byte integer corresponding to `int`, and `string`—corresponding to `varchar`. See the MSDN Online topic titled "XML Data Types" for more information.

  The `content` attribute is also of interest. It specifies how the XML for the named element is formed—whether it is `empty` (contains no data), `textOnly` (contains only data but no child elements), `eltOnly` (contains elements only) or `mixed` (contains both data and child elements).

- `AttributeType`—`ElementType` elements contain these elements. They specify the name and type of any attributes that the element specified in its `name` attribute have.
- `attribute`—`ElementType` elements contain these elements. They define an element's attributes and refer back to `AttributeType` via their `type` attribute.

Knowing these things about your XML results before parsing them enables you to write generic processing code that is far more likely to be reused than code that is purely data-specific.

Retrieving Binary Data in XML

You might be wondering: If XML describes only character-based data, how can I retrieve the binary data stored in my columns? You can do this in two ways. The first is by explicitly requesting the binary data in a character-encoded format by specifying the `BINARY BASE64` option at the end of the `FOR XML` clause. The second is by using `FOR XML` without the `BINARY BASE64` option to return an XPath reference to the location of the binary data.

SQL Server 2000 uses the `BASE64` algorithm to encode binary column data into XML-friendly character data. (`BASE64` is defined as part of the Multipurpose Internet Mail Extensions (MIME) types, a set of standards for transmitting data over the Internet.)

NOTE

`BINARY BASE64` works with all three `FOR XML` modes, but it is required unless you use `FOR XML AUTO`, which generates encoded data automatically (detailed in the section "The Basics of XML Path Language (XPath)"). When using `RAW` or `EXPLICIT` mode, SQL Server 2000 requires you to know ahead of time whether a field in your query is binary. If you select a binary field but do not specify `BINARY BASE64`, an error will result that reads, in part, `use BINARY BASE64 to obtain binary data in encoded form.`

Listing 41.7 provides an example of the use of `BINARY BASE64` in conjunction with `AUTO` mode. Note: The resulting Picture element's value is truncated at the ellipses for brevity.

LISTING 41.7 Using `AUTO` Mode with `BINARY BASE64` to Retrieve Base64-Encoded Data from an Image Datatype Column

```
SELECT Picture FROM Categories
WHERE CategoryID=1
FOR XML AUTO, ELEMENTS, BINARY BASE64

go

XML_F52E2B61-18A1-11d1-B105-00805F49916B
<Categories><Picture>FRwvAAIAAAANAA4AFAAhAP////9CaXRtYXA[...]
</Picture></Categories>
```

When using AUTO mode, you can retrieve binary data in two ways:

- Specify BINARY BASE64.
- Add the primary key of the table to the SELECT list in the query.

When you add the primary key to the SELECT list and do not specify BINARY BASE64, SQL Server 2000 won't return base64-encoded data in the XML. Instead, it will create a *URL-encoded* string that points to the relative database location of the binary data using a special XML syntax called XML Path Language (XPath).

The Basics of XML Path Language (XPath)

XPath queries are used to locate and retrieve XML elements, attributes, and their values. XPath's name is derived from its syntactical resemblance to file paths. You can find out more about the XPath standard by consulting the XML standards body on the World Wide Web Consortium at http://www.w3c.org. Because XPath is a standard in its own right, the discussion in this chapter will be limited to the XPath syntax used to address database objects in SQL Server 2000.

The syntax for retrieving the value of a binary column is as follows:

```
dbobject/TableName[@PrimaryKeyName='PrimaryKeyValue']/@ColumnName.
```

In XPath, the @ symbol (think *at*tribute) refers to an XML attribute. The / character indicates element depth—just like it indicates directory depth in file paths. The XPath query Top/belowTop[@pk='1']/@col, for example, indicates that you are requesting the value of an XML attribute called col belonging to an element belowTop that is a child element of Top and has an attribute pk whose value is 1. The square brackets thus indicate a subexpression that is applied to the attribute or element to its left. As usual, attribute names correspond to columns, and element names correspond to tables.

dbobject represents the virtual name of type dbobject. dbobject-type virtual names allow direct access to database objects from the Internet.

TableName represents the name of a table (think XML element) that you are accessing. *PrimaryKeyName* represents the primary key column name (think XML attribute) of the table specified in *TableName*. *PrimaryKeyValue* is the value of *PrimaryKeyName* for the row that contains the selected value. The primary key is specified to guarantee the uniqueness of the object returned when you execute this XPath query.

As an example:

```
http://<myserver>/NorthwindVdir/dataobjects/Categories[@CategoryID='1']/@Picture.
```

dataobjects represents the virtual name called dataobjects of type dbobject that you created when you created the NorthwindVdir virtual directory.

Categories represents the name of the table (think XML element) that you are accessing. *CategoryID* represents the primary key column name (think XML attribute) of the table specified in *TableName*. *'1'* is the value of *CategoryID* for the row that contains this value.

If you change the code in Listing 41.6, adding the primary key to the select list and removing `BINARY BASE` from the `FOR XML` clause, you get the results in Listing 41.8.

LISTING 41.8 `FOR XML AUTO` Generates XPath References to Binary Data

```
SELECT Picture, CategoryID FROM Categories
WHERE CategoryID=1
FOR XML AUTO, ELEMENTS

go

XML_F52E2B61-18A1-11d1-B105-00805F49916B
<Categories><Picture>dbobject/Categories[@CategoryID='1']/@Picture</Picture>
<CategoryID>1</CategoryID></Categories>
```

> **TIP**
>
> You can force SQL Server to return XPath references to binary data in `RAW` and `EXPLICIT` mode in the following way. Select the primary key of the table, and then build a string representation based on the XPath syntax discussed earlier by selecting the primary key again and concatenating it to the `@CategoryID` expression. Listing 41.9 shows how to retrieve data from the Picture column in Categories using this method.

LISTING 41.9 Creating the XPath Manually Using `FOR XML RAW`

```
SELECT CategoryID,
   'dbobject/Categories[@CategoryID='+
       CONVERT(varchar(10), CategoryID)+']/@Picture' Picture
FROM Categories
WHERE CategoryID < 4
FOR XML RAW

go

XML_F52E2B61-18A1-11d1-B105-00805F49916B------------------------------------------
<row CategoryID="1" Picture="dbobject/Categories[@CategoryID=1]/@Picture"/>
<row CategoryID="2" Picture="dbobject/Categories[@CategoryID=2]/@Picture"/>
<row CategoryID="3" Picture="dbobject/Categories[@CategoryID=3]/@Picture"/>
```

Using XML in Stored Procedures

Now that you have seen several ways to produce XML documents from queries, it's time to take a look at how to deal with XML where you are most likely to use it: inside stored procedures. To talk to ActiveX Data Objects (ADO), URL queries, templates, and other data sources, your procedures need to know how to read and write XML. If you are not familiar with stored procedures, please refer to Chapter 28, "Creating and Managing Stored Procedures in SQL Server," before proceeding. Listing 41.10 provides the basis for our discussion.

LISTING 41.10 A Stored Procedure That Reads XML Input and Writes XML Output

```
CREATE PROCEDURE dbo.S_ORDERS_BY_CUSTOMER_AND_EMPLOYEE_XML
(@xml varchar(1000))
as
declare       @ixml int,
       @CustomerID nvarchar(5),
       @EmployeeID int

EXECUTE sp_xml_preparedocument @ixml OUTPUT, @xml

SELECT @CustomerID = CustomerID, @EmployeeID = EmployeeID
FROM OPENXML(@ixml, 'sp/row')
WITH (
       CustomerID nvarchar(5) '@CustomerID',
       EmployeeID int '@EmployeeID'
)

SELECT Customer.CustomerID, OrderID, LastName + ', ' + FirstName as EmployeeName
FROM Customers Customer
JOIN Orders [Order] ON Customer.CustomerID = [Order].CustomerID
AND [Order].CustomerID = @CustomerID
JOIN Employees Employee ON [Order].EmployeeID = Employee.EmployeeID
AND [Order].EmployeeID = @EmployeeID
FOR XML AUTO

IF @@ROWCOUNT > 0
       return 0
else
       return 1
EXEC sp_xml_removedocument @ixml
```

In the `CREATE PROCEDURE` statement, you declare a single input parameter `@xml`. This is a convention I use based on a principle of simplicity. Size `@xml` according to the size of your expected input xml. Your XML input string should contain all the values that, prior to the advent of XML support, would have been found in a complex list of input parameters of varying datatypes.

Next, declare the actual parameters that the procedure will need as local variables. A select statement that uses the `OPENXML` extension will then populate them.

Listing 41.11 shows the execution of our example using Query Analyzer and its result.

LISTING 41.11 The Result of a Call to `S_ORDERS_BY_CUSTOMER_AND_EMPLOYEE_XML`

```
S_ORDERS_BY_CUSTOMER_AND_EMPLOYEE_XML
'<sp>
        <row CustomerID=''ANTON'' EmployeeID=''7''/>
</sp>'

go

XML_F52E2B61-18A1-11d1-B105-00805F49916B
----------------------------------------
<Customer CustomerID="ANTON">
        <Order OrderID="10507" EmployeeName="King, Robert"/>
        <Order OrderID="10573" EmployeeName="King, Robert"/>
</Customer>
```

You should standardize the structure of your XML input by using a common root element name. Then, format its child elements so they look like they could have been produced by the `FOR XML` clause. This is because `OPENXML` works a lot like `FOR XML` in reverse. Following are some suggested conventions:

- When your stored procedure needs input values that correspond to columns in multiple tables, create a flat input XML structure, resembling what `FOR XML RAW` might produce (as exemplified in Listing 41.10).
- When input values can be logically mapped to the columns in a single table and are small in terms of character count (say, 100 or less), name the attributes after the column to which they correspond. Then, name the element that holds these attributes after the table to which they belong, such as `<CUSTOMERS CUSTOMERID='ANTON'/>`. This is known as **attribute-centric data mapping** and it resembles the output produced by `FOR XML AUTO`.
- If input values are larger, store them in elements named after the column to which they correspond. (This is also safer in terms of data processing—XML elements are less restricted than attributes in what characters they can contain.) These elements

should then be child elements of an element named after the table to which they belong, such as <CUSTOMERS><CUSTOMERID>ANTON</CUSTOMERID></CUSTOMERS>. This is known as **element-centric** mapping and it resembles the output produced by FOR XML AUTO, ELEMENTS.

Use these techniques to structure your XML in a logical manner and debugging will be easier because your XML (whenever possible) is both human *and* machine-readable. In addition, XML is input ready for easy use with OPENXML. The more your input XML resembles table structures, the simpler your OPENXML queries will be.

Using OPENXML to Read XML

Inside stored procedures, you retrieve values from your XML input into your local variables using the OPENXML extension. Following is the syntax for OPENXML:

```
OPENXML(ixml int, pattern nvarchar,[flags byte])
[WITH (SchemaDeclaration | TableName)]
```

OPENXML is known as a **rowset provider**: Based on its parameters, it maps XML into a rowset against which you can perform queries by specifying FROM OPENXML as you would FROM *tablename(s)*.

Before you can use OPENXML, you need to call the system-stored procedure sp_xml_preparedocument and pass it @xml as input and @ixml as an OUTPUT parameter. It returns a reference to @xml in @ixml for use as OPENXML's first parameter (*ixml*). Free the memory allocated for this reference when you are finished reading the XML by passing the variable represented by *ixml* to sp_xml_removedocument.

In the second parameter, *pattern*, specify an XPath query that identifies the elements or attributes in the input XML that OPENXML will map into rows. Each element that matches *pattern* creates a row in the rowset that is produced by OPENXML. In this chapter's example, the simple pattern 'sp' generates a single row that has no columns, because only one element is named sp. The example uses the WITH clause to add columns to this row by matching more of the XML input. This happens in the *SchemaDeclaration* parameter—so called because its tuples establish the column names, datatypes, and values of the table that OPENXML creates. The syntax of the tuples is as follows:

```
ColumnName datatype [ColumnPattern | MetaProperty]
[, ColumnName datatype [ColumnPattern | MetaProperty]...]
```

Each tuple adds a column *ColumnName* of type *datatype* to the rowset created by OPENXML when the XPath query specified in *ColumnPattern* matches. This chapter's example has two such tuples: CustomerID nvarchar(5) '@CustomerID' and EmployeeID int '@EmployeeID'.

The select statement below your call to OPENXML then uses the values selected FROM OPENXML into local variables in a subsequent query, which in turn returns an XML document that tells you which Orders were handled by EmployeeID 7 for CustomerID 'ANTON'. (*MetaProperty* is an advanced parameter that provides detailed information about the input XML such as would be found in an XML schema.)

By far, the simplest way to use OPENXML is to specify a *TableName* parameter and no tuples in the WITH clause. Do this if your input XML will match all the required columns in your query in either an attribute or element-centric manner. This comes in handy in the case of insert or update queries, although your input XML is now strongly tied to the underlying table structure. Listing 41.12 provides an example of an insert query using OPENXML and a tablename.

LISTING 41.12 An Insert Query Using OPENXML

```
CREATE PROCEDURE dbo.I_NEW_SHIPPERS_XML
(@xml varchar(1000))
as
declare       @ixml int,
       @ShipperID nvarchar(5),
       @rc int

EXECUTE sp_xml_preparedocument @ixml OUTPUT, @xml

INSERT INTO Shippers
SELECT CompanyName, Phone
FROM OPENXML(@ixml, 'sp/Shippers')
WITH Shippers

SELECT @rc = @@ROWCOUNT

EXEC sp_xml_removedocument @ixml

IF @rc > 0 begin
       select '<Success rv=''0'' msg=''Created ' +
                        cast(@rc as varchar(4)) + ' new Shippers''/>'
       return 0
end
else begin
       select '<Failure rv=''0'' msg=''Failed to create any new Shippers''/>'
       return 1
end
```

The input XML and its result are as follows:

```
I_NEW_SHIPPERS_XML
'<sp>
       <Shippers CompanyName=''House of Shipping'' Phone=''555-5555''/>
       <Shippers CompanyName=''World of Shipping'' Phone=''555-5554''/>
</sp>'

go

XML_F52E2B61-18A1-11d1-B105-00805F49916B
----------------------------------------------
<Success rv='0' msg='Created 2 new Shippers'/>
```

Notice how the example input looks a bit like `AUTO` mode output? The XPath pattern used in `OPENXML` first matches every Shippers element, then uses attribute-centric mapping (the default *flags* parameter) to create a column value for every attribute that matches Shippers columns. In addition, it's a good idea to send an XML-formatted string indicating success or failure back to the calling application.

`OPENXML`'s *flags* parameter can also be changed to alter how you want `OPENXML` to map the various types of XML input you might have into rowsets when you specify *TableName* or use *SchemaPattern* tuples but don't specify a column pattern.

`OPENXML` uses the value of *flags* to map your XML into a rowset based on the following possible values:

- 0—The default: Apply attribute-centric mapping to the XML input.
- 1—Apply attribute-centric mapping to the XML input. Combinable with 2.
- 2—Apply element-centric mapping to the XML input. Combinable with 1.
- 8—For use with metaproperties—Indicates that the XML should not be copied to the overflow metaproperty `@mp:xmltext`. Combinable with 1 or 2.

As you can see, SQL Server 2000 is flexible in terms of the type of XML input you can send to your stored procedures and the ways it can be unpacked and read using `OPENXML`.

Using URL Queries

SQL Server 2000 provides tight integration with IIS via an ISAPI filter called *sqlisapi.dll* that IIS calls on behalf of SQL Server to execute the queries you specify in the text of a URL.

If you haven't already done so, please follow the instructions in the first section of this chapter to create the virtual directory and virtual names you will use to access the Northwind database.

The simplest way to execute T-SQL commands using a URL query is to specify a `select statement` in the URL. Open Internet Explorer and type the following, substituting your Web server name for *<myserver>*:

```
http://<myserver>/NorthwindVdir?sql=SELECT EmployeeID FROM Employees
➥FOR XML AUTO&root=myEmployees
```

The syntax of this address is as follows:

```
http://<myserver>/myVirtualDirectory?sql=[sql statements]&root=[rootElementName]
```

myVirtualDirectory is the name of a virtual directory and the ? character specifies that what follows is a **query string**—a list of name-value pairs of the form name=value&name=value. These pairs are the named parameters that are passed to the virtual directory or template file for processing.

In this example, the value of `sql` is one or more T-SQL statements that return XML using `FOR XML`. `root` tells the URL query processor to enclose the resulting document fragment in a root element named *rootElementName*. The results are shown in Figure 41.10.

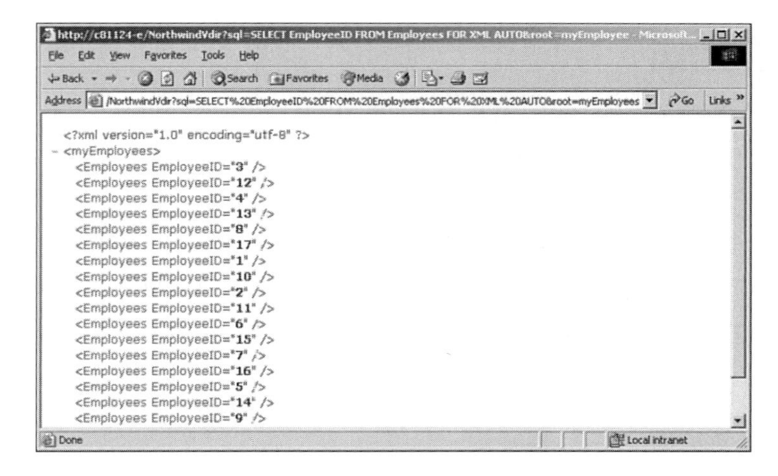

FIGURE 41.10 Using a virtual directory to execute a URL query.

NOTE

Notice how IE automatically converts the spaces in the URL to the string `%20`? This is called *URL-encoding* and it makes the URL safe for transmission from server to server across the Internet. When you type queries by hand into Internet Explorer, you don't have to worry about manually encoding the URL because IE does it for you. You still have to in code.

Fortunately, when writing client or server-side script (the usual method for calling Web pages in code) the JScript language provides the `escape` and `unescape` functions that encode and unencode URLs. In addition, the Active Server Page (ASP) object model's `Server` object provides the `URLEncode` method. Therefore, you really don't need to memorize the list of special characters that need to be encoded.

You can also execute stored procedures that return XML by using the `EXEC` keyword in the `sql` parameter. To try this, open Query Analyzer and, using the Object Browser, navigate to and expand the Stored Procedures node under the Northwind database. Right-click `dbo.CustOrderHist`, navigate to Script Object to New Window As, and select Alter (see Figure 41.11).

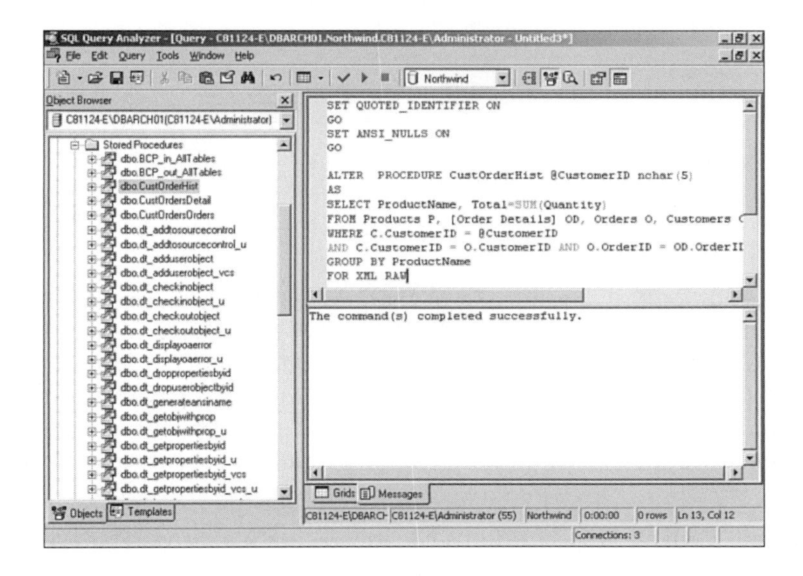

FIGURE 41.11 Altering `CustOrderHist` stored procedure with `FOR XML RAW`.

Add a `FOR XML RAW` clause to the `select statement` (after `GROUP BY`). Press F5 to save your changes. Then test this URL in Internet Explorer by typing the following address:

```
http://<myserver>/NorthwindVdir?sql=exec CustOrderHist @CustomerID='ANTON'
➥&root=OrderHistory
```

The resulting well-formed XML document is found in Figure 41.12.

Allowing URL queries opens up a potential security hole in your system you might not want. Not to give you any bad ideas, but how easy would it be to run a query like `sql=DELETE FROM Customers`? For better security, use XML templates.

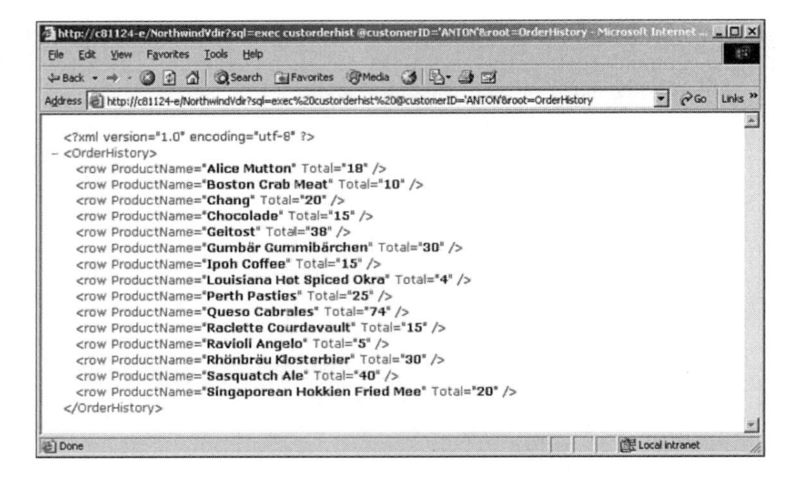

FIGURE 41.12 Executing a stored procedure from a URL query.

Using XML Templates

An XML template is an XML document that contains T-SQL statements that are executed when you specify the template name in the URL. This is handy because you don't want to use URL queries when you have many lines of T-SQL code to execute. Also, if you uncheck the Allow URL Queries option from your Northwind virtual directory (using the IIS Virtual Directory Management for SQL Server tool as explained earlier), the security hole opened by URL queries is closed and URL access is limited to addresses that specify template filenames.

When a template filename is specified in a URL query, the SQL Server 2000 ISAPI filter executes the statements inside. The ISAPI filter uses the virtual name called `Templates` (or any other virtual names of type `template`) that you created earlier to run the template files stored in the Template subdirectory (see Figure 41.13).

Listing 41.13 shows an example of a simple XML template. Save its code in a file called OrdersByEmployee.xml to the Template subdirectory (this code can also be found on the CD-ROM with this book).

LISTING 41.13 A Simple XML Template

```
<OrdersByEmployee xmlns:sql="urn:schemas-microsoft-com:xml-sql">
    <sql:header>
              <sql:param name="CustomerID">ANTON</sql:param>
       </sql:header>
    <sql:query>
              <![CDATA[
              --SQL Comments work here too!
```

41

LISTING 41.13 Continued

```
            SELECT TOP 10 Employee.LastName + ', ' +
                        Employee.FirstName EmployeeName,
                        OrderID,
                        convert(varchar(11),RequiredDate) RequiredDate,
                    [Order].CustomerID
             FROM    Orders [Order]
             JOIN Customers C on C.CustomerID = [Order].CustomerID
             AND C.CustomerID = @CustomerID
             JOIN Employees Employee on
                    Employee.EmployeeID = [Order].EmployeeID
             ORDER BY EmployeeName, RequiredDate
             FOR XML AUTO
             ]]>
        </sql:query>
</OrdersByEmployee>
```

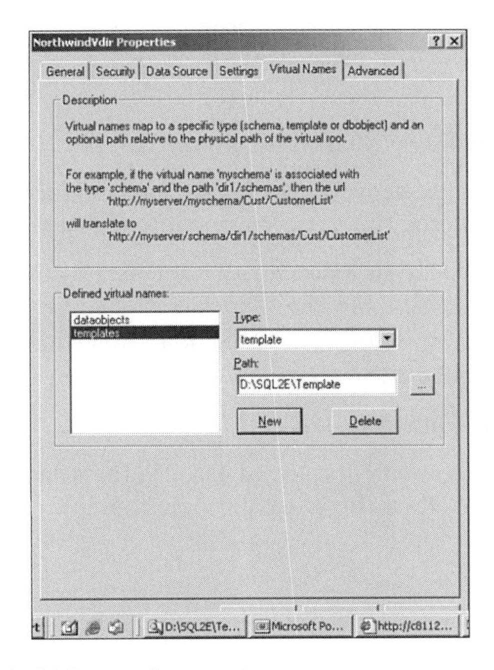

FIGURE 41.13 NorthwindVdir templates path.

Now take a look at the special tags used inside XML templates. They include the following:

- A root element of any name. (Listing 41.13 uses `Customers`). The root element must specify the namespace attribute `xmlns:sql="urn:schemas-microsoft-com:xml-sql"`. It also supports the optional attribute `sql:xsl` whose value is a relative or absolute path to an XSL stylesheet. SQL Server will transform and output the results of the template query using the specified stylesheet before returning it to its calling object.
- `sql:query`—This is the enclosing element for all your T-SQL statements. It can be repeated to organize statements into groups.

> **TIP**
>
> Enclose your `sql:query` statements and `sql:param` values between `<![CDATA[` and `]]>` (known as a CDATA section) to avoid having to manually encode any special characters. This makes things much easier because it instructs the parser to treat comparison characters such as < as *less-than* and not as an indicator of the start of an XML element. For reference, the special characters you need to encode outside of a CDATA section are <, >, &, ', and ". Convert them to the strings (known as entities) `<`, `>`, `&`, `'`, and `"` when you need to use them as element or attribute values.

- `sql:header`—The enclosing element for any `sql:param` tags. Not repeatable.
- `sql:param`—A repeatable element used to define any input parameters (named `name`) you want to pass from the URL's query string into the statements in `sql:query`.
- `sql:xpath-query`—Specify an XPath query in the template.

Execute OrdersByEmployee.xml using IE with the following URL:
`http://<myserver>/NorthwindVdir/templates/OrdersByEmployee.xml?CustomerID=ALFKI`.

The resulting XML is found in Figure 41.14.

The results also show how the default value of ANTON, the value of our `sql:param` tag, is overridden by passing in ALFKI as the value of the CustomerID parameter in the query string.

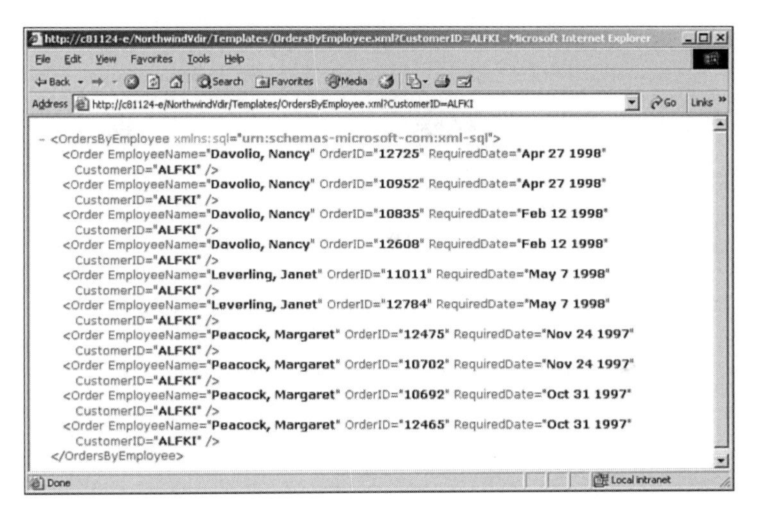

FIGURE 41.14 The results of the template query `http://<myserver>/NorthwindVdir/templates/ OrdersByEmployee.xml?CustomerID=ALFKI`.

Using XML Updategrams

In addition to the template and URL techniques illustrated previously, SQL Server 2000 provides special support for Internet **updategrams**: template queries that insert, update, and delete rows based on special XML elements.

Before you can use updategrams, download and install the XML for SQL Server 2000 Web Release 1 from `http://msdn.microsoft.com/downloads/default.asp?URL=/code/sample.asp?url=/MSDN-FILES/027/001/554/msdncompositedoc.xml`. You also need to have installed Microsoft XML Parser version 3, configured an IIS virtual directory for use with SQL Server 2000, and checked the Allow Template Queries option on the Settings tab of the IIS Virtual Directory Management for SQL Server tool for that directory.

The updategram elements (note the use of the `updg` namespace declared in the root element) are as follows:

- A document root element of any name, having the namespace attribute `xmlns:updg="urn:schemas-microsoft-com:xml-updategram"`.
- `updg:sync`—Like the keyword *TRANSACTION*, the statements enclosed by `updg:sync` are considered a transaction in the template query. `updg:sync` is the parent element of `updg:before` and `updg:after`.
- `updg:before`—When used in a transaction by itself, rows specified as its child elements are deleted. When used with `updg:after`, it identifies the rows to be updated by `updg:after`.

- `updg:after`—When used in a transaction by itself, the rows specified as its child elements are inserted. When used with `updg:before`, it updates the rows identified in `updg:before`.

Listing 41.14 shows template code that uses an updategram to insert a row in the Shippers table. The code is fairly straightforward: Specify the row you want to insert as a child element of `updg:after` using either attribute or element-centric XML-to-table mapping. This example specifies the target row using attribute-centric mapping. Save the following code to your Template directory as an .xml file and test it in your browser.

LISTING 41.14 Inserting a Row in Shippers Using an Updategram

```
<updategramRoot xmlns:updg="urn:schemas-microsoft-com:xml-updategram">
<updg:sync>
       <updg:after>
              <Shippers CompanyName='IShipIt' Phone='555-1212'/>
       </updg:after>
</updg:sync>
</updategramRoot>
```

Deletes work the same way except that the rows that are to be deleted are specified under `updg:before`. Listing 41.15 attempts to delete a row from Shippers. This example specifies the target row using element-centric mapping.

LISTING 41.15 Deleting a Row in Shippers Using an Updategram

```
<updategramRoot xmlns:updg="urn:schemas-microsoft-com:xml-updategram">
<updg:sync>
       <updg:before>
              <Shippers><ShipperID>1</ShipperID></Shippers>
       </updg:before>
</updg:sync>
</updategramRoot>
```

Notice the error message that is returned to the browser. It too is a well-formed XML document containing special tags (beginning with the character sequence <? and ending with ?>) called **processing instructions** that indicate to the calling program any errors that might have occurred.

The final example (shown in Listing 41.16) is an updategram that updates the ContactName field in a row in Customers. It first identifies the rows to be updated in `updg:before`. All matching rows (using attribute-centric mapping) will be updated. New values for the columns in the matching rows are specified in the attributes of the Customer elements in `updg:after`.

LISTING 41.16 Updating a Row in Customers Using an Updategram

```
<updategramRoot xmlns:updg="urn:schemas-microsoft-com:xml-updategram">
<updg:sync>
      <updg:before>
             <Customers CustomerID="ALFKI"/>
      </updg:before>
      <updg:after>
             <Customers CustomerID="ALFKI" ContactName="Alien Life Form"/>
      </updg:after>
</updg:sync>
</updategramRoot>
```

Summary

At this point, your SQL Server 2000 XML toolbox should be just about full. The neat thing is that SQL Server 2000 is only the first version of SQL Server with native XML support. Now more than ever, with the advent of Web Services, Windows XP, the .NET Framework, and other emerging standards, the path to the future is paved with XML. SQL Server 2000 and the techniques illustrated here will help you find your way along it.

In the next chapter, you'll learn about Microsoft SQL Server Analysis Services, a powerful set of tools for data mining and analytical processing.

CHAPTER 42

Microsoft SQL Server Analysis Services

by Paul Bertucci

IN THIS CHAPTER

This version of SQL Server is jam-packed with numerous data warehousing, data mining, and OLAP-rich tools and technology. A Data Warehouse manager from a prominent Silicon Valley company once said, "I can now build [using MS SQL Server 2000 Analysis Services] sound, extremely usable, OLAP cubes myself, faster and smarter than my whole department could do only a few years ago." This is what Microsoft has brought to the table. In past SQL Server versions, it was much harder to turn Online Analytic Processing (OLAP) requirements into viable and scalable OLAP cubes, let alone get a handle on complex data mining models. Things just got a lot better.

What Is Analysis Services and OLAP?

Because OLAP is at the heart of Analysis Services (formerly known as OLAP Services component), it is best to understand what it is and how it solves the requirements of decision makers in a business. As you might already know, data warehousing requirements typically include all the capability needed to report on a business's transactional history, such as with sales history. This transactional history is often organized into subject areas and tiers of aggregated information that can support some online querying and usually much more batch reporting. Data warehouses and data marts typically extract data out of Online Transaction Processing (OLTP) systems and serve it up to these end users and reporting systems. In general, these are all called decision support systems (DSS), and the latency of this data is determined by the business requirements they must support.

OLAP falls squarely into the realm of DSS and what is called business intelligence. The purpose of OLAP is to provide for a "mostly" online reporting environment that can support various end user reporting requirements. Typically, OLAP representations are that of OLAP cubes. A **cube** is a multidimensional representation of basic business facts that can be accessed easily and quickly to provide you with the specific information you need to make a critical decision. It is useful to note that a cube can comprise from 1 to *N* dimensions. However, remember that the business facts represented in the cube must exist for all of the dimensions being defined for the fact.

Figure 42.1 illustrates a Sales_Units historical business fact that is the intersection of time, product, and geography dimensional data. For a particular point in time (February 2001), with a particular product (IBM laptop model 451D), and in a particular country (France), the sales units were 996 units. You can see easily how many of these laptop computers were sold in France in February 2001.

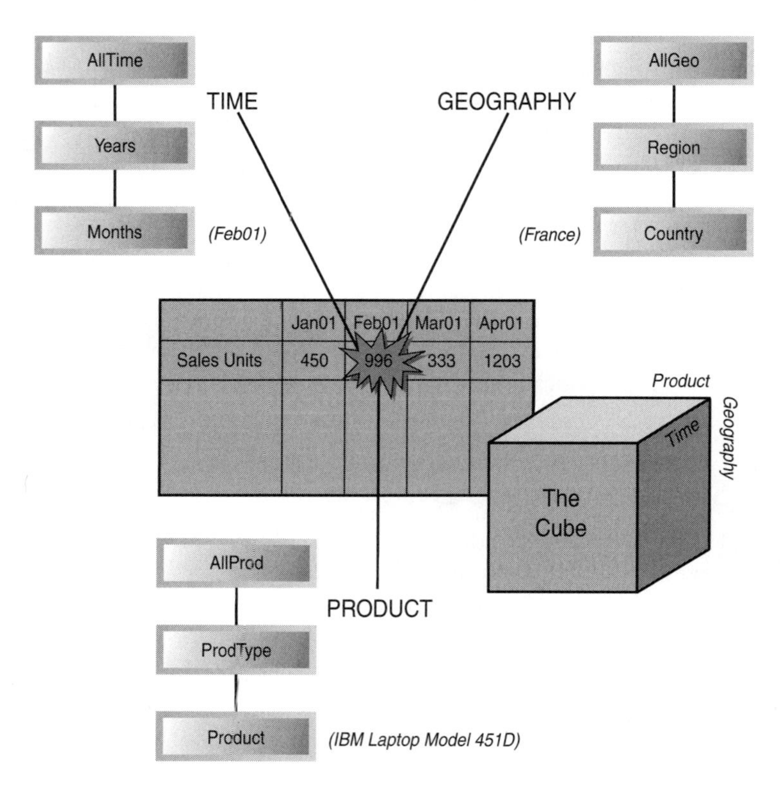

FIGURE 42.1 Multidimensional representation of business facts.

Basically, you are looking at business facts via well-defined and organized dimensions (time, product, and geography dimensions in this example). Note that each of these dimensions is further organized into hierarchical representations that correspond to the way data is looked at from the business point of view. This will provide for the capability to "drill-down" into the next level from a higher, broader level (like drilling down into a specific country's data within a region).

Microsoft Analysis Services (AS) directly supports this and other types of data warehousing capability. In addition, AS allows a designer to implement OLAP cubes using a variety of physical storage techniques that are directly tied to data aggregation requirements and other performance considerations. You can easily access any OLAP cube built with AS via the Pivot Table Service, you can write custom client applications using Multidimensional Extensions (MDX) with OLE DB for OLAP or ActiveX Data Objects Multidimensional (ADO MD), and you can use a number of third-party OLE DB for OLAP-compliant tools. MDX is the multidimensional expression in SQL that enables you to formulate complex multidimensional queries.

The data mining capabilities that are part of AS provide a new avenue for organized data discovery. And, as is always the case with any object built by Microsoft, all OLAP object definitions are externalized into the Microsoft metadata repository (via Unified Modeling Language, or UML). It is also worthy to note that many of the leading OLAP and statistical analysis software vendors have joined the Microsoft Data Warehousing alliance and are building front-end analysis and presentation tools for Microsoft AS.

This chapter takes you through the major components of AS, discusses a mini-methodology for OLAP cube design, and leads you through the creation and management of a robust OLAP cube that can easily be used to meet a company's DSS needs.

Understanding the Analysis Services Environment and the "Land of Wizards"

Welcome to the "land of wizards." This implementation of Analysis Services is heavily wizard oriented. AS has a Cube Wizard, Dimension Wizard, Partition Wizard, Incremental Update Wizard, Storage Design Wizard, Usage Analysis Wizard, Usage-Based Optimization Wizard, Calculated Cells Wizard, Action Wizard, Virtual Cube Wizard, Mining Model Wizard, and Security Roles Wizard. All are useful, and many of the capabilities are also available through editors of one kind or another. The wizard approach helps many who need to have a little structure in the definition process (and who want to rely on the default for much of what they need).

Figure 42.2 depicts how AS fits into the overall scheme of SQL Server 2000. AS has become a natural outgrowth of the baseline capabilities of SQL Server. Utilizing many different mechanisms, such as Data Transformation Services and direct datasource access capabilities, a vast amount of data can be funneled into the AS environment. Most of the cubes that you will build are read-only because they should be in support of DSS. A write-enabled capability is available in AS for situations that meet certain requirements.

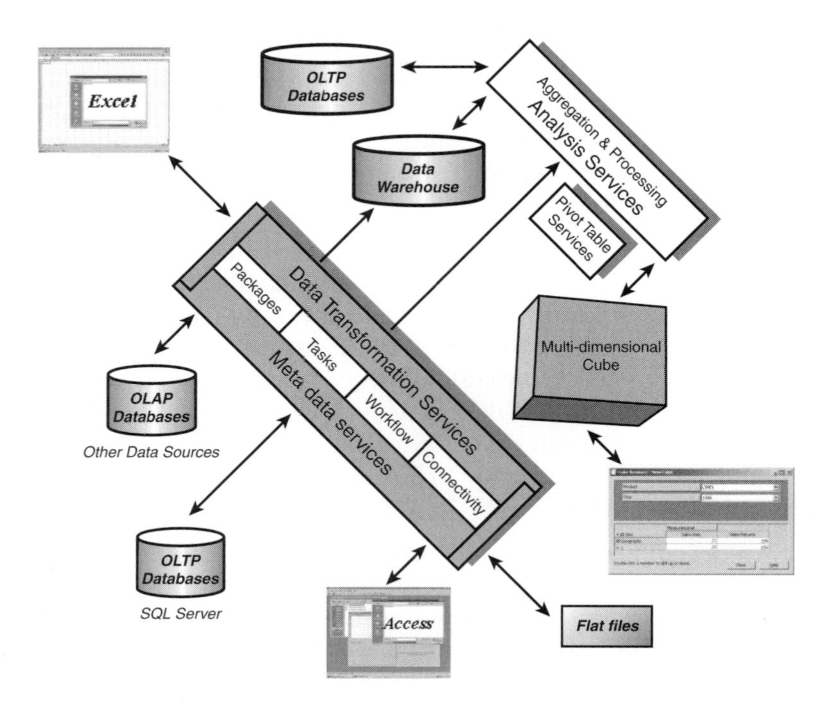

FIGURE 42.2 Analysis Services as part of the MS SQL Server 2000 environment.

The basic components within AS are all focused around building and managing data cubes. AS consists of the Analysis Server and the Pivot Table Service.

Cubes are created by pre-processing aggregations (pre-calculated summary data) that reflect the desired levels within dimensions and support the type of querying that will be done. These aggregations provide the mechanism for rapid and uniform response times to queries. These aggregations are created *before* the user uses the cube. All queries are utilizing either these aggregations, the cube's source data, a copy of this data on the AS, a client cache, or a combination of these sources. A single Analysis Server can manage many cubes.

A cube is defined by the measures and dimensions that it contains. Each cube dimension can contain a hierarchy of levels to specify the natural categorical breakdown that users need to drill down into for more details. Look back at Figure 42.1 and you can see a product hierarchy, time hierarchy, and geography hierarchy representation.

The data values within the cube are represented by measures (the facts). Each measure data might utilize different aggregation options depending on the type of data. Unit data might require SUM (summarization), Date of Receipt data might require the MAX function, and so on. Members of a dimension are the actual level values, such as the particular product number, the particular month, and the particular country. A cube can contain up to 128 dimensions, each with millions of members, and up to 1,024 measures. In reality, you will probably not have more than a handful of dimensions. Remember: The dimensions are the paths to the interesting facts. Dimension members should be textual and are used as criteria for queries and as row and column headers in query results.

Every cube has a schema from which the cube draws its source data. The central table in this schema is the fact table that will yield the cube's data measures. The other tables in the schema are the dimension tables that are the source of the cube dimensions. A classic star-schema data warehouse design will have this central fact table along with multiple dimension tables. This is a great starting point for OLAP cube creation, as you can see in Figure 42.3.

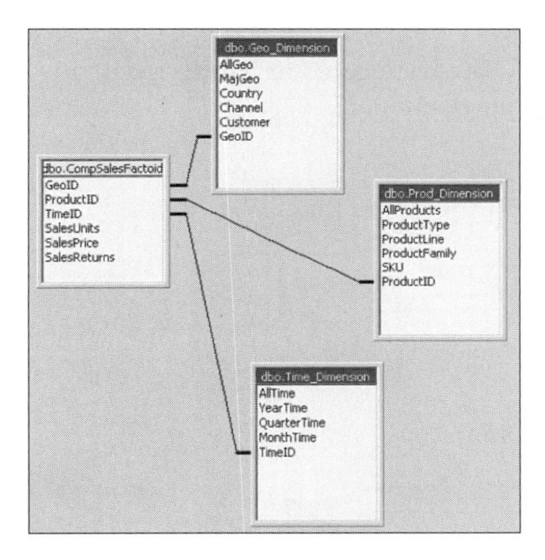

FIGURE 42.3 Central Fact table and multiple dimensions of these facts.

AS allows you to build dimensions and cubes from heterogeneous datasources. It can access relational OLTP databases, multidimensional data databases, text data, and any other source that has an OLE DB provider available. You don't have to move all your data first, just connect to its source.

Essentially, cubes can be regular, virtual, or local cubes. Slight variations on this theme are linked cubes and real-time cubes. The following list explains these cubes in more detail:

- Regular cubes—Regular cubes are based on real tables for their datasource, will have aggregations, and will occupy physical storage space of some kind. If a datasource that contributes to this cube changes, the cube must be reprocessed. Figure 42.4 shows cube representations.
- Virtual cubes—Virtual cubes are logical cubes based on one or more regular cubes (or linked cubes). Virtual cubes use the aggregations of their component regular cubes, in which case storage space is not needed.

- Linked cubes—Linked cubes are based on regular cubes defined and stored on another Analysis Server. Linked cubes also use the aggregations (and storage) of the regular cube they reference.
- Local cubes—Local cubes are entirely contained in portable files (tables) and can be browsed without a connection to an Analysis Server. They do not have aggregations. This is really like being in "disconnected" mode.
- Real-time cubes—These are regular cubes that have dimensions or partitions that have been enabled for "real-time OLAP." In other words, real-time cubes receive updates dynamically from the datasources that are defined in their dimensions/ partitions.
- Write-enabled cubes—These are cubes in which updates (writes) are allowed and can be shared back with the datasources.

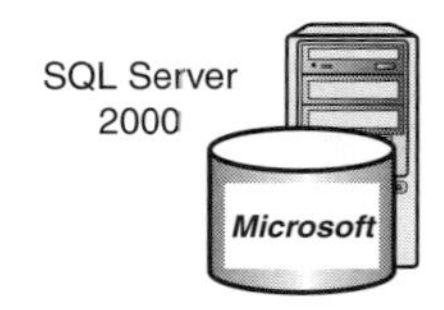

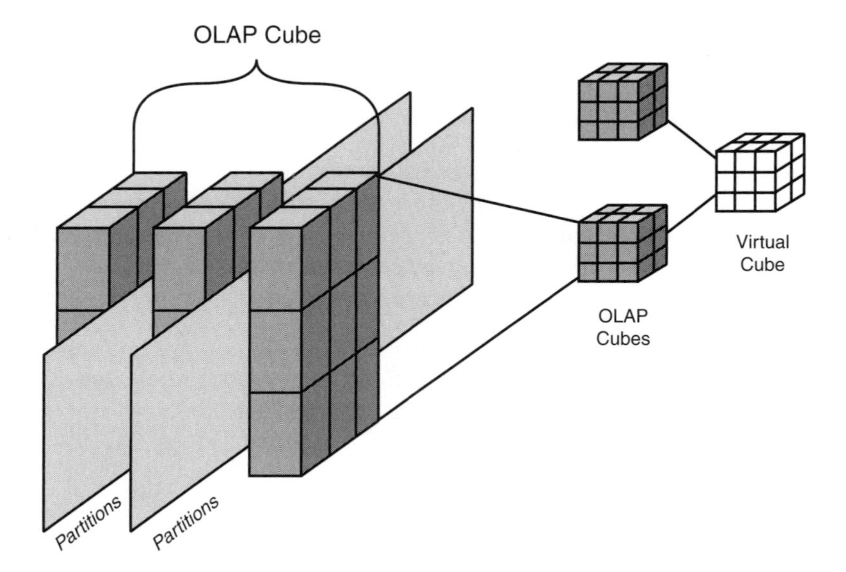

FIGURE 42.4 The AS cube representations—regular OLAP cubes, partitions, and virtual cubes.

Following is a quick summary of all the essential terms in AS:

- Database—The logical container of one or more cubes. Cubes are defined within Analysis Server databases.
- Cube—The multidimensional representation of the business facts. Types of cubes include regular, virtual, linked, and local.
- Datasource—The origin of a cube's data.
- Measure—The data fact representation. A measure is typically a data value fact such as price, unit, quantity, and so on. Up to 1,024 measures can exist per cube.
- Cell—The part of a data measure that is at the intersection of the dimensions. The cell contains the data value. If an intersection (cell) has no value yet, it will not physically exist until it is populated.
- Dimension—A cube's dimension is defined by the aggregation levels of the data that are needed to support your data requirements. A dimension can be shared with other cubes or private to a cube. A cube can have up to 128 dimensions. The structure of a dimension is directly related to the dimension table columns, member properties, or from the structure of OLAP data mining models. This structure becomes the hierarchy and should be organized with this in mind. You can also have strict parent-child dimensions in which two columns are identified as being parent and child, and the dimension is organized according to them. In a regular dimension, each column in the dimension contributes a hierarchy level. In a virtual dimension, each member property or column in the definition of the dimension contributes a hierarchy level.
- Level—A level includes the nodes of the hierarchy or data mining model. Each level contains the members. Millions of members for each level are possible.
- Partition—One or more partitions comprise the cube. A partition is a way to physically separate parts of a cube. This separation essentially lets you deal with individual "slices" of a data cube separately, querying only the relevant datasources. If you partition by dimension, you can perform incremental updates to change that dimension independently of the rest of the cube. Consequently, you only have to reprocess aggregations affected by those changes. This is an excellent feature for scalability.
- Hierarchy—The set of members in a dimension and their position relative to each other. Hierarchies can either be balanced or unbalanced. Being balanced simply means that all branches of the hierarchy descend to the same level. An unbalanced hierarchy allows for branches to descend to different levels. It is also possible to define more than one hierarchy for a single dimension. A great example of this is for "fiscal calendar time" and "Gregorian calendar time" being defined in one dimension (time dimension: time.gregorian and time.fiscal).

As mentioned previously, AS has many wizards. Depending on exactly what you need to create, you will be using one set of wizards or another. Later, in the "Creating an OLAP Database" section, the order and path through these wizards will be outlined.

OLAP Versus OLTP

One of the primary goals of OLAP is to increase data retrieval speed. A multidimensional schema is not a typical normalized relational database; redundant data is stored to facilitate quick retrieval. The data in a multidimensional database should be relatively static; in fact, data is not useful for decision support if it changes constantly. The information in a data warehouse is built out of carefully chosen snapshots of business data from OLTP systems. If you capture data at the right times for transfer to the data warehouse, you can quickly make accurate comparisons of important business activities over time.

In an OLTP system, transaction speed is paramount. Data modification operations must be quick, must deal with concurrency, and must provide transactional consistency. An OLTP system is constantly changing; every snapshot of the system, even if taken only a few seconds apart, will be different. Although historical information is certainly available in an OLTP system, it might be impractical to use it for DSS-type analysis. Storing old data in an OLTP system becomes expensive, and you might need to reconstruct history dynamically from a series of transactions.

AS supports three OLAP storage methods, providing flexibility to the data warehousing solution and enabling powerful partitioning and aggregation optimization capabilities. These OLAP storage methods are MOLAP, ROLAP, and HOLAP. The following sections will take a closer look at these.

MOLAP

Multidimensional OLAP (MOLAP) is an approach in which cubes are built directly from OLTP datasources or from dimensional databases and downloaded to a persistent store.

In Microsoft Analysis Services, data is downloaded to the server, and these details and aggregations are stored in a native Microsoft OLAP format. No zero-activity records are stored.

The dimension keys in the fact tables are compressed, and bitmap indexing is used. A high-speed MOLAP query processor retrieves the data.

ROLAP

Relational OLAP (ROLAP) uses fact data in summary tables in the OLTP datasource to speed retrieval. The summary tables are populated by processes in the OLTP system and are not downloaded to AS. The summary tables are known as materialized views and contain various levels of aggregation, depending on the options you select when building data cubes with AS. AS builds the summary tables with a column for each dimension and each measure. It indexes each dimension column and creates an additional index on all the dimension columns.

HOLAP

AS also implements a combination of MOLAP and ROLAP called hybrid OLAP (HOLAP). Here, the facts are left in the OLTP datasource, and aggregations are stored in the AS server. You use AS to boost query performance. This approach helps avoid data duplication, but performance suffers a bit when you query fact data in the OLTP summary tables. The amount of performance degradation depends on the level of aggregation you selected.

ROLAP and HOLAP are useful in situations where an organization wants to leverage its investment in relational database technology and existing infrastructure. The summary tables of facts are also accessible in the OLTP system via normal data access methods. However, keep in mind that when using AS, both ROLAP and HOLAP require more storage space because they don't use the storage optimizations of the pure MOLAP-compressed implementation.

An Analytics Design Methodology

A data warehouse can be built top down or bottom up. To build a top-down warehouse, you need to form a complete picture or logical data model for the entire organization (or all the subsystems that are within the scope of the project, such as all financial systems). In contrast, building a warehouse from the bottom up takes a much more departmental or specific business-area focus (such as Sales Order system only). This breaks the task of modeling the data into more manageable chunks. Such a departmental approach produces data marts that are potentially subsets of the overall data warehouse. The bottom-up approach can simplify implementation. It helps get departmental or business-area information to the people who need it, makes it easier to protect sensitive data, and results in better query response times because data marts deal with less data. The potential risk in the data mart approach is that disparity in data-mart implementation can result in a logically disjointed enterprise data warehouse if efforts aren't carefully coordinated across the organization.

Before you embark on an OLAP database creation effort, the time you spend understanding the underlying requirements is the best time you can give your effort. If scope is set correctly, you will be able to achieve an industrial-strength OLAP design without much difficulty.

First, you need to take care of some ground work:

1. Assess the scope of what you want to represent in the DSS environment carefully. Start small, as the bottom-up approach suggests. For instance, just tackle the Sales data facts.
2. Coordinate your efforts with other related DSS efforts. Let people know that you are carving out a specific subject area or departmental data and, when you finish, publish your design to everyone.

3. Seek out any shared dimensions that might have already been created for other cubes. You will want to leverage these as much as possible for data consistency and non-redundant processing sake.

4. Understand your datasources. The OLAP cube you create will only be as good as the data you put into it. It's best to understand the dirty data issues of what you are about to touch long before you try to build an OLAP cube with it.

An Analytics Mini-Methodology

Assumption: You are building a business-area focused OLAP cube.

Requirements Phase:

1. Identify the processing requirements for this decision-support system. What analysis do you need to do? Are trend reporting, forecasting, and so on necessary? These can often be represented in Use Case form (via UML).
    a. Ask each user what business decision questions he needs to have answered.
    b. Ask each user how often he needs these questions answered and exactly when the questions must be answered.
    c. Ask each user how current the data must be to get accurate answers. This is data latency.
2. Identify the data needed to fulfill these requirements. What must be touched to provide answers? The best way to capture this type of information is a logical data model. Even a rough model is better than none at all. It is here that you focus on the "facts" that need to be analyzed.
3. Identify all possible hierarchies and level representations (aggregations). This is the "how data is used" question. Most users will tell you that they want to see product data in the product hierarchy structure that has already been set up (such as product family, product groups, and so on).
4. Identify the time hierarchies that the users need. Because time is usually implicit, it will just need to be clarified in terms of levels of aggregation (years, quarters, months, weeks, days, and so on) and if they need fiscal versus Gregorian calendar, both, or others.
5. Understand the data that each user can view from a security point of view.

Design Phase:

1. Analyze which datasources are needed to fulfill the requirements. See if dimensions or OLAP cubes already in existence can be shared.

2. Understand what data transformations need to be done to the source data to provide it to the OLAP world. This might include pre-aggregation, reformatting, data integrity verifications, and so on.
3. Translate these requirements into an OLAP model design:
   a. Translate to MOLAP if your datasources are not going to be leveraged at all and you will be taking full advantage of OLAP storage.
   b. Translate to ROLAP if you are going to leverage off of an existing relational design and storage.
   c. Translate to HOLAP if you are going to partially utilize the source data storage and partially utilize OLAP storage. This is the most frequently used approach.

Construction Phase:

1. Implement data extract/transformation logic (via SQL, DTS, or other methods).
2. Create the data sources to be used.
3. Create the dimensions.
4. Create the cube.
5. Select data measures (the data "facts") for the cube.
6. Design the storage and aggregations.
7. Process the cube. This brings the data into the OLAP environment.
8. Verify data integrity.

Implementation Phase:

1. Define the security roles in the cube.
2. Train the user to use the system.
3. Process the data into the OLAP environment (from production datasources).
4. Verify data integrity.
5. Turn the OLAP cube loose to the user.

Maintenance Phase:

1. Evaluate access optimization in the OLAP cube via usage analysis.
2. Do data mining discovery if desired.
3. Make schema changes/enhancements as necessary.

An OLAP Requirements Example

Following is an abbreviated requirement that reflects an actual implementation that was done for a large Silicon Valley company. You will follow the mini-methodology as closely as possible to implement this requirement in AS, pointing out which facilities of AS should be used for which purpose along the way.

CompSales International

A large computer manufacturer named CompSales International needs to do basic analytical processing of its product data in a new DSS environment. The main business issues at hand are related to minimizing channel inventory and better understanding market demand for the company's most popular products. The detailed data processing requirements are as follows:

1. View sales unit actuals and sales returns for system and non-system products for the past two years via the product hierarchy (All Products, Product Types, Product Lines, Product Families, SKUs), geography hierarchy (All Geos, Major Geos, Countries, Channels, Customers) and for different time levels (All Time, Years, Quarters, Months).
2. View data primarily at the yearly and monthly levels, although the finance department also uses it a little bit at quarterly levels.
3. View net sales (sales – returns) at all levels of the hierarchy.
4. Viewing of the fiscal and Gregorian calendar are the same for CompSales International.
5. One day past "month end" processing, all "actuals" data from the prior month is available (sales units and returns).

You will implement some general design decisions using AS, including the following:

- Hierarchies (dimensions)—This includes product, geography, and time.
- Facts (measures)—This includes sales units, sales returns, and net sales (units – returns) calculated.

Figure 42.5 illustrates the desired hierarchies and facts for CompSales International's requirements.

- OLAP storage—This includes HOLAP (to leverage off of the star-schema data mart that already contains most of what you want).
- Physical tables that exist—This includes Geo_Dimension, Prod_Dimension, Time_Dimension, and CompSalesFacts. This data is updated monthly. Each of these tables uses an artificial key into the main facts table for performance reasons (GeoID, ProductID, TimeID).

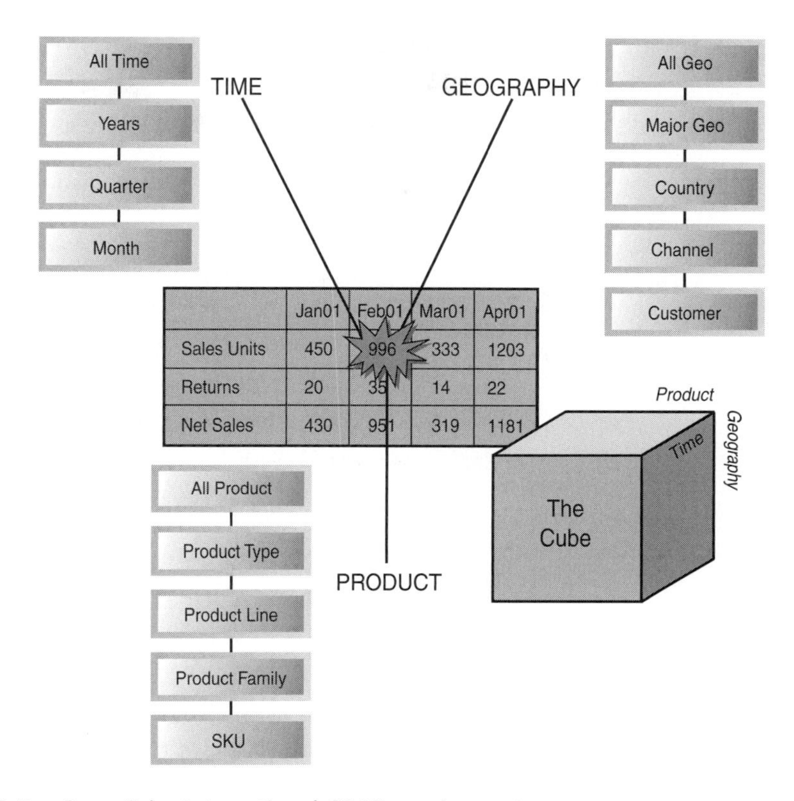

FIGURE 42.5 CompSales International OLAP requirements.

OLAP Cube Creation

You are almost ready to create the OLAP cube to fulfill the DSS needs of the users. Most of your construction phase will be spent using Analysis Manager. All wizards and editors are invoked from there. When you first fire up Analysis Manager, you must, of course, already have installed AS.

The Analysis Manager

The Analysis Manager is launched from the AS Services Program group on the Start menu. You will typically keep the Meta Data tab active as your current tab rather than the Getting Started tab. One of the first things that must be done is to create an Analysis Server database through the Action menu option. (You can also do this by right-clicking when your mouse is positioned at a connected Analysis Server.) Figure 42.6 shows the Analysis Manager with a Microsoft sample cube called FoodMart 2000.

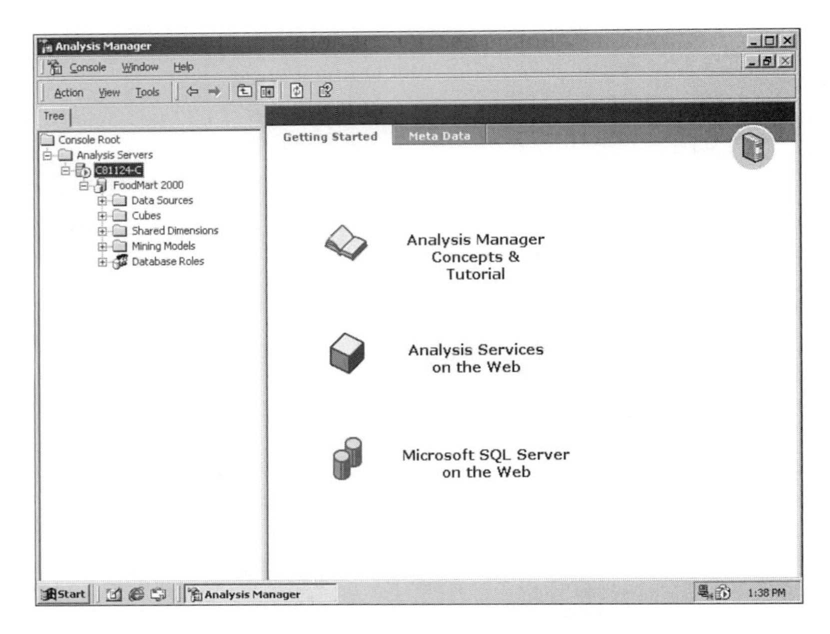

FIGURE 42.6 The Microsoft Analysis Manager console.

After you have created an Analysis Services database, it will appear in the console window with five subfolders (Data Sources, Cubes, Shared Dimensions, Mining Models, and Database Roles). As you can see from Figure 42.6, options are available for an online Concepts and Tutorial tour, Analysis Services on the Web, and Microsoft SQL Server on the Web. The latter two will connect you directly to Microsoft's Web site for up-to-the-minute information on these subjects.

Figure 42.7 shows what it looks like after a database (CompSales in this example) and its subfolders have been created. Everything for this particular database—including datasources, dimensions, cubes, mining models, and roles—will be managed from here.

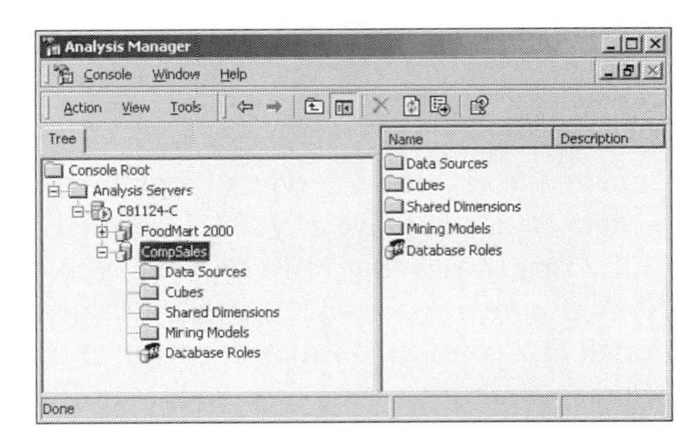

FIGURE 42.7 Database view in Analysis Manager.

Creating an OLAP Database

Remember: An OLAP database is made up of datasources, dimensions, and cubes. A datasource is simply a pointer to data somewhere, such as via a Jet OLE DB provider, an OLE DB provider, MSDataShape, MS Directory Services, and even DTS packages. Dimensions are constructed of columns from tables that you select that will be used to build and filter data cubes. Cubes are combinations of dimensions whose intersections contain strategically significant measures of business performance, such as quantities, units, and so on. Virtual cubes are joins of regular cubes, but they don't use storage space. (Virtual cubes are analogous to views in SQL Server.) You can join cubes this way with no more than one dimension in common. In addition, linked cubes are the way you include cube data from remotely defined OLAP cubes. You will need to identify any datasources on which your OLAP cube will now be based.

Adding a Datasource

To add datasources for this database, expand the database you have created (CompSales in your example) and right-click the Data Sources subfolder. The Choose New Data Source dialog box opens. Again, you can get the same menu by highlighting Data Sources and clicking Action on the Management Console toolbar. Select the data provider you will be using for this datasource and click Next. Then specify all needed connection information for that datasource. In this example, you will be connecting to a database named CompSales using the sa user ID. Click the Test Connection button; it should report the message `Test completed successfully`. Figure 42.8 shows this Data Link Properties dialog box.

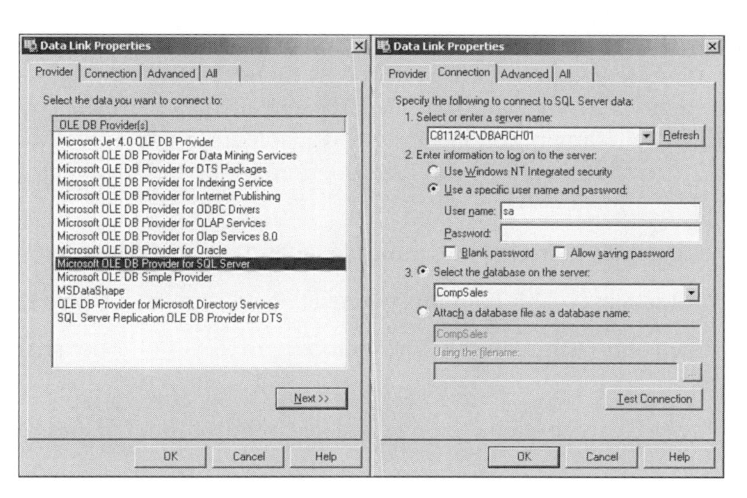

FIGURE 42.8 The Data Link Properties dialog box.

Adding Dimensions

You are now ready to start adding dimensions to your database. Dimensions are the building blocks for cubes in AS. Start by right-clicking Shared Dimensions in the CompSales database, right-click New Dimension, and select Wizard to open the Dimension Wizard. You will be welcomed to the Dimension Wizard, as shown in Figure 42.9. From there, you should probably just check the Skip This Screen in the Future box so that you are taken directly to the Dimension Creation screen the next time you come this way.

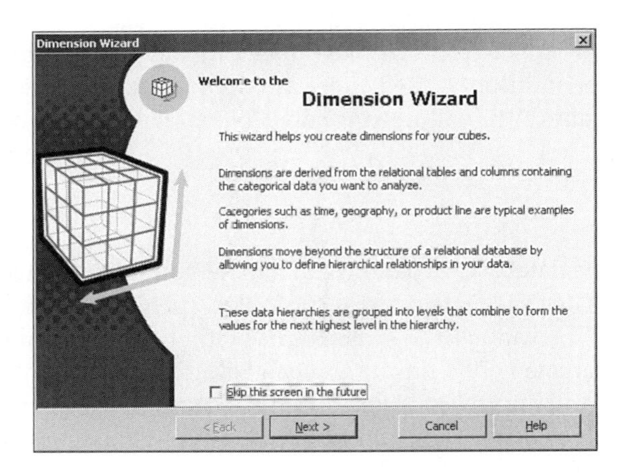

FIGURE 42.9 The Dimension Wizard welcome.

After you have reached the Dimension Creation screen, you will select the option Star Schema: A Single Dimension Table for the CompSales example. What you are saying is that you want to create a dimension and define its hierarchy from a single, star schema table. This is going to be from the CompSales star schema data mart that you are using as the basis of your cube. Many other options are available from which to choose, as shown in Figure 42.10. These other options can base the dimension and hierarchy from the following:

- Snowflake schema—This contains multiple tables that are related to each other.
- Parent-Child schema—This contains two related columns in a single table.
- Virtual Dimension—This contains the member properties of other shared dimensions.
- Mining Model—This contains the predictable column (node) of an OLAP mining model.

The CompSales requirement allows you to start from the Star Schema option.

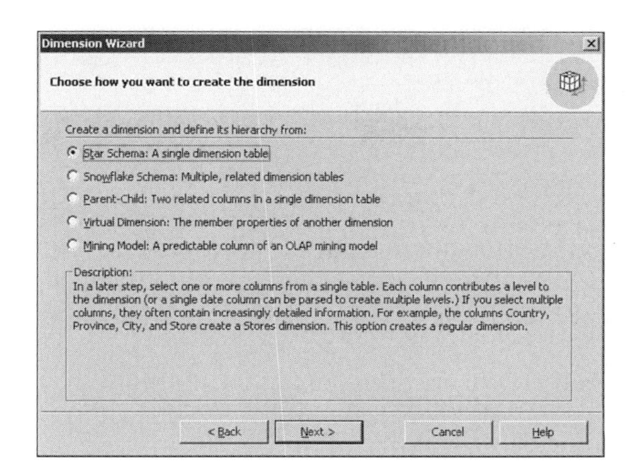

FIGURE 42.10 How to create the cube's dimension: Star Schema option.

The wizard offers a Select the Dimension Table dialog box where you can add a new datasource and use its tables for this dimension or access existing datasources you have already defined. You will simply expand the CompSales datasource and select the Geo_Dimension table (of the CompSales data mart) as the basis of your current dimension. You can browse the first 1,000 rows of data here. Figure 42.11 shows this dialog box along with the data browsing of the current Geo_Dimension tables data.

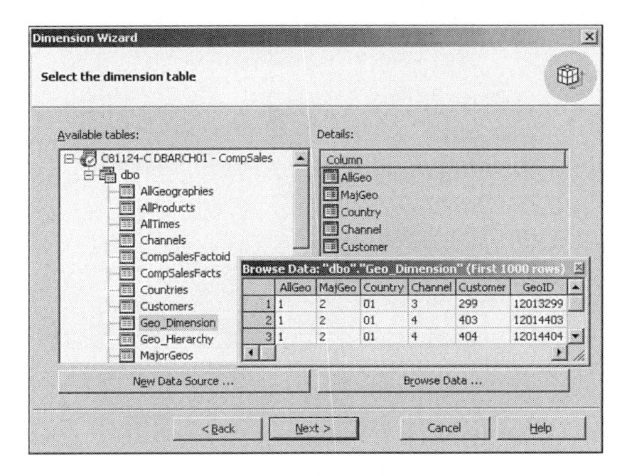

FIGURE 42.11 Selecting the datasources for dimensions.

The next step is to select the dimension levels. In the CompSales example, you will select all levels of this data mart dimension table for this OLAP dimension hierarchy and in the order you want them to be based from top to bottom. Figure 42.12 shows this selection. Remember that each column will correspond to a level of this OLAP dimension.

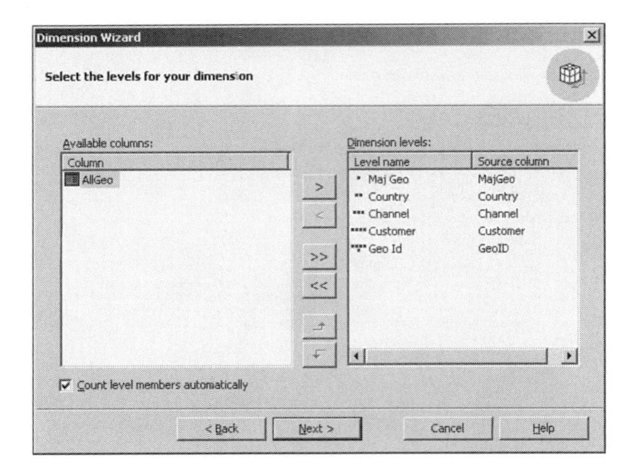

FIGURE 42.12 Selecting the levels for a dimension.

Next comes the Member Key Columns dialog box, as shown in Figure 42.13. Remember that members are the data values of the levels. In this example, the columns and the member name column are the same.

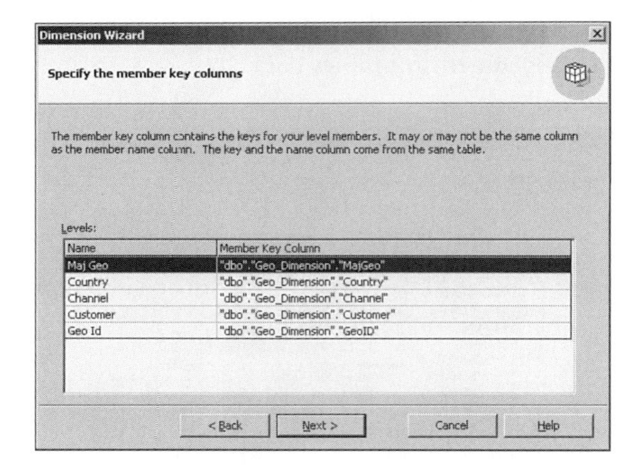

FIGURE 42.13 Specifying the keys for the level members.

A few advanced options need to be specified for the dimension. Figure 42.14 shows the advanced options that might apply for this dimension definition. These options include the following:

- Changing Dimension—This option allows members to change, update, or move without reprocessing the cube. This option is highly recommended.
- Ordering and Uniqueness of Members—Ordering specifies member sorting (ascending, descending), and uniqueness specifies how unique the level keys and names are. This option is recommended.

- Storage Mode and Member Groups—Storage mode determines the storage location for the dimension members. Member groups can be associated with a large level to facilitate navigation within a dimension. This method is optional.

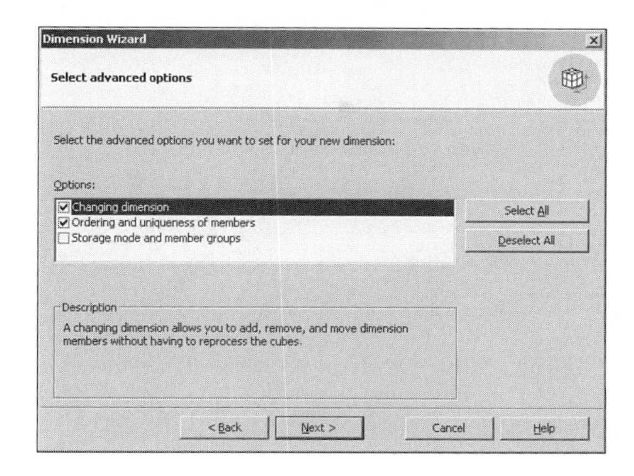

FIGURE 42.14 Specifying advanced options for a dimension.

The Set Change Property dialog box should be set to Yes to indicate that you indeed want to allow additions, updates, and moves of members between levels without reprocessing the cube.

The Specify Ordering and Uniqueness dialog box (see Figure 42.15) allows you to specify, level-by-level, whether the following conditions occur:

- The level keys are unique with the member level or within the entire dimension.
- The names of the level members are unique among the level members, within the entire dimension, just among siblings, or not unique at all.
- Whether you prefer to order the dimension levels by the names, keys, or based on the column. By default, the dimension levels will be ordered by keys.

As you can see in Figure 42.16, the Dimension Wizard will display the final wizard dialog box allowing you to name the dimension and to preview the dimension levels. It also gives you a chance to create multiple-hierarchy dimensions if you need to provide similar, yet alternate views of the cube data. These hierarchies can be created for new or existing dimensions.

After this, you will be in the Dimension Editor, where you can create dimensions directly by adding tables, levels, and so on. You can also process the dimension here.

The upper-left pane of the Dimension Editor has the dimension structure hierarchy. Figure 42.17 shows the Dimension Editor with this dimension built. The right pane shows the tables that contribute to the dimension.

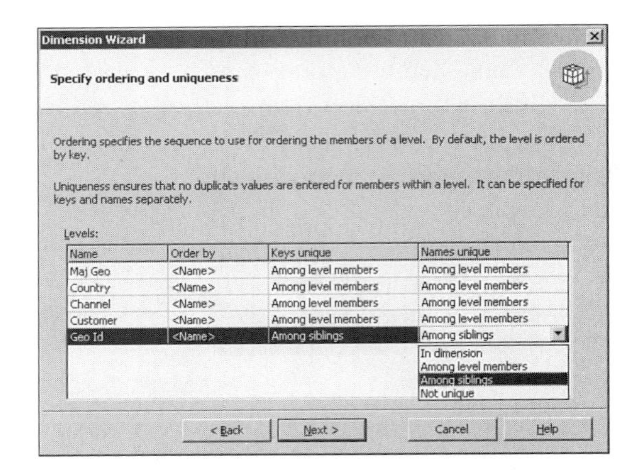

FIGURE 42.15 Specifying ordering and uniqueness for dimensions.

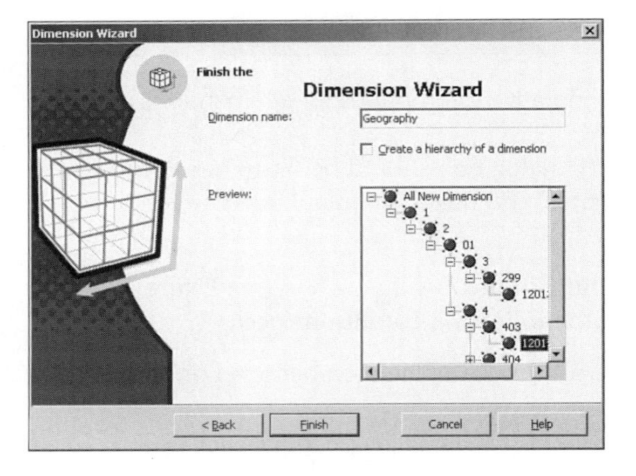

FIGURE 42.16 Finish the Dimension Wizard: Naming and Preview.

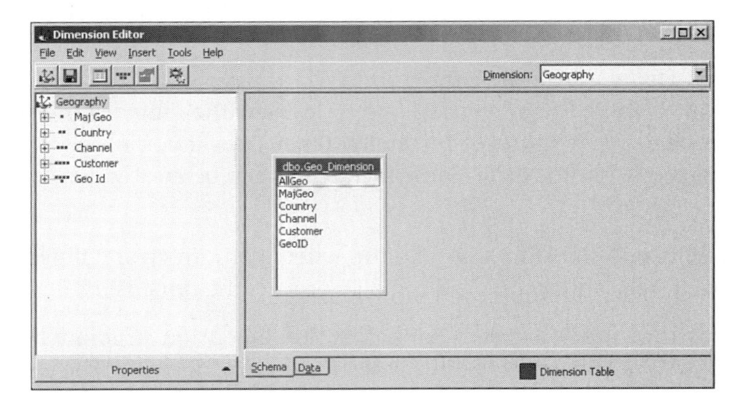

FIGURE 42.17 Dimension Editor showing the geography dimension.

By going to the Data tab of the Dimension Editor, you can preview exactly what the dimension level's members will be. Before you can use this dimension, it must be processed and have real data populated from its datasource. Simply choose the Tools option pull-down menu and click on Process Dimension to execute this. Notice that you can also initiate a count of dimension members (which is stored as a property) and even do a dynamic validation of the dimension structure if you are editing it. Figure 42.18 shows the Data tab in the Dimension Editor of the processed dimension geography.

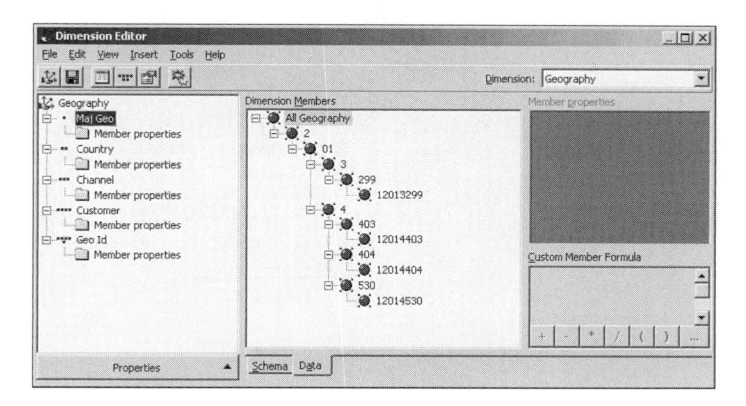

FIGURE 42.18 Data tab of the Dimension Editor.

After closing all Dimension Editors, you can view all the shared dimensions from the main Analysis Manager console under the database in which you are working (CompSales in this example). Figure 42.19 shows that three shared dimensions have been created to reflect the requirements given to you (Geography, Product, and Time dimensions).

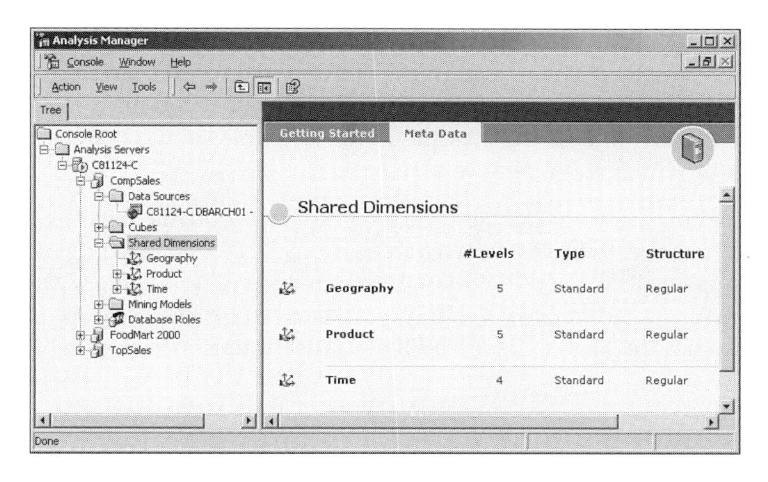

FIGURE 42.19 Meta Data view of Shared Dimensions: Geography, Product, and Time.

Building a Cube

Now that you have all of the dimensions that you need to fulfill your requirement, you can proceed to building the OLAP cube. This will entail defining the data measures you want in the cube along with the storage mode and aggregations you desire. As you can see from Figure 42.20, the Analysis Manager console shows no cubes defined for this database yet. The CompSales requirement will call for a regular cube that will be using the HOLAP storage mode to be created. To start the Cube Wizard, simply right-click the Cubes folder under a database (CompSales in your example) and select New Cube and Wizard.

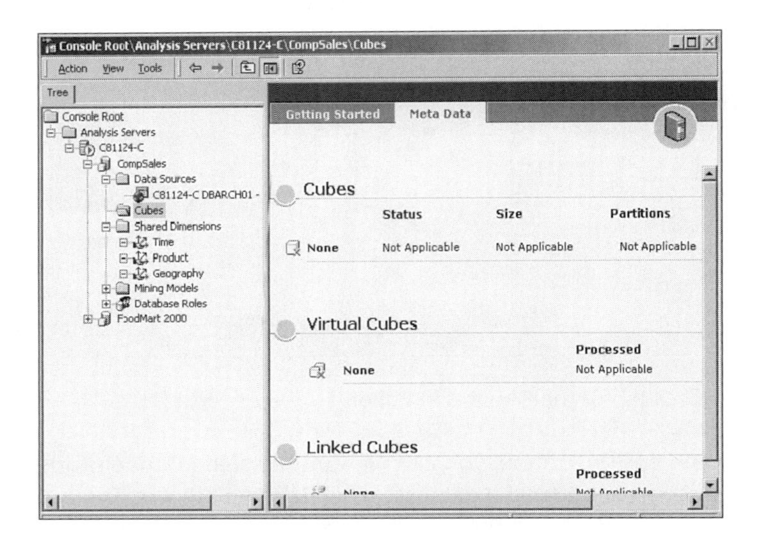

FIGURE 42.20 AS console view of cubes: None created yet!

If it is your first time in the Cube Wizard, a Welcome dialog box will greet you. (You will want to check the box Skip This Screen in the Future so you won't have to see the Welcome dialog box on subsequent visits.) In creating a cube, you must have identified a "fact" table from which to base the measures. This fact table should correlate to each of the dimensions by which you intend to access the fact.

You must be able to get to this fact table via a datasource. If one is not yet defined, add it now. Figure 42.21 shows the Select a Fact Table From a Data Source dialog box. Your CompSales example calls for you to choose the CompSalesFactoid table as the basis of your fact (measure). For any table you choose, its data can be easily browsed here as well. Figure 42.21 also has the Browse Data window of this CompSalesFactoid table's data.

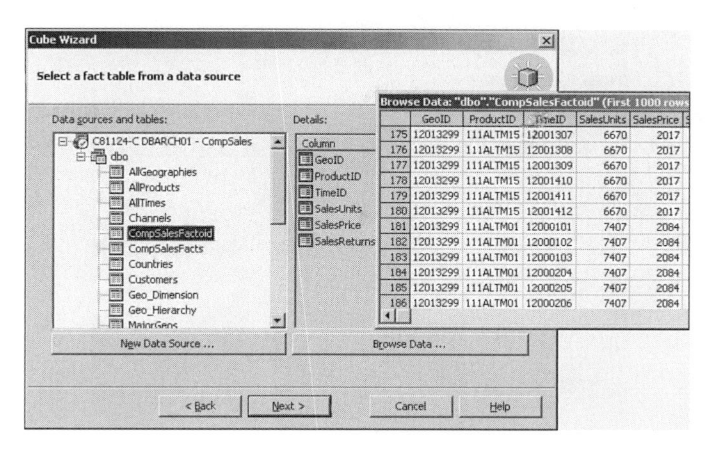

FIGURE 42.21 Selecting the datasource for a fact table and browsing data from that datasource.

Measures

The Cube Wizard now prompts you to select the numeric columns that will define your data measures in this cube. The columns that meet the CompSales requirements are the Sales_units and Sales_returns columns of the CompSalesFactoid table. Figure 42.22 shows the cube measures as you have selected them and also shows a column that you did not choose (SalesPrice). SalesPrice was not in your requirements so it won't be selected here!

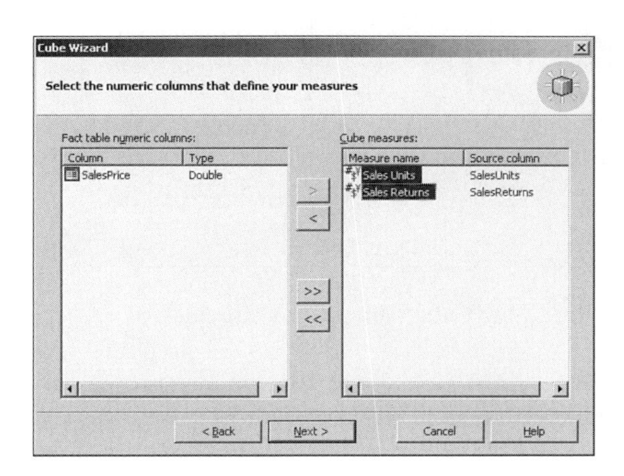

FIGURE 42.22 Identifying the numeric columns that define data measures.

At this point, you must specify the dimensions that the cube will use for these data measures. Your CompSales requirement is calling for the measures to be accessed via all three of the dimensions you defined earlier. As you can see from Figure 42.23, you select these dimensions by making them the Cube dimensions. (From the Shared Dimensions list on the left, click on the > button to move them to the right side.)

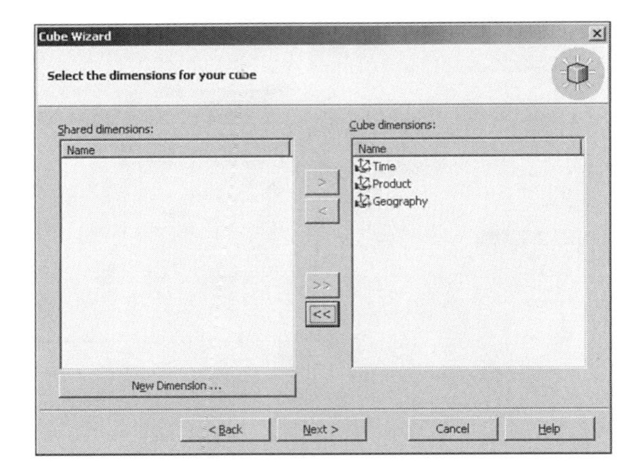

FIGURE 42.23 Specifying all dimensions for the cube.

After you are finished, the Finish the Cube Wizard screen appears, which allows you to name the cube and shows you what you have defined (see Figure 42.24).

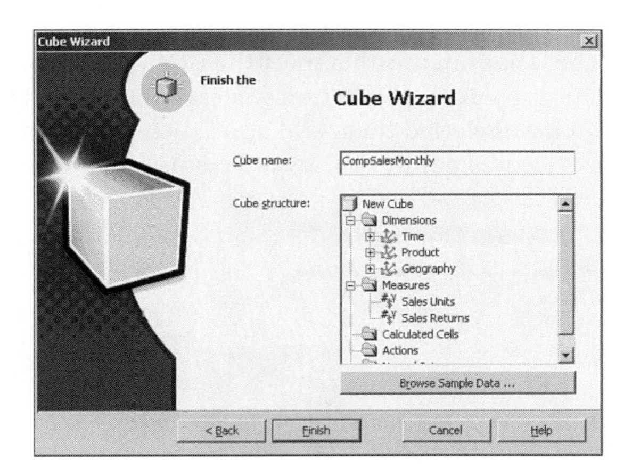

FIGURE 42.24 Finish the Cube: Cube name, Cube structure.

From the Finish the Cube Wizard dialog box, you can also browse sample data. Note that this is artificial data because the Cube has not been processed yet. Figure 42.25 illustrates this sample browsing in the Cube browser. Two out of the three dimensions are placed in the upper window pane of the Cube browser and can be manipulated easily for a particular level at which to view data. In addition, one dimension (the geography dimension in this example) has been chosen as the dimension in the lower (spreadsheet) portion of the Cube browser. The browser also displays the measures that you had defined in the Cube up to this point (sales units and sales returns). Again, remember that this data is artificial and does not reflect live data from your datasources yet. You have positioned the cube to look at product (SKU level) LTM01, for the time (year level) 1999. The geography dimension is positioned at the highest point (All Geography level).

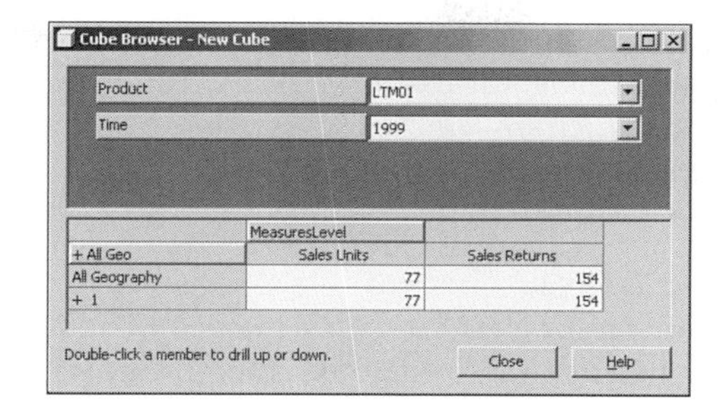

FIGURE 42.25 Browsing sample data in a cube.

After the Cube Wizard finishes, it puts you automatically into the Cube Editor (see Figure 42.26). From here, you can see the physical schema on which this cube is based and also use the data browser to drill down into data. The schema diagram shows the relationships that are being used from the dimension tables to the fact table (the keys). This diagram is often the one I share with the end user and the programmers so that they understand how the facts in the cube are represented.

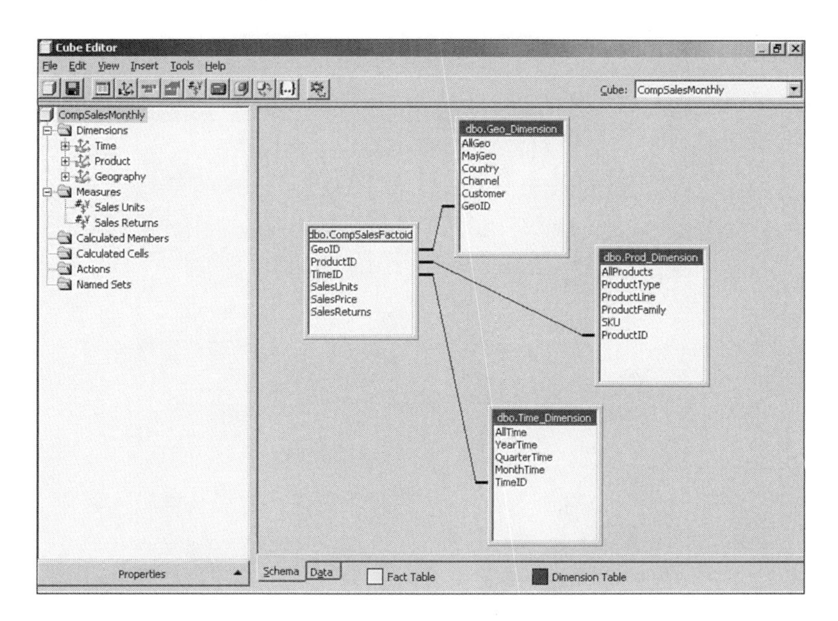

FIGURE 42.26 Cube Editor for CompSalesMonthly cube.

You must complete your requirements for this cube by adding a Calculated Member (measure) to this cube for net sales units. If you remember from the CompSales requirements, this value is the difference between sales units and sales returns (Sales_Units – Sales_Returns). Calculated member definitions are automatically stored in the Measures parent dimension. These will behave just like a physical data measure except that they are just calculated from values or functions—including registered functions—that are physically stored for data measures or available for use for functions.

Calculated Members

To create a calculated member, right-click on the Calculated Member folder or choose it from the Tools option. This takes you into the Calculated Member Builder. To fulfill your CompSales requirement, you will need to create a value expression that reflects this difference calculation (Sales_Units – Sales_Returns). Figure 42.27 illustrates how this is specified. You simply expand the Measures folder, choose the first measure you want as part of the calculation (double-clicking on it moves it into the Value Expression window). You then double-click on the minus sign (–) in the keypad for the difference calculation needed, followed by the other measure to complete the value expression. Many functions are available for use that should meet your individual calculation needs. Don't forget to name this new calculated member. (The new CompSales calculated member was named Net Sales Units.)

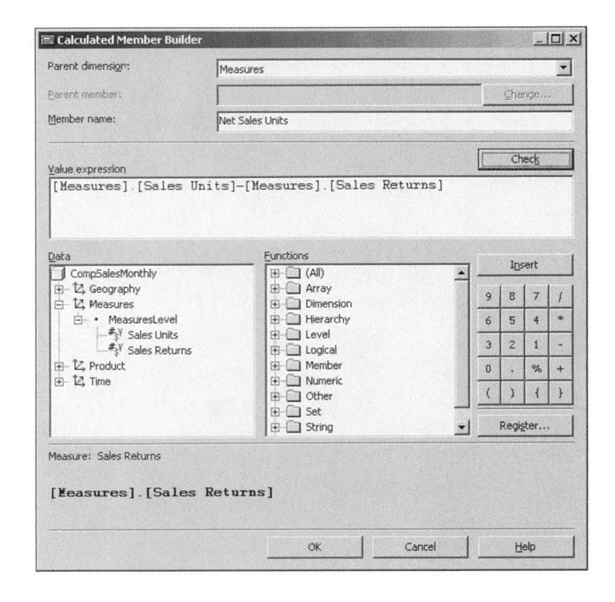

FIGURE 42.27 Calculated Member Builder.

In the Cube Editor, choose the Data tab to see how this new calculated member will look. As you can see in Figure 42.28, the Net Sales Units reflects your calculation perfectly and appears as if it is just another data measure. This fulfills the data measure requirements of CompSales.

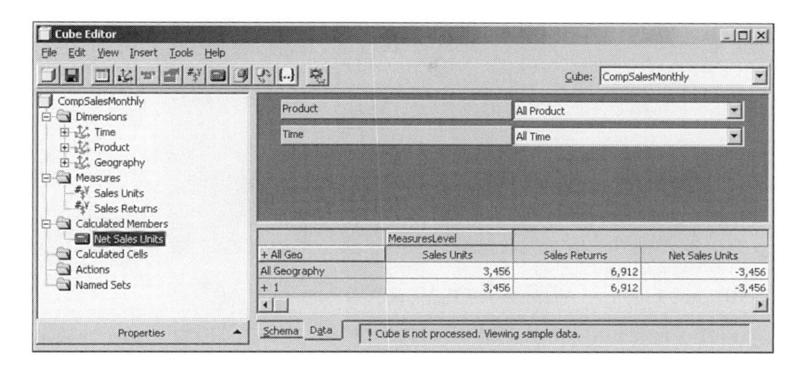

FIGURE 42.28 Cube Editor showing the newly created calculated member Net Sales Units.

All that is left to do is to design the storage for the cube and process the cube so others can use it. Here is where you decide on MOLAP, ROLAP, or HOLAP, and the degree of aggregation. The cube will physically be built differently based on these choices. If you choose to process the cube now, no storage decisions have been decided yet, so it will automatically force you to enter the Storage Design Wizard. So, why not go to this step directly?

Designing Storage

The initial Storage Design Wizard dialog box is where the primary storage method is decided. Your choices are MOLAP, ROLAP, or HOLAP storage. If you choose MOLAP, Analysis Services will build a complete multidimensional structure of detail facts, with the granularity based on the time dimension, other dimensions as you have defined them, and aggregations to the degree you select. ROLAP will use the fact table you identified in the source database and build new summary tables with dimension and fact data in the source database for aggregations. HOLAP will use the table you identified as the fact table in the source database for the detail facts and build and store the dimensions and aggregations on the Analysis Server. Figure 42.29 shows the initial Design Storage choice from the Tools menu, along with the three data storage options from which you can select. You had already decided that HOLAP made the most sense for this requirement so that you could leverage off of the existing relational fact table and also take advantage of the OLAP summary files generated by Analysis Services.

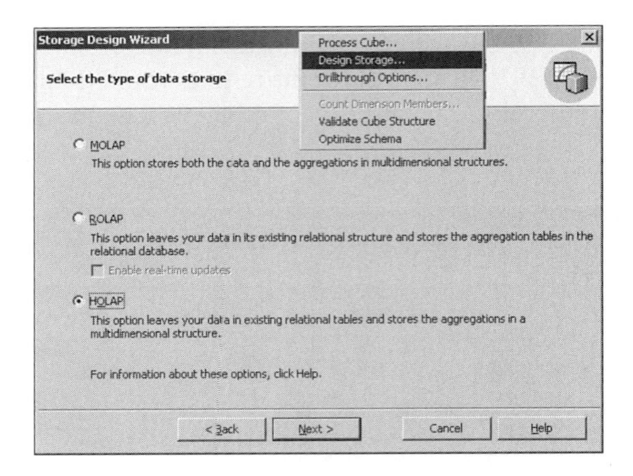

FIGURE 42.29 Storage Design Wizard: MOLAP, ROLAP, or HOLAP.

The next step is to specify the aggregation options. This determines how much data is to be aggregated and stored for use by the queries. The more you aggregate, the more disk space is required; however, you are also allowed to satisfy more queries from these aggregations. (Overall performance will be high, but disk usage will also be high.) The less aggregation you specify, the less disk space is needed; however, very few of the queries will be satisfied by the aggregations, and these will have to be performed online. (You will have less overall performance, but disk usage will be lower.) This decision is solely dependent on the following factors:

- Available disk storage to this application
- CPU power available to Analysis Services
- Processing window of this aggregation

Additionally, the amount of memory available to AS is always a performance factor, but it is not considered during the aggregation storage options.

If your company has sales transaction data for the past 5 years and 250 stores that sell an average of 1,000 items per day, the fact table will have 456,500,000 rows. This is obviously a challenge in terms of disk space by itself without aggregation tables to go along with it. The control that Analysis Services provides here is important in balancing storage and retrieval speed (performance versus size). Aggregations are built to optimize rollup operations so that higher levels of aggregation are easily derived from the existing aggregations to satisfy broader queries. If a high degree of query optimization weren't possible because of limitations in storage space, Analysis Services might choose to build aggregates of monthly or quarterly data only. If a user queried the cube for yearly or multiyear data, those aggregations would be created dynamically from the highest level of pre-aggregated data. With disk storage becoming cheaper and servers becoming more powerful, the tendency here is to opt for meeting performance gains. A recommended approach is to specify between 80–90 percent performance gain here. Figure 42.30 shows the number of aggregations that will be built to support a 100 percent performance gain selection (seven aggregations designed for your cube).

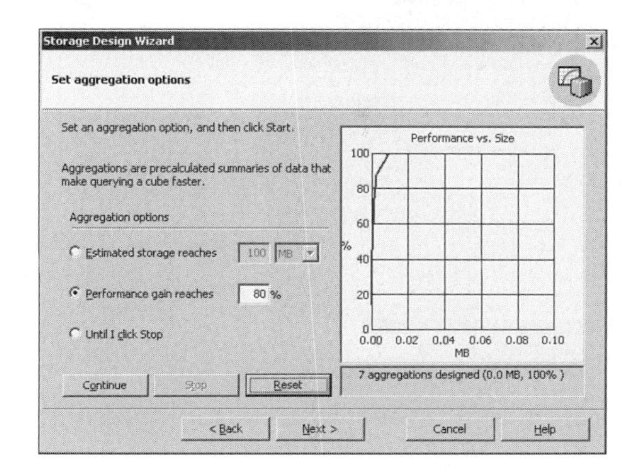

FIGURE 42.30 Number of aggregation options that can be designed for this cube.

In the Set Aggregation Options dialog box (again, refer to Figure 42.30), you could also run the Aggregation Designer and watch the graph, stopping the aggregation level when you reach a point where you are comfortable. You will notice that the performance gain might begin to flatten out at a certain point. This relies on the accuracy of the Analysis Services data estimates; however, there is a point of diminishing returns in using disk space. Going beyond this point gets you increasingly less performance for the space used. Because you can tune individual queries, you might want to cut off aggregations at a point when optimization begins to flatten out, and then tune your queries based on observation as the cube is used.

You can choose to process these aggregations now or later depending on when the cube needs to be materialized. You will certainly be reprocessing it as the data changes over time.

Processing a Cube

For the CompSales—CompSalesMonthly cube, you will choose to process now. You will be thrown into a Process dialog window and actually be able to follow the entire initialization process from start to finish. This includes the SQL statements executed against the datasources needed to generate your cube's dimensions. Depending on the amount of aggregation, this might actually take a while. At the end, all of the generated data will be committed and your cube will be processed. Figure 42.31 shows the CompSales Process dialog window.

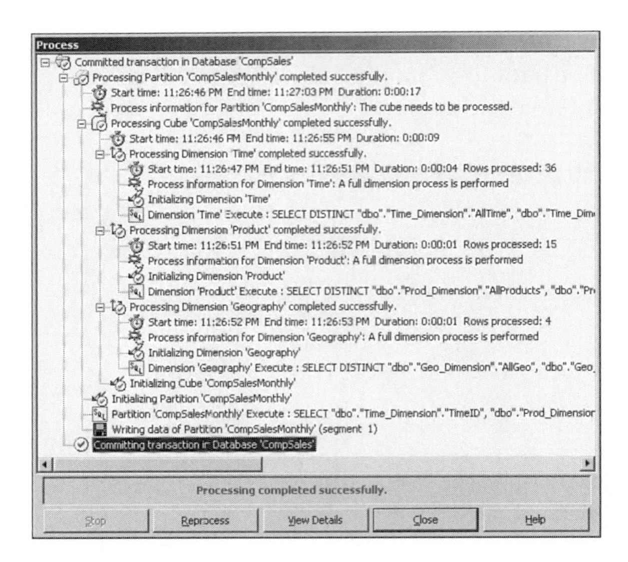

FIGURE 42.31 Process cube information dialog window.

Now you have a data cube that can be browsed from the Analysis Manager's Cube Data browser with its built-in drill-down features. Of course, this can also be browsed via the Cube Editor, Data tab. Figure 42.32 shows the completed cube view from the Analysis Manager with all of its components in place.

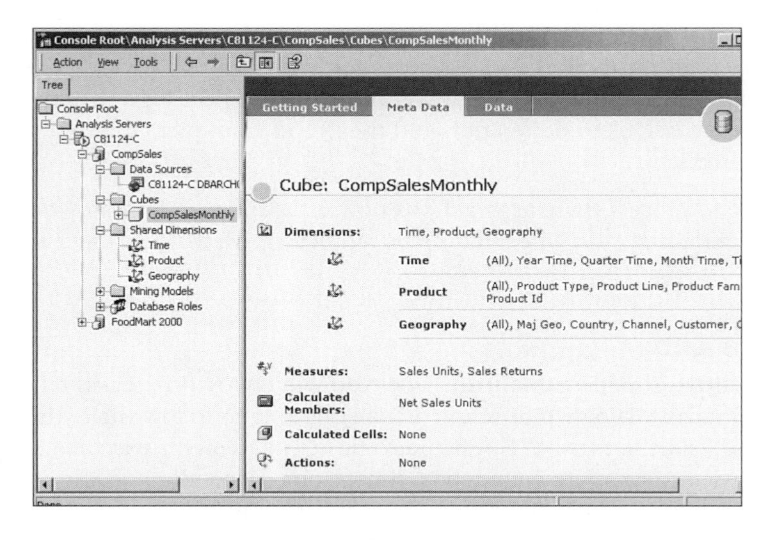

FIGURE 42.32 Meta Data view of CompSalesMonthly cube.

Using the Pivot Table Service, you can write custom client applications using Multidimensional Extensions (MDX) with OLE DB for OLAP or ActiveX Data Objects Multidimensional (ADO MD). You can also use a number of third-party OLE DB for OLAP-compliant tools to access the cube.

Browsing a Data Cube from the Analysis Manager

The Cube browser isn't a robust end user analysis tool, and it only exists on the server side. To browse data in your cube, right-click on your cube in the appropriate database (CompSales database, CompSalesMonthly cube in this example). The Cube browser opens and presents aggregated data. In Figure 42.33, the product and time dimension are in the top pane and the geography dimension and the measures (including the calculated member) are in the lower pane that looks like a spreadsheet. It is easy to move around the cube by simply drilling down deeper into each dimension to the place you want to view the data. The measure data will always reflect the data that is at the intersection of all the dimensions at the same time. In the CompSales example, it is showing measure data for Product (SKU) LTM02, for Time (year) 2000, and in Geography (MajGeo) 01.

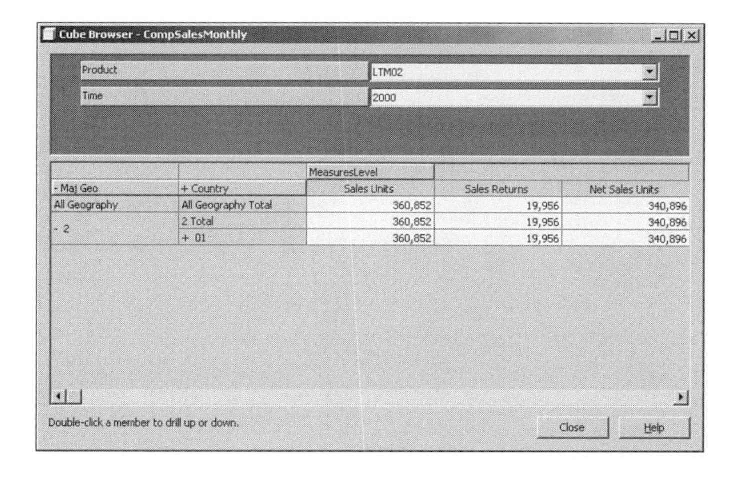

FIGURE 42.33 Cube browser of CompSalesMonthly cube.

In the Cube browser, you can drag dimensions and measures around to change the column and row headings, depending on your preference. Double-clicking Dimension Data drills down into that dimension to lower levels of granularity. Figure 42.34 shows measures along the left side of the spreadsheet, with the geography dimension along the top (the columns).

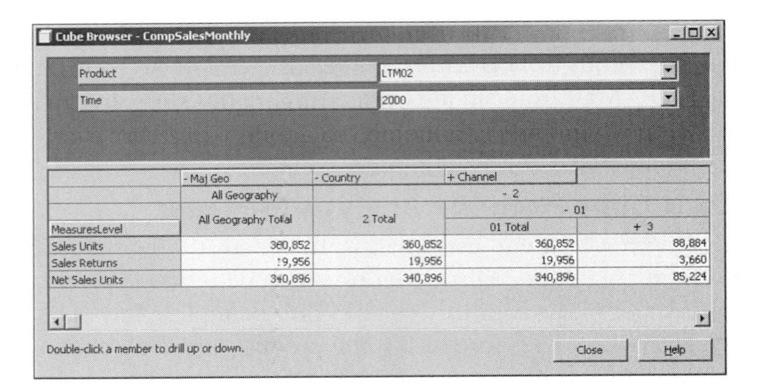

FIGURE 42.34 Cube browser with data measures as rows in the spreadsheet.

You can also drag and drop the dimension in the upper pane to become part of the lower pane spreadsheet. Figure 42.35 shows the geography and time dimensions in the spreadsheet, with measures as the selectable option in the top pane (showing Sales Units data only).

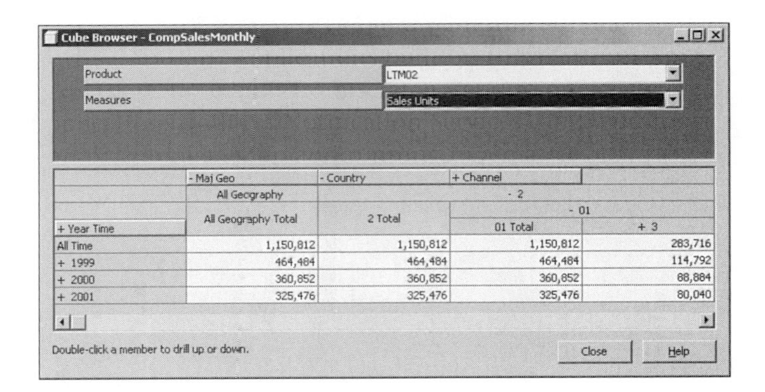

FIGURE 42.35 Cube browser with geography and time dimensions as the rows and columns of the spreadsheet.

The Cube browser shows you what your cube has in it, but also illustrates the utility of a dimensional database. Users can easily analyze data in meaningful ways. The data can also be "mined" by intelligent applications to find hidden relationships and patterns in the data that could have significant business implications.

Analysis Manager allows you to browse individual dimension data as well. Right-click the store dimension and select Browse Dimension. The Dimension browser opens with All. Expanding each level gets you to more detailed information as you move down the dimension hierarchy.

OLE DB for OLAP and ADO MD expose the interfaces to do this kind of data browsing, and many leading vendors have used these interfaces to build front-end analysis tools and ActiveX controls. These tools should prove useful for developers of user interfaces in data warehousing and data mart projects.

Query Analysis and Optimization

In the Analysis Manager, you can look at query utilization and performance in a cube. You can look at queries by user, frequency, and execution time to determine how to better optimize aggregations. If a slow-running query is used frequently by many users, or by the CEO, it might be a good candidate for individual tuning. The Analysis Manager allows you to adjust aggregations based on a query to reduce response time.

The Optimization dialog boxes will allow you to filter queries by user, frequency of execution, time frame, and execution time. You will see a record for each query you have run since the date you began, the number of times it was executed, and the average execution time in seconds. This is like a SQL trace analysis of your OLAP queries.

Because aggregations already exist, the wizard will ask whether you want to replace them or add new ones. If you replace the existing aggregations, the cube will be reprocessed with this particular query in mind.

Partitioning a Cube

Cube partitioning is another powerful feature of Microsoft Analysis Services. It allows you to deal with individual "slices" of a data cube separately, querying only the relevant datasources. If you partition by dimension, you can perform incremental updates to change that dimension independently of the rest of the cube. Consequently, you only have to reprocess aggregations affected by those changes. This is an excellent feature for scalability.

The ability to use multiple datasources is a key feature of Analysis Services because it allows you to access data on clusters of servers, retrieving only what you need from each server to satisfy the request for information. The storage methods can be different on each datasource; the only constraint is that the dimensions and facts are logically compatible in the different sources.

Separating the dimensions allows Analysis Services to query only the datasources that contain the slice of data that was requested.

In Advanced Options, you will get a dialog box that allows you to filter the data in the partition with a `WHERE` clause and to assign a prefix to the aggregation table names to distinguish them from existing aggregation tables if the ROLAP storage mode is used.

Merge combines the aggregations back into the original partition.

With well-designed partitions, a cube can be updated incrementally when it is reprocessed because the partition can be updated independently.

Creating a Virtual Cube

As mentioned previously, a virtual cube is a logical join of physical cubes; it doesn't store data. Virtual cubes are easy to build and provide great data visibility across multiple regular cubes. From within a database, invoke the New Virtual Cube Wizard from the Action menu option. Then perform the following:

1. Select the cubes to include in the virtual cube.
2. Select the measures for the virtual cube.
3. Select one or more dimensions for the virtual cube.
4. Name the virtual cube and choose when to process it. You can choose to process it now or later.

That's it. You will be able to change the virtual cube or view its data via the Virtual Cube Editor.

Working with a Relational Database

The examples you have worked to this point have been from a dimensional database that uses a star or snowflake schema.

NOTE

Designing dimensional databases is an art form and requires not only sound dimensional modeling knowledge, but also knowledge of the business processes with which you are dealing. Data warehousing has several design approaches. Regardless of which approach you take, having a good understanding of the approach's design techniques is critical to the success of a data warehouse project. Although Microsoft provides a powerful set of tools to implement data marts, astute execution of design methods is critical to getting the correct data—the truly business-significant business data—to the end users.

Analysis Services can connect to a relational database and allow you to build dimensions and define measures from it.

You would typically create something like a time dimension using a view as the dimension table and selecting the Time Dimension option. You would, of course, also select any other dimensions that you need that can be fulfilled by the relational table being accessed. After you have the dimensions, you can create a cube.

You just select another view (or the table) as the fact table and the appropriate numeric column(s) for the measures.

Process the cube as HOLAP. Select 80 percent for the Estimated Percentage of Optimization in the Aggregation option and process it. The cube should now be useable (can be browsed).

Limitations of a Relational Database

Even using a tool such as Analysis Services, you have limitations when dealing with a normalized database. Using a view can often solve (or mask) these issues. In some cases, however, more complicated facts and dimensions might require denormalized tables or a dimensional database in the storage component of the data warehouse to bring information together. Data cleansing and transformation are also major considerations before you attempt to present decision makers with data from OLTP systems.

Delivering the Data to Users

Microsoft Analysis Services provides a great deal of flexibility for building scalable OLAP solutions, but how do you present the data to users? The answer lies in the other major component of Microsoft Decision Support Services: the Pivot Table Service. This client-side component delivers much of the functionality of Analysis Services using the same code base for the dimensional calculation engine, caching, and query processing. The Pivot Table Service manages client/server connections and is the layer for user interfaces to access Analysis Services cubes through the OLE DB for OLAP interface. ActiveX Data Objects Multidimensional (ADO MD) provides an application-level programming interface for development of OLAP applications. Third-party tools and future versions of Microsoft Excel and other Microsoft Office products will use the Pivot Table Service to access cubes.

The Pivot Table Service shares metadata with the Analysis Services, so a request for data on the client causes data and metadata to be downloaded to the client. The Pivot Table Service determines whether requests need to be sent to the server or can be satisfied at the client with downloaded data. If a user requests sales information for the first quarter of 1998 and then later decides to query that data for the first quarter of 1997 for comparison, only the request for 1997 data has to go to the server to get more data. The 1998 data is cached on the client.

Slices of data that are retrieved to the client computer can also be saved locally for analysis when the client computer is disconnected from the network. Users can download the data in which they are interested and analyze it offline. The Pivot Table Service can also create simple OLAP databases by accessing OLE-DB–compliant datasources.

With the ADO MD interface, developers will be able to access and manipulate objects in an Analysis Services database, enabling Web-based OLAP application development.

Many independent software vendors (ISVs) such as Brio are working with Microsoft to leverage the rich features of the OLAP Services. They offer robust user interfaces that can access Analysis Services and Pivot Table Service functionality. Versions of Microsoft Office will include the Pivot Table Service to enable built-in analysis in tools such as Excel.

Multidimensional Expressions

The OLE DB for OLAP specification contains Multidimensional Expressions (MDX) syntax that is used to build datasets from cubes. Developers of OLE DB OLAP providers can map MDX syntax to SQL statements or native query languages of other OLAP servers, depending on storage techniques.

MDX statements build datasets by using information about cubes from which the data will be read. This includes the number of axes to include, the dimensions on each axis and the level of nesting, the members or member tuples and sort order of each dimension, and the dimension members used to filter, or slice, the data. **Tuples** are combinations of dimensions such as time and product time that present multidimensional data in a two-dimensional dataset.

An MDX statement has three basic parts:

- Dimension, measure, and axis information in the `SELECT` clause
- The source cube in the `FROM` clause
- Dimension slicing in the `WHERE` clause

Expressions in an MDX statement operate on numbers, strings, members, tuples, and sets. Numbers and strings mean the same thing here as they do in other programming contexts. Members are the values in a dimension, and levels are groups of members. If the dimension were time, then a particular year, quarter, or month would be a member, and month values would belong to the month level. Use the dimension browser in the Analysis Manager to view members of a dimension. Sets are collections of tuple elements to further combine facts.

An example of an MDX statement and its results in the MDX sample application that installs with Microsoft DSS are shown in Figure 42.36. You can launch the sample MDX application from the Analysis Services program group (MDX Sample Application program item).

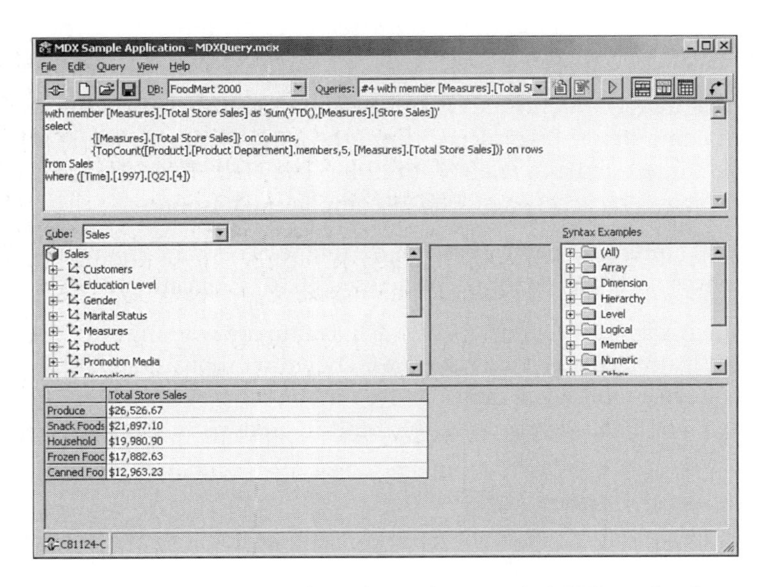

FIGURE 42.36 An MDX statement and results in the sample MDX application.

This is a simple MDX statement that shows the basic parts of a working query. In this case, measures are displayed in columns, and product and store dimension members make up the axes of this multidimensional query and are displayed in rows. The display of multiple dimensions in rows like this is how the term *tuple* is used in the context of Microsoft Analysis Services.

A number of other examples are included in the sample MDX application using the FoodMart2000 sample database.

Much more could be said about MDX syntax, and a complete discussion of MDX is probably worth its own chapter. The OLE DB for OLAP Programmers Reference is available on the Microsoft Web site at `http://msdn.microsoft.com/library/default. asp?url=/libraryen-us/oledb/htm/olapintroduction_to_ole_db_for_olap.asp`. It contains detailed information about MDX.

ActiveX Data Objects Multidimensional

ActiveX Data Objects Multidimensional (ADO MD) is an easy-to-use access method for dimensional data via an OLE DB for OLAP provider. You can use ADO MD in Visual Basic, Visual C++, and Visual J++. Like ADO, ADO MD offers a rich application-development environment that can be used for multitier client/server and Web application development.

You can retrieve information about a cube, or metadata, and execute MDX statements using ADO MD to create "cellsets" to return interesting data to a user. ADO MD is another subject too broad to cover in detail in this chapter. Specifications for OLE DB for OLAP and ADO MD are available on the Microsoft Web site at `www.microsoft.com`.

Files at the Operating System Level

Figure 42.37 shows the underlying data files that are generated for the cube. This is the Windows Explorer window of the directory that is created for the Analysis Services database (CompSales in this example). Do not modify or erase any of these files or subdirectories! You can also see subdirectories for each cube and for data mining models.

Security in Analysis Services

Security is straightforward in Analysis Services. For each database or cube, roles are identified with varying levels of granularity for users. It is these roles that are used when accessing the data in the cubes. The way it works is that a role is defined and then an individual user or group who is a member of that role (at the NT/Windows level) is assigned that role. Figure 42.38 shows the creation of a database role. You can see where the role will be enforced (such as at the server), and what rules should apply at a dimensional level. All users and groups of a database role have the same access unless it was overridden in cube roles of the same name.

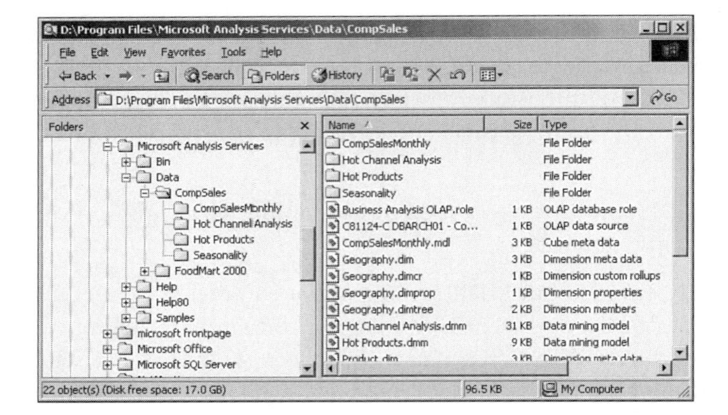

FIGURE 42.37 Physical files of AS at the operating system level.

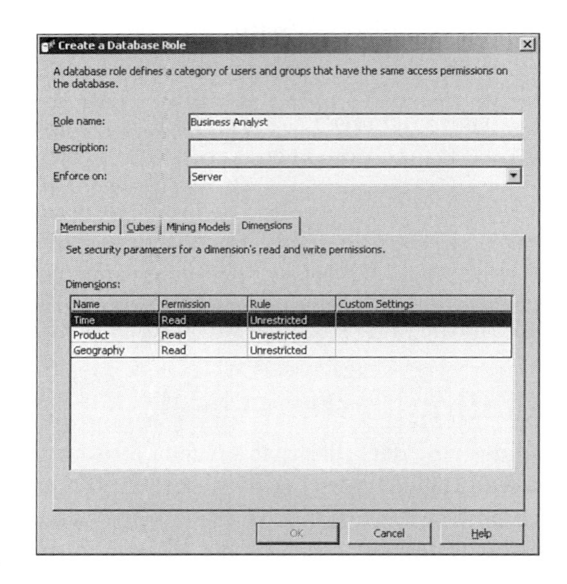

FIGURE 42.38 Creating a database role for cube access.

Data Mining Models

With Analysis Services, the feature of defining OLAP data mining models has arrived. **Data mining** is the process of understanding potentially undiscovered characteristics or distributions of data. Data mining can be extremely useful for OLAP database design in that patterns or values might define different hierarchy levels or dimensions that were not previously known. As you create dimensions, you can even choose a data mining model as the basis for a dimension.

Basically, a data mining model is a virtual structure that represents the grouping and predictive analysis of relational or multidimensional data. It is composed of rules, patterns, and other statistical information of the data that it was analyzing. These are called **cases**. A **case set** is simply a way of viewing the physical data. Different case sets can be constructed from the same physical data. Basically, a case is defined from a particular point of view. If the algorithm you are using supports the view, you can use mining models to make predictions based on these findings.

Another aspect of a data mining model is that of using training data. This is a process that determines the relative importance of each attribute in a data mining model. It does this by recursively partitioning data into smaller groups until no more splitting can occur. During this partitioning process, information is gathered from the attributes used to determine the split. Probability can be established for each categorization of data in these splits. It is this type of data that can be used to help determine factors about other data that is utilizing these probabilities. This training data, in the form of dimensions, levels, member properties and measures, is used to process the OLAP data mining model and further define the data mining column structure for the case set.

In Analysis Services, Microsoft provides two primary types of data mining algorithms; decision trees and clustering. (Other algorithms are accessible via different providers.)

To create an OLAP data mining model, Analysis Services will use a source OLAP cube, a particular data mining technique/algorithm, case dimension and level, predicted entity, and training data. The source OLAP cube provides the information needed to create a case set for the data mining model. It will use a dimension and level that you will choose to establish key columns for the case sets. You then select the data mining technique (decision tree, clustering, or one from another provider). The case dimension and level provide a certain orientation for the data mining model into the cube for creating a case set. The predicted entity can be either a measure from the source OLAP cube, a member property of the case dimension and level, or any member of another dimension in the source OLAP cube.

NOTE

The wizard can also create a new dimension for the source cube or a virtual cube based on the source cube. This enables users to query the data mining data model data just as they would query OLAP data.

By right-clicking on the Mining Model folder, a new mining model can be defined (Wizard). You will be given the option of either creating your mining model from relational data or OLAP data. Figure 42.39 shows this option. The purpose of the new mining model that this example will show you is that of determining product sales characteristics. It will be based on the information you built in your CompSales OLAP cube.

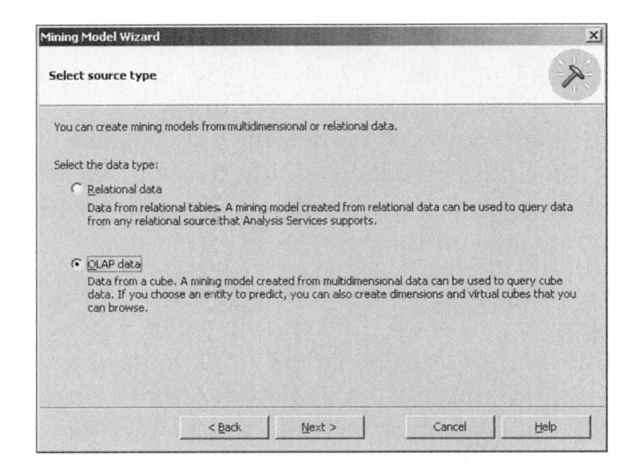

FIGURE 42.39 Creating a mining model from relational data or OLAP data.

You will now select the source OLAP cube in which you want to base your data mining model. Your example will select the CompSalesMonthly cube within the CompSales databases (see Figure 42.40).

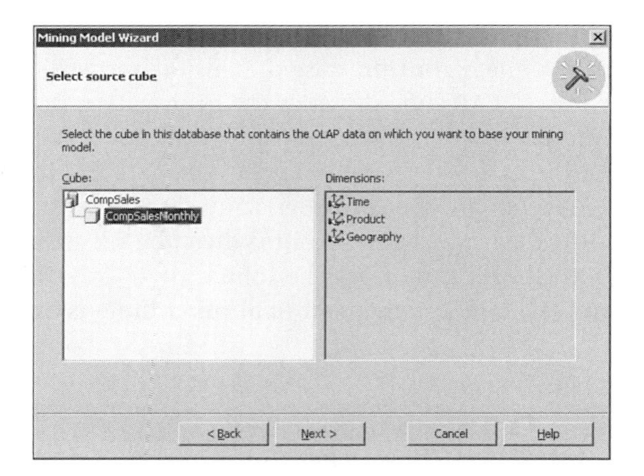

FIGURE 42.40 Identifying the OLAP source cube for the mining model basis.

You must now select the data mining technique of either clustering, or decision trees. The following describes these algorithms in more detail:

- Clustering—This algorithm finds natural groupings of data in a multidimensional space. It is useful when you want to see general groupings in your data, such as hot spots.

- Decision trees—This algorithm chooses significant characteristics in the data and narrows down sets of data based on those characteristics until clear correlations are established. Decision trees are helpful when you want to make specific predictions based on characteristics of the source data, such as products that have similar sales patterns.

You will then select the case or point of view for the analysis. Figure 42.41 illustrates the case to be based on the product dimension and at the SKU level (individual product level).

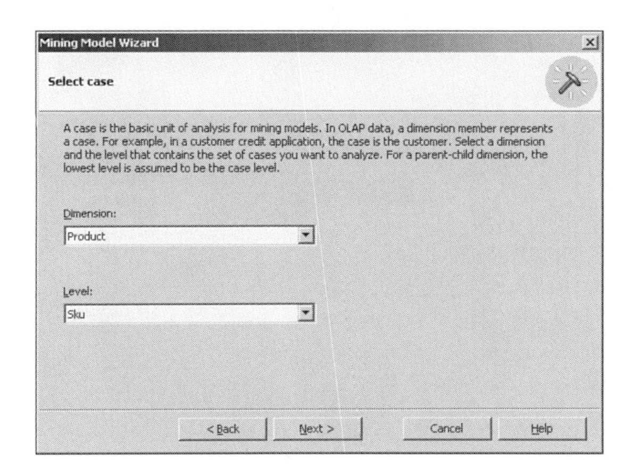

FIGURE 42.41 Identifying the basic unit of analysis for the mining model.

You will now establish the training data for this mining model to be that of the case dimension (the default) and, optionally, at least one other piece of data on which to base it (see Figure 42.42).

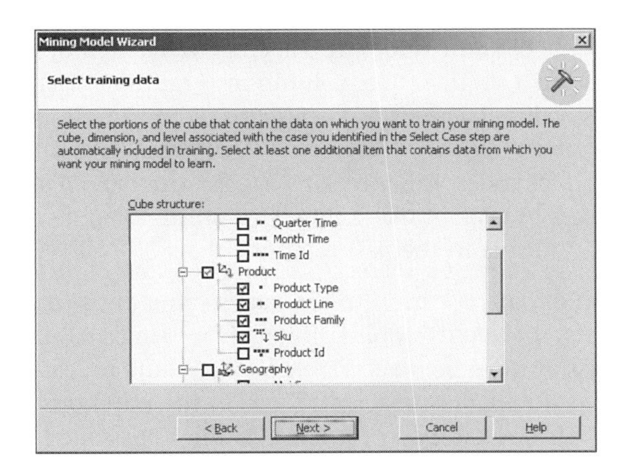

FIGURE 42.42 Identifying the training data for the mining model.

The mining model is now specified and must be processed. When it has finished executing, you will be automatically taken into the Mining Model Editor. Here you can delve into the discovered characteristics of your mining model as well as change options and reprocess the model (see Figure 42.43).

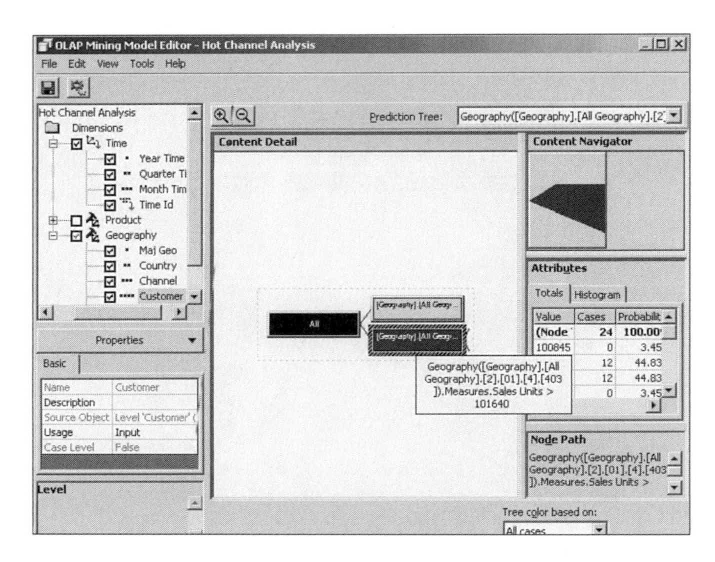

FIGURE 42.43 OLAP Mining Model Editor with results of processing.

Data Transformation Services

Microsoft Data Transformation Services (DTS) provides a means to move data between sources. Data can be exported, validated, cleaned up, consolidated, transformed, and then imported into the destination.

You can combine multiple column values into a single calculated destination column or divide column values from a single source column into multiple destination columns. You might need to translate values in operational systems. For example, many OLTP systems use product codes that are stored as numeric data. Few people are willing to memorize an entire collection of product codes. An entry of 100235 for a type of shampoo in a product dimension table is useless to a VP of marketing who is interested in how much of that shampoo was sold in California in the past quarter.

Cleanup and validation of data is critical to the data's value in the data warehouse. The old saying "garbage in, garbage out" applies. If data is missing, redundant, or inconsistent, then high-level aggregations can be inaccurate, so you should at least know that these conditions exist. Perhaps the data is rejected for use in the warehouse until the source data can be reconciled. If the shampoo of interest to the VP is called "Shamp" in one database and "Shampoo" in another, then aggregations on either value do not produce complete information about the product.

The DTS package defines the steps in a transformation workflow. You can execute the steps serially and in combinations of serial, parallel, or conditional. For more information on Microsoft DTS, refer to Chapter 20, "Importing and Exporting SQL Server Data Using BCP and DTS."

The Metadata Repository

The Repository is a sharable metadata information store that supports the data warehouse environment by maintaining technical information on datasources and targets, transformations and mapping (such as DTS packages), data cleanup and enhancement rules, and scheduling. Business metadata is stored for end users to facilitate use of the data warehouse. You can also store query and report definitions and documentation in the Repository.

The Repository is based on the Unified Modeling Language (UML) with Microsoft Extensions to provide a common data warehousing infrastructure. Object sharing and reuse is implemented in a visual component manager for Visual Studio.

The Repository is installed by default in the msdb database in the Workgroup and Enterprise Editions of SQL Server. A SQL server can contain multiple Repositories, but DTS supports only a single Repository database per server in SQL Server Enterprise Manager.

OLAP Performance Discussions

Recently, a data warehousing manager revealed her frustration with the OLAP performance she was getting (using HOLAP and MOLAP approaches) with Analytic Services. This was put to rest by relocating the OLAP physical storage components on a new Solid State disk device (a persistent memory device). The performance gains were tenfold. The price of this type of technology has dramatically been reduced within the last 12 months and the ease of transparently applying this type of solution to OLAP was a natural fit. It affected both the OLAP data population process as well as the day-to-day "what if" usage by the end users. Keep these types of surgical incisions in mind when faced with OLAP performance issues in this platform. They are easy to apply, the gains are huge, and the ROI is quickly attained.

Summary

This chapter discussed extensively the OLAP approach, OLAP terms, and the tools from Microsoft to enable OLAP cubes. It presented a mini-methodology to follow that should help you get an OLAP project off the ground and running smoothly. These efforts are typically not simple, and a well-trained data warehouse analyst or data architect is usually worth his weight in gold because of the end results (and value) that can be achieved with a good OLAP cube design.

Sometimes it is difficult to engage the end users and get them to use the OLAP cube successfully. Easy-to-use third-party tools can greatly help with this problem.

From an Analysis Services point of view, the ease of control of storage methods, dimension creation, degrees of aggregation, cube partitioning, and usage-based optimization are features that make this product a serious data warehousing tool. Through the Pivot Table Service, easy publication of this data can be achieved via Web sites or other means. AS is truly the "land of the wizards," but having a wizard lead you down through a good OLAP cube design is critical. The expense and complexity of a data warehouse or data mart OLAP solution will be significantly reduced, enabling you to build many more, much needed, solutions for your end users.

The next chapter, "Microsoft Transaction Server," will venture into the realm of the Microsoft Transaction Server (MTS). This powerful feature enables cross-site and cross-dbms transactions to be defined and managed by MTS that are guaranteed to have 100 percent transactional integrity.

CHAPTER **43**

Microsoft Transaction Server

by Paul Bertucci

IN THIS CHAPTER

- MTS Overview
- Building an MTS Component
- Installing an MTS Component
- Configuring Security
- Running an MTS Application
- Using Database Connection Pooling

Microsoft Transaction Server (MTS) is an important foundation of the Microsoft server offerings. MTS is intended to simplify the development and deployment of multitiered applications built using Microsoft Component Object Model (COM) technologies. This is what Enterprise Java Beans (EJB and J2EE) set out to do.

MTS has truly evolved into an architecture, rather than just a transaction server. The name MTS is really a mislabeling of what comes with this feature. As MTS is integrated deeper into COM+ in the future, MTS will probably lose its current name in favor of something more accurate. In fact, MTS has rapidly been folded into the COM+ environment and is becoming the choice of developers for developing scalable, multitiered, production-quality applications with distributed object technologies. And, if you haven't noticed yet, the .NET framework is using the COM+ functionality for much of its capabilities.

One thing that might get a little blurred in this chapter is that SQL Server 2000 is just a companion to MTS (using MS DTC as a cross-server coordinator and SQL Server 2000 as just another resource manager). It is my hope that this will not diminish the essential position of SQL Server 2000 as an important part of the MTS architecture.

MTS Overview

MTS plays a key role in Microsoft's vision for distributed systems. The primary objective of MTS is to take care of many of the functions required to build robust distributed applications that can gracefully handle a large number of requests. Custom software components that are installed under MTS control can take advantage of these MTS features. Figure 43.1 shows a typical three-tiered system architecture that would be deployed using MTS. This illustration shows both standard client applications and Web-based applications sharing a common MTS-based infrastructure.

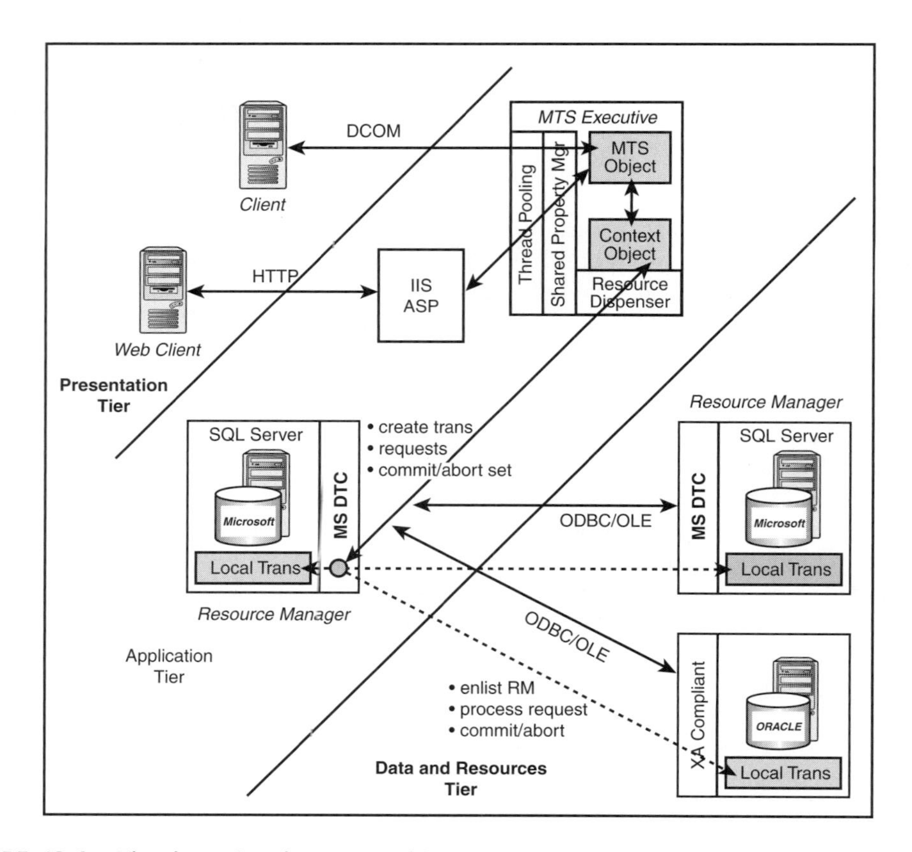

FIGURE 43.1 The three-tiered system architecture using MTS.

The success that Microsoft has experienced with MTS revolves around allowing developers to build these multitiered applications by providing a true component-oriented runtime environment that will all but eliminate writing traditional infrastructure code. This is not a dream. It's reality.

MTS is built entirely on COM. Developers can use many different development tools—such as Visual Basic—easily within this environment. The COM-based architecture simplifies object use and reuse, and administrators perform management tasks via drag-and-drop GUIs. MTS also includes automatic transaction support, role-based security, the ability to access most major databases, message queuing product integration, and mainframe-based application integration. As Figure 43.1 also illustrates, MTS is fully integrated with IIS and Active Server Pages (ASP) for ease of Internet/intranet application development. MTS is also positioned for high performance by tackling the hard subjects of database connection pooling, shared property management, and thread pooling.

Why Use Transaction Server?

MTS is a complex product, and the techniques for building a distributed system that includes MTS are different from standard coding techniques. However, the criteria for whether to use MTS is probably getting fuzzier. First, because MTS comes with most of the high-profile Windows operating systems (Windows NT, Windows 2000, and so on), it is rarely a barrier to just start using MTS. It is already there. Second, because MTS offers such things as connection pooling, automatic transactions, thread pooling, IIS/ASP integration, and MSMQ integration, the reasons not to leverage off of this built-in capability are few. And, third, MTS is essentially a formal system architecture (much like J2EE/EJB is), but it is already available and is production worthy. A short discussion of some of the highlights of MTS will make things more clear.

Connection Pooling

The connection pooling feature of MTS allows multiple clients or components to share a limited pool of database connections. This saves time and resources that would otherwise be used to open, close, and maintain database connections.

Multiserver Transactions

A close working partner of MTS is the Distributed Transaction Coordinator. This is truly the distributed transaction workhorse of MTS. MTS and DTC can coordinate transactions across multiple back-end databases (see Figure 43.1). This allows the developer to commit or roll back all changes with one MTS managed statement. For more information on MS DTC, refer to Chapter 32, "Distributed Transaction Processing."

Automatic Transaction Management

MTS provides automatic transaction management services to components. All the developer or administrator has to do is use a simple property page interface to specify what level of transaction protection is required by a given component. Then, at runtime, MTS performs all required transaction management automatically. This greatly simplifies development and facilitates component reuse.

Shared Property Manager

MTS provides a Shared Property Manager to simplify programming of components that need to save state information or share state with other components.

Thread Pooling

The thread pooling feature of MTS automatically assigns threads to components from a preallocated pool. When a component finishes executing, MTS reclaims the thread. This greatly reduces the overhead of thread creation/deletion for better overall performance and scalability.

Object Instance Management

MTS creates instances of components on the server only when requested and reclaims memory resources when the component finishes executing. This form of just-in-time (JIT) activation and as-soon-as-possible deactivation minimizes memory requirements on server machines.

Validation/Authentication

Client applications and users can be validated/authenticated at the time they call an MTS component. This feature can simplify database administration in an *n*-tier application by moving most security functionality from the database to the middle tier in MTS. For details, see "Configuring Security" later in this chapter.

Client Administration

MTS comes with an automatic client setup feature. Using the client setup program, an administrator can readily configure client machines to access components that are hosted on a remote MTS machine.

MTS Fundamental Processing Basics

Any component in MTS control must create a reference to its MTS Context Object. Creating this reference enables the component to take advantage of MTS services, such as transaction and security support. It is customary *not* to save the state information across transaction boundaries within components. States are best kept in databases or in the Shared Property Manager (SPM) and retrieved by components when needed.

You can also call other objects from within an MTS component call to the `CreateInstance()` method. When components complete execution, they must call the SetComplete method on the MTS Context Object. This tells MTS that the component wants to commit any work it has performed when all components involved in the transaction are finished executing. If a component cannot execute successfully, it must call the SetAbort method on the MTS Context Object. This will tell MTS that it should abort the current transaction and roll back all changes made by components involved in the transaction. A basic MTS component pseudocode template would look like the following:

```
Set ObjectContext = GetObjectContext()
     (some application code here)
Set ObjXYZ = ctxObject.CreateInstance()
     (some application code here)
if (everything OK)
     ObjectContext.SetComplete
Else
     ObjectContext.SetAbort
```

The preceding is not executable code, just a functional template illustration. The exact coding technique will vary depending on the program in which you are coding. Now take a look at how to get started with MTS.

Setting Up Transaction Server

The setup of MTS is fairly straightforward. If you haven't installed software from the option pack associated with your operating system, then you probably don't have MTS yet. Keep the following issues in mind:

- MTS comes bundled with the NT Option Pack. The NT Option Pack is available in the Enterprise Edition of Visual Studio, the Universal MSDN subscription, or from the Microsoft Web site at `www.microsoft.com/windows/downloads/default.asp`.
- MTS can be installed on any of the 32-bit platforms that Microsoft has, just like SQL Server 2000. Check the documentation for restrictions on Windows 95/98 installations of MTS.
- It is safe to install SQL Server 2000 after installing MTS. In previous versions of SQL Server, you had to reinstall MTS.
- It is highly recommended that you install the MTS samples code during this installation. Often, it will require you to choose the Custom Installation option and then make sure you get all MTS boxes checked. Some are not installed as the default. The sample code is great for learning MTS capabilities. A couple of code samples are available, including a banking package called Sample Bank and even Tic-Tac-Toe.
- If MTS is installed on a server whose role is a primary or backup domain controller, a user must be a domain administrator to manage packages in the MTS Explorer.

MTS Explorer

After MTS has been installed, you can use the MTS Explorer to view all services that relate to MTS (including MTS), such as Microsoft SQL Server and OLAP Servers. With MTS Explorer, you have the ability to trace messages, see the active transaction list (and ID), and observe the transaction statistics since the last time MS DTC was started. As you can see in Figure 43.2, the MTS Explorer is simply a snap-in for the Microsoft Management Console.

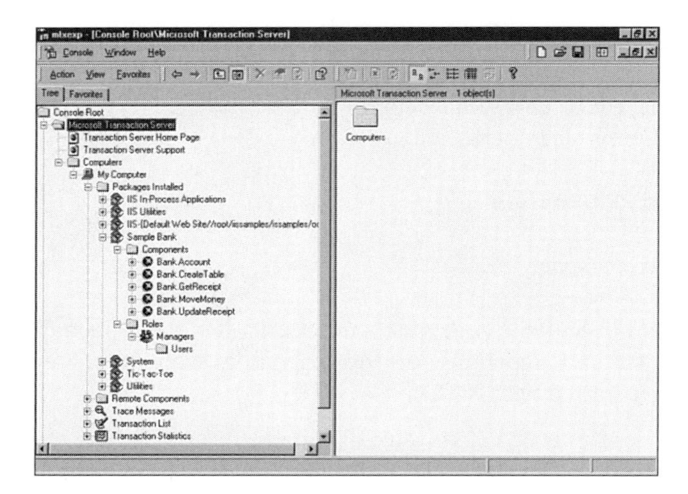

FIGURE 43.2 The MTS Explorer snap-in in Microsoft Management Console.

Learning the MTS Hierarchy

The MTS Explorer is also a good place to view the objects within MTS. These objects are organized into a hierarchy. You should be able to see this hierarchy in Figure 43.2 starting from the Microsoft Transaction Server node and working your way down through the tree to Installed Packages, Components, and Roles.

Some of the important items in the MTS hierarchy are described in Table 43.1.

TABLE 43.1 Items in the MTS Hierarchy

Item	Comments
Computers folder	Several computers with MTS can be managed from one console.
Packages Installed folder	Each computer can have several packages installed; all of these packages are contained in the Packages Installed folder.
Package	One package can contain many components. Components within a package share a process, so calls between them are fast.
Components folder	Each package can contain several components; these components are contained in the Components folder.
Component	A component is the item that outside applications actually call. You can set certain security and transaction support properties at the component level.
Role	A role is the primary security mechanism in MTS. Each package can have its own set of roles defined.

Building an MTS Component

This section examines the fundamentals of building components for MTS. MTS components have several important coding techniques, but describing these techniques is beyond the scope of this book. Earlier, this chapter outlined the basic coding template for MTS components. All examples in this chapter will adhere to this template. To make this even more relevant for SQL Server 2000, this chapter will focus on the pivotal elements of a data access component that allow it to participate in the transactional environment.

You can use several development tools to develop Component Object Model (COM) components for MTS. The examples in this chapter use Visual J++.

The `ObjectContext`

The `ObjectContext` is the mechanism that MTS components use to access the MTS runtime environment. The `ObjectContext` informs a component about the context within which it is operating. For example, a component can discover the security permissions of the client application through the `ObjectContext`.

The most important function of the `ObjectContext` is tying together the work of several components into a logical transaction. You can configure components such that if one component aborts, all the other components in the logical transaction will abort as well.

Listing 43.1 shows how a component can obtain a reference to the `ctxObject` using the `GetObjectContext()` function. The role of the calling user is also checked via the `ctxObject.IsCallerInRole` statement. In this case, the calling user must be in the Manager's role if the users are updating the balance of the Account table with a value greater than $500. The `ctxObject.SetComplete` statement informs the `ObjectContext` that the method was successful; the `ctxObject.SetAbort` statement informs the `ObjectContext` that the method was aborted.

LISTING 43.1 Using `GetObjectContext()`, `IsCallerInRole SetComplete`, and `SetAbort` in Java

```
Filename: Account.java
Package Account;
Import com.ms.mtx.*;
Import com.ms.com.*;
Import msado15.*;
Public class Account implements iAccount {
// Get a reference to the MTS Runtime Environment
   IObjectContext ctxObject = MTx.GetObjectContext()
// Check if user has right role for the bank trans(>$500)
   if ((lngAmount > 500 || lngAmount < -500) &&
    !ctxObject.IsCallerInRole ("Managers"))
                     throw new ComFailException ("need right role")'
```

LISTING 43.1 Continued

```
// more code here that might update database files (later example)

// then finally can set complete or abort the transaction

    if (bSuccess)
                ctxObject.SetComplete();
    else
               ctxObject.SetAbort();
```

Methods for Database Activities

Many MTS components include some type of data access functionality. This chapter will use data access components to demonstrate the interaction between MTS and SQL Server 2000. The same account class with a database update code is in Listing 43.2.

This code establishes a connection to the ODBC datasource named MTSSamples, which is pointing to SQL Server 2000 and the Pubs database. As you can see in Figure 43.3, the MTS installation already provided the ODBC entry. All you have to do is point it to a valid MS SQL Server with a Pubs database.

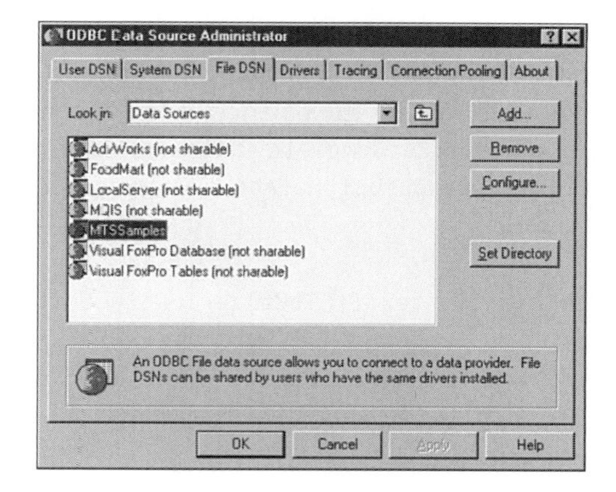

FIGURE 43.3 The ODBC datasource entry for MTSSamples.

At that point, the Account Java class will create the Account table in the Pubs database if the table doesn't exist. Following is the code to update the Account table's balance column with the supplied value.

LISTING 43.2 Using an MTS Component for Database Access

```
Public class Account implements iAccount {
// Get a reference to the MTS run-time environment
   IObjectContext ctxObject = MTx.GetObjectContext()
try {
// Create ADOConnection object and initialize the connection
   adoConn = (_Connection) new Connection();
   String vDSN = "FILEDSN=MTSSamples";
   adoConn.Open (vDSN, null, null, CommandTypeEnum.adCmdUnspecified);
// Obtain the desired record set with an SQL query
    Variant   vRowCount = new Variant();
    String strSQL = "UPDATE Account SET Balance = Balance + " + lngAmount +
                  " WHERE AccountNo = " + lngAccountNo;
    adoConn.Execute (strSQL, vRowCount, - 1);

// other appropriate code like calls to other components
//   (that will be automatically enlisted)

    finally {
// then finally can set complete or abort the transaction
    if (bSuccess)
              ctxObject.SetComplete();
    else
             ctxObject.SetAbort();
```

The details of the syntax are not important here; simply note the sequence of events in the function:

1. The component obtains a reference to MTS.
2. The component connects to needed datasources.
3. The component performs its work, such as updates.
4. Other components are enlisted in the transaction via the `CreateInstance()` function (optional).
5. The component either completes or aborts its transaction.

TIP

A component that is hosted by MTS cannot have more than 1,024 methods.

If you look back at Figure 43.1, you can trace the actual execution path that a request takes as it executes under MTS. It is interesting to note the facility that is being touched and the action that is occurring along the way. A common sequence is as follows:

- An MTS application is invoked from a DCOM client request.
- The MTS application is turned into an MTS transaction request.
- The resource dispenser determines whether any resource managers need to be enlisted and ODBC enlists them as they are referenced in a request.
- Because resource managers are needed by this request, MS DTCs handle all requests at each resource manager location.
- All enlisted resources are known to MTS.
- Each resource manager processes its specific request (updates, inserts, deletes, and so on) and returns an outcome of commit or abort. Remember: MS DTC is the one handling all of the two-phased commits across multiple resource managers.
- MTS then looks at these results before the MTS transaction completes and is either successful as a whole or not, in which case all resource managers would need to abort their individual, local transactions accordingly.
- Finally, the success or failure is returned to the requesting client.

Installing an MTS Component

Microsoft has made it simple to manage components via MTS Explorer. Figure 43.4 readily shows all packages that have been installed. Following are the steps of installing a component under MTS control. For this example, the Sample Bank package that comes with MTS sample code will be used (c:\Program Files\Mts\Samples\Packages\Sample Bank.PAK).

Creating a Package

Before you install a new component in MTS, you must decide on which package you want the component to be a member. This example will show the install of a prebuilt package:

1. Open the MTS Explorer.
2. Open the My Computer icon and select the Packages Installed folder.
3. Right-click the Packages Installed folder, and select New, Package.
4. Select Install Pre-Built Package on the Package Wizard screen. This is for packages that were distributed to you, such as the Sample Banking package with MTS. Figure 43.5 shows these two options.

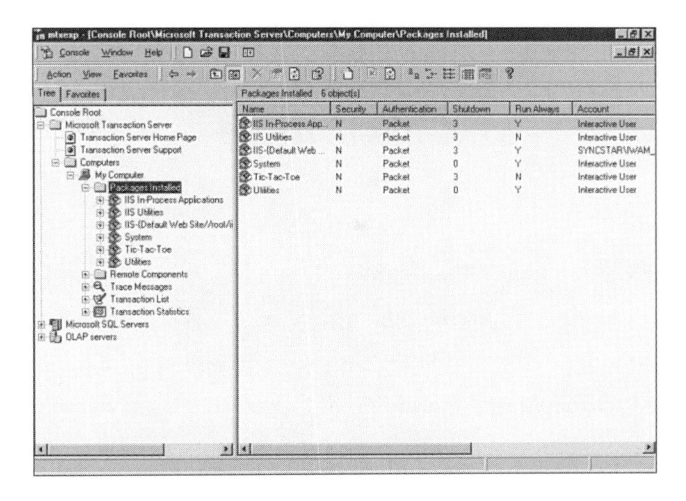

FIGURE 43.4 The MTS Explorer: Packages installed.

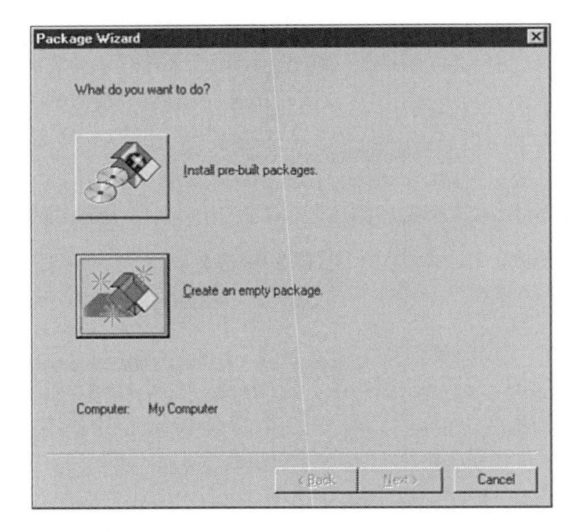

FIGURE 43.5 The Package Wizard: What do you want to do?

NOTE

The other option on the Package Wizard screen is Create an Empty Package. This is used to install packages that you have created using VB, or other development tools.

1. Click on the Add button and browse for the package file you want. Again, in this example, it will be the Sample Bank package located in C:\Program Files\Mts\Samples\Packages\Sample Bank.PAK). Select this file and then click Next. Figure 43.6 shows the package that has been selected to be installed. Alternatively, only a component within this package could have been selected, such as only the Visual Basic components (and not the VJ, and so on components).

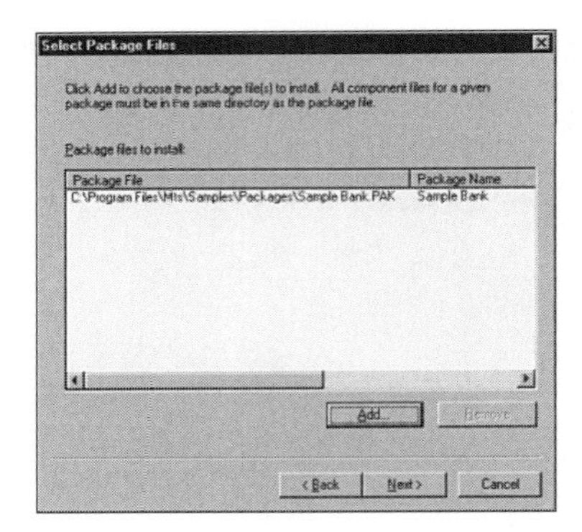

FIGURE 43.6 The Package Wizard: Package Files to Install dialog box.

2. Just click Next on the Set Package Identity dialog box. This screen is used to specify what user identity the package will assume while performing its work. In this case, you want the default option of Interactive User.

3. The component files will be installed into an Install directory of your choice. You might choose the default value of C:\Program Files\Mts\Packages. Click the Next button to finish the install. Figure 43.7 shows a completed install of the Sample Bank package.

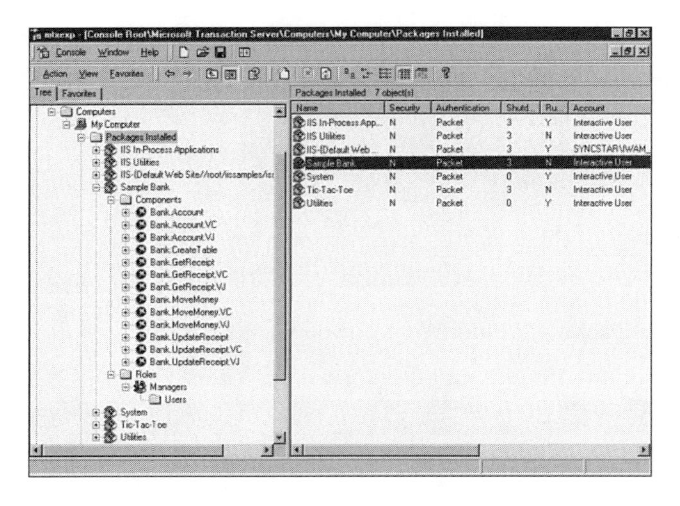

FIGURE 43.7 The MTS Explorer showing installed package: Sample Bank.

Setting Component Properties

After the components have been installed, you can set properties such as what transaction support you want for these components. In this example, the component properties for the `Bank.Account` component that was just installed will be set to Requires a Transaction. The following steps accomplish this:

1. Open the Components folder in Sample Bank.
2. Select the Bank.Account component. Right-click the component and select Properties.
3. Select the Transaction tab.
4. Click Requires a Transaction (see Figure 43.8).
5. Click OK.

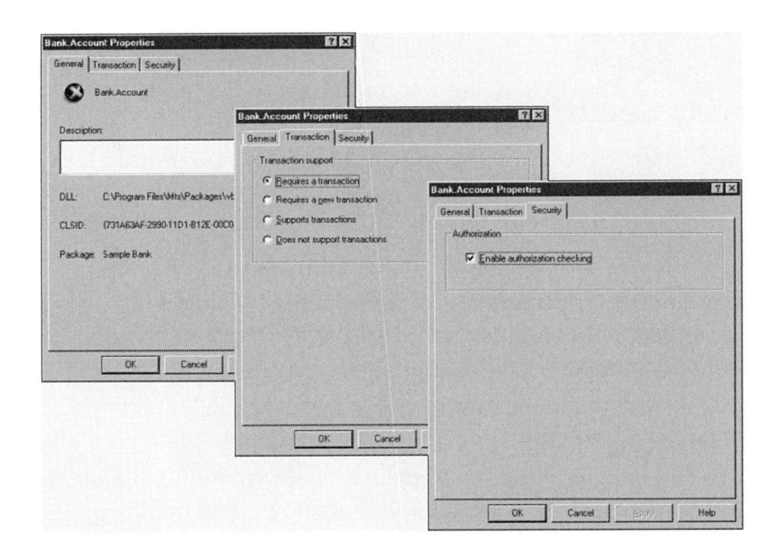

FIGURE 43.8 The Component Properties tab: Transaction property.

> **TIP**
>
> In Visual Basic 6.0, you can set the Transaction Support property during the development of a component by using the `MTSTransactionMode` property of the class.

The behavior of each of the supported transaction modes is as follows:

- Requires a transaction—The component must execute within the context of a transaction, although it does not care where the context originates. If the caller has a transaction already, then the called component will use the existing transaction. If the caller does not have a transaction, then MTS automatically creates a new transaction for the component.
- Requires a new transaction—The component must always establish its own transaction context. Regardless of whether the calling application has a transaction context, MTS automatically creates a new transaction context object for the component.
- Supports transactions—The component does not care whether a transaction context is in place.
- Does not support transactions—The component cannot support a transaction, and the CreateInstance method from within a context object will fail.

Configuring Security

MTS provides a flexible security model. As with most software products, flexibility can lead to complexity. This exploration of MTS security includes setting permissions on components and packages along with the relationship between MTS security and SQL Server 2000 security.

MTS security relies on the configuration of users in the NT domain. Users and groups within an NT domain can be assigned to roles in MTS. These roles are in turn granted permissions on MTS objects.

Package Security Options

Only a couple of steps are necessary to implement security within a package. If you look back at Figure 43.8, the Bank.Account component shows that this component has Authorization Checking enabled, and it was noted that this component didn't have a role set up for it. What this means is that the component will use the security set up for the package.

Creating Roles

Roles are mechanisms in MTS to which permissions are assigned. Roles consist of groups or users from an NT domain. Roles are defined on a per-package basis. In other words, each package might have a different set of roles with which to work. The following example creates a new role called Execs for the Sample Bank package:

1. Select the Roles folder under the Sample Bank Package from MTS Explorer.
2. Right-click the Roles folder, and select New, Role.

3. Type **Execs** in the New Role screen, and click OK.
4. Select the Users folder in the Execs role.
5. Right-click the Users folder and select New, User.
6. Select Everyone as the user for Execs role by clicking the Add button, as shown in Figure 43.9.

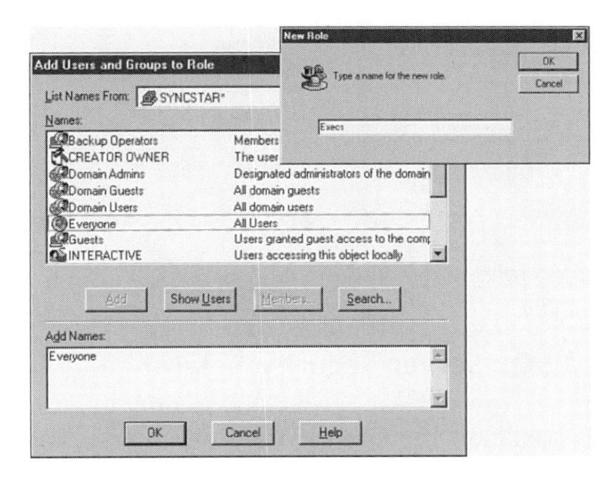

FIGURE 43.9 Adding users to MTS package roles.

7. Click OK.

Setting Role Membership for a Component

Each component within a package can have its own security settings. The Role Membership folder is the mechanism for designating which roles have access to which components. The following example grants the Execs role access to the Bank.Account component only:

1. Open the Bank.Account component in the MTS Explorer.
2. Select the Role Membership folder.
3. Right-click the Role Membership folder and select New, Role.
4. In the Select Roles window, select the Execs role and click OK (see Figure 43.10).

> **TIP**
>
> You should shut down a package after you change its roles or the role memberships of its components. This action will ensure that the new settings take effect. To shut down a package, right-click the package and select Shut Down. The package will restart the next time it is called.

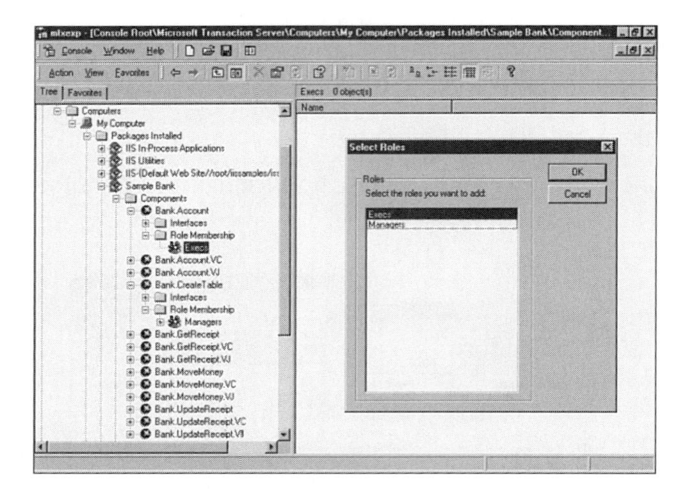

FIGURE 43.10 Selecting roles for a component.

How Do MTS and SQL Server Security Relate?

You can combine MTS security and SQL Server 2000 security in several ways. This section addresses two primary scenarios. The first scenario is when you want to grant access to the database on a per-user basis, and the second scenario is when you want to grant access on a per-package basis. Both of these scenarios assume that SQL Server is using SQL Server and Windows NT security (Mixed Mode Authentication).

Scenario 1: Per User

In this situation, you should build each MTS component to accept database usernames and passwords as parameters. The component can then use these parameters to open a connection. To set up this scenario, you must give access to the MTS component to each user through roles, and you must also give each user a login for the database.

CAUTION

Using this security scheme could severely limit scalability. You must create a unique connection for each user, which cripples the effectiveness of connection pooling.

Scenario 2: Per Package

In this scenario, all components in a package call the database under one database login. MTS can validate individual users by checking a component's role membership. After MTS validates the users, the users then perform all database activities under a single database login. This security scheme enables effective use of connection pooling.

Other Security Considerations

You must keep several other issues in mind regarding MTS security:

- This discussion has only covered declarative security. Programmatic security is also available in MTS. Programmatic security enables an MTS component to determine the authorization of its caller through code.
- It is possible to control who has administrative privileges in MTS. You might want only certain users to be able to make changes to your MTS setup.
- Several different authentication levels are available for MTS components. All of the examples in this chapter use only the Connect authentication level.
- You must enable Distributed COM (DCOM) security on all client machines that will access a component under MTS control. You can use the dcomcnfg.exe utility to configure the client machines.

Running an MTS Application

It's pretty easy to run an MTS application. You will execute the Sample Banking MTS Application supplied with MTS on the NT Server Option Pack. Several prerequisites are necessary before this sample application can run successfully:

1. Use 32-bit ODBC to create a System DSN named MTSSamples. This DSN will point to the Pubs database in SQL Server 2000. Figure 43.11 shows the ODBC DSN dialog box needed for this MTS example.

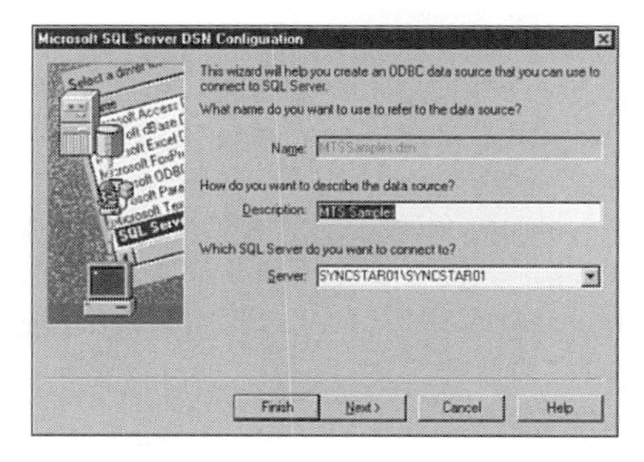

FIGURE 43.11 Configuring ODBC DSN entry: MTS Samples.

2. You should install the Sample Bank.PAK file under MTS control as described in the section "Installing an MTS Component" earlier in this chapter.
3. You should configure security for the Sample Bank package components as described in the section "Configuring Security" earlier in this chapter.

4. In SQL Server, set Authentication to SQL Server and Windows NT. Now, ensure that SQL Server 2000 is running. Figure 43.12 shows a valid NT user/domain login for SQL Server (Windows Authentication).

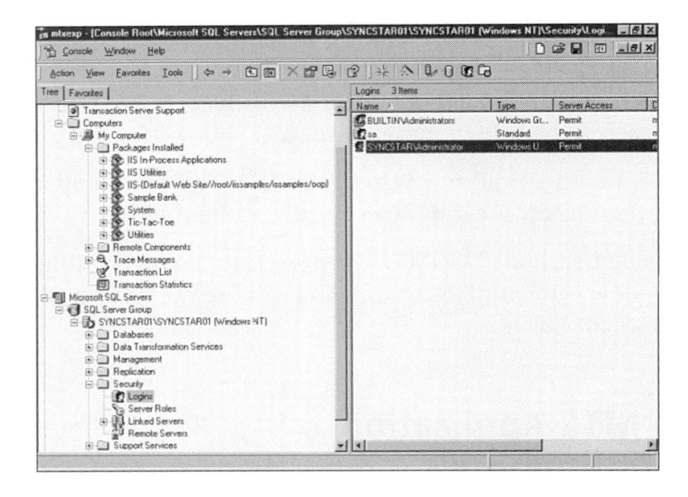

FIGURE 43.12 The Enterprise Manager: Server Logins.

5. Ensure that DTC is running. Figure 43.13 shows both MS DTC and MS SQL services running.

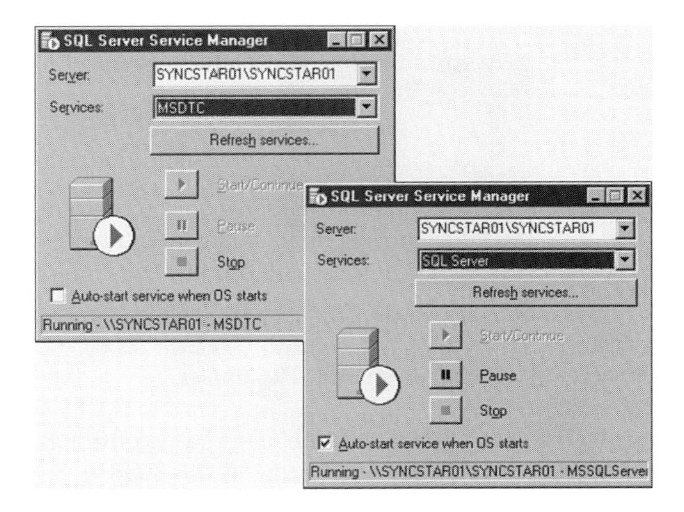

FIGURE 43.13 MS DTC and SQL Server running.

NOTE

All examples illustrated here were run on a Windows NT Server 4.0 platform.

Everything appears to be ready to execute the Sample Banking MTS application.

Executing Sample Banking

This test application can be started via the program item entry in the MTS program group named Bank Client or by directly executing the Bank Client located in C:\Program Files\Mts\vbbank.exe from Windows Explorer. After Bank Client is started, it should display the Sample Bank screen from which you can submit transactions (Figure 43.14).

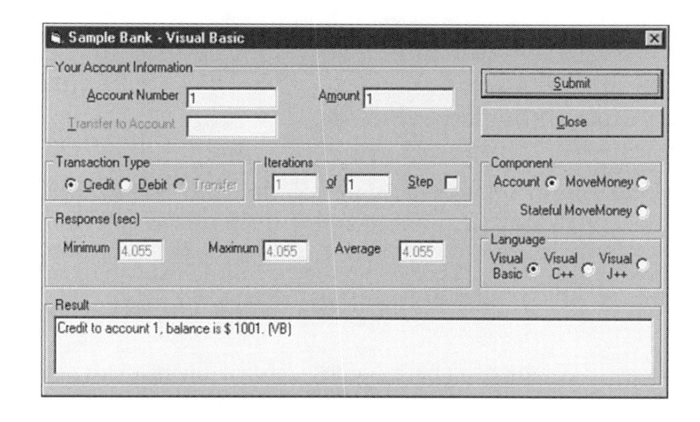

FIGURE 43.14 Bank Client MTS application.

I entered a transaction request that would execute the Account Component and issue a credit transaction. Before I submitted this request, I brought up the MTS Explorer and displayed the Transaction Statistics option. I observed the number of active and aggregated transactions processed by MS DTC and expected to see more committed transactions after I executed the request. Figure 43.15 shows the aggregated MS DTC transaction picture after I executed the request and others.

Troubleshooting

MTS is likely to be in a middle tier in an *n*-tier system, and complex interactions might take place between the MTS software and the software in other tiers.

Table 43.2 lists some of the errors you might encounter when running any MTS application. You will probably see these types of errors in your own system fairly soon after starting to use MTS.

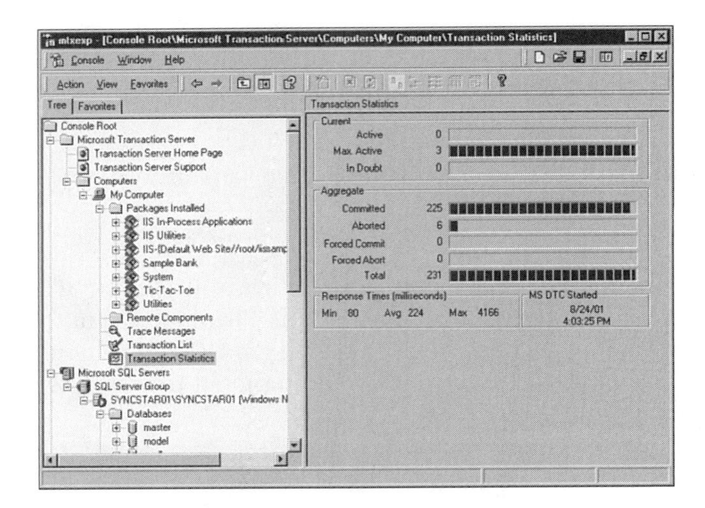

FIGURE 43.15 MTS Explorer: Transaction statistics.

TABLE 43.2 Common Errors in MTS Applications

Error Message	Meaning
`429 ActiveX component can't create object`	The MTS component you are trying to use has not been installed correctly. See the section "Installing an MTS Component" earlier in this chapter.
`70 Permission Denied`	You don't have permission to use the methods of the MTS component. Did you remember to shut down the package after changing MTS permissions?
`13 Type Mismatch`	Your application could not pull results from the database. Check the database configuration. Do you have a proper ODBC System DSN entry and the necessary permissions?

Play with the permissions and configurations in both MTS and SQL Server to see how to cause and fix all these types of errors. This exercise will more clearly reveal the relationship between SQL Server 2000 and MTS.

In general, if you are starting to have trouble with transactions under MTS, verify the following:

- Make sure that MS DTC is up and running on all servers.
- Check network communication by first testing on a local computer to verify that the application works.
- Use ping to verify that each machine is reachable.

- Make sure that SQL Server and MS DTC are either located on the same computer or that the DTC Client Configuration program specifies that the DTC is on another computer. If not, SQLConnect will return an error when called from a transactional component.
- Make sure your ODBC drivers are thread-safe and do not have thread affinity.
- Set the MTS Transaction timeout to a higher number than the default 60 seconds; otherwise, MTS aborts the transaction after this time has passed.
- Perhaps turn off resource pooling (a registry key flag).
- You might have to resolve MTS transactions manually via the Transaction list window of the MTS Explorer. Understand where the failure might be and then force (commit manually) the transaction. You might have to look at each MS DTC involved in the request.

Using Database Connection Pooling

One of the most useful features of MTS is database connection pooling. MTS can hold a connection open for a specified period of time even after a component is finished using the connection. When another component in MTS needs a database connection, MTS already has the connection open and waiting.

Connection pooling will only be effective if many of the database requests occur under the same database login. Note that the database requests can originate from different users as long as they use the same database login. The reason for this restriction is that the database login is a characteristic of a database connection.

If MTS components are written so that they hold open database connections only for a brief time, a limited pool of database connections can serve many client applications. This saves time and server resources and allows a system to scale more gracefully.

Changing the Driver Timeout

After SQL Server 2000 is installed, you can use ODBC to configure connection pooling. Figure 43.16 shows the Connection Pooling tab of the ODBC Administrator. The important parameter here is the Pool Timeout (in seconds). This parameter tells ODBC how long a connection should be held open in the connection pool after a client application is finished with it.

To change the timeout for SQL Server, follow these steps:

1. Open ODBC from the Control Panel. Click the Connection Pooling tab.
2. Double-click SQL Server in the ODBC Drivers box.
3. Select Pool Connections to this driver. The connection pool timeout defaults to 60. For this test, change it to 120. Click OK.

4. Note that the Pool Timeout for SQL Server has changed to 120 in the ODBC Drivers list. Click Apply.
5. Stop and restart the MS SQL Server service.

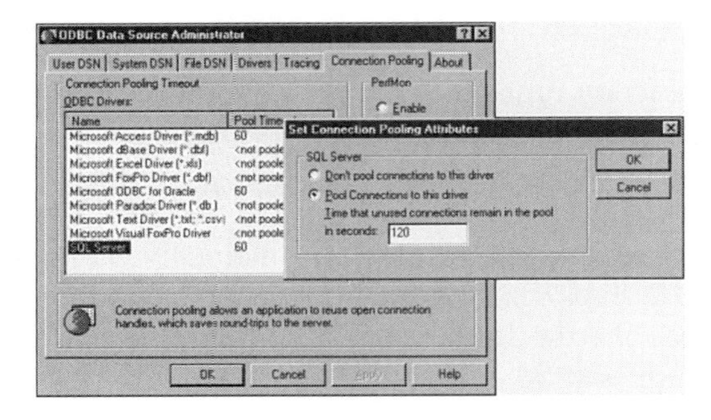

FIGURE 43.16 ODBC: Set connection pooling attributes.

NOTE

Always remember to restart SQL Server after changing the connection pooling timeout setting in ODBC. This action will enable the changes to take effect.

Summary

If you have an environment with hundreds of components running across multiple servers, then you should be running with MTS. MTS allows developers to build transactional integrity into every application, enables safe integration of components from multiple developers and development environments, enables distributed applications across multiple servers and databases, and provides a single point from which to manage the components and their security.

Looking to the future, it is COM+ and the .NET framework that is building on what has already been defined by MTS and other services. COM+ is at the heart of most .NET implementations and is the infrastructure for building enterprise applications for Microsoft. And .NET/COM+ continues to become more highly integrated with each release. And, of course, MTS is a critical player within COM+.

The next chapter, "SQL Server Full-Text Search Services," will highlight the essential services capabilities and show you how easy it is to take advantage of them from within any SQL Server application.

CHAPTER 44

SQL Server Full-Text Search Services

by Bennett McEwan

IN THIS CHAPTER

In this chapter, you will look at how to use the Microsoft Search Server to perform full-text searching capabilities. You are already familiar with how SQL Server supports a basic level of searching in the standard database engine. Search Server provides more robust functions that allow you to find documents containing different word forms, or documents that contain words in close proximity to other words.

Common uses for full-text indexing include the following:

- Robust text-searching capabilities for text data (databases of résumés, internal documents, documentation).
- Text searching on binary documents stored in an **image** column, using document filters to gain access to the actual document data.
- Searching on documents that are maintained outside of SQL Server (for example, a directory of active Word documents on a file server or HTML files on a Web site). Your database can track the locations of these files and provide links to them.

How Search Server Works

Microsoft Search Server is a separate service that is installed as part of the SQL Server 2000 product. It is included with Enterprise, Standard, and Developer Editions, but not Personal Edition. The Search Server runs as a separate service, so you can disable it if you do not make use of it.

The Search Server creates indexes on the Windows file system completely outside of SQL Server. These indexes are similar in structure to the nonclustered indexes used by SQL Server. Search Server uses B-tree indexing for each discrete word, with pointers to the table, column, and location of those words. This allows the index to find specific words very rapidly and with small amounts of work.

The Search Server will pull the data to be indexed out of the SQL tables and break it up into single words. Certain words, called **noise words**, will be dropped from the index. Noise words, which are language-specific, are words that are so common, that any indexing would be counterproductive. You can look at the list of noise words for your language by looking in c:\Program Files\Microsoft SQL Server\FTDATA\SQLServer\Config.

NOTE

The path to the noise word file, and other paths mentioned in this chapter, might be different on your system if you installed SQL Server in a path other than the default.

TIP

If you would like to add to the list of ignored words in the noise files, you can manually edit them by following these steps:

1. Stop the Search Service.
2. Descend to the `\Microsoft SQL Server\MSSQL\FTDATA\SQLServer\Config` directory, and use Notepad or another text editor to open the file for your language. For example, edit noise.enu for American English. (Be sure to make a backup of the file in case the editing goes awry.)
3. Although it is not required, maintain the word list in alphabetical order. You can also remove words from the list, if you choose.
4. Note that phrases are not supported. Separate the words with spaces or add one word per line.
5. Save the file.
6. Restart Search Server.
7. Rebuild your full-text indexes.

The full-text index keeps track of each word and the key values for rows where the word can be found.

Setting Up a Full-Text Index

You can set up a full-text index using system-stored procedures (including sp_fulltext_database, sp_fulltext_table, and so on), or through the SQL Enterprise Manager. The examples here demonstrate how to set up an index using the Enterprise Manager.

Suppose you are working on a project for a technical recruiting firm that wants to have a searchable database of candidate résumés. You have a table called `resume`, with the following definition:

```
create table resume(
       resume_id int identity
              constraint PK_resume primary key clustered,
        contact_id int not null
               constraint FK_resume_contact references contact,
        submitDT datetime not null default CURRENT_TIMESTAMP,
       res_text text null
       )
```

In the preceding definition, `contact_id` refers to a separate table that contains details about the person whose résumé is listed in res_text. You would look in this table to find a person's phone number and email address. The res_text column is the column that will need to be full-text indexed.

To create a full-text index on this table, start by drilling down through the SQL Server's name, Databases, ResumeDB, Tables, then selecting the résumé table from the list. From the Tools menu in Enterprise Manager, select Full-Text Indexing. This will load the Full-Text Wizard. The wizard will lead you through the steps for enabling a full-text index on the table. You must complete each of these steps:

1. Identify the database and table you want to index. In this example, you have selected the résumé table.

2. Identify the unique index you want to use. It is not necessary to have a primary key constraint on the table, but full-text indexing requires a unique index on non-nullable columns to support its own indexes. Each index entry will include a pointer to the primary key record where the word exists.

   In this example, select the primary key `PK_resume`.

3. The next step is to identify the columns containing data to be indexed. Normally, a table contains just a single text column, but it is possible to index more than one column per table.

   In this example, select the text column `res_text`.

4. Select a name and file system location for the new full-text catalog. A catalog can contain information for many tables, and a database can contain many catalogs. The catalog name is used when querying to identify which full-text index should be searched.

   In this example, check the dialog box for Create New Full-Text Catalog. You will have the option to indicate where in the file system to place the full-text catalog.

5. Optionally, you can set up a repopulation schedule for the index. More information on population is provided later in the chapter, in the section titled "Choosing the Best Refresh Schedule."

TIP

The Microsoft Search Server is a separate service. If you are attempting to create full-text indexes from within SQL Enterprise Manager, and the options are grayed out, ensure that the Search Server service is running.

TIP

Full-text search needs a single unique index on a table to be able to work. A composite primary key consisting of two or more columns will not work. If you have tables that do not have a single column unique index, you will need to add a new, unique column to the table. Identity columns work well for this.

If the table has more than one unique index, use the smallest, most narrow available index to get the best performance. For example, if you had a table with a unique GUID column and a unique integer 4 bytes each, instead of the GUID at 16 bytes each.

At this point, you have set up the index, but it is not yet populated. In Figure 44.1, I have set up a full-text index on `resume` in a catalog named FTCatalog. From the Action menu, select Start Full Population. This starts the actual indexing process.

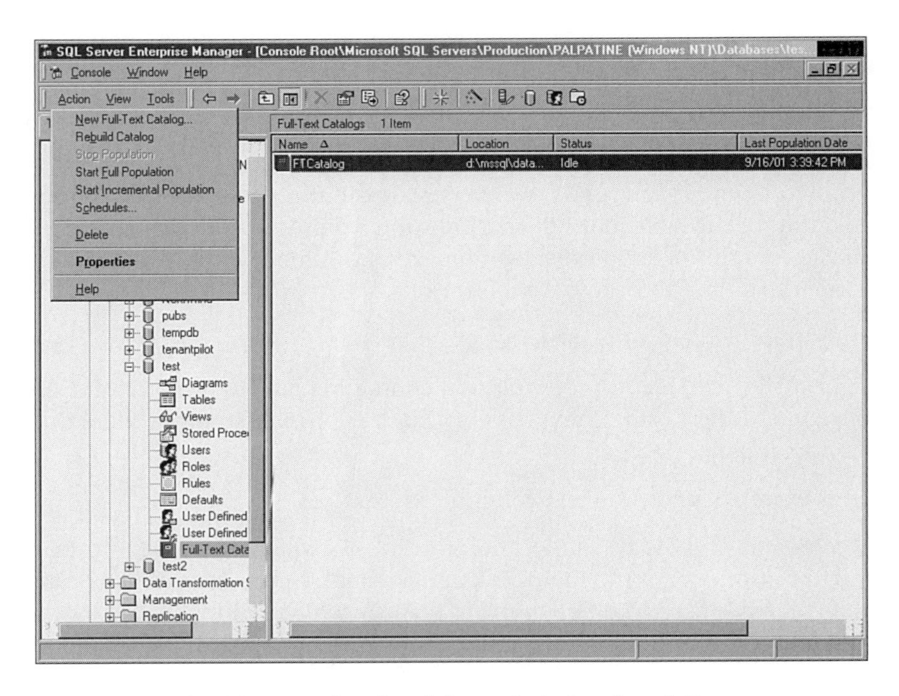

FIGURE 44.1 Enterprise Manager showing full-text Indexing Population menu.

Now that you have a full-text index created and populated, it is ready for use.

Maintaining Full-Text Indexes

Maintaining full-text indexes presents some new challenges to the database administrator. One of the most important choices that must be made with regard to full-text indexes is how to repopulate them.

Choosing the Best Refresh Schedule

Updating a full-text index is an expensive operation. If possible, restrict the refresh periods to an off-peak time window. Complete refreshes are the simplest method for maintaining your indexes, but large data sets (more than a million rows) can be unwieldy. The correct choice for repopulation schedules must be made with application design goals in mind. Do you require real-time indexing? Can you live with one hour, one day, or one week of lag time between updating the index?

You have several options for refreshing full-text data:

- Perform a full repopulation—This option can be scheduled or performed manually when required. This choice is best when you replace all of the full-text data in your indexes at once. For example, if you had a nightly job that truncated the indexed table and imported fresh data, a full repopulation would be the most efficient method. Note that this operation will cause the search server to issue a table scan against each indexed table, although if the table is in use by other processes, it will acquire less intrusive, shared, row-level locks.

- Perform an incremental repopulation—If the number of changes to your table is small relative to the total size, this form of repopulation will take the least amount of resources to complete. You could schedule an incremental repopulation every hour or half hour, which would update the full-text index with all changes to the data at a regular interval. The advantage of incremental repopulation is that it is usually faster than full repopulation. However, if your text data changes frequently, the incremental update could take longer than a full repopulation. In most cases, an incremental repopulation, in which all the text data in the table is not repopulated, will be the most efficient method.

  SQL Server supports this method by using timestamps to identify rows that have changed since the last update. Your table must have a timestamp column to support incremental updates. If anything in the row changes, the timestamp will change and the row will be flagged for reindexing, even if the full-text indexed column didn't change. If you want to avoid the timestamp requirement, investigate change-tracking options.

- Perform a scheduled change-tracking repopulation—If you have a steady stream of updates to your index, and you do not have a timestamp column, this form of repopulation is best.

The difference between change tracking and incremental repopulation is the method used by SQL Server to support them. With incremental repopulation, SQL Server stores only the timestamp of the last successful repopulation, and scans the table during refreshes to identify rows with larger (later) timestamps. Change tracking uses a system table, sysfulltextnotify, to track the table, row, and full-text index key when changes occur.

With either of these last two options, you must choose a scheduled refresh that fits with the design goals of your application.

Backing Up Full-Text Indexes

The ability to back up the full-text indexes depends heavily on the update method you have chosen. In a worst-case scenario, you can restore your database backups (which are kept consistent by a transaction log), rebuild the catalog, and then perform a full repopulation. However, with large full-text indexes, this could be a lengthy process.

If you are using change tracking, it is more difficult to implement a solid backup policy because there are constant changes occurring to the full-text data. You could perform a backup of the files once a day, and restore these partial indexes in the event of a failure. This would provide limited functionality until you could take the system down for a full repopulation.

If you are using incremental updates, you can back up the full-text indexes that are in the file system separately by stopping the MSSearch service, backing up all the files in the catalog, backing up the SQL Server database, and restarting the MSSearch service. In the event of an index corruption or file system failure, stop the search service. Restore these files, restart the search server, and immediately perform an incremental full-text update. Search Server will receive all the changes to the table based on the timestamp from the last update.

> **TIP**
>
> Microsoft maintains a Knowledge Base article on recommended methods for performing full-text Index backups. See KB article #Q240867.

Effects of Inconsistent Data

Maintenance of full-text indexes is an asynchronous process, meaning that your indexes can easily be out of sync with your data. SQL Server uses transactions and locking to prevent inconsistency in its data, but the full-text search engine has neither of these features.

This section describes the effects of inconsistent data with Search Server. Following are descriptions of what would happen if a row is inserted, updated, or deleted in the SQL Server table, but the full-text index has not yet been updated to reflect the change.

Inserted Row

A row that is inserted to the table, but isn't in the index, will not be returned by any search that would normally find it. Because the unique key associated with the word did not exist at the time of the index creation, the new row will not be reachable by Search Server. Of course, you can still get to the row through conventional Transact-SQL commands.

Deleted Row

A deleted row will work correctly, although extra processing will be involved. When you write a query to find certain words, SQL Server asks the Search Server for the key values of rows that satisfy your request. When these results are returned, SQL Server attempts to retrieve the row using this key. If the row has been deleted, no row will be returned.

Updated Row

If the text for an indexed column is modified such that it no longer satisfies the full-text search criteria, the index will still find the old row, but will return the new information. Because the key value is unchanged, and the Search Server only returns the key values that satisfy your query, SQL Server has no way to know that the results are incorrect. This can be confusing to a user.

Full-Text Searches

You hook into the Microsoft Search Server by using four special SQL commands: `CONTAINS`, `CONTAINSTABLE`, `FREETEXT`, and `FREETEXTTABLE`.

To learn how to use these functions, you need to go back to the résumé example you looked at earlier in this chapter. Suppose you wanted to find out how many résumés were in your table that had the word "SQL" somewhere.

CONTAINS()

If you didn't have full-text search working, you would write a query like this:

```
select count(*)
from resume
where res_text like '%SQL%'
```

If your table has many résumés in it, this is going to take a while to complete because the entire table (including all text pages) will be scanned. To perform the same search with Search Server, use `CONTAINS()`:

```
select count(*)
from resume
where contains(*, 'SQL')
```

The first argument to CONTAINS() is the name of the full-text indexed column to search. Using the wildcard searches all columns in all tables in the query that are enabled for full-text indexing.

Here is the full syntax for CONTAINS():

```
CONTAINS
    ( { column | * } , '< contains_search_condition >'
    )
< contains_search_condition > ::=
        { < simple_term >
        | < prefix_term >
        | < generation_term >
        | < proximity_term >
        | < weighted_term >
        }
        | { ( < contains_search_condition > )
        { AND | AND NOT | OR } < contains_search_condition > [ ...n ]
        }
< simple_term > ::=
    word | " phrase "
< prefix term > ::=
    { "word * " | "phrase * " }
< generation_term > ::=
    FORMSOF ( INFLECTIONAL | THESAURUS , < simple_term > [ ,...n ] )
< proximity_term > ::=
    { < simple_term > | < prefix_term > }
    { { NEAR | ~ } { < simple_term > | < prefix_term > } } [ ...n ]
< weighted_term > ::=
    ISABOUT
        ( { {
                < simple_term >
                | < prefix_term >
                | < generation_term >
                | < proximity_term >
                }
            [ WEIGHT ( weight_value ) ]
            } [ ,...n ]
        )
```

CONTAINS() works a lot like a Web search engine, so if you're comfortable with Boolean expressions in Web search engines, you already have most of what you need to get CONTAINS() running. Just as with search engines on the Internet, you can use quotes around exact phrases. For example, to find someone with SQL Server experience, but exclude people with Oracle experience, you could use this query against the résumé table:

```
select *
from resume
where contains(res_text, '"SQL Server" and not Oracle')
```

You can use FORMSOF() with the inflectional argument to match different word forms of the terms in your query. This will match singular and plural word forms and different verb tenses. In this example, I would get anyone who included the word "query" or "queries" in their résumé text:

```
select *
from resume
where contains(*, 'formsof(inflectional, "query")')
```

The Thesaurus argument in formsof() is largely undocumented. As of Service Pack 2, the Thesaurus option was implemented, but disabled. Microsoft did not supply the actual Thesaurus data. The list of words used by the Thesaurus, like the noise words, is stored in c:\Program Files\Microsoft SQL Server\FTDATA\SQLServer\Config. The Thesaurus is stored in XML format. Without real data, Thesaurus works just like a simple expression in CONTAINS.

FREETEXT()

FREETEXT() is a newer and looser ("fuzzy") version of CONTAINS(). Use FREETEXT() when you want to match rows that are near the meaning of the phrases you suggest, but do not necessarily contain specific words or word forms in your expression. FREETEXT() can provide you with more utility, matching plurals, and other verb forms of a root word.

You can pass sentences or even entire paragraphs to FREETEXT() for it to find similar words and phrases.

This following example would match anything containing the word SQL, server, admin, basic, or visual. FREETEXT() does not use phrase matching or Boolean expression evaluation. The query shown next would be broken down into a query that looked for each of the non-noise words appearing in the sentence, and their varying inflectional word forms. It would identify nouns and multiword noun phrases and search for these, as well.

```
select *
from   resume
where  freetext(*, 'Our company requires someone with
experience in SQL Server, Visual Basic, and a
desire to be part of a strong team.')
```

CONTAINSTABLE() and FREETEXTTABLE()

These special forms of CONTAINS and FREETEXT are used in a SQL query as part of the FROM expression. They operate like their basic functions, but they return a table object that lists two columns: KEY and RANK.

The KEY column can be joined to the queries table to retrieve the actual text values; these functions do not return text. The RANK column returns a numerical value describing how closely the row matched the search expression, from 0 to 1,000.

> **NOTE**
>
> Because KEY is an ANSI SQL reserved word, you must enclose it in brackets or double quotes when you reference it as the column name returned by CONTAINSTABLE() or FREETEXTTABLE().

The next example searches for résumés in the résumé table that have SQL Server, Oracle, or Sybase experience. A weighting value is assigned to each of these expressions, with SQL Server experience worth 5 times as much as Sybase, and 10 times as much as Oracle. A résumé that has more than one of these will have a higher rank. The query will then order the results by rank, with the most impressive résumé at the top:

```
select RANK, res_text
from containstable(
        resume, *,
       'isabout(
             "SQL Server" weight (1.0),
                Oracle weight (0.1),
                Sybase weight (0.2)
                )'
        ) a
       join resume b
                on a.[KEY] = b.resume_id
order by RANK desc

RANK        res_text
----------- ---------------------------------------------------------
120         SQL Server Sybase Oracle
113         SQL Server Sybase
106         SQL Server Oracle
99          SQL Server, ASP, Perl, leadership, grace under pressure
99          SQL Server
18          Sybase Oracle
12          Sybase
6           Oracle
```

Limiting Maximum Hits

When using the containstable() and freetexttable() functions, you can optionally specify the maximum number of rows to return from a query. Just as with any large result-set, it can take a long time to get back all the data for a general query.

Here is the previous example, limited to the first three entries:

```
select RANK, res_text
from containstable(
        resume, res_text,
       'isabout(
             "SQL Server" weight (1.0),
              Oracle weight (0.1),
              Sybase weight (0.2)
              )',
        3
        ) a
       join resume b
              on a.[KEY] = b.resume_id
order by RANK desc

RANK        res_text
----------- ---------------------------------------------------------
120         SQL Server Sybase Oracle
113         SQL Server Sybase
106         SQL Server Oracle
```

You could get the same answer by specifying `SELECT TOP 3` in the SQL statement, but this would be much less efficient. Using the optional fourth parameter will instruct the Search service to return immediately upon finding the maximum number of rows specified.

Using Document Filters

You can use SQL Server 2000 to support full-text queries against data in non-text files, too. Document filters that ship with SQL Server 2000 support the capability to search Microsoft Word, Excel, PowerPoint, and HTML files. Other companies have provided document filters to search their products, as well. Adobe, for example, provides a free document filter for indexing .pdf files at `http://www.adobe.com/support/downloads/8122.htm`.

To implement this, you create a table that contains at least two columns: an `image` column to hold the data to be searched, and a char(3) column to hold the document type. You store the document type (.pdf, .doc, .htm, .txt) in this char(3) column. SQL Server relies on the document type to choose the document filter to use during indexing operations.

Summary

Microsoft Search Server that ships with SQL 2000 provides a needed link between the fast, efficient processing of the SQL 2000 database engine and the requirement for robust text-searching features. Full-text indexing creates some different administration requirements for the SQL administrator.

Special thanks to Hilary Cotter for his assistance and feedback on the free-text chapter.

44

CHAPTER 45

SQL Server Notification Services

by Shyam Pather

IN THIS CHAPTER

- Introduction to SQL Notification Services
- Obtaining and Installing SQL Notification Services
- SQL Notification Services Architecture
- Instances and Applications
- Deploying and Configuring a Notificaton Services Instance
- Monitoring and Administering a Notification Services Instance

SQL Notification Services is a set of platform extensions to Microsoft SQL Server 2000. These extensions make it easy to build, deploy, and execute **notification applications**: applications that send notification messages to users at any time and on any device, based on subscriptions that they set up in advance. Notification Services offers both a simple programming model for building notification applications and an efficient and scalable server for executing those applications.

This chapter provides an overview of the Notification Services platform and describes how to configure and deploy a notification application. The details concerning how to build an application on SQL Notification Services are beyond the scope of this chapter.

Introduction to SQL Notification Services

Most methods of obtaining information from a computer involve making an explicit request for that information. Requesting information might mean querying a database, browsing a Web site, or reading information from an Internet newsgroup.

Asking for information works when you know what information to ask for, you remember to ask for it at the appropriate time, and you have access to a computer or other device that can connect you to the appropriate information source. But there are some important cases in everyday life where explicitly asking for information is inconvenient or impossible.

Imagine that you have to meet someone arriving at the airport. Knowing that flights sometimes arrive earlier or later than scheduled, you might call the airline or check its Web site for an update on the flight's arrival time. But if you forget to check with the airline, or don't have access to a phone or computer at the time you need to check, you won't get the latest information about the flight. Even if you are able to get the information, the flight's arrival time might change after your initial check.

It would be more convenient if the airline were to notify you, on whatever device you might be carrying (a mobile phone, pager, or PDA, for example) if the flight arrival time changed. However, doing this manually would be an expensive and impractical proposition for the airline.

What's needed is a notification application: software that allows users to specify the kinds of information that interest them (in this case, the arrival times of particular flights) and sends that information to the users when it becomes available. Such software is simple in concept, but can prove difficult to build from scratch. Making it scale to the expected number of users (often millions) and the volume of incoming data (often large) can be a challenge. Implementing support for multiple target devices and languages, as well as other application features, involves serious development effort.

SQL Notification Services eases the task of building notification applications by providing a platform from which to start. Applications built on this platform can be developed much more quickly than those built from scratch, tend to offer richer features, and scale better. Typical applications built on Notification Services can be prototyped in a single day, and often can be completely up and running in a matter of weeks.

The platform supports a wide variety of notification application scenarios. In addition to the flight status application discussed earlier, others that have been built on this platform include applications that send alerts to customers when certain stock symbols in their portfolios reach target values, applications that alert users when there are traffic problems on roads and highways they use in their commutes, and applications that provide immediate sports score updates for games and teams that users have subscribed for.

The two main offerings in SQL Notification Services are

- a simple, declarative model for developing notification applications
- an efficient, scalable server for executing notification applications

To build an application, you write a little application-specific code. This code is then hosted and executed within the Notification Services framework.

To help you begin understanding the SQL Notification Services platform, let's examine the common elements of a notification application.

Figure 45.1 shows a high-level view of a notification application. On the left side, the inputs to the application are **events**: things that happen in the outside world that might be of interest to a particular set of users. In the case of the airline flight status example, the events would be new flight status information (changes to arrival or departure times, gate changes, or cancellations). The top of the figure shows the other input: **subscriptions**. Subscriptions are users' requests for notifications (for example, "send me a notification when the status of flight XYZ changes," or "alert me when the value of Microsoft stock goes above $100").

The box in the middle is the core of the notification application. It performs matching between the incoming events and the subscriptions that have been entered to determine which users should receive notifications and what the content of those notifications should be. The output of the application, on the right-hand side of the figure, is a set of notifications that go to the subscribers.

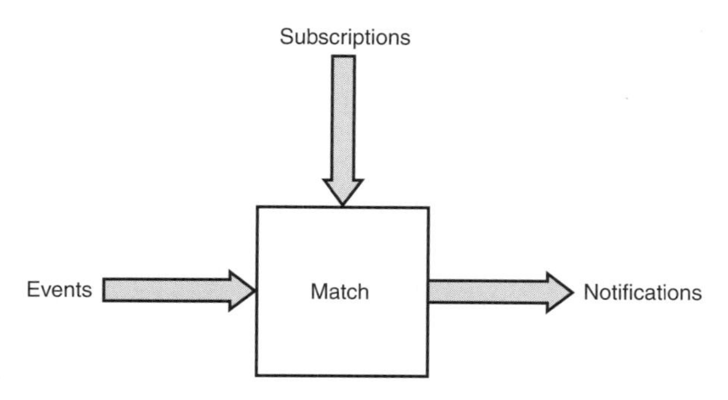

FIGURE 45.1 The high-level view of a notification application.

Applications built on SQL Notification Services can use APIs and components provided by the platform to enter events and subscriptions into the system. The platform provides the matching component, which uses SQL Server as the matching engine and applies application-specific logic to determine whether a match occurs. The application can deliver the resulting notifications via either a delivery mechanism provided by the platform, or one the application developer implements.

The core components of the application run within a Windows Service provided by SQL Notification Services. They can all run on the same computer or on separate computers in order to scale out. The platform provides a set of tools for deploying, managing, and monitoring notification applications.

Obtaining and Installing SQL Notification Services

SQL Notification Services is available as a Web download from Microsoft's Web site at `http://www.microsoft.com/sql/ns`. The Web site lists detailed system requirements, provides links to further information about the product, and specifies the licensing requirements.

After registering, you can download the installer for SQL Notification Services from the Web site. Before attempting to install Notification Services, ensure that you have the prerequisite software installed. The System Requirements page on the Web site lists the required software for various configurations.

Run the installer to launch the Setup Wizard, which will take you through the setup process. You will have to choose the components to install, as well as the SQL Server instance to use.

Successfully completing setup will result in the addition of a group for SQL Notification Services under your Start/Programs menu. This group will contain links to the Notification Services samples, documentation, and a command prompt that is set up to execute the Notification Services commands.

SQL Notification Services Architecture

Understanding the internal architecture of SQL Notification Services will aid you in administering notification applications, as well as in diagnosing problems that may occur. This section provides an overview of the various functional components of a notification application built on SQL Notification Services and distinguishes those supplied by the platform from those implemented by the application developer.

Figure 45.2 shows the functional components of an application. There are three main running elements, represented by the three large boxes in the figure:

- A subscription management application that allows users to enter subscriptions
- A SQL Server that stores data for the notification application, and is used as the basis for the matching engine
- A Windows Service that hosts the event collection, notification generation, and notification distribution components of the application

These three elements can run on the same computer, or on separate computers. The various functional components within the Windows Service can even be distributed onto separate computers. This allows you to scale out the pieces of the application that require the most resources.

The following sections will describe each of the functional components shown in Figure 45.2.

Subscription Management

The component at the top of Figure 45.2 deals with management of subscriptions. Typically, users (subscribers) deal with the notification application by means of a standalone subscriber and subscription management application. This application provides an interface by means of which users can enter, modify, or delete subscriptions and configure the devices to which they want their notifications sent. Often, this application takes the form of an ASP.NET Web application, though it really can be any kind of application, including regular ASP, a Windows application, or even a command-line application.

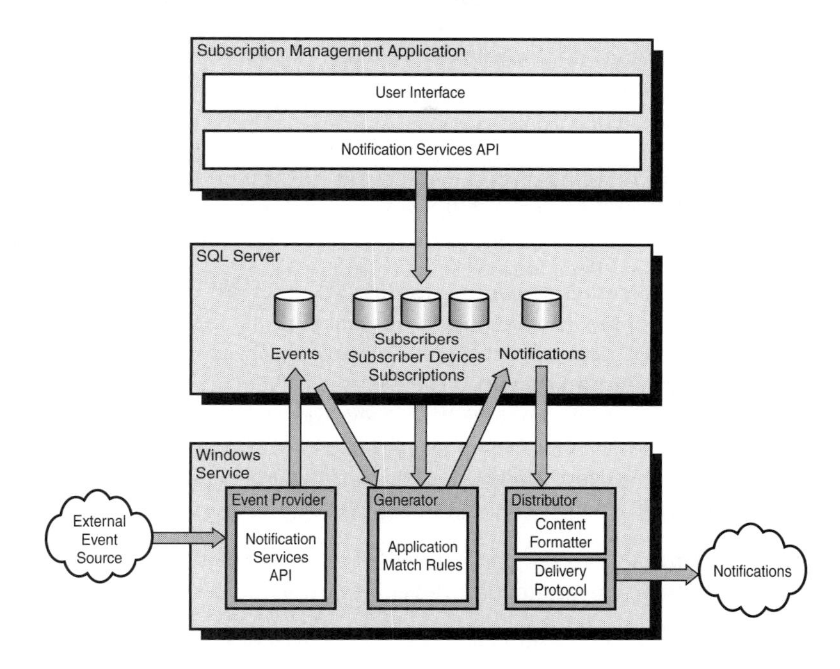

FIGURE 45.2 Functional components of a notification application built on SQL Notification Services.

Whatever form the application takes, internally it uses APIs provided by Notification Services to manage subscriptions. These APIs consist of a set of managed classes that represent subscribers, subscriber devices, and subscriptions. The application creates objects that are instances of these classes, and sets the values of various properties on them. The application then calls a method to submit the property values to Notification Services, where they are ultimately stored in the database.

SQL Server Database

The SQL database shown in the middle of Figure 45.2 is used both as a data store, and as the basis of the matching engine. It contains tables in which subscriber information, event data, and notification data are stored. These tables are created when the application is compiled, and as the various components of the application run, they populate these tables with data. The event data and the subscription data are matched by means of SQL joins written by the application developer.

The Windows Service

The Windows Service, shown at the bottom of Figure 45.2, hosts the core components of the application. These are the components that collect events, perform matching to generate notification data, and then format and deliver that notification data. The following sections detail each of these functional components and their operations.

Event Collection

The leftmost box in the Windows Service shown in Figure 45.2 deals with the input of events into the notification application. Events enter the system by means of an **event provider**: an object that can read event data from a source in the outside world and insert the events into the notification application using APIs provided by Notification Services.

For example, in the flight status application discussed earlier, an event provider might read flight status information out of the existing flight tracking database used by the airline, and then insert these events into the notification application using the Notification Services APIs. For a stock alert application, the event provider would be an object that reads stock prices from the stock provider (the stock exchange, a broker service, or another financial data provider) and submits them as events. Event providers need not be just simple pass-through mechanisms; they can perform filtering or other processing on the input data before submitting it in the form of events.

Event providers are simply managed code classes that implement an interface defined by SQL Notification Services. The application developer implements the class and Notification Services instantiates it when needed. In implementing the event provider class, the developer will build in knowledge of the particulars of the event source: how to connect to it, the protocol used to interact with it, and how to parse the data read.

In the implementation, the event provider submits events via Notification Services APIs. Internally, the APIs write this data to an events table in the application database.

Notification Services ships with several built-in event providers. If these fit the needs of the application, the application developer can use them by simply specifying some configuration information, and thus does not have to write any code.

Event providers can either run within the Notification Services Windows Service, or as standalone applications. If run within the Windows Service, they are referred to as **hosted event providers. Non-hosted event providers** run separately from the Notification Services Windows Service, either as standalone applications or as components of other processes.

An application can have several event providers, possibly distributed across several computers. The event providers can be enabled or disabled independently from the rest of the application.

Notification Generation

Event providers enter events into the application and a subscription management application enters subscriptions into the application. A component of Notification Services called the **generator** does the work to match these events and subscriptions. There is always exactly one generator per application. The generator runs within the Windows Service, but does most of its real work on the SQL Server.

The generator is a periodic component: At an interval specified by the application developer, it polls the database to determine whether there are new event batches ready for processing. The duration of the polling interval is referred to as a **quantum** in Notification Services terminology.

If it finds batches to process, the generator executes **rules** written by the application developer. These rules are SQL statements that operate on the event data and either update application state or produce notifications by matching events with subscriptions. Typically, these rules statements join the events and subscription tables and apply predicates to determine which rows match. The generator inserts the result of these joins into a notifications table.

Notification Distribution

The data in the notifications table is the output of the generator. Each of the rows in the table represents a notification to be sent, but the data in the table is in its raw form. It needs to be formatted so as to be readable by the end recipient, and then delivered via a network protocol. **Distributors** are components of Notification Services that perform the formatting and delivery of notifications.

A distributor applies formatting and delivery instructions specified by the application developer to the notifications in the notifications table. For scale-out reasons, applications can have more than one distributor, and these distributors can run on separate computers.

Within a distributor, formatting is done by means of a **content formatter**: an object that receives raw notification data as input, and returns a formatted notification message as output. Content formatters, like event providers, are managed classes that implement an interface defined by Notification Services. The application developer can implement one or more content formatters to be used by the application. Alternatively, if the requirements of the application permit, the application developer may choose to use a standard content formatter provided by Notification Services.

The application's distributors read rows of data from the notifications table and pass them to the application's content formatter. They then pass the resulting formatted strings to a **delivery protocol** object, along with addressing information about the recipient and target device. The delivery protocol object is an implementation of some network protocol; it delivers the notification and returns status information to the distributor, indicating whether the delivery succeeded or failed. The distributor records this delivery status information in the notifications table. The distributor can reattempt those deliveries that failed, according to a schedule specified by the application developer.

Delivery protocol objects are also just managed classes that implement a Notification Services interface. Notification Services ships with some built-in delivery protocol objects that implement standard protocols, but the application developer can implement a new delivery protocol object if the built-in ones do not fit the needs of the application.

Instances and Applications

Each notification application exists within a single **instance** of Notification Services. An instance is a named entity that groups one or more applications. Multiple instances of Notification Services can run side by side on a single computer, and can be created, started, stopped, managed, and deleted independently.

Instances are defined by an instance **configuration file**, an XML document that defines the properties of the instance. These properties include the name of the SQL Server that the instance uses, the list of applications in the instance, and information about protocols and delivery channels that applications in the instance can use.

Each application in the instance is defined by an **application definition file (ADF)**. The ADF defines the schema of the various entities in the application (events, subscriptions, and notifications), rules that maintain application state and perform matching, and various execution settings that control the runtime behavior of the application. The instance configuration file contains a link to the ADF for each application listed.

When the instance is created, a Notification Services compiler processes the instance configuration file, and each ADF it refers to, and creates databases. The compiler creates one main database for the instance, and one database for each application. Subscriber data is stored in the instance database and is shared by all applications in that instance. Event, subscription, and notification data for each application is stored separately in each application database.

Each instance is associated with its own Windows Service that can be started and stopped independently. The Windows Service for a particular instance is named `NS$<InstanceName>`, where `<InstanceName>` is the name of the instance. For example, the Windows Service in which the functional components of an instance named `MyInst01` will run will be called `NS$MyInst01`.

When the Windows Service for a particular instance is started, it instantiates and runs all the components (event providers, generators, and distributors) for the applications contained in that instance. These interact with the instance and application databases, as described in the previous section.

Just as multiple instances can exist on a single computer, a single instance can span multiple computers. For scale-out purposes, an administrator may wish to run the event collection, generation, and distribution components of an application on separate computers. Though they run on separate computers, these are still considered a single instance from a management point of view. Each computer will run a separate copy of the Windows Service, which will then host only the components configured to run on that computer.

Separate instances can be configured with separate security settings. The Windows Services for each instance can run under separate user accounts, and the databases for each can be configured with different access rights. This is particularly useful when the data in one instance needs to be isolated from the data in another instance.

Deploying and Configuring a Notification Services Instance

Deploying and configuring a Notification Services instance involves several steps:

1. Creating the instance and application databases
2. Installing the Windows Service, registry keys, and performance counters for the instance
3. Granting the appropriate access permissions to the databases

Notification Services provides a command-line utility called `nscontrol` for performing the first two of these steps. The third step can be done using the standard SQL Server tools.

The following sections show how to execute these steps. A key decision in deploying a Notification Services instance is whether or not to use Windows integrated security or SQL Server Authentication. This decision affects how the `nscontrol` utility logs in to the database, as well as how the Windows Service and the subscription management application log in to the database when the application runs. Notification Services supports both authentication modes, although Microsoft recommends using Windows integrated security. The sections that follow will describe the use of both authentication modes.

Creating the Instance and Application Databases

To create the instance and application databases, pass the instance configuration file to the `nscontrol create` command. The syntax of the command is

```
nscontrol create [-nologo] [-help]
    -in <configFile>
    [-sqlusername <sqlUserName> -sqlpassword <sqlPassword>]
    [-argumentkey <key>]
    [param=value ...]
```

The Notification Services Books Online file provides a detailed description of all the command options. The following is a typical example of an invocation of `nscontrol create`:

```
nscontrol create -in C:\MyInstance\MyInstanceConfig.xml
```

The important point to note here is that the name of the configuration file (including the full path, if the file is not in the directory from which the command is run) is passed in the -in argument. The name of the database server is specified in the configuration file itself.

This command will parse the configuration file, as well as the ADF files it refers to, and create the instance and application databases. If you wish to use SQL Server Authentication to log in to the SQL Server to create the databases, provide a SQL user name and password in the -sqlusername and -sqlpassword arguments to nscontrol create. If you do not use these arguments, nscontrol create connects to the database using Windows integrated security, with the credentials of the user running the command.

The user under whose identity nscontrol create logs in to the database (either the user running the command if using Windows integrated security, or the specified SQL user if using SQL Server Authentication) must have permission to create databases. This requires the user to be a member of the dbcreator and sysadmin fixed server roles.

If nscontrol create executes successfully, you will see new databases on your SQL Server. There will be one database for the instance, named <InstanceName>NSMain, where <InstanceName> is the name of the instance. For example, the instance database for an instance named MyInstance will be called MyInstanceNSMain. In addition to the instance database, there will be an application database for each application declared in the configuration file. The application database will be named <InstanceName><ApplicationName>, where <InstanceName> is the name of the instance, and <ApplicationName> is the name of the application. For example, the application database for an application named StockAlerts in the MyInstance instance will be called MyInstanceStockAlerts.

Registering the Instance

After creating the instance and application databases, the next step is to register the instance. Registration installs the Windows Service, registry keys, and performance counters associated with the instance. Registration is performed via the nscontrol register command.

If your instance is distributed across several different computers for scale-out reasons, you will need to perform the registration step on each of the computers that will run the Windows Service.

The syntax of the nscontrol register command is

```
nscontrol register [-nologo] [-help]
    -name <instanceName> [-server <databaseServer>]
    [-service
        [-serviceusername <NSServiceUserName> -servicepassword <NSServicePwd>]
        [-sqlusername <sqlUserName> -sqlpassword <sqlPassword>]
        [-argumentkey <key>]]
```

The Notification Services Books Online file provides a detailed description of all the command options. The following is a typical example of an invocation of `nscontrol register`:

```
nscontrol register -name MyInstance -server MyDBServer
    -service -serviceusername MYDOMAIN\MyUser -servicepassword MyPassword
```

Table 45.1 lists the various arguments used in this sample invocation and their meanings.

TABLE 45.1 Meanings of Some `nscontrol register` Arguments

Argument Name	Meaning
`-name`	Name of the instance being registered
`-server`	Name of the database server for the instance
`-service`	Instructs the command to install the Windows Service for the instance
`-serviceusername`	Windows username under which the Windows Service should run
`-servicepassword`	Password for the username specified in the `-serviceusername` argument

The `nscontrol register` command installs the service and stores the name of the database server for the instance in the registry. When the Windows Service starts, it reads this server name from the registry and uses it to connect to the instance and application databases.

If you wish to have the Windows Service connect to the database server using SQL Server Authentication, specify `-sqlusername` and `-sqlpassword` arguments to the `nscontrol register` command. If specified, the values of these arguments are also stored in the registry, but are encrypted so that they cannot be freely read. If you do not specify `-sqlusername` and `-sqlpassword` arguments to the command, the Windows Service will be configured to log in to the database using Windows integrated security, with the credentials of the user account under which the service runs. This user account is specified by means of the `-serviceusername` and `-servicepassword` arguments.

Microsoft recommends that you configure the Windows Service to run under a weak (non-Administrator) domain account, and use Windows integrated security to log in to the database.

Granting Database Permissions

Access to the instance and application databases in Notification Services is granted via roles. Notification Services defines a set of roles, and the various elements of the databases (tables, views, stored procedures, and functions) are set up in such a way that only members of the appropriate roles can access them. Notification Services defines separate roles for each of the functions that needs to be performed in relation to a Notification Services instance (for example, event collection, generation, distribution, subscriber and subscription management, and administration). These functions can each be run under different user accounts, and each of these user accounts need only be a member of the roles required for its function. You can therefore grant a particular account only the minimum permissions it needs to perform its tasks.

Table 45.2 lists the various database roles that Notification Services defines.

TABLE 45.2 Notification Services Database Roles

Role Name	Allowed Operations
`NSAnalysis`	Executing reporting stored procedures
`NSAdmin`	Enabling and disabling components via `nscontrol enable` and `disable`
`NSDistributor`	Performing distributor functions
`NSEventProvider`	Performing event provider functions
`NSGenerator`	Performing generator functions
`NSMonitor`	Executing stored procedures that collect data used to update the Notification Services performance counters
`NSReader`	Reading information from the configuration tables in the instance and application databases
`NSRunService`	All operations allowed by the `NSDistributor`, `NSEventProvider`, `NSGenerator`, `NSMonitor`, `NSReader`, and `NSVacuum` roles
`NSSubscriberAdmin`	Performing subscriber and subscription management functions
`NSVacuum`	Removal of old data from the Notification Services tables

If you are running all the components of the Notification Services Windows Service (event providers, generator, and distributor) on the same computer, you can simply add the service account to the `NSRunService` role. Note that if you're using Windows integrated security, the service account is the Windows account under which the service runs; if you're using SQL Server Authentication, the service account is the SQL user whose credentials you passed to the `nscontrol register` command when registering the instance.

If you have deployed the various Notification Services components on separate computers for scale-out, you can configure the Windows Service on each of these computers to run under a different account. You can then add these accounts to the various roles (`NSEventProvider`, `NSDistributor`, `NSGenerator`, and so on) separately, as needed. This ensures that each account has only the permissions it needs to perform its designated functions.

The user account under which your subscription management application runs needs to be added to the `NSSubscriberAdmin` role. This account will vary depending on the nature of your subscription management application. If it is an ASP.NET Web application, the user account may be the local ASP.NET account on your Web server computer.

There are two steps in granting database permissions to a user account:

1. Granting database access to the account
2. Adding the account to the required database roles

You can perform both of these steps graphically through Enterprise Manager, or by invoking system-stored procedures. To grant database access, invoke the `sp_grantdbaccess` stored procedure. Note that you must grant access to the instance database and all the application databases that the user account needs to access. To add an account to a role, invoke the `sp_addrolemember` stored procedure. Stored procedures are fully documented in SQL Server 2000 Books Online.

Monitoring and Administering a Notification Services Instance

Once you have deployed your Notification Services instance, it's important to constantly monitor it to ensure that it is running without problems and performing as expected. Notification Services provides monitoring information through the following means:

- The Windows Application Event Log
- Performance monitor objects
- A set of reporting stored procedures in the instance and application databases

The following sections describe how to use these to monitor your instance.

The Windows Application Event Log

The Windows Application Event Log is generally the place to start when checking the behavior of the system. Notification Services writes various types of log entries, including verbose, informational, warning, and error messages. All log entries written by Notification Services will specify "NotificationServices" as the event source. Figure 45.3 shows an example of a typical error message from Notification Services.

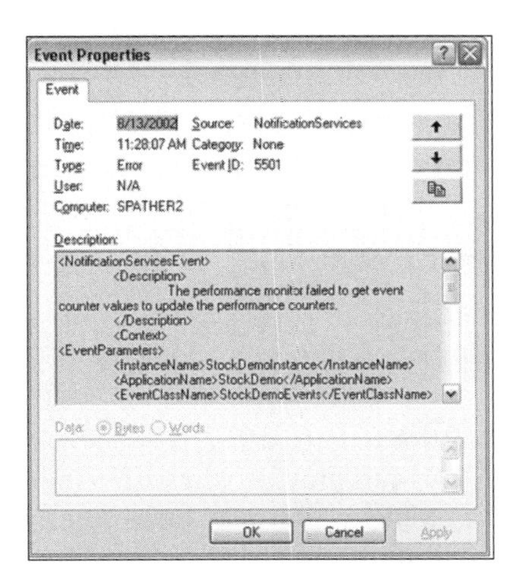

FIGURE 45.3 An error message written to the Windows Application Event Log by Notification Services.

If something abnormal occurs during the running of your notification applications, Notification Services will usually write an error or warning event log entry. These entries all have the same structure: They begin with a description of the issue, and then list the details of the component to which it relates (usually the entry will specify at least the instance name, the application name, and the name of the computer, but it may also contain other information such as the name of a particular event provider), followed by more technical details about the problem. Each event log message contains a link to a Microsoft Web site that provides more information, including possible causes of the problem being described and potential resolutions.

Performance Monitor Objects

Notification Services provides several performance monitor objects that you can use to track various aspects of a running instance. These performance objects can be tracked in the perfmon tool, or any other tool that displays information from Windows performance monitor objects.

The Notification Services objects are classified into three groups:

- **Component-level objects** track the performance of individual components, some of which span multiple applications.
- **Application-level objects** track the performance of applications as a whole.
- **Instance-level** objects track performance at the level of a whole instance.

Notification Services Books Online provides a detailed description of each counter available in the various performance objects.

Reporting Stored Procedures

Notification Services provides a set of stored procedures that provide detailed reporting information about an instance or application. There are three categories of reports:

- **Snapshot reports** provide a view of the immediate state of an instance.
- **Diagnostic reports** provide an in-depth view of the activity of the Notification Services components during specific time periods.
- **Detail reports** provide details about particular Notification Services entities (for instance, a particular event batch or notification batch).

It is a good practice to run snapshot reports at regular intervals to observe the instantaneous behavior of the system. This can provide you with a quick insight into the health of the instance and can highlight problems that may have occurred. For example, one of the data points returned by the application's snapshot report is the amount of time that has elapsed since the last batch of notifications was generated. In an application that generates notifications fairly regularly, one would expect this to always be a fairly small value. If the snapshot report shows that in fact a lot of time has passed since a notification batch was generated, it can be an indication that something is wrong. Perhaps the application isn't receiving any new events, or the generator is not functioning correctly. Having been alerted to the problem, you can make a fuller diagnosis by examining the Windows Application Event Log for error information, or executing other reports to isolate the source of the problem.

The diagnostic reports are useful when you want to examine the behavior of an aspect of an instance or application during a particular time interval. For example, you can execute the diagnostic event class report for a particular event class, passing it a start and end time of interest. The report will return information about activity relating to that event class during the specified time interval. This will include how many event batches of that class were collected, the event collection rate, how long it took for the generator to process those event batches and generate notifications, and how long it took for those notifications to be distributed.

The detail reports can help diagnose problems with a particular Notification Services entity, such as a specific notification or event batch. For example, the notification batch details report can provide details on a particular notification batch. The information returned will include the number of notifications in that batch, how long the batch took to generate, and the delivery status of the notifications in that batch.

Notification Services Books Online provides detailed information about the individual reporting stored procedures, along with the exact information returned by each one.

Summary

SQL Notification Services is a platform for developing and deploying rich, highly scalable notification applications. It greatly reduces the development time required to build applications with sophisticated features, and provides an execution engine for executing those applications efficiently. Applications built on the Notification Services platform are reliable, secure, and can be administered easily.

Notification applications are becoming increasingly important in a world in which people want to receive personalized and timely information on whatever device they may be carrying. Many people recognize the value of notification applications, but underestimate the complexity of building them well. SQL Notification Services offers an elegant solution to the problem, allowing developers to focus on the core logic of their applications rather than the more basic platform issues.

CHAPTER 46

SQL Server and the Microsoft .NET Framework

by Paul Bertucci

IN THIS CHAPTER

- The Microsoft .NET Framework Class Library
- ADO.NET
- .NET SQL Providers
- .NET Concurrency Model (Default)
- XML Externalization in .NET
- A .NET Application Within Visual Studio .NET

The Microsoft .NET Framework has been thrust upon us to address enterprise-wide, largescale application development for both Web-based applications and traditional Windows-based applications. This is one of the most significant technology shifts Microsoft has ever made. It is Microsoft's answer to J2EE/J2SE (Sun's Java-centric multitiered framework).

Like J2EE, the .NET Framework is a multitiered platform that consists of developer tools, Web services, a set of strongly typed programming languages that are syntactically identical whether used to program for the Web or for the desktop, a common language runtime, a set of framework classes encapsulating areas of common functionality, and a greatly improved data access model.

Microsoft SQL Server 2000 sits firmly in the heart of .NET as the major data provider for this framework. You can take advantage of 100 percent of the power of SQL Server 2000 within any .NET application. SQL Server 2000 interacts with any external system as well, easily communicating with other non-Windows platforms via XML.

Microsoft's .NET Framework ships with a set of useful built-in classes. These classes contain many of the objects you'll use to create applications, both for the Web and for the desktop, such as all built-in Web controls, Windows forms controls, and collection objects. Several of these built-in classes make up ADO.NET (the data layer for .NET). It is this layer that we will focus on here because it directly relates to how SQL Server 2000 is used in the .NET Framework.

Figure 46.1 illustrates the basic multitiered components that constitute the .NET Framework and the ADO.NET data layer.

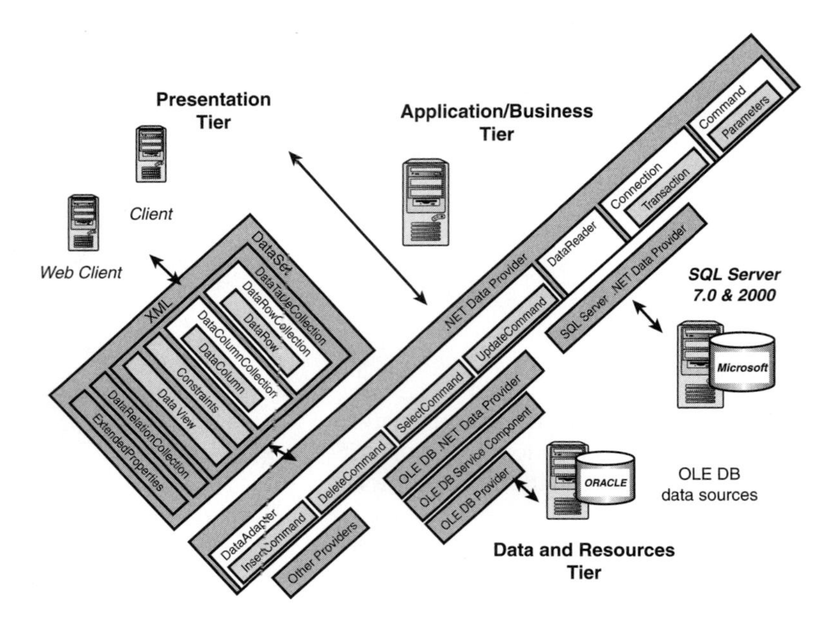

FIGURE 46.1 The Microsoft .NET Framework.

As you can see in Figure 46.1, the .NET SQL Server Data Provider embraces SQL Server (both SQL Server 7.0 and 2000). This data provider layer has been fine-tuned for SQL Server. All other database engines or file systems (such as Oracle and Excel) are addressed via the OLE DB .NET Data Provider or some other data provider unique to a data source. The overall .NET Data Provider spans all the specific data providers and is utilized in programming environments using ADO.NET classes. In other words, ADO.NET is the way SQL (or XML) is invoked from any programming environment (Visual Basic .NET, C# .NET, J# .NET, ASP.NET, and so on).

The Microsoft .NET Framework Class Library

There are a large number of classes and methods inside the Microsoft .NET Framework. The classes are organized into groups called namespaces. A namespace is simply a logical division, and can be as large or small as desired.

NOTE

If you wish to download the Microsoft .NET Framework, navigate to `http://msdn.microsoft.com/net`.

ADO.NET

ADO.NET is Microsoft's platform for data access in the .NET Framework. Out of the box, ADO.NET is scalable, interoperable, and familiar enough to ADO developers to be immediately usable. By design, the ADO.NET object model and many of the ADO.NET code constructs will look very familiar to ADO developers.

At the most basic level, ADO.NET consists of the following set of framework namespaces:

- `System.Data`
- `System.Data.Common`
- `System.Data.SqlClient`
- `System.Data.OleDbClient`
- `System.Data.SqlTypes`

The `System.Data` namespace contains many of the objects on which ADO.NET is built. This is where you'll find the `DataTable`, `DataSet`, `DataRelation`, and `DataView` objects. Additionally, this is where ADO.NET constants are stored. For instance, the `System.Data.SqlDbType` class shown in Figure 46.2 contains all the Microsoft SQL data types.

The `System.Data.SqlClient` namespace contains objects designed to work with a Microsoft SQL database. These are objects such as `SqlCommand`, `SqlConnection`, and `SqlParameter` as well as new faces such as `SqlDataAdapter` and `SqlDataReader`. If you're a SQL developer, this namespace will be your sandbox. The namespace uses a managed SQL provider to work with the database. By working directly with the SQL database APIs, `SqlClient` bypasses ODBC (Open Database Connectivity) and OLE DB (Object Linking and Embedding for Databases) entirely, offering a very robust and efficient interface.

The `System.Data.OleDbClient` namespace is designed to work with any valid OLE DB source. This includes data sources as varied as Oracle databases, Microsoft Excel files, standard ASCII comma-delimited text files, Microsoft Access, and versions of Microsoft SQL Server prior to version 7.0. As mentioned previously, if you're working with Microsoft SQL Server directly, the `System.Data.SqlClient` is the optimal way to go.

The `System.Data.OleDbClient` namespace almost mirrors the `System.Data.SqlClient` namespace. In fact, if you scan the classes in both, you'll notice that the classnames differ only by their preface (for instance, `SqlCommand` versus `OleDbCommand`). Fortunately, once you've worked with one namespace, you'll understand how to use both.

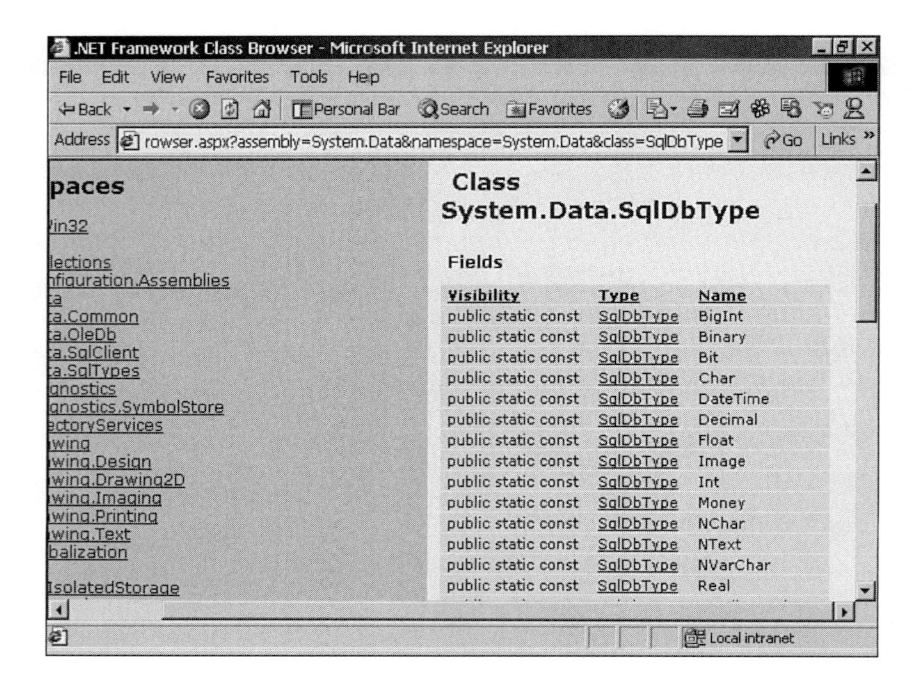

FIGURE 46.2 The `System.Data.SqlDbType` class contains constant values for all the data types in Microsoft SQL versions 7.0 and 2000.

ADO.NET Versus ADO

The relationship between ADO and ADO.NET is analogous to the one between ASP and ASP.NET. Many of the object and method names are similar, but behind the curtains everything has been redesigned and improved.

For instance, the ADO data model is based around the `recordset` object. In essence, the `recordset` is a spreadsheet of data in memory. You are very limited in what you can do with a `recordset` of data. It is difficult to do advanced data filtering or combine two `recordsets`. And, though it is possible to transmit an ADO `recordset` to a remote server, you have to configure all firewalls between the two servers to enable the proprietary ports required for COM marshaling.

Additionally, the remote server must know what an ADO `recordset` is. For all intents and purposes, this means that the remote server must be running a Microsoft operating system. Because of the limitations of the ADO `recordset` object, solutions based on ADO are likewise limited.

Microsoft has fixed these problems with ADO.NET. The centerpiece object of ADO.NET is the `DataSet` (not the old `recordset`). The `DataSet`, as shown in Figure 46.3, is an in-memory (cached) representation of data that provides a consistent relational programming model regardless of the data source.

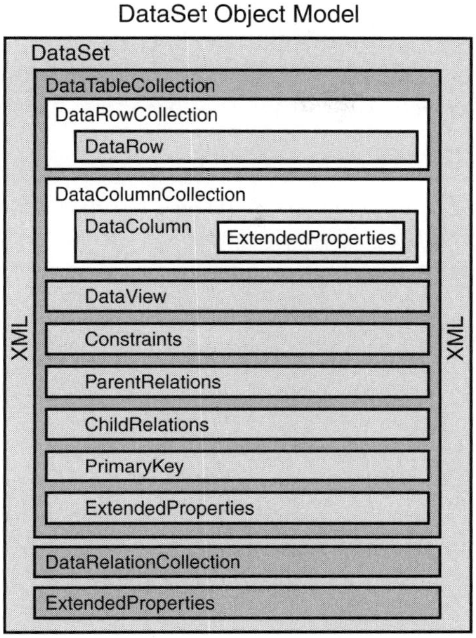

DataSet Object Model
DataSet
DataTableCollection
DataRowCollection
DataRow
DataColumnCollection
DataColumn
ExtendedProperties
DataView
Constraints
ParentRelations
ChildRelations
PrimaryKey
ExtendedProperties
DataRelationCollection
ExtendedProperties
XML
XML

FIGURE 46.3 The ADO.NET `DataSet` object model.

`DataSets`

The `DataSet` contains a collection of `DataTables`, which are very much like `recordsets` in that each `DataTable` is a set of data. However, rather than just serving as a container for various `DataTables`, the `DataSet` can store relations and constraints pertaining to the `DataTables`! Not only can a `DataSet` mirror the relations and constraints in your data source, but you can add new ones as the logic of your application dictates. This gives you complete control over filtering and combining `DataTables`.

Additionally, `DataSets` (and the `DataTables` within them) are represented internally by strongly typed XML. Thus, at any point, it is possible to save a `DataSet` to XML. This might not seem like a major point at first glance. However, this means that any platform that can parse XML—and I don't know of any platform that cannot—can retrieve data from an ADO.NET `DataSet`.

`DataSets` are easily transmitted to remote machines, as well. Web services are designed to transmit XML data via SOAP to remote machines. Because the `DataSet` is represented internally as XML, sending a `DataSet` to a remote server requires no special handling. The remote server could be running any platform that understands XML, including Java-based solutions such as IBM WebSphere. A WebSphere developer would only need to parse the XML.

The `DataSet` object is the parent object of most of the other objects in the `System.Data` namespace. Its primary role is to store a collection of `DataTables`, the relations, and constraints between those `DataTables`. The `DataSet` also contains several methods for reading and writing XML, as well as merging other `DataSets`, `DataTables`, and `DataRows`.

The `DataTable`

The `DataTable` stores a table of information, typically retrieved from a data source. In addition to simply containing the various `DataColumns` and `DataRows`, however, the `DataTable` also stores metatable information such as the primary key and constraints.

The `DataRow` and `DataColumn`

The `DataRow` and `DataColumn` objects are at the bottom of the ADO.NET "food chain," so to speak. These instances are where you can drill down to the actual columns and rows in a `DataTable`.

The `System.Data.SqlClient` and `System.Data.OleDb` Namespaces

As previously mentioned, the `System.Data.SqlClient` and `System.Data.OleDb` namespaces work with data sources. `System.Data.SqlClient` uses a managed provider to interact directly with Microsoft SQL Server Version 7.0 and 2000. `System.Data.OleDb` interacts with any valid OLE DB source. Though the namespaces are separate, the base objects function very similarly. Both namespaces contain `connection`, `command`, `DataAdapter`, and `DataReader` objects.

The `connection` Object

As you might have guessed, the `connection` object opens a connection to your data source. All the configurable aspects of a database connection are represented in the `connection` object, including `ConnectionString` and `ConnectionTimeout`. Also, database transactions are still dependent on the `connection` object.

The `command` Object

The `command` object performs actions on the data source. You can use the `command` object to execute stored procedures, or any valid T-SQL command understood by your datasource. This is the object that performs the standard `SELECT`, `INSERT`, `UPDATE`, and `DELETE` T-SQL operations.

The `DataAdapter` Object

The `DataAdapter` object is brand-new in ADO.NET. The `DataAdapter` takes the results of a database query from a `command` object and pushes them into a `DataSet` using the `DataAdapter.Fill()` method. Additionally, the `DataAdapter.Update()` method will communicate any changes to a `DataSet` back to the original data source. Unlike with ADO, updating the original data source with modified data works reliably well.

The `DataReader` Object

The `DataReader` object is also brand-new in ADO.NET. The `DataReader` provides a very fast, forward-only view of the data returned from a data source. In most instances, to display a set of data in a Web or Windows form, this is the object you'll use, because there is very little overhead. No `DataSet` is created; in fact, no more than one row of information from the data source is in memory at a time. This makes the `DataReader` quite efficient at returning large amounts of data. You can think of the `DataReader` as a direct route from the data source to the final destination. However, if you need to manipulate schema or use some advanced display features such as automatic data paging, you must use a `DataAdapter` and `DataSet`.

.NET SQL Providers

By the late 1980s, several vendors (including IBM and Microsoft) realized that it would be a good idea to offer programmers a standardized database interface. By factoring a standard interface from the mire of proprietary APIs used by the database system, these vendors created an environment in which programmers only had to learn one API. This standard API is known as ODBC (Open Database Connectivity).

OLE DB (Object Linking and Embedding for Databases) is a COM (Component Object Model)-based version of ODBC. OLE DB offers much better performance than ODBC.

Both ODBC and OLE DB are layers that exist between application code and the database. As such, they are not as fast as interfacing with the database system directly. The developers of ADO.NET created a namespace that works with Microsoft SQL Server (versions 7.0 and 2000) using its native APIs. Because the code connects directly to SQL Server and is managed by the framework, it's known as a managed provider.

Regardless of which method is used to connect to the database, ADO.NET provides a single interface for retrieving data. You don't need to worry about the underlying connection method.

.NET Concurrency Model (Default)

Concurrency is critical in any multiuser environment where data is to be updated. Concurrency, as you can see in Figure 46.4, is best described as "multiple users vying to update data without affecting each other as they update it." In this illustration, each client application (Windows Client A, Web Client B, and Web Client C) has read the same customer data values at approximately the same time. They all see the same customer data, and some will choose to update this data and will expect their updates to be successful. The type of concurrency model you utilize will directly determine how these data resources are treated (whether they are held, locked, or enqueued), what type of performance to expect, and how scalable your application will be.

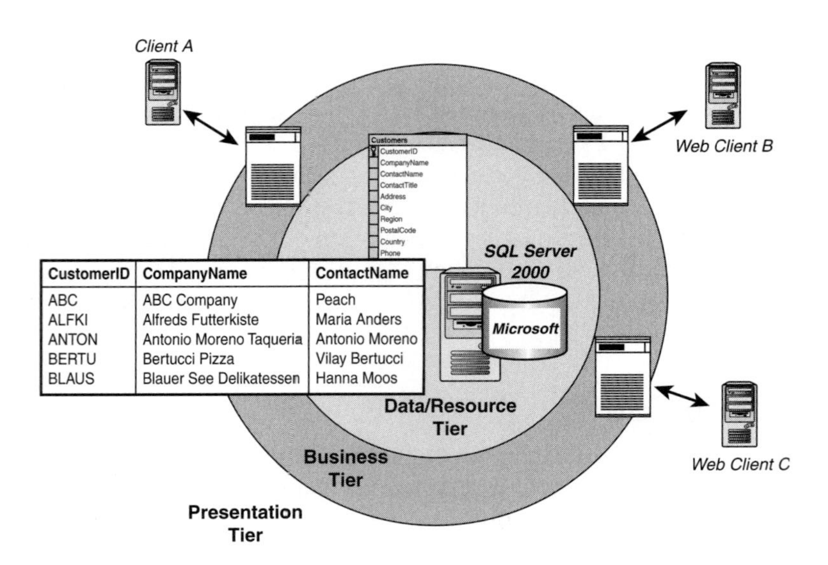

CustomerID	CompanyName	ContactName
ABC	ABC Company	Peach
ALFKI	Alfreds Futterkiste	Maria Anders
ANTON	Antonio Moreno Taqueria	Antonio Moreno
BERTU	Bertucci Pizza	Vilay Bertucci
BLAUS	Blauer See Delikatessen	Hanna Moos

FIGURE 46.4 A typical multiuser data access in a .NET architecture. Here, three clients are accessing customer data stored in Microsoft SQL Server 2000.

In classic client/server architectures, most programming languages and database servers support multiple types of concurrency models—optimistic, pessimistic, and everything in between (different isolation levels). In the multitiered .NET architecture, the focus is on utilizing a "disconnected" mode of data retrieval to minimize data concurrency issues and to increase scalability. This correlates well with using the optimistic concurrency approach and is the default approach used in the .NET Framework.

Optimistic concurrency enables multiple users to read the same data row at the same time without having to lock it. Any one of the users can change (update) the data values. An optimistic concurrency violation will occur when a user tries to update the previously read data if another user has already updated it since the last time the first user read it. This can really be a disaster if not understood well or not handled properly.

What is so significant here is that *not* locking the data resource (the data row) for update leads to an improvement in the overall performance of your system due to the major reduction of additional server resources needed to lock data. For an application to hold a lock on a data resource, it must also maintain a persistent connection to the database server that houses the data. Because this is not happening in optimistic concurrency (no persistent connection is needed and no data lock is used), connections to the database server are available to handle many more clients in less time. This directly achieves the scalability and performance goals of multitiered architectures.

Coding for Optimistic Concurrency

In general, there are two basic coding techniques you can use to implement the optimistic concurrency approach within ADO.NET. The default approach is to compare each column of data in the database table to the original data values you read into your DataSet as part of your UPDATE statement. This will detect any optimistic concurrency violations. If any of the database data values have changed since you last read the data row, your UPDATE statement will fail (as you would probably want it to). At a minimum, this forces you to reread the data values from the database, see what they are, and see whether you want to update some data value further.

Another, quicker method of doing the same thing is to utilize a timestamp column that may be available in the data table you are working with. (Such a column is available in MS SQL Server tables that have defined one.) This technique allows you to read a timestamp value that is part of the database data row and then compare timestamps at the time you want to update the data in the database. If the timestamp value has changed since the last time you read the data values, your UPDATE statement will fail (again, as you would want it to do).

The following is a short piece of Visual Basic code that you can execute for practice. This example uses the ADO.NET DataSet fill-and-update approach from the Customers table in the Northwind database that comes with Microsoft SQL Server:

```
  CustomerAdapter.Fill(CustomerDataSet, "Customers")
  CustomerAdapter.Update(CustomerDataSet, "Customers")
```


It will save the original data row values as they were originally read from the database:

```
OldParms = CustomerAdapter.UpdateCommand.Parameters.Add("@oldCustomerID",
        SqlDbType.NChar, 5, "CustomerID")
  OldParms.SourceVersion = DataRowVersion.Original
```

These will be used in a comparison (WHERE clause) that will be part of the UPDATE statement:

```
CustomerAdapter.UpdateCommand = New SqlCommand(
"UPDATE Customers (CustomerID, CompanyName, ContactName) " &
"VALUES(@CustomerID, @CompanyName, @ContactName) " & _
"WHERE CustomerID = @oldCustomerID AND CompanyName = @oldCompanyName " &
" AND ContactName = @oldContactName", nwindConn)
```

By doing this comparison of the original data values read from the database with what's in the database at the time the update is issued, you will guarantee that no other user has slipped in and updated something before you. This is optimistic concurrency, and is shown in its complete form in Listing 46.1.

LISTING 46.1 Optimistic Concurrency (File 46OptCon.vb)

```
Imports System
Imports System.Data
Imports System.Data.SqlClient
Imports Microsoft.VisualBasic
namespace HowTo.ADONET24.Samples
Public Class OptConSample
  Public Shared Sub Main()
    Dim nwindConn As SqlConnection = New SqlConnection
  ("Data Source=localhost;Integrated Security=SSPI;Initial Catalog=northwind")
    Dim CustomerAdapter As SqlDataAdapter = New SqlDataAdapter
        ("SELECT CustomerID, CompanyName, ContactName " &
         " FROM Customers ORDER BY CustomerID", nwindConn)
  CustomerAdapter.UpdateCommand = New SqlCommand
        ("UPDATE Customers (CustomerID, CompanyName, ContactName) " &
         "VALUES(@CustomerID, @CompanyName, @ContactName) " & _
        "WHERE CustomerID = @oldCustomerID AND CompanyName = @oldCompanyName " &
        " AND ContactName = @oldContactName", nwindConn)
  CustomerAdapter.UpdateCommand.Parameters.Add
        ("@CustomerID", SqlDbType.NChar, 5, "CustomerID")
  CustomerAdapter.UpdateCommand.Parameters.Add
        ("@CompanyName", SqlDbType.NVarChar, 40, "CompanyName")
  CustomerAdapter.UpdateCommand.Parameters.Add
        ("@ContactName", SqlDbType.NVarChar, 30, "ContactName")
 'Set up OldParms to hold the rows original values
 'These are then used in the WHERE clause for the
 'optimistic concurrency comparison
  Dim OldParms As SqlParameter
  OldParms = CustomerAdapter.UpdateCommand.Parameters.Add
        ("@oldCustomerID", SqlDbType.NChar, 5, "CustomerID")
  OldParms.SourceVersion = DataRowVersion.Original
  OldParms = CustomerAdapter.UpdateCommand.Parameters.Add
        ("@oldCompanyName", SqlDbType.NVarChar, 40, "CompanyName")
  OldParms.SourceVersion = DataRowVersion.Original
  OldParms = CustomerAdapter.UpdateCommand.Parameters.Add
        ("@oldContactName", SqlDbType.NVarChar, 30, "ContactName")
  OldParms.SourceVersion = DataRowVersion.Original
  Dim CustomerDataSet As DataSet = New DataSet()
  Console.Writeline ("Go get some customer data - Fill")
  CustomerAdapter.Fill(CustomerDataSet, "Customers")
  Console.Writeline ("Update the rows")
  CustomerAdapter.Update(CustomerDataSet, "Customers")
  Dim CustRow As DataRow
```

LISTING 46.1 Continued

```
  Console.Writeline ("Look for optimistic concurrency violations")
  For Each CustRow In CustomerDataSet.Tables("Customers").Rows
    Console.Writeline ("Looking for errors for row with CustomerID of " &
        CustRow(0) )
    If CustRow.HasErrors Then Console.WriteLine(CustRow(0) &
        vbCrLf & CustRow.RowError)
    if not CustRow.HasErrors then Console.Writeline
        ("No optimistic concurrency error found")
  Next
  Console.Writeline ("Show contents of DataSet")
  For each CustRow in CustomerDataSet.Tables("Customers").Rows
      Console.Writeline("Customer Contacts Selected: "
        + CustRow("ContactName").ToString())
  Next
 End Sub
End Class
End namespace
```


XML Externalization in .NET

As mentioned before, all data communication within .NET and outside of .NET can be done via XML. By definition, any `DataSet` can be transported anywhere via its XML externalization. In fact, the `DataSet` is stored at all times in its XML form.

Figure 46.5 shows the Customers table in the Northwind database. Listing 46.2 is the associated XML Schema Definition for Customers (compliant with the XML Schema definition language standards). This is easily generated in Visual Studio .NET or via the ADO.NET XML Schema generation command (the `WriteXMLSchema` method of the `DataSet`).

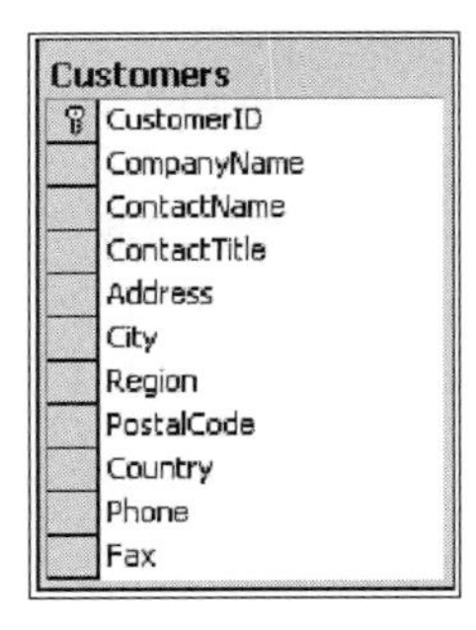

FIGURE 46.5 The Customers table.

LISTING 46.2 The XML Schema File for the Customers DataSet

```
<?xml version="1.0" encoding="utf-8"?>
<xs:schema id="CustDataSet" xmlns=""
    xmlns:xs="http://www.w3.org/2001/XMLSchema"
    xmlns:msdata="urn:schemas-microsoft-com:xml-msdata">
  <xs:element name="CustDataSet" msdata:IsDataSet="true">
    <xs:complexType>
      <xs:choice maxOccurs="unbounded">
        <xs:element name="Customers">
          <xs:complexType>
            <xs:sequence>
              <xs:element name="CustomerID" type="xs:string" minOccurs="0" />
              <xs:element name="CompanyName" type="xs:string" minOccurs="0" />
              <xs:element name="ContactName" type="xs:string" minOccurs="0" />
              <xs:element name="ContactTitle" type="xs:string" minOccurs="0" />
              <xs:element name="Address" type="xs:string" minOccurs="0" />
              <xs:element name="City" type="xs:string" minOccurs="0" />
              <xs:element name="Region" type="xs:string" minOccurs="0" />
              <xs:element name="PostalCode" type="xs:string" minOccurs="0" />
              <xs:element name="Country" type="xs:string" minOccurs="0" />
              <xs:element name="Phone" type="xs:string" minOccurs="0" />
              <xs:element name="Fax" type="xs:string" minOccurs="0" />
            </xs:sequence>
          </xs:complexType>
        </xs:element>
      </xs:choice>
    </xs:complexType>
  </xs:element>
</xs:schema>
```

If you need a much more complex `DataSet` that, for instance, includes customers (all elements) and their associated orders (all elements), the XML coding is a bit longer. Figure 46.6 shows the relationship that must be traversed from the Customers table to the Orders table. This translates into a more complex XML Schema definition that contains both customers and orders. Remember, it must allow you to traverse a relationship (from parent customers to their child orders) using one `DataSet` (as shown in Listing 46.3).

LISTING 46.3 The XML Schema File for the Customers and Orders DataSet

```
<?xml version="1.0" encoding="utf-8"?>
<xs:schema id="CustDataSet0" xmlns=""
    xmlns:xs="http://www.w3.org/2001/XMLSchema"
    xmlns:msdata="urn:schemas-microsoft-com:xml-msdata">
```

LISTING 46.3 Continued

```
<xs:element name="CustDataSet0" msdata:IsDataSet="true">
  <xs:complexType>
    <xs:choice maxOccurs="unbounded">
      <xs:element name="Customers">
        <xs:complexType>
          <xs:sequence>
            <xs:element name="CustomerID" type="xs:string" minOccurs="0" />
            <xs:element name="CompanyName" type="xs:string" minOccurs="0" />
            <xs:element name="ContactName" type="xs:string" minOccurs="0" />
            <xs:element name="ContactTitle" type="xs:string" minOccurs="0"/>
            <xs:element name="Address" type="xs:string" minOccurs="0" />
            <xs:element name="City" type="xs:string" minOccurs="0" />
            <xs:element name="Region" type="xs:string" minOccurs="0" />
            <xs:element name="PostalCode" type="xs:string" minOccurs="0"/>
            <xs:element name="Country" type="xs:string" minOccurs="0" />
            <xs:element name="Phone" type="xs:string" minOccurs="0" />
            <xs:element name="Fax" type="xs:string" minOccurs="0" />
          </xs:sequence>
        </xs:complexType>
      </xs:element>
      <xs:element name="Orders">
        <xs:complexType>
          <xs:sequence>
            <xs:element name="OrderID" type="xs:int" minOccurs="0" />
            <xs:element name="CustomerID" type="xs:string" minOccurs="0" />
            <xs:element name="EmployeeID" type="xs:int" minOccurs="0" />
            <xs:element name="OrderDate" type="xs:dateTime" minOccurs="0" />
            <xs:element name="RequiredDate" type="xs:dateTime" minOccurs="0"/>
            <xs:element name="ShippedDate" type="xs:dateTime" minOccurs="0" />
            <xs:element name="ShipVia" type="xs:int" minOccurs="0" />
            <xs:element name="Freight" type="xs:decimal" minOccurs="0" />
            <xs:element name="ShipName" type="xs:string" minOccurs="0" />
            <xs:element name="ShipAddress" type="xs:string" minOccurs="0"/>
            <xs:element name="ShipCity" type="xs:string" minOccurs="0" />
            <xs:element name="ShipRegion" type="xs:string" minOccurs="0" />
            <xs:element name="ShipPostalCode" type="xs:string" minOccurs="0"/>
            <xs:element name="ShipCountry" type="xs:string" minOccurs="0" />
          </xs:sequence>
        </xs:complexType>
      </xs:element>
    </xs:choice>
```

LISTING 46.3 Continued

```
    </xs:complexType>
  </xs:element>
</xs:schema>
```

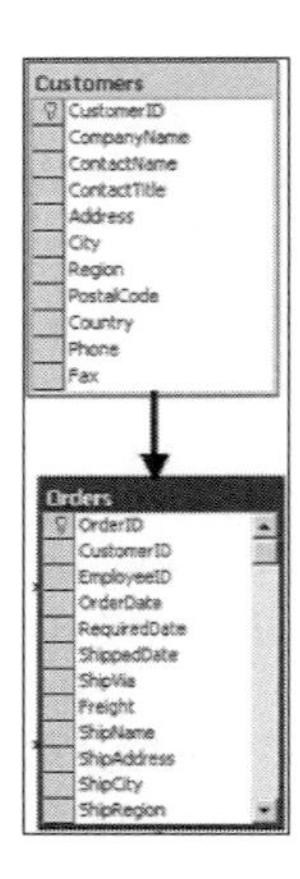

FIGURE 46.6 The relationship between the Customers and Orders tables.

The .NET Framework SDK supplies the `XSD.exe` (XML Schema Definition) tool. The XSD tool can generate XML Schema or common language runtime classes from XDR, XML, and XSD files, or from classes in a runtime assembly. You simply provide the XML Schema file as input (`Customers.xsd` in this example) along with a few directives. The file extensions drive the XSD tool logic. Thus, if you specify (and provide) an XML file, `XSD.exe` will infer a schema from the data in the file and produce an associated schema file (`.xsd`). If you specify (and provide) an XSD file (schema file), `XSD.exe` will generate source code for runtime objects that correspond to the XML Schema.

NOTE

To generate a typed `DataSet` that can be used by many programs (and languages such as VB and C#), you must start with an XML Schema representation of the `DataSet`. This will be the `.xsd` (XML Schema Definition) XML file. After you have created this, you can turn it into a typed `DataSet` and make it available to programs that reference it properly (via a generated `.dll`). This `.xsd` schema of the `DataSet` must be compliant with the XML Schema definition language standards, available at `http://www.w3.org/2001/XMLSchema` and `http://w3c.org`.

A .NET Application Within Visual Studio .NET

Just to give you a taste of what it is like creating applications in Visual Studio .NET and SQL Server 2000, let's build a simple Windows Forms .NET application. Our example will query customer contact names for customers in the Customers table of the Northwind SQL Server database. Of course, you must have already downloaded .NET and installed it before you can follow along with this example. In case you don't have .NET installed, I've provided enough figures here to give you a very good idea of what the process entails.

Creating a New Project in Visual Studio .NET

Following is a Visual Studio .NET project example that will query customer contact names for customers in the Customers table of the Northwind SQL Server database. It is very easy to re-create, and we suggest you take a stab at it here.

1. Create a new project in Visual Studio .NET by choosing File, New, and then choosing the Project option.

2. When the New Project dialog box appears (see Figure 46.7), choose Visual Basic Projects (or Visual C# Projects) and Windows Applications. Name this project "Unleashed.NET".

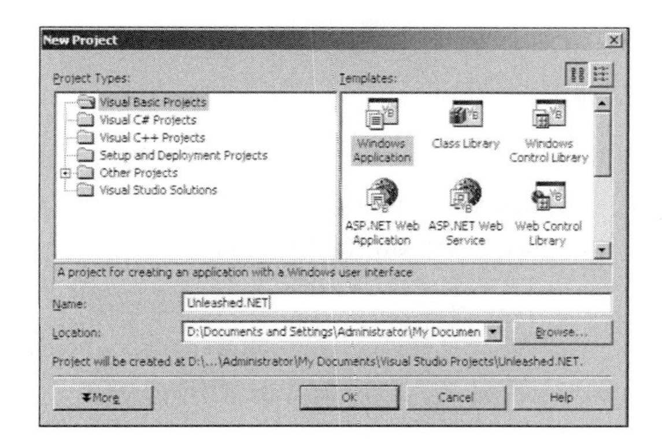

FIGURE 46.7 Visual Studio .NET New Project dialog box.

3. This creates a default form from which you can start.

Adding the Data Connection and Data Adapter

We will be accessing the Customers table in SQL Server's Northwind database, so we will first need to create a data connection and a data adapter to Microsoft SQL Server.

1. From the Data tab of the Toolbox, drag a `SQLDataAdapter` object into your form (see Figure 46.8).

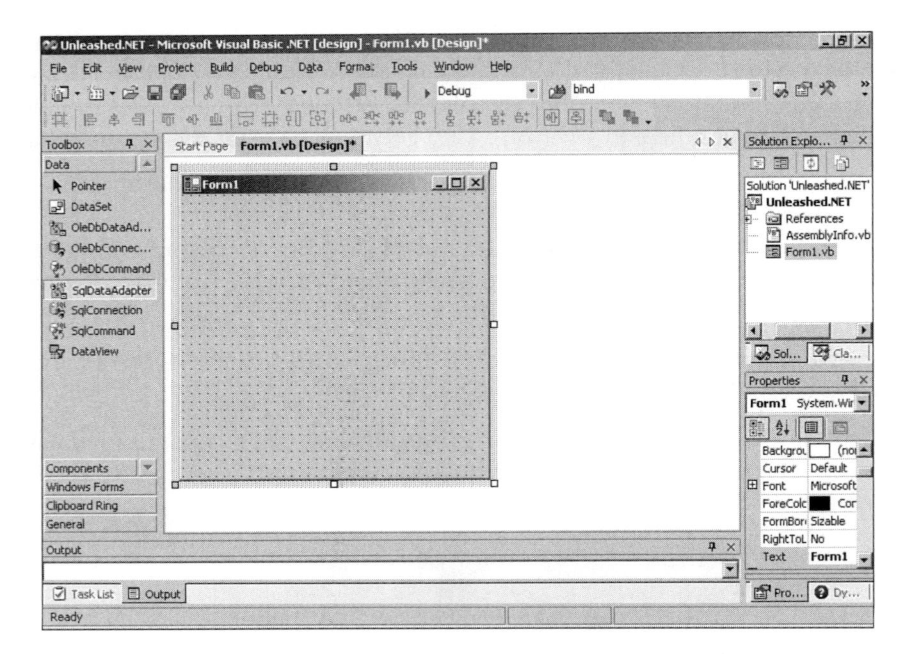

FIGURE 46.8 A Visual Studio .NET Form with a Data Toolbox `SqlDataAdapter` object selected.

2. This will automatically invoke the Data Adapter Configuration Wizard. Both the data connection and the data adapter can be fully configured here.

   a. The wizard starts with the Choose Your Data Connection dialog box (see Figure 46.9). If you already have a connection defined in your project, it will be placed in the dialog box; otherwise, choose to create a new connection and specify the appropriate connection information. (Test the connection as well.)

   b. You will have to decide whether to supply SQL statements, build a new stored procedure, or give the name of an existing stored procedure for the data access. In our example we will use the Use SQL Statements option.

   c. You will be presented with a Generate the SQL Statements dialog box where you can simply type in a valid SQL statement. Alternatively, you can use the Query Builder option to formulate the SQL query. What you are really doing is defining what data the data adapter will load into the `DataSet`. For this example, just type in the following query:

```
SELECT CustomerID, ContactName FROM Customers
WHERE (CustomerID = @param1)
```

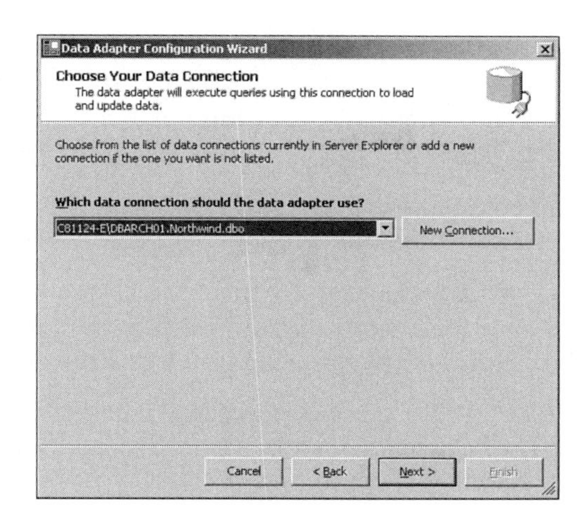

FIGURE 46.9 The Choose Your Data Connection dialog box of the Data Adapter Configuration Wizard.

You should also note that for `SqlDataAdapters`, you will use a named parameter (`@param...`) for any values that are to be substituted into the `WHERE` clause. The `OleDBDataAdapter`'s SQL statements would use a question mark (`?`). This dialog box looks like Figure 46.10.

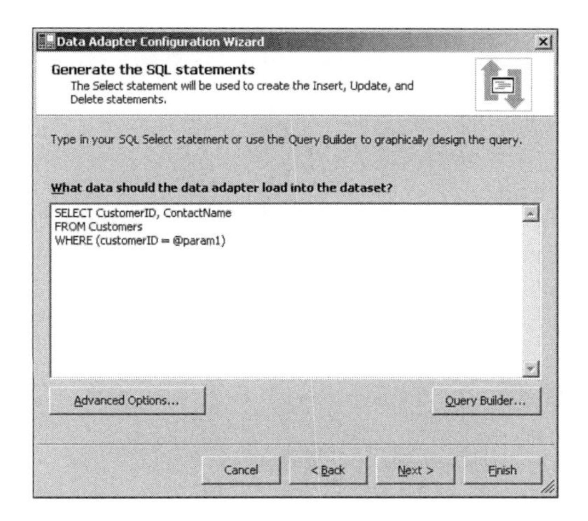

FIGURE 46.10 The Generate the SQL Statements dialog box of the Data Adapter Configuration Wizard.

d. The wizard will show you the tasks it has done and indicate whether the `SqlDataAdapter` has been configured successfully. The details will show you that it generated a `SELECT` statement, Table mappings, an `INSERT` statement (which corresponds to the `SELECT`), an `UPDATE` statement (which also corresponds to the `SELECT`), and a `DELETE` statement. Wow!

After the `SqlDataAdapter` and `DataConnection` objects have been configured and added to the form, you must generate a `DataSet` and then add an instance of this `DataSet` to the form. We will be binding our `TextBox` properties to the columns in the `DataSet`.

e. Right-click on the `SqlDataAdapter` (`SqlDataAdapter1`) that is on your form and choose the Generate Dataset menu option, as shown in Figure 46.11.

f. Choose to create a *new* `DataSet` using the default name that Visual Studio .NET provides (`DataSet1`). Make sure you have checked the Customers table and checked the box indicating that it will be added to the designer.

When the process finishes, a `DataSet` instance named `DataSet11` will be on the form and a `DataSet` schema named `DataSet1.xsd` will be in the `SolutionsExplorer`.

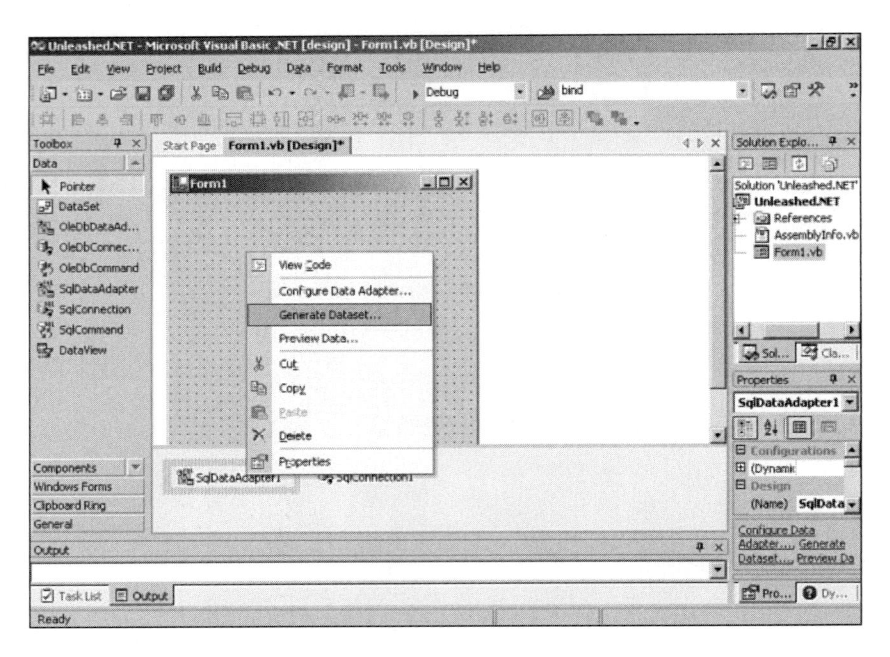

FIGURE 46.11 Generating the DataSet menu option.

Adding Some Controls to Display the Data

The next step is to update the small form example to include a couple of text boxes and a control button. From the Windows Forms tab of the Toolbox, add the following:

- A blank `Textbox` named `txtCustParameter`
- A blank `Textbox` named `txtContactName`
- A `Button` named `btnGet` with the `text` "Get Contact"

Go ahead and add a label in front of each text box so that the form looks like Figure 46.12.

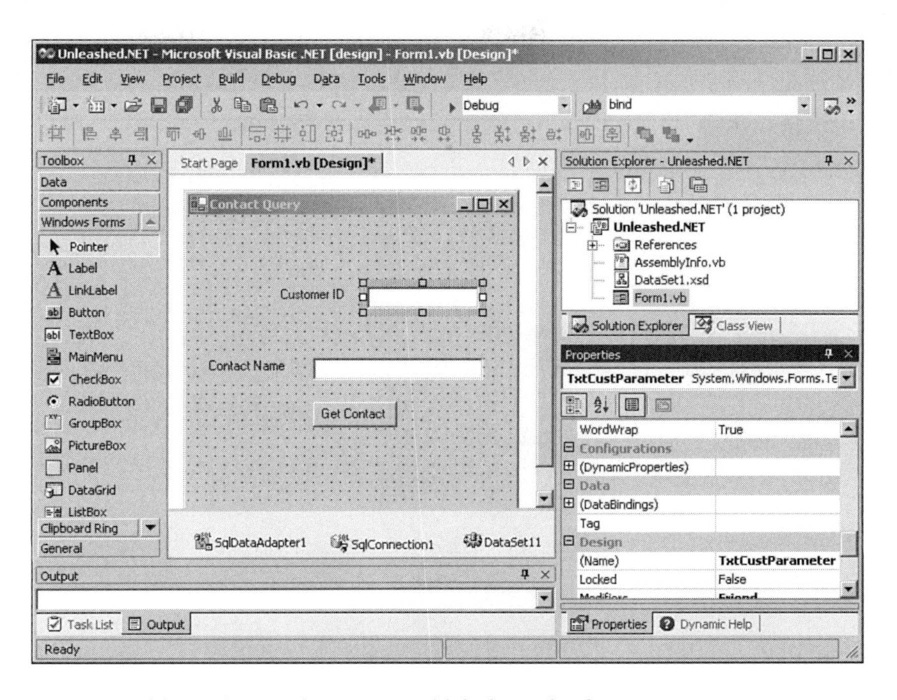

FIGURE 46.12 Add text boxes, buttons, and labels to the form.

Adding Code to Populate the DataSet

Now we are ready to complete the application by adding the code to fill the `DataSet` based on the parameterized value we get from the `txtCustParameter` text box. This will be plugged into the SQL statement and executed to fill the `DataSet` (and displayed in the `txtContactName` text box.

Just double-click on the Get Contact button to create a method for the `Click` event. You will have to add code to the handler to set the value of the single parameter required by the SQL statement (from `txtCustParameter`), make a call to the `DataSet`'s `Clear` method to clear the `DataSet` (`DataSet11`) between iterations, and call the data adapter's `Fill` method, passing the reference to the `DataSet` and the parameter value for the query. The following code is added:

```
SqlDataAdapter1.SelectCommand.Parameters("@param1").Value =
    txtCustParameter.Text
DataSet11.Clear()
SqlDataAdapter1.Fill(DataSet11)
```

Binding the Text Box to the DataSet

The only thing left to do is to bind the text box to the `DataSet` and run the application.

1. From the Forms designer, select the `txtContactName` text box and press F4. This will position you in the Properties window for this text box.
2. Expand the `(DataBindings)` node in the Properties list and its `text` property.
3. Expand the `DataSet11` and `Customers` nodes and select the `ContactName`.

Testing It!

That's it. Now just press the F5 key and test your application by putting in a customer ID value that is in the Customers table. Try the value *ALFKI*. In Figure 46.13 you can see that the form has successfully retrieved a valid contact name from the Customers database.

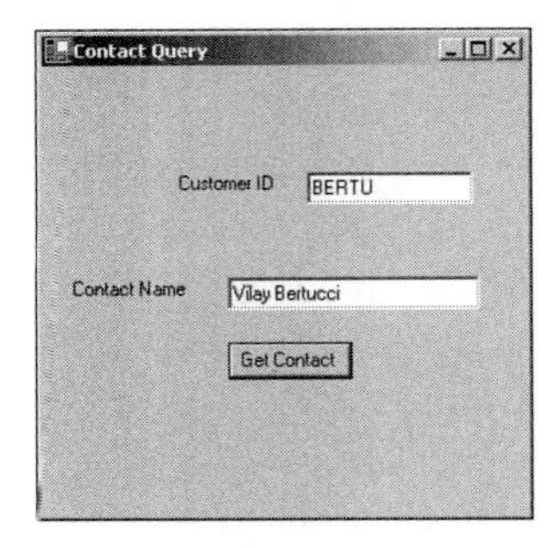

FIGURE 46.13 Form execution—retrieving a valid contact name from the Customers table.

Summary

This brief Visual Studio .NET example has shown you how easy it is to create applications in the .NET Framework and how tightly coupled SQL Server 2000 is as well. All data access is achievable via ADO.NET and the very robust `DataSet` representation. (The `DataSet` contains the `DataTable`, which contains `DataRows` and `DataColumns`.) Programmers are no longer at the mercy of the very restrictive `recordset` and can now write applications that span platforms via XML. *Sams Teach Yourself ADO.NET in 24 Hours* (Lefebvre/Bertucci) provides many more details about how to code using ADO.NET.

Remember, the .NET Framework is a multitiered platform that consists of developer tools, Web services, and a set of strongly typed programming languages that allow you to deploy applications for the Web or for the desktop in a single bound. Microsoft has positioned .NET to be a scalable architecture with many features such as optimistic concurrency, connection pooling, and XML interoperability. Microsoft SQL Server 2000 is at the heart of .NET and serves as the major data provider for this framework.

CHAPTER 47

English Query

by Bennett McEwan

IN THIS CHAPTER

English Query first shipped with MS SQL Server 7.0. The implementation in SQL 2000 improves on most of the early problems with the first release. Although English Query is not very widely used, it provides some interesting functionality that can be applied in certain specific circumstances.

What Is English Query?

English Query is a natural language-query processor. Using simple English sentences, you and your users can write queries that return results just like SQL queries do. Behind the scenes, English Query interprets the sentences, converts them to SQL queries (or, in the case of OLAP datasources, MDX), and then presents the results.

English Query applications can be built with Visual Studio tools (Visual Basic 6.0, for example) and deployed on the Web or in a standard .exe format.

English Query can interface with your standard relational databases or with OLAP cubes.

For Whom Is English Query Designed?

The target consumer for English Query applications is a user who doesn't know or doesn't want to use standard SQL to interface with a SQL Server database. Most applications that are designed for these kinds of users can produce reports and provide static answers easily, but they are often rigid and don't allow a user to browse, mine, or discover a database or OLAP cube with the freedom that English Query does.

English Query is not designed for developers, administrators, or power users who are willing to learn the SQL language. One of the problems with English Query is that it is based on the English language—and that language (like all Germanic languages) is notoriously inexact. English Query attempts to interpret what you want to know based on the rules that you, as the project developer, describe. But mistakes can occur in the interpretation of contextual information that wouldn't happen with a precise language such as SQL.

Getting Started with English Query

Before you can get started building an English Query application, you need to install the English Query designer. This is not installed by default when you install the SQL Server database software. The English Query packages should be installed on your personal workstation for development, not the database server.

> **TIP**
>
> English Query is included in the Standard, Enterprise, and Developer editions of SQL Server 2000.

Throughout this chapter, I will be referencing a movie database. It is a very simple database that contains only three tables used by the English Query application: Customers, Movies, and Rentals. The Customers table lists all the customers for a mythical video store. The Movies table lists all the movies in the inventory. The Rentals table is a transaction table that describes who rented which movies, when the movies were rented, and when they were returned to the store.

Installation

Installation is done from the original SQL Server 2000 distribution CD. From the splash screen, you have an option to Install English Query.

After selecting English Query installation, you have the option to install complete or runtime packages. The runtime packages are necessary only when distributing a finished English Query application. Installation of these packages would not be required if you deployed a Web application that used English Query.

For development, select the complete installation. This installs the English Query processor and snap-in designer for Visual Studio 6.0. Approximately 25–40Mb of disk space is required, depending on whether you already have VS 6.0 installed and which options you have.

Microsoft includes a very well-developed set of English Query tutorials with the complete installation. These packages leverage the Northwind database and Food Mart 2000 OLAP cubes for their examples.

How Does English Query Work?

English Query harnesses a natural language processor to interpret sentences and process them into SQL queries that are sent to SQL Server for processing. If you had a table named Customers that contained a list of all your customers and their addresses, telephone numbers, ages, and email, you could issue the following requests for information:

```
Show me all the customers.
How many customers are there?
Show customers with their address and phone and email.
```

English Query examines these queries and converts them into standard SQL queries:

```
select CustomerID from customers
select count(distinct CustomerID) from customers
select CustomerID, address, phone, email from customers
```

Notice that in these examples, English Query didn't get all the columns from the Customers table. Instead, it returned just the customer identifier (in this case, the `CustomerID`). You can define which column identifies a row in a table, but, by default, English Query assumes that the primary key should be used.

In the case of an OLAP cube, English Query converts your questions into MDX to query directly against the cube.

Translating English Commands

The English Query parser is fairly robust. With a little help, it can understand commands as vague as "Who rented the most movies last week?" Although the parser can understand a wide range of questions, users will quickly learn the most efficient way to get the answers they need. The following sentences all generate the same SQL query in English Query:

```
Show me a list of all of the customers in my database.
Are there any customers?
Give me a complete list of my customers, please.
List all customers.
Customers.
```

All of these sentences produce this SQL query:

```
Select CustomerID from Customers
```

SQL Clauses and Their English Query Equivalents

If you already know SQL, you are familiar with the rules that enable you to get answers to your questions. Listed here is a table that shows you how to translate the components of a SQL `SELECT` statement into the appropriate English Query words or phrases that provides the same result.

SQL Clause	Corresponding English Query Word or Phrase
`SELECT`	`Show` or `list`, as in the following: `List the customers`
`<column list>`	Specify each column name in a `with` clause, separated by `and`: `Show customers with email and phone.`
`FROM`	Include the table name as the noun in your sentence: `List customers.`
`WHERE`	A wide variety of verbs or prepositions can be used to specify the search criteria, depending on the type of relationship between the entities, such as `have`, `in` (existence), `between` (range), `before`, `after` (date/time). The definition of the relationships is the largest part of an English Query application.

`count()` or `sum()`	Specify `How many`, as in:
	`How many customers are there?`
	`How many customers have not rented movies this month?`
	`How many movies are romances?`

`avg()`	Specify the word `average`, as in: `What is the average age of people who rented movies directed by Stanley Kubrick?`

`min()` or `max()`	Ask for `smallest/largest`, `lowest/highest`, `earliest/latest`, `least/most`, or `oldest/youngest`:
	`Which is the oldest store?`
	`What is the latest date that a person rented the movie 'Full Metal Jacket'?`

`GROUP BY`	Specify `for each` or `per`:
	`How many movies for each customer?`
	`What is the average number of rentals per customer?`

TOP	Specify a number or percentage of records to return:
	`List the ten oldest stores`
	`List the 5 oldest stores`
	`List the 5 customers with the most rentals`

Building a Simple English Query Application

An easy way to get started with the English Query designer is to point it at a copy of your database and start a new EQ project with the Project Wizard. Because you are most familiar with the data in your database, exploring this data with the designer shows you the benefits and limitations of English Query better than with the Tutorial databases.

Requirements for an English Query Application

English Query works best on a normalized database. When you use the Project Wizard, it makes assumptions about the relationships between your tables based on the referential integrity constraints between them. For example, a database containing customers and rentals with a one-to-many relationship will assume that "customers have rentals." Likewise, movies that reference a Genres lookup table will create the relationship "movies have genres."

If your database is not well normalized, English Query will return inaccurate results. Suppose that you had customers with more than one address. One way to solve this problem would be to add an "addresses" table with the `CustomerID` in it. However, your predecessor (lazy administrator that he was) decided to take the easy way out and violate first normal form. He coded the application to make a duplicate entry with a new `CustomerID`, identical customer name, and the second address.

English Query would then count this customer twice when asked the question "How many customers are there?"

47

TIP

You can use views to solve most of the problems that English Query encounters in databases that lack good normalization rules. After creating the views, you need to manually add the entities to your solution and then add the relationships between the entities based on those views.

Entities

You are probably used to hearing of an Entity as a table in a relational database. An entity in an English Query application is any noun-object that can be referenced in the database. Entities can be tables or specific columns in a table. For example, a Customer table would comprise an entity. Suppose there was another table, VisitLog, that tracked dates when a customer visited a store. Instead of adding the table, you could instead add just the VisitDate column as an entity. You would then describe this relationship as "Customers make a visit."

When you use the Project Wizard, it creates entities based on each table you select. You can choose to include or not include each table in your database.

TIP

English Query doesn't allow you to take entities based on tables in other databases. Remember that it does allow you to reference views, however, so you can get around this limitation by building views that reference other databases, and use those in your English Query project.

Relationships

An English Query relationship defines how the English Query entities in your project relate to each other. In a relational database, there are only a few types of relationships. A typical parent/child relationship could be one-to-one (which could be either one-to-zero-or-one or one-to-exactly-one), or one-to-many. In an English Query relationship, you must define how the words your users will use map to the relationships between your tables.

"Customers have rentals" means that there is a relationship between the customers and rentals entities. Each entity could have many subentities (a table to a column, for example). A customer could have an address, a phone number, and a ZIP code. Each of these relationships will be represented in the application.

The Project Wizard infers most of these relationships for you. However, you must go through and define relationships needed by your users that the Project Wizard didn't guess. The relationships that will be guessed include the relationship between a table and its columns (customers have addresses and phone numbers; movies have directors, run times, and genres) and relationships that are defined by primary and foreign keys (a customer rents a movie; a customer relates to rentals).

To define these relationships, you must select a phrasing type that describes the relationship. Here are the different types of phrases that can be defined in an English Query application.

Prepositional Phrasing

Prepositional phrases include a preposition, such as `from`. Here is an example of a prepositional phrase in an English Query:

```
Which customers are from NY?
```

To create a prepositional phrase, follow these steps:

1. Select the entity that will be described by the phrase. In this case, select the Customers entity.
2. Click the Add button for phrasings.

3. Select Prepositional Phrasing from the Phrasing Type dialog box.
4. Enter the prepositions that will be used to describe the relationship. In this case, `from` will be used.
5. Select the entity that contains the appropriate measurement. In this case, select Customer_state, which is a column in the Customers table.

Verb Phrasing

By default, English Query assumes that the basic verb `have` will describe the relationships between entities. In many cases, this is sufficient. However, users will employ additional verb phrases to ask questions about the data. All of the following questions are verb phrases:

```
Who bought oranges last month?
How many movies were rented yesterday?
How many customers visited stores in NY?
```

The verbs in these questions are `bought`, `rented`, and `visited`.

Adjective Phrasing

The English language contains adjectives that describe, in inexact ways, traits of the nouns in sentences. For example, `tall person` or `large store` are adjective phrases that a user could ask your application to quantify.

To make this work, you need to specify both the adjectives that describe the measurements and what discrete measurement constitutes these adjectives. Suppose you had a movie rental database with renters' ages in it. This database would allow you to ask questions like in this example:

```
Which movies were rented by young customers?
```

To answer this question, the application needs to know what `young` means:

1. Edit the rentals relationship.
2. Add a phrase and select Adjective Phrase.
3. Of the three types of adjective phrases, select Measurement.
4. Four pieces of data are required to quantify what `young` means. Enter **`young`** in the Low Value box. Add synonyms such as **`teenager`**, **`kid`**, and **`children`**. Enter the numerical cutoff for `young` in the Numerical Threshold box. (Use **`18`** here.)
5. Finish by entering the same information for the High Threshold, using **`old`**, **`mature`**, and **`senior`**. Select an appropriate age for the high age threshold.

Trait Phrasing

Trait phrasing most often describes the relationships between a table and its columns. A customer has an address, a phone number, and an age.

```
List customer address and age
```

The Project Wizard normally imports this for you.

Name and ID Phrasing

Use these phrases to indicate the unique IDs of an entity and the descriptive names of an entity—for example:

```
Who are the customers?
What are the customer's IDs?
```

The Project Wizard normally imports this for you.

Subset Phrasing

A subset is another way of describing a type. For example, the genre of a movie is a subset of movies. You would need to define a subset phrase to answer the questions:

```
Which movies are science fiction?
Who rented romances or dramas?
```

To create a subset phrasing, follow these steps:

1. Add a relationship to the entity referencing the subset. In this case, use movies.
2. Add genres to the list of entities participating in the reference. Add a phrasing.
3. Select subset phrasing.
4. The subject is movies. The entity containing category values is genres.

Entity Synonyms

Every business has special words to describe things that are not in public parlance. If you were developing an English Query application for a movie rental store, for example, a movie type (genre) could have four or five different names: horror, thriller, and gore, for example.

You can make synonym entries to map any word to any other word in your application, as long as the entity type represents a field. By default, the English Query processor creates links between common English words.

NOTE

You can add synonyms to your application in two ways. Entity synonyms are in effect only for the data values in the entity for which you enter the synonym. Application synonyms are active throughout the application. If conflicts arise, entity synonyms override the priority of application synonyms.

To add a synonym, follow these steps:

1. Edit the entity. In this example, edit the genre_descriptions entity because it contains the actual words for which you want to provide synonyms.
2. Click Advanced Properties.
3. Select the Name Synonyms tab.
4. The left column is a list of synonyms for words in the right column. The words in the right column are the actual database values.
5. For this example, enter **`Chick Flicks and Drama`**, **`Thriller and Horror`**, and **`Gore and Horror`**. You can enter as many synonyms for a word as you like.

It now is possible to ask this question:

```
List all the chick flicks and their running times.
```

Dictionary Entries

Dictionary entries enable you to add to the existing English Query dictionary, define application-wide synonyms, adjust how the application interprets specific words, and adjust what the application returns in its results.

Three kinds of dictionary entries exist:

- Words (synonyms)
- Read synonyms (remap what the query processor sees)
- Write synonyms (remap what the user sees)

Words

Because the dictionary contains only the root forms of words and uses generalized grammatical rules to interpret tenses and plural nouns, any irregular words must be defined with a dictionary entry. The plural of the word `person` is `people`. `Persons` is also valid, but this is handled properly by the English Query language processor.

In the movie database example, `People` means "Customer." Here is how to add the word to the dictionary:

1. Select the menu option "Add Dictionary Entry."
2. In the Root form drop-down, select Person.
3. In the Part of speech drop-down, select Common Noun.
4. For this example, check the Irregular Plural check box and enter **`people`**.

Read Synonym

This enables you to invisibly map a word to another word for the entire application. For example, anytime you see the word `person`, you could interpret that to mean `customer`. Any queries that contain `person` would be fed into the processor as `customer`, and the returned results would reference the word `customer`. Assuming that you defined `people` as in the previous example, this question:

```
Which people rented science fiction?
```

gives this answer:

```
The customers that rented science fiction are:

David Wordsmith        2001: A Space Odyssey
Rachel Welch           2001: A Space Odyssey
John Black             A Clockwork Orange
```

Write Synonym

If you want to return different words from a question but you still want the processor to interpret them in their original form, you can create a write synonym. Creating a write synonym that maps `Customer` to `Guest` gives this slightly different result,

```
Who rented science fiction?
```

that gives this answer:

```
The guests that rented science fiction are:

David Wordsmith        2001: A Space Odyssey
Rachel Welch           2001: A Space Odyssey
John Black             A Clockwork Orange
```

Contextual Information

The English Query processor remembers the questions that have been recently asked. If you use pronouns to refer to information that you are examining, it remembers the previous results and uses those to interpret follow-up questions. For example, suppose that you start off with this query:

```
Who rented movies in the last 30 days?
```

Using this list as a starting point, you can then ask questions that relate only to the data returned by these follow-up queries:

```
How many were Science Fiction?
Of those, which movies were directed by Stanley Kubrick?
Which of those had a running time over two hours?
```

Summary

English Query applications enable you to deploy open-ended client/server or Web-based applications to users who do not know the SQL language. The English Query add-on includes a sophisticated natural-language processor. To get the most out of it, you must train the processor to understand how to interpret the data in your database.

Index

Symbols

A

B

C

D

E

F

G

H

I

M

N

O

P

Q

R

T

U

V

W

X–Y–Z

What's on the CD-ROM

The companion CD-ROM contains all the sample files used in the book and related software.

Windows Installation Instructions

1. Insert the disc into your CD-ROM drive.
2. From the Windows desktop, double-click the My Computer icon.
3. Double-click the icon representing your CD-ROM drive.
4. Double-click `start.exe`. Follow the onscreen prompts to finish the installation.

> **NOTE**
>
> If you have the AutoPlay feature enabled, `default.htm` will be launched automatically whenever you insert the disc into your CD-ROM drive.

By opening this package, you are also agreeing to be bound by the following agreement:

You may not copy or redistribute the entire CD-ROM as a whole. Copying and redistribution of individual software programs on the CD-ROM is governed by terms set by individual copyright holders.

The installer and code from the author(s) are copyrighted by the publisher and the author(s). Individual programs and other items on the CD-ROM are copyrighted by their various authors or other copyright holders.

This software is sold as-is without warranty of any kind, either expressed or implied, including but not limited to the implied warranties of merchantability and fitness for a particular purpose. Neither the publisher nor its dealers or distributors assumes any liability for any alleged or actual damages arising from the use of this program. (Some states do not allow for the exclusion of implied warranties, so the exclusion may not apply to you.)

NOTE: This CD-ROM uses long and mixed-case filenames requiring the use of a protected-mode CD-ROM Driver.